INTERNATIONAL INTELLECTUAL PROPERTY IN AN INTEGRATED WORLD ECONOMY

ASPEN CASEBOOK SERIES

INTERNATIONAL INTELLECTUAL PROPERTY IN AN INTEGRATED WORLD ECONOMY

Second Edition

Frederick M. Abbott
Edward Ball Eminent Scholar
Professor of International Law
Florida State University, Tallahassee

Thomas Cottier
Professor of European and International Economic Law
University of Berne and
Director, World Trade Institute, Berne

Francis Gurry
Director General
World Intellectual Property Organization, Geneva

Copyright © 2011 CCH Incorporated.

Published by Wolters Kluwer Law & Business in New York.

Wolters Kluwer Law & Business serves customers worldwide with CCH, Aspen Publishers, and Kluwer Law International products. (www.wolterskluwerlb.com)

To contact Customer Service, e-mail customer.service@wolterskluwer.com, call 1-800-234-1660, fax 1-800-901-9075, or mail correspondence to:

> Wolters Kluwer Law & Business
> Attn: Order Department
> PO Box 990
> Frederick, MD 21705

Printed in the United States of America.

1 2 3 4 5 6 7 8 9 0

ISBN 978-0-7355-9966-6

Library of Congress Cataloging-in-Publication Data

Abbott, Frederick M.
  International intellectual property in an integrated world economy /
Frederick M. Abbott, Thomas Cottier, Francis Gurry. — 2nd ed.
    p. cm. — (Aspen casebook series)
  Includes bibliographical references and index.
  ISBN 978-0-7355-9966-6
1. Intellectual property (International law) I. Cottier, Thomas. II.
Gurry, Francis. III. Title.
  K1401.A922 2011
  346.04′8-dc22

                                                          2011013848

About Wolters Kluwer Law & Business

Wolters Kluwer Law & Business is a leading global provider of intelligent information and digital solutions for legal and business professionals in key specialty areas, and respected educational resources for professors and law students. Wolters Kluwer Law & Business connects legal and business professionals as well as those in the education market with timely, specialized authoritative content and information-enabled solutions to support success through productivity, accuracy and mobility.

Serving customers worldwide, Wolters Kluwer Law & Business products include those under the Aspen Publishers, CCH, Kluwer Law International, Loislaw, Best Case, ftwilliam.com and MediRegs family of products.

CCH products have been a trusted resource since 1913, and are highly regarded resources for legal, securities, antitrust and trade regulation, government contracting, banking, pension, payroll, employment and labor, and healthcare reimbursement and compliance professionals.

Aspen Publishers products provide essential information to attorneys, business professionals and law students. Written by preeminent authorities, the product line offers analytical and practical information in a range of specialty practice areas from securities law and intellectual property to mergers and acquisitions and pension/benefits. Aspen's trusted legal education resources provide professors and students with high-quality, up-to-date and effective resources for successful instruction and study in all areas of the law.

Kluwer Law International products provide the global business community with reliable international legal information in English. Legal practitioners, corporate counsel and business executives around the world rely on Kluwer Law journals, loose-leafs, books, and electronic products for comprehensive information in many areas of international legal practice.

Loislaw is a comprehensive online legal research product providing legal content to law firm practitioners of various specializations. Loislaw provides attorneys with the ability to quickly and efficiently find the necessary legal information they need, when and where they need it, by facilitating access to primary law as well as state-specific law, records, forms and treatises.

Best Case Solutions is the leading bankruptcy software product to the bankruptcy industry. It provides software and workflow tools to flawlessly streamline petition preparation and the electronic filing process, while timely incorporating ever-changing court requirements.

ftwilliam.com offers employee benefits professionals the highest quality plan documents (retirement, welfare and non-qualified) and government forms (5500/PBGC, 1099 and IRS) software at highly competitive prices.

MediRegs products provide integrated health care compliance content and software solutions for professionals in healthcare, higher education and life sciences, including professionals in accounting, law and consulting.

Wolters Kluwer Law & Business, a division of Wolters Kluwer, is headquartered in New York. Wolters Kluwer is a market-leading global information services company focused on professionals.

To our children

Annie

Céline

Devin

Emma

Maurice

Ryan

Samuel

and

Thomas

SUMMARY OF CONTENTS

CONTENTS

CHAPTER 1

STRUCTURAL FRAMEWORK, BASIC PRINCIPLES, AND POLICIES   1

CHAPTER 2

THE INTERNATIONAL PATENT SYSTEM 165

CHAPTER 3

THE INTERNATIONAL TRADEMARK AND
IDENTIFIER SYSTEM   317

CHAPTER 4

THE INTERNATIONAL COPYRIGHT SYSTEM 477

CHAPTER 5

COMPETITION LAW AND *SUI GENERIS* SYSTEMS OF INTELLECTUAL PROPERTY PROTECTION: TRADITIONAL KNOWLEDGE, PLANT VARIETY PROTECTION, UNDISCLOSED INFORMATION, INDUSTRIAL DESIGNS, AND INTEGRATED CIRCUITS

643

CHAPTER 6

THE INTERNATIONAL SYSTEM FOR THE ENFORCEMENT OF
INTELLECTUAL PROPERTY RIGHTS   717

PREFACE TO THE SECOND EDITION

The international intellectual property system is continuously evolving. This book evolves with it.

Intellectual property (IP) remains at center stage in developments responding to globalization. Innovation and marketing skills define the competiveness of companies and nations. The quest for a proper balance between the grant of exclusive rights and protection of the public domain remains at the heart of legal developments. The authors continue to take particular interest in the social welfare dimensions of intellectual property. IP laws ultimately are mechanisms to achieve desirable social welfare objectives for people around the world. We continuously draw attention to the "whole effect" of the international IP system.

Since the first edition was published in 2007, four major trends or developments may be highlighted.

First, the IP policies of large emerging economy countries — including Brazil, China, and India — have been the subject of considerable political and legal attention. As industry based in these countries invests more heavily in developing innovative products and brands, government institutions in these countries are gradually leaning toward strengthening domestic IP protection, while hesitating to do so at the international level. So far, this trend only implicitly alters the international IP landscape, but this may change in coming years.

Second, as emerging economy industries start to seriously challenge those of Europe, the United States and Japan, political leadership in the latter demand stronger global IP enforcement to maintain technological advantage. Intensifying attention to global enforcement of IP was manifest in the first WTO dispute settlement case interpreting the rules of the TRIPS Agreement enforcement chapter. The *China-Enforcement* case, decided in 2009, involved US claims that China's criminal IP enforcement laws provided insufficient deterrence. The United States did not succeed with its claims, but the report of the WTO panel began to flesh out TRIPS Agreement enforcement standards. Key excerpts are introduced in Chapters 4 and 6. In a related development, the government of India was sued by a Swiss pharmaceutical company in Indian court for allegedly introducing patentability standards inconsistent with its TRIPS Agreement obligations. The late 2007 decision of the Indian High Court in the *Novartis* case, rejecting the allegation, is introduced in Chapters 1 and 2. Consistent with policies in the U.S. and the European Union, the *Novartis* decision is another example of denying direct effect to the TRIPS Agreement.

Third, the slow pace of IP norm-making at the multilateral level — already evident in 2007 — has led some governments to voice serious concern about the role of existing multilateral IP institutions, with an implicit threat to move international IP subject matter elsewhere. That "elsewhere" already is manifest in efforts to negotiate in *ad hoc* forums, as well as in bilateral trade agreement settings. This third major trend — a continuation — is evidenced by a proposed plurilateral Anti-Counterfeiting Trade Agreement or ACTA designed to provide more extensive rights to private IP holders and customs authorities to act at the border. The proposed agreement goes well beyond traditional notions of "counterfeiting" and has met with considerable political pushback from NGOs and developing country governments. We discuss the ACTA in various chapters. There is hardly a free trade agreement lacking provisions relating to the protection of IPRs. As to bilateral agreements, it is increasingly difficult to keep track of the many diverging IPRs provisions, most of which deploy MFN obligations to contribute to global increases in IP protection. Whether plurilateral or bilateral efforts led by the 20th century economic powers will succeed in pressuring the emerging 21st-century powers to give more serious attention to heightened IP standards and enforcement is not clear. It seems unlikely that Brazil, China, India and other major emerging economy countries will succumb to such pressure. Yet it is certainly possible that the perspective of emerging economy industrialists will ultimately converge with those of European, U.S., and Japanese industrialists, all seeking to protect investments in innovation. Perhaps the global need for climate change mitigation and adaption will lead to more balanced approaches for protecting IPRs and promoting transfer of technology.

A fourth major development was the December 2009 entry into force of the Lisbon Treaty for the European Union (EU). Through this treaty, the EU has firmly secured comprehensive jurisdiction to address intellectual property rights (IPRs), both internally and in external relations. Importantly, the Lisbon Treaty altered the allocation of internal EU competences to conclude international agreements in the field of IP, strengthening the role of the European Parliament. Significant new powers relating to IP also were given to the EU in the field of investment protection. These developments are explained in chapter 1. Further progress was also made towards a single EU patent. It has been on the drawing board since the early 1970s, and it seemed almost certain that it would finally come into being in time for publication of this Second Edition. But, once again, language issues and questions regarding allocation of judicial competences continue to frustrate this objective.

Although there has been a great deal of IP-related activity taking place at WIPO, refining international registration systems and seeking to make progress on substantive issues, there has been limited progress in the area of multilateral IP norm-making. The WIPO Development Agenda has not yet shaped legal developments. As an exception to the general lack of progress at the multilateral level, the Nagoya Protocol on Access and Benefit Sharing to the Convention on Biological Diversity (CBD) was concluded in November 2010. The Nagoya Protocol seeks to clarify CBD IP-related obligations. It is introduced in Chapters 1 and 5.

This Second Edition introduces new cases addressing IP subject matter from various jurisdictions, with increasing attention to jurisprudence emanating from outside Europe and the United States. Chapter 2 provides an update on patent-related legislative developments in China. Chapter 5 introduces new material addressing protection of traditional knowledge, as well as the intersection between IP and competition law, and principles of unfair competition more generally.

Despite all the changes, the fundamentals of intellectual property have remained stable and witness gradual challenges from new technologies, in particular in the field of copyright protection. We are mindful of the evolution of Internet-based content, most notably social network content, that once again challenges copyright and unfair competition law to adapt to changing forms of expression. So far, this has not led to any paradigm shift in norms or the way they are applied, but we monitor these developments.

We once again welcome your comments and suggestions for the next edition.

Frederick M. Abbott
Thomas Cottier
Francis Gurry

April 2011

Author's Statement: The views expressed in this book are personal and, in respect of Francis Gurry, do not necessarily reflect the views of the World Intellectual Property Organization (WIPO).

PREFACE TO THE FIRST EDITION

The title of this book reflects reality for lawyers involved in the field of intellectual property (IP). The world economy is highly integrated, and intellectual property law is playing an increasingly important role in this global environment. Intellectual property rights (IPRs) regulation in Brazil, China, India, and Russia affects not only those countries, but has important effects on the businesses and economies of the United States and European Union. IPRs regulation affects social welfare, such as by influencing the quantum of information available in the public domain and by influencing the development and pricing of medicines. Because markets for socially important goods and services are international, IPRs rules established for one country (or a group of countries) may well affect social welfare in other countries. Multilateral and regional IPRs rules provide the framework in which the multinational business community operates. The same rules have important implications for social welfare throughout the world.

This book is designed as a detailed introduction to the international system that regulates intellectual property rights. Chapter 1 introduces the forms of intellectual property from a cosmopolitan perspective, taking into account decisions from various jurisdictions. It identifies and explains the multilateral organizations in which rules are negotiated and applied, such as the World Intellectual Property Organization (WIPO), the World Trade Organization (WTO), and other organizations with subject matter interest in IPRs, such as the Food and Agriculture Organization (FAO) and World Health Organization (WHO). Regional agreements and institutions, which play an important role in IPRs regulation, are introduced in the first chapter, and the role of regional institutions in IPRs regulation is covered throughout the book. Chapter 1 then turns to basic principles, such as national and most favored nation treatment, exhaustion, independence, territoriality, extraterritoriality, and human rights, which have systemic effects across the IPRs landscape. At the conclusion of the first chapter, the policies underlying the protection of IPRs at the multilateral level are considered.

The book approaches the detailed subject matter of international IPRs regulation by addressing the three main categories of IPRs, with their respective subcategories, in separate chapters on the international patent system (Chapter 2), the international trademark and identifier system (Chapter 3), and the international copyright system (Chapter 4). Each chapter starts with a more detailed consideration of the IP form. It then proceeds to identify the multilateral rules that apply to that IP form, how rights are secured on a wide geographic basis, and how rules have been applied in dispute settlement. Relevant regional institutions and rules, select national rules, and special policy considerations follow. Chapter 5 addresses protection of industrial design, plant varieties, trade secret, and regulatory data, using a similar approach. One of the most significant developments regarding the international IPRs system over the past decade is heightened attention to matters of enforcement. Chapter 6 covers the subject in some detail, including how enforcement is being addressed at the WTO, in other international organizations, at the regional level, and in national law.

Throughout the book we pay strong attention to the public policy implications of international IPRs rules and enforcement, with special attention to the different interests and perspectives of developed and developing countries. For law students, as well as practitioners, judges, government officials, representatives of international organizations and nongovernmental organizations, it is essential to understand technical aspects of how the international IPRs system works and to understand — as well as our collective state of knowledge allows — how the system affects economic and social welfare. A full appreciation of the technical details and social welfare implications of the international IPRs system among those who shape and apply the rules is critical to continued improvement of the system. Properly designed and implemented, the system should benefit us all.

Frederick M. Abbott
Thomas Cottier
Francis Gurry

May 2007

ACKNOWLEDGMENTS

For the second edition, the authors are grateful to Tetayna Payosova, doctoral student research fellow, and Andrea Kienast, junior research fellow, both at the Department of Economic Law and the World Trade Institute of the University of Bern for careful support and assistance. Both ardent students using the first edition, they offered valuable advice from a student's perspective in improving the book for teaching purposes. The authors are also grateful to Maegan McCann, Kelly Shaw and Charles Whittington, students at Florida State University College of Law, for their able assistance with research, including their help in identifying recent judicial decisions of interest. The authors are indebted to faculty users of the first edition for their questions and comments that help refine the ongoing work. They also very much appreciate the commitment and effort of John Devins and Jessica Barmack, Assistant Managing Editor and Developmental Editor, respectively, at Aspen Publishers.

For the first edition, authors wish to thank the anonymous reviewers on behalf of Aspen Publishers who contributed to improving the organization of this book. They wish to thank Cathy Abbott, who has again demonstrated her excellent editing skills. They thank Leslie Jennings for her able assistance in securing permissions to reprint. Thomas Cottier acknowledges the research assistance of Christophe Germann with respect to his contribution. They also very much appreciate the commitment and effort of Richard Mixter and Eric Holt, the Acquisitions Editor and Managing Editor, respectively, at Aspen Publishers. The authors finally wish to thank Professor Jerry Reichman for his encouraging words.

The authors very much appreciate the assistance of Troy Froebe, who coordinated the editing for the first and second editions.

In addition, we gratefully acknowledge permission to reprint materials from the following authors and publishers:

Abbott, Frederick M. Intellectual Property Rights in World Trade, in Research Handbook in International Economic Law (Andrew Guzman & Alan Sykes eds.), Edward Elgar Publishing 2007. Reprinted by permission of Edward Elgar Publishing.

Abbott, Frederick M. Non-Violation Nullification or Impairment Causes of Action under the TRIPS Agreement and the Fifth Ministerial Conference: A Warning and Reminder. Quaker United Nations Office, Occasional Paper No. 11, July 2003. Reprinted by permission of the Quaker United Nations Office.

Abbott, Frederick M. China in the WTO 2006: "Law and Its Limitations" in the Context of TRIPS, in Developing Countries in the WTO: A Law and Economics Analysis (George Bermann & Petros Mavroidis eds.), Cambridge

University Press: forthcoming 2007. Reprinted by permission of Cambridge University Press.

Abbott, Frederick M. The North American Integration Regime and Its Implications for the World Trading System, IX:1 Collected Courses of the Academy of European Law: The EU, the WTO and the NAFTA (JHH Weiler ed., 2000), Oxford Univ. Press. Reprinted by permission of Oxford University Press.

Abbott, Frederick M. Intellectual Property Provisions of Bilateral and Regional Trade Agreements in Light of U.S. Federal Law. Issue Paper No. 12, February 2006, UNCTAD—ICTSD Project on IPRs and Sustainable Development. Reprinted by permission of the International Centre for Trade and Sustainable Development.

Barlow, John Perry. The Economy of Ideas: A Framework for Patents and Copyrights in the Digital Age (Everything you know about intellectual property is wrong.), Wired 2.03, Mar. 1994. Reprinted by permission of Wired Magazine.

Barton, John H. The Economics of TRIPS: International Trade in Information-Intensive Products, 33 Geo. Wash. Int'l L. Rev. 473 (2001). Reprinted by permission of John Barton and the George Washington International Law Review.

Barton, John. New Trends in Technology Transfer; Implications for National and International Policy, ICTSD Intellectual Property and Sustainable Development Series, Issue Paper No. 18, Feb. 2007. Reprinted by permission of John Barton and the International Centre for Trade and Sustainable Development.

Battling HIV-AIDS: A Decision-Maker's Guide to the Procurement of Medicines and Related Supplies (Yolanda Tayler ed.), World Bank, 2004. Reprinted by permission of World Bank Publishing.

Beier, Freidrich-Karl. The European Patent System, 14 Vand. J. Transnat'l L. 1 (1981). Reprinted by permission of the Vanderbilt Journal of International Law.

Cottier, Thomas. The Agreement on Trade-Related Aspects of Intellectual Property Rights (TRIPs), in The World Trade Organization: Legal, Economic and Political Analysis, Vol. I 1040-1120, at 1082-1085 (Patrick F. J. Macroy, Arthur E. Appleton & Micheal G Plummer eds.), Springer: New York 2005. Reprinted by permission of Springer Publishing.

Cottier, Thomas. Industrial Property, International Law, http://www.mpepil. com/. Reprinted by permission of Max Planck Institute.

Cottier, Thomas & Jevtic Ana. The Protection Against Unfair Competition in WTO Law: Status, Potential and Prospects, Drexl Josef (ed.). Technology and Competition. Contributions in Honour of Hanns Ullrich. Bruxelles 2009, at 669-695.

Cottier, Thomas & Germann Christophe. Teaching Intellectual Property, Unfair Competition and Anti-Trust Law, in Yo Takagi, Larry Allman & Mpazi A. Sinjela (eds.), Teaching of Intellectual Property. Principles and Methods (Cambridge University Press 2008), at 130-166. Reprinted by permission of Cambridge University Press.

Cottier, Thomas & Panizzon Marion. Legal Perspectives on Traditional Knowledge: The Case for Intellectual Property Protection, 7 J Int'l Economic Law 371-399 (2004). Reprinted by permission of Journal of International Economic Law.

Fink, Carsten, and Patrick Reichenmiller. Tightening TRIPS: The Intellectual Property Provisions of Recent US Free Trade Agreements. World Bank Group, International Trade Development, Trade Note 20, Feb. 7, 2005. Reprinted by permission of Carsten Fink and the World Bank Group.

Helfer, Laurence R. Toward a Human Rights Framework for Intellectual Property, 40 U.C. Davis Law Review 971, 1017-1020 (2007). Reprinted by permission of U.C. Davis Law Review.

Hoeren, Thomas. The European Union Commission and Recent Trends in European Information Law, 29 Rutgers Computer & Tech. L.J. 1 (2003). Reprinted by permission of Thomas Hoeren and the Rutgers Computer and Technology Law Journal.

Kiewiet, Bart. Plant Variety Protection in the European Community, World Patent Information 27 (2005). Reprinted by permission.

Lessig, Lawrence. Open Source Baselines: Compared to What?, in Government Policy toward Open Source Software (Robert W. Hahn ed.), AEI-Brookings Joint Center: January 2003. Reprinted by permission of Lawrence Lessig.

Maskus, Keith. Intellectual Property Rights in the Global Economy, Institute for International Economics (2000). Reprinted by permission of Keith Maskus.

Maskus, Keith E., & J. H. Reichman. The Globalization of Private Knowledge Goods and the Privatization of Global Public Goods, 7 J. Int'l Econ. L. 279 (2004). Reprinted by permission of Keith Maskus and Jerome Reichman.

Mondini, A. & P. Groz. New Developments in Swiss Patent Law, September 2009 Newsletter of law firm Schellenberg/Wittmer.

Moyer-Henry, Kari, Ph.D. Patenting Neem and Hoodia: Conflicting Decisions Issued by the Opposition Board of the European Patent Office, 27 Biotechnology Law Report 6-9 (2008). Reprinted by permission of Mary Ann Leibert Inc.

Musungu, Sisule F., & Graham Dutfield. Multilateral Agreements and a TRIPS-Plus World: The World Intellectual Property Organisation (WIPO), TRIPS Issues Papers 3, Quaker United Nations Office (QUNO), Geneva Quaker International Affairs Programme (QIAP), Ottawa. Reprinted by permission of Sisule F. Musungu and the Quaker United Nations Office.

Penrose, Edith. Economics of the International Patent System. pp.101-107, 162-169. Copyright © 1961 by The Johns Hopkins University Press. Reprinted by permission of The Johns Hopkins University Press.

Ricketson, Sam. The Birth of the Berne Union, The Centenary of The Berne Convention, Conference (Intellectual Property Law Unit, Queen Mary College, University of London and British Literary and Artistic Copyright Association London, April 17-18, 1986). Reprinted by permission of Sam Ricketson.

Samuelson, Pamela. The U.S. Digital Agenda at WIPO, 37 Va. J. Int'l L 369 (1997), Reprinted by permission of Pamela Samuelson.

Sell, Susan K. The Global IP Upward Ratchet, Anti-Counterfeiting and Piracy Enforcement Efforts: The State of Play, paper presented at George Washington University, June 9, 2008. Licensed under a Creative Commons Attribution 3.0 License. See http://creativecommons.org/licenses/by/3.0/. Reprinted with permission.

Stiglitz, Joseph E. Knowledge as a Public Good, http://www.worldbank.org/
knowledge/chiefecon/articles/undpk2/index.htm (1998), World Bank Group.
Reprinted by permission of Joseph Stiglitz.

Sykes, Alan O. Public Health and International Law: TRIPS, Pharmaceuticals,
Developing Countries, and the Doha "Solution," 3 Chi. J. Int'l L. 47
(2002). Reprinted by permission of the Chicago Journal of International
Law.

UNCTAD/ICTSD Resource Book on TRIPS and Development. Cambridge
University Press (2005). Reprinted by permission of Cambridge University Press.

WIPO. The WIPO Copyright Treaty (WCT), WIPO Intellectual Property Handbook (2006). Reprinted by permission of the World Intellectual Property
Organization.

WIPO. The Hague Agreement Concerning the International Registration of
Industrial Designs: Main Features and Advantages. WIPO Publication,
No. 911(E). Reprinted by permission of the World Intellectual Property
Organization.

WIPO. The Madrid Agreement Concerning the International Registration of
Marks and the Protocol Relating to that Agreement, WIPO Intellectual
Property Handbook (2006). Reprinted by permission of the World
Intellectual Property Organization.

WIPO. Technical Study on Disclosure Requirements in Patent Systems Related
to Genetic Resources and Traditional Knowledge, WIPO Intergovernmental Committee on Intellectual Property and Genetic Resources, Traditional Knowledge and Folklore, Study No. 3, Feb. 2004, Reprinted by
permission of the World Intellectual Property Organization.

WIPO. Summary of the Convention Establishing the World Intellectual
Property Organization (WIPO Convention), http://www.wipo.int (2006).
Reprinted by permission of the World Intellectual Property Organization.

WIPO. WIPO Arbitration and Mediation Center New Generic Top-Level
Domains: Intellectual Property Considerations, http://www.wipo.int (2007).
Reprinted by permission of the World Intellectual Property Organization.

Xintian, Yin. A Brief Introduction to the Patent Practice in China, 9 Duke J. of
Comp. & Int'l L. 253. Reprinted by permission of the Duke Journal of
Comparative & International Law.

INTERNATIONAL INTELLECTUAL PROPERTY IN AN INTEGRATED WORLD ECONOMY

CHAPTER

1

Structural Framework, Basic Principles, and Policies

I. INTRODUCTION

A. *International Intellectual Property as a Discipline*

Technology is bringing the international community together. The business sector functions globally, collecting and assembling inputs from factories and employees around the world, and distributing products and services to a global consumer. Scientists and academicians exchange ideas over the Internet and at international conferences where national identity plays a modest role. Social networking web sites change the way individuals and communities are interacting locally and globally. Diseases show limited regard for national borders as pandemic and threats of pandemic challenge the global public health system. We collectively share a planetary environment that requires multilateral attention.

Innovation is driving the global economy. Biotechnology is transforming agriculture and medicine. Materials and propulsion technologies are creating new global transportation infrastructure. Development of new environmentally friendly sources of energy is one of the great technological challenges of the twenty-first century. Less exotic innovation in areas such as supply-chain management has a profound effect on efficiencies of production and distribution, making life better for a very large number of people.

Expression in the form of music, film, and video game provides content for new generations of personal entertainment technologies. Books are digitized and increasingly read on portable electronic devices embodying constantly changing technologies. Product design has captured the imagination of consumers and is leading to renewed corporate attention to the role of aesthetics in consumer behavior. A defining characteristic of technological development in the twenty-first century is acceleration in the rate of change. New technology markets develop rapidly, and technologies likewise "obsolesce" quickly. Intellectual property law must keep pace. Whether the subject is a life or death matter, such as the availability of drugs to treat disease, or one of personal entertainment, such as access to MP3 files, the scope and terms of intellectual property protection are of great interest to the researcher, artist, producer, and consumer. And, because the market for drugs, MP3 files, agricultural products, civilian aircraft, and energy is global, the lawyer should not and really cannot be satisfied with understanding only the nature of that protection in a single national market. Yet, the nation-state continues to be the principal geographical and political entity around which the world community is organized. The critical role that national governments play in regulating political, economic, and social activity must be acknowledged.

In principle, the international legal treatment of each form of intellectual property right (IPR) can be studied as an extension of the domestic law applicable to that IPR. A course on patent law, for example, can include a component on patenting in foreign countries. But understanding the international regulatory framework that governs IPRs involves more than appreciating that the same IPR can or should be protected in more than one country. International institutions make law that governs IPRs, and they play a key role in administering that law. Increasingly, the domestic IPR norms that all countries apply are shaped by rules made in Geneva, Switzerland, at the World Trade Organization and the World Intellectual Property Organization, or in other international fora, whether by other multilateral institutions or by regional and bilateral treaty. Intellectual property emerged as an important component of international trade regulation, addressing both trade in goods and services, as well as of the international law of international investment protection. It needs to be studied in close relation to these fields.[1]

The member states of the European Union have adopted a new constitutional framework with the Lisbon Treaty, entered into force in December 2009, that further consolidates the regulation of IPRs in regional institutions and rules. When disputes arise concerning the application of these international and regional rules, they may be settled by dispute settlement mechanisms unique to these organizations. A technical understanding of how a patent application filed in the United States may also be filed in other countries does not fully convey an appreciation of how the international patent system affects the inventor. Moreover, each form of intellectual property is regulated differently in the international legal framework.

Many students of the international intellectual property system will go on to represent the intellectual property interests of large corporations with the money to take advantage of legal rules. Much of the time, their work may be devoted to seeking protection for and enforcing IP rights. But this is only part of what international intellectual property lawyers do. Businesses large and small have defensive, as well as offensive, interests in IP. The largest industrial companies may wish to challenge claims to exclusive rights by their equally large competitors. IP lawyers may be contesting rights in IP — for example, by challenging the validity of patents — as well as seeking to protect them.

Public interest groups like Doctors without Borders (Médecins Sans Frontières) take a great interest in how the international IPRs system affects access to the medicines its patients desperately require. Multilateral organizations like the World Health Organization and the World Bank are concerned with the way that intellectual property affects public health and development. Questions surrounding the development of "green energy" technologies, their protection by IPRs, and providing access to them are debated in the

---

1. For a comprehensive discussion, *see* THOMAS COTTIER & MATTHIAS OESCH, INTERNATIONAL TRADE REGULATION: LAW AND POLICY IN THE WTO, THE EUROPEAN UNION AND SWITZERLAND (London: Cameron May and Bern: Staempfli Publishers 2005).

United Nations Framework Convention on Climate Change. The parties to the Convention on Biological Diversity are concerned with how patents may affect the preservation and exploitation of genetic resources. The Food and Agriculture Organization is concerned with how intellectual property rights affect the world food supply. To make a long story short, it is not only multinational corporations or business enterprises more generally that are concerned with international intellectual property rules and how they are applied. These rules affect everyone. Lawyers who understand the system are needed to represent the interests of all stakeholders in it.

B. *Trends in the International IP System*

1. Harmonization, Integration, and Countervailing Trends

The first major multilateral treaty regulating intellectual property was the Paris Convention for the Protection of Industrial Property concluded in 1883. During negotiation for that Convention, proposals were considered for a substantially harmonized international patent system. Owing to major differences between countries in the way that patents were granted and regulated, such proposals did not gain traction. The Paris Convention established a framework of basic principles and a mechanism for facilitating applications for patent and trademark in more than one country, but it did not create harmonized patent or trademark law. The Berne Convention for the Protection of Literary and Artistic Works, establishing international rules on copyright, was concluded in 1886. It established a higher level of substantive harmonization than the Paris Convention, and its rules provide much of the basis for international copyright protection today.

During the first half of the twentieth century, a number of revisions were made to the Paris and Berne Conventions, and several additional international agreements covering different forms of intellectual property were adopted. While the Paris and Berne Conventions were widely adopted (with the United States joining the latter convention only in 1986), other agreements achieved considerably less acceptance.

In the early 1970s, a new specialized agency of the United Nations was created — the World Intellectual Property Organization (or WIPO). The WIPO charter expressly envisioned the promotion of intellectual property rights. Administration of the Paris and Berne Conventions was transferred to and consolidated in WIPO. In 1977, the Patent Cooperation Treaty (PCT) was adopted under the auspices of WIPO with the objective of providing a more efficient means for inventors to secure patents in different countries. This was a significant step toward harmonization and integration of the international IP system, even though the PCT system does not establish an "international patent" or replace national patent offices.

In the late 1970s and early 1980s, two conflicting trends in IP were converging. Developing countries were demanding increased access to the technology owned and controlled by developed countries within the framework of their demands for a New International Economic Order. At the same time, industry interests in the United States, Europe, and Japan were growing increasingly frustrated with what they perceived as the misappropriation of their intellectual property interests in developing countries. Developing countries demanded reforms at WIPO intended to limit the scope of intellectual property protection, while developed countries demanded stronger rules. This produced a stalemate at WIPO.

The United States, the European Union, and Japan made a strategic decision to shift the focus of the intellectual property debate to another forum, the General Agreement on Tariffs and Trade (GATT). The GATT, up until the mid-1980s, was concerned with regulating international trade in goods, and took little interest in intellectual property matters. However, the trilateral group of industrialized countries perceived that pressure could be exerted on developing countries to accommodate demands for stronger IP protection within GATT because the developing countries were dependent on access to developed country markets for their exports. Thus, in 1986, the Uruguay Round of trade negotiations, including as one of its key components Trade-Related Aspects of Intellectual Property Rights (TRIPS), was launched. After seven years of highly contentious negotiations, the Agreement on Trade-Related Aspects of Intellectual Property Rights (TRIPS Agreement) was concluded in 1993, signed in 1994, and came into force on January 1, 1995. The TRIPS Agreement represented a sea change in the international regulation of IPRs, shifting the central forum for rulemaking to the newly created World Trade Organization (WTO) and transforming the substantive rules. For the time being, the TRIPS Agreement represents the furthest reach of multilateral harmonization efforts.

The results of the TRIPS negotiations were intensely controversial, and remain so. We will be examining the basis for WTO controversy at various points throughout the book. There remain significant differences, particularly as between developed and developing countries, regarding the consequences of the adoption of higher levels of IP protection, notably for areas such as public health. In 2001, WTO Member countries adopted the Doha Declaration on the TRIPS Agreement and Public Health, which emphasized the right of governments to take measures to protect public health and expanded certain TRIPS Agreement flexibilities.

But the fact of controversy at the WTO does not ameliorate the concerns of industry in developed countries, including the United States, the European Union, Switzerland, and Japan, about the level of IP protection and its enforcement around the world. At the present time, it is unrealistic for these countries to seek to strengthen IP protection multilaterally under the auspices of the WTO, again for reasons we will examine. Once again, the principal forum for negotiation may be shifting. While there is an ongoing effort at WIPO to negotiate a Substantive Patent Law Treaty (SPLT), which would result in harmonization of the criteria of patentability, the difference in perspective among developed and developing countries at the WTO manifests itself in the WIPO SPLT negotiations, which negotiations are making slow progress. Efforts to bridge the gaps and render IPRs more conducive to the interests of developing countries has been undertaken within the WIPO Development Agenda, so far without tangible results.

More significantly, IPRs rulemaking has shifted to regional and bilateral trade agreements, and even to plurilateral efforts, involving like-minded groups of countries addressing common IPR substantive and procedural standards. Recently negotiated regional and bilateral trade agreements include detailed commitments on intellectual property rights that are significantly more stringent than TRIPS Agreement rules. These regional and bilateral trade agreements are being pursued by the United States and the European Union with many of their trading partners (including accession partners), and in most instances with success. Concern among developed countries with a perceived lack of attention to IPRs enforcement in developing countries has manifested itself in negotiations among a group of developed countries on an Anti-Counterfeiting Trade Agreement (or ACTA) designed to make it easier to enforce IPRs at the border, as well as to enhance the role of government authorities (e.g., customs) in enforcement. Whether the ACTA negotiations will yield an agreement, and whether these regional and bilateral agreements will serve as "precursors" to new multilateral rules at the WTO or WIPO is not clear. There remain several key major developing country actors, including Argentina, Brazil, China, India, and South Africa, which continue to resist pressures for stronger protection of IPRs, but the national interest changes over time and one should be cautious about predictions.

Bilateral and regional trade agreements should be distinguished from another phenomenon, which is the establishment of regional systems for the grant and/or enforcement of IPRs. The most highly evolved such system is in Europe, where the European Patent Office reviews and grants patents under the European Patent Convention, which might be transformed into a system for the grant of an EU-wide Patent. The European Union has also created a Community Trade Mark (CTM) and harmonized rules across a broad spectrum of IP interests. The Lisbon Treaty has extended the internal authority of the EU institutions in the field of IPRs. Somewhat less evolved regional systems are in place or under development elsewhere.

As a general proposition, there is a broad historical trend toward harmonization, strengthening, and integration of the international intellectual property system at the multilateral level, but this trend is slow-moving owing to differences among the interests of stakeholders in the system. When movement toward integration is blocked at the multilateral level, industrialists attempt to pursue their varying agendas in alternative settings, such as through regional and bilateral trade agreements, and plurilateral agreements. So far, there are limited instances where countries have moved away from the broad trend, in favor of national autonomy. However, there is a substantial interest among some stakeholders in expansion of the public domain. This represents a counterweight to the forces urging strengthening and integration of the international system and increases uncertainty about the speed and future direction of the trend. The current debate on intellectual property protection is characterized by the ongoing search for a proper balance between appropriation and the public domain in the process of shaping the public good of IPRs.

2. Stakeholder Interests

Pressures have long been exerted by multinational industry to move the international system for the regulation of intellectual property toward harmonization and integration. Major multinational corporations assume that a globally harmonized and integrated intellectual property system will serve their interests by allowing them to more efficiently secure protection for their innovations and expressive works, and expand the geographic scope of their rights to exclude others from the market. These enterprises recognize that they are better able to take advantage of a fragmented system (because of their extensive financial resources) than some potential competitors, but this advantage would not seem to outweigh the value of a more integrated system. Major multi-national corporations are the primary driver for stronger intellectual property rights protection around the world.

Yet, even within this multinational stakeholder community concerns are arising about whether proliferation of IPRs and "overprotection" in fields such as computer software may, in fact, be stifling the capacity to innovate and to market new products. More thought is being given to restoring competitive working space. The multinational corporate community is not quite a one-way street in favor of stronger protection.

The IP-protection objectives of the major multinational companies may not be shared by competitors and potential competitors in diverse national markets who want to preserve their own positions on the market. A Korean, Taiwanese, Nigerian, or Chilean manufacturer may not be interested in the more efficient grant of patent rights to a German or American multinational corporation.

National governments tend to promote the interests of enterprises owned and controlled by their own nationals. There are a number of reasons for this. One is that locally owned enterprises are more likely to contribute to national economic development by returning income and profits to the local economy, paying taxes, and employing local labor. There is a widely held belief, evidenced by national government policies around the world, that local ownership and control of business is preferable to foreign control from the standpoint of national economic development and security. Just as local business enterprises are not necessarily keen to further the interests of foreign national competitors by making it easier to protect innovation developed abroad, so the national government for its own economic reasons may not be interested in promoting the interests of foreigners. Also, domestically owned businesses are more likely to make contributions to and further the aspirations of local politicians. Government delegates represent the national constituency in multilateral negotiating fora, and they are likely to be advocating the interests of local national stakeholders on whom they depend for political support.

Yet, there is a counter pressure to acting on protectionist policies in favor of local industry. This is an era of global competition for investment capital, and failure to provide comparable levels of protection for foreign investors (and IP holders) may act as a disincentive to investment. China provides an example of a country with an internal market that is so large and dynamic that it can attract capital even with IPRs policies that to some extent may favor the development of local industry. Most countries do not offer the same market opportunities, and in the competition for capital investment have an incentive for protecting IPRs.

Research communities, including universities and government institutions, increasingly look to IPRs protection as a source of revenue and funding for their work, and take an international perspective. It is not only industrial enterprises that seek to maximize revenues from research and development (R&D), but parts of the public sector and individual researchers as well. The interest of research communities in maximizing revenues from innovation is not limited to the more highly developed countries. Research institutions in developing countries such as India are increasingly active in patenting their innovations in many countries.

There is a countervailing perspective regarding publicly funded R&D. Non-governmental organizations and legislators are asking whether governments and supporting taxpayers are securing adequate benefits when the results of publicly funded research are not made more readily accessible.

There is also a substantial group of public intellectuals who argue that expansion of the "public domain" of knowledge may be preferable to further privatization and exclusion. Whether exclusive control of knowledge is exercised on behalf of government research institutions or the private sector does not change the negative impact of limiting the diffusion of knowledge.

NGOs with widely varying interests are taking an increasingly active role in the international intellectual property system. Whether the issue is protection of the environment, access to medicines, the rights of indigenous farmers, or more equitable distribution of global wealth, NGOs appreciate that the ownership of technology and its implementation may substantially influence their subject matter areas. Civil society is taking part in IP-related discussions and negotiations at multilateral fora in a very active way and acting to offset the narrower interests of industrialists.

The role of intellectual property lawyers should not be overlooked. Patent and trademark lawyers who represent clients before the local IP office do not necessarily have an interest in a "seamless electronically integrated international patent application and granting system." Much of the resistance to extension of the international trademark registration system is based on protecting the financial interests of local IP lawyers.

The foregoing factors, among others, exert pushes and pulls on the evolution of the international intellectual property system.

C. A Brief Introduction to the Forms and Functions of Intellectual Property

Intellectual property is a defined set of the intangible products of human creative activity. Unlike real property and personal property, which is often protected by means of physical security devices (such as fences and other enclosures), intellectual property is mainly protected by sets of enforceable legal rights granted to "owners" or "holders." These legal rights are intended to solve the economic problem described by Kenneth Arrow as the "incomplete appropriability of knowledge."[2] Because intellectual property is intangible and typically easy to copy and transport, it is difficult for business enterprises to capture the full value of investments in it (i.e., competitors can easily appropriate it). Intellectual property rights are an effort to solve this incomplete appropriability problem.

Intellectual property is usually referred to by the form of "right" (or IPR) granted to the holder. So, for example, a "patent" is a set of legal rights granted to an inventor. It is not the invention itself. Historically, the patent and trademark were referred to as "industrial property rights," while the copyright and related rights were referred to as "authors' and artists' rights." However, with the advent of the protection of computer software by copyright, the line between industrial property rights and authors and artists rights blurred and this distinction is no longer particularly relevant.

---

2. Kenneth J. Arrow, *Economic Welfare and the Allocation of Resources for Invention*, in THE RATE AND DIRECTION OF INVENTIVE ACTIVITY: ECONOMIC AND SOCIAL FACTORS 609 (Richard R. Nelson ed., 1962).

Before we introduce the institutions and basic principles that govern the international IP system, it may be useful to briefly introduce or review the forms of IP and the functions they are intended to serve.[3] Bear in mind that these brief introductions are expanded upon in subsequent chapters of the book discussing patents, trademarks, copyright, unfair competition, and *sui generis* forms of protection. The nuances are not introduced here.

1. Patent

The "patent" is a set of rights granted to the inventor of a product or process that is "new" (or "novel"), involves an "inventive step" (or is "nonobvious") and is "capable of industrial application" (or "useful").[4] The inventor must disclose the invention in the patent application in a way that enables others to make the invention without undue experimentation. The minimum term of a patent under the TRIPS Agreement is 20 years from the filing of the application. The holder of a patent may prevent others from making, using, offering for sale, selling, or importing for those purposes the invention during the patent term. As with other IPRs, the rights of the patent holder are qualified by certain important exceptions. The patent is typically referred to as a "hard" form of intellectual property because it generally excludes another person from using the invention without the consent of the patent holder even if the other person independently found the same invention.

The patent is intended to perform three functions: (1) to stimulate inventive activity; (2) to encourage investment in the products of inventive activity; and (3) to disseminate technical information to the public. The extent to which the patent effectively performs these functions has been the subject of long debate. The principal alternative to using patents to stimulate inventive activity is government subsidy (or the establishment of "prize funds"). Economists generally believe that patents are a more efficient policy instrument than government subsidies for promoting investment in innovation, while allowing that in certain circumstances subsidies can be more effective. There is recent concern that an over-proliferation of patents may impede inventive activity, at least in certain fields, as a "patent thicket" grows.

Patents have a cost to society in terms of allowing higher than competitive prices to be charged to consumers, and this cost must be weighed against their positive invention-encouraging effects. In some areas, the social cost of allowing market exclusivity may be quite high. By way of illustration, allowing the inventor of a new cancer drug to prevent others from making it may significantly increase its price and reduce patient access to it. To offset the social cost, the patent term is limited. After some years, generic producers are allowed to copy the drug and enter the market. Nonetheless, there is intense debate about the extent to which patents on pharmaceutical products should be permitted to restrict access to medicines. Prior to the TRIPS Agreement, many countries

---

3. This section is excerpted from Frederick M. Abbott, *Intellectual Property Rights in World Trade*, in HANDBOOK OF INTERNATIONAL TRADE (A. Guzman & A. Sykes eds., 2007) (footnotes partly omitted).

4. The criteria of patentability are referred to by different words in European and American law. European law refers to new, involving an inventive step, and capable of industrial application, while American law refers to novel, nonobvious, and useful.

excluded pharmaceutical and food-related inventions from patenting, or sharply curtailed the rights granted to patent holders.

The social benefits and costs of patenting inventions in different fields of technology differ. High-definition television and cancer treatment serve different social functions, and limiting consumer access to these products has different social effects.

2. Trademark

The "trademark" is a sign or symbol that distinguishes the goods or services of one enterprise from another in commerce. Trademarks may consist of virtually any form of sign, including letters and words, designs, colors, shapes, sounds, and scents.[5] A trademark allows its holder to prevent others from using an identical or confusingly similar sign to identify its goods or services in commerce. Trademark rights may last as long as the right holder continues to use the mark in commerce. In civil law jurisdictions, trademark rights are typically based on registration. In common law jurisdictions, trademark rights may be based either on registration or on use in commerce (the latter referred to as "common law" trademarks).[6] In some jurisdictions, trademark rights may extend beyond the prevention of consumer confusion to encompass the prevention of "dilution" of the trademark holder's interests, that is, third parties may be prevented from "tarnishing" or "blurring" the trademark.

It is generally believed that trademarks serve an efficiency-enhancing function by providing consumers with an easy way to identify products with preferred qualities or characteristics. Consumers come to identify certain "brands" that they prefer, and make purchasing decisions based on brand identification (as a substitute for more costly and time-consuming product testing). Trademarks also provide a vehicle into which business enterprises can invest advertising dollars, stimulating brand identification and "goodwill." Economists are divided as to whether it is useful to encourage investments in goodwill since there is not necessarily a correlation between the usefulness and quality of products and the amount of advertising invested in them. This can lead to market distortions (in which consumers make purchases based on artificially stimulated demand).

3. Copyright

"Copyright" is granted to authors and artists to protect expressive works against unauthorized reproduction or distribution by third parties. Expressive works are broadly defined, and include such things as books, films, music recordings, and computer software. There is, in fact, no express limit on what material might be considered to embody protectable artistic expression. However, copyright does not extend to functional works or ideas. This

---

5. Some jurisdictions impose limitations on the use of single colors as trademarks. The TRIPS Agreement does not mandate the acceptance of single colors, sounds, or scents as trademarks.

6. In both civil law and common law systems, trademark rights are dependent upon "use" of the mark, but registration affects presumptions in favor of the party asserting rights.

principle is often referred to as the "idea-expression dichotomy," with the "idea" excluded from copyright protection. Under the TRIPS Agreement, the minimum term of copyright protection is the life of the author plus 50 years. However, in a number of places, including the United States and the European Union, the duration of copyright has been extended to the life of the author plus 70 years. Copyright also extends to the rights of performers in the fixation of their unfixed performances, and to rights of producers of sound recordings and broadcasters. These latter rights traditionally were protected as "neighboring rights" in European law, but as a consequence of more recent treaty developments are generally now considered the subject of copyright. Copyright also protects the "moral" rights of authors and artists, the extent of protection varying among jurisdictions. Moral rights extend at least to right of the author to be identified with the work, and not to suffer from the mutilation or distortion of the work with which he or she is identified. Copyright is considered a "soft" form of IPR because it does not preclude independent creation by third parties.

Copyright is intended to benefit the public by encouraging authors and artists to create and disseminate their works. As with other forms of IP, it is difficult to assess the economic effects of copyright protection. It is not easy to measure how much creative expression is gained (or lost) as a result of copyright, and what the economic value of that expression is. While movie and music producing companies routinely offer data regarding losses suffered as a result of inadequate enforcement of copyright protection, the figures typically do not reveal the extent to which the claimed losses — which usually refer to lost opportunity costs — should be offset by the economic and social benefit to consumers of unauthorized copies, or of the economic gains/benefits to "pirates." In the well-known Napster court battle between music producers and an online file-sharing service, economists had considerable difficulty estimating what the effect of nonenforcement of copyright protection was on music producers because of difficulties assessing the extent to which losses from uncompensated file sharing were offset by gains from increased artist exposure and consequent CD sales.

4. Design Protection

Designs are covered by various forms of IPRs, including design patent, copyright, trademark and trade dress, and *sui generis* registration systems. The protection of nonutilitarian designs has long been a problematic area for intellectual property law. The traditional "utility patent" is granted with respect to a useful or functional invention. It is not suited to nonfunctional aesthetic design. In a number of jurisdictions, this led to the creation of a separate "design patent" specifically granted to nonfunctional product elements. However, design patenting has a number of drawbacks, including that securing protection is time-consuming and costly. Copyright protection covers expressive works and in principle is suitable for design protection, but many designs include potentially functional elements, resulting in uncertainty at the enforcement stage. Trademark and trade dress also protect design. The design or shape of a product or its packaging may be distinctive and associated with a particular enterprise. However, as with copyright, trademark and trade dress offer protection only for nonfunctional design, and this aspect also creates enforcement uncertainty. To overcome problems with design protection by traditional forms of IP, jurisdictions such as the European Union have established design registration systems with somewhat more flexible standards than those associated with the traditional IPRs.

One of the industries most concerned with design protection is the textile or clothing industry. In this sector consumer preferences change very rapidly, and an expensive time-consuming process for securing protection would not be particularly helpful to the industry. The TRIPS Agreement acknowledges this and obligates Members not to impede the grant of protection by costly examination or publication requirements. The major economic issues associated with design protection arise when industries blur the line between form and function. For example, the most controversial issue in European design protection is the treatment of automobile spare parts, including body panels and motor parts. In its 2001 Design Regulation, the European Union excluded engine components from design protection and put off for future negotiation a decision on whether automobile body parts were covered.[7]

5. Geographical Indication

Geographical indications (GIs) are identifiers that associate a product with a place based on the quality or characteristics of the product or goodwill associated with the place.[8] The classic illustrative GI is "Champagne," that is, the name of a region in France known for producing quality sparkling wines by a specific method. GIs are protected in a variety of ways in different national jurisdictions. The United States protects them by collective and certification trademarks, as well as by a special labeling system for wines and spirits administered by the Treasury Department. The European Union protects them by special registration systems, which typically include elaborate monitoring of production methods. Many Latin American countries protect "appellations of origin" separately from trademarks. In addition, geographical indications are also protected by common and civil law unfair competition regimes.

GIs are controversial. The European Union has been pressing at the WTO to increase the level of GI protection for agricultural products other than wines and spirits (which already enjoy comparatively high protection), but this is resisted by the United States, among others. The European Union is a high cost producer of specialized agricultural products and is seeking higher prices for those products based on GI protection. The United States is a low-cost producer of bulk agricultural products and is concerned about potential market access restrictions from stronger GI protection. Whether other countries support one or the other "camp" in this GIs debate largely depends on whether they are efficient large-scale agricultural producers, on one hand, or are producers of specialized niche products, on the other.

---

7. Council Regulation (EC) No 6/2002 of 12 December 2001 on Community designs, at recitals 12-13.

8. A geographical indication is distinguished from a "mark of origin," which merely identifies the place where a good is produced. The latter is not intended to denote characteristics.

6. Protection of Layout-Design of Integrated Circuits

Integrated circuits (or semiconductors) (IC) are produced on the basis of three-dimensional maps or "mask works" that are used to direct sophisticated equipment that etches circuits on semiconductor materials. In the 1980s, it was unclear whether such mask works could be protected by copyright (since they perform a function), and patent protection is often unsuitable to incremental innovations in IC design. *Sui generis* (or unique) systems of IC layout protection were developed. Such systems can be given effect either through registration or automatic protection. There has been little enforcement activity based on *sui generis* IC layout-design protection, but it is the subject of TRIPS Agreement rules.

7. Protection of Undisclosed Information

Undisclosed information is generally protectable if it is commercially valuable, undisclosed, and the business claiming rights takes reasonable steps to protect it. Protection of undisclosed information is generally (but not exclusively) synonymous with "trade secret" protection. Such protection is provided in a variety of ways, including by specific statute or by unfair competition law. Trade secret protection generally lasts as long as the relevant information remains secret. The TRIPS Agreement specifically requires protection of undisclosed data with respect to new chemical entities in pharmaceutical and agricultural chemical products that is submitted for government regulatory purposes, requiring protection against "unfair commercial use."

Trade secret protection enables businesses to develop and maintain production processes, customer lists, recipes, and other valuable information that provide advantages over competitors. Allowing businesses to protect such information encourages competition and is generally thought to be healthy from an economic standpoint. Trade secret protection is controversial principally when it is abused, such as when businesses demand payment for information that is in the public domain as a condition to providing necessary products or services. The scope of protection of data submitted for regulatory purposes in the pharmaceutical and agricultural sector is highly controversial because the extent of protection helps to determine the speed at which copies (or "generic" versions of "originator" products) can be granted regulatory approval and brought to market.

II. SOURCES OF INTERNATIONAL IP LAW

Intellectual property protection essentially relies on a combination of national, regional, and international law. While specific rights and obligations are mainly — and variably — defined and put into operation by national law (and increasingly also by regional law), international law provides the over-arching framework for interfacing national and regional regulatory systems. It governs the transnational aspects of IPRs. It establishes basic principles for the international IPRs system, and it increasingly plays a role in harmonizing substantive and procedural rules in the process of globalization. The international law of intellectual property is one of the most advanced areas of law of global integration. Though often neglected in general courses on public international law, it offers an impressive body of international law reflected in a number of sources within and beyond those listed in Article 38 of the Statute of the International Court of Justice.[9]

ARTICLE 38

1. The Court, whose function is to decide in accordance with international law such disputes as are submitted to it, shall apply:
   a. international conventions, whether general or particular, establishing rules expressly recognized by the contesting states;
   b. international custom, as evidence of a general practice accepted as law;
   c. the general principles of law recognized by civilized nations;
   d. subject to the provisions of Article 59 [which *inter alia* allows the Court to call witnesses and experts] judicial decisions and the teachings of the most highly qualified publicists of the various nations, as subsidiary means for the determination of rules of law.
2. This provision shall not prejudice the power of the Court to decide a case *ex aequo et bono,* if the parties agree thereto.

This list of sources still reflects the main contemporary sources of international law. At the same time, it may not adequately capture certain of the more recent evolutions in recognized principles of law. It is difficult, for example, to classify basic constitutional principles of international law such as the right to self-determination as purely matters of treaty or customary law. The same holds true for the concept of basic human rights. Moreover, Article 38 does not address the legal nature of recommendations and decisions of international organizations, nor does it capture the phenomenon of soft law. Finally, this list does not establish any formal hierarchy of sources. It leaves the relationship between treaty law and customary law open.

In the context of the international IPRs system, the uncertain relationship among different sources of international law has not so far raised serious difficulties since it has been predominantly grounded in treaty norms. Questions of interpretation and application of these norms have been addressed by reference to the law of treaties. In the future, other sources of international law — in particular "general principles of law" such as good faith — may play a more important role in the international IPRs system, especially as this system is now effectively open to quasi-judicial dispute settlement under the umbrella of the WTO.

A.   Treaty Law

Intellectual property protection in international law is essentially based upon treaty law, both multilateral and bilateral, and both global and regional. The bulk of multilateral agreements relating to intellectual property and administrated by WIPO are classified in terms of intellectual property treaties, global

---

9. The text below is adapted from Thomas Cottier, *Industrial Property, International Law,* in MAX PLANCK ENCYCLOPEDIA OF INTERNATIONAL PUBLIC LAW, available at http://www.mpepil.com/updates.

protection system treaties, and classification treaties. The WIPO web site offers a complete listing, including institutional arrangements and membership of the Convention Establishing the World Intellectual Property Organization, intellectual property protection treaties, and global protection system treaties.[10]

Major treaties are located outside WIPO. The TRIPS Agreement of the WTO establishes the modern backbone of international intellectual standards in all fields of intellectual property, including enforcement mechanisms with which Members of the WTO have to comply. The TRIPS Agreement refers to different treaties, such as the International Convention for the Protection of Performers, Producers of Phonograms and Broadcasting Organizations (Rome Convention) and the Treaty on Intellectual Property in Respect of Integrated Circuits (Washington Treaty). Most importantly, it incorporates the Paris and Berne Conventions (Articles 2 and 9(1), TRIPS Agreement). The TRIPS Agreement builds upon these Conventions, and substantially develops their standards. Incorporation — considered at the time as an act of unfriendly takeover by WIPO — was mainly undertaken in order to link the provisions of the Berne and Paris Conventions to the WTO dispute settlement and render them enforceable within the multilateral trading system. This puts the TRIPS Agreement, with its substantive and procedural standards, at the heart of multilateral and global law relating to intellectual property. The relationship of the Paris Convention and the TRIPS Agreement is found in the *U.S.-Havana Club* decision (discussed *infra,* in various chapters of this book). An introduction to the function and provisions of the TRIPS Agreement is presented later in this chapter (*infra,* p. 28).

Many agreements, like the Convention on the Grant of European Patents (EPC), administered by the European Patent Office in Munich, and comparable systems under the Eurasian Patent Organization, the African Regional Intellectual Property Organization (ARIPO), and the African Intellectual Property Organization (OAPI) are of major regional importance.

Numerous bilateral agreements complete what amounts to one of the most elaborate and complex fields of international law, albeit often neglected and hardly mentioned in general treatises and doctrine. We note that relevant treaty law is not limited to IPRs and trade agreements. An increasing number of agreements provide relevant context, ranging from human rights to environmental agreements. We address them later in this book. Finally, treaty law also encompasses the Vienna Convention on the Law of Treaties, which sets out the relevant provisions on treaty interpretation and also the interrelationship of different agreements.

Beyond treaty law, decisions, recommendations, guidelines, and other forms of soft law play an important role in administrating IPRs, in particular by international organizations such as WIPO or the European Patent Office. It is important to note the importance of reports and recommendations issued by policy making bodies, such as the Organization for Economic Co-operation and Development (OECD) and the United Nations Conference on Trade and Development (UNCTAD). These instruments often amount to soft law and influence the shaping of national law and the interpretation of international agreements.

10. http://www.wipo.int/treaties/en/.

B. Customary International Law

To date, the sources of international law other than treaty law, as expressed in Article 38 of the ICJ Statute, have been of much less importance to the international IPRs system than to the classical domains of international law. Indeed, it would appear that the link between international IP law and the full body of international law has not been fully established. This is not only because IP law has, for a long time, been highly specialized and contained. It is also because international lawyers, as a general proposition, have not exhibited interest in IPRs subject matter comparable to interest exhibited in other areas (e.g., regarding international security law or the law of natural resources), and interdisciplinary links between international lawyers and IP lawyers remain to be further developed in doctrine and practice.

Customary international law is defined both by evidence of state practice and by shared perceptions of law (*opinio iuris sive necessitatis*). Traditionally, rules of customary international law evolve over substantial periods of time as nations engage in more or less consistent patterns of conduct that reflect their shared perception of the required behavior in particular situations.

Nationally and internationally, regulation of IPRs has been a domain of legislation (including treaty). This "positivist" tradition in the IPRs field is likely to change. Regulation of IPRs is subject to the effects of rapid technological change and to interfaces with other regulatory areas. New problems often cannot be solved by recourse to positive rules relating to past technologies. But it may, for that matter, be quite difficult to resolve IP regulatory issues by traditional recourse to customary international law. Pace and circumstances are at odds with customary law, which by tradition has required longstanding practice, and an essentially stable societal and economic environment, to evolve. An example of modern forms of customary protection is the Uniform Domain Name Dispute Resolution Policy at WIPO established through the practice of a full-fledged dispute resolution system short of relying upon treaty law.

C. Precedents and Doctrine

Judicial decisions provide a backbone for the IPRs system. Yet, almost all of the decisions we examine emanate either from national or regional courts, in particular the Court of Justice of the European Union. Outside the EU, the field suffered from a lack of appropriate avenues of international dispute settlement. Until the inception of the WTO, the international IPRs system produced virtually no international legal precedents in the sense of decisions by international adjudicatory authorities. While the ICJ has jurisdiction to adjudicate matters relating to international IPRs conventions (Article 28, Paris Convention and Article 33, Berne Convention), no cases were brought before the Permanent Court of International Justice, and no cases have been brought so far before the ICJ, mainly due to their perceived weakness concerning the enforcement of decisions.

1. WTO Dispute Settlement

With the advent of the TRIPS Agreement, disputes became subject to WTO dispute settlement. From 1995 to December 2010, a total of 168 panel reports and 97 Appellate Body reports were adopted. Most of the 11 cases relating to the TRIPS Agreement that were settled by panels and the Appellate Body (of 28 disputes notified and subject to consultation) by the end of 2010 dealt with issues between industrialized States, limiting disputes with developing countries to initial stages and mainly to matters of law enforcement.

While the decisions of the Dispute Settlement Body are binding, the reasoning of the panel or Appellate Body does not amount to *stare decisis,* as this concept is generally unknown in international law.[11] Future panels are obliged to consider the arguments and reasoning of past GATT panels and WTO panels and AB recommendations, but they may deviate, for good cause, from prior decisions.

National and regional courts giving effect to decisions of WTO panels and the Appellate Body when such decisions specifically affect matters under their jurisdiction would substantially promote the rule of law in the international economic system. Even though not bound by them, national and regional courts should also take into account the reasoning and interpretations of panels and the Appellate Body. It is recommended to follow such reasoning and interpretations unless there are compelling reasons to do otherwise, since it is important to build a coherent system. Overall, the precedents set by the bodies of the WTO will be of more than a merely subsidiary character, as might appear contemplated by Article 38(1)(d) of the Statute of the ICJ.

2. Domestic Court Decisions

Today, most precedents of general importance in the IPRs field stem from national or regional courts. These rulings are not primary sources of international law under Article 38 of the Statute of the ICJ, though they are important in constituting the body of general principles of law and may be used as subsidiary sources. Core concepts, such as the doctrine of exhaustion, are primarily shaped and framed by national and regional courts, and it is important that courts make their decisions while fully informed about trends and developments in other jurisdictions. National and regional court precedents are of key importance to bringing about judicial coherence of the overall system. The international IPRs field could not have evolved without a strong comparativist approach, and such an approach will likely serve well in the future.

3. Doctrine

Article 38 of the ICJ Statute refers to the writings of highly qualified jurists as a subsidiary or secondary source of international law. Recourse to the international academic community could be an important element in bringing about an overall coherence of the IPRs system. Yet, it is too early to tell what influence

---

11. *Stare decisis* doctrine, as it is known in national legal systems, generally requires that legal rules be applied by one nation's courts in a consistent manner in equivalent sets of circumstances. Once a determination has been made as to the proper interpretation of a rule of law, that determination should be applied in comparable cases involving different parties. However, in international law each state is sovereign and, in recognition of this sovereignty, it is accepted that the method of application of a legal rule in one set of circumstances involving a sovereign entity(ies) does not require an identical application of the same legal rule to an equivalent set of circumstances involving another sovereign entity. That is, judicial interpretations in respect of one sovereign entity do not automatically bind another sovereign entity.

prominent authors will have in international IPRs adjudication. The WTO Appellate Body occasionally refers to leading authors. Common law courts (e.g., British and U.S. courts) refer to scholarly works, though this occurs much more frequently in the civil law tradition. The Swiss Federal Court, as example, frequently refers to scholars in order to explore different views, and to substantiate its own decisions.

D.   General Principles of Law

General principles apply extensively to national, regional, and international law, and they have the potential of substantially contributing to the coherence of the overall system. Beyond positive law, these principles are of paramount importance in the operation of intellectual property protection as in any other field of law. They assist in balancing the relationship between private rights and public domain as they are applicable to the conduct of private parties. As IPRs are mainly held and used by private operators, general principles of law are well suited to be applied to the IPRs field in order to assist in preventing and remedying the abuse of rights.

The term "general principles of law," as found in Article 38(1)(c) Statute of the ICJ, does not refer to principles of international law that are formally part of customary or treaty law (such as the principle that treaties should be performed in good faith), but refers instead to principles of law common to the different legal systems of the world. These general principles operate in all areas of the law, including IP regulation. They contain the most valuable general body of law — a record of human nature, experience, and wisdom, often essential to resolving difficult conflicts. It is not intended that national laws be adopted "lock, stock, and barrel," but the principles underlying such laws can be important in filling gaps and lacunae, and they may guide courts in the process of interpreting international and regional law.[12]

General principles of law, recognized in international law, comprise a considerable body of rules that are important to the interpretation and administration of IPRs. There are, to begin with, principles relating to good faith and equity.[13] Most importantly, the doctrines of abuse of rights (*abus de droit*, important in the relationship between IPRs and competition law[14]) and estoppel and acquiescence flow from the principle of good faith.[15] General principles of equity also include: "no one may transfer more than he has"[16] (arguably

---

12. *See generally* OSCAR SCHACHTER, INTERNATIONAL LAW IN THEORY AND PRACTICE 49-58 (Martinus Nijhof Publishers: Dordrecht, Boston, New York 1991); for a comprehensive classical analysis *see* WILFRIED JENKS, THE PROSPECTS OF INTERNATIONAL ADJUDICATION 316-427 (1964); B. CHENG, GENERAL PRINCIPLES OF LAW APPLIED BY INTERNATIONAL COURTS AND TRIBUNALS (1953); CHARLES DE VISSCHER, DE L'ÉQUITÉ DANS LE RÈGLEMENT ARBITRAL OU JUDICIAIRE DES LITIGES DE DROIT INTERNATIONAL PUBLIC (Editions A. Pedone, Paris 1972).

13. For a comprehensive review and analysis, *see* Ralph A. Newman, *The General Principles of Equity,* in EQUITY IN THE WORLD'S LEGAL SYSTEMS: A COMPARATIVE STUDY 599-604 (R.A. Newman ed., Emile Brylant: Brussels 1973).

14. Doctrines regarding abuse of rights flow from the idea that legal entitlements do not confer unfettered discretion regarding the uses that may be made of such entitlements. *See infra.*

15. Closely related doctrines of estoppel and acquiescence refer to circumstances in which parties may as a consequence of their own conduct be precluded from asserting rights that might otherwise have been available to them. *See* Thomas Cottier & Jörg Paul Müller, *Estoppel,* in ENCYCLOPEDIA OF PUBLIC INTERNATIONAL LAW, www.mpepil.com.

16. *Nemo plus iuris transfere potest quam ipse habet.*

important in trademarks and parallel importation); the principle of *lex specialis;*[17] the latter in time rule;[18] the prohibition against retroactive laws;[19] and the principle of proportionality.[20]

General principles have not figured prominently in IPRs adjudication, but some decisions have employed them extensively. For example, the decision of an EPO Technical Board of Appeal (*Procter & Gamble v. Unilever,* discussed below) in which general principles of law in relation to the doctrine of *res judicata* are used as a central source of law in interpreting the EPC. The advent of efficient dispute settlement under the umbrella of the WTO should also enhance the role of general principles.

There are recent evolutions in the field of equity, addressing in particular the goals of sustainable development and human rights. However, concepts such as intergenerational equity are not part of general principles of law common to different legal systems. They will be addressed later in this book.

NOTES AND QUESTIONS

1. Some of the principles of equity may, at least initially, appear somewhat dated — or naive — in the present global business environment, in which the sharp operator is often applauded for taking advantage of opportunity. Yet, consider these principles from the standpoint of the arbitrator called upon to resolve a dispute between enterprises with an interest in maintaining long-term relations. Might the application of some of these principles of fairness help to fashion decisions that accommodate longer-term interests?

III.   THE INTERNATIONAL IP INSTITUTIONS

Governance of the international intellectual property system at the multilateral level is today principally shared by two institutions: the World Intellectual Property Organization (WIPO) and the World Trade Organization (WTO). The relationship between these two institutions and their respective subject matter authorities is not well defined.[21] The existence of two fora with overlapping jurisdiction regarding the same subject matter presents possibilities for inconsistent rulemaking and oversight of implementation. It also raises room for "forum shopping" by all groups with interests in intellectual property matters. A group of countries may conclude that progress on a particular matter

17. Specific rules take precedence over general rules. *Lex specialis derogat generalis.*
18. Absent an intervening rule, a law adopted later in time is presumed to take precedence over a law earlier in time to the extent of a conflict. (*Lex posterior derogat priori.*)
19. Laws should not impose new obligations or displace rights with respect to acts that have already occurred.
20. The rule that laws should not impose obligations in excess of those reasonably necessary to address circumstances that give rise to them. The doctrine of proportionality is a centerpiece of European Court of Justice jurisprudence.
21. Recall that the WTO became involved in IPRs matters because U.S., European, and Japanese business groups grew frustrated with their inability to negotiate higher standards of protection at WIPO. During the GATT Uruguay Round, senior officials at WIPO were not anxious to see another institution assume major responsibility for IPRs subject matter, and there was not a good "spirit of cooperation" between the two institutions during the negotiations.

cannot be made at the WTO, and look to WIPO as an alternative forum. WIPO presents the possibility for reaching agreements among a limited number of states. While its members also favor action by consensus where possible, it will conclude substantive agreements with acceptance by less than all its members. Negotiation at WIPO also has disadvantages. Governments are only negotiating about intellectual property and cannot offer "cross-concessions" in areas such as agricultural trade. In addition, WIPO agreements are not enforceable by withdrawal of trade concessions.

Despite the potential problems raised by the overlap of authority, there are some fairly clear distinctions between the roles of WIPO and the WTO. WIPO administers various treaties that facilitate the grant of IP rights in multiple jurisdictions. These include the Patent Cooperation Treaty and the Madrid Agreement and Protocol (on trademarks). The WTO does not perform a comparable administrative function. In addition, WIPO has substantially more staff devoted to IP matters than the WTO, and a substantial part of WIPO staff efforts are directed at training IP office personnel at the national level, as well as providing assistance with the drafting of national legislation. WIPO tends to engage in negotiations regarding more detailed "technical" aspects of IP regulation, such as defining the criteria for identification of well-known trademarks or on harmonization of patentability criteria. But this more technical facet of WIPO activity might also be undertaken at the WTO where, for example, governments have been negotiating on details concerning geographical indications and the potential for patent application disclosures regarding the source and origin of genetic resources. It perhaps should not be assumed that one of the two fora has a more extensive competence regarding rulemaking on "technical" IP matters than the other. (As a matter of geography, the headquarters of WIPO and the WTO are about a ten-minute walk from each other in Geneva. It is not so difficult for human technical expertise to move between the two organizations.)

We will examine the shared competence of WIPO and the WTO further after briefly introducing the two organizations.

A. WIPO

1. Overview

WIPO introduces its organizational structure and objectives in the following excerpt.

**SUMMARY OF THE CONVENTION ESTABLISHING
THE WORLD INTELLECTUAL PROPERTY ORGANIZATION**

WIPO Convention*

The WIPO Convention, the constituent instrument of the World Intellectual Property Organization (WIPO), was signed at Stockholm on July 14, 1967, entered into force in 1970 and was amended in 1979. WIPO is an

---

* From http://www.wipo.int (01-29-06).

intergovernmental organization that became in 1974 one of the specialized agencies of the United Nations system of organizations.

The origins of WIPO go back to 1883 and 1886 when the Paris Convention for the Protection of Industrial Property and the Berne Convention for the Protection of Literary and Artistic Works, respectively, were concluded. Both Conventions provided for the establishment of an "international bureau." The two bureaus were united in 1893 and, in 1970, were replaced by the International Bureau, by virtue of the WIPO Convention.

WIPO has mainly two objectives. The first is to promote the protection of intellectual property throughout the world through cooperation among States and, where appropriate, in collaboration with any other international organization. The second is to ensure administrative cooperation among the intellectual property Unions established by the treaties that WIPO administers.

In order to attain these objectives, WIPO, in addition to performing the administrative tasks of the Unions, undertakes a number of activities, including:

i.   normative activities, involving the setting of norms and standards for the protection and enforcement of intellectual property rights through the conclusion of international treaties;
ii. program activities, involving legal technical assistance to States in the field of intellectual property;
iii. international classification and standardization activities, involving cooperation among industrial property offices concerning patents, trademarks and industrial design documentation; and
iv. registration activities, involving services related to international applications for patents for inventions and the registration of international marks and industrial designs.

Membership in WIPO is open to any State which is a member of any of the Unions and to any other State satisfying one of the following conditions:

(i) it is a member of the United Nations, any of the specialized agencies brought into relationship with the United Nations, or the International Atomic Energy Agency;
(ii) it is a party to the Statute of the International Court of Justice; or
(iii) it has been invited by the General Assembly of WIPO to become a party to the Convention.

There are no obligations arising from membership of WIPO concerning other treaties administered by WIPO. Accession to WIPO is effected by means of the deposit with the Director General of WIPO in Geneva of an instrument of Accession to the WIPO Convention.

The WIPO Convention establishes three main organs: The WIPO General Assembly, the WIPO Conference and the WIPO Coordination Committee. The WIPO General Assembly is composed of the member States of WIPO which are also members of any of the Unions. Its main functions are, inter alia, the appointment of the Director General upon nomination by the Coordination Committee, review and approval of the reports of the Director General and the reports and activities of the Coordination Committee, adoption of the biennial budget common to the Unions, and adoption of the financial regulations of the Organization.

The WIPO Conference is composed of parties to the WIPO Convention. It is, inter alia, the competent body for adopting amendments to the Convention, for all matters relating to legal-technical assistance and establishes the biennial program of such assistance. It is also competent to discuss matters of general interest in the fields of intellectual property and it may adopt recommendations relating to such matters.

The WIPO Coordination Committee is composed of members elected from among the members of the Executive Committee of the Paris Union and the Executive Committee of the Berne Union. Its main functions are to give advice to the organs of the Unions, the General Assembly, the Conference, and the Director General, on all administrative and financial matters of interest to these bodies. It also prepares the draft agenda of the General Assembly and the draft agenda and draft program and budget of the Conference. The Coordination Committee also, when appropriate, nominates a candidate for the post of Director General for appointment by the General Assembly.

The principal sources of income of the regular budget of WIPO are the fees paid by the private users of the international registration services, and the contributions paid by the Governments of the member States. For the purposes of determining the amount of its contribution, each State belongs to one of 14 classes. . . .

The Secretariat of the Organization is called the International Bureau. The executive head of the International Bureau is the Director General who is appointed by the WIPO General Assembly and is assisted by two or more Deputy Directors General.

The headquarters of the Organization are in Geneva, Switzerland. The Organization has Liaison Offices in Brussels, Belgium, Singapore, at the United Nations in New York and in Washington D.C., United States of America.

The Organization benefits from the privileges and immunities granted to international organizations and their officials to facilitate the fulfillment of its objectives and exercise of its functions and has concluded a headquarters agreement with the Swiss Confederation to that effect.

NOTES AND QUESTIONS

1. A number of developing countries and NGOs have expressed concern about the policy direction of WIPO. They argue that WIPO has been mainly concerned with promoting higher levels of IPRs protection, without adequately accounting for the different roles that IPRs play at varying levels of development. The efforts of these countries and NGOs resulted in the establishment at WIPO of a Provisional Committee on Proposals Related to a WIPO Development Agenda. The Fourth Session of the Provisional Committee on Proposals Related to a WIPO Development Agenda (PCDA) met on June 11-15, 2007. At that meeting, the PCDA approved a list of 45 proposals in a number of areas, including capacity building, technical assistance, norm-setting, and technology transfer, in addition to proposing establishment of a permanent Committee on Development and Intellectual Property at WIPO.[22] In October 2007, the proposal for the Committee was

22. http://www.wipo.int/ip-development/en/agenda/pcda07_session4.html.

adopted by the WIPO General Assembly. The Committee on Development and Intellectual Property held its first meeting in Geneva on March 3-7, 2008.[23] This Committee has a broad mandate to study and make recommendations with respect to improving the intellectual property framework in order to better promote the development and use of technology, especially by developing countries. Documents with respect to the WIPO Development Agenda may be found at http://www.wipo.int.

2. Consider the relationship of industrialized and developing countries in WIPO and the role of emerging economies. Does the Development Agenda entail the return to blocs, or does it rather reflect a constellation of changing coalitions and variable geometry? What is the likely effect of an increasing interest of emerging economy industries in enhanced levels of protection? Where could be particular interests and potentials for developing countries with a large agricultural sector?

2. Substantive and Administrative Rules

The WIPO Convention does not include substantive rules. The rules administered by WIPO are established in separate treaties or conventions between its members.[24] Some of those treaties, such as the Paris and Berne Conventions, principally codify substantive law applicable to the member states; others, such as the PCT, establish procedures for the review of patent applications. The Paris and Berne Conventions are widely adhered to by states, but most of the WIPO treaties, such as the Madrid Agreement on False Indications of Source, have significantly more limited membership. Of the administrative treaties, the PCT has wide membership, but other agreements, such as the Hague Convention on Industrial Design, have more limited membership.

Significant parts of the Paris and Berne Conventions are incorporated by reference in the WTO TRIPS Agreement, as are some references to the Rome Convention and the Treaty on Intellectual Property in Respect of Integrated Circuits.[25] This creates a concrete substantive link between WIPO and the WTO.

The rules of treaties and conventions administered by WIPO are examined throughout this book, so detailed treatment is not given here. The treaties and conventions share certain basic principles, which are discussed later in this chapter.

WIPO plays an active role in the negotiation of new intellectual property rules and agreements. This is typically done through the initial establishment of a committee of experts to analyze and make recommendations about the possibilities for such rules or agreements. This is followed by a drafting phase in which the WIPO members and observers periodically meet to make recommendations and review progress, and in which the Secretariat plays a major drafting

---

23. *New Body on Development and IP Wraps up Inaugural Meeting*, Geneva, March 10, 2008 PR/ 2008/540, WIPO Press Release, http://www.wipo.int/pressroom/en/articles/2008/article_0012. html.

24. The full texts of all treaties administered by WIPO and up-to-date lists of the state parties to them are available at http://www.wipo.int.

25. The Treaty on Intellectual Property in Respect of Integrated Circuits has not come into force because it lacks sufficient ratification by signatories. Nonetheless, its rules are incorporated with modifications into the TRIPS Agreement.

role. If negotiations are sufficiently successful, a diplomatic conference will be convened to consider adoption of the proposed agreement.

3. Dispute Settlement

The WIPO treaties and conventions do not establish their own dispute settlement mechanisms. The Paris and Berne Conventions permit members to initiate dispute settlement before the International Court of Justice (a United Nations body). Up until 2011, no such claim had been brought before the ICJ. In the late 1990s, proposals were made for a stand-alone WIPO interstate dispute settlement mechanism, but these proposals did not move forward largely because of concerns with overlapping jurisdiction with the WTO dispute settlement mechanism. The lack of an internal state-to-state dispute settlement mechanism at WIPO without doubt reduces the possibilities for conflict with the WTO. At the same time, it may leave WIPO as a less attractive forum from an industry standpoint as the possibilities for rule enforcement are less than at the WTO.

There is, however, a robust arbitration mechanism established under the auspices of the WIPO Arbitration and Mediation Center. The initial focus of the Center was to serve as a dispute resolution service provider under the Internet Corporation for Assigned Names and Numbers (ICANN) Uniform Domain Name Dispute Resolution Policy (UDRP). The Center has enjoyed considerable success in this regard, being the leading provider of domain name dispute settlement services. More recently, the Center has increased attention to settlement of more traditional types of intellectual property disputes, such as patent and trademark infringement and licensing disputes, and its arbitration caseload is growing. The role of the Center is considered further in Chapter 3, in connection with domain name disputes, and in Chapter 6 regarding enforcement.

B. WTO

1. Institutional Framework

The World Trade Organization (WTO) is the primary multilateral institution regulating international trade.[26] It was established on January 1, 1995, by the Agreement Establishing the World Trade Organization (WTO Agreement). The WTO succeeded the General Agreement on Tariffs and Trade (GATT), established in 1947, also to regulate trade. The GATT 1947 was concerned almost exclusively with trade in goods and the various regulatory mechanisms, such as tariffs, quotas, and subsidies, which affect such trade. The WTO extends subject matter coverage to trade in services, such as banking and other financial services, and telecommunications. The WTO also extends subject matter coverage to trade-related aspects of intellectual property rights (TRIPS). This is accomplished by the incorporation of the TRIPS Agreement as one of the three "Multilateral Trade Agreements" (MTAs) (along with the GATT 1994

---

26. Information concerning the WTO, including a list of Members, texts of agreements, and dispute settlement decisions, as well as information concerning ongoing work programs and instructional aids, is available at http://www.wto.org.

and the General Agreement on Trade in Services (GATS)) accepted by all WTO Members as part of their participation in the WTO Agreement.[27]

The WTO formally is a one country, one vote organization.[28] Under the WTO Agreement, the countries participating are referred to as "Members." As of December 2010, the WTO had 153 Members, with 30 countries in the process of accession. The WTO Agreement provides voting requirements for making various types of decisions, including majority voting on ordinary decisions[29] and three-quarter majority voting on waivers of compliance.[30] However, the WTO by customary practice (which is referred to in the WTO Agreement and derives from GATT 1947 practice) acts by "consensus" of its Members. Decisions are thus taken if none of the Members present formally objects to the motion.[31] There is an important reason for the consensus voting practice. Unlike the United Nations, which concentrates voting power in the Security Council, the WTO has no mechanism for weighting the vote of its Members, such as by aggregate volume of trade or gross domestic product. In principle, the United States or China has the same voting weight or power as Burundi or Ecuador. The great majority of WTO Members are developing countries. The United States, the European Union, and other high-income economies are not willing to subject their trade policy to majority rule, particularly when they might regularly be outvoted by a bloc of developing countries. It is also doubtful that developing countries would be willing to subject themselves to majority rule in determining their trade interests. They are particularly concerned to protect their sovereignty.

The WTO Agreement obligates the Members to meet at least once every two years in a Ministerial Conference.[32] Since its inception, Ministerial Conferences have been held in Singapore, Seattle, Doha, Cancun, Hong Kong and Geneva. As the name implies, the Ministerial Conference is a gathering of the trade ministers of the Members. The business of the WTO outside the Ministerial Conference is conducted by the General Council, which exercises the powers of the Ministerial Conference when it is not in session.[33] The General Council meets regularly at the headquarters of the WTO in Geneva. In addition to the General Council, there are subsidiary councils for each of the MTAs, including a Council for Trade-Related Aspects of Intellectual Property (TRIPS Council).[34] The TRIPS Council meets in regular session to oversee the implementation of the TRIPS Agreement and conduct other business, including negotiation further to an agenda "built in" to the TRIPS Agreement, and on proposals put forward by the Members. The TRIPS Council according to its rules of procedure acts only by consensus.[35] A matter that might be voted on other than by consensus must be referred to the General Council.

27. Art. II:2, WTO Agreement.
28. Art. IX:1, *id.*
29. Art. IX:1, *id.*
30. Art. IX:3, *id.*
31. Footnote 1 to the WTO Agreement: "The body concerned shall be deemed to have decided by consensus on a matter submitted for its consideration, if no Member, present at the meeting when the decision is taken, formally objects to the proposed decision."
32. Art. IV:1, *id.*
33. Art. IV:2, *id.*
34. Art. IV:5, *id.*
35. Rules of Procedure for Meetings of the Council for TRIPS, Rule 33, WTO Doc. IP/C/1 (1995). In default of consensus in the TRIPS Council, the matter is referred to the General Council.

The consensus voting rule of the WTO and TRIPS Council has advantages and disadvantages. The advantages include that the interests of all Members need to be taken into account in decision making. The smallest and economically weakest country, at least in principle, can veto a decision. On the other hand, the requirement to achieve consensus means that decisions are very difficult to arrive at. It is not easy for 150 countries to agree on anything, much less highly complex international agreements. As the GATT has grown into the highly inclusive WTO, collective decision making has become one of the great challenges. It should not be surprising that there are proposals to reform the decision-making process to allow the possibility for action by less-than-consensus, with appropriate safeguards.

The WTO provides a forum for the Members to negotiate the progressive liberalization of barriers to trade in goods and services with the objectives of increasing global productivity, enhancing employment, encouraging development, and recognizing the importance of doing this in a sustainable way.[36] The WTO seeks to accomplish these objectives through "rounds" of trade negotiations, which are initiated with particular negotiating mandates, and which involve the exchange of offers of trade concessions among the various Members. Ultimately, the results of a round are embodied in new agreements and changes in schedules of commitments of Members in existing agreements.[37] The current round of negotiations was launched in November 2001 in Doha, Qatar, and is referred to as the Doha Development Round (DDR).[38] While the DDR initially was proposed to be completed by 2005, it is difficult to predict when it may be concluded. The prior GATT Uruguay Round lasted seven years (1986-1993).

Changes to the WTO Agreements can also take place outside the context of a negotiating round. For example, the first amendment to the TRIPS Agreement, relating to public health, was agreed upon by the Members in a session of the General Council in December 2005.[39]

The administration of the WTO is carried out by the Secretariat, which is headed by a Director-General (DG), who is appointed by the Members.[40] The DG appoints several Deputy DGs and Directors of various Divisions, including the Intellectual Property Division.

2. Substantive Rules

The WTO Agreements set forth the basic substantive rules governing international trade and the specific commitments of Members on trade liberalization. The entire network of rules regarding trade in goods, services, and TRIPS is extremely complex, reflecting the complexity of the modern global economy. That said, there are two basic principles that underlie the entire system. These

---

36. Preamble, *id.*

37. For example, the GATT 1994 incorporates an annex with the maximum tariff rate commitments or bindings of each Member. The conclusion of the DDR presumably will include revised (and reduced) tariff rate commitments by Members.

38. For a description of the issues at stake in the DDR, *see* 2006 Report of the Committee on International Trade Law of the International Law Association, available at http://www.ila-hq.org.

39. See discussion in Chapter 2, *infra.* The amendment effectively operates as a "waiver" until it is ratified by two-thirds of WTO Members. The waiver will continue in effect until the amendment is accepted by all WTO Members.

40. Art. VI, WTO Agreement.

are the principles of "most favored nation treatment" (MFN) and "national treatment." The MFN principle obligates each Member to extend the same trade concessions to all other Members.[41] The national treatment principle obligates each Member to treat goods imported from other Members the same way it treats domestically produced goods,[42] and to treat foreign services and service providers in covered sectors in the same way that domestic services and service providers are treated.[43] The MFN and national treatment principles also operate with respect to TRIPS, obligating Members to extend the same IP protection to all WTO Members (MFN)[44] and to treat foreign IP applicants and holders on the same basis as domestic applicants and holders (national treatment).[45] We will return to these principles later in this chapter.

In addition to the basic MFN and national treatment principles, the GATT 1994 provides for elimination of quotas (or quantitative restrictions) on trade in goods,[46] and provides for the binding of national tariffs.[47] There are special rules applicable to trade in agricultural products.[48] The WTO Agreements include obligations with respect to the application of antidumping and countervailing duty laws,[49] the application of sanitary and phytosanitary measures with respect to trade in food and agricultural products,[50] and the way that governments procure goods and services.[51] The TRIPS Agreement establishes minimum substantive standards of intellectual property rights protection and enforcement.

Throughout the WTO Agreements, special attention is given to the needs of developing countries, though there is considerable debate about how effective this attention is. As its name would indicate, one of the main objectives of the DDR is to address development-related issues.

3.   Dispute Settlement

One of the main functions of the WTO is to settle disputes among its Members regarding compliance with its rules. The WTO Agreement incorporates the Dispute Settlement Understanding (DSU) applicable to all Members.[52] The DSU provides for the appointment of "panels" to initially decide cases,[53] and establishes an Appellate Body (AB) to decide appeals on questions of law.[54] The decisions of panels and the AB must be formally adopted by Members sitting as the "Dispute Settlement Body" (DSB),[55] but because only a consensus against

---

41. Art. I, GATT 1994, Art. II, GATS and Art. 4, TRIPS Agreement.
42. Art. III, GATT 1994.
43. Art. XVII, GATS.
44. Art. 4, TRIPS Agreement.
45. Art. 3, *id.*
46. Art. XI, GATT 1994.
47. Art. II, *id.*
48. *See, e.g.,* Agreement on Agriculture.
49. *See* Articles VI & XVI, GATT 1994, Agreement on Implementation of Article VI of the General Agreement on Tariffs and Trade 1994, and Agreement on Subsidies and Countervailing Measures.
50. Agreement on Sanitary and Phytosanitary Measures.
51. Agreement on Government Procurement.
52. Art. III:3, WTO Agreement, and Annex 2 (Understanding on Rules and Procedures Governing the Settlement of Disputes).
53. *E.g.,* Art. 6, DSU.
54. Art. 17, DSU.
55. Arts. 16 & 17.14, DSU.

adoption (a so-called negative consensus) defeats the adoption of a panel or AB "report," for all practical purposes the panel and AB decisions are automatically adopted.[56]

The DSU applies to cases arising in relation to intellectual property rights. Before the adoption of the TRIPS Agreement, issues relating to intellectual property protection were litigated under the provisions of the GATT, and issues may continue to arise under all the WTO agreements. Today, the TRIPS Agreement is the main instrument addressing intellectual property rights and subject to dispute settlement,[57] although there are certain qualifications relating to complaints involving "nonviolation nullification or impairment" causes of action.[58] We will examine the non-violation complaint in Chapter 6, section II.

The DSU establishes rules of procedure relating to the establishment of panels, the powers of panels and the AB, and the time frame for decision making. In general, the time period from the initiation of a complaint by a Member to the rendering of a decision by the AB should not exceed two years.[59] Panels of three members are appointed by the agreement of the parties to a dispute, but if the parties cannot agree on the panelists (which is commonly the case), they are appointed by the Director-General of the WTO.[60] The panels hold hearings where the complaining and responding parties argue their cases and present evidence. Members other than the complainant and respondent may participate as third-party observers in the proceedings.[61] The panels issue preliminary and final reports that decide issues of law and fact and may make recommendations.[62] The usual form of recommendation is to request a Member whose law or practice is found to violate WTO law to bring its measures into conformity.[63] Panels do not typically make specific recommendations regarding changes to law or practice.

A complaining or responding party may request Appellate Body review of a panel decision.[64] The AB automatically accepts the case for review — it is not discretionary like the U.S. Supreme Court certiorari process — and examines the legal analysis of the panel. The AB is not expressly authorized to reexamine factual determinations, but as with domestic court processes it is often difficult to separate review of law and review of fact.

When the AB issues its report (or if the panel decision is not appealed), the DSB adopts it. A Member against which findings have been made has a reasonable period of time (rebuttably presumed to be a maximum of 15 months) to bring its measures into conformity.[65] If it fails to do this, the complaining Member is authorized to withdraw trade concessions up to the level of harm it is suffering as a consequence of the noncompliance.[66] The withdrawal of concessions preferably is directed to the same category — goods, services, or

---

56. In theory, the WTO membership could find some decision of a panel or the AB sufficiently offensive that even the party that won the case would object to its adoption.

57. Art. 64, TRIPS Agreement.

58. Art. 64.2-3, *id.*

59. Art. 20, DSU (including extensions).

60. Art. 8, *id.*

61. Art. 10, *id.*

62. Art. 11, *id.*

63. Art. 19, *id.*

64. Art. 17, *id.*

65. Art. 21, *id.*

66. Art. 22, *id.*

IPRs — as the complained-against measure, but Members are allowed to with-draw "cross-concessions" when withdrawing a measure in the same category would not be effective. The questions of whether a Member has brought its measures into conformity or withdrawn an appropriate level of concessions are each subject to arbitration, generally by the same panel that decided the dispute.[67]

The possibility for enforcement of WTO dispute settlement decisions by withdrawal of trade concessions was one of the factors that motivated the United States, the European Union, and Japan to select the WTO as the alternative forum to WIPO. WTO dispute settlement has "teeth," although those teeth are more likely to favor strong economies. Small economies may find it very diffi-cult to withdraw trade concessions against large economies with which they trade for at least two reasons. First, their imports tend to constitute only a small part of the exports of the larger economies, so the impact on the larger economies may be very minor. Second, by imposing higher tariffs or quotas on imports from their trading partners, small economies may damage their own producers and consumers, making the exercise counterproductive. On the other hand, when a country like the United States or an entity like the European Union withdraws concessions from a small economy country, the impact on the small economy country may be quite severe because it is dependent on exports to the country withdrawing concessions. Recently, following success in separate dispute settlement actions, Ecuador threatened to withdraw TRIPS concessions from the European Union, and Brazil threatened to withdraw TRIPS conces-sions from the United States, and in each case the complaining developing country party appears to have achieved a favorable negotiated outcome.[68]

4. The TRIPS Agreement

The TRIPS Agreement performs a number of functions in the WTO legal system. First, the Agreement adopts certain generally applicable principles. These principles include national treatment,[69] most favored nation (MFN) treatment,[70] and the right of each Member to determine its own policy and rules with respect to "exhaustion of rights."[71] These general principles are applicable to all forms of intellectual property covered by the Agreement, and are discussed in the next section.

Second, the TRIPS Agreement prescribes minimum substantive standards of IPRs protection for all WTO Members.[72] It does this by incorporating parts of the Paris, Berne, Rome, and Washington[73] Conventions[74] and by prescribing

---

67. Art. 22.6-7, *id.*

68. *See* Frederick M. Abbott, Cross-Retaliation in TRIPS: Options for Developing Countries, ICTSD Programme on Dispute Settlement and Legal Aspects of International Trade, Issue Paper No. 8, April 2009, International Centre for Trade and Sustainable Development, Geneva. Antigua and Barbuda similarly won a WTO case against the United States and has threatened to withdraw concessions in TRIPS, but so far there is no settlement.

69. Art. 3, TRIPS Agreement.

70. Art. 4, *id.*

71. Art. 6, *id.*

72. Part II, *id.*

73. The Treaty on Intellectual Property in Respect of Integrated Circuits was concluded in Washington, D.C., and is sometimes referred to as the "Washington Convention."

74. *E.g.*, arts. 2 & 9.1, TRIPS Agreement.

additional norms. It recognizes that Members may implement the substantive standards in accordance with their own customs and practices, leaving flexibility as to the manner in which the norms are translated into national law.[75] The Agreement refers to seven categories of intellectual property and its subject matter scope is generally limited to those categories.[76] However, because the Agreement incorporates rules of WIPO Conventions that refer to forms of IP not specifically mentioned in the TRIPS Agreement (e.g., Article 8 of the Paris Convention regulates "trade names," which are not specifically mentioned in the TRIPS Agreement), the scope of subject matter coverage is somewhat broader than would be ascertained by reference only to the TRIPS Agreement text.[77]

Third, the TRIPS Agreement requires that Members make provision for adequate and effective enforcement of IP rights, and it lays out a number of express requirements in terms of availability of administrative or judicial processes and remedies.[78] The Agreement also seeks to provide due process protection for those against whom IP claims are asserted. The preamble of the TRIPS Agreement indicates that intellectual property rights are "private" rights. This was included to reinforce that private holders of IPRs are expected to pursue enforcement of their rights in administrative and judicial proceedings, and that governments (with some limited exceptions spelled out in the Agreement) are not expected to "police" IPRs enforcement.

Fourth, the TRIPS Agreement recognizes the importance of maintaining competitive markets. It expressly authorizes Members to regulate IPRs by application of competition laws.[79] It also encourages cooperation among competition authorities.[80]

Fifth, the TRIPS Agreement gives special attention to the situation of developing and least developed countries.[81] For the most part, this was accomplished by incorporation of transitional arrangements that extended the time for compliance with various obligations. It is also reflected in the preamble and the provisions on objectives and principles.

Sixth, the TRIPS Agreement establishes institutional arrangements.[82] This includes defining the role of the TRIPS Council and making provision for further negotiations on prescribed subject matter (the "built-in" agenda) as well as subject matter put forward by the Members.[83] The responsibilities of the TRIPS Council include review of the implementation of TRIPS commitments by the Members.

Seventh, the TRIPS Agreement incorporates dispute settlement under the DSU.[84] As noted earlier, this includes a moratorium on non-violation nullification or impairment complaints, which remains in effect in 2011.

The substantive and procedural rules of the TRIPS Agreement will be examined throughout the book.

---

75. Art. 1.1, *id.*
76. Art. 1.2, TRIPS Agreement.
77. The WTO Appellate Body addressed this issue in respect to trade names in the *U.S.-Havana Club* decision, *infra* Chapter 3.
78. Part III, *id.*
79. *E.g.,* arts. 8.2 & 40, *id.*
80. Arts. 40.3-4, *id.*
81. *E.g.,* Preamble, arts. 7-8, 65-67, *id.*
82. Part VII, *id.*
83. Art. 71, *id.*
84. Art. 64, *id.*

Before doing so, the following excerpts address the relationship of the IP standards and traditional trade rules of the GATT and the WTO and the history of negotiations.

THE AGREEMENT ON TRADE RELATED ASPECTS OF INTELLECTUAL PROPERTY RIGHTS (TRIPS)

Thomas Cottier*

FROM TARIFFS TO INTELLECTUAL PROPERTY

It is important to describe at the outset the inherent linkages between trade regulation and intellectual property protection and to understand the sequencing and the reasons thereof. The lack of appropriate protection of IPRs results in trade restrictions. This should be addressed in the proper context of what I call third generation trade barriers.

Trade policy in the early post-World War II era focused on the gradual reduction of tariffs and the elimination of preferential systems. Tariffs, the first generation of barriers, were high, stemming from the protectionist policies of the great depression of the 1930s. In addition, preferential tariffs existed within the colonial systems. After the failure to establish the International Trade Organization, based upon the Havana Charter, the 1947 General Agreement on Tariffs and Trade ("GATT") provided, in essence, a framework for a gradual and, as it turned out, successful process of tariff reductions. In seven rounds of multilateral negotiations, tariffs on manufactured goods, which averaged forty percent in 1947, were reduced by the conclusion of the Tokyo Round in 1979 to an average of 4.7 percent in the main industrialized nations. Further cuts were achieved in the Uruguay Round, the eighth round of multilateral trade negotiations, and the Round resulted in the decision of developing countries to bind many tariffs. Importantly, all quantitative restrictions were tariffied under the new Agreement on Agriculture. The average tariff reduction achieved by the 117 participants during the Uruguay Round negotiations amounted to forty percent.

The provisions of the GATT were designed to accompany tariff reductions and to prevent circumvention of tariff bindings by other means, in particular quantitative import restrictions, subsidies or discriminatory taxes on imports. Indeed, the gradual reduction (and even the elimination of tariffs within customs unions and free trade arrangements) increasingly shifted the emphasis in the negotiations to non-tariff measures, which began to replace tariffs as the main instrument of governmental trade policy in order to protect domestic industries and products. Quantitative restrictions, export subsidies, anti-dumping measures, technical norms and standards, balance of payment measures, labeling requirements, import licensing, rules on government procurement, "voluntary" import obligations or export restrictions ("grey area" measures such as voluntary export restraints or "VERs," and orderly marketing arrangements or "OMAs") and other imaginative tools became widely-used instruments for economic and political ends, both in developing and industrialized countries. They form a second generation of barriers. Such non-tariff

* AB-1997-5, WT/DS50/AB/R, 15 Dec. 1997.

measures became, in addition to the classical process of tariff reductions, the main subject of trade negotiations in the Tokyo Round. The Tokyo Round agreements on non-tariff measures were further developed in the Uruguay Round, and new ones, in particular on safeguards (including a prohibition of grey area measures) and textiles were added.

As a result of the substantial tariff reductions and increasing legal disciplines in the field of non-tariff measures, a third generation of non-tariff barriers emerged during the 1980s. These barriers encompassed a number of issues, ranging from domestic farm support, to the restrictive regulation of service industries and investments, and finally, the protection of intellectual property. What do these subjects share in common? They stem from different fields of law, public and private, but the common trait is that they all are foremost part of *domestic* legal systems. They are not directly geared to border measures and classical international trade relations, but they have been affecting such relations more and more in terms of limiting market access while other barriers were gradually dismantled or at least legally disciplined. The great political difficulty in reaching final agreement on important issues in the Uruguay Round, such as the reduction of agricultural support, but also the failure to achieve substantial streamlining of conditions for investment, or to bring about significant liberalization of trade in services beyond binding existing levels of market access (a first and important step to establish a framework for liberalization), all stemmed from this development — turning more and more to areas of domestic law, beyond simple regulation of imports and exports.

The main difficulties to be settled in the area of intellectual property had similar roots. The patentability of pharmaceuticals, foodstuffs or living matter, i.e., how far exceptions to patentability should be allowed to go, or, in copyright, how the relationships of authors, producers, performers and users should be arranged, are primarily matters of domestic law and policy. At the same time, they are perhaps the most prominent examples of how far international negotiations and regulations have penetrated socially, ethically or culturally sensitive contemporary issues concerning the domestic political process.

International trade law has come a long way. It has left the area of mere transboundary action. More than ever before, international trade regulation now seeks to assure fair competition in a globalizing market economy. Foreign and domestic economic affairs can no longer be separated; and the increasing importance and attention paid to foreign policy in general is a natural effect of such developments. Today, efforts under the Doha Development Agenda aim, *inter alia,* at developing disciplines on anti-trust rules, on investment and enhanced transparency in government procurement.[85] These new areas continue the move towards the development of global rules on domestic conditions of competition beyond border measures, which essentially began in the Uruguay Round with the intellectual property and services negotiations.

The Uruguay Round mandate to negotiate on intellectual property resulted in what amounts to the most comprehensive instrument ever adopted in the field. Many consider it to be one of the main, if not the main, achievement of the

---

85. *Ministerial Declaration,* adopted on November 14, 2001 at the Ministerial Conference, Fourth Session, Doha, November 9-14, 2001, WT/MIN(01)/DEC/1, November 20, 2001, ¶¶20-26. The so-called Singapore issues also contain a future mandate on trade facilitation; *see* THE SINGAPORE ISSUES AND THE WORLD TRADING SYSTEM: THE ROAD TO CANCUN (Swiss State Secretariat of Economic Affairs and S. Evenett eds., 2003).

Round. Others in hindsight, for reasons already discussed, identify a fundamental and fatal error in placing IPRs under the umbrella of the WTO; it is argued that trade rules in favor of freer trade and market access are fundamentally at odds with the allocation of exclusive rights and monopolies under the very same instrument. Many economists fear that the balance tipped too much towards exclusive or monopoly rights, profoundly at odds with freer trade. For them, as mentioned before, the negotiating history suggests that many countries were forced into a strange agreement under the single undertaking approach of the Uruguay Round in return for other benefits expected, but without an inherent linkage to trade liberalization. The TRIPs Agreement is thus seen by some as an alien and misplaced body of law in the WTO.

Two counter-arguments should be made and stressed. First, the negative point of view ignores the fact that intellectual property is not the only field encompassing what was described above as a new generation of trade regulation. Other areas are in principle, equally structured and follow the patterns of positive or prescriptive integration. Rules relating to safeguards, dumping, subsidies, and agriculture are equally harmonizing, albeit setting maximum, and not minimum standards. To the extent that Members make use of such policy instruments, they are obliged to respect a set of well-defined disciplines aimed at excluding excessive recourse and use. Second, the contradiction between trade liberalization and exclusive rights is a formal one. In substance, there is no difference in principle between exclusive rights and freer trade. Intellectual property rights are an inherent part of the international trading system. The evolution of intellectual property disciplines in the European Communities both under free movement of goods and competition rules, despite the rule that property rights *per se* remain within the competence of the Member States, proves the point on an international level. Every rule-based trading system depends on intellectual property protection, to the extent that it presupposes property rights over traded goods and services. Whether or not the effects are beneficial or detrimental to national and global welfare depends on the balance achieved. Lack of, or insufficient protection amounts to *de facto* restrictions on market access, as exported products will be replaced by both generic and copied products that free-ride on research and development, investment in creative activities and in quality control and product differentiation undertaken elsewhere. On the other hand, lack of appropriate limitations on rights may unduly hamper the flow of goods and services. The real issue is one of balancing different policy goals. This is the core of the matter, upon which fruitful discussions between proponents and critics of intellectual property protection should focus. The proper debate is one of degrees and levels of protection, rather than protection *per se* or the existence of the TRIPs Agreement in the WTO.

URUGUAY ROUND NEGOTIATIONS

The complexity and comprehensiveness of the TRIPs Agreement cannot be fully understood without recalling the negotiating process through which it was concluded. It may be described as one of the most successful operations in building coalitions, partnerships and, above all, creating a mutual learning process.

At the end of the Tokyo Round, the United States and the European Community launched negotiations on a draft Anti-Counterfeit Code. That effort ceased when intellectual property was included in the 1986 negotiating mandate for the Uruguay Round, which as a political compromise was limited to its "trade-related aspects." The initiative was eventually supported by U.S. estimates that its industries suffered losses of some 24 billion dollars in 1986 as a result of inadequate protection of intellectual property and related investments. At that time, no estimates were available for other countries, in particular for European industries. In the beginning, the European Community was reluctant to commit itself on the issue, but in the course of the negotiations, it gradually became one of the major *demandeurs*.

The seven-year negotiations went through three phases. A long process of fact-finding, which also worked as a tool for mutual education, led to comprehensive proposals by various contracting parties. In the second phase, intensive negotiations took place after the Montreal mid-term review (December 1989) and the April 1990 Ministerial Decision. The work was successfully concluded in December 1991, when the draft TRIPs Agreement was included in the "Dunkel text." During the last phase, efforts were aimed at preserving the results achieved and avoiding jeopardizing the results by counterproductive new IP proposals, as well as avoiding a deadlock in the negotiations on other IP issues, relating to agriculture or audiovisual services. Unlike the first two phases, the last phase was marked by conflicting interests between the United States and the EC on copyright issues (cultural aspects, levies on blank tapes, and national treatment of collecting societies).

The results were made possible by various factors, many of which are interesting for the purposes of a general assessment of the importance of intellectual property. To a great extent the results exceeded the initial expectations.

The educational process in the first phase led to a change in the attitude of a majority of developing countries toward the traditional UNCTAD approach of regarding higher protection of intellectual property as detrimental to the development of those countries. Negotiations were frank, and conducted by well-informed delegations. Complaints that many developing countries could not fully grasp the scope of obligations entailed by an IP agreement are not well founded, perhaps with the exception of complaints from some African States that were not prepared or able to make the necessary resources available during the negotiations. But there was a strong group of countries, including Brazil and India, which resolutely defended their interests, as well as those of small and often absent delegations. The efforts of these countries were reflected in key provisions, such as those relating to the recognition of social and developmental goals, compulsory licensing, and restrictive business practices.

The developing countries eventually recognized the importance of intellectual property protection as a prerequisite, albeit not the only one, for foreign direct investment and transfer of technology. In that respect, the decisive position in favor of IPRs maintained by the newly industrialized Asian economies, the political and economic transformation of Central and Eastern European countries, as well as the growing competition between those countries in order to make their markets more attractive, undoubtedly played an important role, within the context of a globalizing world economy, in reaching an agreement. Developing countries subsequently discovered the virtue of the multilateral system as a bulwark against unilateral pressure, in particular that of the United States (through the Super 301 procedure of the Trade Act). They also saw the TRIPs Agreement as a means to reinforce their position with respect to trade in goods: the potential of reprisals through the withdrawal of concessions in the field of intellectual property enhanced their negotiating power on market access to Europe and the United States. Last, there was a clear linkage, albeit not openly and formally stated as such, between the TRIPs negotiations and those in the fields of agriculture and textiles. No breakthrough on TRIPs would have been possible without middle and long-term prospects of better market access conditions for developing countries in those two areas.

NOTES AND QUESTIONS

1. It is important to note that the TRIPS Agreement is not the only instrument in WTO addressing intellectual property rights. The provisions of GATT and other agreements may also be of relevance in assessing national IP-related regulations. Prior to the adoption of the TRIPs Agreement, important cases were dealt with under the rules of the General Agreement on Tariffs and Trade which, *inter alia*, addresses the protection of IPRs in terms of an exception in Article XX(d).
2. IP-related cases decided under the GATT regime included *The United States Manufacturing Clause*, Report of the Panel adopted 15 June 1983, L/5609–31 S/74 (renewal of import restrictions for copyright protected works not consistent with the Provisional Protocol of Accession); and *United States–Section 337 of the Tariff Act of 1930*, Report by the Panel, adopted 7 November 1989, L/6439–36 S/345 (special administrative and judicial proceedings for imported patent protected products inconsistent with principle of national treatment under Article III and not justified under exceptions of GATT Article XX).
3. Consider whether the rules of GATT are still of relevance for IPRs, or whether all the pertinent issues today are absorbed by the TRIPS Agreement. The issue will be of particular relevance in the context of exhaustion of rights, which pertains both to the TRIPS Agreement and to GATT as a matter of import restriction under Article XI. Consider also the important role that GATT Article V prescribing freedom of transit may continue to play.

C. Other Multilateral Institutions

WIPO and the WTO are the principal regulatory institutions for the international intellectual property system, but do not possess a shared monopoly (or duopoly) over the regulation of IPRs at the multilateral level. A substantial number of other multilateral institutions play a regulatory role. Ultimately, this raises questions of "coherence" among all of these legal regimes.

A significant number of United Nations agencies are active in IPRs regulation. UN human rights treaties, such as the UN Convention on Economic, Social, and Cultural Rights, address IPRs, and the UN Human Rights Commission has issued a number of reports on IPRs matters. The United Nations Conference on Trade and Development (UNCTAD) provides technical assistance and training in the IPRs area, as well as preparing analytic studies. The UN Development Programme (UNDP) and the UN Environment Programme (UNEP) each study the impact of IPRs on their respective area of competence. UNESCO adopted in 2005 a Convention on the Protection of Cultural Diversity, which promotes the protection of national cultural institutions and may affect trade in intellectual property-protected goods and services. UNAIDS and

UNICEF assist in supplying pharmaceutical products to developing countries and become involved in IPRs issues in this context.

The Food and Agriculture Organization (FAO) has addressed IPRs in its International Treaty on Plant Genetic Resources in Food and Agriculture.

The Convention on Biological Diversity (CBD) obligates bio-prospectors to obtain the prior informed consent of the host government before exploring for and/or removing genetic resources, and to make provision for the equitable sharing of benefits from their exploitation. These requirements are closely related to patenting of genetic resources.

The World Health Organization (WHO) is considering mechanisms for promoting pharmaceutical research and development using mechanisms in addition to the patent, and has called attention to the potential conflict between trade-related intellectual property rules and access to medicines.

The World Bank studies and provides guidance on intellectual property matters, including with respect to the use of bank funding to purchase medicines and the role of IPRs in transfer of technology for addressing climate change.

The Organization for Economic Cooperation and Development (OECD), which is limited in membership to developed countries, studies and reports on intellectual property issues.

We will revert to policy issues addressed by these various multilateral institutions throughout this book.

IV. REGIONAL AND BILATERAL ARRANGEMENTS

There are different kinds of regional institutions relating to intellectual property. Some, like the European Patent Office, are specifically concerned with intellectual property matters. However, this is not the most common type of regional IP institution. Many, if not most, regional integration agreements — including customs unions and free trade areas — include chapters or provisions relating to intellectual property. These provisions may be implemented by regional institutions, or by national governments carrying out their regional obligations.

The role of regional and bilateral trade and investment agreements in establishing intellectual property standards must be emphasized. These limited membership agreements have dramatically grown in number and scope over the past decade. For the past several years, negotiations at the regional and bilateral level constituted the most dynamic part of IPRs rulemaking. WIPO conventions and the TRIPS Agreement do not alone provide a comprehensive sense of the rules governing the international IP system.

Representative terms of regional and bilateral agreements will be examined throughout the book. In the next section, we will consider how the regional and bilateral agreements fit (or fail to fit) within the context of a multilateral trading system based on most favored nation treatment, which is a principle of non-discrimination among countries.

A significant number of recent regional and bilateral agreements have been negotiated in circumstances of asymmetric bargaining power. By this we mean that one country involved in the negotiations had a much larger economy than, and provided a major source of export revenue for, other countries involved in the negotiations. This gave the first country effective power to control the terms of the resulting agreement — a "take it or leave it" situation.

A. *Regional Integration Arrangements*

Regional integration arrangements differ substantially in terms of their political, economic, and social objectives. Some regional integration efforts embody strong political commitments, including the creation of regional governing institutions. Others are principally directed toward more narrow trade objectives, such as elimination of regional tariffs. Furthest along among the former, in terms of institutional development, is the European Union, which now encompasses 27 member states, and regional institutions including the Council, Commission, Parliament, and Court of Justice.

1. European Union

The European Union, or EU, as it is known today, is the most fully integrated among the many regional arrangements functioning around the world. The inception of the EU generally can be traced to the entry into force of the Treaty of Rome in 1958 establishing the European Economic Community (EEC) among six European states. From the late 1950s until December 2009, the arrangement initially constituted by the Treaty of Rome was referred to by various different names depending on which of the constitutive agreements and related institutions were being invoked (e.g., European Community, European Communities, or European Union). However, with the entry into force of the Lisbon Treaty in December 2009, the name "European Union" is now settled to identify the regional arrangement presently constituted by 27 member states in Europe.[86] There are two principal constituent instruments, the Treaty on European Union (TEU) and the Treaty on the Functioning of the European Union (TFEU). The two Treaties have the same "legal value."[87] Although it is tempting to ascribe the TEU a more "political" character and the TFEU a more legal or instrumental character, the distinction between the two Treaties is not so clear, and the use of two constitutive documents, as opposed to use of a single consolidated document, appears mainly to derive from historical factors.

We discuss the naming convention to help alleviate confusion by references in legislative and judicial decisions throughout the remainder of the book. Until 2010, the EU was a Member of the WTO under the name "European Communities," and WTO dispute settlement decisions refer to the "EC." The European Court of Justice (ECJ), now referred to as the Court of Justice of the European Union (the abbreviation ECJ is still used in practice as no consensus on an alternative has been established until now), mainly decided cases involving the "EC Treaty," but also some other instruments depending on the specific subject matter at issue. The history of the transformation from the EEC in 1958 to the EU in 2009 is the subject of a voluminous literature. For present

---

86. *See* Article 1, Treaty on European Union.
87. *Id.*

purposes, we focus on key developments and issues that affect regional and international IP law. Questions regarding how the EU makes and implements internal IP law, and how EU IP policy is given effect internationally, remain very much alive. The evolution of the EU has not simplified matters regarding IP law very much.

The EU is presently comprised of 27 member states, and there are procedures for accession of new members. There are four principal institutions of the EU: the European Council/Council, the European Parliament, the European Commission, and the ECJ. The European Council is comprised of the heads of state of the member states, but this body meets relatively infrequently, and day-to-day business from the member state perspective is conducted by the "Council" that is made up of senior representatives of the member states that may vary depending on the subject matter under consideration. The Council is essentially the EU institutional body of the governments of the member states. The Council plays a key role in legislating for the EU, and at least through the late 1980s was principally responsible for promulgating EU legislation. The Council votes in different ways depending on the circumstances spelled out in the Treaties, whether by majority, qualified majority, or unanimity. Each member state has a single representative on the Council, yet the population and economic weight of the member states is quite different. "Qualified majority" assigns different weights to votes of the member states to take these differences into account.

The role of the European Parliament has grown steadily since the late 1980s. In early days of the EU, the Parliament was largely a consultative body that did not have authority to control the adoption of legislation. With the entry into force of the Lisbon Treaty, the Parliament is now effectively a full partner with the Council in the adoption of EU legislation, and this has changed the dynamic of EU lawmaking considerably. The Parliament is composed of members (MEPs) directly elected by the citizens of the member states. The Parliament typically acts by majority vote of its members.

The Commission is the executive arm of the EU, composed of "Directorates General" headed by "Commissioners." For purposes of international IP law, the most relevant Directorates are "Internal Markets" (responsible for internal EU IP law), "Trade" (responsible for external IP relations), and "Competition" (responsible for competition law), though certainly other Directorates can be and are important in some IP-related discussions. The Commission is responsible for proposing EU legislation to the Council and Parliament, and for overseeing the implementation of EU law. The Directorates and Directors General (DGs) are roughly analogous to the Cabinet-level Departments (or Executive Agencies) of the U.S. federal government (e.g., the Commerce, State, and Treasury Departments), and their "Secretaries."[88] In the EU, legislative proposals must originate with the Commission (unlike in the United States where Congress is free to initiate legislation on its own).

The Court of Justice of the European Union or ECJ is responsible for the definitive interpretation of the EU Treaties. The ECJ is comprised of one judge from each member state, so presently 27 judges, though cases are typically heard by smaller panels or "chambers." The ECJ adopts decisions by a collegial process, and opinions are rendered by the Court. There are no "minority" or

---

88. Bear in mind that in the United States, the conduct of external trade negotiations is the responsibility of the United States Trade Representative (USTR), also a Cabinet-level official.

dissenting opinions. This collegial procedure was adopted early on to avoid even the appearance of potential bias based on the nationality of the judges that might have undermined the role of the Court. Most cases come before the ECJ as referrals or references from the courts of the member states that seek definitive interpretation of the EU Treaties. This is the procedure by which cases involving individuals (individual and corporate) come before the Court. The ECJ also hears challenges to the validity of EU legislation or implementing acts. The Council, Commission, Parliament, and member states may initiate claims before the ECJ, including against each other. There is a subsidiary body to the ECJ, the "General Court" (formerly known as the "Court of First Instance"). The General Court generally hears claims involving administrative actions taken at the EU level, and which are generally subject to further appeal to the ECJ. Important to the discussion of intellectual property, the TFEU includes a provision authorizing the establishment of specialized courts associated with the General Court (Article 257), and authorizes adoption of legislation conferring jurisdiction on the ECJ "in disputes relating to the application of acts adopted on the basis of the Treaties which create European intellectual property rights. These provisions shall enter into force after their approval by the Member States in accordance with their respective constitutional requirements" (Article 262). These provisions will be further addressed as we consider the status of the EU Patent Regulation and associated judicial arrangements.

The EU institutions legislate with three types of acts: the "regulation," "directive," and "decision."[89] A "regulation" is a legislative act that is directly effective in the law of the member states. A "directive" is an instruction to the member states to achieve a specified result, but leaving the "form and methods" to accomplish the result to the member states to which it is addressed. A "decision" is an order binding on the particular persons to whom it is addressed.

After the GATT Uruguay Round was concluded and it was time for countries to formally notify their ratification and acceptance, the Commission sought an advisory opinion from the ECJ regarding whether the European Union had the exclusive authority to formally enter into the WTO Agreements, including the TRIPS Agreement, or whether the member states must also become parties to the various agreements.[90] Referring to the common commercial policy (Article 113 of the EC Treaty, which subsequently became Article 133 of the EC Treaty and today is found in Article 207 of the TFEU), the ECJ refused to acknowledge exclusive competence of the Union governing organs in the field of IPRs on the basis of its *ERTA* decision.[91]

In said case, the Court held that if the European Union had adopted harmonizing measures in a particular area, then even in the absence of an express grant of exclusive competence in the EC Treaty, the European Union organs would assume exclusive competence for the conduct of external relations in that area to avoid conflict with the internal harmonizing measures. In this decision concerning the TRIPS Agreement, the Court said that the European Union had not yet achieved a sufficient level of harmonization in the IPRs area for the *ERTA* rationale to be applicable.

---

89. *See* Article 288, TFEU.

90. Opinion 1/94, Re The Uruguay Round Treaties. The Court of Justice of the European Communities [1995] 1 CMLR 20515 November 1994.

91. Case 22/70, *Commission of the European Communities v. Council of the European Communities,* 1971 E.C.R. 263.

The Lisbon Treaty brought about some significant changes to the way intellectual property rights are treated in the EU Treaties, although to a certain extent these changes already were anticipated by developments in the EU. First, Article 118 of the TFEU clarifies that EU institutions have the authority to regulate with respect to all forms of IPRs, including patents. It provides, in relevant part:

> In the context of the establishment and functioning of the internal market, the European Parliament and the Council, acting in accordance with the ordinary legislative procedure, shall establish measures for the creation of European intellectual property rights to provide uniform protection of intellectual property rights throughout the Union and for the setting up of centralised Union-wide authorisation, coordination and supervision arrangements.

This is particularly important in the context of the potential establishment of a proposed EU Patent Regulation, a subject we will visit later.[92] From the inception of the EU in 1958, there was controversy surrounding whether the powers of the EU extended to legislating on internal IP matters, and especially with respect to patents. This accounts for the existence of a European Patent Office and European Patent that are not part of the EU institutional or legislative structure.

Second, Article 207 of the TFEU, which establishes the "common commercial policy" that governs external trade relations of the EU, addresses the institutional mechanisms for negotiating and concluding agreements concerning trade related aspects of intellectual property rights, as well as the implementation of those agreements. Since the 1990s, the ECJ has considered purely external trade aspects of IPRs to be within the exclusive jurisdiction of the EU. However, because the member states retain authority to regulate internal IP matters, the general situation of IPRs was considered "mixed," dividing authority between the EU and the member states.

Today, the EU has the authority to harmonize internal IP legislation (per Article 118, above), and commercial aspects of IPRs are within the common commercial policy (per Article 207). These provisions concede important competences in relation to the conclusion and modification of international and bilateral trade agreements to the European Parliament and the Council. The member states' freedom to negotiate new agreements and amend existing ones is limited to a degree where the "mixed competence assumption" the ECJ has established may no longer be sustained.

However, much of EU IPRs regulation is undertaken by way of implementation at the member state level, and to what extent the controversy concerning the allocation of authority to legislate in the field of IPRs in ways that affect international trade persists remains to be seen.

NOTES AND QUESTIONS

1. As noted earlier, the European Union legislates in three different ways. The "directive" is a form of legislation at a more general level that instructs the member states to bring their own legislation into conformity as they see fit.

---

92. See *infra*, Chapter 2.

The "regulation" is directly effective as law throughout the European Union and does not require member state legislation to be given effect. The "decision" is an order directed to a specific person(s). Some EU IPRs legislation takes the form of directive, such as the First Trade Marks Directive. The First Trade Marks Directive contemplated that each member state would maintain its own trademark law and trademark office, under general guidance from the European Union. EU IPRs legislation also takes the form of regulation, such as the Community Trade Mark Regulation (CTMR). The CTMR established a single unitary trademark for the European Union that operates through an EU trademark office (the Office for Harmonization in the Internal Market or OHIM).

2. Note that regional intellectual property law in Europe is not exclusively European Union Law. The European Patent Convention is formally located outside the European Union and forms an international organization in its own right with membership beyond Members of the EU.

3. Note that the European Court of Justice abbreviates the TRIPS Agreement as "TRIPs," as do other EU institutions. This is *not* the abbreviation used by the WTO, including its Appellate Body.

4. The status of the EU and its member states as parties to the WTO, and their respective roles in the dispute settlement process, continues to be contentious. The EU consistently takes the position that it alone is responsible for representing the interests of the member states in dispute settlement, notwithstanding that the member states are independently Members of the WTO. When a third country Member initiates consultations with an EU member state, it receives a letter from the EU WTO delegation indicating that the EU will act as the sole representative in dispute settlement on behalf of the member state, and will be responsible for assuring implementation of any resulting decision. However, dispute settlement panels have been formed to include individual member states as named parties. In the recently decided *EU-Aircraft Subsidies* case, the panel made specific findings against individual EU member states and specifically recommended that they bring their measures into conformity.[93] The EU has indicated its intention to appeal the panel decision, but has not yet indicated whether it will challenge the practice of individual findings against member states. In consultations initiated by India and Brazil with the EU and the Netherlands regarding seizures of generic pharmaceuticals in transit, India and Brazil each named the Netherlands as a party to the consultations.[94] Consistent with the practice discussed above, the EU notified India and Brazil that it is solely responsible for representing the interests of the member states in WTO dispute settlement. The Netherlands did not agree to participate in consultations, but did send several representatives to the consultations held between India and Brazil and the EU.

5. EU institutions and rules are further discussed throughout the book, including the status of the TRIPS Agreement within EU law.

---

93. WT/DS316/R, 30 June 2010.
94. *See* Request for Consultations by India, WT/DS408/1, G/L/921, IP/D/28, 19 May 2010 and Request for Consultations by Brazil, WT/DS409/1, IP/D/29, G/L/922, 19 May 2010.

2. Andean Community

The Andean Community was created in 1969 pursuant to the Treaty of Cartegena.[95] The members of the Community as of the beginning of 2006 were Bolivia, Colombia, Ecuador, Peru, and Venezuela. However, as a consequence of the signing of free trade agreements between the United States, on one side, and Colombia and Peru, on the other, Venezuela announced its withdrawal from the Community in April 2006. The Andean Community establishes a free trade area among its member countries and a common external tariff. It maintains common institutions, including a Council of Ministers, Presidential Council, Parliament, Commission, and Court of Justice. The Andean Community in the early 1970s adopted common provisions relating to intellectual property and transfer of technology, which sought to limit the influence of foreign right holders in the regional economy. The legislation, principally Decisions 84 and 85 of the Andean Commission, required approval of technology licensing agreements and limited the royalty outflows that could be paid to foreign technology suppliers.[96] However, by the early 1990s, the Andean Community largely abandoned this experiment in rebalancing the terms of technology transfer with the adoption of Decision 344, which was superseded in 2000 by Decision 486. Noteworthy among Andean Community IP-related legislation is Decision 391, establishing the Common Regime on Access to Genetic Resources, adopted in 1996. Decision 391 is intended to implement the provisions of the Convention on Biological Diversity and, among other things, requires prospective bio-prospectors to obtain the prior informed consent of the host country before commencing their activities.

3. Mercosur

Argentina and Brazil are large economy developing countries, which, together with Paraguay and Uruguay, formed the Mercosur in 1991. Bolivia, Chile, Colombia, Ecuador, and Peru are "associated" members of the Mercosur. The Mercosur countries had made substantial progress toward reduction of traditional trade barriers between them. Harmonization or approximation of intellectual property rights rules has not so far been a priority.

4. Free Trade Area of the Americas

The Mercosur countries, along with the countries of the Andean Community and the NAFTA (discussed below), were taking part in negotiations intended to lead to the formation of a Free Trade Area of the Americas (FTAA). The FTAA negotiations were initiated in 1994 and encompassed all countries of the Western Hemisphere with the exception of Cuba. There was a Negotiating Group on Intellectual Property Rights. IPRs are among the most contentious subject matter of the negotiations, as a number of Latin American countries have substantially different views than the United States regarding appropriate

---

95. Information regarding the Andean Community, including its constitutive texts, can be found at http://www.comunidadandina.org.

96. *See generally* Frederick M. Abbott, *Bargaining Power and Strategy in the Foreign Investment Process: A Current Andean Code Analysis*, 3 SYRACUSE J. INT'L L. & COM. 319 (1975).

levels of protection, such as in the area of pharmaceuticals. As of 2011, the FTAA negotiations appear to have come to an end without an agreement. Information concerning the FTAA negotiations, including with respect to intellectual property, may be found at the web site of the Organization of American States, at http://www.oas.org. The OAS web site provides an excellent access point for information about laws and institutions in Latin America, including those with respect to IPRs. The web site includes links to various national laws and IP offices.

5. UNASUR

In May 2008, members of the Andean Community and Mercosur, along with Venezuela, signed the constitutive treaty of the Union of South American Nations (Unión de Naciones Suramericanas), or UNASUR. This treaty foresees the eventual integration of the two existing customs unions. It is premature to predict what impact this may have with respect to rules regarding IPRs protection, but it is certainly possible that this new integration mechanism will play a significant role in the approximation of regional IPRs rules.

6. NAFTA

The North American Free Trade Agreement (NAFTA) between Canada, Mexico, and the United States entered into force on January 1, 1994. The NAFTA includes a detailed Chapter 17 on intellectual property. This chapter was negotiated at roughly the same time as the WTO TRIPS Agreement and is similar in most respects. However, there were some notable differences. These included "pipeline" patent protection for pharmaceutical and agricultural chemical products that could not previously be patented in Mexico,[97] and more restrictive protection of data submitted in connection with regulatory approval of pharmaceutical and agricultural products.[98] Outside of the IP chapter, Canada and Mexico insisted on measures allowing protection of local cultural institutions. Mexico, for example, limited foreign participation in its broadcast and film sectors.

The following excerpt briefly explains the difference between the NAFTA and EU institutional arrangements.

THE NORTH AMERICAN INTEGRATION REGIME AND ITS IMPLICATIONS FOR THE WORLD TRADING SYSTEM
Frederick M. Abbott*

I. The NAFTA Mutation of the EC Model Revisited

The NAFTA is a significantly different model of regional economic integration than the European Union. The EU is loosely based on the concept of a federal

---

97. NAFTA, art. 1709(4).
98. NAFTA, art. 1711(6).
* IX:1 Collected Courses of the Academy of European Law: The EU, the WTO and the NAFTA 170 (J.H.H. Weiler ed., 2000) (Oxford Univ. Press).

polity with an allocation of power between Union organs — the Council, Commission, Parliament and Court of Justice — on one side, and member state governments on the other side. The NAFTA is in the nature of a confederation among independent sovereigns, each maintaining autonomous political decision-making authority within constraints defined by agreement. The political decision-making apparatus of the NAFTA is closely circumscribed to roughly include within the boundaries of its central authority (the Free Trade Commission) the powers traditionally conferred upon trade ministers by their governments. The European Court of Justice has referred to the EC Treaty as a constitutional charter, and the Court has viewed its role as the guardian of that constitution. The NAFTA does not purport to serve as a constitution in the sense of altering the distribution of powers among its Parties.

The EC Treaty provides for the adoption of directives, regulations and decisions by the Union political organs. These enactments are customarily referred to as "secondary legislation" reflecting their status underneath the "primary legislation" of the EC Treaty. The relationship between primary and secondary Union legislation is similar to the traditional relationship between the constitution and parliamentary enactments of a national federal government. The EC Treaty and secondary legislation may have direct effect in the EU member states, meaning that this legislation may be relied on by individuals in the courts of the member states in appropriate circumstances.

The NAFTA political institutions are not empowered to enact secondary legislation except in very limited circumstances prescribed by the agreement (such as in adopting rules of procedure for NAFTA dispute settlement panels). There is no general legislative power allocated to the NAFTA political institutions. The NAFTA is in theory capable of direct effect within the national courts of its Parties. The United States has by legislation deprived the NAFTA of potential direct effect in U.S. courts.

The economic undertakings of the Parties were negotiated in detail. The results of these negotiations were expressed in the NAFTA text. The Parties have so far carried out the economic undertakings of the NAFTA substantially in accordance with its terms. Though a few matters are disputed, in the context of the overall undertaking, these disputes are modest.

The NAFTA prescribes mechanisms for the resolution of disputes between its Parties, and in limited circumstances for the resolution of disputes between the nationals of its Parties and Party governments. The general dispute settlement mechanism of the NAFTA is an arbitral procedure that refers determinations to Party governments for political resolution. This is consistent with the NAFTA's limited design in respect to intrusion on Party autonomy. The NAFTA's anti-dumping and countervailing duty dispute settlement apparatus directly binds Party governments.[9] Party nationals are entitled to pursue third party

9. The NAFTA includes a separate dispute settlement mechanism in respect to antidumping and countervailing duty (AD/CVD) related complaints (Chapter 19, NAFTA). The NAFTA contains no rules regarding the substance of the AD/CVD laws of the Parties, requiring only that each Party act in domestic AD/CVD actions in compliance with its own laws. In the AD/CVD dispute settlement system, arbitral panels constituted on a case-by-case basis make decisions as to whether a country Party has complied with its own AD/CVD laws in a particular action. The decisions of AD/CVD panels are directly binding on the country Parties. There are approximately 30 completed or active Chapter 19 panels reviewing AD/CVD decisions of Canadian, Mexican and U.S. administrative authorities. NAFTA Secretariat, www.nafta-sec-alena.org.

arbitration of investment-related claims at ICSID or under UNCITRAL rules.[10] Each of these dispute settlement mechanisms is operational.

The European Union is a customs union. The EC Treaty prescribes the elimination of tariffs and other restrictive regulations of commerce on trade between its member states, and prescribes the establishment of common tariffs applicable to goods originating outside EU territory. The EC Treaty prescribes that goods originating outside its territory are in free circulation within its territory following the payment of the applicable common tariff upon entry into any member state. The EC Treaty prescribes a common commercial policy which binds its member states to follow a coordinated trade policy program. The EC Treaty prescribes the free movement of services, capital and persons between its member states.

The NAFTA is a free trade area. The NAFTA prescribes the elimination of tariffs and other restrictive regulations of commerce between its Parties, but does not prescribe common tariffs applicable to goods originating outside NAFTA territory. Except in so far as goods originating outside the NAFTA are transformed within a Party(s) so as to assume a regional character, such third country goods are subject to the payment of tariffs upon entry into each NAFTA Party. The NAFTA prescribes the free movement of services and capital, and limited free movement of business persons, between its members. Except in so far as the Parties are limited in their relations with third countries by the terms of the NAFTA, the agreement does not mandate that the Parties pursue a common commercial policy.

NOTES AND QUESTIONS

1.   The NAFTA includes Chapter 17 on Intellectual Property. When Mexico agreed to provide "pipeline" protection for pharmaceutical products that had been patented previously in the United States or Canada, but had not yet been patented or marketed in Mexico (NAFTA, art. 1709(4)), this raised concern for countries outside the NAFTA that were not entitled to MFN treatment by Mexico. It was this type of special treatment under a regional agreement that led countries to insist on an MFN provision in the TRIPS Agreement. We discuss the MFN treatment principle *infra*, at V.B.
2.   What advantages would you see to harmonization of IPRs legislation among the United States, Canada, and Mexico? Do you think this would be a good idea?
3.   Assuming for the sake of argument that the United States, Canada, and Mexico intended to harmonize their IP legislation, what should be the legislative process? Should the trade negotiators handle this and put the results before the legislatures of each country? How would this differ from the customary legislative process in the United States?

---

10. The NAFTA permits investors of Parties to pursue third party arbitration against a host government in the International Centre for the Settlement of Investment Disputes (ICSID) or under UNCITRAL rules. NAFTA, arts. 1115, *et seq.* ... The NAFTA obligates the Parties to make adequate provision for the enforcement of resulting arbitral awards. Several proceedings based on NAFTA investment rules have been initiated in the ICSID by U.S. nationals against the government of Mexico, and claims both by U.S. nationals against the government of Canada and by Canadian nationals against the government of the United States have been initiated or threatened.

4. Should businesses in the United States be able to sue Mexican companies for violations of NAFTA IP rules in the courts of the United States? What hurdles would you foresee?

5. We will examine some additional specific provisions from the NAFTA IP chapter later in the book.

B.   Regional IP Offices in Africa

Prior to World War II, much of the African continent was governed by European colonial powers. IP laws and administrative systems reflected that situation. This legacy is mentioned because it accounts for a continued similarity between the IP laws of a number of African countries and former colonial powers. The achievement of independent statehood resulted in the creation of new IP infrastructure, including the establishment of regional IP institutions. The establishment of these institutions was strongly supported and influenced by WIPO (and by European IP advisers). Reform of national IP laws has also taken place, particularly as a consequence of the adoption of the WTO TRIPS Agreement.

There are two principal regional IP institutions in Africa, ARIPO and OAPI. It was originally conceived that ARIPO would be constituted by English-speaking African states, and OAPI by the French-speaking, though this bifurcation is not rigid. Detailed information concerning the organizational structure and operation of ARIPO and OAPI may be found at their respective web sites, http://www.aripo.org and http://www.oapi.wipo.net. Each of them provides a mechanism for securing patent protection across the regional territory of its membership, but with different procedural and substantive characteristics.

In addition to the regional IP institutions of ARIPO and OAPI, there are a significant number of more general regional institutions in Africa, including the African Union, the New Partnership for Africa's Development (NEPAD), and the Southern African Customs Union (SACU). Each of these institutions includes some aspects of intellectual property regulation within its range of activities.

C.   Regional Consultation (APEC)

The Asia-Pacific Economic Cooperation forum (APEC) is essentially a consultative body among countries of the Pacific region, including the United States. Unlike the European Union or Mercosur, APEC does not establish governmental institutions or common legislation. It is rather a consultative body. It does, however, encourage transparency with respect to intellectual property rules and enforcement. An Intellectual Property Rights Experts Group (IPEG) was created in 1996 that coordinates and undertakes the work related to IPRs (*see* http://www.apecsec.org.sg).

In addition to APEC, there are a number of regional institutions in Asia that include aspects of intellectual property regulation within the range of their activities, including ASEAN, AFTA, and SAFTA. *See generally* United Nations Economic and Social Commission for Asia and the Pacific (UNESCAP),

Asia-Pacific Trade and Investment Agreements Database (APTIAD), at http://www.unescap.org/tid/pta_app/.

D. Bilateral, Regional, and Plurilateral Trade Agreements

There is, at present, limited possibility for the United States or the European Union to negotiate higher standards of protection at the WTO or WIPO because a substantial number of developing countries consider that the standards already in place create administrative and economic burdens for them. Nonetheless, major industry groups in the United States perceive gaps in the TRIPS Agreement and place constant pressure on U.S. trade negotiators to remedy this situation. The result is pursuit of a "second-best" solution (from an industry standpoint) of pursuing higher standards in bilateral, regional, and more recently, "plurilateral" negotiations.

1. Bilateral and Regional Trade Agreements

In bilateral and regional settings, the United States offers market access concessions in areas such as agriculture and textiles in exchange for tightening IP protection. This raises important public policy questions. For example, is it appropriate for developing countries to limit their possibility to lower domestic drug prices by preventing generic drugs from entering the market in exchange for improved access to the U.S. market for their agricultural producers? If poorer segments of developing country populations are unable to afford medicines, does providing owners of developing country agricultural exporting businesses remedy this? A number of policy issues are considered by economists in the following World Bank Trade Note. Carsten Fink is presently Chief Economist at WIPO.

TIGHTENING TRIPS: THE INTELLECTUAL PROPERTY PROVISIONS OF RECENT U.S. FREE TRADE AGREEMENTS

Carsten Fink & Patrick Reichenmiller*

INTRODUCTION

Over the past few years, the United States has pursued an increasing number of bilateral and regional free trade agreements (FTAs) in different parts of the world. This has marked a considerable shift in US international trade diplomacy. While the US Government entered into regional trade agreements in the past — notably in the case of the North American Free Trade Agreement (NAFTA) — it relied mostly on the multilateral trading system to advance the progressive opening of world markets and to create legally enforceable trading rules.

* World Bank Group, International Trade Development, Trade Note 20, Feb. 7, 2005.

A central element of the recent set of bilateral FTAs is the establishment of strong rules for the protection of intellectual property rights (IPRs). This is a key offensive market access interest of the United States — supported by private sector constituents for whom the export of intangible assets is commercially gainful. Indeed, the Trade Promotion Authority, under which these agreements were negotiated, explicitly states as a negotiating objective to promote intellectual property rules that "... *reflect a standard of protection similar to that found in United States law.*"[1] US trading partners generally have more defensive negotiating interests in intellectual property, but are willing to commit to stronger intellectual property rules as a quid pro quo for concessions in other areas — most notably, preferential access to US markets for agricultural and manufactured goods. ...

Intellectual Property Rights and Investment Rules

In addition to the rules contained in the intellectual property chapters of the FTAs, IPRs are subject to separate investment disciplines. As illustrated in Table 3 [not reproduced here — Eds.], six of the bilateral agreements have separate chapters on investment. The US-Bahrain and US-Jordan FTAs do not have such chapters, but the respective governments have negotiated bilateral investment treaties (BITs) with similar provisions. As no multilateral agreement on investment exists at the WTO or elsewhere, these bilateral investment rules break new ground.

A common element of the recent US FTA investment chapters and BITs is that intellectual property rights are explicitly listed in the definition of what is considered an investment. Thus, the agreements' specific investment disciplines apply, in principle, to government measures affecting the intellectual property portfolios of foreign investors. This raises, for example, the question of whether granting a compulsory license is considered an act of expropriation. Five of the FTA investment chapters explicitly remove compulsory licenses from the scope of expropriation, as long as such licenses comply with the obligations of the TRIPS Agreement and the intellectual property chapter of the respective FTA. However, the US-Vietnam FTA and the two BITs with Bahrain and Jordan do not have a comparable safeguard. Thus, as an example, if Vietnam were to issue a compulsory license in case of a national emergency, could the patent holder challenge such a decision as an act of investment expropriation?

Questions like this may be important, as these investment agreements provide for direct investor-to-state dispute settlement — going beyond the more traditional state-to-state dispute settlement procedures included in trade agreements. An exception is the investment chapter of the US-Australia FTA, which only allows for the possibility that investor-to-state dispute settlement procedures be negotiated in future. Investor-to-state dispute settlement may be more attractive to foreign investors, who can seek arbitration awards for uncompensated expropriation. By contrast, state-to-state dispute settlement can typically authorize only the imposition of punitive trade sanctions.

1. See the Bipartisan Trade Promotion Authority Act of 2002, available at http://www.tpa.gov.

Notwithstanding these considerations, the reach of investment agreements into the intellectual property domain is still untested and remains in many ways legally uncertain (Correa, 2004).

A GOOD BARGAIN?

Whether an FTA's package of commitments produces net welfare gains to all parties is an empirical question. However, FTAs with stronger rules on intellectual property complicate an assessment of economic benefits and costs, for three reasons.

First, the traditional logic economists apply to mercantilist trade bargaining does not straightforwardly extend to intellectual property. While reduced import protection is seen as a concession by trade negotiators, it is generally regarded as a welfare-enhancing policy change by trade economists. Nonetheless, economists have supported mercantilist bargaining, as it helps governments to make a stronger case for import liberalization: exporters that gain from improved access to foreign markets can become a political counterweight to firms that would lose out from more intense import competition.

From an economic perspective, IPRs are different. Put simply, they imply a trade-off between incentives for innovation and competitive access to new technologies. To balance these tradeoffs, governments limit the length and scope of the market exclusivity conferred by IPRs, according to national policy objectives. In particular, there is no assurance that stronger intellectual property rules will always be welfare enhancing, and the direction and size of the welfare effect will depend on a country's level of economic development. While there is undoubtedly a market access dimension to IPRs, subjecting standards of protection to mercantilist bargaining cannot be viewed in the same light as subjecting import barriers to such bargaining.

Second, improved access to US markets for agricultural and manufactured goods is of a preferential nature. These preferences are time-bound because they will be eroded once the US reduces remaining tariffs and quotas on a non-discriminatory basis in the current or future multilateral trading rounds (or signs additional FTAs). By contrast, a commitment to stronger IPRs rules is permanent and likely to be implemented on a non-preferential basis. Even if preferential treatment in the area of IPRs were technically feasible, it would likely be inconsistent with the TRIPS Agreement which mandates most-favored nation (MFN) treatment of IPRs holders. In contrast to the WTO's agreements on trade in goods and trade in services, the TRIPS Agreement does not provide for an exception to the MFN principle for FTAs.

Third, it is inherently difficult to quantify the implications of changing intellectual property standards, let alone to compare them in monetary values to the gains derived from improved market access abroad. As will be explained further below, certain effects of stronger IPRs are conceptually not well-understood. But even where they are well-understood, the direction and size of net welfare changes depend on future developments that are difficult to predict — such as the nature of future innovations and their relevance to the country concerned.

Economic and Social Implications

As just pointed out, evaluating the social and economic implications of the FTAs in the area of intellectual property is a difficult task. First of all, this requires an understanding of the changes in laws and regulations required by obligations in the FTAs that do not already reflect actual legal practice in the countries concerned.

For example, both Morocco and the United States had legislation in place prohibiting parallel imports of pharmaceutical products before they signed the FTA. To be sure, trade agreements are still relevant even if they do not require changes in laws, because they make it difficult for countries to change their minds and amend laws. Indeed, in the specific case of parallel importation many countries — including the United States — re-examine from time to time existing policies and sometimes decide to change course. Certainly, if policy changes were not conceivable, there would be no need to lock policy into trade agreements. A full economic assessment of the new intellectual property obligations in the FTAs would require in-depth study in each of the affected countries and goes beyond the scope of this note.

Still, what are some of the general benefits and costs that may come with the new intellectual property standards outlined above?

A commitment to stronger intellectual property protection may send a welcoming signal to foreign investors, contributing to a country's increased participation in international commerce. The empirical evidence on this question is mixed, however. Fink and Maskus (2004) review studies undertaken to gauge the link between the strength of intellectual property protection and the attraction of foreign direct investment flows. They conclude that countries that strengthen their IPRs regime are unlikely to experience a sudden boost in inflows of foreign investment. Other factors account for most of the variation across countries in the activity of multinational enterprises. At the same time, the empirical evidence does point to a positive role of IPRs in stimulating cross-border licensing activity, affecting the nature of formal technology transfers.

Moving on to sector-specific implications, the role of patent protection in the pharmaceutical industry is conceptually well-understood. Patents create an incentive to invest in pharmaceutical research and development (R&D), but the market exclusivity they confer leads to prices above marginal production costs — as illustrated by sharp price falls when patents expire and generic competition emerges. The benefits and costs associated with protecting pharmaceutical patents differ from country to country. Among other things, they depend on the relevance of drug discoveries to national disease patterns, the purchasing power of patients, and the availability of health insurance programs that cover drug expenses. As already pointed out, insufficient flexibility in over-riding drug patents can have a detrimental impact on the protection of public health. The need for such flexibility has not been widespread so far, as generic sources for most medicines have still been available. However, it is likely to become more important in the future, as the implementation of TRIPS obligations will lead newly invented drugs to be protected by patents in most developing countries that host generic pharmaceutical industries.

The benefits and costs of stronger and new copyright protection standards are less clear cut. Most countries have industries that rely on copyright protection and that may benefit from strengthened protection. And new technologies that greatly facilitate the copying of digital works pose challenges that policymakers need to address. At the same time, copyright laws have historically sought to strike a balance between the interests of copyright producers and the interests of the general public. So-called fair use exemptions allow the copying of protected works for educational or research purposes. There are concerns that new rules on the term of protection, technological protection measures, the liability of Internet services providers, and the burden of proof in case of copyright infringement could diminish the rights of consumers and the general public (CIPR, 2002). Such concerns have also been voiced in the United States itself, not only by consumer rights advocates and academic institutions, but also by computer manufacturers and communications service providers that distribute copyrighted works. For example, specific amendments to the Digital Millennium Copyright Act have been proposed that would permit the circumvention of technological protection measures if such action does not result in an infringement of a copyrighted work. Ensuring fair use of copyrighted material seems particularly important for accessing educational material. The opportunities and gains from the use of digital libraries, Internet-based distance learning programs, or online databases would be limited if access to such tools is unaffordable or otherwise restricted by copyright law.

Finally, strengthening the enforcement of intellectual property rights can be a costly exercise — both in terms of budgetary outlays and the employment of skilled personnel. For developing countries that face many institutional deficiencies, a critical question is whether stronger enforcement of IPRs would draw away financial and human resources from other development priorities.

LESSONS LEARNED

. . . [T]he United States is in the process of negotiating FTAs with additional — mostly developing — countries, and new negotiations are likely to be launched in the foreseeable future. Given the importance of intellectual property as a market access interest for the US, it will likely be difficult for US trading partners to avoid negotiating new IPRs rules.

What are the lessons learned from the recently signed agreements? First, while there are common elements in the eight intellectual property chapters discussed here, there are also important differences . . . . To varying degrees of success, US trading partners were able to advance their own, mostly defensive interests. Of particular importance is the preservation of flexibilities to protect public health. Indeed, the US is obligated by its own Trade Promotion Authority ". . . *to respect the Declaration on the TRIPS Agreement and Public Health, adopted by the World Trade Organization at the Fourth Ministerial Conference at Doha* [. . .]."

Second, the intellectual property chapters of the eight FTAs mostly reflect proposals put forward by the US. It may be possible to change the negotiating dynamics in future FTAs, if US trading partners put forward [their] own proposals on new intellectual property rules and related incentive mechanisms. These may pertain to policy areas in which developing countries have offensive interests, such as the protection of biodiversity and traditional knowledge. But they may also consist of alternative mechanisms of addressing the problems new intellectual property rules intend to fix.

Finally, countries need to carefully assess the economic and social effects of tightened IPRs standards, ideally before new agreements are negotiated. As pointed out above, these effects are multifaceted and depend on country-specific circumstances. An assessment should therefore involve consultations with relevant ministries, the private sector, consumer groups, and other stakeholders.

2. The Protection of IPRs Through International Investment Agreements

The Protection of IPRs Through Bilateral Investment Treaties

As mentioned above, similarly as through FTAs, IPRs are also protected through disciplines of bilateral investment treaties (BITs). BITs have been concluded since 1959, as they emerged in a historical context of internationally diverging views on private property rights, ownership over national resources, and the sovereign right of states to regulate. At the time, Western market economies developed and negotiated BITs in order to broadly protect their investors' assets in those countries in which investors had to fear expropriation or unfair treatment.

BITs feature a number of broadly formulated treatment standards basically aiming to ensure that the treatment investors receive in a host country does not fall under a certain floor set in light of international law. Treatment standards that BITs enshrine today include standards on most favored nation treatment, national treatment, and fair and equitable treatment. Rules on expropriation in the agreements do not prohibit expropriation of investors or their investments as such, but condition it to the adherence to certain standards such as full and prompt compensation. The arguably most distinct feature of today's BITs, stipulated by the overwhelming majority of agreements, lies in their investor-state dispute settlement (ISDS) clauses, creating a dispute settlement system in which investors can sue the host countries of their investments directly before an international panel, in case they see their rights under the applicable BIT violated.

These features of investment agreements also apply to investments taking the form of intellectual property rights, since the broadly formulated definitions of BITs bring intangible assets such as IPRs virtually always under the scope of the agreements. Given that the protection clauses in BITs are usually formulated broadly, and clear evidence from case law on the matter is lacking, the precise level of protection offered by BITs for investments taking the form of IP is contested. However, in light of the fact that BITs have never been harmonized with the large body of international IP law such as the TRIPS Agreement, it cannot be excluded that protection standards for IPRs in investment agreements make available more stringent or more far-reaching protection for IPRs than dedicated, international intellectual property agreements. As such, there is a certain risk that protection of IPRs under investment agreements could force governments to allow in individual cases for higher IP protection standards "through the backdoor," meaning, via claims brought against the government of the host state by an investor.

INTELLECTUAL PROPERTY RIGHTS IN INTERNATIONAL INVESTMENT AGREEMENTS

OECD Working Papers on International Investment 2010/1 Lahra Liberti

. . .

III. ENHANCING IPR PROTECTION THROUGH INTERNATIONAL INVESTMENT AGREEMENTS

IPRS AS COVERED INVESTMENT UNDER INTERNATIONAL INVESTMENT AGREEMENTS

Beyond the trade context, IPRs as a form of investment also fall under the scope of application of BITs and investment chapters of RTAs (including FTAs and Economic Partnership Agreements).

The qualification of IPRs as covered investments under most international investment agreements is far from being a novelty. The reference to intellectual property rights was already a common feature of the US Friendship Commerce and Navigation (FCN) Agreements before the expansion of BITs. As early as 1903, the US had negotiated a FCN treaty with China that included copyright protection. In some treaties, the term property was simply extended to such intangible rights, while in others explicit reference was made to patents, copyrights and trademarks.

In some cases the reference to IPRs appears in the preamble of BITs. For example, the 1999 US-Turkey BIT recognises the importance of providing adequate and effective protection and enforcement of intellectual property rights and of adherence to intellectual property rights conventions.

. . .

TREATMENT OF IPRS AS INVESTMENT UNDER INTERNATIONAL INVESTMENT AGREEMENTS

Unlike RTAs' IP chapters, bilateral and multilateral investment treaties and investment chapters of RTAs do not set specific substantial standards on intellectual property, but they protect the rights of investors who use intellectual property as a mode of investment.

A first issue regarding the scope of the definition of investment is whether patent applications, though not an IPR, would qualify as an intangible property. Since for some IPRs the holder is entitled to enjoy them only after completion of the registration process (patents, trademarks, industrial designs), the holder is required to file an application. Although a patent application creates a mere expectation of obtaining an exclusive right, it entitles the holder with certain prerogatives such as the ability to act against infringers. It has been argued that the wording of certain investment treaties referring to the rights with respect to copyrights, patents, [. . .] or to copyright and related rights would qualify for coverage [see, for example, the 1991 Canada-Argentina BIT, Article 1(a)(iv), 1996 Canada-Barbados BIT, Article 1(f)(v)].

. . .

IIAs [international investment agreements] can also strengthen IPR protection through the unqualified operation of Most-Favoured-Nation (MFN) and National Treatment (NT) obligations and expropriation provisions, which would trigger a wider impact for IPR protection. Under an unqualified MFN treatment of IPRs, a state party to a BIT should accord to the investors and investments (including IPRs) of the other contracting party no less favourable treatment than it accords in like circumstances to a third country under any other bilateral or multilateral agreement in respect of the protection of intellectual property rights.

In this regard, Article 18(2) of the Japan-Vietnam BIT and Article 6(2) of the Japan-Korea BIT expressly clarify that — [n]othing in this Agreement shall be construed so as to oblige either Contracting Party to extend to investors of the other Contracting Party and their investments treatment accorded to investors of any third country and their investments by virtue of multilateral agreements in respect of protection of intellectual property rights, to which the former Contracting Party is a party.

A further question relates to the operation of the MFN treatment when a WTO-TRIPS member country enters into a bilateral investment treaty or a free trade agreement providing for TRIPS-Plus obligations. Since under the TRIPS agreement there is no equivalent of Article XXIV providing for an exception to MFN for free trade agreements and customs unions, further analysis would be needed to appreciate whether states parties to the WTO-TRIPS Agreement will be required to extend the same benefits deriving from BITs or FTAs with TRIPS-Plus provisions to all TRIPS-WTO members.

In order to appreciate whether International Investment Agreements [IIAs] actually provide for extended IPR protection, a distinction could be drawn between pre-TRIPS and post-TRIPS IIAs. With respect to MFN and NT, the TRIPS Agreement offers WTO members the possibility of using the various exceptions which were negotiated during the years of the Uruguay Round.

Most of the pre-1994 North-South BITs do not cover all the exceptions to national or most-favoured nation treatment provided under WTO-TRIPS and IP treaties. As a result, most of pre-TRIPS investment agreements allow for a broader application of both standards. For example, NAFTA Article 1108(5) stipulates that articles 1102 (national treatment) and 1103 (MFN clause) — do not apply to any measure that is an exception to, or derogation from, the obligations under the IP chapter, article 1703 (Intellectual Property-National Treatment) as specifically provided in that article. Article 1703 (4) is, however, limited to procedural laws relating to treaties negotiated under WIPO.

. . .

WHAT HAPPENS IF SPECIFIC EXCEPTIONS AND EXCLUSIONS ARE LACKING?
Reference to TRIPS under IIAs ensures that there is no breach of investment protection standards to the extent that domestic measures derogating from MFN, national treatment and expropriation conform to TRIPS exceptions and waivers. By so doing, foreign investors will have guarantee that the exception from the duty to compensate for expropriation or other treatment would be predictable and measured with an agreed yardstick. At the same time, states will have the flexibility to adopt IPR measures in line with TRIPS exceptions and waivers (e.g. the decision of the WTO General Council on 30 August 2003, which authorized countries that lack the capacity to manufacture generic substitutes for patented medicines under locally granted compulsory licences, to obtain imports of these medicines) (including subsequent decisions). Should such measures be challenged under investor-state dispute settlement,

arbitrators will get clear guidance to distinguish *bona fide* regulatory measures from compensable expropriations.

It may be argued that without express reference to TRIPS provisions, the balance could be upset by unqualified MFN, national treatment and expropriation requirements in a subsequent investment treaty.

IV. ENFORCING IPRs THROUGH INVESTOR-STATE ARBITRATION

Under the TRIPS Agreement, only member states can resort to the WTO dispute settlement procedure. TRIPS Article 64 (Dispute Settlement) provides for consultations and settlement of TRIPS disputes under the WTO Understanding on Rules and Procedures Governing the Settlement of Disputes, which in turn specifically applies to TRIPS. But WTO rules do not require disputes arising under TRIPS-Plus provisions to be settled by the mandatory WTO dispute settlement mechanism, since these provisions lie outside the WTO Agreements.

The possibility for an IPR holder to bring a claim against a state under the investor-state dispute settlement mechanism for breach of TRIPS-Plus provisions is a further element which should be taken into account while appreciating IIAs potential for expanding IPR protection beyond the standards prescribed under multilateral IPR instruments.

In addition to the possibility of a state-to-state dispute, FTAs' investment chapter vests the IP owner as an investor with the right to bring the host state to binding international arbitration. For instance, as an investment, IPRs are protected as intangible property under NAFTA Chapter 11 providing for investor-state dispute settlement, in addition to the possibility of state-state dispute settlement under NAFTA Chapter 20. Except for the US-Australia FTA, which only provides for state-to-state dispute settlement, international investment agreements generally allow private investors to sue a state party to an investment treaty before an international arbitration tribunal, should a breach of IPR protection standards under the treaty occur.

A few claims have been brought by private investors under both NAFTA and BITs on the basis of an alleged violation of IPRs. None of them has been adjudicated so far.

NOTES AND QUESTIONS

1. Many NGOs have criticized the United States for its approach to IP in bilateral trade negotiations, particularly with developing countries. *See, e.g.,* Oxfam Briefing Note, Undermining Access to Medicines: Comparison of Five US FTAs (June 2004), available at http://www.twnside.org.sg/title2/FTAs/Intellectual_Property/IP_and_Access_to_Medicines/Undermining AccessToMedicines.pdf; CPTech, Table of Selected Provisions Related to Healthcare in the Free Trade Agreement Texts That Have Been Made Public [as of Apr. 6, 2005], available at http://www.cptech.org/ip/health/trade; see also MSF Briefing Note, Access to Medicines at Risk Across the Globe: What to Watch Out for in Free Trade Agreements with the United States (May 2004), available at http://www.accessmed-msf.org. An excellent analysis of the U.S.-Chile FTA is Pedro Roffe, Bilateral

Agreements and a TRIPS-plus World: The Chile-USA Free Trade Agreement (Quaker International Affairs Programme, Ottawa, TRIPS Issues Paper No. 4, 2004).

2. Developing countries are sovereign. Their governments have the right under customary international law to make agreements binding on their people. But is there some international legal baseline against which such agreements must be assessed? Do human rights norms, such as a "right to health," inform this discussion? See the human rights discussion in the next section.

3. The major reason why IPRs enforcement through investor-state arbitration does not occur that often is mainly because most IPR infringements are the result of the conduct of private individuals and thus are not attributable to the states. What could be the other reasons?

3. Plurilateral Trade Agreements (The Anti-Counterfeiting Trade Agreement)

Recent years have seen a trend toward reverting to plurilateral efforts beyond the WTO and WIPO framework. Given the difficulties in making progress within international organizations, initiatives have been taken up by like-minded countries with a view toward creating a critical mass for future standards. These efforts mainly relate to enhancing the effectiveness of international enforcement of IPRs. Efforts have been made within the OECD countries. The most controversial initiative aimed at heightened enforcement of IPRs protection in recent years involves the Anti-Counterfeiting Trade Agreement (or ACTA). The Agreement is discussed in Chapter 6.

V. INTERPRETATION AND STATUS OF IPR AGREEMENTS IN DOMESTIC LAW

A. Interpretation

International agreements in intellectual property protection pertain to the realm of international law and thus are subject to the customary rules of interpretation in accordance with Article 31 of the 1969 Vienna Convention on the Law of Treaties. The following case discusses the relevance of these rules for the interpretation of the TRIPs Agreement.

The TRIPS Agreement, at Article 1.1, provides flexibility for WTO Members regarding the manner in which they implement their obligations. The first WTO dispute settlement complaint under the TRIPS Agreement was brought by the United States against India. In its complaint, the United States alleged that India had failed to implement its obligation to provide a so-called mailbox for the filing of patent applications during India's ten-year transition period for providing protection for pharmaceutical products. The panel found that India had, in fact, failed to establish the mailbox. But in doing so, the panel emphasized the expectations of the United States and its private sector pharmaceutical constituency regarding the outcome of the Uruguay Round negotiations. The Appellate Body affirmed the panel's conclusion, but took exception to its methodology. (We will further explore the substance of the patent "mailbox" system established by the TRIPS Agreement in Chapter 2.)

The following case expounds the main principles of interpretation and assesses the role of domestic law in assessing compatibility with WTO obligations. It illustrates that the TRIPS Agreement establishes an overarching set of rules, but leaves WTO Members with discretion regarding the precise manner in which these rules are implemented and enforced.

INDIA — PATENT PROTECTION FOR PHARMACEUTICAL AND AGRICULTURAL CHEMICAL PRODUCTS*
WTO Appellate Body (1997)

43. In addition to relying on the GATT *acquis*, the Panel relies also on the customary rules of interpretation of public international law as a basis for the interpretative principle it offers for the *TRIPS Agreement*. Specifically, the Panel relies on Article 31 of the *Vienna Convention*, which provides in part:

> 1. A treaty shall be interpreted in good faith in accordance with the ordinary meaning to be given to the terms of the treaty in their context and in the light of its object and purpose.

44. With this customary rule of interpretation in mind, the Panel stated that:

> In our view, good faith interpretation requires the protection of legitimate expectations derived from the protection of intellectual property rights provided for in the Agreement.

45. The Panel misapplies Article 31 of the *Vienna Convention*. The Panel misunderstands the concept of legitimate expectations in the context of the customary rules of interpretation of public international law. The legitimate expectations of the parties to a treaty are reflected in the language of the treaty itself. The duty of a treaty interpreter is to examine the words of the treaty to determine the intentions of the parties. This should be done in accordance with the principles of treaty interpretation set out in Article 31 of the *Vienna Convention*. But these principles of interpretation neither require nor condone the imputation into a treaty of words that are not there or the importation into a treaty of concepts that were not intended.

46. In *United States — Standards for Reformulated and Conventional Gasoline*, we set out the proper approach to be applied in interpreting the *WTO Agreement* in accordance with the rules in Article 31 of the *Vienna Convention*. These rules must be respected and applied in interpreting the *TRIPS Agreement* or any other covered agreement. The Panel in this case has created its own interpretative principle, which is consistent with neither the customary rules of interpretation of public international law nor established GATT/WTO practice. Both panels and the Appellate Body must be guided by the rules of treaty

* AB-1997-5, WT/DS50/AB/R, 15 Dec. 1997.

interpretation set out in the *Vienna Convention,* and must not add to or diminish rights and obligations provided in the *WTO Agreement.*

47.   This conclusion is dictated by two separate and very specific provisions of the DSU. Article 3.2 of the DSU provides that the dispute settlement system of the WTO:

> . . . serves to preserve the rights and obligations of the Members under the covered agreements, and to clarify the existing provisions of those agreements in accordance with customary rules of interpretation of public international law. Recommendations and rulings of the DSB cannot add to or diminish the rights and obligations provided in the covered agreements.

Furthermore, Article 19.2 of the DSU provides:

> In accordance with paragraph 2 of Article 3, in their findings and recommendations, the panel and Appellate Body cannot add to or diminish the rights and obligations provided in the covered agreements.

These provisions speak for themselves. Unquestionably, both panels and the Appellate Body are bound by them.

48.   For these reasons, we do not agree with the Panel that the legitimate expectations of Members *and* private rights holders concerning conditions of competition must always be taken into account in interpreting the *TRIPS Agreement.* . . .

57.   . . . The Agreement takes into account, *inter alia,* "the need to promote effective and adequate protection of intellectual property rights." We believe the Panel was correct in finding that the "means" that the Member concerned is obliged to provide under Article 70.8(a) must allow for "the entitlement to file mailbox applications and the allocation of filing and priority dates to them." Furthermore, the Panel was correct in finding that the "means" established under Article 70.8(a) must also provide "a sound legal basis to preserve novelty and priority as of those dates." These findings flow inescapably from the necessary operation of paragraphs (b) and (c) of Article 70.8.

58.   However, we do *not* agree with the Panel that Article 70.8(a) requires a Member to establish a means "so as to eliminate any reasonable doubts regarding whether mailbox applications and eventual patents based on them could be rejected or invalidated because, at the filing or priority date, the matter for which protection was sought was unpatentable in the country in question." India is *entitled,* by the "transitional arrangements" in paragraphs 1, 2 and 4 of Article 65, to delay application of Article 27 for patents for pharmaceutical and agricultural chemical products until 1 January 2005. In our view, India is obliged, by Article 70.8(a), to provide a legal mechanism for the filing of mailbox applications that provides a sound legal basis to preserve both the novelty of the inventions and the priority of the applications as of the relevant filing and priority dates. No more.

59.   But what constitutes such a sound legal basis in Indian law? To answer this question, we must recall first an important general rule in the *TRIPS Agreement.* Article 1.1 of the *TRIPS Agreement* states, in pertinent part:

> . . . Members shall be free to determine the appropriate method of implementing the provisions of this Agreement within their own legal system and practice.

Members, therefore, are free to determine how best to meet their obligations under the *TRIPS Agreement* within the context of their own legal systems. And, as a Member, India is "free to determine the appropriate method of implementing" its obligations under the *TRIPS Agreement* within the context of its own legal system.

NOTES AND QUESTIONS

1.   Article 1.1 of the TRIPS Agreement is one of the provisions that establish that WTO Members enjoy "flexibility" in the manner in which they implement their obligations under the Agreement. This flexibility was later confirmed in the Doha Declaration on the TRIPS Agreement and Public Health (adopted by the WTO Ministerial Conference on November 14, 2001), which provides:

> 4. We agree that the TRIPS Agreement does not and should not prevent Members from taking measures to protect public health. Accordingly, while reiterating our commitment to the TRIPS Agreement, we affirm that the Agreement can and should be interpreted and implemented in a manner supportive of WTO Members' right to protect public health and, in particular, to promote access to medicines for all.
>
> In this connection, we reaffirm the right of WTO Members to use, to the full, the provisions in the TRIPS Agreement, which provide flexibility for this purpose.

2.   Why do you think the Appellate Body is so intent on distinguishing a process of interpretation that relies on the express language of the Agreement, as opposed to a process that relies on the legitimate expectations of the parties? What is the practical difference between reliance on the wording, and reliance on legitimate expectations? Is the former an objective, and the later a subjective standard? How do you assess the role of good faith in treaty interpretation in accordance with Article 311(1) of the Vienna Convention?

3.   The doctrine of protecting legitimate expectations derives from GATT practice of protecting legitimate expectations as to conditions of competition. It is an emanation of good faith and seeks to rely upon an interpretation that a party to an agreement is reasonably entitled to in light of the conduct exercised by the other party to an agreement. It is meant to be an objective standard. Did the Appellate Body fail to appreciate the panels' underlying reasoning in its so-called *India-Mailbox* decision?

Flexibility provides policy space for governments in the field of IP. Certain industry interests, however, consider that this same flexibility may be used to unreasonably limit their return on investment. Much of the conflict over the TRIPS Agreement concerns defining the breadth of government policy space. This in turn brings us back to the discussion earlier in the chapter about efforts to harmonize the international IP system. Is flexibility the "enemy" of harmonization? Or might providing some "play in the joints" of international IP agreements make it more likely that governments would join them? An indepth study commissioned by the United Nations Conference on Trade and Development (UNCTAD) and the International Centre for Trade and Sustainable Development (ICTSD) regarding the negotiating history and interpretation of the TRIPS Agreement focuses on explaining the policy space or flexibilities within the Agreement.

VI. BASIC PRINCIPLES OF INTERNATIONAL IP PROTECTION

All forms of IPRs embody certain cornerstones and shared concepts, such as territoriality, ubiquity, exhaustion, and limited duration. The need to achieve some level of coherence and transnational uniformity resulted in various treaties, which in turn include important general principles like national treatment, most favored nation (MFN) treatment, and (in the context of registered rights) the right of priority. Addressing such features beforehand will help us navigate through the detailed provisions of the legal framework.

A. National Treatment

It is appropriate to start with the principle of national treatment, which is one of the oldest organizing principles found in international trade and investment agreements. This was a core feature of nineteenth-century bilateral agreements, establishing the fundamental tenet of nondiscrimination: Foreign nationals or entitled subject matter (such as goods, services, or investment) shall not be treated less favorably than domestic nationals or subject matter. This principle, eventually enshrined in the GATT 1947 and the 1995 WTO agreements, including Article 3 of the TRIPS Agreement, is of paramount importance in bringing about level playing fields and fair conditions of competition for foreign products. It is equally a fundamental principle of political economy: As political systems tend to favor domestic constituencies and voters, it is the task of international agreements to bring about a proper rebalancing of these shortcomings. Mutual interest in furthering fair conditions of competition in foreign markets provides ample incentive for this rebalancing.

National treatment also effectively functions as a substitute for international harmonization. To the extent that states concentrate on national law, and progress in international law is slow (as it was after decolonization and before the Uruguay Round), the principle of national treatment allows the international community to automatically benefit from improved standards in municipal law or regional law introduced mainly for the welfare (and at request) of domestic right holders.

In the field of IPRs, national treatment has been part of the international system from the very beginning. Article 2 and 3 of the 1883 Paris Convention enshrined the principle, and ever since it has been part of all multilateral IPRs agreements.

Art. 2(1) Paris Convention [National Treatment for Nationals of Countries of the Union]

Nationals of any country of the Union shall, as regards the protection of industrial property, enjoy in all the other countries of the Union the advantages that their respective laws now grant, or may hereafter grant, to nationals; all without prejudice to the rights specially provided by this Convention. Consequently, they shall have the same protection as the latter, and the same legal remedy against any infringement of their rights, provided that the conditions and formalities imposed upon nationals are complied with.

Article 3 of the TRIPS Agreement contains the most comprehensive statement of the principle and its exceptions under existing and partially incorporated international agreements. Its formulation is based on Article III of the GATT 1947 and requires member states to "accord to the nationals of other Members treatment no less favourable than that it accords to its own nationals with regard to the protection of intellectual property." The obligation extends to all parts of the Agreement, including the availability, acquisition, scope, maintenance, and enforcement of IPRs as well as those matters affecting the use of intellectual property rights specifically addressed in the Agreement.

ART. 3 TRIPS AGREEMENT: NATIONAL TREATMENT

1.   Each Member shall accord to the nationals of other Members treatment no less favourable than that it accords to its own nationals with regard to the protection[3] of intellectual property, subject to the exceptions already provided in, respectively, the Paris Convention (1967), the Berne Convention (1971), the Rome Convention or the Treaty on Intellectual Property in Respect of Integrated Circuits. In respect of performers, producers of phonograms and broadcasting organizations, this obligation only applies in respect of the rights provided under this Agreement. Any Member availing itself of the possibilities provided in Article 6 of the Berne Convention (1971) or paragraph 1(b) of Article 16 of the Rome Convention shall make a notification as foreseen in those provisions to the Council for TRIPS.

2.   Members may avail themselves of the exceptions permitted under paragraph 1 in relation to judicial and administrative procedures, including the designation of an address for service or the appointment of an agent within the jurisdiction of a Member, only where such exceptions are necessary to secure compliance with laws and regulations which are not inconsistent with the provisions of this Agreement and where such practices are not applied in a manner which would constitute a disguised restriction on trade.

The wording of the provision deviates from Article 2 of the Paris Convention, which requires equal treatment ("the same protection"). Differences between the two provisions are limited. While treatment no less favorable, in theory and practice, allows for reverse discrimination (discrimination à rebours) in favor of non-nationals, intellectual property laws normally provide, as abstract rules, for equal protection of all right holders alike and neither privilege nor disadvantage nationals, although exceptions to this finding exist. Moreover, Article 3 of the Paris Convention provides for equal protection also of resident nationals of non-members, thus extending protection beyond the TRIPS Agreement.

---

3. For the purposes of Articles 3 and 4, "protection" shall include matters affecting the availability, acquisition, scope, maintenance and enforcement of intellectual property rights as well as those matters affecting the use of intellectual property rights specifically addressed in this Agreement.

Finally, national treatment obligations under Article III of the GATT also apply in regard to procedures affecting the importation of products protected by intellectual property rights.

In a case usually referred to as *U.S.-Havana Club,* the WTO Appellate Body has applied the national treatment principle. At the heart of the dispute were U.S. rules applied to trademarks nationalized by the government of Cuba in the 1960s. A more extensive excerpt from the decision appears in Chapter 3 with specific reference to the trademark law questions. Here the AB rigorously applies a standard that appears to preclude virtually any distinction between foreign and domestic national trademark applicants.

UNITED STATES — SECTION 211
OMNIBUS APPROPRIATIONS ACT OF 1998*

WTO Appellate Body

233.   We turn now to the issue of national treatment. In this appeal we have been asked to address, for the first time, this fundamental principle of the world trading system as it relates to intellectual property. There are two separate national treatment provisions that cover trademarks as well as other intellectual property rights covered by the *TRIPS Agreement.* The European Communities claims, on appeal, that Sections 211(a)(2) and (b) violate both.

234.   One national treatment provision at issue in this appeal is Article 2(1) of the Paris Convention (1967), which states:

> Nationals of any country of the Union shall, as regards the protection of industrial property, enjoy in all the other countries of the Union the advantages that their respective laws now grant, or may hereafter grant, to nationals; all without prejudice to the rights specially provided for by this Convention. Consequently, they shall have the same protection as the latter, and the same legal remedy against any infringement of their rights, provided that the conditions and formalities imposed upon nationals are complied with.

235.   As we have already explained, the Stockholm Act of the Paris Convention, dated 14 July 1967, is but the most recent version of that important international intellectual property convention. Article 2(1) was part of the Paris Convention in 1883. Since that time, it has remained a treaty obligation of all the countries that have been party to the Paris Convention.

236.   The parties to this dispute are not unacquainted with the national treatment obligation and other protections for trademarks and other forms of industrial property provided by the Paris Convention. Every one of the fifteen Member States of the European Union has long been a country of the Paris Union. Most of the current Member States of the European Union became party to the Paris Convention in the 1880's. The most recent did so in 1925 — seventy-seven years ago. Likewise, the United States has, from almost the very beginning, been a country of the Paris Union. The United States became a country of the Paris Union on 30 May 1887 — one hundred and fifteen years ago.

---

* WT/DS176/AB/R, 2 Jan. 2002.

237.   Thus, the national treatment obligation is a longstanding obligation under international law for all the countries directly involved in this dispute, as well as for many more countries of the Paris Union that, like the parties to this dispute, are also Members of the WTO. If there were no *TRIPS Agreement*, if there were no WTO, the parties to this dispute would be bound, nevertheless, under Article 2(1) of the Paris Convention (1967), to accord national treatment to other countries of the Paris Union.

238.   As we have explained, what *is* new is that, as a consequence of the Uruguay Round, Article 2(1) of the Paris Convention (1967) was made part of the *WTO Agreement*. And, as we have previously explained, by virtue of Article 2.1 of the *TRIPS Agreement*, Article 2(1) of the Paris Convention (1967), as well as certain other specified provisions of the Paris Convention (1967), have been incorporated into the *TRIPS Agreement* and, thus, the *WTO Agreement*. Consequently, these obligations of countries of the Paris Union under the Paris Convention (1967) are also now obligations of all WTO Members, whether they are countries of the Paris Union or not, under the *WTO Agreement*, and, thus, are enforceable under the DSU.

239.   In addition to Article 2(1) of the Paris Convention (1967), there is also another national treatment provision in the *TRIPS Agreement*. The other national treatment provision at issue in this appeal is Article 3.1 of the *TRIPS Agreement*, which states in relevant part:

> Each Member shall accord to the nationals of other Members treatment no less favourable than that it accords to its own nationals with regard to the protection [footnote 3] of intellectual property, subject to the exceptions already provided in, respectively, the Paris Convention (1967), the Berne Convention (1971), the Rome Convention or the Treaty on Intellectual Property in Respect of Integrated Circuits.
>
> Footnote 3: For the purposes of Articles 3 and 4, "protection" shall include matters affecting the availability, acquisition, scope, maintenance and enforcement of intellectual property rights as well as those matters affecting the use of intellectual property rights specifically addressed in this Agreement.

240.   Thus, in drafting the *TRIPS Agreement*, the framers of the *WTO Agreement* saw fit to include an additional provision on national treatment. Clearly, this emphasizes the fundamental significance of the obligation of national treatment to their purposes in the *TRIPS Agreement*.

241.   Indeed, the significance of the national treatment obligation can hardly be overstated. Not only has the national treatment obligation long been a cornerstone of the Paris Convention and other international intellectual property conventions. So, too, has the national treatment obligation long been a cornerstone of the world trading system that is served by the WTO.

242.   As we see it, the national treatment obligation is a fundamental principle underlying the *TRIPS Agreement*, just as it has been in what is now the GATT 1994. The Panel was correct in concluding that, as the language of Article 3.1 of the *TRIPS Agreement*, in particular, is similar to that of Article III:4 of the GATT 1994, the jurisprudence on Article III:4 of the GATT 1994 may be useful in interpreting the national treatment obligation in the *TRIPS Agreement*.

243.   As articulated in Article 3.1 of the *TRIPS Agreement*, the national treatment principle calls on WTO Members to accord no less favourable treatment

to non-nationals than to nationals in the "protection" of trade-related intellectual property rights. The footnote to Article 3.1 clarifies that this "protection" extends to "matters affecting the availability, acquisition, scope, maintenance and enforcement of intellectual property rights as well as those matters affecting the use of intellectual property rights specifically addressed" in the *TRIPS Agreement*. . . .

1. National Treatment and Discrimination

Several sets of issues tend to be raised in cases involving intellectual property and the national treatment principle. The national treatment principle is one of "nondiscrimination" between foreigners and domestic nationals. It is important at the outset to distinguish between "discrimination" and "differentiation." The national treatment principle does not prevent a government from establishing different rules that apply to foreigners and domestic nationals, that is, rules that take into account legitimate differences. What is prohibited are measures that adversely affect foreigners without justification, thereby creating an imbalance in conditions of competition. The WTO panel decision in the *EU-Geographical Indications* case, excerpted below, addresses various claims by the European Union regarding legitimate differentiation between the treatment of EU and foreign nationals. The possibility to differentiate between foreign and domestic nationals with respect to application procedures is expressly addressed in the relevant international agreements.

Another set of issues involves the distinction between *de jure* and *de facto* discrimination. Some legislation or regulation expressly addresses rights of foreigners in a way that is different from the way the rights of domestic nationals are addressed. Differences are stated as a matter of law or *de jure*. Some legislation or regulation does not make overt distinction between foreigners and domestic nationals, yet operates in a way that creates a difference that is discriminatory. This situation was addressed by a GATT panel in a 1989 case involving a European challenge to Section 337 of the U.S. Trade Act of 1930.[99] Section 337 allows holders of registered IP rights in the United States to seek remedies before the International Trade Commission (ITC) from imports that would infringe their rights. In 1989, the Section 337 procedures made it faster and easier for U.S. patent holders to block importation of infringing imports before the ITC than to obtain remedies for infringement in federal court. The Section 337 procedure was available to foreign nationals holding registered U.S. patents, and on its face did not differentiate between foreigners and domestic U.S. patent holders. However, the GATT panel did not think this *de jure* nondiscrimination insulated the legislation because imported products are preponderantly produced by foreigners.

If the term of copyright protection in two countries varies in duration (70 versus 50 years, the latter being a minimum standard under Article 12, TRIPS Agreement), the principle of national treatment generally would not allow the country with the longer term to accord only the shorter term to the other's nationals. IPRs holders would equally enjoy a term of 70 years in one country, and 50 years in the other. The Berne Convention deviates from the

---

99. GATT Panel Report, *United States Section 337 of the Tariff Act of 1930*, adopted 7 November 1989, BISD 36S/345.

principle of national treatment in regard to the duration of copyright, stating that foreigners need only be accorded the term of their home country (Article 7, Berne Convention).

2. National Treatment and Reciprocity

A national treatment obligation requires that a state grant to nationals of other states (enjoying protection) treatment equivalent to that which it grants its own nationals. Under WTO rules, the national treatment obligation is essentially unconditional. That is, once a WTO Member agrees to provide national treatment to another Member, it may not require any further "concession" in order to make that obligation operational.

Another potential approach to the treatment of foreign nationals is "material reciprocity" or "conditional national treatment." Under such an approach, a country would agree to provide national treatment to persons (or products) from foreign countries, but only on the condition that the foreign countries provide an equivalent level of protection as the first country. (Hypothetically, the United States might agree to provide the same form of "patent term extension" to foreign applicants as it provides to U.S. patent applicants, but only on the condition that the home countries of relevant foreign applicants provide equivalent patent term extension to U.S. national patent applicants.[100])

Material reciprocity is not permitted under the TRIPS or GATT national treatment provisions. However, a number of IPRs in the field of copyright remain subject to the requirement of reciprocity. Here, national treatment of rights is only granted if applied mutually by both Parties. Such exceptions are referred to in Article 3.1 of the TRIPS Agreement. Corresponding rules are contained in Articles 6.1 and 20 of the Berne Convention and Article 13.d and 16.1 of the Rome Convention. They essentially relate to the predominantly European system of collecting societies by which authors and performers obtain remuneration on the basis of membership and overall income from royalties, rather than on the basis of individual contracts. The extension of national treatment to collecting societies was a major goal of the United States, since much of the revenue of these societies is generated from works of U.S. authors and artists but does not reach these persons if they are not members of the societies. The United States did not prevail on this point, partly due to its lack of corresponding societies and a system based on individual contracts, and partly due to European resistance to sharing income that was used in Nordic countries to support general cultural activities.

Article 3.2 of the TRIPS Agreement qualifies those exceptions referred to in Article 3.1 that relate to judicial and administrative procedures, including the designation of an address for service or the appointment of an agent for foreign right holders (which does not exist for domiciled persons), thus facilitating intercourse with the authorities. Exceptions are only permitted where necessary to secure compliance with laws and regulations that are not inconsistent with the Agreement, and they must not be applied in a way that constitutes a disguised restriction on trade. The wording of these exceptions is very narrow. Obligations to appoint an agent for service are common in all fields of

---

100. This is "hypothetical" because the United States does not restrict patent term extension to U.S. national patent applicants.

registered IPRs, such as trademarks or patents, and it is difficult to see why they should be limited to the exceptions set out in paragraph 1 of the provision. The text does not reflect the purpose of the provision and should be read in its overall context to encompass all rights that are subject to registration.

In a dispute over the treatment of geographical indications with the United States,[101] the European Union attempted to defend a provision in its legislation that made protection under its GIs legislation conditional upon an equivalent level of treatment being provided by third countries. The WTO dispute settlement panel rejected the EU approach, as discussed in the following excerpt.[102] The panel also rejected the European Union's claim that its regulations provided equivalent opportunity for non-nationals to register GIs for products produced within the territory of the European Union. The panel's decision was not appealed to the Appellate Body.

EUROPEAN COMMUNITIES — PROTECTION OF TRADEMARKS AND GEOGRAPHICAL INDICATIONS FOR AGRICULTURAL PRODUCTS AND FOODSTUFFS COMPLAINT BY THE UNITED STATES

Report of the Panel*

B. National Treatment Claims . . .

LESS FAVOURABLE TREATMENT ACCORDED TO THE NATIONALS OF OTHER MEMBERS

Less Favourable Treatment

7.131 The Panel now examines the second element of this claim which is whether the nationals of other Members are accorded less favourable treatment than the European Communities' own nationals. It is useful to recall that Article 3.1 of the TRIPS Agreement combines elements of national treatment both from pre-existing intellectual property agreements and GATT 1994.[166] Like the pre-existing intellectual property conventions, Article 3.1 applies to "nationals," not products. Like GATT 1994, Article 3.1 refers to "no less favourable" treatment, not the advantages or rights that laws now grant or may hereafter grant, but it does not refer to likeness. This combination of elements is reflected in the preamble to the TRIPS Agreement which explains the purpose of the "basic principles" in Articles 3 and 4 (a term highlighted in the title of Part I) as follows:

> "*Recognizing,* to this end, the need for new rules and disciplines concerning:
> (a) the applicability of the basic principles of GATT 1994 and of relevant international intellectual property agreements or conventions;" . . .

---

101. Australia brought a separate complaint against the European Union.

102. Another part of the EU-GIs WTO panel report, addressing the relationship between trademarks and GIs, appears in Chapter 3.

* WT/DS174/R, 15 Mar. 2005.

166. Three of these national treatment obligations are incorporated in the TRIPS Agreement itself: Article 2 of the Paris Convention (1967) . . . , Article 5 of the Berne Convention (1971) and Article 5 of the IPIC Treaty, which are incorporated by Articles 2.1, 9.1 and 35 of the TRIPS Agreement, respectively.

7.133 We recall that the Panel in *US — Section 211 Appropriations Act*, in a finding with which the Appellate Body agreed, found that the appropriate standard of examination under Article 3.1 of the TRIPS Agreement is that enunciated by the GATT Panel in *US — Section 337*. That GATT Panel made the following findings on the "no less favourable" treatment standard under Article III:4 of GATT 1947:

> "The words 'treatment no less favourable' in paragraph 4 call for effective equality of opportunities for imported products in respect of the application of laws, regulations and requirements affecting the internal sale, offering for sale, purchase, transportation, distribution or use of products. This clearly sets a minimum permissible standard as a basis."

Therefore, the Panel will examine whether the difference in treatment affects the "effective equality of opportunities" between the nationals of other Members and the European Communities' own nationals with regard to the "protection" of intellectual property rights, to the detriment of nationals of other Members. . . .

7.139 Although the parties disagree on whether the equivalence and reciprocity conditions in Article 12(1) of the Regulation discriminate in a manner inconsistent with the covered agreements, it is not disputed that those conditions accord less favourable treatment to persons with interests in the *GIs* to which those conditions apply.[172] The Panel considers that those conditions modify the effective equality of opportunities to obtain protection with respect to intellectual property in two ways. First, GI protection is not available under the Regulation in respect of geographical areas located in third countries which the Commission has not recognized under Article 12(3). The European Communities confirms that the Commission has not recognized any third countries. Second, GI protection under the Regulation may become available if the third country in which the GI is located enters into an international agreement or satisfies the conditions in Article 12(1). Both of those requirements represent a significant "extra hurdle" in obtaining GI protection that does not apply to geographical areas located in the European Communities.[173] The significance of the hurdle is reflected in the fact that currently no third country has entered into such an agreement or satisfied those conditions.

7.140 Accordingly, the Panel finds that the equivalence and reciprocity conditions modify the effective equality of opportunities with respect to the availability of protection to persons who wish to obtain GI protection under the Regulation, to the detriment of those who wish to obtain protection in respect of geographical areas located in third countries, including WTO Members. This is less favourable treatment. . . .

---

172. . . . Note that the European Communities asserts only that the product specifications and inspection regimes for individual GIs do not constitute less favourable treatment. With respect to the equivalence and reciprocity conditions, it asserts that it does not apply them and that they do not depend on nationality, but *not* that they do not accord less favourable treatment where they apply: see its first written submission, paras. 113-126, and paras. 62-69. It also concedes that they constitute less favourable treatment for the purposes of Article III:4 of GATT 1994, but does not consider that the meaning of the phrase is necessarily the same as in Article 3.1 of the TRIPS Agreement: see its responses to Panel question Nos. 94(a) and 113.

173. This was also the approach of the Appellate Body in *US — Section 211 Appropriations Act* to an "extra hurdle" imposed only on foreign nationals: see para. 268 of its report.

Formally Identical Provisions

7.172 The issue for the Panel remains that of determining the treatment accorded to the nationals of other Members and to the European Communities' own nationals. On its face, the Regulation contains formally identical provisions vis-à-vis the nationals of different Members, with respect to the availability of GI protection.

7.173 It is well recognized that the concept of "no less favourable" treatment under Article III:4 of GATT 1994 is sufficiently broad to include situations where the application of formally identical legal provisions would in practice accord less favourable treatment. The GATT Panel in *US—Section 337,* which considered an intellectual property enforcement measure prior to the conclusion of the TRIPS Agreement, interpreted the "no less favourable" standard under Article III:4 as follows:

> "On the one hand, contracting parties may apply to imported products different formal legal requirements if doing so would accord imported products more favourable treatment. On the other hand, it also has to be recognised that there may be cases where application of formally identical legal provisions would in practice accord less favourable treatment to imported products and a contracting party might thus have to apply different legal provisions to imported products to ensure that the treatment accorded them is in fact no less favourable." . . .

7.182 The Panel therefore considers it appropriate for the purposes of this claim to compare the effective equality of opportunities for the group of nationals of other Members who may wish to seek GI protection under the Regulation and the group of the European Communities' own nationals who may wish to seek GI protection under the Regulation. On this approach, there is no need to make a factual assumption that every person who wishes to obtain protection for a GI in a particular Member is a national of that Member.[202] . . .

7.189 The[se] provisions create a link between persons, the territory of a particular Member, and the availability of protection. The definition of a "designation of origin" requires that the applicant and users must produce, process and prepare the products covered by a registration in the relevant geographical area, whilst the definition of a "geographical indication" requires that the applicant and users must carry out at least one, or some combination, of these three activities in the geographical area, and must do so in accordance with a specification.

---

202. The Panel notes that its approach based on the respective treatment accorded to groups (of nationals) is consistent with an approach based on the respective treatment accorded to groups (of products) contemplated by the Appellate Body in *EC — Asbestos,* in the context of the national treatment obligation in Article III:4 of GATT 1994:

> "(. . .) A complaining Member must still establish that the measure accords to the group of 'like' *imported* products "less favourable treatment" than it accords to the group of 'like' *domestic* products. The term 'less favourable treatment' expresses the general principle, in Article III:1, that internal regulations 'should not be applied . . . so as to afford protection to domestic production.' If there is 'less favourable treatment' of the group of 'like' imported products, there is, conversely, 'protection' of the group of 'like' domestic products. However, a Member may draw distinctions between products which have been found to be 'like,' without, for this reason alone, according to the group of 'like' *imported* products 'less favourable treatment' than that accorded to the group of 'like' *domestic* products. (. . .)", at para. 100.

7.190 Accordingly, insofar as the Regulation discriminates with respect to the availability of protection between GIs located in the European Communities, on the one hand, and those located in third countries, including WTO Members, on the other hand, it formally discriminates between those persons who produce, process and/or prepare a product in accordance with a specification, in the European Communities, on the one hand, and those persons who produce, process and/or prepare a product in accordance with a specification, in third countries, including WTO Members, on the other hand. . . .

7.194 The Panel agrees that the vast majority of natural and legal persons who produce, process and/or prepare products according to a GI specification within the territory of a WTO Member party to this dispute will be nationals of that Member. The fact that there may be cases where such a person does not qualify as a national — and none has been brought to its attention — does not alter the fact that the distinction made by the Regulation on the basis of the location of a GI will operate in practice to discriminate between the group of nationals of other Members who wish to obtain GI protection, and the group of the European Communities' own nationals who wish to obtain GI protection, to the detriment of the nationals of other Members. This will not occur as a random outcome in a particular case but as a feature of the design and structure of the system. This design is evident in the Regulation's objective characteristics, in particular, the definitions of "designation of origin" and "geographical indication" and the requirements of the product specifications. The structure is evident in the different registration procedures.

7.195 Complete data on the persons who have actually availed themselves of protection under the Regulation is not available. Any person who produces, processes and/or prepares a product according to the specification in a GI registration is entitled to use the GI. Data on the persons who have applied for, and obtained, protection under the Regulation and their respective addresses is available but their nationality is not recorded. However, there is no clear evidence that even a single person who has applied for or is entitled to use a registered GI is not one of the European Communities' own nationals. . . .

7.197 The European Communities presented evidence intended to show that certain foreign nationals have actually obtained protection under the Regulation. The Panel notes that all its examples consist of a foreign national, or a corporation incorporated under the laws of an EC member State, that acquired another corporation incorporated under the laws of an EC member State, which produces products entitled to GI protection.[209] Those subsidiary corporations obtaining the benefit of protection appear to be the European

---

209. The evidence is as follows: Mr. Jens-Reidar Larsen, a Norwegian national, acquired a French cognac firm in 1928. Cognac is not a product covered by the Regulation at issue; Sara Lee Personal Products SpA, an Italian corporation under common control with Sara Lee Charcuterie SA, a French corporation belonging to the Sara Lee group, acquired Al Ponte Prosciutto SRL, an Italian corporation; Kraft Foods Group, which has an Italian subsidiary, acquired the business of Giovanni Invernizzi, an Italian, and partly sold it to Lactalis, a French dairy company with an Italian subsidiary; Nestlé sold Vismara, a salami firm, to an Italian company. The persons who acquired GI protection in these three examples may all be the European Communities' own nationals. The European Communities also refers to the website of a private beer label collector who disclaims accuracy but suggests that a Belgian company used to produce a beer with a German GI, possibly before the Regulation entered into force. The Panel considers this example unreliable. See Exhibits EC-36, EC-61, EC-62, EC-63 and EC-89 and the United States' response to Panel question No. 102.

Communities' own nationals, according to a place of incorporation test. Evidence is not available on the place of their company seat but such cases appear to be rare. This evidence confirms, rather than contradicts, the link between the treatment accorded to GIs located in the European Communities and EC nationality. . . .

7.203 . . . Whilst the Regulation does not prevent a foreign national from producing goods within the territory of the European Communities which would be entitled to use a GI, the implications of its design and structure on the opportunities for protection are such that its different procedures will operate to accord different treatment to the European Communities' own nationals and to the nationals of other Members, to the detriment of the nationals of other Members.[214]

7.204 Accordingly, the Panel's preliminary conclusion is that, with respect to the availability of protection, the treatment accorded to the group of nationals of other Members is different from, and less favourable than, that accorded to the European Communities' own nationals. . . .

NOTES AND QUESTIONS

1. EU regulations governing geographical indications are extraordinarily complex, and for this reason (among others), the decision of the WTO panel in this case is also complex. However, the two aspects of the case presented above are not so difficult. First, the European Union argued that nationals of foreign countries would be treated the same as EU nationals with respect to recognition of their GIs, but only if the European Union decided that the foreign countries maintained GI protection systems equivalent to those in place in the European Union (such as by maintaining systems that monitored the production processes used for GI-protected products). In the alternative, a foreign country could negotiate an agreement with the European Union for the recognition of specific GIs. The panel said that the TRIPS Agreement national treatment provision did not allow the European Union to condition its provision of national treatment in these ways. Second, the European Union argued that foreigners were accorded the same *de jure* legal treatment as EU nationals according to the terms of its legislation, and were equally entitled to register GIs that met the requirements for protection within the European Union. The panel said that might be so, but was essentially beside the point. As a *de facto* matter, foreign applicants would almost exclusively seek to register GIs for products produced abroad, and the EU regulations effectively precluded that by imposing restrictive conditions. The only instances in which foreign nationals had become holders of EU-registered GIs involved foreign takeovers of existing EU businesses that had previously registered them. In sum, the European Union conferred the benefits of GI protection on its own nationals, and not on foreign nationals.

214. Article 8a of the EC Treaty provides that every citizen of the European Union shall have the right to move and reside freely within the territory of the EC member States. Article 52 (in conjunction with Article 58) provides for the progressive abolition of restrictions on the freedom of establishment of nationals of an EC member State. These provisions remove obstacles to persons who wish to produce products according to a GI specification within the territory of the European Communities, but apply to the European Communities' own nationals only.

2. Assume that an American scientist invents a new chemical compound at a laboratory in California. The scientist files a patent application in the United States, and a U.S. patent is granted. The European Patent Office receives the same application and applies a (hypothetical) European Patent Convention rule that says that only inventive activity taking place in Europe can form the basis for a valid European patent. It says that it will grant patents to American inventors in Europe (so that it does not discriminate on the basis of nationality), but rejects the instant application because the invention was made in the United States. Is this permitted under the TRIPS Agreement national treatment rule?

3. The entire WTO negotiating process (save for exceptions in favor of developing countries) is based on the principle of reciprocity. (*See* OLIVIER LONG, LAW AND ITS LIMITATIONS IN THE GATT MULTILATERAL TRADING SYSTEM 1987.) That is, no Member is expected to make a concession without receiving a concession from another Member in return. But, once the negotiating is complete, the agreements are drafted so as to make obligations unconditional. Why do WTO Members consistently reject establishing legal obligations based on the concept of reciprocity?

4. The EU Database Directive, discussed *infra* Chapter 4, similarly provides that nationals of third countries will only enjoy protection for their databases if their home countries provide equivalent protection for EU nationals. The European Union has sometimes attempted to defend this reciprocity condition on grounds that *sui generis* database protection is not the subject of the TRIPS Agreement, and therefore this part of the Database Directive is not subject to the TRIPS Agreement national treatment rule. In the *U.S.-Havana Club* case, excerpted *infra*, Chapter 3, II.D.2, the WTO Appellate Body discusses the scope of intellectual property subject matter covered by the TRIPS Agreement, though not this specific issue. Do you think the EU Database Directive condition is consistent with its TRIPS Agreement national treatment obligation?

5. The GATT 1994 addresses trade in goods, including agricultural products. It includes its own national treatment provision at Article III, which has a substantial history of interpretation in dispute settlement tracing all the way back to the formation of the GATT 1947. While the WTO Agreement takes precedence over its subsidiary agreements, such as GATT 1994 and the TRIPS Agreement, in the event of a conflict (Article XVI:4, WTO Agreement), it does not otherwise establish a hierarchy among these agreements. In parts of the text decision not reproduced here, the WTO panel in the text case analyzes the EU legislation under both national treatment rules. Why might it have done this?

B. Most Favored Nation Treatment (MFN)

Most favored nation treatment (MFN) is a second mainstay of nondiscrimination in international trade and investment regulation. It has accompanied national treatment in many bilateral agreements, and it became the main conceptual and legal pillar of the GATT 1947. This classical principle prescribes in Article I, GATT 1994, that "any advantage, favour, privilege or immunity granted by any contracting party to any product originating in or destined for any other country shall be accorded immediately and unconditionally to

the like product originating or destined for the territories of all other contracting parties." The MFN principle has been important to the successful reduction
of tariff barriers during the last 50 years. Unlike national treatment, this cornerstone of the international trading system did not apply to intellectual property under the Paris and Berne Conventions. Neither of them contained
comparable rights and obligations.

There was an important political motive for adoption of an unconditional
MFN rule for the international trading system. In the pre-Second World War
environment, trade concessions were widely used as an instrument of diplomacy. Political alliances were created and maintained through economic preferences. Since diplomatic decisions were often made for reasons apart from
improving world prosperity, an economic system in which trade concessions
were used as political instruments would be unlikely to generate a global
welfare-optimizing result. The MFN principle was and is intended to de-
politicize the international economic system so as to reduce the chances of
breakdown into a system of diplomacy-based alliances. The net effect should
be to distribute the benefits of trade widely. The MFN principle was the key
multilateralism provision in the GATT 1947, and it remains a cornerstone of
the WTO system, including in the TRIPS context.

So far as the Paris and Berne Conventions were concerned, the MFN principle appeared to be dispensable as nondiscrimination could be largely achieved
on the basis of national treatment in the regulatory context of IPRs. As all
foreign national IPRs holders are entitled to equal treatment with nationals,
discrimination among foreign IPRs holders was unlikely to arise. In the 1980s
and early 1990s, however, the United States pursued bilateral and regional
agreements to obtain IPRs protection that went beyond national standards,
particularly in the field of patent "pipeline" protection for pharmaceutical
and chemical products.[103] This raised concerns during the Uruguay Round,
and lead to the introduction of the MFN principle in the international IPRs
system — Article 4 of the TRIPS Agreement. An intention to maintain consistency within the WTO system also played a role in the adoption of Article 4.

Article 4 of the TRIPS Agreement establishes the obligation of most favored
nation treatment. This obligation reflects the influence of GATT Article I and
obliges all WTO members to extend privileges accorded to one Member immediately and unconditionally to all other Members. Importantly, the provision is
not limited to TRIPS obligations, but extends to all protection granted to
intellectual property, with the exception of rights of performers, producers
of phonograms, and broadcasting organizations not provided under the
TRIPS Agreement. The MFN provision strengthens, in particular, the position
of smaller IP-owner countries such as Switzerland vis-à-vis the large IP-owner
trading powers in third markets. As a result of the TRIPS Agreement and its
MFN clause, unilateral practices, or a bilateral agreement concluded between
two Members, granting and providing greater protection (TRIPS-plus), or the
improvement of registration procedures, may need to be extended to all

---

103. "Pipeline" protection refers to several variations on a similar theme. Essentially, it connotes agreement by a country to provide patent (or equivalent) protection to products that already
have been granted patent protection in a second country, or which are in the process of regulatory
approval in that second country, even though patent (or equivalent) protection has not been
available in the first country prior to expiration of the Paris Convention priority period.

Members, but this conclusion is controversial because of the potential adverse impact on non-IP-owner member exports.

ART. 4 TRIPS AGREEMENT: MOST-FAVOURED-NATION TREATMENT

With regard to the protection of intellectual property, any advantage, favour, privilege or immunity granted by a Member to the nationals of any other country shall be accorded immediately and unconditionally to the nationals of all other Members. Exempted from this obligation are any advantage, favour, privilege or immunity accorded by a Member:

(a) deriving from international agreements on judicial assistance or law enforce-ment of a general nature and not particularly confined to the protection of intellectual property;
(b) granted in accordance with the provisions of the Berne Convention (1971) or the Rome Convention authorizing that the treatment accorded be a function not of national treatment but of the treatment accorded in another country;
(c) in respect of the rights of performers, producers of phonograms and broad-casting organizations not provided under this Agreement;
(d) deriving from international agreements related to the protection of intellec-tual property which entered into force prior to the entry into force of the WTO Agreement, provided that such agreements are notified to the Council for TRIPS and do not constitute an arbitrary or unjustifiable discrimination against nationals of other Members.

Article 4 thus provides for a number of enumerated exceptions to MFN, which relate to privileged, non-IPR-specific judicial assistance or law enforcement. Again, the provision refers to relevant privileges contained in the Berne Con-vention and the Rome Convention providing for reciprocity and that, logically not only exclude national treatment, but also MFN. Finally, privileges existing prior to the entry into force of the TRIPS Agreement in all areas of intellectual property are grandfathered to the extent that respective agreements were for-mally notified to the TRIPS Council and, in addition, do not amount to "arbi-trary and unjustifiable discrimination" against nationals of other Members. The interpretation of this proviso will be influenced by the jurisprudence relating to the chapeau of GATT Article XX, which uses similar language. Special arrange-ments and practices therefore will only be lawful if they are based upon relevant factual differences between Members.

The TRIPS Agreement does not contain a "forward-looking" exception corresponding to Article XXIV of GATT and Article V of GATS allowing for privileges in the context of newly-concluded free trade agreements, customs unions, and regional economic integration. Negotiators agreed that preferen-tial treatment in terms of intellectual property protection was neither advisable, nor necessary. However, the agreements of customs unions and free trade areas in force when the TRIPS Agreement was adopted were notified to the TRIPS Council as falling under the Article 4(d) MFN exemption, and certain of the arrangements (including the EU) provided in the notification that the exemption from MFN would apply to future rules adopted by the customs union.

In the following brief excerpt, again from the *U.S.-Havana Club* case, the WTO Appellate Body stresses the importance of the MFN principle in TRIPS.

UNITED STATES — SECTION 211
OMNIBUS APPROPRIATIONS ACT OF 1998*

WTO Appellate Body

297. Like the national treatment obligation, the obligation to provide most-favoured-nation treatment has long been one of the cornerstones of the world trading system. For more than fifty years, the obligation to provide most-favoured-nation treatment in Article I of the GATT 1994 has been both central and essential to assuring the success of a global rules-based system for trade in goods. Unlike the national treatment principle, there is no provision in the Paris Convention (1967) that establishes a most-favoured-nation obligation with respect to rights in trademarks or other industrial property. However, the framers of the *TRIPS Agreement* decided to extend the most-favoured-nation obligation to the protection of intellectual property rights covered by that Agreement. As a cornerstone of the world trading system, the most-favoured-nation obligation must be accorded the same significance with respect to intellectual property rights under the *TRIPS Agreement* that it has long been accorded with respect to trade in goods under the GATT. It is, in a word, fundamental.

NOTES AND QUESTIONS

1. Assume that you are representing a small developing country in trade negotiations with the European Union. The EU representative says that she would like your client country to provide EU national patent holders with a patent term of 25 years, instead of the 20 years your client country currently provides to all patent holders. In exchange, the European Union will allow duty and quota free access to the EU market for agricultural products produced in your client's country. This will provide a major competitive advantage for its exports. If your client extends an additional term of patent protection to EU nationals, can it refuse to extend it for U.S. nationals? Can your client require the United States to provide duty and quota free access for its agricultural products as a condition to extending patent protection for U.S. nationals? If not, how does the MFN treatment principle benefit your client country? Is it giving up something for nothing, or is there more to it than that? How does a small developing country benefit from MFN? Does the principle serve different functions when applied to protection of patents than when applied to exports of bananas?

C. Transparency

Transparency amounts to one of the fundamental and basic principles and equations of intellectual property protection. Exclusive rights are granted in return for the publication of inventions, which in return allows competitors to assess the state of the art and explore the possibilities of obtaining a voluntary license by the right holder. In addition, transparency assumes functions of legal

---

* WT/DS176/AB/R, 2 Jan. 2002.

security, which is essentially served by registration of IPRs. Conversely, the principles of transparency are not served in the field of copyright, which is not subject to registration and in the protection of undisclosed information. Trade secrets enjoy a growing importance. Unlike patents, they do not require publication. Yet, they equally fail to benefit from legal security. The principle of transparency therefore remains specific to different forms of IPRs. General rules of transparency, however, equally exist and follow the principles of WTO law.

THE AGREEMENT ON TRADE RELATED ASPECTS OF INTELLECTUAL PROPERTY RIGHTS (TRIPs)

Thomas Cottier*

TRANSPARENCY AND GOOD GOVERNANCE

Transparency is one of the core principles of WTO law. Building upon the tradition of Article X GATT, Article 63 of the TRIPs Agreement contains important obligations in this regard. Members are obliged to publish not only laws and regulations, but also final judicial decisions and administrative rulings of general application, subject to the protection of undisclosed information affecting trade and commercial secrets of companies involved. Moreover, WTO notification requirements assist in ensuring that new legislation complies with TRIPs obligations. Members are obliged to notify the Council for TRIPs of their laws and regulations for the purpose of facilitating the Council's review of the operation of the TRIPs Agreement. In practice, some of these tasks are already fulfilled through WIPO's Collection of Laws for Electronic Access,[104] a database on the intellectual property-related legislation of most countries in English translation. In addition, under Article 63:3, each Member must be prepared to supply information on its relevant national rules and case law in response to a request from another Member. Article 63 aims at implementing transparency as a prerequisite for dispute prevention and settlement, and as a tool to assess the effectiveness of the TRIPs agreement.

A major portion of the work of the TRIPs Council in its first years consisted in exercising its review function and asserting a certain amount of peer pressure with a view to bringing about compliance. Further support for this effort is provided by regular trade policy reviews of Members under the Trade Policy Review Mechanism ("TPRM").[105] The TPRM reports reflect complaints of Members and responses to those complaints. They contain additional information on the state of play and problems relating to intellectual property protection in the concerned Members.

Perhaps more than any other agreement, the TRIPs Agreement promotes the doctrine of good governance through its rules on procedural standards in Part III of the Agreement.[106] . . . It is important to note that the many

---

* The World Trade Organization: Legal Economic and Political Analysis. Vol I., p. 1041 (Patrick F.J. Macrory, Arthur E. Appleton, Michael G. Plummer eds., Springer 2005).
  104. [This database has been renamed "WIPO Lex." — EDS.]
  105. [See Chapter 6 of this book. — EDS.]
  106. [*See* Thomas Cottier, *Emerging Doctrines of Good Governance: The Impact of the WTO and China's Accession,* in CHINA IN THE WORLD TRADING SYSTEM — DEFINING THE PRINCIPLES OF ENGAGEMENT 119 (Frederick M. Abbott ed., 1998). — EDS.]

provisions in the Agreement on civil, administrative and penal procedures applicable to intellectual property protection not only benefit foreign right holders, but also domestic right holders as the benefit of these rules would normally be made available to them as well. Finally, we note that improvements in these procedures will not be limited to intellectual property, but will carry over to other areas of civil and administrative law enforcement. *De facto,* the TRIPs Agreement makes a general contribution to good governance in the field of judicial administration.

D. *Territoriality and Independence*

1. Territoriality

It is not infrequently said that intellectual property rights are "territorial" in nature. This is understood to mean that the grant of an IP right by a particular country has effect only within the territory of that country (see, e.g., citations and references in *NTP v. Research in Motion,* below). Thus, for example, a patent granted within the United States is understood only to give the inventor rights within the United States to prevent enumerated acts (i.e., making, using, selling, offering for sale, and importing).

The concept of territoriality plays an enormously important role in the international IP system. In order to secure IPRs protection for one invention, expressive work, or indication of origin, the creator must obtain protection in each territory where protection is considered necessary. The grounding of the international IPRs system in the nation-state, and the principle of territoriality, was a logical consequence of the world political order of the late nineteenth century, when the Paris and Berne Conventions were negotiated and concluded. In that era, and to a large extent today, the sovereignty of each national government within its own territory was considered the paramount principle by which the international legal and political order was constituted.

To some extent, the notion of IP "territoriality" appears to be based on the Paris Convention rule of independence (see below), which prescribes that regulatory or judicial actions with respect to a patent or trademark in one country do not affect the validity or enforceability of a patent or trademark in another country. However, the blending of the concepts of "independence" and "territoriality" is not based on express terms of the Paris Convention. Neither the Paris nor Berne Convention uses the term "territorial" or "territoriality," nor do they expressly prescribe a jurisdictional limitation on the effect of the grant of a patent, trademark, or copyright.

Public international law, on the other hand, does impose limits on the jurisdictional reach of the laws and regulatory actions of countries. For the following, we use the United States as an example. The U.S. Congress does not ordinarily legislate for the territory of Canada or France, nor do U.S. courts ordinarily enforce Canadian or French law.[107] As a general rule, countries prescribe and enforce legislation with respect to conduct taking place within their own territories (the principle of "subjective territoriality"), to conduct that has a direct, foreseeable, and substantial effect within their own territories

---

107. They may, however, more generally recognize and enforce judgments of Canadian and French courts on the basis of comity.

(the principle of "objective territoriality"), and to conduct of their nationals wherever those nationals may be located (the "nationality" principle).[108]

U.S. courts ordinarily refrain from enforcing French patents in American courts, and likewise French courts ordinarily refrain from enforcing U.S. patents. Each of these countries reserves to itself the right to determine whether a patent should be granted for its own territory and the terms under which it will enforce that patent. Moreover, the rule of "independence" prescribed by the Paris Convention prevents a U.S. court from directly applying a French administrative or judicial decision to invalidate or render unenforceable an American patent.

The observation that IPRs are territorial should not be understood categorically. There is some jurisprudence in the United States, particularly in the field of trademarks, which suggests that holders of rights in one nation (e.g., the United States) may on that basis assert rights to protect against injury suffered in other nations or regions. Doctrines asserting so-called extraterritorial IPRs are controversial, and to date have been used in very limited contexts. We could not from this limited experience generalize a departure from the accepted territorial nature of IPRs.

Microsoft v. AT&T concerned the potential extraterritorial application of U.S. patent law. The decision of the Supreme Court reverses the Court of Appeals for the Federal Circuit. Microsoft exported a master disk incorporating its Windows program to a personal computer manufacturer in Taiwan. In order to install the Windows program on a volume of personal computers, the Taiwanese manufacturer made Windows CD copies from the master disk and installed the Windows program from the copies.

AT&T holds a patent on computer software used in voice recognition. Microsoft infringed that patent in the United States by incorporating the software in its Windows program.

An amendment to the U.S. Patent Act was adopted by Congress in 1984 to overturn a 1972 decision of the Supreme Court (*Deepsouth Packing Co. v. Laitram Corp.*, 406 U.S. 518 (1972)). In *Deepsouth Packing*, the Supreme Court held that it was not a violation of the Patent Act to collect and export components of a machine protected by a patent in the United States (along with instructions on their assembly) because the machine was not "made" in the United States. The Patent Act amendment established this type of activity as contributory infringement, providing, *inter alia*:

> Sec. 271(f)(1) Whoever without authority supplies or causes to be supplied in or from the United States all or a substantial portion of the components of a patented invention, where such components are uncombined in whole or in part, in such manner as to actively induce the combination of such components outside of the United States in a manner that would infringe the patent if such combination occurred within the United States, shall be liable as an infringer.

In *Microsoft v. AT&T*, the Supreme Court repeatedly stresses that the U.S. Patent Act is not intended to have extraterritorial effect, and that the amended Patent Act provision cited above is an exception to this general rule (that therefore should be construed narrowly). Applying this general principle to

---

108. Two additional recognized bases of jurisdiction are the "protective" and "universal" principles, but those are of limited relevance to this discussion. *See generally* Restatement 3d Foreign Relations, Part IV.

Microsoft's activities (that are not clearly prohibited by the statute), the Court held that it would not extend the statute to cover them. The factual basis for its ruling was that the "master disk" exported by Microsoft was not itself a component that was installed on a computer. Instead, CD copies were first made of the master disk, and those CD copies were used to install the program that infringed AT&T's software patent (in the United States). The decision turned on the definition of a "component" as used in the statute. The Court expressly refrained from deciding whether Microsoft would have violated AT&T's patent if it had directly exported the CD copies used to install the program on the computers.

MICROSOFT CORP. v. AT&T CORP.
550 U.S. 437 (2007)

Justice GINSBERG for the Court:

Any doubt that Microsoft's conduct falls outside § 271(f)'s compass would be resolved by the presumption against extraterritoriality, on which we have already touched. See *supra* . . . The presumption that United States law governs domestically but does not rule the world applies with particular force in patent law. The traditional understanding that our patent law "operate[s] only domestically and d[oes] not extend to foreign activities," Fisch & Allen, [The Application of Domestic Patent Law to Exported Software: 35 U.S.C. § 271(f), 25 U. Pa. J. Int'l Econ. L. 557, 565 (2004)] at 559, is embedded in the Patent Act itself, which provides that a patent confers exclusive rights in an invention within the United States. 35 U.S.C. § 154(a)(1) (patentee's rights over invention apply to manufacture, use, or sale "throughout the United States" and to importation "into the United States"). See *Deepsouth*, 406 U.S., at 531, 92 S. Ct. 1700 ("Our patent system makes no claim to extraterritorial effect"; our legislation "d[oes] not, and [was] not intended to, operate beyond the limits of the United States, and we correspondingly reject the claims of others to such control over our markets." (quoting *Brown*, 19 How., at 195, 15 L. Ed. 595)).

As a principle of general application, moreover, we have stated that courts should "assume that legislators take account of the legitimate sovereign interests of other nations when they write American laws." *F. Hoffmann-La Roche Ltd. v. Empagran S.A.*, 542 U.S. 155, 164, 124 S. Ct. 2359, 159 L. Ed. 2d 226 (2004); see *EEOC v. Arabian American Oil Co.*, 499 U.S. 244, 248, 111 S. Ct. 1227, 113 L. Ed. 2d 274 (1991). Thus, the United States accurately conveyed in this case: "Foreign conduct is [generally] the domain of foreign law," and in the area here involved, in particular, foreign law "may embody different policy judgments about the relative rights of inventors, competitors, and the public in patented inventions." Brief for United States as *Amicus Curiae* 28. Applied to this case, the presumption tugs strongly against construction of § 271(f) to encompass as a "component" not only a physical copy of software, but also software's intangible code, and to render "supplie[d] . . . from the United States" not only exported copies of software, but also duplicates made abroad.

AT&T argues that the presumption is inapplicable because Congress enacted § 271(f) specifically to extend the reach of United States patent law to cover certain activity abroad. But as this Court has explained, "the presumption is not defeated . . . just because [a statute] specifically addresses [an] issue of extraterritorial application," *Smith v. United States*, 507 U.S. 197, 204, 113 S. Ct. 1178, 122 L. Ed. 2d 548 (1993); it remains instructive in determining the *extent* of the statutory exception. See *Empagran*, 542 U.S., at 161-162, 164-165, 124 S. Ct. 2359; *Smith*, 507 U.S., at 204, 113 S. Ct. 1178.

AT&T alternately contends that the presumption holds no sway here given that § 271(f), by its terms, applies only to domestic conduct, *i.e.*, to the supply of a patented invention's components "from the United States." § 271(f)(1). AT&T's reading, however, "converts a single act of supply from the United States into a springboard for liability each time a copy of the software is subsequently made [abroad] and combined with computer hardware [abroad] for sale [abroad.]" Brief for United States as *Amicus Curiae* 29; see 414 F.3d, at 1373, 1375 (Rader, J., dissenting). In short, foreign law alone, not United States law, currently governs the manufacture and sale of components of patented inventions in foreign countries. If AT&T desires to prevent copying in foreign countries, its remedy today lies in obtaining and enforcing foreign patents. See *Deepsouth*, 406 U.S., at 531, 92 S. Ct. 1700.[17]

NOTES AND QUESTIONS

1. The Supreme Court limits the geographical scope of the U.S. Patent Act. As a matter of principle, it refuses to adopt an expansive interpretation of the statutory provision adopted by the Congress. In your view, does the fact that Microsoft is exporting a disk with embedded object code, which is copied onto a personal computer in a foreign country, provide a basis for placing the export outside the reach of Section 271(f)? What are the economic policy implications of the decision by the Supreme Court? Does it surprise you that Microsoft, which so actively campaigns against copyright piracy in China and Russia, is seeking to limit the geographic range of patent law?

2. Returning to the WTO consultations initiated by India and Brazil with the European Union and the Netherlands regarding transit seizures of generic pharmaceutical products based on patents only in the transit country (i.e., at the Dutch airport during transshipment), do you think the U.S. Supreme Court would be sympathetic to applying a U.S. patent to a pharmaceutical product shipment moving from India to Brazil solely on the basis of transit through a U.S. airport? Does it help to know that the United States is party to a GATT/WTO Article V obligation to allow "freedom of transit" through its ports and airports, and not to unreasonably interfere with such transit?

In the *NTP v. Research in Motion* case, decided before *Microsoft v. AT&T*, the U.S. Court of Appeals for the Federal Circuit examined whether a U.S. patent is infringed when part of the infringing action occurs in Canada. It also examined whether a U.S. process patent is infringed when part of the patented process is performed in Canada.

An issue related to the territorial scope of application of patents (and other IPRs) is whether the courts of one country should enforce judgments rendered by the courts of other countries. Should, for example, an award of damages for

17. AT & T has secured patents for its speech processor in Canada, France, Germany, Great Britain, Japan, and Sweden. App. in No. 04-1285 (CA Fed.), p. 1477. AT & T and its *amici* do not relate what protections and remedies are, or are not, available under these foreign regimes. Cf. Brief for Respondent 46 (observing that "foreign patent protections are *sometimes* weaker than their U.S. counterparts" (emphasis added)).

infringement of a patent rendered by a French court be enforceable in a U.S. court? We will examine this issue in Chapter 6.

The formation of regional institutions (such as the EU), and the development of regional and multilateral mechanisms that facilitate the granting of IPRs on a multi-country basis, have not so far fundamentally altered the reliance of the international IPRs system on the principle of territoriality. The major area in which an evolution away from strict reliance on territoriality can be seen is in the EU, where some forms of IPR are now granted and regulated on a Union-wide level. Note, however, that the EU is somewhat exceptional in the sense of its organization as a quasi-federal polity. An evolution away from the strict nation-state IPRs territoriality principle in the EU in some ways reflects a consolidation of that principle within a new and larger political unit.

Whether the principle of territoriality continues to serve well the international IPRs system, or the international economic and political systems, is another question entirely. Many important challenges to territoriality are already present, and more are on the horizon. The inherent tension between territorially based IPRs, on one side, and the free movement of goods and services, on the other, is a subject that we address extensively in this book. Resolving this conflict may not necessarily involve a diminished stature for the basic principle of territoriality of IPRs, but may instead involve more adequately elaborating the goals that territoriality is expected to accomplish.

Another important challenge to the territoriality of IPRs is raised by the Internet and other forms of high-speed data transmission, as well as the concomitant evolution of global electronic commerce. As it has become possible to simultaneously and instantaneously transmit copyrighted works to all countries of the world, the utility of maintaining different rule systems and bundles of rights in each country is called into question. The Internet domain name is a globally employed identifier that has limited relevance as a creature of national law, and its regulation on a nation-to-nation basis raises a host of law and policy issues.

While the territorial basis of the international IPRs system may be under challenge, for present purposes the principle of the territorial nature of IPRs remains basic to the system. Neither the Paris, Berne, or Rome Conventions, nor any other instrument under the umbrella of WIPO, nor the TRIPS Agreement, creates a supranational system of IPRs protection. These international agreements are instruments to bring about minimum standards — to harmonize or approximate national and regional intellectual property law.

NTP v. RESEARCH IN MOTION

418 F.3d 1282 (Fed. Cir. 2005), rehearing en banc denied

LINN, Circuit Judge. . . .

2. SECTION 271(A)

Section 271(a) of title 35 sets forth the requirements for a claim of direct infringement of a patent. It provides:

> Except as otherwise provided in this title, whoever without authority makes, uses, offers to sell, or sells any patented invention, within the United States or

imports into the United States any patented invention during the term of the patent therefore, infringes the patent.

35 U.S.C. § 271(a) (2000). The territorial reach of section 271 is limited. Section 271(a) is only actionable against patent infringement that occurs within the United States. . . .

Ordinarily, whether an infringing activity under section 271(a) occurs within the United States can be determined without difficulty. This case presents an added degree of complexity, however, in that: (1) the "patented invention" is not one single device, but rather a system comprising multiple distinct components or a method with multiple distinct steps; and (2) the nature of those components or steps permits their function and use to be separated from their physical location.

In its complaint, NTP alleged that RIM had infringed its patents by "making, using, selling, offering to sell and importing into the United States products and services, including the Defendant's BlackBerry TM products and their related software. . . ." . . . According to RIM, the statutory requirement that the allegedly infringing activity occur "within the United States" was not satisfied because the BlackBerry Relay component of the accused system is located in Canada.[11] . . .

The district court declined to grant summary judgment in RIM's favor. . . .

. . . RIM has . . . appealed whether any direct infringement, by it or its customers, can be considered "within the United States" for purposes of section 271(a). Citing the Supreme Court's decision in [*Deepsouth Packing Co. v. Laitram Corp.*, 406 U.S. 518 (1972)], RIM contends that an action for infringement under section 271(a) may lie only if the allegedly infringing activity occurs within the United States. RIM urges that, in this case, that standard is not met because the BlackBerry Relay component, described by RIM as the "control point" of the accused system, is housed in Canada. For section 271(a) to apply, RIM asserts that the entire accused system and method must be contained or conducted within the territorial bounds of the United States. RIM thus contends that there can be no direct infringement as a matter of law because the location of RIM's Relay outside the United States precludes a finding of an infringing act occurring within the United States. . . .

The question before us is whether the using, offering to sell, or selling of a patented invention is an infringement under section 271(a) if a component or step of the patented invention is located or performed abroad. . . . [I]t is unclear from the statutory language how the territoriality requirement limits direct infringement where the location of at least a part of the "patented invention" is not the same as the location of the infringing act.

RIM argues that *Deepsouth* answers this question. However, *Deepsouth* did not address this issue. In *Deepsouth*, the Supreme Court considered whether section 271(a) prevented, as direct infringement, the domestic production of all component parts of a patented combination for export, assembly, and use abroad. 406 U.S. 518 at 527, 92 S. Ct. 1700, 32 L. Ed. 2d 273 (1972). The Court held

---

11. There was a question below as to whether the Relay was also operated out of Virginia. This question appears to have been resolved in RIM's favor; on appeal, NTP does not contest the location of the BlackBerry Relay in Canada. For the purposes of our discussion, we assume that the BlackBerry Relay is located only in Canada. If, in fact, a Relay is also located in the United States, the need for this analysis would of course be obviated.

that the export of unassembled components of an invention could not infringe the patent. *Id.* at 529. The Court said that it could not "endorse the view that the 'substantial manufacture of the constituent parts of a machine' constitutes direct infringement when we have so often held that a combination patent protects only against the operable assembly of the whole and not the manufacture of its parts." *Id.* at 528. Thus, the Court concluded that the complete manufacture of the operable assembly of the whole within the United States was required for infringement by making under section 271(a). In that case, however, both the act of making and the resulting patented invention were wholly outside the United States. By contrast, this case involves a system that is partly within and partly outside the United States and relates to acts that may be occurring within or outside the United States.

Although *Deepsouth* does not resolve these issues, our predecessor court's decision in *Decca Ltd. v. United States*, 210 Ct. Cl. 546, 544 F.2d 1070 (Ct. Cl. 1976), is instructive. In *Decca*, the plaintiff sued the United States for use and manufacture of its patented invention under 28 U.S.C. § 1498. The claimed invention was a radio navigation system requiring stations transmitting signals that are received by a receiver, which then calculates position by the time difference in the signals. At the time of the suit, the United States was operating three such transmitting stations, one of which was located in Norway and thus was outside the territorial limits of the United States. Only asserted claim 11 required three transmitting stations. Thus, in considering infringement of claim 11, the court considered the extraterritorial reach of the patent laws as applied to a system in which a component was located outside the United States. The court recognized that *Deepsouth* did not address this issue. *Id.* at 1081. In analyzing whether such a system was "made" in the United States, however, the court focused on the "operable assembly of the whole" language from *Deepsouth* and concluded that "the plain fact is that one of the claimed elements is outside of the United States so that the combination, as an operable assembly, simply is not to be found solely within the territorial limits of this country." *Id.* at 1082. The court recognized that what was located within the United States was as much of the system as was possible, but the court reached no clear resolution of whether the accused system was "made" within the United States. Nevertheless, the court said, "Analyzed from the standpoint of a use instead of a making by the United States, a somewhat clearer picture emerges." *Id.* The court concluded that "it is obvious that, although the Norwegian station is located on Norwegian soil, a navigator employing signals from that station is, in fact, 'using' that station and such use occurs wherever the signals are received and used in the manner claimed." *Id.* at 1083. In reaching its decision, the court found particularly significant "the ownership of the equipment by the United States, the control of the equipment from the United States and . . . the actual beneficial use of the system within the United States." *Id.* Although *Decca* was decided within the context of section 1498, which raises questions of use by the United States, the question of use within the United States also was implicated because direct infringement under section 271(a) is a necessary predicate for government liability under section 1498. *Motorola, Inc. v. United States*, 729 F.2d 765, 768 n.3 (Fed. Cir. 1984).

Decca provides a legal framework for analyzing this case. As our predecessor court concluded, infringement under section 271(a) is not necessarily precluded even though a component of a patented system is located outside the United States. However, as is also evident from *Decca*, the effect of the extraterritorial component may be different for different infringing acts. In *Decca*, the court found it difficult to conclude that the system had been made within the United States but concluded that the system had been used in the United States even though one of the claim limitations was only met by including a component located in Norway. Not only will the analysis differ for different types of infringing acts, it will also differ as the result of differences between different types of claims. *See Minton v. Nat'l Ass'n of Sec. Dealers, Inc.*, 336 F.3d 1373, 1378 (Fed. Cir. 2003) ("It is not correct that nothing in § 102(b) compels different treatment between an invention that is a tangible item and an invention that describes a series of steps in a process. The very nature of the invention may compel a difference." (quotation marks omitted)). Because the analytical frameworks differ, we will separately analyze the alleged infringing acts, considering first the system claims and then the claimed methods.

A. "USES . . . WITHIN THE UNITED STATES"

The situs of the infringement "is wherever an offending act [of infringement] is committed." *N. Am. Philips Corp. v. Am. Vending Sales, Inc.*, 35 F.3d 1576, 1579 (Fed. Cir. 1994) ("[Section 271] on its face clearly suggests the conception that the 'tort' of patent infringement occurs where the offending act is committed and not where the injury is felt."). The situs of the infringing act is a "purely physical occurrence[]." *Id.* In terms of the infringing act of "use," courts have interpreted the term "use" broadly. In *Bauer & Cie v. O'Donnell*, 229 U.S. 1, 57 L. Ed. 1041, 33 S. Ct. 616, 1913 Dec. Comm'r Pat. 533 (1913), the Supreme Court stated that "use," as used in a predecessor to title 35, is a "comprehensive term and embraces within its meaning the right to put into service any given invention." *Id.* at 10-11. The ordinary meaning of "use" is to "put into action or service." Webster's Third New International Dictionary 2523 (1993). The few court decisions that address the meaning of "use" have consistently followed the Supreme Court's lead in giving the term a broad interpretation. E.g., *Roche Prods., Inc. v. Bolar Pharm. Co.*, 733 F.2d 858, 863 (Fed. Cir. 1984), superseded-in-part by 35 U.S.C. § 271(e) (holding that testing is a "use").

The use of a claimed system under section 271(a) is the place at which the system as a whole is put into service, i.e., the place where control of the system is exercised and beneficial use of the system obtained. *See Decca*, 544 F.2d at 1083. Based on this interpretation of section 271(a), it was proper for the jury to have found that use of NTP's asserted system claims occurred within the United States. RIM's customers located within the United States controlled the transmission of the originated information and also benefited from such an exchange of information. Thus, the location of the Relay in Canada did not, as a matter of law, preclude infringement of the asserted system claims in this case.

RIM argues that the BlackBerry system is distinguishable from the system in *Decca* because the RIM Relay, which controls the accused systems and is necessary for the other components of the system to function properly, is not located within the United States. While this distinction recognizes technical differences between the two systems, it fails to appreciate the way in which the claimed NTP system is actually used by RIM's customers. When RIM's United States customers send and receive messages by manipulating the handheld devices in their possession in the United States, the location of the use of the communication system as a whole occurs in the United States. This satisfactorily establishes that the situs of the "use" of RIM's system by RIM's United States customers for purposes of section 271(a) is the United States. Therefore, we conclude that the jury was properly presented with questions of infringement as to NTP's system claims containing the "interface" or "interface switch" limitation; namely, claim 15 of the '960 patent; claim 8 of the '670 patent; and claims 28 and 248 of the '451 patent.

4. Section 271(g)

The next question is whether RIM can be said to "import[] into . . . or offer[] to sell, sell[], or use[] within the United States a product which is made by a process patented in the United States" and thus infringe under 35 U.S.C. § 271(g). The district court held that "wireless electronic mail" specially formatted by a patented process can be a "product" under section 271(g). Section 271 Order at 13-14. The district court compared the breadth of "product" to the breadth of patentable subject matter, cited to *Diamond v. Chakrabarty*, 447 U.S. 303, 65 L. Ed. 2d 144, 100 S. Ct. 2204 (1980), and explained that specially formatted wireless email is not naturally occurring, an abstract idea, or a physical phenomenon. Section 271 Order at 14.

RIM argues that the product created by the NTP process is data or information, and that *Bayer AG v. Housey Pharmaceuticals, Inc.*, 340 F.3d 1367 (Fed. Cir. 2003), held that section 271(g) does not cover the production of intangible items. NTP counters that *Bayer* held only that a "product" cannot be "information in the abstract." NTP asserts that the "email packets" flowing from the BES, to the interface, and back to the RF receiver, have a "tangible" structure which includes the interface address, an RF address, and the inputted message. NTP argues that *AT&T Corp. v. Excel Communications, Inc.*, 172 F.3d 1352 (Fed. Cir. 1999); *State Street Bank & Trust Co. v. Signature Financial Group*, 149 F.3d 1368 (Fed. Cir. 1998); and *In re Alappat*, 33 F.3d 1526 (Fed. Cir. 1994), illustrate that the transformation of data can produce a tangible result, that RIM transforms data by moving email through the network, and that the tangible result of the transformation is a product under section 271(g). NTP adds that RIM "manufactures" email into its tangible structure and "imports" email using patented methods, in part, by replacing the interface address with the RF receiver address at the interface Relay. RIM responds that the email packets that it may transfer into the United States are not manufactured, physical goods, and therefore are not "products" under section 271(g).

In *Bayer*, we considered whether research data from the performance of a method to identify substances, which inhibit or activate a protein affecting characteristics of the cell, was "a product which is made by a process." 340 F.3d at 1370. We held that "the production of information is not covered" by section 271(g), explaining that the process must be for the "manufacturing" of "a physical article." Id. at 1377. In this case, the relevant claims are directed to methods for the transmission of information in the form of email messages. See '960 patent, col. 52, ll. 12-50; col. 54, ll. 31-36, 59-68; col. 55, ll. 10-14 (claiming methods for "transmitting" information from an originating processor to a destination processor); '172 patent, col. 82, ll. 11-33, 57-64 (claiming a method for "transmitting and distributing an inputted message" through an email system and an RF system); '451 patent, col. 51, ll. 41-60; col. 58, ll. 8-26, 34-63; col. 59, ll. 1-6, 24-30 (claiming methods for "transmitting information" contained in email using a communication system and RF system, and for "transmitting and distributing inputted information through a distributed system"). Because the "transmission of information," like the "production of information," does not entail the manufacturing of a physical product, section 271(g) does not apply to the asserted method claims in this case any more than it did in *Bayer*.

AT&T, State Street Bank, Alappat, and *Chakrabarty* do not command a different result because sections 101 and 271(g) are not coextensive in their coverage of process inventions. Although section 101 extends to "any process that applies an equation to a new and useful end," *AT&T,* 172 F.3d at 1357, section 271(g) does not cover every patented process and its purported result, *Bayer,* 340 F.3d at 1370. In *Bayer,* we expressed no doubt that a process producing research data is patentable under section 101. See 340 F.3d at 1371-78. However, we held that section 271(g) was inapplicable because research data is not a physical product. *Id.* at 1378. NTP's argument that the transformation of data and the manipulation of addresses qualify the asserted processes for section 271(g) protection is unpersuasive. The requirement that a process transform data and produce a "tangible result" was a standard devised to prevent patenting of mathematical abstractions. *AT&T,* 172 F.3d at 1359. We rejected this "tangible result" test for section 271(g) in *Bayer* when we held that research data — a "tangible result" for section 101 purposes — did not garner the protection of section 271(g).

For the foregoing reasons, the district court erred in not holding as a matter of law that § 271(g) was inapplicable to the asserted method claims.

NOTES AND QUESTIONS

1. Assume that the German national holder of a patent in Germany, Thailand, and the United States on a computer component licenses the manufacture and sale of that component to a producer in Thailand. The license says nothing about exports. The Thai producer sells the component to a Japanese computer manufacturer, which ships the completed computer product to the United States. Should the German holder of the U.S. patent be able to block importation of the Japanese computer into the United States? *See, e.g., Minebea v. Pabst,* 444 F. Supp. 2d 68 (D.D.C. 2006).

2. Independence

The Paris Convention establishes a rule of "independence" of patents.

ARTICLE 4*BIS*

PATENTS: *INDEPENDENCE OF PATENTS OBTAINED FOR THE SAME INVENTION IN DIFFERENT COUNTRIES*

(1) Patents applied for in the various countries of the Union by nationals of countries of the Union shall be independent of patents obtained for the same invention in other countries, whether members of the Union or not.

(2) The foregoing provision is to be understood in an unrestricted sense, in particular, in the sense that patents applied for during the period of priority are independent, both as regards the grounds for nullity and forfeiture, and as regards their normal duration. . . .

(5) Patents obtained with the benefit of priority shall, in the various countries of the Union, have a duration equal to that which they would have, had they been applied for or granted without the benefit of priority.

The Paris Convention also establishes a rule of independence of trademarks.

ARTICLE 6

MARKS: *CONDITIONS OF REGISTRATION; INDEPENDENCE OF PROTECTION OF SAME MARK IN DIFFERENT COUNTRIES*

. . . (3) A mark duly registered in a country of the Union shall be regarded as independent of marks registered in the other countries of the Union, including the country of origin.

The basic principle of independence states that a decision by the regulatory authorities or courts of any country with respect to the grant, denial, or invalidation of a patent or trademark does not have effects on corresponding patent or trademark proceedings or rights in any other country party to the Paris Convention. The reason for adoption of such a principle was fairly straightforward. There was concern that authorities in one country might use patent or trademark proceedings as a mechanism to gain commercial advantage by invalidating patents or trademarks of foreign owners. If the decisions were effective in other counties party to the Paris Convention, the interests of foreigners might be injured throughout the system. With the rule of independence, one country might behave "badly," but the effects on the right holder would be limited to that country.

Even today, among the close-knit countries of the European Union, one of the major obstacles to establishing a EU-wide patent is determining what institutions are sufficiently trustworthy to make decisions binding for all members of the European Union. The Paris Convention rule of independence of patents means that there is no mechanism for a "central attack" on either patents or trademarks under that Convention. That is, invalidating a patent or trademark in one national patent and trademark office will not invalidate parallel patents or trademarks in other national offices. (However, this observation has an exception under the Madrid Agreement Concerning the International Registration of Marks, which does provide a form of central attack with respect to trademarks (discussed in Chapter 3, *infra*).)

3.   Independence in the Courts

In the *Cuno v. Pall* decision that follows, a U.S. federal district court judge has occasion to give concrete effect to the principle of the *independence of patents* established by the Paris Convention. An English court had already ruled on the validity of various competing patent claims after prolonged litigation, and the U.S. federal court is in essence asked to repeat the process, but in a different national jurisdiction. The party that succeeded in England would for obvious reasons prefer that the U.S. judge decide that there is no point to reconsidering the same issues at what will undoubtedly be of considerable cost both in terms of money and wasted time. The U.S. judge seems to share this perspective, but must consider the relevant provisions of the Paris Convention.

CUNO, INC. v. PALL CORPORATION
729 F. Supp. 234 (E.D.N.Y. 1989)

JACK B. WEINSTEIN, J.

The production of microporous nylon membrane filters generates hundreds of millions of dollars in worldwide revenues. It is vital to pharmaceutical, microchip and other industries requiring filtration of impurities the size of the smallest microbes. Plaintiff Cuno and defendants Pall and its associated companies are major competitors in this field. They press claims and counterclaims relating to the validity, infringement and enforceability of a number of key patents teaching methods of producing these filters.

Defendants move for partial summary judgment based on the collateral estoppel effect of factual findings made by a Justice of the United Kingdom Court of Chancery, Patent Division, in a prior adjudication between the parties. The European Patent Office's counterpart of defendants' United States patent at issue here was there found to be valid and non-infringing. Defendants argue that the findings of fact made by the foreign court are entitled to preclusive effect since the patent issued by the European Patent Office on behalf of the countries of the European Economic Community describes the same technological invention and makes claims that are in all material ways identical to those contained in defendants' United States patent.

Plaintiff argues that the traditional requirements for granting collateral estoppel are not present here and that the application of preclusive effect to findings made by a foreign court runs counter to policies underlying both domestic and foreign patent law. For the reasons noted below, the court denies defendants' motion.

I. FACTS . . .

On July 25, 1989 the British judge, Justice Falconer, ruled in Pall's favor, making extensive findings and construing critical terms in the claims made in Pall's EPC patent. In a 64-page opinion, he concluded, inter alia, 1) that Pall's patent was valid; 2) that Cuno's Zetapor membranes infringed claims in Pall's EPC patent; 3) that there was no merit to the anticipation defense raised by Cuno based on its United States Marinaccio patent; and 4) that there had been no invalidating prior public use when Pall utilized some of its filters in 1976 and 1977 in tests by prospective customers. An order enjoining Cuno from infringing the Pall EPC patent was entered on August 1, 1989. Shortly thereafter Cuno filed a notice of appeal.

Cuno continues to prosecute its opposition to the Pall EPC patent in the European Patent Office. It is unclear what, if any effect a decision revoking or modifying Pall's EPC patent would have on the British court's ruling should Cuno's opposition prove successful. The court's order contained a "liberty to apply" provision, which apparently allows either party to return to the court to make further applications in the event that matters are elicited "concerning or arising out of [Cuno's] Opposition in the [European Patent Office]." In any event, the parties have informed the court that the European Patent Office may not render a decision for years.

This court originally ordered a jury trial to begin in September. As a result of the United Kingdom decision, the court tentatively suggested that collateral estoppel might permit shortening of the trial. It became apparent, however, that the procedural and technical problems associated with a motion for application of collateral estoppel on the basis of findings made in the English judgment were so difficult and required so much further briefing and argument that it would be impossible to start the jury trial as scheduled.

In support and opposition to the motion for partial summary judgment, several days of hearings were conducted at which experts on patent and procedural law from the United States, the United Kingdom and Germany testified. Experts from both sides described the technology and development of a variety of patents in this field over the last 20 years. Extensive briefing and argument followed.

II. Law . . .

Where the prior adjudication was by a foreign nation's court applying its patent law to its patents, the barriers to reliance on the foreign judgment for collateral estoppel purposes become almost insurmountable. Differences in the law of the two nations and in the detailed language of the patent are emphasized to avoid issue preclusion in a patent case pending in this country even where the invention, the technological and economic competition between the parties, and the consequences of the judgments are for all practical purposes the same. *See, e.g., Medtronic, Inc. v. Daig Corp.*, 789 F.2d 903, 907-08 (Fed. Cir.), *cert. denied*, 479 U.S. 931, 107 S. Ct. 402, 93 L. Ed. 2d 355 (1986) (prior conclusion of German tribunal as to obviousness of counterpart German patent does not control issue of obviousness in action involving United States patent); *Stein Associates, Inc. v. Heat and Control, Inc.*, 748 F.2d 653 (Fed. Cir. 1984) (denying motion to enjoin efforts to enforce British patent in Britain) (citing cases); *In re Yarn Processing Patent Validity Litigation*, 498 F.2d 271, 278-85 (5th Cir. 1974) (issue in United States of date of "reduction to practice" not the same as issue of "date of invention" decided in previous Canada case); *Ditto, Inc. v. Minnesota Mining & Manufacturing Co.*, 336 F.2d 67, 70-71 (8th Cir. 1964) (prior adjudication in which West German Federal Patent Court found German counterpart patent invalid is not controlling authority); *Baracuda International Corp. v. F.N.D. Enterprises, Inc.*, 222 U.S.P.Q. 134, 135 (S.D. Fla. 1982) ("The South African courts' judgments are, of course, not binding upon our own where patent validity is at issue."). As Chief Judge Markey remarked in *Stein Associates v. Heat and Control, Inc.*, 748 F.2d 653 (Fed. Cir. 1984):

> British law being different from our own, and British and United States courts being independent of each other, resolution of the question of whether the United States patents are valid could have no binding effect on the British court's decision.

Id. at 658. The converse is equally true.

Even if this court were to apply collateral estoppel to certain factual findings made by the British court — as opposed to importing its legal conclusions wholesale — it is not clear that trial time would be significantly shortened. Furthermore, the Federal Circuit's reluctance to give collateral estoppel effect to foreign judgments would seem to apply here to foreign findings of fact insofar as those findings involve mixed questions of fact and foreign law. It is a quiddity of our law that a well and thoroughly reasoned decision reached by a highly skilled and scientifically informed justice of the Patent Court, Chancery Division, in the High Court of Justice of Great Britain after four weeks of trial must be ignored and essentially the same issues with the same evidence must now be retried by American jurors with no background in science or patents, whose average formal education will be no more than high school. This curious event is the result of the world's chauvinistic view of patents.

The law's absurdity as revealed by this case lends force to recommendations for a universal patent system that recognizes that ours is a worldwide technological and economic community. *See, e.g.,* Note, International Patent Cooperation: The Next Step, 16 Cornell Int'l L.J. 229, 248-49, 252-68 (1983) (recommending unified international patent law); Beier, The European Patent System, Vand. J. Transnat'l L. 1, 14-15 (1981) (recommending greater cooperation along lines of European system). Obviously there are grave difficulties in devising a system that will not disadvantage the old fashioned single craftsman-inventor or citizens of countries with patent offices that are careful in investigating before issuing patents. But the European Patent Office furnishes a model that appears to be working. Perhaps paragraph (1) of Article 4*bis* of the Paris Convention, with its emphasis on nationality, needs to be reconsidered. It reads:

> (1) Patents applied for in the various countries of the Union by nationals of countries of the Union shall be independent of patents obtained for the same invention in other countries, whether members of the Union or not.

Convention of Paris for the Protection of Industrial Property, article 4*bis* (1), 21 U.S.T. 1583, 1635, T.I.A.S. No. 6923 (text), 24 U.S.T. 2140, T.I.A.S. No. 7727 (ratification).

There would appear to be no constitutional inhibition against a reconsideration of international patent policy. Clause 8 of Article I of the Constitution grants Congress power over patents. But, just as Congress delegates much of its patenting power to the patent office and the courts, the government may, under Article II, section 2, clause 2 of the Constitution, provide a role for international bodies through the treaty making powers. *See, e.g.,* 39 U.S.C. § 407(a) (authorizing Postal Service, with consent of President, to negotiate and conclude postal treaties or conventions); *Universal Postal Union,* 16 U.S.T. 1291, T.I.A.S. 5881 (international treaty ratified and approved by United States Postmaster, approved by President). Cf. Casad, Issue Preclusion and Foreign Country Judgments: Whose Law?, 70 Iowa L. Rev. 53, 79-80 (1984) (suggesting treaty or exercise of federal common law power of Supreme Court to resolve issues of recognizing and enforcing foreign judgments).

III. OTHER GROUNDS FOR SUMMARY JUDGMENT

As an alternative ground for summary judgment the court could rely on the evidence produced on the motion for summary judgment. It includes extensive affidavits, testimony before this court of scientific and legal experts, the transcript of the trial in Great Britain, patent files and extensive materials for judicial notice. Taken together this mass of evidence still depends somewhat on evaluation of the credibility of prospective witnesses. The issue must be left for the jury.

Should the jury decide in a way inconsistent with the United Kingdom court's decision or the record, the court could, after the trial, grant what would be in effect a delayed summary judgment motion. *See County of Suffolk v. Long Island Lighting Co.*, 710 F. Supp. 1387, 1393 (E.D.N.Y. 1989) (citing *DeRosa v. Remington Arms Co.*, 509 F. Supp. 762 (E.D.N.Y. 1981)).

IV. CONCLUSION

The motion for summary judgment is denied. . . .

NOTES AND QUESTIONS

1. Judge Weinstein says it is not clear what effect revocation of Pall's European patent would have on the British judge's finding of patent infringement in favor of Pall. Examine Articles 68 and 99 of the EPC and consider why the result may be unclear to Judge Weinstein. Is the result unclear to you?
2. Cuno claimed that Pall's patent was invalid because Pall had publicly used the patented product more than one year before applying for a patent in the United States. The rules in different jurisdictions vary on the extent to which an invention may be publicly disclosed prior to filing an application without undermining its patentability. In the United States, public disclosure within one year of filing does not affect patentability.[109] Under the EPC, public disclosure made within six months of an EPC filing does not affect novelty, but only in the limited cases of abuse in relation to the patent applicant or display at an officially recognized international exhibition.[110]
3. Judge Weinstein observes that it is a "quiddity" of U.S. patent law that the opinion of a specialized British judge must be ignored in favor of a decision by a jury with an average of high school education and no background in science. The question whether the U.S. patent system is adequately served by trying facts before a lay jury is a longstanding one. What do you think?
4. The key to Judge Weinstein's decision is Article *4bis* of the Paris Convention. The drafters of the Paris Convention adopted the principle of independence, among other reasons, out of concern that national sentiment might cause administrators or courts in one country to refuse or revoke a foreigner's patent. The effects of such national sentiment would at least be limited if that decision applied only in one territory. Would such concerns about national sentiment be valid today? If so, how might a more efficient international patent system cope with such sentiment?

109. 35 U.S.C. § 102(b).
110. EPC, Art. 55.

4. Independence at the WTO

India and Brazil initiated dispute settlement consultations with the European Union and the Netherlands at the WTO on grounds that seizures of generic pharmaceuticals in transit between countries where there is no patent protection cannot be justified on the basis of a patent in the transit country. One of the legal grounds relied upon by India and Brazil is that extending the patent of a country where goods are merely passing through the airport to otherwise unpatented goods effectively deprives the exporting and importing countries of the right to make their own determinations regarding the grant or denial of patent protection, thereby interfering with the principle of independence. In fact, the Court of Justice of the European Union has strongly affirmed, in *Commission v. France*, Case C-23/99, decided 26 Sept. 2000, that applying an IPR to goods based on "mere transit" interferes with the right of other countries to grant or deny IP rights. *Commission v. France* involved trade between member states of the EU, and design rights, so the analogy to international trade and patents is not perfect, but it is difficult to identify a policy distinction.

E. *Ubiquity and Exhaustion of Rights*

Intellectual property is characterized by a unique feature that clearly distinguishes it from real and tangible property. Ownership of IPRs is fundamentally different from ownership of a chair, a house, or a car. IPRs are of a "ubiquitous" nature. They exist independently of the specific material good in which they are incorporated. Yet, each and every copy of a protected product contains these IPRs. IPRs follow the product downstream and potentially control the use of the product. In an age in which goods increasingly contain IPRs-protected components (such as a refrigerator with a silicon chip), the potential effects of IPRs are extremely far-reaching.

Perhaps the most telling example is in the field of biotechnology. The patented technical rule in this field is an abstract idea. Yet, it is incorporated in each and every copy of a product that, moreover, produces its own offspring. Logically, the patent right could expand endlessly, interfering in downstream markets infinitely. It therefore is necessary, at some point, to put an end to the effect on the market of IPRs. This concept is called exhaustion of rights.

The question of when and where the rights of an intellectual property holder are "exhausted" is central to defining the economic effect of such rights.[111] An IPR is exhausted when the holder or owner may no longer exercise control over the use or movement of the good or service embodying that right. In the United States, exhaustion typically occurs upon the "first sale" of a good, and this principle is referred to as the "first sale rule." In other countries, exhaustion is typically referred to as occurring upon "placing the good on the market."[112] This is the "when" of exhaustion.

---

111. On the economics of exhaustion and parallel imports, *see, e.g.,* Keith Maskus, *Parallel Imports in Pharmaceuticals: Implications for Competition and Prices in Developing Countries, Final Report to World Intellectual Property Organization,* April 2001; Mattias Ganslandt & Keith E. Maskus, *Parallel Imports and the Pricing of Pharmaceutical Products: Evidence from the European Union,* Research Institute of Industrial Economics, Working Paper No. 622 (2004).

112. The answer to "when" exhaustion occurs is not necessarily clear even within a single country. A manufacturer may sell goods to the ultimate end-user through a distribution chain

To illustrate, consider the ubiquitous can of Coca-Cola. The Coca-Cola Company owns the trademark that it places on the can. It has the right to prevent third parties from making the first sale of the can under its trademark. Once it sells that can to a consumer, the consumer has the right to drink the soda inside it, and the right to sell or give the can of soda to someone else. That is, the Coca-Cola Company's right in its trademark has been "exhausted" by the sale. But, by purchasing the can of soda, the consumer does not acquire rights in the Coca-Cola trademark. It does not have the right to open a Coca-Cola bottling plant and to begin selling its own cans of Coca-Cola. That right remains with the trademark owner.

A country is free to decide whether exhaustion of an IPR takes place only upon the lawful first sale of a good within its own territory, a lawful first sale within a particular region, or a lawful first sale anywhere in the world. In other words, exhaustion may be take place on a national, regional, or international basis. Moreover, a country may apply a different rule of the "where" of exhaustion to different forms of intellectual property. There are conceptual bases for treating different forms of IP differently from the standpoint of the applicable geographic rule of exhaustion, although the validity of the distinctions can be debated.

A rule of "national" exhaustion provides that the IP right holder's power to control movement of the good is only extinguished upon a first sale or placing on the market within the national territory. Using the Coca-Cola can to illustrate, the first sale of the product in New York will prevent the Coca-Cola Company from blocking a resale to California. On the other hand, a first sale of the product in Bangkok will not prevent the Coca-Cola Company from blocking importation into California.

A rule of "regional" exhaustion provides that the IP right holder's power to control movement of the good is only extinguished upon a first sale or placing on the market within the defined regional territory of an integration arrangement. The first sale of a can of Coca-Cola in Berlin will prevent the Coca-Cola Company from blocking import of the can into France or Poland (both EU member states). On the other hand, a first sale of the product in Bangkok will not prevent the Coca-Cola Company from blocking importation into any country of the European Union.

A rule of "international" exhaustion provides that the IP right holder's power to control movement of the good is extinguished upon a first sale or placing on the market anywhere in the world. The first sale of a can of Coca-Cola in New York, Bangkok, or Berlin will prevent the Coca-Cola Company from blocking importation into the United States, Germany, France, or Poland. In other words, after a first sale anywhere in the world, the good moves freely.

A rule of international exhaustion may be an important stimulant to achieving the benefit of open markets because it precludes producers from segmenting markets on the basis of IP rights.[113] Producers have to set their prices for the

---

that involves a number of purchases and sales by intermediaries. It is certain that the manufacturer does not exercise control through an IP right once the good has been purchased by the end user. The case law is less definitive about the right of control through the intermediary chain. In EU law where the European Court of Justice refers to placing the goods on the market, it appears that exhaustion takes place when the goods are purchased outside the manufacturer's distribution chain.

113. *See, e.g.,* Frederick M. Abbott, *First Report (Final) to the International Trade Law Committee of the International Law Association on the Subject of Parallel Importation,* 1 J. INT'L ECON. L. 607 (1998)

global market. This should exert downward pressure on those prices as producers seek to maximize global demand. In essence, a rule of international exhaustion is a tool for promoting competition and the efficient allocation of resources.

On the other hand, allowing producers to set different prices for different markets on the basis of IP rights increases their profit-making capacity, and some see benefits to greater returns for IPRs holders.[114] It is also argued that consumers benefit because retailers who can charge higher prices will provide better service and support for products.

There are different factors that influence the choice of an exhaustion rule for different forms of IPR. Because trademark, copyright, and patent perform different economic and social functions, it may be possible to justify distinguishing how they are treated from the standpoint of an exhaustion rule. Some commentators believe that it is easier to justify market segmentation, for example, applying national exhaustion to patents,[115] while it is very difficult to justify that for trademarks,[116] and that copyright falls somewhere in between.[117] Because many countries have, in fact, adopted different rules of exhaustion for different IPRs subject matter, the arguments for different rules of exhaustion will be considered in the subject matter chapters on patents, trademark, and copyright. Suffice it to say at this stage that exhaustion rules are a subject of intense international debate.

It should be noted here that in November 2001, the WTO expressly confirmed, in paragraph 5(d) of the Doha Declaration on the TRIPS Agreement and Public Health, that the TRIPS Agreement permits Member countries to adopt their own policies and rules on the subject of exhaustion. Each WTO

(Oxford Univ. Press) and *Second Report (Final) to the Committee on International Trade Law of the International Law Association on the Subject of the Exhaustion of Intellectual Property Rights and Parallel Importation,* presented in London, July 2000, at the 69th Conference of the International Law Association, rev. 1.1.

114. *See, e.g.,* Alan O. Sykes, *TRIPS, Pharmaceuticals, Developing Countries, and the Doha "Solution,"* CHI. J. INT'L L. (2002).

115. See views of various commentators summarized in Second Report, *supra* note 108, and conclusions of ILA International Trade Law Committee.

In some industry sectors, such as pharmaceuticals, producers might refrain from providing lower priced products in some markets if they are charging much higher prices in other markets. Assume that an anticancer drug can be manufactured for $300 per patient per year. It can be sold in Europe for $10,000 per patient per year. Because of personal income differentials, the same drug can be sold in Africa for no more than $500 per patient per year. If the pharmaceutical manufacturer has to choose a single global price because the anticancer drug can move freely under a rule of international exhaustion, it may choose to offer the drug to Africa at $10,000 per patient per year, even though very few people in Africa can purchase it. It will make more money from high-price sales in Europe than it could from low-price sales in Africa and Europe.

Whether pharmaceutical companies should be able to charge widely different prices to consumers in different markets is the subject of a great deal of policy debate. The industry argues that only by charging high prices in affluent markets can it recover its research and development costs. If low-price sales are to be made in other markets, the affluent markets should be protected against imports.

Perhaps the economic picture painted by the industry reflects a distortion in the way the drug sector operates. If advertising, promotion, lobbying, and administrative costs were reduced, perhaps it might be possible to sell drugs at prices more affordable to the global consumer.

116. Virtually all products traded on international markets are protected by trademark, and allowing producers to segment markets on the basis of those marks may severely inhibit trade and competition. There is limited social utility in dividing up markets on the basis of trademark rights.

117. Copyrighted expression presents some interesting issues in regard to exhaustion. Books, CDs, and DVDs are very much like traditional commodities traded on world markets, and there is limited reason to think that it is useful to divide up the world market based on the price of these products. Computer software has a significant utility function, and an argument can be made in favor of offering lower prices in less affluent markets.

Member is free to choose international, regional, or national exhaustion without interference based on TRIPS Agreement rules.

The issue of exhaustion of rights is addressed in Article 6 of the TRIPS Agreement.

ARTICLE 6: EXHAUSTION

For the purposes of dispute settlement under this Agreement, subject to the provisions of Articles 3 and 4 nothing in this Agreement shall be used to address the issue of the exhaustion of intellectual property rights.

In the final stages of the Uruguay Round, the GATT Contracting Parties were unable to address in great detail the complex issue of exhaustion of rights and to agree on a common standard. Whereas the scope and content of Article 6 appear to be simple, the provision is not devoid of normative content and poses a number of puzzling problems.

First, exhaustion rules are subject to the provisions of nondiscrimination, that is, national treatment and most favored nation treatment. While Members remain free to adopt whichever doctrine of exhaustion they wish (national, regional, or international), this has to be done on a consistent basis. The practical relevance of national treatment is limited in this context. For example, Members would be precluded from providing rules less favorable to foreign right holders than for nationals on the enforcement of contracts establishing marketing territories. The implications of MFN treatment are more important as Members are basically not allowed to treat other WTO Members differently in terms of exhaustion of rights of products originating from these countries. To what extent does MFN treatment affect and restrict the use of regional exhaustion?

Second, as noted above, customs territories and thus customs unions are deemed to be a single territorial entity for the purposes of the TRIPS Agreement. The use of regional exhaustion within such an entity therefore does not amount to a violation of MFN.

Third — and this is of importance to free trade agreements — differential treatment of parallel trade based upon exhaustion or other rules is dealt with primarily as a matter of trade in goods and thus falls under the GATT, as will be discussed below. The country of exportation, rather than the nationality of the right holder, is decisive in determining the exhaustion of rights in relation to the product at stake. For example, a product exported from Switzerland to the EU will be subject to the doctrine of exhaustion applied by the EU to third countries (or on the basis of specific bilateral treaty provisions) even if the right holder is a national of a member state of the European Union. MFN treatment as to the nationality of the right holder therefore does not exclude differential and preferential treatment of parallel imports based upon categories other than IPRs, in particular provisions relating to free movement of goods in trade agreements.

Finally, provisions other than national treatment and MFN are arguably exempted from invocation, in the context of Article 6, for purposes of WTO dispute settlement between Members. However, Article 6 does not preclude recourse to such other provisions of the Agreement in domestic dispute settlement for the purpose of construing national or regional law relating to exhaustion and parallel trade in accordance with WTO rules.

When it first proposed the Trade Marks Directive, the European Commission recommended that the European Union adopt a uniform rule of international exhaustion. However, EU industry strongly opposed this move. The Commission retreated to seemingly neutral ground in Article 7 of the directive, which appears only to codify the rule of intra-Union exhaustion. Nevertheless, without a referral to the ECJ, the German Federal Supreme Court in the *Dyed Jeans*[118] case eliminated the longstanding German rule of international exhaustion for trademarks based on its interpretation of Article 7. This was followed by a referral from the Austrian Supreme Court to the ECJ in the *Silhouette* case. At the time of the events giving rise to the litigation, Austria was a member of the European Economic Area (EEA). The EEA is a free trade area established among the EU and European Free Trade Association (EFTA) countries. EEA members are obligated to follow the rules of the Trade Marks Directive, and the ECJ approaches interpretation of the Trade Marks Directive as if Austria were an EU member. By the time of the ECJ's decision in *Silhouette*, Austria had, in fact, become a full-fledged EU member.

SILHOUETTE INTERNATIONAL SCHMIED GMBH & CO. KG v. HARTLAUER HANDELSGESELLSCHAFT MBH

(Case C-355/96) Court of Justice of the European Communities [1998] 2 CMLR 953 16 July 1998

Headnote:
Reference from Austria by the Oberster Gerichtshof under Article 177 EC. . . .

Decision:
By order of 15 October 1996, received at the Court on 30 October 1996, the Oberster Gerichtshof referred to the Court for a preliminary ruling under Article 177 EC two questions on the interpretation of Article 7 of the First Council Directive 89/104 to approximate the laws of the Member States relating to trade marks ("the Directive") ([1989] OJ L40/1) as amended by the Agreement on the European Economic Area of 2 May 1992 ("the EEA Agreement") ([1994] OJ L1/3.).

Those questions were raised in proceedings between two Austrian companies, Silhouette International Schmied GmbH & Co KG ("Silhouette") and Hartlauer Handelsgesellschaft mbH ("Hartlauer"). . . .

Silhouette produces spectacles in the higher price ranges. It markets them worldwide under the trade mark "Silhouette," registered in Austria and most countries of the world. In Austria, Silhouette itself supplies spectacles to opticians; in other States it has subsidiary companies or distributors.

Hartlauer sells inter alia spectacles through its numerous subsidiaries in Austria, and its low prices are its chief selling point. It is not supplied by Silhouette because that company considers that distribution of its products by Hartlauer would be harmful to its image as a manufacturer of top-quality fashion spectacles.

118. BGH, Urt. v.14.12.1995-1 ZR 210/93 (Stuttgart), NJW 1996, Heft 15, 994-97.

In October 1995, Silhouette sold 21,000 out-of-fashion spectacle frames to a Bulgarian company, Union Trading, for the sum of US$261,450. It had directed its representative to instruct the purchasers to sell the spectacle frames in Bulgaria or the states of the former USSR only, and not to export them to other countries. The representative assured Silhouette that it had so instructed the purchaser. However, the Oberster Gerichtshof noted that it had not proved possible to ascertain whether that had actually been done.

In November 1995, Silhouette delivered the frames in question to Union Trading in Sofia. Hartlauer bought those goods — it has not, according to the Oberster Gerichtshof, been possible to find out from whom — and offered them for sale in Austria from December 1995. In a press campaign Hartlauer announced that, despite not being supplied by Silhouette, it had managed to acquire 21,000 Silhouette frames abroad.

Silhouette brought an action for interim relief before the Landesgericht Steyr, seeking an injunction restraining Hartlauer from offering spectacles or spectacle frames for sale in Austria under its trade mark, where they had not been put on the market in the European Economic Area ("EEA") by Silhouette itself or by third parties with its consent. It claims that it has not exhausted its trade mark rights, since, in terms of the Directive, trade-mark rights are exhausted only when the products have been put on the market in the EEA by the proprietor or with his consent. It based its claim on paragraph 10a of the Markenschutzgesetz and on paragraphs 1 and 9 of the Gesetz gegen den Unlauteren Wettbewerb (Law against Unfair Competition) and paragraph 43 of the Allgemeines Burgerliches Gesetzbuch (General Civil Code, "the ABGB").

Hartlauer contended that the action should be dismissed since Silhouette had not sold the frames subject to any prohibition of reimportation into the Community. In its view, paragraph 43 of the ABGB was not applicable. Moreover, it observed that the Markenschutzgesetz does not grant a right to seek prohibitory injunctions and that, given that the legal position was unclear, its conduct was not contrary to established customs.

Silhouette's action was dismissed by the Landesgericht Steyr and, on appeal, by the Oberlandesgericht Linz. Silhouette appealed to the Oberster Gerichtshof on a point of law.

The Gerichtshof noted, first, that the case before it concerned the reimportation of goods originally produced by the proprietor of the trade mark and put on the market by the proprietor in a non-member country. It went on to point out that before paragraph 10a of the Markenschutzgesetz entered into force Austrian courts applied the principle of international exhaustion of the right conferred by a trade mark (the principle that the proprietor's rights are exhausted once the trade-marked product has been put on the market, no matter where that takes place). Finally, the Oberster Gerichtshof stated that the explanatory memorandum to the Austrian law implementing Article 7 of the Directive indicated that it was intended to leave the resolution of the question of the validity of the principle of international exhaustion to judicial decision.

Accordingly, the Oberster Gerichtshof decided to stay proceedings and refer the following questions to the Court for a preliminary ruling:

(1) Is Article 7(1) of the First Council Directive 89/104 to approximate the laws of the Member States relating to trade marks ([1989] OJ L401) to be interpreted as meaning that the trade mark entitles its proprietor to prohibit a third party

from using the mark for goods which have been put on the market under that mark in a State which is not a Contracting State? . . .

QUESTION 1

By its first question the Oberster Gerichtshof is in substance asking whether national rules providing for exhaustion of trade-mark rights in respect of products put on the market outside the EEA under that mark by the proprietor or with his consent are contrary to Article 7(1) of the Directive.

It is to be noted at the outset that Article 5 of the Directive defines the "rights conferred by a trade mark" and Article 7 contains the rule concerning "exhaustion of the rights conferred by a trade mark."

According to Article 5(1) of the Directive, the registered trade mark confers on the proprietor exclusive rights therein. In addition, Article 5(1)(a) provides that those exclusive rights entitle the proprietor to prevent all third parties not having his consent from use in the course of trade of, inter alia, any sign identical with the trade mark in relation to goods or services which are identical to those for which the trade mark is registered. Article 5(3) sets out a non-exhaustive list of the kinds of practice which the proprietor is entitled to prohibit under paragraph 1, including, in particular, importing or exporting goods under the trade mark concerned.

Like the rules laid down in Article 6 of the Directive, which set certain limits to the effects of a trade mark, Article 7 states that, in the circumstances which it specifies, the exclusive rights conferred by the trade mark are exhausted, with the result that the proprietor is no longer entitled to prohibit use of the mark. Exhaustion is subject first of all to the condition that the goods have been put on the market by the proprietor or with his consent. According to the text of the Directive itself, exhaustion occurs only where the products have been put on the market in the Community (and in the EEA since the EEA Agreement entered into force).

No argument has been presented to the Court that the Directive could be interpreted as providing for the exhaustion of the rights conferred by a trade mark in respect of goods put on the market by the proprietor or with his consent irrespective of where they were put on the market.

On the contrary, Hartlauer and the Swedish Government have maintained that the Directive left the Member States free to provide in their national law for exhaustion, not only in respect of products put on the market in the EEA but also of those put on the market in non-member countries.

The interpretation of the Directive proposed by Hartlauer and the Swedish Government assumes, having regard to the wording of Article 7, that the Directive, like the Court's case law concerning Articles 30 and 36 EC, is limited to requiring the Member States to provide for exhaustion within the Community, but that Article 7 does not comprehensively resolve the question of exhaustion of rights conferred by the trade mark, thus leaving it open to the Member States to adopt rules on exhaustion going further than those explicitly laid down in Article 7 of the Directive.

As Silhouette, the Austrian, French, German, Italian and United Kingdom Governments and the Commission have all argued, such an interpretation is contrary to the wording of Article 7 and to the scheme and purpose of the rules of the Directive concerning the rights which a trade mark confers on its proprietor.

In that respect, although the third recital in the preamble to the Directive states that "it does not appear to be necessary at present to undertake full-scale approximation of the trade mark laws of the Member States," the Directive none the less provides for harmonisation in relation to substantive rules of central importance in this sphere, that is to say, according to that same recital, the rules concerning those provisions of national law which most directly affect the functioning of the internal market, and that that recital does not preclude the harmonisation relating to those rules from being complete.

The first recital in the preamble to the Directive notes that the trade mark laws applicable in the Member States contain disparities which may impede the free movement of goods and freedom to provide services and may distort competition within the Common Market, so that it is necessary, in view of the establishment and functioning of the internal market, to approximate the laws of Member States. The ninth recital emphasises that it is fundamental, in order to facilitate the free movement of goods and services, to ensure that registered trade marks enjoy the same protection under the legal systems of all the Member States, but that this should not prevent Member States from granting at their option extensive protection to those trade marks which have a reputation.

In the light of those recitals, Articles 5 to 7 of the Directive must be construed as embodying a complete harmonisation of the rules relating to the rights conferred by a trade mark. That interpretation, it may be added, is borne out by the fact that Article 5 expressly leaves it open to the Member States to maintain or introduce certain rules specifically defined by the Community legislature. Thus, in accordance with Article 5(2), to which the ninth recital refers, the Member States have the option to grant more extensive protection to trade marks with a reputation.

Accordingly, the Directive cannot be interpreted as leaving it open to the Member States to provide in their domestic law for exhaustion of the rights conferred by a trade mark in respect of products put on the market in non-member countries.

This, moreover, is the only interpretation which is fully capable of ensuring that the purpose of the Directive is achieved, namely to safeguard the functioning of the internal market. A situation in which some Member States could provide for international exhaustion while others provided for Community exhaustion only, would inevitably give rise to barriers to the free movement of goods and the freedom to provide services.

Contrary to the arguments of the Swedish Government, it is no objection to that interpretation that since the Directive was adopted on the basis of Article 100a EC, which governs the approximation of the laws of the Member States concerning the functioning of the internal market, it cannot regulate relations between the Member States and non-member countries, with the result that Article 7 is to be interpreted as meaning that the Directive applies only to intra-Community relations.

Even if Article 100a of the Treaty were to be construed in the sense argued for by the Swedish Government, the fact remains that Article 7, as has been pointed out in this judgment, is not intended to regulate relations between Member States and non-member countries but to define the rights of proprietors of trade marks in the Community.

Finally, the Community authorities could always extend the exhaustion provided for by Article 7 to products put on the market in non-member countries by entering into international agreements in that sphere, as was done in the context of the EEA Agreement.

In the light of the foregoing, the answer to be given to the first question must be that national rules providing for exhaustion of trade-mark rights in respect of products put on the market outside the EEA under that mark by the proprietor or with his consent, are contrary to Article 7(1) of the Directive, as amended by the EEA Agreement. . . .

On those grounds, THE COURT, in answer to the questions referred to it by the Oberster Gerichtshof by order of 15 October 1996,

Hereby Rules:

1. National rules providing for exhaustion of trade mark rights in respect of products put on the market outside the EEA under that mark by the proprietor or with its consent are contrary to Article 7(1) of First Council Directive 89/104 to approximate the laws of the Member States relating to trade marks, as amended by the Agreement on the European Economic Area of 2 May 1992. . . .

NOTES AND QUESTIONS

1. Advocate General Jacobs had urged the Court to interpret Article 7 to prohibit individual member states from adopting a rule of international exhaustion. He said that while the language of Article 7 may not be clear on this question, such an interpretation could be "reasonably inferred." Do you agree? Does codifying the doctrine of intra-Union exhaustion "infer" the preclusion of international exhaustion? Recall that no mention is made of international exhaustion either in the recitals or text of the Directive, and that the Commission had initially proposed a uniform rule of international exhaustion.

2. The ECJ says that Article 7 does not address the subject of international exhaustion, so EU trademark holders must retain rights specified in Article 5. The Court then interprets Article 5 to mandate a right to block parallel imports (subject to the intra-Union "exception" of Article 7). Article 5(1) entitles the trademark holder to prohibit "third parties not having his consent from using [the mark] in the course of trade." In *Silhouette*, what party placed the goods on the market?

3. The Court says that Article 5(3) mandates a right to block imports as part of the holder's protection arsenal. Might the Court have chosen to interpret the right to block imports under the mark in a more limited way? Might it have interpreted that right to apply in circumstances in which the mark had been applied without the consent of the right holder, that is, so as to preclude imports of counterfeit trademarked goods?

F.   Duration of Intellectual Property Rights

The different disciplines of IPRs have in common that the duration of protection is — in general — limited. This principle is based, first, on the idea that IPRs are granted to allow the author or inventor to secure an appropriate return on investment, but that they should not unnecessarily impair the diffusion of knowledge. Second, limitations in time are motivated by competition policies that require a balancing of exclusive rights and open markets. Third, and related to the doctrine of exhaustion, IPRs inhering in products must at some point give way to legal security for the owner of the product.

Exceptions to the principle of limited duration are found in trademarks and trade secrets. The protection of trademarks generally can be indefinitely extended if certain conditions are met. Trade secrets are protected as long as the conditions of secrecy are satisfied. The unlimited duration of trademarks relates to their prime function, which is to allow consumers to distinguish between products of competitors, and to identify their origin.

The duration of IPRs protection varies in different legal systems. Specific mechanisms for extending duration exist in the field of patents to offset time spent during government approvals and clinical trials.[119]

Efforts to harmonize the duration of protection at the international level have met with difficulty. The Paris Convention failed to regulate duration. The results achieved in the TRIPS Agreement were a major advance, particularly in the fields of copyright and patent law, and have lead — or will lead — to the substantial extension of protection in many countries.

Relevant provisions on minimal standards provided for different IPRs can be found in Articles 12, 18, 26(3), 33, and 38 of the TRIPS Agreement and Article 7 of the Berne Convention.

However, while the TRIPS Agreement has resulted in harmonization of minimum terms of protection, the TRIPS Agreement does not specifically prescribe, and it has not led to, harmonized maximum terms of protection. There has been a persistent trend within the EU to extend the duration of IPRs protection beyond that mandated by the TRIPS Agreement and the United States has largely followed the EU in this regard.

NOTES AND QUESTIONS

1. Unlimited duration of trade secret protection is controversial. Some argue that it is not so apparent why the trade secret is more worthy of restriction on the diffusion of knowledge than other forms of IPR. On the other hand, unlimited duration seems inherent to the concept of trade secret since a trade secret exists as long as valuable information is not disclosed. Are trade secrets in practice really of unlimited duration? Why is the protection of intellectual property as undisclosed information a risky strategy?

G. Right of Priority

The coexistence of national (or regional) systems of intellectual property, each based upon the principle of territoriality, requires appropriate tools of interconnection. One of the key instruments to bring about interconnection is the right of priority. Because the validity of IPRs generally depends on an intellectual step, filing and registration of rights theoretically should take place simultaneously in all countries where protection is sought. A failure to act simultaneously would risk that novelty, originality, or creativity would be lost, either as a later act of creation rendered the earlier act non-original, or as

---

119. *See, e.g.*, EC Council Regulation 1768/92 of 18 June 1992 on the creation of a supplementary protection certificate for medicinal products [1992] O.J. L182/1.

disclosure or public use of a covered product in one country undermined novelty in another.

The international IPRs system guards against the undermining of an intellectual step by means of the principle of right of priority. The principle prescribes the preservation of novelty, originality, and creativity upon the filing of an application for the grant of protection in one country of the Paris Union — for a limited period of time of twelve months (patents) and six months (trademarks and industrial designs). During that limited period, a more recent invention, creation, or disclosure cannot legally destroy novelty, and the creator may file in other countries of the Paris Union based upon the priority date. This right of interconnection is contained in Article 4 of the Paris Convention:

ARTICLE 4, PARIS CONVENTION (1967)

A.

(1) Any person who has duly filed an application for a patent, or for the registration of a utility model, or of an industrial design, or of a trademark, in one of the countries of the Union, or his successor in title, shall enjoy, for the purpose of filing in the other countries, a right of priority during the periods hereinafter fixed.

(2) Any filing that is equivalent to a regular national filing under the domestic legislation of any country of the Union or under bilateral or multilateral treaties concluded between countries of the Union shall be recognized as giving rise to the right of priority.

(3) By a regular national filing is meant any filing that is adequate to establish the date on which the application was filed in the country concerned, whatever may be the subsequent fate of the application.

B.

Consequently, any subsequent filing in any of the other countries of the Union before the expiration of the periods referred to above shall not be invalidated by reason of any acts accomplished in the interval, in particular, another filing, the publication or exploitation of the invention, the putting on sale of copies of the design, or the use of the mark, and such acts cannot give rise to any third-party right or any right of personal possession. Rights acquired by third parties before the date of the first application that serves as the basis for the right of priority are reserved in accordance with the domestic legislation of each country of the Union.

The right of priority is more or less unknown in the copyright field since copyright adheres upon the creation of an expressive work, and, according to the Berne Convention, without the necessity of complying with formalities. Copyright adheres in countries throughout the Berne Union simultaneously.

While the right of priority is of paramount importance to the daily operation of the international IPRs system, the basic concept has rarely raised controversy or been the subject of court decision.

H. Direct Effect and Consistent Interpretation

When a nation enters into an international agreement, it may assume obligations that require implementation in national law. The way this implementation takes place is defined by the national Constitution, which acts as the interface between international law and domestic law. For countries following a so-called monist tradition, an international agreement (including a treaty or convention) automatically becomes part of domestic law without further action by the national parliament or legislature. For countries following a so-called dualist tradition, an international agreement only becomes part of domestic law when it is implemented by the national legislature. Some countries determine whether an international agreement has direct effect or must be implemented into national law on a case-by-case basis.

Under European Union law, as interpreted by the Court of Justice of the European Union, the determination whether an international agreement has direct effect is made on a case-by-case basis. This is also the case under the U.S. Constitution. Although the Constitution expressly provides that treaties are the supreme law of the land, the Supreme Court has long interpreted this to mean that international agreements will be given direct or "self-executing" effect depending on a number of factors.

1. In EU Law

In the following case, *Parfums Christian Dior v. Tuk,* the ECJ examines whether the WTO TRIPS Agreement is directly effective in EU law. If it is, private parties may rely on its provisions in courts within the European Union. If it is not, private parties may only rely on EU or member state implementing legislation. But note that the Court also discusses what is called the doctrine of consistent interpretation. Even if direct effect is lacking, courts are obliged to construe domestic law as far as possible in accordance with international law.

PARFUMS CHRISTIAN DIOR SA v. TUK CONSULTANCY BV

**Judgment of the Court of Justice of the European Communities 14 Dec. 2000
In Joined Cases C-300/98 and C-392/98**

REFERENCES to the Court under Article 177 of the EC Treaty (now Article 234 EC) by the Arrondissementsrechtbank's-Gravenhage (Netherlands) (C-300/98) and the Hoge Raad der Nederlanden (Netherlands) (C-392/98) for preliminary rulings in the proceedings pending before those courts. . . .

DIRECT EFFECT OF ARTICLE 50(6) OF TRIPs

41. By the second question in Case C-392/98 and the only question in Case C-300/98, the national courts seek in essence to ascertain whether, and to what extent, the procedural requirements of Article 50(6) of TRIPs have entered the sphere of Community law so that, whether on application by the parties or of their own motion, the national courts are required to apply them.

42. It is settled case-law that a provision of an agreement entered into by the Community with non-member countries must be regarded as being directly applicable when, regard being had to the wording, purpose and nature of the agreement, it may be concluded that the provision contains a clear, precise

and unconditional obligation which is not subject, in its implementation or effects, to the adoption of any subsequent measure (see, in that regard, Case 12/86 *Demirel* v *Stadt Schwäbisch Gmünd* [1987] ECR 3719, paragraph 14, and Case C-162/96 *Racke* v *Hauptzollamt Mainz* [1998] ECR I-3655, paragraph 31).

43. The Court has already held that, having regard to their nature and structure, the WTO Agreement and the annexes thereto are not in principle among the rules in the light of which the Court is to review measures of the Community institutions pursuant to the first paragraph of Article 173 of the EC Treaty (now, after amendment, the first paragraph of Article 230 EC) (see Case C-149/96 *Portugal* v *Council* [1999] ECR I-8395, paragraph 47).

44. For the same reasons as those set out by the Court in paragraphs 42 to 46 of the judgment in *Portugal* v *Council,* the provisions of TRIPs, an annex to the WTO Agreement, are not such as to create rights upon which individuals may rely directly before the courts by virtue of Community law.

45. However, the finding that the provisions of TRIPs do not have direct effect in that sense does not fully resolve the problem raised by the national courts.

46. Article 50(6) of TRIPs is a procedural provision intended to be applied by Community and national courts in accordance with obligations assumed both by the Community and by the Member States.

47. In a field to which TRIPs applies and in respect of which the Community has already legislated, as is the case with the field of trade marks, it follows from the judgment in *Hermès,* in particular paragraph 28 thereof, that the judicial authorities of the Member States are required by virtue of Community law, when called upon to apply national rules with a view to ordering provisional measures for the protection of rights falling within such a field, to do so as far as possible in the light of the wording and purpose of Article 50 of TRIPs.

48. On the other hand, in a field in respect of which the Community has not yet legislated and which consequently falls within the competence of the Member States, the protection of intellectual property rights, and measures adopted for that purpose by the judicial authorities, do not fall within the scope of Community law. Accordingly, Community law neither requires nor forbids that the legal order of a Member State should accord to individuals the right to rely directly on the rule laid down by Article 50(6) of TRIPs or that it should oblige the courts to apply that rule of their own motion.

49. The answer to the second question in Case C-392/98 and the only question in Case C-300/98 must therefore be that:

— in a field to which TRIPs applies and in respect of which the Community has already legislated, the judicial authorities of the Member States are required by virtue of Community law, when called upon to apply national rules with a view to ordering provisional measures for the protection of rights falling within such a field, to do so as far as possible in the light of the wording and purpose of Article 50 of TRIPs, but

— in a field in respect of which the Community has not yet legislated and which consequently falls within the competence of the Member States, the protection of intellectual property rights, and measures adopted for that purpose by the judicial authorities, do not fall within the scope of Community law. Accordingly, Community law neither requires nor forbids that the legal order of a Member State should accord to individuals the right to rely directly on the rule laid down by Article 50(6) of TRIPs or that it should oblige the courts to apply that rule of their own motion.

NOTES AND QUESTIONS

1. The ECJ decides that the TRIPS Agreement is not directly effective as a matter of EU law, but this is not the end of the matter. First, the Court expounds the doctrine of consistent interpretation. Both authorities and courts of the EU and of member states are obliged to construe EU law to the utmost extent possible in accordance with WTO law (*supra,* at VI.H.). Moreover, member states, and their Courts, are free to give direct effect to TRIPS provisions in areas that have not been fully harmonized and where Members retain regulatory powers. What is the difference between the doctrine of consistent interpretation and the doctrine of direct effect?

2. The Court generally excludes direct effect of the TRIPS Agreement. In *Portugal v. Council* [1999] ECR I-8395, the Court also referred to the lack of granting direct effect to WTO law in major trading partners, by which it mainly addressed the United States (see below). Are reasons based upon reciprocity convincing? Is it convincing to exclude direct effect on the level of EU law, but to allow for it within national law, by referring the nature and structure of the WTO Agreements?

3. Most provisions of the TRIPS Agreement are perfectly suitable for direct effect as they deal with matters that pertain to the provinces of the courts and of case law. Instead of denying direct effect in general terms, is it more appropriate to assess whether a particular provision is justiciable in a particular context?

4. Direct effect is suitable for so-called monist countries, which consider international law to be part of the law of the land, applicable without further transformation. It is not suitable, unless prescribed by an international agreement or domestic legislation, in countries with a dualist tradition. These countries generally require transformation of international agreements to domestic law prior to their application by domestic authorities and courts in a domestic context. The approach of the U.S. Supreme Court falls between the monist and dualist traditions because direct effect is permitted in some circumstances, and not in others.

5. Novartis, a multinational originator pharmaceutical company, sued the government of India in the courts of India alleging that a provision of the amended Indian Patent Act violated India's obligations under the TRIPS Agreement. Article 3(d) of the Indian Patent Act requires that applicants for drug patents based on modifications of existing chemical compounds demonstrate that the claimed inventions result in a significant enhancement in efficacy. Novartis contended that this adds an additional criterion for patentability not provided for in the TRIPS Agreement, and discriminates against the pharmaceutical sector.[120] However, India's constitutional structure is based on the dualist British Commonwealth model,

---

120. An excerpt of the *Novartis* case relating to the introduction of the efficacy standard is reprinted in Chapter 2, IV.B.

which denies direct effect to treaties such that Novartis could not base a claim under Indian law on the TRIPS Agreement. Not surprisingly, the Indian courts rejected Novartis' claim based on the lack of direct effect of the TRIPS Agreement (see decision of the Madras High Court, *Novartis v. India,* W.P. Nos. 24759 of 2006 and 24760 of 2006, decided Aug. 6, 2007 excerpted regarding a constitutional/delegation issue in Chapter 2, IV.B. *infra*). Knowledgeable observers both within and outside India remain perplexed as to what prompted Novartis to pursue a cause of action that clearly could not succeed in India, spending a great deal of money on legal fees to do so. Why do you think Novartis might have pursued a claim that it could not win? Is it possible that Novartis' entire team of lawyers was unfamiliar with Indian constitutional law? That does seem unlikely, doesn't it?

2. In U.S. Law

U.S. law allows for the possibility of direct or "self-executing" effect for international agreements, including trade agreements. However, since 1979 when Congress approved the results of the GATT Tokyo Round, it has included language in implementing legislation for trade agreements that expressly deprives them of self-executing effect. This means that the agreements do not change federal law unless Congress expressly does so through legislation. It also means that individuals may not directly rely on the agreements in court. Congress apparently wants to carefully control any impact international commitments have in the domestic legal sphere. The following excerpt describes the situation as it applies to the intellectual property provisions of bilateral and regional trade agreements of the United States.

INTELLECTUAL PROPERTY PROVISIONS
OF BILATERAL AND REGIONAL TRADE
AGREEMENTS IN LIGHT OF U.S. FEDERAL LAW
Frederick M. Abbott*

. . . Under the U.S. Constitution, treaties and other international agreements may be "self-executing" in domestic law. Whether an international agreement is self-executing depends on its terms and context. When the provisions of an international agreement are self-executing, they do not require additional implementing legislation to have effect in national law, and they may be directly relied on by private parties in the courts as a source of law. Congress approves the FTAs in legislation which also implements the agreements in domestic law to the extent deemed appropriate. Congress has made a practice of expressly denying self-executing effect to the FTAs in its implementing legislation. Section 102 of the Dominican Republic-Central America-United States Free Trade

---

* Issue Paper No. 12, February 2006 UNCTAD-ICTSD Project on IPRs and Sustainable Development, available at www.iprsonline.org.

Agreement Implementation Act is typical of the provisions denying self-executing effect:

SEC. 102. RELATIONSHIP OF THE AGREEMENT TO UNITED STATES AND STATE LAW.

(a) RELATIONSHIP OF AGREEMENT TO UNITED STATES LAW. —

(1) UNITED STATES LAW TO PREVAIL IN CONFLICT. — No provision of the Agreement, nor the application of any such provision to any person or circumstance, which is inconsistent with any law of the United States shall have effect.

(2) CONSTRUCTION. — Nothing in this Act shall be construed —

(A) to amend or modify any law of the United States, or

(B) to limit any authority conferred under any law of the United States, unless specifically provided for in this Act.

(b) RELATIONSHIP OF AGREEMENT TO STATE LAW. —

(1) LEGAL CHALLENGE. — No State law, or the application thereof, may be declared invalid as to any person or circumstance on the ground that the provision or application is inconsistent with the Agreement, except in an action brought by the United States for the purpose of declaring such law or application invalid.

(2) DEFINITION OF STATE LAW. — For purposes of this subsection, the term "State law" includes —

(A) any law of a political subdivision of a State; and

(B) any State law regulating or taxing the business of insurance.

(c) EFFECT OF AGREEMENT WITH RESPECT TO PRIVATE REMEDIES. — No person other than the United States —

(1) shall have any cause of action or defense under the Agreement or by virtue of congressional approval thereof; or

(2) may challenge, in any action brought under any provision of law, any action or inaction by any department, agency, or other instrumentality of the United States, any State, or any political subdivision of a State, on the ground that such action or inaction is inconsistent with the Agreement.

Based on this type of implementing legislation, the FTAs do not change existing federal law unless specifically mandated by Congress. An individual may not directly invoke the provisions of an FTA in a court of the United States. To the extent that FTAs may impose obligations on the United States that are inconsistent with existing federal law, this is not relevant for domestic legal purposes (even if the United States may incur international legal liability).

U.S. practice with respect to the treatment of international agreements in domestic law is not unusual. Many countries do not directly apply treaties in domestic law, requiring implementing legislation to give them local effect. The European Court of Justice has denied direct effect to the WTO Agreement in EU law. It is nonetheless useful for developing countries to be aware that a provision in an FTA negotiated with the United States does not automatically become the domestic law of the United States.

For developed countries and regions, allowing international trade agreements to have direct effect may facilitate the process of integration by allowing private operators to challenge government conduct inconsistent with the agreements. Developing countries must recognize that directly effective international agreements allow private operators to challenge pre-existing legislation that is inconsistent with them. If a government wants to control the terms of implementation of the agreement, it must be prepared to adopt implementing changes to domestic law that are consistent with the agreement. Also, for developing countries, allowing direct effect presents risks because large multinational companies often have substantially greater access to legal resources than even the national government. Governments may find themselves faced with court challenges based on international agreements which are given direct or self-executing effect. Even though governments may also be challenged on the basis of ordinary domestic legislation, the terms of domestic law typically will not have been negotiated with a foreign government.

USTR has expressly advised Congress that it may adopt subsequent legislation inconsistent with the terms of an FTA. USTR has advised Congress that decisions of dispute settlement panels under the FTAs do not affect U.S. federal law unless those decisions are expressly given effect by the Congress.

This is consistent with U.S. constitutional practice. Congress may adopt legislation inconsistent with prior international agreements. This is referred to as the "last in time" rule; meaning that the later-adopted of a statute or international agreement will govern. Also, the terms of the FTAs do not strictly obligate the parties to implement the decisions of dispute settlement panels. They may instead elect to offer compensation. In any case, most countries will not give direct effect to the decisions of dispute settlement panels of FTAs (or, for that matter, of the WTO (including the Appellate Body)). In order to give domestic effect to a dispute settlement decision, government implementing action is required.

The legislatures of U.S. FTA partners whose constitutions allow subsequent domestic legislation to conflict with the terms of an international agreement (i.e., those which do not follow a so-called "monist" approach), may also legislate inconsistently with the terms of the FTA. In doing so, they may breach an international obligation to the United States. Because of the large imbalance in effective political and economic power between the United States and its FTA partners, countries other than the United States may find the breach of such obligations problematic. The economy of the United States is significantly dependent on only a few foreign countries, meaning that the United States can afford to strain its political and economic relations with almost all other countries. For many smaller and developing country economies, denial of access to the U.S. market would create very serious adverse effects. Therefore, it is likely that the legislatures of most U.S. FTA partners will be significantly more reluctant to legislate inconsistently with an FTA than the U.S. Congress.

NOTES AND QUESTIONS

1. Do you think it is a good idea for the United States to limit the effect of its international agreements in national law? Does this help or hinder U.S. influence on foreign IP systems? What factors go into your analysis?
2. Assess the reasons why the U.S. Congress would rule out direct effect in U.S. courts. What is the implication of direct effect on the balance of power between the different branches of government?
3. Does denial of direct effect equally exclude the doctrine of consistent interpretation, which in the United States is called the Charming Betsy doctrine? (*Murray v. The Schooner Charming Betsy*, 6 U.S. (2 Cranch) 64 (1804).) The matter has not been settled for intellectual property. In the trade remedy

area in the United States, there seems to be a contest between the Charming Betsy doctrine and the canon of interpretation deriving from the Chevron case (*Chevron U.S.A., Inc. v. Natural Res. Def. Council, Inc.*, 467 U.S. 837 (1984)), which divides the process of review into two stages: If the intention of Congress is clearly reflected in the statute, there is no room for interpretation. If a statute is ambiguous or incomplete, the court will defer to any agency interpretation that is reasonable (Davies 2007; Barceló 2006). In the Corus case (*Corus Staal BV and Corus Steel USA Inc. v. United States Department of Commerce*, 259 F. Supp. 2d 1253 CIT, 2003), the Court of International Trade found that U.S. legislation neither requires nor prohibits the practice of zeroing and therefore the Charming Betsy doctrine was of no use.

4. Abbott suggests that the same factors that might make direct effect a good idea for the United States or the European Union may not make this a good idea for Thailand or Ecuador. Why the distinction? How does the annual revenue of General Electric compare with the Gross Domestic Product (GDP) of Ecuador? Which legal entity has more money to spend on IP litigation?

VII. INTELLECTUAL PROPERTY AND OTHER POLICY GOALS

Intellectual property rights form part of the larger body of economic law and of law in general. IPRs do not exist and stand in isolation. They require coordination with other and related policy instruments and rules. Much of the body of rules on intellectual property seeks to establish a proper balance between diverging and competing rules and interests: the limited scope of rights, the limited duration of rights, the proviso for exceptions, and so forth. In terms of principles, the relationship to other policy goals is expressed by the TRIPs Agreement itself in Article 7 and 8 of the Agreement.

THE AGREEMENT ON TRADE RELATED ASPECTS OF INTELLECTUAL PROPERTY RIGHTS (TRIPs)

Thomas Cottier*

DEVELOPMENT AND SOCIAL POLICY GOALS IN THE TRIPs AGREEMENT

THE GOALS AND PRINCIPLES

The TRIPs Agreement reflects the importance of effective protection of intellectual property rights for social and economic development. This is an important ingredient of the rule of law and good governance. At the same time, the Agreement emphasizes that the goals of social and economic development need to be considered in shaping intellectual property regimes. The preamble of the Agreement explicitly recognizes "the underlying public policy objectives

* The World Trade Organization: Legal Economic and Political Analysis, Vol I, p. 1041 (Patrick F.J. Macrory, Arthur E. Appleton & Michael G. Plummer eds., Springer 2005).

of national systems for the protection of intellectual property, including developmental and technological objectives." It equally recognizes "the special needs of the least-developed country Members in respect of maximum flexibility in the domestic implementation of laws and regulations in order to enable them to create a sound and viable technological base."

In addition to the right to exceed the mandatory standards discussed above, the TRIPs Agreement allows Members to limit protection for certain specific reasons which are enumerated in Articles 7 and 8. Each provision of the TRIPs Agreement is to be read in light of the object and purpose of the Agreement as expressed in the preamble and, in particular vested in these two provisions.

Article 7, addressing the "objectives" of the TRIPs Agreement, states that:

> The protection and enforcement of intellectual property rights should contribute to the promotion of technological innovation and to the transfer and dissemination of technology, to the mutual advantage of producers and users of technological knowledge and in a manner conducive to social and economic welfare, and to a balance of rights and obligations.

Article 8:1, addressing "principles," states that:

> Members may, in formulating or amending their laws and regulations, adopt measures necessary to protect public health and nutrition, and to promote the public interest in sectors of vital importance to their socio-economic and technological development, provided that such measures are consistent with the provisions of this Agreement.

Article 8 acknowledges in paragraph 2 that:

> Appropriate measures, provided that they are consistent with the provisions of this Agreement, may be needed to prevent the abuse of intellectual property rights by right holders or the resort to practices which unreasonably restrain trade or adversely affect the international transfer of technology.

The wording of these provisions seeks to strike a careful balance between these objectives and principles and the rights protected in the Agreement. Recourse to the requirement that measures need to be consistent with the provisions of the Agreement, however, appears tautological and circular to some extent as this stipulates a predominance of the other provisions of the Agreement. It may support the view that the provisions of Article 7 and 8 merely express that necessary public policy measures do not amount to nonviolation nullification and impairment of benefits to the extent that such policies may affect market access and protection of investment. However, subsequent developments in state practice relating to access to essential drugs suggest that the objectives and principles of Articles 7 and 8 are given a preferred position as they define important public policy goals which must not be prevented by over-extensive protection of intellectual property rights.

In the Doha Ministerial Declaration the Members stressed that the TRIPs Agreement must be implemented and interpreted in a manner supportive of public health, by promoting both access to existing medicines and research and development into new medicines. In a separate Doha Ministerial Declaration on TRIPs and Public Health, the Members agreed that the TRIPs Agreement does not and should not prevent Members from taking measures to protect public health. This document is of considerable importance in defining the balance between exclusive rights and the needs associated with public health care. It recognizes the importance of protecting intellectual property rights for research-based industries while making it clear that these rights are subject to public health policies. While not officially an "interpretation" in accordance with Article IX:2 of the WTO Agreement, the Declaration will nevertheless influence the interpretation of the TRIPs Agreement beyond the waiver adopted in 2003 in the field of compulsory licenses for essential drugs.

The objectives and principles set forth in Articles 7 and 8 of the Agreement not only apply with respect to the protection of technological subject matter but extend to all intellectual property elements that are related to the socio-economic development of the Members. They are not limited to developing countries. States therefore are entitled to shape domestic intellectual property standards by taking into account, for example, the need to protect and preserve cultural diversity.[121] The long-term impact of these provisions remains to be explored more deeply. So far, the provisions have not yet been fully explored in jurisprudence. In *United States–Section 110(5) of the U.S. Copyright Act* the Panel had to deal with two U.S. copyright provisions exempting certain transmissions from copyright infringement. The Panel focused mainly on Article 13 of the TRIPs Agreement in order to decide whether these exemptions were permissible. In interpreting Article 13 of the Agreement it failed to make any explicit reference to the objectives and purposes of the Agreement as embodied in Articles 7 and 8.[122] In *Canada-Patent Protection of Pharmaceutical Products*, despite a general reference to Articles 7 and 8, the Panel did not specifically address these provisions in the process of interpreting Article 30. Commentators have identified in these two cases a trend in TRIPs interpretation that does not sufficiently take into account the balance of rights and obligations embodied in Articles 7 and 8.[123] The argument was made that the Panel mainly interprets Article 30 from the perspective of IPR holders, thereby "largely dismissing competing social interests, and reducing considerably the range of regulatory diversity permitted under TRIPs."[124] This concern for appropriate balance is valid. It also applies to industrialized countries and reflects the wording of Article 7 that the protection of intellectual property rights should contribute, *inter alia,* to the transfer of technology for the *mutual* advantage of producers and *users.* Both need to be taken into account in shaping and fine-tuning WTO obligations in the process of treaty interpretation.

TECHNICAL COOPERATION AND TRANSFER OF TECHNOLOGY

Article 67 requires industrial countries to provide, upon request, technical and financial cooperation in building the IP system. The task not only implies preparation of legislation, but also training and institution building. It does not extend to the transfer of knowledge and technology on the part of the private sector. Substantial efforts to build and reinforce IPR systems in developing

---

121. For the audiovisual sector, *see* Christophe Germann, *Content Industries and Cultural Diversity: The Case of Motion Pictures,* CULTURELINK, June 2003.

122. *Id.* ¶¶6.71-6.101.

123. *See* R. Howse, *The Canadian Generic Medicines Panel: A Dangerous Precedent in Dangerous Times,* 3 JOURNAL OF WORLD INTELLECTUAL PROPERTY 493, 497 (2000); D. Williams, *The First Six Years and Beyond,* 4 JOURNAL OF WORLD INTELLECTUAL PROPERTY 177, 204 (2001).

124. *Id.* at 494.

countries have been made by Members, and in cooperation with WIPO, over the last decade on the basis of these provisions.

The goals of transfer of technology set forth in Article 7 are understood to be achieved over time as developing countries implement IPR legislation and improve conditions for foreign direct investment. Explicit provisions only exist in relation to least developed countries.

Under Article 66:2 developed countries are obliged to provide incentives to enterprises and institutions at home for the purpose of promoting and encouraging technology transfer to least developed countries. The provision has remained largely without effect. No significant efforts have been made to discuss and introduce governmental measures supporting transfer of technology, such as tax breaks for investing firms, or any other benefits. It remains one of the problems of the TRIPs Agreement that this obligation has not yet been taken seriously, which to some extent undermines the legitimacy of the TRIPs Agreement. Bringing about a more effective transfer of knowledge, information and technology may require more proactive policies. Leaving the matter to the private sector and the market may not be sufficient to achieve the goals of Article 7 of the TRIPs Agreement. Appropriate incentives in the domestic law of industrialized Members should be created to this effect. It is hoped that upon the entry into force of all the provisions of the TRIPs Agreement upon the expiry of transitional periods these efforts will be increased.

A. Intellectual Property and Human Rights

Worldwide attention to international human rights standards includes interest in whether — and the extent to which — the right to IPRs protection is part of the panoply of human rights that individuals enjoy. The protection of human creativity and the fruits of one's labor seem closely related to human rights concerns, and the question arises how the two fields are related. References to IPRs in human rights instruments are not extensive and, until recently, IPRs issues were rarely discussed by the human rights community. Efforts to bring about a better understanding of the relationship between human rights and intellectual property rights are currently under way. Also, it will be necessary to clarify their relationship to the principles set forth in Article 7 and 8 of the TRIPS Agreement.

A number of provisions in international and regional human rights treaties provide a starting point of analysis. Explicit references to IPRs can be found in the Universal Declaration of Human Rights and the International Covenant on Social, Economic and Cultural Rights.

ARTICLE 27(2), UNIVERSAL DECLARATION OF HUMAN RIGHTS (1948)

Everyone has the right to protection of the moral and material interests resulting from any scientific, literary or artistic production of which he is the author.

ARTICLE 15, INTERNATIONAL COVENANT ON ECONOMIC, SOCIAL AND CULTURAL RIGHTS (1966)

1. The States parties to the present Covenant recognize the right of everyone: . . .

c. To benefit from the protection of the moral and material interests resulting from any scientific, literary or artistic production of which he is the author.

2. The steps to be taken by the States Parties to the present Covenant to achieve the full realization of this right shall include those necessary for the conservation, the development and the diffusion of science and culture.

In addition, the protection of property rights is addressed in regional human rights instruments,[125] while a new generation of IPR rights is proclaimed by way of the natural resources rights of indigenous peoples.[126]

In analyzing the relationship of human rights and intellectual property, two basic questions should be distinguished: (1) what is the foundation and legitimizing source of IPRs and (2) what is the impact of human rights norms in shaping and applying existing IPRs?

1. Is Intellectual Property Based upon Human Rights?

Based upon the broad statements contained in the Universal Declaration of Human Rights and the International Covenant on Economic, Social and Cultural Rights as well as other instruments, it would seem possible to argue that the international IPRs system is at least partially based in human rights. From this point of view, it would follow that protection of moral and material interests resulting from scientific, literary, and artistic activities would exist independently of legislation, and be protected even in its absence. From a practical point of view, the key question would amount to whether IPRs protection could

---

125.

ARTICLE 1 OF THE FIRST PROTOCOL TO THE EUROPEAN CONVENTION ON HUMAN RIGHTS

Protection of property
Every natural or legal person is entitled to the peaceful enjoyment of his possessions. No one shall be deprived of his possessions except in the public interest and subject to the conditions provided for by law and by the general principles of international law.

The preceding provisions shall not, however, in any way impair the right of a State to enforce such laws as it deems necessary to control the use of property in accordance with the general interest or to secure the payment of taxes or other contributions or penalties.

ARTICLE 21, AMERICAN CONVENTION ON HUMAN RIGHTS (1969)

1. Everyone has the right to the use and enjoyment of his property. The law may subordinate such use and enjoyment to the interest of society.

. . .

ARTICLE 14, AFRICAN CHARTER ON HUMAN RIGHTS AND PEOPLES RIGHTS (1981)

The right to property shall be guaranteed. It may only be encroached upon in the interest of public need or in the general interest of the community and in accordance with the provisions of appropriate laws.

126.

ARTICLE 31, DECLARATION ON THE RIGHTS OF INDIGENOUS PEOPLES (2007)

Indigenous peoples are entitled to the recognition of the full ownership, control and protection of their cultural and intellectual property.

They have the right to special measures to control, develop and protect their sciences, technologies and cultural manifestations, including human and other genetic resources, seeds, medicines, knowledge of the properties of fauna and flora, oral traditions, literatures, designs and visual and performing arts.

be claimed solely on the basis of human rights standards, and in the absence of a corresponding national or regional IPRs legislative regime. The answer would depend on whether the rights are self-executing.[127] With respect to rights subject to a registration and filing system, it would seem unlikely that they would be considered self-executing. On the other hand, this would seem possible in relation to copyright. In any case, a human rights standard might imply an obligation on the state to provide an appropriate IPRs system, and to enact necessary legislation and establish administrative machinery.

It remains unclear how far IPRs protection expands as a matter of human rights. Would it envelop the rights of corporations, and thus juridical persons? Or, more likely, is the right limited to the human individual seeking protection of his or her own work and efforts? It would seem evident that such protection would only encompass a fraction of the entire IPRs system, and could hardly provide its entire foundation. Consider also the limited duration of most IPRs. How can limited duration be reconciled with a concept of inalienable fundamental rights?

Indeed, both from a historical and a functional angle, it is difficult to argue that national IPRs systems or the international IPRs system are based upon the concept of human rights. Human rights have been answers to specific and fundamental threats to individuals in human history. They establish specific zones of protection and cannot entail the design of an overall economic concept. They do not, and must not, cover the entire range of human activities. Moreover, the international IPRs system may conversely be argued to amount to a system of limitations on fundamental rights. It is a part of economic law and market regulation, which in effect limits economic liberties and trade to the extent these are recognized in constitutional law (e.g., *Wirtschaftsfreiheit* or *liberté économique* in Germany and Switzerland). From this perspective, the granting of intellectual IPRs amounts to a monopoly, for which a sound legal basis is required in statutory law.

IPR protection emerged on a functional basis, expanding in accordance with the economic needs of different industries and countries. A utilitarian approach can now be observed in the ongoing development of the system, as new technologies and markets arise. The fundamental debates on private versus public ownership of knowledge are informed by perceived economic advantage and disadvantage and the need to balance different interests. These debates are likely to persist, and little ground can be gained by recourse to human rights standards for most of the problems involved.

Since the international IPRs system exists at a fairly high level of refinement, debate concerning its foundation may seem rather esoteric. However, issues of premise or foundation may appear more relevant as we consider the justification for entirely new types of rights, in particular the right of protection for traditional knowledge (so-called Traditional Intellectual Property Rights (TIPRs)). These are claims based on broad concepts of equity and justice. Moreover, they often address communities, more so than individuals, and human

---

127. The doctrine of direct effect is also referred to as the doctrine of "self-executing" effect, particularly in U.S. jurisprudence. Arguably, there are several meanings to the doctrine of self-executing effect. For present purposes, suffice it to say that an individual may directly rely on a norm of international law as a source of rights (i.e., it is "self-executing") if the norm is intended to serve as a direct source of rights and if the norm is sufficiently precise that it may be applied by a court. Whether an international norm is self-executing depends both on the character of the norm, and on the constitutional regime of the state in which it is invoked (see *supra* section VII.H).

rights pertaining to individuals may not provide an adequate philosophical foundation for these aspirational norms.

2.   The Relationship of Intellectual Property and Human Rights

While human rights norms may not provide an adequate foundation for IPRs except for moral rights, these standards may eventually influence the shaping and interpretation of IPRs to a larger extent than they currently do.

a.   *Consistent Interpretation*

First, it is submitted that as with any other rules, those regarding existing IPRs should be construed so as to be consistent with fundamental rights. To the extent that treaty or statutory language allows, the scope and contents of rights should be construed in light of related human rights values and provisions. In specific contexts — in particular when addressing the status of individuals and their personalities — the invocation of human rights may well make a difference. For example, trademark protection may be grounded in the protection of a person's reputation, and not only in the avoidance of consumer confusion. An inventor may retain his or her rights to some degree, even if the economic potential of the invention in question has been transferred to an employer. Such effects may flow not just from human rights standards that explicitly refer to IPRs, but from a host of rights, including freedom of the press or freedom of expression. In particular cases, it may be necessary to explore how such rights influence the international IPRs system with a view to preserving basic human rights within a utilitarian concept of IPRs protection.

Conversely, intellectual property may not remain without an impact on construing and applying human rights standards. The relationship is a new field, which still requires in-depth analysis. It forms part of the broader agenda of defining the relationship of trade and human rights. In domestic law, the matter has hardly come up. Utilitarian commercial law, on the one hand, and fundamental rights based on idealism on the other hand, have coexisted without major interaction.

b.   *Do Human Rights Trump Intellectual Property Rights?*

The impact of human rights, however, does not stop here. Beyond interpretation, they increasingly influence the shaping and making of other rights. This second dimension is complex and controversial.

Many countries in Western Europe have witnessed a domestic debate on patenting life forms. The debate on patenting human genes is, as much as the debate on cloning, a debate on human dignity. Patent rules are merely used instrumentally to encourage or discourage investment and thus activities in the field. Human rights issues therefore are controversially discussed focusing on patent law; in wider public opinion, patent law is often, and unrightfully so, blamed as such and has suffered in credibility, legitimacy, and political acceptance and support. The second problem that brought about discussions on the relationship of human rights and IPRs is access to essential drugs.

Importantly, and unlike the field of patenting life forms, access to essential drugs directly relates to the expansion of the relatively high intellectual property standards to developing countries by means of the TRIPS Agreement, being a mandatory commitment of all the member states of the World Trade Organization. The advent of patent protection for pharmaceuticals gave rise to concerns that this would undermine access to essential drugs at low costs and thus the right of health of a great number of people around the world. The scourge of HIV-AIDS in particular fuelled debate. Tensions arose when industrialized country governments sought the restriction of parallel imports or imports of generic medicaments, invoking the provisions of the TRIPS Agreement. Even though the TRIPS Agreement does not legally prevent developing countries from taking such measures in most, if not in all, cases upon an appropriate interpretation of the Agreement, the problem stirred an important political debate in the context of the WTO Ministerial Conference of Doha in November 2001.

At this stage, we merely wish to note that discussion of the relationship of intellectual property and human rights has been triggered by this political debate. It has not yet reached deeper levels of the legal problem. To what extent do intellectual property rights, emanating from the fundamental concept of private property and being part of the human rights tradition in relation to the protection of moral rights in copyrights, foster or impede the cause of human rights? Are there any general answers to this, or does it always depend on the particular context? What, for example, is the economic role of copyright protection for the enhancement of freedom of expression, free speech, freedom of the press, freedom of information, freedom of the arts, and for the right to education? What is the impact of patenting drugs on the right to health in general? What is the impact of patenting life forms on human dignity? It would seem that we can hardly find general and easy answers. Effects may be beneficial in one constellation of rights, and detrimental in another. Human rights and intellectual property rights coexist, both with their own legitimacy. It will be important to explore to what extent human rights standards can and should influence the interpretation of intellectual property norms, for example, in assessing the scope or limitations of an intellectual property right.

3.   The Role of the WTO

At the normative level, the question arises whether the WTO is an appropriate forum for negotiation of rules that affect human rights. Two points seem appropriate in reply. First, there are structural imbalances at the WTO that make it a poor choice of institution in which to negotiate rules with effects on social welfare. Negotiations at the WTO are conducted by trade delegations that largely represent producer group interests. This inevitably leads to solutions that are weighted in favor of the most economically powerful producers.[128] In short, the WTO is not an optimal forum for the negotiation of TRIPS rules that have human rights consequences. Nonetheless, WTO negotiations will inevitably result in rules that affect human rights, so it is important that

---

128. *See* Eric Stein, *International Integration and Democracy: No Love at First Sight*, 95 Am. J. Int'l L. 489 (2001).

better approaches be devised for assuring that human rights interests are taken into account there.

Second, governments do not so far appear inclined to reform the WTO decision-making processes so as to better account for human rights interests. This suggests that it may be necessary to continue negotiating rules attuned to human rights in alternative forums where such interests may be better accommodated. Even here the options are limited because of two phenomena: (1) most or all international institutions reflect to some degree the same problem of imbalanced governance as the WTO, and (2) the international institutions with more balanced decision-making structures tend to lack the effective power of the WTO, and therefore to present less forceful possibilities for improvement.

TOWARD A HUMAN RIGHTS
FRAMEWORK FOR INTELLECTUAL PROPERTY
Laurence R. Helfer*

CONCLUSION

The creation of a human rights framework for intellectual property is still in an early stage of development. During this gestational period, government officials, international jurists, NGOs, and commentators — many of whom have divergent views concerning the appropriate relationship between human rights and intellectual property — have a window of opportunity to influence the framework's substantive content and the procedural rules that mediate relationships among its component parts. In this conclusion, I briefly sketch three hypothetical futures for the framework and explain why each of these predictions is both plausible and likely to be contested by states and non-state actors.

A. USING HUMAN RIGHTS TO EXPAND INTELLECTUAL PROPERTY

One possible future relationship between human rights and intellectual property is an expansion of intellectual property protection standards at the expense of other human rights and the interests of licensees, users, and consumers. In this vision of the future (a dystopian one, to be sure), industries and interest groups that rely upon intellectual property for their economic well-being would invoke the authors' rights and property rights provisions in human rights treaties to further augment existing standards of protection. The fear of such expansions helps to explain why some commentators are skeptical of attempts to analyze intellectual property issues in human rights terms.

Early intimations of this version of the framework's future are already apparent. The authors' rights clauses of the UDHR and ICESCR share a close affinity with the natural rights tradition of droit d'auteur prominent in civil law jurisdictions. Constitutional courts in several European countries have recently relied on fundamental rights guarantees in their respective domestic constitutions to justify intellectual property protection. It would be but a short step for these courts to turn to international human rights law to enhance this protection still further. Whether these expansionist tendencies take root or not may

* 40 U.C. Davis L. Rev. 971 (2007).

depend upon the outcome of a dispute pending before the European Court of Human Rights ("ECHR"), the international tribunal charged with adjudicating complaints under the European Convention on Human Rights ("European Convention") and its Protocols. In *Anheuser-Busch, Inc. v. Portugal,* a decision issued in late 2005, the ECHR concluded that registered trademarks are protected by the property rights clause of the European Convention's first Protocol. Using forceful and unequivocal language, the ECHR stated that "intellectual property as such incontestably enjoys the protection of Article 1 of Protocol No. 1." On the facts presented, however, a majority of the ECHR found no violation of the right to property because the American brewer's trademark application was contested by a rival Czech beer distributor whose products were protected by a registered geographical indication. Given the importance of these issues, the ECHR referred the case to a Grand Chamber for re-argument in 2006. The Grand Chamber held that the right to property includes intellectual property as well as applications to register trademarks. On the unique facts presented, however, it concluded that the government had not violated article 1. (Article 1 expressly authorizes governments to regulate private property in the public interest. Article 1, (. . .) at 262 ("The preceding provisions shall not, however, in any way impair the right of a State to enforce such laws as it deems necessary to control the use of property in accordance with the general interest . . ."). It does not, however, specify how the ECHR is to assess the legality of such regulations.) The Grand Chamber thus left unresolved the more difficult issue of when governments may regulate or restrict intellectual property in the public interest.

B. USING HUMAN RIGHTS TO IMPOSE EXTERNAL LIMITS ON INTELLECTUAL PROPERTY

Patent, trademark, and copyright owners who invoke the property rights and authors' rights provisions of human rights law to demand additional legal protections will likely face stiff resistance from user groups. These groups can draw upon other fundamental rights and freedoms to press for a competing version of the framework, one that relies on human rights law to restrict intellectual property. National courts in Europe are using the right to freedom of expression protected by the European Convention for precisely this purpose. "In particular, there have been a number of decisions in the field of copyright in which the freedom of expression has been invoked to justify a use that is not covered by an exception provided for in the law." These decisions rely on human rights law to overcome the "malfunctions" of the intellectual property system, using them as a "corrective when [intellectual property] rights are used excessively and contrary to their functions." In effect, these cases reach beyond intellectual property's own safety valves — such as fair use, fair dealing, and other exceptions and limitations — to impose external limits, or maximum standards of protection, upon rights holders.

How might user groups increase the likelihood that national courts will invoke human rights law to constrain intellectual property in this way? One plausible method would be to extend . . . to other international lawmaking venues. (Regime Shifting . . . (a) strategy whereby states and non-state actors shifted lawmaking initiatives into biodiversity, plant genetic resources, public health, and human rights regimes as way to create "counterregime intellectual property norms" in tension with TRIPS.) Increasing the number of new treaties and soft law standards that contain precise, subject-specific limits on intellectual property improves the odds that domestic judges will refer to those limits when resolving the disputes that come before them. Such an approach also creates "strategic inconsistency" that increases pressure on government representatives in other international organizations to acknowledge these new rules and standards.

This tactic has considerable risks, however. The international legal system is disaggregated and decentralized and lacks the comprehensive normative hierarchies and enforcements mechanisms found in national laws. A surfeit of conflicting rules will further diminish the system's coherence. This could make international rules less amenable to incorporation into national law, especially for judges unsure of their authority to construe domestic statutes in harmony with those rules.

C. ACHIEVING HUMAN RIGHTS ENDS THROUGH INTELLECTUAL PROPERTY MEANS

The two future frameworks described above share a common strategy. They each take the existing baseline of intellectual property protection as a given and then invoke human rights law to bolster arguments for moving that baseline in one direction or the other.

A third human rights framework for intellectual property proceeds from a very different premise. It first specifies the minimum outcomes — in terms of health, poverty, education, and so forth — that human rights law requires of states. The framework next works backwards to identify different mechanisms available to states to achieve those outcomes. Intellectual property plays only a secondary role in this version of the framework. Where intellectual property laws help to achieve human rights outcomes, governments should embrace it. Where it hinders those outcomes, its rules should be modified (but not necessarily restricted, as I indicate below). But the focus remains on the minimum levels of human well-being that states must provide, using either appropriate intellectual property rules or other means.

A 2001 report by the U.N. High Commissioner for Human Rights analyzing the impact of TRIPS on the right to health exemplifies this outcome-focused, inductive approach. The report reviews the components of the right to health protected by article 12 of the ICESCR. According to a general comment issued by the CESCR Committee, the right to health includes an obligation for states to promote medical research and to provide access to affordable treatments, including essential drugs.

The High Commissioner's report analyzes how intellectual property affects these two obligations. It acknowledges that patents help governments promote medical research by providing an incentive to invent new medical technologies, including new drugs. But the report also asserts that pharmaceutical companies' "commercial motivation . . . means that research is directed, first and foremost, towards 'profitable' disease. Diseases that predominantly affect people in poorer countries . . . remain relatively under-researched." One way to remedy this market imperfection is to create incentives for innovation outside of the patent system.

A similar perspective informs the High Commissioner's discussion of access to essential medicines. The report states that patent protection decreases the affordability of drugs. But affordability also depends on factors unrelated to intellectual property, "such as the level of import duties, taxes, and local market approval costs." In light of these dual impediments, governments can improve access to patented pharmaceuticals in two ways. First, they can exploit the flexibilities already embedded in TRIPS, such as issuing compulsory licenses to manufacturers of generic drugs and importing cheaper drugs from other countries. Second, they can adopt affordability enhancing mechanisms outside of the intellectual property system, for example through differential pricing, "the exchange of price information, price competition and price negotiation with public procurement and insurance schemes." Strikingly, the efficacy of these mechanisms may require augmenting existing intellectual property protection rules, such as negotiating "drug licensing agreements with geographical restrictions[,] . . . so that cheaper drugs do not leak back to wealthier markets." It is too early to predict which of these three versions of the human rights framework for intellectual property, or others yet to be identified, will emerge as dominant. What is certain is that the rules, institutions, and discourse of international human rights are now increasingly relevant to intellectual property law and policy and that the two fields, once isolated from each other, are becoming ever more intertwined.

NOTES AND QUESTIONS

1. Scholarly attention has increasingly turned to the relationship between the norm-system regulating international economic activity, on one hand, and the norm-system regulating human rights, on the other. Two recent compilations that address this relationship in some detail are INTERNATIONAL TRADE AND HUMAN RIGHTS: FOUNDATIONS AND CONCEPTUAL ISSUES (F. Abbott, C. Breining-Kaufmann & T. Cottier eds., U. Mich. Press 2006), and HUMAN RIGHTS AND INTERNATIONAL TRADE (T. Cottier, J. Pauwelyn & E. Bürgi eds., Oxford Univ. Press 2006). IPRs are an important subset of the more general relationship between economic regulation and human rights. Several chapters of these books address IPRs and include references to the work of UN human rights organs on this subject.

2. Is the WTO Ministerial Conference, or are trade negotiating rounds, suited to addressing human rights interests, particularly in light of the reciprocity-based character of the negotiations? Consider, for example, whether it is appropriate for Country A to exchange a concession on the terms of patent protection for pharmaceuticals with a concession by Country B to allow market access for textile products. Does the fact that higher pharmaceutical prices and limited access will result in a deterioration of public health conditions in Country A factor into these negotiations? How does the fact that improved market access for textiles may offset the price increase for pharmaceuticals affect this equation?

3. What is the relationship of the principles expounded in Article 7 and Article 8 to the protection of human rights? Do these principles offer a door of entry for human rights consideration within the WTO and the TRIPS Agreement?

4. Does a multinational corporation have human rights? If an individual inventor has a human right to enjoy the fruits of his or her creative work, does that extend to the individual inventor's corporate patent assignee?

B. *Intellectual Property and Sustainable Development*

With general objectives in Articles 7 and 8 of the TRIPS Agreement and human rights closely interacting with intellectual property rights, broad and somewhat elusive ideas of justice are equally important in shaping the international IPRs system. All laws and regulations, whatever the field, are grounded in (often unspoken) concepts and precepts of justice and equity. IPRs regimes evolved on the basis of utilitarian concepts, and justice was seen in furthering the common good by honoring investment and creativity.

Technological advances throughout the last century were facilitated by the emerging international IPRs system. Yet, to what extent did the system also contribute to the depletion of natural resources and to endangering the global environment and commons? Since adoption of the Stockholm principles in 1972, and the principles of the Rio Declaration in 1992, attention has been directed to the goals of sustainable development, and what the idea of intergenerational equity means to the international IPRs system. How should these concepts and principles affect the evolution of the IPRs system? How do they affect the field of biotechnology? It is important to observe in connection with sources of international law that the international IPRs system cannot be considered in isolation. It has to be responsive to prevailing concepts of justice. It has to adapt to the emerging aspirational norms of international law.

In a comparable manner to the relationship of intellectual property and human rights, the relationship of intellectual property and the principles of sustainable development in environmental law and policies of social and economic development amounts to a new issue that was also brought about by the process of globalization of lawmaking in the two fields. Again, in domestic law, the matter has hardly come up. Intellectual property rights coexist with the emerging field of environmental law and no explicit overlaps or tensions can be reported. This began to change with the advent of the 1992 Rio Summit on Sustainable Development, of Agenda 21, and foremost, of the Convention on Biological Diversity (CBD), which was adopted at this time and which entered into force on 29 December 1993. Negotiations leading to the Convention were in the closing days of the negotiations of the TRIPS Agreement. Protection required for the plant varieties in the TRIPS Agreement was considered to be detrimental for the advancement of important goals of the CBD, in particular benefit sharing and access to technology. Intellectual property was also considered to be detrimental to achieving the protection of traditional knowledge of indigenous peoples and rural populations at large. Indeed, patenting genetically modified organisms that are based upon non-protectable traditional varieties or landraces risks creating a serious and inequitable balance. Moreover, it was felt that IPRs would seriously hamper the free flow of genetic material stored in gene banks, and this concern largely stimulated the efforts to bring about the new International Treaty on Plant Genetic Resources for Food and Agriculture adopted by the FAO Conference in 2001.

Beyond this area, the debate on IPRs and sustainable development has not really developed. Again, we should ask in a broader context: What is the relevance of patent or trademark laws for the creation and promotion of environmentally friendly products? Does sustainable development call for a "greening" of intellectual property? What, beyond the areas of traditional knowledge and genetic engineering, could be pertinent issues relating to other forms of IPR? What could and should be the impact of environmental law on the interpretation of intellectual property? Again, it is difficult to discuss these matters on a highly abstract level. It takes a particular context to advance insights and arguments. But what can be said is that the globalization of law-making, the expansion of IPR in developing countries, and relations of North and South have brought about new issues that previously were not present in the highly specialized world of national intellectual property law. The international system has added new and important dimensions that require, more than before, an integrated approach to addressing these relationships.

One of the international legal instruments that gives shape to sustainable development is the Convention on Biological Diversity (CBD). Virtually all countries of the world are parties to the CBD, with the notable exception of the United States, which has signed but not ratified the agreement. One of the main reasons given by the United States for refusing to ratify the agreement is concern about the way in which provisions regarding intellectual property rights will be implemented. The TRIPS Agreement and the CBD were concluded at roughly the same time. Ever since, questions have been raised as to whether the two agreements are compatible. The following excerpt considers the objectives of the two agreements and how those objectives are sought to be accomplished.

PRESERVATION AND USE OF GENETIC RESOURCE ASSETS AND THE INTERNATIONAL PATENT SYSTEM

Study for the Ministry of Foreign Affairs of Norway Draft of March 31, 2005 rev 1.2 Hong Kong Ministerial Revision Frederick M. Abbott

. . . In 1992 the Convention on Biological Diversity (CBD) was adopted at the Rio Conference.[1] In 1994 the Agreement on Trade-Related Aspects of Intellectual Property Rights (TRIPS Agreement) was adopted in Marrakech.[2] From the outset, questions were raised as to whether there are conflicts or potential conflicts between the objectives and rules of these two international undertakings. These questions have been on the agenda of the WTO TRIPS Council[3] and the Committee on Trade and Environment,[4] they have been raised in the context of work programs and negotiations at the World Intellectual Property Organization (WIPO),[5] they have been considered by the Conference of the

---

1. Convention on Biological Diversity (CBD), adopted June 5, 1992, available at http://www.biodiv.org/convention/articles.asp. As of March 26, 2005, there are 188 state parties to the CBD. The United States signed the CBD on June 4, 1993, but has not ratified the Convention. *See generally* Françoise Burhenne-Guilmin & Susan Casey-Lefkowitz, *The Convention on Biological Diversity: A Hard Won Global Achievement*, 3 (1992) YbIEL 43 (1993) and Edith Brown Weiss, *Introductory Note, United Nations Conference on Environment and Development*, 31 I.L.M. 814 (1992) (and agreement texts following, including Convention on Biological Diversity at 31 I.L.M. 818 (1992)).

2. Agreement Establishing the World Trade Organization, adopted April 15, 1994, available at http://www.wto.org/english/docs_e/legal_e/04-wto_e.htm. As of February 26, 2005, there are 148 Members of the WTO.

3. *See, e.g.,* documents collected at WTO TRIPS Trade Topics web page for Article 27.3(b), traditional knowledge, biodiversity at http://www.wto.org/english/tratop_e/trips_e/art27_3b_e.htm.

4. *See, e.g.,* Committee on Trade and Environment, Report to the Fifth Session of the Ministerial Conference in Cancún, WT/CTE/8, July 11, 2003, at paras. 25-29.

5. *See, e.g.,* WIPO International Bureau, Draft Substantive Patent Law Treaty, SCP/10/2, Sept. 30, 2003, at article 14(3), and note 11; WIPO Secretariat, Genetic Resources: Draft Intellectual Property Guidelines for Access and Equitable Benefit-Sharing, WIPO/GRTKF/IC/7/9, July 30, 2004.

Parties of the CBD,[6] and they are the subject of numerous studies and reports by governments, intergovernmental and non-governmental organizations.[7] This study attempts to clarify the issues at stake in analysis of the relationship between the TRIPS Agreement, related international patent system rules and the CBD. It examines the conflicts or potential conflicts between the objectives and rules of these international undertakings, and it makes certain recommendations regarding the promotion of complementarity among these systems. . . .

III. The Goals of the Convention on Biological Diversity and Related Treaties Governing Genetic Resources

A. PRESERVATION OF GENETIC RESOURCE STOCKS

The first objective of the CBD is preservation of the diversity of genetic resources found in nature, including in animals and plants.[23] There are various reasons for promoting such preservation, including to allow continuity in the natural evolution of species (including adaptation to new environmental conditions), for use in research and development as a source of primary material for direct and recombinant use (taking advantage of natural development and adaptation of biological systems), and maintaining the quality of life from the presence of a diverse biological environment.

Determining the "economic value" of genetic resource stocks is a problematic exercise because it involves anticipating what technological capacities will evolve to exploit such resources, as well as what technological capacities will evolve as alternatives to the exploitation of genetic resources. The world community remains at early stages in assessing the economic value of genetic

---

6. *See, e.g.,* Decision VII/19 of the COP of the CBD requesting technical assistance from WIPO on matters relating, *inter alia,* to the relationship between the CBD and international patent system disclosure, which:

> invited WIPO to examine, and where appropriate address, taking into account the need to ensure that this work is supportive of and does not run counter to the objectives of the CBD, issues regarding the interrelation of access to genetic resources and disclosure requirements in intellectual property rights applications, including, *inter alia:*
>
> (a) Options for model provisions on proposed disclosure requirements;
> (b) Practical options for intellectual property rights application procedures with regard to the triggers of disclosure requirements;
> (c) Options for incentive measures for applicants;
> (d) Identification of the implications for the functioning of disclosure requirements in various WIPO-administered treaties;
> (e) Intellectual property-related issues raised by a proposed international certificate of origin/source/legal provenance;
> and regularly provide reports to the CBD on its work, in particular on actions or steps proposed to address the above issues, in order for the CBD to provide additional information to WIPO for its consideration in the spirit of mutual supportiveness.

See WIPO Secretariat, Patent Disclosure Requirements Relating to Genetic Resources and Traditional Knowledge: Update, WIPO/GRTKF/IC/7/10, at para. 11.

7. *See, e.g.,* Carlos Correa, Establishing a Disclosure of Origin Obligation in the TRIPS Agreement, Quaker United Nations Office (QUNO) Occasional Paper No. 12, 2003 and The Politics and Practicalities of a Disclosure of Origin Obligation, QUNO, Occasional Paper 16, January 2005.

23. *See, e.g.,* Secretariat of Convention on Biological Diversity, Sustaining Life on Earth, April 2000 ("CBD Secretariat Summary").

resource stocks and strong assumptions concerning their future value should be avoided.[24] Anecdotal references to a comparatively small number of "biopiracy" cases are not a proper framework for evaluating the economic value of genetic resource stocks. The economic value of genetic resources may remain stable, or increase or decrease dramatically in the future. Notwithstanding caveats regarding indeterminacy in valuing genetic resources, there is a reasonable likelihood that such resources are of "material" value.

Developing countries are the preponderant owners of diverse genetic resources.[25] The special interest of the international community in encouraging development suggests that a presumption in favor of recognizing rights in genetic resources on the part of developing countries is appropriate. In other words, to the extent that developing countries are able to effectively exploit economic interests in genetic resources it is in the interests of the wider international community to support this.

B. RECOGNIZING OWNERSHIP AND CONTROL

1. CBD-Based Rules

The second objective of the CBD is to recognize state ownership and control over genetic resources located within territorial boundaries. This basic objective has at least two grounds: first, to provide an economic incentive to countries for preserving genetic resources by assuring compensation for their use, and; second, to enhance economic welfare in countries that house existing stocks of genetic resources by assuring compensation for genetic assets.

These objectives are implemented by (i) broadly recognizing sovereignty over genetic resources,[26] (ii) requiring prior informed consent (PIC) of the host country as a condition of access to genetic resources,[27] and (iii) providing for the equitable sharing of benefits from the exploitation of such resources.[28]

---

24. *See, e.g.,* Thomas Cottier, *The Protection of Genetic Resources and Traditional Knowledge: Towards More Specific Rights and Obligations in World Trade Law,* 1 J. Int'l Econ. L. 555 (1998) and Joshua P. Rosenthal, Fogarty International Center, National Institutes of Health, United States of America, *A Benefit-sharing Case Study for the Conference of Parties to Convention on Biological Diversity,* The International Cooperative Biodiversity Groups Program (ICBG).

25. *See* FIC-Economic Development and Biodiversity, Table-Economic Development and Biodiversity, available at http://www.fic.nih.gov/programs/countries.html and UN list of Megadiverse countries.

26. The CBD provides:

ARTICLE 15. ACCESS TO GENETIC RESOURCES
1. Recognizing the sovereign rights of States over their natural resources, the authority to determine access to genetic resources rests with the national governments and is subject to national legislation.

27. The CBD provides:

ARTICLE 15. ACCESS TO GENETIC RESOURCES
5. Access to genetic resources shall be subject to prior informed consent of the Contracting Party providing such resources, unless otherwise determined by that Party.

28. The CBD provides:

ARTICLE 15. ACCESS TO GENETIC RESOURCES
7. Each Contracting Party shall take legislative, administrative or policy measures, as appropriate, and in accordance with Articles 16 and 19 and, where necessary, through the financial mechanism established by Articles 20 and 21 with the aim of sharing in a fair and equitable way the results of research and development and the benefits arising from the commercial and other utilization of genetic resources with the Contracting Party providing such resources. Such sharing shall be upon mutually agreed terms.

Methods for implementation of PIC and equitable benefit sharing are elaborated in the Bonn Guidelines on Access to Genetic Resources and Fair and Equitable Sharing of the Benefits Arising Out of Their Utilization.

The CBD is implemented in national and regional legislation in various ways. Explicit legislation has been adopted by the Andean Community, Brazil, Costa Rica and India, among other countries.[29] In addition, a number of countries through regulatory guidance offer some form of protection for genetic resources.

2. Public International Law

Because some countries are not parties to the CBD, and particularly from an economic standpoint the United States which has signed but not ratified the agreement, it is important to clarify that the principle of sovereignty of states over resources located within their territory did not arise in the CBD but was only codified in that agreement.[30] The United States has in multilateral fora acknowledged its acceptance of this principle.[31] Therefore, to the extent that the rules of the international patent system are reviewed for promoting compliance with the objective of national sovereignty over genetic resource stocks, the review is not directed only to countries that are party to the CBD.

IV. Complementarity and Potential Conflicts in Implementation of the CBD with the TRIPS Agreement and WIPO Conventions

A. Complementarity and its Limits

In adopting the CBD and in development of public international law states have decided that ownership and control over genetic resources is vested in the territory where those resources are located.[32] The CBD is intended to protect rights in genetic resources and promote the equitable sharing of benefits from the exploitation of such resources. The patent is an instrument that provides legal protection for intangible interests in inventive activity. It facilitates the commercialization of such interests. At a fundamental level the objectives of the CBD and international patent system are complementary. The international patent system should facilitate the objectives of the CBD by allowing states to legally protect their recognized interests in genetic resources, including inventions derived from genetic resources, including through commercialization.

However, to recognize that rule systems are conceptually complementary does not mean that they are properly aligned so as to achieve that complementarity. For example, if the international patent system as currently

---

29. *See* WIPO database of CBD implementing legislation.

30. The United States is a signatory to the CBD. Therefore, in accordance with the Vienna Convention, it has an obligation not to take measures inconsistent with the object and purpose of the agreement even if it is not obligated to specifically comply with the agreement.

31. *See, e.g.,* Communication from the United States, Views of the United States on the Relationship between the Convention on Biological Diversity and the TRIPS Agreement dated 24 April 2001, IP/C/W/257, 13 June 2001 (implicitly acknowledging right of state to control access to genetic resources). *See also* U.S. statements in WIPO Intergovernmental Committee on Intellectual Property and Genetic Resources, Traditional Knowledge and Folklore.

32. An argument may be made in favor of treating genetic resources as the "common heritage of mankind" over which no state or person exercises ownership or control. Since the parties to the CBD have rejected that premise, this study does not analyze whether a regime based on common heritage may be preferable.

implemented facilitates circumvention of the CBD by allowing patent applicants to secure patents based on incomplete or misleading information, this may undermine the objectives of the CBD. Similarly, if the CBD is implemented in a way which adds an unnecessary level of insecurity to patent rights, this may undermine the commercial value of patents and incentives for the development of new products. The CBD and the international patent system have not been subject to "conscious alignment" and that is the reason for the present international dialogue.

The protection of genetic resource stocks presupposes the capacity of countries to enforce the sovereign right of ownership and control recognized by the CBD. The CBD adopts PIC and equitable benefit sharing as the mechanism for protecting and exploiting ownership interests. The commercial exploitation of genetic resources may (but does not necessarily) entail securing patent protection. With respect to patents, options for enforcing CBD-based rules include providing evidence of compliance with the requirements of that agreement as a condition of patentability.

NOTES AND QUESTIONS

1. In the Doha Ministerial Declaration,[129] the TRIPS Council was instructed "to examine, *inter alia*, the relationship between the TRIPS Agreement and the Convention on Biological Diversity, the protection of traditional knowledge and folklore, and other relevant new developments raised by Members pursuant to Article 71.1."[130] At the Hong Kong Ministerial Conference, the WTO Director-General was directed to intensify consultations on this subject, among others. The General Council would "review progress and take any appropriate action no later than 31 July 2006."[131] Proposals by WTO Members to further the objectives of the CBD by mandating disclosure of the source and origin of genetic resources in patent applications, as well as by requiring evidence of compliance with prior informed consent (PIC) and equitable benefit sharing (EBS) requirements, remain controversial.[132] Members of this Committee have authored a number of contributions on this subject matter.[133] The positions of WTO Members fall roughly into three categories:

    a. A substantial group of developing countries argues that mandatory disclosure of source and origin is necessary to assure that patent examiners take into account information relevant to assessment of patentability (including novelty and inventive step), as well as in making determinations of inventorship. Evidence of compliance with PIC

---

129. This note is adapted from the 2006 and 2010 Reports of the Committee on International Trade Law to the International Law Association.

130. Adopted 14 Nov. 2001, WT/MIN(01)/DEC/1 (20 Nov. 2001), at para. 19.

131. WT/MIN(05)/DEC (18 Dec. 2005), at para. 39.

132. *See* Note by the WTO Secretariat, *The Relationship Between the TRIPS Agreement and the Convention on Biological Diversity, Summary of Issues Raised and Points Made, Revision,* IP/C/W/368/ Rev. 1, 8 Feb. 2006.

133. *See, e.g.,* Frederick M. Abbott, *Preservation and Use of Genetic Resource Assets and the International Patent System, A Study for the Ministry of Foreign Affairs of Norway,* Mar. 31, 2005; Thomas Cottier & Marion Pannizon, *Legal Perspectives on Traditional Knowledge: The Case for Intellectual Property Protection,* in INTERNATIONAL PUBLIC GOODS AND TRANSFER OF TECHNOLOGY 565 (K. Maskus & J. Reichman eds., 2005).

and EBS is argued to assure consistent implementation of TRIPS Agreement and CBD requirements. The penalty for failure to comply with mandatory disclosure and evidence requirements may include patent forfeiture.

b. A second group of countries sees merit in the proposal to impose a requirement to disclose the source and origin of genetic resources, but expresses concern with the potential remedy of patent forfeiture. Alternative remedies are suggested to include the civil assessment of compensation (e.g., royalties). Concern is also expressed with the potential bureaucratic complexities involved in evidencing compliance with PIC and EBS.

c. A third group of countries considers that complementarity between the TRIPS Agreement and CBD can be adequately addressed through contractual arrangements between countries housing genetic resource stocks and bio-prospecting enterprises and argues against the imposition of a mandatory disclosure and/or evidence requirement. This group argues that the source and origin of genetic resources are not relevant to determinations of patentability or inventorship, and that disclosure and/or evidence requirements would be unduly burdensome and create harmful uncertainty regarding the enforceability of patents.

d. Since the Hong Kong Ministerial, the Director-General of the WTO has convened a series of consultations with interested Members further to a request made there. The results of those consultations were reported by the Director-General at the Geneva March 2010 stock-taking of the Doha Round. He reported only that "while my consultations have not created convergence they have certainly shed clearer light on the divergences."[134] Although the constellation of Members supporting one or another position may have shifted over the past two years, there has been (as per the report of the Director-General) no material progress toward substantive agreement.

e. Progress, however, was achieved in addressing fair and equitable sharing of benefits under the Nagoya Protocol on Access to Genetic Resources and the Fair and Equitable Sharing of Benefits Arising from Their Utilization to the Convention on Biological Diversity, adopted 29 October 2010, and opened for signature. The Protocol sets forth mechanisms to bring about fair and equitable benefit sharing with holders of traditional knowledge. It provides for clearing house mechanisms and funding, but does not address or alter intellectual property rights per se. In recognizing traditional knowledge, the Protocol will be of importance in further developing *sui generis* rights on plant genetic resources.

2. In the course of addressing climate change mitigation and climate change adaption, particular attention has been paid to the relevance of intellectual property rights. See UNEP, EPO, ICTSD, Patents and Clean Energy: Bridging the Gap Between Evidence and Policy (2010). The question arises as to whether combating climate change requires substantial changes in intellectual property protection in order to meet the challenges. While

---

134. WTO: 2010 News Items, 22 March 2010, Trade Negotiations Committee, Lamy Opens Stocktaking Week with Hope for Strong Signal on Concluding the Round, available at http://www.wto.org/english/news_e/news10_e/tnc_dg_stat_22mar10_e.htm.

patents are of great importance in developing green technologies, main regulatory efforts need to address transfer of technology between developed and developing countries. The Clean Development Mechanism (CDM) within the Kyoto Protocol of the UN Framework Convention on Climate Change offers the potential to enhance transfer of climate change–related technology in coming years.

VIII. POLICIES UNDERLYING THE INTERNATIONAL IPRs SYSTEM

The characteristics and scope of IPRs are defined by law. In adopting and implementing IP laws, government authorities are seeking to balance a wide range of interests. The legislator deals with a multidimensional problem set.

The legislator may seek to promote investments in creativity by inventors, authors, and artists by providing legal mechanisms that allow them to secure a reward in the marketplace. Although a substantial amount of research has been devoted to identifying the causal relationship between the grant of IPRs and the output of creative works, correlations remain elusive. The legislator is working under conditions of substantial uncertainty.

The beneficiaries of IPRs, such as inventors, authors, and artists, generally have an interest in maximizing the economic benefits they derive from their investments in creativity. Yet, the interest in maximizing economic returns will, for some inventors and artists, be tempered or overtaken by a personal desire to confer a public benefit by making their contribution widely accessible (i.e., at low cost).

The legislator may seek to promote the public welfare by making the results of creative efforts widely available. "Stronger" IP protection, whether in terms of precluding independent creation, extending the scope of claims, or extending the duration of protection, may limit public access by enhancing pricing power. "Weaker" IP protection may allow greater dissemination to the public, but the legislator also considers whether underprotection may reduce the quantity of new creative works.

Questions about the characteristics and scope of IP protection take on different sensitivities depending on the field of regulation. The question of whether a new audio recording will be protected against free downloading from the Internet is much different than the question of whether a new anti-cancer drug will be protected against low-cost use by developing countries.

During most of the historical development of IP law, major decisions regarding the characteristics and scope of IPRs were made at the national level. In some areas, particularly copyright, international rules exercised an influence over the choices that the national legislature might make, yet, by and large the international system reserved wide discretion to each country in adopting and implementing IP law. With the entry into force of the TRIPS Agreement in 1995, that framework underwent a dramatic change, and the international IP system metamorphosed toward greater direct control at the multilateral level.

There was very little empirical or objective theoretical research concerning the possible effects of transforming the international IP regulatory system from one reserving substantial discretion to national authorities to one imposing a set of fairly comprehensive multilateral rules. Deeper inquiry into the implications of the TRIPS Agreement and the new multilateral "top down" regulatory system largely post-dated transformation of the rules, and is continuing.

As we examine the policies underlying IP protection at the international or multilateral level, a few basic questions might be kept in mind. Who is making the decisions regarding appropriate levels of IP protection? Where are these decisions being made? What are the objectives of the new rules? What are the interests at stake? Who is benefiting from the new rules? Who may be losing? Assuming that there are risks from underprotecting and overprotecting IP, and that decision makers are acting under conditions of uncertainty, on which side are risks better taken? Should we err on the side of underprotection or overprotection?

Without IP protection, information may be widely disseminated and used. It typically forms part of a "public commons." IP rules fence off parts of this public commons. In the first contribution, Joseph Stiglitz examines the rationale for building fences, and asks whether it is appropriate to build the same fences for the developed and developing countries.

A.   Public Welfare and Private Rights

KNOWLEDGE AS A GLOBAL PUBLIC GOOD

Joseph E. Stiglitz*

Thomas Jefferson, the third President of the United States, described knowledge in the following way: "He who receives an idea from me, receives instruction himself without lessening mine; as he who lights his taper at mine, receives light without darkening me." In doing so, Jefferson anticipated the modern concept of a public good. Today, we recognize that knowledge is not only a public good, but a *global* or *international* public good. We have also come to recognize that knowledge is central to successful development. The international community, through institutions like the World Bank, has a collective responsibility for the creation and dissemination of one global public good — knowledge for development.

The purpose of this paper is to review the concept of global public goods, to explain the sense in which knowledge is a public good, and to explore the implications for *international* public policy that derive from the fact that knowledge is a global public good. In particular, I shall emphasize the role of knowledge for development, articulated forcefully in this year's World Development Report, and the consequences that follow.

I. Basic Concepts

This paper combines two concepts developed over the past quarter of century: the concept of global public goods and the notion of knowledge as a global public good.

* Joseph Stiglitz, then Senior Vice President and Chief Economist at the World Bank, presently Professor at Columbia University. http://www.worldbank.org/knowledge/chiefecon/articles/undpk2/index.htm (1998).

A public good has two critical properties, non-rivalrous consumption — the consumption of one individual does not detract from that of another — and non-excludability — it is difficult if not impossible to exclude an individual from enjoying the good. Knowledge of a mathematical theorem clearly satisfies both attributes: if I teach you the theorem, I continue to enjoy the knowledge of the theorem at the same time that you do. By the same token, once I publish the theorem, anyone can enjoy the theorem. No one can be excluded. They can use the theorem as the basis of their own further research. The "ideas" contained in the theorem may even stimulate others to have an idea with large commercial value.

NON-RIVALROUSNESS

The fact that knowledge is non-rivalrous — there is a zero marginal cost from an additional individual enjoying the benefits of the knowledge — has a strong implication. Even if one could exclude someone from enjoying the benefits of knowledge, it would be undesirable to do so because there are no marginal costs to sharing its benefits. If information is to be efficiently utilized, it cannot be privately provided as efficiency implies charging a price of zero — the marginal cost of another individual enjoying the knowledge. However, at zero price, only knowledge that could be produced at zero cost would be produced.

To be sure, to acquire and use knowledge, individuals may have to expend resources — just as they might have to expend resources to retrieve water from a public lake. That there may be significant costs associated with transmission of knowledge does not in any way affect the public good nature of knowledge itself: private providers can provide the "transmission" for a charge reflecting the marginal cost of transmission while at the same time, the good itself can remain free.

EXCLUDABILITY

While its non-rivalrous property says that no one *should* be excluded from the enjoyment of a public good (since the marginal cost of benefiting from it is zero), non-excludability implies that no one *can* be excluded. This too has important implications: it means that knowledge cannot be provided privately. For assume someone produced, say, a theorem. Assume the theorem is valuable in providing insights into how to solve practical problems. But assume also that the theorem cannot be kept secret and must be immediately available. Then, since anyone can immediately enjoy the theorem, the individual could make no profit from it. Competition would drive its price to zero. At any positive price, it would pay someone to get the information (which by assumption he could do) and undercut the seller.

Some forms of knowledge are (or can be made) "excludable." For example, in some industries, such as metallurgy, trade secrets are used. To be sure, the firms run a risk: a competitor, observing the new alloy, could analyze its composition and infer the mix of metals (and with modern techniques, even the relative proportion of the atoms). The firm might have a hard time inferring precisely how the alloy is made, but there is no way that rivals can be excluded from knowledge of the chemical composition and the properties of the alloy. By the same reasoning, when a firm discovers that consumers love, say, yogurt, others cannot be excluded from using that knowledge to put on the market their own yogurts.

Patents provide the exclusive right to the inventor to enjoy the fruits of his innovative activity over a limited period of time [20 years], but in return, the inventor must disclose the details of his invention. The *fact* of the invention, let alone the details provided in the patent application, make an enormous amount of knowledge freely available. The development of rayon provided other researchers with enormous information: it demonstrated the feasibility of a synthetic fiber — knowledge which itself was of enormous commercial value and which enhanced incentives for others to look for other synthetic fibers. Indeed, research in chemicals often consists of looking for slight variations of the original chemical.

It is precisely because of the high value of the knowledge disclosed through the patent process (and the limited duration of the patent) that some firms prefer the seemingly less protective route of trade secrecy.

But because the returns to some knowledge can, to some extent, be appropriated (there is some degree of non-excludability) knowledge is often thought of as an *impure* public good.

GLOBAL PUBLIC GOODS

Shortly after [Paul] Samuelson articulated the general theory of pure public goods, it became recognized that the benefits of some public goods were limited geographically. These were called local public goods. Of course, the public goods earlier theory had focused on — such as national defense — were also limited geographically to a particular country. At the same time there are several public goods which are not so limited — the benefits of which accrue to everyone in the world. In my earlier paper, I identified five such global public goods: international economic stability, international security (political stability), the international environment, international humanitarian assistance, and knowledge.

Most knowledge is a global public good: a mathematical theorem is as "true" in Russia as it is in the United States, in Africa as it is in Australia. To be sure, there are some kinds of knowledge which are of value only or mostly to those living in the country, e.g. knowledge particular to a country's institutions, weather, or even geography. But scientific truths — including many of the propositions of the social sciences — are universal in nature. The problems with which economics deals, such as scarcity, are ubiquitous, and the "laws" of economics are accordingly universally applicable, even if idiosyncratic institutions exist within each country.

THE ROLE OF THE STATE

The central public policy implication of public goods is that the state must play some role in the provision of such goods; otherwise they will be undersupplied. If firms cannot appropriate the returns to producing knowledge, then they will have limited incentive to do so: in deciding how much to invest, they will only look at the return that they acquire, not the benefits that accrue to others. The benefits that have accrued from the development of the transistor, the laser, or the mathematical algorithms that underlay the modern computer have been enormous, extending well beyond benefits accruing to those who made or financed these innovations and discoveries.

Governments have pursued two different strategies in addressing these concerns. The first is to increase the degree of appropriability of the return to knowledge, by issuing patents and copyright protection. In doing so, governments are engaged in a careful balancing act: after all, one of the basic properties of knowledge as a public good is that the marginal cost of usage is zero (non-rivalrous consumption). Inventors obtain a return on their innovative activity, either through charging through the use of a patent (licensing) or by charging a monopoly price on the product. In either case, there is an inefficiency. The gain in *dynamic* efficiency, as a result of the greater innovative activity, is intended to balance out the losses from *static inefficiency*, from the under-utilization of the knowledge, or the underproduction of the good protected by the patent.

One part of the "balancing" act is to limit the duration of the patent. A very short patent life would imply a low level of appropriability — such that the limited returns to innovative activity would imply low levels of innovation. A very long life to a patent would mean large losses in static efficiency; most of the fruits of the innovation would accrue to the innovator, with little passed on to consumers say in the form of lower prices, since the inventor would never be subjected to competitive pressure. Typically, patents last for [20] years, and as it turns out, in many cases, by the time the patent has expired, its value is limited, as new products and innovations have superseded it. This is *not* the case, however, for many drugs (partly because there may be a long testing period before the drug is actually marketed).

But there are other aspects of the patent system that play an important role in how the dynamic efficiencies are balanced with the static inefficiencies: the breadth and scope of a patent claim (whether a patent for a new genetically altered tomato covers all genetically altered vegetables, all genetically altered tomatoes, or only this particular genetically altered variety) can obviously have profound implications.

Initial knowledge is a key input into the production of further knowledge, and the design of the patent system can thus affect dramatically the overall pace of innovation. An excessively broad patent system (e.g. with long-lived patents of broad scope) can raise the price of one of the most vital inputs into the innovative process and thus reduce the pace of follow-on innovations, even as it may provide returns to those making the original innovation. As a result, the overall pace of technical progress may be slowed. Worries about the adverse effects of excessively strong intellectual property protection have been brought home by the recent anti-trust suit against Microsoft, which (it is alleged) has attempted to leverage the power associated with its control of the dominant operating system (itself a consequence of important network externalities which result in huge advantages associated with the establishment of an industry standard) to a broader dominance in application software. Many industry experts believe that in doing so, the overall pace of innovation in the industry may have been retarded.

These concerns are of particular importance to developing countries. New innovations (research and development expenditures) are even more concentrated in the advanced industrial countries than are incomes, and many of the advances in less developed countries consist of adapting the technologies of the more advanced countries to the circumstances of the developing world.

The second strategy for dealing with the appropriability problem entails direct government support. *If* government could costlessly raise revenues for financing the support and *if* government were effective in discriminating between good and bad research projects, clearly this strategy would dominate that of enhancing intellectual property rights; for the latter strategy entails static distortions (the monopoly prices associated with patent rights result in prices exceeding marginal costs) and the inefficient utilization of knowledge. The static distortions can be thought of as a "tax" used to finance the R&D; but the tax is not an "optimal tax." But the patent system provides an effective "self-selection" mechanism: those who are convinced that they have a good idea invest their own money, and the money of those whom they can persuade of the attractiveness of their idea. Such selection mechanisms may not only be more effective than, say, government bureaucrats attempting to assess various applications, but the costs of mistakes are borne by those making the misjudgment, not by the public at large. The system thus provides strong incentives for individuals to engage in due diligence in assessing the merits of alternative research proposals. It is because of these strong incentive/selection properties that most economists believe that for a wide range of areas, the strategy of enhancing intellectual property rights is preferable to that of government subsidization.

But there are some important situations where the costs of the improved appropriability strategy are high. This is particularly true in the case of basic research because its benefits are widespread and diffuse and because attempts to appropriate its returns may significantly slow the overall pace of innovation. Indeed, many advances in basic knowledge — such as mathematical theorems — are not patentable, in spite of their importance and their potential practical applications.

This discussion should have made clear one central point: the concept of "intellectual property" — the breadth, scope, and applicability of patent protection — is not just a technical matter. There are judgment calls and trade-offs, with different people and different countries all affected differently by alternative decisions. There are conflicts of interests between the developed and the less developed countries. But unfortunately, many of the key issues cannot even be summarized by a set of simply stated principles; in practice, decisions are made on a case-by-case approach.

The stance sometimes taken by the producers of knowledge, that we need "strong" intellectual property rights, masks this underlying debate. Strong, in this context, becomes equivalent to "good"; with the implication that the "stronger" the better. But I hope this discussion has brought out that issues are far more implicated [*sic*]: stronger, in the sense of "tighter" protection, could not only have large distributive consequences (between say developed and less developed countries), but also large efficiency consequences, with the pace of innovation actually impeded and living standards in less developed countries diminished.

Within some of the advanced industrialized countries there are effective competition policies, which work to mitigate the risks that results from the abuse of monopoly power associated with a patent. But most countries do not have comparably effective anti-trust policies. For instance, drug companies can, and have an incentive to, act like discriminating monopolists, charging higher prices where the consumer surplus is higher, and/or where they can extract more of the consumer surplus. Some European countries have policies that offset these monopolistic powers: given the large role of government in the health care sector, they can effectively exercise their monopsonistic powers. It is thus conceivable (and there are anecdotes supporting this possibility) that consumers in less developed countries be charged higher prices for drugs than consumers in far richer countries. (In doing so, it is the consumers in the less developed countries that, in effect, are paying the fixed cost of research; consumers in the more developed countries are partial free riders.) Within the United States, such price discrimination (not *fully* justified by differences in transactions costs) would probably be illegal. But there is no international competition policy which protects the poor country. Well-designed (not "excessively strong") intellectual property regimes can provide some protection. It is not clear the extent to which effective competition policies *within a country* might provide safeguards: presumably a country could pass a "most favored nation" provision — no firm, enjoying the benefit of intellectual property protection, could charge the consumers of that country a higher price than the price charged for the same good elsewhere in the world.

There are other issues in the design of an intellectual property regime. Every innovation makes use of previously accumulated knowledge — it draws on the global commons of pre-existing knowledge. How much of the returns to the innovation should be credited to this use of the global commons? Current practice says zero — because it is a commons, there is no price. But this is not the way things need be. In many parts of the world, there is a recognition that charges can and should be imposed for the use of commons (whether they are forests, grazing lands, or fisheries). Such charges can be justified on both efficiency and equity grounds. The international community could similarly claim the right to charge for the use of the global knowledge commons. Because knowledge is a pure public good, the argument for charging a fee is largely based upon an equity rationale. However, by recycling funds to support further research, an efficiency argument could also be developed. There are obvious practical problems in the implementation of such a scheme: what fraction of the returns to the innovation are due to the use of the global commons? But even a rough rule of thumb, in which a certain fraction of the returns to innovations is used to finance a "replenishment" of the global knowledge commons, might be an improvement.

This issue of the use of the global knowledge commons has been brought home forcefully in the context of bio-diversity, where private firms have prospected for valuable drugs in natural settings. In many cases, local people have long recognized the value of these local drugs, though they have not identified the particular chemicals within the plants which give the desired effects.

The contrast between the way this unpatented knowledge is treated, and the way adaptations of innovations in developing countries of patented ideas from developed countries are treated could not be more stark. In the former case, all of the return is credited to the "discoverer," with none to the pre-existing knowledge; in the latter, the patent holder is allowed to act as a perfectly discriminating monopolist, regardless of the extent to which his own innovation built on pre-existing knowledge.

The effective use of knowledge developed in the advanced industrialized countries typically involves substantial elements of adaptation — combining global and local knowledge. Yet the intellectual property regime, as it has been evolving, assigns most of the bargaining power associated with how the fruits of these combinations are shared to the developed country, especially in larger developing countries, where there may be effective competition for the use of the patented idea.

An international intellectual property regime, designed to facilitate the production and use of the global public good — knowledge — in a way that sustains high rates of growth and is consistent with broad notions of equity, must balance a variety of subtle concerns, including dynamic and static efficiency and the use of the global knowledge commons.

NOTES AND QUESTIONS

1. Joseph Stiglitz points out, and it should be emphasized, that patents are not the only mechanism by which governments can and do promote inventive activity. The principal alternative to the patent is the government "subsidy," that is, payment (direct or indirect) by the government to a person to support research.[135] Subsidies are frequently used to direct research in a particular direction, such as toward the development of a military application. Subsidies are also used when the government recognizes that the "market" does not offer an adequate incentive, such as in the development of a new vaccine to defend against a bioweapon threat. Moreover, governments use research and development subsidies to gain advantages in commercial sectors, for example, by promoting R&D in the large commercial aircraft sector.

     Stiglitz also notes that use of subsidies as a policy instrument for the promotion of invention has certain limitations or drawbacks. Who decides whether to grant a subsidy and under what conditions? Are government policymakers likely to be successful at predicting the most promising areas for research? Assuming that "neutral" policymakers might make good decisions, are there risks that government policymakers may be "captured" by special interests?

     Is it possible that patents may be a better policy instrument for encouraging research in some areas, and that subsidies may be a better policy instrument for encouraging research in others? In what fields of application do you think subsidies may be preferable?

2. In advanced industrial societies, competition or antitrust laws play an essential role in maintaining the balance between the interests of IPRs holders and the general public. Few developing countries have the resources to monitor, investigate, and prosecute competitive market abuses, so this vital part of the balancing equation is missing. How would you suggest compensating for this defect in the system? Is it realistic to expect developing countries to put sophisticated competition enforcement offices into place in the near to medium term? Should developing countries rely on competition authorities in the European Union or the United States to protect them? Do these authorities have developing country interests in mind? The United Nations Conference on Trade and Development (UNCTAD) has done a good deal of work in drawing attention to the imbalance in the field of competitive market regulation.

3. At the conclusion of his essay (not reprinted above), Stiglitz notes a risk that some countries may prefer to "free ride" on investments in invention undertaken elsewhere, and that unchecked free riding could ultimately prevent the replenishment of the public commons. Might it be useful to draw distinctions between those countries that can afford to pay for new inventions and those that might be allowed to use inventions without contributing toward their development? In his article, *From Free Riders to Fair Followers,* Jerome Reichman explored this idea.[136] In section VIII.C *infra,*

---

135. Perhaps the leading work on policy instruments for promoting invention is WILLIAM D. NORDHAUS, INVENTION, GROWTH AND WELFARE (1969).

136. *See* J.H. Reichman, *From Free Riders to Fair Followers: Global Competition Under the TRIPs Agreement,* 29 N.Y.U. J. INT'L L. & POL. 11 (1997).

Keith Maskus's work on correlating levels of IP protection with stages of economic and social development may suggest some answers.

B.   The Economics of the International Patent System

The seminal work on the economics of the patent system for an industrialized country was authored by Fritz Machlup as a report to the U.S. Senate in 1956.[137] We urge students who have not read Machlup's study as part of a course on patent law to do this. Machlup rejected a "natural rights" approach to patent protection since there was no way to resolve the philosophical question of entitlement to ownership of ideas, and since an answer did not in any case provide guidance to the appropriate design of a patent system. Machlup also discounted the view that patents are necessary to encourage invention since there was little empirical evidence to support such a correlation. Inventors do what they do with complex motives. In Machlup's view, the most persuasive economic case for the grant of patents was found in its encouragement of the commercialization of new products; that is, patents encourage investors to provide capital for manufacturing and distribution facilities because they believe that a patent ensures a better return. Machlup largely considered this effect a beneficial illusion since he thought investors tended to overvalue patents. Finally, Machlup discounted the importance of publication and disclosure to society because, *inter alia,* inventors seek patent protection precisely because their inventions can otherwise be copied.

Machlup was dismissive of the idea that a pharmaceutical company with an invention critical to public health — such as the polio vaccine — would be allowed to freely exploit it at monopoly prices. Is this a reflection of Machlup's naiveté, or have attitudes toward the virtues of the market shifted since the late 1950s?

Machlup's conclusion for the United States is well known: Based on what is known, if there were no patent system, he could not recommend creating one; yet, because the United States has a patent system and the economy appears to be functioning relatively well, based on what is known, he could not recommend getting rid of it.

Machlup limited his conclusion to a large industrial country such as the United States — it may *not*, he says, apply to "a small country and not [apply to] a predominantly nonindustrial country, where a different weight of argument might well suggest another conclusion."

Edith Tilton Penrose was a long-time colleague and collaborator with Fritz Machlup. Machlup observed in his forward to her book, THE ECONOMICS OF THE INTERNATIONAL PATENT SYSTEM (1951):

> The discussion of the economics of the international patent system, and in particular of the international patent [Paris] Convention, has been almost devoid of contributions by *bona fide* economists. The international patent Convention is now 67 years old and the literature on it is by no means small. But scrutinize it and

---

137. Fritz Machlup, *An Economic Review of the Patent System,* Subcomm. on Patents, Trademarks and Copyrights, of the Committee on the Judiciary, 85th Congress, 2d Sess. (excerpts *reprinted in* F. ABBOTT, T. COTTIER & F. GURRY, THE INTERNATIONAL INTELLECTUAL PROPERTY SYSTEM: COMMENTARY AND MATERIALS, at 224-46).

you will find only a handful of economists writing on this subject, even as they address themselves more to peripheral issues than to the fundamental economic issue — the balance of costs and gains.

The book by Dr. Edith Penrose is the first of its kind. ... [T]he economic analysis of the international patent system is both novel and controversial. The parts of the study that deal with the economic evaluation of various provisions will undoubtedly draw fire, because several dogmas which legal experts have held in great respect are exposed to the bright searchlight of a skilled economic analyst and are shown to be untenable. One may safely predict that many members of the American patent bar, and especially international patent lawyers, will intensely dislike some of the views expressed and perhaps all of the suggestions contained in this book.

But the views and suggestions of Mrs. Penrose are not out of line with the current thinking of the more enlightened patent experts.

Following are the Summary and Conclusions of the pioneering work by Edith Tilton Penrose. Her observations and questions from 1951 have not lost their relevance.

THE ECONOMICS OF THE INTERNATIONAL PATENT SYSTEM

Edith Tilton Penrose*

CHAPTER XI SUMMARY AND CONCLUSIONS

In this chapter I shall briefly recapitulate the argument of this study, the propositions I have tried to establish and the implications of the prevailing assumptions about the international extension of the patent system.

I.

The patent of invention is a monopoly privilege of ancient origin granted for the purpose of encouraging innovation. It was first systematically used in Venice in the 14th and 15th centuries and has today been adopted by nearly all countries. The only serious attack on the principle of the patent system took place in the 19th century under the influence of the free trade movement. It was defeated but it served to emphasize the economic effects of the restrictions on industry that are inherent in the patent system and that most countries try to reduce by placing specific limitations on the monopoly granted.

II.

The origin of the patent system is clearly economic. In the 19th century attempts were made to justify it by appealing to a "natural" property right in ideas and to an inventor's moral right to receive a reward for his services. Although vestiges of the latter still crop up in patent discussions, today the primary arguments for the patent system are economic. Patents are held to be necessary to persuade inventors to disclose their secrets and to encourage the making and introduction of inventions.[1]

---

* ECONOMICS OF THE INTERNATIONAL PATENT SYSTEM, 101-107, 162-169. ©1951 The Johns Hopkins Press.
1. I have not in this study attempted to appraise the influence of national patent systems on the rate of invention. Most countries have adopted some form of patent law under which patents are

III.

Theories of natural property rights, idealistic visions of a world drawn together in international unity, and pressures from manufacturers in industrial countries combined to advance the cause of the international protection of patentees. After a series of conferences the International Convention for the Protection of Industrial Property was signed in 1883 creating the International Union for the Protection of Industrial Property. Today forty countries are members of the Union.

The Convention is founded on two basic principles: 1) that foreigners should receive in each country the same treatment as the nationals of that country; and 2) that the first applicant for a patent on an invention in one country should have a right of priority over all other applicants to obtain patents on the same invention in other countries. Most countries have always felt, however, that the grant of unconditional patents to foreigners would retard their economic development and the most controversial issues in the international conferences have centered around the question of what restrictions a country should be permitted to place on its patents.

IV.

Before the International Convention was created a patentee in one country could generally obtain patents on his invention in other countries, but he faced many special difficulties in those countries and was frequently discriminated against. The purpose of the Convention is to reduce the difficulties and eliminate the discrimination. It thus formally sanctions the principle that a patentee in one country ought to be able to obtain patents on his invention in all other countries with a minimum of difficulty. In other words, the Convention rests on the assumption that it is insufficient for a patentee to obtain a monopoly on his invention in one country only and that he ought to obtain a worldwide monopoly.

The deliberate adoption of this economic policy can be justified on economic grounds only if the gains that accrue to society from it exceed the costs incurred because of it. It is indeed awkward that the costs cannot be measured nor the gains counted. As a result the optimum limits of the patent system, whether with respect to time, space, patentability or restrictions on the use of the grant, must always remain a subject of controversy. There is no doubt, however, that the costs have been underestimated.

It is generally assumed that the economic justification for the international extension of the patent system lies in its effects upon the advance of technology and the development of industry. Upon analysis, however, it appears that if one were to rely on this justification one would have to conclude that on balance the social cost of extending the patent system internationally exceeds the gain to be derived from it for the world as a whole. Nearly all foreign patenting is done by already industrialized countries, and the question of the effect of the prospect of patents in foreign markets on the rate of invention is a question of the extent to which the expected increment of profit arising from the geographical extension of the limits of patent protection will stimulate additional invention. There are many factors to be taken into consideration: the size of the national market, the nature of national industry, the types of invention, the motivation of

---

also granted on inventions already patented and worked in other countries and I am only concerned with the economics of this arrangement.

inventors and the methods of financing invention. I have concluded that on balance the effect on invention of a system in which patents in many countries can be obtained is probably negligible for the world as a whole although it may be important for some firms and for some inventions. With respect to the introduction of inventions, there is little evidence that business men in industrial countries require patent protection to encourage them to adopt inventions which have already been developed to a commercial stage elsewhere.

But whatever may be the effect of the international extension of the patent system on the rate of invention or innovation, a heavy social cost is incurred. The patent method of encouraging invention operates by restricting the use of new inventions in order that a monopoly rent may be earned by the patentees to recompense them for the expenses and risks of making or introducing new inventions. The social costs to which this restriction gives rise appear in the first instance as increased prices and royalty payments. The more fundamental and important cost, however, is the production lost through the less efficient use of resources when new techniques cannot be freely used and when monopoly power is extended by means of patent agreements.[5]

v.

A few individual countries may gain from the system in which foreign patents are permitted. Industrial exporting countries obtain monopoly profits resulting from the increased price of exports; in some instances patent protection may enable exporting countries to retain a market against competitors or to surmount tariff barriers. The majority of countries, however, probably lose, since the higher price of patented imports, royalty payments to foreign patentees and in particular the restriction on their own use of new techniques constitute a cost much greater than is generally realized and the benefit derived from patent protection in foreign countries is much less than is usually assumed.

Under these circumstances if individual countries weigh the costs and gains of granting patents on inventions already patented and primarily used in other countries, most of them could easily conclude that the costs exceed the gains and that it is not to their benefit to grant them. The reasons why any particular country has adopted a policy of granting such patents can, of course, be explained only in terms of its history and of the pressures that have influenced its government. These pressures include those of exporting firms who wish to obtain protection abroad, of patent lawyers, of spokesmen for "internationalism," and — of particular importance for many of the smaller countries — the pressure exerted by the larger industrial countries to persuade the smaller ones to adopt "suitable" patent laws. On the other hand, most countries have realized that the social costs of granting unrestricted patents on inventions primarily worked abroad would exceed any benefit to be obtained and have accordingly placed special restrictions on such patents.[9]

---

5. See discussion of the sources of costs and gains in an international extension of the patent system. . . . The costs with which we are concerned are not the costs of making the inventions but the social cost of the patent method of encouraging them.

9. This is particularly brought out in the Swiss controversy over the inauguration of patent protection. . . .

VI.

From the point of view of the world economy and of the economies of individual countries, the usual justification for the establishment of an international patent system — that it promotes technological progress — is not convincing. But the mere existence of national laws creates an economic problem which can only be met by an international extension of patent protection. In order to show this clearly I have examined what would be the economic consequences of a prohibition of international patenting, that is, of a system in which a patentee could obtain a patent in one national market only. Such a system would have the effect of enabling producers of patented products to obtain as a result of their patents higher profits in one country than in other countries. The prospect of such profits, which are unrelated to the underlying economic factors, would, therefore, exert an uneconomic influence on the international location of industry.[10]

Let us assume for the moment that a patentee is permitted to obtain a patent on his invention only in the country in which he produces. There is nothing, however, to prevent him from deciding to produce only in the country in which he wants a patent; the choice of plant location in many industries is not independent of market considerations. If the location of a plant in one area would permit monopoly profits to be obtained which would be foregone if the plant were located in another area, an intelligent producer would include the possibility of obtaining these profits in his calculations regarding the most profitable location of his plant. Thus a strong incentive would be created for patentees to locate their plants in larger industrial countries merely because they could there obtain a monopoly profit greater than elsewhere. If the expected monopoly profits were very great, a producer might well find it desirable to incur considerably higher costs of production in order to obtain the protected market. In addition, industrial research and technical innovations would tend to concentrate in these countries.

This tendency for patentees who wish to sell in the larger markets to take out their patents in those markets would have still other consequences. A patent has a double effect within the territory in which it is valid: it prevents others from producing or selling in that territory. But outside that territory the products or processes are free from the patent restrictions. Hence if an invention could only be patented in one country, there would be an incentive for firms who wished to use the invention, to establish plants outside the territory covered by the patent and there produce for the rest of the world. Thus the exporting industries of the countries in which the larger number of patents were taken out would suffer, since when one firm holds a patent on an important new process, all other firms producing competitive products in that industry are at a disadvantage. In industries where all firms produce largely for foreign markets and are in competition with foreign firms in foreign markets, the firms without access to new developments would not only be at a disadvantage compared with the firm holding the patent in the domestic market but also with respect to the rest of the world: firms in the rest of the world could freely use any of the new techniques. Not only is the monopolistic position of the patentee firm increased within the domestic industry, but for

---

10. Because a short summary statement of the argument in this section would be misleading, I am giving a large part of the argument just as it appears in Chapter VI. . . .

no sound economic reason the domestic industry, other than the patentee firm is handicapped in relation to foreign industry.[11]

If the patentee were not required to produce in the country in which he takes out his patent, the fear of losing and the hope of safeguarding his patent monopoly in this or that market would not enter into the calculations of the producer in determining the location of his plant. Yet the position of the countries containing the larger markets would be even more adversely affected. The tendency for patents to be concentrated in these markets would be strengthened and the restrictions on industry in these countries would consequently be increased. It is part of the purpose of the patent system to retard the development of competitors of the patentee in order to enable him to earn a reward for his innovating enterprise, but it is difficult to justify a discrimination between these competitors by which one group is retarded — the group unfortunate enough to be in the country selected for the patent — while all others are left free. The patentee firm may gain very little by this secondary effect since it may be selling in markets which would not be served by the restricted group of firms and the latter may suffer very much. If the patentee is not allowed to extend his monopoly over the greater part of his market, the patent, in securing protection to him against competitors, automatically discriminates between these competitors. This alone is sufficient to justify some international arrangement regarding foreign patents.

Because of the social costs of the international extension of patenting, however, any international arrangement regarding foreign patenting should meet three conditions: 1) It should prevent the exploitation of the weaker industrial countries by the stronger. 2) It should reduce the influence of patents on the location of industrial activity. 3) It should reduce the social cost to each country of granting patents on inventions developed and primarily worked abroad. The present International Convention has made considerable advances in all three directions but with respect to the third, much more needs to be done.

VII.

Two methods of reducing the social costs to a country of granting patents on inventions developed and primarily worked abroad have been widely used. The oldest is compulsory working.[12] Most countries have at some time adopted compulsory working laws in order to ensure that all patents granted are worked in the country granting them. This method is not only ineffective and frequently nothing but a clumsy way of obtaining access to foreign inventions for domestic firms, but it also conflicts with the second of the functions of an international patent arrangement since it establishes an uneconomic influence on the location of industry of the sort discussed in the previous section. The efforts of the International Union for the Protection of Industrial Property to eliminate such requirements are therefore in the right direction.

---

11. Foreign branch plants of domestic firms are of course here considered as part of "foreign industry."

12. Compulsory working means that the law requires a patentee or his licensee to produce under the patent in the country granting the patent, although a patentee is usually exempt from this requirement if he can produce "acceptable excuses" instead. Until recently revocation of the patent was the chief penalty for failure to work. Now compulsory licensing is becoming more commonly adopted.

VIII.

The second method of reducing the cost of the patent monopoly is that of compulsory licensing.[138] This is by far the most effective and flexible method and enables the state to prevent most of the more serious restrictions on industry. It could be used very effectively to undermine the monopoly power of several of the more powerful international cartels whose position is largely based on their control of the patent rights to industrial processes in the larger industrial countries; and it could be used to ensure that patented new techniques developed abroad are available to domestic industries wishing to use them.

The International Convention places restrictions on the right of countries to subject patents to compulsory licensing. These restrictions should be eliminated and countries should be encouraged to use this device to break up some of the more serious of the monopolistic restrictions on the use of new techniques.

IX.

The Convention has been attacked by those who are concerned about the rise of international monopolistic practices, especially of international cartels. Although it is true that the Convention is one-sided, being more concerned with the rights of patentees than with the public interest in these rights, and that undue restrictions are placed on the use of compulsory licensing, the Convention itself cannot be held responsible for the existing evils of international patent practices merely because it has not outlawed them, for, conversely, it certainly has not sanctioned them. The difficulty lies with the national patent laws and national policies existing independently of the Convention. So long as national patent laws exist, an international convention on patents is desirable, but the patent policies of national governments and their trade and monopoly policies have not been very well coordinated and this lack of coordination is reflected in the one-sided nature of the Convention.

The Convention has also been criticised by the friends of international patent protection because it does not establish uniformity of patent practice in administrative matters. The laws and practices of different countries are very different and it has not yet proved possible to obtain substantial agreement on any uniform provisions. This is indeed a real weakness of the Convention, for if international patenting is to be permitted, a reduction of legal and administrative difficulties is desirable not only from the point of view of patentees but also in the general interest. The more difficult and expensive international patenting is, the more the large, well financed, and legally equipped firms have an advantage over smaller firms. Indeed a single international patent valid in all Union countries, long the ideal of ardent supporters of international patenting, is a desirable, though far-distant goal, providing that the patented technique is made easily available at a reasonable royalty to all who wish to use it.

X.

Although an international patent Convention between the industrial countries of the world is desirable, the non-industrial countries, few of whose nationals want patents in foreign countries, have nothing to gain from granting patents to foreign firms. In view of the desirability of encouraging the development of these countries and of the fact that foreign patents tend more to restrict than to

---

138. Under compulsory licensing a patentee is required by law to license his patent to another producer who wishes to use it upon payment of a reasonable royalty. . . .

advance their industrial techniques, such countries should be exempt from any international patent arrangements.

XI.

Up to the present, the regime for the international protection of patent rights has been developed primarily in the interest of patentees. The gains to be derived from an extension of the patent system have been stressed, but the concomitant increase in social costs has been seriously neglected. So far as it goes, the International Convention has not been to any important extent incompatible with the best interests of the world economy. Nonetheless, the Convention in no way helps to alleviate the restrictions on trade and industrial activity which unregulated international patenting permits. A reconsideration of its provisions from this point of view is in order.

NOTES AND QUESTIONS

1. Edith Tilton Penrose supports the early international patent system established by the Paris Convention mainly because it should prevent a distortion in the international allocation of productive resources. If inventors could effectively patent their inventions in only one country, they would be likely to locate their production facilities in densely populated industrialized countries where they could maximize their monopoly returns. Penrose explains that this would have a number of undesirable effects. It might well lead to a concentration of R&D activities in already well-off countries. It would also place domestic competitors of the patent holder that might otherwise export to other countries at a disadvantage vis-à-vis foreign producers of the same product, unhindered by patent.
2. Penrose sees little reason why developing countries should find it desirable to provide patent protection to foreign inventors, and proposes to exempt developing countries from any international patent arrangements.
3. Penrose introduces us to the concept of the compulsory patent license. A compulsory patent license is granted by a government without the consent of the patent holder, and it permits the exploitation of rights otherwise controlled by the patent holder. The license may be granted in favor of a private enterprise or in favor of the government itself. Compulsory licensing will be considered further in Chapter 2.
4. Penrose alerts us to the question whether international patent protection may foster higher levels of industrial concentration. Again, this question is probably more trenchant today than it was when Penrose raised it in 1951.
5. Penrose's perspective on the value of an international patenting system for developing countries is out of synch with current OECD industry views, and perhaps with the predominant current trend in opinion among international economists.

    Nevertheless, Penrose returns us to the question of whether the same level of IPRs protection is appropriate for all countries.

C.   *Intellectual Property Rights and International Trade*

The most significant development in the regulation of IPRs since the conclusion of the Paris and Berne Conventions was the conclusion of the TRIPS

Agreement. John Barton considers the economic implications of moving IP into the trade arena.

THE ECONOMICS OF TRIPS: INTERNATIONAL TRADE IN INFORMATION-INTENSIVE PRODUCTS

John H. Barton*

The Agreement on the Trade Related Aspects of Intellectual Property Rights (TRIPs) has become highly controversial. Although trade in the most directly affected products is still a small portion of overall international trade, it is becoming more and more important. U.S. pharmaceutical firms sell products abroad totaling over $40 billion annually. Further, the U.S. trade surplus in software is expected to be over $20 billion for the year 2000; movie exports total approximately $6.5 billion and database service exports are on the order of $2 billion.

Solid numbers in this area are extremely difficult to obtain, in part because data collection systems are more oriented toward trade in goods. It is also partly due to definitional problems. For example, the "real royalty" for a sale of a pharmaceutical in a foreign nation may appear as a royalty from the foreign firm that sold it, or it may appear as a higher price on the exported product itself. Economically, these two cases are similar but there is a significant difference in balance of payments accounting. Nonetheless, the flow of royalties and payments is significant — and strongly favors the United States, which received over $36 billion in royalties in 1998 and paid out less than a third of that. Moreover, international trade in these areas affects fundamental values including cultural sensitivities and human health.

The World Trade Organization (WTO) has taken jurisdiction over these products, here called information-intensive products (IIPs), through the Uruguay Round's General Agreement on Trade in Services, as well as through TRIPs. The debate over TRIPs has been unusually sharp, ranging from those who view the failure to observe U.S.-style intellectual property arrangements as piracy to those who see TRIPs as a form of neo-imperialism.

As a result of TRIPs, the WTO panel process is now available for disputes in the area of IIPs. This process allows for resolution of international trade disputes by an expert panel that interprets the relevant treaty documents — its decisions are enforceable through trade sanctions. In 1999, there were sixteen WTO dispute settlement filings based on TRIPs, amounting to ten percent of all filings before the WTO panel. The United States brought eleven of these sixteen filings.

Integrating trade law and intellectual property law creates problems because the economics of IIPs can be significantly different from that of the products traditionally the subject of international trade law. In general economic trade theory, we think of trade as equalizing prices near the world's lowest available marginal cost, which benefits the world's consumers in the form of lower prices. For IIPs, however, market prices are necessarily significantly different from marginal cost. Intellectual property protection exists precisely to maintain that difference, as an incentive for innovation and creativity.

* 33 Geo. Wash. Int'l L. Rev. 473 (2001).

At the same time, technology is a crucial accelerator to the global economy. It is responsible for at least one to two percent per year of the long-term growth in the U.S. economy, and is likely to have a comparable contribution to global growth. The advance of technology and authorship is supported by intellectual property law, which necessarily distorts market prices. However, a balance must be struck between encouraging future development and making the benefits of past development available at as low a price as possible.

Consequently, as the WTO and the world move into this new area of regulation, it is important to examine the extent to which the non-zero-sum mutual benefit assumptions of traditional free trade theory are satisfied for IIPs. This paper attempts such an examination and identifies certain necessary and important modifications of the traditional free trade theory. The paper then explores the implications of this modified theory for several important WTO issue areas, including intellectual property protection itself, differential pricing, and market protection devices such as subsidies. Finally, this paper suggests ways in which the WTO might strengthen its supporting statistical and study programs to ensure that TRIPs actually leads to global benefit. . . .

III. IMPLICATIONS FOR THE PROTECTION OF INTELLECTUAL PROPERTY RIGHTS

The United States and other exporters of IIPs saw that they would benefit from higher global standards for intellectual property rights and sought such an agreement in the Uruguay Round. They were successful in achieving TRIPs, which sets significantly higher minimum standards for intellectual property protection than the various prior multilateral treaties. TRIPs arranges for the enforcement of these standards through the WTO panel process, which can impose trade sanctions against nations that do not comply with panel decisions. WTO panels have thus become the ultimate international authority on intellectual property standards.

There is a strong pragmatic argument for this evolution. The trade of IIPs is greatly growing in importance — for example, royalties received by U.S. firms have increased from roughly $8 billion in 1986 to roughly $37 billion in 1998. In addition, such trade brings many disputes of a type amenable to the WTO dispute settlement panel process. Further, the agreement clearly benefits several U.S. sectors, especially the audio-visual and pharmaceutical sectors, in a way parallel to that of other trade agreements. Finally, at least to these exporters, a failure to provide intellectual property protection appears very similar to a trade barrier.

As the above analysis shows, however, there is an important difference between a failure to provide intellectual property protection and a more traditional trade barrier. In the traditional trade barrier, such as a tariff erected by the European widget industry against cheap U.S. widget imports, the European consumer is clearly harmed. The United States, acting under the pressure of its widget exporters, will protest this barrier, and either negotiate its removal (presumably balanced politically by removing some U.S. trade barrier) or attack Europe before a WTO panel. Once the barrier is removed by negotiation or dispute settlement, the European consumer will get cheaper widgets, widget production will shift to the lower-cost U.S. producers, and the European widget industry will shrink. We can, under principles of free-trade theory, be quite confident that the world has moved to a Pareto-superior state in which, even for

Europe viewed as an economy on its own, the benefits to consumers outweigh the costs to the European widget industry. The WTO dispute settlement process serves as an engine through which the achievement of free trade, as well as the concept of negotiating reciprocal reductions in trade barriers on a package basis, is more politically feasible.

The same analysis can next be considered in the case of an IIP, such as a pharmaceutical whose European patent was, according to the U.S. firm, not enforced. If the patent is enforced in response to trade negotiations or a WTO panel decision, the price of the product will go up in Europe and the European consumer will pay more. This result is the reverse of the widget tariff case. The U.S. industry gains additional rent, and therefore, increased incentive to innovate and invest in research and development.

Free trade theory tells us that, for "normal" products, the world, as well as each nation, will be better off with free trade. Under the theory, free trade is best because the price of goods will equalize closest to their lowest marginal cost, minimizing consumer cost. With IIPs, however, intellectual property rights increase sales prices away from the lowest marginal cost, creating an economic misallocation. But it is generally believed that intellectual property rights are necessary to stimulate innovation and creativity. Thus, in determining whether the world is better off with intellectual property rights, one must ask whether the intellectual property right produces a favorable trade-off between the short-term cost to consumers through higher prices and long-term benefit to consumers through increased innovation. In other words, the relevant question for determining global benefit when considering IIPs is whether the overall incentive benefits outweigh the price costs. This political question often depends on social evaluations of which types of IIPs should be encouraged. It can also depend on the extent to which the intellectual property rents are used for research or content creation rather than for marketing. Systematic differences in perspective between developed and developing nations may also exist, arising from differing discount rates in comparing present costs and future benefits.

There is a second question, however, as to what is best for each individual nation. With free trade, each nation is benefited by falling trade barriers because consumer prices are minimized. But this is not necessarily the case with intellectual property rights. In the pharmaceutical industry, the United States certainly benefits from free trade through increased exports and a larger pharmaceutical market that can lead to more pharmaceutical products. The imposition of intellectual property rights in Europe may also benefit the United States through increased consumer prices and royalty outflow. For the European, however, these are considered to be costs of imposing intellectual property rights because the importers must pay for the higher prices and royalties. The benefits, however, are increased incentives for the global industry to produce new pharmaceuticals that may benefit Europeans. The analysis here must consider two perspectives — the world and the European community. The world analysis compares the European price increases with the benefits of the increased research to the entire world. The European analysis compares the European price increases and the royalty outflow with the research benefits accruing to Europe alone. Through this analysis, it is quite possible for the European balance to be unfavorable, while the world balance is favorable.

It is clear then that the political dynamics of the international intellectual property system are different from those of the international trade system. The

WTO panel process is institutionally adapted to resolving disputes in intellectual property, and the traditional WTO plaintiffs, generally the home nations of exporting industries, have a strong incentive to uphold international standards. But, one cannot be quite sure that those standards serve the global interest; and often they will not serve the local interest. However, even in the latter case, there may be a global benefit in avoiding free riders — the fewer the number of nations willing to pay for research or authorship, the fewer and lower-quality IIPs there will be.

What does this mean for TRIPs and for dispute settlement panels enforcing it? First of all, it counsels care to ensure that the forms of intellectual property protection applied are actually beneficial. The issue is not whether the rents from an IIP will go to an entity that is politically powerful (i.e., software or movie industries) or to one that appears politically deserving (i.e., originators of traditional knowledge), but whether the long term benefits to innovation and authorship outweigh the costs to the world's consumers. This issue raises many questions which are the subject of substantial debate. What proportion of their rents is the movie or pharmaceutical industry using for innovative production or research? Should copyrights over software include protection against reverse engineering? Should database protection be enacted? The last two questions have been recent subjects of sharp domestic debate and of international trade discussion. In the software case, U.S. trade officials have sought to compel third nations to accept forms of intellectual property protection that have been rejected by U.S. courts. Such debates are important to consider in negotiating new international intellectual property agreements; and can be important to WTO panels to the extent that they are free to consider such arguments, as well as in interpreting TRIPs.

At the same time, the free-rider point is solid. The world benefits from certain intellectual property protections that do not benefit specific nations. The integration of intellectual property issues into the WTO provides a mechanism for managing this free-rider problem and for compelling nations to do what is in the group interest if not in their individual interest were they acting alone. But if legitimacy and loyalty are to be maintained, the burdens must be reasonably balanced.

The real issue here is the global allocation of the authorship and innovation costs. For example, the costs of pharmaceutical research must be reasonably balanced across different economies, which means that the developed-world patient should pay a much larger per-capita share of those costs than does the developing-world patient. This must be done in the background of the definition and interpretation of provisions such as those governing compulsory license arrangements. It also affects the differential pricing analysis to be undertaken in the next section. If an importing nation fails to provide a form of intellectual property protection that is required by TRIPs, there is no reason not to adopt the standard measure. However, there is a real risk that the amount involved may be overestimated, as by assuming that all sales would be made at a world price or at a price comparable to that of the highest price sales in the particular nation. Clearly, reasonable principles must be applied in estimating the actual rent lost.

These are particularly important issues for developing nations. It seems unfair to ask the consumers of these nations to contribute to investments that are unlikely to benefit them. In addition, it is difficult to encourage investment for pharmaceuticals oriented specifically toward developing world needs because the great cost of developing a pharmaceutical is unlikely to be recoverable from developing world markets. Such investment may, however, be feasible with partial public-sector support. In some cases, product development may be undertaken with an expectation that costs will be recovered from the developed-world market. If there is developing-country patent protection in such a case, the producer gets the additional benefit of the developing-world rents. Developing nations also often benefit from such pharmaceuticals, but there remains the question of whether they should contribute a share of the royalty and what that royalty should be.

Presumably, to the extent feasible, producers will also set Ramsey prices, in which the price is set inversely to the elasticity of the market. Thus, those who are willing to pay almost any price will do so, and those who are unlikely to buy without low prices will have the benefit of low prices. This seems fair for luxury products (such as some forms of entertainment), but may be unfair for pharmaceuticals.

NOTES AND QUESTIONS

1. John Barton served as Chair of the British Commission on Intellectual Property Rights that examined the implications of the TRIPS Agreement for developing countries. *See Integrating Intellectual Property Rights and Development Policy,* Report of the Commission on Intellectual Property Rights, London, Sept. 2002.[139] That Commission concluded, *inter alia:*

> The difficulty for developing countries in this context is that they are "second comers" in a world that has been shaped by the "first comers." And because of that, it is a very different world from that in which the "first comers" developed. It is a cliché to say that we live in an age of globalisation, when the world economy is becoming more integrated. It is an article of faith in the international community that integration on appropriate terms into the world economy is a necessary condition for development. The question from our point of view is what are the appropriate terms for that integration in the field of IPRs. Just as the now-developed countries moulded their IP regimes to suit their particular economic, social and technological circumstances, so developing countries should in principle now be able to do the same.
>
> We therefore conclude that far more attention needs to be accorded to the needs of the developing countries in the making of international IP policy. Consistent with recent decisions of the international community at Doha and Monterrey, the development objectives need to be integrated into the making of IP rules and practice. At Monterrey in March 2002, governments welcomed "the decisions of the World Trade Organization to place the needs and interests of developing countries at the heart of its work programme." They also acknowledged the concerns of developing countries, including:
>
>> the lack of recognition of intellectual property rights for the protection of traditional knowledge and folklore; the transfer of knowledge and technology; the implementation and interpretation of the Agreement

---

139. http://www.iprcommission.org/graphic/documents/final_report.htm.

on Trade-Related Aspects of Intellectual Property Rights in a manner supportive of public health ..." [Monterrey Consensus, March 2002].

We believe this is a satisfactory but partial agenda. There is far more that needs to be thought about and done in considering the impact of the existing system upon developing countries. It is our contention that intellectual property systems may, if we are not careful, introduce distortions that are detrimental to the interests of developing countries. Very "high" standards of protection may be in the public interest in developed countries with highly sophisticated scientific and technological infrastructures (although we note, as above, that this is controversial in several respects), but this does not mean the same standards are appropriate in all developing countries. In fact we consider that developed countries should pay more attention to reconciling their own perceived commercial self-interest, with their own interest in the reduction of poverty in developing countries.

To achieve that end, so far as possible developing countries should not be deprived of the flexibility to design their IP systems that developed countries enjoyed in earlier stages of their own development, and higher IP standards should not be pressed on them without a serious and objective assessment of their development impact. We need to ensure that the global IP systems evolve so that they may contribute to the development of developing countries, by stimulating innovation and technology transfer relevant to them, while also making available the products of technology at the most competitive prices possible. We need to make sure that the IP system facilitates, rather than hinders, the application of the rapid advances in science and technology for the benefit of developing countries. (Report, at Introduction).

One of the major difficulties facing policymakers dealing with the TRIPS Agreement is the relative absence of reliable data and analysis concerning its present and future effects. Keith Maskus has played a lead role in seeking to close the information gap.

INTELLECTUAL PROPERTY RIGHTS IN THE GLOBAL ECONOMY
Keith E. Maskus*

CHAPTER FOUR

EVIDENCE ON THE GLOBAL IMPACTS OF INTELLECTUAL PROPERTY RIGHTS: MEASURING WHAT CANNOT BE SEEN

Determinants of Intellectual Property Rights

It is obvious from the figures above [not reproduced here — EDS.] that the strength of IPRs tends to rise with levels of economic development and income. That optimal protection of intellectual property is an increasing function of income and technological capacity is easy to explain. As incomes rise the demand for higher-quality, differentiated products also rises, leading to growing preferences for protection of trademarks and copyrights or, in political economy terms, an increasing supply of IPRs. As an economy's technological sophistication increases, inventors and creators require stronger and deeper protection for their works, implying a rising demand for IPRs. Of course, causation may go both ways, with stronger property rights also contributing to

---

* Institute for International Economics (2000).

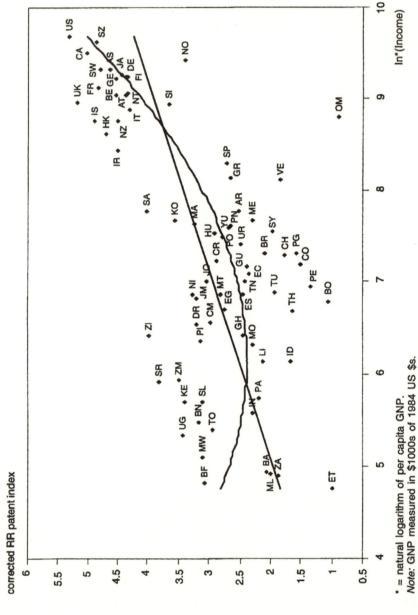

Figure 1.1 Relationship Between Patent Rights and Per-Capita GNP

* = natural logarithm of per capita GNP.
Note: GNP measured in $1000s of 1984 US $s.

Sources: Maskus and Penubarti (1995) and author's calculations.

growth in incomes. The latter point remains subject to debate and is not yet well understood in empirical terms. I elaborate these points in the following chapter on IPRs and economic development. . . .

Inspection of Figure 1.1 actually suggests that patent rights decline as incomes rise from low levels, then accelerate sharply at highest income levels. Thus, there seems to be a quadratic relationship between IPRs and GNP per capita. . . . This specification strongly suggests that countries tend to weaken their patent laws as incomes rise to some point and then strengthen them after that. This U-shaped curve is reminiscent of the so-called "environmental Kuznets curve," which indicated that countries reduce their environmental standards up to some level of per-capita income and then raise them continuously after that point (Grossman and Krueger, 1993). . . .

. . . I add further explanatory variables that account for other influences on patent rights. One of these is the economy's size, as measured by real GDP. It could be hypothesized that countries do not begin to provide strong IPRs until they reach a minimum size, because there are fixed costs in organizing and administering a patent system. In the regression . . . market size has no detectable impact on patent rights. This finding is potentially important in policy terms. It suggests that the economy's GDP itself is not a determinant of IPRs reform, as opposed to per-capita income and economic development. Because U.S. trade authorities are concerned with the strength of IPRs protection in large but poor economies, such as India and China, they have mounted considerable pressure for change. This finding suggests that, despite such pressure, effective patent rights may remain limited until incomes grow well beyond current levels. Putting it differently, the higher standards required by TRIPS may well command limited enforcement attention in a wide swath of nations. . . .

NOTES AND QUESTIONS

1. The data assembled by Keith Maskus highlights a phenomenon that is consistent with previous discussions of IP history and intuition. That is, as countries begin to move up the development curve, they borrow technology from more advanced countries to make their industries competitive. When a country reaches a certain point in its development, local interests in protecting new technologies begin to outweigh more diffuse interests in borrowing technologies, and the legislature is pressed to strengthen IP protection. The examples of the United States as "technology borrower" in the 1800s and early 1900s (the period of the "industrial revolution"), Japan in the 1950s through 1970s, and Taiwan in the 1980s and 1990s, are commonly used to illustrate this phenomenon.

   The TRIPS Agreement is essentially an effort to eliminate that part of the development curve during which technology borrowing takes place. Yet, the consequences of eliminating the flexibility that the United States and other similarly situated countries enjoyed is unpredictable, and could be decidedly negative from the standpoint of developing countries. If local industries in these countries are precluded from using foreign technologies, and cannot afford to develop their own, they may find themselves in a perpetual circumstance of technological dependence. Foreign investors may dominate local industry as only they will be able to establish globally competitive businesses.

In an alternative scenario, developing countries benefit from the introduction of foreign-owned technology as knowledge and training diffuses locally (through employment, leakage, etc.). Over the long term, as this diffusion results in greater local capacity for innovation, and as local entrepreneurs are able to access a more highly skilled labor force, developing country-based enterprises will become globally competitive.

In another alternative scenario, since most multinational enterprises are publicly traded, and "ownership" can as well be vested in individuals from developed as well as developing countries, the whole notion of "local ownership" and control is irrelevant. Individuals in Bolivia and Tanzania can just as well own shares in General Electric and profit from the introduction of new technologies as individuals in the United States and Switzerland. Of course, this last scenario fails to identify how an individual in Bolivia or Tanzania would find the money to buy into General Electric, but it demonstrates how far one could go in attempting to rationalize technological dependence.

2. As both John Barton and Keith Maskus have suggested, one of the principal difficulties in analyzing the role of IP in development involves the impracticability of disaggregating or isolating IP from other factors. China and Taiwan have experienced major inflows of foreign capital and high rates of economic growth while essentially ignoring foreign-held IPRs. But China has an enormous internal market that holds tremendous appeal for foreign investors, and Taiwan (during its low protection period in the 1980s and 1990s) excelled as a low-cost producer with a highly educated work force and proximity to major Asian markets. Would higher standards of IP protection have hurt either of these two economies? Would higher standards have helped? There is no "counter-factual" by which to test such hypotheses. What we do know is that low standards of IP protection did not create a "doomsday scenario" for these developing countries.

D. Intellectual Property in a Digital Age

The invention of the microprocessor transformed the world in profound ways. The cost of building computers rapidly dropped, processing capacities expanded exponentially, and information became "digital." The Internet — a network of networks — connects the far reaches of the world community with vast information resources. A remote village today has a library resource capacity unthought of by even the greatest university libraries only two decades ago.

It is a common axiom that intellectual property law continuously adapts to new technologies. Yet, intellectual property law has rarely been confronted with a challenge as complex as the Internet. If works protected by copyright can be uploaded to a server and accessed by individuals throughout the world instantaneously, the ability of copyright holders to control distribution of their work is challenged.

On one hand, the world has developed an information resource with incalculable capacity to disseminate information and promote understanding (though, as we know, information is not used only for "good" ends). On the other hand, the interests of copyright holders may be compromised (though copyright holders also have access to greatly expanded markets).

John Perry Barlow, a songwriter for the Grateful Dead and co-founder of the Electronic Frontier Foundation (EFF), was one of the first to suggest ways that the digitization of information and the Internet might challenge existing intellectual property paradigms. Barlow asks the reader to think of information in new ways — as a "living" entity whose characteristics fluctuate across time and space.

Barlow foresaw difficulties that would increasingly confront content providers and software developers, but likewise foresaw that enterprises would adapt their products to address new environments. His observations in 1994 anticipate to a large extent Microsoft's adaptation of its operating system technology (in Windows XP) to ongoing interaction between the end-user and Microsoft's server system.

He also suggested that legal rules might not provide the answers that content providers would seek. In recent years, copyright-dependent industries initiated major court battles against online distributors such as Napster. More recently, university administrators have, at the insistence of copyright holders, pursued intrusive actions against their own students to punish them for taking advantage of materials readily accessible on the Internet. Where will this end? Will the inability of the copyright industries to protect their content lead to an Orwellian social order where access to information is strictly controlled by authorities? Will the Internet, hailed as a global good, become a tool of social control in the name of protecting against the downloading of rock and roll music? There must be better answers to reconciling the interests of copyright holders with the capacity of new information technologies.

THE ECONOMY OF IDEAS: A FRAMEWORK FOR PATENTS AND COPYRIGHTS IN THE DIGITAL AGE. (EVERYTHING YOU KNOW ABOUT INTELLECTUAL PROPERTY IS WRONG.)

John Perry Barlow*

. . . INTERACTION AND PROTECTION

Direct interaction will provide a lot of intellectual property protection in the future, and, indeed, already has. No one knows how many software pirates have bought legitimate copies of a program after calling its publisher for technical support and offering some proof of purchase, but I would guess the number is very high.

The same kind of controls will be applicable to "question and answer" relationships between authorities (or artists) and those who seek their expertise. Newsletters, magazines, and books will be supplemented by the ability of their subscribers to ask direct questions of authors. . . .

---

* WIRED, 2.03 — March 1994.

CRYPTO BOTTLING

Cryptography, as I've said perhaps too many times, is the "material" from which the walls, boundaries — and bottles — of cyberspace will be fashioned.

Of course there are problems with cryptography or any other purely technical method of property protection. It has always appeared to me that the more security you hide your goods behind, the more likely you are to turn your sanctuary into a target. Having come from a place where people leave their keys in their cars and don't even have keys to their houses, I remain convinced that the best obstacle to crime is a society with its ethics intact.

While I admit that this is not the kind of society most of us live in, I also believe that a social over reliance on protection by barricades rather than conscience will eventually wither the latter by turning intrusion and theft into a sport, rather than a crime. This is already occurring in the digital domain as is evident in the activities of computer crackers. . . .

But cryptography will not be used simply for making locks. It is also at the heart of both digital signatures and the aforementioned digital cash, both of which I believe will be central to the future protection of intellectual property.

I believe that the generally acknowledged failure of the shareware model in software had less to do with dishonesty than with the simple inconvenience of paying for shareware. If the payment process can be automated, as digital cash and signature will make possible, I believe that soft product creators will reap a much higher return from the bread they cast upon the waters of cyberspace.

Moreover, they will be spared much of the overhead presently attached to the marketing, manufacture, sales, and distribution of information products, whether those products are computer programs, books, CDs, or motion pictures. This will reduce prices and further increase the likelihood of noncompulsory payment.

But of course there is a fundamental problem with a system that requires, through technology, payment for every access to a particular expression. It defeats the original Jeffersonian purpose of seeing that ideas were available to everyone regardless of their economic station. I am not comfortable with a model that will restrict inquiry to the wealthy.

AN ECONOMY OF VERBS

The future forms and protections of intellectual property are densely obscured at this entrance to the Virtual Age. Nevertheless, I can make (or reiterate) a few flat statements that I earnestly believe won't look too silly in 50 years.

- In the absence of the old containers, almost everything we think we know about intellectual property is wrong. We're going to have to unlearn it. We're going to have to look at information as though we'd never seen the stuff before.
- The protections that we will develop will rely far more on ethics and technology than on law.
- Encryption will be the technical basis for most intellectual property protection. (And should, for many reasons, be made more widely available.)
- The economy of the future will be based on relationship rather than possession. It will be continuous rather than sequential.

• And finally, in the years to come, most human exchange will be virtual rather than physical, consisting not of stuff but the stuff of which dreams are made. Our future business will be conducted in a world made more of verbs than nouns.

NOTES AND QUESTIONS

1. In a discussion of Lotus 1-2-3 and WordPerfect, Barlow notes that software products generate increasing returns as they are more widely adopted and that to some extent piracy may serve a useful purpose from the creator's standpoint. Another side to the value of widespread adoption concerns a phenomenon known as "network effects." This phenomenon is the subject of considerable discourse in the antitrust field. Certain products, such as computer operating systems, are thought to generate increasing social returns as they are more widely adopted. It may be a mistake from a social welfare standpoint to inhibit the emergence of a dominant operating system since consumers benefit from the capacity of programmers to write to a single standard (thereby encouraging the creation of new applications), and they benefit from being able to more easily share their digital work. Would the conclusion that a single standard for computer operating systems is socially beneficial justify private monopoly control over that standard, or would it argue for the regulation of that standard as an "essential facility," access to which must be assured under defined terms and conditions? In the Microsoft case, the Court of Appeals for the District of Columbia Circuit considered Microsoft's argument that analysis of its behavior under the laws against monopolization should take into account network effects. The Court said:

> Whether or not Microsoft's characterization of the operating system market is correct does not appreciably alter our mission in assessing the alleged antitrust violations in the present case. As an initial matter, we note that there is no consensus among commentators on the question of whether, and to what extent, current monopolization doctrine should be amended to account for competition in technologically dynamic markets characterized by network effects. . . . Indeed, there is some suggestion that the economic consequences of network effects and technological dynamism act to offset one another, thereby making it difficult to formulate categorical antitrust rules absent a particularized analysis of a given market.
>
> Moreover, it should be clear that Microsoft makes no claim that anticompetitive conduct should be assessed differently in technologically dynamic markets. It claims only that the measure of monopoly power should be different. For reasons fully discussed below, we reject Microsoft's monopoly power argument.

United States v. Microsoft, 253 F.3d 34, 50 (D.C. Cir. 2001).

2. Barlow did not precisely anticipate the current controversies surrounding file sharing and downloading of music and movies from the Internet. He did, however, anticipate through the intellectual property policies of the Grateful Dead one of the main economic arguments in favor of file sharing made by Napster in its much-publicized dispute with the recording industry

— namely, that wide availability of free music on the Internet stimulates consumer demand for CDs, and therefore is not antithetical to recording industry interests. This argument did not particularly impress the district court or the Court of Appeals. *See A & M Records v. Napster,* 239 F.3d 1004, 1016-17 (9th Cir. 2001).

3. Barlow observed the fundamental problem that technology is enabling activities that interfere with rights in intellectual property as traditionally understood, and he suggested that technological measures may, in the long run, be more effective than law in controlling those activities. Yet, Barlow knew then, and we know today, that envisioning technological controls and effectively implementing them are different matters. Since early days in California's Silicon Valley, computer software creators have sought to protect their works against unauthorized duplication by technological means. No sooner had a new method of preventing access been encoded than methods of circumventing the code were found. Anticopying devices often made the ordinary use of programs difficult for authorized users, leading to frustration and dissatisfied customers. Are more sophisticated encryption technologies the answer to the problems faced by copyright holders?

4. As recently as 20 years ago, the distribution and sale of a copyright-protected work throughout the world was an expensive process that required the development and maintenance of a substantial physical distribution network. Today, a copyright-protected work can be sent by an IPRs holder anywhere in the world virtually cost-free with the click of a button. Conceptually at least, the potential profit that can be obtained from global distribution vastly exceeds what was possible in the past. Should this potential windfall for copyright holders affect the level of protection their works are afforded?

E. *The Future of Global IP Policy*

Few individuals have been so perceptively involved in the study of the relationship between intellectual property rights and economic development as Keith Maskus and Jerome Reichman. They here combine their experience and skills as economist and lawyer to assess the current state of the IP world and its implications for developed and developing countries. They make several important recommendations, a few of which are included within the following excerpt.

THE GLOBALIZATION OF PRIVATE KNOWLEDGE GOODS AND THE PRIVATIZATION OF GLOBAL PUBLIC GOODS

Keith E. Maskus & J. H. Reichman*

. . . TECHNOLOGY TRANSFER AFTER THE TRIPS AGREEMENT

The international flow of technological information and its successful integration into domestic production and management processes are central to the

* 7 J. INT'L ECON. L. 279 (2004).

ability of firms in developing countries to compete in the global economy. Technological change is a principal source of sustained growth in living standards and is essential for the transformation and modernization of economic structures. In most instances, developing countries find it cheaper and faster to acquire foreign technologies than to develop them with domestic resources. Such technologies may "spill over" into wider improvements in productivity and follow-on innovation in the domestic economy.

International technology transfer (ITT) is a comprehensive term covering mechanisms for shifting information across borders and its effective diffusion into recipient economies. It refers to numerous complex processes, which range from innovation and international marketing of technology to its absorption and imitation. There are also many different channels through which technology may be transferred. One major conduit consists of trade in goods, especially capital goods and technological inputs. A second is foreign direct investment (FDI), which generally transfers technological information that is newer or more productive than that available from local firms. A third is technology licensing, which may occur either within firms or between unrelated firms. Licenses typically involve the purchase of production or distribution rights and the technical information and know-how required to exploit them.

There are also important non-market channels of ITT. Perhaps most significant is the process of imitation through product inspection, reverse engineering, and trial and error. A related mechanism is triggered when technical and managerial personnel leave a firm and start a rival firm based on information learned in the original location. Still another means is to study information available from patent applications. Thus, patents provide both a direct source of technology transfer, through FDI and licensing, and an indirect source through legally regulated disclosures. Indeed, "trade in ideas" is a significant factor in world economic growth, and developing economies could gain considerably more access to foreign technologies as international firms take out patents in their locations. Nevertheless, this benefit remains dependent on local abilities to learn from incoming technological information, and on the diffusion practices or strategies of technology-exporting firms.

Much knowledge appears to be transferred through the temporary migration of students, scientists, and managerial and technical personnel to universities, laboratories, and conferences located mainly in the developed economies. Finally, technical information may be available from the public domain, making it free for taking, or from a research commons accessible with certain restrictions.

International markets for trading technologies are inherently subject to failure due to distortions attributable to concerns about appropriability, problems of valuing information by buyers and sellers, and market power, all strong justifications for public intervention at both the domestic and global levels. Technology developers are interested in reducing the costs and risks of making transfers, along with protecting their rights to profit from them. They argue that effective protection and policy supports for markets are necessary to increase the willingness of innovative firms to provide knowledge about their production processes to firms in developing countries. Technology importers are interested in acquiring knowledge and products at minimal cost. Some observers argue that this objective is best met by limiting the exclusive rights to exploit technology.

While the close and complex relationships between intellectual property rights and ITT cannot be fully discussed here, it is useful to consider some of the main impacts, both positive and negative, that stronger global IPRs may have on international information flows. First, the preponderance of econometric studies suggests that market-mediated flows of technology respond positively to the strengthening of patent laws across countries. This finding applies to international trade flows, especially in patent-sensitive industries and capital goods, as regards patents in middle-income and large developing countries. However, trade flows to poor countries seem unresponsive to patent laws. Similarly, recent studies of patents and inward FDI find positive impacts on more advanced and larger developing countries, but not on poor and small countries. Licensing volumes between U.S. firms and unrelated concerns in larger developing countries also expand with the rigor of local patent regimes.

A reasonable interpretation of these findings is that there are threshold effects in market-based licensing. Economies with low incomes and limited technological capacity present neither attractive markets nor a competitive imitation threat. Because their intellectual property regimes are not particularly important in attracting ITT, it seems unlikely that the standards implemented in compliance with TRIPS will encourage additional technology transfer to the poorest countries. However, at higher incomes and technological capacities, IPRs become an important factor in this regard, even though they are only one of a list of variables that influence ITT. Other important factors include effective infrastructure, efficient governance, market size and growth, and proximity to suppliers and demanders.

The literature also suggests that stronger patent rights may be expected to raise considerably the rents earned by international firms as patents become more valuable, with the result that firms in developing countries would pay more for the average inward protected technology. Expansion of breadth, scope, and length of patents would tend to amplify this result. Thus, there are countervailing impacts in middle-income countries: higher volumes of ITT but increased payments per unit of technology. Moreover, recipient countries are more likely to benefit where the supply of technologies is competitive and local firms are capable of adapting them effectively into production processes.

While the evidence supports the claim that TRIPS standards could enhance ITT (at least into the larger and more advanced developing economies) through better performing technology markets, it should be weighed against national historic experience. Few now-developed economies underwent significant technological learning and industrial transformation without the benefit of weak intellectual property protection. A good example is Japan, which from the 1950s through the 1980s pursued an industrial property regime that favored small-scale innovation, adaptation and diffusion, and the licensing of new technologies. Key features of this system included pre-grant disclosure, rapid opposition to patent grants, narrow patent claims, local reliance on utility models and advantages for licensing. Another example is South Korea, which in the 1970s encouraged domestic firms to acquire and adapt mature technologies available on international markets for purposes of developing local innovation capacities.

The extent to which the emerging global IP regime may be expected to enhance or impede ITT thus poses a complicated question. Answering it is made even harder because technology transfer across borders involves a mixture of private activities and public measures of encouragement (or discouragement). This mixture varies in cost and efficiency by sector, country, and over time, which suggests that globalized IP protection could have both complex and sub-optimal effects unless accompanied by appropriate complementary policy approaches.

The new system raises entry barriers for firms and competition in the poorest countries, while even the middle-income nations find their scope of action limited. Market distortions due to misuses of intellectual property rights may also be harder to detect or police in developing than in developed countries. Moreover, new or relatively untested forms of intellectual property protection that choke access to upstream information inputs — including scientific and technical data as such — could narrow access to the research commons and limit other transfer mechanisms, with incalculable long-term effects on ITT as it used to occur.

In our view, governments in developing countries need to be pro-active in ensuring that the net effect of expanded IP protection is to enhance access to technology and to encourage its domestic adaptation and diffusion. Potential gains in dynamic competition are reason enough for this approach. An additional important factor is that tightened protection raises significant questions regarding the ability to access international technology and information to improve the provision of broader public goods. In the rest of this article we explore these issues in more detail. . . .

INSTABILITY AND LOSS OF BALANCE IN DEVELOPED INTELLECTUAL PROPERTY REGIMES

The drive to stamp out free-riding practices thus tends to obscure serious problems engendered by the radical transformation of IP policies that has occurred in developed countries. This transformation constitutes a prolonged effort to strengthen the protection of investors in cutting-edge technologies, especially computer programs and biogenetically engineered products, which fit imperfectly within the classical patent and copyright paradigms.

Under the classical IP system, as implemented in the United States through the mid-1960s, for example, the strong legal monopolies of the patent law protected only a narrow layer of discontinuous inventions that fell outside the technical trajectories guiding the day-to-day application of normal scientific discoveries. Entrepreneurs constrained to innovate in a highly competitive economy looked to the liability rules of unfair competition law, especially trade secret law, to provide natural lead time in which to recoup their investments, and to the rules of trademark law to maintain a foothold in the market based on their reputations as producers of quality goods. Because copyright law excluded industrial products in virtually every form, their producers could not hope to avoid the rigors of competition by masquerading as authors of literary and artistic works. As for the rest, vigorously enforced antitrust laws, supplemented by a robust doctrine of patent misuse, rid the market of deleterious patent pools and other barriers to entry and, in the view of Professors Mowery and Rosenberg, by disciplining Bell Labs and IBM, paved the way for the technological leaps of the 1970s and 1980s.

This classical system of intellectual property protection obliged innovators to look to the public domain for the basic inputs of most technological development. They took the availability of vast amounts of government-generated or government-funded scientific data and technical information for granted; and they assumed that facts and data generated by non-confidential public research endeavors at universities and other nonprofit institutions would become public goods available to all. Investors also assumed that sub-patentable innovations could be reverse-engineered by proper means that would endow competitors with improvements and lower cost modes of production. They further assumed that even patented inventions would enter the public domain at fairly short intervals and that it was not inordinately difficult to work around these inventions if the commercial payoffs justified the effort. However, basic underlying scientific discoveries would remain freely available.

If we now fast forward to a descriptive analysis of the current U.S. system, one could hardly imagine a starker contrast. The United States Court of Appeals for the Federal Circuit, entrusted by Congress to manage the patent system, has deliberately remolded that system to protect investment as such, rather than discontinuous technical achievements that elevate the level of competition. The patent system has accordingly degenerated to protecting incremental slivers of know-how applied to industry, including those very business methods that were formerly the building blocks of the free-enterprise economy.

The copyright system, expanding in the same direction, now confers virtually perpetual protection on computer software and digital productions of all kinds, and it encourages creators to surround even their unprotectible technical ideas and components with untouchable electronic fences. Once surrounded by these fences, even the underlying facts and data may be put off limits; while one-sided electronic adhesion contracts may override public interest exceptions favoring education and public research, and they may even prohibit reverse engineering by honest means.

As hybrid IP regimes multiply to fill still other perceived gaps in the system, there are virtually no products sold on the general products market that do not come freighted with a bewildering and overlapping array of exclusive property rights that discourage follow-on applications of routine technical know-how. Weak enforcement of antitrust laws then further reinforces the barriers to entry erected upon this thicket of rights, while the need to stimulate and coordinate investment in complex innovation projects justifies patent pools, concentrations of research efforts, and predatory practices formerly thought to constitute misuses of the patent monopoly.

The end results of this process, which James Boyle has felicitously called the Second Enclosure Movement, are not fully known, but the problems it is already causing for developed systems of innovation shed light on the larger problems facing the international economy. The availability of upstream data and scientific information from the public domain is shrinking at the very moment when advances in Internet technologies make it possible to link both centrally located and distributed data repositories as never before. A growing thicket of rights surrounds gene fragments, research tools, and other upstream inputs of scientific research, and the resulting transaction costs impede and delay research and development undertaken in both the public and private sectors. Lost research and competitive opportunities appear to be mushrooming as exchanges of even government funded research results become problematic. As well-known economists point out, complex research and development projects at every level — whether public or private — will become increasingly impracticable if too many owners of too many rights have to be tithed along the way.

Meanwhile, the sharing norms of science and the principle of open access to data have begun to break down as universities commercialize publicly funded research products. New intellectual property rights in collections of data — adopted in the EU and pending adoption in the U.S. — further undermine these norms by enabling scientists, universities and entrepreneurs to retain control of data and technical information even after the publication of research results in articles or after public disclosure for purposes of filing patent applications on such results.

These and other social disutilities cast light on the problems afflicting the international system and raise serious questions about its future prospects. They represent the unintended consequences of an excess of regulation and interference with market forces. In allowing large multinational firms to lock in temporary advantages, the IP system could discourage innovation by those same small and medium-sized firms that depend on access to public domain inputs for developing applications of new technologies.

In this environment, economists fear that the ratcheting up of intellectual property standards will boomerang against the capacity to innovate in developed countries. They ask whether the breakthrough inventions of the recent past would still be possible in a protectionist environment and in the presence of a shrinking public domain. They make us question whether future innovation will flourish in a dynamic, transnational system of innovation liberated from excessive governmental regulation or flounder in a re-regulated, ever more anti-competitive market that increasingly resembles the top-down economies that trailed behind U.S. high-tech industries in the past.

EXPORTING A DYSFUNCTIONAL SYSTEM TO THE REST OF THE WORLD?

Logically, the shift to a high-protectionist agenda in the developed countries should spark a cautious and skeptical response from the rest of the world for a number of reasons. First, the TRIPS Agreement itself, coupled with the WIPO Copyright Treaties of 1996, foreshadowed a revolutionary transformation of the legal and economic infrastructures in developing countries, and they need a lengthy period of time in which to digest and adjust to these reforms. These countries can hardly absorb the unknown social costs of new intellectual property burdens when the real costs of the last round of legislative initiatives are still making themselves felt. Yet, this reality has not attenuated the pressures for TRIPS-plus standards in both multilateral and bilateral forums.

A second reason for diffidence in developing countries is the scholarly debate that the high-protectionist agenda has generated in both the United States and Europe, and the corresponding fears that this agenda could harm investment and research-based innovation in the long run. If the critics prove right, then the last thing the developing countries should want to do is to emulate these policies.

Consider, for example, that the drive to further harmonize the international minimum standards of patent protection at WIPO has occurred at the very time when the domestic standards of the United States and the operations of its patent system are under critical assault. That country's patent system has been subject to scathing criticism in numerous law journal articles, in the scientific literature, and even in magazines of general circulation. New proposals to reform both the domestic and international patent systems appear frequently, and commissions to study or propose reform are operating on numerous fronts. How, under such circumstances, could it be timely to harmonize and elevate international standards of patent protection — even if that were demonstrably beneficial — when there is so little agreement in the U.S. itself on how to rectify a dysfunctional apparatus that often seems out of control?

Even in the courts themselves, which, in the United States, still operate at some degree of removal from lobbying and other political pressures, there are elements of change, uncertainty, and disarray that do not bode well for an international standard-setting exercise. In the past few years, for example, the U.S. federal courts have significantly changed the way patent claims are interpreted; narrowed the doctrine of equivalents in patent infringement actions; practically eliminated the research exemption under which universities had operated for fifty years or more; expanded patent protection of computer programs in ways that both the domestic and European authorities had previously opposed; and opened patent law to the protection of business methods in ways that have disrupted settled commercial activities.

These events should make U.S. authorities cautious about surrendering the power to undertake adjustments in the future, and policy makers in the rest of the world should become wary of locking themselves into the untested results of ad hoc judicial tinkering in a single country. It is therefore disconcerting to think of "harmonizing" the international patent system at such a time, when the risks of unintended harm to worldwide competition seem high, and when the only basis for a consensus on harmonization might be to squeeze out the remaining flexibilities in the TRIPS Agreement.

One can paint a similar picture with respect to copyright and related rights laws. Here, the developing countries, acting in concert with user interests in the developed countries, managed to ensure that the 1996 WIPO treaties governing works transmitted in digital media continued to allow certain privileged uses and exceptions permitted by prior law. Notwithstanding this outcome at the international level, the United States and the European Union both ignored these provisions and cut well back on permitted uses in their domestic implementation laws; and they have been pressing developing countries for still higher standards of protection in bilateral negotiations.

Yet, these domestic initiatives to expand and strengthen copyright protection of works transmitted over digital telecommunications networks have generated popular resistance to copyright norms in the United States as well as strenuous academic concerns about free competition, free speech, privacy, and the need to ensure access to inputs for future creative works. Further harmonization efforts in this climate thus amount to a gamble from which bad decisions and bad laws are far more likely to emerge than good laws that appropriately balance public and private interests.

There are still other risks of participating in further harmonization exercises that are even more sobering. First, certain new initiatives — such as the European database protection right — could radically subvert the classical intellectual property tradition built around patents and copyrights, with unintended consequences that could elevate the costs of research and development across the entire knowledge economy. While pressures to adopt similar legislation in the United States mount, legal and economic analysis of database protection as a generator of anti-competitive effects and of potential obstacles to innovation also grow more refined and alarming. Such premature initiatives could undermine sound economic development everywhere, and action in this regard at the international level would require great caution under the best of circumstances.

In this climate, it is difficult to see that developing countries have anything to gain from new efforts to strengthen IP standards. As matters stand, these international standard-setting exercises are not being conducted either to promote their interests or the global public interest. On the contrary, the developing countries play virtually no role in norm formation (partly due to their disorganized institutional apparatus), and the global public interest is hardly represented at the negotiating tables in the developed countries themselves, much less in international forums where hard law is enacted. From this perspective, even if the developing countries possessed more bargaining power than they do, they should remain wary of further harmonization exercises in the absence of effective strategies for preserving and enhancing the public good side of the equation. Until this gap in international lawmaking has been suitably addressed, such initiatives will continue to suffer from a basic design defect.

Any gains in efficiency of operations and lower transaction costs that greater harmonization might entail are likely to be offset by losses of sovereign power to control the single states' own innovation policies; by a shrinking public domain; by still higher costs of technological inputs and reverse engineering; and by growing thickets of rights that will make transfer of technology harder for those operating outside patent and IP pools (pools that could soon include major research universities as well as corporate holding companies). With every rise in international IP standards, moreover, there will likely be a corresponding loss of flexibility under the TRIPS Agreement and still greater risks deriving from the possible claims of nonviolatory acts of nullification that new standards may engender in the future. . . .

A Moratorium on Stronger International Intellectual Property Standards

Building an effective transnational system of innovation is a sobering task because the choice and disposition of optimal incentive structures has become increasingly uncertain in both theory and practice, especially as regards new technologies, and because neither high-protectionist interests in developed countries nor low-protectionist interests in developing countries could be expected to advocate principles appropriately balancing the needs of innovators with those of followers. From this perspective, further harmonization is not an improper goal, but rather a premature exercise under the new and uncertain conditions that attend the development of cutting-edge technologies generally and information-based technologies in particular.

Here the single most daunting problem is how to allocate public and private interests in such goods, given that their raw materials — information — necessarily perform a dual function as both outputs and inputs of a "cumulative and sequential" innovation process. As matters stand, the complex nature and pace of cutting-edge innovation so outstrips the conventional assumptions of the patent and copyright paradigms handed down from the nineteenth century that disinterested economists and policymakers in the most technologically advanced countries lack both the experience and the evidence to draw these lines with confidence.

Contrary to the special interests' relentless propaganda, in other words, intellectual property law has not arrived at the end of history. On the contrary, the turmoil generated by the TRIPS Agreement and its aftermath, including the WIPO Copyright Treaties, suggests that we stand at the threshold of an era in which unanswered questions about the role of IPRs in a networked information economy demand a lengthy period of "trial and error" experimentation, like that which ensued after the adoption of the Paris and Berne Conventions in the 1890s.

In order to validate empirically the loose claims made for and against different modes of protection, we will thus need a period of time in which states at different levels of development accommodate existing international standards to their own nascent or evolving systems of innovation. This would yield a new body of "laboratory effects," to use Ladas' phrase, with which to compare and test different development strategies. In the long run, the resulting empirical data could make it possible for states to trade further intellectual property concessions on a win-win basis, without coercion and with fewer risks that powerful interest groups had rigged the rules to lock in fleeting competitive advantages.

The time has come, in short, to take intellectual property off the international law-making agenda and to foster measures that better enabled developing countries to adapt to the challenges that prior rounds of harmonization had already bred. Such a moratorium would then enable both high and low protectionist countries to test their respective strategies against actual results without fear that the market openings nominally available to developing country entrepreneurs would be foreclosed by premature, ill-advised or unbalanced efforts to re-regulate that same marketplace at their expense.

A "time out" along these lines would make it possible, for example, to evaluate growing fears that overprotection of research results in developed countries will produce anticommons effects and lost competitive opportunities likely to retard the pace of innovation over time. It would allow room for any countries so inclined to experiment with alternative forms of protecting investment, including proposals for more open-source initiatives and for compensatory liability regimes that could reconstitute the shrinking semicommons that historically mediated between exclusive intellectual property rights and the public domain. It would allow time for the worldwide scientific community to reformulate its data exchange policies and to reconstruct contractually the public domain for scientific and technical information that has recently come under a privatizing assault.

A moratorium on stronger international intellectual property standards would especially help developing countries shift their attention and limited resources away from compliance-driven initiatives toward programs to potentiate their national and regional systems of innovation. It would, for example, give them time to adapt promising new initiatives to their own environments, such as programs to encourage the transfer of technology from universities and public research centers to the private sector, which have produced mixed results in the United States. It would also give them breathing room in which to formulate competition laws and policies rooted in fairness, in concerns to lower barriers to entry, and in the need to ensure that market-induced transfers of technology were not thwarted by refusals to deal and unreasonable licensing terms or conditions.

Efforts to institute such a moratorium could, however, run up against legitimate concerns in developed countries to prohibit free riding on investments in new technologies that enter the global marketplace. Developing countries that demand a moratorium on stronger intellectual property standards must therefore remain willing to oppose free-riding practices that undermine incentives to invest in new technologies everywhere. A willingness to accommodate legitimate concerns about free riding could defuse potentially heated conflicts and remove controversial topics, such as database protection, from a more ambitious standard-setting agenda. It would also reinforce the credibility of a demand for a moratorium on further harmonization efforts by accompanying it with a "clean hands" doctrine that would reassure investors in all countries. . . .

NOTES AND QUESTIONS

1. As a general proposition, the academic community is substantially more skeptical of claims that strong intellectual property protection advances the interests of developing countries — or, for that matter, developed countries — than developed country business interests. What accounts for this difference in perspective? Are economists and law professors ignoring benefits conferred by the industrial community? Is the perspective of the business community too heavily shaped by narrow short-term interests in rent collection? What suggestions might you have for resolving the tension between the two perspectives?

2. When the international IPRs system was taking shape in the late 1800s, the possibilities for exploiting inventions and expressive works internationally were rather limited. A right to exclude others from practicing an invention or exploiting an expressive work on a global scale was in most cases a theoretical benefit. Does the fact that an inventive or expressive work can today *actually* be exploited among a very large base of consumers/end-users, and earn large amounts of money, affect how you think the balance should be struck between IPRs holders and the general public, or is it all the same?

CHAPTER
2

The International Patent System

I. THE PATENT AS INTELLECTUAL PROPERTY FORM

A. *Discovery and Invention*

There is a fundamental distinction in patent law between the concepts of "discovery" of properties of nature or principles governing natural phenomena, and "invention," which presupposes human intervention to make use of or alter natural things or phenomena. The boundary line between these two types of activity may at times be blurred.

Imagine that a scientist discovers that a certain previously unknown form of magnetic wave strikes the earth's atmosphere from deep space, and that this kind of wave has an adverse effect on the transmission of data between the earth and communications satellites. Such a discovery may have enormous commercial implications, perhaps leading to the invention of a device that filters out the harmful effect of the wave. The inventor of the filtering device may be entitled to a patent. The discoverer of the magnetic wave cannot patent his or her discovery. Today, the distinction between discovery and invention is of particular importance in the fields of biotechnology and genetic engineering.

The U.S. Supreme Court acknowledged the discovery-invention distinction in a seminal decision on the patenting of life forms.[1]

---

1. In the United States there is a federal court system, and there are court systems for the separate states. Patents are the subject of federal legislation, and patent cases are exclusively subject to the jurisdiction of the federal courts. Patent cases may arise either in the form of appeals from determinations by the Patent and Trademark Office (PTO), or in the form of private civil litigation, such as private suits for patent infringement. Civil claims are brought in one of the many federal district courts located throughout the United States, depending upon the amenability of a defendant to suit in a particular location. While most decisions of federal district courts are appealed to one of twelve Circuit Courts of Appeal located in different regions of the country (the First through Eleventh Circuits and the District of Columbia Circuit), appeals from district court patent decisions may be heard only by the Court of Appeals for the Federal Circuit (CAFC), located in Washington, D.C. (a thirteenth appeals court). Decisions of the PTO (a federal agency) are directly and indirectly appealed to the CAFC. Also, the International Trade Commission (ITC) has initial jurisdiction over patent claims brought under Section 337 of the Trade Act of 1930, and appeals are taken to the CAFC. The federal court system as it applies to patent cases is therefore more centralized than it is in respect to most other kinds of cases. In most other areas of federal law, the various Courts of Appeal may divide on common questions, and a good portion of the Supreme Court's time is generally occupied with resolving splits among the Courts of Appeal. Since there is only one federal appeals court that decides patent appeals (the CAFC), the Supreme Court need not occupy itself with resolving splits among the Circuits on patent questions.

DIAMOND v. CHAKRABARTY
447 U.S. 303 (1980)

Mr. Chief Justice BURGER[:] . . .

This is not to suggest that § 101 [of the U.S. Patent Act] has no limits or that it embraces every discovery. The laws of nature, physical phenomena, and abstract ideas have been held not patentable. *See Parker v. Flook*, 437 U.S. 584 (1978); *Gottschalk v. Benson*, 409 U.S. 63, 67 (1972); *Funk Brothers Seed Co. v. Kalo Inoculant Co.*, 333 U.S. 127, 130 (1948); *O'Reilly v. Morse*, 15 How. 62, 112-121 (1854); *Le Roy v. Tatham*, 14 How. 156, 175 (1853). Thus, a new mineral discovered in the earth or a new plant found in the wild is not patentable subject matter. Likewise, Einstein could not patent his celebrated law that $E = mc^2$; nor could Newton have patented the law of gravity. Such discoveries are "manifestations of . . . nature, free to all men and reserved exclusively to none." *Funk, supra*, at 130.

Judged in this light, respondent's micro-organism plainly qualifies as patentable subject matter. His claim is not to a hitherto unknown natural phenomenon, but to a nonnaturally occurring manufacture or composition of matter — a product of human ingenuity "having a distinctive name, character [and] use." *Hartranft v. Wiegmann*, 121 U.S. 609, 615 (1887). The point is underscored dramatically by comparison of the invention here with that in *Funk*. There, the patentee had discovered that there existed in nature certain species of root-nodule bacteria which did not exert a mutually inhibitive effect on each other. He used that discovery to produce a mixed culture capable of inoculating the seeds of leguminous plants. Concluding that the patentee had discovered "only some of the handiwork of nature," the Court ruled the product nonpatentable:

> "Each of the species of root-nodule bacteria contained in the package infects the same group of leguminous plants which it always infected. No species acquires a different use. The combination of species produces no new bacteria, no change in the six species of bacteria, and no enlargement of the range of their utility. Each species has the same effect it always had. The bacteria perform in their natural way. Their use in combination does not improve in any way their natural functioning. They serve the ends nature originally provided and act quite independently of any effort of the patentee." 333 U.S., at 131.

Here, by contrast, the patentee has produced a new bacterium with markedly different characteristics from any found in nature and one having the potential for significant utility. His discovery is not nature's handiwork, but his own; accordingly it is patentable subject matter under § 101.

NOTES AND QUESTIONS

1. The Supreme Court distinguishes between the creation by Dr. Chakrabarty of a new bacterium and an earlier claim (in *Funk Brothers*) for use of existing root-nodule bacteria in combination to inhibit plant disease. The Court uses the latter to illustrate the unpatentable discovery of properties of nature. As we look further into patent claims for biotechnological inventions, consider them in light of the Supreme Court's distinction in

Diamond v. Chakrabarty between the creation of new products and the use of known ones (as in *Funk Brothers*).

2.   The decoding of the human genome raised the "discovery-invention" issue in a most profound way. For an introduction to the human genome and its various components, *see generally* John Sulston & Georgina Ferry, The Common Thread (2002). Questions regarding the basic information of the genetic code were largely resolved by the decision of the Wellcome Trust to place its work in the public domain, thereby preventing its competitor in the race to unravel the code (Celera Genomics) from patenting its results (*see* the web site of the Wellcome Trust for information regarding public access to the human genome, http://www.wellcome.ac.uk). However, this represents only one subset of issues regarding the patentability of genetic information and materials.

While it might seem that sequencing (or mapping) the DNA of a material found in the human body involves "discovering" a property of nature, courts in the United States[2] and the European Union in its Biotechnology Directive[3] have accepted that synthesizing the end product of a DNA sequence (using identical genetic information with previously known methods of synthesis) represents "invention" (*see Amgen v. Hoechst Marion Roussel*, 457 F.3d 1293 (Fed. Cir. 2006), *rehearing en banc denied*, 469 F.3d 1039 (Fed. Cir. 2006), *cert. denied*, 550 U.S. 953 (2007)). This decision seems largely based on argument from the commercial biotechnology sector that investment in the discovery of new medicines and compounds will not take place in the absence of adequate financial incentive, and that patents for DNA-based products will provide that financial incentive. The "legal" approach so far adopted is that the act of reproducing naturally occurring substances via sequenced DNA through laboratory processes (e.g., purifying, isolating, and producing in quantity) involves human intervention, and therefore is inventive. The laboratory process is different than the "natural" process of creation.

One limit to the patenting of genetic information has been recognized in respect to expressed sequence tags (ESTs) used as genetic "markers" for research purposes based on an absence of specific utility (see criterion of utility, *infra*), *In re Fisher*, 421 F.3d 1365 (Fed. Cir. 2005). In *Association for Molecular Pathology v. U.S. Patent and Trademark Office*, 702 F. Supp. 2d 181 (S.D.N.Y. 2010), a federal district court invalidated patents held by Myriad Genetics. The court noted that "the challenged patent claims are directed to (1) isolated DNA containing all or portions of the *BRCA1* and *BRCA2* gene sequence and (2) methods for 'comparing' or 'analyzing' *BRCA1* and *BRCA2* gene sequences

---

2. *See, e.g., Amgen v. Chugai Pharmaceutical*, 927 F.2d 1200 (Fed. Cir. 1991).

3. Directive 98/44/EC of the European Parliament and of the Council of 6 July 1998 on the legal protection of biotechnological inventions, OJ L 213, 30/07/1998 p. 0013-0021, provides:

Article 5

1. The human body, at the various stages of its formation and development, and the simple discovery of one of its elements, including the sequence or partial sequence of a gene, cannot constitute patentable inventions.

2. An element isolated from the human body or otherwise produced by means of a technical process, including the sequence or partial sequence of a gene, may constitute a patentable invention, even if the structure of that element is identical to that of a natural element.

3. The industrial application of a sequence or a partial sequence of a gene must be disclosed in the patent application.

to identify the presence of mutations correlating with a predisposition to breast or ovarian cancer." The court concluded that

> DNA's existence in an "isolated" form alters neither this fundamental quality of DNA as it exists in the body nor the information it encodes. Therefore, the patents at issue directed to "isolated DNA" containing sequences found in nature are unsustainable as a matter of law and are deemed unpatentable subject matter under 35 U.S.C. § 101. 702 F. Supp. 2d at 185.

As of January 2011, this district court decision is on appeal to the Court of Appeals for the Federal Circuit. The fundamental assumption of the district court, that is, that DNA sequences as found in nature are unpatentable discoveries, appears consistent with traditional patent law concepts and understanding. It goes without saying that the decision of the CAFC is much anticipated by interested stakeholders on all sides, and that further appeal to the Supreme Court would not be unexpected.

A decision that uses of naturally occurring genetic code are patentable raises a host of questions regarding access and use of information by researchers, the extent to which an effect must be demonstrated (or merely suggested) to justify the grant of a patent, the ethical and moral implications of granting private rights in genetic code, and more.

B. Patentable Subject Matter

An invention will involve a "subject matter," such as a machine or chemical compound. Generally speaking, the subject matter scope of patent protection is intended to be broad. Predetermining the subject matter scope of patent protection is inherently difficult since "invention" contemplates the doing of something not done before. Legislators are naturally constrained in their capacity to predict what will be invented and so to establish rules for things that have not been done. Yet, this does not preclude setting boundaries around patentable subject matter. For example, advances in reproductive technologies make it scientifically possible to modify the genetic structure of existing human beings such that "new" humans might be created through laboratory processes. It is generally accepted that such new humans, should they be made, will not be patentable subject matter.[4]

As with most areas of law, patentability tends to be formulated in terms of "rules" and "exceptions" to them. The TRIPS Agreement patent rules, which we examine closely in this chapter, initially establish a comprehensive scope of patentable subject matter.[5] The Agreement then permits each national government to adopt certain types of exception, such as to protect public order, and also includes a general provision addressing "limited exceptions."

---

4. The "Harvard Mouse" cases made clear that the ethical question of patenting humans was one that needed to be addressed with some immediacy, not as a science fiction question. *See, e.g.,* EU Biotechnology Directive, at art. 5 (precluding patenting of the human body as such). Directive 98/44/EC of the European Parliament and of the Council of 6 July 1998 on the legal protection of biotechnological inventions, Official Journal L 213, 30/07/1998 p. 0013-0021.

5. TRIPS Agreement, art. 27.1 ("patents shall be available for any inventions, whether products or processes, in all fields of technology").

In the first passages quoted below, the U.S. Supreme Court states the case for a broad scope of patent subject matter protection, invoking Thomas Jefferson, one of America's Founding Fathers (and an early "garage inventor").

DIAMOND v. CHAKRABARTY

447 U.S. 303 (1980)

Mr. Chief Justice BURGER [for the majority. . . .]

Guided by these canons of construction, this Court has read the term "manufacture" in § 101 in accordance with its dictionary definition to mean "the production of articles for use from raw or prepared materials by giving to these materials new forms, qualities, properties, or combinations, whether by hand-labor or by machinery." *American Fruit Growers, Inc. v. Brogdex Co.*, 283 U.S. 1, 11 (1931). Similarly, "composition of matter" has been construed consistent with its common usage to include "all compositions of two or more substances and . . . all composite articles, whether they be the results of chemical union, or of mechanical mixture, or whether they be gases, fluids, powders or solids." *Shell Development Co. v. Watson*, 149 F. Supp. 279, 280 (DC 1957) (citing 1 A. Deller, Walker on Patents § 14, p. 55 (1st ed. 1937)). In choosing such expansive terms as "manufacture" and "composition of matter," modified by the comprehensive "any," Congress plainly contemplated that the patent laws would be given wide scope.

The relevant legislative history also supports a broad construction. The Patent Act of 1793, authored by Thomas Jefferson, defined statutory subject matter as "any new and useful art, machine, manufacture, or composition of matter, or any new or useful improvement [thereof]." Act of Feb. 21, 1793, § 1, 1 Stat. 319. The Act embodied Jefferson's philosophy that "ingenuity should receive a liberal encouragement." 5 Writings of Thomas Jefferson 75-76 (Washington ed. 1871). *See Graham v. John Deere Co.*, 383 U.S. 1, 7-10 (1966). Subsequent patent statutes in 1836, 1870, and 1874 employed this same broad language. In 1952, when the patent laws were recodified, Congress replaced the word "art" with "process," but otherwise left Jefferson's language intact. The Committee Reports accompanying the 1952 Act inform us that Congress intended statutory subject matter to "include anything under the sun that is made by man." S. Rep. No. 1979, 82d Cong., 2d Sess., 5 (1952); H.R. Rep. No. 1923, 82d Cong., 2d Sess., 6 (1952).[6] . . .

. . . A rule that unanticipated inventions are without protection would conflict with the core concept of the patent law that anticipation undermines patentability. *See Graham v. John Deere Co.*, 383 U.S., at 12-17. Mr. Justice Douglas reminded that the inventions most benefiting mankind are those that "push back the frontiers of chemistry, physics, and the like." *Great A. & P. Tea Co. v. Supermarket Corp.*, 340 U.S. 147, 154 (1950) (concurring opinion). Congress

---

6. This same language was employed by P.J. Federico, a principal draftsman of the 1952 recodification, in his testimony regarding that legislation: "[Under] section 101 a person may have invented a machine or a manufacture, which may include anything under the sun that is made by man. . . ." Hearings on H.R. 3760 before Subcommittee No. 3 of the House Committee on the Judiciary, 82d Cong., 1st Sess., 37 (1951).

employed broad general language in drafting § 101 precisely because such inventions are often unforeseeable.[10]

NOTES AND QUESTIONS

1. In a later part of its opinion, the U.S. Supreme Court said that it was up to the Congress (the U.S. legislative branch) to establish limits on the subject matter scope of patent protection. Generally speaking, a legislature or parliament is the branch of government considered to most directly reflect the "voice of the people." At the international level, patent rules are generally made by treaty. Treaties are typically negotiated by the executive branch of government, subject to subsequent approval by the legislative branch. Is there a difference in the democratic input into the two processes? What impact might these differences be expected to have on the outcome of the rulemaking?

Canada's Patent Act uses the same language as the U.S. Patent Act to define patentable subject matter. Yet, in a decision concerning the patentability of higher life forms, Canada's Supreme Court was able to discern limits without waiting for legislative intervention. The essence of the decision is that a higher life form is something greater than the sum of its parts.

HARVARD COLLEGE v. CANADA (COMMISSIONER OF PATENTS)

Supreme Court of Canada
2002 SCC 76 File No.: 28155
2002: May 21, 2002: December 5

BASTARACHE J. —

157. . . . In *Chakrabarty*, the majority attributed the widest meaning possible to the phrases "composition of matter" and "manufacture" for the reason that inventions are, necessarily, unanticipated and unforeseeable. Burger C.J., at p. 307, also referred to the fact that the categories of invention are prefaced by the word "any" ("any new and useful process, machine, manufacture, or composition of matter"). Finally, the Court referred to extrinsic evidence of Congressional intent to adopt a broad concept of patentability, noting at p. 309 that: "The Committee Reports accompanying the 1952 Act inform us that Congress intended statutory subject matter to 'include anything under the sun that is made by man.'"

158. I agree that the definition of invention in the [Canadian] *Patent Act* is broad. Because the Act was designed in part to promote innovation, it is only reasonable to expect the definition of invention to be broad enough to encompass unforeseen and unanticipated technology. I cannot however agree with the suggestion that the definition is unlimited in the sense that it includes "anything under the sun that is made by man." In drafting the *Patent Act*,

---

10. Even an abbreviated list of patented inventions underscores the point: telegraph (Morse, No. 1,647); telephone (Bell, No. 174,465); electric lamp (Edison, No. 223,898); airplane (the Wrights, No. 821,393); transistor (Bardeen & Brattain, No. 2,524,035); neutronic reactor (Fermi & Szilard, No. 2,708,656); laser (Schawlow & Townes, No. 2,929,922). *See generally* Revolutionary Ideas, Patents & Progress in America, United States Patent and Trademark Office (1976).

Parliament chose to adopt an exhaustive definition that limits invention to any "art, process, machine, manufacture or composition of matter." Parliament did not define "invention" as "anything new and useful made by man." By choosing to define invention in this way, Parliament signalled a clear intention to include certain subject matter as patentable and to exclude other subject matter as being outside the confines of the Act. This should be kept in mind when determining whether the words "manufacture" and "composition of matter" include higher life forms.

159. With respect to the meaning of the word "manufacture" (*fabrication*), although it may be attributed a very broad meaning, I am of the opinion that the word would commonly be understood to denote a non-living mechanistic product or process. . . .

These definitions use the terminology of "article," "material," and *objet technique.*" Is a mouse an "article," "material," or an "*objet technique*"? In my view, while a mouse may be analogized to a "manufacture" when it is produced in an industrial setting, the word in its vernacular sense does not include a higher life form. The definition in *Hornblower v. Boulton* (1799), 8 T.R. 95, 101 E.R. 1285 (K.B.), cited by the respondent, is equally problematic when applied to higher life forms. In that case, the English courts defined "manufacture" as "something made by the hands of man" (at p. 1288). In my opinion, a complex life form such as a mouse or a chimpanzee cannot easily be characterized as "something made by the hands of man."

160. As regards the meaning of the words "composition of matter," I believe that they must be defined more narrowly than was the case in *Chakrabarty, supra*, at p. 308 [—] namely "all compositions of two or more substances and . . . all composite articles." If the words "composition of matter" are understood this broadly, then the other listed categories of invention, including "machine" and "manufacture," become redundant. This implies that "composition of matter" must be limited in some way. Although I do not express an opinion as to where the line should be drawn, I conclude that "composition of matter" does not include a higher life form such as the oncomouse.

161. The phrase "composition of matter" (*composition de matières*) is somewhat broader than the term "manufacture" (*fabrication*). . . .

163. It also is significant that the word "matter" captures but one aspect of a higher life form. As defined by the *Oxford English Dictionary, supra*, vol. IX, at p. 480, "matter" is a "[p]hysical or corporeal substance in general . . . , contradistinguished from immaterial or incorporeal substance (spirit, soul, mind), and from qualities, actions, or conditions." "*Matière*" is defined by the *Grand Robert de la langue française, supra*, vol. 4, p. 1260, as "[TRANSLATION] corporeal substance 'that is perceptible in space and has mechanical mass.'" Although some in society may hold the view that higher life forms are mere "composition[s] of matter," the phrase does not fit well with common understandings of human and animal life. Higher life forms are generally regarded as possessing qualities and characteristics that transcend the particular genetic material of which they are composed. A person whose genetic make-up is modified by radiation does not cease to be him or herself. Likewise, the same mouse would exist absent the injection of the oncogene into the fertilized egg cell; it simply would not be predisposed to cancer. The fact that it has this predisposition to cancer that makes it valuable to humans does not mean that the mouse, along with other animal life forms, can be defined solely with reference to the genetic matter of which it is composed. The fact that animal life forms have

numerous unique qualities that transcend the particular matter of which they are composed makes it difficult to conceptualize higher life forms as mere "composition[s] of matter." It is a phrase that seems inadequate as a description of a higher life form.

164. Lastly, I wish also to address Rothstein, J.A.'s assertion that "[t]he language of patent law is broad and general and is to be given wide scope because inventions are, necessarily, unanticipated and unforeseeable" (para. 116). In my view, it does not thereby follow that all proposed inventions are patentable. On the one hand, it might be argued that, in this instance, Parliament could foresee that patents might be sought in higher life forms. Although Parliament would not have foreseen the genetically altered mouse and the process of genetic engineering used to produce it, Parliament was well aware of animal husbandry or breeding. While the technologies used to produce a crossbred animal and a genetically engineered animal differ substantially, the end result, an animal with a new or several new features, is the same. Yet Parliament chose to define the categories of invention using language that does not, in common usage, refer to higher life forms. One might thus infer that Parliament did not intend to include higher life forms in the definition of "invention." . . .

166. Patenting higher life forms would involve a radical departure from the traditional patent regime. Moreover, the patentability of such life forms is a highly contentious matter that raises a number of extremely complex issues. If higher life forms are to be patentable, it must be under the clear and unequivocal direction of Parliament. For the reasons discussed above, I conclude that the current Act does not clearly indicate that higher life forms are patentable. Far from it. Rather, I believe that the best reading of the words of the Act supports the opposite conclusion — that higher life forms such as the oncomouse are not currently patentable in Canada.

NOTES AND QUESTIONS

1. The decision by the Canadian Supreme Court is based on the express language of Canada's Patent Act. The Court appears to have left it open for the Parliament to allow for the patenting of higher life forms.

    Would such a decision by the Parliament be consistent with the Canadian Supreme Court's conception of patentable subject matter? If the Court is saying that higher life forms incorporate noncorporeal elements that are not encompassed by a "composition of matter," then on what would the Parliament be allowing patents?

    Perhaps what Canada's Supreme Court meant to say was, "We think it is wrong to allow for the patenting of higher life forms because these are creations of a divine spirit. We do not think that human beings should purport to own such creations. The patenting of higher life forms is inconsistent with the strong public policy of Canada." Why do you think Canada's Supreme Court chose to decide based on the language of the Patent Act? Was it attempting to force an ethical debate?

2. Justice Binnie of the Canadian Supreme Court noted in a dissenting opinion:

    "The oncomouse has been held patentable, and is now patented in jurisdictions that cover Austria, Belgium, Denmark, Finland, France, Germany,

> Greece, Ireland, Italy, Luxembourg, The Netherlands, Portugal, Spain, Sweden, the United Kingdom and the United States. A similar patent has been issued in Japan. New Zealand has issued a patent for a transgenic mouse that has been genetically modified to be susceptible to HIV infection. Indeed, we were not told of any country with a patent system comparable to Canada's (or otherwise) in which a patent on the oncomouse had been applied for and been refused." (at para. 2).

What consequences might flow from differential treatment of higher life forms in national patent laws?

The patent system, essentially developed for mechanics and chemistry, presents difficulties in fields other than genetic engineering. Established criteria also face difficulties when applied to business application software, which normally has been protected under copyright law. The U.S. Supreme Court considered the patentability of computer software used to perform "mental processes" in the following case.

BILSKI v. KAPPOS [DIRECTOR OF THE U.S. PTO]
130 S. Ct. 3218 (2010)

Justice KENNEDY delivered the opinion of the Court . . . :*

The question in this case turns on whether a patent can be issued for a claimed invention designed for the business world. The patent application claims a procedure for instructing buyers and sellers how to protect against the risk of price fluctuations in a discrete section of the economy. Three arguments are advanced for the proposition that the claimed invention is outside the scope of patent law: (1) it is not tied to a machine and does not transform an article; (2) it involves a method of conducting business; and (3) it is merely an abstract idea. The Court of Appeals ruled that the first mentioned of these, the so-called machine-or-transformation test, was the sole test to be used for determining the patentability of a "process" under the Patent Act, 35 U.S.C. § 101.

. . .

The Court of Appeals incorrectly concluded that this Court has endorsed the machine-or-transformation test as the exclusive test. It is true that *Cochrane v. Deener*, 94 U.S. 780, 788, 24 L. Ed. 139 (1877), explained that a "process" is "an act, or a series of acts, performed upon the subject-matter to be transformed and reduced to a different state or thing." More recent cases, however, have rejected the broad implications of this dictum; and, in all events, later authority shows that it was not intended to be an exhaustive or exclusive test. *Gottschalk v. Benson*, 409 U.S. 63, 70, 93 S. Ct. 253, 34 L. Ed. 2d 273 (1972), noted that "[t]ransformation and reduction of an article 'to a different state or thing' is the clue to the patentability of a process claim that does not include particular machines." At the same time, it explicitly declined to "hold that no process patent could ever qualify if it did not meet [machine or transformation] requirements." *Id.*, at 71, 93 S. Ct. 253. *Flook* took a similar approach, "assum[ing] that

---

* [Justice Scalia did not join two parts of the majority opinion. See discussion *infra*. — EDS.]

a valid process patent may issue even if it does not meet [the machine-or-transformation test]." 437 U.S., at 588, n. 9, 98 S. Ct. 2522.

This Court's precedents establish that the machine-or-transformation test is a useful and important clue, an investigative tool, for determining whether some claimed inventions are processes under § 101. The machine-or-transformation test is not the sole test for deciding whether an invention is a patent-eligible "process."

. . .

Section 101 similarly precludes the broad contention that the term "process" categorically excludes business methods. The term "method," which is within § 100(b)'s definition of "process," at least as a textual matter and before consulting other limitations in the Patent Act and this Court's precedents, may include at least some methods of doing business. *See, e.g.*, Webster's New International Dictionary 1548 (2d ed. 1954) (defining "method" as "[a]n orderly procedure or process . . . regular way or manner of doing anything; hence, a set form of procedure adopted in investigation or instruction"). The Court is unaware of any argument that the " 'ordinary, contemporary, common meaning,' " *Diehr, supra*, at 182, 101 S. Ct. 1048, of "method" excludes business methods. Nor is it clear how far a prohibition on business method patents would reach, and whether it would exclude technologies for conducting a business more efficiently. *See, e.g.*, Hall, Business and Financial Method Patents, Innovation, and Policy, 56 Scottish J. Pol. Econ. 443, 445 (2009) ("There is no precise definition of . . . business method patents").

. . .

Even though petitioners' application is not categorically outside of § 101 under the two broad and atextual approaches the Court rejects today, that does not mean it is a "process" under § 101. Petitioners seek to patent both the concept of hedging risk and the application of that concept to energy markets. App. 19-20. Rather than adopting categorical rules that might have wide-ranging and unforeseen impacts, the Court resolves this case narrowly on the basis of this Court's decisions in *Benson, Flook*, and *Diehr*, which show that petitioners' claims are not patentable processes because they are attempts to patent abstract ideas. Indeed, all members of the Court agree that the patent application at issue here falls outside of § 101 because it claims an abstract idea.

. . .

Today, the Court once again declines to impose limitations on the Patent Act that are inconsistent with the Act's text. The patent application here can be rejected under our precedents on the unpatentability of abstract ideas. The Court, therefore, need not define further what constitutes a patentable "process," beyond pointing to the definition of that term provided in § 100(b) and looking to the guideposts in *Benson, Flook*, and *Diehr*.

And nothing in today's opinion should be read as endorsing interpretations of § 101 that the Court of Appeals for the Federal Circuit has used in the past. *See, e.g., State Street*, 149 F.3d, at 1373; *AT & T Corp.*, 172 F.3d, at 1357. It may be that the Court of Appeals thought it needed to make the machine-or-transformation test exclusive precisely because its case law had not adequately identified less extreme means of restricting business method patents, including (but not limited to) application of our opinions in *Benson, Flook*, and *Diehr*. In disapproving an exclusive machine-or-transformation test, we by no means foreclose the Federal Circuit's development of other limiting criteria that further the purposes of the Patent Act and are not inconsistent with its text.

The judgment of the Court of Appeals is affirmed.

[Justice Scalia joined the majority of the Court, but did not join those parts of the opinion in which Justice Kennedy might be understood to question the utility of the machine-or-transformation test, which, in Justice Scalia's view, the CAFC had not suggested was the exclusive test of patentable process subject matter.

Justice Stevens, writing for a four-Justice minority, vigorously dissented, summarizing the view of the dissenting Justices:]

The Court correctly holds that the machine-or-transformation test is not the sole test for what constitutes a patentable process; rather, it is a critical clue. But the Court is quite wrong, in my view, to suggest that any series of steps that is not itself an abstract idea or law of nature may constitute a "process" within the meaning of § 101. The language in the Court's opinion to this effect can only cause mischief. The wiser course would have been to hold that petitioners' method is not a "process" because it describes only a general method of engaging in business transactions — and business methods are not patentable. More precisely, although a process is not patent-ineligible simply because it is useful for conducting business, a claim that merely describes a method of doing business does not qualify as a "process" under § 101.

NOTES AND QUESTIONS

1. Justice Kennedy emphasizes that the world of the Internet is different than the world of brick-and-mortar, and suggests that more flexibility must be extended to the definition of patentable "processes" in this new environment. Justice Stevens is concerned that this will result in an unmanageable flood of patents on abstract ideas. Who is right?

C. Four Criteria

Establishing patentability is often framed in terms of satisfying three criteria: novelty, usefulness, and inventive step. However, enablement (i.e., disclosing means for producing the invention) is so fundamental to patentability that it should be considered a fourth basic criterion. The advance of science and technical skill during the past century, along with the proliferation of information, has made the application of the four criteria of patentability an enormously complex affair. This complexity is exacerbated by differences among national and regional patent laws, and the way in which they are applied by patent authorities (including patent offices and courts). There are political, social, economic, moral, and cultural dimensions to patents that transcend the domain of the patent law specialist.

Although the concept of invention is central to the law of patents, the U.K. House of Lords explains in *Biogen v. Medeva* that the determination of whether a product or process is patentable is nevertheless based on whether the applicant's claim(s) satisfies certain criteria.

In the United Kingdom, the House of Lords referred both to the upper chamber of the Parliament and to the highest judicial body of the land. Since October 1, 2009, jurisdiction of the House of Lords was transferred to the newly established Supreme Court, the highest appeal court of the United Kingdom.

BIOGEN, INC. v. MEDEVA PLC

House of Lords [1997] RPC 1 31 October 1996

Lord HOFFMANN: . . .

9. WHAT IS AN INVENTION?

The [U.K Patent Act] thus lays down various conditions, both positive . . . and negative . . . which an invention must satisfy in order to be a "patentable invention." This scheme might suggest that logically one should first decide whether the claimed invention can properly be described as an invention at all. Only if this question receives an affirmative answer would it be necessary to go on to consider whether the invention satisfies the prescribed conditions for being "patentable." In practice, however, I have no doubt that in most cases this would be a mistake and cause unnecessary difficulty.

The Act does not define the concept of an invention. Section 1(1) was intended to reflect, "as nearly as practicable," article 52 of the European Patent Convention ("EPC"): *see* section 130(7) of the 1977 Act. Article 52 also has no definition of an invention. It seems that the parties to the EPC were unable to agree upon one: . . . But the reason why the parties were content to do without a definition was that they recognised that the question would almost invariably be academic. The four conditions in section 1(1) do a great deal more than restrict the class of "inventions" which may be patented. They probably also contain every element of the concept of an invention in ordinary speech. I say probably, because in the absence of a definition one cannot say with certainty that one might not come across something which satisfied all the conditions but could not be described as an invention. But the draftsmen of the Convention and the Act, as well as counsel at the bar, were unable to think of any examples. Just in case one should appear, section 1(5) gives the Secretary of State power to vary the list of matters excluded by paragraph (d) "for the purpose of maintaining them in conformity with developments in science and technology."

As the four conditions are relatively familiar ground, elucidated by definitions in the Act and the jurisprudence of the courts and the EPO, it will normally be more convenient to start by deciding whether they are satisfied. In virtually every case this will be the end of the inquiry. There may one day be a case in which it is necessary to decide whether something which satisfies the conditions can be called an invention, but that question can wait until it arises.

One can of course imagine cases in which the alleged subject-matter is so obviously not an invention that it is tempting to take an axe to the problem by dismissing the claim without inquiring too closely into which of the conditions has not been satisfied. So in Genentech Inc's Patent [1989] RPC 147, 264, Mustill LJ said, by reference to the ordinary speech meaning of "invention":

> You cannot invent water, although you certainly can invent ways in which it may be distilled or synthesised.

This is obviously right and in such a case it may seem pedantic to say that water fails the condition in paragraph (a) of section 1(1) because it is not new. Unfortunately, most cases which come before the courts are more difficult. Judges would therefore be well advised to put on one side their intuitive sense of what constitutes an invention until they have considered the questions of novelty, inventiveness and so forth. In the present case, I think that Medeva's counsel was right to resist the invitation of the Court of Appeal to make submissions on whether the claims constituted an invention.

NOTES AND QUESTIONS

1. U.K. patent law accepts that the separate concept of "invention" is too broad to be analytically useful as the basis for assessing patentability. Yet, a number of countries expressly limit the subject matter of patentable "invention," even post-TRIPS Agreement. For example, in the European Patent Convention, at Article 52(2), "(c) schemes, rules and methods for performing mental acts, playing games or doing business, and programs for computers" are expressly excluded from the definition of "invention."[6] Decision 486 of the Andean Community, at Article 15, expressly excludes from the definition of "inventions": "(d) plans, rules, and methods for the pursuit of intellectual activities, playing of games, or economic and business activities; (e) computer programs and software, as such."[7] India, in Section 3 of the Patents Act, excludes business methods and computer software programs (as such) from the definition of "invention."[8] It is important therefore to distinguish Lord Hoffmann's proposition that "invention" is not useful as a separate analytic criteria of patentability from a suggestion that "invention" may not be used to define patentable subject matter.

2. As we review the criteria of patentability in the next pages, consider whether there is something you would consider an "invention" that would not be captured by these criteria.

---

6. For Article 52, see *infra* section III.

7. Andean Community, Decision 486—Common Provisions on Industrial Property (of September 14, 2000), available at WIPO Collection of Laws for Electronic Access (CLEA) database.

8. Section 3, as amended by the Patents (Amendments) Act, 2002, provides:

> The following are not inventions within the meaning of this Act, — (k) a mathematical or business method or a computer programme *per se* or algorithms.

1. Novelty

The first criterion and major qualification for a patent is that an invention be "new" or "novel." This means that the invention (product or process) has not been anticipated by prior art. In other words, the invention has not been disclosed or described before the date of the patent application filing. Although national patent rules differ regarding the form of disclosure that will be considered to anticipate an invention,[9] novelty will generally be defeated by an anticipating disclosure (in a covered form) anywhere in the world.[10] The patent applicant is usually obligated to identify prior art of which he or she is aware. One role of the patent examiner is to conduct a "prior art search" that attempts to identify relevant anticipating disclosure.

Naturally, there may be disagreement between an inventor and the patent examiner about whether a particular prior art disclosure in fact anticipates an invention. A prior inventor may have described a device similar, but not identical, to the subsequent inventor's device. The patent examiner must determine whether the second device is sufficiently different from the first device to be "new" or "novel" in the sense of not being encompassed by the prior art. Some inventions are considered "inherent" in the prior art, even if not specifically disclosed (*see, e.g., Abbott Labs. v. Baxter Pharms.*, 471 F.3d 1363 (Fed. Cir. 2006), rehearing *en banc* denied.

The European Patent Office (EPO) is established under the terms of the European Patent Convention (EPC) and issues patents with respect to more than 30 countries in Europe (not limited to EU countries).[11] A European Patent is granted with effect in EPC members that have been designated by an applicant, following an examination by the EPO. Once the patent is granted, it is governed by the law of the country in which it is practiced. In the EPC system, there is a post-grant opposition procedure that permits parties believing a patent should not have been granted to challenge the grant within a set time period. We examine the EPC/EPO arrangement in section III.A-B, *infra*, as well as the proposed Community Patent Regulation.

The following passage from a decision by the Technical Board of Appeal of the EPO in *Motorola v. Agence Spatiale Européenne* illustrates the issue of novelty. In this case, Motorola had been granted a patent by the EPO, but the patent was revoked by the Opposition Division. The opponent alleged that a document published before the initial filing (and priority date) of the patent application disclosed a means for controlling cellular telephone transmissions that included Motorola's claimed invention, at least insofar as Motorola's patent application described the invention. Motorola argued that the Opposition Division had not properly understood its claim. Motorola appealed the decision of the Opposition Division to the Technical Board, arguing that its claim was in fact new.

---

9. Some countries, for example, require that a disclosure be in writing to constitute prior art, while for others oral disclosure will suffice.

10. The patent laws of a few countries limit anticipating disclosure to those that occur within their territory. This rule is largely a remnant of the colonial era, and is generally being replaced.

11. As of November 2010, there are 38 EPO member states: Albania, Austria, Belgium, Bulgaria, Switzerland, Croatia, Cyprus, Czech Republic, Germany, Denmark, Estonia, Spain, Finland, France, United Kingdom, Greece, Hungary, Ireland, Iceland, Italy, Latvia, Liechtenstein, Lithuania, Luxembourg, Former Yugoslav Republic of Macedonia, Malta, Monaco, Netherlands, Norway, Poland, Portugal, Romania, San Marino, Serbia, Sweden, Slovenia, Slovakia, and Turkey. *See* http://www.epo.org/about-us/epo/member-states.html.

MOTOROLA, INC. v. AGENCE SPATIALE EUROPÉENNE, ALCATEL SPACE INDUSTRIES

Satellite cellular telephone and data communication system
T 0365/98
Technical Board of Appeal, Electricity I
April 28, 1999

OPINION:

Summary of Facts and Submissions

1. THIS IS AN APPEAL BY THE PROPRIETOR OF EUROPEAN PATENT NO. 0 365 885 AGAINST THE DECISION OF THE OPPOSITION DIVISION TO REVOKE THE PATENT. . . .

III. The Opposition Division decided on the proprietor's main request (the patent as granted) and two auxiliary requests. The main request and the first auxiliary request were refused for lack of novelty with respect to E3. . . .

IV. On 26 March 1999 the appellant [Motorola] filed four new requests. . . .

Reasons for the Decision

1. construction of the invention

1.1. The invention is a satellite cellular system. This system comprises satellites in low-earth orbit, i.e. at a height at which satellites are not geostationary but have a period of perhaps a few hours. The satellites are capable of switching telephone calls from users on earth. Since the satellites are constantly moving, a communication link set up between two users needs generally to be redefined during the call. This process, a kind of dynamic re-routing, is referred to as handing-off. The handing-off can be between different "cells"—corresponding to different antenna beams—of one and the same satellite, or between two satellites. In the first case one speaks of intra-satellite handing-off, in the second case of inter-satellite handing-off. According to claim 1 (of all requests) the inter-satellite handing-off is performed by a "first means for handing-off" and the intra-satellite handing-off by "second means for handing-off."

1.2. A crucial point throughout the opposition proceedings has been how the term "handing-off" in claim 1 should be understood, taking into account the way it is used in the description. Briefly stated, the appellant [Motorola] is of the opinion that the expression not merely implies that the physical switching is performed in the satellites, but that the complete control of the handing-off process is located there. In particular, the invention comprises no external control on earth or in a geostationary satellite. The respondents, on the other hand, argue that there is no basis for such a restricted interpretation since the whole specification is silent on what kind of handing-off control is used and where it might be situated. . . .

1.6. . . . [T]he Board [cannot] see that an overall consideration of the specification supports the appellant's understanding of the invention. It is true that there is no mention of any kind of switching control besides the satellites. It is also true that the appellant's interpretation is consistent with the teaching of the patent. This is however not conclusive. The fact that a controlling earth station is not described does not necessarily mean that there is none or could not be one — it may just as well be that the issue of handing-off control was never contemplated at the time the application was drafted. Nor is consistency sufficient — in fact, neither the appellant's nor the respondents' interpretations of the invention seem to contradict the patent specification in any way.

1.7. The Board thus finds that the invention as it has been disclosed concerns a satellite cellular system comprising satellites which are capable of establishing calls autonomously and which contain (some) means for intra-satellite and inter-satellite handing-off. The invention is however not limited . . . to a system in which the complete handing-off control is contained in the satellites.

2. THE APPELLANT'S MAIN REQUEST

The closest prior art document, and the only one considered in the decision of the Opposition Division, is E3. It deals in particular with a system called MSS (Multiple Satellite System). This system comprises satellites which are in low earth orbits and employ packet switching technology, which implies that the satellites contain switching means. As to handing-off, it is said on page 1671 that when "a cell passes over, the user's receiving/transmitting antenna would adjust to its new frequency and an on-board computer in the satellite, perhaps under the direction of a traffic routing (and billing) ground station, would ensure that communication is not interrupted." The Board is satisfied that the skilled person would regard this statement as an indication that means for intra-satellite handing-off are present in the satellites. It is further said on page 1674 that "satellite changeover is required" as satellites move. This is regarded as referring to inter-satellite handing-off. Since, trivially, handing-off is not possible without "handing-off means" (of some kind) within the satellites, such means are also disclosed in E3. It is not clearly disclosed that the complete control of handing-off could be performed by the satellites, but this becomes irrelevant with the Board's understanding of the invention according to the patent in suit.

The Board thus concludes, as did the Opposition Division, that the subject-matter of claim 1 is not new. . . .

ORDER

For these reasons it is decided that:
The appeal is dismissed.

NOTES AND QUESTIONS

1. In the text case, the Technical Board of Appeals has confirmed the revocation of Motorola's patent because the subject matter of the invention was disclosed prior to its application for the patent. Motorola was claiming that its invention was limited to a particular kind of "handing off" of signals within satellites, and Agence Spatiale was arguing that Motorola's patent claim was broader. The reason for these positions? If Agence Spatiale's broader construction was accepted, the invention had been disclosed earlier (and "anticipated").

2. One of the most controversial issues in respect to novelty concerns the availability of patent protection for "new uses" of existing products.[12] In terms of product patent subject matter, the inventor of a new use does not create a new manufacture or composition of matter. The invention has been disclosed and constitutes prior art in so far as the product "as such" is concerned. However, patent examiners and courts have been receptive to the argument that a new use for a known product may constitute an inventive process or method of use. While there is not unanimity among national jurisdictions on the patenting of new uses, the trend in decisions so far is largely to accept the novelty (and subject matter patentability) of new uses of known products.[13]

3. There are obvious practical difficulties associated with the patenting of new uses. Conceptually, the patent holder should not be able to prevent the manufacture, sale, or use of the compound outside the scope of the new use claim. In fact, the product for which a new use patent is granted may be patented by a third party and the new use patent holder may not make the product itself. But how does the new use patent holder address the situation in which a producer offers to sell its products for one purpose, yet buyers decide to use the product for the patented purpose? Should the patent holder be able to enjoin sales by the producer? Would not this extend patent protection beyond the scope of the claims? Should the way in which third-party producers advertise or promote their products matter?[14]

4. A critical aspect of the new use question involves so-called second medical indication or second medical use patents. A compound or material that is known to be effective in the treatment of one medical condition or disease is found to be effective in the treatment of another condition or disease. The patenting of second medical uses has been allowed in a number of jurisdictions under the heading of "method of use" ("the use of compound X for the treatment of disease Y") or "Swiss claim" ("the use of compound X for the manufacture of a treatment for disease Y"). Such patenting has been rejected in other jurisdictions; for example, Section 3(d) of the India Patents Act (as amended 2005) provides:

> 3. What are not inventions
> The following are not inventions within the meaning of this Act, —
> (d) the mere discovery of a new form of a known substance which does not result in the enhancement of the known efficacy of that substance or *the mere discovery of any new property or new use for a known substance* or of the mere use of

---

12. The issue of "new use" might also be considered a question of patentable "subject matter" since it concerns whether a particular type of invention is patentable, or a question of inventive step since a new use may be obvious in light of prior art. *See* discussion of analytic possibilities in CHISUM ON PATENTS, § 1.03[8] (2002).

13. *See, e.g.,* U.S cases collected, *id.,* at § 1.03[8][c]. The "new use" of a known compound is considered by the Canadian Supreme Court in *Apotek v. Wellcome Foundation,* excerpted in the section on "Utility." In that case, the court assumed that a new use for an existing compound was patentable. The question was the point at which the patent applicant had in fact invented the new use.

14. *See, e.g., Warner-Lambert v. Apotexcorp.,* 316 F. 3d 1348 (Fed. Cir. 2003), in which the holder of a method of use patent for a pharmaceutical compound asserted patent infringement based on a generic manufacturer's alleged inducement to doctors to prescribe for treatment of a medical condition outside the scope of the method of use claims. The U.S. Court of Appeals rejected the infringement claim for lack of proof of "specific intent" and "action to induce infringement."

a known process, machine or apparatus unless such known process results in a
new product or employs at least one new reactant.
Explanation. — For the purposes of this clause, salts, esters, ethers, poly-
morphs, metabolites, pure form, particle size, isomers, mixtures of isomers,
complexes, combinations and other derivatives of known substance shall be
considered to be the same substance, unless they differ significantly in properties with regard to efficacy; . . . [italics added].

We examine a decision of the Indian High Court of Madras addressing the
constitutionality of Section 3(d) later in this chapter.

5. If the premise of patentability of second medical indications is accepted (as
    in the United States and at the EPO), an issue arises regarding what con-
    stitutes a new use. In *Perricone v. Medicis Pharmaceutical*, 432 F.3d 1368 (Fed.
    Cir. 2005), the CAFC permitted an inventor to claim a method of using the
    same pharmaceutical product for preventing sunburn as distinct from a
    claim for treating sunburn (432 F.3d at 1378-79).

6. The granting of second medical use patents on pharmaceutical products
    has important social and economic implications. On one hand, the disco-
    verers of second medical uses argue that the expense of obtaining regula-
    tory approval for new uses necessitates patent protection be granted to
    permit them to recover such expenses (e.g., in conducting clinical trials);
    otherwise, newly discovered uses would not make it to the market of doctors
    and patients. On the other hand, patents for new uses may be used as means
    to prevent the emergence of competition in the pharmaceutical market
    (and the lowering of prices) as patent holders place costly and time-
    consuming legal obstacles in the way of generic producers.[15]

    Pfizer's Viagra (sildenafil citrate) has been one of the most profitable
    medicines patented over the past decade. Pfizer's original patent for the
    compound disclosed its use in the treatment of cardiovascular disease. The
    property of treating erectile dysfunction was discovered as a "side effect" of
    cardiovascular treatment.[16] Pfizer did not discover a compound. It discov-
    ered that a known compound (on which it already held a product patent)
    possessed certain beneficial properties. Is this an "invention"?[17] An inter-
    esting discussion of the treatment of the Viagra patent in China can be
    found in Note, *Patent Law for New Medical Uses of Known Compounds and
    Pfizer's Viagra Patent*, 46 IDEA 283 (2006).

7. Viagra is sometimes referred to as a "lifestyle drug" since it does not involve
    a "life or death" medical condition. But the "new use" issue extends to many
    other compounds, including for the treatment of HIV-AIDS. Consider, for
    example, the discovery that combining certain known antiretroviral med-
    icines into a triple combination therapy "cocktail" dramatically improves

15. *See Warner-Lambert, id.* The U.S. Federal Trade Commission has expressed concern about
the ways that a range of patenting techniques are used to block generic competition (*see* FTC,
Generic Drug Entry Prior to Patent Expiration: An FTC Study, July 2002).
    16. *See Lilly Icos v. Pfizer*, 2002 WL 45115 (CA) (2002) 25(4) I.P.D. 25, 022, [2002] EWCA Civ 1,
23 Jan. 2002. Judgment by Lord Justice Aldous, at para. 59.
    17. As it happens, Pfizer's second use patent for treatment of erectile dysfunction was invali-
dated in the United Kingdom on the basis of obviousness in light of prior art. That prior art
included the suggestion published prior to submission of the patent application that the class of
compounds of which sildenafil citrate is a part may be effective in the treatment of erectile dysfunction. *Id.*, at, e.g., para. 44.

the effectiveness of treatment. Should the person who discovered that combining antiretroviral medicines results in more effective treatment of HIV-AIDS receive a patent on triple combination therapy?

2.   Inventive Step

Inventive step or nonobviousness might be said to refer to the conceptual distance between prior art and invention. One way that legislators and courts have approached this criterion is to ask whether a claimed invention would have been obvious to a person reasonably skilled in the art practiced by the invention. However, this is not the only method by which inventive step might reasonably be assessed. For example, in certain fields it may be possible to limit inventive step by excluding certain classes of "easy" manipulations of subject matter.

To illustrate the criterion, imagine that someone has been granted a patent on the clip that is used to keep ballpoint pens fastened to shirt pockets. Suppose that the patent application described a clip with a pointed tip, and that such clips as described in the application were soon found to tear holes in shirt pockets. A second person submits a patent application describing the same clip, but with a rounded end. The rounded end prevents shirt pockets from tearing. Such an invention may be new and useful, but it is probably too obvious to qualify for a patent (it lacks an inventive step).

The objective of the patent system is to reward invention. The patent grant allows its holder to exclude others from a range of activity with respect to the invention for a period of time. Because grants of exclusive rights in technology impose burdens on society, there is a need to limit such grants. The criterion of inventive step is intended to limit the grant of exclusive rights to those that have made a significant contribution to the development of new and useful technologies.

In *Biogen v. Medeva*, the U.K. House of Lords discussed the concept of inventive step in the complex environment of recombinant DNA research. What happens when many scientists share a general idea, but only one of them pursues concrete realization of that idea in the face of widely feared obstacles? Are the actions of the more-determined scientist "inventive," or merely industrious?

BIOGEN, INC. v. MEDEVA PLC

House of Lords
[1997] RPC 1
31 October 1996

Lord HOFFMANN: . . .

10. INVENTIVE STEP

I will therefore first consider the question of whether what Professor Murray did in 1978 involved, as at the date of Biogen 1, an inventive step. Section 3 says:

> An invention shall be taken to involve an inventive step if it is not obvious to a person skilled in the art, having regard to any matter which forms part of the state of the art by virtue only of section 2(2) above. . . .

Section 2(2) defines the state of the art:

> The state of the art in the case of an invention shall be taken to comprise all matter (whether a product, a process, information about either or anything else) which has at any time before the priority date of that invention been made available to the public (whether in the United Kingdom or elsewhere) by written or oral description, by use or in any other way.

The question is therefore whether what Professor Murray did was obvious having regard to all matter which had been made available to the public before 22 December 1978. Aldous J, after hearing expert evidence about what people skilled in the art of recombinant DNA technology would have thought and done at the time, held that it was not. I will summarise his reasoning. He followed the procedure suggested by Oliver LJ in *Windsurfing International Inc v Tabur Marine* (Great Britain) Ltd [1985] RPC 59, 73-74 by dividing the inquiry into four steps:

> The first is to identify the inventive concept embodied in the patent in suit. Thereafter, the court has to assume the mantle of the normally skilled but unimaginative addressee in the art at the priority date and impute to him what was, at that date, common general knowledge in the art in question. The third step is to identify what, if any, differences exist between the matter cited as being "known or used" and the alleged invention. Finally, the court has to ask itself whether, viewed without any knowledge of the alleged invention, those differences constitute steps which would have been obvious to the skilled man or whether they require any degree of invention.

Aldous J identified the inventive concept as "the idea or decision to express a polypeptide displaying HBV antigen specificity in a suitable host." The identification of the inventive concept is, as I have said, critical to this case and I shall have more to say about it later. At this stage I only observe that as formulated by Aldous J, the inventive concept means, in effect, having the idea of making HBV antigens by recombinant DNA technology.[18] But that seems to me to be putting the matter far too wide. The idea of making HBV antigens by recombinant DNA technology was shared by everyone at the Geneva meeting of Biogen in February 1978 and no doubt by others working in the field, just as the idea of flying in an heavier-than-air machine had existed for centuries before the Wright brothers. The problem which required invention was to find a way of doing it.

Aldous J then considered what would have been known to the man skilled in the art. I have already summarised what relevant information would have been available to the public in 1978. In particular, Aldous J considered the importance of the Villa-Komaroff paper and said:

> "It is accepted that once a decision [had] been made to try expression of the HBV genome, the technique set out in Villa-Komaroff would have been sufficient to enable it to be carried out. Thus the difference between the prior art and the

---

18. [WILSON & GISVOLD'S TEXTBOOK OF ORGANIC MEDICINAL AND PHARMACEUTICAL CHEMISTRY (J. Delgado & W. Remers eds., 10th ed. 1998) says: "An antigen (Ag) is a substance that induces antibody formation, and then reacts with that antibody. Inherent in the definition is a chemical reaction." (at p. 154). Antigens are used in vaccines. *Id.*, at 164-65. — EDS.]

inventive concept is the idea or decision to express a polypeptide displaying HBV antigen specificity in a suitable host." ([1995] RPC 25, 58.)

Again, I think that this is not a sufficiently specific way of stating the inventive concept. The general idea of expressing the gene for a polypeptide[19] displaying HBV antigen specificity in a suitable host was, as I have said, fairly widely entertained. The inventive concept was the notion that Professor Murray's method of achieving the goal—creating large fragments of genomic DNA, ligating them to pBR322 and introducing the hybrid molecule into E coli—would work.

Aldous J then considered what strategies would have been available in 1978 to a skilled man who wanted to achieve the goal of making HBV antigens by recombinant DNA technology. One (strategy A) was to try to find out more about HBV and its DNA. In particular, one would sequence the genome. This would provide the information upon which a decision could be made as to whether and if so how to express the relevant genes. The alternative (strategy B) was, as Professor Murray had done, to take the genomic DNA and try to express it in E coli. Biogen's case, as recorded by the judge, was that—"it was not until the sequence had been obtained, with the knowledge that introns would not be a problem, that the skilled man would seriously consider expression of HBV antigens." ([1995] RPC 25, 64.)

The judge accepted this submission and held that strategy B would not have been obvious in 1978. He said:

"In the present case, there is no evidence to suggest that anyone, other than Biogen, contemplated expression of the HBV antigen in December 1978, despite the fact that the skilled man must have read the Villa-Komaroff paper and there was an incentive to do so. The reason may well be that stated in the patent, namely the skilled man was put off by introns." ([1995] RPC 25, 65.)

He also rejected the argument that strategy A was an obvious way of making the antigens. The evidence showed only that sequencing might show that there were no introns[20] and that the gene could be expressed in bacteria but there was no ground for assuming that it would.

In the Court of Appeal, Hobhouse LJ held that strategy B was obvious. The decision to adopt it was a "matter of business judgment," a "mere commercial decision." Biogen had made a decision "to pursue an identified goal by known means." I think, with all respect to the closely-reasoned judgment of Hobhouse LJ, that the reference to a commercial decision is an irrelevancy. The fact that a given experimental strategy was adopted for commercial reasons, because the anticipated rewards seemed to justify the necessary expenditure, is no reason why that strategy should not involve an inventive step. An inventor need not pursue his experiment untouched by thoughts of gain. Most patents are the result of research programmes undertaken on the basis of hard-headed cost-benefit analysis. Nor do I think that the analogy of a bet is particularly helpful.

---

19. [REMINGTON, THE SCIENCE AND PRACTICE OF PHARMACY (20th ed. 2000), states: "Peptides are very small hydrolytic fragments of their original proteins. They contain from 2 to possibly 20 or so amino acids and commonly are subdivided into di-, tri-, etc., peptides according to the number of amino acid residues they contain. Collectively, the higher members are often termed *polypeptides*" (at p. 419).—EDS.]

20. ["Introns" are portions of DNA sequence that are presently thought not to code for proteins. *See, e.g.,* Wilson & Gisvold, *supra* note 18, and SULSTON & FERRY, THE COMMON THREAD (2002).—EDS.]

In Genentech Inc's Patent [1989] RPC 147, 281, Mustill LJ said, in my opinion rightly, that "it cannot . . . be assumed that inventiveness must have been involved somewhere, just because a wager on success could have been placed at long odds." The question is not what the odds were but whether there was an inventive step.

Having said this, I do think that Hobhouse LJ was substantially correct in saying that Professor Murray had chosen to pursue an identified goal by known means. The goal of obtaining HBV antigens by recombinant DNA technology was obvious and the Villa-Komaroff method was by then part of the state of the art. If, therefore, the inventive concept was simply, as Aldous J said, "the idea or decision to express a polypeptide displaying HBV antigen specificity in a suitable host," I would agree with Hobhouse LJ that, so stated, the concept was obvious. It is however clear from the reasoning of Aldous J that in order to explain why he regarded the decision as involving an inventive step it is necessary to describe it with rather more particularity. A proper statement of the inventive concept needs to include some express or implied reference to the problem which it required invention to overcome. The reasons why the expert witnesses thought it was not obvious to try the expression of genomic HBV DNA in E coli were for the most part concerned with the uncertainties, in the absence of sequence information, about the presence of the HBV antigen genes in the Dane particle DNA, the perceived difficulties of expressing genomic eukaryotic DNA in a prokaryotic host, and, specifically, the problem of introns. It seems to me, therefore, that a more accurate way of stating the inventive concept as it appeared to Aldous J is to say that it was the idea of trying to express unsequenced eukaryotic DNA in a prokaryotic host.

The question of whether an invention was obvious had been called "a kind of jury question" (*see* Jenkins LJ in *Allmanna Svenska Elektriska A/B v The Burntisland Shipbuilding Co Ltd* (1952) 69 RPC 63, 70) and should be treated with appropriate respect by an appellate court. . . . Where the application of a legal standard such as negligence or obviousness involves no question of principle but is simply a matter of degree, an appellate court should be very cautious in differing from the judge's evaluation.

In the present case I think that the reason why Hobhouse LJ differed from the judge on the question of obviousness was not because of any failure to give sufficient weight to the judge's evaluation of the evidence but because he took at face value the judge's statement of the inventive concept. On the other hand, if the concept is reformulated in accordance with the judge's reasoning as I have suggested, the argument for the existence of an inventive step is much stronger. If no question of principle were involved, I think it would be wrong to interfere with the judge's assessment. But the inventiveness alleged in this case is of a very unusual kind. It is said to consist in attempting something which a man less skilled in the art might have regarded as obvious, but which the expert would have thought so beset by obstacles as not to be worth trying. In *Raleigh Cycle Co Ltd v H Miller & Co Ltd* (1946) 63 RPC 113 the Court of Appeal was prepared to assume that it could be inventive to realise that a bicycle hub dynamo of conventional design could function satisfactorily even though it rotated at a lower speed than was previously thought essential. There may be a question of principle here but, like the Court of Appeal in that case, I shall not pursue the question of whether this amounts to an inventive step for the purposes of patent law because I am content to assume, without deciding, that what Professor Murray did was not obvious.

NOTES AND QUESTIONS

1. The patent system is often justified as a stimulus to inventive activity through enhanced financial reward (or potential reward). If an invention is achieved by a commercial decision to invest capital in pursuit of a widely identified goal, can the patent grant be said to have stimulated inventive activity? Has it instead stimulated the investment of capital? Is there a difference?

2. In *KSR v. Teleflex*, 550 U.S. 398 (2007), the U.S. Supreme Court addressed the test to be used in assessing the patent criteria of "nonobviousness" (referred to in most countries as the "inventive step" requirement). There is a long history of Supreme Court jurisprudence emphasizing the importance of granting patents only for genuinely creative inventions (those that would not be "obvious" to a person reasonably skilled in the art).

    In U.S. law, a patent examiner in making determinations regarding "novelty" may find that an invention has been "anticipated" only if the invention is disclosed in a single piece of prior art. In making a determination regarding nonobviousness, an examiner has more latitude because a number of prior art references may be combined to establish that a person reasonably skilled in the art would have considered the technical step as obvious. The Federal Circuit developed a "teaching, suggestion or motivation" (or "TSM") test for evaluating whether a combination of "prior art" represents a bar to a finding of nonobviousness. In the TSM test, the Federal Circuit said that at least one piece of combined prior art must have given some instruction to the reasonably skilled person that would direct him or her to combine the prior art. Unless such a teaching, suggestion, or motivation was demonstrated, the reasonably skilled person would presumably not have thought to put together the prior art. This was a highly limiting requirement for disqualifying an invention on the basis of obviousness. It is often difficult to find an express teaching, suggestion, or motivation.

    KSR v. Teleflex involved combining prior art in the development of a digitally controlled truck accelerator pedal. The Supreme Court rejected the Federal Circuit's view that an explicit teaching, suggestion, or motivation to combine prior art must be demonstrated for a finding of obviousness. The Supreme Court said that a person reasonably skilled in the art should be assumed to be familiar with the general state of development in his or her field of technology, and should be understood to be capable of adapting technologies that are generally known, even if a specific suggestion to combine them is not found. Among the questions that the patent examiner may consider are whether it was "obvious to try" a combination of prior art (a question that the Federal Circuit said was not relevant). The Supreme Court therefore broadened in a very substantial way the factors that patent examiners may consider when assessing whether a claimed invention is obvious. This decision effectively makes it more difficult to secure a patent in the United States because it extends the grounds upon which patent examiners may reject applications.

3. It is sometimes suggested that patents should be granted only for "major" or "important" inventions since a proliferation of "minor" improvement patents does more to inhibit productivity and competition than to stimulate creative activity. The inventive step criterion in a limited way serves to

distinguish between major and minor inventions. Development and application of a "major-minor" test for patentability presents some conceptual and practical issues, including how it might be applied across a broad spectrum of inventive subject matter and how to take into account uncertainty about the future value of inventions. Might a more rigorous application of the inventive step criterion be a useful way to address the problem of a proliferation of weak patents? *See* U.S. Federal Trade Commission, To Promote Innovation: The Proper Balance of Competition and Patent Law and Policy, ch. 3 (2003).

4. As suggested in the introduction to this inventive step criterion, alternatives to the case-by-case "person reasonably skilled in the art" approach may be feasible in some fields. For example, certain kinds of modifications to molecular structure may be sufficiently commonplace to warrant exclusion — or a least a strong presumption of exclusion — from inventiveness. This kind of approach has been suggested as a means to limit pharmaceutical patents for minor changes in chemical structure that may yield some patient benefit, but may not justify a new 20-year patent.

3.   Utility

The third criterion for patenting is that an invention be "useful" or "capable of industrial application." Until fairly recently, it seemed that the requirement of utility was not terribly important to the patenting process since very few otherwise patentable inventions failed to meet this criterion. Some commercial use, it seemed, could be found for most anything. However, developments in the fields of biotechnology and chemistry have made it possible for researchers to develop new materials, molecules, and compounds with relative ease, yet without, at least initially, any good idea whether these might be useful. The question then arises to what extent patents should be granted on these "speculative" inventions, since a proliferation of patent grants might impede research by other persons. The criterion of utility has thus reemerged as a critical one in the evaluation of claims for inventions.

In *Apotek v. Wellcome Foundation*, the Supreme Court of Canada considered the point at which a concept turns from mere speculation to utility. If a scientist speculates that a certain substance might be useful in the treatment of a particular disease, does that speculation establish the usefulness of the substance? What objective evidence of effect, or at least potential effect, in the treatment of disease is needed to cross the utility barrier?

APOTEX, INC. v. WELLCOME FOUNDATION LTD.

Supreme Court of Canada
2002 SCC 77 File No.: 28287
2002: February 14, 2002: December 5

Binnie J. —

35. AZT has earned for the respondents hundreds of millions of dollars in worldwide sales since its usefulness was discovered for the treatment of HIV and AIDS. In the United States alone, it is estimated that AZT earned for the patent

owner a profit of $592 million between 1987 and 1993: J. Yardley, "Industry Giant Owns Right to AIDS Drug? N.C. Trial to Decide," *Atlanta Constitution*, June 27, 1993 at p. 14, quoted in "Case Comment: *Burroughs Wellcome Co. v. Barr Laboratories, Inc.*" (1995), 108 *Harv. L. Rev.* 2053, at note 17.

36. It is not surprising that the appellants, being generic drug manufacturers, would like to obtain at least a percentage of the AZT market in Canada. To do so they must somehow have the patent declared invalid. Yet their challenge, understandably motivated by the hope of private profit, raises broader issues of public interest.

37. A patent, as has been said many times, is not intended as an accolade or civic award for ingenuity. It is a method by which inventive solutions to practical problems are coaxed into the public domain by the promise of a limited monopoly for a limited time. Disclosure is the *quid pro quo* for valuable proprietary rights to exclusivity which are entirely the statutory creature of the *Patent Act*. Monopolies are associated in the public mind with higher prices. The public should not be expected to pay an elevated price in exchange for speculation, or for the statement of "any mere scientific principle or abstract theorem" (s. 27(3)), or for the "discovery" of things that already exist, or are obvious. The patent monopoly should be purchased with the hard coinage of new, ingenious, useful and unobvious disclosures. The appellants' argument here is that the identification in March of 1985 of AZT as a treatment and prophylaxis for HIV/AIDS was a shot in the dark, a speculation based on inadequate information and testing, a lottery ticket for which the public in general and HIV and AIDS sufferers in particular have paid an exorbitant price. AZT works, but for reasons both unknown and unknowable by Glaxo/Wellcome at the time it filed its patent application, the appellants argue. A lucky guess is not, they say, patentable.

38. Furthermore, if credit is to be given, the appellants argue, it should go to Drs. Broder and Mitsuya at the NIH who actually established the utility of AZT in human T-cells. If the patent on AZT was owned by the NIH or even by a co-ownership of Glaxo/Wellcome and the NIH, they say, the commercial history of AZT would have been vastly more oriented to the public interest.

39. The public interest arguments were not advanced in the U.S. just by advocates of rights for AIDS patients. The NIH itself in 1991 granted a non-exclusive licence to Barr Laboratories "to exploit any patent rights" the NIH "might have" in Glaxo/Wellcome's AZT patents. *See* Case Comment, *supra*, at p. 2054. *See also* "Agency Wants to End AIDS Drug Monopoly," *The New York Times*, May 29, 1991, p. A24. However, the U.S. patent owner successfully defeated this challenge in *Burroughs Wellcome v. Barr Laboratories*, *supra*, and *see* Case Comment, *supra*.

40. Under United States law, the Court of Appeals for the Federal Circuit said, it was irrelevant that Glaxo/Wellcome had no evidence of AZT's effectiveness against the HIV/AIDS virus in humans and no reasonable basis for believing that the invention would work (*Burroughs Wellcome Co. v. Barr Laboratories Inc.*, *supra*, at p. 1921) until it subsequently received the NIH results. It was sufficient that on February 6, 1985, Glaxo/Wellcome scientists had a concept that was "definite and permanent" which could be applied by a person skilled in the art "without extensive research or experimentation" (p. 1919). In order for there to be an invention in the United States, U.S. law requires "reduction to practice." "Constructive reduction to practice" may occur when a patent application is filed in which an untested invention is adequately disclosed: *Travis v.*

Baker, 137 F.2d 109, at p. 111. This seems to have some affinity with our doctrine of "sound prediction" discussed below. However, given the differences in our respective patent laws, the outcome of the U.S. litigation on this patent is of limited interest here. . . .

51. The *Patent Act* defines an "invention" as, amongst other criteria, "new and useful" (s. 2). If it is not useful, it is not an invention within the meaning of the Act.

52. It is important to reiterate that the only contribution made by Glaxo/Wellcome in the case of AZT was to identify a new use. The compound itself was not novel. Its chemical composition had been described 20 years earlier by Dr. Jerome Horwitz. Glaxo/Wellcome claimed a hitherto unrecognized utility but if it had not established such utility by tests or sound prediction at the time it applied for its patent, then it was offering nothing to the public but wishful thinking in exchange for locking up potentially valuable research turf for (then) 17 years. As Jackett C.J. observed in *Procter & Gamble Co. v. Bristol-Myers Canada Ltd.* (1979), 42 C.P.R. (2d) 33 (F.C.A.), at p. 39:

> By definition an "invention" includes a "new and useful process." A "new" process is not an invention unless it is "useful" in some practical sense. Knowing a new process without knowing its utility is not in my view knowledge of an "invention."

53. Glaxo-Wellcome says the invention was complete when the draft patent application was circulated internally on February 6, 1985. Its argument here, as in the United States, was that the written description identified the drug and its new use sufficiently to give the invention "definite and practical shape." It taught persons skilled in the art how the invention could be practised. This, however, misses the point. The question on February 6, 1985 was not whether or how the invention could be practised. The question was whether AZT did the job against HIV that was claimed; in other words, whether on February 6, 1985, there was *any* invention at all within the meaning of s. 2 of the *Patent Act*.

54. Canadian case law dealing with inventorship has to be read keeping the particular factual context in mind. In *Christiani v. Rice*, [1930] S.C.R. 443, this Court held, *per* Rinfret J. (as he then was), at p. 454:

> . . . for the purpose of section 7 [now s. 27] "it is not enough for a man to say that an idea floated through his brain; *he must at least have reduced it to a definite and practical shape* before he can be said to have invented a process." [Emphasis added.] . . .

55. In the present case, by contrast, if the utility of AZT for the treatment of HIV/AIDS was unpredictable at the time of the patent application, then the inventors had not made an invention and had offered nothing to the public in exchange for a 17-year monopoly except wishful thinking.

56. Where the new use is the *gravamen* of the invention, the utility required for patentability (s. 2) must, as of the priority date, either be demonstrated or be a sound prediction based on the information and expertise then available. If a patent sought to be supported on the basis of sound prediction is subsequently challenged, the challenge will succeed if, *per* Pigeon J. in *Monsanto Co. v. Commissioner of Patents*, [1979] 2 S.C.R. 1108, at p. 1117, the prediction at the date of application was not sound, or, irrespective of the soundness of the prediction, "[t]here is evidence of lack of utility in respect of some of the area covered." . . .

66. The doctrine of "sound prediction" balances the public interest in early disclosure of new and useful inventions, even before their utility has been verified by tests (which in the case of pharmaceutical products may take years) and the public interest in avoiding cluttering the public domain with useless patents, and granting monopoly rights in exchange for misinformation. . . .

70. The doctrine of sound prediction has three components. Firstly, as here, there must be a factual basis for the prediction. In *Monsanto* and *Burton Parsons*, the factual basis was supplied by the tested compounds, but other factual underpinnings, depending on the nature of the invention, may suffice. Secondly, the inventor must have at the date of the patent application an articulable and "sound" line of reasoning from which the desired result can be inferred from the factual basis. In *Monsanto* and *Burton Parsons*, the line of reasoning was grounded in the known "architecture of chemical compounds" (*Monsanto*, at p. 1119), but other lines of reasoning, again depending on the subject matter, may be legitimate. Thirdly, there must be proper disclosure. Normally, it is sufficient if the specification provides a full, clear and exact description of the nature of the invention and the manner in which it can be practised: H. G. Fox, *The Canadian Law and Practice Relating to Letters Patent for Inventions* (4th ed. 1969), at p. 167. It is generally not necessary for an inventor to provide a theory of *why* the invention works. Practical readers merely want to know that it does work and how to work it. In this sort of case, however, the sound prediction is to some extent the *quid pro quo* the applicant offers in exchange for the patent monopoly. Precise disclosure requirements in this regard do not arise for decision in this case because both the underlying facts (the test data) and the line of reasoning (the chain terminator effect) were in fact disclosed, and disclosure in this respect did not become an issue between the parties. I therefore say no more about it.

71. It bears repetition that the soundness (or otherwise) of the prediction is a question of fact. Evidence must be led about what was known or not known at the priority date, as was done here. Each case will turn on the particularities of the discipline to which it relates. In this case, the findings of fact necessary for the application of "sound prediction" were made and the appellants have not, in my view, demonstrated any overriding or palpable error.

72. On March 1, 1985, Glaxo/Wellcome received from the NIH the key results of the *in vitro* test of AZT against the HIV in a human cell line. This, taken together with Glaxo/Wellcome's own data on AZT, including the mouse tests, provided a factual foundation. Glaxo/Wellcome's knowledge of the mechanism by which a retrovirus reproduces, and the "chain terminator effect" of AZT, as disclosed in the patent, was found by the trial judge to provide a line of reasoning by which utility could be established as of the date of the U.K. patent application, March 16, 1985, which is also the priority date by which the invention must be evaluated for purposes of the Canadian patent. Although "sound prediction" was not the precise approach followed by the trial judge, his reasoning as well as his ultimate ruling is entirely consistent with its application. . . .

76. Not all predictions, even sound ones, turn out to be correct. If the Glaxo/Wellcome prediction had subsequently been shown to be wrong, the patent would have been invalidated for want of utility. But, as Pigeon J. remarked in *Monsanto*, *supra*, at p. 1116, commenting on *Société des usines chimiques Rhône-Poulenc v. Jules R. Gilbert Ltd.*, [1968] S.C.R. 950, "while the substances without utility had not been tested, the true cause of the invalidity was the fact

that they were without utility, not that they had not been tested before the patent was applied for."

77. The appellants take issue with the trial judge's conclusion. In their factum (though not in oral argument), they argue that utility must be demonstrated by prior human clinical trials establishing toxicity, metabolic features, bioavailability and other factors. These factors track the requirements of the Minister of Health when dealing with a new drug submission to assess its "safety" and "effectiveness." *See now*: *Food and Drug Regulations*, C.R.C., c. 870, s. C.08.002.(2) as amended by SOR/95-411, s. 4, which provides in part:

> A new drug submission shall contain sufficient information and material to enable the Minister to assess the safety and effectiveness of the new drug. . . .

The prerequisites of proof for a manufacturer who wishes to market a new drug are directed to a different purpose than patent law. The former deals with safety and effectiveness. The latter looks at utility, but in the context of inventiveness. The doctrine of sound prediction, in its nature, presupposes that further work remains to be done.

78. Glaxo/Wellcome contends that because AZT turned out to have both treatment and (limited) prophylactic properties, its prediction must necessarily have been sound, and the patent upheld on that basis. This argument presupposes that the critical date to establish utility is the state of knowledge when the patent is attacked, even though the attack may come years after its issuance, rather than as of the date the patent application is filed. The patent in this case was applied for in 1986, and issued in 1988. The trial did not occur until 1997, almost a decade after the grant of the AZT patent in Canada.

79. The "after-the-fact" validation theory was accepted by the Federal Court of Appeal, at para. 51:

> In other words, so long as an inventor can demonstrate utility or a sound prediction at the time a patent is attacked, the patent will not fail for lack of utility. The time at which usefulness is to be established is when required by the Commissioner of Patents or in court proceedings when the validity of the patent is challenged on that ground.

80. In my view, with respect, Glaxo/Wellcome's proposition is consistent neither with the Act (which does not postpone the requirement of utility to the vagaries of when such proof might actually be demanded) nor with patent policy (which does not encourage the stockpiling of useless or misleading patent disclosures). Were the law to be otherwise, major pharmaceutical corporations could (subject to cost considerations) patent whole stables of chemical compounds for all sorts of desirable but unrealized purposes in a shot-gun approach hoping that, as in a lottery, a certain percentage of compounds will serendipitously turn out to be useful for the purposes claimed. Such a patent system would reward deep pockets and the ingenuity of patent agents rather than the ingenuity of true inventors.

81. The Federal Court of Appeal was concerned that patents based on "instinct and intuition (and) gut reaction" might be invalidated in a case where the ignorance that passed at the time for "sound prediction" turned out to be wrong and the inventor eventually vindicated. An example was given of a hypothetical patent on the Wright brothers' airplane. Perhaps all

the "experts" thought it would not fly, but it did. Would it not be illogical, it was asked, to invalidate a hypothetical patent on a heavier-than-air flying machine because scientific opinion in the pre-flight era was wrong?

82. The hypothetical Wright brothers patent relates to a new and useful product, rather than (as here) to a new *use* for an old product, but all the same it illustrates, I think, the flaw in the Glaxo/Wellcome argument. The mere idea of a "heavier-than-air flying machine" is no more patentable than would be "*anything* that grows hair on bald men" (emphasis in original): *Free World Trust v. Electro Santé Inc.*, [2000] 2 S.C.R. 1024, 2000 SCC 66, at para. 32. The patent (even in this improbable scenario) would have to teach precisely *how* the machine could be made to fly. Section 34(1)(*b*) requires the applicant to set out in the specification "the method of constructing, making . . . or using a machine . . . in such full, clear, concise and exact terms as to enable any person skilled in the art . . . to make, construct . . . or use it." This means the Wright brothers' hypothetical patent would have to describe, amongst other things, how to design an air foil that creates "lift" by reducing the air pressure on the upper surface of the wing as the air rushes over it, as well as a suitable airborne method of forward locomotion. If the essentials of the heavier-than-air flying machine were set out with sufficient precision to allow the reader actually to make a flying machine that flies, it is hard to accept the "hypothetical" that experts would continue to insist, after it had flown, that the prediction was unsound. (Of course, if the prediction turned out to be wrong, the patent would be struck down for inutility. Leonardo da Vinci's elegant drawings showed exactly how to make a "bird man" machine but it never could, would or did sustain a person in flight.)

83. On the other hand, if the patent failed to disclose the essentials of a heavier-than-air flying machine, such that no one could "soundly predict" whether or not the ill-defined thing could get off the ground, then the patent would be rightly invalidated, even though the inventors had eventually flown some sort of machine in the meantime. It goes back to the same point. The public is entitled to accurate and meaningful teaching in exchange for suffering the patent monopoly. The patent claims must be supported by the disclosure. Speculation, even if it afterwards proves justified, does not provide valid consideration. As Lord Mustill pointed out in *Genetech Inc.'s Patent*, [1989] R.P.C. 147 (Eng. C.A.), at p. 275:

> Many years ago, an inventor could not have patented a heavier-than-air flying machine simply by writing down the concept, but equally the fact that the concept was capable of being written down in advance could not, in itself, exclude the rights of a person who had actually made one fly.

NOTES AND QUESTIONS

1.   The Canadian Supreme Court refers to an earlier decision on the same subject matter by the U.S. Court of Appeals for the Federal Circuit in *Burroughs Wellcome v. Barr Laboratories*, 40 F.3d 1223 (Fed. Cir. 1994), 32 U.S.P.Q. (2d) 1915 (1994). According to the Canadian Court, the CAFC said "it was irrelevant that Glaxo/Wellcome had no evidence of AZT's effectiveness against the HIV/AIDS virus in humans and no reasonable basis for believing that the invention would work . . . until it subsequently received

the NIH results. It was sufficient that on February 6, 1985, Glaxo/Wellcome scientists had a concept that was 'definite and permanent' which could be applied by a person skilled in the art 'without extensive research or experimentation' (p. 1919)."

The U.S. CAFC said in *Barr Laboratories*:

"Conception is the touchstone of inventorship, the completion of the mental part of invention. *Sewall v. Walters*, 21 F.3d 411, 415, 30 U.S.P.Q.2d (BNA) 1356, 1359 (Fed. Cir. 1994). It is 'the formation in the mind of the inventor, of a definite and permanent idea of the complete and operative invention, as it is hereafter to be applied in practice.' *Hybritech Inc. v. Monoclonal Antibodies, Inc.*, 802 F.2d 1367, 1376, 231 U.S.P.Q. (BNA) 81, 87 (Fed. Cir. 1986) (citation omitted). Conception is complete only when the idea is so clearly defined in the inventor's mind that only ordinary skill would be necessary to reduce the invention to practice, without extensive research or experimentation. *Sewall*, 21 F.3d at 415, 30 U.S.P.Q.2d (BNA) at 1359; *see also Coleman v. Dines*, 754 F.2d 353, 359, 224 U.S.P.Q. (BNA) 857, 862 (Fed. Cir. 1985) (conception must include every feature of claimed invention). Because it is a mental act, courts require corroborating evidence of a contemporaneous disclosure that would enable one skilled in the art to make the invention. *Coleman v. Dines*, 754 F.2d at 359, 224 U.S.P.Q. (BNA) at 862.

Thus, the test for conception is whether the inventor had an idea that was definite and permanent enough that one skilled in the art could understand the invention; the inventor must prove his conception by corroborating evidence, preferably by showing a contemporaneous disclosure. An idea is definite and permanent when the inventor has a specific, settled idea, a particular solution to the problem at hand, not just a general goal or research plan he hopes to pursue. *See Fiers v. Revel*, 984 F.2d 1164, 1169, 25 U.S.P.Q.2d (BNA) 1601, 1605 (Fed. Cir. 1993); *Amgen, Inc. v. Chugai Pharmaceutical Co.*, 927 F.2d 1200, 1206, 18 U.S.P.Q.2d (BNA) 1016, 1021 (Fed. Cir. 1989) (no conception of chemical compound based solely on its biological activity). The conception analysis necessarily turns on the inventor's ability to describe his invention with particularity. Until he can do so, he cannot prove possession of the complete mental picture of the invention. These rules ensure that patent rights attach only when an idea is so far developed that the inventor can point to a definite, particular invention.

But an inventor need not know that his invention will work for conception to be complete. *Applegate v. Scherer*, 51 C.C.P.A. 1416, 332 F.2d 571, 573, 141 U.S.P.Q. (BNA) 796, 799 (CCPA 1964). He need only show that he had the idea; the discovery that an invention actually works is part of its reduction to practice. *Id.; see also Oka v. Youssefyeh*, 849 F.2d 581, 584 n.1, 7 U.S.P.Q.2d (BNA) 1169, 1171 n.1 (Fed. Cir. 1988)." 40 F.3d at 1227-28.

The Canadian and U.S. courts follow different approaches in reaching the same result. The Canadian Supreme Court is principally concerned with whether Glaxo satisfied the criterion of utility through by making a sound prediction. The CAFC is concerned with whether Glaxo (successor to Burroughs-Wellcome) had a definite and permanent idea. Are the decisions consistent? In what contexts do you think the approaches might yield different results?

2. The Canadian Supreme Court notes that the U.S. CAFC considered conception as of February 6, 1985 (para. 40). In Canada, analysis of sound

prediction depended on Glaxo's knowledge as of the "priority date" of the U.K. patent application, March 16, 1985. Attention to these different dates in part reflects a difference between U.S. "first-to-invent" rules for determining inventorship, as compared with "first-to-file" rules prevailing in the rest of the world.

3. Pharmaceutical Company *X* discovers a genetic sequence that causes "biological activity" to occur in human cells, but it cannot identify the function of that biological activity, including whether that activity might have some therapeutic effect generated by a medicine taking advantage of the sequence. Should the discovery of the "biological activity" be sufficient to meet the utility criterion?

4. Enablement

The fourth criterion with respect to the grant of the patent is that an inventor shall have disclosed in the patent application either a means for enabling the practice of the invention (generally for most of the world), or the best known means for practicing the invention (for the United States). One objective of this criterion is that persons other than the inventor should be able to benefit from the inventor's disclosure, and this is most likely to happen if others are well informed with respect to the means of making or using the invention. Another objective of this requirement is to distinguish true inventions from speculative concepts of would-be inventors about future possibilities. A claimed invention should function as described. Of course, many inventors would prefer to secure their patents without telling others just exactly how to go about making or using the invention. Third parties seeking to practice inventions based only on enabling disclosure made to the patent office not infrequently find this difficult.

The requirement of enabling disclosure played the decisive role in the decision of the U.K. House of Lords (now the Supreme Court) in *Biogen v. Medeva*. The patent applicant showed that its invention would produce a specified result. Was this enough to exclude others from achieving the same result through a better means?

BIOGEN, INC. v. MEDEVA PLC

House of Lords [1997] RPC 1 31 October 1996

Lord HOFFMANN: . . .

I think that in concentrating upon the question of whether Professor Murray's invention could, so to speak, deliver the goods across the full width of the patent or priority document, the courts and the EPO allowed their attention to be diverted from what seems to me in this particular case the critical issue. It is not whether the claimed invention could deliver the goods, but whether the claims cover other ways in which they might be delivered: ways which owe nothing to the teaching of the patent or any principle which it disclosed.

It will be remembered that in Genentech I/Polypeptide expression the Technical Board spoke of the need for the patent to give protection against other ways of achieving the same effect "in a manner which could not have been envisaged without the invention." This shows that there is more than one way in which the breadth of a claim may exceed the technical contribution to the art embodied in the invention. The patent may claim results which it does not enable, such as making a wide class of products when it enables only one of those products and discloses no principle which would enable others to be made. Or it may claim every way of achieving a result when it enables only one way and it is possible to envisage other ways of achieving that result which make no use of the invention.

One example of an excessive claim of the latter kind is the famous case of *O'Reilly v Morse* (1854) 56 US (15 How) 62 in the Supreme Court of the United States. Samuel Morse was the first person to discover a practical method of electric telegraphy and took out a patent in which he claimed any use of electricity for "making or printing intelligible characters, signs, or letter, at any distances." The Supreme Court rejected the claim as too broad. Professor Chisum, in his book on Patents (vol 1, § 1.03 [2]) summarises the decision as follows:

> Before Morse's invention, the scientific community saw the possibility of achieving communication by the "galvanic" current but did not know any means of achieving that result. Morse discovered one means and attempted to claim all others.

A similar English case is *British United Shoe Machinery Co Ltd v Simon Collier Ltd* (1908) 26 RPC 21. The patentee invented a piece of machinery for automatically trimming the soles of boots and shoes by means of a cam. One of the claims was in general terms for automatic means of trimming soles. Parker J said, at pages 49-50:

> (The) problem was simply how to do automatically what could already be done by the skill of the workman. On the other hand, the principle which the inventor applies for the solution of the problem is the capacity of a cam to vary the relative positions of two parts of a machine while the machine is running. Assuming this principle to be new, it might be possible for the inventor, having shown one method of applying it to the solution of the problem, to protect himself during the life of his patent from any other method of applying it for the same purpose, but I do not think that the novelty of the principle applied would enable him to make a valid claim for all means of solving the problem whether the same or a different principle were applied to its solution.

I return therefore to consider the technical contribution to the art which Professor Murray made in 1978 and disclosed in Biogen 1. As it seems to me, it consisted in showing that despite the uncertainties which then existed over the DNA of the Dane particle — in particular whether it included the antigen genes and whether it had introns — known recombinant techniques could nevertheless be used to make the antigens in a prokaryotic host cell. As I have said, I accept the judge's findings that the method was shown to be capable of making both antigens and I am willing to accept that it would work in any otherwise suitable host cell. Does this contribution justify a claim to a monopoly of any recombinant method of making the antigens? In my view it does not. The claimed invention is too broad. Its excessive breadth is due, not to the inability of the teaching to produce all the promised results, but to the fact that the same results could be produced by different means. Professor Murray had won a brilliant Napoleonic victory in cutting through the uncertainties which existed in his day to achieve the desired result. But his success did not in my view establish any new principle which his successors had to follow if they were to achieve the same results. The inventive step, as I have said, was the idea of trying to express unsequenced eukaryotic DNA in a prokaryotic host. Biogen 1 discloses that the way to do it is to choose the restriction enzymes likely to cleave the Dane particle DNA into the largest fragments. This, if anything, was the original element in what Professor Murray did. But once the DNA had been sequenced, no one would choose restriction enzymes on this basis. They would choose those which digested the sites closest to the relevant gene or the part of the gene which expressed an antigenic fragment of the polypeptide. The metaphor used by one of the witnesses was that before the genome had been sequenced everyone was working in the dark. Professor Murray invented a way of working with the genome in the dark. But he did not switch on the light and once the light was on his method was no longer needed. Nor, once they could use vectors for mammalian cells, would they be concerned with the same problem of introns which had so exercised those skilled in the art in 1978. Of course there might be other problems, but Biogen 1 did not teach how to solve them. The respondents Medeva, who use restriction enzymes based on knowledge of the HBV genome and mammalian host cells, owe nothing to Professor Murray's invention.

It is said that what Professor Murray showed by his invention was that it could be done. HBV antigens could be produced by expressing Dane particle DNA in a host cell. Those who followed, even by different routes, could have greater confidence by reason of his success. I do not think that this is enough to justify a monopoly of the whole field. I suppose it could be said that Samuel Morse had shown that electric telegraphy could be done. The Wright Brothers showed that heavier-than-air flight was possible, but that did not entitle them to a monopoly of heavier-than-air flying machines. It is inevitable in a young science, like electricity in the early nineteenth century or flying at the turn of the last century or recombinant DNA technology in the 1970s, that dramatically new things will be done for the first time. The technical contribution made in such cases deserves to be recognised. But care is needed not to stifle further research and healthy competition by allowing the first person who has found a way of achieving an obviously desirable goal to monopolise every other way of doing so. (*See* Merges and Nelson, On the Complex Economics of Patent Scope (1990) 90 Columbia Law Review 839.)

I would therefore hold that Biogen 1 did not support the invention as claimed in the European Patent and that it is therefore not entitled to the priority date of Biogen 1. As it is conceded that the invention was obvious when the patent application was filed, it is invalid.

NOTES AND QUESTIONS

1. In the well-known Star Trek science fiction series, people (including alien people) are moved about from one point in space to another by means of the "transporter." The transporter has become so much a part of global culture that most of us likely assume it is only a matter of time (even if a very long time) before people are "beaming" from one place to another. Should the producers of the Star Trek series have filed a patent application on the transporter before they first publicly introduced it?

When it was introduced, was the concept of the transporter new?[21]

When it was introduced, was the concept of the transporter capable of industrial application?

When it was introduced, did the concept of the transporter involve an inventive step?

If the Star Trek transporter were new, capable of industrial application, and involved an inventive step, why should not a patent examiner have recommended the grant of a patent? Could the producers of the Star Trek series have provided an enabling disclosure?

D. Term of Protection

The Paris Convention on the Protection of Industrial Property did not establish a minimum or maximum term of patent protection and, prior to the negotiation of the TRIPS Agreement, there was considerable variation among countries regarding the term of protection. The TRIPS Agreement (Article 33) prescribed a minimum patent term of 20 years from filing of the patent application, and did not prescribe a maximum term of protection.

The legislation of a number of countries provides for extension of the term of the patent on the occurrence of certain conditions. For example, the U.S. Patent Act provides for extension based on unreasonable delay by the Patent Office in processing applications,[22] and for pharmaceutical patents based on the length of the Food and Drug Administration (FDA) regulatory review process (at 35 U.S.C. § 156). The latter provision is complex and subject to a substantial number of conditions and qualifications. The regulatory review is divided into two phases: (1) the phase during which the drug is subject to clinical testing (which is dated from authorization to test by the FDA) (the "testing" phase) and (2) the phase during which the FDA evaluates the test (and other) data (the "approval" phase). One half of the period of the testing phase plus the approval phase are subject to compensation (35 U.S.C. § 156(c) & (g)). In no event may the duration of the extension exceed five years (35 U.S.C. § 156(g)(6)(A)). The total period of effective patent protection may not exceed 14 years (the original patent term, shortened by the regulatory review period, plus the extension) (35 U.S.C. § 156(c)(3)). There are a substantial number of additional conditions, including a limitation to the first commercial marketing of the product.

The European Union effectively extends the term of patents in the pharmaceutical sector, also based on the regulatory review period. However, it refers to this extension as the provision of a Supplementary Protection Certificate (SPC).[23]

21. Staying within the science fiction genre, consider, for example, the teleportation device that played a prominent role in a 1958 science fiction film, *The Fly*, with Vincent Price.

22. The U.S. Patent Act provides (at 35 U.S.C. § 154) for extension of the patent term based on delay of the Patent Office, generally more than three years from the filing of the application. Unlike an extension based on drug regulatory approval, the extension based on delay of the Patent Office applies to all fields of technology. However, there are several important exceptions to the general rule of extension. Thus, for example, if an interference is declared under 35 U.S.C. § 135(a) and a proceeding is held to determine the rightful claimant to a patent among competing claimants, the interference period is excluded from the processing time (as are appeals from decisions of the patent examiner). Likewise delays based on national security review are excluded.

23. *See* Council Regulation (EEC) No. 1768/92 of 18 June 1992, concerning the creation of a supplementary protection certificate for medicinal products. Available at http://eur-lex.europa.eu/LexUriServ/LexUriServ.do?uri = CELEX:31992R1768:EN:HTML.

In the WTO *Canada-Generic Pharmaceuticals* panel decision,[24] excerpted *infra* section II.B.1, the European Union unsuccessfully argued that a mechanism for patent term extension was a necessary element in laws that permit early working of patents for regulatory review purposes.

II.   THE MULTILATERAL PATENT AGREEMENTS

A.   *The Paris Convention*

1.   Historical Perspective

As we have previously noted, efforts to create an international intellectual property rights (IPRs) system date back to the late 1800s, when two treaties that continue to form the backbone of the system were agreed upon—the Paris Convention for the Protection of Industrial Property (1883) and the Berne Convention for the Protection of Literary and Artistic Works (1886). The Paris Convention addresses patents, and we begin with a historical perspective on that Convention.

The Paris Convention has been subject to a series of revisions since its adoption in 1883. The most recent revision was undertaken at Stockholm in 1967 (and amended in 1979), and the Stockholm revision of the Paris Convention is the most widely adopted among its contracting parties.

As part of her economic analysis (recall the excerpt in Chapter 1), Edith Penrose described the negotiating history of the Paris Convention.

THE ECONOMICS OF THE INTERNATIONAL PATENT SYSTEM
Edith Tilton Penrose*

CHAPTER III

THE DEVELOPMENT OF THE INTERNATIONAL CONVENTION FOR THE PROTECTION OF INDUSTRIAL PROPERTY

As the patent system spread into one country after another in the 19th century, demands from various quarters for the adoption of international regulations increased. Commercial interests are no respecters of national boundaries and while the law of each country prevails only within the jurisdiction of that country, the interest of the patentees in the use of their inventions frequently extends beyond the jurisdiction of any one country. As might be expected, the patent laws adopted by the various countries, though designed broadly for the same purposes, varied considerably in their detailed provisions. Although few discriminated against foreigners specifically, the difficulty of complying with

---

24. Canada—Patent Protection of Pharmaceutical Products, Report of the Panel, WT/DS114/R, March 17, 2000 ("Canada-Generic Pharmaceuticals").

* Economics of the International Patent System, 101-107, 162-169. ©1951 The Johns Hopkins University Press.

many different regulations made it almost impossible for a patentee to get protection in many countries.

The definition of what was considered a patentable invention differed between the laws of different countries and consequently a patent might be obtained on an invention in some countries while in others the invention was excluded from patent protection. This was — and is — particularly true with regard to medicines, foods, drugs and chemical products. Novelty of the invention was required in most countries and an invention was frequently not considered new if it had been published or publicly used abroad. When an inventor applied for a patent in his own country he had to disclose the nature of his invention, and the publication of the specification attached to this patent application was held by a few other countries to destroy the newness of the invention for patent purposes. In applying for a patent in several countries an inventor had to draw up applications conforming to widely different and extremely detailed rules; he had strictly to observe complicated procedures, and he had to do all of these things within short periods of time. In the meantime, others might learn of his invention through the patent application in his own country and patent the invention themselves, if permitted. Or they might simply use it, thus either destroying its novelty for patent purposes or acquiring a legal right to its use which could not be touched even if the original inventor succeeded eventually in obtaining a patent. Taxes had to be paid on time or the patent would be forfeited. In many countries the invention had to be put into commercial use within a limited period of time. Thus, to obtain and maintain patents in foreign countries, a patentee was usually forced to incur the expense of obtaining and maintaining patent agents in each country to defend his interests.

Hence a patentee who wished to exploit his invention abroad, or to obtain a revenue from its exploitation abroad by others, or to prevent others from using his invention to compete with him in foreign markets, had a strong incentive to press for international agreements which would eliminate the difficulties of obtaining protection in countries other than his own. Patent lawyers, jurists and manufacturers joined in the demand for international legislation. The "rights of man" were freely invoked in the cause and at times the movement took on the tone of a religious crusade. One of the crusaders, for example, wrote:

> The striving of the individual human and the interest of the social organism join in a common cause to justify the juridical institution of the right of the inventor or of the creator. . . . But a right which has its source in a human aspiration as profound as that we have just revealed extends to the entire community of men who live and think. . . . How contain the explosion of a new principle in the narrow confines of a single country without permitting it to expand across the universe?

Nor was invention the only type of industrial property for which international arrangements were being asked. Trade marks, industrial designs and models were included. The only international protection existing when the International Convention for the Protection of Industrial Property was created in 1880 was such as had been written into bipartite treaties most of which were concerned primarily with other matters. Of these there were some 69 that included provisions affecting industrial property, but only two of them contained provisions for the protection of patents. This type of protection was generally considered to be unsatisfactory since it had no separate existence apart from the general commercial arrangements with which it was usually associated. Hence the protection was apt to be *"brève et précaire."*

The Vienna Congress of 1873

The first conference to consider the protection of inventors on an international scale met in Vienna in 1873. An international Exposition under the auspices of the Austria-Hungarian Government was to be held in that year and the inventors in some countries, particularly the United States, feared that their inventions would be inadequately protected under Austrian law. The United States took the lead in pressing Austria to protect more adequately inventions exhibited at the Exposition and, in addition, to revise her patent laws to give more complete protection to foreign patentees in general. Among those provisions of the Austrian law which met the disapproval of the United States was the compulsory working requirement, under which a patented article had to be manufactured in Austria within a year from the issue of the patent. The American Minister in Vienna even referred the Austrian Foreign Ministry to an article in the Scientific American which complained of Austrian treatment of American inventors and ended with a veiled threat of refusal to join in the Exposition if the Austrian law were not changed.

The Austrians passed a special law protecting exhibited inventions. In addition, on the suggestion of the United States, it was decided to hold an international conference on patent reform immediately after the Exposition. Thus, the first international conference on patents was held while the controversy between the patent and anti-patent forces throughout Europe was still lively and bitter. It was not an official conference although representatives from 13 countries were included among the 158 participants. The majority of those attending the conference were from Germany and the acute difference of opinion in Germany as to whether a patent law was desirable and whether Germany should adopt one was reflected in the debates of the conference.

The resolutions were very general but clearly endorsed the principle of patent protection. The first resolution, consisting of seven reasons why "the protection of inventions should be guaranteed by the laws of all civilized nations under the condition of a complete publication of the same," was violently debated but was adopted by a vote of 80 to 4. The second resolution, setting out the principles on which an "effective and useful patent law should be based" was even more controversial. The most notable decision of the conference was paragraph (f) of this resolution which recommended compulsory licensing of patents "in cases in which the public interest should require it." This principle was not again to be accepted by an international conference for 50 years but the anti-patent movement in the 19th century had created such an awareness of the possible monopolistic and restrictive effects of the patent system that some limitation of the patent monopoly had to be conceded by the patent advocates. The official United States position was strongly opposed to any concessions but the resolution was carried by a vote of 42 to 17.

Finally the conference resolved that it was "of pressing moment that governments should endeavor to bring about an international understanding upon patent protection as soon as possible" and empowered a preparatory committee "to continue the work commenced by this first international congress, and to use all their influence that the principles adopted be made known as widely as possible, and carried into practice." Five years later the conference that was to establish the basis of an international agreement was called.

The Paris Conference of 1878

Under the auspices of the French Government, and again in connection with an international Exposition, a conference of nearly 500 participants, including eleven government delegates and delegates from 48 Chambers of Commerce and industrial and technical societies was called in Paris. Like the Vienna conference, this conference was an unofficial affair, although called by the French government and attended by some official delegates. More than three-fifths of the delegates were French industrialists and thus the French point of view completely dominated the conference. This is one of the reasons why the views of this conference in many respects contrasted strongly with those of the Vienna conference in which the German element was predominant. Malapert, a French jurist and patent authority, complained that, although invitations were widely sent out, the scope of the conference was so restricted by its promoters that people with a critical point of view did not attend:

> The acts of the organizing committee had restricted too much a field which ought to be open. There was no place where one could take account of the social position of different populations of the globe, although all were invited to engage in a common task. The radius of the circle was too short, the circumference inscribed a cell in which it was not possible to breathe. It was for this reason that many jurists and economists, expert in the study of patent laws, refrained from attending the conference where they would have nothing to learn and nothing to do or teach, since limits had been set outside of which it was forbidden to go.

The stenographic report of the conference shows clearly that critics of the operation of the patent system were not well received. "Vice applandissements" occur after speeches in which the strongest and most far-reaching claims were made for inventors' rights, while "rumeurs" are reported when remarks such as the following were made:

> Messieurs, after the eloquent words which you have just heard, it takes great temerity on my part to mount this platform; but I consider it my duty to arise here to tell you of the dangers and inconveniences which result from the monopoly of exploitation granted by the French law to patentees for fifteen years. (Murmurs)

It is not surprising, therefore, that the resolutions of the conference reflect almost exclusively the patentees' point of view. In addition to the exaltation of the rights of inventors was the exaltation of the spirit of international union. The dream of many who attended the conference was complete uniformity of the laws protecting industrial property in all nations. At this time the formation of unions of many kinds was being discussed in conferences all over Europe. The most important of these referred to postal matters, the telegraph, weights and measures, and literary and artistic property. A patent union analogous to these other unions, with a uniform international law, was the goal.

There were a few participants, however, who were aware of the social implications of the patent law and who felt that some recognition of the interest of society should be explicitly stated other than the general assertion that society benefitted because of the encouragement of invention. The very first debate of the conference was on the nature of the inventor's right and the proposition before the conference was as follows:

> The right of inventors and of industrial creators in their work, or of manufacturers and business men in their marks is a right of property, the civil law does not create it, it only regulates it.

M. Clunet, a French jurist, presented a "counter-proposition"[:]

> The right of inventors and of industrial creators is an equitable and useful creation of the civil law, which reconciles the rights of inventors and of society by the concession of a temporary monopoly.

The debate on this issue was heated and involved, but the conference came out decisively in favor of the first proposition. It adopted in effect the "natural property" theory of inventors' rights. Nonetheless, in spite of this extreme position, it was not possible for the participants in the discussions to escape the fact that at times there might be a serious interference with the welfare of society if this "most sacred of all property" was subject to no limitations. Hence it was proposed that "the principle of expropriation in the public interest is applicable to patents." The adoption of this proposal was opposed on the ground that it was not necessary; if a matter of public health or military necessity existed, the state obviously had the power to override private interests. The majority of the conference, however, felt it was worthwhile to make this principle explicit and adopted the proposal.

On the principle of expropriation in the public interest, the conference admitted the right of the state to revoke a patent if manufacture was not undertaken in the country in a specified time, at least if the patentee could not justify his inaction. In other words, the conference approved what is now known as compulsory working revocation of the patent if it was not worked. Even compulsory licensing as the sanction for failure to work was rejected. In later conferences, revocation of the patent was considered to be too harsh on the inventor, and its replacement by compulsory licensing was fought for and obtained. The Vienna conference had rejected the principle that a patent must be worked in the country granting it and had therefore not even proposed compulsory licensing as a sanction for non-working although it had approved compulsory licensing whenever the public interest required it. In both respects, the Vienna conference was far ahead of the times.

It seems curious, however, that in the 1878 conference, where the rights of inventors were upheld in the most extreme forms, the principle of compulsory licensing for failure to work was rejected in favor of outright revocation of the patent. This position was the direct result of the natural property theory of patents adopted by the conference. M. Charles Lyon-Caën, a prominent French lawyer, argued heatedly that compulsory licensing was a derogation of the right of property and compared the inventor subject to such licensing to a man who owned his house but was required to allow all who requested it, to live with him on the payment of a rental. Compulsory licensing only aided other private groups and could not be tolerated, although he would accept expropriation "*pour cause d'utilité publique*" if necessary:

> If one thinks that industry would have to suffer because of the monopoly, the remedy should not be to impose the obligation on the patentee to concede

licenses, but to eliminate patents. . . . It is to completely misunderstand the absolute character of the right of property of the inventor to impose on him the obligation to concede licenses.

The conference accepted M. Lyon-Caën's point of view and approved the resolution that:

Patents ought to assure, during their entire duration, to inventors or their assigns, the exclusive right to the exploitation of the invention and not a mere right to a royalty paid to them by third parties.

The conference adopted a number of other resolutions which were much more practical than those so far discussed. Some of them were subsequently taken over as the basis of the international Convention when it was finally agreed. These included the principle that foreigners should be treated equally with nationals in each country; that the laws of each country should apply to its colonies; that the importation of patented products by a patentee should not cause revocation of his patent; and that the rights acquired for the same invention in different countries should be independent of each others. It was also agreed that it should be possible for a patent claim to be made simultaneously at the appropriate national office and at the consulates of the various foreign nations in which a patent was desired.

When it came, however, to the problem of devising the framework of uniform legislation, the conference was obliged to recognize the realism of those who had insisted that uniformity was impossible in a world of national states with different interests, different legal structures and different economic histories, aspirations and ideologies. The participants contested vigorously over their different positions, but it soon became clear that the ideal of uniformity of legislation would have to give way to lesser goals. To the orators the ideal was good but the practical problems of achieving it were too great, since no state would admit that its own legal framework was not the best from which to take the international model.

The biggest obstacle to agreement on uniform patent laws was the question of the "previous examination" of the invention. Under the law of France and some other countries a patent was issued on the claim of the inventor, without examination of the merits or validity of his claim or of the novelty of the invention. Many other countries, on the other hand, required that the novelty, utility, patentability, etc. of the invention be scrutinized before the patent could be issued. Although most of the non-French delegates supported the latter system, the French were in the majority and the conference passed a resolution that a patent should be delivered to all claimants at their own risk and thus without governmental examination.

Nor was there unanimous agreement on what products should be patentable. "Batailles très chaudes" took place on whether chemical products, pharmaceutical preparations and foodstuffs should be patentable and, although the conference decided in the affirmative, an important minority was left dissatisfied.

These various differences prevented the conference from coming to any final agreement on the nature of an international patent law, and it was decided to charge a permanent international commission with the task of carrying out the resolutions of the conference and of arranging an official international conference called by a government to lay the basis for uniform international legislation. In spite of the violent differences of opinion, the promoters of the conference had not yet lost hope of seeing such uniform legislation adopted.

The First Draft Convention

The commission set up by the conference of 1878 set to work immediately after the conference was over and the French section, which formed the executive committee of the commission, produced a long draft which constituted in effect an extensive universal law. The French Minister of Commerce, to whom the draft was presented, recognized that such a far-reaching proposal could never command universal acceptance, and requested the section to draft a convention of more modest proportions. A "Projet d'une Union Internationale pour la protection de la propriété industrielle" was then drafted by the French delegate Jagerschmidt.

In the drafting of this project an eye was kept on existing national laws; uniform international legislation was no longer the goal and the convention was admittedly designed to encroach as little as possible on existing laws. Since the next step was a governmental one, it became necessary to produce specific proposals that would be politically viable. Thus the delegates had come down from the stars, and concentrated on provisions that they hoped would overcome the worst difficulties facing patentees with international interests, and would at the same time be politically practical. Gone was the talk of "natural property rights," or any attempt to define the nature of an inventor's right; gone were attempts to eliminate compulsory working, which was provided for in the laws of nearly all countries; and gone were attempts to impose a uniform standard of patentability devised in the interest of patentees. M. Jagerschmidt showed remarkable political acumen in the draft, most of the essentials of which were eventually accepted in the Convention.

The Conference at Paris in 1880

The draft together with an invitation to an international diplomatic conference was sent by the French government to other governments. The response was favorable, and in 1880 the official conference met in Paris with representatives from 19 governments. The draft convention was adopted with some amendments and the amended draft was submitted to governments for their comment and approval. Provision was made for the protection of other forms of industrial property as well as for patents, for the organization of an International Bureau for the Protection of Industrial Property, for amendments to the Convention and for the adhesion of new member states.

The provisions on patents were confined to specific issues on which it was hoped sufficient agreement could be obtained to form a union. The important ones were as follows:

> Art. 2. The subjects or citizens of each of the contracting states shall enjoy, in all of the other States of the Union, so far as patents, industrial designs or models, trade marks, and commercial names are concerned, the advantages that their respective laws now grant, or may hereafter grant to their own nationals. Consequently they shall have the same protection as the latter, and the same legal remedy against any infringement of their rights, provided they comply with the formalities and conditions imposed on nationals by the domestic legislation of each State.
>
> Art. 3. The subjects of States not forming part of the Union who are domiciled or who have industrial or commercial establishments in the territory of one of the States of the Union are assimilated to the subjects or citizens of the contracting States.

Art. 4. Any person who has duly applied for a patent, the registration of an industrial design or model, or a trade mark in one of the contracting States, shall enjoy for the purpose of registration in other countries and subject to the rights of third parties, a right of priority during the periods hereinafter stated.

Consequently, subsequent filing in one of the other States of the Union, before the expiration of these periods shall not be invalidated through any acts accomplished in the interval, as, for instance, by another filing, by publication of the invention or the working thereof, by the sale of copies of the design or model, or by the use of the trade mark.

The above-mentioned periods of priority shall be six months for patents and three months for industrial designs or models and for trade marks they shall be increased by one month for countries overseas.

Art. 5. The introduction by the patentee into the country where the patent has been granted of objects manufactured in any of the countries of the Union shall not entail forfeiture. Nevertheless the patentee is subject to the obligation to work his patent in accordance with the laws of the country into which he introduces the patented articles.

The International Union for the Protection of Industrial Property

In 1883 a brief conference was held at which the Convention was finally approved and signed. Ratifications were exchanged and in 1884 the International Union for the Protection of Industrial Property came into being. The Union was first composed of eleven countries, to which another twenty-nine were successively added.

Amendments to the Convention are made by Conferences of Revision, of which there have been six so far. These conferences meet periodically and are called when it seems desirable to the countries concerned. All amendments must have the unanimous approval of the members of the Union. If unanimity is not forthcoming Special Arrangements between the countries agreeing to the provisions under discussion may be adopted. The principle of special arrangements or "restricted unions" is not looked upon with favor, since it destroys the uniformity of the international regulations affecting members of the Union, and only three special arrangements have been established, none for patents.

The text of the Convention, as revised in the conferences of revision, comes into effect for each country when it deposits its ratification. The old text remains in force for countries that have not ratified the new text. Hence at any given time there may be several regimes in effect depending upon the progress of ratification of the latest revised texts.

NOTES AND QUESTIONS

1. Edith Penrose discusses the factors that underlay the negotiation of the Paris Convention for the Protection of Industrial Property. She attributes the motivation for the negotiations to concerns surrounding the Austria-Hungarian International Exposition of 1873. What were American inventors concerned about? How could the display of an invention affect their economic rights?

   Generally speaking, disclosure of an invention would undermine its novelty, a critical element in determining patentability. Thus, disclosure of an invention in a country where a patent had not yet been granted may have prevented patent protection from ever being obtained there, or from being obtained in any other country whose patent office took into account foreign disclosures in determining novelty.

If disclosure did not preclude patentability, someone other than the inventor may nevertheless have sought a patent on the invention before the original inventor. Some patent systems would have awarded a patent only to the true inventor, but it may not always have been easy to disprove another party's claim to inventive activity.

2. Edith Penrose notes that during the negotiation of the Paris Convention, there were some proposals to adopt a far more ambitious system of harmonized rules than those that eventually resulted. She observes that each country was persuaded that its own rules were the best, and that this made harmonization efforts difficult. Are matters so different today?

3. In the late 1800s many countries' patent systems did not provide for the pre-grant examination of patent applications (and some still do not, including the Swiss). These systems relied instead on post-grant opposition to patents by parties challenging the entitlement of the grantees. Such challenges may have taken the form of administrative or judicial proceedings seeking revocation of patents, or may have taken the form of defense against the enforcement of patents in civil litigation (claiming defects in the original patent grants). The absence of a pre-grant examination procedure reduces the *ex ante* cost of administering a patent system, but might impose substantial *ex post* costs, particularly on the general public, which may face a proliferation of product markets monopolized by patent holders.

4. The architects of the Paris Convention employed certain fundamental rules in the new international patent protection system. These were:
   1. National treatment;
   2. Independence of patents; and
   3. Right of priority.

   These fundamental principles continue to underlay the international patent protection system.

2. Paris Convention Rules

WIPO administers the Paris Convention on behalf of the Paris Union. The WIPO Secretariat describes below the main features of the Convention.

THE PARIS CONVENTION FOR THE PROTECTION OF INDUSTRIAL PROPERTY*

PRINCIPAL PROVISIONS

5.9 The provisions of the Paris Convention may be sub-divided into four main categories:

— a first category contains rules of substantive law which guarantee a basic right known as the right to national treatment in each of the member countries;

---

* From WIPO Handbook on Intellectual Property, at http://www.wipo.int.

— a second category establishes another basic right known as the right of priority;

— a third category defines a certain number of common rules in the field of substantive law which contain either rules establishing rights and obligations of natural persons and legal entities, or rules requiring or permitting the member countries to enact legislation following those rules;

— a fourth category deals with the administrative framework which has been set up to implement the Convention, and includes the final clauses of the Convention.

NATIONAL TREATMENT

5.10 National treatment means that, as regards the protection of industrial property, each country party to the Paris Convention must grant the same protection to nationals of the other member countries as it grants to its own nationals. The relevant provisions are contained in Articles 2 and 3 of the Convention.

5.11 The same national treatment must be granted to nationals of countries which are not party to the Paris Convention if they are domiciled in a member country or if they have a "real and effective" industrial or commercial establishment in such a country. However, no requirement as to domicile or establishment in the country where protection is claimed may be imposed upon nationals of member countries as a condition for benefiting from an industrial property right.

5.12 This national treatment rule guarantees not only that foreigners will be protected, but also that they will not be discriminated against in any way. Without this, it would frequently be very difficult and sometimes even impossible to obtain adequate protection in foreign countries for inventions, trademarks and other subjects of industrial property. . . .

5.14 This means furthermore, that any requirement of reciprocity of protection is excluded. Supposing that a given member country has a longer term of patent protection than another member country: the former country will not have the right to provide that nationals of the latter country will enjoy a term of protection of the same length as the term of protection is in the law of their own country. This principle applies not only to codified law but also to the practice of the courts (jurisprudence), and to the practice of the Patent Office or other administrative governmental institutions as it is applied to the nationals of the country.

5.15 The application of the national law to the national of another member country does not, however, prevent him from invoking more beneficial rights specially provided in the Paris Convention. These rights are expressly reserved. The national treatment principle must be applied without prejudice to such rights.

5.16 Article 2(3) states an exception to the national treatment rule. The national law relating to judicial and administrative procedure, to jurisdiction and to requirements of representation is expressly "reserved." This means that certain requirements of a mere procedural nature which impose special conditions on foreigners for purposes of judicial and administrative procedure, may also validly be invoked against foreigners who are nationals of member countries. An example is a requirement for foreigners to deposit a certain sum as security or bail for the costs of litigation. Another example is expressly stated: the requirement that foreigners should either designate an address for service or appoint an agent in the country in which protection is requested. This latter is perhaps the most common special requirement imposed on foreigners. . . .

THE RIGHT OF PRIORITY

5.20 The right of priority means that, on the basis of a regular application for an industrial property right filed by a given applicant in one of the member countries, the same applicant (or its or his successor in title) may, within a specified period of time (six or 12 months), apply for protection in all the other member countries. These later applications will then be regarded as if they had been filed on the same day as the earliest application. Hence, these later applications enjoy a priority status with respect to all applications relating to the same invention filed after the date of the first application. They also enjoy a priority status with respect to all acts accomplished after that date which would normally be apt to destroy the rights of the applicant or the patentability of his invention. The provisions concerning the right of priority are contained in Article 4 of the Convention.

5.21 The right of priority offers great practical advantages to the applicant desiring protection in several countries. The applicant is not required to present all applications at home and in foreign countries at the same time, since he has six [for industrial designs and trademarks] or 12 [for patents and utility models] months at his disposal to decide in which countries to request protection. The applicant can use that period to organize the steps to be taken to secure protection in the various countries of interest in the particular case.

5.22 The beneficiary of the right of priority is any person entitled to benefit from the national treatment rule who has duly filed an application for a patent for invention or another industrial property right in one of the member countries.

5.23 The right of priority can be based only on the *first* application for the same industrial property right which must have been filed in a member country. It is therefore not possible to follow a first application by a second, possibly improved application and then to use that second application as a basis of priority. The reason for this rule is obvious: one cannot permit an endless chain of successive claims of priority for the same subject, as this could, in fact, considerably prolong the term of protection for that subject. . . .

5.26 The first application must be "duly filed" in order to give rise to the right of priority. Any filing, which is equivalent to a regular national filing, is a valid basis for the right of priority. A regular national filing means any filing that is adequate to establish the date on which the application was filed in the country concerned. The notion of "national" filing is qualified by including also applications filed under bilateral or multilateral treaties concluded between member countries.

5.27 Withdrawal, abandonment or rejection of the first application does not destroy its capacity to serve as a priority basis. The right of priority subsists even where the first application generating that right is no longer existent.

5.28 The effect of the right of priority is regulated in Article 4B. One can summarize this effect by saying that, as a consequence of the priority claim, the later application must be treated as if it had been filed already at the time of the filing, in another member country, of the first application the priority of which is claimed. By virtue of the right of priority, all the acts accomplished during the time between the filing dates of the first and the later applications, the so-called priority period, cannot destroy the rights which are the subject of the later application.

5.29 In terms of concrete examples, this means that a patent application for the same invention filed by a third party during the priority period will not give a prior right, although it was filed before the later application. Likewise, a publication or public use of the invention, which is the subject of the later application, during the priority period would not destroy the novelty or inventive character of that invention. It is insignificant for that purpose whether that publication is made by the applicant or the inventor himself or by a third party.

5.30 The length of the priority period is different according to the various kinds of industrial property rights. For patents for invention and utility models the priority period is 12 months, for industrial designs and trademarks it is six months. In determining the length of the priority period, the Paris Convention had to take into account the conflicting interests of the applicant and of third parties. The priority periods now prescribed by the Paris Convention seem to strike an adequate balance between them.

5.31 The right of priority as recognized by the Convention permits the claiming of "multiple priorities" and of "partial priorities." Therefore, the later application may not only claim the priority of one earlier application, but it may also combine the priority of several earlier applications, each of which pertaining to different features of the subject matter of the later application. Furthermore, in the later application, elements for which priority is claimed may be combined with elements for which no priority is claimed. In all these cases, the later application must of course comply with the requirement of unity of invention.

5.32 These possibilities correspond to a practical need. Frequently after a first filing further improvements and additions to the invention are the subject of further applications in the country of origin. In such cases, it is very practical to be able to combine these various earlier applications into one later application, when filing before the end of the priority year in another member country. This combination is even possible if the multiple priorities come from different member countries.

PROVISIONS CONCERNING PATENTS
Independence of Patents

5.33 Patents for invention granted in member countries to nationals or residents of member countries must be treated as independent of patents for invention obtained for the same invention in other countries, including nonmember countries. The rule concerning the "independence" of patents for invention is contained in Article 4*bis*.

5.34 This principle is to be understood in its broadest sense. It means that the grant of a patent for invention in one country for a given invention does not oblige any other member country to grant a patent for invention for the same invention. Furthermore, the principle means that a patent for invention cannot be refused, invalidated or otherwise terminated in any member country on the ground that a patent for invention for the same invention has been refused or invalidated, or that it is no longer maintained or has terminated, in any other country. In this respect, the fate of a particular patent for invention in any given country has no influence whatsoever on the fate of a patent for the same invention in any of the other countries.

5.35 The underlying reason and main argument in favor of this principle is that national laws and administrative practices are usually quite different from country to country. A decision not to grant or to invalidate a patent for invention in a particular country on the basis of its law will frequently not have any bearing on the different legal situation in the other countries. It would not be justified to make the owner lose the patent for invention in other countries, on the ground that he or she lost a patent in a given country as a consequence of not having paid an annual fee in that country, or as a consequence of the patent's invalidation in that country, on a ground which does not exist in the laws of the other countries.

5.36 A special feature of the principle of independence of patents for invention is contained in Article 4*bis*(5). This provision requires that a patent granted on an application which claimed the priority of one or more foreign applications, must be given the same duration which it would have according to the national law if no priority had been claimed. In other words, it is not permitted to deduct the priority period from the term of a patent invoking the priority of a first application. For instance, a provision in a national law starting the term of the patent for invention from the (foreign) priority date, and not from the filing date of the application in the country, would be in violation of this rule.

The Right of the Inventor to Be Mentioned

5.37 A general rule states that the inventor must have the right to be mentioned as such in the patent for invention. This is stated in Article 4*ter*.

5.38 National laws have implemented this provision in several ways. Some give the inventor only the right for civil action against the applicant or owner in order to obtain the inclusion of his name in the patent for invention. Others — and that tendency seems to be increasing — enforce the naming of the inventor during the procedure for the grant of a patent for invention on an *ex officio* basis. In the United States of America, for example, it is even required that the applicant for a patent be the inventor himself.

Importation, Failure to Work and Compulsory Licenses

5.39 The questions of importation of articles covered by patents, of failure to work the patented invention and of compulsory licenses, are dealt with in Article 5A of the Convention.

5.40 With respect to importation, the provision states that importation by the patentee, into the country where the patent has been granted, of articles covered by the patent and manufactured in any of the countries of the Union will not entail forfeiture of the patent. This provision is quite narrowly worded, and hence only applies when several conditions are met. Consequently the countries of the Union have considerable leeway to legislate with respect to importation of patented goods under any of the circumstances which are different to those foreseen in this provision. . . .

5.44 With respect to the working of patents and compulsory licenses, the essence of the provisions contained in Article 5A is that each country may take legislative measures providing for which might result from the exclusive rights conferred by a patent for invention, for example failure to work or insufficient working.

5.45 Compulsory licenses on the ground of failure to work or insufficient working are the most common kind of coercive measure against the patent owner to prevent abuses of the rights conferred by the patent for invention. They are expressly dealt with by Article 5A.

5.46 The main argument for enforcing working of the invention in a particular country is the consideration that, in order to promote the industrialization of the country, patents for invention should not be used merely to block the working of the invention in the country or to monopolize importation of the patented article by the patent owner. They should rather be used to introduce the use of the new technology into the country. Whether the patent owner can really be expected to do so, is first of all an economic consideration and then also a question of time. Working in all countries is generally not economical. Moreover, it is generally recognized that immediate working in all countries is impossible. Article 5A therefore tries to strike a balance between these conflicting interests.

5.47 Compulsory licenses for failure to work or insufficient working of the invention may not be requested before a certain period of time has elapsed. This time limit expires either four years from the date of filing of the patent application or three years from the date of the grant of the patent for invention. The applicable time is the one which, in the individual case, expires last.

5.48 The time limit of three or four years is a minimum time limit. The patent owner must be given a longer time limit, if he can give legitimate reasons for his inaction—for example, that legal, economic or technical obstacles prevent working, or working more intensively, the invention in the country. If that is proven, the request for a compulsory license must be rejected, at least for a certain period. The time limit of three or four years is a minimum also in the sense that national law can provide for a longer time limit.

5.49 The compulsory license for non-working or insufficient working must be a non-exclusive license and can only be transferred together with the part of the enterprise benefiting from the compulsory license. The patent owner must retain the right to grant other non-exclusive licenses and to work the invention himself. Moreover, as the compulsory license has been granted to a particular enterprise on the basis of its known capacities, it is bound to that enterprise and cannot be transferred separately from that enterprise. These limitations are intended to prevent a compulsory licensee from obtaining a stronger position on the market than is warranted by the purpose of the compulsory license, namely, to ensure sufficient working of the invention in the country.

5.50 All these special provisions for compulsory licenses in Article 5A(4) are only applicable to compulsory licenses for non-working or insufficient working. They are not applicable to the other types of compulsory licenses for which the national law is free to provide. Such other types may be granted to prevent other abuses, for example, excessive prices or unreasonable terms for contractual licenses or other restrictive measures which hamper industrial development.

5.51 Compulsory licenses may also be granted for reasons of the public interest, in cases where there is no abuse by the patent owner of his rights—for example, in the fields of military security or public health.

5.52 There are also cases where a compulsory license is provided for to protect the public interest in unhampered technological progress. This is the case of the compulsory license in favor of the patent for invention granted to another person, then the owner of the dependent patent, in certain circumstances, may have the right to request a compulsory license for the use of that invention. If the owner of the dependent patent for invention obtains the compulsory license, he may in turn be obliged to grant a license to the owner of the earlier patent for invention.

5.53 All these other types of compulsory licenses can be grouped together under the general heading of compulsory licenses *in the public interest*. National laws are not prevented by the Paris Convention from providing for such compulsory licenses, and they are not subject to the restrictions provided for in Article 5A. This means in particular that compulsory licenses in the public interest can be granted without waiting for the expiration of the time limits provided for compulsory licenses that relate to failure to work or insufficient working.

5.54 It should be noted, however, that Article 31 of the TRIPS Agreement further provides a number of conditions with respect to the use of subject matter of a patent without the authorization of the right-holder.

Grace Period for the Payment of Maintenance Fees

5.55 Article 5*bis* provides for a grace period for the payment of maintenance fees for industrial property rights and deals with the restoration of patents for invention in case of non-payment of fees. . . .

Patents in International Traffic

5.58 Another common rule of substantive importance, containing a limitation of the rights of the patent owner in special circumstances, is contained in Article 5*ter*. It deals with the transit of devices on ships, aircraft or land vehicles through a member country in which such device is patented.

5.59 Where ships, aircraft or land vehicles of other member countries enter temporarily or accidentally a given member country and have on board devices patented in that country, the owner of the means of transportation is not required to obtain prior approval or a license from the patent owner. Temporary or accidental entry of the patented device into the country in such cases constitutes no infringement of the patent for invention. . . .

Inventions Shown at International Exhibitions

5.62 A further common rule of a substantive nature is the provision concerning temporary protection in respect of goods exhibited at international exhibitions, contained in Article 11 of the Convention.

5.63 The principle stated in Article 11 is that the member countries are obliged to grant, in conformity with their domestic legislation, temporary protection to patentable inventions, utility models, industrial designs and trademarks in respect of goods exhibited at official or officially recognized international exhibitions held in the territory of any member country. . . .

NOTES AND QUESTIONS

1. In promoting the TRIPS Agreement, OECD country industries pointed to several weaknesses of the Paris Convention in respect to patents. One such weakness is that the Paris Convention does not prescribe the subject matter areas or fields of invention for which a government must offer patent protection. Article 1(3) prescribes a broad scope of subject matter coverage for "industrial property," but this prescription does not extend specifically to patents. Why do you think that the drafters of the Paris Convention may have limited their subject matter definition to "industrial property"?

2. Note that the Paris Convention does not attempt to set forth any criteria of
    patentability. Edith Penrose has told us that efforts to harmonize substan-
    tive criteria for patenting proved too controversial. Do you think it is
    unusual to find a treaty (e.g., this one on "patents") that does not establish
    a definition for its most basic element?
        In fact, it is common for treaties to leave the meaning of basic terms open.
    The United Nations Charter allows the Security Council to take action after
    it has determined that a threat to the "peace" exists, but its does not attempt
    to define what a threat to the peace may be. Human rights treaties often
    (though certainly not always) refer to basic human rights in general terms.
    Reaching agreement on the specific content of rights may be quite difficult
    in a wide number of international contexts. Much of the Uruguay Round
    negotiations involved reducing broadly drafted GATT provisions to more
    precise rules.
3. Another provision of the Paris Convention criticized by OECD industry
    groups was the compulsory licensing provision. Article 5 refers only to
    preventing "abuses" of the patent right. There is no reference in Article 5
    to compensation for the right holder.
4. Article 28 of the Paris Convention provides for dispute settlement before
    the International Court of Justice (ICJ). No complaint under the Paris (or
    Berne) Convention has ever been filed in the ICJ. In the TRIPS negotia-
    tions, OECD industry groups contended that referral to the ICJ is a "weak"
    means of settling IPRs-related disputes. Why is the ICJ perceived as weak?
    International dispute settlement bodies almost always rely on the persua-
    sive force of their decisions (and not on gunboats) to assure compliance. ICJ
    judges are certainly as capable as WTO panel members of understanding
    the issues at stake in an IPRs-related dispute. Might the real concern of
    OECD industry groups with the Paris Convention have been that the ICJ
    would have too much flexibility in interpreting the Paris Convention since
    its provisions are rather broad? The real key to the perceived weakness of
    the Paris Convention perhaps lay more in its lack of substantive definition.

3. Paris and the Independence of Patents

See Chapter 1, section V.C on the establishment of independence, including
the *Cuno v. Pall* decision, as well as the recent dispute between India/Brazil and
the EU regarding seizures of pharmaceutical products in transit.

4. Patent Exhaustion and the Free Movement of Goods

We have previously introduced the subject of exhaustion of rights and
parallel trade. Each country has the freedom to determine whether exhaustion
of patent rights under its national law takes place when patented goods are first
placed on the market anywhere in the world (i.e., international exhaustion), are
first placed on the market within a regional territory (i.e., regional exhaustion),
or are first placed on the market within that country (i.e., national exhaustion).
We examine below the attitudes of the national courts of Japan and the United
States, and a legislative provision from South Africa.

a. Japan

The Supreme Court of Japan in 1997 decided a case involving the parallel importation into Japan of a product patented both in Japan and Germany. The product was first sold in Germany with the consent of the German patent holder. A Japanese affiliate of the German patent holder held a license under a parallel patent in Japan. The Japanese patent holder/licensee thereafter attempted to block importation into Japan of the product first sold in Germany. The Supreme Court of Japan held that, pursuant to the Paris Convention principle of independence of patents, a first sale of the product in Germany did not exhaust the rights of the patent holder in Japan. However, it went on to hold that the close integration of the global economy leads to the presumption that a patent holder in Japan that consents to the placement of its product on the market in a foreign country does so with the expectation that such product may be exported to Japan or another third country. Consequently, unless the Japanese patent holder establishes a contractual obligation on the part of the first purchaser not to export the patented product to Japan, the Japanese patent holder may not block importation of the product into Japan. By entering into a restrictive agreement with the first purchaser, and by affixing a notice to the product itself declaring this restriction, the Japanese patent holder may apparently extend the restriction to subsequent purchasers. The Court says it is not relevant whether the product is patented in the country of first sale outside of Japan.

Following is an excerpt from the opinion of the Japanese Supreme Court in the *BBS* case.

BBS KRAFTFAHRZEUGTECHNIK AG
AND BBS JAPAN, INC. v. RASIMEX JAPAN, INC.

**Supreme Court Heisei 7(o) No. 1988 (July 1, 1997), J. of S. Ct., No. 1198
(July 15, 1997), pages 8-10***

The following is the summary of the Supreme Court decision in the *BBS* case, Part 3, Chapter 4, which, according to the translator, is translated as accurately as possible even at the sacrifice of ease of reading:

The Judgment is in favor of the importer (Rasimex) of a patented product (aluminum wheels) rejecting an appeal made by the patent holder (BBS). Part 1 of the Opinion relates the factual and procedural background of the case. Part 2 summarizes the arguments heretofore made by both parties. Part 3, occupying majority of pages of the decision, gives the opinion of the court in reaching the decision. Chapter 1 of Part 3 concludes that the present case should be decided only in light of the Japanese Patent Act and not by the Paris Convention or by the doctrine of territoriality. Chapter 2 states that the doctrine of exhaustion is based on Article 1 of the Japanese Patent Act ("The purpose of the Act is to promote invention and thereby to contribute to the development of industries"). Chapter 3 denies so-called international exhaustion, saying that patent rights in Japan and in the exporting country are different rights. Chapter 5 is the conclusion of the opinion.

Brackets [] are added for contextual clarity.

---

* Translation with introductory synopsis by Tadayoshi Homma, Professor of Law, Chiba University, Japan.

4

Now, considering the balance between the distribution of products in international trade and the right of a patentee, it is safely to be said that, in light of the situation that international trade is progressing extremely widely and highly in modern society, the highest degree of respect to the freedom of distribution of products including importation is required, even where a Japanese trader imports into Japan the product [first] sold in other countries and puts the same into distribution into the [Japanese] market. And whereas, even in economic transactions in other countries, a transaction is achieved on the basis that a seller generally transfers all of his rights in the merchandise to the purchaser and the purchaser acquires all of the rights owned by the seller, it is naturally expected that, where a patentee has sold a patented product in other countries, the [first] purchaser or the third parties who purchased the same from the [first] purchaser may import into Japan, use or further sell to others as a business, in light of the abovementioned situation of international trade in modern society. Considering the above points, the patentee is not permitted to enforce his patent right in Japan [1] against the [first] purchaser of the product except where the patentee has agreed with the [first] purchaser to exclude Japan from the territories for sale or use or [2] against the third parties or subsequent purchasers who purchased the product from the [first] purchaser except where the patentee has agreed with the [first] purchaser as abovementioned and has explicitly indicated the same on the patented product. In other words, (1) in light of the abovementioned fact that a patented product sold in other countries is naturally expected to be imported into Japan subsequently, the sale of a product by the patentee in other countries without any reservation should be interpreted as a grant of rights to the [first] and subsequent purchasers to control the product in Japan without any patent restriction. (2) Focusing upon the right of the patentee on the other hand, it should be permitted for a patentee to make a reservation of right upon the sale of a patented product in other countries, to enforce his patent right in Japan, and where the patentee has agreed with the [first] purchaser and has explicitly indicated the same on the patented product, the subsequent purchasers can recognize the attached restriction to that effect even if third parties have intervened during the distribution of the product and can decide at his free will whether or not to purchase the product in the face of such restriction. (3) And the sale of the patented product in other countries by subsidiaries or affiliates who can be regarded as same as the patentee should be interpreted as the sale of the product by the patentee himself, and (4) the need to protect the belief in free trade of the purchaser of a patented product does not differ depending upon whether or not the patentee has a parallel patent right at the place of first sale of the patented product.

NOTES AND QUESTIONS

1. The Japanese Supreme Court says that the rights of the Japanese patent holder are not exhausted by the first sale of the product outside Japan, but that the purchaser of the product outside Japan has a legitimate expectation that it will be able to resell the product in international commerce free of the patent restriction. Thus, the Court accepts a basic territorial nature

for the patent grant, but seeks to limit the consequences of this territorial nature for the free movement of goods in world trade. What changes in business practices might you expect as a consequence of this decision? Might these changes add transparency to the effects of the international patent system? Are they likely to materially affect the flow of goods in world commerce?

2. As noted earlier, independence of patents should not be confused with a principle of territoriality (*see* Christopher Heath, *Parallel Imports and International Trade*, 28 IIC 623, 627-28 (1997)). The Japanese Supreme Court invokes independence as a ground for not expressly recognizing that exhaustion takes place when the products are placed on the German market. Yet, it reaches a conclusion consistent with the principle of international exhaustion. Japan was under some pressure from the United States not to accept international exhaustion of patents in this case. Might this help explain the Supreme Court's "interesting" reasoning?

b.   United States

In 1890, the U.S. Supreme Court decided *Boesch v. Graff*, 133 U.S. 697 (1890). In *Boesch*, the inventor of a lamp burner held parallel patents in Germany and the United States. Under German law, there was a "prior user" exception that allowed a third party to lawfully manufacture and sell a patented product in Germany. Under a prior user exemption, a third party that has manufactured or made serious preparations to manufacture the subject product prior to the application for a patent is entitled to continue its activities.[25] Goods (lamp burners) that were sold in Germany and sent to the United States were lawfully made and sold by a third party (not the patent holder) under the German prior user exemption. The U.S. Supreme Court held that the first sale in Germany did not affect the rights of the patent holder within the United States, enabling the U.S. patent holder to block the sale of imported lamp burners. However, it is essential to note that the U.S. patent holder had not placed, or authorized placement of, the patented goods on the market in Germany.

Following *Boesch*, there were several important Court of Appeals decisions holding that the United States follows a doctrine of international exhaustion of patent rights, distinguishing *Boesch* based on the absence of the patent holder's consent to the first sale. Among the most important of these is the decision of the Court of Appeals for the Second Circuit in *Curtiss Aeroplane v. United Aircraft*, 266 F. 71 (2d Cir. 1920). In that case, a holder of U.S. patents on aircraft components had licensed the British government to produce aircraft in Canada (for use in the First World War). After the war, the British government sold some of the aircraft it had produced to a third party that imported them into the United States for resale. The Second Circuit held that the U.S. patent holder, in consenting to the use of its patent for the manufacture of airplanes in Canada, had exhausted its right to control the importation of the resulting aircraft into the United States.

---

25. In countries other than the United States where patents are awarded based on the first filing, the prior user exemption may avoid injustice to earlier inventors who are not the first to the patent office.

While there had been some conflicting case law at the district court level on the question of international exhaustion of patent rights, the most comprehensive analysis of the case law found that the United States followed a doctrine of international exhaustion in respect to patents. (*See* Margreth Barrett, *The United States Doctrine of Exhaustion: Parallel Imports of Patented Goods*, 27 N. KY. L. REV. 911 (2000)). That is, at least until *Jazz Photo v. ITC*, 264 F.3d 1094 (Fed. Cir. 2001). In *Jazz Photo*, the Court of Appeals for the Federal Circuit articulated a national exhaustion principle for the United States said to derive from *Boesch v. Graff*. But the CAFC did not take note of contrary preexisting case law (which had appropriately distinguished that case), nor did it even nod to the potential implications of its decision, for example, in respect to patented medicines first sold outside the United States.

Jazz Photo involved an appeal to the CAFC of a decision by the International Trade Commission in a Section 337 action initiated by Fuji Photo. Fuji sought to prevent importation of used disposable cameras in which third parties had replaced film. Some of those disposable cameras were first sold in the United States (and exported for film replacement), and some were first sold abroad. Fuji holds a number of patents on the disposable cameras in the United States and elsewhere.

Much of the CAFC decision involved the question of whether the actions by third parties constitute "repair" or "reconstruction" as a matter of U.S. patent law. Under existing doctrine, a patent holder may not prevent a third party from "repairing" a patented product that has been first sold, but may prevent the "reconstruction" of a product. Reconstruction is treated as the equivalent of "making" a new product, and therefore to be within the acts the patent holder may prevent.

The ITC decided that the acts performed by third parties constituted reconstruction, and that importation of the used and reconstructed disposable cameras should be generally prohibited. The CAFC disagreed with the ITC's legal analysis, holding that the acts performed by third parties constituted "repair," and therefore were permitted as to disposable cameras that had been first sold. That is, the rights of the patent holders to exercise control over repair of the cameras had been "exhausted" when they were first sold.

However, the CAFC went on to hold that exhaustion of the patent holder's rights only took place regarding products that had been first sold in the United States, stating:

> Fuji states that some of the imported LFFP cameras originated and were sold only overseas, but are included in the refurbished importations by some of the respondents. The record supports this statement, which does not appear to be disputed. United States patent rights are not exhausted by products of foreign provenance. To invoke the protection of the first sale doctrine, the authorized first sale must have occurred under the United States patent. *See Boesch v. Graff*, 133 U.S. 697, 701-703, 33 L. Ed. 787, 10 S. Ct. 378 (1890) (a lawful foreign purchase does not obviate the need for license from the United States patentee before importation into and sale in the United States). Our decision applies only to LFFPs for which the United States patent right has been exhausted by first sale in the United States. Imported LFFPs of solely foreign provenance are not immunized from infringement of United States patents by the nature of their refurbishment.

264 F.3d at 1105. The CAFC held that Fuji could not prevent importation of cameras that had first been sold in the United States, exported for repair, then

re-imported. However, since U.S. patent rights as to cameras first sold outside the United States were not exhausted, importation of cameras first sold and repaired outside the United States could be blocked. That is, it prescribed a rule of national exhaustion.

The *Jazz Photo* case followed a somewhat unusual route. In addition to initiating a Section 337 action against Jazz Photo (which was the subject of the CAFC appeal), the plaintiff Fuji Film pursued a civil patent infringement case. We will examine Section 337 of the Trade Act of 1930 further in Chapter 6. A Section 337 proceeding may result in an order blocking imports, but not an award of damages. Based on the CAFC's holding that Jazz Photo violated Fuji's patent, the district court in the infringement case considered, *inter alia*, the issue of damages. In doing so, it devoted more attention to the exhaustion question than had the CAFC. Unlike the CAFC, the district court recognized that *Jazz Photo* involved a matter of first impression (i.e., it recognized that *Boesch* had not addressed the central issue).

FUJI PHOTO FILM v. JAZZ PHOTO
249 F. Supp. 2d 434 (D.N.J. 2003)

HOCHBERG, District Judge: . . .

II. "EXHAUSTION" BY FIRST SALE

This Court's finding of repair with respect to approximately 4 million cameras does not end the inquiry, because a refurbished disposable camera infringes unless it was permissibly repaired from an empty camera shell first sold in the *United States. Jazz v. ITC*, 264 F.3d at 1098-99, 1103-1107, 1110-11). This requirement of domestic first sale derives from the principle of patent "exhaustion."

"EXHAUSTION" — LEGAL PRINCIPLES

The principle of exhaustion holds that a patentee's rights in a patented article are "exhausted" after the first sale of the article by the patentee or under the patentee's authority. *Jazz v. ITC*, 264 F.3d at 1105. In exchange for the royalty received, the patentee ceases to have the ability to use its patent monopoly to restrict the further sale, use, or lawful modification or repair of the product. *See id.; see also, e.g., Mitchell v. Hawley*, 83 U.S. 544, 547, 21 L. Ed. 322 (1872); *Boesch v. Graff*, 133 U.S. 697, 703, 33 L. Ed. 787, 10 S. Ct. 378, 1890 Dec. Comm'r Pat. 287 (1890) ("when the machine passes to the hands of the purchaser it is no longer within the limits of the monopoly. It passes outside it, and it is no longer under the protection of the act of congress."). This principle flows logically from the common-sense notion that a patentee is "entitled to but one royalty for a patented machine." *Mitchell*, 83 U.S. at 547.[18]

18. While several decisions of the Federal Circuit, including *Jazz v. ITC*, have addressed the repair/reconstruction question as implicating the doctrine of "exhaustion" (*see, e.g., Jazz v. ITC*, 264 F.3d at 1105; *Surfco Hawaii v. Fin Control Sys Pty., Ltd.*, 264 F.3d 1062, 1065 (Fed. Cir. 2001); *Kendall Co. v. Progressive Med. Tech., Inc.*, 85 F.3d 1570, 1573 (Fed. Cir. 1996)), other Federal Circuit decisions have addressed the issue under the rubric of implied license. *See, e.g., Bottom Line*

As the Federal Circuit noted in *Jazz v. ITC*, however, there is a significant exception to this general principle of exhaustion by first sale: A patentee's United States patent rights are not exhausted unless the patented product is first sold "under the United States patent." *Jazz v. ITC*, 264 F.3d at 1105. This exception traces its origins to the Supreme Court's decision in *Boesch v. Graff*, in which the Court held that the sale or use in the United States of a patented product purchased abroad, even from an authorized seller of the product in the foreign country, constitutes patent infringement. *See* 10 S. Ct. at 380.

The patentee in *Boesch* owned both United States and German patents for lamp burners. The defendant acquired the burners in Germany from an individual who was not licensed by the patentee to make or sell the product in either country, but was permitted to make or sell the burners under *German law*. 10 S. Ct. at 379-80. The Supreme Court found the defendant's sale of the product in the United States to be infringement. *Id.* at 380.

The Supreme Court's decision in *Boesch* left open the question whether a foreign sale by the holder of both United States and foreign patents (or its licensee with a license to sell in both countries) "exhausts" the patentee's rights "under the United States patent." *See* 5 CHISUM ON PATENTS § 16.05[3][a][ii]. Several courts thereafter distinguished *Boesch* on this ground, concluding that, on the one hand, the foreign sale of a patented article by the patentee (or a licensee) constituted exhaustion, while on the other hand the patentee retained its monopoly over items sold abroad by a licensee with no authority to sell the product in the United States. *See Dickerson v. Matheson*, 57 F. 524 (2d Cir. 1893); *Curtiss Aeroplane & Motor Corp.*, 266 F. 71, 78 (2d Cir. 1920); *Sanofi, SA v. Med-Tech Veterinarian Products, Inc.*, 565 F. Supp. 931 (D.N.J. 1983). *See also Dickerson v. Tinling*, 84 F. 192, 1898 Dec. Comm'r Pat. 503 (8th Cir. 1897) (dictum); *Kabushiki Kaisha Hattori Seiko v. Refac Tech. Devel. Corp.*, 690 F. Supp. 1339, 1342 (S.D.N.Y. 1988) (dictum); *PCI Parfumes et Cosmetiques Int'l v. Perfumania Inc.*, 1995 U.S. Dist. LEXIS 3462, No. 93 Civ. 9009, 35 U.S.P.Q.2d 1159, 1160, 1995 WL 121298, at *1 (S.D.N.Y. Mar. 21, 1995).

Prior to its decision in *Jazz v. ITC*, the Federal Circuit was never called upon to address this distinction.[19] The record on appeal in *Jazz v. ITC*, however, placed the issue before the Circuit, which held that in order for a sale to be "under the United States Patent" such that the patentee's rights are exhausted, the sale must be "in the United States." 264 F.3d at 1105.

Mgmt. Inc. v. Pan Man, Inc., 228 F.3d 1352, 1354 (Fed. Cir. 2000); *Hewlett-Packard Co. v. Repeat-O-Type Stencil Mfg. Corp., Inc.*, 123 F.3d 1445, 1451 (1997)). While these two doctrines are not always congruent, in the instant case they can be viewed as opposite sides of the same coin; i.e., where a patentee's rights are "exhausted" through first sale, subsequent purchasers could be said to have an implied license to repair the purchased article. *See, e.g.*, Michael D. Lake, Patent & Know-How (Technology). Licensees and Licensing Strategies, 722 PLI/Pat 353, 371 (Practicing Law Institute, 2002) (exhaustion and implied license rationalized identically). Because the Federal Circuit treated the repair/reconstruction issue as implicating the "exhaustion" doctrine, reserving its discussion of implied license for its analysis of whether subsequent purchasers' rights of repair were limited by the circumstances of sale under principles of contract law (*Jazz v. ITC*, 264 F.3d at 1107-08), this Court similarly treats the repair/reconstruction question as one of "exhaustion," rather than "implied license."

19. Compare *Ajinomoto Co., Inc. v. Archer-Daniels-Midland Co.*, 228 F.3d 1338, 1348 (Fed. Cir. 2000) (importation into United States of a product made abroad by a patented process is infringement under Product Process Amendments Act, 35 U.S.C. § 271(g), even though product was authorized to be produced outside the United States).

United States patent rights are not exhausted by products of foreign provenance. To invoke the protection of the [exhaustion by first sale] doctrine, the authorized first sale must have occurred under the United States patent [citing *Boesch*]. . . . Our decision applies only to LFFPs for which the United States patent right has been exhausted by first sale *in the United States*.

Id. (emphasis added). The Federal Circuit explicitly stated this holding four times in the *Jazz v. ITC* opinion. *See id.* at 1098 (reaching repair issue only with respect to used cameras whose first sale was "in the United States" with the patentee's authorization); *id.* at 1105 (exhaustion applies "when a patented device has been lawfully sold in the United States"); *id.* at 1110 (same, and affirming the ITC's finding of infringement for "LFFPs whose prior sale was not in the United States"). Thus, the Federal Circuit has ruled that Fuji's patent rights are exhausted only with respect to cameras refurbished from shells first sold in the United States. This court is bound by that ruling.[20]

"EXHAUSTION" — THE JURY'S VERDICT

In the stipulated Special Verdict form, the jury was asked to determine: (1) the total number of refurbished cameras sold by Jazz Photo and Jazz Hong Kong in or to the United States during the relevant period (Question 1); (2) the number of those cameras refurbished from shells of cameras first sold in the United States (Question 2); and (3) the number of those cameras made from shells of cameras first sold abroad (Question 3).[21] In response to these questions, the jury rendered the following verdict:

TOTAL NUMBER OF REFURBISHED CAMERAS:	40,099,369
TOTAL NUMBER FIRST SOLD IN THE U.S.:	3,809,442
TOTAL NUMBER FIRST SOLD ABROAD:	36,289,927

. . .

---

20. Jazz sought a stay of the Federal Circuit's ruling, rehearing en banc, and certiorari to the Supreme Court on the exhaustion issue. In its various petitions, Jazz argued that the Federal Circuit improperly changed the law and that foreign exhaustion should remain viable if the patented article is sold by the holder of a license in both the United States and the foreign country. Jazz's petitions were denied. The Circuit's decision is therefore stare decisis in this case. Nor is the proposition that foreign sales should not eviscerate United States patent rights without substantial justification. Indeed, it follows directly from the territorial nature of the patent laws themselves. Cf. *Deepsouth Packing Co., Inc. v. Laitram Corp.*, 406 U.S. 518, 531, 32 L. Ed. 2d 273, 92 S. Ct. 1700 (1972) (patent laws "do not, and were not intended to, operate beyond the limits of the United States"). As one leading commentator has noted, "since a patent only extends to the borders of the country using it, it makes sense to limit the right to make, use or sell the product to the same borders." Martin J. Adelman, PATENT LAW PERSPECTIVES § 3.6[1]. Thus, "anyone purchasing a product in the territory of one sovereign country ought to be on notice that the use or sale of that product in another sovereign country may be impermissible." *Id.* This was precisely the balance struck by the Federal Circuit in *Jazz v. ITC*.

21. Specifically, Question 3 asked the jury to determine the number of cameras sold by Jazz in or to the United States made from refurbished shells of cameras first sold outside the United States by Fuji or a licensee with the right to sell in both countries. This question was asked solely in an abundance of caution: after the appeal of this matter, should the Federal Circuit sitting en banc or the Supreme Court overrule the panel decision in Jazz v. ITC on the issue of foreign first sale, a retrial of this matter would be unnecessary.

Conclusion

For the reasons stated in this Opinion, this Court finds that Jazz is liable for infringement of Fuji's patents with respect to 40,928,185 cameras sold by Jazz during the period 1995 through August 21, 2001. [This sum reflects findings of infringement in addition to those further to the exhaustion ruling. — EDS.] Multiplying this number by the jury's reasonable royalty award of 56 cents per infringing camera, this Court finds that Fuji was damaged by Jazz's infringing sales in the amount of $22,919,783.60. . . . An appropriate Final Order and Judgment will issue forthwith.

HON. FAITH S. HOCHBERG, U.S.D.J.

NOTES AND QUESTIONS

1. The consequence of the *Jazz Photo* decision is that U.S. patent holders are able to charge prices in the United States different from the prices they charge in foreign markets without having to worry that the products placed on the market abroad will affect their U.S. prices. Do you think it is a good idea to shield the U.S. market from price competition?

2. The U.S. Congress has had a number of bills before it to overrule the *Jazz Photo* decision in so far as that prevents import of pharmaceutical products put on the market in other developed countries, such as in Australia, Canada, or the European Union. The major pharmaceutical companies actively oppose such legislation principally on grounds that countries outside the United States usually maintain some form of price controls on drugs, so that in effect the United States would be importing price controls. They further argue that because the United States has no controls on drug prices, American consumers are effectively subsidizing research and development for foreign consumers. The argument is that foreign consumers should be paying higher prices for drugs. The major pharmaceutical companies spend about 15 percent of their revenues on research and development, and a much higher portion on advertising and promotion. Should foreign consumers be asked to invest more in American television advertising?

3. As noted earlier, a rule against international exhaustion raises some very difficult practical problems. A typical high technology product, such as a computer or DVD player, contains components manufactured under patents held in many countries. How can a foreign manufacturer (or U.S. importer) be sure that one of many components is not subject to a U.S. patent, and that the patent holder will not seek to block the importation? U.S. patent holders have sought to block imports in this way. They are, in effect, seeking an additional royalty on technology they already licensed abroad. U.S. courts have yet to settle whether there is an implied license in some such cases, as recognized by the Japanese Supreme Court in the *BBS* case. *See, e.g., Minebea v. Pabst*, 444 F. Supp. 2d 68 (D.D.C. 2006).

4. In *Quanta Computers v. LG Electronics*, 553 U.S. 617 (2008), the U.S. Supreme Court addressed the question of exhaustion of patent rights in the domestic context, specifically whether the sale of a product embodying a "method patent" exhausts the patent holder's rights in that method. The Supreme Court answered in the affirmative.

    LG Electronics licensed several method patents to Intel. The patented methods were used to improve the operation of Intel microprocessors.

In its license agreement with Intel, LG Electronics required Intel to provide notice to third-party purchasers of Intel parts that they were not acquiring rights to practice LG's method patents when Intel products were combined with the products of third parties. Quanta Computers purchased microprocessors incorporating LG's method patents from Intel and incorporated those microprocessors in computers along with third-party parts. LG sued Quanta for violation of its method patents.

LG argued that because the Intel microprocessors continued to use its method patents even after the purchase by Quanta, the sale to Quanta did not exhaust LG's patent rights (as might be anticipated if LG's patents covered a product). LG contended that method patents are not subject to traditional exhaustion because the purchaser practices the invention after the sale.

The Supreme Court disagreed, holding that method patents involving processes incorporated in products are exhausted upon first sale, just as patented machine components would be. The Supreme Court noted that if method patents were permitted to escape the application of exhaustion doctrine, inventors would be encouraged to file patent applications in the form of method patents. The Supreme Court noted that LG was not in a contract relationship with the third-party purchasers from Intel. The third-party purchasers were entitled to expect they could use the Intel microprocessors without facing pass-through patent claims from LG.

The Supreme Court in this case reversed the Federal Circuit, and in doing so limited the scope of rights that may be asserted by patent holders. This case was closely watched by product resellers in the United States. The resellers feared that an extension of the exhaustion doctrine would limit their ability to market products to end-users. The Supreme Court did not in any way address "international" exhaustion issues in this decision.

5.   You are advising the owner of a chain of pharmacies located in the United States. The owner tells you that popular cholesterol-lowering drugs are available in Canada at wholesale prices about half the wholesale prices of the same drugs available in the United States. The owner wants to know whether the pharmacy chain will face any patent-related problems if it purchases and imports the drugs from Canada for sale to U.S. consumers. How would you answer that question? What additional facts will be important to your analysis?

c.   *South Africa*

Section 15C of South Africa's Medicines Amendments Act was the subject of threats by the European Union and the United States to impose trade sanctions for violation of the TRIPS agreement, and a lawsuit by 39 pharmaceutical companies.[26] The European Union and the United States eventually withdrew their objections, recognizing the TRIPS consistency of authorizing parallel imports. The pharmaceutical companies eventually withdrew their case and paid the legal fees of the South African government. This incident marked a

---

26. *See* discussion in Frederick M. Abbott, *WTO TRIPS Agreement and Its Implications for Access to Medicines in Developing Countries*, prepared for the British Commission on Intellectual Property Rights (Study Paper 2a, Feb. 2002).

low point for patent law as it had been used to threaten the legitimate interests of the South African government and people in the midst of the HIV-AIDS pandemic. The legitimacy of the international intellectual property system has yet to fully recover from this.

PARALLEL IMPORTS IN SOUTH AFRICA— UNDER THE RULE OF INTERNATIONAL EXHAUSTION

Y. Tayler, ed.*

South Africa has adopted legislation (Section 15C of the Medicines and Related Substances Control Amendment Act, No. 90 of 1997) pursuant to which its Minister of Health (through the Medicines Control Council) has issued regulations that establish the conditions for the parallel importation of medicines into the country. In addition to the regulations, the Council has issued a Guideline for Parallel Importation of Medicines in South Africa.

The regulations provide that: "parallel importation" means the importation into the Republic of a medicine protected under patent and/or registered in the Republic that has been put on to the market outside the Republic by or with the consent of such patent holder.

The regulations and guideline provide procedures under which a parallel importer must obtain a permit to undertake importation. These procedures are intended to assure that parallel import medicines are duly approved and registered by the Department of Health, and that the parallel importer will comply with requirements ordinarily imposed on vendors of medicine in South Africa, such as using an approved storage facility and having in place a recall procedure. The guideline also establishes that, "The parallel importer may use the proprietary name approved in South Africa as well as any trade marks applicable to the medicine in order to ensure the public health interests."

d. Switzerland

Switzerland is not a member state of the European Union. However, it adapts its own laws to the Union's standards in specific sectors. In 2009, Switzerland unilaterally introduced the concept of regional exhaustion for patents in relation to the EEA member states while keeping up national exhaustion for third countries.

SWITZERLAND: NEW DEVELOPMENTS IN SWISS PATENT LAW

P. Groz & A. Mondini

1.3 PRESENT EXHAUSTION REGIME IN SWISS INTELLECTUAL PROPERTY LAW

Until now, the exhaustion regime in Swiss copyright, trademark, and patent law was solely determined by case law. The Swiss Federal Court ruled that, under Swiss law, the principle of international exhaustion applies to copyrights (BGE

---

* Battling HIV-AIDS, World Bank, Annex 2, Box B.2.

124 III 321, Nintendo) and to trademark rights (BGE 122 III 469, Chanel). However, patent rights were subject to national exhaustion (BGE 126 III 129, Kodak). No relevant Swiss Federal Court decision exists as yet concerning design rights.

Under the concept of national exhaustion, patent rights could be asserted to prevent parallel imports to Switzerland of patent-protected products first sold abroad, provided that the patent owner did not engage in a restriction of trade amounting to a violation of competition law. Since the Kodak judgment, the national exhaustion of patent rights has been the subject of much controversy.

On one hand it was argued, inter alia, that national exhaustion enables the patent holder to charge different prices in different countries depending on the demand. This allows further financing of research and development activities. A move away from the system of national exhaustion would harm Switzerland as a place for research. Similarly, with a transition to international exhaustion, there would be a danger that developing countries might no longer be supplied with drugs or other patent-protected products because of the fear that products sold in those countries at a lower price would then be re-imported to Switzerland.

On the other hand, it was broadly criticized that the restriction of intra-brand competition that follows from a system of national exhaustion is one of the main reasons that prices in Switzerland for some products are higher than in neighboring countries.

1.4 REGIONAL EXHAUSTION IN PATENT LAW SINCE 1 JULY 2009

After a highly publicized political debate, the Swiss Parliament decided to amend the Patent Act (PatA) by introducing the regional exhaustion concept in relation to the contracting States of the European Economic Area. This patent law revision went into effect on 1 July 2009. This means that patented products first put on the market in the European Economic Area with the consent of the patent holder may now be imported into Switzerland without the patent holder's consent (Art. 9a PatA).

If a patented product is first put on the market outside the European Economic Area, the patent holder continues to be able to defend against possible parallel imports into Switzerland. The patent holder may not prevent the importation, however, where the patent in question does not pertain to the main function of the product (e.g., a perfume) to be imported, but is instead only of secondary importance (e.g., a patented closure on a perfume bottle, Art. 9a para 4 PatA).

It is noteworthy that the concept of national exhaustion continues to apply for patented goods with government-administered prices (particularly pharmaceuticals) in Switzerland or in the country of sale (Art. 9a para 5 PatA). This exception (introduced as a result of the efforts of the strongly-represented Swiss pharmaceutical industry) is of great practical relevance. First, patent protection is of fundamental importance to the pharmaceutical industry. Second, the price of pharmaceuticals differs greatly among European countries due to national regulations.

It should finally be noted that, exceptionally, international (not just regional) exhaustion applies to agricultural means of production and investment goods.

1.5 SIMPLIFIED APPROVAL OF PARALLEL-IMPORTED DRUGS

The Swiss Therapeutic Products Act provides for a simplified marketing authorization procedure for parallel-imported drugs that are already approved in Switzerland. Previously, simplified approval was not possible as long as the already-approved therapeutic product (i.e., the original preparation) was still patent-protected. The first applicant was allowed to assert its patent rights during the marketing authorization procedure for the parallel-imported drug before the Swiss Agency for Therapeutic Products (Swissmedic).

With the revision of patent law effective 1 July 2009, the Therapeutic Products Act was also amended. It is no longer possible to claim patent protection in the administrative marketing authorization procedure for a parallel-imported drug. This results in a shortening and simplification of the marketing authorization procedure for parallel-imported drugs.

In the future, the owner of the original preparation will only be able to assert its patent rights against a parallel importer in civil court proceedings.

NOTES AND QUESTIONS

1. How would you classify Switzerland's new exhaustion policy in the context of the multilateral trading system? Do you see any issues arising in connection with the nondiscrimination provisions of the TRIPS Agreement? Which parties could be subject to *de facto* discrimination and how likely is it that they are going to challenge Switzerland's new policy?

2. In an advisory opinion for the Swiss Federal Institute of Intellectual Property, Thomas Cottier and Rachel Liechti produced evidence that the exhaustion rules applied by Switzerland, which provide for regional exhaustion in connection with EU countries with simultaneous maintenance of national exhaustion toward other countries, result in a *de lege* discrimination of parallel exports from third countries under the GATT Agreement.[27] What are the prospects of justifying the Swiss patent exhaustion policy under Articles XXIV and XX(d) of GATT?

e. The Doha Declaration

The WTO Doha Declaration on the TRIPS Agreement and Public Health, discussed in section II.B.1.c, *infra*, expressly confirms the right of each WTO Member to determine its own policy and rules with respect to exhaustion of rights and thus whether to permit parallel importation of medicines.

B. The WTO TRIPS Agreement

We have previously examined the factors that brought about negotiation and conclusion of the TRIPS Agreement. Pharmaceutical and agricultural chemical

---

27. Thomas Cottier & Rachel Liechti, "Ist die einseitig statuierte regionale Erschöpfung im schweizerischen Patentrecht mit dem WTO-Recht vereinbar?," available at https://www.ige.ch/fileadmin/user_upload/Juristische_Infos/d/j10071d.pdf, or in Astrid Epiney & Tamara Civitella (eds.), *Schweizerisches Jahrbuch für Europarecht/Annuaire suisse de droit européen (2007/2008)*, Zürich: Stämpfli, 2007.

producers were among the leading lobbying groups advocating higher standards of patent protection. Prior to the TRIPS Agreement, a substantial
number of developing countries did not provide patent subject matter protection for pharmaceutical and food-related products. The TRIPS Agreement
changed that: Articles 27 to 34 of the Agreement specifically address patents,
in addition to incorporating the substantive provisions of the Paris Convention.
The international system thus prescribes minimal standards requiring that,
inter alia, patents be granted in all fields of technology, including chemicals
and pharmaceutical products, both product and process patents (the latter with
the burden of proof reversed); the minimum term of protection is 20 years from
the filing of the application; and that the invention be sufficiently disclosed.

INTELLECTUAL PROPERTY RIGHTS IN WORLD TRADE

Frederick M. Abbott*

The most significant changes to the international IP regulatory system brought
about by the TRIPS Agreement were in the field of patents. The Paris Convention provides rules regarding the mechanisms by which patents are granted,
and prescribes national treatment. It does not, however, define the subject
matter scope of patent protection, the criteria of patentability or the term of
patent protection. It includes a limited set of rules applicable to the compulsory
licensing of patents.

The TRIPS Agreement provides that patents should be available for products
and processes in all fields of technology on the basis of the criteria of novelty,
inventive step and capability of industrial application.[58] It also provides for
sufficiency of disclosure.[59] Taken together, these criteria reflect the basic
rules of developed country patent systems. The Agreement provides that
patents rights shall be available and enjoyed without discrimination based on
place of invention, field of technology, and whether products are imported or
locally produced.[60] The TRIPS Agreement prescribes a minimum 20 year term
of protection counted from the filing of the patent application.[61]

The TRIPS Agreement allows for certain exclusions from patentability, such
as for the protection of public order and for diagnostic or therapeutic procedures.[62] It permits Members to refuse patenting of animals and plants, but
requires that some form of plant variety protection be provided.[63] This may
be through patent or a *sui generis* form of protection. Also, the exclusion for
animals and plants does not extend to non-biological and microbiological
processes.

The TRIPS Agreement expands upon the compulsory licensing rules found
in the Paris Convention, prescribing substantive and procedural conditions for
the grant of such licenses.[64] However, it does not limit the grounds upon which

---

* In Research Handbook in International Economic Law (A. Guzman & A. Sykes eds., Elgar
2007).
58. Article 27, TRIPS Agreement.
59. Article 29, *id.*
60. Article 27, *id.*
61. Article 33, *id.*
62. Article 27.2-3(a), *id.*
63. Article 27.3(b), *id.*
64. Article 31, *id.*

compulsory licenses may be granted, and it provides for a waiver of procedural prerequisites in cases of national emergency, extreme urgency, or for public non-commercial use. In addition to the provision on compulsory licensing, the TRIPS Agreement incorporates a general provision concerning exceptions to patent rights.[65] This allows a Member to adopt limited exceptions that do not unreasonably conflict with the normal exploitation of the patent or the legitimate interests of patent holders, taking into account the legitimate interests of third parties. This general exception provision is the subject of an important panel decision to be discussed later.[66]

The requirement that countries subject inventions in all fields of technology to patent protection required a major change to the patent laws of many countries. Developing countries were granted a ten year transition period in which to provide patent protection for subject matter areas not previously covered.[67] In respect to pharmaceutical and agricultural chemical product patents, special "mailbox" rules required developing Members to accept applications filed during the transition period and preserve them for review when protection became available. If and when a patent was eventually granted the term would be limited based on the original filing date of the mailbox application.[68] This rather complex system was the subject of the first AB decision concerning TRIPS,[69] [see *supra* Chapter 1, section II.B.4. The ten-year transition period expired on January 1, 2005, but continues to be of interest as India has grappled with a large number of mailbox applications.[28]]

1. Fair Use Under the TRIPS Agreement

The grant of a patent involves a bargain between the inventor and society. In some circumstances, important social interests dictate an alteration to the "business as usual" patent bargain. National security interests typically are found to take precedence over individual inventor interests, and provisions are routinely made in patent laws to allow governments to keep security-related inventions secret, or to use them under compulsory license.

The field of public health raises difficult patent-related issues that in recent years have garnered considerable attention. The most visible issues have involved the HIV-AIDS pandemic and efforts by developing countries to address this crisis in ways they can afford, as well as concerns among developed

65. Article 30, *id.*

66. Canada — Patent Protection of Pharmaceutical Products, WT/DS114, 17 Mar. 2000 ("Canada-Generic Pharmaceuticals").

67. The change would have a particularly significant effect in countries which did not provide patent protection for pharmaceutical products since bringing such products under patent protection would affect generic producers and almost certainly increase the price of medicines. Article 64.4, TRIPS Agreement.

68. Article 70.8, TRIPS Agreement.

69. India — Patent Protection for Pharmaceutical and Agricultural Chemical Products, WT/DS50, 5 Sept. 1997 ("India-Mailbox").

28. [A large number of mailbox applications were filed in India. Pre-grant opposition is possible in India, and a significant number of pre-grant oppositions have been filed. India's amended Patents Act also incorporates a *sui generis* prior user right to permit the continued production of medicines on which patents are granted, conditional on payment of a reasonable royalty. For an overview of the situation in India, *see* Frederick M. Abbott, *The WTO Medicines Decision: World Pharmaceutical Trade and the Protection of Public Health*, 99 AM. J. INT'L L. 317, 320-22 (2005), and the excerpt *infra* section III.C from *TRIPS II, Asia and the Mercantile Pharmaceutical War.* — EDS.]

and developing countries regarding access to medicines for the treatment of avian bird flu. But there are systemic issues involving patents and public health that do not involve immediate crises and that will continue to be the source of debate.

The objective of the TRIPS Agreement negotiations was to require all WTO Member countries to adopt and enforce high levels of patent protection. Nonetheless, it was accepted that the TRIPS Agreement would need to accommodate exceptions to the broad right of patent holders to exclude others from making use of patented inventions. As with most aspects of the TRIPS Agreement negotiations, the scope of exceptions and safeguards was controversial.

a. Article 30 (Exceptions)

In WTO-GATT jurisprudence, a provision that allows an "exception" acts to waive compliance with an otherwise applicable requirement. For example, in traditional GATT-WTO jurisprudence, restrictions placed on imports to protect public health were considered an "exception" from the general requirement to freely allow imports.[29]

Article 30 of the TRIPS Agreement is headed "Exceptions to Rights Conferred." It provides for "limited exceptions" to the rights of patent holders. Since the Paris Convention contained no antecedent to Article 30 of the TRIPS Agreement, WTO dispute settlement panels interpreting Article 30 find themselves in largely uncharted legal territory.[30] The WTO panel in the *Canada-Generic Pharmaceuticals* decision that follows described Article 30 as imposing a three-prong test. An exception (1) should be "limited"; (2) should "not unreasonably conflict with a normal exploitation of the patent"; and (3) should "not unreasonably prejudice the legitimate interests of the patent owner, taking account of the legitimate interests of third parties."

In the *Canada-Generic Pharmaceuticals* case,[31] the European Union complained against Canadian legislation that (1) allowed generic drug manufacturers to stockpile drugs prior to the expiration of patents (so that the generic drugs could immediately enter the market immediately after the expiration of patents), and (2) allowed use of patented technology for purposes of securing regulatory approval prior to the expiration of patent terms.

The WTO panel found that Canada's stockpiling legislation was inconsistent with its TRIPS obligations. Bulk stockpiling of generic pharmaceuticals did not constitute a limited exception to the rights of patent holders in the sense of Article 30. However, the panel found that the provisions allowing product testing and submission of data for regulatory approval was an allowable limited

---

29. In its *EC-Asbestos* decision, the Appellate Body determined that the GATT does not require WTO Members to treat products posing health risks as being "like" products that do not pose such risks. Import barriers to unsafe imports may no longer be considered "exceptional." European Communities—Measures Affecting Asbestos and Asbestos-Containing Products, Report of the Appellate Body, AB-2000-11, WT/DS135/AB/R, 12 March 2001.

30. The three-pronged test has an antecedent in Article 9(2) of the Berne Convention dealing with copyright, and decisions of national courts under the Berne Convention might provide some guidance to panels considering the scope of exceptions to patent protection. However, patents and copyright serve substantially different functions and the utility of the analogies is uncertain.

31. Canada—Patent Protection of Pharmaceutical Products, Report of the Panel, WT/DS114/R, March 17, 2000 ("Canada-Generic Pharmaceuticals"). WTO dispute settlement decisions are often referred to by names that identify their essential subject matter in lieu of the formal titles.

exception. Having made this finding, the panel was confronted with the European Union's argument that limited exceptions under Article 30 remain subject to the TRIPS Article 27.1 prohibition of discrimination as to "field of technology." The panel's response follows.

CANADA—PATENT PROTECTION OF PHARMACEUTICAL PRODUCTS, REPORT OF THE PANEL
WT/DS114/R, March 17, 2000

. . . (A) APPLICABILITY OF ARTICLE 27.1 TO ARTICLE 30 EXCEPTIONS

7.88 Canada took the position that Article 27.1's reference to "patent rights" that must be enjoyable without discrimination as to field of technology refers to the basic rights enumerated in Article 28.1 subject to any exceptions that might be made under Article 30. In other words, governments may discriminate when making the "limited" exceptions allowed under Article 30, but they may not discriminate as to patent rights as modified by such exceptions.

7.89 In support of this position, Canada argued that the scope of Article 30 would be reduced to insignificance if governments were required to treat all fields of technology the same, for if all exceptions had to apply to every product it would be far more difficult to meet the requirement that Article 30 exceptions be "limited." It would also be more difficult to target particular social problems, as are anticipated, according to Canada, by Articles 7 and 8 of the TRIPS Agreement. Conversely, Canada argued, requiring that exceptions be applied to all products would cause needless deprivation of patent rights for those products as to which full enforcement of patent rights causes no problem.

7.90 Canada acknowledged that there are certain textual difficulties with this position. It acknowledged that two of the primary purposes of Article 27.1 were to eliminate two types of discrimination that had been practised against pharmaceuticals and certain other products—either a denial of patentability for such products, or, if patents were granted, automatic compulsory licences permitting others to manufacture such products for a fee. Canada acknowledged that, in order to preclude discrimination as to compulsory licences, the non-discrimination rule of Article 27 was made applicable to Article 31 of the TRIPS Agreement, which grants a limited exception for compulsory licences under specified conditions. To defend its position, therefore, Canada was required to explain how Article 27.1 could apply to exceptions made under Article 31, but not to exceptions made under its neighbouring exception provision in Article 30. Canada argued that Article 31 was "mandatory" in character while Article 30 was "permissive," and that this distinction made it appropriate to apply the non-discrimination provision to the former but not the latter.

7.91 The Panel was unable to agree with Canada's contention that Article 27.1 did not apply to exceptions granted under Article 30. The text of the TRIPS Agreement offers no support for such an interpretation. Article 27.1 prohibits discrimination as to enjoyment of "patent rights" without qualifying that term. Article 30 exceptions are explicitly described as "exceptions to the exclusive rights conferred by a patent" and contain no indication that any exemption from non-discrimination rules is intended. A discriminatory exception that takes away enjoyment of a patent right is discrimination as much as is discrimination in the basic rights themselves. The acknowledged fact that the Article 31 exception for compulsory licences and government use is understood to be subject to the non-discrimination rule of Article 27.1, without the need for any textual provision so providing, further strengthens the case for treating the non-discrimination rules as applicable to Article 30. Articles 30 and 31 are linked together by the opening words of Article 31 which define the scope of Article 31 in terms of exceptions not covered by Article 30. Finally, the Panel could not agree with Canada's attempt to distinguish between Articles 30 and 31 on the basis of their mandatory/permissive character; both provisions permit exceptions to patent rights subject to certain mandatory conditions. Nor could the Panel understand how such a "mandatory/permissive" distinction, even if present, would logically support making the kind of distinction Canada was arguing. In the Panel's view, what was important was that in the rights available under national law, that is to say those resulting from the basic rights and any permissible exceptions to them, the forms of discrimination referred to in Article 27.1 should not be present.

7.92 Nor was the Panel able to agree with the policy arguments in support of Canada's interpretation of Article 27. To begin with, it is not true that being able to discriminate against particular patents will make it possible to meet Article 30's requirement that the exception be "limited." An Article 30 exception cannot be made "limited" by limiting it to one field of technology, because the effects of each exception must be found to be "limited" when measured against each affected patent. Beyond that, it is not true that Article 27 requires all Article 30 exceptions to be applied to all products. Article 27 prohibits only discrimination as to the place of invention, the field of technology, and whether products are imported or produced locally. Article 27 does not prohibit bona fide exceptions to deal with problems that may exist only in certain product areas. Moreover, to the extent the prohibition of discrimination does limit the ability to target certain products in dealing with certain of the important national policies referred to in Articles 7 and 8.1, that fact may well constitute a deliberate limitation rather than a frustration of purpose. It is quite plausible, as the EC argued, that the TRIPS Agreement would want to require governments to apply exceptions in a non-discriminatory manner, in order to ensure that governments do not succumb to domestic pressures to limit exceptions to areas where right holders tend to be foreign producers.

7.93 The Panel concluded, therefore, that the anti-discrimination rule of Article 27.1 does apply to exceptions of the kind authorized by Article 30. We turn, accordingly, to the question of whether Section 55.2(1) of the Canadian Patent Act discriminates as to fields of technology.

(B) DISCRIMINATION AS TO THE FIELD OF TECHNOLOGY

7.94 The primary TRIPS provisions that deal with discrimination, such as the national treatment and most-favoured-nation provisions of Articles 3 and 4, do not use the term "discrimination." They speak in more precise terms. The ordinary meaning of the word "discriminate" is potentially broader than these more specific definitions. It certainly extends beyond the concept of differential treatment. It is a normative term, pejorative in connotation, referring to results of the unjustified imposition of differentially disadvantageous treatment. Discrimination may arise from explicitly different treatment, sometimes called "*de jure* discrimination," but it may also arise from ostensibly identical treatment which, due to differences in circumstances, produces differentially disadvantageous effects, sometimes called "de facto discrimination."

The standards by which the justification for differential treatment is measured are a subject of infinite complexity. "Discrimination" is a term to be avoided whenever more precise standards are available, and, when employed, it is a term to be interpreted with caution, and with care to add no more precision than the concept contains.

7.95 The European Communities acknowledged that the words of the regulatory review exception of Section 55.2(1) do not limit its application to pharmaceutical products. The terms of the exception protect potentially infringing conduct:

> solely for uses reasonably related to the development and submission of information required under any law [. . .] that regulates the manufacture, construction, use or sale of any product.

Applied literally, these words apply to any of a wide range of products that require regulatory approval for marketing. The EC itself mentioned agricultural chemicals, foodstuffs, cosmetics, automobiles, vessels and aircraft as products that often require regulatory approval.

7.96 The EC pointed out, however, that pharmaceuticals were the only products mentioned in Canada's 1991 legislative debates on the enactment of Sections 55.2(1). It also asserted that Section 55.2(1) was "in effect applied only to pharmaceuticals products." These assertions led to two distinct allegations of discrimination. The first claim of discrimination was the claim that the legislative history's concentration on pharmaceuticals actually governs the legal scope of the measure, so that, as a matter of law, Section 55.2(1) applied only to pharmaceuticals. If that is so, it could be said that Section 55.2(1) imposes *de jure* discrimination against pharmaceuticals. The second claim of discrimination was the claim that, whatever the *de jure* scope of Section 55.2(1), the actual effects of Section 55.2(1) are limited to pharmaceutical producers, and these differential effects amount to a case of de facto discrimination.

7.97 Canada denied that the *de jure* scope of Section 55.2(1) is limited to pharmaceuticals. It pointed to the words of that provision making the exception available to "any product" for which marketing approval was needed. . . .

7.98 In considering how to address these conflicting claims of discrimination, the Panel recalled that various claims of discrimination, *de jure* and de facto, have been the subject of legal rulings under GATT or the WTO. These rulings have addressed the question whether measures were in conflict with various GATT or WTO provisions prohibiting variously defined forms of discrimination. As the Appellate Body has repeatedly made clear, each of these rulings has necessarily been based on the precise legal text in issue, so that it is not possible to treat them as applications of a general concept of discrimination. Given the very broad range of issues that might be involved in defining the word "discrimination" in Article 27.1 of the TRIPS Agreement, the Panel decided that it would be better to defer attempting to define that term at the outset, but instead to determine which issues were raised by the record before the Panel, and to define the concept of discrimination to the extent necessary to resolve those issues.

7.99 With regard to the issue of *de jure* discrimination, the Panel concluded that the European Communities had not presented sufficient evidence to raise the issue in the face of Canada's formal declaration that the exception of Section 55.2(1) was not limited to pharmaceutical products. Absent other evidence, the words of the statute compelled the Panel to accept Canada's assurance that the exception was legally available to every product that was subject to marketing approval requirements. In reaching this conclusion, the Panel took note that its legal finding of conformity on this point was based on a finding as to the meaning of the Canadian law that was in turn based on Canada's representations as to the meaning of that law, and that this finding of conformity would no longer be warranted if, and to the extent that, Canada's representations as to the meaning of that law were to prove wrong.

7.100 The Panel then turned to the question of de facto discrimination. Although the EC's response to the Panel's questions indicated that it did intend to raise the issue of de facto discrimination, the EC did not propose a formal definition of de facto discrimination, nor did it submit a systematic exposition of the evidence satisfying the elements of such a concept.

NOTES AND QUESTIONS

1. The *Canada-Generics* panel was chaired by Professor Robert Hudec, one of the world's most highly respected trade law experts, now deceased.[32] Although this was not an Appellate Body decision, it is bound to exercise an important influence on future WTO jurisprudence.

2. Do you find the logic in paragraph 7.92 of the panel report persuasive? The panel finds that Article 30 is subject to Article 27.1 because Article 27.1 applies the rule of nondiscrimination to the enjoyment of "patent rights," and Article 30 addresses "exceptions to the exclusive rights conferred by a patent." Does it follow that a limited exception to the exclusive rights conferred by a patent could not be defined in terms of a particular subject matter? Why? Is there some logical step missing?

3. The panel also finds that Article 30 is subject to Article 27.1 because the parties agree that Article 31 (compulsory licensing) is subject to Article 27.1. (This is based on Article 70.6, which limits retroactive application of Article 27.1 with respect to compulsory licenses granted before the TRIPS Agreement became known.) The panel says that no party provided it with a reason why Article 30 exceptions should be treated differently than Article 31 compulsory licensing. The parties agreed that Canadian legislation authorizing automatic compulsory licensing of pharmaceutical patents was intended by TRIPS negotiators to be prohibited by the Agreement.

    Does this imply that Canada's legislation that automatically authorized compulsory licensing for pharmaceutical patents was discriminatory? If so, does it follow that applying different rules to the compulsory licensing of pharmaceutical patents than to patents in other fields of technology cannot be justified? This seems a very doubtful result in light of the panel's subsequent indication that WTO Members may differentiate among patented products for *bona fide* reasons.

    What may TRIPS negotiators have found particularly objectionable about Canada's automatic compulsory licensing of pharmaceutical patents? Might the absence of a requirement for justifying a compulsory license in each case have been the failing of the Canadian legislation? If this is the case, how does the United States justify its government use legislation (28 U.S.C. § 1498), which applies automatically to all patents? This legislation

---

32. *See* Frederick M. Abbott, Bob Hudec as Chair of the *Canada-Generic Pharmaceuticals Panel* — The WTO Gets Something Right, 6 J. INT'L ECON. L. 733 (2003).

allows the U.S. federal government to use any patent and prohibits patent holders from obtaining injunctions. The only remedy is a suit for compensation before the Court of Claims in Washington, D.C.

4. The panel's decision focuses on the term "discrimination" and makes clear that this means something other than "differentiation." The panel does not attempt to provide a general definition of "discrimination" or what elements must be demonstrated to prove it. It does say that the term is "pejorative in connotation, referring to results of the unjustified imposition of differentially disadvantageous treatment." The panel clearly leaves open the possibility that patented technologies may be treated differently for regulatory purposes if the differences are justified.

5. The panel draws a distinction between *de jure* and *de facto* discrimination, noting that a number of GATT-WTO panels have addressed this distinction. These panels have held that legislation that is nondiscriminatory on its face (and therefore *de jure* nondiscriminatory) may nevertheless discriminate in its "operational effect" (and therefore be *de facto* discriminatory). *See*, *e.g.*, United States — Section 337 of the Tariff Act of 1930, BISD 36S/345, Report by the Panel adopted Nov. 7, 1989.

6. In *Merck v. Integra Lifesciences*, 545 U.S. 193 (2005), the U.S. Supreme Court interpreted 35 U.S.C. § 271(e) to allow the use of patented inventions for the purpose of conducting research with respect to drugs as to which there is some reasonable prospect that an application to the FDA may be submitted, regardless whether an application is, in fact, eventually submitted or successful. The relevant research may be conducted at the pre-clinical trial phase. The Supreme Court made clear that the regulatory review exception is not limited to the development by generic producers of information necessary to show bioequivalence in the abbreviated new drug application (ANDA) process. It said, among other things:

> Properly construed, § 271(e)(1) leaves adequate space for experimentation and failure on the road to regulatory approval: At least where a drugmaker has a reasonable basis for believing that a patented compound may work, through a particular biological process, to produce a particular physiological effect, and uses the compound in research that, if successful, would be appropriate to include in a submission to the FDA, that use is "reasonably related" to the "development and submission of information under . . . Federal law." § 271(e)(1).
>
> For similar reasons, the use of a patented compound in experiments that are not themselves included in a "submission of information" to the FDA does not, standing alone, render the use infringing. The relationship of the use of a patented compound in a particular experiment to the "development and submission of information" to the FDA does not become more attenuated (or less reasonable) simply because the data from that experiment are left out of the submission that is ultimately passed along to the FDA. 545 U.S. at 207.

The exception broadly allows third-party use of patented technology for research and experimentation toward the development of new drugs. In reaching this decision, the Supreme Court overruled a highly restrictive interpretation of the regulatory review exception adopted by the Court of Appeals for the Federal Circuit in the same case.[33]

---

33. *Integra Lifesciences I v. Merck*, 331 F.3d 860 (Fed. Cir. 2003).

Article 271(e), interpreted by the Supreme Court in *Merck v. Integra Life-sciences*, applies only to drugs and to veterinary biological products. Does Article 271(e) discriminate as to field of technology, or does it constitute legitimate differentiation in the sense accepted by the *Canada-Generic Pharmaceuticals* panel?

In 2002, the CAFC rendered a highly restrictive interpretation of the common law "experimental use exception" in *Madey v. Duke University*, 307 F.3d 1351 (Fed. Cir. 2002). It restricted experimental use to actions performed "for amusement, to satisfy idle curiosity, or for strictly philosophical inquiry" (citing *Embrex v. Service Engineering*, 216 F.3d 1343 (Fed. Cir. 2000)). It observed that universities are in the business of providing education and that as a consequence their activities are conducted with a commercial aim. For that reason, research activities conducted by universities do not generally fall under an experimental use exception. *Madey*, 307 F.3d at 1362. The common law "experimental use exception" interpreted by the CAFC in *Madey* is different than the statutory "regulatory review exception" interpreted by the Supreme Court in *Merck v. Integra*. For all intents and purposes, however, the Supreme Court has in the field of drug research and development created a broad experimental use exception that takes precedence over the narrow CAFC interpretation.

b. Article 31 (Compulsory Licensing)

A stark illustration of the tension between the rights of patent holders to prevent third-party use of their inventions and the public interest in obtaining the benefits of those inventions at an affordable price involves efforts to address the HIV-AIDS pandemic. The World Bank provides loans and grants to countries seeking to purchase antiretroviral treatment. The Bank's primary interest is to aid in the supply of medicines to the largest number of individuals. To help accomplish this objective, it has provided guidance on the use of TRIPS Agreement flexibilities that may help overcome patent-related obstacles. An excerpt from the Bank's Technical Guide dealing with compulsory licensing follows.

BATTLING HIV-AIDS: A DECISION-MAKER'S GUIDE TO THE PROCUREMENT OF MEDICINES AND RELATED SUPPLIES
Y. Tayler, ed.*

ANNEX B — INTELLECTUAL PROPERTY RIGHTS: HOW THEY AFFECT PROCUREMENT AND WHAT STEPS CAN BE TAKEN

COMPULSORY LICENSING AND GOVERNMENT USE

Most or all countries — developed and developing — allow the government to make use of patented inventions for public purposes with fewer bureaucratic obstacles than apply to the private sector. The procurement authority may find

---

* World Bank, 2004.

it useful to invoke this authority in obtaining HIV/AIDS medicines. There remains an obligation to pay the patent holder "adequate remuneration in the circumstances of each case, taking into account the economic value of the authorization." The remuneration may be determined after the fact.

To overcome obstacles that may be presented by patents, developing country governments and their procurement authorities can secure access to HIV/AIDS-related medicines, including ARVs, through a "compulsory license" or "government use" authorization. Recall that a patent is a government grant that permits its holder to exclude third parties from the market for a product, such as an HIV/AIDS-related medicine. A "compulsory license" is an authorization by the government to itself or to a third party to use the patent without the permission of the patent holder. A compulsory license authorizing the government to use the patent for its own purposes is also referred to as a "government use" authorization (in British terminology, "Crown use"). The term "compulsory licensing" is used here to refer to compulsory licensing and government use authorization, unless expressly indicated otherwise.

The legal concept of compulsory licensing is long embedded in international patent law. The patent system involves a tradeoff between the interests of society in encouraging new invention (and disclosure) and the interests of society in promoting competitive markets, access to products, and affordable prices. Since the earliest discussions of an international patent system, it was recognized that governments would encounter circumstances in which social interests in access and affordability would override longer term interests in encouraging invention (by granting exclusive rights to patent holders). It was also recognized that the government would be entitled to use or authorize the use of the patent without the consent of the patent holder. The law of every country allows for some form of compulsory licensing of patents.

Important HIV/AIDS medicines or supplies are covered by one or more patents in many countries. If the procurement authority wishes to procure a bioequivalent medicine (a generic version) from a party other than the patent holder or its authorized distributor, including by importing the medicine, it may need to authorize procurement under a compulsory license. The TRIPS Agreement, in Article 31, authorizes every government to grant compulsory licenses without restriction as to purpose.

This authority was confirmed in paragraph 5(b) of the Doha Declaration. Article 31 establishes certain procedural and substantive requirements regarding compulsory licensing. For government procurement authorities dealing with HIV/AIDS medicines, the procedural requirements are minimized in important ways. Note that the procurement authority is not required to use these "fast track" options, and may decide to seek a voluntary license, waiver of enforcement, or price concessions from the patent holder prior to granting a compulsory license. The special rules, in any case, provide assurance that the procurement authority can act rapidly when the situation calls for it.

Under Article 31(b) of the TRIPS Agreement, a party seeking a compulsory license must first have sought a license from the patent holder "on reasonable commercial terms and conditions and [indicate] that such efforts have not been successful within a reasonable period of time." But government procurement authorities do not need to comply with this precondition in respect of HIV/AIDS medicines, on two separate grounds: First, the precondition may be waived for national emergency or other circumstances of extreme urgency.

And the Doha Declaration has expressly recognized that "HIV/AIDS, tuberculosis, malaria and other epidemics, can represent a national emergency or other circumstances of extreme urgency." To take advantage of the right to waive the precondition under these circumstances, the government does not need to "declare" a general national emergency under legislation or constitutional authority that may allow it to suspend a citizen's rights on a temporary basis. It is legally sufficient that the national health authority state that a compulsory license be granted because of a national health emergency or an extremely urgent public health circumstance. It is highly unlikely that any patent holder or foreign government would seek to challenge the validity of such a statement in the HIV/AIDS context, particularly in view of the Doha Declaration.

Second, the precondition may also be waived "in cases of public noncommercial use." The precise meaning or limit of "public non-commercial use" is not spelled out in the TRIPS Agreement, leaving developing countries to interpret the term in good faith. It is clear, however, that a government procurement authority purchasing HIV/AIDS medicines for distribution through public clinics and without seeking to make a commercial profit from such distribution, will be engaging in "public noncommercial use." If members of the public are required to bear all or a portion of the cost of the medicines either directly or through health insurance, this should not affect the public noncommercial character of the transaction as long as the government was not seeking to profit from the arrangement (that is, if the arrangement is essentially revenue neutral).

There may well be further flexibility inherent in the "public noncommercial use" language of the TRIPS Agreement. The situation for HIV/AIDS is expressly recognized in the Doha Declaration. The HIV/AIDS pandemic is a national emergency and circumstance of extreme urgency in every developing country confronting it.

From a practical standpoint, it may be easiest and most efficient for a government and its procurement authority to rely on the ground of national emergency or extreme urgency as the basis for a waiver under TRIPS Article 31(b). For HIV/AIDS, the ground of public noncommercial use may work just as well in view of the pandemic and urgent need to address it. But if patent holders should fear that the public noncommercial use grounds may be used by procurement authorities "down the road" in more nuanced circumstances, some patent holders might choose to challenge its use even for HIV/AIDS as a "matter of legal principle," thereby inviting delays. To sum up, a government may issue a compulsory license to its procurement authority to acquire generic HIV/AIDS medicines, including by import, despite the presence of a local patent by stating that it is doing so to address a national emergency or circumstance of extreme urgency.

As a matter of general practice, it is preferable that national patent or public health laws or regulations expressly provide a basis for such action. But if such laws or regulations are not in place, this does not prevent a government from taking this action. Inherent in the sovereignty of every government is the right to protect the public interest in a national emergency or circumstance of extreme urgency, and the government does not need to refer to specific national legislation to exercise this authority. Nothing in the TRIPS Agreement requires that the steps a government takes in these circumstances be laid out in advance.

Article 31(h) of the TRIPS Agreement requires that "the right holder shall be paid adequate remuneration in the circumstances of each case, taking into account the economic value of the authorization." The TRIPS Agreement does not attempt to define "adequate remuneration," leaving it to each government to determine this amount in good faith. The government does not need to determine this amount in advance of granting the compulsory license, and its legislation may specifically refuse to allow a patent holder the right to seek an injunction to block the granting of a license for government use.

When a compulsory license is granted for procurement of a generic version of an HIV/AIDS medicine or supply, the government will be dealing with the circumstance of attempting to maximize the quantity of medicines it can procure, and with the highest level of public interest at stake. Under these circumstances, the government may be justified in limiting "adequate remuneration" to the patent holder to a low royalty based on the purchase price of the generic medicines.

Article 31 of the TRIPS Agreement includes other procedural and substantive requirements for granting compulsory licenses. Because national legislation and regulations have been, or will be, revised to take into account these requirements, the procurement authority should be able to ascertain the requirements of national law. Certainly, however, implementation of the TRIPS Agreement is an ongoing process. And as developing members gain experience, they will be evaluating their laws and regulations to determine whether they adequately account for the public interest.

Government use and compulsory licensing are the principal means enabling procurement authorities to overcome patent barriers to obtaining lower priced generic medicines and related supplies. But for many developing countries the option to use such licensing is illusory. They do not have sufficient local production capacity to make needed medicines at a reasonable cost.

The TRIPS Agreement generally allows WTO members to grant compulsory licenses and to satisfy those licenses by importing. However, there is a catch. There must be medicines lawfully available for import. In other words, even if patent barriers are overcome domestically, there may be patents in prospective exporting countries that prevent the manufacture and export of needed medicines and supplies. This problem will become very serious after January 1, 2005, when all developing countries are required to have patent protection for pharmaceutical products in place, and when "mailbox" pipeline applications that have accumulated during the past 10 years are given effect. The availability of newer off-patent medicines from India, as the most notable illustration, will be reduced.

The WTO addressed the problem of countries with insufficient or no capacity in the pharmaceutical sector and their inability to make effective use of compulsory licensing in "Paragraph 6" negotiations that concluded on August 30, 2003. The result of these negotiations was a "waiver" of the provision of the TRIPS Agreement that otherwise might limit exports under compulsory license (Article 31(f)). A procuring-importing country (except a least developed country, which is automatically eligible) needs to notify the WTO that it intends to take advantage of the waiver. It may then request that a producer in an exporting country supply it. The producer may be a private enterprise, or it may be the government (or a private enterprise acting on its behalf). The exporting country must grant a license authorizing use of the patent for export.

When imports commence there should also be a license in the importing country (if a license is needed to overcome a domestically granted patent).

The waiver also exempts the importing country from an obligation under Article 31(h) of the TRIPS Agreement to pay remuneration since the patent holder will be compensated in the exporting country "taking into account the economic value to the importing Member of the use that has been authorized in the exporting Member."

The August 30, 2003, decision of the General Council and the accompanying statement of the Chairperson contain further detailed provisions for its implementation. Because the Paragraph 6 solution is new as of August 2003, there will be a start-up period as prospective exporting countries decide on the best way to implement the rules.

c. *The Doha Declaration on the TRIPS Agreement and Public Health*

The WTO Council for TRIPS held sessions in June and September 2001 specifically devoted to issues concerning access to medicines. A substantial group of developing countries submitted a detailed proposal for a declaration on TRIPS and Public Health to be adopted at the Doha Ministerial.[34] The United States and a small group of like-minded countries submitted an alternate proposal. Following extensive negotiations based on a compromise text prepared by the WTO Secretariat, Ministers in Doha adopted a Declaration on the TRIPS Agreement and Public Health (WT/MIN(01)/DEC/2).

THE DOHA DECLARATION ON THE TRIPS AGREEMENT AND PUBLIC HEALTH: LIGHTING A DARK CORNER AT THE WTO

Frederick M. Abbott*

. . . III. THE LEGAL EFFECTS OF THE DOHA DECLARATION

A. PARAGRAPH-BY-PARAGRAPH COMMENTARY

The discussion and analysis of the TRIPS Agreement that preceded the Doha Ministerial was itself of legal significance. The Members of the WTO evidenced a concrete interest in addressing the complex set of issues surrounding the effects of the TRIPS Agreement on access to medicines. The expressions of interest represent action by states to direct implementation of the agreement along more particularized lines, and in this sense represent a form of state practice that may be taken into account when interpreting the agreement.

The title "Declaration on the TRIPS Agreement and Public Health" incorporates the language of the initial developing Member draft, and rejects narrower formulations directed at "intellectual property," "pandemics" and other

---

34. Issues raised by developing countries in regard to the TRIPS Agreement and access to medicines were identified and analyzed in F.M. Abbott, *The TRIPS Agreement, Access to Medicines and the WTO Doha Ministerial Conference*, 5 J. WORLD INTELLECTUAL PROP. 15 (2002), first published as Quaker United Nations Office Occasional Paper No. 7, Sept. 8, 2001.

* 5 J. INT'L ECON. L. 469 (2002).

limiting terms. This signals that the Declaration applies to a broad scope of public health concerns, and not to a limited set of special circumstances.

1. *We recognize the gravity of the public health problems afflicting many developing and least-developed countries, especially those resulting from HIV/AIDS, tuberculosis, malaria and other epidemics.*

Comment: The first three paragraphs (1-3) of the Declaration are in the nature of preambles to the operative paragraphs 4-7. Preambular language in an international agreement is used to ascertain the intention of the parties in the process of interpretation, and is part of the context of the agreement. By recognizing the seriousness of the public health difficulties facing the developing and least developed countries, Ministers place decisions made in the Declaration at a high level in the hierarchy of norms should there be a conflict between rules.

2. *We stress the need for the WTO Agreement on Trade-Related Aspects of Intellectual Property Rights (TRIPS Agreement) to be part of the wider national and international action to address these problems.*

Comment: This paragraph can be interpreted to indicate that the TRIPS Agreement should not stand as an obstacle to addressing public health concerns, and in that sense to reinforce paragraph 4. It also suggests an effort by Ministers to disperse or shift the burden for addressing public health to other multilateral and national actors. This provision might be interpreted to recognize the primary role of the WHO in matters relating to the prevention and treatment of disease. It might provide a basis to argue against the practice of the WTO Secretariat and certain Members from excluding representatives of other organizations such as WHO from informal meetings relating to access to medicines.

3. *We recognize that intellectual property protection is important for the development of new medicines. We also recognize the concerns about its effects on prices.*

Comment: This paragraph represents a modest developing country concession to Pharma in two senses. As indicated in their draft Declaration, developing Members have serious concerns regarding whether patent protection does indeed encourage research and development on drugs for diseases especially relevant to them. The unqualified text of the first sentence does not touch on this issue. The second sentence is a relatively weak way of acknowledging that patents have negative consequences in the form of higher prices, thereby reducing access to medicines, particularly among the poor. It is a controversial juxtaposition: patents are "important," high prices raise "concerns."

4. *We agree that the TRIPS Agreement does not and should not prevent Members from taking measures to protect public health. Accordingly, while reiterating our commitment to the TRIPS Agreement, we affirm that the Agreement can and should be interpreted and implemented in a manner supportive of WTO Members' right to protect public health and, in particular, to promote access to medicines for all.*

    In this connection, we reaffirm the right of WTO Members to use, to the full, the provisions in the TRIPS Agreement, which provide flexibility for this purpose.

Comment: The first important point regarding this paragraph is that it is stated in the form of an agreement (i.e., "we agree"). Since this statement was adopted by consensus of the Ministers, and since the operative language is in the form of an agreement, this may be interpreted as a "decision" of the Members under article IX:1 of the WTO Agreement. This decision of WTO Members would appear to constitute an agreement on the method of application of the agreement within the meaning of Article 31(3)(a) of the Vienna Convention on the Law of Treaties ("VCLT"), and to be the substantive equivalent of an interpretation of the TRIPS Agreement.

Although paragraph 4 is not an "interpretation" in the formal sense since it was not based on a recommendation of the TRIPS Council pursuant to article IX:2 of the WTO Agreement, a decision that states a meaning of the Agreement may be considered as a very close approximation of an interpretation and, from a functional standpoint, may be indistinguishable.

Ministers in Doha should be assumed to have acted with a purpose. The only apparent purpose for agreeing on a method of application of the TRIPS Agreement is to have an effect on the way in which the agreement is implemented by WTO Members.

There are different ways that paragraph 4 might be understood, and it is perhaps premature to venture interpretations in the absence of concrete cases. However, there is already one concrete case on the horizon, and a few words might be addressed to that.

Paragraph 6 of the Declaration, as discussed in further detail below, directs the TRIPS Council to seek a solution to the problem of use of compulsory licensing by Members with insufficient or no manufacturing capacity. This is a complex undertaking and is addressed in some detail by this author in another paper.[81] To summarize analysis, establishing a productive interpretation of Article 31(f), TRIPS Agreement, may be sufficiently difficult that Members will decide that the best route for addressing imports of low priced drugs from countries where they are under patent is to formally recognize that Article 30 "limited exceptions" to patent rights may be authorized for the making and export of drugs. Article 30 has been interpreted by a panel in the *Canada-Generic Pharmaceuticals* case.[82] However, the WTO Agreements make clear that the Ministerial Conference and General Council are not bound in their formal interpretation of the TRIPS Agreement by a panel report. The Conference and Council are instead bound to respect the terms and context in light of the object and purpose of the agreement. In considering a formal interpretation of Article 30, the TRIPS Council (in its recommendation), and the General Council and Ministerial Conference, should give effect to the decision taken in the Doha Declaration that the TRIPS Agreement "can and should be interpreted and implemented in a manner supportive of WTO Members' right to protect public health and, in particular, to promote access to medicines for all." This may include recognition that Members may authorize the making and export of drugs in appropriate contexts.

---

81. *See* Frederick M. Abbott, *Compulsory Licensing for Public Health Needs: The TRIPS Agenda at the WTO After the Doha Declaration on Public Health*, Quaker United Nations Office—Geneva, Occasional Paper 9, February 2002, available at http://www.quno.org.

82. Canada-Patent Protection of Pharmaceutical Products, Report of the Panel, WT/DS114/R, March 17, 2000.

5. *Accordingly and in the light of paragraph 4 above, while maintaining our commitments in the TRIPS Agreement, we recognize that these flexibilities include:*

    (a) *In applying the customary rules of interpretation of public international law, each provision of the TRIPS Agreement shall be read in the light of the object and purpose of the Agreement as expressed, in particular, in its objectives and principles.*

Comment: Paragraph 5(a) states an interpretative principle that has been enunciated by the panel in the *Canada-Generic Pharmaceuticals* case, and that would already be understood by operation of Article 31 of the Vienna Convention on the Law of Treaties. By particularizing reference to objective and principles, the Declaration appears indirectly to reference Articles 7 (Objectives) and 8 (Principles) of the TRIPS Agreement. This might to a certain extent elevate those provisions above the preamble of the TRIPS Agreement for interpretative purposes.

    (b) *Each Member has the right to grant compulsory licences and the freedom to determine the grounds upon which such licences are granted.*

Comment: Paragraph 5(b) states propositions that are clear from the text of Article 31 of the TRIPS Agreement, but which the pharmaceutical sector, among others, has attempted to put in doubt. There has been a great deal of misperception in the public press concerning the bases upon which compulsory licenses may be issued, and this inaccurate press reporting may influence national government officials who are not conversant with intellectual property law. For this reason, it is very helpful to have a direct and unequivocal statement regarding the right of Members to grant compulsory licenses.

    (c) *Each Member has the right to determine what constitutes a national emergency or other circumstances of extreme urgency, it being understood that public health crises, including those relating to HIV/AIDS, tuberculosis, malaria and other epidemics, can represent a national emergency or other circumstances of extreme urgency.*

Comment: This is a strong statement of Member sovereignty in regard to implementation of the waiver of negotiation with patent holders prior to the grant of compulsory licenses. As such, it should act as a strong defense against any assertion in dispute settlement that a Member declared an emergency, etc., without justification. Framing the determination as one reserved to each Member ("can represent"), rather than as a joint determination, makes clear that the determination is a matter to be undertaken by each Member in its sovereign discretion.

    (d) *The effect of the provisions in the TRIPS Agreement that are relevant to the exhaustion of intellectual property rights is to leave each Member free to establish its own regime for such exhaustion without challenge, subject to the MFN and national treatment provisions of Articles 3 and 4.*

Comment: This is an unequivocal recognition of the right of each Member to permit parallel importation of medicines. This should foreclose further argument from the U.S., Switzerland, and the pharmaceutical sector that while Article 6 of the TRIPS Agreement precludes TRIPS dispute settlement on the issue of exhaustion, Article 28 nonetheless prevents parallel importation of patented drugs. The formulation of paragraph 5(d) does not foreclose the interpretation advanced by some commentators that parallel importation may be based on compulsory licensing.

The EU and U.S. each proposed to incorporate in the Declaration on the TRIPS Agreement and Public Health a limit on international exhaustion to marketing with the consent of the patent holder. Such limitation was not included in the Doha Declaration. Instead, paragraph 5(d) leaves each Member "free to establish its own regime for such exhaustion without challenge." This appears to leave each Member with the discretion to determine whether it will recognize compulsory-licensed marketing or sale of a product in a country of export as exhausting the patent holder's rights in the country of import to consent to importation and resale.

Although the Doha Declaration appears to resolve the issue of exhaustion based on marketing under compulsory license, it may be useful to consider the legal issues in more detail since they are likely to be further discussed by Members.

There are circumstances under which patented products may be first sold or put onto the market under compulsion of government authority. This is typically through the grant to the government itself, or to a third party, of a compulsory license to make and dispose of the product. Such licenses may be authorized because the government determines that public interests will be met by the grants, including as a remedy for anticompetitive practices by patent holders.

When patent holders are required to license third parties to produce and dispose of patented drugs, and the licensees put the drugs on the market, buyers are entitled to use or dispose of those drugs just as if the drugs had been put onto the market by the patent holders. In other words, first sales by the licensees have the same effects (in the local market) as first sales by patent holders. The right of the patent holders to control subsequent sales or transfers is extinguished or exhausted by the licensees' acts.

The question has been raised whether drugs (or other patented products) put onto the market under compulsory license in one country may be parallel imported into another country without the consent of the patent holder in that other country. Two textual bases in the TRIPS Agreement suggest a basis for authorizing parallel importation in this context. The first is article 6, TRIPS Agreement, providing that the exhaustion issue may not be subject to dispute settlement. Since "exhaustion" is not a specifically defined term, it would appear that each WTO Member is permitted to adopt the definition it reasonably considers appropriate. This definition might include exhaustion by first sale under compulsory license. The second textual basis is article 31(f), providing that compulsory licenses "shall be authorized predominantly for the supply of the domestic market of the Member authorizing such use." If some drugs produced by compulsory licensees may be exported (i.e. the non-predominant portion), then logically they may [be] imported somewhere, and parallel importation is a mechanism for allowing this without the consent of the patent holder.

The Appellate Body has emphasized that the express language of the WTO Agreement (including the TRIPS Agreement) is its principal source for interpretative guidance, giving terms their ordinary meaning in their context, and in light of the object and purpose of the agreement. Only if the text is unclear does the Appellate Body resort to supplementary means of interpretation. If "exhaustion" can reasonably be interpreted to take place upon the first sale by a compulsory licensee, then the Appellate Body might well determine that a WTO Member is not subject to WTO dispute settlement for authorizing parallel importation based on sales made by compulsory licensees.

In addition, although (as noted below) there is some case law in the developed country WTO Members holding that exhaustion of patent rights is based on the "consent" of the patent holder to placement of goods on the market, the Appellate Body is not under an international legal obligation to interpret the TRIPS Agreement to reflect the traditional practices of developed country Members. Practice in developing Members may well evolve in an alternative direction, provided that such practice is not inconsistent with the express terms of the TRIPS Agreement.

Arguments that run counter to the suggestion that Members may authorize parallel importation based on the acts of compulsory licensees are:

- Though the exhaustion issue is not subject to dispute settlement, as reinforced by paragraph 5(d) of the Doha Declaration, the question what constitutes exhaustion might be determined by dispute settlement since there are limits to how the term may be interpreted.
- Article 28, TRIPS Agreement, expressly establishes the rights of patent holders to "consent" to the enumerated acts, including importation. "Consent" to placement on the market anywhere in the world may exhaust the import right under Article 28.
- There is a body of case law in the EU, Japan, Switzerland and the United States holding that the notion of patent right exhaustion is based on the consent of the patent holder to first sale. There is a specific holding by the European Court of Justice that intra-Union exhaustion of pharmaceutical patent holder rights does not occur on the basis of a compulsory licensee's placement of drugs on the market. Although international exhaustion of patent rights is accepted in the United States, the U.S. Supreme Court has barred imports of goods lawfully produced under patent abroad without the consent of the U.S. patent holder (under a so-called prior users' right).
- Although article 31(f) allows export of the non-predominant portion of compulsory licensee production, there are at least two contexts in which corresponding importation does not require consent of the patent holder: (a) where the drug is not patented in the country of import, and (b) where the country of import has issued a compulsory license for importation.

From a practical standpoint, why is the question whether international exhaustion may take place under compulsory license important?

Developing countries that provide patent protection for medicines have limited potential supply of those drugs. They may be purchased locally at on-patent prices, or they may be purchased following placement on the market abroad by the patent holder (or its agent). Although parallel importation may allow price savings, these savings are not likely to be on the order of magnitude seen in the relationship between on-patent versus off-patent medicines.

A drug produced under compulsory license is effectively an off-patent drug (though payment of an adequate royalty will add to the price). If parallel importation of compulsory licensed drugs is accepted, then in principle a single compulsory licensee in a major market (e.g., Brazil or India) could export a substantial (though "non-predominant") quantity of low-price drugs, and no action would be required by importing developing countries other than to recognize a broad doctrine of exhaustion and parallel importation. Provided that one or two major market Members were willing to grant compulsory licenses, a part of the worldwide solution to the problem of low-price medicines might be found.

It is clear that WTO Members may authorize parallel importation of patented medicines placed on the market by or with the consent of the patent holder. It is not clear whether the Appellate Body will construe exhaustion doctrine to authorize parallel importation of medicines placed on the market by compulsory licensees. It is likely that developed Members such as the U.S., EU and Switzerland will resist an interpretation of exhaustion doctrine that is not based on the consent of the patent holder. Paragraphs 4 and 5(d) of the Doha Declaration, however, support an interpretation that advances the interests of developing Members in obtaining low cost access to pharmaceutical supplies.

6.   *We recognize that WTO Members with insufficient or no manufacturing capacities in the pharmaceutical sector could face difficulties in making effective use of compulsory licensing under the TRIPS Agreement. We instruct the Council for TRIPS to find an expeditious solution to this problem and to report to the General Council before the end of 2002.*

Comment: A substantial change to the TRIPS-imposed legal conditions in developing and least developed countries will occur on January 1, 2005 and January 1, 2016. Among the important consequences of this changed situation will be that developing countries with the present capacity to export off-patent drugs will lose that capacity in regards to newly-developed patented drugs (and drugs in the mailbox pipeline that come under patent). At this juncture, affordable access to on-patent medicines in developing and least developed countries will become increasingly dependent on compulsory licensing. If the prices of medicines offered by patent holders are too high, or if sustainable access is otherwise restricted or threatened, relief will be sought through the issuance of compulsory licenses.

Certain developing countries will have capacity to manufacture under compulsory license, but there will certainly be developing and least developed countries without that capacity. Moreover, developing countries will require a variety of medicines, and it may be important that production of different medicines be allocated among countries. Finally, it may well be that certain developed countries will wish to aid developing and least developed countries by producing under compulsory license to satisfy import requirements.

Article 31 of the TRIPS Agreement permits all WTO Members to grant compulsory licenses regarding, *inter alia*, pharmaceutical products and processes. The terms of Article 31 are in general permissive and flexible. As confirmed by paragraphs 5(b) and (c) of the Doha Declaration, Article 31 does not limit the grounds upon which licenses may be granted, and it permits each Member to determine in its own discretion what constitutes a national emergency or circumstances of extreme urgency (thereby establishing an exception from pre-grant negotiation). There is substantial flexibility in terms of the administrative processes that may be adopted to implement a compulsory licensing regime.

To date, developing countries have made limited use of compulsory licensing as a tool to address public health issues. This stems from a number of causes: (1) the TRIPS Agreement has only recently begun to increase the incidence of patent protection; (2) use has been opposed by developed country WTO Members and interested industry groups within them, and a strong political commitment to act in the face of this opposition is required; (3) some developing countries have expressed concern regarding a potential backlash from foreign direct investors; (4) developing country enterprises may find it easier to reach accommodation with foreign patent holders than to challenge them through the compulsory licensing process for various economic and administrative reasons and, as noted earlier; (5) effectively implementing compulsory licensing requires that certain preconditions relating to administrative, financial and technical capacity be met, and these conditions are often not met in developing countries.

Addressing the limited use by developing countries of the compulsory licensing tool will require that substantial attention be paid to putting into place appropriate legal infrastructure. In this regard, developing countries will need to seek advice and assistance from sources such as UNCTAD, WHO and non-governmental organizations (NGOs) attentive to their interests. Addressing the problem of limited use will also require access to and coordination of financial and technical resources. The solution to the limited use of compulsory licensing by developing countries requires addressing a number of important elements.

Recognizing the multi-dimensional nature of the problem, the TRIPS Agreement nevertheless establishes certain obstacles to effectively addressing access to medicines through compulsory licensing. The most widely noted of these potential obstacles is Article 31(f), which provides:

> (f) any such use shall be authorized predominantly for the supply of the domestic market of the Member authorizing such use;

Article 31(f) establishes a limitation: the terms of the compulsory license should include the condition that the licensee uses the patented invention predominantly to supply the domestic market of the Member granting the license.

The word "predominantly" would generally appear to refer to the major part or majority, and would generally suggest that more than fifty percent of the production by a compulsory licensee should be intended for supply of the domestic market of the Member granting the license.

The limitation imposed by Article 31(f) creates two inter-linked problems:

1. By restricting the availability of export drugs made under compulsory license, it limits countries that are not in a position to support manufacturing under compulsory license (or where patent protection is not in force) in the availability of supply of generic import drugs, and;
2. By requiring compulsory licensees to supply a predominant part of their production to the domestic market, it limits the flexibility of countries to authorize the export of compulsory-licensed drugs and thereby to exploit economies of scale.

Article 31(f) creates difficulties on the demand and supply side of the generic drug pipeline.

The demand side problem is self-evident. If a developing Member lacks manufacturing capacity for a particular drug, and there are no Members that are able to supply it by export under compulsory license (or exception), there may be no affordable supply of the drug. The supply side problem is identified because there are WTO Members, including developing Members, with the capacity to address the drug import needs of a wide range of developing Members under compulsory license, but that may be inhibited from undertaking this role because of the Article 31(f) limitation. . . .

IV. Future Work Program

This issue of availability of low-priced medicines becomes more pressing as the transition timetables in the TRIPS Agreement draw to an end, and the available supply of generic (off-patent) pharmaceutical products is progressively reduced. If there are limited supplies made available for export, there are, by definition, limited supplies available for import. Article 31(f) appears to restrict the right of Members to grant compulsory licenses for export. Although there were several proposals made in advance of the Doha Ministerial to address this situation, including proposals in the developing Member draft Declaration, there was no political consensus to resolve it at that stage, and the matter has been set for further discussion.

[The Paragraph 6 issue was addressed through two years of negotiations at the WTO. The negotiations and result are described and analyzed in Frederick M. Abbott, *The WTO Medicines Decision: World Pharmaceutical Trade and the Protection of Public Health*, 99 Am. J. Int'l L. 317 (2005), and in section d, immediately following, which refers also to the adoption of a proposal for amendment. — Eds.]

  7. *We reaffirm the commitment of developed-country Members to provide incentives to their enterprises and institutions to promote and encourage technology transfer to least-developed country Members pursuant to Article 66.2. We also agree that the least-developed country Members will not be obliged, with respect to pharmaceutical products, to implement or apply Sections 5 and 7 of Part II of the TRIPS Agreement or to enforce rights provided for under these Sections until 1 January 2016, without prejudice to the right of least-developed country Members to seek other extensions of the transition periods as provided for in Article 66.1 of the TRIPS Agreement. We instruct the Council for TRIPS to take the necessary action to give effect to this pursuant to Article 66.1 of the TRIPS Agreement.*

Comment: This paragraph directs the TRIPS Council to authorize the extension until January 1, 2016 of the transition period for least developed Members (hereinafter "LDCs") to implement or enforce pharmaceutical patent protection. The terms of this extension are somewhat ambiguous in that it is not clear from the express text whether LDCs are required to implement mailbox and exclusive marketing rights provisions prior to the end of the transition deadline. There is some indication that paragraph 7 was understood by negotiators in Doha not to require that mailbox and exclusive marketing rights requirements be implemented or enforced.

If an LDC is required to implement mailbox protection, it must establish a procedure under which it will accept for filing pharmaceutical product patent applications filed abroad. Until the LDC establishes patent protection, the patent application remains dormant. However, during the period of dormancy, the LDC is required to grant exclusive marketing rights to the patent holder for a maximum period of five years following marketing approval of its drug. For almost all intents and purposes, the grant of exclusive marketing rights will be as effective as granting a patent in preventing generic drugs from entering the LDC market. Beyond that, however, when the dormancy period of the mailbox application ends, the drug covered by the application will be patented (assuming it meets relevant criteria). An entire "pool" of drugs that may be generic in an LDC during the mailbox transition period will come under patent at the end of the period. If, however, there is no mailbox system in place, holders of patents outside the LDC will not be able to obtain patents after the transition period has ended because the inventions covered by the patents will no longer be novel in the patenting sense. Thus, if there is no mailbox system in place, drugs that are generic (off-patent) during the transition period will remain generic after the transition period ends.

The issue whether mailbox and exclusive marketing rights requirements are applicable to LDCs during the extended transition period is of considerable importance and should be addressed by the TRIPS Council in connection with operationalizing the extension envisaged by paragraph 7.

In a limited set of circumstances, the transition period extension in favor of LDCs will allow them additional access to generic medicines. This will occur when a medicine is off patent in a developing Member such as India (and may be exported), but prior to the extension would be on patent in the LDC. The transition period extension relieves the LDC from the obligation to enforce local patents, so the LDC will be able to import the drug for so long as it remains off-patent in India.[101] For drugs that go on-patent in India (and other developing Members) after January 1, 2005, either because applications filed during the mailbox period are converted to patents, or because of newly-filed applications, no relief will be provided for LDCs that otherwise wish to import drugs. Those drugs will be on-patent in the country of export and more expensive.

LDCs that are not required to implement or enforce pharmaceutical patent protection until 2016 will have a certain added measure of flexibility even as to drugs that are covered by patent in non-LDC Members. LDCs will be free to increase their own capacity to manufacture generic drugs, and export and import those drugs among themselves, without contravening the TRIPS Agreement. Since there are fourteen (14) years until patent protection will be mandated, there is a reasonable amount of time if plans are initiated soon to bring manufacturing facilities within LDCs on-line and recover investment capital prior to the end of the transition period. If the LDCs are not required to implement mailbox protection, drugs for which production is commenced during the transition period will be available indefinitely as generics. If mailbox protection is required, the end of the transition period will also mark the end of access to low priced drugs made available as a consequence of the extension, until such time as patents issued on the basis of mailbox applications expire.

The value of this added flexibility is highly dependent on the capacity of the LDCs to increase manufacturing capacity, and this will depend on factors such as the availability of World Bank grants or loans to provide working capital, and the availability of technical assistance.

---

101. There is an additional complication in that the drug in India may be subject to exclusive marketing rights, and it is not clear whether such rights would entitle the mailbox application holder to block exportation as well as local supply.

Also, paragraph 7 of the Doha Declaration is somewhat ambiguous regarding whether LDCs are relieved from implementing and enforcing pharmaceutical process patent protection during the extended transition period. If LDCs are not so relieved, then under TRIPS Agreement Article 66:1, pharmaceutical process patent coverage must be implemented by January 1, 2006. This may limit the capacity of LDCs to initiate production. In giving effect to paragraph 7, the TRIPS Council should clarify that it extends to pharmaceutical process patents.

NOTES AND QUESTIONS

1. The WTO acted to implement paragraph 7 of the Doha Declaration. The implementing decisions are described by the WTO Secretariat as follows:

> INTELLECTUAL PROPERTY: TRIPS AND PUBLIC HEALTH*
>
> Council approves LDC decision with additional waiver
>   The WTO council responsible for intellectual property, on 27 June 2002, approved a decision extending until 2016 the transition period during which least-developed countries (LDCs) do not have to provide patent protection for pharmaceuticals.
>   The Council for Trade-Related Aspects of Intellectual Property Rights (TRIPS) also approved a waiver that would exempt least-developed countries from having to provide exclusive marketing rights for any new drugs in the period when they do not provide patent protection.
>   The waiver is to be submitted to the WTO General Council for approval on 8 July 2002.
>   Both decisions are part of WTO members' ongoing efforts to ensure that intellectual property protection supports and does not obstruct poorer countries' need to tackle serious public health problems.
>   "I am pleased that WTO members have acted promptly to implement this important part of the Doha Declaration on TRIPS and public health, and have seen fit to go beyond the strict reading of that declaration by also approving a draft waiver on exclusive marketing rights," said WTO Director-General Mike Moore.
>   The TRIPS Council's decision formalizes part of paragraph 7 of the Declaration on the TRIPS Agreement and Public Health, which WTO ministers adopted on 14 November 2001 at their conference in Doha, Qatar.
>   The relevant part of paragraph 7 of the Doha declaration says: "We . . . agree that the least-developed country members will not be obliged, with respect to pharmaceutical products, to implement or apply Sections 5 and 7 of Part II of the TRIPS Agreement or to enforce rights provided for under these Sections until 1 January 2016, without prejudice to the right of least-developed country members to seek other extensions of the transition periods as provided for in Article 66.1 of the TRIPS Agreement. We instruct the Council for TRIPS to take the necessary action to give effect to this pursuant to Article 66.1 of the TRIPS Agreement."
>   This follows from the ministerial declaration's opening statements: "We recognize the gravity of the public health problems afflicting many developing and least-developed countries, especially those resulting from HIV/AIDS, tuberculosis, malaria and other epidemics.

---

* WTO News: 2002 Press Releases, Press/301, 28 June 2002.

"We stress the need for the WTO Agreement on Trade-Related Aspects of Intellectual Property Rights (TRIPS Agreement) to be part of the wider national and international action to address these problems.

"We recognize that intellectual property protection is important for the development of new medicines. We also recognize the concerns about its effects on prices."

The TRIPS Agreement allows developing countries extra periods to delay providing patent protection for pharmaceuticals. But countries making use of the extra period still have to allow inventors to submit patent applications during the period (Article 70.8, sometimes called the "mailbox" provision). If a country's health authority then approves a new drug for sale, the patent applicant has to be given exclusive marketing rights for five years even though there is no patent (Art. 70.9).

The waiver exempts least developed countries from having to give these exclusive marketing rights.

Do you think the decision by the WTO not to waive the requirement for LDCs to maintain patent "mailboxes" was a positive step? Do you think LDCs have the capacity to maintain such systems? Should this be a priority in countries where poverty is endemic?

d. The WTO August 30, 2003 Decision and December 6, 2005 Amendment

The mandate for resolving the issue of effective use of compulsory licensing by countries with insufficient capacity in the pharmaceutical sector led to an additional two years of negotiations leading to the adoption of a waiver, and another two years of debate leading to adoption of the first proposed amendment of the TRIPS Agreement, which is in the process of being ratified by WTO Members. The amendment will come into force once two-thirds of the Members have formally approved it. The waiver and amendment are described in the following excerpt from a report of the International Law Association Committee on International Trade Law.

REPORT OF THE COMMITTEE ON INTERNATIONAL TRADE LAW OF THE INTERNATIONAL LAW ASSOCIATION AT THE 2006 BIENNIAL MEETING, TORONTO

THE TRIPS AGREEMENT AND PUBLIC HEALTH

On December 6, 2005, shortly before the Hong Kong Ministerial Conference, WTO Members agreed upon the first amendment to the TRIPS Agreement.[7] Once acceptance of the amendment has been notified by two-thirds of Members, Article 31 *bis* will be added to the main text of the Agreement, and an Annex and Appendix to the Annex also will be added.

The Article 31 *bis* amendment (hereinafter the "Medicines Export Amendment") follows on from Paragraph 6 of the Doha Declaration on the TRIPS

---

7. Amendment of the TRIPS Agreement, WTO General Council, Decision of 6 December 2005, WT/L/641, 8 Dec. 2005, available at http://www.wto.org.

Agreement and Public Health.[8] That paragraph recognized that countries with insufficient or no manufacturing capacity in the pharmaceutical sector may have difficulty in making effective use of compulsory licensing, one of the principal flexibilities of the TRIPS Agreement. Paragraph 6 directed Members to find a solution to this problem.

The Committee took an active interest in the negotiations leading to the Medicines Export Amendment. Background is reported in some detail in its 2004 Report. At its biennial meeting in Geneva in 2005, the Committee heard and discussed several reports regarding negotiations on transforming the August 30, 2003 waiver decision into the Amendment.[9]

Developing country *demandeurs* of the Doha Declaration recognized that as of January 1, 2005, the world pharmaceutical supply market would change substantially as the 10-year TRIPS Agreement transition period for introducing pharmaceutical product patent protection ended. India has served as a major supplier of low-priced generic drugs to the developing world because, among other reasons, it did not provide product patent protection for pharmaceuticals. Up until January 1, 2005, a country seeking to import supplies of generic medicines generally could find them for export in India. Even if the product was patented in the importing country, the issuance of a compulsory license in that country would be adequate to permit the importation.

Following the end of the transition period, new drugs—and "older" drugs which are patentable pursuant to the mailbox system—could be protected by patent in all developing countries,[10] including India. Generic supplies would be restricted. If an importing country sought low-cost supplies from a country where products are under patent, the existing text of the TRIPS Agreement created a potential impediment. The exporting country could issue a compulsory license and produce a generic version of the drug, but pursuant to Article 31(f) of the TRIPS Agreement it could only export a non-predominant portion of its production. This might significantly restrain export supply capacity.[11]

Article 31 *bis* authorizes the issuance of compulsory licenses predominantly for the supply of pharmaceutical products to export markets, thereby overcoming the potential obstacle presented by Article 31(f). It also provides that the obligation of Article 31(h) to provide adequate remuneration in the circumstances of the case is satisfied by the payment of remuneration in the exporting country, which should take into account the economic value of the authorization to the importing country.

There are various conditions associated with the grant of compulsory licenses for export under Article 31 *bis*. These include certain notifications to the TRIPS Council, a determination by the importing country that it lacks manufacturing

8. For description and analysis of the negotiating history and text of the August 30, 2003 waiver decision which forms the basis of the Amendment, *see* Frederick M. Abbott, *The WTO Medicines Decision: World Pharmaceutical Trade and the Protection of Public Health*, 99 AM. J. INT'L L. 317 (2005).

9. These included reports by the Rapporteur, F.M. Abbott, and the director of the WTO Intellectual Property Division, A. Otten.

10. This does not include least developed countries, which, further to the Paragraph 7 of the Doha Declaration and WTO implementing measures, have at least until January 1, 2016 to introduce or enforce pharmaceutical patent and data protection.

11. Article 30 of the TRIPS Agreement on Exceptions to Rights Conferred may also provide the basis for third-party exports of patented pharmaceuticals. The Amendment reserves the position of Members on this question. Medicines Export Amendment, Article 31 *bis* (5).

capacity,[12] and identification of the exported products as supplied pursuant to the Article 31 *bis* system. The conditions have been the subject of considerable debate. A number of NGOs, generic producers and some developing countries argue that the conditions make the system overly difficult to use. Some developed countries and pharmaceutical industry constituencies argue that the system is too open-ended. These arguments may be better assessed once the system is used, or attempts have been made to use it.

A substantial number of developed and emerging market countries "opted out" of the system as importing countries, either wholly or by limiting their usage to certain circumstances. As the threat of an avian flu pandemic has emerged in 2005-06, and as there are shortages of patented antiviral drug therapy for the flu in many developed countries, question has been raised regarding the wisdom of opting out of a system that facilitates the importation of drugs necessary to protect public health.

Canada and Norway were the first countries to adopt legislation and regulations implementing the August 30 waiver decision. China, the European Union, India, South Korea and Switzerland each have adopted (or are soon to adopt) implementing legislation or regulations.

The Committee welcomes adoption of the Medicines Export Amendment. However, the Committee recognizes that effective use of the Amendment can be adversely influenced by political pressure from Members and their industry constituencies. It therefore urges WTO Members to refrain from seeking to prevent use of the Amendment by the application of political pressure. It also urges Members not to seek terms in bilateral and regional trade agreements which undermine the letter or spirit of the Amendment.

NOTES AND QUESTIONS

1. The Canadian Commissioner of Patents issued the first compulsory license for export to Apotex, Inc., a Canadian manufacturer of pharmaceutical products, pursuant to Canada's Access to Medicines Regime (CAMR) on September 19, 2007. The license covers export to Rwanda, a least-developed African country, of a fixed dose combination of antiretroviral medicines used in the treatment of HIV-AIDS. The Apotex formulation, referred to as Apo-Triaver, combines 300 mg Zidovudine (AZT), 150 mg Lamivudine (3TC), and 200 mg Nevirapine. Canadian patents on the separate antiretroviral components were held by the Glaxo Group, Shire Biochem, and Boehringer Engelheim, respectively. The license authorized the manufacture of 15,600,000 Triaver tablets, and was initially valid for two years from the date of issuance. *See* Introductory Note to World Trade Organization Canada First Notice to Manufacture Generic Drug for Export, by Frederick M. Abbott, International Legal Materials, Nov. 2007.

2. As of January 2011, the August 30, 2003 waiver, or Article 31 *bis*, has been used only once, and for this reason has been subject to criticism as being ineffective. However, this criticism may be premature for two reasons. First, one of the principal reasons the waiver/amendment was negotiated was to address the global pharmaceutical supply situation following India's

---

12. Least developed countries are automatically determined to lack manufacturing capacity.

implementation of pharmaceutical product patent protection. That protection was only initiated on January 1, 2005, and even then provided a transition mechanism that allows generic drug makers to continue producing products that were already under production (and in which investment had been made) prior to the grant of a patent, upon payment of a reasonable royalty. Because India is still producing a wide range of generic drugs, need for the new system has not truly materialized. Second, when worries over an avian bird flu pandemic circulated, and global demand for Roche's patented Tamiflu (oseltemovir) escalated, a number of countries indicated that they would produce the drug under compulsory license. Roche responded by offering to quickly negotiate voluntary licenses. While the August 30, 2003 waiver has been used only once, it provided important "background" for the announcements regarding compulsory licensing and almost certainly affected Roche's decision making.

3. The preceding discussion of patent rules affecting access to medicines reflects serious concern about the potential impact on developing countries, and supports recognizing exceptions to strong patent protection in order to promote lower-cost access. There are other points of view promoting the idea that stronger protection is better. *See* Harvey E. Bale Jr., *The Conflicts Between Parallel Trade and Product Access and Innovation: The Case of Pharmaceuticals*, 1 J. INT'L ECON. L. 637, 640 (1998); J.A. DiMasi, R.W. Hansen & H.G. Grabowski, *The Price of Innovation: New Estimates of Drug Development Costs*, 22 J. HEALTH ECON. 151 (2003).

The following is an excerpt from Alan O. Sykes, *Public Health and International Law: TRIPS, Pharmaceuticals, Developing Countries, and the Doha "Solution,"* 3 CHI. J. INT'L L. 47 (2002):

> The precise impact of the Doha Declaration on the policies of developing nations remains to be seen, but it seems likely that the Declaration will embolden them to enact measures that will reduce the returns to pharmaceutical patent holders, at least with respect to drugs that are used to treat certain diseases. Such measures will likely include the award of compulsory licenses for the production of patented medications (with minimal royalties payable to the patent holder), and the allowance of "parallel imports" of medications from nations where prices are lower. This essay will take a preliminary look at the merits of such policies from an economic perspective, and draw on this analysis to suggest some directions for the resolution of legal issues that remain on the table after Doha.
>
> The ultimate wisdom of measures that relax intellectual property protection for pharmaceuticals in developing countries turns on complex matters, including empirical issues about which one can only hazard an educated guess. It is conceivable that patent rights in the developing world have negligible impact on research incentives. They may simply raise prices on patented drugs, transferring rents to foreign pharmaceutical patent holders, and creating deadweight losses by pricing consumers out of the market who are willing to pay the marginal cost of medicines but not the monopoly markup charged by the patent holder.
>
> But there is another possibility, one which in my view better accords with what we know about the importance of patents to pharmaceutical research, and with the extraordinary value to consumers of medicines that successfully treat serious conditions. Developing nations have long had little intellectual property protection for pharmaceuticals, and we have concurrently witnessed an apparent dearth of research into diseases such as malaria and

drug-resistant tuberculosis that are of particular importance to these nations. The lack of patent protection may have resulted, at least in part, from an acute collective action problem — developing nations reap the full benefits from lower prices when they do not create pharmaceutical patents, yet the costs in terms of diminished research incentives are largely externalized to the rest of the developing world. The WTO TRIPS agreement held out some promise of overcoming part of this problem. Yet, just as the obligations of developing nations under TRIPS are beginning to take hold, the Doha Declaration casts great doubt on the future credibility of patent rights for pharmaceuticals in developing nations. The result may be quite unfortunate for research incentives, especially those relating to particular diseases. *Id.*, at 48-49.

Many experts on pharmaceutical R&D disagree strongly with Sykes' suggestion that an absence of patent protection in developing countries is discouraging research on so-called neglected diseases. The main problem, instead, is an absence of "demand pull." That is, pharmaceutical companies simply will not invest in treatments for individuals who do not have the capacity to pay, especially when there is an abundance of patients in wealthier countries who will pay for costly treatments for diseases affecting them. The WHO Commission on Intellectual Property Rights, Innovation and Public Health agreed with that assessment, citing absence of demand pull as the key problem limiting research on neglected diseases. *See Public Health: Innovation and Intellectual Property Rights*, Report of the Commission on Intellectual Property Rights, Innovation and Public Health, April 2006, at 28-32.

4. The revised system allowing member states to grant compulsory licensing under Article 31(f) of TRIPS has not been widely used. Moreover, the corresponding amendment to the TRIPS Agreement has not yet entered into force. Do you think issues connected with the patenting of pharmaceuticals have received too much public attention, or perhaps not enough? What you do think has been the main effect of the August 30, 2003 Waiver on the conduct of right holders and research-based companies relating to the supply of drugs to least developed countries?

C. The Patent Cooperation Treaty

Securing a patent generally requires submitting an application that describes an invention to a governmental authority, an examination of that application by the authority in respect to formal requirements (such as mention of the inventor), an examination in respect to whether the claimed invention meets the criteria of patentability, publication of the application (in most countries and regions prior to the grant of a patent), and the grant (or denial) of a patent by the authority. These procedures may vary along a number of different lines among nations and regions. Formal requirements differ — some nations allow applications only by natural persons, others by both natural and legal persons. Some nations, such as South Africa and Switzerland, do not subject applications to pre-grant examination regarding the criteria of patentability. Some nations, such as India, permit third parties to pursue pre-grant opposition.

The United States is the only major economy in the world to employ a "first to invent" rather than a "first to file" criterion for determining which inventor among competing applicants will be awarded a patent. In the United States, though certain presumptions are established in favor of the first inventor to submit an application to the Patent Office, another inventor may rebut those presumptions by proving that he or she was the first to conceive and reduce an invention to practice (with reasonable diligence). In other countries and regions, the first inventor to submit to the patent office an application for the same invention is awarded a patent.

The main instrument and innovation at the multilateral level concerning the grant of patents is the Patent Cooperation Treaty (PCT). The PCT is widely used by businesses seeking a broad territorial scope of patent protection for their inventions.

The Patent Cooperation Treaty represented the first major step following conclusion of the Paris Convention toward a truly internationalized patent system. First and foremost, it must be stressed that use of the PCT system does not result in the grant of an "international patent." Rather, the PCT facilitates the grant of national and regional patents, which remain substantively governed by national and regional patent laws. However, there are many reasons why use of the PCT system has grown dramatically over the past decade, and why its use has now become standard operating procedure among many, if not most, multinational enterprises.

Before the advent of the PCT, an inventor seeking to patent his or her invention in many countries would file a patent application in a first country. Assuming that this inventor was entitled to the benefits of the Paris Convention, this inventor would then have a 12-month priority period in which to file corresponding patent applications in all other countries in which he or she sought protection. Since filing a patent application in a foreign country would usually require the appointment of a foreign agent, translation of the patent application and compliance with a different set of formalities than applied to the first filed application, a great deal of time pressure was involved in the process, as well as a great deal of expense. After expiration of the priority period, the inventor faced a variety of risks that might result in loss of the ability to obtain a patent. If a third party had filed an application on the same invention during the priority period (and the inventor had not), that third-party application would now take precedence (in a first to file country). If the inventor had disclosed the invention during the priority period, novelty might be lost. For these reasons, the 12-month priority period was treated as something of an "all or nothing" proposition.

The PCT made dramatic changes to the old Paris Convention system. First, the patent applicant need comply with only one set of formal requirements when filing the PCT application, and only a limited number of national and regional formal requirements become applicable at subsequent stages in the process. The patent applicant generally files his or her PCT application in a Receiving Office (RO), which is a national or regional patent office where the first filing would ordinarily take place. The PCT also permits initial filing of a patent application with the International Bureau at WIPO (which filing results in a grant of priority under the Paris Convention). However, many countries (including the United States) do not allow patent applications for local inventions to be filed abroad until a national security review is completed. As a consequence, the first filing of patent applications with the International Bureau is not very common.

Before the end of the priority period, the RO transmits the application to the International Bureau at WIPO, and also transmits a copy to the International

Search Authority (ISA). In its PCT application, the inventor specifies or "designates" the countries in which he or she will seek a patent. PCT fees are structured such that once a certain number of countries are designated, the applicant may designate all PCT countries with no additional designation fees payable.

The PCT procedure is more fully described below.

One of the major advantages of the PCT procedure is that it delays decisions with respect to the payment of fees, preparation of translations (and so forth) up to 30 months from the priority date. This allows applicants to prepare their international strategies with more deliberation. When applications are ready to enter the National Phase, the applicant has a much better idea whether the invention will be commercialized (as will justify the expense of patenting in national offices), and whether a patent will, in fact, be granted.

WIPO PCT APPLICANT'S GUIDE— VOLUME I—INTERNATIONAL PHASE*

CHAPTER 2. WHAT IS THE PCT?

2.001. The Patent Cooperation Treaty or PCT is a multilateral treaty that was concluded in Washington in 1970 and entered into force in 1978. It is administered by the International Bureau of the World Intellectual Property Organization (WIPO), whose headquarters are in Geneva (Switzerland).

2.002. The PCT facilitates the obtaining of protection for inventions where such protection is sought in any or all of the PCT Contracting States. . . . It provides for the filing of one patent application ("the international application"), with effect in several States, instead of filing several separate national and/or regional patent applications. In addition to designations of PCT Contracting States for the purposes of obtaining national patents and similar titles, an international application includes designations for regional patents in respect of States party to any of the following regional patent treaties: the Protocol on Patents and Industrial Designs within the framework of the African Regional Intellectual Property Organization (ARIPO) (hereinafter referred to as "the ARIPO Harare Protocol"), the Eurasian Patent Convention, the European Patent Convention, and the Agreement establishing the African Intellectual Property Organization (OAPI) (hereinafter referred to as "the OAPI Agreement"). The PCT does not eliminate the necessity of prosecuting the international application in the national phase of processing before the national or regional Offices, but it does facilitate such prosecution in several important respects by virtue of the procedures carried out on all international applications during the international phase of processing. The formalities check, the international search and the optional supplementary international search(es) and the likewise optional international preliminary examination carried out during the international phase, as well as the automatic deferral of national processing which is entailed, give the applicant more time and a better basis for deciding whether and in which countries to further pursue the application.

* As of October 2010.

CHAPTER 3. THE "INTERNATIONAL PHASE" AND THE "NATIONAL PHASE" OF THE PCT PROCEDURE

3.001. The PCT procedure consists of two main phases. It begins with the filing of an international application and ends (in the case of a favorable outcome for the applicant) with the grant of a number of national and/or regional patents: hence the terms "international phase" and "national phase." (The expression "national phase" is used even if the Office before which it takes place is a regional Office.) The expressions "international phase" and "national phase" are not actually used in the PCT, but they are convenient, short expressions which have become customary. . . .

3.002. The international phase . . . consists of five stages. The first three occur automatically for all international applications and the last two are optional. The first three Steps consist of the filing of the international application by the applicant and its processing by the "receiving Office" . . . , the establishment of the international search report and written opinion by one of the "International Searching Authorities" . . . , and the publication of the international application together with the international search report by the International Bureau of WIPO (hereinafter referred to as "the International Bureau"). The fourth step includes the establishment of a supplementary international search which may be carried out by one or more of the International Searching Authorities (other than the one that carried out the main international search) resulting in the establishment of a supplementary international search report. . . . Hereinafter, reference to the "(main) international search" alone does not include reference to the "supplementary international search," and reference to "international search report" alone does not include reference to "supplementary international search report," except where otherwise indicated. The third step includes communication of the published international application and the international search report and, where applicable, the supplementary international search report(s), as well as the international preliminary report on patentability (Chapter I of the PCT), by the International Bureau to the national (or regional) Offices which the applicant wishes to grant him a patent on the basis of his international application (the so-called "designated Offices"). The communication occurs upon request by the designated Office to the International Bureau.

3.003. The optional fifth step involves what is known as international preliminary examination (under Chapter II of the PCT), and is concluded with the establishment of the international preliminary report on patentability (Chapter II of the PCT) by one of the "International Preliminary Examining Authorities." . . . The international preliminary report on patentability (Chapter II of the PCT) analyzes aspects of the general patentability of the invention. Together with the published international application, the international search report and any supplementary international search report, the international preliminary report on patentability (Chapter II of the PCT) is communicated to the national (or regional) Offices which the applicant wishes to grant him a patent on the basis of his international application (the so-called "elected Offices"). The communication occurs upon request by the elected Office to the International Bureau. International preliminary examination is available subject to certain conditions and qualifications being met; . . .

3.004. On completion of the international phase, further action is required before and in each of the national (or regional) Offices which the applicant wishes to grant him a patent on the basis of his international application. In particular, the applicant has to pay to those Offices the required national (or regional) fees, furnish them with any translations that are required and appoint a representative (patent agent) where required. There are time limits by which those steps must be taken if the application is to proceed in the national phase. . . . If the steps are not taken within the applicable time limit, the effect of the international application may cease in any State where the time limit has not been met. The national (or regional) Offices then examine the application and grant or refuse the national (or regional) patent on the basis of their national laws. (In the PCT and in this Guide, any reference to "national law" is also a reference to a regional treaty such as the ARIPO Harare Protocol, the Eurasian Patent Convention, the European Patent Convention and the OAPI Agreement. . . .) These procedures before the national (or regional) Offices constitute what is usually referred to as the "national phase" of the PCT procedure and are considered in that part of this Guide.

3.005. It is up to the applicant to decide whether and when to enter the national phase before each national (or regional) Office. The international phase continues, for any particular State, until entry into the national phase before the national (or regional) Office concerned or until the expiration of the applicable time limit for entering the national phase before that Office. Since the national phase may be entered before different Offices at different times, the international application may simultaneously be in the international phase for some States and the national phase for others. Where national phase processing or examination has begun before a particular Office, any actions taken on the international application remaining in the international phase have no effect on the proceedings before that Office.

Chapter 4. Usefulness of the PCT for Applicants

4.001. Use of the PCT saves effort — time, work — for any person or firm ("the applicant") seeking protection for an invention in a number of countries.

4.002. Use of the PCT also helps the applicant to make decisions about the prosecution of the application before the various national Patent Offices in the national phase of processing.

4.003. The saving arises primarily from the fact that, under the PCT, the applicant files one application — the international application — in one place, in one language and pays one initial set of fees, and that this international application has the effect of a national or regional application, which, without the PCT, he would have to file separately for each country or region.

4.004. The help to the applicant in the national phase prosecution of the application follows from the "advice" he obtains from the international search report, a report which is established for each international application, according to high, internationally regulated standards, by one of the Patent Offices that are highly experienced in examining patent applications and that have been specially appointed to carry out international searches. Those Offices are listed in Annex D ("International Searching Authorities"). Detailed advice may also be obtained from the written opinion established by the International Searching Authority which gives a preliminary nonbinding opinion on whether the claimed invention appears to be novel, to involve inventive step and to be industrially applicable.

4.005. If the applicant so requests (see Form PCT/IB/375), a supplementary international search may be carried out, by one or more of the participating International Searching Authorities (see Annex SISA) other than the one which carried out the main international search. The supplementary international search report(s) (see Form PCT/SISA/501), thus obtained will provide the applicant with a more comprehensive overview of the relevant prior art and enable him to better assess his chances of obtaining patent protection for his invention (see Chapter 8).

4.006. If the applicant files a demand under Chapter II, international preliminary examination is carried out on the basis of the international search report and the written opinion of the International Searching Authority, and concludes with the international preliminary report on patentability (Chapter II of the PCT). Offices qualified to prepare such reports are specifically appointed to carry out international preliminary examinations. . . . [I]n order to be appointed International Searching Authority, an Office must also hold an appointment as International Preliminary Examining Authority, and vice versa. The additional benefit for applicants of filing a demand for international preliminary examination is that it provides the applicant with an opportunity to enter into a dialogue with the examiner at the International Preliminary Examining Authority and to possibly amend the international application in order to influence the content of the international preliminary report on patentability (Chapter II of the PCT).

4.007. The advantages offered by the PCT are given in more detail below.

4.008. By the single act of filing an international application under the PCT, it is possible to secure the very effect that, without the PCT, would require as many filings of separate applications as there are countries or regions in which the applicant seeks protection.

4.009. The filing of an international application takes place in one of the languages accepted by the Office with which the application is filed; for many applicants that will be the language, or one of the languages, used by the national or regional Patent Office of, or acting for, their country.

4.010. The international application is filed in a single place; it is generally filed at the national Patent Office of the applicant's country or at a regional Patent Office acting for the applicant's country, or it may be filed direct with the International Bureau in its capacity as a receiving Office under the PCT.

4.011. There is a prescribed form for the international application. This form must be accepted by all designated Offices for the purposes of the national phase, so that there is no need to comply with a great variety of widely differing formal requirements in the many countries in which protection may be sought.

4.012. The international fees payable in respect of the filing of an international application may be paid at one time, at one Office and in one currency. The costs and possible complications connected with the payment, on filing, of many fees in many countries, and generally in different currencies, are thus avoided.

4.013. Before the applicant goes to the effort and expense of having translations prepared, paying the national or regional fees and appointing agents in the various countries, his views are able to mature to a greater extent than would be possible without the PCT, not only because he has more time, but also because the international search report, the written opinion of the International Searching Authority, the supplementary international search report(s), and the international preliminary report on patentability

(Chapter II of the PCT) constitute a solid basis on which he can judge his chances of obtaining protection. Furthermore, any patents subsequently granted by the designated or elected Offices can be relied on by the applicant to a greater extent than would have been the case without the benefit of the international search report, the written opinion of the International Searching Authority, the supplementary international search report(s), and the international preliminary report on patentability (Chapter II of the PCT). Moreover, because of the longer time the applicant has for making decisions, he is better placed to assess the technical value and economic interest of patent protection and to select the particular countries in which he desires to continue seeking protection for his invention. As a result, substantial savings can be made in both translation and filing costs for those countries which are no longer of interest to the applicant.

4.014. If an international application is filed in a language which is not both a language accepted by the International Searching Authority which is to carry out the international search and a language of publication, it needs to be translated into an appropriate language shortly after filing, but all the translations required by the Offices of or acting for the countries in which the applicant ultimately wishes to obtain protection need to be prepared only much later. Instead of having to be filed within the 12-month priority period, they are generally not required until the expiration of the time limit referred to in paragraph 4.016.

4.015. Fees payable to national or regional Patent Offices similarly become due later than they do without the PCT, and only in the case where the applicant decides to go ahead with the processing of his international application at the national or regional Patent Office. Generally, such national or regional fees must be paid within the same time limit as referred to in paragraph 4.016.

4.016. Since 1 April 2002, the applicable time limit for entering the national phase is 30 months from the priority date (or even later in some cases) for all Offices except those in respect of which the former 20-month time limit remains applicable unless the applicant files a demand for international preliminary examination before the expiration of 19 months from the priority date, in which case the 30-month time limit (or even later in some cases) will also apply. For regular updates on these applicable time limits, refer to the Official Notices (*PCT Gazette*), the *PCT Newsletter*, and the relevant National Chapters; a cumulative table is also available from WIPO's website at: www.wipo.int/pct/en/texts/time_limits.html.

4.017. An international search report (and any supplementary international search report) which is favorable from the applicant's viewpoint strengthens his position vis-à-vis the various national or regional Patent Offices, and his arguments for the grant of a patent by those Offices are likely to be more convincing.

4.018. This is even more true in the case of a favorable international preliminary report on patentability under either Chapter I or II, which contains far more material on which to base an opinion on the chances of obtaining patents than does an international search report.

4.019. If the international search report and the written opinion of the International Searching Authority are partly favorable and partly unfavorable, the applicant can modify his claims so as to maintain only those which are likely to result in the grant of a patent. If the international search report and the written opinion are unfavorable, and the applicant consequently decides not to proceed any further, he saves the cost of having the application processed in the various countries. The same applies to supplementary international search report(s).

4.020. The preceding paragraph also applies in the case of international preliminary reports on patentability under Chapter II of the PCT.

4.021. Important other advantages resulting from use of the PCT route are referred to in this text. They consist, among other things, in savings in the procedure before the designated Offices (for instance, there is no need to provide each Office with original drawings, or certified copies of the priority application, there is a reduction in national fees in several countries and the European Patent Office, etc.).

REGIONAL PATENTS VIA THE PCT

4.022. Important additional advantages for applicants wishing to protect their inventions in countries party both to any of the various regional patent treaties (see paragraph 2.002) and to the PCT result from combined use of the PCT system and those regional systems. Not only is the PCT fully compatible with the regional patent systems, but there are possibilities for advantageous combined use of both kinds of system by the applicant, irrespective of the country in which he files. . . .

GLOBAL TREND[3]

1.1 Trends in PCT Applications

In 2009, an estimated 155,900 PCT applications were filed worldwide, representing a 4.5% decrease compared to 2008. For the first time, the PCT System witnessed a decline over the previous year. This can be explained largely by the negative impact, for many countries, of the global economic downturn on international patenting activity.

Figure 1.1. Trends in PCT Applications, 1978-2009

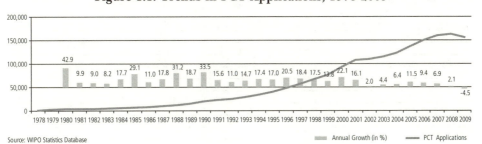

Source: WIPO Statistics Database

Annual Growth (in %)   PCT Applications

---

3. PCT Annual 2009 Review, available at: http://www.wipo.int/export/sites/www/ipstats/en/statistics/pct/pdf/901e_2009.pdf.

Figure 1.2. Distribution of PCT applications by country of origin, 2005 and 2009

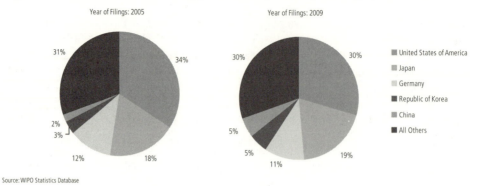

Source: WIPO Statistics Database

Applicants from the US filed the largest share (30%) of PCT applications in 2009, followed by applicants from Japan and Germany. The combined share of the top 5 countries has remained the same, around 70%, between 2005 and 2009. However, US and German shares of total PCT applications in 2009 decreased by 4 and 1 percentage points, respectively; whereas, China, the Republic of Korea and Japan each saw their shares of PCT applications increase by 3, 2 and 1 percentage points, respectively.

Table 1.1 shows the number of PCT applications filed by the top 15 countries of origin from 2005 to 2009.

Note: In 1979 (the first year after PCT came into force) there were around 2600 applications, by 1990 the number of applications had increased six-fold.

Table 1.2 shows the number of PCT applications filed by a selection of developing countries and countries in transition from 2005 to 2009.

Table 1.1. Applications by country of Origin, 2005–2009

Country of Origin	Year of Filing					2009 Share (%)	Changed compared to 2008 (%)
	2005	2006	2007	2008	2009		
United States of America	46,858	51,296	54,044	51,673	46,079	29.6	-10.8
Japan	24,870	27,023	27,749	28,785	29,807	19.1	3.6
Germany	15,987	16,734	17,825	18,854	16,732	10.7	-11.3
Republic of Korea	4,689	5,946	7,065	7,900	8,049	5.2	1.9
China	2,512	3,937	5,465	6,126	7,906	5.1	29.1
France	5,756	6,264	6,570	7,073	7,163	4.6	1.3
United Kingdom	5,096	5,093	5,539	5,513	5,326	3.4	-3.4
Netherlands	4,504	4,550	4,422	4,341	4,445	2.9	2.4
Switzerland	3,294	3,613	3,814	3,749	3,673	2.4	-2.0
Sweden	2,887	3,334	3,658	4,136	3,581	2.3	-13.4
Italy	2,349	2,702	2,948	2,885	2,664	1.7	-7.7
Canada	2,320	2,573	2,848	2,913	2,569	1.6	-11.8
Finland	1,893	1,844	1,994	2,223	2,133	1.4	-4.0
Australia	2,001	2,003	2,053	1,946	1,754	1.1	-9.9
Israel	1,461	1,599	1,747	1,905	1,577	1.0	-17.2
All Others	10,277	11,159	12,216	13,230	12,442	8.0	-6.0
Total	136,754	149,670	159,957	163,252	155,900	100	-4.5

Source: WIPO Statistics Database

**Table 1.2. PCT Applications by Developing Countries and Countries
in Transition, 2005–2009**

Countries of Origin among Selected Developing Countries/Countries in Transition	Year of Filing				
	2005	2006	2007	2008	2009
Republic of Korea	4,689	5,946	7,065	7,900	8,049
China	2,512	3,937	5,465	6,126	7,906
India	679	836	901	1,070	835
Russian Federation	660	697	735	803	662
Singapore	455	483	522	563	578
Brazil	270	334	398	472	496
Turkey	174	269	359	393	385
South Africa	360	424	406	399	376
Malaysia	38	60	111	205	226
Mexico	141	168	186	213	193
Poland	97	101	107	128	174
Ukraine	60	77	94	99	77
Colombia	23	29	44	37	64
Chile	9	12	17	27	54
Egypt	51	41	40	43	33
Serbia		8	23	37	26
Bulgaria	22	26	30	27	25
Latvia	16	17	21	20	24
Lithuania	8	10	13	18	22
Morocco	9	10	18	16	22
All Others	186	258	224	244	246
Total	10,459	13,743	16,779	18,840	20,473

Source: WIPO Statistics Database

The majority of developing countries and countries in transition saw increases in 2009 compared to the previous year, despite the onset of the economic crisis. However, the percentage increases are lower than those experienced in 2008, with the notable exception of Chinese PCT applications, which grew by 29.1% in 2009, compared to 12.1% in 2008.

Since 2005, PCT applications from all developing countries and countries in transition combined show annual increases, although each annual increment is smaller than the previous one, i.e., 2006 growth was 31.4% followed by 22.1% in 2007, 12.3% in 2008 and 8.7% in 2009.

The following table reflects the top-ten PCT applicants in 2009.

2009 Rank	Position Changed	PCT Applicant's Name	Country of Origin	Number of PCT applications published
1	1	Panasonic Corp.	Japan	1,891
2	-1	Huawei Tech. Co., LTD.	China	1,847
3	2	Robert Bosch GmbH	Germany	1,587
4	-1	Koninklijke Philips Electronics N.V.	Netherlands	1,295
5	6	Qualcomm Incorporated	United States of America	1,280
6	3	Telefonaktiebolaget LM Ericsson (Publ)	Sweden	1,240
7	1	LG Electronics Inc.	Republic of Korea	1,090
8	4	NEC Corporation	Japan	1,069
9	-5	Toyota Jidosha Kabushiki Kaisha	Japan	1,068
10	3	Sharp Kabushiki Kaisha	Japan	

D. *Substantive Patent Law Harmonization in WIPO*

Discussion of case law at the outset of this chapter reveals that patent law, despite common foundations, largely varies among different jurisdictions. As noted earlier in the excerpt by Edith Penrose, differences among national approaches to patenting precluded any serious pursuit of harmonized patent law in the late 1800s. Common rules in the Paris Convention and the TRIPS Agreement are still far from constituting a harmonized international patent system. Following the adoption of the TRIPS Agreement, a new effort to make progress on harmonizing key concepts of patent law has been underway.

A work program for a draft Substantive Patent Law Treaty (SPLT) was initiated at the WIPO in 2000 under the auspices of the Standing Committee on the Law of Patents (SCP). The WIPO Secretariat (International Bureau) has prepared treaty drafts, as well as draft regulations and practice guidelines, along with explanatory notes. However, this work program has generated substantial controversy.

There is considerable resistance, particularly among some developing countries, to harmonizing national patent laws based closely on models employed by highly developed countries. There is a perception that this would act to solidify the dominance of developed country enterprises in the technology-dependent global economy. While developed countries have characterized their limited areas of harmonization interest as "technical" matters, the resistant developing countries argue this does not adequately characterize the potential welfare impact of the proposed rules. What is sought by developing countries is to maintain "flexibility" or "policy space." Some developing countries have insisted that the SPLT negotiations, if they are to proceed, must not ignore subject matter of interest to them, including control of anticompetitive practices.

It is not only developing country resistance that blocks movement toward a more harmonized patent system. There remain some serious differences between the United States and the European Union on issues such as "first to file" and "first to invent," and grace periods for disclosure.

The following excerpt expressed the viewpoint shared by a number of developing countries concerning the SPLT negotiations.

MULTILATERAL AGREEMENTS AND A TRIPS-PLUS WORLD: THE WORLD INTELLECTUAL PROPERTY ORGANISATION (WIPO)

Sisule F. Musungu & Graham Dutfield*

. . . The negotiations on the SPLT, on the other hand, are aimed at initially creating uniform substantive patent law standards on prior art, novelty, utility and inventiveness, requirements relating to sufficient disclosure and the drafting of claims and, possibly, to facilitate the mutual recognition of patent search

* TRIPS Issues Papers 3, Quaker United Nations Office (QUNO), Geneva Quaker International Affairs Programme (QIAP), Ottawa.

and examination results. After this first phase of work, further harmonisation is envisaged in areas where the main players, the USA and the Europeans, do not agree such as the first to file versus first to invent principles and post grant opposition proceedings.

Harmonisation as proposed in the SPLT drafts is likely to result in TRIPS-plus standards for developing countries. While most of the proposed standards will benefit international industries, they will make it more difficult for developing countries to adapt their patent laws to local conditions and needs[,] including adapting their laws to take into account their critical public health and other needs. Such a result will undermine the achievements in Doha on public health and elsewhere on the other issues of intellectual property and development. One can conclude that the process of patent law harmonisation, coupled with various bilateral agreements that contain TRIPS-plus standards, will seriously compromise the ability of developing countries to use the various TRIPS flexibilities for development objectives.

Harmonised patent law standards will also make it more difficult for these countries to seek amendments to the TRIPS Agreement, for example, to introduce disclosure requirements with respect to genetic resources and traditional knowledge.

Some of the proposals in the SPLT negotiations that have implications for TRIPS flexibilities include those aimed at:

— reducing the flexibility of countries to define patentability requirements by, for example, eliminating the requirements for a technical character in inventions;
— introducing matters of equivalence in international patent rules; and
— prohibiting countries from imposing any further conditions, other than those specifically provided for in the treaty, on patent applicants.

The draft SPLT under article 12 seeks to harmonise the conditions for patentability. An important aspect of the draft deals with industrial applicability or utility. One proposed approach is to define industrially applicable inventions as those which "can be made or used for exploitation in any field of [commercial] [economic] activity." Considering that after the adoption of the SPLT contracting parties would not be allowed to impose any further conditions on applicants other than those specifically spelt out in the SPLT, if accepted, this proposal would mean that anything used in commercial and/or economic activity except mere discoveries, abstract ideas as such, scientific and mathematical theories and laws of nature as such and purely aesthetic creations, would be patentable. This would pave the way for the mandatory patenting of such things as business methods and software and eliminate the current flexibility under TRIPS which allows each country to define what an invention is, including requiring that inventions have a technical character. The possibility of introducing matters of equivalence under this treaty also poses TRIPS-plus risks. If, for example, equivalence for purposes of infringement proceedings, was harmonised based on the approach that a process or product would be considered as equivalent if it performs substantially the same function as the protected process or product, then the freedom under TRIPS to define equivalence so as to allow inventing around patented inventions would be eliminated.

NOTES AND QUESTIONS

1. In October 2010, a compromise was reached that may permit some nego-
    tiations on a SPLT to move forward. The WIPO press release announced:

    SCP AGREES ON FUTURE WORK ON PATENT-RELATED ISSUES

    Geneva, October 15, 2010
       PR/2010/666
       The WIPO Standing Committee on the Law of Patents (SCP) agreed on late
    Friday at the close of its week-long session from October 11-15, 2010 to
    include a number of key substantive issues relating to patent law and practice
    in its future work. Delegations from 86 countries, 5 international organiza-
    tions and 25 non-governmental organizations participated in the session of
    the Committee, which was characterized by a very positive and constructive
    atmosphere among member states that resulted in significant progress in the
    Organization's substantive agenda with respect to the further development of
    the international patent system.
       WIPO Director General Francis Gurry expressed satisfaction about the
    progress achieved and highlighted the importance for WIPO to be able to
    offer a consensus-based and a multilateral forum to all member states for
    patent-related matters.
       In summarizing the work of the Committee, SCP Chairperson Maximi-
    liano Santa Cruz from Chile said the SCP decided to include the following
    issues into its future work:
       (i)   Exceptions and limitations to patent rights;
       (ii) Quality of patents, including opposition systems;
       (iii) Patents and health;
       (iv) Client-patent advisor privilege;
       (v)   Transfer of technology.
    The Committee also agreed that the non-exhaustive list of issues first iden-
    tified at its June 2008 meeting will remain open for further elaboration and
    discussion at its next session, and that four more issues will be included in the
    list, namely, "Impact of the patent system on developing countries and
    LDCs," "Patents and food security," "Strategic use of patents in business"
    and "Enhancing IT infrastructure for patent processing."

2. A great deal of information concerning the SPLT negotiations, including
    draft texts and explanatory notes prepared by the Secretariat, can be found
    at the WIPO web site, at http://www.wipo.int. *See, e.g.,* WIPO International
    Bureau, Draft Substantive Patent Law Treaty, SCP/10/2, Sept. 30, 2003.

3. Assess the reasons why patent law harmonization is slow and meets resis-
    tance, looking back through this chapter. How do you assess differences in
    economic interests, rooted in the structure of different economies? Is it
    suitable to harmonize what perhaps is best left to the process of trial and
    error in case law and among different jurisdictions? Which are the elements
    that should be harmonized in addition to the TRIPS Agreement from the
    point of view of the international trading system?

4. Are developing countries right to be worried about solidifying developed
    country technological dominance? Does the patent system play a significant
    role in the global economic imbalance? Does the fact that the patent system
    is complex and expensive to use argue for or against harmonization from
    the standpoint of developing countries? Might developing country

inventors gain from a harmonized system, which might reduce their trans-action costs? Recall that today nothing prevents developing country inven-tors from filing patent applications in developed countries.

5. Some industry interests in the United States, Europe, and Japan suggest that because of the slow pace of harmonization efforts at WIPO, developed and "like-minded" developing countries should abandon that effort and undertake their own harmonization effort in a forum like the OECD. Do you think this is a useful suggestion? What would be the drawbacks?

E. Territorial Reach

See Chapter 1, section IV.E, including the *Microsoft v. AT&T* and *NTP v. Research in Motion* decisions.

The question of the territorial reach of patents took on considerable signif-icance in the context of seizures by customs authorities in the Netherlands of medicines in transit between India and other developing countries, where the medicines were not patented in the exporting or importing countries, but where Dutch customs authorities undertook seizures of the generic drugs based on claims under local Dutch patents. India and Brazil eventually initiated consultations with the EU and the Netherlands pursuant to the WTO Dispute Settlement Understanding. On December 10, 2010, senior political officials of the EU and India announced that this matter had been settled with an under-taking by the EU to change its relevant legislation to make clear detention/seizures of generic medicines in transit based on patents is not permitted, and committing the EU to a cessation of the practice pending amendment of the legislation. India signaled that it would suspend further dispute settlement action at the WTO. See *EU and India Resolve Dispute over Generic Drugs*, Reuters, Brussels, December 10, 2010. As of January 2011 the parties had not yet for-mally notified the WTO of a settlement, though there is every indication that the parties intend to fulfill the aforesaid political commitments.

SEIZURE OF GENERIC PHARMACEUTICALS IN TRANSIT BASED ON ALLEGATIONS OF PATENT INFRINGEMENT: A THREAT TO INTERNATIONAL TRADE, DEVELOPMENT AND PUBLIC WELFARE

Frederick M. Abbott*

The European Union amended its border control regulations in 2003 in a way that allegedly signaled permission to EU patent holders to demand seizure of goods in transit through EU ports and airports. The precise intention of the EU IP Border Regulation has been the subject of some controversy among European courts. What has generated intense controversy, however, is the use of the regulation as the basis for seizure of pharmaceutical products alleged to be infringing "local" patents on their way through European airports. Although the next steps at the inter-governmental level remain to be

* 1 W.I.P.O. J. 43 (2009).

determined, the fundamental IP related issues raised by the seizures are worthy of attention because of their long-term implications for the international economic system, economic development and public welfare.

Implementation of the EU IP Border Regulation represents a challenge to fundamental ideas about the way the international intellectual property system operates. The Paris Convention on the Protection of Industrial Property incorporates "independence" of patents as a core principle. The principle is framed in terms of protecting national institutions and decision-making against intrusive determinations by foreign authorities. The principle of independence of patents preserves the sovereign authority of states to adopt and implement patent protections as they consider appropriate, within the framework of a general set of rules. Each member of the Paris Convention decides whether to grant or deny patent protection, and that determination is not dependent on decisions of foreign courts or administrative bodies. The principle of "independence" is corollary to the "act of state doctrine" in international law pursuant to which the courts in one country do not sit in judgment on the acts of foreign governments taken within their own territory based on considerations of comity and restraint.

The principle of independence is sometimes equated with a "territorial" nature of the international patent system. The Paris Convention does not prescribe the jurisdictional scope of patents, nor does it prescribe or define "territoriality." The scope, extension or limitation of patent jurisdiction is determined by national legislatures and courts within boundaries prescribed by public international law. Traditionally, national legislatures and courts have approached potential extraterritorial application of patent law with considerable caution, recognising the problems that would arise in attempting to extend local control to economic activity taking place (and fundamentally regulated by) foreign legislatures and courts. (A territorial nature of the international patent system is recognised in the WTO Decision of August 30, 2003, at para. 6(i), and in the corresponding TRIPS Agreement Amendment, at art. 31*bis*.3, each expressly referring to the "territorial nature of [. . .] patent rights.")

In recent years, some national courts have begun to move away from a rigid understanding of the "territoriality" of patent law. In the Blackberry case, the United States Court of Appeals for the Federal Circuit recognised that advances in technology may create situations in which an invention operates through actions carried out in more than one country, and that the issue of infringement within a country may not always be assessed only by examination of actions within that single national territory.

A modest extension into extraterritorial application of patent law in the Blackberry case was grounded in traditional international law concepts of jurisdiction whereby an act undertaken outside the territorial limits of a state that has a direct and substantial effect within that state may lead its courts to take cognisance of those acts. In cases such as Blackberry, the infringement affects most directly and substantially the country where the allegedly infringed patent is held. Following the US Supreme Court decision in *Microsoft v AT&T*, which stressed limitation of patent infringement to the national territory (and cautioned against extraterritorial extension), the Federal Circuit acknowledged a strong presumption against extraterritorial effect in excluding process patents from the scope of a US statutory prohibition on exporting infringement-capable components.

It is an axiom of public international law that sovereign nations exercise exclusive control over activities taking place within their own territory (although international human rights law challenges certain aspects of that axiom). The European Union bases its exercise of jurisdiction over pharmaceutical products moving in transit through EU airports on its right as sovereign to control activity taking place within EU (and Member State) territory. This extension of jurisdiction is said to be codified in EU customs regulations.

Yet a corollary of the axiom of sovereign control over activities within the national territory is that states have the right to cede elements of exclusive control through international agreement and custom. Thus, through a long history of international agreements and custom, states of the international community have adopted exceptions from exercise of jurisdiction in favor of immunity for diplomats, for naval vessels from in rem admiralty actions and for activities taking place on foreign operated military bases established under basing agreements.

Since 1947, Member States of the European Union have been members of the GATT, now the World Trade Organization (WTO). The EU is a Member of the WTO. The WTO provides the legal framework under which international trade is conducted. From its inception, the GATT/WTO has recognised in GATT art. V the principle of "freedom of transit" for goods moving through ports and airports in international trade. This fundamental principle has been so widely and consistently implemented that there has been virtually no controversy about it in the history of the GATT/WTO, despite the fact that goods are constantly moving in transit through its Members. It is simply a "given" in international trade law that the customs authorities of a country do not seize or detain goods passing through their ports and airports en route to foreign destinations without a good reason. GATT art. V prohibits Members from imposing unreasonable regulatory requirements on goods in transit.

The WTO TRIPS Agreement did not purport to modify the three core principles of the Paris Convention: national treatment, independence and right of priority. The TRIPS Agreement obligates WTO Members to extend patent subject matter coverage to all fields of technology. But the authority to grant or deny patent protection remains with national patent offices of Members based on relevant national legislation. An inventor may lack patent protection in a WTO Member for a number of reasons, including: (1) no patent was ever sought; (2) a patent has expired; (3) a patent application was rejected because the claimed invention was deemed not to meet the criteria of patentability; (4) the claimed invention did not constitute patentable subject matter under the law of the particular Member (e.g. computer software as such in Europe). India, as a case in point, was not required by the TRIPS Agreement to provide pharmaceutical product patent protection until January 1, 2005, and many pharmaceutical products patented in Europe are not patented in India.

* * *

The European Court of Justice in *Montex Holdings v Diesel* raised serious doubt whether seizure of IP protected goods in transit and not intended for the European internal market was permissible. The Court of Justice noted that violation of the 1994 IP Border Regulation (predecessor of the 2003 IP Border Regulation) was predicated upon infringement of an EU intellectual property right (in that case a trade mark), and that the Trademark Directive predicated trade mark infringement on entry into the EU stream of commerce. The ECJ said that unless direct evidence of third party action to place the goods into the EU stream of commerce was present, there could be no infringement under EU law; thus no seizure was authorised. The High Court of England and Wales recently affirmed this line of reasoning in *Nokia v UK Customs*, also with respect to trademarks, but on this occasion expressly interpreting the 2003 EU IP Border Regulation. Dutch authorities and pharmaceutical patent holders, on the other hand, have relied on a decision of the Court of The Hague in the Netherlands, *Sisvel v Sosecal*, grounded in recital 8 of the 2003 IP Border Regulation. The Court of The Hague interprets the recital to establish a "manufacturing fiction." Using this "fiction," an act of patent infringement takes place by "use" of the patent for manufacturing in the Netherlands, even though it is absolutely clear that no such manufacturing takes place. It is a truly remarkable theory under which Dutch law is deemed to be violated by actions taking place in another country, e.g. India, as if those actions had taken place in the Netherlands.

It is hard to imagine a greater departure from the principle of independence of patents than the "manufacturing fiction" that is said to support a finding of infringement of a Netherlands patent by an action in India. The absence of a patent in India where the manufacturing takes place (and which is independent of the Netherlands) is completely ignored. There is no direct or substantial effect on the Netherlands that might be deemed to constitute a reasonable substitute for actual manufacturing. There is no harm in or to the Netherlands unless one reaches to the farthest levels of attenuation (which the European Commission has soundly rejected in the area of competition law).

It is also difficult to imagine what the international legal system will be like if the "fictional acts" theory of jurisdiction becomes widely adopted. American manufacturers might be sued in Europe for violating EU environmental law standards when manufacturing in the United States in compliance with US environmental law. Chinese companies could be sued in the EU for failing to provide EU-standard paid vacation for their workers on the fiction that they were manufacturing in France. A doctor performing a legal abortion in Germany could be prosecuted in Ireland on the theory that the abortion would have been illegal if performed in Ireland. An 18-year-old student drinking beer in Germany could be prosecuted in Florida because 21 is the legal drinking age in Florida. The concept of national sovereignty would be completely meaningless in this new "fictional acts" environment.

* * *

It is neither the responsibility nor the right of WTO Members outside a country that has not granted patent protection to "cure" that situation in favor of a local patent holder by disregarding the decisions taken by authorities in the country that has not provided protection. The European Union has elected to disregard the sovereign rights of foreign WTO Members by refusing to give effect to their decisions as to patent status by the use of force — the seizure and detention by customs authorities of goods in transit. The allegations of infringement are purely for the convenience of a patent holder that happens to have chosen a particular transit country as a place to obtain a patent. This is a form of "long-arm" extension of jurisdiction that the European Union has claimed to abhor when adopted by US antitrust authorities.

While the threat to the international economic system and foundations of international law are serious enough, an even more important negative consequence of the EU policy with respect to the seizure of generic pharmaceuticals in transit is the breach of the understanding reached at the WTO regarding access to medicines as embodied in the Doha Declaration on the TRIPS Agreement and Public Health. There was a bargain reached at the conclusion of the GATT Uruguay Round of trade negotiations in 1993 that provided a 10-year transition period for countries such as India that did not provide pharmaceutical patent protection to institute that protection. That bargain acknowledged that public health systems and patients throughout the developing world relied on countries such as India to provide low-cost generic versions of pharmaceutical products on patent in the developed countries, and that a rapid transition to globalised patent protection would have significant adverse effects on public health. In good measure as a consequence of India's decision to take full advantage of the transition period, a significant part of the developing world can and does continue to rely on that country for the supply of low-cost generic medicines.

NOTES AND QUESTIONS

1. You may wish to consult the requests for consultations transmitted by India and Brazil to the EU and the Netherlands, available on the WTO web site (European Union and a Member State — Seizure of Generic Drugs in Transit, Request for Consultations by India, WT/DS408/1, G/L/921, IP/D/28, 19 May 2010 (initiated May 11, 2010); Request for Consultations by Brazil, WT/DS409/1, IP/D/29, G/L/922, 19 May 2010 (initiated May 12, 2010)). From the requests for consultations, can you identify the differences in approach between India and Brazil on the legal issues?

III. REGIONAL SYSTEMS

In Chapter 1, we introduced various regional institutions that play a role in the international intellectual property system. The country members of the European Patent Convention have developed the most comprehensive regional system for the granting of patents, though the system does not result in the grant of a patent with effect throughout Europe. Because of limitations built into the original treaty upon which the European Union was founded, the regional patent law effort was not a "European Union" (then "European Community") enterprise, but was rather separate and included countries such as Switzerland, which were (and still are) not members of the European Union. Since the earliest discussions of a European patent system, there has been strong interest in a single unified European patent, and as we will see, a complete draft for such an instrument has been under consideration for some time. Nonetheless, as of January 2011, adoption remains elusive.

In the EPC system, the application for a patent is examined by the search authority of the EPO located in The Hague. The EPC establishes the criteria of patentability, which are that the invention be new, capable of industrial application, and involve an inventive step. The key provision, Article 52, provides:

(1) European patents shall be granted for any inventions which are susceptible of industrial application, which are new and which involve an inventive step.
(2) The following in particular shall not be regarded as inventions within the meaning of paragraph 1:
    (a) discoveries, scientific theories and mathematical methods;
    (b) aesthetic creations;
    (c) schemes, rules and methods for performing mental acts, playing games or doing business, and programs for computers;
    (d) presentations of information.
(3) The provisions of paragraph 2 shall exclude patentability of the subject-matter or activities referred to in that provision only to the extent to which a European patent application or European patent relates to such subject-matter or activities as such.
(4) Methods of treatment of the human or animal body by surgery or therapy and diagnostic methods practiced on the human or animal body shall not be regarded as inventions which are susceptible of industrial application within the meaning of paragraph 1. This provision shall not apply to products, in particular substances or compositions, for use in any of these methods.

If an EPC patent is granted, the inventor obtains a separate bundle of patent rights in each EPC country that was designated in the application. There are a number of important differences in the process by which patents are granted as between the United States and EPC-Europe. These differences include, in respect to the EPC, that the first applicant to file an application for the same invention is entitled to the patent and that there is a post-grant opposition period during which third parties may seek revocation of a patent that has been granted. The EPC establishes an administrative and judicial system for resolving disputes that may arise throughout the patenting process, from the time the application is submitted until any opposition has run its course (and even after). At each stage, decisions of bureaucrats may be appealed to various Boards of Appeal.

We begin with an excerpt from Friedrich-Karl Beier introducing the basic rules of the EPC concerning patentability and the application procedure.

THE EUROPEAN PATENT SYSTEM
Friedrich-Karl Beier*

. . . IV. THE MUNICH PATENT CONVENTION

B. CONDITIONS OF PATENTABILITY

Part II of the Munich Convention contains the provisions of substantive patent law of which the chapter on patentability is the most important one. Under article 52(1), European patents shall be granted for inventions which are new, involve an inventive step, and are susceptible of industrial applications. Since the basic provisions on patentability mention only these four criteria, namely:

---

* 14 VAND. J. TRANSNAT'L L. 1 (1981).

invention, novelty, inventive step or nonobviousness, and industrial applicability, and are to be understood as containing an exhaustive enumeration, no other criteria of patentability can be applied to European patent applications, in particular the requirement that the invention achieve technical progress as was required in the Federal Republic of Germany and is still required in many other countries. At first glance, it seems contrary to the basic philosophy of patent protection to abandon the very requirement of technical progress whose promotion is the main purpose of the patent system. We must admit, however, that the requirement of technical progress as a separate object of examination, in addition to novelty and nonobviousness, is of minor importance in practice and that its proof in some fields leads to practical difficulties. It is, therefore, no great loss if European patent law relinquishes the requirement of technical progress as an independent examination criterion and proceeds from the general presumption that an invention which is susceptible of industrial application and which is not obvious to the average man skilled in the art constitutes an enrichment of technology and thus contributes to technical progress, without the applicant's having to prove in each case that the invention is more advantageous than all other known technical solutions. This does not mean, however, that we should totally forget that patents are granted to advance the art, stimulating not only technical but also economic and social progress. If, therefore, the invention actually achieves such progress, it should be taken into consideration as a positive criterion for patentability, be it as a general rule derived from the main objective of patent protection or as the most important indicia in proving an inventive step.

The Munich Convention avoids the questionable attempt to give a positive definition to the term "invention." Article 52(2) gives only a negative, non-exhaustive enumeration of subjects which should not be considered inventions. Excluded are discoveries, scientific theories, mathematical methods, aesthetic creations, presentations of information, and, in particular, non-technical mental processes, including computer programs. With that provision, the contracting states have, under the motto of "no experiments," adopted a very conservative concept of patentable inventions which leaves little room for the future adaptation of the European patent system to new scientific and technical developments. This is, in my opinion, a short-sighted view which can only be explained, not justified, by the administrative consideration that the newly-created EPO should not be burdened with additional and difficult problems of substantive patent law and search.

Much more forward looking is article 53, containing the other exceptions to patentability. The catalogue is, fortunately, very small. Only inventions whose publication or exploitation would be contrary to the *ordre public* or morality and inventions in the area of plant cultivation and animal breeding are excluded. The latter exclusion does not, however, apply to microbiological processes and the products thereof. Thus, the patentability of microbiological inventions, which play an important role in the field of antibiotics, is expressly acknowledged. Rule 28 of the Implementing Regulations contains specific provisions concerning the disclosure of such inventions and regulating the details of microorganism deposit, culture collection, and the release of samples to the public. Although the content of rule 28 was improved during the Munich Diplomatic Conference, the pharmaceutical industry was not completely satisfied. It therefore urged a further amendment, which, after an interesting discussion, was recently adopted by the Administrative Council.

The most important feature of article 53, however, is that it does not exclude or restrict patent protection for chemical and pharmaceutical inventions, foods, or agricultural products. This is a complete deviation from the existing national law of many contracting states, which, for reasons of economic, health, or agricultural policy, have restricted patent protection in these fields to the manufacturing process only or even, for pharmaceutical inventions, have granted no protection at all, as in Italy. In all these fields, full patent protection will be available at the end of a transition period. Exceptions may be claimed by the contracting states by way of reservation. Up to now, only Austria has used that possibility to maintain provisionally its existing restrictions for chemical products, medicines, and foods.

With respect to novelty, the basic patentability criterion, the French law concept of absolute novelty has been adopted. According to article 54, an invention is considered new if it does not belong to the state of the art. The state of the art comprises everything made available to the public before the priority date through written or oral description, use, or any other method. All substantive, temporal, and territorial limitations of the novelty concept, which are known from various national patent laws, have become obsolete. The European novelty examination is based on the strictest world wide novelty standard.

According to article 64(3), the content of prior applications, which on the priority date of a later publication have not yet been published, will also belong to the state of the art. Such a rule was necessary in order to prevent double patenting. But how this objective was to be accomplished has been extraordinarily controversial in the last twenty years. After a long discussion of the advantages and disadvantages of the traditional prior claim approach, its modern counterpart, the so-called whole contents approach, and many intermediate solutions, the contracting states adopted the whole contents approach to avoid a separate identity test by the simple inclusion of the prior application in the normal novelty test. Therefore, not only the claims, but the entire disclosure contained in the prior application, will hinder the grant of a subsequently filed patent application. These prior applications, however, are considered only as a bar to novelty; they will not be considered in deciding whether the later application involves an inventive step. To be patented, a subsequent application, in other words, can therefore be obvious in view of the contents of an earlier, not yet published application; it must not be fully anticipated. This solution constitutes a reasonable compromise which facilitates the granting procedure and meets the demands of patent practice.

Unfortunately, the same cannot be said with respect to article 55 dealing with non-prejudicial disclosures. In contrast to the German, Japanese, and United States patent laws, which provide a grace period of six or twelve months during which the inventor or his legal successor is protected against the anticipatory effects of his own disclosures, article 65 restricts that protection to disclosures by third parties which may be considered as evident abuse. This very narrowly defined exception, together with the introduction of the absolute novelty concept and the requirement of nonobviousness, will certainly lead to great disadvantages for independent inventors, scientists, and small and medium-sized enterprises which are used to test, exhibit, or give other information on their inventions before filing a patent application. The grace period accorded them sufficient time to evaluate the technical and economic value of the invention, and, if necessary, to improve the invention without fear of losing patent protection. If these possibilities no longer exist, serious disadvantages for many inventors will be the consequence. A more liberal solution which should preferably be an international, worldwide solution would be highly desirable.

My final comments on patentability concern the concept of nonobviousness, for which the Munich Convention utilizes the somewhat unfortunate expressions "inventive step," "*activité inventive*," and "*erfinderische Tätigkeit*" adopted by the Strasbourg Patent Convention of 1963. These terms, at least the German and French versions, are unfortunate since they mis-state the real meaning of this important criterion of patentability. It is not the activity of inventing which is decisive to the concept, but rather the product of that activity, the invention, and its distance from the state of the art. It is nevertheless a welcome development that this judge-made condition of patentability, whose practical importance is much greater than that of novelty, is now firmly anchored in the European patent law. According to the legal definition in article 56, an invention shall be considered to involve an inventive step if, having regard to the state of the art it is not obvious to a person skilled in the art. This definition corresponds to the definitions developed by United States and German courts for nonobviousness or *Erfindungshöhe* respectively. It is to be hoped that this criterion, upon which the quality of future European patent examination will largely depend, will find reasonable interpretation by the European Patent Office and the national courts. After thorough discussions within interested circles, the European Patent Office recently announced its intention to follow the middle line practiced by the German Patent Office rather than the too liberal English or too strict Dutch standard of evaluating nonobviousness.

V. The European Granting Procedures

Most of the remaining articles of the Munich Patent Convention deal with the European patent granting procedure. It is not possible in this article to comment on the details of that procedure. It will be sufficient to say that the European Patent Office will practice one of the most elaborate, modern examination procedures based on the experiences of large, national patent offices and provide all the necessary legal guarantees for the patent applicant as well as for competitors and the general public. This procedure contains the following steps:

(1) The filing of a European patent application designating the member states for which protection is sought, in one of the three official languages, English, French, or German;

(2) the examination on filing and formal requirements;

(3) the drawing up of a search report revealing the relevant state of the art;

(4) the publication of the application, together with the search report, eighteen months after the date of priority;

(5) the examination of the published patent application as to patentability, dependent on a written request by the applicant which can be filed within six months after publication; otherwise the application will be deemed to be withdrawn;

(6) the grant of the European patent or its refusal, with the possibility of appeal; and

(7) a post-grant opposition procedure to give third parties the opportunity to raise objections against patentability; if the opposition is successful, the

patent will be revoked, with retroactive effect; if the opposition fails or no opposition is raised during the nine month period after publication of the grant, the European patent will be given full effect within the territories of all contracting states for which it has been granted.

NOTES AND QUESTIONS

1. In *Biogen*,[35] the House of Lords observed the conceptual difficulties sur-rounding attempts to define "invention" beyond the requirements of new-ness, industrial applicability, and inventive step. Note that the drafters of the EPC did not overcome these conceptual difficulties.
2. The EPC expressly excludes computer software from the scope of patent-able subject matter. The EPO has nevertheless found some room for patent-ing computer software that forms part of an otherwise patentable invention. This is consistent with the approach that the U.S. Supreme Court adopted in *Diamond v. Diehr*.[36] The U.S. Patent and Trademark Office today grants, and the CAFC confirms, patents on computer software standing alone.
3. Debate over the grant of patents on computer software has been going on within the European Union for a number of years. The European Commission submitted a proposal to allow such patenting to the Council and Parliament. (*See* Proposal for a Directive of the European Parliament and of the Council on the patentability of computer-implemented inven-tions, Brussels, 20.02.2002, COM(2002) 92 final.) On July 6, 2005, the European Parliament rejected the proposal after intensive discussion and lobbying from various stakeholder groups.
4. Friedrich-Karl Beier is quite critical of the EPC rule on nonprejudicial disclosures, suggesting that it will substantially disadvantage small and medium-sized businesses. Recall that the U.S. Patent Act provides a broad one-year grace period for prior public disclosure. At least part of the patent bargain between inventors and the public at large is that inven-tors receive a grant of exclusivity in exchange for disclosing their inventions to the public. If an inventor has already publicly disclosed an invention prior to filing a patent application, for what is the public bargaining?

A. The European Patent Office

The EPC establishes a number of divisions at the European Patent Office, which are the Receiving Section, Search Divisions, Examining Divisions, Opposition Divisions, Legal Division, Boards of Appeal, and Enlarged Board of Appeals (art. 15 EPC). The Boards of Appeal, as their name suggests, review the deci-sions of the various divisions. The Boards of Appeal and the President of the EPO may refer questions of law to the Enlarged Board of Appeals. In deciding a case, a Board of Appeal may exercise any of the powers conferred by the EPC on the department from which an appeal is taken, or it may remit a case back to that department for further action consistent with its decision (art. 111 EPC).

---

35. See *supra* section I.C.2.
36. 450 U.S. 175 (1981).

The Boards of Appeal and Enlarged Board of Appeals have developed a substantial case law regarding the interpretation and application of the EPC. In the *Procter & Gamble* decision of a Technical Board of Appeal that follows, the relationship among the various examining and opposition divisions, and the Boards, is considered. The decision includes a very useful discussion of the doctrine of *res judicata*, which plays an important role in IPRs law generally. Under what circumstances have two parties exhausted their IPRs claims against each other in the courts? Under what circumstances, if any, does the decision in a case involving two parties bind a third party not represented in that case? For example, does a finding that a patent is valid in one proceeding preclude a challenge to the patent in another proceeding? The principles elucidated in the following decision may be helpful to answering these questions.

PROCTER & GAMBLE v. UNILEVER

Decision of Technical Board of Appeal 3.3.1
Dated 3 May 1996 T
167/93 - 3.3.1

Composition of the board:
Chairman: A. J. Nuss
Members: J. M. Jonk, S. C. Perryman
Patent proprietor/Appellant: The Procter & Gamble Company

Opponent/Respondent: Unilever PLC/Unilever N.V. . . . .
Article: 54, 56, 111(2), 113(1), 125 EPC . . .

HEADNOTE

A decision of a Board of Appeal on appeal from an Examining Division has no binding effect in subsequent opposition proceedings or on appeal therefrom, having regard both to the EPC and "res judicata" principle(s).

SUMMARY OF FACTS AND SUBMISSIONS

I. The Appellant (proprietor of the patent) lodged an appeal against the decision of the Opposition Division by which European patent No. 0 098 021 was revoked in response to an opposition, based on Article 100(a) EPC, which had been filed against the patent as a whole. . . .

IV. The Opposition Division held that the subject matter of Claim 1 as granted lacked novelty and that of the claims of the auxiliary request did not involve an inventive step in the light of the document (3). . . .

V. Oral proceedings were held on 3 May 1996.

VI. The Appellant argued in view of the decision T 298/87 of another Board of Appeal, setting aside the decision of the Examining Division refusing the present patent application, in which the then deciding Board concluded that neither of the documents considered (i.e. the present documents (3) and (9)), taken alone or in combination, had been shown to lead in an obvious manner to the subject matter claimed . . . , that the issues considered by the Opposition Division on which their decision was based were res judicata. In support of this view he referred to the decisions T 934/91 and T 843/91.

The Appellant also argued that the subject matter of Claim 1 of the disputed patent was novel in view of document (3). . . .

VII. The Respondents disputed that the issues considered by the Opposition Division would be res judicata. In their view an Opposition Division was entitled to disagree with a Board's decision in examining proceedings. Moreover, res judicata could only apply in cases involving the same parties. Furthermore, the Respondents fully agreed with the reasoning of the Opposition Division regarding lack of novelty for the main request and lack of inventive step for the auxiliary request.

IX. At the conclusion of the oral proceedings the Board's decision to allow the Appellant's auxiliary request was pronounced.

REASONS FOR THE DECISION

1. The appeal is admissible.

2. The first issue to be dealt with is the Appellant's submission on res judicata. The Appellant was arguing that the Opposition Division was bound by the ratio decidendi of the remitting decision T 298/87 of the Board of Appeal, setting aside the decision of the Examining Division refusing the present patent application on the ground of lack of inventive step in view of document (3). In the Appellant's view, this also meant that all findings of facts from document (3) on which the binding part of the decision rested were not open to reconsideration and thus equally binding.

2.1 This issue requires a preliminary investigation of whether there is any legal basis under the European Patent Convention for such a binding effect.

The only explicit reference to any binding effect of a decision of a Board of Appeal (other than the Enlarged Board) is in Article 111(2) EPC stating:

> "If the Board of Appeal remits the case for further prosecution to the department whose decision was appealed, that department shall be bound by the ratio decidendi of the Board of Appeal, in so far as the facts are the same. If the decision which was appealed emanated from the Receiving Section, the Examining Division shall similarly be bound by the ratio decidendi of the Board of Appeal." (Emphasis by the Board)

2.2 There is no reference here to an Opposition Division being bound by a decision of a Board of Appeal on appeal from an Examining Division. The basis, if any, for such binding effect could thus only be under Article 125 EPC stating

> In the absence of procedural provisions in this Convention, the European Patent Office shall take into account the principles of procedural law generally recognized in the Contracting States,

or some principle developed by interpretation of the European Patent Convention.

2.3 To discover principles of procedural law generally recognized in the Contracting States it is useful first to turn to maxims of Roman Law, as these have proved themselves in practice over many centuries, have fundamentally influenced the laws of all Contracting States, and survive, though possibly in slightly modified form, in these laws today. In this case, where the Appellant has referred to a principle of res judicata to support his argument, relevant maxims are:

(1) Res inter alios judicata alii non praejudicat.
(Dig, 2, 7, § 2 in Corpus iuris civilis, editio stereotypa, Bd. 1, Berlin 1908)

A matter adjudged between others does not prejudice third parties.

(2) Res judicata pro veritate accipitur.
(Digest 1, 5, 25 in Op. cit.)

The adjudged matter is to be accepted as truth.

(3) Res judicatas restaurari exemplo grave est.
(Codex Just. 7, 52, 4 in Corpus iuris civilis, editio stereotypa, Bd. 2, Berlin 1877)

To reopen adjudged matters is undesirable because of the [bad] example set.

(4) Expedit rei publicae, ut finis sit litium.
(Cod. Just. 7, 52, 2 (Caracalla); 2, 4, 10 (Philipp); 3, 1, 16 (Justinian) in Corpus iuris civilis, editio stereotypa, Bd. 1, Berlin 1908)

It is in the public interest that there be an end to litigation.

The principle of res judicata is thus a compromise between the right of all parties to a fair hearing (maxim (1)), and a desire to bring litigation to a speedy end (maxims (2) to (4)).

2.4 This is also accepted under the national laws of at least certain Contracting States as set out below:

2.4.1 For the purpose of English law it is useful to quote the following definitions taken from Halsbury's Laws of England, Fourth Edition Reissue 1992, Volume 16:

> "There is said to be an estoppel where a party is not allowed to say that a certain statement of fact is untrue, whether in reality it is true or not. Estoppel may therefore be defined as a disability whereby a party is precluded from alleging or proving in legal proceedings that a fact is otherwise than it has been made to appear by the matter giving rise to that disability." (§ 951)

> "Estoppel per rem judicatam arises:

> (1) where an issue of fact has been judicially determined in a final manner between the parties by a tribunal having jurisdiction, concurrent or exclusive in the matter, and the same issue comes directly in question in subsequent proceedings between the same parties (this is sometimes known as cause of action estoppel);
> (2) where the first determination was by a court having exclusive jurisdiction, and the same issue comes incidentally in question in subsequent proceedings between the same parties (this is sometimes known as issue estoppel)" (§ 953)

2.4.2 For French law, the Code Civil Art. 1351 states:

> L'autorité de la chose jugée n'a lieu qu'à l'égard de ce qui a fait l'objet du jugement. Il faut que la chose demandée soit fondée sur la même cause; que la

demande soit entre les mêmes parties, et formée par elles et contre elles en la même qualité.

The binding effect of the adjudged matter only exists for what was the object of the judgment. It is necessary that the relief sought is based on the same cause of action; that the suit is between the same parties, and for and against them in the same legal capacity.

2.4.3 In respect of German law § 325 Zivilprozeßordnung (Rechtskraft und Rechtsnachfolge) states that:

Das rechtskräftige Urteil wirkt für und gegen die Parteien und die Personen, die nach dem Eintritt der Rechtshängigkeit Rechtsnachfolger der Parteien geworden sind oder den Besitz der in Streit befangenen Sache in solcher Weise erlangt haben, daß eine der Parteien oder ihr Rechtsnachfolger mittelbarer Besitzer geworden ist.

A legally binding judgment has force for and against the parties and persons, who after the start of litigation became successors of the parties or obtained possession of the thing in dispute in such a manner, that one of the parties or its successors has become the mediate owner.

2.5 Without needing to consider the laws of the Contracting States in more detail, in the Board's judgment, it can be seen from the above that any generally recognized principle of estoppel by rem judicatam for the Contracting States is of extremely narrow scope as it will involve something that has been:

(a) judicially determined
(b) in a final manner
(c) by a tribunal of competent jurisdiction,
(d) where the issues of fact are the same,
(e) the parties (or their successors in title) are the same, and
(f) the legal capacities of the parties are the same.

2.6 In cases T 843/91 (OJ EPO 1994, 832) and T 934/91 (OJ EPO 1994, 184) relied on by the Appellant, all criteria (a) to (f) were met, as the proceedings in both cases involved a second appeal in the same opposition proceedings. Here, however at least criterion (e) is not met, as the Respondent was not a party to the application proceedings in which decision T 298/87 issued.

2.7 As stated above, the principle of res judicata is based on public policy that there should be an end to litigation. But the European Patent Convention specifically provides that the grant of a patent should be considered both at a first examination stage (Articles 96 and 97) and at an opposition stage (Articles 99 to 102), and Article 113(1) EPC provides that "The decisions of the European Patent Office may only be based on grounds or evidence on which the parties concerned have had an opportunity to present their comments." In the Board's view these explicit provisions of the Convention preclude any implicit public policy preventing a matter being considered a second time in judicial proceedings, that is estoppel per rem judicatam, from being applicable. Further, to consider in opposition proceedings whether certain lines of argument are precluded on some principle of res judicata, would itself be an undue complication. As a party in opposition proceedings is free to adopt as its own argument the reasons given in a decision of a Board of Appeal in ex parte proceedings, it is this Board's view that the aim of speedy proceedings is best served, if all the issues in opposition proceedings are decided by the relevant tribunal on its own view of the facts, free from res judicata considerations relating to decisions made during the examination proceedings.

2.8 It should be stated that until the beginning of 1996 it was the generally accepted view that Boards of Appeal are not in inter partes proceedings bound by decisions in ex parte proceedings (see, for example, the categoric statement to this effect in the commentary on the basis of German and European jurisprudence, Schulte, "Patentgesetz mit EPÜ, 5. Auflage" (Carl Heymanns Verlag KG 1994), last sentence on page 710). This could have been justified as consistent with the above criteria for res judicata not only on the basis of criterion (e), but also on criterion (c) since an examining division has no jurisdiction to decide an inter partes case, its decision could not bind the opposition division.

2.9 However in decision T 386/94 of 11 January 1996 (OJ EPO 1996, 658), it has been said by Board 3.3.4 that a document may not be taken into account when assessing novelty under Article 54(3)(4) EPC (in circumstances where this document was an application in the name of an opponent, who was arguing that it was entitled to its priority and therefore destroyed the novelty of the opposed patent) because in two earlier appeal proceedings on the opponent's application firstly Board 3.3.2 had decided (T 269/87 of 24 January 1989 (not published in the OJ EPO)) that the application was not entitled to such priority and secondly Board 3.3.4 in decision T 690/91 of 10 January 1996 (not published in the OJ EPO) had reached the conclusion that the findings of T 269/87 with regard to priority were res judicata and not amenable to being reinvestigated.

2.9.1 It is worth observing that the patent under consideration in T 386/94 was in fact revoked for lack of inventive step over other prior art, so the part of this decision (points 19, 21 and 22) stating that this opponent was precluded by earlier decisions from relying on his own application to destroy novelty of the opposed patent was not necessary to support the order made.

2.9.2 There is no discussion in decision T 386/94 of why the matter is res judicata in the opposition proceedings, or whether the change in capacity from applicant to opponent might not require that the merits of the argument be looked at afresh. Other opponents could have raised the same argument, so it is not clear why in the public interest the allegation should not be considered on its merits. Further, while on the facts of T 386/94 the opponent had at least been heard in some proceedings, this Board would not agree that this is sufficient to invoke the principle of res judicata to preclude an opponent raising a particular issue which he has lost in the capacity of applicant in different proceedings.

2.10 Thus, this Board can see no basis for res judicata in the present case, either under the wording of Article 111 or 125 EPC, or on the basis of any interpretation of the European Patent Convention.

2.11 This is a situation where in accordance with the Enlarged Board Decision G 5/83 (OJ EPO 1985, 64, point 5), it is legitimate to take into account the preparatory documents and the circumstances of the conclusion of the treaty in order to confirm the meaning that the Board believes correct.

2.11.1 The penultimate version of what is now Article 111(2) EPC read:

"All further decisions on the same application or patent involving the same facts shall be based on the ratio decidendi of the Board of Appeal" (see document BR/

184 e/72 of the Historical documentation relating to the European Patent Convention).

2.11.2 The reason for the change from that version to the present one appears from document BR/209 e/72 zat/QU/K of the Historical documentation relating to the European Patent Convention. This shows that it resulted from a joint proposal of the German, British, French and Dutch delegations, in which the committee agreed basically with their suggestion to avoid having a decision of a Board of Appeal from being binding on the Opposition Division or the courts of the individual states or the revocation divisions of the second convention. The committee however approved a change to make clear that the department to which the matter is remitted is bound by the ratio decidendi in so far as the facts are the same.

2.11.3 The Board thus concludes that a decision of a Board of Appeal on appeal from an Examining Division has no binding effect in subsequent Opposition proceedings or on appeal therefrom, having regard both to the European Patent Convention and "res judicata" principle(s).

2.12 The question of the circumstances, if any, in which the principle of res judicata can be relied on to achieve a binding effect of an Appeal Board Decision going beyond that specifically provided for by Article 111(2) EPC is one which may at some time have to be considered by the Enlarged Board. However in decision T 298/87, on which the res judicata argument of the appellant is based and which was a decision on appeal from the Examining Division, while the Board concerned had admittedly considered that inventive step was established for the Claim 1 before it, it also considered that feature (a) of this Claim 1, introduced during the examination procedure to remove an objection of lack of novelty, and which had been accepted without comment by the Examining Division, did not seem, on closer review, to meet the formal requirements of Article 123(2) EPC. As that Board was unable to trace any explicit disclosure of feature (a) in the originally filed documents, it found it necessary to remit the matter to the Examining Division for a full examination of the matter of the amended claims, especially as regards Article 123 EPC, on which the decision of the Examining Division then under appeal was completely silent. The Examining Division on the referral then found these claims unallowable under Article 123(2) EPC, but granted the patent on the basis of a different set of claims. The claims considered by the Board of Appeal in T 298/87 thus differed significantly from the claims before the Opposition Division, and now before this Board, so that on any view of the law no estoppel arises, and an independent consideration of novelty and inventive step is necessary. In these circumstances, this Board does not consider that a referral to the Enlarged Board relating to an issue of estoppel by rem judicatam is necessary in the present case.

2.13 The Board accordingly holds that the Respondent's arguments on all issues must be decided anew on the facts as determined.

3. Main request

3.1 The first substantive issue to be dealt with is whether the subject matter of the claims of the patent in suit as granted is novel in view of the novelty objections indicated above under points IV and VII.

4. Auxiliary request . . .

ORDER

For these reasons it is decided that:

1. The decision under appeal is set aside.
2. The case is remitted to the first instance with the order to maintain the patent on the basis of the set of claims submitted as auxiliary request at the oral proceedings on 3 May 1996, and a description to be adapted.

NOTES AND QUESTIONS

1. The Board of Appeal invokes maxims of Roman law since, according to the Board, these maxims "have fundamentally influenced the law of all Contracting States, and survive, though possibly in slightly modified form, in these laws today." Do you think this was an appropriate way for the Board to determine the procedural rules common to the contracting states of the EPC? What other method(s) might you have suggested?
2. It is interesting to note that the drafters of the EPC finally undertook to narrow the effect of decisions of the Boards of Appeal. In *Biogen, supra* section I.C.2, the House of Lords held that the decision of the EPO Board of Appeal regarding the same patent was not binding on the U.K. courts. If the penultimate version of Article 111(2) EPC referred to by the Board of Appeal (in *Procter & Gamble*) had been adopted, do you think the result in *Biogen* would have been different? Would it be preferable that national courts in EPC states be required to follow the decisions of Boards of Appeal?

B. A New European Union Patent?

The EU patent system is still fragmented to a large extent, notwithstanding the fact that national patent laws (especially provisions on conditions of patentability and invalidity of patents) have been mainly harmonized. The existence of a single market, as well as a desire to increase competitiveness internationally, are the main driving forces for the creation of the single EU Patent. Moreover, at the same time, there are important drawbacks related to patent litigation in the EU: simultaneous litigations against the same patent in different member states, high costs for these litigations, forum shopping, and possible contradictory decisions weaken legal security, pushing toward a single system of patent litigation within the EU (conditioned upon the existence of an EU Patent).

The first steps toward the creation of a European Patent were made as early as 1949. The French senator Longchambon presented to the Consultative Assembly of the Council of Europe a plan for a European Patent Office, which, however, was rejected. In 1959, according to a proposal of the Commission of the European Economic Community (EEC), its member states started drafting a patent law for the Common Market to overcome territorial limitations. However, due to the political situation at that time and the position of the United Kingdom (still not a member of the EEC), these efforts were unsuccessful.

Four years later France submitted its proposal for restarting negotiations on European patent law based on drafting two separate conventions. The first was to establish a European Patent Office with a single European patent grant procedure for a number of national patents. The second convention was seen to deal with a European patent for the Common Market. After successful conferences in Luxemburg and Munich, the EPC (1973) (discussed above) came into effect.

In 1975, the Convention on the European Patent for the Common Market was signed in Luxemburg. It provided not only for the creation of the Community Patent but also for a litigation procedure within the EPO system. Newly created Nullity Boards would have dealt with claims as to patent granting procedure, while the national courts would retain jurisdiction over infringement actions. Appeals on decisions of the Nullity Boards would have been lodged with the European Court of Justice (ECJ). At the very end, due to an insufficient number of ratifications by the signatory states, it never entered into force. Two further draft Conventions followed in 1985 and 1989; however, neither of them entered into force.

In March 2000, the European Council called for the creation of a Community patent system. Following this, the Commission put forward a proposal for a Council regulation on the Community Patent. According to this proposal, the EPO would have been the granting authority to issue this patent. However, to make this possible, membership of the EU in the EPC was required. At the same time, the creation of a specialized patent court system was planned to deal with questions of validity and infringement of the Community Patent. The ECJ would also have had jurisdiction in these matters. In the following excerpt, the European Commission discusses its proposal for a Community — now EU (see *infra*) — Patent.

PROPOSAL FOR A COUNCIL REGULATION ON THE COMMUNITY PATENT

(Presented by the Commission) Brussels, 1.8.2000 COM(2000) 412 Final 2000/0177 (CNS)

. . .

2.4. THE MAIN FEATURES OF THE COMMUNITY PATENT

The Community patent must be of a unitary and autonomous nature (2.4.1.). It must stem from a body of Community patent law (2.4.2.), be affordable (2.4.3.), have appropriate language arrangements and meet information requirements (2.4.4.), guarantee legal certainty (2.4.5.) and coexist with existing patent systems (2.4.6.).

2.4.1. *Unitary and Autonomous Nature of the Community Patent*

The Community patent must be unitary in nature. It will produce the same effect throughout the territory of the Community and may be granted, transferred, declared invalid or allowed to lapse only in respect of the whole of the Community.

The Community patent must be of an autonomous nature. It shall be subject only to the provisions of the proposed Regulation and to the general principles of Community law.

2.4.2. Law Applicable to the Community Patent

The proposed Regulation introduces specific provisions applicable to Community patents. It is important to note that the Regulation does not set out to depart substantially from the principles embodied in national patent law already in force in the Member States; these have all acceded to the Munich Convention and have, moreover, largely harmonised substantive patent law in accordance with the Luxembourg Convention, even though the latter Convention has never entered into force. The same applies concerning the specific rules of the TRIPS Agreement, which links the Community and the Member States.

On this basis, the provisions of the Munich Convention concerning such subjects as conditions of patentability, for example, will be applicable to the Community patent.

Thus, in accordance with the provisions of the Munich Convention, Community patents will be granted in respect of inventions, whether products or processes, provided that they are new, involve an inventive step and are capable of industrial application. Similarly, exceptions to patentability will be covered by the Munich Convention. Amendments made to the Convention in the course of the intergovernmental conference currently under way for the revision of the Convention will of course be applicable to the Community patent.

By contrast, the effects of the Community patent, once granted, will be governed by the provisions of this Regulation. This applies, for instance, to the limitations of the effects of the Community patent.

As regards the use of a patented invention without the patent proprietor's authorisation, the proposed Regulation would incorporate the best practice in force in the Member States: the granting of compulsory licences would thus be possible. . . .

2.4.4. Language Arrangements—Access to Information

. . . [T]he universal language in the field of patents is, in reality, English. Translations are very rarely consulted. For example, at the *Institut National de la Propriété Industrielle*, the French national institute of industrial property rights, translations are consulted in only 2% of cases. Moreover, any obligation to translate the patent into all the Community languages would not necessarily guarantee easy access to this information for all economic operators established in the Community. Incidentally, separate information and assistance systems can be put in place or upgraded in order to help small and medium-sized enterprises, in particular, in searching for information on patent applications and patents published.

NOTES AND QUESTIONS

1. In the end, the Council failed to adopt this proposal in 2004. Simultaneously, there were attempts to create a patent litigation system outside the EU framework. The Working Party on Litigation of the Intergovernmental Conference of the EPC States presented the first drafts of the Agreement on the establishment of a European Patent Litigation Agreement (EPLA), and a Statute of the European Patent Court in 2003 (the latest draft was submitted in 2005). The proposal in itself was characterized as well balanced between centralized and locally oriented systems; however,

due to legal constraints for EU member states to participate in such an international agreement, it never entered into force.

2. A considerable part of the Commission's discussion (above) addresses translation costs and dispute settlement. Recall that the European Union in 2011 includes 27 member states, most of which do not share a common language. The Commission observed that the common language of patent applications is English, but refrained from proposing adoption of a single language for use in EU matters relating to patents. This is not surprising from a social and cultural standpoint, but it does impose costs on inventors.

Since 2004, work on the (now) "EU Patent" and the relevant patent court system has continued. Developments in 2009 included a General Approach to the Proposal for a Council Regulation on the Community Patent and a proposal for a Unified Patent Litigation System for Europe, which would take a form of an Agreement. The latter proposal has been submitted to the ECJ for consideration on compatibility with EU law.

In the following excerpts, the Council of the EU expresses its general approach to the Proposal for a Council Regulation on the EU Patent.

PROPOSAL FOR A COUNCIL REGULATION
ON THE COMMUNITY PATENT — GENERAL APPROACH

(Addendum to the Note from General Secretariat of the Council to the Council (Competitiveness)) Council of the European Union, Brussels 27 November 2009 16113/09, ADD 1, 2000/0177 (CNS)

Delegations will find in Annex a revised proposal for a Council Regulation on the European Union patent drawn up by the Presidency for discussion at the meeting of the Council (Competitiveness) on 4 December 2009.

In view of the entry into force on 1 December 2009 of the Lisbon Treaty, the term "Community" has been replaced by "European Union," where appropriate, throughout the text (see Art. 1 of the Treaty on European Union as amended by the Lisbon Treaty).

ANNEX

Proposal for a COUNCIL REGULATION on the European Union patent (Text with EEA relevance)

THE COUNCIL OF THE EUROPEAN UNION,
Having regard to the Treaty on European Union and the Treaty on the Functioning of the European Union and in particular Article 118, first subparagraph, of the latter,
Having regard to the proposal from the Commission,[4]
Having regard to the opinion of the European Parliament,[5]

---

4. Proposal for a Council Regulation on the Community patent, COM/2000/0412 final - CNS 2000/0177 *, OJ C 337, 28.11.2000, p. 278.

5. European Parliament legislative resolution on the proposal for a Council Regulation on the Community patent (COM(2000) 412 - C5-0461/2000 - 2000/0177(CNS), OJ C 127E, p. 519-526.

Having regard to the opinion of the European Economic and Social Committee,[6]

Whereas:

(1) The activities of the European Union (hereafter "EU") include the establishment of an internal market characterized by the abolition of obstacles to the free movement of goods and the creation of a system ensuring that competition in the internal market is not distorted. The creation of the legal conditions enabling undertakings to adapt their activities in manufacturing and distributing products to an EU dimension helps to attain these objectives. A patent to which uniform protection is given and which produces uniform effects throughout the EU should feature amongst the legal instruments which undertakings have at their disposal.

(1a) A cost effective, legally secure European Union patent (hereafter "EU patent") would in particular benefit Small and Medium-Sized Enterprises (hereafter: SMEs) and would be complementary to the Small Business Act for Europe. The creation of such a unitary title should make access to the patent system easier, less costly and less risky, which would be of particular importance for SMEs.

(1b) The availability of a unitary title providing for equal protection throughout the entire territory of the EU would enhance and help raise effectiveness of the fight against counterfeiting and patent infringement to the benefit of inventors, businesses and society at large. A complete geographical coverage without any loopholes would ensure effective patent protection at all external borders of the EU and would help to prevent the entry of counterfeit products into the European Single Market on the basis of Council Regulation (EC) No 1383/2003 of 22 July 2003 concerning customs action against goods suspected of infringing certain intellectual property rights and the measures to be taken against goods found to have infringed such rights.[7]

(2) The Convention on the Grant of European Patents of 5 October 1973 as amended by a revision act of 29 November 2000 (hereafter: EPC) established the European Patent Office (hereafter: EPO) and entrusted it with the task of granting European patents. The expertise offered by the EPO should be used in the granting of the EU patent.

(2a) The EPO would play a central role in the administration of EU patents and would alone be responsible for examination of applications and the grant of EU patents. Enhanced partnership should however enable for the European Patent Office to make regular use, where appropriate, of the result of any search carried out by central industrial property offices of the member states of the European Patent Organisation on a national patent application the priority of which is claimed in a subsequent filing of a European patent application.

(2aa) All central industrial property offices, including those which do not perform searches in the course of a national patent granting procedure can have an essential role under the enhanced partnership, *inter alia* by giving advice and support to potential applicants for EU patents, in particular SMEs, by receiving applications, by forwarding applications to the EPO, and

---

6. Opinion of the Economic and Social Committee on the Proposal for a Council Regulation on the Community patent, OJ C 2001 155, p. 80.

7. OJ L 196, 2.8.2003, p. 7.

by disseminating patent information. National patent offices should be compensated for these activities through the distribution of annual renewal fees.

(2b) Applications for EU patents should be filed directly with the EPO or via the national patent office of a Member State.

(2c) The level of procedural fees for processing an application for an EU patent should be the same regardless of where the application is filed and should be related to the costs of handling the EU patent.

(3) The accession of the EU to the EPC would enable it to be included in the system of law established by the EPC as a territory for which a unitary patent can be granted. The pre-grant stage of the EU patent should thus principally be governed by the EPC. This Regulation should in particular establish the law applicable to the EU patent once granted.

(3a) The EPO should also be entrusted with the task of administering the EU patent in the postgrant stage, for example, as regards the collection and distribution of renewal fees to Member States and the management of the Register of EU Patents.

(4a) To the extent that this Regulation does not provide otherwise the substantive law applicable to the EU patent, for example as regards patentability, the scope of patent protection and the limitation of the effects of the patent, should be governed by the pertinent provisions of the EPC and national law where this complies with EU law.

(4b) The EU patent should constitute a third option. Applicants should remain free to apply instead for a national or a European patent. This Regulation is without prejudice to the right of the Member States to grant national patents and should not replace Member States' laws on patents or European patent law as established by the EPC.

(6) Negative effects of an exclusive right created by an EU patent should be mitigable through a system of compulsory licences. This is without prejudice to the application of EU competition law by the Commission or national authorities. The [European and EU Patents Court] should be entrusted with the grant of compulsory licences in situations not falling under EU competition law.

(7) The jurisdictional system for the EU patent should be part of the [European and EU Patents Court] having jurisdiction for both European and EU patents. This jurisdiction is established and governed by [quote title of the legal instrument].

(8) In accordance with the principles of subsidiarity and proportionality as set out in Article 5 of the Treaty, the objectives of the proposed action, in particular the creation of a unitary right with effect throughout the EU can be achieved only by the EU. This Regulation confines itself to the minimum required in order to achieve those objectives and does not go beyond what is necessary for that purpose.

(9) Whereas the creation of the EU patent by this Regulation is part of a comprehensive patent reform, which also involves changes to the EPC and the establishment of a unified patent litigation system based upon an international agreement to be concluded between the EU, its Member States and certain other Contracting Parties to the EPC, ratified in accordance with the Member States' Constitutional requirements.

[The text of the operative provisions of the draft regulation is not reproduced here, but may be found at http://http://ec.europa.eu/internal_market/indprop/patent/index_en.htm — EDS.]

NOTES AND QUESTIONS

1.   A considerable part of the discussions on the EU Patent and the new patent
     litigation system addresses translation issues. Recall that the European
     Union in 2011 includes 27 member states, most of which do not share a
     common language. What could be the arguments for and against the trans-
     lations of the patent applications and patent specifications into one of the
     EPO official languages sustained by the new proposed EU patent regime?
     Read the following provisions of the Draft Agreement on the European and
     EU Patent Court on language of the proceedings and consider the right to
     be heard.

> CHAPTER II — LANGUAGES OF PROCEEDINGS ARTICLE 29
>
> **Language of proceedings at the Court of First Instance**
> (1) The language of proceedings before any local or regional division shall
> be the official European Union language(s) of the Member State or the
> official language(s) of other Contracting States hosting the relevant division,
> or the official language(s) designated by Contracting States sharing a regional
> division.
> (2) Notwithstanding paragraph 1, Contracting States may designate one or
> more of the official languages of the European Patent Office as the language
> of proceedings of their local or regional division.
> (3) Parties may agree on the use of the language in which the patent was
> granted as language of proceedings, subject to approval by the competent
> division. If the division concerned does not approve their choice, the parties
> may request that the case be referred to the central division.
> (4) [At the request of one of the parties and after having heard the other
> parties]/[With the agreement of the parties] the competent local or regional
> division may, on grounds of convenience and fairness, decide on the use of
> the language in which the patent was granted as language of proceedings.
> (5) The language of proceedings at the central division is the language in
> which the patent concerned was granted.
>
> ARTICLE 30
>
> **Language of proceedings at the Court of Appeal**
> (1) The language of proceedings before the Court of Appeal shall be the
> language of proceedings before the Court of First Instance.
> (2) Parties may agree on the use of the language in which the patent was
> granted as language of proceedings.
> (3) In exceptional cases and to the extent deemed appropriate, the Court
> of Appeal may decide on another official language of a Contracting State as
> the language of proceedings for the whole or part of the proceedings, subject
> to agreement by the parties.
>
> ARTICLE 31
>
> **Other language arrangements**
> (1) Any division of the Court of First Instance and the Court of Appeal may,
> to the extent deemed appropriate, dispense with translation requirements.
> (2) At the request of one of the parties, and to the extent deemed appro-
> priate, any division of the Court of First Instance and the Court of Appeal
> shall provide interpretation facilities to assist the parties concerned at oral
> proceedings.

2. This Agreement will be open for accession not only for the EU member countries, but also to other EPC members, since it will be dealing not only with the EU Patent, but also with the European patent. The Court will comprise a Court of First Instance, a Court of Appeal, and a Registry. Both instances will be vested with a right to submit questions for interpretation to the ECJ.

3. The adoption of common patent rules will deprive the member states of legislative discretion. For example, the unitary EU Patent would be subject to compulsory licensing only as prescribed in the regulation. At present, the EU member states have their own rules on compulsory licensing, which vary quite considerably. They also have significant legislative and judicial differences in respect of the scope of exemptions, such as for experimental use.

C. Regional Trade Agreements and Patent Norms

The United States has been unable to persuade governments participating in multilateral organizations, including the WTO, to provide higher levels of patent protection to its technology-based industries. As a "second best" solution, it has sought to negotiate higher levels of protection in bilateral and regional negotiations where it maintains greater leverage. This phenomenon is described in the following excerpt.

TRIPS II, ASIA AND THE MERCANTILE PHARMACEUTICAL WAR: IMPLICATIONS FOR INNOVATION AND ACCESS

Frederick M. Abbott*

I. THE TRIPS II AGENDA

A powerful agenda for adoption of high levels of intellectual property protection, including related regulatory protection, is being advanced by the United States (and certain other developed countries) for developing countries, including developing and emerging market countries of Asia.[1] This agenda essentially reflects a TRIPS II exercise, but is largely being carried out in bilateral and regional negotiations, as well as in WTO accession negotiations.

The TRIPS II agenda, as the TRIPS I agenda, is explained by strong mercantile interests seeking to increase technology and expression rents. Circumstances since the launch of the GATT Uruguay Round in 1986 have changed substantially. In 1986, OECD industries were principally concerned with preventing weak developing country industries from substituting low-cost and often lower quality "copied" versions of products on local markets, but were

---

* Stanford Center for International Development, Working Paper No. 308, Dec. 2006.

1. *See* discussion and analysis of the phenomenon in Frederick M. Abbott, *The WTO Medicines Decision: World Pharmaceutical Trade and the Protection of Public Health*, 99 Am. J. Int'l L. 317, 348-58 (2005) and Frederick M. Abbott, *Toward a New Era of Objective Assessment in the Field of TRIPS* and *Variable Geometry for the Preservation of Multilateralism*, 8 J. Int'l Econ. L. 77, 88-98 (2005); Peter Drahos, *Developing Countries and International Intellectual Property Standards-Setting*, 5 J. World Intell. Prop. 765 (2002); Carsten Fink & Patrick Reichenmiller, *Tightening TRIPS: The Intellectual Property Provisions of Recent US Free Trade Agreements* (World Bank Trade Note No. 20, 2005); World Bank, Global Economic Prospects 2005, ch. 5, at 98-110.

not threatened with competition in their home markets or with respect to originator and high-quality products.[2]

The OECD industry groups driving the TRIPS II agenda are (1) the copyright-dependent audio-visual industry concerned with unauthorized duplication and distribution of video and audio content and (2) the pharmaceutical (and agricultural chemical) industry concerned with competition from generic producers and, in a forward-looking sense, emerging originator enterprises. . . .

III. THE **TRIPS II** COMMITMENTS

A. THE AGREEMENTS

The TRIPS II agenda is principally manifest in bilateral and regional trade agreements negotiated by the United States, in force or signed with Jordan, Singapore, Chile, Australia, Morocco, Central America — DR, Bahrain, Oman, Peru, and Colombia, and under negotiation with Thailand, Southern Africa Customs Union (SACU), South Korea and others.[46] The proposed Free Trade Agreement of the Americas, negotiations on which are presently stalled, includes IP commitments.[47] The TRIPS II agenda is also carried out in WTO accession negotiations which are characterized by bilateral demands for concessions, and which in recent years have witnessed increasing demands for pharmaceutical related protections.[48] Negotiations ongoing between the United States and Russia are awaiting movement on IP issues.[49]

---

2. Frederick M. Abbott, *Protecting First World Assets in the Third World: Intellectual Property Negotiations in the GATT Multilateral Framework*, 22 VAND. J. TRANSNAT'L L. 689 (1989); contributions by Silvia Ostry and J. Michael Finger in THE POLITICAL ECONOMY OF INTERNATIONAL TRADE LAW: ESSAYS IN HONOR OF ROBERT E. HUDEC (Daniel Kennedy and James Southwick, eds.) (Cambridge University Press 2002); SUSAN SELL, PRIVATE POWER, PUBLIC LAW, THE GLOBALIZATION OF INTELLECTUAL PROPERTY RIGHTS 121-62 (2003) (Cambridge).

46. Texts available at http://www.ustr.gov.

47. Texts available at http://www.oas.org (http://www.ftaa-alca.org/NGroups/WGroups_e.asp#IntellectualPropertyRights).

48. *See, e.g.*, WTO, Working Party on the Accession of Cambodia, Report of the Working Party on the Accession of Cambodia, WT/ACC/KHM/21, 15 Aug. 2003, at para. 205:

> [The representative of Cambodia] . . . further confirmed that during the transition period, that Cambodia would protect against unfair commercial use of undisclosed test or other data submitted in support of applications for marketing approval of pharmaceutical or of agricultural chemical products which utilize new chemical entities, by providing that no person other than the person who submitted such data may, without the permission of the latter person, rely on such data in support of an application for product approval for a period of at least five years from the date on which Cambodia granted marketing approval to the person that produced the data. Prior to the issuance of marketing approval of any pharmaceutical and agricultural chemical products, the relevant Ministries in Cambodia will determine the existence of a patent covering a product for which an application for marketing approval had been filed by a party other than the patentee, and will not approve such application for marketing approval until the date of the expiration of such patent. He added that Cambodia would seek out all available technical assistance to ensure that its capacity to fully enforce its TRIPS-consistent legal regime upon expiration of the transition periods is assured and that Cambodia would make available all legislation in draft and promulgated form to WTO Members so that advice on TRIPS-consistency can be obtained.

49. *See, e.g.*, Trade Committees to Oppose PNTR for Russia Without IPR, SPS Fixes, INSIDE US TRADE, May 12, 2006.

Pharmaceutical-related commitments in bilateral and regional agreements extend well beyond TRIPS I requirements.[50] Patents must be granted for new uses of known substances (including second medical indication patents), the scope of biotechnology patenting is extended (e.g., by requiring plant and animal variety patenting), patents must be extended to compensate for delays based on regulatory review, and the TRIPS I patent regulatory review exception is reformulated in a more restrictive way. For some countries (i.e., Jordan, Singapore and Australia), the grounds for issuing compulsory licenses are restricted. Parallel importation of patented products is blocked. In a section of the IPRs chapter labeled "Certain Regulated Products," marketing exclusivity and data protection is extended for a five-year period based not only on submission of regulatory data in the country where registration is undertaken, but extended to foreign submission of regulatory data, or reliance on foreign marketing approval. Covered products are expanded beyond "new chemical entities" to products not previously approved. Three-year extensions of marketing exclusivity are available for new clinical studies (including those undertaken abroad). Patents are linked to the health department medicines registration process, precluding approval of market entry effective prior to expiration of the patent term. In the US-Australia FTA, the US secured entry into Australia's pharmaceutical price control system,[51] and the US is seeking similar entry into the South Korean price control system.

The international intellectual property system prior to the TRIPS II regime relied on private patent holders to enforce rights through civil litigation. While an imperfect system, patent holders were required to overcome challenges to the validity of their patents. A significant portion of litigated patents are, in OECD jurisdictions, determined to be invalid.[52] The objective of the TRIPS II exercise is to provide grants of marketing exclusivity without the necessity of validating the patent, and or even maintaining a patent. This is accomplished through data protection rules and patent-regulatory review linkage. The combined effect is to shift the burden of enforcement from the private patent holder to government authorities. Because of the complexity of the rule systems, developing country governments are likely to rely on Pharma industry representations concerning the validity of claims.[53] Developing country government authorities are susceptible to inter-governmental pressure, further reinforcing the effect of market exclusivity rules.

NOTES AND QUESTIONS

1. Do you think the U.S. practice of a forum shifting on IPRs matters from the WTO and WIPO is a good idea? Does it make a difference whether the country or countries the United States is negotiating with are developed or developing countries? *See, e.g.,* Keith E. Maskus, *Reforming U.S. Patent*

---

50. *See* references in note 1, *supra.*

51. Ely Lilly has initiated the first challenge to a determination made under Australia's PBS. Mark Metherell, *Drug subsidy appeal to test new review,* http://www.smh.com.au/news/national/drug-subsidy-appeal-to-test-new-review/2006/05/07/1146940413807.html, May 8, 2006.

52. Kimberly A. Moore, *Judges, Juries, and Patent Cases — An Empirical Peek Inside the Black Box,* 99 Mich. L. Rev. 365, 392 (2002).

53. *See* Frederick M. Abbott, *Intellectual Property Provisions of Bilateral and Regional Trade Agreements in Light of U.S. Federal Law,* UNCTAD/ICTSD Issue Paper 12, Feb. 2006.

Policy: Getting the Incentives Right, CSR No. 19, Nov. 2006, U.S. Council on Foreign Relations.

2. Patent provisions in recently negotiated bilateral trade agreements of the United States are largely consistent with U.S. law and practice. But U.S. patent law continuously changes through acts of the executive, legislative, and judicial branches. How will entering into binding international agreements affect U.S. domestic evolution of patent norms?

IV.   SELECTED NATIONAL PATENT SYSTEMS

A.   *China*

Since it began to liberalize its domestic market in the late 1980s, China has undergone one of the most rapid and profound economic transformations in world history. This has certainly *not* been because China introduced strong intellectual property protection. While China introduced a wide range of IP legislation and joined the major international IP agreements, at least until recently, China's record on IP enforcement has been weak. China has been under constant pressure from the United States and Europe to more vigorously enforce IP law. It is almost certain that China will gradually do this as its domestic producers begin to rely more heavily on locally generated technology. In light of China's emergence as a major economic power it is important to study its patent law.

A BRIEF INTRODUCTION TO THE PATENT PRACTICE IN CHINA
Yin Xintian*

The Patent Law of the People's Republic of China was adopted in 1984 and entered into force on April 1, 1985. It was revised in 1992, and the revised law entered into force on January 1, 1993. Through this revision, the patent system in China has been improved and protection for patent rights has been strengthened in the following ways:

(1) The technological fields of patent protection have been broadened to cover pharmaceutical products, food, beverages, flavorings, and substances obtained by means of chemical processes.

(2) The duration of a patent right has been extended. The duration of patent rights for inventions has been extended from fifteen years to twenty years, and the duration of patent rights for utility models and design has been extended from five years to ten years.

(3) The exclusive right has been enhanced. The patent protection for a manufacturing process has been extended to the product directly obtained by the patented process and a patentee has the right to prevent any other

* Deputy Principle Director, Administrative Department for Patent Examination, Chinese Patent Office. 9 DUKE J. COMP. & INT'L L. 253 (1998).

person from importing, without his authorization, the patented product or products obtained directly by his patented process.

(4) The grounds for granting a compulsory license have been restricted. The situations in which a compulsory license may be granted only include those where (a) an entity qualified to utilize the invention or utility model made a request for authorization from the patentee to utilize the patent on reasonable terms and such efforts have not been successful within a reasonable period of time, and (b) a national emergency, an extraordinary state of affairs, or the public interest requires it.[1]

(5) The original pre-granting opposition procedure has been replaced by the post-granting revocation procedure. As a result, the entire approval procedure of a patent right has been shortened by an average time period of three to four months. The retroactive effect of a declaration of invalidation has been restricted.

(6) According to the former Patent Law, any patent right declared invalid was deemed to be non-existent from the beginning. The revised Chinese Patent Law keeps this provision, but at the same time stipulates the following:

The decision of invalidation shall have no retroactive effect on any judgment or order on patent infringement that has been pronounced and enforced by the People's Court, on any decision concerning the handling of patent infringement that has been made and enforced by the administrative authority for patent affairs, and on any contract of a patent license and of an assignment of a patent right which has been performed, prior to the decision of invalidation. However, the damage caused by other persons in bad faith on the part of the patentee shall be compensated. This new provision is helpful for maintaining a stable economic order.

The revised Chinese Patent Law is fully in line with the requirements of the Agreement on Trade-Related Aspects of Intellectual Property Rights (TRIPS Agreement). Moreover, in light of experiences since the enforcement of the revised Chinese Patent Law, the preparation work for the second revision of the Chinese Patent Law is in progress. In addition, the drafting and approval of the Regulations on Protection of Plant Varieties and the Regulations on Protection of Layout Design of Integrated Circuits have been completed. These two regulations are independent legislation, as allowed by the TRIPS Agreement, and patent applications in these fields will be handled by governmental authorities separate from the Chinese Patent Office.[2]

––––––––––––

Currently, Chinese patent law is at a further stage of revision. A third revision was adopted in 2008 and the following text describes the most recent changes of the Patent Law in China.

1. Article 51 of the old Patent Law stipulated that a patentee has the obligation to utilize or otherwise to authorize other persons to employ the patented invention or utility model in China, and Article 52 of the old Patent Law stipulated that the Patent Office may grant a compulsory license where the patentee fails, without a justified reason, to fulfill the obligation set forth in Article 51 within three years from the date of the grant of the patent right. Clearly, a grant of a compulsory license at present is limited. In fact, the Chinese Patent Office has never granted a compulsory license since its establishment.

2. The Chinese Patent Law simultaneously provides three kinds of patent rights: patents for inventions, patents for utility models, and patents for design. This is one of the distinct characteristics of the Chinese Patent Law.

THIRD REVISION OF CHINA'S PATENT LAW

EU-China IPR2 Project[8]

The adoption of the amendments to the Chinese Patent Law by the Standing Committee of the National People's Congress (NPC) on 27 December 2008 (Patent Law 2008) marked the first major legislative step in the field of IP law after the release of the National IP Strategy (NIPS) in June 2008. The announcement of NIPS noticeably accelerated the legislative procedure for the patent law revision as NIPS defines the revision of the Patent Law as a key requirement for the achievement of its working targets for 2013 as well as for the overall objective of fully improving the creation, utilization, protection and administration of IP by 2020. This introductory article gives a brief overview of the legislative process for the revision of the law as well as the main new features of the revised law. It should be read in conjunction with the documents compiled in this publication for a valuable insight and a better understanding of the whole revision process.

MOTIVATIONS BEHIND THE AMENDMENT

The Patent Law of the People's Republic of China was first enacted in 1985 and successively amended three times. The first amendment, that inaugurated China's membership in the Patent Cooperation Treaty (PCT), was endorsed in 1992. The second amendment in 2000 focused on the alignment of the Chinese Patent Law system with the provisions of the Trade Related Aspects of Intellectual Property Rights Agreement (TRIPs) prior China's accession to the WTO. These changes included the strengthening of the patent owner's rights against infringement and the provision of new means of protection such as injunctions. At a first glance, it is clear that the first two revisions of the Patent Law followed the country's bid to join the international system of protection for IPRs and the World Trade Organization (WTO) with the aim of fostering domestic industrial property development as well as attracting foreign investments by endorsing a system of law as familiar as possible to that of foreign investors. However, problems connected with the enforcement of the law and with the special social cultural environment in China hindered, to a certain extent, the realization of the legislative goal, the effective protection of patent rights. Insofar, one must always consider that the country's IP law system is remarkably new compared to the respective systems in European countries. Many of the currently existing problems in the Chinese IP system are typical features of the transition from a centrally planned economy to a market economy.

In recent years, the protection of Intellectual Property rights has increased its significance on the political agenda with the consequent need of developing a strategy that balances IPRs, public interests and international obligations. Particularly the promotion of technological innovation is stated as being directly related with the economic development. Based on the comprehensive understanding of the importance of self-innovation the need for greater efforts to improve China's capacity for independent innovation and the respective perfection of the IPR protection system was made absolutely clear at 17th

---

8. Available at: http://www.ipr2.org/images/eu_patent_law-final.pdf.

Congress of China's Communist Party in November 2007 and le[d] to the adoption of NIPS in June 2008. Given this background, the drafters for the third revision of the patent law focused on two areas. Firstly, the strengthening of the protection of the legitimate rights and interests of right holders, the encouragement of innovation and the promotion of timely implementation und utilization of patented technology. Secondly, the harmonization of the Chinese Patent Law with international patent treaties by taking into due accounts the specific national conditions and the actual needs of the country.

Legislative Process for Revision

The actual process for the third revision of the Patent Law started as early as 2005. In accordance with the provisions of the Chinese Legislation Law, the State Intellectual Property Office (SIPO) commissioned research in more than 10 fields related to patent legislation considered to be in urgent need of an update and revision. . . .

. . . The delicate final phase of the drafting proceeding conducted by the Legislative Affairs Commission of the Standing Committee of NPC included again researches and a number of consultations with domestic and foreign experts before the Standing Committee of NPC adopted the revision after the second reading of the law in December 2008. The revision will only enter into force on 1 October 2009 in order to provide sufficient time for consequent amendments to the Implementing Regulations of the Patent Law.

Major Changes

The third amendment revised a substantial number of provisions in the Patent Law and also added completely new articles to the law. Important changes include the following:

1. Patent Granting Procedure
a. Foreign Filing Requirements

The requirement that inventions completed in China must be first filed in China has been deleted. The new Patent Law replaces such filing requirement with a mandatory advance confidentiality examination. Article 20 Patent Law 2008 requires an advance application for confidentiality examination with SIPO before any patent filing abroad for inventions completed in China. Failure to comply with this requirement will result in the non-patentability of the respective invention in China. It has to be noted that the earlier drafts of revised law contained a much more detailed mechanism to implement this foreign filing license which cannot be found in the final text of the law. Insofar, it is expected that these rules will be incorporated in the Implementing Regulations of the Patent Law.

b. Domestic Filing by Foreigners

The old Patent Law established that all foreign applicants who applied for patents in China shall delegate patent agencies that are designated by the SIPO. This requirement to appoint only designated patent agencies has been abolished in the new law due to the growth of the Chinese patent agency industry and competences. Article 19 Patent Law 2008 allows foreign companies to appoint any patent agency established in accordance with the law to act as his or its agent.

c. Absolute Novelty Standard

One of the most important changes in the new law is the adoption of the absolute novelty requirement that will raise the standard for patentability compared to the requirement of relative novelty that was laid down in the old legislation. Insofar, the mere use abroad did not destroy the novelty of an invention under the old law. Articles 23 and 24 Patent Law 2008 endorse now the absolute novelty requirement which offers no territorial restrictions on the prior art and the prior design. Prior art and prior design are defined as any technology/design known to the public before the date of filing by way of public disclosure in publications, public use or any other means in China or abroad. It must be pointed out that the standard of absolute novelty is still restricted by the provision of Article 25 Patent Law 2008 that expounds the terms of the so called grace period of 6 months when an invention creation was exhibited for the first time at an international exhibition sponsored or recognized by the Chinese Government or it was made public for the first time at a "prescribed academic or technical conference."

2. OWNERSHIP AND MANAGEMENT OF PATENT RIGHTS

a. Co-owned Rights

The previous law did not contain any article on the exercise of jointly owned rights. To overcome the problems related with the absence of a regulatory framework for such significant subject matter, Article 15 Patent Law 2008 establishes that the parameters for the exploitation of co-owned rights shall be, in first instance, enclosed in an agreement between the parties. However, if such agreement has not been signed, each co-owner is free to independently utilize and license the patent through common license. Any royalties obtained through the licensing shall be distributed amongst all the co-owners.

b. Coexistence of Patents for Invention Creations and Patents for Utility Models

The new first paragraph of Article 9 Patent Law 2008 stipulates that for one identical invention creation, only one patent right shall be granted. However, if the same applicant applies for both a utility model patent and an invention patent for the identical invention-creation on the same day, the invention patent can only be granted if the applicant declares to abandon the obtained utility model patent.

3. BALANCING PATENT RIGHTS AND PUBLIC INTEREST

a. Protection of Genetic Resources

Due to the complexity and importance of the matter, which relates to one of the tactical resources for the sustained development of one of the countries with the richest genetic resources in the world, the changes related to the protection of genetic resources were quite controversial. The new law provides that no patent shall be granted for an invention based on genetic resources, if the latter are obtained or utilized illegitimately (Article 5 Paragraph 2 Patent Law 2008). Where such resources are used, their initial/direct origin must be disclosed in the patent application; and reasons must be given if the disclosure cannot be provided (Article 26 Paragraph 6 Patent Law 2008). SIPO explained insofar that it is in the interest of China to follow the same practice of developing countries in an area where international treaties have always focused on the interest of developed countries. The impact of this provision will depend on how the terms will be defined and what will constitute illegal acquisition and use.

b. Compulsory Licensing

Issues related with compulsory licensing have always been [the] object of heated debates because of their ability to strike at the core of the scope of intellectual property rights or, in other words, government-granted temporary monopolies. However, the granting of compulsory licenses is a common practice, although barely used, nearly everywhere in the world. Insofar, the revised Patent Law introduces a number of additional grounds for granting of compulsory licenses. According to Article 48 (1) Patent Law 2008 SIPO may, upon the request of the entity or the individual which is qualified for exploitation, grant a compulsory license to exploit a patent for an invention or utility model, when the patentee has not or not sufficiently exploited the same, without any justified reason, within three years from the grant of the patent right or four years from the date of filing such patent. A compulsory license can also be granted in order to avoid or eliminate the adverse effects caused to competition in cases where it has been legally determined that the enforcement of the patent right by the patentee constitutes a monopolistic act (Article 48 (2) Patent Law 2008).

A compulsory license may under the new law also be granted in favour of a least developed country or a WTO Member which has no or insufficient means to manufacture such indispensable drug (Article 50 Patent Law 2008).

c. International Exhaustion of Rights and Bolar Exemption

Article 69 Patent Law 2008 provides a series of exemption for acts that shall not be considered as infringing upon a patent right. According to Article 69 (1) Patent Law 2008 parallel importation will not constitute patent infringement if the product first entered the international market with authorization or consent by the patent owner. Such international exhaustion will reduce the scope of the patent law protection in China as inventors' rights will be exhausted once the product is sold in another country. The so called Bolar Exemption is introduced in Article 69 (5) Patent Law 2008. Manufacture, import or use of a patented drug or patented medical apparatus by any person in order to acquire information necessary for regulatory approval as well as manufacture or import of the drug/apparatus by any person solely for others to acquire such information will be deemed as an exception to patent infringement. Consequently, a pharmaceutical firm will be able to start the procedure for obtaining the requested authorization for the generic chemical compound of the patented drug without seeking to acquire the right owner's consent. It is interesting to note that the Bolar Exemption in the new law is not combined with the possibility of extending the term for patent protection as it is usually provided for in the patent legislation of other countries in order to balance the different interests involved.

4. PATENT ENFORCEMENT

a. Evidence Preservation

The revised law introduces a new provision on pre-litigation preservation measures (Article 67 Patent Law 2008). Insofar, the existing Article 74 Civil

Procedural Law which is dealing with the preservation of evidence does not explicitly permit to seize infringing goods prior to the litigation. However, the new provision in the patent law on pre-litigation evidence preservation will not have a significant impact on the patent litigation practice as the Supreme People's Court issued already in 2001 provisions which allowed the court, at request of the party, to preserve the evidence before the actual litigation on the merits by referring to the provision of Article 74 Civil Procedural Law.

b. Administrative Enforcement of IP Rights . . .

c. Prior Art Defence
The new law codifies the current practice that if the alleged infringer in a patent infringement dispute has evidence proving its or his technology or design belongs to the prior art or design, it will not constitute patent infringement (Article 62 Patent Law 2008).

d. Damage Compensation
Article 65 Paragraph 2 Patent Law 2008 also codifies the possibility of statutory compensation into the patent law. Courts will under the new law be able to grant statutory damage compensation of up to a maximum of RMB 1,000,000 in cases where the losses of the patentee, the profit of the infringer or the appropriate exploitation fee are difficult to determine. Respective existing provisions issued by SPC provided for compensation of up to RMB 500,000 only.

5. DESIGN PATENTS
The new law extends the exclusive right of the patentee to exploit a design patent to also include offering to sell the patented product for production or business purposes (Article 11 Paragraph 2 Patent Law 2008). Previously, an offer to sell did not constitute an infringement of a registered design. However, patent protection will no longer be available for two-dimensional designs of images, colours or combinations of the two that mainly serve as identifiers (Article 25 (6) Patent Law 2008). The Chinese legislator deemed such exclusion from patentability of designs necessary in order to avoid the registration of copied trademarks as designs. Although the new law allows multiple applications for similar or related designs of products belonging to a single category and sold or used in sets, the standard rule is that each patent application for design has to be limited to a single design (Article 31 Paragraph 2 Patent Law 2008). A clarification on how to determine the extent of similarity required for a design to constitute a related design is expected in the Implementing Regulations of the Patent Law.

The discretion of the court to ask the patentee to provide a search report issued by SIPO has been extended to design patents. Article 61 Paragraph 2 Patent Law 2008 stipulates that the court may require the patentee in utility model or design patent infringement cases to submit an evaluation report made by SIPO which may be used as evidence to settle the dispute. This system provides an effective mean to avoid malicious litigation and to speed up the invalidation procedure.

The new features of the Chinese patent system introduced in the Patent Law 2008 will be further defined and explained in the respective amendments to the Implementing Regulations of the Patent Law which are currently being drafted and are expected to be passed by the State Council in due time before the revised law takes effect in October 2009. The changes will, once implemented, surely have a significant impact on the patent system and practice. Insofar, it has to be seen whether the revised legal framework will ultimately also increase the effectiveness of patent enforcement in China.

It is interesting to follow the dynamics of the number of applications for all three kinds of patents in China. In comparison to 2006, in 2009 the total amount of applications (both domestic and foreign) almost doubled. As to the total granted patents—the number also doubled showing, however, an interesting trend towards increased approval of foreign applications. Thus, in 2006 less than 50% of foreign applications resulted in a grant of patents, while in 2009 the ratio increased up to 80%.[9]

On the part of enforcement the most recent changes were marked by the establishment of the first IP court in Guangdong Province in the late 2009.[10]

NOTES AND COMMENTS

1. *See* Note, *Patent Law for New Medical Uses of Known Compounds and Pfizer's Viagra Patent*, 46 IDEA 283 (2006), for additional details regarding application of China's patent legislation.
2. Unlike in the United States with the right to a patent of the first inventor, China adheres to the first-to-file system, meaning that inventors or those owning the rights to inventions should file their patent applications as soon as possible to secure their rights. To determine who was the first applicant, priority dates (both domestic and foreign) within 12 months are considered.

B. *India*

The adoption by India of a more market-oriented economic approach includes amendments to its Patents Act, which were mandated by the TRIPS Agreement. Like China, the acceleration of economic growth in India in the late 1990s and early twenty-first century can hardly be attributed to the introduction of strong intellectual property protection. In fact, India developed its highly successful generic pharmaceutical sector largely because it had elected not to provide pharmaceutical product patent protection until 2005. Now India also seeks to be among the countries that house "originators" of new pharmaceutical products.

TRIPS II, ASIA AND THE MERCANTILE PHARMACEUTICAL WAR: IMPLICATIONS FOR INNOVATION AND ACCESS

Frederick M. Abbott*

The internal Indian regulatory structure is undergoing a transformation, largely based on implementation of TRIPS I requirements as the ten-year

---

9. The most recent statistics [are] available at: http://www.sipo.gov.cn/sipo_English/statistics/.

10. See: http://www.china-briefing.com/news/2009/12/10/first-ip-court-set-up-in-guangdong. html. China IP litigation cases analysis can be found at: http://www.ciela.cn/Default.aspx? pageId=1&ppId=1&language=en.

* Stanford Center for International Development Conference, Working Paper No. 308, Dec. 2006.

pharmaceutical transition period ended on December 31, 2004.[24] Amendments to the Patents Act included implementation of pharmaceutical product patent protection.[25] Nine thousand "mailbox" applications are under review. The Act retained the institution of pre-grant opposition proceedings. The WTO August 30, 2003 waiver for exports under compulsory license was implemented.[26] A *sui generis* form of prior user right was adopted to permit continued production of generic versions of mailbox-patented products, with payment of reasonable royalty. India is taking steps to rapidly expand the capacity of its patent office and to increase regulatory oversight of pharmaceutical producers. The government seeks to ameliorate the public welfare impact of introducing product patents by extending price controls for a prescribed list of drugs.[27]

When India amended its Patent Act effective January 1, 2005 to extend to pharmaceutical product patents to comply with its TRIPS Agreement obligations, it included in Section 3(d) a limitation as to the circumstances in which new forms of known substances might be considered inventive, requiring an enhancement of known efficacy by the new form, and adding an explanation regarding the types of changes to pharmaceutical substances that would be considered new forms subject to the enhanced efficacy requirement. The Swiss pharmaceutical firm Novartis challenged the legislation principally on the grounds that it was inconsistent with Article 27.1 of the TRIPS Agreement, and also contravened the Indian Constitution. In the first part of its opinion on an appeal from the court of first instance, the High Court at Madras ruled that the TRIPS Agreement is not directly effective in Indian law based on the traditional treatment of treaties by the Indian Constitution. In the following excerpt, the High Court considers Novartis' claim that the legislative standard suffered from excessive vagueness and constituted an improper delegation of authority

24. *See* Frederick M. Abbott, *The WTO Medicines Decision: World Pharmaceutical Trade and the Protection of Public Health*, 99 AJIL 317, at 320-23.

25. On April 5, 2005, the Patents (Amendment) Act was published as law. Gaz. India Extraordinary pt. II, sec. 1 (2005), Patents (Amendment) Act, 2005, No. 15, New Delhi, 5 Apr. 2005 (An Act further to amend the Patents Act, 1970). In addition to introducing pharmaceutical product patent protection, the 2005 amendments (1) defined "inventive step" to require technical advance as compared to existing knowledge, or having economic significance; (2) expressly limited patentability of different forms of the same substance absent a showing of a significant difference in efficacy; (3) maintained a reasonably strong form of pre-grant opposition; (4) eliminated an unnecessary hurdle to the grant of compulsory licenses under the WTO August 30, 2003 Decision; (5) clarified exports permitted under the general compulsory licensing provision (e.g., expressly authorizing export of the nonpredominant part of production), as well as establishing certain presumptive time frames used in that provision; (6) improved a provision intended to permit parallel importation of patented products; and (7) allowed continued production in India of generic versions of medicines already on the market (if now patented by third parties under the mailbox system), with payment of a reasonable royalty—a form of "prior user right"—adapted to India's unique situation. Text available at http://patentoffice.nic.in/ipr/patent/patents.htm. *See also* D. G. Shah, Secretary General, Indian Pharmaceutical Alliance, *The New Indian Patent Law and August 30 Decision: The Response of the Generic Industry*, presentation to WHO-CIPIH Commission on Intellectual Property Rights, Innovation and Public Health, Geneva, Mar. 1, 2005 (PowerPoint), and Frederick M. Abbott, *India at the Crossroads: The Patents (Amendment) Bill 2003 and the Future of Public Health*, Proceedings of the India Federation of Chambers of Commerce and Industry (2004) and *Beginning of a New Policy Chapter*, FINANCIAL EXPRESS (INDIA), June 4, 2005.

26. Regarding the WTO waiver, *see generally* Abbott, *WTO Medicines Decision, supra* note 24. The waiver provisions are only relevant when compulsory licenses are granted to export the predominant part of local production.

27. Deepali Gupta, *At what price?*, EXPRESSPHARMA, April 16-30, 2006.

from the Indian Parliament. In doing so, it refers to the standards of the TRIPS Agreement in the context of discussing the object and purpose of the legislation.

NOVARTIS v. UNION OF INDIA

In the High Court of Judicature at Madras
Dated: 06.08.2007
The Hon'ble Mr. Justice R. Balasubramanian
and
The Hon'ble Mrs. Justice Prabha Sridevan
W.P. Nos. 24759 and 24760 of 2006

. . .

13. Let us now test the argument advanced before this court by learned Senior Counsels on the validity of the amended section on the touchstone of Article 14 of the Constitution of India. As we understand the amended section, it only declares that the very discovery of a new form of a known substance which does not result in the enhancement of the known efficacy of that substance, will not be treated as an invention. The position therefore is, if the discovery of a new form of a known substance must be treated as an invention, then the Patent applicant should show that the substance so discovered has a better therapeutic effect. Darland's Medical Dictionary defines the expression "efficacy" in the field of Pharmacology as "the ability of a drug to produce the desired thera- peutic effect" and "efficacy" is independent of potency of the drug. Dictionary meaning of "Therapeutic," is "healing of disease — having a good effect on the body." Going by the meaning for the word "efficacy" and "therapeutic" extracted above, what the patent applicant is expected to show is, how effective the new discovery made would be in healing a disease/having a good effect on the body? In other words, the patent applicant is definitely aware as to what is the "therapeutic effect" of the drug for which he had already got a patent and what is the difference between the therapeutic effect of the patented drug and the drug in respect of which patent is asked for. Therefore it is a simple exercise of, though preceded by research, — we state — for any Patent applicant to place on record what is the therapeutic effect/efficacy of a known substance and what is the enhancement in that known efficacy. The amended section not only covers the field of pharmacology but also the other fields. As we could see from the amended section, it is made applicable to even machine, apparatus or known process with a rider that mere use of a known process is not an invention unless such a known process results in a new product or employs at least one new reactant. Therefore the amended Section is a comprehensive provision covering all fields of technology, including the field of pharmacology. In our opinion, the explanation would come in aid only to understand what is meant by the expression "resulting in the enhancement of a known efficacy" in the amended section and therefore we have no doubt at all that the Explanation would operate only when discovery is made in the pharmacology field. In 1989 (4) SCC Pg. 378 (*Aphali Pharma. Ltd. Vs. State of Maharashtra*), in laying down the law on "Explanation," the Supreme Court held as hereunder:

"33. An Explanation, as was found in *Bihta Marketing Union vs. Bank of Bihar*, may only explain and may not expand or add to the scope of the original section. . . ."

. . .

In this case we find that the Explanation creates a deeming fiction of derivatives of a known substance are deemed to be the same substance unless they differ significantly in properties with regard to efficacy. Therefore it is clear from the amended section and the Explanation that in the pharmacology field, if a discovery is made from a known substance, a duty is cast upon the patent applicant to show that the discovery had resulted in the enhancement of a known efficacy of that substance and in deciding whether to grant a Patent or not on such new discovery, the Explanation creates a deeming fiction that all derivatives of a known substance would be deemed to be the same substance unless it differ[s] significantly in properties with regard to efficacy. In our opinion, the amended section and Explanation give importance to efficacy. We have already referred to the meaning of "efficacy" as given in Dorland's Medical Dictionary. Scientifically it is possible to show with certainty what are the properties of a "substance." Therefore when the Explanation to the amended section says that any derivatives must differ significantly in properties with regard to efficacy, it only means that the derivatives should contain such properties which are significantly different with regard to efficacy to the substance from which the derivative is made. Therefore in sum and substance what the amended section with the Explanation prescribes is the test to decide whether the discovery is an invention or not is that the Patent applicant should show the discovery has resulted in the enhancement of the known efficacy of that substance and if the discovery is nothing other than the derivative of a known substance, then, it must be shown that the properties in the derivatives differ significantly with regard to efficacy. As we stated earlier, due to the advanced technology in all fields of science, it is possible to show by giving necessary comparative details based on such science that the discovery of a new form a of known substance had resulted in the enhancement of the known efficacy of the original substance and the derivative so derived will not be the same substance, since the properties of the derivatives differ significantly with regard to efficacy. As rightly contended by learned Additional Solicitor General India and the lea[r]ned Senior Counsels and learned counsels for the Pharmaceutical Company opposing the Writ that the writ petitioner is not a novice to the pharmacology field but it, being [a] pharmaceutical giant in the whole of the world, cannot plead that they do not know what is meant by enhancement of a known efficacy and they cannot [k]now that the derivatives differ significantly in properties with regard to efficacy. Mr. P.S. Raman learned senior counsel argued that the Legislature, while enacting a Law, is entitled to create a deeming fiction and for that purpose, brought to our notice a judgment of the Supreme Court reported in AIR 1988 SC 191 (M/s. J.K.Cotton Spinning and Weaving Mills Ltd. vs. Union of India) where, in paragraph 40, the Supreme Court had said that "the Legislature is quite competent to enact a deeming provision for the purpose of assuming the existence of a fact which does not really exist." It is also stated in the very same paragraph that "it is well settled that a deeming provision is an admission of the non-existence of the fact deemed."

14. It is argued by learned Senior Counsels for the writ petitioners that it is possible for the Parliament to define in the Act itself what is meant by enhancement of a known efficacy and what is meant by differing significantly in properties with regard to efficacy. The above expressions are vague and ambiguous by themselves and therefore the meaning of such expressions ought to have been given in the Act or the amended section. Therefore when the meaning is

not so given, then the vagueness and ambiguity in the provision would result in arbitrary exercise of power by the statutory authority. Opposing this argument, learned Additional Solicitor General of India would contend that Parliament is not an expert; it cannot foresee the future contingencies which may arise, when they enact an Act; therefore the Parliament always thinks it wise to use only general expressions in the Statute leaving it to the Court to interpret it depending upon the context in which it is used and the facts that are made available in each case. For this purpose, learned Additional Solicitor General brought to our notice the judgment of the Supreme Court reported in 1995 Supp. (1) SCC 235 (*Benilal vs. State of Maharashtra*) and 1980 (1) SCC 340 (*Registrar of Co-op. Societies vs. K. Kunjabmu*). Mr. P.S. Raman, learned senior counsel in supporting the argument of learned Additional Solicitor General that the Parliament cannot foresee things that may arise in the future, brought to our notice the judgment of the English Court reported in (1949) 2 All England Law Reports 155 (*Seaford Court Estates vs. Asher*), to understand and realise whether it would be possible at all to foresee things that may arise in the future when a Statute comes up for consideration before the Houses and what would be the duty of the Judge before whom interpretation of such a Statute arise for consideration. . . .

In 1980 (1) SCC 340 referred to supra the Supreme Court had held as hereunder:

> "(1) Parliament and the State Legislatures function best when they concern themselves with general principles, broad objectives and fundamental issues, instead of technical or situational intricacies which are better left to better equipped full time expert executive bodies and specialist public servants. Parliament and the State Legislatures have neither the time or expertise to be involved in detail or circumstance, nor can visualise and provide for new strange unforeseen or unpredictable situations. That is the raison d'etre for delegated legislation. The power to legislate carries with it the power to delegate. But excessive delegation may amount to abdication. Delegation unlimited may invite despotism uninhibited. So the theory has been evolved that the legislature cannot delegate its essential legislative function. Legislate it must, by laying down policy and principle and delegate it may to fill in detail and carry out policy. The legislature may guide the delegate by speaking through the express provision empowering delegation or the other provisions of the statute such as the preamble, the scheme or even the very subject-matter of the statute. If guidance there is, wherever it may be found, the delegation is valid. A good deal of latitude has been held to be permissible in the case of taxing statutes and on the same principle generous degree of latitude must be permissible in the case of welfare legislation, particularly those statutes which are designed to further the Directive Principles of State Policy."

. . .

Therefore it is clear from the case laws referred to above that Parliament[] expresses its object and purpose in general terms when enacting a Statute and does not foresee the minute details that are likely to arise in the future and provide a solution for the same at the time when the Act itself is enacted. On the other hand, they would be acting wiser if they make only general expressions, leaving it to the experts/Statutory Authorities and then courts, to understand the general expressions used in the Statute in the context in which they are used in a case to case basis depending upon the facts available in each case. Using general expressions in a Statute, leaving the court to understand its meaning, would not be a ground to declare a section or an Act ultra vires, is the law laid down by the Supreme Court in Benilal's case referred to supra. Interpretation of a Statute must be to advance the object which the Act wants to achieve.

15. Now, we went through the statements of objects and reasons of Amending Act 15/2005. As rightly emphasized by Mr. Soli Sorabji learned senior counsel for the petitioners, the statement of objects and reasons for Amending Act 15/2005 emphasises in more than one place that the amendment is in the discharge of India's obligation to "TRIPS," which forms part of the "WTO" agreement. Therefore a need has arisen for us to look into the relevant Articles of "TRIPS" for the limited purpose of what obligations are created under "TRIPS," which, India was attempting to discharge by bringing in Amending Act 15/2005. Article 7 of "TRIPS" provides enough elbow room to a member country in complying with "TRIPS" obligations by bringing a law in a manner conducive to social and economic welfare and to a balance of rights and obligations. Article 1 of "TRIPS" enables a member country free to determine the appropriate method of implementing the provisions of this agreement within their own legal system and practice. But however, any protection which a member country provides, which is more extensive in nature than is required under "TRIPS," shall not contravene "TRIPS." Article 27 speaks about patentability. Lengthy arguments have been advanced by learned Additional Solicitor General appearing for the Government of India, learned senior counsels and learned counsels appearing for the pharmaceutical companies that India, being a welfare and a developing country, which is predominantly occupied by people below poverty line, it has a constitutional duty to provide good health care to its citizens by giving them easy access to life saving drugs. In so doing, the Union of India would be right, it is argued, to take into account the various factual aspects prevailing in this big country and prevent evergreening by allowing generic medicine to be available in the market. As rightly contended by the learned Additional Solicitor General of India, the Parliamentary debates show that welfare of the people of the country was in the mind of the Parliamentarians when Ordinance 7/2004 was in the House. They also had in mind the International obligations of India arising under "TRIPS" and under "WTO" agreement. Therefore the validity of the amended section on the touchstone of Article 14 of the Constitution of India must be decided having regard to the object which Amending Act 15/2005 wanted to achieve.

16. It is argued by the learned senior counsels for the petitioners that since the amended section uses only general expressions, leaving it to the Statutory Authority to understand what it means, the Statutory Authority is likely to act arbitrarily in exercising its discretion, since it has no guidelines. We have already held that the amended section cannot be said to be vague or ambiguous. We reiterate here at this stage that the amended section with its Explanation is capable of being understood and worked out in a normal manner not only by the Patent applicant but also by the Patent controller. In other words, the patent controller would be guided by various relevant details which every patent applicant is expected to produce before him showing that the new discovery had resulted in the enhancement of the known efficacy; the derivatives differ significantly in properties with regard to efficacy and therefore it cannot be said that the patent controller had an uncanalised power to exercise, leading to arbitrariness. The argument that the amended section must be held to be bad in Law since for want of guidelines it gives scope to the Statutory Authority to exercise its power arbitrarily, has to be necessarily rejected since, we find that

there are in-built materials in the amended section and the Explanation itself, which would control/guide the discretion to be exercised by the Statutory Authority. In other words, the Statutory Authority would be definitely guided by the materials to be placed before it for arriving at a decision. . . .

NOTES AND QUESTIONS

1. The U.S. Patent and Trademark Office based decisions regarding the utility of pharmaceutical compounds on assessment of efficacy until it was precluded from doing so by the Court of Appeals for the Federal Circuit. In *In re Brana*, 51 F.3d 1560 (Fed. Cir. 1995), the U.S. PTO had rejected a patent application for an anticancer treatment on grounds that the applicant failed to demonstrate utility of the claimed compound through clinical testing on human beings intended to show efficacy. The Federal Circuit rejected efficacy in humans as the benchmark of utility of pharmaceutical substances in the following passages:

> "The Commissioner counters that such in vivo tests in animals are only pre-clinical tests to determine whether a compound is suitable for processing in the second stage of testing, by which he apparently means in vivo testing in humans, and therefore are not reasonably predictive of the success of the claimed compounds for treating cancer in humans. The Commissioner, as did the Board, confuses the requirements under the law for obtaining a patent with the requirements for obtaining government approval to market a particular drug for human consumption. See *Scott v. Finney*, 34 F.3d 1058, 1063, 32 U.S.P.Q.2D (BNA) 1115, 1120 (Fed. Cir. 1994) ('Testing for the full safety and effectiveness of a prosthetic device is more properly left to the Food and Drug Administration (FDA). Title 35 does not demand that such human testing occur within the confines of Patent and Trademark Office (PTO) proceedings.').
>
> . . .
>
> Our court's predecessor has determined that proof of an alleged pharmaceutical property for a compound by statistically significant tests with standard experimental animals is sufficient to establish utility. *In re Krimmel*, 48 C.C.P.A. 1116, 292 F.2d 948, 953, 130 U.S.P.Q. (BNA) 215, 219 (CCPA 1961); see also *In re Bergel*, 48 C.C.P.A. 1101, 292 F.2d 958, 130 U.S.P.Q. (BNA) 205 (CCPA 1961). In concluding that similar in vivo tests were adequate proof of utility the court in *In re Krimmel* stated:
>
>> We hold as we do because it is our firm conviction that one who has taught the public that a compound exhibits some desirable pharmaceutical property in a standard experimental animal has made a significant and useful contribution to the art, even though it may eventually appear that the compound is without value in the treatment in humans.
>
> *Krimmel*, 292 F.2d at 953, 130 U.S.P.Q. (BNA) at 219. . . .
>
> . . .
>
> On the basis of animal studies, and controlled testing in a limited number of humans (referred to as Phase I testing), the Food and Drug Administration may authorize Phase II clinical studies. See 21 U.S.C. § 355(i)(1); 5 C.F.R. § 312.23(a)(5), (a)(8) (1994). Authorization for a Phase II study means that the drug may be administered to a larger number of humans, but still under strictly supervised conditions. The purpose of the Phase II study is to

determine primarily the safety of the drug when administered to a larger human population, as well as its potential efficacy under different dosage regimes. See 21 C.F.R. § 312.21(b).

FDA approval, however, is not a prerequisite for finding a compound useful within the meaning of the patent laws. *Scott*, 34 F.3d 1058, 1063, 32 U.S.P.Q.2D (BNA) 1115, 1120. Usefulness in patent law, and in particular in the context of pharmaceutical inventions, necessarily includes the expectation of further research and development. The stage at which an invention in this field becomes useful is well before it is ready to be administered to humans. Were we to require Phase II testing in order to prove utility, the associated costs would prevent many companies from obtaining patent protection on promising new inventions, thereby eliminating an incentive to pursue, through research and development, potential cures in many crucial areas such as the treatment of cancer." *Id.*, at 1567-68 [footnotes omitted].

The reasoning of the Federal Circuit may certainly be questioned. The question of whether a claimed invention is "useful" can be assessed across the spectrum of endpoints. Is a drug compound useful because it can be tested on mice, or is it useful because it can be used to treat humans? Do you find the answer self-evident?

V. PATENTS AND THE CONVENTION ON BIOLOGICAL DIVERSITY (CBD)

A. The CBD and the WTO TRIPS Agreement

See Chapter 1, section V, including Note summary of recent developments adapted from the 2006 Report of the Committee on International Trade Law to the International Law Association.

B. The CBD at WIPO

The relationship between the CBD and international patent system has been the subject of extensive dialogue and study within WIPO as well as the WTO. The following is part of a WIPO study of disclosure requirements and how they might further the objectives of the CBD.

TECHNICAL STUDY ON DISCLOSURE REQUIREMENTS IN PATENT SYSTEMS RELATED TO GENETIC RESOURCES AND TRADITIONAL KNOWLEDGE*

WIPO Intergovernmental Committee on Intellectual Property and Genetic Resources, Traditional Knowledge and Folklore

. . . The underlying, key issue is how to characterize the necessary relationship between the genetic resource and traditional knowledge on the one hand, and

---

* Study No. 3, Feb. 2004, available at www.wipo.int.

the claimed invention on the other. Discussion of possible disclosure requirements has already covered many ways of expressing this linkage. Better characterizing this linkage should also clarify the range and duration of obligations that
may attach to such resources and knowledge, within the source country and in
foreign jurisdictions, and how far these obligations "reach through" subsequent
inventive activities and ensuing patent applications. General patent law principles provide certain more specific ways of expressing this relationship, even if
the objective of the requirement is not conceived in traditional patent terms.
Patent law may also be drawn on to clarify or implement more generally stated
disclosure requirements: for example, a general requirement to disclose genetic
resources used in the invention may be difficult to define in practice, and may
[be] implemented through a more precise test that requires disclosure only when
access to the resources would be necessary to reproduce the invention.

Another key issue is the legal basis of the disclosure requirement in question,
and its relationship with the processing of patent applications, the grant of
patents and the exercise of patent rights. This raises also the legal and practical
interaction of the disclosure requirement with other areas of law beyond the
patent system, including the law of other jurisdictions. Some of the legal and
policy questions that arise are:

— the potential role of the patent system in one country in monitoring and
   giving effect to contracts, licenses, and regulations in other areas of law and
   in other jurisdictions, and the resolution of private international law or
   "choice of law" issues that arise in interpreting and applying across jurisdictions contract obligations and laws determining legitimacy of access and
   downstream use of GR/TK;
— the nature of the disclosure obligation, in particular whether it is essentially
   a transparency mechanism to assist with the monitoring of compliance with
   non-patent laws and regulations, or whether it incorporates compliance;
— the ways in which patent law and procedure can take account of the circumstances and context of inventive activity that are unrelated to the assessment
   of the invention itself and the eligibility of the applicant to be granted a
   patent;
— the situations in which national authorities can impose additional administrative, procedural or substantive legal requirements on patent applicants, within existing international legal standards applying to patent
   procedures, and the role of non-IP international law and legal principles
   in this regard;
— the legal and operational distinction (to the extent one can be drawn)
   between patent formalities or procedural requirements, and substantive
   criteria for patentability, and ways of characterizing the legal implications
   of such distinctions;
— clarification of the implications of issues such as the concept of "country of
   origin" in relation to genetic resources covered by multilateral access and
   benefit-sharing systems, differing approaches to setting and enforcing conditions for access and benefit sharing in the context of patent disclosure
   requirements, and coherence between mechanisms for recording or certi-
   fying conditions of access and the patent system.

A further area for clarification is what actions of the inventor or patent applicant are to be monitored or regulated through a disclosure requirement — the

actual use of the GR/TK (including its use in the inventive process), or the act of filing a patent application as such. The policy concern may relate to the legitimacy of the research or commercial behavior that makes use of the GR/TK (including prior informed consent of TK or GR holders). In this case, the patent application has a secondary role in providing evidence of such behavior. The concern may relate to the very filing [of] a patent application or holding a patent (for instance, where prior informed consent is given to research but not seeking IP, or prior informed consent includes agreement on assignment, coownership or similar disposition of ensuing IP).

The study concludes by noting that the core issues raised are the subjects of ongoing international policy debate. They may involve specific policy choices, such as the distinction between formal requirements or "form or contents" and substantive patent law and how to certify the basis of prior informed consent or legitimacy of access to GR/TK. It observes that some key legal concepts and approaches raised in the debate are so far untested, are the subject of policy development, or are in the early stages of implementation and practical experience, and thus cannot be definitively analyzed. Accordingly, the study is offered as a resource to facilitate the continuing debate, not to prescribe any particular approach.

NOTES AND QUESTIONS

1. An important U.S. federal decision concerning bio-prospecting in Yellowstone National Park is *Edmonds Institute v. Babbitt*, 93 F. Supp. 2d 63 (D.D.C. 2000). There has been increasing attention to the subject of access to biological resources and benefit sharing in the United States since that decision.

2. A detailed study of national implementation of patent disclosure requirements regarding access to and benefit sharing with respect to biological resources is Chatham House, Disclosure of Origin in IPR Applications: Options and Perspectives of Users and Providers of Genetic Resources, IPDEV, Work Programme 8: Final Report, May 2006. This study includes extensive surveying of various stakeholders.

3. You represent a nongovernmental organization in India that is concerned with preventing foreign enterprises from patenting indigenous Indian plant varieties that exhibit commercially useful properties. Will requiring patent applicants in Europe, Japan, the United States, and elsewhere to disclose to the Patent Office the geographic location from where biological specimens were obtained adequately serve your client's interests? What other mechanisms might you suggest? How do potential enforcement costs affect your analysis?

4. Whether and to what extent patents should be granted on pathogenic biological materials as found in nature and/or as modified by human intervention is a significant issue in WHO negotiations regarding "pathogen sharing," as well as under the CBD and its recently negotiated Access and Benefit-Sharing Protocol. See Frederick M. Abbott, *An International Legal Framework for the Sharing of Pathogens: Issues and Challenges*, ICTSD Programme on IPRs and Sustainable Development, Issue Paper No. 30, October 2010.

VI.   PATENT LICENSING, TRANSFER OF TECHNOLOGY, AND COMPETITION

The patent right is exploited in a number of different ways. Licensing plays a significant role in many of the ways a patent is used. The role of patent licensing, as well as possibilities for misuse, are considered in the following presentation made to the WIPO Open Forum on the draft Substantive Patent Law Treaty in March 2006.

PATENT LICENSING, COMPETITION LAW AND THE DRAFT SUBSTANTIVE PATENT LAW TREATY

Frederick M. Abbott*

1. Patent licensing may enhance the development of new technologies and making them available to the public.
    a. Patent licensing may facilitate access by researchers to third-party technologies and facilitate experimentation with a view toward commercialization or public use;[1]
    b. Patent licensing may facilitate movement of new technologies from the research phase to the commercialization phase as small and medium enterprises out-license inventions to more highly capitalized enterprises;
    c. Patent licensing may provide a means for enterprises to negotiate the "patent thicket" so as to overcome obstacles to incremental innovation
        i. In areas such as standards-setting, sharing of patented technologies may be necessary to maintenance of competitive markets. . . .
    d. Patent licensing may facilitate joint research and development, accelerating technology development and spreading risk;
    e. Patent licensing may facilitate partitioning of R & D and production functions, allowing production at most efficient locations without corollary investments in R & D.
2. Patent licensing is a tool for the transfer of technology between developed and developing countries.
    a. Positive welfare effects dependent on validity of underlying patent. Licensing and payment of royalties on technology otherwise in the public domain is unjustified social expense, [although services payment for training of personnel using public domain information may be justifiable — Eds.];
    b. "Securitization" of invention encourages sharing of information based on rent or royalty stream expectation;
    c. Forms of enterprise combination and licensing arrangements highly variable — parent-subsidiary, joint venture, independent entities, etc.;

---

* March 2, 2006, Open Forum on the Draft Substantive Patent Law Treaty, World Intellectual Property Organization, Geneva, available at http://www.wipo.int.

1. Note that U.S. Supreme Court in *Merck v. Integra Lifesciences*, [545 U.S. 193 (2005)] dramatically expanded scope of permissible noninfringing uses of patented pharmaceutical technologies during drug research and development phase, reducing need for licensing prior to market entry.

    d.   Extent to which patent licensing generates improvement to local technology capacity is context specific

        i.   Patent licensing may take place in closely-guarded intracorporate setting which may limit local diffusion, or may take place in open setting (e.g., to university research institution) which may encourage diffusion

        ii. Associated "know-how" licensing affects level of technology transfer

        iii. Restrictive licensing terms may substantially affect economic and social value of patent license to transferee country.

3. Patent licensing is subject to anticompetitive abuse.

    a.   "Patent pools" into which enterprises combine their technologies may be used to create prohibitive market entry barriers, facilitating cartelization of markets;

    b.   Restrictive third-party licensing terms (e.g., exclusive grantbacks) may be used to foreclose emergence of competitors;

    c.   Patent licensing terms can be used to leverage market power, such as through product tying arrangements and block licensing;

    d.   Patent licensing agreements may include terms generally disfavored in competition law, such as fixing of resale prices, restricting output and dividing territories among horizontal competitors;

    e.   No-challenge clauses in patent licenses encourage unearned surplus payments to holders of invalid patents;

    f.   Patent licensing agreements merit particular scrutiny in the context of licensors holding dominant position on the relevant market.

4. Control of anticompetitive patent licensing is a generally accepted practice among states.

    a.   The WTO TRIPS Agreement includes provisions which recognize that intellectual property rights may be abused, that authorize Members to regulate anticompetitive licensing practices and that encourage cooperation in enforcement (e.g., Articles 8.2, 31(k)-(l), 40).[2] Concern with anticompetitive patent licensing is reflected in the original International Trade Organization Charter;

    b.   Paris Convention recognizes abuse of patents as grounds for compulsory licensing (Article 5A(2));

    c.   Developed country regulation specifically addresses anticompetitive patent licensing arrangements

        i.   *See, e.g.*, U.S. Department of Justice/Federal Trade Commission, Antitrust Guidelines for the Licensing of Intellectual Property (1995). Also, the Supreme Court has ruled that patent misuse is an equitable defense to the enforcement of patents (e.g., in the case of certain product tying arrangements). *See also* U.S. Federal Trade Commission, To Promote Innovation: The Proper Balance of Competition and Patent Law and Policy (2003)

        ii. *See, e.g.*, European Commission Regulation No 772/2004 of 27 April 2004 on the application of Article 81(3) of the Treaty to categories of technology transfer agreements and Guidelines on the application of Article 81 of the EC Treaty to technology transfer agreements (2004/C/101/02)

---

2. *See* Frederick M. Abbott, *Are the Competition Rules in the WTO TRIPS Agreement Adequate?*, 7 J. INT'L ECON. L. 685 (2005 Oxford).

   iii. *See, e.g.,* Fair Trade Commission of Japan (FTCJ), Antimonopoly Act Guidelines Concerning Joint Research and Development, 20 April 1993.

  d. Developing countries address anticompetitive patent licensing through regulation and court decision

   i. *See, e.g.,* Andean Community, Decision 291, Article 14

   ii. Abuse of patent is common grounds in developing country patent legislation for grant of compulsory license

   iii. As a general proposition, developing countries have a lower level of competition law enforcement capacity than the OECD countries. Competition law enforcement tends to be fact intensive, complex and expensive.

  e. Proposals from leading experts on competition law for international antitrust regulation routinely address anticompetitive patent licensing practices, *see* International Antitrust Working Group (W. Fikentscher, et al.), Draft International Antitrust Code, at Article 6: Restraints in Connection with Intellectual Property Rights[3];

  f. Trend of regulation in OECD is to evaluate patent licensing restrictions under "rule of reason" approach and to limit inquiry where market share of parties is below defined threshold. Nonetheless, certain *per se* (or hardcore) prohibitions remain (e.g., in EU, against exclusive grantbacks)

   i. Specific doctrinal issues are continuously re-examined. For example, U.S. Supreme Court currently considering presumption of patent-based market power in context of tying arrangements (*Illinois Tool Works v. Independent Ink*, No. 04-1329). . . .

  g. Current regulatory approach of OECD competition law authorities is not necessarily the best approach for developing countries which tend to have lower levels of enforcement capacity;

  h. Developing countries may benefit from greater use of *per se* rules and other positive prohibitions such as characterized EU competition and technology law until 2004[4]

   i. Developing countries are more likely to be patented-technology importers than exporters

   ii. Developing country markets are generally more susceptible to market power concentration among dominant enterprises than developed country markets

    a. Competition law risk assessment should account for these factors. . . .

5. Rules regarding anticompetitive aspects of patent licensing are within the reasonable potential subject matter scope of a Substantive Patent Law Treaty. Such rules might take a positive form, prescribing certain types of conduct or establishing presumptions regarding certain types of conduct. Such rules might take a negative form, making clear that governments are permitted to regulate anticompetitive licensing practices notwithstanding positive obligations regarding the grant of patents. Such

---

3. *Reprinted in* Public Policy and Global Technological Integration (F. Abbott & D. Gerber eds., 1997) (Kluwer), at Appendix 2. *See also* Wolfgang Fikentscher, *The Draft International Antitrust Code (DIAC) in the Context of International Technological Integration, id.* at 211.

 4. *See* elaboration in F. Abbott, *supra* note 2.

rules might include illustrative list of potentially anticompetitive licensing practices.

a.   The negotiating history of the GATT Uruguay Round and subsequent efforts within the WTO to establish mandatory positive competition rules suggest obstacles to that approach in the context of SPLT negotiations

   i.   In TRIPS Agreement Art. 40, listing of anticompetitive licensing conditions is illustrative of subject matter that may be addressed, not prohibited as mandatory positive obligation

   ii.   WTO Trade and Competition Working Group manifested disagreement on limited set of positive rules, with differences between governments at all levels of development.

b.   Approaches to regulation of competition tend to vary over time within the same jurisdiction as industrial policy considerations shift. This may argue in favor of preserving regulatory flexibility;

c.   Industrial policy considerations of developed and developing countries with respect to application of competition law to patent licensing may differ. Developing countries at different stages of development may also maintain differing industrial policy interests;

d.   A negative approach would permit maintenance of regulatory flexibility. For example:

> Nothing in this [SPLT] shall prevent or hinder a member state from prescribing or enforcing measures to address patent licensing conditions or practices determined to be anticompetitive. Such measures, which may be preventive and remedial, may be enforceable by private and government action, and may include civil damages and criminal penalties.

Note that the foregoing does not address patent misuse in general because the subject matter of this presentation concerns patent licensing. However, it is reasonable to assume that additional negative provision should be included in SPLT to permit maintenance of regulatory flexibility regarding patent abuse in other contexts, such as abuse of patents by dominant enterprises;

e.   A combination approach might negatively preserve regulatory flexibility and positively list potentially anticompetitive practices, along the lines of the WTO TRIPS Agreement

   i.   An SPLT provision might also address enhanced enforcement cooperation and capacity-building. . . .

NEW TRENDS IN TECHNOLOGY TRANSFER: IMPLICATIONS FOR NATIONAL AND INTERNATIONAL POLICY

John Barton*

LICENSING

Very often, a developing-world firm will need to license in some or all of the technology it needs for a particular product. This is especially likely with

* ICTSD Intellectual Property and Sustainable Development Series, Issue Paper No. 18, Feb. 2007.

globalization, for a firm that hopes to export to the developed world may need a license of developed-world patent rights covering the technology. Even [if] it is marketing locally, it may face local competition from developed nation firms who hold local patents; the firm needs to obtain a license to use the relevant technology, unless it can find a way to design around those patents. And, the licensing of existing technology will often be cheaper and faster than re-engineering that technology.

In negotiating to obtain such a license, the bargaining position of the local firm depends on the economics of the specific situation. For the licensor (and to a certain extent for the developing nation's economy as well), licensed production is an alternative to FDI—a foreign firm can supply a global or a local market through its own facility in a developing nation or alternatively through license to a firm in a developing nation. Economics favors FDI over the license when technologies are changing very rapidly. This is because the relationship between the foreign supplier and the local manufacturer can be updated more easily through managerial negotiations within one entity than through formal revisions of a contract between two entities. The license is favored when the licensee brings special knowledge of the local environment, or when the technologies are changing in such a way that new licensors or licensees with new core expertise are needed from time to time. Thus, if the local firm holds important comparative advantages, such as the semiconductor production skills held by Taiwanese firms, then it is in a position to negotiate effectively for a cooperative agreement under which it obtains the necessary licenses. And, TRIPS probably favors FDI over licensing.[65]

If the agreement is to produce a product for a global market, the licensor will be interested in providing the best possible and most up-to-date technology. The globalization paradigm overrides the traditional product cycle model. In some cases, however, the purpose of the license will be for production for a local market. This is likely for service industries; it is also likely for very large markets such as China. In such a situation, the traditional 1970s concerns still apply: a foreign firm may be motivated to supply a less advanced technology for production for the local market, while holding its more advanced technologies for use for global markets and seeking to protect itself from local production with more advanced technologies. Such reticence to supply technology is also likely when the local license is compelled by regulations that, for example, require local partners and restrict FDI. These are contexts in which especially careful negotiation of specific licenses is essential, for the economic incentives of the two parties are less closely aligned than for production for export.

For many of today's technologies, particularly in the computer and communications sectors, new products require a variety of skills, more than available in any single firm. Hence, there is a need for strategic alliances and innovative licensing arrangements in order to produce a product — and a new developing-world firm may be able to develop and contribute one of the relevant areas of expertise. To make these efforts work, it is important to facilitate cooperative research efforts between firms and research entities of different nations. In many industries, strategic research alliances are a measure of the success of firms; they demonstrate that the science and technology are moving faster than can industrial organizations alone. In the biotechnology sector, these are

---

65. *See* J. Barton, Patents and the Transfer of Technology to Developing Countries, presented at OECD, Conference on IPR, Innovation and Economic Performance, Paris (Oct. 2003).

both national and international and lead to what amounts to an integrated North Atlantic industry. In the semiconductor sector, the same kind of integration occurs across the Pacific. Such arrangements will be even more important for developing nations, who will often need access to foreign centers of excellence.

NOTES AND QUESTIONS

1. Technology licensing certainly plays an important role in technology transfer but, as the foregoing discussion notes, the extent of technology diffusion is dependent on the terms of licenses and business contexts in which licensing is used. In the 1970s and 1980s, a substantial number of developing countries attempted to compel licensors to employ licensing terms that would encourage diffusion of technology into the local economy. The trend in the 1990s and early 2000s has been away from such efforts and reliance on the "free market" to determine the terms of technology licensing. Why do you think developing countries were largely unsuccessful during the 1970s and 1980s in directing the terms of technology transfer? Is it because developed country enterprises own the vast preponderance of patents and thereby are in a stronger position to direct the terms of transfer? Or is it because governments are not well equipped to intervene in business decision making? What other factors may determine the success or failure of attempts by governments to control the terms of technology transfer?

2. Might "neutral" consultants working on behalf of international or national development agencies seek to identify targets of opportunity for developing country industries to cooperate with developed country industries and help negotiate the terms of patent licensing arrangements?

3. Under the auspices of UNITAID, an independent Medicines Patent Pool has been established with the objective of improving access to medicines in developing countries. The Patent Pool has briefly described its operation and objectives as follows:

> How the Pool Works
>
> - **Pooling patents:**
>   The idea behind a patent pool is that patent holders — companies, researchers, universities and governments — voluntarily license their patents to the Pool under certain conditions. The Pool then makes licenses to the patents available to qualified third parties, such as generic drug manufacturers, which then pay appropriate royalties on the sale of the medicines for use in developing countries.
> - **Stimulus to innovation:**
>   The Pool aims to foster the development of needed formulations. For example, a company wishing to develop a fixed-dose combination (FDC) might need to obtain licenses from at least three different patent holders to be able to develop, produce, export and sell the product. With the Pool offering the relevant patent licenses, however, the company would only have to deal with the Pool, which serves as a one-stop shop for all parties involved. The Pool facilitates legal and administrative processes involved in obtaining licenses, reduces expenses, and increases access to patents essential to making urgently-needed medicines.

- **Making medicines more affordable, faster:**
  The Pool will help to speed up the availability of lower-priced, newer medicines in developing countries because there will be no need to wait out the 20-year patent term. With licenses covering low- and middle-income countries, the scope of the market would be attractively large to encourage multiple producers to compete in the market and sustainably drive down prices.

FEATURES OF THE POOL

The Medicines Patent Pool:

- Focuses on **HIV medicines:** the Pool focuses on products for which prices are too high and/or suppliers too few (such as newer HIV medicines), and on products that have not yet been developed (such as paediatric and heat-stable formulations).
- Is a **voluntary mechanism:** the willingness of pharmaceutical patent holders to participate and license their patents to the Pool is critical.
- Targets **developing countries:** License agreements should make medicines available to people in both low- and middle-income countries, where the need for more affordable and adapted medicines is widespread. It is also important that markets for generic products are large enough to achieve economies of scale and generate price reductions.
- Will require that producers getting licenses from the Pool meet agreed **quality standards**.
- Offers **benefits to everyone involved:** medicine patent holders are compensated for the use of their technology; generic pharmaceutical companies are able to obtain licenses more easily to produce and sell medicines; people in developing countries get faster access to better, more affordable treatments.

CHAPTER
3

The International Trademark and Identifier System

I. BASIC CHARACTERISTICS OF THE TRADEMARK, SERVICE MARK, TRADE NAME, DOMAIN NAME, AND GEOGRAPHICAL INDICATION

A. *Trademark Subject Matter*

A trademark is a sign or symbol used to distinguish the goods or services of one enterprise from those of other enterprises in commerce. The function is fundamentally different from patents. While the latter protect innovation, the former essentially serves the purpose of allowing consumers to distinguish different products on the market. As a corollary, it forms the basis for investment in advertising and marketing of goods and services. Human beings are capable of identifying many different kinds of signs or symbols, including words, other alphanumeric combinations, designs, colors, sounds, scents, shapes, and even textures. Conceptually, all of these types of signs or symbols are capable of allowing consumers to distinguish the goods or services of one enterprise from another. However, even within the broad definition of trademark established by the WTO TRIPS Agreement, some limitations may be placed on the types of signs or symbols constituting trademarks.

Trademarks may be used to identify and distinguish goods or services. The term "service mark" is specifically used with respect to services, such as accounting, banking, travel, and tourism services. While the term "trademark" may be used in a narrow sense in connection only with goods, it may also be used in a broader sense to encompass services.

In many national jurisdictions, principally those of civil law countries, trademark rights are granted solely on the basis of registration at a national (or regional) trademark office, except in the case of so-called well-known and famous trademarks, and without prejudice to protection under the laws of unfair competition. In other national jurisdictions, principally those of common law countries, trademark rights may also be acquired by use in commerce, without the need for registration. Yet, in common law countries, the trademark registration available provides significant litigation advantages, and trademarks are ordinarily registered in these countries for reasons of legal security

The trademark provides its holder with the right to prevent others from using the protected sign on identical or similar goods where such use is likely to cause consumer confusion. There are typically two key questions in a trademark infringement proceeding: first, whether the complainant holds a valid trademark; and second, whether the complained-against party is using it in a way likely to confuse consumers. There are a substantial number of elements that go into answering these questions.

In order for a sign or symbol to serve as a trademark, it must be capable of distinguishing goods or services; that is, it must be "distinctive." A term that is commonly used in a language to identify a genus or class of thing (i.e., a "generic" term) may not serve as a trademark to identify that genus or class of thing. In English, the word "apple" may not be used as a trademark to identify a type of fruit because that is the generic term for a type of fruit. (On the other hand, "apple" may be used to identify a computer because the term has no inherent connection to electronic goods.)

Some trademarks are "inherently distinctive." These are "arbitrary," "fanciful," or "suggestive" terms that do not have an established connection with a good or service. If a mark is inherently distinctive, the trademark holder does not need to prove that consumers identify it with its product. Trademarks may also be "descriptive," meaning consumers would ordinarily draw connections between the marks and the goods or services on which they are used (i.e., the marks, at least in part, describe the goods or services). In order for a descriptive term to be recognized as a trademark, its holder must demonstrate that it has become associated in the mind of consumers with the holder's good or service; that is, it has become "distinctive." This is often referred to as acquiring "secondary meaning." A trademark holder may demonstrate acquired distinctiveness or secondary meaning in a number of ways, including by conducting a consumer survey.

Once a complainant in a trademark infringement proceeding shows that it is the holder of a valid trademark, it must still demonstrate that the complained-against party is using the mark in a way that is likely to confuse consumers. When an identical mark is used on identical goods or services, a likelihood of confusion is typically presumed. However, more difficult cases arise when the sign used by the complained-against party is different than the trademark holder's mark — for example, when the spelling of a word is changed — or when the sign is used in connection with different goods or services — for example, when a trademark ordinarily used to identify automobiles is used to identify refrigerators.

The trademark right is limited. Trademark rights, like other intellectual property rights, are subject to exhaustion. In addition, a trademark does not prevent "fair use" by third parties. There are other recognized limitations on the scope of trademark holder rights.

In the following decision, the U.S. Supreme Court considers whether a single color may serve as a trademark and, in doing so, provides a very useful introduction to the subject matter of the trademark.

QUALITEX CO. v. JACOBSON PRODUCTS CO., INC.
514 U.S. 159 (1995)

BREYER, J., delivered the opinion for a unanimous Court.

The question in this case is whether the Lanham Trademark Act of 1946 (Lanham Act), 15 U.S.C. §§ 1051-1127 (1988 ed. and Supp. V), permits the registration of a trademark that consists, purely and simply, of a color. We conclude that, sometimes, a color will meet ordinary legal trademark requirements. And, when it does so, no special legal rule prevents color alone from serving as a trademark. . . .

The Lanham Act gives a seller or producer the exclusive right to "register" a trademark, 15 U.S.C. § 1052 (1988 ed. and Supp. V), and to prevent his or her competitors from using that trademark, § 1114(1). Both the language of the Act and the basic underlying principles of trademark law would seem to include color within the universe of things that can qualify as a trademark. The language of the Lanham Act describes that universe in the broadest of terms. It says that trademarks "include any word, name, symbol, or device, or any combination thereof," § 1127. Since human beings might use as a "symbol" or "device" almost anything at all that is capable of carrying meaning, this language, read literally, is not restrictive. The courts and the Patent and Trademark Office have authorized for use as a mark a particular shape (of a Coca-Cola bottle), a particular sound (of NBC's three chimes), and even a particular scent (of plumeria blossoms on sewing thread). . . . If a shape, a sound, and a fragrance can act as symbols why, one might ask, can a color not do the same?

A color is also capable of satisfying the more important part of the statutory definition of a trademark, which requires that a person "use" or "intend to use" the mark

> "to identify and distinguish his or her goods, including a unique product, from those manufactured or sold by others and to indicate the source of the goods, even if that source is unknown." 15 U.S.C. § 1127.

True, a product's color is unlike "fanciful," "arbitrary," or "suggestive" words or designs, which almost automatically tell a customer that they refer to a brand. *Abercrombie & Fitch Co. v. Hunting World, Inc.*, 537 F.2d 4, 9-10 (CA2 1976) (Friendly, J.); *see Two Pesos, Inc. v. Taco Cabana, Inc.*, 505 U.S. 763 (1992) (slip op., at 6-7). The imaginary word "Suntost," or the words "Suntost Marmalade," on a jar of orange jam immediately would signal a brand or a product "source"; the jam's orange color does not do so. But, over time, customers may come to treat a particular color on a product or its packaging (say, a color that in context seems unusual, such as pink on a firm's insulating material or red on the head of a large industrial bolt) as signifying a brand. And, if so, that color would have come to identify and distinguish the goods—i.e. to "indicate" their "source"—much in the way that descriptive words on a product (say, "Trim" on nail clippers or "Car-Freshner" on deodorizer) can come to indicate a product's origin. *See, e.g., J. Wiss & Sons Co. v. W. E. Bassett Co.*, 462 F.2d 567, 59 C.C.P.A. 1269, 1271 (Pat.), 462 F.2d 567, 569 (1972); *Car-Freshner Corp. v. Turtle Wax, Inc.*, 268 F. Supp. 162, 164 (SDNY 1967). In this circumstance, trademark law says that the word (e.g., "Trim"), although not inherently distinctive, has developed "secondary meaning." *See Inwood Laboratories, Inc. v. Ives Laboratories, Inc.*, 456 U.S. 844, 851, n. 11, 72 L. Ed. 2d 606, 102 S. Ct. 2182 (1982) ("secondary meaning" is acquired when "in the minds of the public, the primary significance of a product feature . . . is to identify the source of the product rather than the product itself"). Again, one might ask, if trademark law permits a descriptive word with secondary meaning to act as a mark, why would it not permit a color, under similar circumstances, to do the same?

We cannot find in the basic objectives of trademark law any obvious theoretical objection to the use of color alone as a trademark, where that color has attained "secondary meaning" and therefore identifies and distinguishes a particular brand (and thus indicates its "source"). In principle, trademark law, by preventing others from copying a source-identifying mark, "reduces the customer's costs of shopping and making purchasing decisions," 1 J. McCarthy, McCarthy on Trademarks and Unfair Competition § 2.01[2], p. 2-3 (3d ed. 1994) (hereinafter McCarthy), for it quickly and easily assures a potential customer that this item — the item with this mark — is made by the same producer as other similarly marked items that he or she liked (or disliked) in the past. At the same time, the law helps assure a producer that it (and not an imitating competitor) will reap the financial, reputation-related rewards associated with a desirable product. The law thereby "encourages the production of quality products," *ibid.*, and simultaneously discourages those who hope to sell inferior products by capitalizing on a consumer's inability quickly to evaluate the quality of an item offered for sale. *See, e.g.*, 3 L. Altman, Callmann on Unfair Competition, Trademarks and Monopolies § 17.03 (4th ed. 1983); Landes & Posner, The Economics of Trademark Law, 78 T. M. Rep. 267, 271-272 (1988); *Park 'N Fly, Inc. v. Dollar Park and Fly, Inc.*, 469 U.S. 189, 198, 83 L. Ed. 2d 582, 105 S. Ct. 658 (1985); S. Rep. No. 100-515, p. 4 (1988). It is the source-distinguishing ability of a mark — not its ontological status as color, shape, fragrance, word, or sign — that permits it to serve these basic purposes. *See* Landes & Posner, Trademark Law: An Economic Perspective, 30 J. Law & Econ. 265, 290 (1987). And, for that reason, it is difficult to find, in basic trademark objectives, a reason to disqualify absolutely the use of a color as a mark.

Neither can we find a principled objection to the use of color as a mark in the important "functionality" doctrine of trademark law. The functionality doctrine prevents trademark law, which seeks to promote competition by protecting a firm's reputation, from instead inhibiting legitimate competition by allowing a producer to control a useful product feature. It is the province of patent law, not trademark law, to encourage invention by granting inventors a monopoly over new product designs or functions for a limited time, 35 U.S.C. §§ 154, 173, after which competitors are free to use the innovation. If a product's functional features could be used as trademarks, however, a monopoly over such features could be obtained without regard to whether they qualify as patents and could be extended forever (because trademarks may be renewed in perpetuity). *See Kellogg Co. v. National Biscuit Co.*, 305 U.S. 111, 119-120, 83 L. Ed. 73, 59 S. Ct. 109 (1938) (Brandeis, J.); *Inwood Laboratories, Inc., supra,* at 863 (White, J., concurring in result) ("A functional characteristic is 'an important ingredient in the commercial success of the product,' and, after expiration of a patent, it is no more the property of the originator than the product itself") (citation omitted). Functionality doctrine therefore would require, to take an imaginary example, that even if customers have come to identify the special illumination-enhancing shape of a new patented light bulb with a particular manufacturer, the manufacturer may not use that shape as a trademark, for doing so, after the patent had expired, would impede competition — not by protecting the reputation of the original bulb maker, but by frustrating competitors' legitimate efforts to produce an equivalent illumination-enhancing bulb. *See, e.g., Kellogg Co., supra,* at 119-120 (trademark law cannot be used to extend monopoly over "pillow" shape of shredded wheat biscuit after the patent for that shape had expired). This Court consequently has explained that, "in general terms, a product feature is functional," and cannot serve as a trademark, "if it is essential to the use or purpose of the article or if it affects the cost or quality of the article," that is, if exclusive use of the feature would put competitors at a significant non-reputation-related disadvantage. *Inwood Laboratories, Inc.*, 456 U.S. at 850, n. 10.

Although sometimes color plays an important role (unrelated to source identification) in making a product more desirable, sometimes it does not. And, this latter fact — the fact that sometimes color is not essential to a product's use or purpose and does not affect cost or quality — indicates that the doctrine of "functionality" does not create an absolute bar to the use of color alone as a mark. *See Owens-Corning,* 774 F.2d at 1123 (pink color of insulation in wall "performs no non-trademark function"). It would seem, then, that color alone, at least sometimes, can meet the basic legal requirements for use as a trademark. It can act as a symbol that distinguishes a firm's goods and identifies their source, without serving any other significant function. *See* U.S. Dept. of Commerce, Patent and Trademark Office, Trademark Manual of Examining Procedure § 1202.04(e), p. 1202-13 (2d ed. May, 1993) (hereinafter PTO Manual) (approving trademark registration of color alone where it "has become distinctive of the applicant's goods in commerce," provided that "there is [no] competitive need for colors to remain available in the industry" and the color is not "functional"); *see also* 1 McCarthy §§ 3.01[1], 7.26 ("requirements for qualification of a word or symbol as a trademark" are that it be (1) a "symbol" (2) "used . . . as a mark," (3) "to identify and distinguish the seller's goods from goods made or sold by others" but that it not be "functional"). Indeed, the District Court, in this case, entered findings (accepted by the Ninth Circuit) that show Qualitex's green-gold press pad color has met these requirements. The green-gold color acts as a symbol. Having developed secondary meaning (for customers identified the green-gold color as Qualitex's), it identifies the press pads' source. And, the green-gold color serves no other function. (Although it is important to use some color on press pads to avoid noticeable stains, the court found "no competitive need in the press pad industry for the green-gold color, since other colors are equally usable" 21 U.S.P.Q.2D (BNA) at 1460. Accordingly, unless there is some special reason that convincingly militates against the use of color alone as a trademark, trademark law would protect Qualitex's use of the green-gold color on its press pads. . . .

The functionality doctrine, as we have said, forbids the use of a product's feature as a trademark where doing so will put a competitor at a significant disadvantage because the feature is "essential to the use or purpose of the article" or "affects [its] cost or quality." *Inwood Laboratories, Inc.*, 456 U.S. at 850, n. 10. The functionality doctrine thus protects competitors against a disadvantage (unrelated to recognition or reputation) that trademark protection might otherwise impose, namely their inability reasonably to replicate important non-reputation-related product features. For example, this Court has written that competitors might be free to copy the color of a medical pill where that color serves to identify the kind of medication (e.g., a type of blood medicine) in addition to its source. *See id.*, at 853, 858, n. 20 ("Some patients commingle medications in a container and rely on color to differentiate one from another"); *see also* J. Ginsburg, D. Goldberg, & A. Greenbaum, Trademark and Unfair Competition Law 194-195 (1991) (noting that drug color cases "have more to do with public health policy" regarding generic drug substitution "than with trademark law"). And, the federal courts have demonstrated that they can apply this doctrine in a careful and reasoned manner, with sensitivity to the effect on competition. Although we need not comment on the merits of specific cases, we note that lower courts have permitted competitors to copy the green color of farm machinery (because customers wanted their farm equipment to match) and have barred the use of black as a trademark on outboard boat motors (because black has the special functional attributes of decreasing the apparent size of the motor and ensuring compatibility with many different boat colors). *See Deere & Co. v. Farmhand, Inc.*, 560 F. Supp. 85, 98 (SD Iowa 1982), *aff'd*, 721 F.2d 253 (CA8 1983); *Brunswick Corp. v. British Seagull Ltd.*, 35 F.3d 1527, 1532 (CA Fed. 1994), *cert. pending*, No. 94-1075; *see also Nor-Am Chemical v. O. M. Scott & Sons Co.*, 4 U.S.P.Q.2D (BNA) 1316, 1320 (ED Pa. 1987) (blue color of fertilizer held functional because it indicated the presence of nitrogen). The Restatement (Third) of Unfair Competition adds that, if a design's "aesthetic value" lies in its ability to "confer a significant benefit that cannot practically be duplicated by the use of alternative designs," then the design is "functional." Restatement (Third) of Unfair Competition § 17, Comment c, pp. 175-176 (1995). The "ultimate test of aesthetic functionality," it explains, "is whether the recognition of trademark rights would significantly hinder competition." *Id.*, at 176.

The upshot is that, where a color serves a significant nontrademark function—whether to distinguish a heart pill from a digestive medicine or to satisfy the "noble instinct for giving the right touch of beauty to common and necessary things" G. K. Chesterton, Simplicity and Tolstoy 61 (1912)— courts will examine whether its use as a mark would permit one competitor (or a group) to interfere with legitimate (nontrademark-related) competition through actual or potential exclusive use of an important product ingredient. That examination should not discourage firms from creating aesthetically pleasing mark designs, for it is open to their competitors to do the same. *See, e.g., W. T. Rogers Co. v. Keene*, 778 F.2d 334, 343 (CA7 1985) (Posner, J.). But, ordinarily, it should prevent the anticompetitive consequences of Jacobson's hypothetical "color depletion" argument, when, and if, the circumstances of a particular case threaten "color depletion."

NOTES AND QUESTIONS

1. In *Qualitex*, the Supreme Court refers to the potential functionality of color, and specifically addresses the use of color to identify types of medicines. After the patent on a medicine has expired, generic producers may enter the market with the same product, bringing competition to the market for the medicine. Generic producers may prefer to use the same color used by the former patent holder because doctors and patients will identify the medicine with its original coloring. Has the Supreme Court endorsed this practice in *Qualitex*?

2. The term "generic" in the context of medicines has more than one meaning. The term is often used to distinguish between patented and off-patent versions of the same medicine, with "generic" referring to the off-patent version. The term is also used to distinguish between "branded" and "unbranded" versions of off-patent medicines. For example "Bayer" is a brand name for "aspirin," which is unpatented. "Bayer Aspirin" is a branded medicine. Many chain stores also sell aspirin under a house label, typically at a lower price than branded aspirin. The medicine sold under the house label is often referred to as a "generic."

In the following 2002 decision, the Court of Justice of the European Union (ECJ) considers a question similar to that addressed by the U.S. Supreme Court in *Qualitex v. Jacobsen*, but with reference to the TRIPS Agreement and European legislation. The ECJ places particular emphasis on the role trademark registration plays in providing information to competitors in the economic marketplace. As you read the ECJ decision, consider whether it is approving the use of a single color as a trademark, as the U.S. Supreme Court has in *Qualitex*.

HEIDELBERGER BAUCHEMIE GMBH

Judgment of the Court (Second Chamber)
24 June 2004

In Case C-49/02,

REFERENCE to the Court under Article 234 EC by the Bundespatentgericht (Germany) for a preliminary ruling in the proceedings brought before that court by

Heidelberger Bauchemie GmbH

on the interpretation of Article 2 of the First Council Directive (89/104/EEC) of 21 December 1988 to approximate the laws of the Member States relating to trade marks (OJ 1989 L 40, p. 1),

THE COURT (Second Chamber),
composed of: C.W.A. TIMMERMANS, President of the Chamber, J.-P. PUISSOCHET, J.N. CUNHA RODRIGUES (Rapporteur), R. SCHINTGEN and N. COLNERIC, Judges, gives the following:

JUDGMENT

1. By order of 22 January 2002, received at the Court on 20 February 2002, the Bundespatentgericht (Federal Patents Court) referred to the Court for a preliminary ruling under Article 234 EC two questions on the interpretation of Article 2 of the First Council Directive (89/104/EEC) of 21 December 1988 to approximate the laws of the Member States relating to trade marks (OJ 1989 L 40, p. 1) (hereinafter "the Directive").

2. Those questions were raised in proceedings brought by Heidelberger Bauchemie GmbH (hereinafter "Heidelberger Bauchemie") against the refusal by the Deutsches Patentamt (German Patent Office) (hereinafter "the Patent Office") to register the colours blue and yellow as a trade mark for certain products used in the building trade.

LEGAL FRAMEWORK . . .

COMMUNITY LEGISLATION

5. Article 2 of the Directive, headed "Signs of which a trade mark may consist," is worded as follows:

A trade mark may consist of any sign capable of being represented graphically, particularly words, including personal names, designs, letters, numerals, the shape of goods or of their packaging, provided that such signs are capable of distinguishing the goods or services of one undertaking from those of other undertakings.

6. Article 3 of the Directive, headed "Grounds for refusal or invalidity" provides:

> . . . 3. A trade mark shall not be refused registration or be declared invalid in accordance with paragraph 1(b), (c) or (d) if, before the date of application for registration and following the use which has been made of it, it has acquired a distinctive character. Any Member State may in addition provide that this provision shall also apply where the distinctive character was acquired after the date of application for registration or after the date of registration. . . .

The Main Proceedings and the Questions Referred

10. On 22 March 1995, Heidelberger Bauchemie applied to the Patent Office for the registration of the colours blue and yellow as a trade mark. The section headed "reproduction of the mark" comprised a rectangular piece of paper, the upper part of which was blue and the lower half yellow. The following description of the mark accompanied the application:

> The trade mark applied for consists of the applicant's corporate colours which are used in every conceivable form, in particular on packaging and labels.
>   The specification of the colours is:
> RAL 5015/HKS 47 — blue
> RAL 1016/HKS 3 — yellow.

11. Registration of the mark was applied for in relation to a list of various products used in the building trade, including adhesives, solvents, varnishes, paints, lubricants and insulating materials.

12. By decision of 18 September 1996, the Patent Office rejected that application on the grounds, first, that the sign which it was sought to register was not capable of constituting a trade mark and was not capable of being represented graphically and, secondly, that the mark was devoid of any distinctive character. However, following the "black/yellow colour mark" decision of the Bundesgerichtshof (Federal Court of Justice) (Germany) of 10 December 1998, the Patent Office reviewed its position. By decision of 2 May 2000, it accepted that colours are in principle able to constitute a trade mark, but rejected the application on the ground of lack of any distinctive character. Heidelberger Bauchemie brought an appeal against that decision before the Bundespatentgericht.

13. The Bundespatentgericht considered that it was uncertain whether abstract, undelineated marks could be treated as "signs" capable of being represented graphically within the meaning of Article 2 of the Directive. . . .

14. In those circumstances, the Bundespatentgericht decided to stay the proceedings and to refer the following questions to the Court for a preliminary ruling. . . .

The Questions Referred

15. By its questions, which should be dealt with together, the national court is essentially asking whether, and if so under what conditions, colours or

combinations of colours designated in the abstract and without contours are capable of constituting a trade mark for the purposes of Article 2 of the Directive. . . .

19. Article 15(1) of the TRIPS Agreement provides that "combinations of colours . . . shall be eligible for registration as trade marks." However, that Agreement does not define a "combination of colours."

20. Since the Community is a party to the TRIPS Agreement, it is required to interpret its legislation on trade marks so far as possible in the light of the wording and purpose of that Agreement (*see,* to that effect, Case C-53/96 *Hermès* [1998] ECR I-3603, paragraph 28).

21. It should therefore be established whether Article 2 of the Directive can be interpreted as meaning that "combinations of colours" are capable of constituting a trade mark.

22. To constitute a trade mark under Article 2 of the Directive, colours or combinations of colours must satisfy three conditions. First, they must be a sign. Secondly, that sign must be capable of being represented graphically. Thirdly, the sign must be capable of distinguishing the goods or services of one undertaking from those of other undertakings (*see,* to that effect, [Case C-104/01] *Libertel* [2003] ECR I-3793, paragraph 23).

23. As the Court has already held, colours are normally a simple property of things (*Libertel,* paragraph 27). Even in the particular field of trade, colours and combinations of colours are generally used for their attractive or decorative powers, and do not convey any meaning. However, it is possible that colours or combinations of colours may be capable, when used in relation to a product or a service, of being a sign.

24. For the purposes of the application of Article 2 of the Directive, it is necessary to establish that in the context in which they are used colours or combinations of colours which it is sought to register in fact represent a sign. The purpose of that requirement is in particular to prevent the abuse of trademark law in order to obtain an unfair competitive advantage.

25. Moreover, it is clear from the Court's case-law (Case C-273/00 *Sieckmann* [2002] ECR I-11737, paragraphs 46 to 55, and *Libertel,* paragraphs 28 and 29) that a graphic representation in terms of Article 2 of the Directive must enable the sign to be represented visually, particularly by means of images, lines or characters, so that it can be precisely identified.

26. Such an interpretation is necessary for the proper working of the trade mark registration system.

27. The function of the requirement of graphic representation is in particular to define the mark itself in order to determine the precise subject of the protection afforded by the registered mark to its proprietor.

28. The entry of the mark in a public register has the aim of making it accessible to the competent authorities and to the public, particularly to economic operators.

29. On the one hand, the competent authorities must know with clarity and precision the nature of the signs of which a mark consists in order to be able to fulfill their obligations in relation to the prior examination of applications for registration and the publication and maintenance of an appropriate and precise register of trade marks.

30. On the other hand, economic operators must be able to acquaint themselves, with clarity and precision, with registrations or applications for registration made by their actual or potential competitors, and thus to obtain relevant information about the rights of third parties.

31. In those circumstances, in order to fulfil its role as a registered trade mark, a sign must always be perceived unambiguously and uniformly, so that the function of mark as an indication of origin is guaranteed. In the light of the duration of a mark's registration and the fact that, as the Directive provides, it can be renewed for varying periods, the representation must also be durable.

32. It follows from the above that a graphic representation for the purpose of Article 2 of the Directive must be, in particular, precise and durable.

33. Accordingly, a graphic representation consisting of two or more colours, designated in the abstract and without contours, must be systematically arranged by associating the colours concerned in a predetermined and uniform way.

34. The mere juxtaposition of two or more colours, without shape or contours, or a reference to two or more colours "in every conceivable form," as is the case with the trade mark which is the subject of the main proceedings, does not exhibit the qualities of precision and uniformity required by Article 2 of the Directive, as construed in paragraphs 25 to 32 of this judgment.

35. Such representations would allow numerous different combinations, which would not permit the consumer to perceive and recall a particular combination, thereby enabling him to repeat with certainty the experience of a purchase, any more than they would allow the competent authorities and economic operators to know the scope of the protection afforded to the proprietor of the trade mark.

36. As regards the manner in which each of the colours concerned is represented, it is clear from paragraphs 33, 34, 37, 38 and 68 of *Libertel* that a sample of the colour concerned, accompanied by a designation using an internationally recognised identification code, may constitute a graphic representation for the purposes of Article 2 of the Directive.

37. As regards the question whether, for the purposes of this provision, colours or combinations of colours are capable of distinguishing the goods or services of one undertaking from those of other undertakings, it must be determined whether or not those colours or combinations of colours are capable of conveying precise information, particularly as regards the origin of a product or service.

38. It follows from paragraphs 40, 41 and 65 to 67 of *Libertel* that, whilst colours are capable of conveying certain associations of ideas, and of arousing feelings, they possess little inherent capacity for communicating specific information, especially since they are commonly and widely used, because of their appeal, in order to advertise and market goods or services, without any specific message.

39. Save in exceptional cases, colours do not initially have a distinctive character, but may be capable of acquiring such character as the result of the use made of them in relation to the goods or services claimed.

40. Subject to the above, it must be accepted that for the purposes of Article 2 of the Directive colours and combinations of colours, designated in the abstract and without contours, may be capable of distinguishing the goods or services of one undertaking from those of other undertakings.

41. It should be added that, even if a combination of colours which it is sought to register as a trade mark satisfies the requirements for constituting a trade mark for the purposes of Article 2 of the Directive, it is still necessary for the competent authority for registering trade marks to decide whether the combination claimed satisfies the other requirements laid down, particularly in

Article 3 of the Directive, for registration as a trade mark in relation to the goods or services of the undertaking which has applied for its registration. That examination must take account of all the relevant circumstances of the case, including any use which has been made of the sign in respect of which trade mark registration is sought (*Libertel,* paragraph 76, and Case 363/99 *Koninklijke KPN Nederland* [2004] ECR I-0000, paragraph 37). That examination must also take account of the public interest in not unduly restricting the availability of colours for other traders who market goods or services of the same type as those in respect of which registration is sought (*Libertel,* paragraphs 52 to 56).

42. In light of the above, the answer to the questions must be that colours or combinations of colours which are the subject of an application for registration as a trade mark, claimed in the abstract, without contours, and in shades which are named in words by reference to a colour sample and specified according to an internationally recognised colour classification system may constitute a trade mark for the purposes of Article 2 of the Directive where:

— it has been established that, in the context in which they are used, those colours or combinations of colours in fact represent a sign, and
— the application for registration includes a systematic arrangement associating the colours concerned in a predetermined and uniform way.

Even if a combination of colours satisfies the requirements for constituting a trade mark for the purposes of Article 2 of the Directive, it is still necessary for the competent authority for registering trade marks to decide whether the combination claimed fulfils the other requirements laid down, particularly in Article 3 of the Directive, for registration as a trade mark in relation to the goods or services of the undertaking which has applied for its registration. Such an examination must take account of all the relevant circumstances of the case, including any use which has been made of the sign in respect of which trade mark registration is sought. That examination must also take account of the public interest in not unduly restricting the availability of colours for other traders who market goods or services of the same type as those in respect of which registration is sought. . . .

NOTES AND QUESTIONS

1. The *Heidelberger Bauchemie* decision introduces some of the complexities of the EU trademark regime. Each of the 27 EU member states has its own trademark law, which law must be compatible with the First Trade Marks Directive, which in 1988 acted to approximate the EU trademark law but left in place the national regulatory and judicial systems. As we examine below, in 1993, the European Union adopted the Community Trade Mark Regulation, which created a unitary mark (the "Community Trade Mark" or CTM) for the European Union and a new institution, the Office for Harmonization in the Internal Market (OHIM). At the judicial "top" of both the member state and CTMR systems is the ECJ, which has ultimate authority to interpret the law governing each of them. Though technically the two systems are separate, a decision by the ECJ regarding a question such as whether colors are appropriate trademark subject matter may apply with equal force to both trademark systems since each similarly defines

trademark subject matter. Answers to some other trademark questions will be relevant to only one of the two systems.

2. Has the ECJ, like the U.S. Supreme Court in *Qualitex,* approved the use of a single color as a trademark?

3. A common form of media advertising involves combining the visual and aural image of an exciting or interesting event with a trademark — without conveying any direct information about a product. The objective is to associate a particular trademark with a positive (or even a negative) feeling such that when the consumer is faced with a choice among products, he or she will be drawn to the one that was advertised. In these circumstances, what function is the trademark performing?

4. In *Lego Juris A/S v. Office for Harmonisation in the Internal Market (Trade Marks and Designs) (OHIM)*, ECJ Case C-48/09 P, 14 Sept. 2010, the ECJ addressed the relationship between shape and function in the context of a product (the Lego building block), subject of an expired patent, saying:

> 38. According to settled case-law, trade mark law constitutes an essential element in the system of competition in the European Union. In that system, each undertaking must, in order to attract and retain customers by the quality of its goods or services, be able to have registered as trade marks signs enabling the consumer, without any possibility of confusion, to distinguish those goods or services from others which have another origin (see, to that effect, Case C-517/99 *Merz & Krell* [2001] ECR I-6959, paragraphs 21 and 22; Case C-206/01 *Arsenal Football Club* [2002] ECR I-10273, paragraphs 47 and 48; and Case C-412/05 P *Alcon* v *OHIM* [2007] ECR I-3569, paragraphs 53 and 54).
>
> 39. A product's shape is a sign which may constitute a trade mark. . . .
>
> 40. In the present case, it has not been disputed that the shape of the Lego brick has become distinctive in consequence of the use which has been made of it and is therefore a sign capable of distinguishing the appellant's goods from others which have another origin.
>
> . . .
>
> 45. First, the inclusion in Article 7(1) of Regulation No 40/94 of the prohibition on registration as a trade mark of any sign consisting of the shape of goods which is necessary to obtain a technical result ensures that undertakings may not use trade mark law in order to perpetuate, indefinitely, exclusive rights relating to technical solutions.
>
> 46. When the shape of a product merely incorporates the technical solution developed by the manufacturer of that product and patented by it, protection of that shape as a trade mark once the patent has expired would considerably and permanently reduce the opportunity for other undertakings to use that technical solution. In the system of intellectual property rights developed in the European Union, technical solutions are capable of protection only for a limited period, so that subsequently they may be freely used by all economic operators. . . .
>
> 47. Furthermore, the legislature has laid down with particular strictness that shapes necessary to obtain a technical result are unsuitable for registration as trade marks, since it has excluded the grounds for refusal listed in Article 7(1)(e) of Regulation No 40/94 from the scope of the exception under Article 7(3). If follows, therefore, from Article 7(3) of the regulation that, even if a shape of goods which is necessary to obtain a technical result has become distinctive in consequence of the use which has been made of it, it is prohibited from being registered as a trade mark (see by analogy, in relation to Article 3(3) of Directive 89/104, which is essentially identical to Article 7(3)

of Regulation No 40/94, *Philips,* paragraph 57, and Case C-371/06 *Benetton Group* [2007] ECR I-7709, paragraphs 25 to 27).

48. Second, by restricting the ground for refusal set out in Article 7(1)(e)(ii) of Regulation No 40/94 to signs which consist "exclusively" of the shape of goods which is "necessary" to obtain a technical result, the legislature duly took into account that any shape of goods is, to a certain extent, functional and that it would therefore be inappropriate to refuse to register a shape of goods as a trade mark solely on the ground that it has functional characteristics. By the terms "exclusively" and "necessary," that provision ensures that solely shapes of goods which only incorporate a technical solution, and whose registration as a trade mark would therefore actually impede the use of that technical solution by other undertakings, are not to be registered.

5. In *Audi AG v. Office for Harmonisation in the Internal Market (Trade Marks and Designs) (OHIM),* ECJ Case C-398/08 P, 21 Jan. 2010, the ECJ addressed trademark protection for advertising slogans, holding that such identifiers are subject to the same standards of assessment as other trademarks, stating:

> 39. The Court has therefore held, in particular, that an advertising slogan cannot be required to display "imaginativeness" or even "conceptual tension which would create surprise and so make a striking impression" in order to have the minimal level of distinctiveness required under Article 7(1)(b) of Regulation No 40/94 (*OHIM* v *Erpo Möbelwerk,* paragraphs 31 and 32; see also Case C-392/02 P *SAT.1* v *OHIM* [2004] ECR I-8317, paragraph 41).
>
> 40. In the present case, the reasoning followed by the General Court derives from an erroneous interpretation of the principles set out in paragraphs 36 to 39 of the present judgment.
>
> 41. It must be held that, even though the General Court stated in paragraph 36 of the judgment under appeal that it is clear from the case-law that registration of a mark cannot be excluded because of that mark's laudatory or advertising use, it went on to explain that the reason for its finding that the mark applied for lacks distinctive character was, in essence, the fact that that mark is perceived as a promotional formula: that is to say, its finding was made precisely on the basis of the mark's laudatory or advertising use.
>
> . . .
>
> 53. As the Board of Appeal stated in the contested decision, the expression "Vorsprung durch Technik" [meaning, *inter alia,* advance or advantage through technology] is a widely known slogan which Audi has been using for years to promote the sale of its motor vehicles. It was registered in 2001 as a Community trade mark for goods in Class 12 on the basis of proof that that slogan was widely known in German-speaking regions.
>
> 54. As regards the goods and services in question, other than those in Class 12, the Board of Appeal based its refusal of registration on the fact that the slogan "Vorsprung durch Technik" conveys an objective message to the effect that technological superiority enables the manufacture and supply of better goods and services. According to the Board of Appeal, a combination of words which limits itself to that banal objective message is, in principle, devoid of any inherently distinctive character and cannot therefore be registered unless it is shown that the public has come to perceive it as a trade mark.
>
> 55. That analysis shows that Article 7(1)(b) of Regulation No 40/94 was misapplied.
>
> 56. In that regard, it must be stated that all marks made up of signs or indications that are also used as advertising slogans, indications of quality or incitements to purchase the goods or services covered by those marks convey by definition, to a greater or lesser extent, an objective message. It is clear,

however, from the case-law set out in paragraphs 35 and 36 of the present judgment that those marks are not, by virtue of that fact alone, devoid of distinctive character.

The following recent decision by the trial court judge in India illustrates that an identical trademark may be used by independent parties with respect to different classes of goods, in this case beer and self-defense pepper spray. The plaintiff proceeded on grounds of trademark dilution or disparagement as compared with strict trademark infringement. In a dilution or disparagement cause of action, the trademark holder is not alleging that the complained-against party is competing for sales in the same market. The trademark holder is instead alleging that the complained-against party is causing injury to its brand.

SKOL BREWERIES v. UNISAFE TECHNOLOGIES

In the High Court of Delhi at New Delhi
CS(OS) 472/2006, I.A. No. 3194/2006
Pronounced on: 25.08.2010

Mr. Justice S. Ravindra Bhat, J

1. The plaintiff, in this suit, seeks the relief of permanent injunction against the defendant alleging infringement, passing off and unfair competition in respect of its trade mark, "KNOCK OUT." Other consequential reliefs are also claimed.

2. The suit avers that the plaintiff is proprietor of the brand, KNOCK OUT for beer by virtue of an assignment deed dated 27.05. . . . It is stated that the said brand has been in existence for over two decades and enjoys large and established reputation both in the domestic, as well as international markets. The plaintiff, inter alia, is engaged in the business of brewing, distilling and marketing beer under various trademarks (Haywards 2000, Haywards 5000, Royal Challenge and Knockout). The brand KNOCK OUT has been in existence and continuous use since 1986 (by the plaintiff's predecessor in interest). . . . The registered trademarks of the plaintiff are:

Trade Mark Class Regn. No. Date Goods KNOCK OUT HIGH PUNCH WITH LOGO 32 450938 11.03.1986 Beer KNOCK OUT LABEL 32 450939 11.03.1986 Beer. The said trademark-registrations are subsisting and valid.

3. Further, it is stated that the KNOCK OUT beer is India's leading brand selling over 7 million cases. . . .

5. It is alleged that the defendant is manufacturing a self defence pepper spray under the trademark "KNOCK OUT," using the plaintiff's brand in entirety. The domain name of defendant's website, i.e. www.knockoutspray.com also amounts to violation of the plaintiff's rights. . . .

6. The plaintiff alleges that the actions of the defendant are with an intention to take unfair advantage of the goodwill and reputation enjoyed by its (the plaintiff's) trademark "KNOCK OUT." . . .

7. In its defence, the defendant states that it has been using the trade mark KNOCK OUT, since April, 2004 in respect of a self defence pepper spray. It has spent substantial amounts to popularize its product, but the plaintiff sought this injunctive relief only in March, 2006 almost two years after the defendant started its operations. Further, the goods of the plaintiff are entirely different from those of the defendant. The plaintiff's goods fall under class 32 and the

defendant's goods fall under classes 5 and 9. The defendant asserts that the plaintiff's trademark cannot become a well-known trade mark within the meaning of Section 11 (Sic 2 (1)(zg)) of the Trade Marks Act, 1999. The defendant submits that "Knock out" being a common dictionary word, which means — punch to the forehead or a strike to the head to cause unconsciousness, cannot be monopolized by the plaintiff in the manner, as is sought. The adoption of the said mark by the defendant is stated to be bonafide, as the meaning of the said word is descriptive of the characteristic of the product, i.e. it is meant for self defence, and when used, it knocks-out (incapacitates) the attacker for some time, giving the victim opportunity to escape or get help.

. . .

9. What the plaintiff complains of here is trademark infringement, by dilution. Although, dilution is not expressly alluded to in the Act, the relevant provision is Section 29(4); it reads as follows:

SECTION 29. INFRINGEMENT OF REGISTERED TRADE MARKS

(1) A Registered trade mark is infringed by a person who, not being registered proprietor or a person using by way of permitted use, uses in the course of trade, a mark which is identical with, or deceptively similar to, the trade mark in relation to goods or services in respect of which the trade mark is registered and in such manner as to render the use of the mark likely to be taken as being used as a trade mark.

. . .

(4) A registered trade mark is infringed by a person who, not being a registered proprietor or a person using by way of permitted use, uses in the course of trade, a mark which —

(a) is identical with or similar to the registered trade mark; and (b) is used in relation to goods or services which are not similar to those for which the trade mark is registered; and (c) the registered trade mark has a reputation in India and the use of the mark without due cause takes unfair advantage of or is detrimental to, the distinctive character or repute of the registered trade mark.

10. In trademark dilution claims, the plaintiff has to establish the identity or similarity with the registered trademark; the goods, in question, of course, necessarily are dissimilar to the plaintiff's goods; the plaintiff has to also prove that his mark has "a reputation in India" and the use of that mark "without due cause" takes unfair advantage, or is "detrimental to" the distinctive character or repute of his (the plaintiff's) mark. At the heart of the claim is the duty to establish that the mark has "a reputation in India" which is not a requirement in the normal class of infringement. This duty is underscored by the circumstance that infringement (i.e. competing similar mark, in relation to similar goods) is presumed, by virtue of the mandate of Section 29(3); there is no such presumption in trademark dilution claims, and all the elements prescribed under Section 29(4) are to be made good, for a claim of infringement, through dilution, to succeed.

. . .

12. Dealing with whether, and to what extent a trader can claim exclusivity in relation to common words, this Court in *SBL Limited v. Himalaya Drug Company,* 67 (1997) DLT 803 (DB), through a division Bench said that:

Nobody can claim exclusive right to use any generic word, abbreviation, or acronym which has become publici juris. In the trade of drugs it is common practice to name a drug by the name of the organ or ailment which it treats or the main ingredient of the drug. Such an organ ailment or ingredient being public jurisdiction or generic cannot be owned by anyone for use as a trademark.

. . .

Recently, in *Rhizome Distilleries P. Ltd. & Ors. v. Pernod Ricard S.A. France & Ors.*, 165 (2009) DLT 474 too, another Division Bench underlined that common words, generic or descriptive names, do not automatically evoke protection of the Court unless a plaintiff establishes that such marks have acquired secondary meaning: . . .

. . .

14. Another consideration which has to weigh with the Court is that the term Knock Out does not inherently describe the plaintiff's product. On the other hand, the defendant's pepper spray, it is claimed, has the attribute or ability to "knock out" the unwanted physical advances of a man, which may threaten the user. The defendant's mark, in the opinion of the Court, has greater degree of association or claim to descriptiveness of the product, than the plaintiff's. Here, the observations in *British Petroleum Company Ltd v. European Petroleum Distributors Ltd.*, [1968 RPC 54], are relevant:

> "In considering whether or not the mark is 'inherently adapted' to distinguish the goods it is relevant to ask oneself whether and to what extent if the proposed mark was not given a statutory protection, other producers of the goods would be likely in the normal course of events to wish to use the mark themselves. . . ."

. . .

17. There is no evidence on record, to establish that the plaintiffs KNOCK OUT has acquired distinctiveness and association with its product of such nature or fame that the consumer or user only thinks of the plaintiff's brand of beer on any reference to the expression, Knock Out. The Court is evaluating the evidence, on the basis of material on record; it is essential that the plaintiff should rely on materials, which are not conjectural, but based on reality. The plaintiff has not led any evidence to show that there was likelihood of consumer confusion, or that the defendant, knowing the plaintiff's mark, deliberately chose to use it. The plaintiff was under an obligation to prove confusion, and not rely merely on the averments in the suit, and the documents filed, which it has failed to discharge.

18. Apart from the above considerations, there are some unusual elements to this case, which the Court cannot but help noticing. The lynchpin of the plaintiff's case is the strong message of "manliness" or machismo associated with the consumer of its KNOCK OUT beer. The plaintiff complains that this masculinity, as it were, is severely damaged by the defendant's use of the same KNOCK OUT term or mark, for the pepper spray it markets. The plaintiff is piqued, because of the manner by which the defendant is marketing, i.e. as an effective deterrent to aggressive or persistent unwanted male attention or physical advances, when it tends to threaten the (female) user. As mentioned earlier, the defendant's mark is closer in description of the product than the plaintiff's. If such is the case, the use of such an inherently descriptive mark is proper and legitimate. Furthermore, the speciousness of the plaintiff's argument is revealed if one examines it closely, for countenancing it would mean accepting that it is "masculine" or "manly" to indulge and persist in such

unwarranted attentions towards women. If the argument implies that the plaintiff's product results in such "machismo" its utter untenability is laid bare, because it would amount to saying that consumption of the KNOCK OUT beer would result in such manliness that would need the use of pepper spray to stave of[f] uncalled[-for] physical advances. Surely that is not the result desired by the plaintiff, while advancing its contentions.

19. The Court is conscious that though the competing marks are similar, the consumer base is entirely different, as is the product. There is nothing to show that trade channels are common, or that the plaintiff's marks have acquired such degree of secondary distinctiveness that the term KNOCK OUT certainly, or almost invariably implies it or its product.

20. In view of the above conclusions, the Court is of opinion that the suit cannot succeed; it is accordingly dismissed. In the circumstances of the case, the parties are left to bear their costs.

NOTES AND QUESTIONS

1. Why does the plaintiff beer producer proceed on a dilution or disparagement claim rather than strict trademark infringement?
2. The Delhi High Court's decision appears grounded in several factors: (1) the trademark at issue has a descriptive meaning; (2) the plaintiff has failed to establish that its mark has become well known in association with its product; (3) the defendant has plausible descriptive grounds for adopting the trademark in connection with its product; and (4) the plaintiff's theory of dilution or disparagement is contrary to good public policy.
3. India is part of the common law legal tradition. In this respect, the trial court may place greater reliance on precedent than statutory language as compared, for example, with the ECJ, whose decisions are more grounded in the civil law tradition.

B. The Limits of the Trademark

The trademark is defined in terms of rights granted to the holder to prevent others from using without the right holder's consent identical or similar signs in the course of trade. This right is limited in a number of ways.

1. Exhaustion of Trademark Rights and Fair Use

The doctrine of exhaustion addresses the point at which the trademark holder's control over the good or service ceases. This termination of control is critical to the functioning of any market economy because it permits the free transfer of goods and services. Without an exhaustion doctrine, the original trademark holder would perpetually exercise control over the sale, transfer, or use of a good or service associated with the mark, and would control economic life.

A trademark is typically exhausted by the "first sale" (U.S. doctrine) or "placing on the market" (EU doctrine) of the good or service embodying it. The basic idea is that once the right holder has been able to obtain an economic return from the first sale or placing on the market, the purchaser or transferee of the good or service is entitled to use and dispose of it without further restriction.

As illustration, consider a can of soda labeled with the famous "Coca-Cola" trademark. Because the Coca-Cola Company holds rights to that mark, it may prevent others from first-selling the can of soda without its consent. If a person buys the can of soda from an authorized first-seller, the Coca-Cola Company's right in its trademark is exhausted, and it cannot prevent the purchaser from drinking the soda, or from giving or selling the can of soda to someone else. The trademark holder has lost its right to control further disposition of the product. The purchase of the can of Coca-Cola does not authorize the purchaser to begin making cans of Coca-Cola, or licensing the mark to others. In other words, the first sale does not grant a purchaser rights in the trademark, but rather it extinguishes the Coca Cola Company's entitlement to control movement of that particular can of soda.

The trademark gives its holder the exclusive right to place the good or service on the market, but it does not give the holder a right to control all uses of the trademark. Third parties are entitled to make "fair use" of the mark. There are a variety of contexts in which fair use may take place, some of which already were alluded to in the *Qualitex v. Jacobsen* decision. Resellers of trademarked products, or sellers of spare parts, typically must make some use of the trademark in order to make purchasers aware of the nature of the goods offered. Trademarks also may be used fairly in comparative advertisement and news reporting. Whether third-party use is "fair" will depend on the specific context of the use: A third party may be fairly using the mark to make consumers aware of the nature of the product, or a third party may be unfairly taking advantage by deliberately implying its own connection to the trademark holder. Trademarks are used in news reporting and in literary and academic references to refer to the "thing itself." A news reporter cannot very well be expected to refer to "the football club based in Manchester, England" every time he or she wishes to report on the exploits of Manchester United. Fair reference to the thing being described is sometimes referred to as "nominative fair use."

In the following decision, the Court of Justice of the European Union considers the extent to which a trademark holder, the maker of BMW automobiles, may prevent third parties from using its BMW mark in advertising second-hand BMWs and servicing them. In doing so, it sets limits on the rights of the trademark holder to control the secondary market in its products.

JUDGMENT OF THE COURT
23 February 1999

(Trade-marks directive — Unauthorised use of the BMW trade mark in advertisements for a garage business)

In Case C-63/97,

REFERENCE to the Court under Article 177 of the EC Treaty by the Hoge Raad der Nederlanden (Netherlands) for a preliminary ruling in the proceedings pending before that court . . .

Bayerische Motorenwerke AG (BMW) and BMW Nederland BV
and
Ronald Karel Deenik

on the interpretation of Articles 5 to 7 of First Council Directive 89/104/EEC of 21 December 1988 to approximate the laws of the Member States relating to trade marks (OJ 1989 L 40, p. 1),

THE COURT,
composed of: G.C. Rodríguez Iglesias, President, P.J.G. Kapteyn, J.-P. Puisso-chet and P. Jann (Presidents of Chambers), C. Gulmann (Rapporteur), J.L. Murray, D.A.O. Edward, H. Ragnemalm, L. Sevón, M. Wathelet and R. Schint-gen, Judges, gives the following:

Judgment

1. By judgment of 7 February 1997, received at the Court on 13 February 1997, the Hoge Raad der Nederlanden (Supreme Court of the Netherlands) referred to the Court for a preliminary ruling under Article 177 of the EC Treaty five questions on the interpretation of Articles 5 to 7 of First Council Directive 89/104/EEC of 21 December 1988 to approximate the laws of the Member States relating to trade marks (OJ 1989 L 40, p. 1, "the directive").

2. Those questions were raised in proceedings between the German company Bayerische Motorenwerke AG (BMW) and the Netherlands company BMW Nederland BV (referred to separately as "BMW AG" and "BMW BV" and jointly as "BMW") and Mr Deenik, the owner of a garage, residing in Almere (Netherlands), concerning his advertisements for the sale of second-hand BMW cars and repairs and maintenance of BMW cars. . . .

6. In many countries, including, since 1930, the Benelux States, BMW AG markets vehicles which it has manufactured and in respect of which it has registered with the Benelux Trade Marks Office the trade name BMW and two figurative trade marks for, *inter alia,* engines and motor vehicles as well as for spare parts and accessories ("the BMW mark").

7. BMW AG markets its vehicles through a network of dealers. In the Netherlands it supervises the network with the help of BMW BV. Dealers are entitled to use the BMW mark for the purposes of their business, but are required to meet the high standards of technical quality deemed necessary by BMW in the provision of service and warranties and in sales promotion.

8. Mr Deenik runs a garage and has specialised in the sale of second-hand BMW cars and in repairing and maintaining BMW cars. He is not part of the BMW dealer network.

9. In the main proceedings BMW claimed that, in carrying on his business, Mr Deenik made unlawful use, in advertisements, of the BMW mark or, at the very least, of similar signs. By writ of 21 February 1994 it accordingly sought an order from the Rechtbank (District Court), Zwolle, restraining Mr Deenik from, in particular, using the BMW mark or any similar sign in advertisements, publicity statements or other announcements emanating from him, or in any other way in connection with his business, and claimed damages from him. BMW relied on its rights under Article 13A of the Uniform Benelux Law on Trade Marks in the version then in force.

10. The Rechtbank took the view that a number of statements made by Mr Deenik in his advertisements constituted unlawful use of the BMW mark, on the ground that they could give rise to the impression that they were put out by an undertaking entitled to use that mark, that is to say, an undertaking affiliated to the BMW dealer network. It therefore made an order prohibiting him from making such use of the BMW mark. However, the Rechtbank considered that Mr Deenik was entitled to use expressions such as "Repairs and maintenance of BMWs" in his advertisements, since it was sufficiently clear that these referred only to products bearing the BMW mark. Furthermore, the Rechtbank deemed permissible statements such as "BMW specialist" or "Specialised in BMWs," on the ground that BMW had not disputed the fact that Mr Deenik had specialist experience of BMW vehicles and it was not for BMW to decide who were entitled to describe themselves as BMW specialists. The Rechtbank dismissed BMW's claim for damages.

11. BMW appealed against that judgment, requesting the Gerechtshof (Regional Court of Appeal), Arnhem, to rule that, by referring in advertisements to "Repairs and maintenance of BMWs" and by describing himself as a "BMW specialist" or as "Specialised in BMWs," Mr Deenik was infringing the trade-mark rights belonging to BMW. Upon the Gerechtshof's confirmation of the Rechtbank's judgment, BMW lodged an appeal in cassation against that decision on 10 November 1995 with the Hoge Raad.

12. In the circumstances the Hoge Raad decided to stay proceedings and refer the . . . questions to the Court for a preliminary ruling: . . .

29. It should in addition be borne in mind that Articles 6 and 7 of the directive contain rules limiting the right of the proprietor of a trade mark, under Article 5, to prohibit a third party from using his mark. In this connection, Article 6 provides *inter alia* that the proprietor of a trade mark may not prohibit a third party from using the mark where it is necessary to indicate the intended purpose of a product, provided that he uses it in accordance with honest practices in industrial or commercial matters. Article 7 provides that the proprietor is not entitled to prohibit the use of a trade mark in relation to goods which have been put on the market in the Community under that trade mark by the proprietor or with his consent, unless there exist legitimate reasons for him to oppose further commercialisation of the goods. . . .

QUESTIONS 2 AND 3

31. By its second and third questions, which should be considered together, the national court is in substance asking whether the use of a trade mark, without the proprietor's authorisation, in order to inform the public that another undertaking carries out repairs and maintenance of goods covered by that trade mark or that it has specialised, or is a specialist, in such goods constitutes a use of that mark for the purposes of one of the provisions of Article 5 of the directive. . . .

42. Accordingly, the answer to be given to the second and third questions must be that the use of a trade mark, without the proprietor's authorisation, for the purpose of informing the public that another undertaking carries out the repair and maintenance of goods covered by that mark or that it has specialised or is a specialist in such goods constitutes, in circumstances such as those described in the judgment making the reference, use of the mark within the meaning of Article 5(1)(a) of the directive.

QUESTIONS 4 AND 5

43. By its fourth and fifth questions, which should be considered together, the national court is in substance asking whether Articles 5 to 7 of the directive entitle the proprietor of a trade mark to prevent another person from using that mark for the purpose of informing the public that he carries out the repair and maintenance of goods covered by a trade mark and put on the market under that mark by the proprietor or with his consent, or that he has specialised or is a specialist in the sale or the repair and maintenance of such goods.

44. The Court is asked to rule, in particular, on the question whether the trade mark proprietor may prevent such use only where the advertiser creates the impression that his undertaking is affiliated to the trade mark proprietor's distribution network, or whether he may also prevent such use where, because of the manner in which the trade mark is used in the advertisements, there is a good chance that the public might be given the impression that the advertiser is using the trade mark in that regard to an appreciable extent for the purpose of advertising his own business as such, by creating a specific suggestion of quality.

45. In order to reply to that question, it must be pointed out that, in view of the answer given to the second and third questions that the use of the trade mark in the advertisements concerned in the main proceedings falls within the scope of Article 5(1)(a) of the directive, the use in issue may be prohibited by the trade mark proprietor unless Article 6, concerning the limitation of the effects of a trade mark, or Article 7, concerning exhaustion of the rights conferred by a trade mark, are applicable.

46. That question must be considered, first, in relation to the advertisements for the sale of second-hand cars and, second, in relation to the advertisements for the repair and maintenance of cars.

THE ADVERTISEMENTS FOR THE SALE OF SECOND-HAND BMW CARS

47. As regards the advertisements for the sale of second-hand BMW cars put on the market under that trade mark by the trade mark proprietor or with his consent, the case-law of the Court should be borne in mind concerning the use of a trade mark to inform the public of the resale of goods covered by a trade mark.

48. In Case C-337/95 *Parfums Christian Dior v Evora* [1997] ECR I-6013, the Court first held, at paragraph 38, that on a proper interpretation of Articles 5 and 7 of the directive, when trade-marked goods have been put on the Community market by the proprietor of the trade mark or with his consent, a reseller, besides being free to resell those goods, is also free to make use of the trade mark in order to bring to the public's attention the further commercialisation of those goods.

49. In the same judgment, the Court then found, at paragraph 43, that damage done to the reputation of a trade mark may, in principle, be a legitimate reason, within the meaning of Article 7(2) of the directive, allowing the proprietor to oppose the use of his trade mark for further commercialisation of goods put on the Community market by him or with his consent. As regards prestige goods, the Court stated, at paragraph 45, that the reseller must not act unfairly in relation to the legitimate interests of the trade mark owner, but must endeavour to prevent his advertising from affecting the value of the trade mark by detracting from the prestigious image of the goods in question. At paragraph 48, the Court concluded that the proprietor of a trade mark may

not rely on Article 7(2) to oppose the use of the trade mark, in ways customary in the reseller's sector of trade, for the purpose of bringing to the public's attention the further commercialisation of the trade-marked goods, unless it is established that such use seriously damages the reputation of the trade mark.

50. In the context of the present case, the consequence of that decision is that it is contrary to Article 7 of the directive for the proprietor of the BMW mark to prohibit the use of its mark by another person for the purpose of informing the public that he has specialised or is a specialist in the sale of second-hand BMW cars, provided that the advertising concerns cars which have been put on the Community market under that mark by the proprietor or with its consent and that the way in which the mark is used in that advertising does not constitute a legitimate reason, within the meaning of Article 7(2), for the proprietor's opposition.

51. The fact that the trade mark is used in a reseller's advertising in such a way that it may give rise to the impression that there is a commercial connection between the reseller and the trade mark proprietor, and in particular that the reseller's business is affiliated to the trade mark proprietor's distribution network or that there is a special relationship between the two undertakings, may constitute a legitimate reason within the meaning of Article 7(2) of the directive.

52. Such advertising is not essential to the further commercialisation of goods put on the Community market under the trade mark by its proprietor or with his consent or, therefore, to the purpose of the exhaustion rule laid down in Article 7 of the directive. Moreover, it is contrary to the obligation to act fairly in relation to the legitimate interests of the trade mark owner and it affects the value of the trade mark by taking unfair advantage of its distinctive character or repute. It is also incompatible with the specific object of a trade mark which is, according to the case-law of the Court, to protect the proprietor against competitors wishing to take advantage of the status and reputation of the trade mark (*see, inter alia,* Case C-10/89 *HAG GF* [1990] ECR I-3711, "*HAG II*," paragraph 14).

53. If, on the other hand, there is no risk that the public will be led to believe that there is a commercial connection between the reseller and the trade mark proprietor, the mere fact that the reseller derives an advantage from using the trade mark in that advertisements for the sale of goods covered by the mark, which are in other respects honest and fair, lend an aura of quality to his own business does not constitute a legitimate reason within the meaning of Article 7(2) of the directive.

54. In that connection, it is sufficient to state that a reseller who sells second-hand BMW cars and who genuinely has specialised or is a specialist in the sale of those vehicles cannot in practice communicate such information to his customers without using the BMW mark. In consequence, such an informative use of the BMW mark is necessary to guarantee the right of resale under Article 7 of the directive and does not take unfair advantage of the distinctive character or repute of that trade mark.

55. Whether advertising may create the impression that there is a commercial connection between the reseller and the trade mark proprietor is a question of fact for the national court to decide in the light of the circumstances of each case.

THE ADVERTISEMENTS RELATING TO REPAIR AND MAINTENANCE OF BMW CARS

56. First, the Court finds that the rule concerning exhaustion of the rights conferred by a trade mark laid down in Article 7 of the directive is not applicable to the advertisements relating to repair and maintenance of BMW cars.

57. Article 7 is intended to reconcile the interests of trade-mark protection and those of free movement of goods within the Community by making the further commercialisation of a product bearing a trade mark possible and preventing opposition by the proprietor of the mark (*see*, to that effect, *Parfums Christian Dior*, paragraphs 37 and 38). Advertisements relating to car repair and maintenance do not affect further commercialisation of the goods in question.

58. None the less, so far as those advertisements are concerned, it is still necessary to consider whether use of the trade mark may be legitimate in the light of the rule laid down in Article 6(1)(c) of the directive, that the proprietor may not prohibit a third party from using the trade mark to indicate the intended purpose of a product or service, in particular as accessories or spare parts, provided that the use is necessary to indicate that purpose and is in accordance with honest practices in industrial or commercial matters.

59. In that regard, as the United Kingdom Government has observed, the use of the trade mark to inform the public that the advertiser repairs and maintains trade-marked goods must be held to constitute use indicating the intended purpose of the service within the meaning of Article 6(1)(c). Like the use of a trade mark intended to identify the vehicles which a non-original spare part will fit, the use in question is intended to identify the goods in respect of which the service is provided.

60. Furthermore, the use concerned must be held to be necessary to indicate the intended purpose of the service. It is sufficient to note, as the Advocate General did at point 54 of his Opinion, that if an independent trader carries out the maintenance and repair of BMW cars or is in fact a specialist in that field, that fact cannot in practice be communicated to his customers without using the BMW mark.

61. Lastly, the condition requiring use of the trade mark to be made in accordance with honest practices in industrial or commercial matters must be regarded as constituting in substance the expression of a duty to act fairly in relation to the legitimate interests of the trade mark owner, similar to that imposed on the reseller where he uses another's trade mark to advertise the resale of products covered by that mark.

62. Just like Article 7, Article 6 seeks to reconcile the fundamental interests of trade-mark protection with those of free movement of goods and freedom to provide services in the common market in such a way that trade mark rights are able to fulfil their essential role in the system of undistorted competition which the Treaty seeks to establish and maintain (*see*, in particular, *HAG II*, paragraph 13).

63. Consequently, for the reasons set out in paragraphs 51 to 54 of this judgment, which apply *mutatis mutandis*, the use of another's trade mark for the purpose of informing the public of the repair and maintenance of goods covered by that mark is authorised on the same conditions as those applying where the mark is used for the purpose of informing the public of the resale of goods covered by that mark.

64. In the light of the foregoing, the answer to be given to the fourth and fifth questions must be that Articles 5 to 7 of the directive do not entitle the proprietor of a trade mark to prohibit a third party from using the mark for the purpose of informing the public that he carries out the repair and maintenance of goods covered by that trade mark and put on the market under that mark by the proprietor or with his consent, or that he has specialised or is a specialist in the sale or the repair and maintenance of such goods, unless the mark is used in

a way that may create the impression that there is a commercial connection between the other undertaking and the trade mark proprietor, and in particular that the reseller's business is affiliated to the trade mark proprietor's distribution network or that there is a special relationship between the two undertakings. . . .

NOTES AND QUESTIONS

1. The Court of Justice of the European Union (ECJ) serves as guardian and ultimate interpreter of the Treaty on the Functioning of the European Union (TFEU) and subsidiary EU legislation. The courts of the EU member states ordinarily interpret and apply community legislation in litigation, but if the national courts are uncertain with respect to a proper interpretation, they may refer the matter to the ECJ. In the text case, the Supreme Court of the Netherlands (the "Hoge Raad") has referred the question of interpretation of the First Trade Marks Directive to the ECJ. When it renders its decision, the ECJ does not "direct" the national court, but rather provides an answer to the question that has been asked and relies on the national court to properly apply it in the case. This reflects the separation of EU and member state powers at the judicial level.

2. The ECJ has referred both to Article 7 of the Trade Marks Directive that provides for exhaustion of rights and Article 6 that addresses fair use. The two doctrines are closely related in that each places a limit on the scope of the rights of the trademark holder. Would BMW gain by exercising more control over downstream uses of its trademark? Who would lose?

3. Consider individuals who have purchased automobiles and wish to sell them by posting advertisements in newspapers or on the Internet. Is it feasible to sell a used car without referring to the manufacturer's trademark?

4. We examine the fair use of trademark in the context of an Internet domain name dispute, *infra* section V.B, *Pfizer Inc. v. Van Robichaux*.

2. National, Regional, and International Exhaustion

Trademark rights are typically granted by national (or regional) authorities. With the registration or acquisition of a trademark, the holder obtains a "bundle of rights" that it may exercise within the territory of the granting authority. When a good or service is first sold or marketed within the country, this exhausts the trademark right embodied in it. Yet, the same trademark holder may hold equivalent or "parallel" rights in many countries. The Coca-Cola Company, again for illustrative purposes, may hold trademark registrations for the Coca-Cola mark in virtually every country of the world.

A country may choose to recognize that exhaustion of a trademark occurs when a good or service is first sold or marketed outside (as well as within) its own borders. That is, the first sale or marketing under a "parallel" trademark anywhere in the world exhausts the intellectual property right holder's rights within that country. If exhaustion occurs when a good or service is first sold or marketed outside a country, the trademark holder within the country may not oppose importation on the basis of its mark. The importation of a good or service as to which exhaustion of a trademark has occurred abroad is commonly referred to as "parallel importation," and the goods and services subject to such trade are commonly referred to as "parallel imports." Since goods and services subject to exhaustion of IPRs (including trademarks) are exported as well as imported, the subject matter of trade in such goods is commonly referred to as "parallel trade."

As a matter of terminology, when a trademark holder's right to control movement of a good or service is only extinguished by the first sale or marketing of a good or service within the territory of a country, that country recognizes a doctrine of "national" trademark exhaustion. When a holder's right to control movement is extinguished when a good or service is first sold or marketed within a region, that region (and its member countries) recognize a doctrine of "regional" trademark exhaustion. When a trademark holder's right to control movement is extinguished when a good or service is first sold or marketed anywhere in the world, that country recognizes a doctrine of "international exhaustion" of trademark rights.

Trademark holder groups have long sought to shift the terminology of parallel trade so as to label parallel imports "gray market" goods. The implication is that such goods, while not "black market" or "illicit" goods, are somehow tainted. This campaign has enjoyed some success, and courts in the United States not infrequently refer to parallel imports as the "gray market." But there is nothing illegal or illicit in parallel trade. It provides significant benefits to consumers in the form of enhanced price competition, and parallel imports are commonly purchased by the largest retail stores in the United States. We do not adopt the "gray market" terminology here.

Countries need not, and often do not, adopt the same exhaustion rule across the spectrum of IPRs.[1] The United States, for example, follows a rule of international exhaustion among commonly controlled enterprises in trademarks (*see K mart v. Cartier, infra*), a rule of national exhaustion with respect to patents (*see Jazz Photo, supra* Chapter 2), and has yet to make a definitive determination with respect to copyright (*see Quality King v. L'Anza, infra* Chapter 4. The U.S. Supreme Court had the occasion, but did not substantively re-address the issue in *Costco v. Omega,* also discussed *infra,* as it affirmed the Court of Appeals for the Ninth Circuit based on a 4-4 split among the Justices). Switzerland follows a rule of international exhaustion for copyright[2] and trademark,[3] but national exhaustion with respect to patent.[4] The European Union appears to follow a rule of regional exhaustion for copyright, patent, and trademark.[5] Consider that the preponderance of goods traded in world commerce is identified by a trademark. Far fewer goods are patented. All other things being equal, a rule that permits the segregation of national markets

1. *See generally* Frederick M. Abbott, First Report (Final) to the International Trade Law Committee of the International Law Association on the Subject of Parallel Importation (June 1997), 1 J. INT'L ECON. L. 607 (1998) (Oxford Univ. Press); Frederick M. Abbott, Second Report (Final) to the Committee on International Trade Law of the International Law Association on the Subject of the Exhaustion of Intellectual Property Rights and Parallel Importation, presented in London, July 2000, at the 69th Conference of the International Law Association, rev. 1.1.

2. *Chanel SA, Geneva and Chanel SA, Glarus v. EPA SA,* BGE 122 II 469, Oct. 23, 1996.

3. *Imprafot AG v. Nintendo Co. et al.*, Swiss Federal Supreme Court, No. 4C.45/1998/zus, July 20, 1998.

4. *Kodak SA v. Jumbo-Markt AG,* 4C.24/1999/rnd, Dec. 7, 1999.

5. *See Silhouette, infra,* regarding trademarks, and First and Second Reports, *supra,* regarding copyright and patent.

(i.e., national exhaustion) *may* have a broader impact on world trade if it applies to trademarked goods than if it is limited to patented goods.[6]

We examine the question of national, regional, and international exhaustion of trademark rights in some detail later in this chapter.

3. Term of Protection

There is no inherent limit on the term of protection for a trademark or service mark. A mark will remain valid for so long as it is used to identify goods or services in commerce, and provided that the mark does not lose its distinctive character. Trademark registration authorities typically require that registrations be renewed on a periodic basis, and the TRIPS Agreement (Art. 18) has set a minimum term of seven years for such renewals (as well as for the initial term of registration).

C. Trade Names

A trade name is also an identifier. While a trademark identifies a good or service of an enterprise, the trade name identifies the enterprise itself. It is not uncommon for an enterprise to use the same trade name and trademark. As a well-known example, IBM is the trade name of a multinational enterprise, and it is also the trademark that this enterprise uses to identify its products and services. There is, however, no necessary link between a trade name and trademark. The name "Emily's Flower Shop" may serve as the identifier of a business, without also serving as the identifier of products or services of that business.

Article 8 of the Paris Convention on the Protection of Industrial Property establishes a general obligation for the protection of trade names, and specifies that such protection should be granted "without the obligation of filing or registration, whether or not it forms part of a trademark." The WTO Appellate Body has interpreted the subject matter "intellectual property" as used in the TRIPS Agreement to include trade names because Article 8 of the Paris Convention is incorporated by reference in the TRIPS Agreement. See discussion in *U.S.-Havana Club, infra* pages 386-93.

Holders of registered trademarks typically enjoy exclusive rights within a national or regional territory. The proprietors of trade names may enjoy more limited protection, confined even to a single town or part of a town. The owner of a local restaurant or cafe, for example, may be able to prevent a newcomer from using the same trade name in the same town. That restaurant or cafe owner may not be able to prevent a competitor from using the same trade name in a nearby town. This depends on principles of unfair competition law generally used to protect trade names.

D. Domain Names

In recent years the "domain name" has taken its place alongside the trademark, service mark, and trade name as an important identifier for enterprises and their

---

6. Patented goods may, on average, be more expensive than trademarked goods, so the extrapolation regarding overall impact on world trade would be complicated. Data collection by government authorities with respect to parallel trade is inadequate to permit an empirical assessment of this issue.

products and services. A domain name is a human-friendly identifier of a location on the Internet,[7] and is composed of a registrant-specific term, followed by
period or "dot" and a "generic Top Level Domain" (gTLD) (e.g., amazon.com).

Domain names are used to identify all manner of web sites on the Internet.
Some of those web sites are commercially oriented. Many are not. From a
business standpoint, the ability to establish an easily recognizable location on
the Internet may have a very high commercial value. If a well-known trademark
or service mark is incorporated in a domain name, this virtually assures a high
volume of Internet traffic at the associated web site. A web site such as cnn.com
may receive millions of visits every day. Yet, this propensity of trademarks and
service marks to attract Internet users also offers an opportunity for third
parties to take advantage of the commercial draw for their own benefit. If a
person other than the trademark holder is successful in registering the same or
a confusingly similar domain name, that third party may divert Internet traffic
to its own web site, which may offer competing products, pornographic
material, or other information not sponsored by or affiliated with the mark
holder. Sometimes the successful third-party registrant of a mark in a domain
name will attempt to sell it to the trademark holder.

Yet, determining who is entitled to use a particular term in a domain name
may be a complex matter. There are legitimate ways marks may be used without
the consent of their holders in domain names, such as under "fair use" doctrine.
A trademark may be identical to an individual's name, and individuals are
generally allowed to use their own names in domain names, though this
right is not unqualified.[8]

A domain name may identify a business enterprise without identifying a
product or service in a trademark sense. In such cases, the domain name
may perform a function much like that of a trade name.

The domain name may share characteristics of the trademark, service mark,
and trade name, but it is a different form of identifier used in its own unique
environment. The law surrounding the use and protection of domain names is
explored in section V of this chapter.

E.   Geographical Indications

A geographical indication is the name of a territory that conveys an attribute of
a product or the goodwill of producers of that place. The right to use a geographical indication is typically shared by a community of producers. An
example of a geographical indication is "Champagne." That term refers to a
region of France where quality sparkling wines are produced, and is used by
wine makers of that region to identify their product. By virtue of long usage of
the term "Champagne" by regional producers exercising control over production, consumers have come to associate the geographical name "Champagne"
with certain qualities, and the term embodies the "goodwill" of its producers.

The right to use a geographical indication does not depend on objectively
demonstrating a particular level of quality or characteristics of a product.

---

7. The domain name is associated with an Internet Protocol (IP) number that identifies the
location of a particular address typically including a host computer (or server) and a sub-location
on that host.
8. Individuals with names that are identical to trademarks may be prevented from taking
unfair commercial advantage of that fact.

Although consumers or experts might (or might not) be able to objectively distinguish between "Champagne" made by wine producers in France and "Sekt" made by wine producers in Germany (using the same bottle-fermenting process), legal reliance on such objective differentiation may not be feasible. Although Champagne might (or might not) have different characteristics than Sekt, it is not necessarily those characteristics that are protected by the geographical indication. Also protected is the goodwill or reputation of wine producers in the Champagne region built up over a long period of time.

In *Wineworths Group Ltd. v. Comite Interprofessionel du Vin de Champagne*, 2 NZLR 327 [1991] (*Wineworths v. CIVC*),[9] decided by the New Zealand Court of Appeal, an importer of Australian sparkling wines was sued by a French semi-official protective body for misuse of the term "Champagne" in connection with its marketing and sales activities. In finding for the French complainant, the court held that the name "Champagne" had acquired distinctiveness among New Zealand consumers as associating a particular product with certain qualities, and that the producers of the "Champagne" region of France had acquired legally protectable goodwill in that name. Judge J. Gault stated:

> "Champagne is a geographical name. When used in relation to wine the primary significance it would convey to persons who know that would be as the geographical origin of the product. If the name conveys something of the characteristics of the wine it is because those familiar with wine sold by reference to the name associate those characteristics with it. . . . For suppliers the attracting force in the name constitutes a part of the goodwill of their business. That will be so whether the name is associated solely with one supplier or with a class of suppliers who stand in the same position to the name. The goodwill may be enjoyed among the whole population or among a particular market segment.
>
> That goodwill will be damaged if someone else uses the name in relation to a product in such a manner as to deceive purchasers into believing the product has the characteristics of products normally associated with the name when it does not. The damage may give rise to a claim for 'passing off' although deceptive trading would be a more accurate designation." (2 NZLR 327, 336)

Geographical indications are protected in different ways. Many countries protect them under unfair competition law, essentially prohibiting their use by persons not appropriately connected with the subject region. Other countries provide for the registration and protection of geographical indications, as such, and may include administrative systems for their regulation. Still, other countries treat geographical indications as trademarks, including collective and certification marks.

Because the geographical indication is associated with a territory and may be used only by those with sufficient connection to the territory, it may not be licensed, assigned, or transferred in the sense of most other IPRs. The extent to which elements of the production process relating to the GI-protected good may be carried on outside the territory identified by the GI is not well settled.

The TRIPS Agreement established the first multilateral set of rules specifically directed to geographical indications, though this set of rules largely relied on the unfair competition provisions of the Paris Convention, and added a few enumerated requirements in respect to wines and spirits. The TRIPS

---

9. This discussion and reference is taken from *Her Majesty the Queen, in right of her Government in New Zealand v. iSMER*, WIPO Case No. DBIZ2002-00270, decided October 2, 2002.

Agreement mandated future negotiations on geographical indications. These negotiations are discussed later in this section.

The geographical indication is an identifier and, like the trademark and trade name, is capable of conferring exclusive rights for so long as the conditions that give rise to its protection endure.

The geographical indication as a form of intellectual property is distinguished from a "mark of origin" (sometimes referred to as an "indication of source") that is typically required to be placed on goods in international trade to allow customs and other regulatory authorities to identify the place where a product is made. The marking "made in China" allows customs authorities in the United States to determine the appropriate tariff applicable to goods that originate in China. This marking might be used to determine whether goods are subject to antidumping duties. As a matter of international trade law, it is unlawful to misdescribe the country of origin of goods because this practice may impede the application of various regulatory controls. The Paris Convention (Article 10) requires that governments provide for the seizure of goods bearing false indications of source, including country of origin markings, upon importation, and provides that producers from the falsely attributed territory should have the right to initiate actions for seizure.

The scope of protection to be extended to products associated with a geographical region is controversial. The European Union accords extensive subject matter protection, including to traditional agricultural products. In the following case, the ECJ decides on the extent of protection accorded to producers of ham in the Parma region of Italy.

CONSORZIO DEL PROSCIUTTO DI PARMA

Judgment of the Court
20 May 2003

(Protected designations of origin — Regulation (EEC) No 2081/92 —
Regulation (EC) No 1107/96 — Prosciutto di Parma — Specification —
Requirement for ham to be sliced and packaged in the region
of production — Articles 29 EC and 30 EC — Justification —
Whether requirement may be relied on against third parties —
Legal certainty — Publicity)

In Case C-108/01,
REFERENCE to the Court under Article 234 EC by the House of Lords (United Kingdom) for a preliminary ruling in the proceedings pending before that court between

Consorzio del Prosciutto di Parma,
Salumificio S. Rita SpA
And
Asda Stores Ltd,
Hygrade Foods Ltd,

on the interpretation of Council Regulation (EEC) No 2081/92 of 14 July 1992 on the protection of geographical indications and designations of origin for agricultural products and foodstuffs (OJ 1992 L 208, p. 1), as amended . . . , and of Commission Regulation (EC) No 1107/96 of 12 June 1996 on the registration of geographical indications and designations of origin under the procedure laid down in Article 17 of Regulation No 2081/92 (OJ 1996 L 148, p. 1),

THE COURT,
composed of: G.C. Rodríguez Iglesias, President, J.-P. Puissochet, M. Wathelet, R. Schintgen and C.W.A. Timmermans (Presidents of Chambers), C. Gulmann (Rapporteur), D.A.O. Edward, P. Jann, V. Skouris, F. Macken, N. Colneric, S. von Bahr and J.N. Cunha Rodrigues, Judges, gives the following:

Judgment . . .

The Main Proceedings

22. Asda operates a chain of supermarkets in the United Kingdom. It sells among other things ham bearing the description Parma ham, purchased pre-sliced from Hygrade, which itself purchases the ham boned but not sliced from an Italian producer who is a member of the Consorzio. The ham is sliced and hermetically sealed by Hygrade in packets each containing five slices.

23. The packets bear the wording ASDA A taste of Italy PARMA HAM Genuine Italian Parma Ham.

24. The back of the packets states PARMA HAM All authentic Asda continental meats are made by traditional methods to guarantee their authentic flavour and quality and Produced in Italy, packed in the UK for Asda Stores Limited.

25. On 14 November 1997 the Consorzio brought proceedings by writ in the United Kingdom against Asda and Hygrade seeking various injunctions against them, essentially requiring them to cease their activities, on the ground that they were contrary to the rules applicable to Parma ham.

26. On 17 November 1997 it issued a notice of motion seeking the injunctions claimed in its writ and statement of claim.

27. Asda and Hygrade opposed the applications, arguing in particular that Regulation No 2081/92 and/or Regulation No 1107/96 did not confer on the Consorzio the rights it alleged.

28. The applications were dismissed.

29. The Consorzio appealed to the Court of Appeal (England and Wales). Salumificio was granted leave to intervene in the proceedings. The appeal was dismissed on 1 December 1998.

30. The Consorzio and Salumificio thereupon appealed to the House of Lords.

31. Since the House of Lords considered that the outcome of the case depended on the interpretation of Regulation No 2081/92 and Regulation No 1107/96, it decided to stay the proceedings and refer the following question to the Court for a preliminary ruling:

As a matter of Community law, does Council Regulation (EEC) No 2081/92 read with Commission Regulation (EC) No 1107/96 and the specification for the PDO [protected designation of origin] Prosciutto di Parma create a valid Community right, directly enforceable in the court of a Member State, to restrain the retail sale as Parma ham of sliced and packaged ham derived from hams duly exported from Parma in compliance with the conditions of the PDO but which have not been thereafter sliced, packaged and labelled in accordance with the specification? . . .

Whether the use of a PDO may be subjected to a condition that operations such as the slicing and packaging of the product be carried out in the region of production

50. It must [first] be concluded that Regulation No 2081/92 must be interpreted as not precluding the use of a PDO from being subject to the condition that operations such as the slicing and packaging of the product take place in the region of production, where such a condition is laid down in the specification.

Whether the condition for the PDO Prosciutto di Parma that the product must be sliced and packaged in the region of production constitutes a measure having equivalent effect to a quantitative restriction on exports. . . .

59. . . . [W]here the use of the PDO Prosciutto di Parma for ham marketed in slices is made subject to the condition that slicing and packaging operations be carried out in the region of production, this constitutes a measure having equivalent effect to a quantitative restriction on exports within the meaning of Article 29 EC.

Whether the condition that the product is sliced and packaged in the region of production is justified . . .

62. It should be noted that, in accordance with Article 30 EC, Article 29 EC does not preclude prohibitions or restrictions on exports which are justified *inter alia* on grounds of the protection of industrial and commercial property.

63. Community legislation displays a general tendency to enhance the quality of products within the framework of the common agricultural policy, in order to promote the reputation of those products through *inter alia* the use of designations of origin which enjoy special protection (*see Belgium* v *Spain*, paragraph 53). That tendency took the form in the quality wines sector of the adoption of Council Regulation (EEC) No 823/87 of 16 March 1987 laying down special provisions relating to quality wines produced in specified regions (OJ 1987 L 84, p. 59), repealed and replaced by Council Regulation (EC) No 1493/1999 of 17 May 1999 on the common organisation of the market in wine (OJ 1999 L 179, p. 1). It was also manifested, in relation to other agricultural products, in the adoption of Regulation No 2081/92, which, according to its preamble, is intended *inter alia* to meet consumers' expectations as regards products of quality and an identifiable geographical origin and to enable producers, in conditions of fair competition, to secure higher incomes in return for a genuine effort to improve quality.

64. Designations of origin fall within the scope of industrial and commercial property rights. The applicable rules protect those entitled to use them against improper use of those designations by third parties seeking to profit from the reputation which they have acquired. They are intended to guarantee that the product bearing them comes from a specified geographical area and displays

certain particular characteristics. They may enjoy a high reputation amongst consumers and constitute for producers who fulfil the conditions for using them an essential means of attracting customers. The reputation of designations of origin depends on their image in the minds of consumers. That image in turn depends essentially on particular characteristics and more generally on the quality of the product. It is on the latter, ultimately, that the product's reputation is based (*see Belgium* v *Spain,* paragraphs 54 to 56). For consumers, the link between the reputation of the producers and the quality of the products also depends on his being assured that products sold under the designation of origin are authentic.

65. The specification of the PDO Prosciutto di Parma, by requiring the slicing and packaging to be carried out in the region of production, is intended to allow the persons entitled to use the PDO to keep under their control one of the ways in which the product appears on the market. The condition it lays down aims better to safeguard the quality and authenticity of the product, and consequently the reputation of the PDO, for which those who are entitled to use it assume full and collective responsibility.

66. Against that background, a condition such as at issue must be regarded as compatible with Community law despite its restrictive effects on trade if it is shown that it is necessary and proportionate and capable of upholding the reputation of the PDO Prosciutto di Parma (*see,* to that effect, *Belgium* v *Spain,* paragraphs 58 and 59).

67. Parma ham is consumed mainly in slices and the operations leading to that presentation are all designed to obtain in particular a specific flavour, colour and texture which will be appreciated by consumers.

68. The slicing and packaging of the ham thus constitute important operations which may harm the quality and hence the reputation of the PDO if they are carried out in conditions that result in a product not possessing the organoleptic qualities expected. Those operations may also compromise the guarantee of the product's authenticity, because they necessarily involve removal of the mark of origin of the whole hams used.

69. By the rules it lays down and the requirements of the national provisions to which it refers, the specification of the PDO Prosciutto di Parma establishes a set of detailed and strict rules regulating the three stages which lead to the placing on the market of prepackaged sliced ham. The first stage consists of boning the ham, making bricks, and refrigerating and freezing them for slicing. The second stage corresponds to the slicing operations. The third stage is the packaging of the sliced ham, under vacuum or protected atmosphere. . . .

75. In this context, it must be accepted that checks performed outside the region of production would provide fewer guarantees of the quality and authenticity of the product than checks carried out in the region of production in accordance with the procedure laid down in the specification (*see,* to that effect, *Belgium* v *Spain,* paragraph 67). First, checks performed in accordance with that procedure are thorough and systematic in nature and are done by experts who have specialised knowledge of the characteristics of Parma ham. Second, it is hardly conceivable that representatives of the persons entitled to use the PDO could effectively introduce such checks in other Member States.

76. The risk to the quality and authenticity of the product finally offered to consumers is consequently greater where it has been sliced and packaged

outside the region of production than when that has been done within the region (*see,* to that effect, *Belgium* v *Spain,* paragraph 74).

77. That conclusion is not affected by the fact, pointed out in the present case, that the ham may be sliced, at least under certain conditions, by retailers and restaurateurs outside the region of production. That operation must in principle be performed in front of the consumer, or at least the consumer can require that it is, in order to verify in particular that the ham used bears the mark of origin. Above all, slicing and packaging operations carried out upstream of the retail sale or restaurant stage constitute, because of the quantities of products concerned, a much more real risk to the reputation of a PDO, where there is inadequate control of the authenticity and quality of the product, than operations carried out by retailers and restaurateurs.

78. Consequently, the condition of slicing and packaging in the region of production, whose aim is to preserve the reputation of Parma ham by strengthening control over its particular characteristics and its quality, may be regarded as justified as a measure protecting the PDO which may be used by all the operators concerned and is of decisive importance to them (*see,* to that effect, *Belgium* v *Spain,* paragraph 75).

79. The resulting restriction may be regarded as necessary for attaining the objective pursued, in that there are no alternative less restrictive measures capable of attaining it.

80. The PDO Prosciutto di Parma would not receive comparable protection from an obligation imposed on operators established outside the region of production to inform consumers, by means of appropriate labelling, that the slicing and packaging has taken place outside that region. Any deterioration in the quality or authenticity of ham sliced and packaged outside the region of production, resulting from materialisation of the risks associated with slicing and packaging, might harm the reputation of all ham marketed under the PDO Prosciutto di Parma, including that sliced and packaged in the region of production under the control of the group of producers entitled to use the PDO (*see,* to that effect, *Belgium* v *Spain,* paragraphs 76 and 77).

81. Accordingly, the fact that the use of the PDO Prosciutto di Parma for ham marketed in slices is conditional on the slicing and packaging operations being carried out in the region of production may be regarded as justified, and hence compatible with Article 29 EC. . . .

NOTES AND QUESTIONS

1. The ECJ decision permits meatpackers in Italy to exercise "downstream" control over the way their product is distributed. Do you think this control is justified to protect the "integrity" of Parma ham? As an EU consumer, are you willing to pay a higher price for this type of ham because Italian meatpackers have sliced it?

2. The Parma ham decision may help illuminate why U.S. farmers and the food services industry are reluctant to extend the scope of protection for geographical indications. It may affect not only primary producers, but also food processors and marketers. *See also Federal Republic of Germany and Kingdom of Denmark v. Commission,* joined cases, C-465/02 and C-466/02, Oct. 2005, regarding protection of "feta" for a type of cheese.

GEOGRAPHICAL INDICATIONS
AT THE HONG KONG MINISTERIAL

Frederick M. Abbott*

1. Negotiations on geographical indications in the TRIPS Council illustrate the basic fact that intellectual property rights are instruments of industrial policy and that states express preferences not based on moral philosophy, but rather on whether they believe their national interests are maximized by granting or denying rights. Their expressed interests tend to be defined by larger producers who have the financial resources to make demands on the political process. . . .

4. WTO members each have offensive and defensive interests with respect to GIs and these interests vary along a spectrum. The fault line between offensive and defensive interests is sometimes characterized as "Old World" versus "New World," although it might also be characterized along efficiencies of agricultural production, marketing and franchising.

5. The EU and Swiss are the core demandeurs for more extensive GIs protection because they have historical designations applicable to their agricultural production and have heavily subsidized farm sectors designed to protect cultural institutions; that is, smaller business operators in agriculture. The EU has recently made its demands explicit, i.e., it will not complete a deal on the removal of agricultural subsidies and market protection without a deal on GIs (*see* Making Hong Kong a Success: Europe's Contribution—Brussels, 28 October 2005). Why, because a high-cost producer will be competitive with consumers if brands are sufficiently attractive to outweigh price differentials. So, the EU is seeking an extended system of GI registration for wines and spirits and agricultural products that will effectively operate as a worldwide grant of rights in a name or symbol, subject to challenge by other members or ultimately in national courts (based on challenging of presumptions). The EU has also proposed a claw back to recover certain designations that may have fallen into generic or commonly descriptive names, or even been trademarked by third parties elsewhere (although some of the details of this are not yet clear). In light of the EU's recent moves to criminalize IP violations, including patent infringement, I expect the EU also to demand criminal penalties for infringing geographical indications.

6. The US and the Cairns group of agricultural producers have opposed the EU plan for a variety of reasons. For example, US agribusiness and foodservice industries do not want to be encumbered with litigation over rights to names. They have fears that the EU will seek to prevent use of designations already in common use in the United States and worldwide; and businesses are very uncertain about the extent to which claims might be advanced. To illustrate:

The classic accepted GI is "Champagne" for a region in France producing quality sparkling wines made through a specific fermentation method. There was significant litigation within the EU over the recapture, i.e. a claw back, of this name involving German Sekt producers who had referred, at the least, to using the "Champagne-method" of production. There were substantial costs of litigation and transition. But you can readily go beyond limited areas of

---

* Presented at WTO Hong Kong Ministerial, ICSTD Session on Recovering Multilateralism in IP Policy Making: Can the WTO Deliver?, Dec. 15, 2005.

geographical production, such as for "Parma" ham and French Champagne. Does Italy have a claim to Italian-style breadcrumbs? Does Switzerland have a claim to Swiss cheese? Does someone hold a claim to French roast coffee? Does a region of Italy have a claim to chicken Parmesan as a style of cooked meal? What would happen to Subway's new Parmesan Chicken Sandwich? The possibilities are virtually endless, and while we can have a technical discussion about how realistic the protection of the foregoing designations might be, US agribusiness and the foodservice industries are quite worried about what they don't know.

It is both a question of a known list of demands and concerns about just how far claims might be extended and what they would mean for US farm exports, grocery store shelf space and the foodservice business that is causing industry reaction.

Nonetheless, it is important to be aware that the US has in place a sophisticated registration system for the names of wines and spirits, including geographic designations, and that in this area the establishment of an enforceable multilateral register would not be such a stretch for the United States.

7. In a relatively simple economic calculation we can say that the EU interests in GIs are primarily offense, and the US interest primarily defensive, but there are US agricultural businesses which would welcome more protection such as the producers of Idaho potatoes and Washington apples.

8. For developing countries the picture is similar. Some developing countries have what they perceive as relatively strong offensive interests. Some in wine, some in teas and spices, some in rice varieties, some in spirit drinks. For most countries, the calculation is not easily made: but like the US, the large efficient agricultural producers like Argentina and Brazil oppose extension. The producers with major export markets in specific products, including smaller producing countries, occupy a movable middle ground.

9. For developing countries there is a factor that is less significant for the EU and the United States; and that is what the regulatory costs will be both on the offense and defensive sides. The creation of legal rights or interests — even if filing fees are reduced by a multilateral registration system — still require enforcement, which is predominantly under TRIPS a private matter. Considerable care must be taken not to conflate a system which theoretically allows protection in foreign markets and the costs of litigation in these foreign markets. There may be a tendency to overvalue the offensive interests and minimize the defensive costs. . . .

10. Because the picture is mixed, there is at present a stalemate. The United States will only move if the food — agriculture and food services — industries are willing to move, and this is not yet prepared. But over some period of time an accommodation a system meeting the EU part way could be worked out. If the EU makes GIs the sine qua non of agricultural reform, developing countries are put in a very serious posture of attempting to calculate the gains from expanded access to the EU market and reduction of damaging EU subsidies, versus the cost of giving EU agricultural products special protection in the market. This is a very difficult equation to solve. The US presumably will protect against a truly terrible deal.

11. I should also mention a paradox of GIs protection, which is that excessive reliance on branding may ultimately harm an industry, a case in point being the French wine industry. Here you have seen application of rigorous standards

defining production methods coupled with branding reliance and high prices. Consumers around the world have rejected this combination in favor of wines made by producers in Australia, Chile and elsewhere sold in supermarkets at substantially lower prices. Ultimately consumers, if given a choice, may not be willing to maintain or shift preferences to inefficiently produced agricultural products, regardless of the name placed on them. In other words, the EU may also be overrelying on GIs protection.

12. What will happen in Hong Kong in GIs depends on what happens of agriculture, which is not a significant revelation. If the EU does not make a major concession of agriculture, neither the US nor the Cairns group will be under pressure to make a move on GIs extension. Even with a move by the EU, it is not clear that the US will be forthcoming since it is not clear that the position of US domestic industry has yet shifted. . . .

NOTES AND QUESTIONS

1. The TRIPS Agreement includes, as part of its built-in agenda, negotiations toward the establishment of a multilateral register for geographical indications for wines and spirits for members participating in the system.[10] These negotiations have been going on for some time. At the Hong Kong Ministerial, WTO Members "agree[d] to intensify these negotiations in order to complete them within the overall time-frame for the conclusion of the negotiations that were foreseen in the Doha Ministerial Declaration."[11] There is also reference in Article 24.1 of the TRIPS Agreement to the possibility of further negotiation on specific indications following the Uruguay Round, but whether this refers to extension to products beyond wines and spirits is the subject of debate in the TRIPS Council. As with the relationship between the TRIPS Agreement and CBD, in Hong Kong, Members agreed that the Director-General should intensify negotiations on the subject and report to the General Council "no later than 31 July 2006." As of January 2011, while a substantial number of developing countries have moved to generally support the EU position on the extension of GIs protection, there had been no significant movement toward agreement at the WTO on the subject of geographical indications. The Director-General at the Geneva March 2010 stock-taking of the Doha Round reported only that "while my consultations have not created convergence they have certainly shed clearer light on the divergences."[12]

2. While the geographical connection of some products is fairly well defined, this does not hold true in many cases. Thus, the introduction of additional layers of protection for geographical indications would almost certainly lead to controversies among important producing regions. Some of those conflicts would involve different developing countries with strong interests in geographic names.

---

10. Article 23.4, TRIPS Agreement.

11. Hong Kong Ministerial Declaration, at para. 29.

12. WTO: 2010 News Items, 22 March 2010, Trade Negotiations Committee, Lamy opens stocktaking week with hope for strong signal on concluding the Round, available at http://www.wto.org/english/news_e/news10_e/tnc_dg_stat_22mar10_e.htm.

3. There is also a question regarding the extent to which "country names" are protectable as intellectual property. New Zealand, for example, unsuccessfully claimed common law trademark rights in its country name "as such" in two domain name disputes (*see Her Majesty the Queen, in right of her Government in New Zealand v. iSMER*, WIPO Case No. DBIZ2002-00270, decided Oct. 2, 2002[13] and *Her Majesty the Queen, in right of her Government in New Zealand, as Trustee for the Citizens, Organizations and State of New Zealand, acting by and through the Honourable Jim Sutton, the Associate Minister of Foreign Affairs and Trade v. Virtual Countries, Inc*, Case No. D2002-0754, decided Nov. 27, 2002). Yet, while country names may not be trademarks "as such," there is interest among many governments in establishing some form of recognition of rights in country names beyond a right to protect against false attribution.

4. One controversial issue under the TRIPS Agreement is whether there is a hierarchy or priority between trademarks and geographical indications. In other words, what happens when a trademark and geographical indication appear to be in conflict? This issue was addressed in a WTO panel decision involving a dispute between United States and the European Union, *European Communities — Protection of Trademarks and Geographical Indications for Agricultural Products and Foodstuffs, Report of the Panel*, WT/DS174/R, 15 Mar. 2005, presented *infra*.

II. TRADEMARKS AT THE MULTILATERAL LEVEL

A. Introduction

The evolution of the multilateral system for the protection of trademarks has been substantially less controversial than the evolution of the system with respect to patents. Virtually all countries have recognized the basic economic and social value of allowing producers and suppliers of services to identify their output with distinctive markings. Trademarks enable consumers to make efficient and informed decisions about what they are buying. They encourage producers to invest in quality as repeat purchasing is facilitated. This is not to suggest the absence of economic and social issues as trademark holders seek to extend the scope of exclusive rights embodied in marks. It is only to suggest that there are good reasons why trademarks are not the subject of the same level of policy concern as patents, and why the evolution of multilateral protection has run more smoothly.

Two recent trends in the evolution of multilateral trademark rules include (1) increased attention to protection for "well known" trademarks and (2) more permissive rules concerning the licensing and transfer of marks (as the trademark itself has turned into a marketable commodity). Of course, the proliferation of

---

13. This decision was rendered under the .biz sunrise procedure (a process under which domain name applications within a new gTLD are subject to pre-registration challenge), and while New Zealand did not succeed on the trademark issue, it was awarded the domain name because it had some legitimate interest in it, which the respondent lacked (and conceded).

the Internet and e-commerce has raised a host of new questions regarding the role of distinctive marks in this fluid environment.

B.   The Paris Convention and Trademarks

Multilateral rules for the protection of trademarks were adopted in the Paris Convention of 1883 along with rules for the protection of patents and industrial designs. As newspapers, magazines, and the word of mouth of travelers made consumers aware of the reputation of foreign products, it became increasingly important to consumers and producers that trademarks associated with products be genuine. This objective could be achieved by granting producers the opportunity to locally register and protect their trademarks. The Paris Convention incorporated provisions on national treatment, right of priority, and independence of trademarks similar to the provisions with regard to patents. We begin with a WIPO introduction to the provisions of the Paris Convention regarding trademarks.

THE PARIS CONVENTION FOR THE PROTECTION OF INDUSTRIAL PROPERTY
WIPO Intellectual Property Handbook, Chapter 5

PRINCIPAL PROVISIONS

[See the Paris Convention introduction in Chapter 2 for a description of general provisions, including national treatment. — EDS.]

THE RIGHT OF PRIORITY . . .

5.30 The length of the priority period is different according to the various kinds of industrial property rights. For . . . trademarks it is six months. . . .

PROVISIONS CONCERNING TRADEMARKS
Use of Trademarks

5.67 The Convention touches on the issue of the use of marks in Article 5C(1), (2) and (3).

5.68 Article 5C(1) relates to the compulsory use of registered trademarks. Some of the countries which provide for the registration of trademarks also require that the trademark, once registered, be used within a certain period. If this use is not complied with, the trademark may be expunged from the register. For this purpose, "use" is generally understood as meaning the sale of goods bearing the trademark, although national legislation may regulate more broadly the manner in which use of the trademark is to be complied with. The Article states that where compulsory use is required, the trademark's registration may be cancelled for failure to use the trademark only after a reasonable period has elapsed, and then only if the owner does not justify such failure.

5.69 The definition of what is meant by "reasonable period" is left to the national legislation of the countries concerned, or otherwise to the authorities competent for resolving such cases. This reasonable period is intended to give the owner of the mark enough time and opportunity to arrange for its proper use, considering that in many cases the owner has to use his mark in several countries.

5.70 The trademark owner's justification of non-use would be acceptable if it were based on legal or economic circumstances beyond the owner's control, for example if importation of the marked goods had been prohibited or delayed by governmental regulations.

5.71 The Convention also establishes in Article 5C(2) that the use of a trademark by its proprietor, in a form differing in elements which do not alter the distinctive character of the mark as it was when formerly registered in one of the countries of the Union, shall not entail invalidation of the registration nor diminish the protection granted to the mark. The purpose of this provision is to allow for unessential differences between the form of the mark as it is registered and the form in which it is used, for example in cases of adaptation or translation of certain elements for such use. This rule applies also to differences in the form of the mark as used in the country of its original registration.

5.72 Whether in a given case the differences between the mark as registered and the mark as actually used alter the distinctive character is a matter to be decided by the competent national authorities.

Concurrent Use of the Same Trademark by Different Enterprises

5.73 Article 5C(3) of the Convention deals with the case where the same mark is used for identical or similar goods by two or more establishments considered as co-proprietors of the trademark. It is provided that such concurrent use will not impede the registration of the trademark nor diminish the protection in any country of the Union, except where the said use results in misleading the public or is contrary to the public interest. Such cases could occur if the concurrent use misleads the public as to the origin or source of the goods sold under the same trademark, or if the quality of such goods differs to the point where it may be contrary to the public interest to allow the continuation of such use.

5.74 This provision does not, however, cover the case of concurrent use of the mark by enterprises which are not co-proprietors of the mark, for instance when use is made concurrently by the owner and a licensee or a franchisee. These cases are left for the national legislation of the various countries to regulate.

Grace Period for the Payment of Renewal Fees

5.75 Article 5bis requires that a period of grace be allowed for the payment of fees due for the maintenance of industrial property rights. . . .

5.76 The countries of the Paris Union are obliged to accord a period of grace of at least six months for the payment of the renewal fees, but are free to provide for the payment of a surcharge when such renewal fees are paid within the period of grace. Moreover, the countries are free to provide for a period of grace longer than the minimum six months prescribed by the Convention.

5.77 During the period of grace, the registration remains provisionally in force. If the payment of the renewal fees (and surcharge where appropriate) is not made during the period of grace, the registration will lapse with retroactive effect to the original date of expiration.

Independence of Trademarks

5.78 Article 6 of the Convention establishes the important principle of the independence of trademarks in the different countries of the Union, and in particular the independence of trademarks filed or registered in the country of origin from those filed or registered in other countries of the Union.

5.79 The first part of Article 6 states the application of the basic principle of national treatment to the filing and registration of marks in the countries of the Union. Regardless of the origin of the mark whose registration is sought, a country of the Union may apply only its domestic legislation when determining the conditions for the filing and registration of the mark. The application of the principle of national treatment asserts the rule of independence of marks, since their registration and maintenance will depend only on each domestic law.

5.80 This Article also provides that an application for the registration of a mark, filed in any country of the Union by a person who is entitled to the benefits of the Convention, may not be refused, nor may a registration be canceled, on the ground that filing, registration or renewal of the mark has not been effected in the country of origin. This provision lays down the express rule that obtaining and maintaining a trademark registration in any country of the Union may not be made dependent on the application, registration or renewal of the same mark in the country of origin of the mark. Therefore no action with respect to the mark in the country of origin may be required as a prerequisite for obtaining a registration of the mark in that country.

5.81 Finally, Article 6 states that a mark duly registered in a country of the Union shall be regarded as independent of marks registered in the other countries of the Union, including the country of origin. This means that a mark once registered will not be automatically affected by any decision taken with respect to similar registrations for the same marks in other countries. In this respect, the fact that one or more such similar registrations are, for example, renounced, cancelled or abandoned will not, *eo ipso,* affect the registrations of the mark in other countries. The validity of these registrations will depend only on the provisions applicable in accordance with the legislation of each of the countries concerned.

Well-Known Trademarks

5.82 The Convention deals with well-known trademarks in Article 6*bis*. This Article obliges a member country to refuse or cancel the registration and to prohibit the use of a trademark that is liable to create confusion with another trademark already well known in that member country. The effect of this Article is to extend protection to a trademark that is well-known in a member country even though it is not registered or used in that country. The protection of the well-known trademark results not from its registration, which prevents the registration or use of a conflicting trademark, but from the mere fact of its reputation.

5.83 The protection of well-known trademarks is deemed justified on the grounds that a trademark that has acquired goodwill and a reputation in a member country ought to give rise to a right for its owner. The registration or use of a confusingly similar trademark would, in most cases, amount to an act of unfair competition and be prejudicial to the interests of the public, who would be misled by the use of a conflicting trademark for the same or identical goods than those in connection with which the well-known trademark is registered.

5.84 The trademark that is protected by Article 6*bis* must be a "well-known" trademark, as determined in a member country by its competent administrative or judicial authorities. A trademark may not have been used in a country, in the sense that goods bearing that trademark have not been sold there; yet that trademark may be well-known in the country because of publicity there or the repercussions in that country of advertising in other countries.

5.85 The protection of a well-known trademark under Article 6*bis* exists only where the conflicting trademark has been filed, registered or used for identical or similar goods, as determined by the administrative or judicial authorities of the country in which protection is claimed.

5.86 The protection of a well-known trademark under Article 6*bis* results from the obligation of a member country to take *ex officio*, where its legislation so permits, or at the request of an interested party, the following type of action:

— first, refusal of the application for registration of the conflicting trademark;
— second, cancellation of the registration of a conflicting trademark, allowing at least a period of five years from the date of registration within which a request for cancellation of the conflicting trademark may be made, unless that trademark was registered in bad faith, in which event no time limit may be fixed;
— third, prohibition of the use of the conflicting trademark, the request for which may be within a period of time prescribed by a member country; however, no time limit may be fixed for such a request in the case of a conflicting trademark used in bad faith.

State Emblems, Official Hallmarks and Emblems of International Organizations

5.87 The Convention deals with distinctive signs of States and international intergovernmental organizations in Article 6*ter.* . . .

Assignment of Trademarks

5.93 Article 6*quater* of the Convention deals with the assignment of trademarks. The rule of Article 6*quater* arises because of the situation where a trademark is used by an enterprise in various countries and it is desired to make a transfer of the right to the trademark in one or more of those countries.

5.94 Some national legislations allow an assignment without a simultaneous or corresponding transfer of the enterprise to which the trademark belongs. Others make the validity of the assignment depend on the simultaneous or corresponding transfer of the enterprise.

5.95 Article 6*quater* states that it shall suffice for the recognition of the validity of the assignment of a trademark in a member country, that the portion of the business or goodwill located in that country be transferred to the assignee, together with the exclusive right to manufacture in the said country, or to sell therein, the goods bearing the trademark assigned. Thus, a member country is free to require, for the validity of the assignment of the trademark, the simultaneous transfer of the enterprise to which the trademark belongs, but such a requirement must not extend to parts of the enterprise that are located in other countries.

5.96 It should be noted that Article 6*quater* leaves a member country free not to regard as valid the assignment of a trademark with the relevant part of the enterprise, if the use of that trademark by the assignee would be of such a nature as to mislead the public, particularly as regards important features of the goods to which the trademark is applied. This freedom may be exercised, for example, if a trademark is assigned for part only of the goods to which it is applied, and if those goods are similar to other goods for which the trademark is not assigned. In such cases, the public may be misled as to the origin or essential qualities of similar goods to which the assignor and assignee will apply the same trademark independently.

Protection of Trademarks Registered in One Country of the Union in Other Countries of the Union

5.97 Parallel to the principle of independence of marks which is embodied in the provisions of Article 6, the Convention establishes a special rule for the benefit of owners of trademarks registered in their country of origin. This exceptional rule is governed by Article 6*quinquies* of the Convention.

5.98 The provisions of Article 6*quinquies* come into operation in the case where a registration in the country of origin is invoked in the country where protection is sought. Whereas the principle of national treatment of applications calls for the normal rule of complete independence of trademarks (as recognized in Article 6), in the exceptional situation regulated by Article 6*quinquies* the opposite rule prevails, providing for extraterritorial effects of the registration in the country of origin.

5.99 There are two main reasons for this special rule. On the one hand, it is in the interest of both owners of trademarks and the public to have the *same* trademark apply to the *same* goods in various countries. On the other hand, there are some important differences in the domestic legislation of the member countries regarding the registration of trademarks. As a consequence, the differences in domestic legislation could prevent this uniform use of the same trademark.

5.100 In order to diminish the impact of those differences on the registration of trademarks in respect of goods in international trade, Article 6*quinquies* of the Paris Convention establishes certain effects where registration in the country of origin has taken place and is invoked in another member country where registration and protection is sought. This provision has the effect of bringing about a certain uniformity of the law of the various countries as to the concept of trademarks.

5.101 For Article 6*quinquies* to apply it is necessary that the trademark concerned should be duly registered in the country of origin. A mere filing or use of the trademark in that country is not sufficient. Moreover, the country of origin must be a country of the Union in which the applicant has a real and effective industrial or commercial establishment or, alternatively, in which he has his domicile, or otherwise, the country of the Union of which he is a national.

5.102 The rule established by Article 6*quinquies* provides that a trademark which fulfils the required conditions must be accepted for filing and protected—*as is* (to use the expression found in the English version) or *telle quelle* (to use the expression adopted in the original French text)—in the other member countries, subject to certain exceptions. This rule is often called the "telle quelle" principle.

5.103 It is to be noted that the rule only concerns the form of the trademark. In this respect, the rule in this Article does not affect the questions relating to the nature or the function of the trademarks as conceived in the countries where protection is sought. Thus a member country is not obliged to register and extend protection to subject matter that does not fall within the meaning of a trademark as defined in the law of that country. If, for example, under the law of a member country, a three-dimensional object or musical notes indicating tunes is not considered a trademark in that country, it is not obliged to accept that subject matter for registration and protection.

5.104 Article 6*quinquies*, Section B, contains certain exceptions to the obligation of accepting a registered trademark "as is" for registration in the other countries of the Union. That list of exceptions is exhaustive so that no other grounds may be invoked to refuse or invalidate the registration of the trademark. However, the list does not exclude any ground for refusal of protection for which there is a need in national legislation.

5.105 The first permitted ground for refusal or invalidation of a trademark exists where the trademark infringes rights of third parties acquired in the country where protection is claimed. These rights can be either rights in trademarks already protected in the country concerned or other rights, such as the right to a trade name or a copyright.

5.106 The second permitted ground for refusal or invalidation is when the trademark is devoid of distinctive character, or is purely descriptive, or consists of a generic name.

5.107 The third permissible ground for refusal or invalidation exists where the trademark is contrary to morality or public order, as considered in the country where protection is claimed. This ground includes, as a special category, trademarks which are of such a nature as to deceive the public.

5.108 A fourth permissible ground for refusal or invalidation exists if the registration of the trademark would constitute an act of unfair competition.

5.109 A fifth and last permissible ground for refusal or invalidation exists where the trademark is used by the owner in a form which is essentially different from that in which it has been registered in the country of origin. Unessential differences may not be used as grounds for refusal or invalidation.

Service Marks

5.110 A service mark is a sign used by enterprises offering services, for example, hotels, restaurants, airlines, tourist agencies, car-rental agencies, employment agencies, laundries and cleaners, etc., in order to distinguish their services from those of other enterprises. Thus service marks have the same function as trademarks, the only difference being that they apply to services instead of products or goods.

5.111 Article 6*sexies* was introduced into the Paris Convention in 1958 to deal specifically with service marks, but the revision Conference did not accept a more ambitious proposal to assimilate service marks to trademarks entirely. However, a member country is free to apply the same rules it applies for trademarks also to service marks in analogous situations or circumstances.

5.112 By virtue of Article 6*sexies*, member countries undertake to protect service marks, but are not required to provide for the registration of such marks. This provision does not oblige a member country to legislate expressly on the subject of service marks. A member country may comply with the provision not only by introducing special legislation for the protection of service marks, but also by granting such protection by other means, for example, in its laws against unfair competition.

Registration in the Name of the Agent Without the Proprietor's Authorization

5.113 Article 6*septies* of the Convention deals with the relationship between the owner of a trademark and his agent or representative regarding registration or use of the trademark by the latter. . . .

Nature of the Goods to Which a Trademark Is Applied

5.115 Article 7 of the Convention stipulates that the nature of the goods to which a trademark is to be applied shall in no case be an obstacle to the registration of the mark.

5.116 The purpose of this rule, and also the comparable rule in Article 4*quater* regarding patents for invention, is to make the protection of industrial property independent of the question whether goods in respect of which such protection would apply may or may not be sold in the country concerned.

5.117 It sometimes occurs that a trademark concerns goods which, for example, do not conform to the safety requirements of the law of a particular country. For instance, the food and drug laws of a country may prescribe requirements concerning the ingredients of a food product or the effects of a pharmaceutical product and allow its sale only after approval of the competent authorities, on the basis of an examination of the food product or of clinical trials as to the effect of the use of the pharmaceutical product on human beings or animals.

5.118 In all such cases, it would be unjust to refuse registration of a trademark concerning such goods. The safety or quality regulations may change and the product may be permitted for sale later on. In those cases where no such change is contemplated but the approval of the competent authorities of the country concerned is still pending, such approval, if imposed as a condition of filing or registration in that country, may be prejudicial to an applicant who wishes to make a timely filing for protection in another member country.

Collective Marks

5.119 A collective mark may be defined as a sign which serves to distinguish the geographical origin, material, mode of manufacture, quality or other common characteristics of goods or services of different enterprises that simultaneously use the collective mark under the control of its owner. The owner may be either an association of which those enterprises are members or any other entity, including a public body.

5.120 Article 7*bis* of the Convention deals with collective marks. It obliges a member country to accept for filing and to protect, in accordance with the particular conditions set by that country, collective marks belonging to "associations." These will generally be associations of producers, manufacturers, distributors, sellers or other merchants, of goods that are produced or manufactured in a certain country, region or locality or that have other common characteristics. Collective marks of States or other public bodies are not covered by the provision.

5.121 In order that Article 7*bis* be applicable, the existence of the association to which the collective mark belongs must not be contrary to the law of the country of origin. The association does not have to prove that it conforms to the legislation of its country of origin, but registration and protection of its collective mark may be refused if the existence of the association is found to be contrary to that legislation.

5.122 Refusal of registration and protection of the collective mark is not possible on the ground that the association is not established in the country where protection is sought, or is not constituted according to the law of that country. Article 7*bis* adds a further stipulation that the association may not even be required to possess an industrial or commercial establishment anywhere. In other words, an association, without possessing any industrial or commercial establishment itself, may be one that simply controls the use of a collective mark by others.

Trademarks Shown at International Exhibitions

5.123 The provision concerning marks shown at international exhibitions is contained in Article 11 of the Convention, which also applies to other titles of industrial property. . . .

PROVISIONS CONCERNING INDUSTRIAL DESIGNS, TRADE NAMES, APPELLATIONS
OF ORIGIN AND INDICATIONS OF SOURCE AND UNFAIR COMPETITION . . .

Trade Names

5.131 Trade names are dealt with by the Convention in Article 8. This Article states that trade names shall be protected in all the countries of the Union without the obligation of filing or of registration, whether or not they form part of a trademark.

5.132 The definition of a trade name for the purposes of protection, and the manner in which such protection is to be afforded, are both matters left to the national legislation of the countries concerned. Therefore, protection may result from special legislation on trade names or from more general legislation on unfair competition or the rights of personality.

5.133 In no case can protection be made conditional upon filing or registration of the trade name. However, if in a member country protection of trade names were dependent on the use of the name and to the extent that another trade name may cause confusion or prejudice with respect to the first trade name, such a requirement and criterion could be applied by that member country.

Appellations of Origin and Indications of Source

5.134 Appellations of origin and indications of source are included among the various objects of protection of industrial property under the Paris Convention (Article 1(2)).

5.135 Both these objects can be referred to under the broader concept of geographical indications, although traditionally, and for the purposes of certain special treaties (e.g., the Madrid Agreement for the Repression of False or Deceptive Indications of Source on Goods and the Lisbon Agreement for the Protection of Appellations of Origin and their International Registration), both concepts have been distinguished.

5.136 Indications of source include any name, designation, sign or other indication which refers to a given country or to a place located therein, which has the effect of conveying the notion that the goods bearing the indication originate in that country or place. Examples of indications of source are the names of countries (e.g., Germany, Japan, etc.) or of cities (e.g., Hong Kong, Paris, etc.) when used on or in connection with goods in order to indicate their place of manufacture or their provenance.

5.137 Appellations of origin have a more limited meaning, and may be considered a special type of indication of source. An appellation of origin is the geographical name of a country, region or locality which serves to designate a product originating therein, the quality and characteristics of which are due exclusively or essentially to the geographical environment, including natural and human factors.

5.138 The Paris Convention contains in Articles 10 and 10*bis* provisions on the protection of indications of source. These provisions cover in general any direct or indirect use of a false indication of the source (including, where applicable, the appellation of origin) of the goods or the identity of the producer, manufacturer or merchant, as well as any act of unfair competition by the use of indications or allegations which are liable to mislead the public as to the nature or the characteristics of the goods for which they are applied.

5.139 The Convention requires the countries to seize the goods bearing false indications or to prohibit their importation, or otherwise to apply any other measures that may be available in order to prevent or stop the use of such indications. However, the obligation to seize goods on importation only applies to the extent that such a sanction is provided for under the national law.

5.140 The Convention provides that action may be taken not only by the public prosecutor but also by any interested party. In this connection, Article 10(2) states that any producer, manufacturer or merchant, whether a natural person or a legal entity, engaged in the production, manufacture or trade in such goods established in the locality, region or country falsely indicated as the source or in the country where such false indications are used, is in any case deemed to be an interested party. Moreover, Article 10*ter*, requires the countries to enable federations and associations representing interested industrialists, producers and merchants to take action before the competent authorities with a view to the repression of the acts referred to above.

Unfair Competition

5.141 The Convention provides in Article 10*bis* that the countries of the Union are bound to assure to persons entitled to benefit from the Convention effective protection against unfair competition. The Convention does not specify the manner in which such protection should be granted, leaving this to the laws existing in each of the member countries.

5.142 Article 10*bis* defines acts of unfair competition as those acts of competition which are contrary to honest practices in industrial or commercial matters. Further, the Article gives some typical examples of acts of unfair competition which should be prohibited in particular.

5.143 The first example refers to all acts of such a nature as to create confusion by any means whatever with the establishment, the goods or the industrial or commercial activities of a competitor. These acts cover not only the use of identical or similar marks or names, which could be attacked as an infringement of proprietary rights, but also the use of other means which can create confusion. Such could be the form of packages, the presentation or style used on products and on their corresponding outlets or points of distribution, titles of publicity, etc.

5.144 The second example relates to false allegations in the course of trade of such a nature as to discredit the establishment, the goods, or the industrial or commercial activities of a competitor. It has been left to the domestic legislation or case law of each country to decide whether, and in what circumstances, discrediting allegations which are not strictly untrue may also be considered acts of unfair competition.

5.145 The third example of acts of unfair competition concerns indications and allegations which are liable to mislead the public as to the nature, the manufacturing process, the characteristics, the suitability for their purpose or the quality of their goods. This provision may be distinguished from the previous cases to the extent that it is concerned with the interests and well-being of the public and is one of the provisions in the Convention that is more directly related to the consumer protection role of industrial property.

NOTES AND QUESTIONS

1. Just as the Paris Convention does not define the patent, so it does not define the trademark. Just as for patents, several gaps regarding trademarks are addressed in the TRIPS Agreement.
2. The Paris Convention (art. 6) provides for the independence of trademarks. Note, however, that the Madrid Agreement Concerning the Registration of Marks (which is discussed later in this chapter) requires that a trademark be granted registration in one Madrid Agreement member country prior to the extension of that registration to other member countries via the Madrid registration system. (This rule is modified for the Madrid Protocol system, discussed *infra*.) For a five-year period following the Madrid Agreement international registration, cancellation of the initial national registration leads to invalidation of the mark in all Madrid Agreement countries. The independence of trademarks is therefore subject to certain limitations for trademark holders that make use of the Madrid Agreement registration system.
3. As noted earlier, Article 8 of the Paris Convention requires that all members provide protection for "trade names" (without imposing a registration requirement). The nature and scope of such protection is not defined.

C. The Paris Convention and Well-Known Marks

1. Joint Recommendation Concerning Provisions on the Protection of Well-Known Marks

Article 6*bis* of the Paris Convention provides limited guidance regarding how state parties are to determine whether marks are well known. In September 1999, the Assembly of the Paris Union and the WIPO General Assembly adopted a Joint Recommendation Concerning Provisions on the Protection of Well-Known Marks.[14] The preface to the Recommendation observed, "The Recommendation is the first implementation of WIPO's policy to adapt to the pace of change in the field of industrial property by considering new

---

14. Joint Recommendation Concerning Provisions on the Protection of Well-Known Marks, *adopted by* the Assembly of the Paris Union for the Protection of Industrial Property and the General Assembly of the World Intellectual Property Organization (WIPO) at the Thirty-Fourth Series of Meetings of the Assemblies of the Member States of WIPO, September 20 to 29, 1999 (WIPO 2000), available at http:www.wipo.int.

options for accelerating the development of international harmonized common principles." Article 2 of the Joint Recommendation provides, in part:

ARTICLE 2

DETERMINATION OF WHETHER A MARK IS A WELL-KNOWN MARK IN A MEMBER STATE

(1) [*Factors for Consideration*] (a) In determining whether a mark is a well-known mark, the competent authority shall take into account any circumstances from which it may be inferred that the mark is well known.

(b) In particular, the competent authority shall consider information submitted to it with respect to factors from which it may be inferred that the mark is, or is not, well known, including, but not limited to, information concerning the following:

1. the degree of knowledge or recognition of the mark in the relevant sector of the public;
2. the duration, extent and geographical area of any use of the mark;
3. the duration, extent and geographical area of any promotion of the mark, including advertising or publicity and the presentation, at fairs or exhibitions, of the goods and/or services to which the mark applies;
4. the duration and geographical area of any registrations, and/or any applications for registration, of the mark, to the extent that they reflect use or recognition of the mark;
5. the record of successful enforcement of rights in the mark, in particular, the extent to which the mark was recognized as well known by competent authorities;
6. the value associated with the mark.

(c) The above factors, which are guidelines to assist the competent authority to determine whether the mark is a well-known mark, are not pre-conditions for reaching that determination. Rather, the determination in each case will depend upon the particular circumstances of that case. In some cases all of the factors may be relevant. In other cases some of the factors may be relevant. In still other cases none of the factors may be relevant, and the decision may be based on additional factors that are not listed in subparagraph (b), above. Such additional factors may be relevant, alone, or in combination with one or more of the factors listed in subparagraph (b), above.

NOTES AND QUESTIONS

1. A WIPO Joint Recommendation is not a new international agreement, and it is not a revision to, or amendment of, the Paris Convention. Its legal status is unclear. Nonetheless, it is likely to have influence on court decisions that consider the factors for establishing the well-known character of marks. Is there reason to be concerned that Joint Recommendations could be used as a means to circumvent the more cumbersome treaty-making and amendment processes at WIPO? What might you want to know about the process by which such Joint Recommendations are approved?

2. The Doctrine of Well-Known Marks in National Law

In the following decision, the U.S. Court of Appeals for the Second Circuit examines the extent to which the well-known marks doctrine of the Paris Convention may control national law. The United States has maintained a longstanding embargo against Cuban enterprises doing business with or holding assets in the United States. A U.S.-based cigar company (General Cigar) registered in the United States a trademark ("Cohiba") widely known throughout the world in connection with cigar products of a Cuban enterprise (Cubatabaco). The Cuban enterprise sought to cancel the registration held by the U.S. company on the basis of its rights in the well-known mark, as well as to prevent the U.S. cigar company from advertising and selling cigars under the mark.

This is not the first time a Cuban claim of rights in a well-known trademark has been tested against the U.S. legislative and regulatory embargo scheme. The first major case, involving the "Havana Club" mark for rum, eventually was the subject of a WTO Appellate Body decision, although the well-known marks doctrine played a limited role on that occasion. The Paris Convention rule at the center of the *U.S.-Havana Club* case was the "telle quelle" or "as is" rule of Article 6*quinquies*. We examine the decision of the Appellate Body in section II.D.2, *infra*.

EMPRESA CUBANA DEL TABACO v. CULBRO
399 F.3d 462 (2d Cir. 2005)

STRAUB, Circuit Judge:

Defendants-Counterclaimants-Appellants-Cross-Appellees, General Cigar Co., Inc., and General Cigar Holdings, Inc. ("General Cigar"), appeal from a judgment and permanent injunction of the United States District Court for the Southern District of New York (Robert W. Sweet, Judge), entered on May 6, 2004, finding in favor of Plaintiff-Counter-Defendant-Appellee-Cross-Appellant, Empresa Cubana del Tabaco, doing business as Cubatabaco ("Cubatabaco"), on its claim of trademark infringement under Section 43(a) of the Lanham Act, ordering cancellation of General Cigar's United States trademark registration for COHIBA cigars, permanently enjoining General Cigar from further use of the COHIBA mark, and ordering General Cigar to deliver to Cubatabaco all merchandise, packaging and other materials bearing the COHIBA name, to recall from retail customers and distributors products bearing the mark, and to inform customers and distributors that they could not sell General Cigar's COHIBA-labeled products in the United States. Cubatabaco has cross-appealed from the District Court's dismissal of its treaty-based and state law claims.

This appeal arises from a dispute between Cubatabaco, a Cuban company, and General Cigar, an American company, over who has the right to use the COHIBA mark on cigars. After filing an application to register the COHIBA mark in Cuba in 1969, Cubatabaco began selling COHIBA cigars in Cuba. Cubatabaco has sold COHIBA cigars outside of Cuba since 1982, but, because of the United States embargo against Cuban goods, imposed in 1963, Cubatabaco has never sold COHIBA cigars in the United States. General Cigar obtained a registration for the COHIBA mark in the United States in 1981 and sold COHIBA cigars in the United States from 1978 until late 1987. In 1992, General Cigar relaunched a COHIBA cigar in the United States and has sold cigars under that mark in the United States since that time.

Cubatabaco claims that it owns the U.S. COHIBA trademark because General Cigar abandoned its 1981 registration in 1987 and that, by the time General Cigar resumed use of the mark in 1992, the Cuban COHIBA mark was sufficiently well known in the United States that it deserved protection under the so-called "famous marks doctrine." The District Court agreed and found that, although Cubatabaco had never used the mark in the United States and was prohibited from doing so under the embargo, it nonetheless owned the U.S. COHIBA mark. The District Court concluded that by failing to use the COHIBA mark from late 1987 to 1992, General Cigar abandoned its 1981 registration. It found further that because the Cuban COHIBA mark was sufficiently well known in the United States by November 1992, the date General Cigar resumed its use of the mark, Cubatabaco was entitled to priority in asserting ownership of the mark. After finding that there was a likelihood of confusion between the Cuban COHIBA mark and the General Cigar COHIBA mark, the court granted judgment to Cubatabaco on its claim for trademark infringement under Section 43(a) of the Lanham Act, 15 U.S.C. § 1125(a), cancelled General Cigar's registration of the mark, and enjoined General Cigar from using the mark. The court dismissed all other claims brought by Cubatabaco, including claims under international trademark treaties and New York law.

We do not reach the question of whether an entity that has not used a mark on products sold in the United States can nonetheless acquire a U.S. trademark through operation of the famous marks doctrine. We need not reach that question in this case because even were we to recognize and apply the famous marks doctrine, the Cuban embargo bars Cubatabaco's acquisition of the COHIBA mark via the famous marks doctrine. Therefore, we reverse the District Court's grant of judgment to Cubatabaco on its claim of trademark infringement under Section 43(a) of the Lanham Act. We affirm the District Court's dismissal of all other claims brought by Cubatabaco. . . .

A. THE TRADEMARK INFRINGEMENT CLAIM FAILS BECAUSE ACQUISITION OF THE MARK VIA THE FAMOUS MARKS DOCTRINE IS PROHIBITED BY THE EMBARGO REGULATIONS . . .

A transaction involving property in which a Cuban entity has an interest includes a transfer of property to a Cuban entity. "Property" includes trademarks, *id.* § 515.311, and "transfers outside the United States" of United States trademark rights to Cuban entities are prohibited by § 515.201(b)(2). "Transfer" is broadly defined to include "any . . . act . . . the . . . effect of which is to create . . . any right, remedy, power, privilege, or interest with respect to property." *Id.* § 515.310. Cubatabaco's acquisition of the mark is a "transfer[] outside the United States with regard to any property or property interest subject to the jurisdiction of the United States," *id.* § 515.201(b)(2), because Cubatabaco's acquisition of the mark is a transfer of U.S. property rights from inside the United States to Cuba—a location "outside of the United States." Therefore, Cubatabaco's acquisition of the U.S. COHIBA mark through the famous marks doctrine is barred by § 515.201(b)(2). . . .

B. CUBATABACO'S CLAIMS FOR INJUNCTIVE RELIEF BASED ON SECTION 43(A) AND THE PARIS CONVENTION FAIL BECAUSE THEY ENTAIL A TRANSFER OF PROPERTY RIGHTS TO CUBATABACO IN VIOLATION OF THE EMBARGO . . .

1. Section 43(a) Claim for Unfair Competition . . .

Cubatabaco's theory is that General Cigar's sale of COHIBA cigars in the United States violates Section 43(a) because it is likely to cause consumer confusion as to the source or attribution of those cigars. The confusion alleged by Cubatabaco in support of its Section 43(a) claim is derived solely from General Cigar's use of the COHIBA mark: Cubatabaco cannot obtain relief on a theory that General Cigar's use of the mark causes confusion, because, pursuant to our holding today, General Cigar's legal right to the COHIBA mark has been established as against Cubatabaco. General Cigar has a right to use the mark in the United States because it owns the mark in the United States.

In Part IA of this opinion we held that General Cigar has priority rights to the COHIBA mark in the United States as against Cubatabaco. . . . To allow Cubatabaco to prevail on a claim of unfair competition against General Cigar and to obtain an injunction prohibiting General Cigar from using the mark would turn the law of trademark on its head. None of United States law, the facts in this case, or international treaties warrants such acrobatics in this case. We therefore find that, on the facts of this case, Cubatabaco's Section 43(a) claim seeking an injunction against General Cigar's use of its duly registered COHIBA mark cannot succeed as a matter of law.

We do not find the analysis offered by the government and by Cubatabaco in defense of the recast Section 43(a) claim persuasive. It may be true that, as the government argues, "Cubatabaco's foreign registrations give it the right to register its COHIBA mark [in the United States], absent General Cigar's registration." Amicus Curiae Br. at 12. That is, however, a hypothetical circumstance upon which we need not speculate. As we hold today, General Cigar does have a valid registration on the COHIBA mark in the United States. Further, while it may be true, as the government points out, that Cubatabaco's COHIBA mark "was 'famous' and had secondary meaning in the United States before General Cigar's first use [of its COHIBA mark]," *id.*, we have already held that this fact cannot justify a transfer of property rights in the COHIBA mark to Cubatabaco via the "famous marks doctrine." We see no reason to alter that holding to allow Cubatabaco to achieve the same transfer via a route that is one step more circuitous than the path rejected above.

2. Article 6bis Paris Convention

Cubatabaco maintains that even if the Regulations bar its acquisition of the mark, and even if it cannot obtain relief for an unfair competition claim under Section 43(a), it has a right under Article 6*bis* of the Paris Convention, in conjunction with Sections 44(b) and (h) of the Lanham Act, to obtain cancellation of General Cigar's mark and an injunction against its use.

Article 6*bis* of the Paris Convention provides that:

(1) The countries of the Union undertake, ex officio if their legislation so permits, or at the request of an interested party, to refuse or to cancel the registration, and to prohibit the use, of a trademark which constitutes a reproduction, an imitation, or a translation, liable to create confusion, of a mark considered by the competent authority of the country of registration or use to be well known in that country as being already the mark of a person entitled to the benefits of this Convention and used for identical or similar goods. These provisions shall also apply when the essential part of the mark constitutes a reproduction of any such well-known mark or an imitation liable to create confusion therewith.

(2) A period of at least five years from the date of registration shall be allowed for requesting the cancellation of such a mark. The countries of the Union may provide for a period within which the prohibition of use must be requested.

(3) No time limit shall be fixed for requesting the cancellation or the prohibition of the use of marks registered or used in bad faith.

Paris Convention, Art. 6*bis*, 21 U.S.T. at 1640.

Both the United States and Cuba are parties to the Paris Convention. *Id.* at 1669, 1676.

According to Cubatabaco, Sections 44(b) and (h) incorporate treaty provisions relating to the "repression of unfair competition," and rights under Article 6*bis* fall into that category. Section 44(b) provides that:

> Any person whose country of origin is a party to any convention or treaty relating to trademarks, trade or commercial names, or the repression of unfair competition, to which the United States is also a party, or extends reciprocal rights to nationals of the United States by law, shall be entitled to the benefits of this section under the conditions expressed herein to the extent necessary to give effect to any provision of such convention, treaty or reciprocal law, in addition to the rights to which any owner of a mark is otherwise entitled by this chapter. . . .

Cubatabaco may be correct that Sections 44(b) and (h) incorporate Article 6*bis* and allow foreign entities to acquire U.S. trademark rights in the United States if their marks are sufficiently famous in the United States before they are used in this country. That is the view expressed by some commentators. *See* 4 McCarthy on Trademarks and Unfair Competition § 29:4 (4th ed. 2004) ("In the author's view, the well-known or famous marks doctrine of Paris Convention Article 6*bis* is incorporated into United States domestic law though the operation of Lanham Act § 43(a), § 44(b) and § 44(h)." (footnote omitted)).[10] However, we need not decide that broad question here because even assuming that the famous marks doctrine is otherwise viable and applicable, the embargo bars Cubatabaco from acquiring property rights in the U.S. COHIBA mark through the doctrine. The Embargo Regulations do not permit Cubatabaco to acquire the power to exclude General Cigar from using the mark in the United States. We do not read Article 6*bis* and Section 44(b) and (h) of the Lanham Act to require cancellation of General Cigar's properly registered trademark or an injunction against its use of the mark in the United States under these circumstances.

In any event, to the extent that the Paris Convention, standing alone, might pose an irreconcilable conflict to the Regulations, the latter will prevail. "An act of congress ought never to be construed to violate the law of nations, if any other possible construction remains." *Weinberger v. Rossi,* 456 U.S. 25, 32, 71 L. Ed. 2d 715, 102 S. Ct. 1510 (1982) (quotations and citations omitted). However, as we have recently recalled, "legislative acts trump treaty-made international law" when those acts are passed subsequent to ratification of the treaty and clearly contradict treaty obligations. *United States v. Yousef,* 327 F.3d 56, 110 (2d Cir. 2003) (citing *Breard v. Greene,* 523 U.S. 371, 376, 140 L. Ed. 2d 529, 118 S. Ct. 1352 (1998); *see also Whitney v. Robertson,* 124 U.S. 190, 194, 31 L. Ed. 386, 8 S. Ct. 456 (1888) (if a treaty and a federal statute conflict, "the one last in date will control the other"). The most recent iteration of the Paris Convention was ratified by the United States in 1970, *see* 21 U.S.T. 1583; whereas the Regulations were

10. McCarthy asserts that claims for protection of "famous" marks should be brought under *Section 43(a). See* 4 McCarthy on Trademarks and Unfair Competition § 29:4 ("Lanham Act § 43(a) gives a foreign national without a federal registration of its mark standing to sue in a federal court, invoke the well-known marks doctrine of the Paris Convention Article 6*bis,* and prevail if its mark is so well-known in the U.S. that confusion is likely."). To the extent that a foreign entity attempts to utilize the famous marks doctrine as basis for its right to a U.S. trademark and seeks to prevent another entity from using the mark in the United States, the claim should be brought under Section 43(a). Under Section 43(a), both foreign and domestic entities can seek relief for infringement of unregistered marks.

reaffirmed and codified in 1996 with the passage of the LIBERTAD Act, 110 Stat. 792 (1996), 22 U.S.C. § 6032(h). In these circumstances, any claim grounded in the Paris Convention that presented an irreconcilable conflict with the Regulations would be rendered "null" by the Regulations. *Breard*, 523 U.S. at 376.

II. OTHER TREATY CLAIMS BROUGHT UNDER SECTIONS 44(B) AND (H) OF THE LANHAM ACT . . .

B. TREATY-BASED UNFAIR COMPETITION CLAIMS . . .

In addition, Cubatabaco cannot maintain a claim for unfair competition under Article 10*bis* of the Paris Convention pursuant to Sections 44(b) and (h) of the Lanham Act. The Paris Convention requires that "foreign nationals . . . be given the same treatment in each of the member countries as that country makes available to its own citizens." *Vanity Fair Mills v. T. Eaton Co.*, 234 F.2d 633, 640 (2d Cir.), *cert. denied*, 352 U.S. 871, 1 L. Ed. 2d 76, 77 S. Ct. 96 (1956). "The Paris Convention provides for national treatment, and does not define the substantive law of unfair competition." *Mattel, Inc. v. MCA Records, Inc.*, 296 F.3d 894, 908 (9th Cir. 2002). As the Eleventh Circuit has explained:

> We agree that section 44 of the Lanham Act incorporated, to some degree, the Paris Convention. But we disagree that the Paris Convention creates substantive rights beyond those independently provided in the Lanham Act. As other courts of appeals have noted, the rights articulated in the Paris Convention do not exceed the rights conferred by the Lanham Act. Instead, we conclude that the Paris Convention, as incorporated by the Lanham Act, only requires "national treatment."

National treatment means that "foreign nationals should be given the same treatment in each of the member countries as that country makes available to its own citizens." So, section 44 of the Lanham Act gives foreign nationals the same rights and protections provided to United States citizens by the Lanham Act. As such, foreign nationals like Plaintiff may seek protection in United States courts for violations of the Lanham Act. But the Paris Convention, as incorporated by section 44 of the Lanham Act, creates no new cause of action for unfair competition. Any cause of action based on unfair competition must be grounded in the substantive provisions of the Lanham Act. *Int'l Cafe, S.A.L. v. Hard Rock Cafe Int'l (U.S.A.), Inc.*, 252 F.3d 1274, 1277-78 (11th Cir. 2001) (citations omitted). Therefore, we conclude that Cubatabaco cannot maintain a separate claim for unfair competition under Article 10*bis* and Sections 44(b) and (h). Rather, a claim for unfair competition must be brought under Section 43(a) or state law. *See Mattel*, 296 F.3d at 908.[14]

NOTES AND QUESTIONS

1. The U.S. Supreme Court denied certiorari in *Empresa Cubana del Tabaco v. General Cigar Co.*, 547 U.S. 1205 (2006).
2. The rule that the later in time of a treaty or statute controls as a matter of internal law is longstanding U.S. constitutional doctrine. In this sense, it is

---

14. In any event, as noted above, any irreconcilable conflict between the Paris Convention and the Regulations would be resolved in favor of the Regulations.

unsurprising that the Court of Appeals decided that the embargo regulations take precedence over an inconsistent rule of the Paris Convention.
But, without going further and transferring the mark to Cubatabaco, why
did the Court of Appeals refuse to cancel General Cigar's "Cohiba"
trademark registration?

3. It is central to the Court of Appeals decision to classify the trademark
holder's right to exclude others as a "property" right, and thus subject to
the embargo. Are "negative" rights to exclude "property"? Under any
particular set of conditions?

4. U.S. business groups were almost uniformly opposed to the Court of
Appeals decision because they fear that other governments will similarly
refuse to acknowledge rights in well-known marks. *See, e.g.*, Amicus Brief of
the National Foreign Trade Council to Supreme Court, filed Dec. 2, 2005.

D.   The WTO TRIPS Agreement and Trademarks

Negotiations during the GATT Uruguay Round with respect to trademarks
were far less controversial than negotiations with respect to patents. In fact,
many developing countries viewed an agreement protecting against trademark
counterfeiting and copyright piracy as a preferable alternative to the more
comprehensive TRIPS Agreement that was concluded. All (or virtually all)
countries involved in the negotiations maintained trademark registration systems. There was little opposition to the premise that trademarks serve a useful
economic function.

1.   The TRIPS Agreement Text Analyzed

The WTO TRIPS Agreement includes a section (Part II, sec. 2) with respect to
trademarks. The following is from the UNCTAD/ICTSD TRIPS and Development Resource Book (2005), which explains the negotiating history of each
provision of the TRIPS Agreement and provides interpretative guidance.
Only the interpretative part of the chapter on trademarks is presented here,
and then only in an excerpted format. The full text of the Resource Book is
available online at http://www.iprsonline.org.

UNCTAD/ICTSD RESOURCE BOOK ON TRIPS AND DEVELOPMENT

http://www.iprsonline.org*

3.1. ARTICLE 15

3.1.1 ARTICLE 15.1: DEFINITION

Article 15 Protectable Subject Matter
    1. Any sign, or any combination of signs, capable of distinguishing the goods or
    services of one undertaking from those of other undertakings, shall be capable of

---

* In hardcover from Cambridge University Press (2005), at 228. The text has been adapted
from the original by its author (who is also an author of this book).

constituting a trademark. Such signs, in particular words including personal names, letters, numerals, figurative elements and combinations of colours as well as any combination of such signs, shall be eligible for registration as trademarks. Where signs are not inherently capable of distinguishing the relevant goods or services, Members may make registrability depend on distinctiveness acquired through use. Members may require, as a condition of registration, that signs be visually perceptible. . . .

3.1.2 ARTICLE 15.2

2. Paragraph 1 shall not be understood to prevent a Member from denying registration of a trademark on other grounds, provided that they do not derogate from the provisions of the Paris Convention (1967).

A Member might elect to refuse registration of a trademark on grounds other than that it does not distinguish the goods or services of an undertaking. For example, in the *U.S.-Havana Club* case decided by the WTO Appellate Body (AB), the United States had refused to register a mark on grounds that the party claiming ownership of the mark was not its rightful owner. The U.S. refusal was upheld by the AB as being within U.S. discretion to make determinations regarding the lawful holders of marks.[251]

Article *6quinquies* of the Paris Convention, which was at issue in the *U.S.-Havana Club* case, obligates Members to accept marks for registration in the same form ("as is," or "*telle quelle*") as registered in the country of origin. This rule was designed to prevent trademark registration authorities from requiring translations or other adaptations of marks to meet local preferences or rules. Under Article 15.2, a Member must comply with the "as is" obligation, and in that way it may not derogate from the Paris Convention. There are exceptions even to the "as is" obligation. That is, Article *6quinquies*, Paris Convention, recognizes certain bases even for refusing to accept the same form of the mark.[15]

The Paris Convention enumerates other bases on which the registration of trademarks may be denied (Article *6bis* and *6ter*). Article *6bis* establishes an obligation to refuse third party registration of well-known marks. Treatment of well-known marks is addressed in sub-Section 3.2.2 below. Article *6ter* creates obligations to refuse trademark registration for state flags and symbols.

---

251. The *U.S.-Havana Club* decision of the AB is discussed [later in this chapter, at section II.D.2].

15. [These are:

B. . . . 1. when they are of such a nature as to infringe rights acquired by third parties in the country where protection is claimed;

2. when they are devoid of any distinctive character, or consist exclusively of signs or indications which may serve, in trade, to designate the kind, quality, quantity, intended purpose, value, place of origin, of the goods, or the time of production, or have become customary in the current language or in the bona fide and established practices of the trade of the country where protection is claimed;

3. when they are contrary to morality or public order and, in particular, of such a nature as to deceive the public. It is understood that a mark may not be considered contrary to public order for the sole reason that it does not conform to a provision of the legislation on marks, except if such provision itself relates to public order. This provision is subject, however, to the application of Article 10*bis*.

— EDS.]

3.1.3 ARTICLE 15.3: USE OF TRADEMARKS

3. Members may make registrability depend on use. However, actual use of a trademark shall not be a condition for filing an application for registration. An application shall not be refused solely on the ground that intended use has not taken place before the expiry of a period of three years from the date of application.

Trademark protection originated as a form of unfair competition law. The tort of "passing off" in Commonwealth jurisdictions evolved to address claims of taking unfair advantage of another person's trademark or business name. This cause of action did not depend on the registration of a mark. The concept is broader than trademark infringement, and could encompass misuse of trade names as well as other distinctive characteristics of a business. It was and remains the subject matter of common law. [On the common law doctrine of "passing off," see W.R. CORNISH, INTELLECTUAL PROPERTY: PATENTS, COPYRIGHT, TRADE MARKS AND ALLIED RIGHTS (4th ed. 1999), at Chapter 16.] Protection of trademarks developed in the United States as a part of the law of unfair competition. Although trademarks long ago came to benefit from registration in the Commonwealth and U.S. legal systems, there remains the possibility to establish and enforce "common law" trademarks from use in commerce.

Before the TRIPS Agreement was negotiated, the United States required use of a trademark in commerce as a precondition to federal registration. This precondition was intended to assure that trademarks were associated only with real goods or services. Among other objectives, this would avoid a proliferation of unused marks on the records of the Patent and Trademark Office (USPTO). The use precondition also served as a reward to business enterprises that acted swiftly to put their goods and services on the market.

However, even without the complications that this use-based registration system created at the international level (since there was a basic incompatibility with most other countries that allowed registration without use), the precondition came to be seen as an impediment to more modern marketing strategies that involved the advertisement to the public of new goods and services before they were actually placed on the market. If use were a precondition for registration, business enterprises would face risks by advertising in advance of product and service introduction. Other businesses might actually use a mark on a good or service before the enterprise advertising it placed its own good or service on the market.

The U.S. moved to a modified use-based registration during the Uruguay Round as the advantages of a more globally-integrated trademark registration system became apparent to U.S. businesses. A Madrid Protocol-based registration system (administered by WIPO) could be employed to reduce registration inefficiencies, and some of the domestic difficulties that the use-based system presented for marketing strategies could be overcome. The U.S. system remains grounded in "use" as a condition of registration, but it is now acceptable to file for registration declaring "intent to use" a mark, and subsequently filing within a prescribed period a verification that the mark has actually been used in commerce.[253] Formal registration of the mark does not occur until the

---

253. *See* 15 U.S.C. § 1051(b)-(d). The prescribed period for filing a verification of use is within six months of a "notice of allowance," extendable by an additional 24 months. Because a notice of allowance is issued after examination, period for response, publication, and an opposition period,

applicant submits verification of actual use to the USPTO. In the meantime, the applicant benefits from priority "constructive use" of the mark that in effect precludes a third party from acquiring competing federal trademark rights during the intent-to-use period, and also allows infringement claims based on that constructive use.[254]

Article 15.3, third sentence, provides that registration may not be denied during a three-year application period solely on the grounds of non-use. This in effect requires that a form of priority be established for unused marks included in filed applications since for a period of three years the mark should be treated (for application purposes) as if it is being used. However, this does not appear to require that an applicant be given rights as against an alleged infringer of an unused mark during the "priority" period since it refers only to the ultimate grant of registration, not to the interim period. It is for each Member to determine the effect of an application under national law. Article 4 of the Paris Convention provides a six-month right of priority in respect to the filing of trademark applications outside the country of first application. This prevents the intervening use of a mark or filing of an application from interfering with the rights of the priority holder.

Article 15.3, TRIPS Agreement, accommodates the U.S.-style registration system that continues to require use as a precondition to completion of registration, but permits an application to be filed prior to actual use. It is of interest that non-use cannot be the sole grounds for refusing registration during a three-year period, but otherwise the effects of an application are not stated.

3.1.4 ARTICLE 15.4

> 4. The nature of the goods or services to which a trademark is to be applied shall in no case form an obstacle to registration of the trademark.

Article 15.4 of the TRIPS Agreement essentially restates Article 7 of the Paris Convention, adding express reference to service marks.[255] . . . IPRs are not "market access" rights. The fact that Article 15.4 states that trademark registration must be granted in connection with all kinds of goods and services does not require that a Member allow such goods and services to be sold.

Article 6*quinquies* of the Paris Convention ("as is" or "*telle quelle*") permits trademark registration to be refused on grounds that the mark is "contrary to morality or public order and, in particular, of such a nature as to deceive the public." Note that reference is to the mark itself, and not to associated goods or services.

The question of morality or public order might arise in connection with goods such as cigarettes that are known to be harmful to health, the advertising or sale of which Members might choose to heavily regulate or even ban. Article 15.4 suggests that a mark used in connection with cigarettes may not be refused registration because of the product with which it is associated. This

---

it is very doubtful that registration would be denied for non-use within the three-year period prescribed by Article 15.3, TRIPS Agreement.

254. *See* 15 U.S.C. § 1057(c). The benefits of "constructive use" do not arise until registration is granted, but can be applied with retroactive effect.

255. Article 7 of the Paris Convention provides:

> The nature of the goods to which a trademark is to be applied shall in no case form an obstacle to the registration of the mark.

appears to create a tension with Article 6*quinquies* that permits refusal of registration of a mark on morality and public order grounds. This apparent tension might be resolved by interpreting Article 6*quinquies* to be limited to refusals for signs or symbols that are offensive "as such." Yet this is a difficult line to draw since a sign or symbol inherently acts to draw (or stimulate) a connection in the public mind to some good, service, activity or belief. A Member might argue that it is entitled to block the registration of a mark used on cigarettes not because of the product, but because promotion of the mark itself has adverse consequences for the public; that is, the mark "as such" is injurious to public order because it encourages a type of behaviour known to cause serious injury (and the behaviour is not linked or limited to the products of a particular enterprise). Whether or not this argument is persuasive, the critical point from a public policy perspective is that allowing registration of a trademark or service mark does not impair the government's authority to regulate the product associated with the mark. Even if a Member must allow registration of trademarks for cigarettes, it may ban (or limit) the sale of the cigarettes on public health grounds.

3.1.5 ARTICLE 15.5

5. Members shall publish each trademark either before it is registered or promptly after it is registered and shall afford a reasonable opportunity for petitions to cancel the registration. In addition, Members may afford an opportunity for the registration of a trademark to be opposed.

Article 15.5 addresses the procedural issues of publication, cancellation and opposition. It is fairly straightforward. . . .

3.2. ARTICLE 16

3.2.1 ARTICLE 16.1: EXCLUSIVE RIGHTS

1. The owner of a registered trademark shall have the exclusive right to prevent all third parties not having the owner's consent from using in the course of trade identical or similar signs for goods or services which are identical or similar to those in respect of which the trademark is registered where such use would result in a likelihood of confusion. In case of the use of an identical sign for identical goods or services, a likelihood of confusion shall be presumed. The rights described above shall not prejudice any existing prior rights, nor shall they affect the possibility of Members making rights available on the basis of use. . . .

The rights are attributable to owners of "registered" trademarks. Members may, but need not, protect "common law" trademarks. In the *U.S.-Havana Club* case the United States was defending its right to determine who the "owner" of the subject trademark was, as a condition predicate to determining what the rights of that owner might be. . . .

The second sentence of Article 16.1 provides that, "In case of the use of an identical sign for identical goods or services, a likelihood of confusion shall be presumed." This provision should facilitate the successful prosecution of infringement claims where the intent to directly take advantage of the trademark owner is evident (*e.g.*, straightforward trademark counterfeiting). By establishing a presumption of likelihood of confusion where the signs and goods/services are identical, the burden is shifted to the alleged infringer to prove the absence of likelihood. This removes a significant evidentiary task from the trademark owner. It is, however, possible to rebut the presumption. Professor T. Cottier has noted that in cases of parallel importation (in countries following a rule of international exhaustion of trademarks), the presumption may be rebutted by showing that the goods were put on the market with the trademark owner's consent in another country.[258] . . .

3.2.2 ARTICLE 16.2: WELL-KNOWN TRADEMARKS

2. Article 6*bis* of the Paris Convention (1967) shall apply, *mutatis mutandis*, to services. In determining whether a trademark is well-known, Members shall take account of the knowledge of the trademark in the relevant sector of the public, including knowledge in the Member concerned which has been obtained as a result of the promotion of the trademark.

Article 6*bis* of the Paris Convention addresses the subject of so-called "well-known" trademarks.[259] A special regime for such marks has the objective of providing protection for trademarks that are well known in a country as already belonging to a certain person, even though they are not, or not yet, protected in that country through a registration. In the absence of registration of the well-known mark, the conflicting mark could theoretically be registered and enforced to the detriment of the well-known mark, which would in most cases result in consumer confusion. Such practice is widely regarded as constituting an act of unfair competition, thus requiring the protection of the well-known trademark.

The necessity of protection of well-known marks usually arises in new markets, i.e. in countries previously closed to foreign traders or which, through an increase in economic development become attractive for the suppliers of branded products. In those cases, the owner of the well-known, but unregistered trademark is considered as worth of protection as if she/he had actually registered the mark. This shows that registration is not considered the ultimate criterion of protection. It is considered more important that the registration of

---

258. Thomas Cottier, *Das Problem der Parallelimporte im Freihandelsabkommen Schweiz-EG und im Recht der WTO-GATT,* REVUE SUISSE DE LA PROPRIÉTÉ INTELLECTUELLE, I/1995, 37, 53-56 [hereinafter "Cottier"]. Note that these cases have to be distinguished from the above example of trademark counterfeiting: In the case of parallel imports, the identical sign originates from the same trademark holder; whereas in the case of counterfeiting, a person different from the right holder uses the latter's trademark for his own products.

259. "Article 6*bis* Marks: Well-Known Marks

(1) The countries of the Union undertake, ex officio if their legislation so permits, or at the request of an interested party, to refuse or to cancel the registration, and to prohibit the use, of a trademark which constitutes a reproduction, an imitation, or a translation, liable to create confusion, of a mark considered by the competent authority of the country of registration or use to be well known in that country as being already the mark of a person entitled to the benefits of this Convention and used for identical or similar goods. These provisions shall also apply when the essential part of the mark constitutes a reproduction of any such well-known mark or an imitation liable to create confusion therewith.

(2) A period of at least five years from the date of registration shall be allowed for requesting the cancellation of such a mark. The countries of the Union may provide for a period within which the prohibition of use must be requested.

(3) No time limit shall be fixed for requesting the cancellation or the prohibition of the use of marks registered or used in bad faith."

As noted earlier, the Paris Convention differentiates between trademarks and service marks. States, for example, are not required to provide for registration of service marks. The TRIPS Agreement requires that registration be made available for service marks.

the same or a similar mark by a third person could lead to *confusion of the public,* who would automatically associate the registered mark with the non-registered, but well-known owner or his products.

To make clear that well-known service marks are subject to protection on the same basis as trademarks (for goods), Article 16.2, TRIPS Agreement, first sentence, explicitly extends the protection of Article *6bis,* Paris Convention, to service marks.

Article *6bis,* Paris Convention, has been understood to leave substantial uncertainty regarding the standards states should apply in determining whether a mark is well known.[261] Article 16.2, TRIPS Agreement, second sentence, addresses one aspect of that uncertainty. It establishes that the question whether a mark is well known should be determined in respect to the "relevant sector of the public." Assume, for example, that an enterprise is the leading manufacturer of sophisticated equipment used by scientific laboratories to determine the chemical composition of materials. The trademark of that enterprise might be very well known among all technical specialists in the field of chemical composition, but would likely be more or less completely unknown to the general public. Article 16.2 indicates that a mark should be considered well known based on the "relevant" sector of the public, which in such circumstances would be the technical specialists. There is a risk that defining "well known" in terms of the relevant sector of the public will lead to a proliferation of well known marks. This risk can be addressed by imposing a relatively high standard regarding the degree of knowledge of the mark among the relevant sector, which possibility is within the scope of the provision.

Article 16.2, second sentence, adds to its relevant sector clarification the phrase, "including knowledge in the Member concerned which has been obtained as a result of the promotion of the trademark."[262] . . . The TRIPS text clarifies that a mark may be well known even if it has not been used on goods and services within the Member concerned, but has become known there through advertisement. . . .

3.2.3 ARTICLE 16.3: WELL-KNOWN TRADEMARKS

3. Article *6bis* of the Paris Convention (1967) shall apply, *mutatis mutandis,* to goods or services which are not similar to those in respect of which a trademark is registered, provided that use of that trademark in relation to those goods or services would indicate a connection between those goods or services and the owner of the registered trademark and provided that the interests of the owner of the registered trademark are likely to be damaged by such use.

Article 16.3, TRIPS Agreement, addresses the situation in which a third party uses a well-known mark in connection with goods or services for which the mark holder is not well known. This provision differs from Article 16.2. in three respects. First, the well-known mark in question is *registered,* as follows from

---

261. In September 1999 WIPO members adopted a Joint Resolution setting out guidance on various aspects of well-known marks, including criteria that might be used in making determinations. See Section 6.2.2 below. *See, e.g.,* Joint Recommendation Concerning Provisions on the Protection of Well-Known Marks, adopted by the WIPO General Assembly and the Assembly of the Paris Union, Sept. 1999.

262. The Brussels Ministerial Text (December 1990) referred to "including knowledge in that PARTY obtained as a result of the promotion of the trademark in international trade."

the language of the provision (see quotation above). Second, the goods or services for which the confusingly similar trademark is used are different from those goods or services that are covered by the well-known mark.[263] Third, this provision emphasizes protection of the *reputation* of the well-known mark. This is indicated by the last part of the paragraph, requiring that the "interests of the owner of the registered trademark are likely to be damaged" by the use of the third party's trademark (see below for details). Articles 16.2 TRIPS and 6*bis* of the Paris Convention do not contain such reference to the interests of the right holder, but focus on the likelihood of confusion of the public. Nevertheless, it has been observed that Article 16.3 TRIPS, by referring to Article 6*bis* of the Paris Convention, also takes account of the concern about confusion of the public.[264]

To illustrate the operation of Article 16.3, consider the situation in which the well-known automobile trademark "AUDI" was used by a third party in connection with the marketing of television sets. To begin with, there would be a difficult question whether television sets might be part of the natural product line expansion of an automobile manufacturer in an ordinary trademark confusion sense (i.e., under Article 16.1). If so, there would be similarity between the television sets potentially covered by the registered trademark and the third party's television sets. Thus, the question of well-known marks might not arise since there may already be a likelihood of confusion between similar goods. However, if there is no likelihood of confusion in the *ordinary* trademark sense, Article 16.3 indicates that the finder of fact should proceed to ask whether a consumer would consider there to be a connection between the goods, even if not part of a natural product line expansion (i.e. the case of non-similarity of the goods). Would a consumer seeing the term "AUDI" on a television set think that there was a connection with the automobile company? In recent years there has been an increasing tendency for producers well known in one area of commerce to market into unrelated lines of commerce. Would it have been anticipated that the "Marlboro" and "Camel" cigarette marks would be used on clothing and shoes? In this context, Article 16.3, TRIPS Agreement, addresses a significant question regarding well-known marks.

Article 16.3 contains an important qualifier. The interests of the owner of the well known trademark must be "likely to be damaged by such use." There are two ways such damage might be foreseen. First, the well known trademark holder might itself have been planning to enter the same market as the third party using the mark. It would therefore be injured by the loss of a revenue opportunity. Second, the third party using the mark might be doing so in a way that would tarnish or injure the reputation of the trademark holder. The burden should presumably be on the trademark holder to establish the likelihood of damage since third party use of a mark in connection with a dissimilar product would not ordinarily be assumed to cause damage.

Subjective questions such as those involving the likelihood of damage from use of a mark on dissimilar goods may be answered differently in various

---

263. This is also what distinguishes this provision from the *first* paragraph of Article 16, which applies in case of identical or similar goods or services protected by a registered trademark (referred to below as "*ordinary* trademark confusion").

264. *See* D. Gervais, [The TRIPS Agreement Drafting History and Analysis, London, 1998,] p. 111.

Members. This is to be expected. In the application of TRIPS Agreement provisions such as Articles 16.2 and 16.3, the issue from a WTO legal standpoint is whether the rules are applied reasonably and in good faith, not whether an exact methodology is used to reach a definitive result.

3.3. Article 17: exceptions

Exceptions

Members may provide limited exceptions to the rights conferred by a trademark, such as fair use of descriptive terms, provided that such exceptions take account of the legitimate interests of the owner of the trademark and of third parties.

Trademark rights involve exclusivity in signs or symbols. In effect a sign or symbol may be taken out of public usage and reserved to private control. When trademarks involve arbitrary combinations of letters and/or designs the effects on the public may be relatively inconsequential. However, there are a variety of contexts in which the effect on the public may be substantial.

When a descriptive word becomes the subject of trademark protection the capacity for expression is restricted. Even though the rights of the trademark holder are nominally limited to use with respect to certain goods or services in the course of trade, there is a chilling effect around the use of the word that discourages others from using it. The impact, both direct and indirect, of granting private rights in words is what motivates the prohibition on the grant of trademark rights in "generic" terms.

It is difficult for one enterprise to compare its goods with those of another without referring to the latter's goods by their trademark name. For this reason, the use of a competitor's mark in comparative advertising is typically allowed as an exception to the rights of the holder.

There are a number of other contexts in which trademarks are referred to without the consent of the owner. A common type of reference is in news reporting and commentary. It is often difficult to make reference to the goods or services of an enterprise without referring to the trademark name. Again consider the "AUDI" trademark. It would be difficult for the publishers of a magazine directed to auto enthusiasts to review the performance of AUDI automobiles without using the term "AUDI." The publisher could, of course, refer to an automobile manufacturer based in Germany with product lines known by certain characteristics, but this would strain writers and the reading public alike. The use by the publisher of the term AUDI in this context is a form of fair use of a trademark, sometimes referred to as "nominative fair use."

Like copyright, trademark protects only the identification of the product and not its function. Pharmaceutical manufacturers market drugs in colored capsules or tablets. Doctors, pharmacists and consumer-patients come to identify those drugs by their distinctive coloring. The users of the drugs come to rely on the color as a principal means for determining what to ingest. The color serves a critical function from a public health standpoint. When generic versions of a drug are produced by second-comers, significant problems for consumer-patients may arise if they are unable to identify the same medication by the same color. Color has taken on an important functional characteristic. The use by third parties of the same color on equivalent drugs may be justified on either of two bases. First, it might be said that the color is not serving a trademark function because it is functional, and thus not protected. Second, it might be said that use of the color is a limited exception to the rights of the trademark owner as a fair use in the public interest.[265]

The Paris Convention does not expressly address the subject of exceptions to trademark rights, and from that standpoint Article 17, TRIPS Agreement, does not have a textual precedent at the multilateral level. This is similar to the circumstances of Article 30, TRIPS Agreement, with respect to patents. . . . While there may be a temptation to analogize because of the similar language of the three exception provisions, it is important to be aware that the forms of IPRs perform very different roles and that the public and private interests in each may be rather different.

The term "limited exception" is capable of different reasonable interpretations. In the *Canada-Generic Pharmaceuticals* case,[266] the panel construed the language to refer to a narrow derogation.[267] Canada had argued that a "limited exception" is an exception with defined boundaries. The text is susceptible to both interpretations.

Article 17 gives "fair use of descriptive terms" as illustration of a limited exception, but clearly not in an exclusive way, as is made clear by the use of the terms "such as." As noted above, there are a number of other types of limited exception that have been recognized in different legal systems.

Article 17 further provides that a limited exception should "take account of the legitimate interests of the owner of the trademark and of third parties." Application of this language will of necessity involve subjective judgments regarding the balance of public and private interests in trademarks. The panel in *Canada-Generic Pharmaceuticals* found that "legitimate interests" was to be understood more broadly than "legal interests" and to take into account broader social interests. Each of the trademark exceptions discussed above should be permissible within the scope of subjective balancing implicit in taking account of the legitimate interests of owners and third parties. [See *EC-Geographical Indications, infra.*]

---

265. Note that use by third parties of the same color on equivalent drugs has recently been admitted by the Court of the European Free Trade Association (EFTA, comprising Iceland, Liechtenstein, Norway, and Switzerland). With the exception of Switzerland, the EFTA countries have concluded with the EC and its member states the Treaty on the European Economic Area (EEA), resulting in their participation in the EC's common market and their being bound by EC law). *See* case E-3/02, *Merck v. Paranova* of 8 July 2003, EFTA Court: One of the biggest European parallel importers, Paranova, imported pharmaceutical products into Norway that the pharmaceutical company Merck had sold before under its trademark in Southern Europe. Before selling the drugs in Norway, Paranova repacked them, leaving the tablets as such untouched. The new packings displayed Merck's name and trademark, and the colors used on Merck's own packings. However, those colors were not in the same place as on Merck's original packings; instead of placing them in the center, Paranova had moved them to the corners of the packings. In response to trademark infringement proceedings initiated by Merck, the EFTA Court decided that under EC law, the holder of a trademark may prevent parallel importers from using a certain design only if such design damages the reputation of the right holder or his mark. The use by the parallel trader of the original colors in a different place with a view to facilitating the identification by consumers of the parallel trader's own product line does not amount to such damage. Contrary to the modeling of a new packing as such, the parallel importer in creating its own design on the packing may go beyond minimum modifications required by the importing country.

266. WT/DS114/R, 17 March 2000.

267. *Canada-Generic Pharmaceuticals* case, at para. 7.30 [see Chapter 2.II.B.1 of this book].

3.4. ARTICLE 18: TERM OF PROTECTION

Term of Protection

Initial registration, and each renewal of registration, of a trademark shall be for a term of no less than seven years. The registration of a trademark shall be renewable indefinitely.

Prior to the TRIPS Agreement, WTO Members maintained significantly disparate renewal periods. Many trademark offices were (and remain) dependent on renewal fees to maintain their operations, and not surprisingly are anxious to collect fees. The seven-year minimum initial and renewal registration period was a compromise between the United States proposal for a minimum ten-year period and a developing country proposal to leave the question of duration to each Member.

Trademarks are capable of indefinite duration. This does not mean that trademark rights last indefinitely based on the mere payment of renewal fees. Trademarks are subject to cancellation on grounds such as non-use (*see* Article 19 below). Article 18, however, makes clear that there is no temporal limit to how long a trademark may remain valid if requirements for maintaining rights are satisfied.

3.5. ARTICLE 19: REQUIREMENT OF USE

Requirement of Use

1. If use is required to maintain a registration, the registration may be cancelled only after an uninterrupted period of at least three years of non-use, unless valid reasons based on the existence of obstacles to such use are shown by the trademark owner. Circumstances arising independently of the will of the owner of the trademark which constitute an obstacle to the use of the trademark, such as import restrictions on or other government requirements for goods or services protected by the trademark, shall be recognized as valid reasons for non-use.

2. When subject to the control of its owner, use of a trademark by another person shall be recognized as use of the trademark for the purpose of maintaining the registration.

Article 19.1, TRIPS Agreement, first sentence, sets a three-year (uninterrupted) minimum term prior to which a registered mark may not be cancelled for non-use. The Paris Convention, at Article 5.C(1), provides that "the registration may be cancelled only after a reasonable period."[269] The TRIPS Agreement thus effectively defines the "reasonable period" of the Paris Convention.

Article 5.C(1), Paris Convention, and Article 19.1, TRIPS Agreement, first sentence, each provide a basis upon which the trademark owner can prevent cancellation. The Paris Convention permits the trademark owner to "justify his inaction." The TRIPS Agreement refers to the "existence of obstacles to such use." Neither formulation is clear as to what types of facts or circumstances might justify non-use, leaving substantial discretion to Members to delimit

---

269. Article 5 of the Paris Convention provides:

C. (1) If, in any country, use of the registered mark is compulsory, the registration may be cancelled only after a reasonable period, and then only if the person concerned does not justify his inaction.

the scope of the grounds. They might be quite broad, for example, allowing the registered holder to justify non-use on grounds that it was unable to put a good into production for technical reasons. On the other hand, they might be narrow, for example, referring only to obstacles arising outside the trademark holder's control, such as a government ban on sales of the subject good.

The Paris Convention rule allowing owners to "justify" non-use might be construed not to provide an excuse when the government acted. The government's action might be construed to de-legitimize the trademark owner's excuse. Article 19.2, TRIPS Agreement, second sentence, makes clear that indeed the obstacle may arise from outside the trademark owner's control, including government-imposed restrictions on the subject goods or services. Thus, an excuse based on a legitimately-imposed government restriction should still constitute a legitimate excuse.

Article 19.2, TRIPS Agreement, provides for the situation in which the trademark is licensed by its owner to a third party. Use by the licensee is equivalent to use by the owner for purposes of preventing cancellation for non-use. However, the licensee's use of the mark is only covered "when subject to the control of its owner." It would appear that a "naked license," that is, a license under which the trademark holder merely collects royalties but does not supervise the licensee, may not constitute use under this provision. This is the logical import of the language and supported by the negotiating history which shows the language concerning control replacing an earlier text according to which only the owner's consent to use of the mark was required.[270] It might alternatively be argued that so long as the trademark owner holds a contractual interest in the mark the licensee is under its control (however loose) and that this may suffice for "control" within the meaning of Article 19.2. This does not seem very persuasive in light of the express language and negotiating history.

3.6. ARTICLE 20: OTHER REQUIREMENTS

Other Requirements
> The use of a trademark in the course of trade shall not be unjustifiably encumbered by special requirements, such as use with another trademark, use in a special form or use in a manner detrimental to its capability to distinguish the goods or services of one undertaking from those of other undertakings. This will not preclude a requirement prescribing the use of the trademark identifying the undertaking producing the goods or services along with, but without linking it to, the trademark distinguishing the specific goods or services in question of that undertaking.

Prior to negotiation of the TRIPS Agreement, it was not unusual for national trademark legislation, particularly in developing countries, to include requirements concerning the manner in which trademarks could be used. The domestic licensee of a foreign-origin trademark might be required to use its own trademark alongside that of the licensor. Additional rules might prescribe the relative placement of local and foreign-origin marks on goods. Despite the

---

270. Note that the Anell text (June 1990) "A" text did not include a requirement of control, providing:

> 6.2A Use of the trademark by another person with the consent of the owner shall be recognized as use of the trademark for the purpose of maintaining the registration.

"telle quelle" or "as is" rule regarding registration in the same form, a foreign-origin trademark owner might be required to transform its mark into a more locally-friendly form, such as by providing a translated version of descriptive terms. The development-oriented objective of such requirements, *inter alia,* was to assure that some name or trademark recognition was established in favour of a local enterprise, assuming that the foreign licensor's presence in the market might be transitory. By requiring the foreign licensor to link its mark with that of a local enterprise, developing country authorities encouraged continuity in business relationships since the licensor might be more reluctant to discontinue its association with a business with whose name or products it had been linked in the public mind. From the perspective of the foreign-origin licensor, this type of requirement presented obstacles to business planning. If the mark or name of a licensee (such as a distributor) was to be linked with the licensor's mark, the licensor risked injury to its own reputation based on actions of the licensee. Also, as the special requirements might discourage foreign-origin licensors from changing or discontinuing business relationships, this was not viewed positively by the licensors.

Article 20 precludes the imposition of "special requirements, such as use with another trademark, use in a special form or use in a manner detrimental to its capability to distinguish the goods or services of one undertaking from those of other undertakings." The first reference is clear, that is "with another trademark." The meaning of "special form" might refer either to a standard format prescribed for all trademark owners (such as "in translation," or in a particular size or colour scheme), or to a case-by-case determination by a trademark authority. It is less clear what is intended by "use in a manner detrimental to its capability to distinguish." Such a result might come about if a mark-owner is required to reduce the size or placement of its mark to a point that consumers would have difficulty recognizing it, or to place it alongside information or materials that likewise would reduce its impact on consumers. Thus, for example, a requirement to include the generic name of a product alongside a trademark might be argued to have such an effect. However, the legal formulation leaves substantial flexibility to the interpreter.

However, Article 20 specifically authorizes rules that require the mark or name of the producing enterprise to be included with that of the trademark owner. Such requirements are intended to serve a development objective by indicating to the public that a local producer is the *de facto* supplier of the goods or services, with the expectation that the local public will gain assurance regarding the capacity of local suppliers. At the same time, Article 20 provides that the local enterprise will use its mark "without linking it to, the trademark" of the subject owner. This is presumably intended to prevent the local enterprise from taking "unfair advantage" of the foreign-origin mark. There should be some form of differentiation, though Article 20 does not provide or suggest a specific means. Although this provision was negotiated in response to developing country insistence that they should be allowed to facilitate awareness of local production capacity, the text does not distinguish between local undertaking-producers and foreign undertaking-producers. If a Chinese producer is making a product on which a U.S. trademark is placed, and the product is being sold in Indonesia, the mark of the Chinese producer should just as well be required to appear (based on the principle of national treatment) as that of an Indonesian producer putting the U.S. mark on the product for sale in Indonesia.

3.7. ARTICLE 21: LICENSING AND ASSIGNMENT

Licensing and Assignment

Members may determine conditions on the licensing and assignment of trade-marks, it being understood that the compulsory licensing of trademarks shall not be permitted and that the owner of a registered trademark shall have the right to assign the trademark with or without the transfer of the business to which the trademark belongs.

Trademarks were traditionally understood to serve as identifiers of the source of goods. The consumer expected that goods placed on the market by a particular producer would conform to the quality standards that the trademark, and thus the producer or source, represented. Consequently, in many legal systems it was not permitted to license a trademark to a third party or, if licensing was permit-ted (and this was largely a development of mid-20th century trademark law), the licensor was required to exercise control over the licensee so as to assure the consumer that the trademark continued to represent an equivalent product.

If a trademark was owned by a business, and the business was sold, there was generally not a legal obstacle to transfer of the mark along with the business. As businesses became more multinational, as well as subdivided into separate operating units, it became commonplace to sell and transfer part of the busi-ness, or business operations in a particular country, as opposed to selling and transferring an entire combined enterprise. National trademark laws, as well as Article 6*quater*(1) of the Paris Convention, acknowledged that assignment and transfer of a mark should be permitted to take place if at least "the portion of the business or goodwill located in that country be transferred to the assignee, together with the exclusive right to manufacture in the said country, or to sell therein, the goods bearing the mark assigned."[271]

Article 21, TRIPS Agreement, acknowledges the right of Members to con-tinue to impose restrictions on the licensing and assignment of trademarks.[272] Members may, for example, continue to require that trademark licensors exercise adequate control over the activities of licensees so as to protect the

---

271. Article 6*quater*

Marks: Assignment of Marks

(1) When, in accordance with the law of a country of the Union, the assignment of a mark is valid only if it takes place at the same time as the transfer of the business or goodwill to which the mark belongs, it shall suffice for the recognition of such validity that the portion of the business or goodwill located in that country be transferred to the assignee, together with the exclusive right to manufacture in the said country, or to sell therein, the goods bearing the mark assigned.

(2) The foregoing provision does not impose upon the countries of the Union any obligation to regard as valid the assignment of any mark the use of which by the assignee would, in fact, be of such a nature as to mislead the public, particularly as regards the origin, nature, or essential qualities, of the goods to which the mark is applied.

272. A "license" is generally understood to refer to a legal arrangement in which a person is given permission to use something owned by another person, but without transfer of ownership interest in the subject matter of the license. An "assignment" is generally understood to refer to a legal arrangement in which ownership interest is effectively transferred from one person to another. However, because the law sometimes imposes restrictions on the formal transfer of ownership of things, an "assignment" of rights might not in all cases involve a formal recordation of change in ownership. For this reason, the words "assignment" and "transfer" are often used to refer first to the change in legal interest in a thing, and second to the formal act involved in recording a change in ownership.

source indication function of the mark (that is, the integrity of the mark from the standpoint of the consumer). The terms of the first clause are not restricted, "Members may determine conditions" on licensing and transfer. The limitations are set out in the second clause.

First, compulsory licensing of trademarks is not permitted. While Article 5.A of the Paris Convention authorizes the compulsory licensing of patents, Article 5.C does not specifically address compulsory licensing of trademarks. It provides that cancellation for non-use should only take place after a "reasonable period" (see sub-Section 2.1.1, *supra*). If a mark is cancelled, it becomes available for use by third parties. In an indirect way cancellation might be viewed as a form of compulsory licensing, but the two concepts are different.

Since trademarks are intended to indicate the source of products, it might seem contradictory to that basic function to permit compulsory licensing to third parties. The source of products would by definition change, and consumers might be misled. Yet there is perhaps more to this question than first meets the eye. Consider the situation in which a compulsory patent license is issued for a medicine. Prior to the introduction of the third-party version of medicine under compulsory license, it is marketed to doctor-pharmacist-consumers under the trademark of the patent holder company. The patent holder asserts that its trademark rights extend to the colour of the medicine tablet. If the colour of the tablet is not licensed along with the patent, this might lead to a situation of confusion in the consuming community (i.e. among doctors, patients and pharmacists). As a practical matter, under the TRIPS Agreement a compulsory license for the claimed mark—which is prohibited by Article 21—is not necessary for two reasons. Trademarks do not cover "function," and if the colour of a medicine tablet is performing a function for doctors, patients and pharmacists, the colour cannot be exclusively reserved to a trademark holder. In addition, Article 17 of the TRIPS Agreement permits limited exceptions to trademark rights, and a Member may recognize a "fair use" right in the mark in these circumstances.[273]

Second, "the owner of a registered trademark shall have the right to assign the trademark with or without the transfer of the business to which the trademark belongs." This formula represents a break with the traditional view of the trademark as an indication of source. There is now permitted the "naked assignment" of marks. The trademark has in essence become a stand-alone commodity that can be traded just as lumber. This acknowledges a major change in the general principles underlying trademark law.

However, the fact that trademarks may be sold and transferred as commodities does not dispense with the basic requirements for the maintenance of marks. In countries where use is required to maintain marks, the new owner must assure that some use in connection with the covered goods or services is made so as to avoid cancellation after the minimum prescribed period has elapsed. Likewise, the mark cannot be allowed to become "generic" and thereby lose its trademark function. (Even a fanciful mark may become generic if it is

273. As noted in the text, when medicines are identified by a single color, that color is often functionally used by consumers as the means to identify it. In these circumstances, there are strong grounds for either (a) denying trademark rights in a single color as it serves a functional (and therefore non-trademark) purpose, or (b) recognizing a fair use right on behalf of third-party producers. Even a limited reference to the "brand name" of the trademark holder may be permitted as fair use when done in a way that does not suggest endorsement of the third-party product by the trademark holder.

widely used in reference to a product and the trademark owner does not take steps to assert its rights and control over the term.)

2. WTO Appellate Body Interpretation of the TRIPS Agreement and Paris Convention

In the *U.S.-Havana Club* case, excerpted below, the WTO Appellate Body for the first time addresses the trademark provisions of the TRIPS Agreement. In doing so, it answers a number of key questions concerning interpretation of the Paris Convention, as well as of the TRIPS Agreement.

The factual setting of the underlying dispute between private operators leading to the WTO case is complex, but may be briefly summarized.[16] Prior to the coming to power of the revolutionary government in Cuba, a family-owned Cuban enterprise made and sold rum under the trademark "Havana Club." That enterprise registered the Havana Club mark in Cuba and the United States. The revolutionary government confiscated the assets of the family-owned business, including the trademarks, and did not compensate the former owners. The former owners did not attempt to renew their trademark registration in the United States, and it lapsed. Subsequently, the Cuban state enterprise that succeeded to the mark in Cuba registered the mark in the United States.

In the 1990s, a France-based multinational liquor manufacturer and distributor (Pernod Ricard) entered into a joint venture with the Cuban state enterprise to sell Havana Club rum worldwide. The joint venture took assignment of the U.S.-registered trademark. In the same period, a U.S.-based (Bermuda incorporated) liquor manufacturer and distributor (Bacardi) purchased the residual interests of the former Cuban-family owners of the Havana Club mark, and began to sell rum under the Havana Club mark in the United States. The Cuban-French joint venture was precluded from selling into the U.S. market because of U.S. legislation and regulations that prevented Cuba and its nationals from doing business in and with the United States. Nonetheless, the Cuban-French joint venture sued the U.S. distributor in federal court in the United States for infringement of its trademark and trade name (and related unfair competition claims) to preserve its rights in the U.S. market.

While the infringement litigation was proceeding, the U.S. Congress passed legislation directed at trademarks and trade names that had been confiscated from Cuban nationals. This legislation retroactively invalidated the assignment of the Havana Club trademark registration to the Cuban-French joint venture, and denied Cuba the right to renew its registration of the Havana Club mark in the United States. In addition, the legislation instructed U.S. courts not to enforce rights in trademarks and trade names asserted by Cuban nationals or their successors-in-interest based on earlier confiscations. The federal court in which the Cuban-French joint venture brought its infringement and unfair competition action rejected the claims based on the newly adopted legislation. This decision was upheld by a federal appeals court, and the U.S. Supreme Court refused to grant a further right of appeal.

---

16. Summary taken from Frederick M. Abbott, *WTO Dispute Settlement Practice Relating to the TRIPS Agreement* in The WTO Dispute Settlement System 1995-2003 (F. Ortino & E.-U. Petersmann eds., 2005).

The European Union challenged the U.S. legislation, regulations, and court decision on a number of grounds. Its main argument was based on the *"telle quelle"* rule of the Paris Convention, which requires that state parties register marks previously registered in other parties "as is." The European Union further argued that the TRIPS Agreement requires WTO Members to recognize trademark ownership determinations made by the state in which a mark is initially registered. The European Union also said that the U.S. scheme deprived Cuba and third countries of national and most favored nation treatment. While the Appellate Body rejected the EU claims regarding the *telle quelle* rule and TRIPS Agreement rules on ownership, it accepted (contrary to the panel) that there were problems on the national treatment and MFN fronts. The portions of the AB decision dealing with national treatment and MFN are not reproduced here because the specific issues respecting the U.S. legislation are highly technical and rather unique to the circumstances. The AB's general pronouncements regarding the importance of the national treatment and MFN rules were excerpted in Chapter 1.

UNITED STATES — SECTION 211 OMNIBUS APPROPRIATIONS ACT OF 1998 AB-2001-7

Report of the Appellate Body*

. . . V. ARTICLE 6*QUINQUIES* OF THE PARIS CONVENTION (1967)

122. We turn now to the claims of the European Communities as they relate to Article 6*quinquies* of the Paris Convention (1967). Article 6*quinquies* A(1) reads:

> Every trademark duly registered in the country of origin shall be accepted for filing and protected *as is* in the other countries of the Union, subject to the reservations indicated in this Article. Such countries may, before proceeding to final registration, require the production of a certificate of registration in the country of origin, issued by the competent authority. No authentication shall be required for this certificate. (emphasis added)

123. Article 6*quinquies* forms part of the Stockholm Act of the Paris Convention, dated 14 July 1967. The Stockholm Act is a revision of the original *Paris Convention for the Protection of Industrial Property*, which entered into force on 7 July 1884. The parties to the Paris Convention, who are commonly described as the "countries of the Paris Union," are obliged to implement the provisions of that Convention.

124. Article 2.1 of the *TRIPS Agreement* provides that: "[i]n respect of Parts II, III and IV of this Agreement, Members shall comply with Articles 1 through 12, and Article 19, of the Paris Convention (1967)." Thus, Article 6*quinquies* of the Paris Convention (1967), as well as certain other specified provisions of the Paris Convention (1967), have been incorporated by reference into the *TRIPS Agreement* and, thus, the *WTO Agreement*.

125. Consequently, WTO Members, whether they are countries of the Paris Union or not, are obliged, under the *WTO Agreement*, to implement those provisions of the Paris Convention (1967) that are incorporated into the

* WT/DS176/AB/R, 2 Jan. 2002.

TRIPS Agreement. As we have already stated, Article 6*quinquies* of the Paris Convention (1967) is one such provision. . . .

130. Before examining the text of Article 6*quinquies,* we note that the Paris Convention (1967) provides two ways in which a national of a country of the Paris Union may obtain registration of a trademark in a country of that Union other than the country of the applicant's origin: one way is by registration under Article 6 of the Paris Convention (1967); the other is by registration under Article 6*quinquies* of that same Convention.

131. Article 6(1) of the Paris Convention (1967) provides:

> The conditions for the filing and registration of trademarks shall be determined in each country of the Union by its domestic legislation.

132. Article 6(1) states the general rule, namely, that each country of the Paris Union has the right to determine the *conditions* for filing and registration of trademarks in its domestic legislation. This is a reservation of considerable discretion to the countries of the Paris Union — and now, by incorporation, the Members of the WTO — to continue, in principle, to determine for themselves the conditions for filing and registration of trademarks. Thus, in our view, the general rule under the Paris Convention (1967) is that national laws apply with respect to trademark registrations within the *territory* of each country of the Paris Union, subject to the requirements of other provisions of that Convention.[72] And, likewise, through incorporation, this is also now the general rule for all WTO Members under the *TRIPS Agreement.*

133. Therefore, an applicant who chooses to seek registration of a trademark in a particular foreign country under Article 6 must comply with the conditions for filing and registration specified in that country's legislation. Such an applicant is *not* obliged to register a trademark first in its country of origin in order to register that trademark in another country of the Paris Union. However, that applicant must comply with the conditions of that other country where registration is sought.

134. As we have stated, Article 6 is not the only way to register a trademark in another country. If an applicant *has* duly registered a trademark in its country of origin, Article 6*quinquies* A(1) provides an alternative way of obtaining protection of that trademark in other countries of the Paris Union. . . .

137. The participants to this dispute disagree on the scope of the requirement imposed by Article 6*quinquies* A(1) to accept for filing and protect trademarks duly registered in the country of origin "as is." Looking first to the text of Article 6*quinquies* A(1), we see that the words "as is" (or, in French, "telle quelle"[77]) relate to the trademark to be "accepted for filing and protected" in another country based on registration in the applicant's country of origin. The ordinary meaning of the words "as is" is "in the existing state."[78] The French

---

72. The discretion of countries of the Paris Union to legislate conditions for filing and registration is not unlimited. It is subject to the international minimum standard of trademark disciplines provided for in other Articles of the Paris Convention (1967). These include, for example, national treatment, as well as internationally agreed reasons for denying trademark registration, such as those provided for in Article 6*ter*. The Paris Convention (1967) limits also the legislative discretion of countries of the Union under Article 6(1) by setting out reasons that countries cannot invoke to deny trademark registration, for example in Article 6(2).

77. Article 29(1)(c) of the Paris Convention (1967) provides: "In case of differences of opinion on the interpretation of the various texts, the French text shall prevail."

78. *The New Shorter Oxford English Dictionary,* L. Brown (ed.), (Clarendon Press, 1993), Vol. I, p. 123.

term "telle quelle" can be defined as "sans arrangement, sans modification."[79] This suggests to us that the requirement of Article 6*quinquies* A(1) to accept for filing and protect a trademark duly registered in the applicant's country of origin relates at least to the *form* of the trademark as registered in the applicant's country of origin.[80] The question before us is whether the scope of this requirement also encompasses other features and aspects of that trademark as registered in the country of origin.

138. According to one expert:

> . . . whenever a trademark is duly registered in the country of origin, the other countries of the Union are obliged to accept and protect it, even if, as regards its form, that is, with regard to the signs of which it is composed, such trademark does not comply with the requirements of the domestic legislation, subject to the additional rules, particularly the grounds for refusal or invalidation of any mark, considered on its individual merits, established in the Article. This rule will therefore apply to trademarks consisting of numbers, letters, surnames, geographical names, words written or not written in a certain language or script, and other signs of which the trademark is composed.[81] (italics and footnotes omitted).

139. However, this view is not determinative of the question before us. To resolve this question, we look to the context of Article 6*quinquies* A(1). We find that there is considerable contextual support for the view that the requirement to register a trademark "as is" under Article 6*quinquies* A(1) does *not* encompass all the features and aspects of that trademark. As we have stressed, Article 6(1) of the Paris Convention (1967) reserves to the countries of the Paris Union the right to determine the *conditions* for filing and registration of trademarks by their domestic legislation.[82] Article 6(1) confirms that the countries of the Paris Union did not relinquish their right to determine the conditions for filing and registration of trademarks by entering into the Paris Convention (1967) — subject, of course, to the other obligations of Paris Union countries under the Paris Convention (1967).[83] Clearly, if Article 6*quinquies* A(1) were interpreted too broadly, the legislative discretion reserved for Members under Article 6(1) would be significantly undermined.

140. To illustrate this point, we will assume for the moment, and solely for the sake of argument, that, as the European Communities argues, Article 6*quinquies* A(1) does require other countries to accept for filing and to protect duly registered trademarks in respect of *all their aspects*, including those other than the form of a trademark. If this were so, an applicant who is a national of a country of the Paris Union would have two choices: that applicant could request trademark registration under Article 6 in another country of the Paris

---

79. *Le Petit Robert Dictionnaire de la Langue Française* (1995), p. 2220. Or in English, as it stands; without adjustments; without modification.

80. The participants agree that the requirement of Article 6*quinquies* A(1) *at the very least* relates to the form of the trademark, but they disagree on what else beyond form, if anything at all, that requirement includes.

81. *See* Bodenhausen, G.H.C, *Guide to the Application of the Paris Convention for the Protection of Industrial Property as revised at Stockholm in 1967* (hereinafter "*Guide to the Paris Convention*"), United International Bureaux for the Protection of Intellectual Property, (1968, reprinted 1991), pp. 110-111.

82. We note that prior to the Revision Conference of Lisbon (1958), the requirements now found in Articles 6 and 6*quinquies* were contained in a single (original) Article 6. At the Revision Conference, it was decided to split the original Article in order to make clear the difference between the two alternative ways to obtain trademark registration explained above.

83. See *supra*, footnote 72.

Union — in which case, that registration would be subject to the trademark law of that other country. Or, that applicant could register the trademark in its country of origin and then invoke the right, pursuant to Article 6*quinquies* A(1), to request acceptance of that trademark for filing and protection in another country. In the latter case, that registration would be governed by the trademark law, not of the country in which the applicant sought registration under Article 6*quinquies* A(1), but of the applicant's country of origin. The "conditions" for registration imposed in the law of the other country of the Paris Union where registration was sought under Article 6*quinquies* A(1) would be irrelevant. If this were so, any such applicant would be able to choose between trademark registration under Article 6 and trademark registration under Article 6*quinquies,* depending on which *conditions* for filing and registration were viewed by the applicant as more favourable to the applicant's interests.[84] Consequently, within the territory of any country of the Paris Union other than the applicant's country of origin, a national of a country of that Union could ensure that it would be subject to *either* the domestic trademark registration requirements of the country of origin (through recourse to Article 6*quinquies*) *or* the domestic trademark registration requirements of the other country where trademark registration is sought (through recourse to Article 6) — *whichever it preferred.* In other words, a national of a Paris Union country could circumvent the "use" requirements of a particular regime by registering in the jurisdiction that does not impose "use" requirements.

141. We are persuaded that the drafters of the Paris Convention did not intend such a result. If, even today, WTO Members have — as the European Communities concedes — reserved the right under the *TRIPS Agreement* to maintain domestic regimes of trademark ownership based on use, then it does not seem credible to us to contend — as the European Communities does — that many of those very same countries intended more than a century ago, in concluding the Paris Convention, or on the occasion of one of the subsequent Revision Conferences of the Paris Convention, to establish a global system for determining trademark ownership that could circumvent, and thereby undermine, a domestic regime of trademark ownership based on use.

142. We note that Article 6*quinquies* B provides that registration of a trademark covered by this Article may be neither denied nor invalidated, except for the reasons listed in subparagraphs B(1) through (3).[85] These exceptions refer,

---

84. As far as trademark protection within the territory of the Paris Union national's country of origin is concerned, such national could not avoid being subject to national trademark law.

85. Article 6*quinquies* B provides:

Trademarks covered by this Article may be neither denied registration nor invalidated except in the following cases:

1. when they are of such a nature as to infringe rights acquired by third parties in the country where protection is claimed;
2. when they are devoid of any distinctive character, or consist exclusively of signs or indications which may serve, in trade, to designate the kind, quality, quantity, intended purpose, value, place of origin, of the goods, or the time of production, or have become customary in the current language or in the bona fide and established practices of the trade of the country where protection is claimed;
3. when they are contrary to morality or public order and, in particular, of such a nature as to deceive the public. It is understood that a mark may not be considered contrary to public order for the sole reason that it does not conform to a provision of the legislation on marks, except if such provision itself relates to public order.

This provision is subject, however, to the application of Article 10*bis.*

inter alia, to acquired rights of third parties; to distinctiveness of character; and to morality, public order ("*ordre public*") and deceptiveness. . . .

145. Finally, we look to an agreed interpretation adopted at the conclusion of the original Paris Convention in 1883. The Final Protocol of the Paris Convention (1883) was considered to form an integral part of that Convention.[88] Paragraph 4 of that Final Protocol in 1883 explained that the provision, which later became Article 6*quinquies* A(1):[89]

> . . . should be understood in the sense that no trademark may be excluded from protection in one of the States of the Union for the sole reason that it does not comply, with regard to the signs of which it is composed, with the conditions of the laws of that State, provided it complies on this point with the laws of the country of origin and that it has been properly filed there. Subject to this exception, *which only concerns the form of the mark,* and subject to the provision of the other Articles of the Convention, *each State shall apply its domestic law.*[90] (emphasis added)

146. As the European Communities has observed, this agreed interpretation was omitted at the Washington Revision Conference of 1911. Yet, like the Panel, we note that no delegation to that conference expressed the view at that time that this omission should change the meaning of the provision.[91] Indeed, as one WIPO publication states, "it is generally believed that such omission did not alter the intended sense of 'telle quelle' as it was made explicit in 1883."[92] On this, we simply observe that our interpretation of Article 6*quinquies* A(1) is not inconsistent with this interpretation.

147. We have already stated that we agree with the Panel that Section 211(a)(1) is a measure dealing, in the particular circumstances in which it applies, with the ownership of a defined category of trademarks. We also agree that the obligation of countries of the Paris Union under Article 6*quinquies* A(1) to accept for filing and protect a trademark duly registered in the country of origin "as is" does not encompass matters related to ownership.

148. For these reasons, we uphold the finding of the Panel in paragraph 8.89 of the Panel Report that Section 211(a)(1) is not inconsistent with Article 2.1 of the *TRIPS Agreement* in conjunction with Article 6*quinquies* A(1) of the Paris Convention (1967). . . .

VII. ARTICLE 16 OF THE *TRIPS Agreement* . . .

185. Article 16 of the *TRIPS Agreement* is entitled "Rights Conferred." Article 16.1 provides:

> The owner of a registered trademark shall have the exclusive right to prevent all third parties not having the owner's consent from using in the course of trade identical or similar signs for goods or services which are identical or similar to those in respect of which the trademark is registered where such use would result in a likelihood of confusion. In case of the use of an identical sign for identical

---

88. Final Protocol of the Paris Convention (1883), para. 7.
89. See *supra,* footnote 82.
90. Final Protocol of the Paris Convention (1883), para. 4.
91. "[I]t is not possible to conclude from this decision [at the Washington Conference of 1911] that agreement was reached regarding a different scope of application of the provision.". Bodenhausen, *Guide to the Paris Convention, supra,* footnote 81, p. 110. Panel Report, para. 8.82.
92. Paris Centenary, 1983, WIPO Publication No. 875. Panel Report, footnote 124 to para. 8.82.

goods or services, a likelihood of confusion shall be presumed. The rights described above shall not prejudice any existing prior rights, nor shall they affect the possibility of Members making rights available on the basis of use.

186. As we read it, Article 16 confers on the *owner* of a registered trademark an internationally agreed minimum level of "exclusive rights" that all WTO Members must guarantee in their domestic legislation. These exclusive rights protect the owner against infringement of the registered trademark by unauthorized third parties.[122]

187. We underscore that Article 16.1 confers these exclusive rights on the "owner" of a registered trademark. As used in this treaty provision, the ordinary meaning of "owner" can be defined as the proprietor or the person who holds the title or dominion of the property constituted by the trademark.[123] We agree with the Panel that this ordinary meaning does not clarify how the ownership of a trademark is to be determined. Also, we agree with the Panel that Article 16.1 does not, in express terms, define how ownership of a registered trademark is to be determined. Article 16.1 confers exclusive rights on the "owner," but Article 16.1 does not tell us who the "owner" *is*.

188. As the United States reminds us, and as the European Communities concedes, the last sentence of Article 16.1 acknowledges that WTO Members may make the rights available "on the basis of use" of the trademark. We read this to permit WTO Members to make the "exclusive rights" contemplated by Article 16.1 available within their respective jurisdictions on the basis of registration or use. The Panel concluded that Article 16.1 contemplates that different forms of entitlement may exist under the laws of different Members, and we agree. However, the *TRIPS Agreement* does not establish or prescribe a regime of ownership of trademarks.

189. In the absence of any *explicit* provisions defining ownership in the *TRIPS Agreement*, it is useful to look also at whether the *TRIPS Agreement* — including the Articles of the Paris Convention (1967) incorporated into it — contains an *implicit* definition of ownership. Turning first to the Paris Convention (1967), we see that, in response to a request for information by the Panel,[126] the Director-General of the International Bureau of the World Intellectual Property Organization ("WIPO") stated that "no provision [of the Paris Convention (1967)] addresses the question how the owner of a trademark has to be determined under the domestic law of States party to the Paris Convention."[127]

---

122. We note that, prior to the entry into force of the *TRIPS Agreement*, only Article 10*bis*(3) of the Paris Convention (1967) provided for a prohibition of "all acts of such a nature as to create confusion by any means whatever with the establishment, the goods, or the industrial or commercial activities of a competitor." *See*, Gervais, D., *The TRIPS Agreement — Drafting History and Analysis*, Sweet & Maxwell, London (1998), pp. 109-110.

123. *The New Shorter Oxford English Dictionary, supra*, footnote 78, Vol. II, p. 2059; *Black's Law Dictionary*, 7th ed., B.A. Garner (ed.), (West Group, 1999), p. 1130.

126. Pursuant to Article 13 of the DSU.

127. The letter from the Director-General of the International Bureau of WIPO, dated 2 March 2001, states:

Even though some provisions of the Paris Convention refer to the concept of trademark ownership (Article 5C(2) and (3), and Article 6*septies:* "proprietor," Article 6*ter*(1)(c): "owner," Article 6*bis*(1) "being already the mark of a person entitled to the benefits of this Convention"), *no provision addresses the question how the owner of a trademark has to be determined under the domestic law of States party to the Paris Convention.* (emphasis added)

Reproduced in relevant part in para. 6.41 of the Panel Report.

The Panel did not discuss this. However, the Panel seems to have taken the view that the definition of the conditions of ownership has been left to the legislative discretion of individual countries of the Paris Union by Article 6(1) of the Paris Convention (1967). We agree. . . .

XI. ARTICLE 8 OF THE PARIS CONVENTION (1967) — TRADE NAMES . . .

333. We disagree with the Panel's reasoning and with the Panel's conclusion on the scope of the *TRIPS Agreement* as it relates to trade names.

334. To explain, we turn first to the Panel's interpretation of Article 1.2 of the *TRIPS Agreement,* which, we recall, provides:

> For the purposes of this Agreement, the term "intellectual property" refers to all categories of intellectual property that are the subject of Sections 1 through 7 of Part II.

335. The Panel interpreted the phrase " 'intellectual property' refers to all categories of intellectual property that are the *subject* of Sections 1 through 7 of Part II" (emphasis added) as if that phrase read "intellectual property means those categories of intellectual property appearing in the *titles* of Sections 1 through 7 of Part II." To our mind, the Panel's interpretation ignores the plain words of Article 1.2, for it fails to take into account that the phrase "the subject of Sections 1 through 7 of Part II" deals not only with the categories of intellectual property indicated in each section *title,* but with other *subjects* as well. For example, in Section 5 of Part II, entitled "Patents," Article 27(3)(b) provides that Members have the option of protecting inventions of plant varieties by *sui generis* rights (such as breeder's rights) instead of through patents.[243] Under the Panel's theory, such *sui generis* rights would not be covered by the *TRIPS Agreement.* The option provided by Article 27(3)(b) would be read out of the *TRIPS Agreement.*

336. Moreover, we do not believe that the Panel's interpretation of Article 1.2 can be reconciled with the plain words of Article 2.1. Article 2.1 explicitly incorporates Article 8 of the Paris Convention (1967) into the *TRIPS Agreement.*

337. The Panel was of the view that the words "in respect of" in Article 2.1 have the effect of "conditioning" Members' obligations under the Articles of the Paris Convention (1967) incorporated into the *TRIPS Agreement,* with the result that trade names are not covered. We disagree.

338. Article 8 of the Paris Convention (1967) covers only the protection of trade names; Article 8 has no other subject. If the intention of the negotiators had been to exclude trade names from protection, there would have been no purpose whatsoever in including Article 8 in the list of Paris Convention (1967)

---

243. Article 27.3(b) of the *TRIPS Agreement* provides:

Members may also exclude from patentability: . . .
    (b) plants and animals other than micro-organisms, and essentially biological processes for the production of plants or animals other than non-biological and microbiological processes. However, Members shall provide for the protection of plant varieties either by patents or by an effective *sui generis* system or by any combination thereof. The provisions of this subparagraph shall be reviewed four years after the date of entry into force of the WTO Agreement.

provisions that were specifically incorporated into the *TRIPS Agreement*. To adopt the Panel's approach would be to deprive Article 8 of the Paris Convention (1967), as incorporated into the *TRIPS Agreement* by virtue of Article 2.1 of that Agreement, of any and all meaning and effect. As we have stated previously:

> One of the corollaries of the "general rule of interpretation" in the *Vienna Convention* is that interpretation must give meaning and effect to all the terms of a treaty. An interpreter is not free to adopt a reading that would result in reducing whole clauses or paragraphs of a treaty to redundancy or inutility.[244]

339. As for the import of the negotiating history, we do not see it as in any way decisive to the issue before us. The documents on which the Panel relied are not conclusive of whether the *TRIPS Agreement* covers trade names. The passages quoted by the Panel from the negotiating history of Article 1.2 do not even refer to trade names. There is nothing at all in those passages to suggest that Members were either for or against their inclusion. Indeed, the only reference to a debate about the categories for coverage in the *TRIPS Agreement* relates, not to trade names, but to trade secrets. The Panel itself acknowledged that "[t]he records do not contain information on the purpose of the addition" of the words "in respect of" at the beginning of Article 2.1. Therefore, we do not consider that any conclusions may be drawn from these records about the interpretation of the words "in respect of" in Article 2.1 as regards trade names.

340. Thus, in our view, the Panel's interpretation of Articles 1.2 and 2.1 of the *TRIPS Agreement* is contrary to the ordinary meaning of the terms of those provisions and is, therefore, not in accordance with the customary rules of interpretation prescribed in Article 31 of the *Vienna Convention*.[247] Moreover, we do not believe that the negotiating history confirms, within the meaning of Article 32 of the *Vienna Convention,* the Panel's interpretation of Articles 1.2 and 2.1.

341. For all these reasons, we reverse the Panel's finding in paragraph 8.41 of the Panel Report that trade names are not covered under the *TRIPS Agreement* and find that WTO Members do have an obligation under the *TRIPS Agreement* to provide protection to trade names.

NOTES AND QUESTIONS

1. The Appellate Body has decisively rejected the European Union's argument that the "telle quelle" or "as is" rule of the Paris Convention addresses more than the form in which the foreign mark must be accepted for registration. There was very little support among international IP experts for that EU position from the outset of this case. A more interesting and debated question in this case was whether, as a matter of public international law, the United States had good grounds for refusing to recognize Cuba's taking of the former Cuban owners' assets, including trademark rights. Recall that the former owners were not U.S. (or other

---

244. Appellate Body Report, *US-Gasoline, supra,* footnote 102, at 21. *See also* Appellate Body Report, *Japan-Alcoholic Beverages II, supra,* footnote 102, at 106.
247. *See* Article 3.2 of the DSU.

foreign) citizens, but rather nationals and residents of Cuba at the time of the confiscation. Thomas Cottier has argued that the U.S. refusal to recognize the acts of the Cuban government with respect to its own citizens may not be valid under international law, and therefore trademark ownership in the United States should properly reside with the Cuban-French joint venture. In the present case, this raises the question of whether the WTO Appellate Body could have invoked general principles of public international law to find U.S. legislation as to trademark ownership inconsistent with WTO norms. It did not. *See* discussion in F.M. Abbott & T. Cottier, *Dispute Prevention and Dispute Settlement in the Field of Intellectual Property Rights and Electronic Commerce: US-Section 211 Omnibus Appropriations Act 1998* ("Havana Club"), in Transatlantic Economic Disputes: The EU, the US, and the WTO (E.-U. Petersmann & M. Pollack eds., Oxford 2005).

2. Throughout the long history of the Paris Convention, the International Court of Justice has never been called upon to interpret its provisions. The WTO Appellate Body has now stepped in to perform this task. Why have states been reluctant to approach the ICJ? Why is the WTO Appellate Body a more attractive forum? Might the experience of litigating the Paris Convention before the WTO encourage some state party to bring a case at the ICJ? Is there a risk from potentially conflicting interpretations?

3. The Appellate Body relies on a former WIPO official's book for interpretive guidance with respect to the meaning of the *telle quelle* rule. This suggests a reasonably strong role for the WIPO Secretariat in the interpretation of the TRIPS Agreement.

4. The United States is a strong advocate of high standards of intellectual property protection. Yet, in the *Havana Club* case, it champions the right of each government to determine who the owner of a trademark is. Does this create risks for U.S. trademark owners?

E. The Interface Between Trademarks and Geographical Indications

The TRIPS Agreement includes a section addressing trademarks (Part II, sec. 2) and a section addressing geographical indications (Part II, sec. 3). The TRIPS Agreement does not, except in a few limited circumstances, address the relationship between the forms of IP protection.

The subject matter of GIs was introduced in section I.E, *supra*. Generally speaking, GIs may be protected by unfair competition law, as trademarks (including as collective and certification marks), by *sui generis* registration systems, and by administrative forms of protection. The TRIPS Agreement requires that wines and spirits receive specified minimum protection, and provides for the establishment of a common register with respect to wines for countries that choose to participate in it (TRIPS Agreement, art. 23).

In the United States, protection of geographical indications is principally provided through collective and certification marks. The United States does provide another form of GIs protection through its system for approving labels on wines and spirits (the Certificate of Labelling Approval or "COLA" system). This system is administered by the Alcohol and Tobacco Tax and Trade Bureau of the Department of the Treasury (TTB). The registration system is established pursuant to the Federal Alcohol Administration Act (27 U.S.C. §§ 201 et seq.), which is supplemented by Chapter 27 of the Code of Federal Regulations (27 C.F.R. §§ 1.1 et seq.).

In the European Union, protection of geographical indications is subject to a complex regulatory system that includes substantial conditions that producers must meet in order to obtain and maintain registration of GIs, and includes substantial oversight by national and EU regulatory authorities.

What happens when the rights of the trademark holder come into conflict with the rights of a holder of a GI? The following is an excerpt from the case brought by the United States against the European Union that addresses the relationship between trademarks and GIs (recall that part of this decision addressing national treatment appeared in Chapter 1).

This WTO panel decision includes the first application in a dispute settlement proceeding of Article 17 of the TRIPS Agreement regarding exceptions to the rights conferred by trademark, and for that reason is the special interest. Neither the European Union nor the United States appealed the panel decision to the Appellate Body.

EUROPEAN COMMUNITIES — PROTECTION OF TRADEMARKS AND GEOGRAPHICAL INDICATIONS FOR AGRICULTURAL PRODUCTS AND FOODSTUFFS COMPLAINT BY THE UNITED STATES

Report of the Panel*

. . . C. Trademark Claim

1. the relationship between GIs and prior trademarks . . .

7.512 The *United States* claims that the Regulation is inconsistent with Article 16.1 of the TRIPS Agreement because it does not ensure that a trademark owner may prevent uses of GIs which would result in a likelihood of confusion with a prior trademark. Its claim only concerns valid prior trademarks, not trademarks liable to invalidation because they lack distinctiveness or mislead consumers as to the origin of goods. It does not dispute that GIs that are identical or similar to trademarks may be used, but only to the extent that they do not result in a likelihood of confusion with respect to prior trademarks.

7.513 The *European Communities* responds that this claim is unfounded for several reasons: (1) Article 14(3) of the Regulation, in fact, prevents the registration of GIs, use of which would result in a likelihood of confusion with a prior trademark; (2) Article 24.5 of the TRIPS Agreement provides for the "coexistence" of GIs and prior trademarks; (3) Article 24.3 of the TRIPS Agreement requires the European Communities to maintain "coexistence"; and (4) in any event, Article 14(2) of the Regulation would be justified as a limited exception under Article 17 of the TRIPS Agreement.

7.514 For the sake of brevity, the Panel uses the term "coexistence" in this report to refer to a legal regime under which a GI and a trademark can both be used concurrently to some extent even though the use of one or both of them

* WT/DS174/R, 15 Mar. 2005.

would otherwise infringe the rights conferred by the other. The use of this term does not imply any view on whether such a regime is justified. . . .

7.562 [T]he Panel considers that the United States has made a prima facie case that Article 14(3) of the Regulation cannot prevent all situations from occurring in which Article 14(2) would, in fact, limit the rights of a trademark owner.

7.563 Consistent with this view, it can be noted that the European Communities specifically rejected a proposal by a Committee of the European Parliament to amend Article 14(2) so as to subject it to the trademark owners' rights when Article 14 was amended in April 2003. This at least suggests that Article 14(3) was considered different from a blanket protection of trademark rights. . . .

7.567 . . . [T]he Panel considers that there is no evidence to show that it is possible to seek invalidation of a GI registration under Article 14(3) in *all* cases in which use of a GI would otherwise be found to infringe a prior trademark. In those cases where it is not possible, it would be necessary for the owner of a prior trademark to be able to anticipate, at the time of the proposed GI registration, all subsequent uses of the proposed GI that would result in a likelihood of confusion. There is no reason to believe that this is possible. The evidence submitted to the Panel shows that GI registrations under the Regulation simply refer to names without limiting the way in which they are used. Indeed, it became apparent in the course of the proceedings that what the United States regards as "trademark-like use" is, in the European Communities, considered perfectly legitimate use as a GI.[452] . . .

7.570 The United States also refers to specific cases in which the Regulation has been applied in support of its claim, as set out in the following paragraphs.

7.571 Article 14(3) of the Regulation has only been applied once. This was the case of "Bayerisches Bier," which was registered as a protected geographical indication in 2001 subject to the proviso that the use of certain prior trademarks, for example, BAVARIA and HØKER BAJER, was permitted to continue under Article 14(2). The GI refers to a beer and the trademarks are registered in respect of beer. The GI and the trademarks are, respectively, the words "Bavaria" or "Bavarian Beer" rendered in the German, English and Danish languages. Upon its registration, the EC Council concluded that the GI would not mislead the public as to the identity of the product, which is the standard embodied in Article 14(3) of the Regulation.

7.572 The United States alleges that the GI "Bayerisches Bier" could be used in a manner that would result in a likelihood of confusion with these prior trademarks. In response to a direct question from the Panel, the European Communities did not deny this specific allegation. It only responded that "in principle" a name registered following the assessment required by Article 14(3) "should not give rise to confusion when used subsequently" and submitted that "in practice" this may happen only when the registered name is used together with other signs or as part of a combination of signs. This was a conspicuous

---

452. The United States submitted copies of the packaging of cheeses bearing the GIs "Esrom," "Bitto," "Bra" and "Tomme de Savoie" in Exhibit US-52. The European Communities submitted the approved specifications for these GIs in Exhibits EC-99 through EC-102. *See* the European Communities' response to Panel question No. 140 and the United States' comment on that response.

choice of words because in the same response it commented in detail on two other specific cases which it considered irrelevant to the dispute.[455]

7.573 The United States also alleges that three Czech beer GIs, "Budejovické pivo," "Cbreveeskobudějovické pivo" and "Budejovický měšt'anský var" could be used in a manner that would result in a likelihood of confusion with the prior trademarks BUDWEISER and BUD, registered in respect of beer.[456] The evidence shows that a court in a non-EC WTO Member found a reasonable probability that a substantial number of persons would be confused if the marks BUDEJOVICKY BUDVAR depicted in a special script, and BUDWEISER and BUD, were used together in relation to beer in a normal and fair manner and in the ordinary course of business, particularly the mark BUD.[457] However, courts in two other non-EC WTO Members found that the use of "Budìjovický Budvar" on specific beer labels did not give rise to a likelihood of confusion with the trademarks BUDWEISER and BUD, registered in respect of beer.[458] In response to a direct question from the Panel, the European Communities did not deny that these GIs could be used in a manner that would result in a likelihood of confusion with these prior trademarks. Instead, it pointed to an endorsement on the three GI registrations that they apply "without prejudice to any beer trademark or other rights existing in the European Union on the date of accession." This might imply that it accepts a likelihood of confusion, but considers that there are other means besides Article 14(3) to deal with that. It also argued that these GIs were outside the terms of reference but the United States expressly clarified that it referred to them only as evidence in support of its claim and did not challenge these individual registrations in this panel proceeding.

7.574 There appears to be an inconsistency between the European Communities' position that Article 14(3) of the Regulation, in practice, prevents the registration of GIs, use of which would result in a likelihood of confusion with a prior trademark, and its decision to avoid contesting that there may be circumstances in which the four specific GIs referred to above could be used which would not result in a likelihood of confusion with these specific prior trademarks.

7.575 For the above reasons, the Panel considers that the European Communities has not rebutted the United States' prima facie case that Article 14(3) of the Regulation cannot prevent all situations from occurring in which

---

455. The European Communities submitted twice that the EC Council had concluded that the registration of this GI would not lead to a likelihood of confusion with these prior trademarks but this is different from the EC Council's conclusion as stated in the decision on registration. The European Communities later indicated in response to a question from the Panel that the EC Council's conclusion was that the signs were not sufficiently similar to mislead the public, which is closer to the wording of the conclusion as stated in the decision, but not necessarily a likelihood of confusion: see European Communities' first written submission, para. 288, fn.140; rebuttal submission, para. 287; and responses to Panel questions Nos. 137 and 143 and compare Council Regulation (EC) No. 1347/2001 reproduced in Exhibits US-41 and EC-9 and the Commission Guide to the Regulation (August 2004 edition, p. 12) in Exhibit EC-64.

456. The evidence indicates that these trademarks are registered in at least two EC member States and rights to them appear to have been acquired through use in another EC member State: see Exhibits US-53, Section 3.6; US-51, para. 26; and US-82.

457. Judgement of the High Court of South Africa in *Budweiser Budvar National Corporation v. Anheuser-Busch Corporation*, dated 3 December 2003, reproduced in Exhibit US-82.

458. Judgement of the Federal Court of Australia in *Anheuser-Busch, Inc. v Budìjovický Budvar, Národní Podnik*,[2002] FCA 390 (dated 5 April 2002); judgement of the Court of Appeal of New Zealand in *Anheuser Busch Incorporated v Budweiser Budwar National Corporation & Ors*[2002] NZCA 264 (dated 19 September 2002) reproduced in Exhibits EC-117 and EC-118, respectively.

a trademark would be subject to Article 14(2) and, hence, in which the Regulation would limit the rights of the owner of such a trademark.

7.576 The Panel will now proceed to examine whether the TRIPS Agreement requires Members to make available to trademark owners rights against the use of GIs.

(d) Relationship between protection of GIs and prior trademarks under the TRIPS Agreement

ARTICLE 16.1 OF THE TRIPS AGREEMENT . . .

7.599 Although each of the Sections in Part II provides for a different category of intellectual property, at times they refer to one another,[547] as certain subject matter may be eligible for protection by more than one category of intellectual property. This is particularly apparent in the case of trademarks and GIs, both of which are, in general terms, forms of distinctive signs. The potential for overlap is expressly confirmed by Articles 22.3 and 23.2, which provide for the refusal or invalidation of the registration of a trademark which contains or consists of a GI.[548] . . .

7.601 The right which must be conferred on the owner of a registered trademark is set out in the first sentence of the text. There are certain limitations on that right which relate to use in the course of trade, the signs, the goods or services for which the signs are used and those with respect to which they are registered and the likelihood of confusion. The ordinary meaning of the text indicates that, basically, this right applies to use in the course of trade of identical or similar signs, on identical or similar goods, where such use would result in a likelihood of confusion. It does not specifically exclude use of signs protected as GIs.

7.602 The text of Article 16.1 stipulates that the right for which it provides is an "exclusive" right. This must signify more than the fact that it is a right to "exclude" others, since that notion is already captured in the use of the word "prevent." Rather, it indicates that this right belongs to the owner of the registered trademark alone, who may exercise it to prevent certain uses by "all third parties" not having the owner's consent. The last sentence provides for an exception to that right, which is that it shall not prejudice any existing prior rights. Otherwise, the text of Article 16.1 is unqualified.

7.603 Other exceptions to the right under Article 16.1 are provided for in Article 17 and possibly elsewhere in the TRIPS Agreement. However, there is no implied limitation vis-à-vis GIs in the text of Article 16.1 on the exclusive right which Members must make available to the owner of a registered trademark. That right may be exercised against a third party not having the owner's consent on the same terms, whether or not the third party uses the sign in accordance with GI protection, subject to any applicable exception. . . .

---

547. For instance, Article 25.2 of the TRIPS Agreement refers to more than one category of intellectual property, as does Article 4 of the IPIC Treaty, as incorporated by Article 35 of the TRIPS Agreement.

548. Articles 22.3 and 23.2, respectively.

(f) Article 17 of the TRIPS Agreement . . .
   7.646 Article 17 provides as follows:

EXCEPTIONS
Members may provide limited exceptions to the rights conferred by a trademark,
such as fair use of descriptive terms, provided that such exceptions take account of
the legitimate interests of the owner of the trademark and of third parties.

7.647 Article 17 expressly permits Members to provide limited exceptions to
the rights conferred by a trademark, which include the right provided for in
Article 16.1 of the TRIPS Agreement. The Panel has already found that the
Regulation limits the availability of the right provided for in Article 16.1.
Therefore, to the extent that it satisfies the conditions in Article 17, this limitation will be permitted under the TRIPS Agreement.
   7.648 Article 17 permits "limited exceptions." It provides an example of a
limited exception, and is subject to a proviso that "such exceptions take account
of the legitimate interests of the owner of the trademark and of third parties."
The ordinary meaning of the terms indicates that an exception must not only be
"limited" but must also comply with the proviso in order to satisfy Article 17.
The example of "fair use of descriptive terms" is illustrative only, but it can
provide interpretative guidance because, *a priori,* it falls within the meaning of a
"limited" exception and must be capable of satisfying the proviso in some
circumstances. Any interpretation of the term "limited" or of the proviso
which excluded the example would be manifestly incorrect.
   7.649 The structure of Article 17 differs from that of other exceptions provisions to which the parties refer. . . .

LIMITED EXCEPTIONS

   7.650 The first issue to decide is the meaning of the term "limited exceptions" as used in Article 17. The United States interprets this in terms of a small
diminution of rights. The European Communities does not disagree with this
approach. The Panel agrees with the views of the Panel in *Canada-
Pharmaceutical Patents,* which interpreted the identical term in Article 30, that
"[t]he word 'exception' by itself connotes a limited derogation, one that does
not undercut the body of rules from which it is made." The addition of the word
"limited" emphasizes that the exception must be narrow and permit only a
small diminution of rights. The limited exceptions apply "to the rights conferred by a trademark." They do not apply to the set of all trademarks or all
trademark owners. Accordingly, the fact that it may affect only few trademarks
or few trademark owners is irrelevant to the question whether an exception is
limited. The issue is whether the exception to the *rights conferred by a trademark* is
narrow.
   7.651 There is only one right conferred by a trademark at issue in this dispute, namely the exclusive right to prevent certain uses of a sign, provided for
in Article 16.1. Therefore, it is necessary to examine the exception on an
individual "per right" basis. This is a legal assessment of the extent to which
the exception curtails that right. There is no indication in the text of Article 17
that this involves an economic assessment, although economic impact can be
taken into account in the proviso. In this regard, we note the absence of any

reference to a "normal exploitation" of the trademark in Article 17, and the absence of any reference in Section 2, to which Article 17 permits exceptions, to rights to exclude legitimate competition. Rather, they confer, *inter alia,* the right to prevent uses that would result in a likelihood of confusion, which can lead to the removal of products from sale where they are marketed using particular signs, but without otherwise restraining the manufacture, sale or importation of competing goods or services.

7.652 The right provided for in Article 16.1 contains several elements and an exception could, in principle, curtail the right in respect of any of them. We recall these elements in the text of that provision as follows:

> "The owner of a registered trademark shall have the exclusive right to prevent *all third parties* not having the owner's consent from using in the course of trade *identical or similar signs* for *goods or services which are identical or similar* to those in respect of which the trademark is registered where such use would result in *a likelihood of confusion*." [emphasis added]

7.653 In principle, an exception could curtail the right of the owner in respect of the third parties concerned, or with respect to the identity or the similarity of the signs or the goods or services concerned or with respect to the degree of likelihood of confusion, or some combination of these. There may be other possibilities as well. The overriding requirement is that the exception must be "limited" and it must also satisfy the proviso, considered below. These elements provide a useful framework for an assessment of the extent to which an exception curtails the right provided for in Article 16.1.

7.654 The example in the text, "fair use of descriptive terms," provides guidance as to what is considered a "limited exception," although it is illustrative only. Fair use of descriptive terms is inherently limited in terms of the sign which may be used and the degree of likelihood of confusion which may result from its use, as a purely descriptive term on its own is not distinctive and is not protectable as a trademark. Fair use of descriptive terms is *not* limited in terms of the number of third parties who may benefit, nor in terms of the quantity of goods or services with respect to which they use the descriptive terms, although implicitly it only applies to those third parties who would use those terms in the course of trade and to those goods or services which those terms describe. The number of trademarks or trademark owners affected is irrelevant, although implicitly it would only affect those marks which can consist of, or include, signs that can be used in a descriptive manner. According to the text, this is a "limited" exception for the purposes of Article 17.

7.655 Turning to the Regulation, it curtails the trademark owner's right in respect of certain goods but not all goods identical or similar to those in respect of which the trademark is registered. It prevents the trademark owner from exercising the right to prevent confusing uses of a sign for the agricultural product or foodstuff produced in accordance with the product specification in the GI registration. We recall that, according to Article 2(2) of the Regulation . . . those goods must all be produced, processed and/or prepared in the region, specific place or, in exceptional cases, country, the name of which is used to describe them. Goods that are not from that geographical area may not use the GI. Further, according to Article 4 of the Regulation, all products using a GI must comply with a product specification. Products that do not so comply may not use the GI even if they are from the geographical area. The trademark owner's right against all other goods is not curtailed. We note that there is no limit in terms of the quantity of goods which may benefit from the exception, as long as they conform to the product specification. However, this cannot prevent the limitation on rights of owners of trademarks subject to Article 14(2) from constituting a limited exception for the purposes of Article 17, as fair use of descriptive terms implies no limit in terms of quantity either, and the text indicates that it is a limited exception for the purposes of Article 17. The quantity of goods which benefits from an exception may be related to the curtailment of the rights to prevent the acts of making, selling or importing a product, but these are not rights conferred by a trademark.

7.656 The Regulation curtails the trademark owner's right against certain third parties, but not "all third parties." It prevents the trademark owner from exercising the right to prevent confusing uses against persons using a registered GI on a good in accordance with its registration. This is a limitation on the third parties who may benefit from the exception. The trademark owner's right is not curtailed with respect to any other third parties.[580]

7.657 The Regulation curtails the trademark owner's right in respect of certain signs but not all signs identical or similar to the one protected as a trademark. It prevents the trademark owner from exercising its right to prevent use of an indication registered as a GI in accordance with its registration. We recall our finding . . . that the GI registration does not confer a positive right to use any other signs or combination of signs nor to use the name in any linguistic versions not entered in the register. The trademark owner's right is not curtailed against any such uses. If the GI registration prevented the trademark owner from exercising its rights against these signs, combinations of signs or linguistic versions, which do not appear expressly in the GI registration, it would seriously expand the exception and undermine the limitations on its scope.

7.658 Under the Regulation, once a GI has been registered and a trademark is subject to the coexistence regime under Article 14(2) . . . the GI may, in principle, be used without regard to the likelihood of confusion that it may cause. However, the Regulation refers to the likelihood or risk of confusion, with a given mark, which would result from use as a GI of an identical or similar sign, in Articles 7(5)(b), 12b(3) and 12d(3), in relation to the decision on whether to register a GI where an objection is admissible. Article 7(4) and, hence, Article 12b(3), provide a ground for objection where registration would jeopardize the existence of a mark, and Article 14(3) provides a ground for refusal of registration which refers to the trademark's reputation and renown and the length of time it has been used. . . .

7.659 The United States submitted that Article 14(2) eliminates the trademark owner's right, granting the owner only the right to continue to use the trademark. However, the European Communities has emphasized

---

580. The United States refers to a case of trademark infringement in which the German Federal Supreme Court held that the concurrent use by Fiat of the SL trademark owned by Mercedes-Benz could put at risk the very existence of that trademark. Note that, in coming to its decision, the Court observed that "it could be expected that other vehicle manufacturers might soon follow the defendant's example." *See* United States' rebuttal submission, para. 173, fn. 167 and Exhibit US-67. The opportunity for all other potential competitors to use a trademark does not arise under the GI Regulation as it only permits use of a GI in accordance with its registration, including the product specifications.

that the trademark owner retains the right to prevent the use of a name registered as a GI by any person in relation to any goods which originate in a different geographical area or which do not comply with the specifications, and that the positive right to use the GI extends only to the linguistic versions that have been entered in the register and not to other names or signs which have not been registered. Accordingly, on the basis of the terms of the GI Regulation and of the Community Trademark Regulation, and the explanation of them provided by the European Communities, the Panel finds that not only may the trademark continue to be used, but that the trademark owner's right to prevent confusing uses, is unaffected except with respect to the use of a GI as entered in the GI register in accordance with its registration. In view of these limitations, the scope of the exception in Article 14(2) falls far short of that which the United States initially claimed.[583]

7.660 Furthermore, the European Communities has explained that the use of a name registered as a GI is subject to the applicable provisions of the food labelling and misleading advertising directives so that the ways in which it may be used are not unlimited.

7.661 For the above reasons, the Panel finds that the Regulation creates a "limited exception" within the meaning of Article 17 of the TRIPS Agreement.

THE PROVISO TO ARTICLE 17

7.662 Limited exceptions must satisfy the proviso that "such exceptions take account of the legitimate interests of the owner of the trademark and of third parties" in order to benefit from Article 17. We must first establish what are "legitimate interests." Read in context, the "legitimate interests" of the trademark owner are contrasted with the "rights conferred by a trademark," which also belong to the trademark owner. Given that Article 17 creates an exception to the rights conferred by a trademark, the "legitimate interests" of the trademark owner must be something different from full enjoyment of those legal rights. The "legitimate interests" of the trademark owner are also compared with those of "third parties," who have no rights conferred by the trademark. Therefore, the "legitimate interests" at least of third parties, are something different from simply the enjoyment of their legal rights. This is confirmed by the use of the verb "take account of," which is less than "protect."

7.663 We agree with the following view of the Panel in *Canada-Pharmaceutical Patents*, which interpreted the term "legitimate interests" of a patent owner and third parties in the context of Article 30 as follows:

> To make sense of the term "legitimate interests" in this context, that term must be defined in the way that it is often used in legal discourse — as a normative claim calling for protection of interests that are "justifiable" in the sense that they are supported by relevant public policies or other social norms. In our view, this is also true of the term "legitimate interests" of a trademark owner and third parties in the context of Article 17.

583. *See* United States' first oral statement, para. 75. The United States appears to acknowledge that the GI registration does not extinguish the trademark owner's rights against other third parties, although it alleges that use of the GI will affect the distinctiveness of the trademark: *see* United States' second oral statement, para. 101. The Panel considers that issue in relation to the proviso to Article 17.

7.664 The legitimacy of some interest of the trademark owner is assumed because the owner of the trademark is specifically identified in Article 17. . . .

7.665 Turning to the Regulation, the evidence shows that the owner's legitimate interest in preserving the distinctiveness, or capacity to distinguish, of its trademark can be taken into account in various ways. Article 7(4) of the Regulation provides that a statement of objection shall be admissible *inter alia* if it shows that the registration of the proposed GI would "jeopardize the existence . . . of a mark." This requires GI registration to be refused.

7.666 Article 14(3) also requires the refusal of GI registration in light of a trademark's reputation and renown and the length of time it has been used, if a particular condition is fulfilled. This addresses the distinctiveness, or capacity to distinguish, of prior trademarks and can ensure that, in cases where trademark owners' legitimate interests would be most likely to be affected, the exception in Article 14(2) simply does not apply. . . .

7.670 Where Articles 7(4) and 14(3) of the Regulation are unavailable, and a trademark is subject to Article 14(2), there remains the possibility that its distinctiveness will be affected by the use of the GI. We do not consider this fatal to the applicability of Article 17 given that, as a provision permitting an exception to the exclusive right to prevent uses that would result in a likelihood of confusion, it presupposes that a certain degree of likelihood of confusion can be permitted. In the light of the provisions of Articles 7(4) and 14(3), we are satisfied that where the likelihood of confusion is relatively high, the exception in Article 14(2) will not apply. In any event, even where the exception does apply, Article 14(2) expressly provides that the trademark may continue to be used, on certain conditions.

7.671 We also note that the proviso to Article 17 requires only that exceptions "take account" of the legitimate interests of the owner of the trademark, and does not refer to "unreasonabl[e] prejudice" to those interests, unlike the provisos in Articles 13, 26.2 and 30 of the TRIPS Agreement and Article 9(2) of the Berne Convention (1971) as incorporated by Article 9.1 of the TRIPS Agreement. This suggests that a lesser standard of regard for the legitimate interests of the owner of the trademark is required.

7.672 The United States submits that Article 17 of the TRIPS Agreement requires a case-by-case analysis and that a blanket exception *a priori* does not take into account the legitimate interests of trademark owners. The Panel observes that Articles 7(4) and 14(3) of the Regulation do require a case-by-case analysis at the time of a decision on GI registration and, even though they do not require a case-by-case analysis at the time of subsequent use, nothing in the text of Article 17 indicates that a case-by-case analysis is a requirement under the TRIPS Agreement. Whilst it may be true that in the United States the doctrine of "fair use" is applied by courts on a case-by-case basis, we do not consider that this is necessarily implied in the use of those words in the TRIPS Agreement.[588]

---

588. If there were any doubt on this point, [one] can observe that this language in Article 17 was proposed in the TRIPS negotiations by the European Communities and Austria, and was not apparently intended to reflect the United States' practice: *see* "Synoptic tables setting out existing international standards and proposed standards and principles," prepared by the GATT Secretariat at the request of the Negotiating Group on Trade-related Aspects of Intellectual Property Rights, including trade in counterfeit goods, (document MTN.GNG/NG11/W/32/Rev.2 dated 2 February 1990, p. 51).

7.673 The Panel notes that there may be situations where, in order to take account of the legitimate interests of the owner of a trademark and third parties, practical conditions may be required to distinguish the goods with the trademark from those using the GI and to distinguish the respective undertakings.

7.674 For these reasons, the Panel considers that the exception created by the Regulation takes account of the legitimate interests of the owner of the trademark within the meaning of Article 17. This finding is confirmed by responses to a question from the Panel which revealed that, of over 600 GIs registered under the Regulation over a period of eight years, the complainants and third parties are unable to identify any that, in their view, could be used in a way that would result in a likelihood of confusion with a prior trademark, with four exceptions. Three of these are the Czech beer GIs, the registration of which is subject to the endorsement set out above. The only remaining example is "Bayerisches Bier," in respect of which the complainants have not shown an example of actual likelihood of confusion with a prior trademark.

7.675 We will now consider whether the exception created by the Regulation takes account of the legitimate interests of third parties.

7.676 The parties to this dispute agree that "third parties" for the purposes of Article 17 include consumers. The function of a trademark is to distinguish goods and services of undertakings in the course of trade. That function is served not only for the owner, but also for consumers. Accordingly, the relevant third parties include consumers.[589] Consumers have a legitimate interest in being able to distinguish the goods and services of one undertaking from those of another, and to avoid confusion.

7.677 Turning to the Regulation, Article 14(3) expressly addresses consumers, by providing for the refusal of GI registration where "registration is liable to mislead the consumer as to the true identity of the product." In the one instance in which Article 14(3) has been applied, the European Communities informs the Panel that:

> In essence, it was concluded that, although the products were similar, the signs were not sufficiently similar to mislead the public, having regard to the degree of recognition of the trademark in the different Member States.

7.678 This indicates to the Panel that Article 14(3) of the Regulation was, in fact, applied to take account *inter alia* of the legitimate interests of consumers. . . .

7.686 For these reasons, the Panel considers that the exception created by the Regulation takes account of the legitimate interests of third parties within the meaning of Article 17.

7.687 On the basis of the evidence presented to the Panel, which is necessarily limited given that Article 14(3) of the Regulation has only been applied once, and for all of the above reasons, the Panel concludes that the European Communities has succeeded in raising a presumption that the exception created by the Regulation to the trademark owner's right provided for in Article 16.1 of the TRIPS Agreement is justified by Article 17 of the TRIPS

---

589. This is confirmed by the reference in Article 16.2 to "the relevant sector of the public," in relation to well-known trademarks.

Agreement. The United States has not succeeded in rebutting that presumption.

7.688 Therefore, the Panel concludes that, with respect to the coexistence of GIs with prior trademarks, the Regulation is inconsistent with Article 16.1 of the TRIPS Agreement but, on the basis of the evidence presented to the Panel, this is justified by Article 17 of the TRIPS Agreement. . . .

NOTES AND QUESTIONS

1. The panel accepts that some consumer confusion between existing trademarks and GIs will occur. Otherwise, there would be no need to invoke an exception. In what type of situation might this occur? If a German beer-producing region was successful in registering the GI "Bürger King," might that conflict with the registered trademark of the U.S.-based fast food chain "Burger King"? Would EU consumers be likely to think that the fast food outlet famous for hamburgers had decided to enter the beer business?

2. What limitations does the panel impose on the use of GIs that are permitted by application of Article 17 of the TRIPS Agreement? *Inter alia,* the European Union explained that "the positive right to use the GI extends only to the linguistic versions that have been entered in the register and not to other names or signs which have not been registered," and the panel noted that limitation. What is the basis for the limitations?

3. Recall from Chapter 1 that the EU GIs Regulation was found to be inconsistent with the TRIPS Agreement and GATT national treatment rules because it imposed burdensome conditions on foreign holders of GIs. These inconsistencies had effectively precluded foreign nationals from registering their GIs in the European Union. The possibility for conflict between prior trademarks and GIs was a relatively minor problem for the United States, which had some difficulty in providing examples where conflicts had arisen or might arise. Though there was one "big-ticket" case involving the "Budweiser" trademark for beer, even that conflict appeared to be at the margin of economic interest for the U.S. "Budweiser" owner, Anheuser-Busch.

4. The continuing saga of Anheuser-Busch and the Budweiser trademark in the European Union can be studied at *Anheuser-Busch v. OHIM*, ECJ Case C-214/09 P, 29 July 2010, where the ECJ refused to overrule the OHIM's decision to refuse Anheuser-Busch's application for registration of a CTM based on opposition by the Czech brewer Budějovický Budvar. Now that Anheuser-Busch is owned by a Belgium-based enterprise, InBev, do you think that the attitude of EU institutions toward full protection of the Budweiser trademark in the EU may change?

5. In the *Canada-Generic Pharmaceuticals* case, *supra* Chapter 2, section II.B.1, the panel found that a provision of Canadian law that allowed stockpiling of generic drugs prior to expiration of the patent was inconsistent with Article 30, mainly because it did not restrict the quantity of drugs that could be stockpiled. Does the panel in the *EC-Geographical Indications* decision address the issue of quantity? Does it impose a limit? Is this consistent with the decision in the *Canada-Generic Pharmaceuticals* case?

6. The panel urges caution in using precedents under the exception provisions from the copyright and patent sections of the TRIPS Agreement in connection with Article 17. Why is this?

F.   Trademark Exhaustion and International Trade

1.   U.S. Law on Trademarks and Parallel Imports

a.   K mart v. Cartier

U.S. law regarding international exhaustion of trademark rights is grounded in Section 526 of the Tariff Act of 1930, as interpreted by the U.S. Supreme Court in *K mart v. Cartier*. In *K mart,* a coalition of U.S. trademark industry groups challenged the Treasury Department's longstanding interpretation of the Tariff Act. Treasury Department regulations generally did not provide for blocking the importation of trademarked goods that had been placed on foreign markets by entities under common control with holders of U.S. registered trademarks, and these regulations did not provide for blocking the importation of trademarked goods that had been placed on foreign markets by authorized licensees of U.S. registered trademarks.

The Supreme Court responded to the challenge from the trademark industry coalition with a complex array of opinions. The practical result in *K mart* is not so complicated. The Court affirms the Treasury Department's interpretation of the Tariff Act insofar as it prevented U.S. trademark holders from blocking parallel imports produced by commonly controlled enterprises (i.e., the "common control exception"). However, the Court rejects that portion of the Treasury regulation that prevented U.S. trademark holders from blocking parallel imports produced by foreign licensees.

It was largely in response to *K mart* that U.S. trademark holders began to assert rights to restrict imports of goods on the basis of copyrights in labels and package design.

K MART v. CARTIER
486 U.S. 281 (1988)

Justice KENNEDY delivered the opinion of the Court with respect to Parts I, II-A, and II-C, and an opinion with respect to Part II-B, in which WHITE, J., joined.

A gray-market good is a foreign-manufactured good, bearing a valid United States trademark, that is imported without the consent of the United States trademark holder. These cases present the issue whether the Secretary of the Treasury's regulation permitting the importation of certain gray-market goods, 19 CFR § 133.21 (1987), is a reasonable agency interpretation of § 526 of the Tariff Act of 1930 (1930 Tariff Act), 46 Stat. 741, as amended, 19 U.S.C. § 1526.

I

A

The gray market arises in any of three general contexts. The prototypical gray-market victim (case 1) is a domestic firm that purchases from an independent foreign firm the rights to register and use the latter's trademark as a United States trademark and to sell its foreign-manufactured products here. Especially where the foreign firm has already registered the trademark in the United

States or where the product has already earned a reputation for quality, the right to use that trademark can be very valuable. If the foreign manufacturer could import the trademarked goods and distribute them here, despite having sold the trademark to a domestic firm, the domestic firm would be forced into sharp intrabrand competition involving the very trademark it purchased. Similar intrabrand competition could arise if the foreign manufacturer markets its wares outside the United States, as is often the case, and a third party who purchases them abroad could legally import them. In either event, the parallel importation, if permitted to proceed, would create a gray market that could jeopardize the trademark holder's investment.

The second context (case 2) is a situation in which a domestic firm registers the United States trademark for goods that are manufactured abroad by an affiliated manufacturer. In its most common variation (case 2a), a foreign firm wishes to control distribution of its wares in this country by incorporating a subsidiary here. The subsidiary then registers under its own name (or the manufacturer assigns to the subsidiary's name) a United States trademark that is identical to its parent's foreign trademark. The parallel importation by a third party who buys the goods abroad (or conceivably even by the affiliated foreign manufacturer itself) creates a gray market. Two other variations on this theme occur when an American-based firm establishes abroad a manufacturing subsidiary corporation (case 2b) or its own unincorporated manufacturing division (case 2c) to produce its United States trademarked goods, and then imports them for domestic distribution. If the trademark holder or its foreign subsidiary sells the trademarked goods abroad, the parallel importation of the goods competes on the gray market with the holder's domestic sales.

In the third context (case 3), the domestic holder of a United States trademark authorizes an independent foreign manufacturer to use it. Usually the holder sells to the foreign manufacturer an exclusive right to use the trademark in a particular foreign location, but conditions the right on the foreign manufacturer's promise not to import its trademarked goods into the United States. Once again, if the foreign manufacturer or a third party imports into the United States, the foreign-manufactured goods will compete on the gray market with the holder's domestic goods.

B

Until 1922, the Federal Government did not regulate the importation of gray-market goods, not even to protect the investment of an independent purchaser of a foreign trademark, and not even in the extreme case where the independent foreign manufacturer breached its agreement to refrain from direct competition with the purchaser. That year, however, Congress was spurred to action by a Court of Appeals decision declining to enjoin the parallel importation of goods bearing a trademark that (as in case 1) a domestic company had purchased from an independent foreign manufacturer at a premium. See A. Bourjois & Co. v. Katzel, 275 F. 539 (CA2 1921), rev'd, 260 U.S. 689, 43 S. Ct. 244, 67 L. Ed. 464 (1923).

In an immediate response to Katzel, Congress enacted § 526 of the Tariff Act of 1922, 42 Stat. 975. That provision, later reenacted in identical form as § 526 of the 1930 Tariff Act, 19 U.S.C. § 1526, prohibits importing

> "into the United States any merchandise of foreign manufacture if such merchandise . . . bears a trademark owned by a citizen of, or by a corporation

or association created or organized within, the United States, and registered in the Patent and Trademark Office by a person domiciled in the United States . . . , unless written consent of the owner of such trademark is produced at the time of making entry." 19 U.S.C. § 1526(a).

The regulations implementing § 526 for the past 50 years have not applied the prohibition to all gray-market goods. The Customs Service regulation now in force provides generally that "foreign-made articles bearing a trademark identical with one owned and recorded by a citizen of the United States or a corporation or association created or organized within the United States are subject to seizure and forfeiture as prohibited importations." 19 CFR § 133.21(b) (1987). But the regulation furnishes a "common-control" exception from the ban, permitting the entry of gray-market goods manufactured abroad by the trademark owner or its affiliate:

> (c) Restrictions not applicable. The restrictions . . . do not apply to imported articles when:
>   (1) Both the foreign and the U.S. trademark or trade name are owned by the same person or business entity; [or]
>   (2) The foreign and domestic trademark or trade name owners are parent and subsidiary companies or are otherwise subject to common ownership or control.

The Customs Service regulation further provides an "authorized-use" exception, which permits importation of gray-market goods where

> "(3) the articles of foreign manufacture bear a recorded trademark or trade name applied under authorization of the U.S. owner. . . ."

19 CFR § 133.21(c) (1987). Respondents, an association of United States trademark holders and two of its members, brought suit in Federal District Court in February 1984, seeking both a declaration that the Customs Service regulation, 19 CFR §§ 133.21(c)(1)-(3) (1987), is invalid and an injunction against its enforcement. . . .
    . . . A majority of this Court now holds that the common-control exception of the Customs Service regulation, 19 CFR §§ 133.21(c)(1)-(2) (1987), is consistent with § 526. *See* post (opinion of Brennan, J.). A different majority, however, holds that the authorized-use exception, 19 CFR § 133.21(c)(3) (1987), is inconsistent with § 526. *See* post (opinion of Scalia, J.). We therefore affirm the Court of Appeals in part and reverse in part.

II

`A

In determining whether a challenged regulation is valid, a reviewing court must first determine if the regulation is consistent with the language of the statute. . . . In ascertaining the plain meaning of the statute, the court must look to the particular statutory language at issue, as well as the language and design of the statute as a whole. . . . If the statute is silent or ambiguous with respect to the specific issue addressed by the regulation, the question becomes whether the agency regulation is a permissible construction of the statute.

See Chevron, supra, at 843; *Chemical Manufacturers Assn. v. Natural Resources Defense Council, Inc.,* 470 U.S. 116, 125, 84 L. Ed. 2d 90, 105 S. Ct. 1102 (1985). If the agency regulation is not in conflict with the plain language of the statute, a reviewing court must give deference to the agency's interpretation of the statute. *United States v. Boyle,* 469 U.S. 241, 246, n. 4, 83 L. Ed. 2d 622, 105 S. Ct. 687 (1985).

B

Following this analysis, I conclude that subsections (c)(1) and (c)(2) of the Customs Service regulation, 19 CFR §§ 133.21 (c)(1) and (c)(2) (1987), are permissible constructions designed to resolve statutory ambiguities. All Members of the Court are in agreement that the agency may interpret the statute to bar importation of gray-market goods in what we have denoted case 1 and to permit the imports under case 2a. *See* post (opinion of Brennan, J.); post (opinion of Scalia, J.). As these writings state, "owned by" is sufficiently ambiguous, in the context of the statute, that it applies to situations involving a foreign parent, which is case 2a. This ambiguity arises from the inability to discern, from the statutory language, which of the two entities involved in case 2a can be said to "own" the United States trademark if, as in some instances, the domestic subsidiary is wholly owned by its foreign parent.

A further statutory ambiguity contained in the phrase "merchandise of foreign manufacture," suffices to sustain the regulations as they apply to cases 2b and 2c. This ambiguity parallels that of "owned by," which sustained case 2a, because it is possible to interpret "merchandise of foreign manufacture" to mean (1) goods manufactured in a foreign country, (2) goods manufactured by a foreign company, or (3) goods manufactured in a foreign country by a foreign company. Given the imprecision in the statute, the agency is entitled to choose any reasonable definition and to interpret the statute to say that goods manufactured by a foreign subsidiary or division of a domestic company are not goods "of foreign manufacture."[4]

4. I disagree with Justice Scalia's reasons for declining to recognize this ambiguity. *See* post. First, the threshold question in ascertaining the correct interpretation of a statute is whether the language of the statute is clear or arguably ambiguous. The purported gloss any party gives to the statute, or any reference to legislative history, is in the first instance irrelevant. Further, I decline to assign any binding or authoritative effect to the particular verbiage Justice Scalia highlights. The quoted phrases are simply the Government's explanation of the practical effect the current regulation has in applying the statute, and come from the statement-of-the-case portion of its petition for a writ of certiorari.

Additionally, I believe that agency regulations may give a varying interpretation of the same phrase when that phrase appears in different statutes and different statutory contexts. There may well be variances in purpose or circumstance that have led the agency to adopt and apply dissimilar interpretations of the phrase "of foreign manufacture" in other regulations implementing different statutes.

I also disagree that our disposition necessarily will engender either enforcement problems for the Customs Service or problems we are unaware of arising out of our commercial treaty commitments to foreign countries. Initially, it is reasonable to think that any such problems or objections would have arisen before now since it is the current interpretation of the regulations we are sustaining. Second, I believe that the regulation speaks to the hypothetical situation Justice Scalia poses, and that the firm with the United States trademark could keep out "gray-market imports manufactured abroad by the other American firms," post, at 320, because the regulation allows a company justifiably invoking the protection of the statute to bar the importation of goods of foreign or domestic manufacture. 19 CFR § 133.21(a) (1987). In this instance, the domestic firm with the United States trademark could invoke the protection of the statute (case 1) and bar the importation of the other domestic firm's product manufactured abroad even though our interpretation of the phrase "of foreign manufacture" would characterize these latter goods to be of domestic manufacture.

(1) Subsection (c)(3), 19 CFR § 133.21(c)(3) (1987), of the regulation, however, cannot stand. The ambiguous statutory phrases that we have already discussed, "owned by" and "merchandise of foreign manufacture," are irrelevant to the proscription contained in subsection (3) of the regulation. This subsection of the regulation denies a domestic trademark holder the power to prohibit the importation of goods made by an independent foreign manufacturer where the domestic trademark holder has authorized the foreign manufacturer to use the trademark. Under no reasonable construction of the statutory language can goods made in a foreign country by an independent foreign manufacturer be removed from the purview of the statute.

(2) The design of the regulation is such that the subsection of the regulation dealing with case 3, § 133.21(c)(3), is severable. . . . The severance and invalidation of this subsection will not impair the function of the statute as a whole, and there is no indication that the regulation would not have been passed but for its inclusion. Accordingly, subsection (c)(3) of § 133.21 must be invalidated for its conflict with the unequivocal language of the statute.

III

We hold that the Customs Service regulation is consistent with § 526 insofar as it exempts from the importation ban goods that are manufactured abroad by the "same person" who holds the United States trademark, 19 CFR § 133.21(c)(1) (1987), or by a person who is "subject to common . . . control" with the United States trademark holder, § 133.21(c)(2). Because the authorized-use exception of the regulation, § 133.21(c)(3), is in conflict with the plain language of the statute, that provision cannot stand. The judgment of the Court of Appeals is therefore reversed insofar as it invalidated §§ 133.21(c)(1) and (c)(2), but affirmed with respect to § 133.21(c)(3).

It is so ordered.

Justice BRENNAN, with whom Justice MARSHALL and Justice STEVENS join, and with whom Justice WHITE joins as to Part IV, concurring in part and dissenting in part. . . .

I turn now to my small area of disagreement with the Court's judgment — the Court's conclusion that the authorized-use exception embodied in 19 CFR § 133.21(c)(3) (1987) is inconsistent with the plain language of § 526. In my view, § 526 does not unambiguously protect from gray-market competition a United States trademark owner who authorizes the use of its trademark abroad by an independent manufacturer (case 3).

Unlike the variations of corporate affiliation in case 2, *see supra* . . . , the ambiguity in § 526, admittedly, is not immediately apparent in case 3. In that situation, the casual reader of the statute might suppose that the domestic firm still "own[s]" its trademark. Any such supposition as to the meaning of "owned by," however, bespeaks stolid anachronism not solid analysis. It follows only from an understanding of trademark law that established itself long after the 1922 enactment and 1930 reenactment of § 526. . . .

When § 526 was before Congress, the prevailing law held that a trademark's sole purpose was to identify for consumers the product's physical source or origin. *See, e.g., Macmahan Pharmacal Co. v. Denver Chemical Mfg. Co.*, 113 F. 468, 475 (CA8 1901). "Under this early 'source theory' of protection, trademark licensing was viewed as philosophically impossible, since licensing meant that the mark was being used by persons not associated with the real manufacturing 'source' in a strict, physical sense of the word." 1 McCarthy, Trademarks and Unfair Competition, at 826; *see Macmahan Pharmacal Co., supra,* at 475 ("An assignment or license without [a] transfer [of the business] is totally inconsistent with the theory upon which the value of a trademark depends"); H. Nims, The Law of Unfair Competition and Trade-Marks 46 (1917) (identifying *Macmahan* as "the usual rule"). Thus, any attempt by a trademark holder to authorize a third party to use its trademark worked an abandonment of the trademark, resulting in a relinquishment of ownership. *See, e.g., Everett O. Fisk & Co. v. Fisk Teachers' Agency, Inc.,* 3 F.2d 7, 9 (CA8 1924).

Nor was it at all obvious then that a trademark owner could authorize the use of its trademark in one geographic area by selling it along with business and goodwill, while retaining ownership of the trademark in another geographic area. There were, as Justice Scalia points out, isolated suggestions that a foreign firm could validly assign to another the exclusive right to distribute the assignor's goods here under the foreign trademark. *See* post, at 326. The cases, however, were rife with suggestions to the contrary.[7] And we have found no contemporaneous case even suggesting that a domestic firm could retain ownership of a trademark after attempting to assign to another the right to use the trademark on goods that the other manufactured abroad. *Cf. Scandinavia Belting Co. v. Asbestos & Rubber Works of America, Inc.,* 257 F. 937, 956 (CA2 1919) (raising similar issue whether assignee of right to use trademark in the United States might use trademark on products not produced by the foreign manufacturer, but concluding "that question is not here and is not decided"). As one commentator writing as late as 1932 observed: "There is much confusion in the books in regard to the transferability of trade marks and trade names. The law on the matter is neither clearly stated nor always uniformly applied." Grismore, The Assignment of Trade Marks and Trade Names, 30 Mich. L. Rev. 490, 491.[8]

Not until the 1930's did a trend develop approving of trademark licensing — so long as the licensor controlled the quality of the licensee's products — on the theory that a trademark might also serve the function of identifying product quality for consumers. 1 McCarthy, Trademarks and Unfair Competition, at 827-829; *see* Grismore, 30 Mich. L. Rev., at 499. And not until the passage of the Lanham Trade-Mark Act in 1946 did that trend become the rule. *See, e.g., Dawn Donut Co. v. Hart's Food Stores, Inc.,* 267 F.2d 358, 366-367 (CA2 1959). Similarly, it was not until well after § 526's enactment that it became clear that a trademark owner could assign rights in a particular territory along with

---

7. *See, e.g., Independent Baking Powder Co. v. Boorman,* 175 F. 448, 454 (CC NJ 1910) ("The assignor cannot, after the assignment, continue the same identical business and at the same places as before, under unassigned trade-marks, and at the same time authorize his assignee to conduct the same business elsewhere under an assigned trade-mark"); *Eiseman v. Schiffer,* 157 F. 473 (CC SDNY 1907) (trademark owner may not assign trademark and then continue to engage in same business under different trademark).

8. Justice Scalia cites *United Drug Co. v. Theodore Rectanus Co.,* 248 U.S. 90, 100-101, 63 L. Ed. 141, 39 S. Ct. 48 (1918), and *Hanover Star Milling Co. v. Metcalf,* 240 U.S. 403, 415, 60 L. Ed. 713, 36 S. Ct. 357 (1916), in support of his contention that the law by 1920 clearly permitted a trademark owner to retain ownership and use a trademark in one territory after assigning the identical trademark along with goodwill in another. . . . Those cases held only that a firm can develop a trademark that is identical to a trademark already in use in a geographically distinct and remote area if the firm is unaware of the identity. Thus, those cases bore on the territorial extent of trademark protection, not on the transferability of a trademark by territory once developed.

goodwill, while retaining ownership in another distinct territory. *See, e.g., California Wine & Liquor Corp. v. William Zakon & Sons, Inc.*, 297 Mass. 373, 378, 8 N.E.2d 812, 814 (1937).

Manifestly, the legislators who chose the term "owned by" viewed trademark ownership differently than we view it today. Any prescient legislator who could have contemplated that a trademark owner might license the use of its trademark would almost certainly have concluded that such a transaction would divest the licensor not only of the benefit of § 526's importation prohibition, but of all trademark protection; and anyone who gave thought to the possibility that a trademark holder might assign rights to use its trademark, along with business and goodwill, to an unrelated manufacturer in another territory had good reason to expect the same result. At the very least, it seems to me plain that Congress did not address case 3 any more clearly than it addressed case 2a, 2b, or 2c. To hold otherwise is to wrench statutory words out of their legislative and historical context and treat legislation as no more than a "collection of English words" rather than "a working instrument of government. . . ." *United States v. Dotterweich*, 320 U.S. 277, 280, 88 L. Ed. 48, 64 S. Ct. 134 (1943). . . .

Since I believe that the application of § 526 to case 3 is ambiguous, the sole remaining question is whether Treasury's decision to exclude case 3 from § 526's prohibition is entitled to deference. . . .

The legislative history that I have already discussed at length confirms Congress' intent to do exactly that, and merely to overrule *Katzel.* There is no more indication that Congress intended to permit a United States trademark holder to prohibit importation of trademarked goods manufactured abroad under its authorization than that Congress intended to permit a United States trademark holder to exclude goods produced by its affiliates or divisions abroad.

Finally, Treasury has, at least since 1951, declined to protect trademark holders who authorize the use of their trademarks abroad. Almost as soon as the Lanham Trade-Mark Act codified the quality theory, enabling trademark holders to license the use of their trademarks without thereby relinquishing ownership, *see supra,* at 311, the Customs Service took the position that § 526's protection would be unavailable to domestic firms that authorized independent foreign firms to use their trademarks. *See* Letter from Customs Commissioner Dow to Sen. Douglas (Mar. 23, 1951), App. 52, 53 ("[A] foreign subsidiary or licensee of the United States trademark is considered to stand in the same shoes as such trademark owner"). *See also* T. D. 69-12(2), 3 Cust. Bull., at 17. Particularly in light of that longstanding agency interpretation, I would uphold the authorized-use exception as reasonable.

Justice Scalia, with whom The Chief Justice, Justice Blackmun, and Justice O'Connor join, concurring in part and dissenting in part.

I agree with the Court's analytic approach to this matter, and with its conclusion that subsection (c)(3) of the regulation, 19 CFR § 133.21(c)(3) (1987), is not a permissible construction of § 526(a) of the Tariff Act of 1930, 19 U.S.C. § 1526(a). I therefore join Parts I, II-A, and II-C of the Court's opinion. In my view, however, subsections (c)(1) and (c)(2) of the regulation are also in conflict with the clear language of § 526(a). I therefore decline to join Parts II-B and III of Justice Kennedy's opinion and dissent from that part of the judgment upholding subsections (c)(1) and (c)(2).

I . . .

Five Members of the Court (hereinafter referred to as "the majority") assert, however, that the regulation's treatment of situations 2b and 2c is attributable to the resolution of yet another ambiguity in § 526(a). *See* ante, . . . (opinion of Kennedy, J.); ante, . . . (opinion of Brennan, J.). The statute excludes only merchandise "of foreign manufacture," which the majority says might mean "manufactured by a foreigner" rather than "manufactured in a foreign country." I think not. . . .

I find it extraordinary for this Court, on the theory of deferring to an agency's judgment, to burden that agency with an interpretation that it not only has never suggested, but that is contrary to ordinary usage, to the purposes of the statute, and to the interpretation the agency appears to have applied consistently for half a century.

II

Section 526(a) also unambiguously embraces a third situation that the regulation excludes — namely, the situation (case 3) in which a domestic trademark owner and registrant authorizes a foreign firm to use its United States trademark abroad. There, the United States trademark is unambiguously "owned by" a United States firm, and registered by a firm "domiciled in the United States," and the goods sought to be imported are "of foreign manufacture." According to Justice Brennan, however, thus reading the words to mean what they say "bespeaks stolid anachronism not solid analysis," because "any prescient legislator who could have contemplated that a trademark owner might license the use of its trademark would almost certainly have concluded that such a transaction would divest the licensor not only of the benefit of § 526's importation prohibition, but of all trademark protection."

There may be an anachronism here, but if so it is the statute itself — which Congress has chosen not to update — and not the faithful reading of it to cover what it covers. Justice Brennan characterizes his view as the resolution of textual "ambiguity," but it has nothing to do with that. . . .

Justice Brennan asserts that legislators in 1922 or 1930 were unlikely to have contemplated that a trademark owner could assign his trademark unless he simultaneously conveyed the goodwill and business associated with the mark. Ante. . . . But the prohibition on assigning a trademark apart from its associated goodwill has not been eliminated. *See* 15 U.S.C. § 1060. And no more in 1922 than today did it preclude assignment of the trademark and goodwill on a region-by-region basis. By 1920, it was firmly established that unrelated businesses could own and use an identical trademark so long as the uses were confined to different and distinct regions. *See United Drug Co. v. Theodore Rectanus Co.*, 248 U.S. 90, 100-101, 63 L. Ed. 141, 39 S. Ct. 48 (1918); *Hanover Star Milling Co. v. Metcalf*, 240 U.S. 403, 415, 60 L. Ed. 713, 36 S. Ct. 357 (1916). As a consequence, a trademark holder doing business in two distinct territories was free to assign the business, goodwill, and rights to the trademark in one of the regions. *See, e.g., Scandinavia Belting Co. v. Asbestos & Rubber Works of America, Inc.*, 257 F. 937, 953-956 (CA2 1919); *Battle Creek Toasted Corn Flake Co. v. Kellogg Toasted Corn Flake Co.*, 54 Ont. L. Rep. 537, 546, 550 (1923); *see also Apollinaris Co. v. Scherer*, 23 Blatchf. 459, 27 F. 18, 19-20 (CC SDNY 1886) (dicta); *cf. Saxlehner v. Eisner & Mendelson Co.*, 179 U.S. 19, 45 L. Ed. 60, 21 S. Ct. 7 (1900) (a trademark owner does not abandon his trademark if he continues to use it domestically while granting another party the exclusive right to sell the product in certain foreign countries).[3] Similarly, a firm that used its trademark in one business, say manufacturing cola syrup, could transfer rights to use the trademark in another business, such as bottling cola-flavored soda. *See Coca-Cola Bottling Co. v. Coca-Cola Co.*, 269 F. 796, 806-808 (DC Del. 1920). It was also well established that different parties using an identical trademark in different regions, or for different purposes, could enter into a consent agreement authorizing each party to continue the nonconflicting uses. *See Waukesha Hygeia Mineral Springs Co. v. Hygeia Sparkling Distilled Water Co.*, 63 F. 438, 441 (CA7 1894). Justice Brennan correctly notes that trademark law now recognizes, as it had only begun to recognize in 1930, that a trademark may be licensed for use by different firms in the same or overlapping regions, ante, at 314-315. That change in the law, however, plays almost no part in the application of § 526(a). Since international trademark licensing is interregional, a statute that applies only to imported goods is hardly affected by a change in trademark law concerning intraregional licensing. Finally, there is direct proof that Congress appreciated the possibility of territorial assignment of trademarks. Justice Brennan acknowledges that the 1922 Congress was well aware of, and indeed was motivated by, the case of *A. Bourjois & Co. v. Katzel,* 275 F. 539 (CA2 1921), which presented a textbook example of an assignment of the right to use a trademark in a distinct market. Although Congress understood that a United States trademark owner could authorize the use of its mark abroad, Congress nonetheless chose not to create an exception to § 526(a) for that situation.

Nor does it seem to me that the second condition for disregarding the words of the statute is met: that the original legislative purpose is not served by its text. I cannot agree that "the equities in case 3 . . . differ significantly from the equities that motivated Congress to protect the prototypical gray-market victim (case 1)," the United States assignee of a foreign trademark. Ante. . . . The United States assignee's innocent vulnerability to gray-market imports is no greater than that of the United States trademark owner who assigns the right to use his trademark abroad—and whom Justice Brennan would deprive of § 526(a)'s protection. I cannot understand why the latter victim "does not have the same sort of investment at stake." . . . If anything, his investment may be even greater, consisting of the entire goodwill associated with his trademark in this country. Nor do I understand why he has more "direct control" over the harm, *ibid.* The means of control available to the United States assignor are precisely those available to the United States assignee: he can

---

3. Justice Brennan's only attempt to provide case-law support for the proposition that regional trademark licensing was impermissible consists of a reference to dicta in *Independent Baking Powder Co. v. Boorman,* 175 F. 448 (CC NJ 1910), and *Eiseman v. Schiffer,* 157 F. 473 (CC SDNY 1907), *see* ante . . . n.7. The latter case contains nothing more than statements of the principle that a trademark cannot be assigned separately from the business to which it pertains—which says nothing about whether business and trademark can be conveyed on a regional basis. The former case does contain the seemingly pertinent remark, quoted by Justice Brennan, that "the assignor cannot, after the assignment, continue the same identical business and at the same places as before, under unassigned trade-marks, and at the same time authorize his assignee to conduct the same business elsewhere under an assigned trade-mark." 175 F. at 454. On the facts of the case, however, "elsewhere" was elsewhere in the same market in which the licensor continued to do business. The basis of the holding and of the dictum was, once again, that a trademark is not assignable separately from the business to which it pertains. There is no reason to believe that the court, even in dictum, was addressing the question of regional licensing.

either decline to participate in the assignment from the beginning, or contractually preclude the other party to the assignment from parallel importation. The latter is as unlikely to be effective in the one case as in the other since the bulk of the gray market is attributable to third parties that are unaffiliated with either the manufacturer or the trademark holder. That same phenomenon renders inexplicable Justice Brennan's perception that all affiliated trademark holders are less in need of, or less deserving of, § 526(a) protection against the products of their foreign affiliates. It is not the affiliates who are doing the damage but third parties.

In sum, while congressional attention to the problem addressed by § 526(a) may have been prompted by the graymarketeering represented by *A. Bourjois & Co. v. Katzel, supra,* the language of the statute goes well beyond that narrow case to cover the same inequity in other contexts. Even if Congress could not have envisioned those other contexts I would find no reasonable basis to disregard what the statute plainly says; but to make the case complete, it surely must have envisioned them.

I of course agree that to the extent § 526(a) is ambiguous we need only determine whether the Customs Service's interpretation of the statute is reasonable, *see Chevron U.S.A. Inc. v. Natural Resources Defense Council, Inc.,* 467 U.S. 837, 842-843, 81 L. Ed. 2d 694, 104 S. Ct. 2778 (1984). But we owe no deference to a construction that is contrary to the interpretation of the agency. I would therefore hold invalid, in addition to subsection (c)(3) of the regulation, subsections (c)(1) and (c)(2).

NOTES AND QUESTIONS

1. The U.S. Treasury Department has consistently opposed limitations on parallel imports of trademarked goods because of its conclusion that parallel imports promote price competition, and that the alleged (but generally unsubstantiated) assertions of injury to consumers can be addressed by means that are less likely to restrict competition.
2. Justice Brennan and Justice Scalia provide a historical perspective on the rights of trademark holders to license or transfer their marks. How does the TRIPS Agreement address these rights to license and transfer? What factors account for the changes?
3. In *Silhouette, supra* Chapter 1.VI.E, the ECJ ruled that holders of trademarks in the European Union may block the importation of goods first placed on the market outside the territory of the European Union. The United States provides less extensive rights to U.S. trademark holders. Based on the history of U.S.-EU IPRs relations, might you expect U.S. trademark holder industry groups to approach Congress with claims of a "parallel imports protection gap"? Does this "gap" adversely affect the United States?

b. The Post-K mart *Material Differences Movement*

In *K mart v. Cartier,* the U.S. Supreme Court interpreted Section 526 of the Tariff Act of 1930. Section 526 provides a basis for recording registered trademarks with the U.S. Customs Service, and for Customs Service blocking of infringing imports. There is another U.S. statute, Section 42 of the Lanham

Act, which performs a function similar to that of Section 526 of the Tariff Act. It likewise provides a basis for recording registered trademarks with the Customs Service, and it is administered under the same rules of Title 19 of the Code of Federal Regulations as Section 526. The Customs Service has treated parallel imports of trademarked goods in the same manner under both statutes.

LEVER BROTHERS v. UNITED STATES
981 F.2d 1330 (D.C. Cir. 1993)

Opinion for the Court filed by Circuit Judge SENTELLE.

The District Court entered a judgment invalidating the "affiliate exception" of 19 C.F.R. § 133.21(c)(2) (1988) as inconsistent with the statutory mandate of the Lanham Act of 1946, 15 U.S.C. § 1124 (1988), prohibiting importation of goods which copy or simulate the mark of a domestic manufacturer, and issued a nationwide injunction barring enforcement of the regulation with respect to any foreign goods bearing a valid United States trademark but materially and physically differing from the United States version of the goods. The United States appeals. We conclude that the District Court, obedient to our limited remand in a prior decision in this same cause, properly determined that the regulation is inconsistent with the statute. However, because we conclude that the remedy the District Court provided is overbroad, we vacate the judgment and remand for entry of an injunction against allowing the importation of the foreign-produced Lever Brothers brand products at issue in this case.

I. BACKGROUND

Lever Brothers Company ("Lever US" or "Lever"), an American company, and its British affiliate, Lever Brothers Limited ("Lever UK"), both manufacture deodorant soap under the "Shield" trademark and hand dishwashing liquid under the "Sunlight" trademark. The trademarks are registered in each country. The products have evidently been formulated differently to suit local tastes and circumstances. The U.S. version lathers more, the soaps smell different, the colorants used in American "Shield" have been certified by the FDA whereas the colorants in British "Shield" have not, and the U.S. version contains a bacteriostat that enhances the deodorant properties of the soap. The British version of "Sunlight" dishwashing soap produces less suds, and the American version is formulated to work best in the "soft water" available in most American cities, whereas the British version is designed for "hard water" common in Britain.

The packaging of the U.S. and U.K. products is also somewhat different. The British "Shield" logo is written in script form and is packaged in foil wrapping and contains a wave motif, whereas the American "Shield" logo is written in block form, does not come in foil wrapping and contains a grid pattern. There is small print on the packages indicating where they were manufactured. The British "Sunlight" comes in a cylindrical bottle labeled "Sunlight Washing Up Liquid." The American "Sunlight" comes in a yellow, hourglass-shaped bottle labeled "Sunlight Dishwashing Liquid."

Lever asserts that the unauthorized influx of these foreign products has created substantial consumer confusion and deception in the United States about the nature and origin of this merchandise, and that it has received numerous consumer complaints from American consumers who unknowingly bought the British products and were disappointed.

Lever argues that the importation of the British products was in violation of section 42 of the Lanham Act, 15 U.S.C. § 1124 which provides that with the exception of goods imported for personal use:

> No article of imported merchandise which shall copy or simulate the name of the [sic] any domestic manufacture, or manufacturer . . . or which shall copy or simulate a trademark registered in accordance with the provisions of this chapter . . . shall be admitted to entry at any customhouse of the United States.

Id. The United States Customs Service ("Customs"), however, was allowing importation of the British goods under the "affiliate exception" created by 19 C.F.R. § 133.21(c)(2), which provides that foreign goods bearing United States trademarks are not forbidden when "the foreign and domestic trademark or tradename owners are parent and subsidiary companies or are otherwise subject to common ownership or control."

In *Lever I,* we concluded that "the natural, virtually inevitable reading of section 42 is that it bars foreign goods bearing a trademark identical to the valid U.S. trademark but physically different," without regard to affiliation between the producing firms or the genuine character of the trademark abroad. . . . [4]

II. ANALYSIS . . .

Here the specific question at Step Two of *Chevron* is whether the intended prohibition of section 42 admits of an exception for materially different goods manufactured by foreign affiliates. . . . When we remanded this case, we indicated that the Government could not prevail unless it produced "persuasive evidence" rebutting our tentative reading of the statute, *Lever I,* 877 F.2d at 111, because the affiliate exception appears to contradict the clear implication of the language of section 42. The legislative history and administrative practice before us, as before the District Court, will not perform that onerous task.

A. LEGISLATIVE HISTORY AND ADMINISTRATIVE PRACTICE PRIOR TO ENACTMENT OF LANHAM ACT . . .

The Supreme Court interpreted section 27 more broadly. In *A. Bourjois & Co. v. Katzel,* 260 U.S. 689, 67 L. Ed. 464, 43 S. Ct. 244 (1923), the Court held that a third party could not import a face powder manufactured in France when the plaintiff owned the United States trademarks for the product, even though the product sold was "the genuine product of the French concern. . . ." *Id.* at 691. The Supreme Court concluded that even an authentic foreign trademark on "genuine" merchandise may infringe a registered United States trademark.

---

4. In *Lever I,* we expressly recognized that our decision was not in conflict with the Supreme Court's decision in *K mart Corp. v. Cartier Inc.,* 486 U.S. 281, 100 L. Ed. 2d 313, 108 S. Ct. 1811 (1988), which upheld the affiliate exception against a challenge based on section 526 of the Tariff Act of 1930, 19 U.S.C. § 1526 (1988), but "did not reach the question of the exception's validity under section 42 of the Lanham Act." *Lever I,* 877 F.2d at 108 & n.8.

In another case that year involving the same Bourjois company, the Supreme Court held in a per curiam memorandum that third-party importation of goods bearing an authentic identical foreign trademark infringed the United States trademark owner's rights under section 27 and must be excluded from entry by Customs. *A. Bourjois & Aldridge*, 263 U.S. 675, 68 L. Ed. 501, 44 S. Ct. 4 (1923) (answering questions certified to it by the Second Circuit at 292 F. 1013 (2d Cir. 1922)).

Until 1936, the regulations implementing section 27 quoted the statute, then provided for an absolute ban on imports bearing trademarks that copied or simulated United States marks. . . .

Section 518(b) of the 1936 regulations also included a "same person" exception, the first precursor of the affiliate exception:

> However, merchandise manufactured or sold in a foreign country under a trade-mark or trade name, which trade-mark is registered and recorded, shall not be deemed for the purpose of these regulations to copy or simulate such United States trade-mark or trade name if such foreign trade-mark or trade name and such United States trade-mark or trade name are owned by the same person, partnership, association, or corporation.

Id. The regulation did not explain the source of this exception, and there is no evidence that Customs considered the issue of physically different imports.

Several conclusions can be drawn from the pre-Lanham Act legislative history and administrative practice. First, at least until 1936, protection from unauthorized importation was consistently based upon ownership of a United States trademark, not upon the nature of the relationship between the trademark owner and the foreign producer. Second, as trademark law became more international, the trend was toward greater protection from foreign importation. Third, although the 1936 regulations implemented the first version of the affiliate exception, the specific question of materially different goods is nowhere addressed. . . .

C. LEGISLATIVE HISTORY AND DEVELOPMENTS SINCE PASSAGE OF LANHAM ACT

The Treasury Department's administrative practice after passage of the Lanham Act has been inconsistent. . . .

After Congress repeatedly considered and failed to enact the affiliate exception, the Treasury Department revived the exception. In 1972 the affiliate exception was adopted in the form at issue here. *See* 37 FR 20677 (1972). Under the 1972 regulations, section 42's protections were rendered inapplicable where:

> (1) Both the foreign and the U.S. trademark or trade name are owned by the same person or business entity;
> (2) The foreign and domestic trademark or trade name owners are parent and subsidiary companies or are otherwise subject to common ownership or control;
> (3) The articles of foreign manufacture bear a recorded trademark or trade name applied under authorization of the U.S. owner.

19 C.F.R. § 133.21(c) (citations omitted).[5]

---

5. In *K mart Corp. v. Cartier, Inc.*, 486 U.S. 281, 100 L. Ed. 2d 313, 108 S. Ct. 1811 (1988), the Supreme Court struck down 19 C.F.R. § 133.21(c)(3), which allowed the importation of

Neither the notice proposing the regulations, 35 FR 19269 (1970), nor the final notice adopting them, Treas. Dec. Int. Rev. 72-266, 6 Cust. B. & Dec. 538 (1972), explained their rationale. The statement accompanying the final rule contained no response to objections raised by several companies and associations. . . .

Customs' main argument from the legislative history is that section 42 of the Lanham Act applies only to imports of goods bearing trademarks that "copy or simulate" a registered mark. Customs thus draws a distinction between "genuine" marks and marks that "copy or simulate." A mark applied by a foreign firm subject to ownership and control common to that of the domestic trademark owner is by definition "genuine." Customs urges, regardless of whether or not the goods are identical. Thus, any importation of goods manufactured by an affiliate of a U.S. trademark owner cannot "copy or simulate" a registered mark because those goods are ipso facto "genuine."

This argument is fatally flawed. It rests on the false premise that foreign trademarks applied to foreign goods are "genuine" in the United States. Trademarks applied to physically different foreign goods are not genuine from the viewpoint of the American consumer. As we stated in *Lever I*:

> On its face . . . section [42] appears to aim at deceit and consumer confusion; when identical trademarks have acquired different meanings in different countries, one who imports the foreign version to sell it under that trademark will (in the absence of some specially differentiating feature) cause the confusion Congress sought to avoid. The fact of affiliation between the producers in no way reduces the probability of that confusion; it is certainly not a constructive consent to importation.

877 F.2d at 111.

There is a larger, more fundamental and ultimately fatal weakness in Customs' position in this case. Section 42 on its face appears to forbid importation of goods that "copy or simulate" a United States trademark. Customs has the burden of adducing evidence from the legislative history of section 42 and its administrative practice of an exception for materially different goods whose similar foreign and domestic trademarks are owned by affiliated companies. At a minimum, this requires that the specific question be addressed in the legislative history and administrative practice. The bottom line, however, is that the issue of materially different goods was not addressed either in the legislative history or the administrative record. It is not enough to posit that silence implies authorization, when the authorization sought runs counter to the evident meaning of the governing statute. Therefore, we conclude that section 42 of the Lanham Act precludes the application of Customs' affiliate exception with respect to physically, materially different goods. . . .

---

foreign-made goods where the United States trademark owner has authorized the use of the mark, as in conflict with the unequivocal language of section 526 of the Tariff Act. Section 526 prohibits the importation of "any merchandise of foreign manufacture" bearing a trademark "owned by" a citizen of, or by a "corporation . . . organized within, the United States" unless written consent of the trademark owner is produced at the time of entry. 19 U.S.C. § 1526. By a different majority, the Supreme Court upheld 19 C.F.R. § 133.21(c)(2), the regulation at issue here, as consistent with section 526. As we noted above, the *K mart* case did not address the validity of these regulations under the Lanham Act. *See supra* note 4.

IV. Conclusion

For the foregoing reasons, we affirm the District Court's ruling that section 42 of the Lanham Act, 15 U.S.C. § 1124, bars the importation of physically different foreign goods bearing a trademark identical to a valid U.S. trademark, regardless of the trademark's genuine character abroad or affiliation between the producing firms. Injunctive relief, however, is limited to the two products which were the subject of this action. We therefore vacate the District Court's prior order to the extent that it renders global relief and remand for the entry of an injunction consistent with this opinion. . . .

NOTES AND QUESTIONS

1. In *Lever Brothers,* the Court of Appeals holds that the common control doctrine adopted by the Supreme Court in *K mart* does not apply when there is a material physical difference between goods imported from an affiliated entity abroad and goods marketed domestically. The court says that *K mart* does not control the outcome of this case because the Supreme Court expressly refrained from addressing the Lanham Act in *K mart.* However, the court rejects the Treasury Department's argument that the scope of the prohibitions in Section 526 of the Tariff Act and Section 42 of the Lanham Act are different (because the Lanham Act appears to be directed to counterfeit trademarks). The court suggests that the scope of the two prohibitions is the same. Under this rationale, does it make sense for the court to say that its decision is not controlled by *K mart*? Conversely, should the Treasury Department assume that the court decision concerning materially different goods governs interpretation of Section 526 of the Tariff Act?
2. In *Lever Brothers,* the U.S. trademark holder has sued the U.S. government, and not the importer. Why?

Following the District of Colombia Circuit's decision in *Lever II,* the Court of Appeals for the Federal Circuit has permitted the blocking of parallel imports of trademark goods based on "material differences." The CAFC's leading decision on this subject is *Gamut Trading v. ITC,* an excerpt from which follows.

GAMUT TRADING v. U.S. INTERNATIONAL TRADE COMMISSION
200 F.3d 775 (Fed. Cir. 1999)

NEWMAN, Circuit Judge.

This action for violation of § 337 of the Tariff Act of 1930, 19 U.S.C. § 1337, was initiated at the United States International Trade Commission ("ITC") on the complaint of the Kubota Corporation, a Japanese company ("Kubota-Japan"), owner of the registered United States trademark "Kubota," and its United States affiliated companies Kubota Tractor Corporation ("Kubota-US") and Kubota Manufacturing of America ("KMA"). Kubota-US is the exclusive licensee of the

"Kubota" trademark in the United States, by agreement with Kubota-Japan which provides that the United States trademark and associated goodwill remain the exclusive property of Kubota-Japan.

The respondents are Gamut Trading Company and other entities (collectively "Gamut") that import from Japan and resell in the United States various models of used tractors of under 50 horsepower, all manufactured in Japan by the Kubota Corporation, used in Japan, and bearing the mark "Kubota" that had been properly affixed in Japan. Gamut was charged with violation of § 337 of the Tariff Act of 1930, 19 U.S.C. § 1337, which provides for exclusion of product bearing infringing marks and other remedies, based on asserted infringement of the United States trademark "Kubota":

19 U.S.C. § 1337 Unfair Practices in Import Trade

(a)(1)(C) The importation into the United States, the sale for importation, or the sale within the United States after importation by the owner, importer, or consignee, of articles that infringe a valid and enforceable United States trademark registered under the Trademark Act of 1946.

Describing this case as one of "gray-market goods," the ITC issued a General Exclusion Order against importation of used Japanese tractors bearing the "Kubota" trademark, and Cease and Desist Orders against sale of such tractors that had already been imported into the United States. The principle of gray market law is that the importation of a product that was produced by the owner of the United States trademark or with its consent, but not authorized for sale in the United States, may, in appropriate cases, infringe the United States trademark.

On Gamut's appeal, we now affirm the decision of the ITC.

Background

Kubota-Japan manufactures in Japan a large number of models of agricultural tractors, for use in Japan and other countries. Various tractor models are custom-designed for a particular use in a particular country. For example, tractor models that are designed for rice paddy farming are constructed for traction and maneuverability under wet, muddy conditions; these tractors have smaller tire separation in order to make tight turns in rice paddies, and are designed to function with rice paddy tillers, which contain narrow, light-weight blades. No corresponding model is designed for export to the United States.

In contrast, some tractor models that are intended to be used in the United States are specially constructed for lifting and transporting earth and rocks, and to function with rear cutters that contain heavy blades capable of cutting rough undergrowth; these models do not have a direct Japanese counterpart. The tractor models intended for sale and use in the United States bear English-language controls and warnings, and have English-language dealers and users manuals. They are imported by Kubota-US and sold through a nationwide dealership network which provides full maintenance and repair service and maintains an inventory of parts for these specific tractor models. Kubota-US conducts training classes for its dealership employees, instructing them on service and maintenance procedures.

Gamut purchases used Kubota tractors in Japan and imports them into the United States. The majority of the imported tractors are described as between 13 and 25 years old. All bear the mark "Kubota." The Kubota companies state that the importation and its extent came to their attention when United States purchasers sought service and repair or maintenance from Kubota-US dealerships.

THE GRAY MARKET

The term "gray market goods" refers to genuine goods that in this case are of foreign manufacture, bearing a legally affixed foreign trademark that is the same mark as is registered in the United States; gray goods are legally acquired abroad and then imported without the consent of the United States trademark holder. *See K Mart Corp. v. Cartier, Inc.*, 486 U.S. 281, 286-87, 6 U.S.P.Q.2D (BNA) 1897, 1899-1900, 100 L. Ed. 2d 313, 108 S. Ct. 1811 (1987) (discussing various gray-market conditions); 4 McCarthy on Trademark and Unfair Competition § 29.46 (4th ed. 1997). The conditions under which gray-market goods have been excluded implement the territorial nature of trademark registration, and reflect a legal recognition of the role of domestic business in establishing and maintaining the reputation and goodwill of a domestic trademark.

Until the Supreme Court's decision in *A. Bourjois & Co. v. Katzel*, 260 U.S. 689, 67 L. Ed. 464, 43 S. Ct. 244 (1923), the prevailing rule in the United States was that the authorized sale of a validly trademarked product, anywhere in the world, exhausted the trademark's exclusionary right; thus the holder of the corresponding registered United States trademark was believed to have no right to bar the importation and sale of authentically marked foreign goods. However, in the *Bourjois* case the Court recognized the territorial boundaries of trademarks, stressing that the reputation and goodwill of the holder of the corresponding United States mark warrants protection against unauthorized importation of goods bearing the same mark, although the mark was validly affixed in the foreign country. In *Bourjois* the foreign-origin goods were produced by an unrelated commercial entity and imported by a third person, although the goods themselves were related in that the United States trademark owner bought its materials from the foreign producer. *See Id.* at 692.

Since the *Bourjois* decision, the regional circuits and the Federal Circuit have drawn a variety of distinctions in applying gray market jurisprudence, primarily in consideration of whether the foreign source of the trademarked goods and the United States trademark holder are related commercial entities and whether the imported goods bearing the foreign mark are the same as (or not materially different from) the goods that are sold under the United States trademark, applying a standard of materiality suitable to considerations of consumer protection and support for the integrity of the trademarks of domestic purveyors, all with due consideration to the territorial nature of registered trademarks in the context of international trade. . . .

THE "KUBOTA" IMPORTATIONS

The ALJ found that twenty-four models of the "Kubota" Japanese tractors imported by Gamut were materially different from any corresponding tractor imported by Kubota-US, and that one model was substantially the same. . . .

The Commission adopted the ALJ's Initial Decision as to the twenty-four models found to be infringing, and reversed the determination of no infringement by the Kubota L200. The Commission also found infringement by twenty additional tractor models not reviewed by the ALJ. For the Kubota L200 and the twenty additional models, the Commission found that the absence of English-language warning and instructional labels constituted a material difference from the "Kubota" brand tractors sold in the United States by Kubota-US, giving rise to trademark infringement by these unauthorized imports and violation of Section 337.

THE QUESTION OF MATERIAL DIFFERENCES

Gamut argues that the ITC erred in finding that there are material differences between their imported tractors and those imported by Kubota-US. Gamut points out that materiality of product differences is determined by the likelihood of confusion of those whose purchasing choice would be affected by knowledge of the differences, *see Nestle*, 982 F.2d at 643, 25 U.S.P.Q.2D (BNA) at 1264, and that its purchasers know that they are purchasing a used Japanese tractor. Gamut states that a purchaser of a used tractor bearing Japanese labels would not be deceived into thinking that he/she is buying a new tractor designed for the United States market. Gamut states that any differences between the imported models and the United States models are readily apparent, and thus can not be a material difference.

The ITC rejected this argument, finding that it is not reasonable to expect that purchasers of used Kubota tractors will be aware of structural differences from the United States models and of the consequences of these differences for purposes of maintenance, service, and parts. This finding was supported by substantial evidence. Indeed, the marking of these tractors with the "Kubota" mark weighs against an inference that purchasers would be expected to be aware of or expect structural differences.

As precedent illustrates, differences that may be readily apparent to consumers may nevertheless be material. In *Nestle* the court found differences in quality, composition, and packaging to be material. In *Martin's Herend* the court found differences in the color, pattern or shape of porcelain figures to be material, although they would be apparent to an observer of the products side-by-side. Differences in labeling and other written materials have been deemed material, on the criteria of likelihood of consumer confusion and concerns for the effect of failed consumer expectations on the trademark holder's reputation and goodwill. *See Original Appalachian Artworks* (Spanish-origin "Cabbage Patch Kids" dolls were materially different because they had Spanish-language instructions and "adoption papers"); *PepsiCo v. Nostalgia Products Corp.*, 1990 U.S. Dist. LEXIS 18990, 18 U.S.P.Q.2D (BNA) 1404, 1405 (N.D. Ill. 1990) (materiality based on Mexican "Pepsi" labels that were in Spanish and did not contain a list of ingredients, along with quality control and marketing differences); *Fender Musical Instruments Corp. v. Unlimited Music Center Inc.*, 1995 U.S. Dist. LEXIS 15746, 35 U.S.P.Q.2D (BNA) 1053, 1056 (D. Conn. 1995) (material difference for guitars with Japanese language owner's manuals); *Osawa & Co. v. B&H Photo*, 589 F. Supp. 1163, 1169, 223 U.S.P.Q. (BNA) 124, 127 (S.D.N.Y. 1984) (material difference for camera equipment with foreign language instruction manuals); *Ferrero U.S.A, Inc. v. Ozak Trading Inc.*, 753 F. Supp. 1240, 1243-44, 18 U.S.P.Q.2D (BNA) 1052, 1055 (D.N.J. 1991) (material differences in the print and content of labels on "Tic-Tac" mints).

The Commission found that the imported used "Kubota" tractors lacked English instructional and warning labels, operator manuals, and service manuals. Labels are attached at various places on the tractor to instruct the user on the proper operation of the tractor and to warn of potential hazards, and include instructions on the direction of the engine speed hand throttle, the function of the transmission, the four-wheel drive, the power take-off speed, hydraulic power lift, and other controls on the tractor. The Commission found that such labels are necessary to safe and effective operation. The authorized "Kubota" tractors bear these labels in English; the permanent labels on the used imported tractors are in Japanese.

While it would be obvious to the purchaser that the warning and instructional labels are in Japanese, there was evidence before the ITC of consumer belief that the used tractors were sponsored by or otherwise associated with the Kubota-US distributorship/service system. . . .

The Kubota companies are not required to arrange to provide service to Gamut's imports in order to ratify these importations by mitigating their injury to the goodwill associated with the "Kubota" trademark. Whether or not the Kubota companies could arrange to service these tractors does not convert an otherwise infringing activity into an authorized importation. *See Osawa,* 589 F. Supp. at 1167-68, 223 U.S.P.Q. (BNA) at 126-27 (trademark holder incurred damage from the unauthorized importation of gray market cameras because it voluntarily bore the warranty expenses for servicing them).

In addition to the differences in labeling, service, and parts, the ALJ found that many of the tractors designed by Kubota for use in the United States are stronger structurally than the corresponding tractors made for use in Japan. For example, the ALJ found that some of the intended United States tractors were made with stronger front and rear axles, front axle brackets, chassis, power trail, and parts contained in the transmission, such as gears. The ALJ found that the stronger gears increase load-bearing capacity and bending strength, thereby reducing wear and tear. The ALJ found that some of the tractor models designed for the United States market have a stronger power take-off shaft, installed to accommodate the heavy load placed on the shaft by implements often used in the United States such as a rear cutter. The ALJ heard evidence that these structural differences significantly increase the likelihood of breakdowns of the less strong Japanese models. Although Gamut points to the absence of evidence of actual breakdown, the conceded or established differences in structural strength are relevant to the finding of material differences, and were properly considered by the Commission, along with the evidence concerning labelling, warnings, service, and parts.

Gamut raises the additional argument that in all events the Commission erred in law by applying the material differences test with the low threshold of precedent, because the imported tractors are not new but used. . . .

Substantial evidence supports the Commission's finding that consumers would consider the differences between the used imported tractors and the authorized Kubota-US tractors to be important to their purchasing decision, and thus material.

EFFECT OF THE FACT THAT THE GOODS ARE USED

Gamut argues that this is not a "gray market" case because the imported tractors are simply durable used goods, rendering it irrelevant whether the trademark owner authorized their sale in the United States. Gamut also argues that imported goods must be sold in competition with the goods of the owner of the United States trademark in order for authentic foreign-marked goods to infringe any trademark rights, citing *K Mart v. Cartier*, 486 U.S. at 286, 6 U.S.P.Q.2D (BNA) at 1899-00. Gamut asserts that because Kubota-US sells new tractors in the United States and the respondents sell only used tractors, the goods are not in direct competition and the imported used tractors can not be held to be infringing gray market goods.

Direct competition between substantially identical goods is a factor to be considered, but it is not a prerequisite to trademark infringement. In *Safety-Kleen Corp. v. Dresser Indus.*, 518 F.2d 1399, 1404, 186 U.S.P.Q. (BNA) 476, 480 (CCPA 1975) the court explained that "While the similarity or dissimilarity of the goods or service should, in appropriate cases, be considered in determining likelihood of confusion . . . the law has long protected the legitimate interests of trademark owners from confusion among noncompetitive, but related, products bearing confusingly similar marks." Similar reasoning applies to products of the gray market.

As we have discussed, trademark law as applied to gray market goods embodies a composite of likelihood of consumer confusion as to the source of the goods, likelihood of consumer confusion arising from differences between the foreign and the domestic goods, impositions on the goodwill and burdens on the integrity of the United States trademark owner due to consumer response to any differences, and recognition of the territorial scope of national trademarks. Various of these factors acquire more or less weight depending on the particular situation. Although it is relevant to consider whether the imported product is new or used, other factors that may affect the reputation and the goodwill enuring to the holder of a trademark are not overridden by the fact that the product is known to be second-hand.

Courts that have considered the question and concluded that used goods can be gray market goods include [citations omitted]. . . .

The ALJ found that Kubota-US has established a reputation for safety, reliability, and service that consumers associate with the "Kubota" mark, and that the used tractors bearing the "Kubota" mark undermine the investment that Kubota-US made in consumer goodwill for "Kubota" products. These findings are supported by substantial evidence. The fact that the imported tractors are used does not prevent a finding of infringement of the United States "Kubota" trademark.

GOODWILL OF THE UNITED STATES TRADEMARK

Gamut points out that according to the trademark license agreement, Kubota-Japan owns the "Kubota" trademark in the United States and associated goodwill. Gamut argues that there can be no infringement of the United States trademark unless Kubota-Japan, as the trademark owner, demonstrates that it "has developed domestic goodwill, that is, independent of the goodwill associated with the mark world wide." The goodwill of a trademark is developed by use of the mark. The ALJ found that Kubota-US, through its large network of authorized dealers in "Kubota"-brand products, had established a reputation for product quality and service throughout the United States, establishing use of the mark accompanied by goodwill. This goodwill enures to the benefit of the trademark owner. Gamut's challenge to the standing of the complainants is not well founded.

REMEDY

The ALJ recommended imposition of a general exclusion order as to the infringing tractor models, barring their importation and sale unless the tractors bore a permanent, non-removable label alerting the consumer to the origin of the used tractors and containing other information deemed necessary to mitigate consumer confusion. The ALJ also recommended that cease and desist orders be issued to bar the respondents from selling infringing used tractors already imported unless the tractors were appropriately labeled. The Commission, on giving full review to the ALJ's Initial Decision, including various modifications thereof, affirmed the ALJ's ruling that the vinyl decal label that was proposed by Gamut would not eliminate the likelihood of consumer confusion because of the high likelihood that the labels would be removed after importation and prior to sale. . . .

The Commission has broad discretion in selecting the form, scope and extent of the remedy in a Section 337 proceeding. . . .

An exclusion order is the Commission's statutory remedy for trademark infringement. 19 U.S.C. § 1337(d). In addition, the Commission may issue cease and desist orders when it has personal jurisdiction over the party against whom the order is directed. 19 U.S.C. § 1337(f). . . .

Accordingly, the Commission's decision is
AFFIRMED.

NOTES AND QUESTIONS

1. In *SKF USA v. International Trade Commission*, 423 F.3d 1307 (Fed. Cir. 2005), the CAFC extended its holding in the *Gamut Trading* decision to differences in after-sales service and support accompanying a product, finding that such differences may be "material" and justify the blocking of parallel imports. However, in that case, the CAFC also said that "all or substantially all" of the trademark goods as to which protection against imports is sought must be accompanied by the relevant service and support. If the trademark owner sold goods both with and without service and support, it would be introducing confusion in the marketplace, and it could not then assert a claim based on consumer confusion against the parallel importer.

2. Both the *Gamut Trading* and *SKF USA* decisions arise under Section 337 of the Trade Act of 1930, a provision that permits actions to prevent importation of goods that infringe U.S.-registered intellectual property. We will examine Section 337 in Chapter 6 on Enforcement.

3. How are trademark holders likely to react to decisions such as *Gamut Trading* and *SKF USA*? Might they introduce low-cost product differences — such as instruction manuals or warning labels in different languages — to meet the CAFC's low material differences threshold? Is the CAFC attempting to provide a bypass around the *K mart* decision?

G. Trademark Exhaustion and the European Union

In its *Ideal Standard* decision, the European Court of Justice describes its "intra-Union" exhaustion doctrine in the field of trademarks.

IHT INTERNATIONALE HEIZTECHNIK GMBH
AND ANOTHER v. IDEAL-STANDARD GMBH AND ANOTHER

(Case C-9/93)
The Court of Justice of the European Communities
[1994] 3 CMLR 857
22 June 1994

Panel: Presiding, DUE CJ; MANCINI, MOITINO DE ALMEIDA, DIEZ DE VELASCO PPC; KAKOURIS, JOLIET

Headnote:
Reference from Germany by the Oberlandesgericht (Regional Court of Appeal), Dusseldorf, under Article 177 EC.

Decision: . . .
The case law on Articles 30 [now renumbered as 34 — EDS.] *and 36 trade mark law and parallel imports.*
On the basis of the second sentence of Article 36 of the Treaty the Court has consistently held:

> Inasmuch as it provides an exception to one of the fundamental principles of the Common Market, Article 36 in fact only admits of derogations from the free movement of goods where such derogations are justified for the purpose of safe-guarding rights which constitute the specific subject-matter of this property.

In relation to trade marks, the specific subject-matter of the industrial property is the guarantee that the owner of the trade mark has the exclusive right to use that trade mark, for the purpose of putting products protected by the trade mark into circulation for the first time, and is therefore intended to protect him against competitors wishing to take advantage of the status and reputation of the trade mark by selling products illegally bearing that trade mark.

An obstacle to the free movement of goods may arise out of the existence, within a national legislation concerning industrial and commercial property, of provisions laying down that a trade mark owner's right is not exhausted when the product protected by the trade mark is marketed in another Member State, with the result that the trade mark owner can [oppose] importation of the product into his own Member State when it has been marketed in another Member State.

Such an obstacle is not justified when the product has been put onto the market in a legal manner in the Member State from which it has been imported, by the trade mark owner himself or with his consent, so that there can be no question of abuse or infringement of the trade mark.

In fact, if a trade mark owner could prevent the import of protected products marketed by him or with his consent in another Member State, he would be able to partition off national markets and thereby restrict trade between Member States, in a situation where no such restriction was necessary to guarantee the essence of the exclusive right flowing from the trade mark (*see* Case 16/74, *CENTRAFARM v WINTHROP*).

So, application of a national law which would give the trade mark owner in the importing State the right to oppose the marketing of products which have been put into circulation in the exporting State by him or with his consent is precluded as contrary to Articles 30 and 36. This principle, known as the exhaustion of rights, applies where the owner of the trade mark in the importing State and the owner of the trade mark in the exporting State are the same or where, even if they are separate persons, they are economically linked. A number of situations are covered: products put into circulation by the same undertaking, by a licensee, by a parent company, by a subsidiary of the same group, or by an exclusive distributor.

There are numerous instances in national case law and Community case law where the trade mark had been assigned to a subsidiary or to an exclusive distributor in order to enable those undertakings to protect their national markets against parallel imports by taking advantage of restrictive approaches to the exhaustion of rights in the national laws of some States.

Articles 30 and 36 defeat such manipulation of trade marks rights since they preclude national laws which enable the holder of the right to oppose imports.

NOTES AND QUESTIONS

1. Article 34 of the TFEU (formerly Article 30) provides:[17]

> Quantitative restrictions on imports and all measures having equivalent effect shall be prohibited between Member States.

Article 36 of the TFEU provides:

> The provisions of Articles 34 and 35 shall not preclude prohibitions or restrictions on imports, exports or goods in transit justified on grounds of public morality, public policy or public security; the protection of health and life of humans, animals or plants; the protection of national treasures possessing artistic, historic or archaeological value; or the protection of industrial and commercial property. Such prohibitions or restrictions shall not, however, constitute a means of arbitrary discrimination or a disguised restriction on trade between Member States.

One of the principal objectives of the European Economic Community (established in 1958) was to eliminate tariffs and quotas that inhibited trade between its member states. Shortly after the Community came into being, the ECJ perceived that the free movement of goods and services might be substantially impaired by forms of regulation more subtle than tariffs and quotas, such as through the adoption of national regulatory schemes that directly or indirectly discriminated against outsiders. The TFEU did not specifically address each more subtle form of discrimination, so the Court began to fashion a jurisprudence based on Article 34 that characterized these other forms of discriminatory regulation as measures with the "equivalent effect" of

---

17. In connection with adopting of the Amsterdam Treaty on European Union in 1997, the EU renumbered the EC Treaty. In an apparent effort to maximize confusion for judges and lawyers, the provision of the EC Treaty that formerly allowed certain restrictions on trade (Article 36), was renumbered as the Article that formerly prohibited restrictions on trade (Article 30). The renumbering, interestingly enough, was purportedly undertaken to make the EC legal system less confusing for the ordinary citizen of the Union.

quotas. There is today an extensive body of ECJ case law interpreting and applying Article 34, and considering its relationship to Article 36.

2. The main issue in the *IHT v. Ideal Standard* case was whether the holder of the IDEAL STANDARD trademark in Germany—which holder was entirely separate from the holder of the same mark in France (due to a series of corporate divestitures and assignments)—could block import from France of goods labeled with the trademark (applied by the separate holder in France). The ECJ said that the absence of an economic link between the trademark holders prevented the German enterprise from exercising control over the quality of the goods made in France. On these grounds, the German enterprise was entitled to block the imports.

3. Another interesting problem was that the products made by the French enterprise differed from those made by the German enterprise. The trademark holder in Germany was using the mark to block imports of different goods. French law would not have permitted the trademark holder in France to prevent the use of its mark on the different goods, but German law allowed such prevention as to different goods (assuming there would be some consumer confusion). The ECJ observed that the First Trade Marks Directive did not harmonize the rules concerning likelihood of confusion, and that the issue of confusion was a matter to be assessed under German law.

In *Revlon,* the U.K. Court of Appeals refused to allow a U.S.-based multinational producer to use a trademark registered in the United Kingdom (by one corporate affiliate) to block importation of goods first sold in the United States with the consent of the U.S. parent company. The judge, whose opinion is set out below, Lord Sydney Templeman, was subsequently appointed a Law Lord of the U.K. House of Lords (now the British Supreme Court).[18] As discussed in Chapter 1.VI.E, *supra,* since this decision was rendered the European Union has adopted common legislation in the field of trademarks and the European Court of Justice has deprived the individual member states of the right to establish their own policies on the subject of international exhaustion.[19] Although the ECJ recognizes a rule of regional or intra-Union exhaustion among the EU member states, it has rejected international exhaustion. While the ruling in *Revlon* has thus been superseded by later developments, it remains a classic articulation of the policies underlying international exhaustion.

REVLON INC. v. CRIPPS & LEE LTD.

Court of Appeal (Civil Division)
[1980] FSR 85
22 November 1979

TEMPLEMAN LJ: This is an action by a multi-national group of companies seeking to prevent products manufactured, named and sold or otherwise disposed of by

---

18. Lord Templeman is skeptical about the claims of intellectual property right-holder groups to benefit society. *See* Lord Sydney Templeman, *Intellectual Property,* 1 J. INT'L ECON. L 603 (1998).
19. *See Silhoutte v. Hartlauer,* Court of Justice of the European Communities, [1998] 2 CMLR 953, 16 July 1998, *supra* Chapter 1.VI.E.

a member of the group in one country from being re-sold to the public in another country under the same name. The Revlon group of companies is organised in a manner which, as Mr. Sparrow, counsel for the Revlon plaintiffs emphasised, is not at all unusual for multi-national groups of companies. The organisation of the Revlon companies and the history and actions of those companies as revealed by the evidence appear to be perfectly proper and commercially prudent and in the exposition which follows I intend no criticism of any of the plaintiffs. The question involved in this interlocutory appeal is whether any of the plaintiffs can plausibly demonstrate a course of action against the defendants for passing-off or infringement of trade mark.

Revlon Inc., the parent company, was incorporated in the State of Delaware, the State that was traditionally lenient to corporations in the imposition of local taxation and charges and traditionally undemanding in the amount of public disclosure required to be made concerning the affairs and ownership of corporations. Revlon Inc. manufacture and sell, "primarily" in the United States, Revlon products under numerous trade names protected under American law, the American trade marks being held by Revlon Inc. Revlon products are also manufactured outside the United States by corporations which are wholly-owned subsidiaries of Revlon Inc. There is no necessary connection between the country of manufacture and the country of incorporation of the company responsible for the manufacture or sale of Revlon products in the country of manufacture. Thus Revlon products were manufactured at a factory in Wales which was owned by Revlon Overseas, a company incorporated in Venezuela. Such an arrangement may enable profits to be extracted from the country of manufacture and may make nationalisation or confiscation more difficult, and may possess other advantages for a multi-national group of companies. Revlon trade names are used for Revlon products sold outside the United States and are protected by trade marks which are registered in the countries where Revlon products are sold. Revlon trade marks in countries outside the United States were originally held by the American parent company, Revlon Inc., but were later transferred to a Swiss corporation named Revlon Suisse. A Swiss company holding trade marks and other assets may be used to accumulate royalties and income in a strong currency under the protection of a country where neither nationalisation nor confiscation nor undue publicity need be feared. The distribution and sale of Revlon products manufactured in countries outside the United States are controlled by Revlon International, a company incorporated in New York and wholly owned by Revlon Inc. The company which holds Revlon trade marks outside the United States, namely Revlon Suisse, is a wholly-owned subsidiary of Revlon International. Revlon Suisse is the registered proprietor of the Revlon British trade marks and granted registered user rights to its American parent company, Revlon International, and to the Venezuelan company, Revlon Overseas, which manufactured Revlon products in Wales. Those user rights were limited so that they could not be exploited by any company which ceased to be under the control of Revlon Inc. . . .

The Revlon Flex shampoos and hair conditioners were first manufactured and sold in the United States and were subsequently manufactured, also in Wales, by Revlon Overseas and sold by Revlon International in the United Kingdom after the Revlon Flex products had proved successful in the United States. The range of Revlon Flex products originally consisted of three types of shampoos and hair conditioners designed for normal, greasy and dry hair. These three types, whether manufactured and sold in the United States or the United Kingdom, all sold under the trade name Revlon Flex in bottles which were similar in appearance. Revlon Flex bottled and manufactured in Wales contained no hint of the country of origin but proclaimed on the bottle that the product emanated from Revlon of New York, Paris and London. The purchaser of Revlon Flex in the United Kingdom would have been surprised to learn that the shampoo bought by him was made in a Welsh factory owned by a Venezuelan company and distributed by a New York company. The purchaser would have been surprised but not alarmed, because Revlon Flex shampoos are all products of an international organisation which has acquired an international reputation. A purchaser of shampoo in London or New York or elsewhere relies on the international reputation of the multi-national group responsible for the manufacture and sale of Revlon Flex all over the world. The purchaser rightly expects, and obtains, the same Revlon Flex shampoo wherever manufactured or purchased in any part of the world. The purchaser himself chooses between the three types of Revlon Flex intended for normal, dry or greasy hair. . . .

The plaintiffs complain that their sales of Revlon Flex products in the United Kingdom will suffer if the defendants sell their Revlon Flex products cheaply in this country. The plaintiffs also complain that the reputation which they have acquired in the United Kingdom by selling expensive goods will be damaged if the defendants sell similar goods cheaply. It is apparently common ground that the difference between brands of shampoos and hair conditioners depends not so much on the ingredients as on advertising and price. Assuming for the purposes of this appeal that Revlon products are expensive in the United Kingdom and are bought because they are expensive, this attempt by the plaintiffs to enforce price fixing by the back door is not sustainable. Revlon Inc. chose to obtain financial advantages by disposing of anti-dandruff medicated Revlon Flex products in such manner that the defendants are now able to sell those products cheaply in the United Kingdom. That choice which benefitted Revlon Inc. in the United States may damage Revlon Inc. through its subsidiaries operating in the United Kingdom. But in my judgment the plaintiff companies form part of a multi-national group, and are not entitled by asserting the English law of passing-off to prevent their own goods, put into circulation by their own group, from being exported from the United States and sold in the United Kingdom at prices determined by the importers. . . .

In my judgment where a parent company chooses to manufacture and sell wholly or partly through a group of subsidiary companies in different parts of the world, products which bear the same trade mark and attract an international reputation, neither the parent nor any subsidiary can complain in the United Kingdom if those products are used, sold and re-sold under that trade mark. A purchaser of a Revlon product from a Revlon company in the United States or the United Kingdom or in any other part of the world, whether a Revlon company operates in that part of the world or not, is at least entitled to assume that he will not be sued by a Revlon company in the United Kingdom, or in Delaware or Venezuela or New York or anywhere else, merely because of the place of manufacture of the product which he has acquired under the name of Revlon. The purchaser may have no idea of the place of manufacture of the Revlon product or of the name of the company responsible for production or distribution, and he will only know that he is buying a Revlon product derived from a Revlon company. The legal ownership of the trade mark enables the proprietor in the interests of the Revlon group in general and Revlon Inc. in particular to protect in the United Kingdom the group Revlon reputation and goodwill by ensuring that no goods are sold under the name Revlon unless they are produced and labelled by a Revlon company. The legal ownership of the trade mark does not go further and enable a Swiss, American or Bermudan subsidiary Revlon company to ensure that the Revlon products of its American parent or other Revlon company are not sold within the territory of the United Kingdom.

For the purposes of section 4(3)(a), if the parent company Revlon Inc. in any part of the world applies a trade mark protected in the United Kingdom by registration in the name of its subsidiary Revlon Suisse as proprietor, the result is exactly the same as if the proprietor had been Revlon Inc. for whose benefit the trade mark is held.

Revlon Inc. can decide where Revlon products can be manufactured, which company shall be responsible for manufacture, which company shall be responsible for distribution in different parts of the world and which company shall be registered in any part of the world as proprietor or user of Revlon trade marks. If Revlon Inc. themselves choose to manufacture and distribute products bearing the Revlon trade marks they cannot complain, and they cannot allow their subsidiary company to complain, of the use of the Revlon trade mark in connection with those products. The registered proprietor or registered user of a Revlon trade mark cannot set up as against Revlon Inc., or against any other member of the Revlon group, any individual claim to the benefit of the trade mark, which is only vested in the registered proprietor so long as Revlon Inc. think fit and is only exploited by the registered user for the ultimate benefit of Revlon Inc.

The reason that none of the plaintiffs can complain in the present case is that by section 4(3)(a) of the Trade Marks Act, 1938 there is no infringement where the trade mark is applied by the proprietor. The object of the section is to prevent the owner of the trade mark claiming infringement in respect of a product which he has produced and to which he has attached the trade mark. In the circumstances of the Revlon group, and applying the approach of Lord Justice Cross in *GE Trade Mark,* [1970] RPC 339 at 395, [1970] FSR 113, use by the parent, Revlon Inc., may fairly be considered as use by the proprietor, the subsidiary Revlon Suisse itself. In more homely language, section 4(3)(a) cannot be evaded by substituting the monkey for the organ-grinder. . . .

Having reached the firm conclusion that the plaintiffs have not established, and on their own evidence cannot establish, a plausible cause of action against any of the defendants in passing-off or trade mark infringement, I too agree that the appeal must be dismissed.

NOTES AND QUESTIONS

1. Lord Templeman says that when an affiliated company within a commonly controlled group of companies makes use of an internationally recognized trademark, the consent of the controlling entity within the corporate group

to use of that mark must be assumed. If trademarked goods are labeled such that consumers may accurately identify the product, and if there is no indication that the goods are of inferior quality to those ordinarily placed on sale by the trademark holder, then there is no trademark infringement or passing off when such goods first sold by a commonly controlled entity are thereafter imported and sold without the consent of an affiliated trademark holder.

Assume there is a U.S.-based multinational company with a Brazilian affiliate subject to U.S. parent control (as in the *Revlon* case). Assume that the Brazilian affiliate manufactures laundry detergent that is formulated to work well with Brazilian water, which is (purely hypothetically) harder than the typical U.S. water. The Brazilian affiliate applies a trademark to its packaging that is identical to the mark used by its parent in the United States. Because Brazilian consumers are generally less well off than U.S. consumers, the Brazilian affiliate sells laundry detergent at a price 30 percent below the price at which comparable detergent is sold in the United States. An unaffiliated wholesaler buys a quantity of packaged laundry detergent from the Brazilian affiliate and ships it to the United States. The detergent packaging is properly labeled in several languages, including English, Portuguese, and Spanish, and the wholesaler adds an additional label stating that the detergent is formulated to work best in hard water. Based on the reasoning in Lord Templeman's opinion, should the U.S. parent be able to block importation from Brazil on the basis of its registered U.S. trademark? What facts are critical to your analysis? Assume that a consumer in a soft water region of the United States buys the detergent, and it does not work particularly well. Should the consumer have been deprived of the opportunity to purchase the less expensive product? What are the interests of the U.S. parent in this transaction? The issue of "material differences" in a parallel import trademarked product was addressed, *supra* pages 415-26 (section F.1.b), in case law from the U.S. Court of Appeals for the District of Colombia Circuit and the U.S. Court of Appeals for the Federal Circuit.

2. Later in this chapter, we examine the Community Trade Mark Regulation (CTMR), which establishes a unitary mark (CTM) valid throughout the European Union. The provision in the CTMR regarding exhaustion provides:

> ARTICLE 13
> Exhaustion of the rights conferred by a Community trade mark
> 1. A Community trade mark shall not entitle the proprietor to prohibit its use in relation to goods which have been put on the market in the Community under that trade mark by the proprietor or with his consent. . . .
> 4. Paragraph 1 shall not apply where there exist legitimate reasons for the proprietor to oppose further commercialization of the goods, especially where the condition of the goods is changed or impaired after they have been put on the market.

Does the express language of the CTMR tell you whether (or not) putting a product on the market outside the European Union with the consent of the trademark holder exhausts the CTM?

III. TRADEMARK REGISTRATION AT THE MULTILATERAL LEVEL

Although business enterprises may acquire certain legal rights in trademarks under common law rules regarding their use in commerce, the principal mechanism for securing legal rights in trademarks is through registration of those marks with national, regional, and international authorities. Historically, businesses have more actively sought international trademark protection than international patent protection. There are a number of reasons for this. First, trademarks are easier to create than patentable inventions. For the most part, trademarks must only be distinct from other marks used on comparable goods or services, whereas patentable inventions must be new, useful, and nonobvious (as well as enabled). There is no requirement that trademarks be associated with innovative products. Trademarks, in short, are easier to come by than patentable inventions. Second, the process of securing patent protection at the international level is time consuming and expensive. Translating documents and appointing local agents generates considerable expense for patent applicants. Although decisions to undertake international trademark registration are not taken lightly, such decisions do not involve financial commitments as significant as those to seek international patent protection. Finally, there is generally a greater risk that trademarks may be misappropriated and misused in foreign countries than patentable inventions. The misappropriation of a patentable invention often requires production of that invention. Such production may be beyond the means of most would-be misappropriators. The misappropriation of a trademark may involve little more than applying a decal or stamp to an existing product — misleading consumers by taking advantage of the reputation of the foreign trademark holder. Trademark registration within each country or region is generally necessary to protect against this simple act of misappropriation.

Trademark protection is less an instrument of national and regional industrial policy than patent protection, and the harmonization of rules on trademark registration has been less controversial than such harmonization regarding patents. Trademark and service mark registrations are generally undertaken in respect to specific classes of goods and services. In 1957, an international agreement was reached on a standard system for classifying goods and services with respect to the registration of marks. The 1957 Nice Agreement Concerning the International Classification for the Purposes of the Registration of Marks provides a common format for designating the classes of goods and services, and is in wide use around the world.

A. The Trade Mark Law Treaty and the Singapore Treaty on the Law of Trademarks

In 1994, the Trade Mark Law Treaty (TLT) was adopted at WIPO. The TLT entered into force in 1996, but as of April 2006 it had attracted only 34 adherents, among which are the United States, Japan, Germany, and Switzerland. The TLT establishes a maximum level of information that national authorities may require from trademark applicants — seeking to reduce the burden on applicants from complying with differing requirements. The TLT also provides an exhaustive list of requirements that may be imposed in connection with certain formalities such as changing the names and addresses of trademark registrants. The TLT adopts certain trademark application forms, which, if used by the applicant, must be accepted by the trademark registration office.

In September 2006, a new Singapore Treaty on the Law of Trademarks was adopted by WIPO members. The Singapore Treaty was signed by over 60 countries when it was adopted. The treaty entered into force on March 16, 2009 and as of December 2010 has 22 Contracting Parties. The Singapore Treaty was intended to remedy certain perceived limitations in the TLT. An excerpt from a summary of the treaty prepared by WIPO follows.

SUMMARY OF THE SINGAPORE TREATY ON THE LAW OF TRADEMARKS
(2006)*

The Singapore Treaty on the Law of Trademarks was adopted by the Diplomatic Conference for the Adoption of a Revised Trademark Law Treaty, that took place in Singapore, from March 13 to 28, 2006.

The objective of the Singapore Treaty is to create a modern and dynamic international framework for the harmonization of administrative trademark registration procedures. Building on the Trademark Law Treaty of 1994 (TLT 1994), the new Treaty has a wider scope of application and addresses new developments in the field of communication technology. As compared with the TLT 1994, the Singapore Treaty is applicable to all types of marks registrable under the law of a given Contracting Party; Contracting Parties are free to choose the means of communication with their Offices (including communications in electronic form or by electronic means of transmittal); relief measures in respect of time limits as well as provisions on the recording of trademark licenses are introduced, and an Assembly of the Contracting Parties is established. Other provisions of the Singapore Treaty (such as the requirements to provide for multi-class applications and registrations, and the use of the International ("Nice") Classification), closely follow the TLT 1994. The two treaties are separate, and may be ratified or adhered to independently.

As opposed to the TLT 1994, the Singapore Treaty applies generally to marks that can be registered under the law of a Contracting Party. Most significantly, it is the first time that non-traditional marks are explicitly recognized in an international instrument dealing with trademark law. The Treaty is applicable to all types of marks, including non-traditional visible marks, such as holograms, three-dimensional marks, color, position and movement marks, and also non-visible marks, such as sound, olfactory or taste and feel marks. The Regulations provide for the mode of representation of these marks in applications, which may include non-graphic or photographic reproductions.

The Singapore Treaty leaves Contracting Parties the freedom to choose the form and means of transmittal of communications and whether they accept communications on paper, communications in electronic form or any other form of communication. This has consequences on formal requirements for applications and requests, such as the signature on communications with the

_____

* International Bureau of WIPO.

Office. The Treaty maintains a very important provision of the TLT 1994, namely that the authentication, certification or attestation of any signature on paper communications cannot be required. However, Contracting Parties are free to determine whether and how they wish to implement a system of authentication of electronic communications.

As a new feature, the Treaty provides for relief measures when an applicant or a holder has missed a time limit in an action for a procedure before the Office. Contracting Parties must make available, at their choice, at least one of the following relief measures: extension of the time limit, continued processing and reinstatement of rights if the failure to meet the time limit was unintentional or occurred in spite of due care required by the circumstances.

The Singapore Treaty includes provisions on the recording of trademark licenses, and establishes maximum requirements for the requests for recordal, amendment or cancellation of the recordal of a license.

The creation of an Assembly of the Contracting Parties introduces a degree of flexibility for the definition of details concerning administrative procedures to be implemented by national trademark offices where it is anticipated that future developments in trademark registration procedures and practice will warrant the amendments of those details. The Assembly is endowed with powers to modify the Regulations and the Model International Forms, where necessary and it can also deal — at a preliminary level — with questions relating to the future development of the Treaty.

Furthermore, the Diplomatic Conference adopted a Resolution Supplementary to the Singapore Treaty on the Law of Trademarks and the Regulations Thereunder, with a view to declaring an understanding by the Contracting Parties on several areas covered by the Treaty, namely: that the Treaty does not impose any obligations on Contracting Parties to (i) register new types of marks, or (ii) implement electronic filing systems or other automation systems. Special provisions are made to provide developing and least developed countries (LDCs) with additional technical assistance and technological support to enable them to take full advantage of the provisions of the Treaty. It was recognized that LDCs shall be the primary and main beneficiaries of technical assistance by Contracting Parties of WIPO. The future Assembly is charged with the task to monitor and evaluate, at every ordinary session, the progress of the assistance granted, and it is provided that any dispute arising with respect to the interpretation or application of the Treaty should be settled amicably through consultation and mediation under the auspices of the Director General of WIPO.

The Singapore Treaty on the Law of Trademarks is open for signature by States members of WIPO and certain intergovernmental organizations until March 27, 2007. Instruments of ratification or accession must be deposited with the Director General of WIPO. The Treaty shall enter into force three months after ten States or intergovernmental organizations having a regional trademark office have deposited their instruments of ratification or accession.

The TLT and Singapore Treaty are employed to promote a uniform set of rules among national trademark authorities and to make the trademark application process more efficient. They are not, however, agreements that provide for a multilateral or international registration system. That objective is addressed by two other multilateral agreements, the Madrid Agreement and Protocol.

B.   *The Madrid Agreement and Protocol*

The Madrid Agreement Concerning the International Registration of Marks was adopted in 1891 — shortly following the Paris and Berne Conventions. This Agreement enables a person who has secured a trademark registration in one contracting state to file an international application for registration with the International Bureau of WIPO. The international application is transmitted to trademark offices of other member countries designated by the applicant, and if there is no objection within an established time period, the international registration becomes effective for the countries designated by such application. Although 56 countries, including many European countries, are party to the Madrid Agreement as of March 2011 and it has been widely used by European trademark holders, the usefulness of the Madrid Agreement was limited because neither the United States, Japan, nor countries of Latin America (with the exception of Cuba) were parties.

In 1989, a Protocol Relating to the Madrid Agreement (Madrid Protocol) was adopted. The Protocol, which entered into force in 1996, is designed to address a number of the perceived defects in the Madrid Agreement. Under the Madrid Protocol, an international application for registration may be filed on the basis of an application in a Madrid Protocol country, dispensing with the require-ment that a trademark be registered prior to filing the international applica-tion. There is the possibility of a longer time period during which a designated Protocol country may object to protection of the mark in that country. Under the Madrid Agreement, cancellation of the trademark in the initial country of registration within the first five years following international registration results in invalidation of the mark in all Madrid countries. Under the Madrid Protocol, upon a cancellation by the initial country of application, the international trademark holder may transform the mark into national applications based on the original filing date of the international application. Finally, the Protocol allows for the participation of the EU Office for Harmonisation in the Internal Market (OHIM) and use of the Community Trade Mark as the basis for an international application.

The relationship between the Madrid Agreement and the Madrid Protocol is defined by Article 9*sexies* of the Protocol.

The United States ratified and became party to the Madrid Protocol on November 3, 2003. The European Union and Japan have also joined. As of March 2011 there are 83 parties to the Madrid Protocol, although Latin American countries (with the exception of Cuba) had yet to become parties.

THE MADRID AGREEMENT CONCERNING THE INTERNATIONAL REGISTRATION OF MARKS AND THE PROTOCOL RELATING TO THAT AGREEMENT*

INTRODUCTION

5.317 The system of international registration of marks is governed by two treaties, the Madrid Agreement Concerning the International Registration of Marks, which dates from 1891, and the Protocol Relating to the Madrid

---

* WIPO Intellectual Property Handbook, as of April 2006.

Agreement, which was adopted in 1989, entered into force on December 1, 1995, and came into operation on April 1, 1996. Common Regulations under the Agreement and Protocol also came into force on that last date. The system is administered by the International Bureau of WIPO, which maintains the International Register and publishes the *WIPO Gazette of International Marks*. . . .

THE FUNCTIONING OF THE SYSTEM OF INTERNATIONAL REGISTRATION

FILING AN INTERNATIONAL REGISTRATION

5.319 An application for international registration (an "international application") may be filed only by a natural person or a legal entity which has a real and effective industrial or commercial establishment in, or is domiciled in, or is a national of, a country which is party to the Madrid Agreement or the Madrid Protocol, or who has such an establishment in, or is domiciled in, the territory of an intergovernmental organization which is a party to the Protocol, or is a national of a member State of such an organization.

5.320 The Madrid system of international registration cannot be used by a person or legal entity which does not have the necessary connection, through establishment, domicile or nationality, with a member of the Madrid Union. Nor can it be used to protect a trademark outside the Madrid Union.

5.321 A mark may be the subject of an international application only if it has already been registered (or, where the international application is governed exclusively by the Protocol, if registration has been applied for) in the Office of origin. In the case of an international application governed exclusively by the Agreement or by both the Agreement and Protocol (see paragraph 5.313), the Office of origin is the Trademark Office of the Contracting State in which the applicant has a real and effective industrial or commercial establishment; if he has no establishment in such a State, it is the Office of the Contracting Party where he has a domicile; if he has no domicile in such a State, it is the Office of the Contracting State of which he is a national. In the case of an international application governed exclusively by the Protocol, these restrictions on the choice of Office of origin (sometimes referred to as the "cascade") do not apply; the Office of origin may be the Office of *any* Contracting Party with respect to which a person or entity fulfills one or more of the above conditions.

5.322 An international application must designate one or more Contracting Parties (not the Contracting Party whose Office is the Office of origin) in which the mark is to be protected. Further Contracting Parties may be designated subsequently. A Contracting Party may be designated only if that Contracting Party and the Contracting Party whose Office is the Office of origin are both party to the same treaty, that is, the Agreement or the Protocol.

5.323 The designation of a given Contracting Party is made under that treaty which is common to that Contracting Party and the Contracting Party whose Office is the Office of origin. Where both Contracting Parties are party to both the Agreement and the Protocol, it is the Agreement which governs the designation; this follows from the so-called "safeguard" clause, Article 9*sexies* of the Protocol. It follows that there are three kinds of international application:

— an international application *governed exclusively by the Agreement;* this means that all the designations are made under the Agreement;

— an international application *governed exclusively by the Protocol;* this means that all the designations are made under the Protocol;
— an international application *governed by both the Agreement and the Protocol;* this means that some of the designations are made under the Agreement and some under the Protocol.

5.324 An international application must be presented to the International Bureau through the Office of origin. It must contain, *inter alia,* a reproduction of the mark (which must be identical with that in the basic registration or basic application) and a list of the goods and services for which protection is sought, classified in accordance with the International Classification of Goods and Services (Nice Classification). If the international application is governed exclusively by the agreement, it must be in French; if it is governed exclusively by the Protocol or by both the Agreement and the Protocol, it may be in either English or French, though the Office of origin may restrict the applicant's choice to one of these languages. . . .

5.327 These fees may be paid direct to the International Bureau or, where the Office of origin accepts to collect and forward such fees, through that Office. . . .

5.328 The Office of origin must certify that the mark is the same as that in the basic registration or basic application, that any indications such as a description of the mark or a claim to color as a distinctive feature of the mark are the same as those contained in the basic registration or basic application, and that the goods and services indicated in the international application are covered by the list of goods and services in the basic registration or basic application. . . .

5.329 The International Bureau checks that the international application complies with the requirements of the Agreement or Protocol and the Common Regulations, including requirements relating to the indication of goods and services and their classification, and that the required fees have been paid. The Office of origin and the holder are informed of any irregularities, which must be remedied within three months, otherwise the application will be considered abandoned. Where the international application complies with the applicable requirements, the mark is recorded in the International Register and published in the *Gazette*. The International Bureau then notifies each Contracting Party in which protection has been requested.

5.330 An international registration is effective for 10 years. It may be renewed for further periods of 10 years on payment of the prescribed fees.

EFFECTS OF THE INTERNATIONAL REGISTRATION

5.331 From the date of the international registration, the protection of the mark in each of the countries of the designated Contracting Parties is the same as if the mark had been the subject of an application for registration filed directly with the Office of that Contracting Party. If no refusal is notified to the International Bureau within the relevant time limit, the protection of the mark in the country of each designated Contracting Party is the same as if it had been registered by the Office of that Contracting Party.

5.332 The effects of an international registration can be extended to a Contracting Party not covered by the international application by filing a subsequent designation. The principles that determine whether such a designation can be made, and whether it is governed by the Agreement or by the Protocol, are as described in paragraphs 5.312 and 5.313 above. A subsequent designation may be made where the Contracting Party concerned was not a party to the Agreement or Protocol at the time of the international application.

5.333 Each designated Contracting Party has the right to refuse protection. Any refusal must be notified to the International Bureau by the Office of the Contracting Party concerned within the time limits specified in the Agreement or Protocol. The refusal is recorded in the International Register and published in the *Gazette* and a copy is transmitted to the holder of the international registration. Any subsequent procedure, such as review or appeal, is carried out directly between the holder and the administration of the Contracting Party concerned, without any involvement on the part of the International Bureau. The Contracting Party concerned must, however, notify the International Bureau of the final decision taken in respect of such review or appeal. This decision is also recorded in the International Register and published in the *Gazette*.

5.334 The time limit for a Contracting Party to notify a refusal is generally 12 months. Under the Protocol, however, a Contracting Party may declare that this period is to be 18 months, or longer in the case of a refusal based on an opposition.

5.335 The Office of the designated Contracting Party has the possibility, under the Common Regulations, to issue a statement of grant of protection. The practical benefit resulting from such a statement of grant of protection is that the holder of the international registration does not have to wait for the expiry of the refusal period to know whether his/her mark is protected in the country concerned.

5.336 For a period of five years from the date of its registration, an international registration remains dependent on the mark registered or applied for in the Office of origin. If, and to the extent that, the basic registration ceases to have effect, whether through cancellation following a decision of the Office of origin or a court, through voluntary cancellation or through non-renewal, within this five-year period, the international registration will no longer be protected. Similarly, where the international registration was based on an application in the Office of origin, it will be canceled if, and to the extent that, that application is refused or withdrawn within the five-year period, or if, and to the extent that, the registration resulting from that application ceases to have effect within that period. The Office of origin is required to notify the International Bureau of facts and decisions concerning such ceasing of effect or refusal and, where appropriate, to request the cancellation (to the extent applicable) of the international registration. Such cancellation is published in the *Gazette* and notified to the designated Contracting Parties.

5.337 After the expiry of this period of five years, the international registration becomes independent of the basic registration or basic application. . . .

5.346 International registration has several advantages for the owner of the mark. After registering the mark, or filing an application for registration, with the Office of origin, he has only to file one application in one language with one Office, and to pay fees to one Office; this is instead of filing separately with the Trademark Offices of the various Contracting Parties in different languages, and paying a separate fee to each Office. Similar advantages exist when the registration has to be renewed or modified.

5.347 International registration is also to the advantage of Trademark Offices. For example, they do not need to examine for compliance with formal requirements, or classify the goods or services, or publish the marks. As stated above, the individual and other designation fees collected by the International Bureau are transferred to the Contracting Parties in which protection is sought. Furthermore, if the International Registration Service closes its biennial accounts with a profit, the proceeds are divided among the Contracting Parties.

5.348 . . . Further information concerning the system of international registrations of marks, including the updated list of Contracting Parties to the Agreement and the Protocol and the fees, the latest annual statistics and the full text of the Agreement, Protocol and Common Regulations, as well as the text of the Guide to the International Registration of Marks, is also available on WIPO's website (www.wipo.int) under the heading "Madrid System."

NOTES AND QUESTIONS

1. The USPTO Trademark Manual of Examining Procedure (TMEP) includes Chapter 1900 with respect to the Madrid Protocol. It begins by observing:

   The Protocol Relating to the Madrid Agreement Concerning the International Registration of Marks ("Madrid Protocol") is an international treaty that allows a trademark owner to seek registration in any of the countries or intergovernmental organizations that have joined the Madrid Protocol by submitting a single application, called an international application. The International Bureau (IB) of the World Intellectual Property Organization (WIPO), in Geneva, Switzerland administers the international registration system.

   The Madrid Protocol became effective in the United States on November 2, 2003. The Madrid Protocol Implementation Act of 2002, Pub. L. 107-273, 116 Stat. 1758, 1913-1921 ("MPIA") amended the Trademark Act to provide that: (1) the owner of a U.S. application or registration may seek protection of its mark in any of the countries or intergovernmental organizations party to the Madrid Protocol by submitting a single international application to the IB through the United States Patent and Trademark Office ("USPTO"); and (2) the holder of an international registration may request an extension of protection of the international registration to the United States.

2. Note that the holder of a U.S. trademark seeking protection in the European Union now has the option of filing an application under the Madrid Protocol designating the European Union and its Community Trade Mark. If the U.S. applicant has a real and effective commercial presence in an EU member state, it may also apply under the Madrid Agreement (assuming it had registered a trademark in a member state). Recall

that application under the Madrid Agreement is predicated on an already-registered trademark.

IV.   REGIONAL TRADEMARK SYSTEMS

A.   The EU Trademark System

The EU program to create a single market in the field of IPRs perhaps finds its furthest development in the field of trademarks. The two central pieces of Union legislation in this regard are the First Trade Marks Directive and the Community Trade Mark Regulation. These two legislative measures take different approaches to the subject matter of trademarks. The First Trade Marks Directive was approved by the Council in 1988 and was intended only as a measure of "partial" approximation (or harmonization). In essence, the Council prescribed a set of basic trademark norms for the EU member states, but left discretion to these states regarding the precise way in which these norms would be implemented in national law. Each member state would remain responsible for granting trademark registrations, and the courts of each member state would interpret national law in light of the Directive (subject to referral to the European Court of Justice (ECJ)). It would be possible for a trademark to be declared valid in the courts of one Union member state and invalid in the courts of another.

The Community Trade Mark Regulation (CTMR), adopted by the Council in 1993, took a substantially different approach to trademark regulation. In the first place, as its name indicates, the CTMR is a "regulation" that is directly applicable in the law of the member states, and to the extent that matters are dealt with by the regulation, the national legislatures do not have discretion as to how the rules will be implemented. Even more important, the regulation provides for the grant of a unitary Community Trade Mark (CTM) valid throughout the European Union. The CTM is granted by a central office — the Office for Harmonisation in the Internal Market (OHIM) — located in Alicante, Spain. The system for resolving disputes concerning CTMs is complex. Generally speaking, actions for invalidation or revocation of trademark registration are brought at the OHIM, while trademark infringement actions are brought in the national courts of the EU member states that have been designated as "Community trade mark courts." While the CTM presents certain obvious advantages to trademark applicants, the unitary character of the mark also presents certain risks (e.g., that a single invalidation action may cause the mark to be lost — at least temporarily — for the whole territory of the European Union).

The First Trade Marks Directive and CTMR function side by side.

1.   The First Trade Marks Directive

The First Trade Marks Directive is introduced with an excerpt from the Opinion of Advocate General Jacobs in *Silhouette v. Hartlauer* (*see also* Chapter 1.VI.E, *supra*) that discusses the intent of the Directive.

SILHOUETTE INTERNATIONAL SCHMIED GMBH & CO. KG v. HARTLAUER HANDELSGESELLSCHAFT MBH

Opinion of Advocate General Jacobs
delivered on 29 January 1998
Case C-355/96

THE TRADE MARKS DIRECTIVE

4. The Trade Marks Directive was adopted under Article 100a of the EC Treaty. Its aim was not "to undertake full-scale approximation of the trade mark laws of the Member States" but simply to approximate "those national provisions of law which most directly affect the functioning of the internal market" (third recital of the preamble to the Directive).

5. The first, third, and ninth recitals of the preamble to the Directive state, respectively:

> Whereas the trade mark laws at present applicable in the Member States contain disparities which may impede the free movement of goods and freedom to provide services and may distort competition within the common market; whereas it is therefore necessary, in view of the establishment and functioning of the internal market, to approximate the laws of Member States; . . .
>
> Whereas it does not appear to be necessary at present to undertake full-scale approximation of the trade mark laws of the Member States and it will be sufficient if approximation is limited to those national provisions of law which most directly affect the functioning of the internal market; . . .
>
> Whereas it is fundamental, in order to facilitate the free circulation of goods and services, to ensure that henceforth registered trade marks enjoy the same protection under the legal systems of all the Member States; whereas this should however not prevent the Member States from granting at their option extensive protection to those trade marks which have a reputation.

6. In summary, the Directive harmonises the general "conditions for obtaining and continuing to hold a registered trade mark" (seventh recital) and the rights conferred by a trade mark (Articles 5, 6 and 7). Thus it specifies signs of which a trade mark may consist (Article 2), the grounds for refusing to register or invalidating a trade mark (Articles 3 and 4), the consequences of acquiescence in the use of a later trade mark (Article 9) and of failure to use a registered trade mark (Articles 10 to 12), and the grounds for revocation of a trade mark (Article 12).

7. However, in certain areas Member States are given a discretion to decide whether to adopt the rules provided for in the Directive: for example, there are certain optional grounds for refusing to register or invalidating a trade mark (Articles 3(2) and 4(4)) and an option as to whether or not to provide protection in certain specified circumstances for a trade mark with a reputation concerning its use in relation to dissimilar goods or services (Article 5(2)). In addition, the seventh recital specifies that:

> Member States will be able to maintain or introduce into their legislation grounds of refusal or invalidity linked to conditions for obtaining and continuing to hold a trade mark for which there is no provision of approximation, concerning, for example, the eligibility for the grant of a trade mark, the renewal of the trade mark or rules on fees, or related to the non-compliance with procedural rules.

The Directive also leaves to the Member States matters such as the procedure concerning the registration, revocation and invalidity of trade marks (fifth recital), the protection of unregistered trade marks (fourth recital) and provisions relating to unfair competition, civil liability and consumer protection (sixth recital).

2.   The Community Trade Mark

The EU Office for Harmonization in the Internal Market introduces the CTM in the following excerpts from its web site.

OFFICE FOR HARMONIZATION IN THE
INTERNAL MARKET (TRADE MARKS AND DESIGNS)*

2.2. The Advantages of the Community Trade Mark

2.2.1. What are the advantages of the Community trade mark?
The Community trade mark gives its proprietor a uniform right applicable in all Member States of the European Union on the strength of a single procedure which simplifies trade mark policies at European level.

It fulfils the three essential functions of a trade mark at European level: it identifies the origin of goods and services, guarantees consistent quality through evidence of the company's commitment vis-à-vis the consumer, and is a form of communication, a basis for publicity and advertising.

The Community trade mark may be used as a manufacturer's mark, a mark for goods of a trading company, or service mark. It may also take the form of a collective trade mark: properly applied, the regulation governing the use of the collective trade mark guarantees the origin, the nature and the quality of goods and services by making them distinguishable, which is beneficial to members of the association or body owning the trade mark.

The Community trade mark covers a market of more than 350 million consumers who enjoy some of the highest living standards in the world. It is the ideal instrument to meet the challenges of this market.

The Community trade mark is obtained by registration in the Register kept by the Harmonization Office. When registered, transferred or allowed to lapse, the effect of such action is Community-wide.

It is valid for a period of 10 years and may be renewed indefinitely.

The rules of law applicable to it are similar to those applied to national trade marks by the Member States. Companies will therefore find themselves in a familiar environment, just on a larger scale.

2.2.2. The Community trade mark and national trade marks
The Community trade mark may be obtained for a sign which is either applied for directly at the Harmonization Office or which has been applied for previously through a national office. It does not imply revocation of previous national or international protection, but merely makes such protection more effective and more manageable.

---

* http://oami.europa.eu/en, visited July 12, 2006.

A newly-created sign adapted to the various languages, cultures and customs within the European market may be protected directly by applying for first registration as a Community trade mark at the Harmonization Office.

A Community trade mark may protect a sign which has already been filed at a national office of a country party to the Paris Convention or to the Agreement on trade-related aspects of intellectual property rights concluded under GATT (TRIPs Agreement). In this case, a right of priority may be claimed for a period of six months.

A national trade mark or series of national trade marks may be registered as a Community trade mark irrespective of their age. The company will thus have the perfect instrument to meet the challenges of the internal market.

Opting for the Community trade mark does not imply the abandonment of national trade marks. The company may retain these as long as it wishes.

The seniority of a national mark may be claimed at the Harmonization Office, even if the national trade mark is subsequently cancelled or surrendered in favour of a Community trade mark. The company enjoys the same rights as if the national trade mark were still registered.

In the event of refusal to register an application, or the revocation or annulment of a Community trade mark, applications for national trade marks may be made in all countries of the European Union in which there are no such grounds for refusal, revocation or annulment. The advantage of priority or seniority is therefore maintained, as are any investment and advertising campaigns previously carried out in these countries.

FREQUENTLY ASKED QUESTIONS
CONCERNING THE COMMUNITY TRADE MARK SYSTEM

1. GENERAL QUESTIONS

1.1. What legislative acts established the Community trade mark system?

The main legal provisions regarding the Community trade mark are contained in three Community regulations, namely:

Council Regulation No 40/94 of 20.12.1993 usually referred to as "the basic Regulation" or the "CTMR";

Commission Regulation No 2868/95 of 13.12.1995 implementing Regulation 40/94, usually referred to as the "Implementing Regulation" or the "IR";

Commission Regulation No 2869/95 of 13.12.1995 on the fees payable to the Office, usually referred to as the "Fees Regulation" or the "FR."

In addition to these three Regulations, on 5.2.1996, the Commission adopted Regulation No 216/96 laying down the rules of procedure of the Boards of Appeal.

The Office has also adopted various guidelines on proceedings before the Office and the President of the Office has taken Decisions and issued Communications.

1.2. What is a Community Trade Mark (CTM)?

A CTM is a sign for identifying and distinguishing goods or services valid across the European Community, registered with the OHIM in accordance with the conditions specified in the CTMR.

1.3. What does it mean when it is stated that the CTM has a unitary character?

A CTM application and a CTM are valid in the European Community as a whole. The application and the ensuing registration extend automatically to all 25 Member States [now 27 — EDS.] of the European Community indivisibly. It is not possible to limit the geographic scope of protection to certain Member States. Furthermore, there is one single registration procedure, which is centrally handled before the OHIM. No actions before the national industrial property offices are necessary. In addition, an invalidation, a refusal or the expiry of the CTM necessarily applies for the whole of the Community. Lastly, the CTM is one single asset of property. It can only be transferred for the whole of the Community and not with respect to individual countries. However, territorially or otherwise limited licences, even limited for a particular Member State, are possible.

1.4. Does the CTM prevail over national trade marks?

The CTM system leaves the national trade mark systems of Member States (as far as Belgium, Luxembourg and the Netherlands are concerned, the Benelux Trade Mark system) unaffected. Business enterprises are free to file national trade mark applications, a CTM application, or both. The large number of national trade marks already existing and registered in the Member States remain valid. It is entirely up to the strategy of the applicants and proprietors of trade marks whether they want to rely exclusively, or in addition to national trade mark rights, on the CTM protection. However, earlier national trade marks constitute earlier rights against a CTM, and vice versa. The Office does not examine such earlier rights of its own motion. Only the proprietor of the earlier right can raise this issue, either by filing an opposition within 3 months of the publication of the CTM application, or following the registration of the CTM by filing an application for a declaration of invalidity on relative grounds.

1.5. Is there an all-or-nothing principle if a ground for refusal applies only with respect to one Member State of the Community?

Yes. The Office refuses a CTM application if a ground for refusal exists only in part of the Community. If, for example, the trade mark consists of the designation of the product in one official language of a Member State of the Community, the Office will refuse the CTM application. Earlier rights, raised in an opposition or in an application for a declaration of invalidity, prejudice the registration of a CTM even if they only exist in one Member State of the Community. The effects of this situation, however, should not be exaggerated. Cases where an application must be refused because the mark constitutes a non distinctive or a descriptive or generic term in only one language of the Community (and not one of their major world trading languages) are not so frequent. If an earlier right in only one Member State exists, it goes without saying that this right can not be invalidated by the later filing of a CTM by another person. The opposition or invalidity procedure before the OHIM will, in such cases, offer ample leeway for an amicable settlement. Lastly, a CTM application which has been refused, or a CTM which has been declared invalid or revoked, may be converted into national trade mark applications in all the Member States of the European Community in which the ground for refusal does not apply. The ensuing national trade mark applications will retain the date of the CTM application.

3. CTMR Institutions in Action

The following decision illustrates how the OHIM system operates, and how the law of the CTMR is applied. The U.S.-based electronics goods retailer "Best Buy" has applied for a Community Trade Mark. The application concerns a word and design service mark, composed of a bright yellow price tag on which the words "Best Buy" are superimposed. Similar marks already have been registered in France and Germany. The OHIM trademark examiner rejected Best Buy's application, and Best Buy lodged an appeal before the OHIM Board of Appeal, which dismissed it. Best Buy further appealed that decision to the European Court of First Instance (which is now renamed the "General Court"), which is designated in the CTMR to hear such appeals. (The ECJ has appellate jurisdiction in such matters.)

BEST BUY CONCEPTS, INC. v. OFFICE FOR HARMONISATION IN THE INTERNAL MARKET

Judgment of the Court of First Instance
(Second Chamber)
3 July 2003 (1)

(Community trade mark — Figurative mark containing the word mark best buy — Absolute ground for refusal — Distinctive character — Article 7(1)(b) of Regulation (EC) No 40/94 In Case T-122/01

APPLICATION for annulment of the decision of the Third Board of Appeal of the Office for Harmonisation in the Internal Market (Trade Marks and Designs) of 21 March 2001 (Case R 44/2000-3) concerning an application for registration of a figurative mark containing the word mark best buy as a Community trade mark,

THE COURT OF FIRST INSTANCE OF THE EUROPEAN COMMUNITIES (Second Chamber), composed of: N.J. Forwood, President, J. Pirrung and A.W.H. Meij, Judges,

Registrar: D. Christensen, Administrator, having regard to the written procedure and further to the hearing on 25 February 2003, gives the following:

JUDGMENT

BACKGROUND TO THE DISPUTE

1. On 7 May 1999, the applicant filed an application under Council Regulation (EC) No 40/94 of 20 December 1993 on the Community trade mark (OJ 1994 L 11, p. 1), as amended, for registration of a Community figurative trade mark at the Office for Harmonisation in the Internal Market (Trade Marks and Designs) (the Office).

2. The trade mark in respect of which registration was sought is the mark . . . with the colours yellow (background) and black (letters, contour, circle)[.]

3. The services in respect of which registration of the mark was sought are in classes 35, 37 and 42 of the Nice Agreement concerning the International Classification of Goods and Services for the Purpose of the Registration of Marks of 15 June 1957, as revised and amended, and, for each of those classes, correspond to the description: . . .

4. By decision of 19 November 1999, the examiner refused the application under Article 38 of Regulation No 40/94 on the ground that the mark applied for was caught by Article 7(1)(b), (c) and (d) of Regulation No 40/94.

5. On 22 December 1999, the applicant filed an appeal at the Office against the examiner's decision in accordance with Article 59 of Regulation No 40/94.

6. By decision of 21 March 2001 (the contested decision), the Board of Appeal dismissed the appeal. It found, essentially, that the sign was devoid of any distinctive character, that it was descriptive and, therefore, came within the scope of Article 7(1)(b) and (c) of Regulation No 40/94. . . .

Law

10. In its application, the applicant makes two pleas in law, alleging infringement of Article 7(1)(b) and (c), respectively, of Regulation No 40/94. . . .

FINDINGS OF THE COURT

19. Under Article 7(1)(b) of Regulation No 40/94, trade marks which are devoid of any distinctive character are not to be registered. Moreover, Article 7(2) of Regulation No 40/94 states that [p]aragraph 1 shall apply notwithstanding that the grounds of non-registrability obtain in only part of the Community.

20. As the Court of First Instance has already held, the marks referred to in Article 7(1)(b) of Regulation No 40/94 are, in particular, those which do not enable the relevant public to repeat the experience of a purchase, if it proves to be positive, or to avoid it, if it proves to be negative, on the occasion of a subsequent acquisition of the goods or services concerned (Case T-79/00 *Rewe-Zentral* v *OHIM (LITE)* [2002] ECR II-705, paragraph 26). Such is the case for *inter alia* signs which are commonly used in connection with the marketing of the goods or services concerned.

21. However, registration of a trade mark which consists of signs or indications that are also used as advertising slogans, indications of quality or incitements to purchase the goods or services covered by that mark is not excluded as such by virtue of such use (*see,* by analogy, Case C-517/99 *Merz & Krell* [2001] ECR I-6959, paragraph 40). A sign which fulfils functions other than that of a trade mark in the traditional sense of the term is only distinctive for the purposes of Article 7(1)(b) of Regulation No 40/94 however if it may be perceived immediately as an indication of the commercial origin of the goods or services in question, so as to enable the relevant public to distinguish, without any possibility of confusion, the goods or services of the owner of the mark from those of a different commercial origin.

22. A sign's distinctiveness can only be assessed, firstly, by reference to the goods or services in respect of which registration is sought and, secondly, on the basis of the perception of that sign by the relevant public.

23. In the present case, the Court notes, firstly, that the business management consultancy and technical assistance and advice for the establishment and management of specialised stores coming under classes 35 and 42 are aimed at a professional public, whilst the installation and maintenance services are intended for the general public. . . .

26. . . . [T]he public should be taken to be normally well-informed and aware for all the services covered. Since the word mark best buy is composed of elements from the English language, the relevant public is the English-speaking public, or even a public which is not English-speaking but has a sufficient grasp of the English language.

27. Second, as regards the assessment of the distinctive character of the mark claimed, it is appropriate, in the case of a complex mark, to examine it in its entirety. That is not incompatible, however, with a prior, separate examination of the different elements which make up the mark.

28. As regards, first, the word mark best buy, the Court notes that it is composed of ordinary English words which clearly indicate an advantageous relation between the price of the services covered by the application and their market value.

29. It is, therefore, perceived immediately by the relevant public as a mere promotional formula or a slogan which indicates that the services in question offer the best buy possible in their category or the best price-quality ratio, as noted by the Board of Appeal. . . .

30. The argument presented by the applicant at the hearing which acknowledged the indubitable semantic content of the word mark in question but maintained that it tells the consumer nothing about the content or the nature of the services offered is irrelevant. For a finding that there is no distinctive character, it is sufficient to note that the semantic content of the word mark, the principal and dominant element of the mark in question, indicates to the consumer a characteristic of the service relating to its market value which, whilst not specific, comes from information designed to promote or advertise which the relevant public will perceive first and foremost as such rather than as an indication of the commercial origin of the services (*see,* to this effect, *REAL PEOPLE, REAL SOLUTIONS,* paragraphs 29 and 30). In addition, the mere fact that the semantic content of the word mark best buy does not convey any information about the nature of the services concerned is not sufficient to make that sign distinctive.

31. Moreover, the applicant, who merely affirmed that the term buy was imprecise and vague, did not indicate which meaning of the word mark in question might be retained by the relevant public, other than that indicating an advantageous relation between the price and market value of the services. Nor did it state whether the word mark could be used in a manner other than in the context of promotion or marketing. Contrary to what the applicant maintains, the meaning of the word mark at issue may relate as much to a service provided as to the distribution of products or services which that service is intended to promote.

32. Moreover, the fact that the two elements constituting the word mark best buy are juxtaposed does not mean that the mere omission of an article in its structure (a best buy or the best buy) is sufficient to make it a lexical invention liable to give it a distinctive character or to give it an original character which, in any event, is not a criterion for assessing the distinctiveness of a sign (*see,* to this

effect, Case T-87/00 *Bank für Arbeit und Wirtschaft* v *OHIM (EASYBANK)* [2001] ECR II-1259, paragraph 40).

33. Turning to the perception of the shape and colour of the price tag by the relevant public, the Court notes that, as stated by the Board of Appeal in paragraph 19 of the contested decision, coloured price tags are commonly used in trade for all kinds of goods and services. Consequently, the applicant's argument that such a tag would attract the public's attention is inopportune.

34. As for the element ®, the Court notes that the presence of this type of element alongside other elements is not sufficient to confer distinctive character on a mark viewed in its entirety.

35. Since the mark claimed is composed of the assembly of the elements examined above, it is appropriate to consider whether the mark is distinctive when viewed as a whole.

36. In the light of the points discussed above, it appears that the mark claimed, as a whole, is merely composed of elements which, when examined separately, are devoid of distinctive character for the marketing of the services concerned. Nor is there any interaction between these different elements which might confer a distinctive character on the whole.

37. The shape of a price tag is not liable to affect the meaning of the dominant word elements. Moreover, far from adding a distinctive element, the shape is figurative and tends to reinforce the promotional character of the word elements in the minds of the relevant public.

38. The trade mark applied for is therefore devoid of distinctive character in respect of the categories of goods and services concerned.

39. As regards the prior registrations in Germany and France, the applicant was unable to provide any clarification of their scope at the hearing. The Court notes that those registrations do not concern either a sign wholly identical to the sign at issue here or similar goods or services.

40. In addition, as rightly pointed out by the Office, references to national registrations conferred by Member States which do not have English as their language, where the sign may well be distinctive without necessarily being so throughout the Community, cannot be accepted as relevant in this case.

41. Lastly, it is appropriate to recall that, according to settled case-law, the Community trade mark regime is an autonomous system and that the legality of the decisions of Boards of Appeal must be assessed solely on the basis of Regulation No 40/94 (Case T-32/00 *Messe München* v *OHIM (electronica)* [2000] ECR II-3289, paragraph 47, and Case T-106/00 *Streamserve* v *OHIM (STREAMSERVE)* [2002] ECR II-723, paragraph 66).

42. The applicant's arguments based solely on the registrations in Germany and France therefore have no bearing on the issue.

43. In the light of all the foregoing considerations, the mark claimed is devoid of distinctive character in a large part of the Community. The plea alleging infringement of Article 7(1)(b) of Regulation No 40/94 must therefore be rejected.

44. Accordingly, it is unnecessary to consider the plea alleging infringement of Article 7(1)(c) of Regulation No 40/94. In accordance with settled case-law, it is sufficient that one of the absolute grounds of refusal applies for the sign to be ineligible for registration as a Community trade mark (Case T-163/98 *Procter & Gamble* v *OHIM (BABY-DRY)* [1999] ECR II-2383,

paragraph 29, and Case T-19/99 *DKV v OHIM (COMPANYLINE)* [2000] ECR II-1, paragraph 30).

45. The action must therefore be dismissed. . . .

NOTES AND QUESTIONS

1. Do you think the General Court gives adequate attention to the claimed mark "as a whole"? Might the bright yellow price tag in combination with what are undoubtedly common descriptive terms stand out in the mind of consumers sufficiently to make the claimed mark distinctive? The Court indicates that the combination word and design mark is merely a collection of otherwise nondistinctive elements, without any "interaction" among the elements—the whole is no greater than the sum of its parts. Do you agree?

2. The General Court emphasizes that decisions of member state trademark offices and courts with respect to national marks do not control decisions under the CTMR.

3. The decision in *Best Buy* illustrates one of the advantages of the dual EU trademark registration system. The fact that Best Buy has not been able to register a CTM does not leave it without trademark protection. It may still be able to register its mark in the individual member states, as it already has done in France and Germany.

4. The First Trade Marks Directive, the EC Treaty, and the Community Trade Mark

The following decision by the Court of Justice of the European Union reflects the complex institutional arrangement governing trademarks in the European Union. Here a German enterprise, Hukla, had registered a trademark in Spain. That registration was undertaken further to the rules established by the First Trade Marks Directive. Another European company, Matratzen Concord, subsequently applied for a Community Trade Mark. That application was rejected following Hukla's opposition based on Hukla's preexisting Spanish trademark registration (the judicial proceedings concerning which proceeded all the way to a judgment by the ECJ). Subsequently, Matratzen Concord sought to invalidate Hukla's Spanish trademark before the courts of Spain on grounds that "Matratzen" is a generic term in German for mattress. The term, however, has no meaning in the Spanish language. A Spanish appeals court was uncertain whether the TFEU—which promotes the free movement of goods between EU member states—precludes granting trademark rights in a term that may be distinctive in Spain, but generic in Germany.

MATRATZEN CONCORD AG v. HUKLA GERMANY SA

Judgment of the Court (First Chamber) 9 March 2006

In Case C-421/04,

REFERENCE for a preliminary ruling under Article 234 EC from the Audiencia Provincial de Barcelona (Spain), made by decision of 28 June 2004, received at the Court on 1 October 2004, in the proceedings

Matratzen Concord AG
v.
Hukla Germany SA

THE COURT (First Chamber), composed of P. Jann, President of the Chamber, N. Colneric, J.N. Cunha Rodrigues, M. Ileŝic (Rapporteur) and E. Levits, Judges . . .

Judgment

1. The reference for a preliminary ruling concerns the interpretation of Articles 28 EC and 30 EC.

2. This reference was made in the context of proceedings between Matratzen Concord AG (hereinafter "Matratzen Concord") and Hukla Germany SA (hereinafter "Hukla") concerning the validity of a national trade mark.

Legal Context

3. Pursuant to Article 28 EC [now 34 — Eds.] "[q]uantitative restrictions on imports and all measures having equivalent effect shall be prohibited between Member States."

4. Article 30 [now 36] EC provides:

The provisions of Articles 28 and 29 [now 34 and 35] shall not preclude prohibitions or restrictions on imports, exports or goods in transit justified on grounds of . . . the protection of industrial and commercial property. Such prohibitions or restrictions shall not, however, constitute a means of arbitrary discrimination or a disguised restriction on trade between Member States.

5. First Council Directive 89/104/EEC of 21 December 1988 to approximate the laws of the Member States relating to trade marks (OJ 1989 L 40, p. 1; hereinafter the "Directive") states, in the seventh recital in the preamble, that "attainment of the objectives at which this approximation of laws is aiming requires that the conditions for obtaining and continuing to hold a registered trade mark are, in general, identical in all Member States" and that "the grounds for refusal or invalidity concerning the trade mark itself . . . are to be listed in an exhaustive manner."

6. Article 3 of the Directive lays down the grounds for refusal to register a trade mark or of invalidity of a registered trade mark. In particular, Article 3(1)(b) and (c) provides:

The following shall not be registered or if registered shall be liable to be declared invalid: . . .
    (b) trade marks which are devoid of any distinctive character;
    (c) trade marks which consist exclusively of signs or indications which may serve, in trade, to designate the kind, quality, quantity, intended purpose, value, geographical origin or the time of production of the goods or of rendering of the service, or other characteristics of the goods or service.

THE MAIN ACTION AND THE QUESTION REFERRED TO THE COURT

7. Hukla is the owner of the national word mark MATRATZEN, registered in Spain on 1 May 1994 to designate, inter alia, "rest furniture such as beds, sofa-beds, camp beds, cradles, divans, hammocks, bunk beds and carrycots, foldaway furniture, casters for beds and furniture, bedside tables, chairs, armchairs and stools, bed frames, straw mattresses, mattresses and pillows," which come within Class 20 of the Nice Agreement concerning the International Classification of Goods and Services for the Purposes of the Registration of Marks of 15 June 1957, as revised and amended.

8. On 10 October 1996 Matratzen Concord filed with the Office for Harmonisation in the Internal Market (Trade Marks and Designs) (OHIM) an application for registration of a composite word and figurative mark including the term "Matratzen," for various products coming within Classes 10, 20 and 24 of the Nice Agreement.

9. Hukla having filed a notice of opposition based on the earlier Spanish mark MATRATZEN, the said application was rejected by a decision of the Second Board of Appeal of OHIM of 31 October 2000. The action brought by Matratzen Concord against this decision was rejected by the judgment of the Court of First Instance of 23 October 2002 in Case T-6/01 *Matratzen Concord* v *OHIM — Hukla Germany (Matratzen)* [2002] ECR II-4335), confirmed on appeal by the order of the Court of Justice of 28 April 2004 in Case C-3/03 P *Matratzen Concord* v *OHIM* [2004] ECR I-3657.

10. In parallel with the opposition procedure before the OHIM bodies and then the Community Courts, Matratzen Concord brought an action for cancellation of the national trade mark MATRATZEN before the Juzgado de Primera Instancia No 22 (Court of First Instance), Barcelona (Spain), on the basis of Article 11(1)(a), (e) and (f) of Ley 32/1988 de 10 de noviembre Marcas, BOE No 272 of 12 November 1988 (Law No 32/1988 of 10 November 1988 on trade marks). It submitted, in substance, that, given that the word "Matratzen" means "mattress" in German, the word of which the trade mark in question consists was generic and could mislead consumers regarding the nature, quality, characteristics or geographical origin of the products bearing the said mark.

11. Its action having been rejected by judgment of 5 February 2002, Matratzen Concord appealed to the Audiencia Provincial de Barcelona (Provincial Court of Barcelona).

12. That court states that the essential function of a trade mark is to enable the commercial origin of the goods and services bearing it to be identified and that, to that effect, Spanish case-law considers names borrowed from foreign languages to be arbitrary, capricious and fanciful, unless they resemble a Spanish word, making it reasonable to assume that the average consumer will be familiar with their meaning, or they have acquired a genuine meaning on the national market.

13. The Audiencia Provincial de Barcelona is nevertheless uncertain as to whether that interpretation is compatible with the concept of the "single market." It considers that generic words from the languages of the Member States must remain available to be used by any undertaking established in these States. Their registration as a trade mark in a Member State would facilitate monopolistic situations, which should be avoided in order to allow normal market forces to prevail, and could be considered an infringement of the

prohibition on quantitative restrictions on imports as between the Member States, laid down in Article 28 EC.

14. The referring court considers that, in the pending case before it, the Spanish trade mark MATRATZEN puts its holder in a position to limit or restrict the import of mattresses from German-speaking Member States and, therefore, to prevent the free movement of goods.

15. That court is, uncertain however, as to whether such limitations or restrictions are capable of justification on the basis of Article 30 EC. In this respect, it points out that, in Case 192/73 *Van Zuylen* [1974] ECR 731, the Court affirmed the pre-eminence of the principle of the free movement of goods over the national protection of industrial property rights and stated that the reverse would lead to an undesirable partitioning of the markets, prejudicial to the free movement of goods and giving rise to disguised restrictions on trade between Member States.

16. Taking the view that the outcome of the dispute pending before it required an interpretation of Article 30 EC, the Audiencia Provincial de Barcelona decided to stay the proceedings and to refer the following question to the Court of Justice for a preliminary ruling:

> Can the validity of the registration of a trade mark in a Member State, when that trade mark is devoid of any distinctive character or serves, in trade, to designate the product which it covers or its kind, quality, quantity, intended purpose, value, geographical origin or other characteristics of goods, in the language of another Member State when that language is not spoken in the first Member State, as may be the case so far as concerns use of the Spanish trade mark "MATRATZEN," to designate mattresses and related products, constitute a disguised restriction on trade between Member States

THE QUESTION REFERRED

17. By its question, the referring court asks, in substance, whether Articles 28 EC and 30 EC must be interpreted as meaning that they preclude the registration in a Member State, as a national trade mark, of a term borrowed from the language of another Member State in which it is devoid of distinctive character or descriptive of the goods or services in respect of which registration is sought.

18. As a preliminary point, it should be noted that, in the context of the procedure established by Article 234 EC providing for cooperation between national courts and the Court of Justice, it is for the latter to provide the national court with an answer which will be of use to it and enable it to determine the case before it. To that end, the Court may find it necessary to consider provisions of Community law to which the national court has not referred in its question (*see*, in particular, Case C-230/98 *Schiavon* [2000] ECR I-3547, paragraph 37, and Case C-469/00 *Ravil* [2003] ECR I-5053, paragraph 27).

19. As is clear from the seventh recital in the preamble, the Directive lists in an exhaustive manner the grounds for refusal or invalidity of registration concerning the trade mark itself.

20. According to settled case-law, in a field which has been exhaustively harmonised at Community level, a national measure must be assessed in the light of the provisions of that harmonizing measure and not of those of primary law (*see*, in particular, Case C-352/95 *Phytheron International* [1997] ECR I-1729,

paragraph 17; Case C-324/99 *DaimlerChrysler* [2001] ECR I-9897, paragraph 32; and Case C-210/03 *Swedish Match* [2004] ECR I-11893, paragraph 81).

21. Consequently, it is the Directive, and in particular Article 3 thereof, on the absolute grounds for refusal or invalidity of registration, and not Articles 28 EC and 30 EC, which must be assessed to determine whether Community law precludes the registration of a national trade mark such as that at issue in the main proceedings.

22. Article 3 of the Directive does not include any ground for refusal to register specifically aimed at trade marks constituted by a term borrowed from the language of a Member State other than the State of registration in which it is devoid of distinctive character or descriptive of the goods or services in respect of which registration is sought.

23. Moreover, such a trade mark does not necessarily fall within the grounds for refusal to register relating to the lack of distinctive character or the descriptive character of the trade mark, referred to in points (b) and (c) respectively of Article 3(1) of the Directive.

24. In fact, to assess whether a national trade mark is devoid of distinctive character or is descriptive of the goods or services in respect of which its registration is sought, it is necessary to take into account the perception of the relevant parties, that is to say in trade and or amongst average consumers of the said goods or services, reasonably well-informed and reasonably observant and circumspect, in the territory in respect of which registration is applied for (*see* Joined Cases C-108/97 and C-109/97 *Windsurfing Chiemsee* [1999] ECR I-2779, paragraph 29; Case C-363/99 *Koninklijke KPNNederland* [2004] ECR I-1619, paragraph 77; and Case C-218/01 *Henkel* [2004] ECR I-1725, paragraph 50).

25. It is possible that, because of linguistic, cultural, social and economic differences between the Member States, a trade mark which is devoid of distinctive character or descriptive of the goods or services concerned in one Member State is not so in another Member State (*see,* by way of analogy, concerning the misleading nature of a trade mark, Case C-313/94 *Graffione* [1996] ECR I-6039, paragraph 22).

26. Consequently, Article 3(1)(b) and (c) of the Directive does not preclude the registration in a Member State, as a national trade mark, of a term borrowed from the language of another Member State in which it is devoid of distinctive character or descriptive of the goods or services in respect of which registration is sought, unless the relevant parties in the Member State in which registration is sought are capable of identifying the meaning of the term.

27. This interpretation of the Directive is in accordance with the Treaty requirements, and in particular those of Articles 28 EC and 30 EC.

28. According to settled case-law, in the context of the application of the principle of the free movement of goods, the Treaty does not affect the existence of rights recognised by the legislation of a Member State in matters of intellectual property, but only restricts, depending on the circumstances, the exercise of those rights (Case 119/75 *Terrapin* [1976] ECR 1039, paragraph 5; Case 58/80 *Dansk Supermarked* [1981] ECR 181, paragraph 11; and order in *Matratzen Concord* v *OHIM,* paragraph 40).

29. Applying that case-law, the Court ruled, at paragraph 42 of the order in *Matratzen Concord* v *OHIM* — in which the Spanish trade mark MATRATZEN was already at issue, being the subject of the main proceedings — that the principle of the free movement of goods does not prohibit a Member State

from registering as a national trade mark a sign which, in the language of another Member State, is descriptive of the goods or services concerned.

30. That also applies if the sign in question is, in the language of a Member State other than that of registration, devoid of distinctive character with regard to the goods or services covered by the application for registration.

31. It should be added that, as the Advocate General observed in points 59 to 64 of his Opinion, registration in a Member State of a trade mark such as that at issue in the main proceedings does not prohibit all use of the term constituting the trade mark by other traders in the said Member State.

32. In conclusion, the answer to the question referred is that Article 3(1)(b) and (c) of the Directive does not preclude the registration in a Member State, as a national trade mark, of a term borrowed from the language of another Member State in which it is devoid of distinctive character or descriptive of the goods or services in respect of which registration is sought, unless the relevant parties in the Member State in which registration is sought are capable of identifying the meaning of the term. . . .

NOTES AND QUESTIONS

1. In paragraph 20, the ECJ says, "in a field which has been exhaustively harmonised at Community level, a national measure must be assessed in the light of the provisions of that harmonizing measure and not of those of primary law." Yet, in paragraphs 28-30, the ECJ assesses its interpretation of the Directive under Articles 28 [34] and 30 [36] of the TFEU. Is the ECJ's analytic approach consistent with its rhetoric?

2. The Advocate General pointed out that, even if trademark rights are granted for a German-language term in Spain, this would not necessarily preclude German exporters from using the relevant term in the Spanish market. Under what doctrine of trademark law might such use be allowed?

B. The Andean Community Trademark System

The intellectual property system of the Andean Community was introduced in Chapter 1. Decision 486 of the Andean Community includes common rules with respect to trademarks.[20] These common rules are applied by national trademark offices in each of the member countries,[21] and litigation to enforce rights is pursued in the national courts of each member country. The Court of Justice of the Andean Community has jurisdiction, *inter alia,* to consider actions by member countries and affected individuals with respect to the compatibility of national legislation and decisions with Andean law.[22]

---

20. Title IV, Decision 486, Common Intellectual Property Regime, Andean Community, available at http://www.comunidadandina.org/ingles/normativa/ande_trie2.htm.

21. *Id., e.g.,* art. 138.

22. Treaty Creating the Court of Justice of the Cartagena Agreement (Amended by the Cochabamba Protocol), at *e.g.,* arts. 17-22.

Decision 486 provides for the international exhaustion of trademark rights at Article 158:

> **Article 158.** — Trademark registration shall not confer on the owner the rights to prevent third parties from engaging in trade in a product protected by registration once the owner of the registered trademark or another party with the consent of or economic ties to that owner has introduced that product into the trade of any country, in particular where any such products, packaging or packing as may have been in direct contact with the product concerned have not undergone any change, alteration, or deterioration.
>
> For the purposes of the preceding paragraph, two persons shall be considered to have economic ties when one of the persons is able to exercise a decisive influence over the other, either directly or indirectly, with respect to use of the trademark right or when a third party is able to exert that influence over both persons.

Colombia and Peru have signed bilateral free trade agreements with the United States. The agreement with Peru has entered into force, while as of March 2011 the Colombia-U.S. agreement awaits approval by the U.S. Congress. These agreements obligate Colombia and Peru to change their trademark legislation in a way that is inconsistent with Decision 486 as it is currently drafted. For example, Decision 486 does not permit a single trademark registration application to cover more than one class of goods or services. Colombia and Peru have each agreed to accede to the Trademark Law Treaty, which requires that one application may relate to more than one class of goods or services (TLT, art. 3(5)). The bilaterals obligate Colombia and Peru to use their best efforts to accede to the Madrid Protocol. The bilaterals do not address the issue of exhaustion with respect to trademarks.

Recall that in April 2006, Venezuela withdrew from the Andean Community, largely because of its objection to the terms of the Colombia-Peru bilateral FTAs with the United States. It remains unclear what position Bolivia and Ecuador will take with respect to the intellectual property provisions in the bilateral agreements, and how Decision 486 might be amended if those countries do not wish to accept obligations similar to those accepted by Colombia and Peru.

V. INTERNET DOMAIN NAMES AT THE MULTILATERAL LEVEL

A. The Uniform Domain Name Dispute Resolution Policy (UDRP)

At the beginning of this chapter, domain names were introduced as a new type of intellectual property. Following is an excerpt from WIPO's Second Report on the Domain Name Process that describes legal rules and a dispute settlement mechanism adopted to address them.

THE RECOGNITION OF RIGHTS AND THE USE
OF NAMES IN THE INTERNET DOMAIN NAME SYSTEM

**Report of the Second
WIPO Internet Domain Name Process
September 3, 2001***

. . . WIPO's PRIOR WORK

1. In June 1998, the National Telecommunications and Information Administration (NTIA), an agency of the United States Department of Commerce, issued a *Statement of Policy on the Management of Internet Names and Addresses* (the "White Paper"). The White Paper called for the creation of a new, private, not-for-profit corporation which would be responsible for coordinating certain DNS functions for the benefit of the Internet as a whole. Following the publication of the White Paper, a process occurred which resulted in the formation of the Internet Corporation for Assigned Names and Numbers (ICANN), a not-for-profit corporation established under the laws of the State of California of the United States of America. The by-laws of ICANN and documentation on the various meetings that it has organized and activities that it has carried out are available on ICANN's web site, www.icann.org.

2. In response to growing publicity and concern over the interface between domain names and trademarks, and the lack of definition of the relation between these two species of identifiers, the White Paper also addressed certain intellectual property questions. In particular, the White Paper stated that the United States Government would "seek international support to call upon the World Intellectual Property Organization (WIPO) to initiate a balanced and transparent process, which includes the participation of trademark holders and members of the Internet community who are not trademark holders," to develop recommendations on certain aspects of the interface between domain names and trademarks, including "a uniform approach to resolving trademark/domain name disputes involving cyberpiracy."

3. Following the publication of the White Paper, and with the subsequent approval of its Member States, WIPO carried out between July 1998 and April 1999 an extensive and intensive process of consultations directed at developing recommendations on the issues which it was requested to address.

4. The WIPO Process, known as the WIPO Internet Domain Name Process, was conducted using a combination of Internet-based consultations, paper-based consultations and 17 physical meetings held in 14 countries. Participation was solicited from governments, intergovernmental organizations, professional and industry associations, corporations and individuals through three Requests for Comments. Responses were received to those Requests for Comments from 40 States, 6 intergovernmental organizations, 72 non-governmental organizations representing professional, industry and other special interests, 181 corporations and law firms and 182 individuals.

5. The Report of the WIPO Internet Domain Name Process, *The Management of Internet Names and Addresses: Intellectual Property Issues,* was published on April 30, 1999. The Report contained a series of recommendations. Chief amongst those recommendations was the establishment of a uniform dispute-resolution policy and procedure for resolving disputes over the alleged bad faith and deliberate

---

* http://wipo2.wipo.int.

misuse of trademarks through the registration of domain names in the generic top-level domains (gTLDs) .com, .net and .org.

THE UNIFORM DOMAIN NAME DISPUTE RESOLUTION POLICY FOR GTLDS

6. Following the publication of the Report of the WIPO Internet Domain Name Process and certain consultation procedures in conformity with the by-laws of ICANN, ICANN adopted, in August 1999, a Uniform Domain Name Dispute Resolution Policy (UDRP), which entered into force for the gTLDs .com, .net and .org on December 1, 1999, and January 1, 2000 (the policy was phased-in for registrars over the two dates).

7. The UDRP establishes a dispute-resolution procedure under which a complainant can seek the transfer or cancellation of a domain name registration in .com, .net or .org on the basis that (i) the domain name is identical or confusingly similar to a trademark in which the complainant has rights; (ii) the domain name holder has no rights or legitimate interests in respect of the domain name; and (iii) the domain name has been registered and is being used in bad faith. The UDRP is a mandatory procedure to which each applicant for a domain name registration in .com, .net or .org is required to submit, in the event that a complaint is lodged in respect of the applicant's registration.

8. ICANN has accredited four dispute-resolution service providers to administer disputes brought under the UDRP: the WIPO Arbitration and Mediation Center, the National Arbitration Forum, e-Resolution and the CPR Institute for Dispute Resolution.[23] Registrars accredited by ICANN to accept registrations in .com, .net or .org are obligated to implement the results of panel decisions under the dispute resolution procedure.

NEW GENERIC TOP-LEVEL DOMAINS:
INTELLECTUAL PROPERTY CONSIDERATIONS*
WIPO Arbitration and Mediation Center

. . . 2.1 Domain Names and Trademarks

9. So far, IP protection in the DNS has focused on trademarks, a specific category of identifiers which serve to distinguish the goods or services of one company from those of another. As stated in the First WIPO Report:

> 11. [. . .] A trademark enables consumers to identify the source of a product, to link the product with its manufacturer in widely distributed markets. The exclusive right to the use of the mark, which may be of indefinite duration, enables the owner to prevent others from misleading consumers into wrongly associating products with an enterprise from which they do not originate.

10. Trademarks serve as a focus for the goodwill associated with a product as a result of investments in quality and marketing. Brand recognition through trademarks enables start-up companies to establish a successful business presence and more established brands to preserve their reputation and value. For a growing number of companies in developed and developing countries,

---

23. [e-Resolution is no longer an active dispute resolution service provider. — Eds.]
* Available at http://www.wipo.int, visited July 11, 2006.

trademarks have become the single most important business asset, their value often exceeding that of such companies' physical assets.

2.2 Domain Names and Other Identifiers

11. Other protected identifiers include trade names, personal names, geographical indications, International Nonproprietary Names (INNs) for pharmaceutical substances and the names and acronyms of international organizations (IGOs). Such identifiers have also become the subject of abusive practices in the DNS. To develop recommendations on means of dealing with such abuse, WIPO conducted the Second WIPO Internet Domain Name Process. The Second WIPO Report was published in September 2001 and discussed by the Member States of WIPO, who in September 2002 recommended to provide protection for country names and for the names and acronyms of IGOs in the UDRP. These recommendations (the "WIPO-2 Recommendations") were transmitted to ICANN in February 2003 and continue to be under ICANN's consideration.

2.3 Intellectual Property Concerns

12. Given the value of trademarks and other identifiers and the importance of the Internet as a commercial communication and marketing channel, rights owners are understandably worried that their identifiers fall victim to deceptive and abusive practices on the Internet. Undermining the status of such identifiers also compromises the credibility of the DNS and consumers' trust in the Internet as a medium for commercial exchange. The First WIPO Report found that:

> 315. [. . .] the priority concern of the trademark community does not relate to conflicts between parties who claim to have competing legitimate rights in the name (for example, different companies with the same trademark in different product lines or operating in different areas of the world), but focuses on cases of clear abuse, often directed at famous and well-known marks.

13. Such concerns are based on previous experience with abusive practices in the existing open gTLDs where domain name registrations are granted purely on a "first come first served" basis. Such abuses have forced trademark owners to invest substantial human and financial resources in defending their interests. The damage that a trademark owner suffers as a result of the abusive registration and use of a domain name may well be extensive by virtue of the global accessibility of domain names. The First WIPO Report notes in this regard:

> 132. [. . .] A considerable disjunction exists between, on the one hand, the cost of obtaining a domain name registration, which is relatively cheap, and, on the other hand, the economic value of the damage that can be done as a result of such a registration and the cost to the intellectual property owner of remedying the situation through litigation, which may be slow and very expensive in some countries.

14. IP owners therefore often adopt a preventive approach by registering their most valuable identifiers (sometimes including misleading variations) in all relevant gTLDs in order to preempt abuse. Such defensive registrations cause substantial cost both for the registration of domain names as well as for the maintenance of large domain name portfolios. . . .

INTERNET DOMAIN NAMES

Prepared by the Secretariat*

I. Domain Name Case Administration

A. Uniform Domain Name Dispute Resolution Policy

3. The WIPO Center administers dispute resolution procedures principally under the Uniform Domain Name Dispute Resolution Policy (UDRP). The UDRP was adopted by the Internet Corporation for Assigned Names and Numbers (ICANN) on the basis of recommendations made by WIPO in the First WIPO Internet Domain Name Process. The UDRP is limited to clear cases of bad-faith, abusive registration and use of domain names. It does not prevent either party from submitting a dispute to a competent court of justice. However, the UDRP has proven highly popular among trademark owners, and very few cases that were decided under the UDRP were also brought before a national court of justice.

4. Since December 1999, the WIPO Center has administered more than 17,500 UDRP and UDRP-based cases. Demand for WIPO's domain name dispute resolution services continued in 2009 with trademark holders filing 2,107 complaints. While this caseload represents a 9.5% decrease over 2008, it covers the highest number of individual domain names in a given year (4,688) since the UDRP was launched ten years ago. Following the introduction by WIPO of its paperless UDRP procedure in December 2009, the first five months of 2010 have seen an increase of some 20% in cases filed compared to the same period in 2009.

5. A diverse mixture of individuals and enterprises, foundations and institutions used the WIPO Center's dispute resolution procedures in 2009. The top five sectors for complainant business activity were Biotechnology and Pharmaceuticals, Banking and Finance, Internet and IT, Retail, and Food, Beverage and Restaurants. Pharmaceutical manufacturers remained the top filers due to numerous permutations of protected names registered for web sites offering or linking to online sales of medications and drugs. WIPO UDRP proceedings have so far involved parties from 155 countries. Reflecting the truly global scope of this dispute mechanism, in 2009 alone, named parties to WIPO cases represented over 110 countries. WIPO UDRP proceedings have so far been conducted in 18 different languages, namely (in alphabetical order), Chinese, Danish, Dutch, English, French, German, Hebrew, Italian, Japanese, Korean, Norwegian, Polish, Portuguese, Romanian, Russian, Spanish, Swedish, Turkish in function of the language of the applicable registration agreement of the domain name at issue.

6. Since the year 2000 all panel decisions are posted on the WIPO Center's website. To facilitate access to these decisions according to subject matter the WIPO Center also offers an online searchable Legal Index. This Index has become a highly-frequented professional resource, allowing panelists, parties, academics or any interested person to familiarize themselves with WIPO case precedent, and is one of the Organization's most visited web pages. The Index is updated periodically to include new search categories that primarily reflect developments in the Domain Name System itself. In addition to its Legal Index, the WIPO Center also offers an overview of broad decision trends on important

---

* WO/GA/39/10, July 20, 2010, prepared for WIPO General Assembly, Thirty-Ninth (20th Extraordinary) Session, Geneva, September 20 to 29, 2010.

case issues, via the WIPO Overview of WIPO Panel Views on Selected UDRP Questions which distills thousands of UDRP cases handled by the WIPO Center. The Overview is a globally used instrument to help maintain the consistency of WIPO UDRP jurisprudence.

7. The WIPO Center also maintains on its web pages an extended statistics search facility in relation to WIPO domain name dispute resolution, intended to assist WIPO case parties and neutrals, trademark attorneys, domain name policy makers, the media and academics. Available statistics cover many categories, such as "areas of complainant activity," "named respondents," "domain name script" and "25 most cited decisions in complaint."

8. In addition, the WIPO Center regularly organizes Domain Name Dispute Resolution Workshops for interested parties and meetings of its Domain Name Panelists. The year 2009 marked the tenth anniversary of the introduction of the UDRP and in recognition of this milestone the WIPO Center turned its annual Panelists Meeting into an open Conference, "10 Years UDRP—What's Next?". This Conference drew lessons from the UDRP experience of the WIPO Center, panelists, parties, and other stakeholders, with a view to informing similar or other processes in the future of the DNS and in the broader context of intellectual property, and exemplifies the WIPO Center's commitment to monitoring and guiding developments in the DNS.

B. *Panel Decisions Under the UDRP*

Following are two panel decisions under the UDRP by one of the authors of this book. They each involve the same complainant, a major multinational pharmaceutical company. The first is a more typical type of complaint against a domain name registrant seeking to take unfair advantage of the trademark holder's rights—this is the prototypical "cybersquatting" case. The second involves a complex issue of fair use with potentially significant public policy implications.

PFIZER, INC. v. MARTIN MARKETING
Case No. D2002-0793, WIPO Arbitration and Mediation Center Administrative Panel Decision

1. THE PARTIES

The Complainant is Pfizer, Inc., a corporation organized in the State of Delaware, United States of America ("USA"), with place of business in New York, New York, USA.

The Respondent is Martin Marketing, with address in New York, New York, USA.

2. THE DOMAIN NAME AND REGISTRAR

The disputed domain name is <viagra-nascar.com>.

The registrar of the disputed domain name is Intercosmos Media Group, Inc. dba directNIC.com ("Intercosmos"), with business address in New Orleans, Louisiana, USA.

3. Procedural History . . .

4. Factual Background

Complainant has registered the term "VIAGRA" as a trademark on the Principal Register at the United States Patent and Trademark Office (USPTO), Reg. No. 2,162,548, dated June 2, 1998, in International Class 5, covering "Compound for treating erectile dysfunction," asserting date of first use and first use in commerce of April 6, 1998 (Complaint, para. 12 & Annex 3). "VIAGRA" is a coined term with no denotative meaning (*id.* para. 12).

Complainant holds registrations for the "VIAGRA" trademark in many countries other than the United States (*id.*, para. 12 & Annex 4).

Complainant has registered the domain name <viagra.com> and maintains an active commercial website at Internet address (URL) <www.viagra.com> (*id.*, para. 12 & Annex 5).

Complainant has advertised its "VIAGRA" brand "sildenafil citrate" widely in the United States and in other countries (*id.*, para. 12). As a consequence of such advertising and news reports, Complainant's "VIAGRA" mark is well known in connection with a drug for the treatment of erectile dysfunction.

The National Association for Stock Car Racing ("NASCAR"), which claims ownership in the "NASCAR" trademark and service mark has consented to the transfer of the disputed domain name to Complainant (*id.*, para. 12 & Annex 6 (Affidavit of Karen B. Leetzow, Intellectual Property Counsel to NASCAR)). NASCAR has not authorized Respondent to use its trademark and service mark in a domain name or otherwise (*id.*).

Complainant is the sponsor of a car that has participated in the NASCAR Winston Cup Series. Such car has prominently displayed the "VIAGRA" mark, enjoyed success in the racing series and been featured in Complainant's television advertisements (*id.*, para. 12).

According to the Registrar's Verification to WIPO, "Martin Marketing" is the registrant of the disputed domain name <viagra-nascar.com>. The administrative contact is "Martin, Jim firstpharmacy@yahoo.com." The record of the disputed domain name was created on September 6, 2001, and was last updated on July 17, 2002.

Respondent has maintained an active commercial website at URL <www.viagra-nascar.com>. The home page of this website is headed with the terms "VIAGRA NASCAR" in large type, with the subheadings "MAIN/VIAGRA INFO/VIAGRA CAR/ORDER VIAGRA." The web pages include detailed information concerning VIAGRA, as well as detailed information concerning the NASCAR race car sponsored by Complainant. At the bottom of the web pages, the following appears in small type: "Copyright(c) 2001. Viagra Nascar. ALL RIGHTS RESERVED. All trademarks and registered trademarks are of their respective companies. Viagra® is a registered trade [unreadable from printout] site is in now [sic] way affiliated with Phizer [sic]. Only a physician should decide if Viagra® is appropriate for you. These pages are only a summary. If you have further questi [unreadable] information about Viagra®, visit viagra.com [hyperlink] or feel free to fill out our contact form or simply e-mail." (Complaint, Annex 11)

As of August 20, 2002, Respondent's website contained a hyperlink to <www.secure-medical.com/viagra-nascar.com/order.html>, which offered to sell VIAGRA product, as well as hyperlinks to websites selling jewelry and sporting tickets. A "pop-up" window also provided click-through links to an on-line gambling website <joebet.com> (*id.*, para. 12 & Annex 12), as well as other websites offering VIAGRA information, herbal virility solutions and tooth whitener (*id.*, para. 12 & Annexes 13-15).

The physical address provided by Respondent in its domain name registration apparently does not exist. The telephone number, as of August 14, 2002, was not working. (*Id.*, Affidavit of Toth, counsel for Complainant, at Annex 10).

The Registration Agreement in effect between Respondent and Intercosmos subjects Respondent to Intercosmos' dispute settlement policy, the Uniform Domain Name Dispute Resolution Policy, as adopted by ICANN on August 26, 1999, and with implementing documents approved by ICANN on October 24, 1999. The Uniform Domain Name Dispute Resolution Policy (the "Policy") requires that domain name Registrants submit to a mandatory Administrative Proceeding conducted by an approved dispute resolution service provider, of which WIPO is one, regarding allegations of abusive domain name registration and use (Policy, paragraph 4(a)).

5. Parties' Contentions . . .

6. Discussion and Findings

The Policy is addressed to resolving disputes concerning allegations of abusive domain name registration and use. The Panel will confine itself to making determinations necessary to resolve this Administrative Proceeding.

It is essential to dispute resolution proceedings that fundamental due process requirements be met. Such requirements include that a respondent have notice of proceedings that may substantially affect its rights. The Policy, and the Rules for Uniform Domain Name Dispute Resolution Policy (the "Rules"), establish procedures intended to ensure that respondents are given adequate notice of proceedings commenced against them, and a reasonable opportunity to respond (*see*, *e.g.*, para. 2(a), Rules).

In this case, the Panel is satisfied that the Center took all steps reasonably necessary to notify the Respondent of the filing of the Complaint and initiation of these proceedings. Respondent transmitted an e-mail to the Center indicating that it was aware of the proceedings.

Paragraph 4(a) of the Policy sets forth three elements that must be established by a complainant to merit a finding that a respondent has engaged in abusive domain name registration and use, and to obtain relief. These elements are that:

i.   Respondent's domain name is identical or confusingly similar to a trademark or service mark in which the Complainant has rights; and
ii. respondent has no rights or legitimate interests in respect of the domain name; and
iii. respondent's domain name has been registered and is being used in bad faith.

Each of the aforesaid three elements must be proved by a complainant to warrant relief.

Complainant is the holder of a trademark registration for the term "VIA-GRA" on the Principal Register of the USPTO. It has registered the mark with other trademark authorities throughout the world. The term "VIAGRA" is arbitrary and distinctive. The "VIAGRA" mark is well known in respect to a drug addressing erectile dysfunction. The Panel determines that Complainant has rights in the trademark "VIAGRA." Those rights arose before Respondent's registration of the disputed domain name.

The disputed domain name <viagra-nascar.com> directly incorporates Complainant's mark as its lead term, and adds a hyphen and the trademark and service mark of a third party (as well as the gTLD ".com"). The addition of the third party mark does not eliminate the visual impression that the disputed domain name is associated with Complainant's trademark. Moreover, in light of Complainant's use of its mark in connection with the third party mark for its own advertising purposes, the combination of the two marks would convey to Internet users familiar with Complainant's advertising an expected association. In the circumstances of this proceeding, the addition of a hyphen and ".com" do not serve to alleviate potential Internet user confusion between the disputed domain name and Complainant's mark. Based on the overall visual impression and expected Internet user association, the Panel determines that the disputed domain name is confusingly similar to Complainant's "VIAGRA" mark.

Complainant has established the first element necessary for a finding of abusive domain name registration and use.

The second element of a claim of abusive domain name registration and use is that the Respondent has no rights or legitimate interests in respect of the domain name (Policy, paragraph 4(a)(ii)). The Policy enumerates several ways in which a Respondent may demonstrate rights or legitimate interests:

> "Any of the following circumstances, in particular but without limitation, if found by the Panel to be proved based on its evaluation of all evidence presented, shall demonstrate your rights or legitimate interests to the domain name for purposes of Paragraph 4(a)(ii)
>
> i. before any notice to you of the dispute, your use of, or demonstrable preparations to use, the domain name or a name corresponding to the domain name in connection with a bona fide offering of goods or services; or
> ii. you (as an individual, business, or other organization) have been commonly known by the domain name, even if you have acquired no trademark or service mark rights; or
> iii. you are making a legitimate noncommercial or fair use of the domain name, without intent for commercial gain to misleadingly divert consumers or to tarnish the trademark or service mark at issue." (Policy, paragraph 4(c)).

Respondent has offered no evidence that it has been commonly known by the disputed domain name. Respondent has no prior business association with Complainant and has used Complainant's mark in the disputed name to attract Internet users to a website where it offers to sell various products and services unconnected with Complainant or its trademarked product. Such use of the disputed domain name is not a fair use of Complainant's mark.

Complainant's mark is arbitrary and well known. Respondent was without doubt aware of Complainant's mark when it registered the disputed domain name, and would likewise be on constructive notice that Complainant would dispute its use of the mark in connection with its website. In the circumstances of this proceeding, in which Respondent has used the marks of two third parties without their consent to attract Internet users to a website where it offers for sale goods and services unconnected with those third parties, Respondent did not make a bona fide offering of goods prior to notice of a dispute.

Complainant has demonstrated that Respondent has no rights or legitimate interests in the disputed domain name, and has established the second element necessary for a finding of abusive domain name registration and use.

Respondent registered and used the disputed domain name to direct Internet users to a commercial website where it directly and indirectly offered for sale a variety of goods and services unconnected with Complainant, as well as offering for sale Complainant's product. Respondent included a small typeface disclaimer of association with Complainant at the bottom of certain web pages. However, that disclaimer is not adequate to overcome the overall impression created by Respondent's use of Complainant's mark in the domain name and again prominently on its home page (and elsewhere on its website) of an association with or sponsorship by Complainant. The Panel finds that Respondent has used the disputed domain name for commercial gain by creating confusion among Internet users as to Complainant's sponsorship of or affiliation with Respondent's website. Such use is in bad faith within the meaning of paragraph 4(b)(iv) of the Policy.

Complainant has satisfied the third element necessary for a finding of abusive domain name registration and use by Respondent.

Complainant has submitted authorization from the holder of the NASCAR trademark and service mark sufficient to relieve potential concern that transfer of the disputed domain name to Complainant would interfere with the rights of the third party trademark holder.

The Panel will therefore direct the registrar to transfer the disputed domain name to Complainant.

7. Decision

Based on its finding that the Respondent, Martin Marketing, has engaged in abusive registration and use of the domain name <viagra-nascar.com> within the meaning of paragraph 4(a) of the Policy, the Panel orders that the domain name <viagra-nascar.com> be transferred to the Complainant, Pfizer, Inc.

Frederick M. Abbott, Sole Panelist
November 15, 2002

PFIZER, INC. v. VAN ROBICHAUX
Case No. D2003-0399, WIPO
Arbitration and Mediation Center
Administrative Panel Decision

1. The Parties

The Complainant is Pfizer Inc, New York, New York, United States of America, represented by Hale and Dorr, LLP of United States of America.

The Respondent is Van Robichaux, of New Orleans, Louisiana, United States of America, represented by Daniel W. Nodurft of New Orleans, Louisiana, United States of America.

2. The Domain Name and Registrar

The disputed domain name <lipitorinfo.com> is registered with TierraNet d/b/a DomainDiscover.

3. Procedural History . . .

4. Factual Background

The Complainant has registered the word trademark "LIPITOR" on the Principal Register of the U.S. Patent and Trademark Office (USPTO), Reg. No. 2,074,561, dated June 24, 1997, in International Class 5, covering "Pharmaceutical preparations for use in the treatment of cardiovascular disorders and cholesterol reduction," claiming date of first use and use in commerce as January 28, 1997.[1] The Complainant has registered the word trademark "LIPITOR" and related word and/or design marks in numerous countries throughout the world, and applications are pending in various countries. "LIPITOR" is an arbitrary term coined by the Complainant. (Complaint, para. 12 & Annexes 3-5)

"LIPITOR" is marketed as a cholesterol-lowering medicine and is "the most prescribed cholesterol-lowering medicine in the United States and is the second largest selling pharmaceutical product of any kind in the world. Last year, worldwide sales of the LIPITOR product were $7.972 billion." The Complainant has spent substantial sums of money advertising and promoting its "LIPITOR" product in the United States and other countries. (*Id.*, para. 12)

According to the Registrar's verification, the Respondent "Van Robichaux" is the registrant of the disputed domain name. According to a Better-Whois.com WHOIS database report submitted by the Complainant, the record of registration for the disputed domain name was created on August 14, 2002, and was last updated on February 12, 2003 (Complaint, Annex 1).

The Respondent, J. Van Robichaux, Jr., is an attorney with offices in New Orleans, Louisiana, USA. He provides information concerning his law practice at a website with Internet address at "www.robichauxlaw.com." This practice includes providing information to prospective clients concerning injuries that may have been caused to them by various medicines, including, for example "Baycol" and "Rezulin." An internal web page at "www.robichauxlaw.com/rezulin.asp" includes information such as a description of the medicine, the problems that have been associated with it, a recommendation to seek medical attention as may be appropriate, and a part that states:

"How can Robichaux Law firm help?
  We will investigate the relevant facts of your case, gather and evaluate your medical records, and take necessary legal steps to protect your legal rights once you become one of our clients.

---

1. The Complainant holds the mark by way of assignment to a wholly-owned subsidiary, Pfizer Ireland Pharmaceuticals. Complaint, para. 12 & Annex 3.

For a free consultation to see how we can help you Click Here" (dated June 24, 2003, Response, Annex 3).

The Respondent indicates that he rejected an offer from the Complainant to purchase the disputed domain name, although no details regarding the nature of that offer were provided by him (Response, para. III).

The disputed domain name has not been used by the Respondent to direct Internet users to an active website. However, the Respondent indicates that he would intend to use it to provide individuals with information about their legal rights and treatment options "should it ultimately be learned that 'lipitor' causes injuries to the consumer" (Response, para. III).

The Registration Agreement in effect between the Respondent and Tierra-Net d/b/a DomainDiscover, subjects the Respondent to dispute settlement under the Policy. The Policy requires that domain name Registrants submit to a mandatory Administrative Proceeding conducted by an approved dispute resolution service provider, of which the Center is one, regarding allegations of abusive domain name registration and use (Policy, paragraph 4(a)).

5. Parties' Contentions . . .

6. Discussion and Findings . . .

A. IDENTICAL OR CONFUSINGLY SIMILAR

The Respondent has conceded that the Complainant has rights in the trademark "LIPITOR" and that the disputed domain name <lipitorinfo.com> is confusingly similar to that mark. The Panel finds that the Complainant has rights in the "LIPITOR" trademark, and that the disputed domain name is confusingly similar to it.

The Respondent has further acknowledged that it included the Complainant's mark in the disputed domain name precisely because it identifies the Complainant's widely sold medicine. This acknowledgement serves for present purposes to address the issue whether the "LIPITOR" mark is well known.[2]

B. RIGHTS OR LEGITIMATE INTERESTS

The second element of a claim of abusive domain name registration is that the respondent has no rights or legitimate interests in respect of the domain name (Policy, para. 4(a)(ii)). The Policy enumerates several ways in which a respondent may demonstrate rights or legitimate interests:

> "Any of the following circumstances, in particular but without limitation, if found by the Panel to be proved based on its evaluation of all evidence presented, shall

---

2. The Complainant has argued that the "LIPITOR" mark is well known, especially in the United States. The main evidence it has put forward to support this is the frequency with which the medicine is prescribed and its high level of sales. Because prescription medicines are prescribed by doctors to patient-consumers, generally by handwriting on a form, and are dispensed by pharmacists with often limited patient-consumer intervention, there is some difficulty in drawing a conclusion concerning consumer identification of a mark based on the volume of prescriptions and sales of a medicine. It will suffice for present purposes for the Panel to conclude that for persons with knowledge of the pharmaceutical sector, such as the Respondent, the mark "LIPITOR" is well known in the United States.

demonstrate your rights or legitimate interests to the domain name for purposes of Paragraph 4(a)(ii):

i.   before any notice to you of the dispute, your use of, or demonstrable prepara-
     tions to use, the domain name or a name corresponding to the domain name
     in connection with a *bona fide* offering of goods or services; or
ii. you (as an individual, business, or other organization) have been commonly
     known by the domain name, even if you have acquired no trademark or service
     mark rights; or
iii. you are making a legitimate noncommercial or fair use of the domain name,
     without intent for commercial gain to misleadingly divert consumers or to
     tarnish the trademark or service mark at issue." (Policy, para. 4(c)).

The Respondent does not contend that it has been commonly known by the disputed domain name.

The Respondent had knowledge of the Complainant's mark when it registered the disputed domain name, and should reasonably have foreseen that the Complainant would object to its use. Whether an offering of legal services using reference to a mark in circumstances such as those present here might be a *bona fide* offering of services need not be decided, as the Panel considers that the Respondent had effective notice of a dispute prior to any such offering.

The Respondent principally claims "fair use" as a defense for using the Complainant's mark in its domain name. The Respondent essentially argues that in order to provide the public with information concerning the Complainant's product, including advice concerning treatment or legal advice, it is necessary or appropriate to use the Complainant's mark in its domain name.

The Respondent is seeking to establish a fair use defense without having actively used the Complainant's mark to identify a website. Paragraph 4(c)(iii) of the Policy refers to a respondent "making . . . fair use of the domain name." This sole panelist has in prior decisions under the Policy noted that the express requirement of "making" does not foreclose the establishment of a fair use defense in circumstances in which the disputed domain name has not been actively used. For example, in *Helen Fielding v. Anthony Corbert aka Anthony Corbett*, WIPO Case No. D2000-1000, (September 25, 2000), this panelist said:

> . . . the Panel notes that while paragraph 4(c)(i) of the Policy refers to "prepara-
> tions to use" a domain name in the context of offering goods or services,
> paragraph 4(c)(iii) refers only to the active "making" of a "legitimate noncom-
> mercial or fair use." The express language of the Policy indicates that its drafters
> intended to limit the circumstances in which legitimate noncommercial or fair use
> could successfully be claimed. Applying the express language of the Policy to the
> Respondent's claim of legitimate noncommercial or fair use, the Panel finds that
> the Respondent is not "making" such legitimate non-commercial or fair use of the
> Complainant's mark in the disputed domain name.
>
> The Panel recognizes that there are contexts in which the registrant of a
> domain name should not be expected to make immediate use of that name,
> including for legitimate noncommercial or fair use purposes. For example, this
> sole panelist on a previous occasion has observed that a requirement of immediate
> use in hosting websites critical of trademark holders might stifle free expression
> by allowing such trademark holders to initiate abusive domain name proceedings

before such domain names could effectively be put to active use.[3] Also, this sole panelist has recognized that a delay in using a domain name for a legitimate noncommercial or fair use purpose in response to a cease and desist demand might be justified.[4] [footnotes numbered 6 and 7, respectively, in quoted decision]

In *Fielding v. Corbert* the respondent had presented no evidence of a plan to make a legitimate noncommercial or fair use of the disputed domain name other than speculative statements in a response filed in the Administrative Proceeding, and had made an offer to sell the name for a substantial sum to the complainant.

The circumstances of the present case are clearly distinguished from those in *Fielding v. Corbert*. Here the Respondent presently maintains a website on which he offers information and representation in connection with potential legal claims associated with pharmaceutical products. He indicates that he does not yet have information concerning the Complainant's trademarked product that he considers would justify adding it to those he presently identifies as the potential subject of legal claims. There is very little reason to doubt that the Respondent will do exactly what he says he intends to do: that is, should he become aware of facts indicating this would be appropriate, he will use the disputed domain name to direct Internet users to a website where he will offer information about the Complainant's trademarked product and recommend that potential clients be in contact with him.

In these circumstances, the absence of active "making" use in connection with a website by the Respondent does not preclude a finding of rights or legitimate interests in the disputed domain name based on fair use. The Respondent is making use of the disputed domain name, but in a passive way. He has reserved it for future use in circumstances in which this is justified.

This does not answer the more fundamental question whether the proposed active use of the name would constitute fair use. If the Complainant has proven that the Respondent's proposed use of the disputed domain name would not be a fair one, the mere fact that the Respondent's present use is of a passive nature cannot establish a defense. In the proceeding, the Complainant bears the burden of proof in establishing the absence of rights or legitimate interests. Paragraph 4(a) of the Policy states "the complainant must prove that each of the[se] three elements are present." One element is that "you [the respondent] have no rights or legitimate interests in respect of the domain name" (Policy, Paragraph 4(a)(ii)).

The Complainant asserts that the Respondent will create initial interest confusion concerning its sponsorship or endorsement of the Respondent's website, and that creating such confusion for purposes of commercial gain precludes the establishment of a fair use defense. It further argues that even if the Respondent intends only noncommercial use of the disputed domain name, attracting Internet users by creating initial interest confusion is not permitted. It refers to the decision in *Banque Cantonale de Genève v. Primatex Group S.A.*, WIPO Case No. D2001-0477, (June 21, 2001), in support of the latter proposition. It suggests that the public interest will be harmed by the Respondent's activities because persons seeking information from the Complainant

---

3. *Wal-Mart Stores, Inc. v. Walsucks and Walmarket Puerto Rico*, WIPO Case No. D2000-0477, (July 20, 2000).
4. *Apple Computer, Inc. v. DomainHouse.com, Inc.*, WIPO Case No. D2000-0341, (July 5, 2000).

about the Complainant's product will find a website on which information is provided by the Respondent.

Before turning to the Respondent's defense, the Panel addresses the *Banque Cantonale de Genève v. Primatex Group S.A.* decision. In that proceeding, a respondent had used the trademark of a well known Swiss bank along with a common term ("-connection") in a domain name to direct Internet users to a noncommercial expression site that was sharply critical of the Bank. The panel in that proceeding suggested that a non-commercial expression site should in some manner identify itself as such in a domain name so that Internet users would not be misled by being transported to a site they had not elected to visit. The panel in that decision said:

> "Transparency starts with choosing a domain name which reflects the protest as opposed to a domain name which implies an affiliation to the trademark holder. If the protest is reflected in the domain name (for instance by adding the component '. . . sucks' or a similar element), Internet users have a choice to follow or not to follow the link. Otherwise, they may be misled.
>
> In this connection, it may be fair to state, however, that no *numerus clausus* of site names indicating protest or parody exists. It may even be legitimate, in some cases, to use a domain name denominating a corporation or public figure without qualifying additions. All depends from the circumstances of the individual case." *Id.*

The panel in *Banque Cantonale de Genève v. Primatex Group S.A.* wisely pointed out that disputes involving questions of fair use are context specific. There is a difference between an aggressive protest site directed at a Bank and a site maintained by a lawyer who is providing information and representation concerning potentially harmful pharmaceutical products. The interests of the public in information are different, and the motivations of the provider of information on the website are different. The complainant in *Banque Cantonale de Genève v. Primatex Group S.A* was Swiss and the respondent Panamanian. In the present proceeding, both parties are based in the United States, and the principal nexus of the Respondent's activities is likely to be in the United States. This decision should take into account the perspective of the U.S. judiciary on questions of fair use. In sum, the facts and circumstances of this proceeding are different than those in *Banque Cantonale de Genève v. Primatex Group S.A.*, and the determination in this proceeding is specific to its context.

The Respondent is essentially claiming "nominative fair use" of the Complainant's mark. In the Respondent's view, he should be able to refer to the Complainant's product by its trademark as a means of identification, rather than being required indirectly to describe the product, and he should be allowed do so in the domain name itself.[5]

This sole panelist, alone or as part of a three-person panel, has on a substantial number of occasions addressed the issue of fair use of marks in

---

5. In *Cairns v. Franklin Mint Co.*, 292 F.3d 1139 (9th Cir. 2002), the Court explained the distinction between a "nominative" fair use and "classic" fair use defense as follows:

> "The nominative fair use analysis is appropriate where a defendant has used the plaintiff's mark to describe the plaintiff's product, even if the defendant's ultimate goal is to describe his own product. Conversely, the classic fair use analysis is appropriate where a defendant has used the plaintiff's mark only to describe his own product, and not at all to describe the plaintiff's product." 292 F.3d, at 1152.

domain names. Each case is different, and the analysis in each is contextual, taking into account a number of factors. Two recent decisions of the U.S. Court of Appeals for the Ninth Circuit, *Playboy Enters. v. Welles*, 279 F.3d 796 (9th Cir. 2002) and *Horphag Research v. Mario Pellegrini*, 328 F.3d 1108 (9th Cir. 2003), reaffirm a useful three-prong approach for determining whether third party use of a mark is "nominative fair use."

> This court looks to three factors in determining whether a defendant is entitled to the nominative fair use defense: (1) the product must not be readily identifiable without use of the mark; (2) only so much of the mark may be used as is reasonably necessary to identify the product; and (3) the user must do nothing that would, in conjunction with the mark, suggest sponsorship or endorsement by the trademark holder. *New Kids,* 971 F.2d at 308.[6]

The Respondent here is an attorney seeking to advise potential clients concerning treatment options and legal rights with respect to a particular medicine. The medicine is known to the public by its trademark name "LIPITOR." Few members of the public would be expected to understand a reference to "Pfizer's atorvastatin calcium product." "LIPITOR" is not readily identifiable without reference to the mark.

The Respondent has not used more of the mark in the domain name than is reasonably necessary to identify the product.[7]

Has the Respondent done anything that would, in conjunction with the mark, suggest sponsorship or endorsement by the trademark holder?

The use of the domain name <lipitorinfo.com> may initially suggest to Internet users who view it that it will direct them to a website sponsored by or affiliated with the Complainant. There may be, as the Complainant suggests, "initial interest confusion."

Some initial interest confusion will be associated with any domain name that incorporates a trademark, whether or not it is conjoined with "sucks" or another signal of impending disaffection. The domain name "LIPITOR-sucks" would initially attract Internet users by virtue of the trademark "LIPITOR" because some users would naturally be curious to find out why.[8] Indeed "LIPITOR-sucks" would provide notice that the referenced site was not sponsored by the Complainant before it was viewed, but there nonetheless would be Internet users who set out to seek information regarding the product from its producer who would visit it because of the mark incorporated in the name. This is a question of degree, and the point at which the Internet user becomes fully aware of the provider of content.[9]

6. As quoted in *Horphag Research v. Mario Pellegrini*, 328 F.3d 1108, at 1112 (9th Cir. 2003).

7. In *Playboy Enters. v. Welles*, 279 F.3d at 802, affirming *New Kids on the Block v. New America Publ'g, Inc.*, 971 F.2d 302, the Court referred to using the word mark of a competitor, but not its distinctive lettering or color scheme, as example of using only necessary parts of the mark.

8. This point was previously made by this sole panelist in *Wal-Mart Stores, Inc. v. Walsucks and Walmarket Puerto Rico*, WIPO Case No. D2000-0477, (July 20, 2000).

9. This sole panelist previously has pointed out the difference between using a trademark on a website and in a domain name from the standpoint of fair use. *See, e.g., Six Continents Hotels, Inc. v. Georgetown Inc.*, WIPO Case No. D2003-0214, (May 18, 2003), and *Six Contents Hotels, Inc. v. eGO*, WIPO Case No. D2003-0341, (July 3, 2003). A domain name that directly incorporates a trademark implicitly suggests an affiliation with the trademark holder. This distinction is recognized by federal courts in the United States. In *Playboy Enters. v. Welles*, the Court noted that its view of the nominative fair use defense might be influenced by whether the use would cause the alleged infringer's website to appear over the trademark holder's in web search results (noting that the

If any nominative fair use of domain names is to be permitted, initial interest confusion cannot standing alone act as a *per se* preclusion. In the context of the third prong of the Ninth Circuit's analytic approach, use of a mark in a domain name does not *standing alone* constitute doing something in conjunction with a mark that suggests sponsorship or endorsement by the trademark holder such as to bar a finding of nominative fair use.

The Respondent suggests that he would use the format of his existing informational web pages, plus a disclaimer, to make clear to any Internet user that the Complainant does not sponsor his website. The Respondent acknowledges by reference to another law firm's website that appropriate nominative fair use may require an express disclaimer of affiliation with the Complainant. Since the Respondent has not established a website addressed by the disputed domain name, the Panel is not in a position to evaluate his actual conduct. Nonetheless, since the Respondent has indicated his awareness of what an appropriate fair use might require, this would be consistent with allowing a passive nominative fair use defense that might later be adversely rebutted by the Respondent's conduct.

As the Complainant observes, the public has an interest in receiving information about medicines directly from their producers. The Complainant can and does maintain an active commercial website on which information concerning its medicine products is available.

The public also has an interest in learning of potential risks posed by medicines, and in securing the assistance of counsel as appropriate. This may be facilitated by the Respondent's proposed use of the disputed domain name.

The Respondent by his proposed use of the disputed domain name would not prevent the public from accessing information directly from the Complainant at the latter's website. The Respondent could provide information concerning "LIPITOR" to the public without using the mark in a domain name, although his communication to the public will be less effective that way. It would be exceedingly difficult for the Respondent to provide information about "LIPITOR" to the public on the Internet, or for the public to receive such information from the Respondent, without some use by the Respondent of the trademark (for example, on web pages addressed by other terms).

The Complainant has a commercial interest that conflicts with that of the Respondent. It is obviously in Complainant's best commercial interests that Internet users seeking information about "LIPITOR" not be directed to a site warning them of risks, and recommending adversary legal counsel.

As the Court of Appeals for the Ninth Circuit noted in *Playboy Enters. v. Welles,* a successful nominative fair use defense is not dependent on whether the party relying on it will make a profit from doing so.[10] The fact that Respondent may profit from use of the disputed domain name does not prevent him from establishing a nominative fair use defense.

---

uses by the alleged infringer were only in metatags). 279 F.3d, at 804. In *PACCAR Inc. v. Telescan Technologies,* 319 F.3d 242 (6th Cir. 2003), the Court of Appeals for the Sixth Circuit noted that domain names very often serve a source identification function, though rejecting a *per se* approach to trademark infringement, adopting instead use of an eight-factor test for determining likelihood of confusion. 319 F.3d, at 249-50. It went on to apply, without adopting, the Ninth Circuit's three-prong test of a nominative fair use defense, rejecting such a claim because of the combined factors of domain name usage and deliberate adoption by the alleged infringer of the trademark holder's distinctive styling on its website. 319 F.3d, at 256.

10.   279 F.3d, at 801.

As noted earlier, the Complainant bears the burden of proving that the Respondent does not have rights or legitimate interests in the disputed domain name (including by establishing a nominative fair use right to use the Complainant's mark in the name).

The Panel is not persuaded that the Complainant has carried its burden. The Complainant has established that it has rights in the mark in the disputed domain name and that the Respondent's proposed use of the name would conflict with its interests. The Respondent has presented a number of reasons why his use of the disputed domain name would be fair under the circumstances. The Respondent's showing has sufficiently rebutted the Complainant's showing so as to preclude the Panel from finding that the Respondent has no rights or legitimate interests in the disputed domain name.

Proceedings under the Policy are intended to address "abusive" domain name registration and use. The Complainant is not suffering immediate harm. The Respondent is not actively using the disputed domain name. The Complainant may further pursue its interests in the courts. In light of the important public interests at stake and the reasonable nature of the Respondent's defense, the Panel does not consider it appropriate to deprive the Respondent of the disputed domain name in this Administrative Proceeding.

Having determined that the Complainant has not proven that the Respondent lacks rights or legitimate interests in the disputed domain name, the Panel will not address the issue of bad faith.

7. Decision

For all the foregoing reasons, the Complaint is denied.

Frederick M. Abbott, Sole Panelist
July 16, 2003

NOTES AND QUESTIONS

1. The *Pfizer v. Van Robichaux* decision makes use of the doctrine of nominative fair use that largely evolved in the U.S. Court of Appeals for the Ninth Circuit. A notable recent decision that elaborates on that doctrine in the context of domain names is *Toyota v. Tabari*, 610 F.3d 1171 (9th Cir. 2010), involving <buy-a-lexus.com> and <buyorleaselexus.com>. This decision describes the typical Internet user as sophisticated, with significant searching skills and ability to rapidly distinguish trademark owner-sponsored and third-party-sponsored web sites (although a concurring opinion says this fact is not established). The Court of Appeals states that a domain name comprised solely of a trademark is presumed likely to cause consumer confusion and identification with the trademark owner, though additional terms may effectively eliminate that presumption. The Court holds that a defendant asserting nominative fair use in the context of an allegedly infringing domain name is subject to the three-prong test of *New Kids* (see text case above). A defendant need only demonstrate that it has used the trademark at issue to refer to the trademark good, and this shifts the burden of proof to the trademark owner to demonstrate likelihood of

confusion (i.e., the trademark owner must prove defendant has suggested sponsorship or affiliation).

2. A respondent that loses a dispute decided by a panel under the Policy has the right to initiate litigation within ten days of notification of the decision, automatically preventing the registrar from transferring or canceling the disputed domain name. This option is used from time to time, though not often. Only in a few cases has a court effectively overturned the decision of a panel. *See Barcelona.Com v. Excelentisimo Ayuntamiento De Barcelona*, 330 F.3d 617 (4th Cir. 2002).

3. There has been modest academic criticism of decision making by panels under the Policy. Some conclude from an imbalance in decisions in favor of complainants that the process must somehow be biased in favor of trademark holders. *See, e.g.*, Michael Geist, *Fair.com?: An Examination of the Allegations of Systemic Unfairness in the ICANN UDRP* (Aug. 2001), and *Fundamentally Fair.Com? An Update on Bias Allegations and the ICANN UDRP* (2002).[24] But this criticism may overlook or discount factors that help explain the imbalance. Compared to the large number of domain names that have been registered, the number of disputes is small. Hundreds of thousands of domain names are registered and maintained without incident. While registering a domain name is very inexpensive (today often less than $10), initiating a dispute under the Policy—while significantly less costly than court litigation—is nevertheless expensive, particularly as many complainants are represented by major law firms. Rational business enterprises do not set out to waste money on frivolous domain name challenges. The vast majority of complaints involve businesses that are able to demonstrate ownership of a trademark, and that have a reasonably good basis for believing they are the subject of abuse by a third-party domain name registrant. A substantial percentage of parties whose domain name registrations are challenged do not file a response, even though this is facilitated by tools provided on the WIPO web site. This context may help explain why the preponderance of UDRP decisions favor trademark holders.[25] The frequency of domain name disputes, and the percentage of trademark holder success, would be cut down by requiring *ex ante* review of domain name registration applications for conflict with existing trademark registrations (which, in fact, is required in some countries). Such a change would make the domain name registration process less efficient, increase its cost, and almost certainly reduce the number of registrations. Trademark holders would need to initiate fewer *ex post* complaints because there would be fewer cases of third-party abuse. The *ex post* percentage of UDRP decisions in favor of trademark holders would almost certainly decline because there would be fewer "obvious" cases of abuse, but at a significant cost to the public, which appears to appreciate the ease and low cost with which domain names may presently be registered.

---

24. For a critique of Geist's almost wholly statistical approach, *see* International Trademark Association (INTA Internet Committee), *The UDRP by All Accounts Works Effectively, Rebuttal to Analysis and Conclusions of Professor Michael Geist in Fair.com and Fundamentally Fair.com* (May 2002).

25. Statistically, three-person panels have supported Respondents at a somewhat more favorable rate than single-person panels. There may, again, be a fairly straightforward explanation for this. Respondents that are prepared to pay the higher fees associated with appointment of a three-person panel may be more likely to believe—and be able to support—that their claims to domain names are justified, and (unsurprisingly) their belief may be correct.

4. What do you see as the costs and benefits of the UDRP process? Would it be preferable for all domain name disputes to be settled by national courts? Does the right to initiate litigation that automatically blocks transfer of a domain name based on a UDRP decision adequately protect the registrant?

5. The potential misuse of trademarks in domain names is not the only area where evolution of the Internet has challenged pre-existing paradigms of international trademark law. Trademark owners are concerned about auction websites where there is the potential for sale of counterfeit goods, with the use of their marks in metatags and in other web content that may be made available to competitors for generating advertising links, and generally with the potential for trademark misuse absent traditional territorial limitations. The WIPO Secretariat has reviewed recent case law and proposals for new rules regarding protection of trademarks on the Internet in a report, "Trademarks and the Internet," prepared for the WIPO Standing Committee on the Law of Trademarks, Industrial Designs and Geographical Indications, SCT/244, August 31, 2010 (Twenty-Fourth Session of the SCT, Nov. 1-4, 2010, available at http://www.wipo.int).

CHAPTER
4

The International Copyright System

I. COPYRIGHT AS AN INTELLECTUAL PROPERTY FORM

A. *Changing Technologies*

During the nineteenth century, and for much of the twentieth, references to IP commonly distinguished between "industrial property" protected by patent and trademark, and artistic or literary property protected by copyright and neighboring rights (such as performers' rights). The former was the province of the business enterprise, while the latter was the province of the artistic community (including publishers and other promoters). While the term of copyright was used ever since in common law countries, originally depicting the crown's paper to authorize printing activities, the focus on rights of authors was expressed by the French term of *droit d' auteur* in the European continental traditions based upon eighteenth-century enlightenment and the advent of human rights. With the adoption of copyright protection by computer software developers in the 1970s, the line between industrial property and artistic property seemed to lose much of its conceptual significance, as do the traditional distinctions between copyright and *droit d'auteur*. The use of copyright to protect the content of commercial Internet web sites may finally be putting all these distinctions to rest.

The Internet has exponentially expanded access to information, and is changing the way people live and work around the world. Whether copyright laws are adequate to control distribution of expressive works on the Internet is an open question. While courts have been receptive to applying traditional copyright doctrine in the Internet arena, and while treaties and national legislation have been adapted, copyright holders face continuing challenges from evolving technologies (see discussion of evolving technologies in *Universal Studios v. Corley* (regarding DeCSS) and *MGM v. Grokster, infra*).

The rise of the Internet may suggest a decline in the relevance of national boundaries in the development and application of copyright and other intellectual property law. Certainly, the Internet gives its users the power to transmit data across national borders with relative ease. Yet, national governments may not be so willing to surrender local regulatory authority. The Internet may be a vector of "globalization," but there remains strong counter-pressure to globalization reflecting values inherent in national sovereignty and the maintenance of local regulatory control.

B. Copyright Subject Matter

Since the advent of the Berne Convention in 1886, copyright subject matter
has been defined very broadly. That subject matter is the creative expression
of artists and authors. Unlike patents, it does not extend to content and
ideas, which remain freely usable. There is no limit on the form copyrightable
expression may take, although national law may condition protection on its
"fixation" in a tangible medium. While commonly thought of in connection
with books, paintings, sculptures, music, and films, copyright may encompass
product labels, computer software, clothing, and jewelry design. The "format"
in which copyrightable expression appears is constantly changing, from film
to videotape to DVD, from vinyl record to CD to MP3 file.

1. Idea/Expression Dichotomy

Copyright protection extends to authors' and artists' creative expression.
Legislatures and courts have consistently interpreted the term "expression"
to exclude the protection of ideas or methods of operation that might be
embodied in an expressive work. This was succinctly put by the U.S. Court of
Appeals for the Second Circuit in *Computer Associates v. Altai.*

COMPUTER ASSOCIATES INTERNATIONAL v. ALTAI
982 F.2d 693 (2d Cir. 1992)

WALKER, Circuit Judge: . . .
    It is a fundamental principle of copyright law that a copyright does not
protect an idea, but only the expression of the idea. *See Baker v. Selden,* 101
U.S. 99, 25 L. Ed. 841 (1879); *Mazer v. Stein,* 347 U.S. 201, 217, 98 L. Ed. 630,
74 S. Ct. 460 (1954). This axiom of common law has been incorporated into
the governing statute. Section 102(b) of the [U.S. Copyright] Act provides:

> In no case does copyright protection for an original work of authorship extend to
> any idea, procedure, process, system, method of operation, concept, principle, or
> discovery, regardless of the form in which it is described, explained, illustrated, or
> embodied in such work.

17 U.S.C. § 102(b). *See also* House Report, at 5670 ("Copyright does not preclude others from using ideas or information revealed by the author's work.").

2. Science and Expression

In the following case, the Swiss Supreme Court considers the distinction
between expression and idea in the realm of science.[1] Frau X filed suit against

---

1. The judicial system in Switzerland, typical for continental Europe, generally consists of three
levels: first the Bezirksgericht (Circuit Court), which has first instance jurisdiction within a small
geographic region. The Obergericht or Kantonsgericht (Court of Appeals) is the second level,
which decides all appeals in one state (a "Canton") of Switzerland. The highest Swiss Court is the

Frau Y and Z Publishing House for infringement of copyright, alleging that Frau Y used written results of Frau X's research in a public presentation before that research was published.[2]

FRAU X v. FRAU Y & Z PUBLISHING HOUSE*

Bundesgericht (Swiss Federal Court)
BGE 113 II 306 ([1989] ECC 232) (translation, as adjusted)
17 June 1987

FACTS . . .

Frau X was a student of psychology at Zurich University. Both her work for a licentiate and her dissertation were concerned with the life and work of the first child psychoanalyst, Hermine von Hug-Hellmuth. At the end of 1983, intending to have the results of her work published, she approached the Z publishing house. The publisher's reader informed her by telephone in March 1984 that publication of the two works in the form in which they then were was not possible but the publisher would be interested in the manuscripts if they were to be reworked. The reader added that she had passed the manuscripts on for an opinion to Frau Y, who, as Frau X knew, had announced a forthcoming lecture at the Zurich Psychoanalytic Seminar on "H Hug-Hellmuth and W Schmidt." Frau Y subsequently also got in touch with Frau X.

The lecture took place on 10 May 1984; it was recorded on a tape which is stored in the library of the Psychoanalytic Seminar. It is not clear whether the lecture has been published in an appropriate form.

In May 1985 Frau X started legal proceedings against Frau Y and the Z publishing house seeking in particular an injunction under threat of penalty on the first defendant against using any quotations or results of scientific research from either of her two unpublished manuscripts unless they were acknowledged as being such. She also asked that the first defendant be ordered to pay her 2,000 Sfr plus interest by way of moral redress and that both defendants be jointly held liable to pay 500 Sfr plus interest by way of damages.

The Zurich Obergericht (court of appeal) dismissed the action on 20 November 1986 on the grounds that the first defendant had not infringed any copyright or droit moral of the plaintiff and had not been guilty of unfair competition, that the second defendant was not responsible for the action of its reader, and that the plaintiff had suffered no harm as a result of the passing on of the manuscript.

The plaintiff has appealed against that judgment in which she maintains her claims.

Federal Court, located in Lausanne. In addition to performing the usual tasks of judicial review, this court, in the area of private law, acts as a court of second appeal with a view to bringing about the uniform interpretation of federal law in the Swiss federalist structure. Unlike the U.S. Supreme Court, the Swiss Federal Court does not have discretion to decide whether or not an appeal should be considered.

2. In section II.A.3.b.i, *infra*, we examine another part of this decision relating to "moral rights."

* In Swiss legal practice, names are deleted from published opinions with a view to protect the plaintiff's and defendant's privacy and integrity.

DECISION: . . .

3. The plaintiff objects that the Obergericht was wrong in finding that there was no infringement by the first defendant of her copyright under section 1(2) of the Copyright Act. She argues in particular that a comparison of her work with the lecture in issue shows that various passages in her manuscripts are quoted and their substantive content is adopted in part. She says that the Court below did not go into the matter at all. Her theses were of an independent character, were the result of a personal intellectual performance and therefore should not have been quoted before publication even in extracts. The content of scientific works was not generally free for copyright purposes, so that, contrary to the view of the court below, it was not admissible to consider individual empirical facts in isolation or to refuse protection in advance in the case of scientific data and theses. Since the individual content of such works had to be sought in the selection and scientific processing of material which they undertook, the aspects relevant for copyright purposes had to be considered as a connected whole before it was possible to make a judgment on whether protection was available to the work.

(a) Literary works fall within the concept of a protected work within the meaning of section 1 of the Copyright Act if the specific presentation does not merely contain what is common property but, when taken as a whole, is to be regarded as a result of intellectual creative activity of an individual character or as the expression of a new original idea; for originality and individuality also count as essential characteristics of a protected work. (*See* 110 IV BGE 105 E 2; 106 II BGE 73-74; 100 II BGE 172, with further references in each case.) A scientific work is also covered by the statutory definition if it shows a minimum standard of creative performance. But for these purposes a scientific idea as such does not come into consideration. What a scientist states about external circumstances, operations or other matters of fact becomes free once it is published so far as the content is concerned, and is not in itself protected for copyright purposes even if it conveys new discoveries or has been worked out with effort (88 IV BGE 127). The content of a scientific idea is not the intellectual work involved therein but consists in the fact that it reveals previously unknown or little known facts. The result of the work, therefore, is freely usable as regards content, as befits the purpose of scientific investigation, which is oriented towards free access. Reservations remain only in the case of scientific discoveries in the technical field, which in appropriate cases can be subject to patent rights or protection by reference to secrecy or confidentiality. (Troller, Immaterialguterrecht I (3rd ed), p 355; Kummer, Das urheberrechtlich schutzbare Werk, pp 106 et seq.)

On the other hand, the specific presentation of a scientific work can be entitled to protection. This includes in the first instance the external form in which the work is communicated if it is clearly distinct from other persons' written work with the same content. For these purposes it evidently cannot be overlooked that for the author of such a work narrow boundaries tend to be set as regards its written formulation because he must adhere to specific sets of facts and in particular to technical language if he wishes to be taken seriously and to be understood (88 IV BGE 129). Where the form of communication is so tightly constricted by the scientific content that there is no longer any room for an individual or original formulation copyright protection disappears for that reason. (Kummer, op cit p 108.) In addition to the form given to it, a scientific work can also exhibit individual characteristics in the way in which it plans, selects and treats, and arranges and articulates the material, and it can thus establish copyright protection (88 IV BGE 127; Troller, op cit I p 356, n 26; Ulmer, Urheber- und Verlsagsrecht (3rd ed), p 123.) Section 70 of the German Copyright Act is interpreted in the same way. (Judgments of the Federal Supreme Court at [1975] GRUR 667 et seq and [1982] UFITA 143 et seq.) Contrary to the plaintiff's view, however, it is not admissible to extend the copyright protection still further to the content of scientific works, as is advocated by some writers on the basis of the German conception. (Haberstumpf zur Individualitat wissenschaftlicher Sprachwerke, p 77 et seq, and at [1983] UFITA 41 et seq.)

Where, as in the present case, scientific works are concerned, an infringement of copyright may accordingly arise as a result of a third person adopting the specific form in which the work is presented or imitating it in its essential aspects. It is necessary to bear in mind in this connection that not only the work's scientific propositions as such but also forms of expression predetermined by them are freely available to the public, and furthermore that the selection, recording and articulation of the subject-matter only qualify for protection as a whole or in relation to connected parts of the work, but not so far as it simply concerns details of the work, such as data, evidence, examples or similar statements. The taking over of such details, even if they are many, is not an infringement of copyright because scientific statements which are common property do not become protected parts of a work as a result of the treatment or presentation of the subject-matter, which can confer copyright protection. Nor is this position altered by the principle that not only the work as a whole but also its individual parts can be entitled to protection if they satisfy the necessary conditions for protection (85 II BGE 123 E 3).

(b) When those criteria are applied there can be no objections under Federal law to the view of the court below that the first defendant did not infringe any copyright owned by the plaintiff. At any rate, in so far as the first defendant adopted quotations and biographic details, one is dealing with pre-existing statements which are therefore in the public domain, nor do they enjoy copyright protection in respect of their content or of the predetermined form in which they are communicated. Accordingly the scientific thesis that the role of Hermine von Hug-Hellmuth must be seen in the light of the dispute between Freud and Jung about the origin of neuroses is not protected as a scientific proposition by reason of its content but at the most by reason of the characteristic written form in which it is expressed. The judgment in question found that in the proceedings at cantonal level the plaintiff did not argue that this thesis was adopted by the first defendant in the external form in which it was communicated in the plaintiff's two works. Accordingly the first defendant was able to consider the scientific propositions of the thesis in her lecture without infringing the plaintiff's copyright.

The position is not altered by the fact the plaintiff's two works were not published at the date when it is alleged that they were taken over. The publication of a protected work is decisive for the ability to quote passages from it or make it known publicly. (Ss 12(1)4 and 42 1(d) of The Copyright Act; Troller op cit II p 704; Ulmer op cit p 313; Lutz Die Schranken des Urheberrechts nach Schweizerischem Recht, Diss Zurich 1964, p 47; E Sciaroni, Das Zitatrecht, Diss

Freiburg 1970 p 28.) But publication does not affect the distinction between
the free and the restricted use of a work. There is therefore no need to decide
whether the plaintiff's two works already counted as published for the purposes of the Act when approved by the faculty. It must still be borne in mind
that the prohibition on quoting from unpublished works does not protect the
author's publishing right, but his or her claim to prevent a distorting representation of the work and to reserve to himself or herself the right to determine the final version; and that condition is sufficiently satisfied if the work is
fixed as regard its essential parts, which is generally the case where the competent body of an institute of further education has passed the work. (*Cf* Lutz,
op cit p 47.)

NOTES AND QUESTIONS

1. How did the Court define the boundary between protectable expression
    and unprotectable content or idea?
2. The Court suggests that the means for expressing scientific ideas may be
    sufficiently constrained such that this expression cannot be an indepen-
    dently creative act for copyright purposes. In what cases are scientific pro-
    positions so clearly "true" in an objective sense that the personality of the
    researcher is not part of the scientific proposition? If a scientific pro-
    position turns out to be false, does this falsity turn the proposition into
    creative expression within the scope of copyright protection?
3. In 1985, the German Federal Supreme Court imposed a minimum require-
    ment of creative spark or innovation on the authors of computer programs
    as a condition of granting copyright protection. In the *Protection of Computer
    Programs*,[3] it said:

> While it must be allowed that copyright protection is in principle possible
> for computer programs, it remains to be considered in individual cases
> whether the program and its preliminary stages do achieve a sufficiently
> creative level of originality within the meaning of section 2(2) of the
> Copyright Act. The question has to be answered in accordance with the prin-
> ciples developed hitherto in judicial decisions. On that basis the question of
> the level of originality is to be assessed according to the total impression of
> intellectual creativity of the specific composition, and that must be done
> moreover through an overall comparison with pre-existing compositions.
> (*See* 27 BGH 351, 356, et seq ("Candida" Script)). Such a comparison does
> not contain any test of novelty (which is not relevant to the question of
> copyright protection (*see* 18 BGHZ 319, 322 (Building Plan)), but answers
> the question whether the specific composition has individual characteristics
> compared with compositions already known. The starting point is known
> programs and the work produced in the individual stages of development
> with such known and usual arrangements, systems and principles of construc-
> tion and treatment as they may have. Any forms of composition which remain
> in proximity to them do not possess a sufficiently creative level of originality;
> merely mechanical or technical advances on and developments of existing

---

3. (I ZR 52/83), Bundesgerichtshof (German Federal Supreme Court), [1986] ECC 498, 9 May
1985.

knowledge remain in this category. (*Cf* von Gamm: [1969] WRP 96, 99). If creative characteristics are established by the test of an overall comparison with what is already known, they must then be set against the products of an average programmer. What the average composer can do, the merely work-manlike mechanical or technical combination and connection of the material, cannot be subject to any protection. Only after a substantial advance does the lower level of protectability begin, and it presupposes a clear superiority of the compositional activity in the matter of the selection, collection, arrange-ment and treatment of the information and instructions over the current average of achievement. (Thus the decided cases, most recently BGH: [1984] GRUR 659, 661, [1985] ECC 562 (Documents in Support of Tender).) Especial originality can also be achieved by the processing, reworking, and working-in of known elements and forms.

The question of the creative level of composition does not in principle depend on the quantitative scope of the program, nor on the expenditure and costs with which it was created or on whether the problem posed was new. Furthermore, it is not decisive for the question of the quality of the work that a number of programmers given the same commission would develop differing programs. (*See* Frankfurt OLG: [1983] GRUR 753, 755).

The approach of the German court was rejected by the European Union in adoption of the Software Directive, discussed *infra*, which forbade the application of any condition of originality other than that the program "is the author's own intellectual creation" (Software Directive, art. 1(3)). The Software Directive was largely a reaction to this German Supreme Court decision.

Yet, the German Federal Supreme Court may merely have been ahead of its time. Courts in the United States have increasingly sought to separate out (as unprotectable) elements of programs that are adopted for reasons having to do with the underlying technology of computers, such as the need for software to address and interact with hardware components, or to take advantage of drafting efficiencies.[4]

4. Compilations of factual material are protected by copyright if their arrangement embodies a creative act by the compiler; see *Feist v. Rural Telephone* below. Why is Frau X's work not protected as a compilation?

3. Fact and Expression

It is generally accepted that "facts" are not protected by copyright. Facts identify persons, places, and events. A person who reports a fact does not create the subject matter he or she is reporting. Distinctive contribution by the author is lacking in the sense of copyright law.

It follows from the lack of protection for facts that mechanically assembled facts are not subject to copyright protection. However, an author may well assemble facts in a creative way and earn copyright protection for the unique characteristics of the arrangement. The U.S. Supreme Court explains this in *Feist v. Rural Telephone*.

---

4. *See, e.g., Computer Associates v. Altai, infra* section V.A.

FEIST PUBLICATIONS v. RURAL TELEPHONE SERVICE
499 U.S. 340 (1991)

Justice O'CONNOR delivered the opinion of the Court.

This case concerns the interaction of two well-established propositions. The first is that facts are not copyrightable; the other, that compilations of facts generally are. Each of these propositions possesses an impeccable pedigree. That there can be no valid copyright in facts is universally understood. The most fundamental axiom of copyright law is that "no author may copyright his ideas or the facts he narrates." *Harper & Row, Publishers, Inc. v. Nation Enterprises,* 471 U.S. 539, 556 (1985). Rural wisely concedes this point, noting in its brief that "facts and discoveries, of course, are not themselves subject to copyright protection". . . . At the same time, however, it is beyond dispute that compilations of facts are within the subject matter of copyright. Compilations were expressly mentioned in the Copyright Act of 1909, and again in the Copyright Act of 1976.

There is an undeniable tension between these two propositions. Many compilations consist of nothing but raw data—i.e., wholly factual information not accompanied by any original written expression. On what basis may one claim a copyright in such a work? Common sense tells us that 100 uncopyrightable facts do not magically change their status when gathered together in one place. Yet copyright law seems to contemplate that compilations that consist exclusively of facts are potentially within its scope.

The key to resolving the tension lies in understanding why facts are not copyrightable. The sine qua non of copyright is originality. To qualify for copyright protection, a work must be original to the author. *See Harper & Row, supra,* at 547-549. Original, as the term is used in copyright, means only that the work was independently created by the author (as opposed to copied from other works), and that it possesses at least some minimal degree of creativity. 1 M. Nimmer & D. Nimmer, Copyright §§ 2.01[A], [B] (1990) (hereinafter Nimmer). To be sure, the requisite level of creativity is extremely low; even a slight amount will suffice. The vast majority of works make the grade quite easily, as they possess some creative spark, "no matter how crude, humble or obvious" it might be. *Id.,* § 1.08[C][1]. Originality does not signify novelty; a work may be original even though it closely resembles other works so long as the similarity is fortuitous, not the result of copying. To illustrate, assume that two poets, each ignorant of the other, compose identical poems. Neither work is novel, yet both are original and, hence, copyrightable. *See Sheldon v. Metro-Goldwyn Pictures Corp.,* 81 F.2d 49, 54 (CA2 1936). . . .

This Court has long recognized that the fact/expression dichotomy limits severely the scope of protection in fact-based works. More than a century ago, the Court observed: "The very object of publishing a book on science or the useful arts is to communicate to the world the useful knowledge which it contains. But this object would be frustrated if the knowledge could not be used without incurring the guilt of piracy of the book." *Baker v. Selden,* 101 U.S. 99, 103 (1880). We reiterated this point in *Harper & Row*:

> "No author may copyright facts or ideas. The copyright is limited to those aspects of the work—termed 'expression'—that display the stamp of the author's originality."
>
> "Copyright does not prevent subsequent users from copying from a prior author's work those constituent elements that are not original—for example . . .

facts, or materials in the public domain—as long as such use does not unfairly appropriate the author's original contributions." 471 U.S., at 547-548 (citation omitted).

This, then, resolves the doctrinal tension: Copyright treats facts and factual compilations in a wholly consistent manner. Facts, whether alone or as part of a compilation, are not original and therefore may not be copyrighted. A factual compilation is eligible for copyright if it features an original selection or arrangement of facts, but the copyright is limited to the particular selection or arrangement. In no event may copyright extend to the facts themselves.

NOTES AND QUESTIONS

1. Later in the *Feist* decision, the U.S. Supreme Court held that the assembly by a telephone company of an alphabetical listing of names and telephone numbers (to form a directory) lacked the minimal creativity necessary to justify protection under copyright law. The decision prompted efforts by "database" compilers to secure additional protection for their work. These efforts succeeded in the European Union with adoption of the Database Directive, discussed further *infra* section III.A.7, which establishes a *sui generis* form of database protection.
2. Librarians and researchers are concerned about the prospects for enhanced database protection. If IP protection for databases becomes commonplace, institutions that currently make information freely available may decide to impose "extraction" fees. This could have a chilling effect on research.
3. Although the mechanical assembly of facts is not protectable by copyright, a database producer may be able to pursue a claim under unfair competition law, depending on the circumstances of the case. In other words, a database compiler may be able to demonstrate that a competitor has taken unfair commercial advantage of its efforts.

C. Copying and Substantial Similarity

Copyright allows its holder to prevent unauthorized copying and distribution. It does not prevent a third party from independently creating the same (or a substantially similar) work. In this sense, copyright is fundamentally different from the patent. The holder of a patent has the right to prevent any third party from making or using the invention, even if the third party developed the invention without knowledge of what the patent holder had done. For this reason, the patent is sometimes referred to as a "hard" form of intellectual property. Because the copyright does not preclude independent creation, it is sometimes referred to as a "soft" form of intellectual property.

In addition to protecting the author's specific form of expression, copyright also protects against the unauthorized reproduction and distribution of derivative works such as translations and adaptations. There are many issues that arise in assessing whether a secondary work is merely an adaptation of an existing work, or is sufficiently transformed so as to constitute a "new" work.

Most copyright infringement lawsuits begin with the question whether the alleged infringer actually copied the relevant subject matter. It is often difficult for the copyright holder to directly prove copying. The act of copying may be "inferred" from the alleged infringer's access to the work and the degree of similarity.

The unauthorized reproduction of an author's work may take the form of direct or literal copying, in which case infringement of the author's rights may be relatively easy to determine (bearing in mind that there are defenses to literal copying, for example, under fair use doctrine). Unauthorized reproduction may also take the form of indirect or nonliteral copying, in which case the copying party is modifying the protected work in order to avoid the appearance of reproducing it. In the case of nonliteral copying, courts apply various tests to determine whether an allegedly infringing work is sufficiently similar to a protected work to violate the author's copyright. In the United States, for example, the traditional legal test is whether an allegedly infringing work is "substantially similar" to the protected work. Application of this test generally requires the use of subjective judgment.

Comparison of copyrighted works for substantial similarity involves determining an appropriate level of "abstraction." At the highest level of abstraction all movies are the same, that is, they are expressive cinematic works. At a lower level of abstraction, movies fall within broad categories (fictional and documentary). At progressively lower levels, movies have broad themes, plot outlines, titles, developed plot lines and characters, sets, and dialogue. At a relatively high level of abstraction — two people fall in love, get married, and endure hardship — hundreds if not thousands of films would be copies of each other. At this high level of abstraction, the movie is a common "idea." A "merger" between idea and expression takes place at this level. Only when an adequate level of detail is achieved may the author's expression become sufficiently distinctive to be protected against misappropriation.

It is not practical to define the appropriate level of abstraction at which comparison between allegedly infringing works should take place. The context in which such comparison takes place is always changing. Some courts have sought to distinguish between "objective" and "subjective" comparison of works. Objective comparison involves analytic dissection of the work — describing the characters, what they are doing, where they are living, and so forth — and seeking to evaluate similarity on the basis of the distilled factors. "Subjective" comparison looks instead to the impression the works make on the finder of fact. Viewing two movies side by side, do they seem to be similar?

Though one might expect courts to have evolved a straightforward body of rules for deciding such important questions, the creativity of authors and artists frustrates the judge. How does one formulate a rule for comparing two similar, but not identical, paintings or films?

In *Computer Associates v. Altai, infra* section V.A, the court assesses substantial similarity between computer programs.

D. Fair Use

The protection afforded by copyright is subject to important exceptions, among the most notable of which are rights of "fair use" accorded to certain copying and distribution. Fair use doctrines permit portions of copyrighted works to be used, for example, for news reference and instructional purposes. The right of fair use is related to freedom of expression.

HARPER & ROW v. NATION
471 U.S. 539 (1985)

Justice O'CONNOR delivered the opinion of the Court. . . .

Fair use was traditionally defined as "a privilege in others than the owner of the copyright to use the copyrighted material in a reasonable manner without his consent." H. Ball, Law of Copyright and Literary Property 260 (1944) (hereinafter Ball). The statutory formulation of the defense of fair use in the Copyright Act reflects the intent of Congress to codify the common-law doctrine. 3 Nimmer § 13.05. Section 107 requires a case-by-case determination whether a particular use is fair, and the statute notes four nonexclusive factors to be considered. This approach was "intended to restate the [preexisting] judicial doctrine of fair use, not to change, narrow, or enlarge it in any way." H. R. Rep. No. 94-1476, p. 66 (1976) (hereinafter House Report).

"[The] author's consent to a reasonable use of his copyrighted works [had] always been implied by the courts as a necessary incident of the constitutional policy of promoting the progress of science and the useful arts, since a prohibition of such use would inhibit subsequent writers from attempting to improve upon prior works and thus . . . frustrate the very ends sought to be attained." Ball 260. Professor Latman, in a study of the doctrine of fair use commissioned by Congress for the revision effort, *see Sony Corp. of America v. Universal City Studios, Inc.*, 464 U.S., at 462-463, n. 9 (dissenting opinion), summarized prior law as turning on the "importance of the material copied or performed from the point of view of the reasonable copyright owner. In other words, would the reasonable copyright owner have consented to the use?" Latman 15.[3]

As early as 1841, Justice Story gave judicial recognition to the doctrine in a case that concerned the letters of another former President, George Washington.

> "[A] reviewer may fairly cite largely from the original work, if his design be really and truly to use the passages for the purposes of fair and reasonable criticism. On the other hand, it is as clear, that if he thus cites the most important parts of the work, with a view, not to criticise, but to supersede the use of the original work, and substitute the review for it, such a use will be deemed in law a piracy." *Folsom v. Marsh*, 9 F. Cas. 342, 344-345 (No. 4,901) (CC Mass.)

As Justice Story's hypothetical illustrates, the fair use doctrine has always precluded a use that "[supersedes] the use of the original." *Ibid. Accord*, S. Rep. No. 94-473, p. 65 (1975) (hereinafter Senate Report).

---

3. Professor Nimmer notes: "[Perhaps] no more precise guide can be stated than Joseph McDonald's clever paraphrase of the Golden Rule: 'Take not from others to such an extent and in such a manner that you would be resentful if they so took from you.'" 3 Nimmer § 13.05[A], at 13-66, quoting McDonald, Non-infringing Uses, 9 Bull. Copyright Soc. 466, 467 (1962). This "equitable rule of reason," *Sony Corp. of America v. Universal City Studios, Inc.*, 464 U.S., at 448, "permits courts to avoid rigid application of the copyright statute when, on occasion, it would stifle the very creativity which that law is designed to foster." *Iowa State University Research Foundation, Inc. v. American Broadcasting Cos.*, 621 F.2d 57, 60 (CA2 1980). *See generally* L. Seltzer, Exemptions and Fair Use in Copyright 18-48 (1978).

NOTES AND QUESTIONS

1. As we will examine, the Berne Convention and TRIPS Agreement permit
    exceptions for fair use of copyrighted works. The availability and scope of
    the exceptions remains, for the most part, subject to national law. We also
    examine, *infra,* a WTO panel decision that gives extensive consideration to
    the permissible scope of the fair use exception under the TRIPS Agreement
    (and the incorporated Berne Convention provisions).

E.   Term of Protection and the Public Domain

The protection afforded by copyright is of substantially longer duration than
that afforded by patent. The Berne Convention and TRIPS Agreement
minimum term of copyright is the author's life plus 50 years. This long duration
is partially justified by the fact that copyright is weaker than the patent right,
since it does not preclude independent creation. The term of copyright was
extended to the author's life plus 70 years by the EU Copyright Directive, and
this extension was followed by the United States. The U.S. term extension
legislation was challenged by a number of groups on grounds, *inter alia,* that
it was inconsistent with the Copyright and Patent Clause of the Constitution,
which refers to the grant of exclusive rights for "limited Times." These groups
worry that term extension has the effect of restricting the "public domain," that
is, works free for all to use.

The following excerpts from the U.S. Supreme Court's decision in *Eldred v.
Ashcroft* highlight the argument put forward on behalf of the U.S. copyright
industries that failure to extend the copyright term would lead to a "protection
gap" with the European Union, encouraging authors to publish outside the
United States.

ELDRED v. ASHCROFT
537 U.S. 186 (2003)

Justice GINSBURG delivered the opinion of the Court.

This case concerns the authority the Constitution assigns to Congress to
prescribe the duration of copyrights. The Copyright and Patent Clause of
the Constitution, Art. I, § 8, cl. 8, provides as to copyrights: "Congress shall
have Power . . . to promote the Progress of Science . . . by securing [to Authors]
for limited Times . . . the exclusive Right to their . . . Writings." In 1998, in the
measure here under inspection, Congress enlarged the duration of copyrights
by 20 years. Copyright Term Extension Act (CTEA), Pub. L. 105-298, § 102(b)
and (d), 112 Stat. 2827-28 (amending 17 U.S.C. §§ 302, 304). As in the case of
prior extensions, principally in 1831, 1909, and 1976, Congress provided for
application of the enlarged terms to existing and future copyrights alike. . . .

The CTEA reflects judgments of a kind Congress typically makes, judgments
we cannot dismiss as outside the Legislature's domain. As respondent
describes, . . . a key factor in the CTEA's passage was a 1993 European
Union (EU) directive instructing EU members to establish a copyright term
of life plus 70 years. EU Council Directive 93/98, p. 4; *see* 144 Cong. Rec.
S12377-S12378 (daily ed. Oct. 12, 1998) (statement of Sen. Hatch). Consistent

with the Berne Convention, the EU directed its members to deny this longer term to the works of any non-EU country whose laws did not secure the same extended term. *See* Berne Conv. Art. 7(8); P. Goldstein, International Copyright § 5.3, p. 239 (2001). By extending the baseline United States copyright term to life plus 70 years, Congress sought to ensure that American authors would receive the same copyright protection in Europe as their European counterparts.[11] The CTEA may also provide greater incentive for American and other authors to create and disseminate their work in the United States. *See* Perlmutter, Participation in the International Copyright System as a Means to Promote the Progress of Science and Useful Arts, 36 Loyola (LA) L. Rev. 323, 330 (2002) ("Matching the level of [copyright] protection in the United States [to that in the European Union] can ensure stronger protection for U.S. works abroad and avoid competitive disadvantages vis-à-vis foreign rightholders."); *see also id.*, at 332 (the United States could not "play a leadership role" in the give-and-take evolution of the international copyright system, indeed it would "lose all flexibility," "if the only way to promote the progress of science were to provide incentives to create new works"). . . .

Petitioners contend that even if the CTEA's 20-year term extension is literally a "limited Time," permitting Congress to extend existing copyrights allows it to evade the "limited Times" constraint by creating effectively perpetual copyrights through repeated extensions. We disagree.

As the Court of Appeals observed, a regime of perpetual copyrights "clearly is not the situation before us." 239 F.3d at 379. . . .

More forcibly, petitioners contend that the CTEA's extension of existing copyrights does not "promote the Progress of Science" as contemplated by the preambular language of the Copyright Clause. Art. I, § 8, cl. 8. To sustain this objection, petitioners do not argue that the Clause's preamble is an independently enforceable limit on *Congress' power*. *See* 239 F.3d at 378. (Petitioners acknowledge that "the preamble of the Copyright Clause is not a substantive limit on Congress' legislative power." (internal quotation marks omitted)). Rather, they maintain that the preambular language identifies the sole end to which Congress may legislate; accordingly, they conclude, the meaning of "limited Times" must be "determined in light of that specified end". . . . The CTEA's extension of existing copyrights categorically fails to "promote the Progress of Science," petitioners argue, because it does not stimulate the creation of new works but merely adds value to works already created. . . .

We have also stressed, however, that it is generally for Congress, not the courts, to decide how best to pursue the Copyright Clause's objectives. . . .

Petitioners separately argue that the CTEA is a content-neutral regulation of speech that fails heightened judicial review under the First Amendment. We reject petitioners' plea for imposition of uncommonly strict scrutiny on a copyright scheme that incorporates its own speech-protective purposes and

---

11. Responding to an inquiry whether copyrights could be extended "forever," Register of Copyrights Marybeth Peters emphasized the dominant reason for the CTEA: "There certainly are proponents of perpetual copyright: We heard that in our proceeding on term extension. The Songwriters Guild suggested a perpetual term. However, our Constitution says limited times, but there really isn't a very good indication on what limited times is. The reason why you're going to life-plus-70 today is because Europe has gone that way. . . ." Copyright Term, Film Labeling, and Film Preservation Legislation: Hearings on H. R. 989 et al. before the Subcommittee on Courts and Intellectual Property of the House Committee on the Judiciary, 104th Cong., 1st Sess., 230 (1995) (hereinafter House Hearings).

safeguards. The Copyright Clause and First Amendment were adopted close in time. This proximity indicates that, in the Framers' view, copyright's limited monopolies are compatible with free speech principles. Indeed, copyright's purpose is to promote the creation and publication of free expression. As *Harper & Row* observed: "The Framers intended copyright itself to be the engine of free expression. By establishing a marketable right to the use of one's expression, copyright supplies the economic incentive to create and disseminate ideas." 471 U.S., at 558.

In addition to spurring the creation and publication of new expression, copyright law contains built-in First Amendment accommodations. *See id.*, at 560. First, it distinguishes between ideas and expression and makes only the latter eligible for copyright protection. . . . Due to this distinction, every idea, theory, and fact in a copyrighted work becomes instantly available for public exploitation at the moment of publication. *See Feist*, 499 U.S., at 349-350.

Second, the "fair use" defense allows the public to use not only facts and ideas contained in a copyrighted work, but also expression itself in certain circumstances. Codified at 17 U.S.C. § 107, the defense provides: "The fair use of a copyrighted work, including such use by reproduction in copies . . . , for purposes such as criticism, comment, news reporting, teaching (including multiple copies for classroom use), scholarship, or research, is not an infringement of copyright." The fair use defense affords considerable "latitude for scholarship and comment," *Harper & Row*, 471 U.S., at 560, and even for parody, *see Campbell v. Acuff-Rose Music, Inc.*, 510 U.S. 569, 127 L. Ed. 2d 500, 114 S. Ct. 1164 (1994) (rap group's musical parody of Roy Orbison's "Oh, Pretty Woman" may be fair use). . . .

Justice BREYER, dissenting.

The Constitution's Copyright Clause grants Congress the power to "promote the Progress of Science . . . by securing for limited Times to Authors . . . the exclusive Right to their respective Writings." Art. I, § 8, cl. 8 (emphasis added). The statute before us, the 1998 Sonny Bono Copyright Term Extension Act, extends the term of most existing copyrights to 95 years and that of many new copyrights to 70 years after the author's death. The economic effect of this 20-year extension—the longest blanket extension since the Nation's founding—is to make the copyright term not limited, but virtually perpetual. Its primary legal effect is to grant the extended term not to authors, but to their heirs, estates, or corporate successors. And most importantly, its practical effect is not to promote, but to inhibit, the progress of "Science"—by which word the Framers meant learning or knowledge, E. Walterscheid, The Nature of the Intellectual Property Clause: A Study in Historical Perspective 125-126 (2002).

The majority believes these conclusions rest upon practical judgments that at most suggest the statute is unwise, not that it is unconstitutional. Legal distinctions, however, are often matters of degree. . . . And in this case the failings of degree are so serious that they amount to failings of constitutional kind. Although the Copyright Clause grants broad legislative power to Congress, that grant has limits. And in my view this statute falls outside them. . . .

Second, the Court relies heavily for justification upon international uniformity of terms. Ante, at 4, 14-15. Although it can be helpful to look to international norms and legal experience in understanding American law, cf. *Printz v. U.S.*, 521 U.S. 898, 977, 138 L. Ed. 2d 914, 117 S. Ct. 2365 (1997) (Breyer, J., dissenting), in this case the justification based upon foreign rules is surprisingly weak. Those who claim that significant copyright-related benefits flow from greater international uniformity of terms point to the fact that the nations of the European Union have adopted a system of copyright terms uniform among themselves. And the extension before this Court implements a term of life plus 70 years that appears to conform with the European standard. But how does "uniformity" help to justify this statute?

Despite appearances, the statute does not create a uniform American-European term with respect to the lion's share of the economically significant works that it affects — all works made "for hire" and all existing works created prior to 1978. . . . With respect to those works the American statute produces an extended term of 95 years while comparable European rights in "for hire" works last for periods that vary from 50 years to 70 years to life plus 70 years. Compare 17 U.S.C. §§ 302(c), 304(a)-(b) with Council Directive 93/98/EEC of 29 October 1993 Harmonizing the Term of Protection of Copyright and Certain Related Rights, Arts. 1-3, 1993 Official J. Eur. Cmty. 290 (hereinafter EU Council Directive 93/98). Neither does the statute create uniformity with respect to anonymous or pseudonymous works. Compare 17 U.S.C. §§ 302(c), 304(a)-(b) with EU Council Directive 93/98, Art. 1.

The statute does produce uniformity with respect to copyrights in new, post-1977 works attributed to natural persons. Compare 17 U.S.C. § 302(a) with EU Council Directive 93/98, Art. 1(1). But these works constitute only a subset (likely a minority) of works that retain commercial value after 75 years. . . . And the fact that uniformity comes so late, if at all, means that bringing American law into conformity with this particular aspect of European law will neither encourage creation nor benefit the long-dead author in any other important way.

What benefit, then, might this partial future uniformity achieve? The majority refers to "greater incentive for American and other authors to create and disseminate their work in the United States," and cites a law review article suggesting a need to "avoid competitive disadvantages." . . . The Solicitor General elaborates on this theme, postulating that because uncorrected disuniformity would permit Europe, not the United States, to hold out the prospect of protection lasting for "life plus 70 years" (instead of "life plus 50 years"), a potential author might decide to publish initially in Europe, delaying American publication. . . . And the statute, by creating a uniformly longer term, corrects for the disincentive that this disuniformity might otherwise produce.

That disincentive, however, could not possibly bring about serious harm of the sort that the Court, the Solicitor General, or the law review author fears. For one thing, it is unclear just who will be hurt and how, should American publication come second — for the Berne Convention still offers full protection as long as a second publication is delayed by 30 days. *See* Berne Conv. Arts. 3(4), 5(4). For another, few, if any, potential authors would turn a "where to publish" decision upon this particular difference in the length of the copyright term. As we have seen, the present commercial value of any such difference amounts at most to comparative pennies. . . . And a commercial decision that turned upon such a difference would have had to have rested previously upon a knife edge so fine as to be invisible. A rational legislature could not give major weight to an invisible, likely nonexistent incentive-related effect.

But if there is no incentive-related benefit, what is the benefit of the future uniformity that the statute only partially achieves? Unlike the Copyright Act of 1976, this statute does not constitute part of an American effort to conform to an important international treaty like the Berne Convention. *See* H. R. Rep. No. 94-1476, pp. 135-136 (1976) (The 1976 Act's life-plus-50 term was "required for adherence to the Berne Convention"); S. Rep. No. 94-473, p. 118 (1975) (same). Nor does European acceptance of the longer term seem to reflect more than special European institutional considerations, i.e., the needs of, and the international politics surrounding, the development of the European Union. House Hearings 230 (statement of the Register of Copyrights); *id.,* at 396-398 (statement of J. Reichman). European and American copyright law have long coexisted despite important differences, including Europe's traditional respect for authors' "moral rights" and the absence in Europe of constitutional restraints that restrict copyrights to "limited Times." *See, e.g.,* Kwall, Copyright and the Moral Right: Is an American Marriage Possible? 38 Vand. L. Rev. 1, 1-3 (1985) (moral rights); House Hearings 187 (testimony of the Register of Copyrights) ("limited Times").

In sum, the partial, future uniformity that the 1998 Act promises cannot reasonably be said to justify extension of the copyright term for new works. And concerns with uniformity cannot possibly justify the extension of the new term to older works, for the statute there creates no uniformity at all. . . .

NOTES AND QUESTIONS

1. In thinking about the "protection gap" argument, it may be helpful to note that the major copyright industry actors are multinational and lobby both in the United States and the European Union. Representatives of the same company will appear at EU Commission-sponsored meetings arguing for stronger protection to improve EU competitiveness vis-à-vis the United States, and fly across the Atlantic to appear at congressional hearings in the United States arguing that it is necessary to close the gap with the European Union.

2. Justice Breyer contends that additional royalty income to U.S. authors and artists creating new works will be very small. Who benefits from the term extension? Large entertainment companies with film and music libraries, as well as holders of copyrights in cartoon characters, lobbied heavily in favor of the extension.

3. The *Eldred v. Ashcroft* decision includes a discussion of the impact of copyright term extension on freedom of speech (or expression).

    Freedom of expression and copyright protection are inherently in tension. Although copyright law makes exception for the fair use of protected works in matters such as critical commentary, the application of the fair use exception is nonetheless subject to limitations. When expression is protected by copyright, it may no longer be used freely in an absolute sense.

    As with other fields of intellectual property protection, society makes a bargain. As encouragement for the creation of works that contribute to public well-being, the author or artist is granted an exclusive right to control his or her expression work for a limited time. A boundary is drawn around the work, and it becomes off limits from the standpoint of free expression (subject to fair use).

    There is always a risk that the public commons may become so cluttered with boundaries that free expression and the public good will suffer. See discussion in *Universal Studios v. Corley, infra.*

The Berne Convention and TRIPS Agreement make provision for fair use, but they do not expressly address freedom of expression or speech. In fact, the Berne Convention provides that it does not interfere with the right of governments to control the distribution of expressive works (art. 17, Berne Convention).[5] The right of free speech or expression will usually be guaranteed by the national constitution. Of course, not all governments or constitutions accord the same scope to this right. Nonetheless, the matter does not end at the national level. Regional and international human rights agreements and principles also recognize rights of speech and expression. (*See, e.g.*, the decision of the European Court of Human Rights in *Hertel v. Switzerland*, 25181/94 [1998] ECHR 77 (25 August 1998). Although this case principally involved conflict between freedom of expression and unfair competition law, the basic principles are similar.)

4. Traditionally, U.S. and British copyright law required registration to obtain a copyright. With adherence to the Berne Convention, both countries abandoned this condition, because the Berne Convention states that copyright may not be bound by any formalities. But, whereas Great Britain fully eliminated the registration requirement, the United States still permits registration and encourages right holders to register by giving them an initial advantage in litigation. Are there reasonable grounds not to require registration of copyrights? Conversely, what justifies registration requirements with respect to patents, plant varieties, industrial designs, integrated circuit layout designs, and trademarks?

II. MULTILATERAL COPYRIGHT NORMS

A. *The Berne Convention*

International norms on copyright are rooted in the Berne Convention for the Protection of Literary and Artistic Work, dating back in its initial form to 1886.[6] The main substantive provisions of the Berne Convention were supplemented by the copyright provisions of the TRIPS Agreement, which incorporates by reference substantial parts of the Berne text. In addition to the TRIPS Agreement, the so-called neighboring rights to copyright are the subject of several separate international agreements, including the Rome Convention for the Protection of Performers, Producers of Phonograms and Broadcasting Organisations (Rome Convention) and the Geneva Convention for the Protection of Producers of Phonograms against Unauthorized Duplication of Their

---

5. The Berne Convention provides:

ARTICLE 17
POSSIBILITY OF CONTROL OF CIRCULATION, PRESENTATION AND EXHIBITION OF WORKS
The provisions of this Convention cannot in any way affect the right of the Government of each country of the Union to permit, to control, or to prohibit, by legislation or regulation, the circulation, presentation, or exhibition of any work or production in regard to which the competent authority may find it necessary to exercise that right.

6. The texts of all WIPO Conventions discussed in this section may be found at http://www.wipo.int.

Phonograms (Geneva Convention). Neighboring rights subject matter that is covered by the Rome and Geneva Conventions is the subject of new rules of the TRIPS Agreement. Moreover, subsequent to entry into force of the TRIPS Agreement, two important new treaties—the WIPO Copyright Treaty and the WIPO Performances and Phonograms Treaty—were concluded. These treaties supplement the rules of the Berne and Rome Conventions. One objective of the negotiators of these new treaties was to create consistency between WTO and WIPO rules. The new WIPO treaties also create rules for the digital environment that are not found in the TRIPS Agreement. This is a complex system of agreements.

As with other areas of international intellectual property rights (IPRs) regulation, the rules of the Berne Convention, TRIPS Agreement, and other multilateral treaties are incorporated and transformed in regional, national, and subnational law. Because the multilateral agreements allow flexibility in implementation, there are variations within national law.

1. Historical Perspective

The following excerpt provides a historical perspective on international copyright protection, including the background of the Berne Convention negotiations. It is of some interest that many of the countries that today are the main advocates of strong copyright protection went through long periods as copyright "pirates." These countries discovered the virtues of copyright protection only after developing a strong local creative community interested in securing copyright protection abroad. Until the 1950s, the United States maintained a "manufacturing clause" in its copyright statute and effectively offered copyright protection only for materials printed in the United States.[7]

THE BIRTH OF THE BERNE UNION
Sam Ricketson[*]

We are celebrating today the centenary of the first true multilateral convention on copyright, the Berne Convention for the Protection of Literary and Artistic Works. I use the adjective "true" advisedly, as prior to the Berne Convention there had been other multilateral conventions on copyright. However, these had been of limited territorial effect and had been entered into in order to overcome particular political problems, such as those that existed in Germany and Italy prior to the unification of those countries. The Berne Convention, on the other hand, was open to all states without restriction, as long as they were prepared to comply with the obligations embodied therein. It is also important to see the Convention in a broader context as it was only one of series of impressive multilateral conventions that came into existence during

---

7. *See* Hamish R. Sandison, *The Berne Convention and the Universal Copyright Convention: The American Experience*, in THE CENTENARY OF THE BERNE CONVENTION, CONFERENCE, at 11-22 (Intellectual Property Law Unit, Queen Mary College, University of London and British Literary and Artistic Copyright Association, London, April 17-18, 1986).

* THE CENTENARY OF THE BERNE CONVENTION, CONFERENCE (Intellectual Property Law Unit, Queen Mary College, University of London and British Literary and Artistic Copyright Association London, April 17-18, 1986).

this period. Of these, the International Telegraph Convention, the Universal Postal Convention, and, of course, the Paris Convention for the Protection of Industrial Property still remain in force today. The Berne Convention, then, can be seen as a manifestation of a period when human society was attempting, in a high-minded but practical spirit, to bring about change and development across a whole range of matters through international cooperation. . . .

In 1886, most national copyright laws were not much more than a few decades old. The United Kingdom was, of course, an exception as it had enacted the first modern copyright statute as far back as 1709 (the "Act of Anne"). The scope of this Act was quite limited, and it was restricted to books, but during the next hundred years protection was extended in piecemeal fashion to other kinds of works, including engravings, sculptures and dramatic works. In most other European countries, however, the situation as regarded the protection of authors was similar to that which had obtained in the United Kingdom prior to 1709: there was no express recognition of authors' rights, and the only protection available was that accorded through the grant of privileges or monopolies for the printing of particular books. These privileges were usually granted by governments to publishers and printers, rather than authors. It is ironic, perhaps, that we should today be meeting in the Hall of the Stationers' Company as this was the trade association whose members traditionally exercised the printing monopolies that were granted by the Crown in the sixteenth and seventeenth centuries in this country.

A similar situation prevailed for longer in most European countries, in particular France, the German and Italian states and Spain. Even in this country, the members of the Stationers' Company strove long and hard throughout the eighteenth century to retain their traditional privileges with respect to the printing of books. Thus, it was not until the end of that century that it was firmly established that the rights accorded under the Act of Anne were authors' rights, rather than publishers' or printers' rights. In France, on the other hand, completely new ground was broken when the ancient regime was swept away by the Revolution of 1789. The rights of man, now enshrined in the new revolutionary laws, were soon recognised to include the rights of authors in their works. A Law of 1791 therefore accorded an exclusive right of public performance to the authors of dramatic and musical works for a period lasting five years after their deaths. A second Law of 1793 granted, in respect of all works, what we would now call an "exclusive reproduction right," enduring for the life of the author. There was a conscious philosophical basis to these laws that was lacking in the Act of Anne, in that the former conceived of the rights of authors as being rooted in natural law, with the consequence that these laws were simply according formal recognition to rights that were already in existence. In the years following the French Revolution this new conception of authors' rights spread to other continental European countries, in particular Belgium, the Netherlands and the Italian states. . . . [B]y 1886 almost all the European states, including the newly unified states of Italy and Germany, had enacted their own copyright laws. Outside of Europe, the United States had had a copyright law since 1791, and laws on copyright were to be found in seven other states of Latin America. A number of other countries, such as Greece, Bulgaria and Turkey, protected authors' rights in a partial or incidental fashion through provisions in their general civil, criminal or press laws.

Many of these new laws drew on the models provided by the two French Laws of 1791 and 1793, although it should be noted that French copyright law continued to develop rapidly throughout the nineteenth century and to do so as much through the jurisprudence as through legislative enactments. Nevertheless, while the principal issues addressed by national laws were the same, the solutions adopted were often quite different. Most laws extended protection to a wide range of productions of a literary and artistic character, including works intended for public presentation, such as musical and dramatic works. But some categories of works, such as architectural, oral and choreographic works, were protected only in a few countries, and there were widely differing approaches to the protection of photographic works. Great diversity also existed in relation to the matter of duration of protection. In two Latin American countries, Guatemala and Mexico, this was perpetual, but in all other countries protection was limited in time. This was usually for a period comprising the life of the author together with a fixed period after his death. France had led the way here with a *post mortem autoris* term of 50 years, but 1879 Spain adopted a period of 80 years, and other nations had terms ranging between 5 and 50. A few other countries, such as the United States of America had terms that were not fixed to the life of the author, and some, including the United Kingdom, accorded different terms of protection to different categories of works. Finally, in Italy there was a system of paying public domain, under which works were protected absolutely for a given period (the author's life or 40 years after publication), and this was followed by a further period of 40 years during which the work might be used by third parties subject to a payment of a compulsory royalty to the author.

The rights protected under these early national laws also varied considerably although the principal ones recognised were those of reproduction and public performance. The right to make translations was recognised to differing degrees and was often of far shorter duration than the other rights, particularly in case of foreign authors. . . . [M]ost laws required that the author comply with some kind of formality before protection would be accorded. The nature and effect of these formalities differed widely from country to country, but the chief ones were registration, the deposit of copies and the making of declarations. In some cases, failure to comply with formalities was fatal, meaning that the work fell into the public domain; in other cases, it meant merely that the copyright owner was unable to enforce his rights until he rectified the omission. By 1886, only a few countries, including Belgium, Germany and Switzerland (but not France), had abolished formalities altogether. . . .

The above sketch has concentrated on the contents of national copyright laws in the pre-1886 period. However, it will be clear that there is an equally important international dimension to the protection of authors' works. Literary and artistic works and musical compositions recognise no national boundaries, even where translation into another language is required for a work to be fully appreciated in a particular country. Thus it was that after the need for protection of authors by national laws had been recognised, the works of these authors still remained vulnerable to copying and exploitation abroad. These activities, commonly referred to as "piracy," had been a long-established feature of European social and cultural life, and this continued to be the case for a considerable time after the enactment of national copyright laws. The attitudes of many countries to these practices were highly anomalous: whilst prepared to protect their own authors, they did not always regard the piracy of foreign authors' works as unfair or immoral. Some countries, in fact, openly countenanced piracy as contributing to their educational and social needs and as reducing the prices of books for their citizens. The particular victims of these practices were the United Kingdom and France. During the eighteenth century English authors suffered from the activities of Irish pirates who could flood both the English and other markets with cheap reprints; after the Act of Union with Ireland in 1800, the chief threat came from the publishing houses of the United States and this continued to be a major problem for the rest of the century. French authors, in turn, suffered from the activities of pirates located in Switzerland, Germany, Holland, and, in particular, Belgium. By the early nineteenth century, Brussels was a major centre for the piracy of French books, and this led to considerable strains in the relations between France and Belgium. Piracy was likewise rampant between the different German and Italian states.

This widespread piracy of foreign works was the principal reason for the development of international copyright relations in the mid-nineteenth century. The arguments that raged both for and against the protection of foreign authors at this time have a surprisingly modern ring to them. On the one hand, it could be said that the activities of the pirates resulted in cheaper copies and the greater availability of the work in question. In countries hungry for knowledge and enlightenment, this could only be to the advantage of the public interest and this, indeed, was the reason for the persistent refusal of the United States to protect foreign works throughout the nineteenth century. On the other hand the moral and practical arguments in the author's favour were obvious: not only was he being robbed of the fruits of his creativity, but this would discourage him from continuing to create, with resultant loss to his own, and other, countries.

It is hard to identify the point at which a country no longer sees advantage in the piracy of foreign works, and decides to extend protection to the authors of such works. It may be that the activities of its own authors have increased, and that the latter now desire protection for their own works abroad. It may also be that, after a while, a country wishes to obtain some kind of international respectability, and to avoid the opprobrium of being labelled as a nation of pirates. Another factor may be that countries with large literary and artistic outputs bring pressure to bear on their more recalcitrant neighbours, promising various forms of trade advantage in return for copyright protection for their authors. Finally, pirate nations may come to recognise that the rights of authors in their works are of a proprietary nature, and that they should therefore be protected internationally in the same way as other property of foreigners. All these factors were certainly applicable in the case of Belgium, which, in the mid-nineteenth century, switched suddenly from being the chief centre of piracy for French works to being one of the most zealous defenders of authors' rights. The same factors applied to many other countries as they began to enter into international copyright relations with each other. Indeed, agreements between states and the formal sanctions of copyright law were not always necessary to achieve protection for foreign authors, at least in a limited form, as systems of "courtesy" copyright operated with some effect during this time and sometimes predated formal international agreements. This was particularly so in the United States, where the major publishing houses observed an unwritten custom whereby each would refrain from publishing editions of foreign works in respect of which another had reached a publishing agreement with the author. This system of mutual self-restraint had several advantages for the parties concerned: it protected the first American publisher of a foreign work from the unfettered copying of his edition, and gave the author the opportunity of earning some remuneration, even if he were unable to prevent the American publication of his work in the first place. As a consequence, authors such as Dickens and Trollope received large sums in respect of the American sales of their works, although they did not enjoy protection under United States copyright law.

"Courtesy copyright," however, is only a partial substitute for full copyright protection, and, in any case, it was not really of great significance outside the American market. . . .

Bilateral copyright agreements . . . had, in fact, become quite common by the middle of the century. . . . The basis of the majority of these conventions was national treatment, but, as stated above, they also contained a number of common rules which each country undertook to apply in its protection of works from the other country. There was usually a statement of the categories of works covered by the agreement, and specific provision was generally made for the protection of translation and performing rights. Restrictions in respect of particular kinds of use were also often allowed relating, for example, to education or the reproduction of newspaper articles. The scope and detail of these provisions differed considerably from one convention to another, but the most "advanced," in terms of protection of authors' interests, were to be found in the conventions made by France, Germany and Italy in the early 1880s. With regard to duration of protection, most of the pre-1886 conventions required material reciprocity, providing that country A was not obliged to protect the works of country B for any longer period than that accorded by state B to its own works, and in any event for no longer than country A protected its own nationals.

There were wider discrepancies with respect to formalities. . . . Matters were further complicated by the fact that the duration of many conventions was uncertain, in that they were linked to some wider treaty of trade or commerce between the countries in question and might suddenly fall to the ground if the latter was revoked or renegotiated. Another source of uncertainty arose from the insertion of "most favoured nation" clauses in many copyright conventions. The effect of these was that the contracting parties agreed to admit each other to the benefits that might be accorded to a third state under another treaty that was made by one of them with that state. The effect of such clauses was that a copyright convention between countries A and B might be abrogated, in whole or in part, by the terms of another convention made by either country A or B with country C if this agreement contained additional measures for the protection of copyright. While these clauses did not mean any loss or protection for authors, they obviously made it difficult for an author from country A to know, at any one time, what level of protection he was entitled to in country B, and vice versa.

It will be clear that this network of bilateral agreements meant that there was little uniformity in the protection that an author might expect to receive in countries other than his own. As far as Europe was concerned, the threat posed by international piracy earlier in the century had largely disappeared by 1886, but quite a number of European states still remained reluctant to enter bilateral agreements on copyright. . . . The most important of these countries was the United States, which throughout the nineteenth century continued to be a major centre for pirated works and resisted efforts by other countries, in particular the United Kingdom, to draw it into bilateral agreements. Several such attempts were made, but the vested interests of publishers and printers, on the one hand, and the voracious appetite for cheap books from the rapidly growing American population, on the other, doomed them to failure. . . .

In the light of the above, it was not surprising that moves for a more widely based and uniform kind of international copyright protection began in the middle of the nineteenth century.

NOTES AND QUESTIONS

1. The early forms of protection granted for books and other printed material were generally in favor of publishers, and not in favor of authors. Today, the largest streams of copyright revenue flow to the producers of films and television programs such as Walt Disney and Comcast/General Electric, and to the large publishing houses such as Time-Warner. The rights of authors are certainly the subject of copyright protection, yet have the basic economics of the copyright industries changed very much from the Middle Ages?

2. The Internet and related digital delivery systems allow authors to bypass large producer/publishers and benefit more directly from their creative acts. Are producers and publishers needed in the new digital environment? Are we in the midst of the next French Revolution in copyright? We will be looking at this digital dimension more closely.

3. Consider the copyright "pirates" of today's China and the copyright pirates of the Industrial Age in the United States. British publishers were unhappy with American pirates in 1870, and U.S. publishers are unhappy with Chinese pirates in 2011. Did the American pirates have a better justification for their conduct than the Chinese pirates?

2. Berne Convention Norms

Next is a description of the terms of the Berne Convention by the International Bureau of WIPO.

THE BERNE CONVENTION FOR THE
PROTECTION OF LITERARY AND ARTISTIC WORKS*

History

5.165 Copyright protection on the international level began by about the middle of the nineteenth century on the basis of bilateral treaties. A number of such treaties providing for mutual recognition of rights were concluded but they were neither comprehensive enough nor of a uniform pattern.

5.166 The need for a uniform system led to the formulation and adoption on September 9, 1886 of the Berne Convention for the Protection of Literary and Artistic Works. The Berne Convention is the oldest international treaty in the field of copyright. . . .

---

* WIPO Intellectual Property Handbook (as of April 2006).

5.167 The Berne Convention has been revised several times in order to improve the international system of protection which the Convention provides. Changes have been effected in order to cope with the challenges of accelerating development of technologies in the field of utilization of authors' works, in order to recognize new rights as also to allow for appropriate revisions of established ones. . . .

5.169 The aim of the Berne Convention, as indicated in its preamble, is "to protect, in as effective and uniform a manner as possible, the rights of authors in their literary and artistic works."

Article 1 lays down that the countries to which the Convention applies constitute a Union for the protection of the rights of authors in their literary and artistic works.

PRINCIPAL PROVISIONS

BASIC PRINCIPLES

5.170 The Convention rests on three basic principles. Firstly, there is the principle of "national treatment," according to which works originating in one of the member States are to be given the same protection in each of the member States as these grant to works of their own nationals.

Secondly, there is automatic protection, according to which such national treatment is not dependent on any formality; in other words protection is granted automatically and is not subject to the formality of registration, deposit or the like. Thirdly, there is independence of protection, according to which enjoyment and exercise of the rights granted is independent of the existence of protection in the country of origin of the work.

WORKS PROTECTED

5.171 Article 2 contains a non-limitative (illustrative and not exhaustive) list of such works, which include any original production in the literary, scientific and artistic domain, whatever may be the mode or form of its expression. Derivative works, that is those based on other pre-existing works, such as translations, adaptations, arrangements of music and other alterations of a literary or artistic work, receive the same protection as original works (Article 2(3)). The protection of some categories of works is optional; thus every State party to the Berne Convention may decide to what extent it wishes to protect official texts of a legislative, administrative and legal nature (Article 2(4)), works of applied art (Article 2(7)), lectures, addresses and other oral works (Article 2*bis*(2)) and works of folklore (Article 15(4)). Furthermore, Article 2(2) provides for the possibility of making the protection of works or any specified categories thereof subject to their being fixed in some material form. For instance, protection of choreographic works may be dependent on their being fixed in some form. . . .

OWNERS OF RIGHTS

5.173 Article 2(6) lays down that protection under the Convention is to operate for the benefit of the author and his successors in title. For some categories of works, however, such as cinematographic works (Article 14*bis*), ownership of copyright is a matter for legislation in the country where protection is claimed.

PERSONS PROTECTED

5.174 Authors of works are protected, in respect of both their unpublished or published works if, according to Article 3, they are nationals or residents of a member country; alternatively, if, not being nationals or residents of a member country, they first publish their works in a member country or simultaneously in a non-member and a member country.

MINIMUM STANDARDS OF PROTECTION

5.175 Certain minimum standards of protection have been prescribed relating to the rights of authors and the duration of protection.

RIGHTS PROTECTED

5.176 The exclusive rights granted to authors under the Convention include the right of translation (Article 8), the right of reproduction in any manner or form, which includes any sound or visual recording, (Article 9), the right to perform dramatic, dramatico-musical and musical works (Article 11), the right to broadcast and communicate to the public, by wire, rebroadcasting or loudspeaker or any other analogous instrument, the broadcast of the work (Article 11*bis*), the right of public recitation (Article 11*ter*), the right to make adaptations, arrangements or other alterations of a work (Article 12) and the right to make cinematographic adaptations and reproductions of a work (Article 14). The so-called "droit de suite" provided for in Article 14*ter* (concerning original works of art and original manuscripts) is optional and applicable only if legislation in the country to which the author belongs permits.

5.177 Independently of the author's economic rights, Article 6*bis* provides for "moral rights" — that is, the right of the author to claim authorship of his work and to object to any distortion, mutilation or other modification of, or other derogatory action in relation to, the work which would be prejudicial to his honor or reputation.

LIMITATIONS

5.178 As a sort of counterbalance to the minimum standards of protection there are also other provisions in the Berne Convention limiting the strict application of the rules regarding exclusive right. It provides for the possibility of using protected works in particular cases without having to obtain the authorization of the owner of the copyright and without having to pay any remuneration for such use. Such exceptions, which are commonly referred to as free use of protected works, are included in Articles 9(2) (reproduction in certain special cases), 10 (quotations and use of works by way of illustration for teaching purposes), 10*bis* (reproduction of newspaper or similar articles and use of works for the purpose of reporting current events) and 11*bis*(3) (ephemeral recordings).

5.179 There are two cases where the Berne Convention provides the possibility of compulsory licenses — in Articles 11*bis*(2), for the right to broadcast and communicate to the public, by wire, rebroadcasting or loudspeaker or any other analogous instrument, the broadcast of the work, and 13(1) for the right of recording musical works.

5.180 As far as the exclusive right of translation is concerned, the Berne Convention offers a choice, in that a developing country may, when acceding to the Convention, make a reservation under the so-called "ten-year rule" (Article 30(2)(b)). This provides for the possibility of reducing the term of protection in respect of the exclusive right of translation; this right, according to the said rule, ceases to exist if the author has not availed himself of it within 10 years from the date of first publication of the original work, by publishing or causing to be published, in one of the member countries, a translation in the language for which protection is claimed.

DURATION OF PROTECTION

5.181 The minimum standards of protection provided for in the Berne Convention also relate to the duration of protection. Article 7 lays down a minimum term of protection, which is the life of the author plus 50 years after his death.

5.182 There are, however, exceptions to this basic rule for certain categories of works. For cinematographic works, the term is 50 years after the work has been made available to the public, or, if not made available, then 50 years after the making of such a work. For photographic works and works of applied art, the minimum term of protection is 25 years from the making of the work (Article 7(4)).

5.183 A majority of countries in the world have legislated for life plus a 50-year term of protection since it is felt fair and right that the lifetime of the author and the lifetime of his children should be covered; this could also provide the incentive necessary to stimulate creativity, and constitute a fair balance between the interests of the authors and the needs of society.

5.184 The term of protection, in so far as moral rights are concerned, extends at least until the expiry of the economic rights.

APPLICATION IN TIME

5.185 The Protection under the Berne Convention is retrospective, since it applies to all works which, at the moment of its coming into force for a specific country, have not yet fallen into the public domain in the country of their origin through the expiry of the term of protection.

The Latest (Paris) Act of the Convention . . .

5.191 The Revision Conference convened in Paris in 1971 was predominantly concerned with finding solutions in order to support the universal effect of the Convention and to establish an appropriate basis for its operation, particularly in relation to developing countries. The question was asked whether it was fair and workable to ask the developing countries to take on obligations under the Convention that were agreed upon by developed countries, without taking into consideration the special circumstances of the former. There was certainly a challenge then posed to international copyright itself and this was, in a manner, sorted out through the give-and-take that culminated in the special provisions concerning developing countries that were incorporated in an Appendix, which now forms an integral part of the Convention, open to developing countries concerning translation and reproduction of works of foreign origin.

The Appendix augments the Convention's existing exceptions to the author's exclusive rights, including those of reproduction and translation (Articles 2*bis*, 9(2), 10(2), 10*bis*) and the ten-year rule (Article 30(2)(b)).

5.193 According to this Appendix, countries which are regarded as developing countries in conformity with the established practice of the General Assembly of the United Nations may, under certain conditions, depart from the minimum standards of protection provided for in the Convention. This exceptional regime concerns two rights, the right of translation and the right of reproduction. . . .

NOTES AND QUESTIONS

1. Organisation for Economic Co-operation and Development (OECD) industry groups criticized the Paris Convention for its lack of adequate subject matter coverage with respect to patents. By contrast, Article 2 of the Berne Convention provides broad subject matter coverage for copyright. In light of Article 2, were the provisions of the TRIPS Agreement on computer programs and compilations necessary? Is there a risk associated with adding express subject matter coverage for new technologies? In other words, if some new subject matter is expressly covered, might it be implied that other new subject matter is not covered without an express reference?

2. Article 2(2), Berne, permits members to require that a copyrighted work be fixed in some tangible form. By way of illustration, the U.S. Copyright Act, Section 102, refers to "original works of expression fixed in any tangible medium of expression, now known or later developed, from which they can be perceived, reproduced, or otherwise communicated, either directly or with the aid of a machine or device." What types of expressive works are not fixed in a tangible medium of expression?

3. Article 2(3), Berne, extends copyright protection to translations (as well as to adaptations, arrangements, and other alterations). In the highly integrated global economy, the economic value of translation rights should be apparent. Article 21, Berne, and the referenced Appendix authorize developing countries to grant compulsory licenses for the translation and reproduction of copyrighted works under specified terms and conditions. The Appendix generally requires that a work has not been translated and made available at a reasonable cost. Berne, Article 21, and the Appendix are incorporated by reference in the TRIPS Agreement (TRIPS, art. 9.1).

4. Note that pursuant to Berne Article 3(1)(a), unpublished works are protected. Article 3(1)(b) provides Berne protection to works first published in a Berne member country even if the author is not a national of a Berne member. This article provides a mechanism that permits Berne protection to be secured "through the back door"; this provision was quite important for American authors so long as the United States had not adhered to the Berne Convention. Now that Berne Convention membership has become virtually universal, this provision is of lesser importance.

5. Article 6*bis* addresses the subject of "moral rights" of authors, a topic we consider in detail later in this chapter. The TRIPS Agreement expressly excludes Article 6*bis*, Berne, from its incorporated provisions (TRIPS Agreement, art. 9.1).

6. The term of copyright protection generally required by Article 7(1), Berne, is the life of the author plus 50 years. However, members may

grant a longer term of protection (art. 7(6)) and, as we saw in *Eldred v. Ashcroft,* the European Union and the United States have extended the term to the author's life plus 70 years. Article 7(8) is of particular importance in the context of nations and regions with differing durations of copyright protection. What is the effect of Article 7(8), Berne?

7. The basic protection of the Berne Convention is set out in Article 9(1), that is, the "exclusive right of authorizing the reproduction of these works, in any manner or form." The most important exceptions to the author's exclusive rights are in Article 9(2), which generally establishes the rights referred to as "fair use" rights. Specific embodiments of fair use rights are set forth in Articles 10 and 10*bis,* Berne.

8. Article 11*bis* establishes the rights to broadcast "to the public" by wireless means, (11*bis*(1)(i)), and by wire or by rebroadcasting when the communication is made by an organization other than the "original one," 11*bis*(1)(ii). The meaning of the various phrases in Article 11*bis* has been the subject of considerable litigation in national and regional courts. For example, Cable News Network (CNN) fought a long court battle in France against a Paris hotel that claimed that its guest rooms were not public areas, and that it was thus entitled to retransmit CNN satellite signals to its guests without payment. CNN eventually prevailed. *See, e.g., Cable News Network Inc. and another v. Novotel SA,* Tribunal de Grande Instance (District Court), Paris, [1991] ECC 492, 14 Feb. 1990, holding that a hotel room is a "private" as opposed to "public" place, subsequently overturned by the Cour de Cassation. *Cable News Network and CNN International Sales Limited v. Novotel Paris-Les Halles SA,* Cour de Cassation (Supreme Court) [1994 ECC 530], 6 Apr. 1994.

9. Article 14*ter*(1) refers to the *droit de suite,* which requires that an author (and his or her heirs) collect an interest in the sale of a work of art or original manuscript in any sale after its first transfer. However, this right only extends to Berne members that choose to prescribe it by legislation, and it only benefits foreign authors whose home country also prescribes such rights (art. 14*ter*(2), Berne).

10. We have previously observed that copyright and other IPRs do not afford market access rights. Article 17, Berne, establishes a right in favor of governments to prohibit the distribution of any copyrighted work. Does the fact that governments exercise that right as they "may find it necessary" suggest any meaningful limitation on the right?

11. Might you have foreseen that Article 18 concerning the retroactive application of Berne protection would be the subject of a major trade dispute? It was. Article 70.2 of the TRIPS Agreement provides that questions relating to copyright in existing works will be governed solely by the terms of Article 18, Berne. Article 14 of the TRIPS Agreement extended the term of protection for performers and producers of phonograms to 50 years from the calendar year of fixation, extending well beyond the 20-year term prescribed by the Rome Convention for such subject matter. When Japan implemented the TRIPS Agreement provisions with respect to performers and producers of phonograms, it presumed that works existing for more than 20 years had fallen into the public domain, and therefore were not subject to TRIPS protection (per art. 18(2), Berne). The United States vehemently objected, arguing that the TRIPS Agreement specifically contemplated the extension of copyright to existing

works. Japan eventually conceded and adopted legislation extending protection, though not because it was convinced of the soundness of any U.S.
legal argument. What do you think?

12. Note again, as in the Paris Convention, the possibility of referral of a
dispute to the International Court of Justice (art. 33, Berne).[8]

3.   Berne Convention in National Law

The Berne Convention may be applied directly by the courts of a contracting
state when the constitution of that state permits the direct application of
treaties. The Convention may also be transformed into national law by the
legislature or parliament of a contracting state. Even when a national legislature
has adopted copyright legislation specifically to implement the provisions of
the Berne Convention, the Convention may be referred to by courts either to
aid in the interpretation of that national legislation, or to fill a gap in the
legislation. The extent to which a court may directly rely on the provisions of
the Convention (e.g., to fill a gap) will depend on the way in which the national
constitution regards treaty law.[9]

a.   Cable Retransmission

In *SUISA v. Rediffusion,* the Swiss Federal Court applies the Berne Convention in a case involving a cable television company that picks up over-air
broadcast signals and retransmits the signals via cable to paying subscribers.
The cable company (Rediffusion) contends that it need not pay a copyright fee
for its retransmissions because it is reaching roughly the same audience as the
over-air broadcast (for which copyright fees are already paid).

---

8. Berne Convention, Article 33:

[Disputes: 1. Jurisdiction of the International Court of Justice; 2. Reservation as to such
jurisdiction; 3. Withdrawal of reservation]

(1) Any dispute between two or more countries of the Union concerning the interpretation or application of this Convention, not settled by negotiation, may, by any one of the
countries concerned, be brought before the International Court of Justice by application in
conformity with the Statute of the Court, unless the countries concerned agree on some
other method of settlement. The country bringing the dispute before the Court shall inform
the International Bureau; the International Bureau shall bring the matter to the attention of
the other countries of the Union.

(2) Each country may, at the time it signs this Act or deposits its instrument of ratification
or accession, declare that it does not consider itself bound by the provisions of paragraph
(1). With regard to any dispute between such country and any other country of the Union,
the provisions of paragraph (1) shall not apply.

(3) Any country having made a declaration in accordance with the provisions of
paragraph (2) may, at any time, withdraw its declaration by notification addressed to the
Director General. . . .

9. In this context, see also the doctrines of consistent interpretation and direct effect, discussed
supra Chapter 1 section IV.D.

SUISA (SWISS SOCIETY OF AUTHORS
AND PUBLISHERS) v. REDIFFUSION AG

Bundesgericht (Swiss Federal Supreme Court)
[1982] ECC 481 (BGE 107 II 57)
20 January 1981

Panel: The President, Judge Chatelain; Judges Ruedi, Stoffel, Messmer and Weyermann

Appeal from the Tribunal Cantonal (Cantonal Court), Zurich.

Judgement: . . .

The issue between the parties is essentially the extent to which the simultaneous retransmission of unaltered broadcasts with the aid of collective aerials requires authorisation from the authors and payment of their royalties. The decision would be the same whether it related only to radio broadcasts or also to television programmes. On the other hand, what must be clarified from the beginning is the meaning to be attached to the term "collective aerial." Indeed it may refer to installations of very different sizes, from the external aerial of an apartment block to a giant network serving an entire town or even region and, in between, a common aerial for several neighbouring houses or a number of districts. (HJ Stern, Die Weiterverbreitung von Radio und Fernsehsendungen, thesis, Zurich 1970, p 36.) In this case there is a large network with wide-spread branches offering some 60,000 subscribers in the Zurich region the broadcasts which are the subject of the dispute.

Section 12 of the Federal Copyright Act (LDA) gives an author the exclusive right to broadcast his work by radio (sub-section (1) no 5) and, in addition, to "communicate [it] publicly either by cable or wireless, if such communication is made by a body other than that which originated it" (no 6), television being treated in the same way as radio broadcasting (sub-section 2). Any person who infringes copyright in respect of any of these provisions is liable, according to section 42, no 1(f) LDA, to civil procedings and prosecution.

In the opinion of the cantonal Court, no such contravention can be found to have occurred in the present case because the defendant does not itself broadcast and confines itself to making technical improvements to reception conditions. The Court's decision argument is that the defendant simultaneously transmits, without alteration, programmes which its subscribers could just as easily receive directly with the aid of private aerials and that, in either case, the user must apply for a licence from the Post Office and pay a fee a share of which intended for authors is already collected by SUISA through the Swiss Radio and Television Corporation (SSR), so that the plaintiff would be seeking to obtain double payment for one and the same service, which constitutes an abuse.

With this reasoning the cantonal Court takes account only of the Federal Copyright Act and neglects, even with regard to foreign broadcasts, the Berne Convention for the protection of literary and artistic works, revised in Brussels on 26 June 1948. . . .

This is why, after all, the parties refer to the origin of the rules adopted by Swiss law, to foreign case law and international attempts to interpret the Convention on these points and to adopt it to technical progress.

(a) In the Rome version of 1928 the Convention reserves to the author the initial radio broadcasting right, and this had to be reconsidered later when it became technically possible to retransmit broadcasts. During the preparatory work of the Brussels Conference on Article 11*bis* of the Berne Convention, there was a proposal to subject any new public communication of the broadcast work, whether by cable or wireless, to a fresh authorisation from the author. This requirement seemed excessive to some delegations, insufficient to others, and was also considered too vague. On a proposal from Belgium, agreement was finally reached on the wording "any public communication," but making the author's authorisation subject to the additional condition: "when this communication is made by a body other than that which originated it" (A Baum, [1949] GRUR 18).

In the plaintiff's opinion this means that there is no requirement for a "new public," but this is disputed by the defendant which considers that the specific words "a body other . . ." aimed, on the contrary, to restrict the author's right even more. However, it does not appear from the proceedings cited by the defendant that the Conference really had this intention. . . . Consequently Article 11*bis,* no 2 of the Berne Convention may apply in cases where the retransmission does not reach a new public, so that it is unnecessary for the reception area of the original broadcast to be enlarged.

Moreover, this is the interpretation given to the preparatory work for the Brussels revision by several writers. . . .

Among Swiss writers, Stern (Thesis, p 58 et seq and in [1975] Film und Recht 773) also accepts that Article 11*bis,* no 2 of the Berne Convention does not presuppose either a new public or an enlargement of the reception area. . . .

(b) The cantonal Court has not taken account of the judgments of foreign courts cited by the parties on the pretext that they cannot constitute precedents in Switzerland. However, in so far as they refer to the Berne Convention they may very well assist in its interpretation. It is true that allowance must be made for the fact that these judgments are based partly on national law which takes priority over the Berne Convention when a contracting State uses the proviso stipulated in Article 11*bis*(2) of the Convention.

The legal situation in Belgium, where the Convention applies as it stands, is instructive. In an action against Coditel, a cable television company, a contravention of Article 11*bis*(1), no 1 of the Berne Convention was sanctioned on 19 June 1979 by the Brussels Appeal Court. Both courts adhered strictly to the letter of the Convention without entering into technical details or into the theory of a new public. . . .

In a case in Feldkirch in Austria judgment was given against a cable television enterprise for infringing copyright. Although the lower courts found that there had only been an enlargement, though only in part, of the direct reception area, the Austrian Supreme Court, in its judgment of 25 June 1974, refused to consider this distinction ([1975] GRUR Int 68-69). In another action against Telesystem, a cable television enterprise, the same Court reached a similar decision on 12 November 1979. The criticism to which these judgments gave rise led to an amendment of the Austrian Act on 2 July 1980. Section 17(3) exempts cable relays of broadcasts by Austrian Radio (ORF) and small collective aerials serving not more than 500 users from authorisation by the author. Section 59 lays down a statutory licence for the rediffusion of foreign broadcasts. These new provisions clearly differ from the Swiss legislation and are therefore of no assistance to the defendant.

On the other hand the defendant can invoke the case law of Holland, where two actions against Amstelveen, a cable television enterprise, were dismissed. It is true that the Amsterdam District Court accepts that there was "public communication" within the meaning of the Berne Convention, without it being necessary for it to involve a public other than the original public. The Court merely found that there was no "own" publication for the purpose of the Dutch Act. On appeal, the Amsterdam Court of Justice rejected this distinction on 12 June 1980 and upheld the decision of the court of first instance, without taking the Berne Convention into consideration, on the ground that the broadcasts in question could have been just as well received direct with the aid of private aerials.

Two decisions by German courts also provide grist for the defendant's mill because they dismiss actions by GEMA, a copyright management society, against the German Post Office concerning its cable networks in Hamburg and Nuremberg. These judgments, which are said to have been affirmed in the meantime by the German Federal Supreme Court, do not however refer to the Berne Convention. . . .

When these foreign judgments do not simply ignore the Berne Convention, as in Germany or Holland, they all interpret Article 11*bis,* no 2 in the manner described above, as moreover E Ulmer agrees (In [1980] GRUR 584). Consequently foreign case law does not permit this Article to be interpreted contrary to its literal meaning by subjecting its effects to the existence of a new public or an enlarged reception area. Furthermore the decisions of the German courts clearly show how difficult it is to find criteria permitting a distinction to be made between cable television enterprises which come within copyright law and those which do not.

(c) Finally, important guidelines will be found in the international efforts at interpretation and adjustment of the controversial provisions of the Berne Convention. First of all we may cite the Guide de la Convention de Berne published in 1978 by the World Intellectual Property Organisation (WIPO). . . . In June 1977 a group of experts appointed by UNESCO and the WIPO had already decided that the concept of a direct reception area was unknown by Article 11 *bis* of the Berne Convention. The same criterion was rejected once again by the same experts in 1980 for the additional reason that cable distribution enterprises always appeal to a different public, even if it remains partly identical, because what use would they have otherwise?

The observations by interest groups are, on the other hand, less convincing. Nevertheless it is clear from their documentation that already for a very long time the international associations of authors' societies of copyright management societies, radio broadcasting organisations and cable distribution enterprises have been conferring together. From this it may be deduced that the rediffusion organisations accept the principle of a copyright fee although, it is true, disputing it in respect of the direct reception area.

As the Federal Copyright Act was amended in 1955 with the specific purpose of harmonising it with the Brussels version of the Berne Convention, which has been said of the latter also applies to the interpretation of section 12(1), no 6 of the Act. . . .

In addition the defendant seeks support in the current proposals for amending the Federal Copyright Act to try to show how the legislature would, according to the defendant, settle the question now by reference to the Convention. . . .

The cantonal Court has not borrowed its theory of the "new public" from the substantive provisions of the Berne Convention, because the point is not referred to at all by the Convention. The Court merely sees it as a suitable opportunity for filling a gap. The defendant also starts from the idea of a gap but the plaintiff, with good reason, denies the gap's existence. . . .

Under no circumstances, therefore, is there any question of providing for a new legal situation which was not regulated either by the Convention or the Federal Copyright Act. What is much more important to decide is whether the protection guaranteed by section 12, no 6 of the Act can be coupled with a new restriction at the expense of authors. As the reply is in the negative, this Court will abide by the Berne Convention and Swiss legislation which, for the retransmission of a work broadcast by radio, lay down no other condition for the exercise of copyright than a public communication by a body other than the originating body, irrespective of whether the direct reception area is enlarged or not. . . .

NOTES AND QUESTIONS

1. The cable company argues that by requiring it to pay a copyright fee, the Court will award the copyright holder a double payment. The Court accepts that this may be true, but says this is a legislative determination based upon the Berne Convention. If a consumer agrees to pay for a subscription service when a public broadcast of the same material is already available, should the copyright holder be entitled to a second payment?
2. The Court refers to decisions in other countries in which the courts have distinguished between larger- and smaller-scale retransmission enterprises. An apartment building owner may install equipment that boosts signal reception from an antenna and retransmits that signal to individual apartments. On what legal basis, if any, might a court or legislature differentiate such small-scale retransmissions from those that require payment of a copyright fee? (The U.S. Copyright Act, for example, makes specific provision for small-scale retransmissions at 17 U.S.C. § 111.)
3. The main purpose for including the text case is to show how the terms of the Berne Convention can be taken into account by a national court, including with reference to decisions of foreign courts, even though the national legislature has already transformed relevant provisions of the Convention into national law.

b. Moral Rights

The Berne Convention requires the recognition of "*droit moral*" or "moral rights" at Article 6*bis*. These include the right of attribution and the right to prevent a mutilation or other abuse of the work that would disparage the reputation of the author. In some legal systems, an author's moral rights are considered inalienable — they cannot be waived or released — and they are not subject to sale or transfer in connection with the author's economic rights in a work. It is often said that one of the greatest differences between Continental European and Anglo-American copyright law is the treatment of moral rights of authors. These differences are often attributed to fundamental disparities in the way in which the respective cultures view the role of the artist in society — the theory being that the Continental European countries place a higher value on artistic expression than do the Anglo-American countries. Moreover, the lack of attention to the moral rights of artists, at least in the United States, is often attributed to the free market capitalist philosophy, which emphasizes the right of individuals to dispose of their possessions as they please.

Whether or not differences arise from profound cultural disparities, it is true that U.S. businesses worry that allowing authors to retain residual rights in copyrighted works may lead to financial uncertainty. A business that contracts for the development of a computer program, and that by contract obtains the copyright to the resulting work, does not want to be faced with demands from the programmer that the work not be altered lest his or her reputation be injured. Likewise, the film producer who invests tens (or hundreds) of millions of dollars in a work does not want the screenwriter or the director objecting to the way the film is marketed on the basis of residual moral rights.

The tension between economics and art is not a new one. We might safely assume that since the very first commercial performances by singers, storytellers, and actors, there has been conflict between artists desiring to perform in their own style and producers of works (e.g., tavern or theater owners) seeking to please the general public and earn a greater return on investment. In a world in which a film studio may invest $200 million in a film and earn a gross return of $1 billion, the stakes in a conflict are heightened.

i. Moral Rights in Continental Europe

The first decision below is by the French Cour de Cassation, the highest civil court in France. The decision involves a widely reported dispute between the corporate owner of the copyright to the film *Asphalt Jungle,* co-directed by John Huston, and the heirs to Huston's estate.

ANGELICA HUSTON v. TURNER ENTERTAINMENT CO.

French Cour de Cassation
[1992] ECC 334
28 May 1991

Panel: Presiding, M Massip; MM Gregoire, Zennaro, Bernard de Sainte-Affrique, Thierry, Averseng, Lemontey and Gelineau-Larrivet, Judges; M Savatier, Associate Judge

Headnote:

Appeal from the Cour d'Appel (Court of Appeal), Paris.
  Copyright. Literary or artistic works. Foreign works. Copyright legislation provides that the integrity of a literary or artistic work must not be violated in France. These provisions are mandatory and apply no matter where in the world the work in question was published for the first time.

The Court allowed the appeal by the plaintiff and others, as heirs to John Huston, against the order of the court below, which refused to enjoin the television company La Cinq from transmitting a coloured version of the film, Asphalt Jungle, made by the defendant, which had succeeded to the producer's rights to the film.

INTRODUCTION: . . .

No cases were cited.

DECISION:

Second ground of appeal, first limb, by Mrs. Angelica Huston, Mr. Daniel Huston and Mr. Walter Huston, and third ground of appeal by SFAI and other legal persons.

The court referred to section 1(2) of Act 64-689 of 8 July 1964, together with section 6 of the Copyright Act of 11 March 1957.

According the former provision, the integrity of a literary or artistic work must not be violated, irrespective of the State in which the work is published for the first time. The person who is the author by the mere fact of creating it is invested with the droit moral granted to him by the latter provision. The application of these rules is mandatory.

Mrs Angelica Huston, Mr Daniel Huston and Mr Walter Huston are the heirs of John Huston, co-director of the film Asphalt Jungle (the French title being Quand la Ville Dort), which was made in black and white, but a colour version of which was made by Turner Entertainment Co, which has succeeded to the producer's rights. Relying on their right to compel respect for the integrity of John Huston's work, the appellant heirs, who have been joined in this appeal on a point of law by the various other appellants which are legal persons, asked the courts dealing with the main issue to prohibit the television company La Cinq from showing this new version. The appeal court dismissed the application on the ground that the factual matters and points of law raised by them "precluded the ouster of American law and setting aside of the contracts" between the producer and directors, which do not acknowledge that the latter are the authors of the film Asphalt Jungle.

In reaching its decision the appeal court infringed the abovementioned provisions by refusing to apply them.

Appeal allowed. Case remitted to the Cour d'Appel, Versailles for rehearing.

NOTES AND QUESTIONS

1. The decision of the Cour de Cassation is to the point: French legislation on the question of moral rights is mandatory—it is not waived by the U.S. contract that transferred the copyright to the film producer. The French rule applies despite the fact that the film is of U.S. origin, and despite the fact that the French Cour d'Appel found that the contract should otherwise be governed by U.S. law. Do you think that this result is unusual from a general conflict of laws standpoint? In other words, do countries commonly mandate the application of their own rules to activities taking place within their territory, despite contractual provisions that might generally call for the application of another country's law?

    In fact, it is not so uncommon for states to mandate the application of their own rules in cases in which important public policy considerations are at stake. A court in one state may, for example, refuse to enforce a judgment rendered by a court in another state if the court in the second state failed to follow a due process rule that is considered essential under the law of the first state.

We earlier examined that part of the Swiss Supreme Court decision in *Frau X v. Frau Y & Z Publishing House* finding that Frau X did not have a copyright in her work because it constituted unprotectable scientific idea. In addition to claiming Frau Y's unlawful reproduction of her expressive work, Frau X claimed that Frau Y infringed her moral rights because she gave the impression to her audience that Frau Y was the author of Frau X's work. The Court also considers Frau X's unfair competition claim.

FRAU X v. FRAU Y & Z PUBLISHING HOUSE

Bundesgericht (Swiss Federal Court)
BGE 113 II 306 ([1989] ECC 232) (translation, as adjusted)
17 June 1987

4. The plaintiff further accuses the first defendant of infringing her droit moral. According to the judgment under appeal that allegation had to be rejected because the quotations, data and propositions which were undoubtedly adopted were nevertheless not of such moment that one could talk of usurpation of the work, and because there was no other prejudice to the plaintiff's scientific reputation.

(a) Under Swiss legal theory and legislation an author is protected not only in his or her power to dispose of the work as the object of property rights, but also as regards his personal relationship to the work, that is as regards his droit moral as author, which are conceived as being a part or special aspect of general droit moral. The protection of that special droit moral arises in part from the provisions of the Copyright Act. . . . The protection arises further from Article 6 *bis* of the Berne Union Convention, and it first occurs in the revision made in Rome in 1928 (96 II BGE 420 E 6, with references).

Under section 28 of the Civil Code it is a condition precedent for claims arising out of droit moral that there is unlawful interference in personal relationships, which are understood as being the sphere of private life and the home, as well as a person's professional and private reputation. That is not to say that any relationship of the author to the work is sufficient to turn an alleged interference into an infringement of a personal right; for the general principle does not grant any claim to an exclusive right of disposal if the author's reputation is not affected; such an approach to the matter would have the end-result of creating a monopoly under section 28 of the Civil Code in something which is designated as freely available to the public under the statutory provisions on the specific subject-matter. The special statutory provision has precedence over the general provisions of the Civil Code and governs the area to which it applies to the exclusion of other rules. It is therefore not admissible to attempt to fill alleged gaps in copyright law by an indirect route through the general principle (110 II BGE 417 E 3a, with references). In the matter of copyright this principle only covers claims which are not subject to the rules of the legislation on the specific subject-matter, such as the author's claim to have his scientific achievement acknowledged, to have his work protected against distortion, or to have access to research documentation. (Engel in [1982] GRUR 709 et seq.) This corresponds to Article 6*bis*(1) of the Berne Union Convention, under which, independently of the author's copyright and even after transfer of such copyright, the author still has the right in particular to object to any distortion, mutilation or other alteration of the work which could be prejudicial to his honour or reputation; under the 1948 Revision the concept also includes anything else which would be prejudicial. For these purposes it is sufficient that the alteration or other prejudicial action is apt to injure his reputation or honour (96 II BGE 421).

(b) The plaintiff attacks the first defendant's manner of proceeding inasmuch as the latter took quotations, data and propositions from her works without stating the source. She supports her claim in this respect with section 26(2) of the Copyright Act, but overlooks the fact that, as shown by heading III, that provision belongs to "Exceptions from Copyright Protection," and therefore presupposes a protected work or a protected part of a work. (Troller, op cit II, p 704; Sciaroni, op cit, pp 28 et seq.) What is available for public use, however, enjoys no copyright protection, and therefore also establishes no duty to attach a statement of source to quotations. The plaintiff, therefore, is likewise unable to derive anything from the general right of personality which will protect her scientific statements, regardless of whether or not her works have to be treated as published.

The Obergericht must also be agreed with in its finding that there was no infringement of the plaintiff's right to acknowledgment of her scientific achievement. It is true that rights of personality give the author a claim in particular to the protection of any reputation and honour which the work may establish for him (84 II BGE 573); he can also oppose the usurpation of authorship by third parties. As the court below correctly held, however, that presupposes that the work is claimed as an individual achievement as regards its essential parts or characteristic features. That cannot be seriously maintained in the present case, especially as according to the findings on the factual aspects the quotations, data and propositions taken over word-for-word or merely in substance cannot qualify for copyright protection.

5. In the same way the accusation that the first defendant's actions are to be regarded as a breach of good faith for the purposes of section 1 of the Unfair Competition Act fails in the first instance by reason of the fact that conduct which is not to be objected to under the specific legislative provisions on intangible property rights also does not in principle contravene the provisions of the Unfair Competition Act (110 IV BGE 107 E 4 and 108 II BGE 331 E 5a, with citation). No doubt on the basis of the general stipulation contained in section 1(1) of the Act an exception would be made for the case of conduct which amounts to a systematic approximation or a deliberate covert approach to another person's work (108 II BGE 74-75 and 332; 104 II BGE 334 E 5b). But this is clearly not such a case. The passages listed by the defendant, consisting of three quotations, five items biographical data and a scientific proposition (thesis), which are allegedly extracted from her two works, make it impossible to conclude that the first defendant, in the exercise of an economic activity, usurped rights in specific parts of the work or even the authorship of the whole presentation, as the plaintiff seeks to argue.

Finally, the plaintiff claims damages for breach of contract and on the grounds of vicarious liability because the reader of the second defendant acting without authority and therefore unlawfully passed her manuscripts on to the first defendant. It is not necessary for present purposes to decide how the facts stand with regard to those claims, for the plaintiff acknowledges in the appeal that she authorised the first defendant to refer to both works under certain "restrictive" conditions. In so doing she herself removes the basis of her objection that the publishing company passed the manuscripts on without authority and thereby made it possible for the first defendant to adopt the passages in question.

Appeal dismissed. Judgment of the lower court reaffirmed.

NOTES AND QUESTIONS

1. Does the author in this case have "personal rights" in her work that copyright has not adequately protected? Do you agree with the Court's view that if material used in the lecture is not protected as creative expression, its author cannot have a moral right in the work?
2. Toward the end of its opinion, the Swiss Federal Court considers the plaintiff's unfair competition claim. While accepting that the usurpation of another person's work might constitute unfair competition, the Court says that the offending conduct must be systematic or involve a deliberate approach to the other person. In this regard, the Court says that appropriation, *inter alia*, of the plaintiff's thesis makes it impossible to conclude that a sufficiently great usurpation occurred. Perhaps the Court was not terribly impressed by the plaintiff's thesis. But as a general proposition, might not a single scientific proposition or thesis be of enormous economic and social value such that its usurpation would constitute a great harm to its creator? What if a rival physicist had broken into Albert Einstein's apartment in Berne and shortly thereafter published Einstein's theory of relativity under a different name?
3. The Swiss Supreme Court emphasizes that general principles of civil law should not be used to address gaps in IP protection deliberately left open by the legislature. Intellectual property law is drafted with exceptions to further the public interest. Is it sensible that courts should not allow those gaps to be closed by general principles of "unfair competition"?
4. Law professors and other academics make their reputations—and thus help determine their living conditions—on the basis of their creative scholarship. Law professors routinely circulate their work to colleagues prior to publication for criticism, editorial suggestion, and so forth, with the aim of improving the final product. Though it is certainly not unheard of, it is in fact rather rare to hear a complaint that one professor has "misappropriated" another's unpublished thesis. What do you think might motivate law professors, or research scientists, to respect the interests of their colleagues in such work? Is it protection by copyright or unfair competition law? Is it high moral standards? Is some other potential "collegial sanctioning mechanism" at work? Does such a sanctioning mechanism operate in the business sector?

ii Moral Rights in the United States

In the 1976 *Monty Python* decision that follows, the U.S. Court of Appeals for the Second Circuit elaborated a basis under the copyright statute of the United States, as well as under a statute on unfair competition, for the attribution of certain moral rights to authors.

GILLIAM v. AMERICAN BROADCASTING COMPANIES, INC.
538 F.2d 14 (2d Cir. 1976)

PRIOR HISTORY:

Appeal from a denial of a preliminary injunction to enjoin broadcast of edited television programs that allegedly infringed appellants' copyright and violated the Lanham Act § 43(a), 15 U.S.C. § 1125(a).

DISPOSITION: REVERSED AND REMANDED . . .

LUMBARD, Circuit Judge:

Plaintiffs, a group of British writers and performers known as Monty Python,[1] appeal from a denial by Judge Lasker in the Southern District of a preliminary injunction to restrain the American Broadcasting Company (ABC) from broadcasting edited versions of three separate programs originally written and performed by Monty Python for broadcast by the British Broadcasting Corporation (BBC). We agree with Judge Lasker that the appellants have demonstrated that the excising done for ABC impairs the integrity of the original work. We further find that the countervailing injuries that Judge Lasker found might have accrued to ABC as a result of an injunction at a prior date no longer exist. We therefore direct the issuance of a preliminary injunction by the district court. . . .

I . . .

American copyright law, as presently written, does not recognize moral rights or provide a cause of action for their violation, since the law seeks to vindicate the economic, rather than the personal, rights of authors. Nevertheless, the economic incentive for artistic and intellectual creation that serves as the foundation for American copyright law, *Goldstein v. California,* 412 U.S. 546, 37 L. Ed. 2d 163, 93 S. Ct. 2303 (1973); *Mazer v. Stein,* 347 U.S. 201, 98 L. Ed. 630, 74 S. Ct. 460 (1954), cannot be reconciled with the inability of artists to obtain relief for mutilation or misrepresentation of their work to the public on which the artists are financially dependent. Thus courts have long granted relief for misrepresentation of an artist's work by relying on theories outside the statutory law of copyright, such as contract law, *Granz v. Harris,* 198 F.2d 585 (2d Cir. 1952) (substantial cutting of original work constitutes misrepresentation), or the tort of unfair competition, *Prouty v. National Broadcasting Co.,* 26 F. Supp. 265 (Mass. 1939). *See* Strauss, The Moral Right of the Author 128-138, in Studies on Copyright (1963). Although such decisions are clothed in terms of proprietary right in one's creation, they also properly vindicate the author's personal right to prevent the presentation of his work to the public in a distorted form. *See Gardella v. Log Cabin Products Co.,* 89 F.2d 891, 895-96 (2d Cir. 1937); Roeder, The Doctrine of Moral Right, 53 Harv. L. Rev. 554, 568 (1940).

---

1. Appellant Gilliam is an American citizen residing in England.

Here, the appellants claim that the editing done for ABC mutilated the original work and that consequently the broadcast of those programs as the creation of Monty Python violated the Lanham Act § 43(a), 15 U.S.C. § 1125(a).[10] This statute, the federal counterpart to state unfair competition laws, has been invoked to prevent misrepresentations that may injure plaintiff's business or personal reputation, even where no registered trademark is concerned. *See Mortellito v. Nina of California*, 335 F. Supp. 1288, 1294 (S.D.N.Y. 1972). It is sufficient to violate the Act that a representation of a product, although technically true, creates a false impression of the product's origin. *See Rich v. RCA Corp.*, 390 F. Supp. 530 (S.D.N.Y. 1975) (recent picture of plaintiff on cover of album containing songs recorded in distant past held to be a false representation that the songs were new); *Geisel v. Poynter Products, Inc.*, 283 F. Supp. 261, 267 (S.D.N.Y. 1968).

These cases cannot be distinguished from the situation in which a television network broadcasts a program properly designated as having been written and performed by a group, but which has been edited, without the writer's consent, into a form that departs substantially from the original work. "To deform his work is to present him to the public as the creator of a work not his own, and thus makes him subject to criticism for work he has not done." Roeder, *supra,* at 569. In such a case, it is the writer or performer, rather than the network, who suffers the consequences of the mutilation, for the public will have only the final product by which to evaluate the work. Thus, an allegation that a defendant has presented to the public a "garbled," *Granz v. Harris, supra* (Frank, J., concurring), distorted version of plaintiff's work seeks to redress the very rights sought to be protected by the Lanham Act, 15 U.S.C. § 1125(a), and should be recognized as stating a cause of action under that statute. *See Autry v. Republic Productions, Inc.*, 213 F.2d 667 (9th Cir. 1954); *Jaeger v. American Intn'l Pictures, Inc.*, 330 F. Supp. 274 (S.D.N.Y. 1971), which suggest the violation of such a right if mutilation could be proven.

During the hearing on the preliminary injunction, Judge Lasker viewed the edited version of the Monty Python program broadcast on December 26 and the original, unedited version. After hearing argument of this appeal, this panel also viewed and compared the two versions. We find that the truncated version at times omitted the climax of the skits to which appellants' rare brand of humor was leading and at other times deleted essential elements in the schematic development of a story line.[12] We therefore agree with Judge Lasker's conclusion that the edited version broadcast by ABC impaired the integrity of appellants' work and represented to the public as the product of appellants what was actually a mere caricature of their talents. We believe that a valid cause of action for such distortion exists and that therefore a preliminary

10. That statute provides in part: Any person who shall affix, apply, or annex, or use in connection with any goods or services, . . . a false designation of origin, or any false description or representation . . . and shall cause such goods or services to enter into commerce . . . shall be liable to a civil action by any person . . . who believes that he is or is likely to be damaged by the use of any such false description or representation.

12. A single example will illustrate the extent of distortion engendered by the editing. In one skit, an upper class English family is engaged in a discussion of the tonal quality of certain words as "woody" or "tinny." The father soon begins to suggest certain words with sexual connotations as either "woody" or "tinny," whereupon the mother fetches a bucket of water and pours it over his head. The skit continues from this point. The ABC edit eliminates this middle sequence so that the father is comfortably dressed at one moment and, in the next moment, is shown in a soaked condition without any explanation for the change in his appearance.

injunction may issue to prevent repetition of the broadcast prior to final determination of the issues.[13] . . .

For these reasons we direct that the district court issue the preliminary injunction sought by the appellants.

GURFEIN, Circuit Judge, concurring:

I concur in my brother Lumbard's scholarly opinion, but I wish to comment on the application of Section 43(a) of the Lanham Act, 15 U.S.C. § 1125(a).

I believe that this is the first case in which a federal appellate court has held that there may be a violation of Section 43(a) of the Lanham Act with respect to a common-law copyright. . . .

In the present case, we are holding that the deletion of portions of the recorded tape constitutes a breach of contract, as well as an infringement of a common-law copyright of the original work. There is literally no need to discuss whether plaintiffs also have a claim for relief under the Lanham Act or for unfair competition under New York law. I agree with Judge Lumbard, however, that it may be an exercise of judicial economy to express our view on the Lanham Act claim, and I do not dissent therefrom. I simply wish to leave it open for the District Court to fashion the remedy.

The Copyright Act provides no recognition of the so-called *droit moral*, or moral rights of authors. Nor are such rights recognized in the field of copyright law in the United States. *See* 1 Nimmer on Copyright, § 110.2 (1975 ed.). If a distortion or truncation in connection with a use constitutes an infringement of copyright, there is no need for an additional cause of action beyond copyright infringement. *Id.* at § 110.3. An obligation to mention the name of the author carries the implied duty, however, as a matter of contract, not to make such changes in the work as would render the credit line a false attribution of authorship, *Granz v. Harris,* 198 F.2d 585 (2 Cir. 1952).

So far as the Lanham Act is concerned, it is not a substitute for droit moral which authors in Europe enjoy. If the licensee may, by contract, distort the recorded work, the Lanham Act does not come into play. If the licensee has no such right by contract, there will be a violation in breach of contract. The Lanham Act can hardly apply literally when the credit line correctly states the work to be that of the plaintiffs which, indeed it is, so far as it goes. The vice complained of is that the truncated version is not what the plaintiffs wrote. But the Lanham Act does not deal with artistic integrity. It only goes to misdescription of origin and the like. *See Societe Comptoir De L'Industrie Cotonniere Etablissements Boussac v. Alexander's Dept. Stores, Inc.,* 299 F.2d 33, 36 (2 Cir. 1962).

The misdescription of origin can be dealt with, as Judge Lasker did below, by devising an appropriate legend to indicate that the plaintiffs had not approved the editing of the ABC version. With such a legend, there is no conceivable violation of the Lanham Act. If plaintiffs complain that their artistic integrity is

---

13. Judge Gurfein's concurring opinion suggests that since the gravamen of a complaint under the Lanham Act is that the origin of goods has been falsely described, a legend disclaiming Monty Python's approval of the edited version would preclude violation of that Act. We are doubtful that a few words could erase the indelible impression that is made by a television broadcast, especially since the viewer has no means of comparing the truncated version with the complete work in order to determine for himself the talents of plaintiffs. Furthermore, a disclaimer such as the one originally suggested by Judge Lasker in the exigencies of an impending broadcast last December would go unnoticed by viewers who tuned into the broadcast a few minutes after it began. We therefore conclude that Judge Gurfein's proposal that the district court could find some form of disclaimer would be sufficient might not provide appropriate relief.

still compromised by the distorted version, their claim does not lie under the Lanham Act, which does not protect the copyrighted work itself but protects only against the misdescription or mislabeling.

So long as it is made clear that the ABC version is not approved by the Monty Python group, there is no misdescription of origin. So far as the content of the broadcast itself is concerned, that is not within the proscription of the Lanham Act when there is no misdescription of the authorship.

I add this brief explanation because I do not believe that the Lanham Act claim necessarily requires the drastic remedy of permanent injunction. That form of ultimate relief must be found in some other fountainhead of equity jurisprudence.

NOTES AND QUESTIONS

1. In discussing the traditional U.S. reluctance to recognize moral rights, the Second Circuit observes that it is difficult to reconcile the economic incentive for creation that American copyright law is intended to provide, on the one hand, with a lack of attention to the reputation of authors and artists. A good reputation, the court suggests, is a predicate of economic success. Do you agree with the court's perspective?

Some 20 years after *Monty Python,* the U.S. Court of Appeals for the Second Circuit again addressed the subject of moral rights in *Carter v. Helmsley-Spear.* In this case, the court is called upon to interpret and apply an amendment to the U.S. Copyright Act, the Visual Artists Rights Act of 1990, which expressly incorporates moral rights into federal law though, as we will see, in a limited way.

CARTER v. HELMSLEY-SPEAR
71 F.3d 77 (2d Cir. 1995)

CARDAMONE, Circuit Judge: . . .

B. VISUAL ARTISTS RIGHTS ACT OF 1990

Although bills protecting artists' moral rights had first been introduced in Congress in 1979, they had drawn little support. *See* Copyright Law at 1018 n.1. The issue of federal protection of moral rights was a prominent hurdle in the debate over whether the United States should join the Berne Convention, the international agreement protecting literary and artistic works. Article 6*bis* of the Berne Convention protects attribution and integrity, stating in relevant part:

> Independently of the author's economic rights, and even after the transfer of the said rights, the author shall have the right to claim authorship of the work and to object to any distortion, mutilation or other modification of, or other derogatory action in relation to, the said work, which would be prejudicial to his honor or reputation.

Berne Convention for the Protection of Literary and Artistic Works, September 9, 1886, art. 6*bis*, S. Treaty Doc. No. 27, 99th Cong., 2d Sess. 41 (1986).

The Berne Convention's protection of moral rights posed a significant difficulty for U.S. adherence. *See* Copyright Law at 1022 ("The obligation of the

United States to provide droit moral . . . was the single most contentious issue surrounding Berne adherence".); Nimmer at 8D-15 ("During the debate over [the Berne Convention Implementation Act], Congress faced an avalanche of opposition to moral rights, including denunciations of moral rights by some of the bill's most vociferous advocates".); H.R. Rep. No. 514, 101st Cong., 2d Sess. 7 (1990), *reprinted in* 1990 U.S.C.C.A.N. 6915, 6917 ("After almost 100 years of debate, the United States joined the Berne Convention. . . . Consensus over United States adherence was slow to develop in large part because of debate over the requirements of Article 6*bis*.").

Congress passed the Berne Convention Implementation Act of 1988, Pub. L. No. 100-568, 102 Stat. 2853 (1988), and side-stepped the difficult question of protecting moral rights. It declared that the Berne Convention is not self-executing, existing law satisfied the United States' obligations in adhering to the Convention, its provisions are not enforceable through any action brought pursuant to the Convention itself, and neither adherence to the Convention nor the implementing legislation expands or reduces any rights under federal, state, or common law to claim authorship of a work or to object to any distortion, mutilation, or other modification of a work. *See id.* §§ 2, 3; *see also* S. Rep. No. 352, 100th Cong., 2d Sess. 9-10 (1988), *reprinted in* 1988 U.S.C.C.A.N. 3706, 3714-15.

Two years later Congress enacted the Visual Artists Rights Act of 1990 (VARA or Act), Pub. L. No. 101-650 (tit. VI), 104 Stat. 5089, 5128-33 (1990). Construing this Act constitutes the subject of the present appeal. The Act protects both the reputations of certain visual artists and the works of art they create. It provides these artists with the rights of "attribution" and "integrity". . . .

> These rights are analogous to those protected by Article 6*bis* of the Berne Convention, which are commonly known as "moral rights." The theory of moral rights is that they result in a climate of artistic worth and honor that encourages the author in the arduous act of creation.

H.R. Rep. No. 514 at 5 (internal quote omitted). The Act brings to fruition Emerson's insightful observation ["[A] country is not truly civilized 'where the arts, such as they have, are all imported, having no indigenous life.'" From earlier in the decision — EDS.].

Its principal provisions afford protection only to authors of works of visual art — a narrow class of art defined to include paintings, drawings, prints, sculptures, or photographs produced for exhibition purposes, existing in a single copy or limited edition of 200 copies or fewer. 17 U.S.C. § 101 (Supp. III 1991). With numerous exceptions, VARA grants three rights: the right of attribution, the right of integrity and, in the case of works of visual art of "recognized stature," the right to prevent destruction. 17 U.S.C. § 106A (Supp. III 1991). For works created on or after June 1, 1991 — the effective date of the Act — the rights provided for endure for the life of the author or, in the case of a joint work, the life of the last surviving author. The rights cannot be transferred, but may be waived by a writing signed by the author. Copyright registration is not required to bring an action for infringement of the rights granted under VARA, or to secure statutory damages and attorney's fees. 17 U.S.C. §§ 411, 412 (1988 & Supp. III 1991). All remedies available under copyright law, other than criminal remedies, are available in an action for infringement of moral rights. 17 U.S.C. § 506 (1988 & Supp. III 1991). With this historical background in hand, we pass to the merits of the present litigation. . . .

III. Work Made for Hire

Also excluded from the definition of a work of visual art is any work made for hire. 17 U.S.C. § 101(B). A "work made for hire" is defined in the Copyright Act, in relevant part, as "a work prepared by an employee within the scope of his or her employment." *Id.* § 101(1). Appellants maintain the work was made for hire and therefore is not a work of visual art under VARA. The district court held otherwise, finding that the plaintiffs were hired as independent contractors. [The court goes on to determine that the work of art at issue in this case was a "work made for hire" and therefore did not benefit from the protection of the VARA.]

NOTES AND QUESTIONS

1. The Court of Appeals recounts the tremendous opposition to incorporation of Article 6*bis* of the Berne Convention into U.S. law. The act approving adherence to the Berne Convention and implementing it into U.S. law expressly precludes direct reliance on the Convention as a source of rights.[10]
2. The "work made for hire" doctrine in U.S. law finds its counterpart in other countries and regions. The essence of the doctrine is that when a work is produced by an author or artist within the course and scope of employment for another person, that other person will hold the copyright to the work. As the court observes in the preceding case, there are a variety of factors that may go into determining whether an author or artist stands in an employee-employer relationship. The work made for hire doctrine is of paramount importance in the business context, and lawyers who represent businesses that contract for expressive works—including computer software—must pay very close attention to which party will hold the copyright at the end of the day.

B. The TRIPS Agreement

Thomas Cottier introduces below the main features of the TRIPS Agreement relating to copyright.

THE AGREEMENT ON TRADE RELATED ASPECTS OF INTELLECTUAL PROPERTY RIGHTS (TRIPS)

Thomas Cottier*

D. STANDARDS CONCERNING THE AVAILABILITY, SCOPE AND USE OF INTELLECTUAL PROPERTY RIGHTS (PART II) . . .

1. Copyright and Related Rights

The provisions related to copyright are set out in Articles 9 to 14 of the TRIPs Agreement. Besides obligating all WTO Members (including prior non-signatories) to comply with the substantive provisions of the Berne Convention,

---

10. 17 U.S.C. § 104(c).

* The World Trade Organization: Legal, Economic and Political Analysis, Vol. I 1040-1120, at 1082-1085 (Patrick F.J. Macrory, Arthur E. Appleton, Michael G. Plummer eds., Springer 2005).

the TRIPs Agreement adds new provisions and clarifies those guaranteed by the Berne Convention. The rights of authors of literary and artistic works are addressed in Articles 9 to 12, the rights of performers, phonogram producers, and broadcasting organizations mainly in Article 14. The protection of performers' rights, which was traditionally limited to European civil law countries, is for the first time dealt with in a multilateral treaty of wider geographical coverage. The TRIPs copyright provisions against counterfeiting and piracy are of particular significance to producers of computer programs and phonograms. . . .

Article 9:2 awards copyright protection only to expressions and not to ideas, procedures, methods of operation, or mathematical concepts as such. The excluded elements are not defined by TRIPs, thus leaving it, subject to treaty interpretation, to Member states and domestic courts to decide what exactly constitutes, for example, a non-protected "procedure" or "method of operation" in software as opposed to protected expression.

Article 10 expands the traditional subject matter of copyright to include computer programs and compilations of data by creating an obligation to protect them as literary works. Like Article 2:5 of the Berne Convention, Article 10:2 of the TRIPs Agreement requires originality in the selection and arrangement of the contents of a compilation. Merely creating a list of works or extracts without engaging in any creative activity is not sufficient to merit copyright protection. If the database is protectable, the copyright protection only extends to the creative elements (e.g., the selection and arrangement of the data) and does not "extend to the material or data itself."

Article 11 provides the exclusive right to authors and their successors to authorize or prohibit the commercial rental of their computer programs and, subject to a so-called impairment test, to their cinematographic works.

Following Article 7:1 of the Berne Convention, Article 12 of the TRIPs Agreement sets the term of protection of most works that are calculated on a basis other than the life of the author to a minimum duration of fifty years from the end of the calendar year of authorized publication, making, or phonogram fixation/performance. Under Article 14:5 a term of twenty years is to apply to the rights of broadcasters, respectively, supplementing the twenty-five year term of protection for photographic works which is provided for in Article 7:4 of the Berne Convention.

Article 13 requires Members to confine limitations or exceptions to exclusive rights to (i) "certain special cases" which (ii) do not conflict with normal exploitation of the work, and (iii) do not unreasonably prejudice the legitimate interests of the right holder. The Panel first applied this test in the case *United States-Section 110(5) of the U.S. Copyright Act*. Since the wording of Article 13 has its roots in Article 9:2 of the Berne Convention, the Panel emphasized that the "preparatory works of Article 9(2) . . . and its application in practice may be of contextual relevance in interpreting Article 13 of the TRIPs Agreement." By applying the above three-prong test to the provisions of the U.S. statute at issue, it held that the exemption in U.S. copyright law from copyright liability for business establishments not exceeding a specified size to transmit or retransmit television or radio broadcasts of non-dramatic musical works failed the first criterion, since too many retail establishments were covered by the exemption to constitute only "certain special cases." However, the Panel found that the home-style exemption, which provided a similar exemption for certain small restaurants and retail outlets using "a single receiving apparatus of a kind commonly used in private homes," satisfied all three conditions of Article 13. The Panel stressed that, in addition to the actual effect on the market, the potential effect of an exemption should be taken into consideration as well when assessing the permissibility of the exemptions. In doing so, the Panel referred to similar concepts and interpretation standards developed in past GATT/WTO dispute settlement practice. It deemed it appropriate to develop an interpretation of the legal protection of IP right holders that is compatible with the treatment of products under GATT and services/service suppliers under GATS.

In the field of neighboring rights, Article 14 grants improved protection of rights of performers, phonogram producers, and broadcasting organizations. With respect to performers, Article 14:1 sets out the protection to be granted (i.e., preventing unauthorized phonogram fixation, reproduction of such fixations, broadcasting by wireless means and communication to the public). Phonogram producers enjoy exclusive rights over the reproduction of their phonograms in Article 14:2 and exclusive rental rights under Article 14:4. Finally, Article 14:3 requires that broadcasting organizations be given the right to prohibit the fixation, reproduction of fixations, wireless re-broadcasting, and communication to the public of television broadcasts in Article 14:3. According to Article 14:6, Members may provide for conditions, limitation, exceptions and reservations to the extent permitted by the Rome Convention, principally those provided for by Articles 12, 15 and 16 of the Convention.

NOTES AND QUESTIONS

1. By way of contrast with the patent provisions of the TRIPS Agreement, the copyright section devotes little attention to the subject matter of protection — addressing computer software and compilations. The main focus of the TRIPS provisions is granting an additional form of distribution right (i.e., the rental right), and enhancing the rights of performers, producers, and broadcast organizations — the traditional beneficiaries of neighboring rights.

    From the standpoint of the copyright industries, the TRIPS Agreement was needed not so much to enhance or clarify the scope of rights, but to provide the leverage by which enforcement of these rights could be secured, particularly in developing countries.

1.   The TRIPS Agreement and Its Relationship to the Berne Convention

Article 9.1 of the TRIPS Agreement establishes the relationship between the Agreement and the Berne Convention. It obliges the member states to comply with Articles 1 through 21 of the Berne Convention. As discussed above, moral rights, however, are explicitly exempted from protection in Article 9, referring to Article 6*bis* of the Berne Convention. In the following case, *United States — Section 110(5) of the U.S. Copyright Act,* the Panel addresses, *inter alia,* the relationship between the TRIPS Agreement and the Berne Convention. In the course of its opinion, the Panel clarifies the relationship between the TRIPS and Berne provisions. It not only states that the rules of the Berne Convention "have to be read as applying to WTO Members," but also that the Berne *acquis* has been incorporated into TRIPS. It held that "the Berne Convention and the TRIPS Agreement form part of the overall framework for multilateral protection." The Panel further points out that, "if the incorporation was not intended to cover the Berne *acquis*, the TRIPS Agreement would have explicitly so provided." Generally, "one should avoid interpreting the TRIPS Agreement to mean something different than the Berne Convention except where this is explicitly provided for."

UNITED STATES—SECTION 110(5) OF THE U.S. COPYRIGHT ACT
Report of the Panel*

II. FACTUAL ASPECTS

2.1 The dispute concerns Section 110(5) of the U.S. Copyright Act of 1976, as amended by the Fairness in Music Licensing Act of 1998 ("the 1998 Amendment"), which entered into force on 26 January 1999. The provisions of Section 110(5) place limitations on the exclusive rights provided to owners of copyright in Section 106 of the Copyright Act in respect of certain performances and displays. . . .

2.4 Subparagraph (A) of Section 110(5) essentially reproduces the text of the original "homestyle" exemption contained in Section 110(5) of the Copyright Act of 1976. When Section 110(5) was amended in 1998, the homestyle exemption was moved to a new subparagraph (A) and the words "except as provided in subparagraph (B)" were added to the beginning of the text. . . .

2.9 The 1998 Amendment has added a new subparagraph (B) to Section 110(5), to which we, for the sake of brevity, hereinafter refer to as a "business" exemption. It exempts, under certain conditions, communication by an establishment of a transmission or retransmission embodying a performance or display of a nondramatic musical work intended to be received by the general public, originated by a radio or television broadcast station licensed as such by the Federal Communications Commission, or, if an audiovisual transmission, by a cable system or satellite carrier.

2.10 The beneficiaries of the business exemption are divided into two categories: establishments other than food service or drinking establishments ("retail establishments"), and food service and drinking establishments. In each category, establishments under a certain size limit are exempted, regardless of the type of equipment they use. The size limits are 2,000 gross square feet (186 m^2) for retail establishments and 3,750 gross square feet (348 m^2) for restaurants. . . .

VI. FINDINGS . . .

D. SUBSTANTIVE ASPECTS OF THE DISPUTE
1. General Considerations About the Exclusive Rights Concerned and Limitations Thereto . . .
(b) Limitations and Exceptions
(i) Introduction
6.30 A major issue in this dispute is the interpretation and application to the facts of this case of Article 13 of the TRIPS Agreement. The U.S. defense is firmly based upon it. . . .

---

* World Trade Organization, Report of the Panel, WT/DS160/R, 15 June 2000.

(iii) The minor exceptions doctrine . . .

The legal status of the minor exceptions doctrine under the TRIPS Agreement

6.60 Having concluded that the minor exceptions doctrine forms part of the "context" of, at least, Articles 11*bis* and 11 of the Berne Convention (1971) by virtue of an agreement within the meaning of Article 31(2)(a) of the Vienna Convention, which was made between the Berne Union members in connection with the conclusion of the respective amendments to that Convention, we next address the second step of our analysis outlined above. This second step deals with the question whether or not the minor exceptions doctrine has been incorporated into the TRIPS Agreement, by virtue of its Article 9.1, together with Articles 1-21 of the Berne Convention (1971) as part of the Berne *acquis*.

6.61 We note that the express wording of Article 9.1 of the TRIPS Agreement neither establishes nor excludes such incorporation into the Agreement of the minor exceptions doctrine as it applies to Articles 11, 11*bis*, 11*ter*, 13 and 14 of the Berne Convention (1971).

6.62 We have shown above that the minor exceptions doctrine forms part of the context, within the meaning of Article 31(2)(a) of the Vienna Convention, of at least Articles 11 and 11*bis* of the Berne Convention (1971). There is no indication in the wording of the TRIPS Agreement that Articles 11 and 11*bis* have been incorporated into the TRIPS Agreement by its Article 9.1 without bringing with them the possibility of providing minor exceptions to the respective exclusive rights. If that incorporation should have covered only the text of Articles 1–21 of the Berne Convention (1971), but not the entire Berne *acquis* relating to these articles, Article 9.1 of the TRIPS Agreement would have explicitly so provided.

6.63 Thus we conclude that, in the absence of any express exclusion in Article 9.1 of the TRIPS Agreement, the incorporation of Articles 11 and 11*bis* of the Berne Convention (1971) into the Agreement includes the entire *acquis* of these provisions, including the possibility of providing minor exceptions to the respective exclusive rights.

6.64 We find confirmation of our interpretation in certain references to the minor exceptions doctrine in the documentation from the GATT Uruguay Round negotiations on the TRIPS Agreement. . . .

6.66 In the area of copyright, the Berne Convention and the TRIPS Agreement form the overall framework for multilateral protection. Most WTO Members are also parties to the Berne Convention. We recall that it is a general principle of interpretation to adopt the meaning that reconciles the texts of different treaties and avoids a conflict between them. Accordingly, one should avoid interpreting the TRIPS Agreement to mean something different than the Berne Convention except where this is explicitly provided for. This principle is in conformity with the public international law presumption against conflicts, which has been applied by WTO panels and the Appellate Body in a number of cases. We believe that our interpretation of the legal status of the minor exceptions doctrine under the TRIPS Agreement is consistent with these general principles. . . .

(vi) Summary of limitations and exceptions

6.92 In the light of the foregoing analysis, we conclude that the context of Articles 11 and 11*bis* of the Berne Convention (1971) comprises, within the meaning of Article 31(2)(a) of the Vienna Convention, the possibility of providing minor exceptions to the exclusive rights in question. This minor exceptions doctrine has been incorporated into the TRIPS Agreement, by virtue of its Article 9.1, together with these provisions of the Berne Convention (1971). Therefore, the doctrine is relevant as forming part of the context of Articles 11(1)(ii) and 11*bis*(1)(iii) of the Berne Convention (1971) as incorporated into the TRIPS Agreement.

6.93 As regards the scope of permissible limitations and exceptions under the minor exceptions doctrine, we conclude that the doctrine is primarily concerned with de minimis use, but that otherwise its application is not limited to the examples contained in the reports of the Berne Convention revision conferences held in Brussels and Stockholm, to exclusively non-commercial uses or to exceptions in national legislation that existed prior to 1967. However, we note that the reports of the Brussels and Stockholm Conferences are inconclusive about the precise scope of exceptions that can be provided in national legislation.

6.94 We conclude that Article 13 of the TRIPS Agreement applies to Articles 11*bis*(1)(iii) and 11(1)(ii) of the Berne Convention (1971) as incorporated into the TRIPS Agreement, given that neither the express wording nor the context of Article 13 or any other provision of the TRIPS Agreement supports the interpretation that the scope of application of Article 13 is limited to the exclusive rights newly introduced under the TRIPS Agreement. . . .

2. The Three Criteria Test under Article 13 of the TRIPS Agreement
(a) General introduction
6.97 Article 13 of the TRIPS Agreement requires that limitations and exceptions to exclusive rights (1) be confined to certain special cases, (2) do not conflict with a normal exploitation of the work, and (3) do not unreasonably prejudice the legitimate interests of the right holder. The principle of effective treaty interpretation requires us to give a distinct meaning to each of the three conditions and to avoid a reading that could reduce any of the conditions to "redundancy or inutility." The three conditions apply on a cumulative basis, each being a separate and independent requirement that must be satisfied. Failure to comply with any one of the three conditions results in the Article 13 exception being disallowed. Both parties agree on the cumulative nature of the three conditions. The Panel shares their view. It may be noted at the outset that Article 13 cannot have more than a narrow or limited operation. Its tenor, consistent as it is with the provisions of Article 9(2) of the Berne Convention (1971), discloses that it was not intended to provide for exceptions or limitations except for those of a limited nature. The narrow sphere of its operation will emerge from our discussion and application of its provisions in the paragraphs which follow. . . .

(c) "Not conflict with a normal exploitation of the work"
(i) General interpretative analysis . . .
6.173 We agree with the European Communities that whether a limitation or an exception conflicts with a normal exploitation of a work should be judged for each exclusive right individually. We recall that this dispute primarily concerns the exclusive right under Article 11*bis*(1)(iii) of the Berne Convention (1971) as incorporated into the TRIPS Agreement, but also the exclusive right under Article 11(1)(ii). In our view, normal exploitation would presuppose the possibility for right holders to exercise separately all three exclusive rights guaranteed under the three subparagraphs of Article 11*bis*(1), as well as the

rights conferred by other provisions, such as Article 11, of the Berne Convention (1971). If it were permissible to limit by a statutory exemption the exploitation of the right conferred by the third subparagraph of Article 11*bis*(1) simply because, in practice, the exploitation of the rights conferred by the first and second subparagraphs of Article 11*bis*(1) would generate the lion's share of royalty revenue, the "normal exploitation" of each of the three rights conferred separately under Article 11*bis*(1) would be undermined.

6.174 An individual analysis of the second condition for each exclusive right conferred by copyright is in line with the GATT/WTO dispute settlement practice. One panel found that GATT non-discrimination clauses do not permit balancing more favourable treatment under some procedure against a less favourable treatment under others. As another panel put it, an element of more favourable treatment would only be relevant if it would always accompany and offset an element of differential treatment causing less favourable treatment. While these cases involved the GATT non-discrimination clauses, we believe that the general principle embodied therein is mutatis mutandis relevant to the issue at hand.

6.175 We also note that the amplification of broadcast music will occur in establishments such as bars, restaurants and retail stores for the commercial benefit of the owner of the establishment. Both parties agree on the commercial nature of playing music even when customers are not directly charged for it. It may be that the amount yielded from any royalty payable as a consequence of this exploitation of the work will not be very great if one looks at the matter in the context of single establishments. But it is the accumulation of establishments which counts. . . .

6.176 That leaves us with the question of how to determine whether a particular use constitutes a normal exploitation of the exclusive rights provided under Articles 11*bis*(1)(iii) and 11(1)(ii) of the Berne Convention (1971). . . .

6.183 We believe that an exception or limitation to an exclusive right in domestic legislation rises to the level of a conflict with a normal exploitation of the work (i.e., the copyright or rather the whole bundle of exclusive rights conferred by the ownership of the copyright), if uses, that in principle are covered by that right but exempted under the exception or limitation, enter into economic competition with the ways that right holders normally extract economic value from that right to the work (i.e., the copyright) and thereby deprive them of significant or tangible commercial gains.

6.184 In developing a benchmark for defining the normative connotation of normal exploitation, we recall the European Communities' emphasis on the potential impact of an exception rather than on its actual effect on the market at a given point in time, given that, in its view, it is the potential effect that determines the market conditions.

6.185 We note that a consideration of both actual and potential effects when assessing the permissibility of the exemptions would be consistent with similar concepts and interpretation standards as developed in the past GATT/WTO dispute settlement practice. . . . Given that the agreements covered by the WTO form a single, integrated legal system, we deem it appropriate to develop interpretations of the legal protection conferred on intellectual property right holders under the TRIPS Agreement which are not incompatible with the treatment conferred to products under the GATT, or in respect of services and service suppliers under the GATS, in the light of pertinent dispute settlement practice.

6.186 Therefore, in respect of the exclusive rights related to musical works, we consider that normal exploitation of such works is not only affected by those who actually use them without an authorization by the right holders due to an exception or limitation, but also by those who may be induced by it to do so at any time without having to obtain a licence from the right holders or the CMOs representing them. Thus we need to take into account those whose use of musical works is free as a result of the exemptions, and also those who may choose to start using broadcast music once its use becomes free of charge.

6.187 We base our appraisal of the actual and potential effects on the commercial and technological conditions that prevail in the market currently or in the near future. What is a normal exploitation in the market-place may evolve as a result of technological developments or changing consumer pre-ferences. Thus, while we do not wish to speculate on future developments, we need to consider the actual and potential effects of the exemptions in question in the current market and technological environment.

6.188 We do acknowledge that the extent of exercise or non-exercise of exclusive rights by right holders at a given point in time is of great relevance for assessing what is the normal exploitation with respect to a particular exclusive right in a particular market. However, in certain circumstances, current licensing practices may not provide a sufficient guideline for assessing the potential impact of an exception or limitation on normal exploitation. For example, where a particular use of works is not covered by the exclusive rights conferred in the law of a jurisdiction, the fact that the right holders do not license such use in that jurisdiction cannot be considered indicative of what constitutes normal exploitation. The same would be true in a situation where, due to lack of effective or affordable means of enforcement, right holders may not find it worthwhile or practical to exercise their rights.

6.189 Both parties are of the view that the "normalcy" of a form of exploi-tation should be analysed primarily by reference to the market of the WTO Member whose measure is in dispute, i.e., the U.S. market in this dispute. The European Communities is also of the view that comparative references to other countries with a similar level of socio-economic development could be relevant to corroborate or contradict data from the country primarily concerned. We note that while the WTO Members are free to choose the method of imple-mentation, the minimum standards of protection are the same for all of them. In the present case it is enough for our purposes to take account of the specific conditions applying in the U.S. market in assessing whether the measure in question conflicts with a normal exploitation in that market, or whether the measure meets the other conditions of Article 13. . . .

[Subsequently, the Panel applied the three conditions contained in Article 13 of the TRIPS Agreement to the exemptions as set forth in Section 110(5) of the U.S. Copyright Act. The Panel held that the homestyle exemption met these requirements, unlike the business exemption, which was therefore considered inconsistent with Articles 11*bis*(1)(iii) and 11(1)(ii) of the Berne Convention (1971) as incorporated into the TRIPS Agreement by Article 9.1 of that Agreement.]

––––––––––––

The following case decided by a WTO Panel in 2009 essentially concerns enforcement of intellectual property rights and will be discussed in Chapter 6. However, the case also entails issues pertaining to the protection of copyright under the TRIPS Agreement and the Berne Convention. The Copyright Law of the People's Republic of China essentially exempted works not authorized for circulation by government authorities from copyright protection. The first sentence of Article 4 of the Chinese law provided that "[w]orks the publication or distribution of which is prohibited by law shall not be protected by this Law."

CHINA — MEASURES AFFECTING THE PROTECTION AND ENFORCEMENT OF INTELLECTUAL PROPERTY RIGHTS

Report of the Panel WT/DS362/R (26 January 2009)*

CLAIM UNDER ARTICLE 5(1) OF THE BERNE CONVENTION (1971), AS INCORPORATED BY ARTICLE 9.1 OF THE TRIPS AGREEMENT

MAIN ARGUMENTS OF THE PARTIES

7.16. The United States claims that Article 4(1) of China's Copyright Law denies the protection of the Copyright Law to certain categories of works, and refers to the text of that sentence. The United States recalls that China, during a review of its legislation in the Council for TRIPS in 2002, explained that this sentence referred to works of which the publication or distribution was prohibited by such laws and regulations as the Criminal Law, the Regulation on the Administration of Publishing Industry, the Regulation on the Administration of Broadcasting, the Regulation on the Administration of Audiovisual Products, the Regulation on the Administration of Films and the Regulations on the Administration of Telecommunication. The United States gives examples of four regulations that prohibit the publication or distribution of works under various circumstances. The United States claims that Article 4(1) of China's Copyright Law denies to the authors of works "the publication or distribution of which is prohibited by law" the broad set of rights enumerated in Article 10 of the Copyright Law, which largely encompasses the rights contemplated by the provisions of the Berne Convention (1971). Nor do authors of works denied protection of the Copyright Law benefit from the remedies specified in Articles 46 and 47 of the Copyright Law. Consequently, the authors of such works do not enjoy the minimum rights that are "specially granted" by the Berne Convention, inconsistently with Article 5(1) of that Convention. The United States submitted more detailed arguments with respect to content review in relation to Article 5(2) of the Berne Convention (1971) . . . .

7.17 China responds that copyright vests upon creation and is independent of publication. Article 2 of the Copyright Law grants full copyright protection by expressly incorporating into Chinese law the rights conferred under international agreements, including the Berne Convention and the TRIPS Agreement. In contrast, Article 4(1) of the Copyright Law is extremely limited in scope. China, like many other countries in the world, bans from publication and dissemination such works as those that consist entirely of unconstitutional or immoral content. Article 4(1) simply provides that such a work shall not be protected by the Copyright Law. China argued in its first written submission that the application of Article 4(1) was not dependent on content review or any other regulatory regime related to publication and that the only result of a finding of prohibited content in that process was a denial of authority to

_____

* Footnotes omitted.

publish, not a denial of copyright. Specifically, China argued that works that fail content review were not denied copyright protection. Article 17 of the Berne Convention (1971) subjects to the sovereign power of governments all of the rights otherwise granted by that Convention.

> . . .

CONSIDERATION BY THE PANEL

Construction of the Measure at Issue

7.28 The Panel notes that this claim challenges China's Copyright Law, in particular Article 4(1), not as it has been applied in any particular instance but "as such." The parties have disagreed on the proper interpretation of that measure since shortly after the first substantive meeting. Therefore, the Panel is obliged, in accordance with its mandate, to make an objective assessment of the meaning of the relevant provisions of that measure. In this context, the Panel is mindful that, objectively, a Member is normally well-placed to explain the meaning of its own law. However, in the context of a dispute, to the extent that either party advances a particular interpretation of a provision of the measure at issue, it bears the burden of proof that its interpretation is correct. The Panel emphasizes that it examines the measure solely for the purpose of determining its conformity with China's obligations under the TRIPS Agreement.

7.29 The United States claims that Article 4(1) of the Copyright Law on its face denies immediate, automatic protection to certain works of creative authorship.

7.30 China responds that this claim is based on the "mistaken view" that copyright protection in China is contingent upon successful completion of content review. In the course of addressing the issue of when copyright vests under Chinese law, China acknowledged that Article 4(1) of the Copyright Law denies protection to certain works due to their content.

7.31 The United States stated at the first substantive meeting that, in view of that acknowledgement, China appeared simply to concede that Article 4 of the Copyright Law was inconsistent with China's obligations under the TRIPS Agreement. Canada and the European Communities, as third parties, took the same view. Argentina considered that the text of Article 4 was straightforward.

7.32 After that meeting, China clarified the terms of its earlier acknowledgement. It clarified that Article 4(1) denies "copyright protection" in the sense of enforcement but does not disturb "copyright."

7.33 The United States dismissed China's clarification as an "artificial distinction."

> . . .

[Following analysis of the provisions of the Copyright Law resolving arguments concerning interpretation of Chinese and English translations, the panel addresses pertinent provisions of the TRIPS Agreement and the Berne Convention:]

ARTICLE 5(1) OF THE BERNE CONVENTION (1971), AS INCORPORATED BY ARTICLE 9.1 OF THE TRIPS AGREEMENT

7.104 This claim is made under Article 9.1 of the TRIPS Agreement, insofar as it incorporates Article 5(1) of the Berne Convention (1971). Article 9.1 of the TRIPS Agreement provides as follows:

"Members shall comply with Articles 1 through 21 of the Berne Convention (1971) and the Appendix thereto. However, Members shall not have rights or obligations under this Agreement in respect of the rights conferred under Article 6*bis* of that Convention or of the rights derived therefrom."

7.105 The United States and China are both WTO Members and, accordingly, both are bound by the TRIPS Agreement, including the incorporated provisions of the Berne Convention (1971). The provisions of the Berne Convention (1971) incorporated by Article 9.1 of the TRIPS Agreement include Article 5(1) of that Convention, which provides as follows:

"(1) Authors shall enjoy, in respect of works for which they are protected under this Convention, in countries of the Union other than the country of origin, the rights which their respective laws do now or may hereafter grant to their nationals, as well as the rights specially granted by this Convention."

7.106 Article 5(1) of the Berne Convention (1971) provides for the enjoyment of two overlapping sets of rights that have been described as "the twin pillars on which protection under the Convention rests." First, there are "the rights which their respective laws do now or may hereafter grant to their nationals." This is a national treatment obligation. The request for establishment of a panel included a claim under this part of Article 5(1) with respect to the Copyright Law in conjunction with certain other measures . . . , but this claim was not pursued.

7.107 Second, there are "the rights specially granted by this Convention." This term is not defined. However, Article 5(1) refers to rights that authors shall enjoy in respect of works. Articles 6*bis*, 8, 9, 11, 11*bis*, 11*ter*, 12, 14, 14*bis* and 14*ter* all provide for such rights. Nevertheless, the incorporation of provisions of the Berne Convention (1971), including Article 5, is subject to the terms of Article 9.1 of the TRIPS Agreement (quoted at paragraph 7.104 above). Therefore, "the rights specially granted by this Convention" as used in Article 5(1) of that Convention, as incorporated by Article 9.1 of the TRIPS Agreement, do not include the rights referred to in Article 6*bis* of the Berne Convention (1971). This Report refers to these rights in that sense.

7.108 The United States' claim relates to these rights, as a group. It makes a separate claim with respect to Article 5(2) of the Berne Convention (1971), which the Panel does not consider in this sub-section of this Report.

7.109 China submits that it has implemented Article 5(1) of the Berne Convention (1971). It offers no defence based on the terms of that Article but rather refers to Article 17 of the Berne Convention (1971), which the Panel addresses at paragraphs 7.120 to 7.139 below.

7.110 The Panel notes that the "rights specially granted" by the Berne Convention (1971), as incorporated by the TRIPS Agreement, include the exclusive right of making and of authorizing translation of works (in Article 8) and the exclusive right of authorizing reproduction of works (in Article 9), to name but the first two substantive rights.

7.111 As regards China's implementation of the "rights specially granted" by the Berne Convention (1971), the United States refers to the rights enumerated in Article 10 of the Copyright Law, as well as Articles 46 and 47 of the same Law. It does not challenge any of these particular Articles of the Copyright Law.

7.112 China agrees that it grants to authors all the substantive protections of the Berne Convention, in addition to others, through Article 10 of the

Copyright Law. It submits that Article 10 of the Copyright Law fully complies with all Berne Convention requirements.

7.113 The Panel notes that many of the rights listed in subparagraphs (5) to (17) of the first paragraph of Article 10 of the Copyright Law provide for rights specially granted by the Berne Convention (1971), that the second paragraph of Article 10 provides that copyright owners may authorize others' exercise of these economic rights, and that these rights appear to be exclusive. . . . Therefore, the Panel finds that it is Article 10 of the Copyright Law that implements rights specially granted by the Berne Convention (1971).

7.114 The Panel recalls its finding . . . that Article 4(1) of the Copyright Law denies the protection of Article 10 to certain works, including those of WTO Member nationals, as the United States claims. The Panel observes that no party alleges that the denial of protection under Article 4(1) of the Copyright Law is permitted by any of the exceptions available with respect to certain specific rights under Articles 9(2), 10 or 10*bis* of the Berne Convention (1971). Nor does any party allege that the denial of protection under Article 4(1) of the Copyright Law is permitted by the exceptions provision in Article 13 of the TRIPS Agreement.

7.115 The Panel notes that both sets of rights under Article 5(1) of the Berne Convention (1971) relate to "works" for which authors are protected under that Convention. The categories of "works" in respect of which authors shall enjoy the rights specially granted by the Convention vary according to the terms of each Article granting the relevant right. For example, the rights of reproduction (Article 9) and of broadcasting (Article 11*bis*) are granted to authors of "literary and artistic works." That expression is defined, in a non-exhaustive manner, in Article 2(1) of the Berne Convention (1971).

7.116 The Panel recalls its finding . . . that the class of works denied protection under Article 4(1) of the Copyright Law includes works that have failed content review and, to the extent that they constitute copyright works, the deleted portions of works edited to satisfy content review. The Panel also recalls its findings . . . regarding the meaning of the word "works" as used in the Copyright Law, in particular in Article 4(1). No party has disputed that the "works" to which the Copyright Law, in particular Article 4(1), applies include at least some, if not all, the categories of works falling within the definition of "literary and artistic works" in Article 2(1) of the Berne Convention (1971). It is not disputed that the "works" to which Article 4(1) of China's Copyright Law applies are more extensive than those for which protection may be refused or limited under other provisions of Article 2, and under Article 2*bis*, of the Berne Convention (1971).

7.117 For the above reasons, the Panel finds that the Copyright Law is sufficiently clear on its face for the United States to have established that the Copyright Law, specifically Article 4(1), is inconsistent with Article 5(1) of the Berne Convention (1971), as incorporated by Article 9.1 of the TRIPS Agreement. This finding is subject to the Panel's consideration of Article 17 of the Berne Convention (1971), set out below.

7.118 The Panel recalls its finding at . . . and confirms that this conclusion does not apply to works never submitted for content review in China, works awaiting the results of content review in China and the unedited versions of works for which an edited version has been approved for distribution in China. However, the Panel recognizes that the potential denial of copyright protection, in the absence of a determination by the content review authorities, implies uncertainty with respect to works that do not satisfy the content criteria prior to a determination under Article 4(1) of the Copyright Law, with the consequent impact on enjoyment of rights described above. Therefore, the Panel reiterates for the record the firm position of China taken in these proceedings that:

> "Copyright vests at the time that a work is created, and is not contingent on publication. Unpublished works are protected, foreign works not yet released in the Chinese market are protected, and works never released in the Chinese market are protected."; and
>
> "Works that are unreviewed are decidedly not 'prohibited by law.'"

7.719 China has an international obligation to protect copyright in such works in accordance with Article 5(1) of the Berne Convention (1971), as incorporated by Article 9.1 of the TRIPS Agreement.

Article 17 of the Berne Convention (1971) as Incorporated by Article 9.1 of the TRIPS Agreement

7.120 China raises a defence under Article 17 of the Berne Convention (1971), as incorporated by Article 9.1 of the TRIPS Agreement. China submits that all rights granted to authors under the Berne Convention (1971) are limited by Article 17 of that Convention, that Article 17 is not an exhaustive codification of the sovereign right to censor and that Article 17 is drafted using very expansive language "that effectively denies WTO jurisdiction in this area."

7.121 The United States responds that Article 17 of the Berne Convention (1971) does not authorize a content review system that denies all enforceable copyright protection to all works that have not been approved for publication or distribution.

7.122 The Panel recalls that Article 9.1 of the TRIPS Agreement, quoted at paragraph 7.104 above, incorporates Article 17 of the Berne Convention (1971). Article 17 of the Berne Convention (1971) provides as follows:

> "The provisions of this Convention cannot in any way affect the right of the Government of each country of the Union to permit, to control, or to prohibit, by legislation or regulation, the circulation, presentation, or exhibition of any work or production in regard to which the competent authority may find it necessary to exercise that right."

7.123 "The provisions of this Convention" as referred to in Article 17 include Article 5(1) of the Berne Convention (1971).

7.124 The parties agree that Article 17 confirms that governments have certain rights to control the exploitation of works. They do not agree as to whether those rights include a denial of all copyright protection with respect to particular works.

7.125 The Panel observes that the terms of Article 17 include certain broad phrases, notably "cannot in any way affect" and "any work or production." The use of the words "any work" (although it is slightly different in the French text) confirms that the subject-matter dealt with by Article 17 is the same as that addressed by the other substantive provisions of the Convention. However, these phrases are not used in isolation but refer to the right of a government to "permit, to control, or to prohibit . . . the circulation, presentation, or exhibition" of any work or production.

7.126 The right of a government "to control, or to prohibit" the "circulation, presentation, or exhibition" of any work or production clearly includes censorship for reasons of public order. Both China and the United States referred to the records of the diplomatic conferences of the Berne Convention, opinions in the academic literature and (in the case of China) to the WIPO Guide to the Berne Convention, that explained that Article 17 relates mainly to censorship and public order.

7.127 The Panel accepts that the three terms "circulation, presentation, or exhibition" are not necessarily an exhaustive list of the forms of exploitation of works covered by Article 17. However, a noticeable feature of these three terms is that they do not correspond to the terms used to define the substantive rights granted by the Berne Convention (1971), although they may be included within some of those rights or they may refer to acts incidental to the exercise of some of those rights. The word "exhibition" is not even used in the provisions setting out the substantive rights granted by the Convention. Therefore, it cannot be inferred that Article 17 authorizes the denial of all copyright protection in any work.

7.128 The Panel appreciates that the position may be somewhat different under Article 10 of China's Copyright Law. Article 10 of the Copyright Law grants in subparagraph (6) "the right of distribution", in subparagraph (8) "the right of exhibition," and in subparagraph (10) "the right of presentation," which may correspond to the "circulation, presentation, or exhibition" of any work in Article 17 of the Berne Convention (1971). Article 10 of the Copyright Law also grants in subparagraph (1) "the right of publication," as well as the "right of distribution," both of which appear to be directly contrary to a prohibition of the publication and/or dissemination of a work due to illegal content, as referenced in Article 4(1) of the Copyright Law. To the extent that Article 10 of the Copyright Law might provide rights additional to, or broader than, those specially granted by the Berne Convention (1971), as incorporated in the TRIPS Agreement and, hence, that Article 4(1) of that Law might deny such rights, the Panel makes no finding.

7.129 The Panel does note that the *second* sentence of Article 4 of the Copyright Law (that is not the subject of the claim in this dispute) may already address China's public policy concerns with respect to some of these rights. The second sentence of Article 4 provides as follows:

> "Copyright owners, in exercising their copyright, shall not violate the Constitution or laws or prejudice the public interests."

7.130 This provision does not deny copyright protection but, as China acknowledges, obliges copyright owners and authorized parties to respect the law in the exercise of their rights. In contrast, the first sentence of Article 4 of the Copyright Law denies all copyright protection with respect to particular works.

7.131 China draws the Panel's attention to the WIPO Guide to the Berne Convention, which states as follows regarding Article 17 of the Berne Convention (1971):

> "It covers the right of governments to take the necessary steps to maintain public order. On this point, the sovereignty of member countries is not affected

by the rights given by the Convention. Authors may exercise their rights only if that exercise does not conflict with public order. The former must give way to the latter. The Article therefore gives Union countries certain powers to control."

7.132 The Panel agrees with this interpretation. A government's right to permit, to control, or to prohibit the circulation, presentation, or exhibition of a work may interfere with the exercise of certain rights with respect to a protected work by the copyright owner or a third party authorized by the copyright owner. However, there is no reason to suppose that censorship will eliminate those rights entirely with respect to a particular work.

7.133 With respect to those rights that are granted by the Berne Convention (1971), China is unable to explain why Article 4(1) of its Copyright Law provides for the complete denial of their protection with respect to particular works. Without prejudice to the range of rights that are granted by the Berne Convention (1971), it suffices to note that they are mostly exclusive rights of authorizing certain acts with respect to protected works. An exclusive right of authorizing necessarily entails the right to prevent others from carrying out the relevant acts with respect to protected works. China is unable to explain why censorship interferes with copyright owners' rights to prevent third parties from exploiting prohibited works.

7.134 China argues that such copyright protection is a "legal and material nullity," as economic rights are pre-empted by public prohibition. It also argues that copyright enforcement is meaningless in this context. China asks the Panel to note that Article 4(1) of the Copyright Law is an exceedingly narrow provision of law with negligible implications in the marketplace and in terms of any nullification or impairment of benefits to Members.

7.135 The Panel notes that copyright and government censorship address different rights and interests. Copyright protects private rights, as reflected in the fourth recital of the preamble to the TRIPS Agreement, whilst government censorship addresses public interests.

7.136 In response to a question from the Panel, China indicated that it "will always enforce copyrights against infringing edited versions, even when there is no edited version authorized by the author." It did not explain how this was possible under its law. In response to another question from the Panel, China indicated that if an unprotected, prohibited work later becomes legal, it will protect copyright in the work going forward. This might require a new court or NCAC determination but, in China's view, such a requirement does not constitute a formality under Article 5(2) of the Berne Convention (1971). In any event, the Panel recalls that Article 4(1) of the Copyright Law produces commercial uncertainty prior to a determination that a work is prohibited.

7.137 China maintains that public censorship renders private enforcement unnecessary, that it enforces prohibitions on content seriously, and that this removes banned content from the public domain more securely than would be possible through copyright enforcement. The Panel notes that these assertions, even if they were relevant, are not substantiated.

7.138 The Panel also recalls that if a measure infringes China's obligations under a covered agreement, in accordance with Article 3.8 of the DSU, this is considered prima facie to constitute a case of nullification or impairment. Even if the measure at issue has had no actual impact on foreign works to date, it has a *potential* impact on works of WTO Member nationals.

7.139 For the above reasons, the Panel confirms its finding . . . and concludes that, notwithstanding China's rights recognized in Article 17 of the Berne Convention (1971), the Copyright Law, specifically Article 4(1), is inconsistent with Article 5(1) of the Berne Convention (1971), as incorporated by Article 9.1 of the TRIPS Agreement.

NOTES AND QUESTIONS

1. We now have WTO dispute settlement panel decisions addressing the scope of exceptions in the fields of patent (*Canada — Generic Pharmaceuticals, supra* Chapter 2), trademark (*EC — Geographical Indications, supra* Chapter 3) and copyright (*U.S. — Copyright Act, China — Measures Affecting the Protection and Enforcement of Intellectual Property Rights, supra*). It is of some interest that none of these panel decisions were appealed to the Appellate Body, even though most WTO dispute settlement decisions are appealed and the Appellate Body often disagrees with the panel on issues of legal doctrine (even if, less frequently, on the practical outcome). What do you think accounts for the absence of appeals on decisions relating to IP exceptions? Are governments reluctant to request the "last word" on the scope of exceptions from the Appellate Body? Is it just a coincidence that in these three cases both governments were satisfied with the outcome? Could it be that the inconsistencies of domestic law with international law are more obvious than in other cases?

2. The WTO dispute settlement system is effectively determining the international scope of permissible exceptions in copyright law. Does the WTO adequately replicate national constitutional systems and courts such that you are comfortable with allocating this decision making "upward" to the global level of judicial governance?

3. What can we learn from *China — Measures Affecting the Protection and Enforcement of Intellectual Property Rights* for the trade and human rights debate? While the authorization of content cannot exclude copyright protection, it nevertheless inhibits the circulation of copyright protected material. How does that relate to freedom of expression and freedom of information? The same problem arose in relation to authorization exclusively reserved to state-controlled enterprises of audiovisual services in *China — Measures Affecting Trading Rights and Distribution Services and Certain Publications and Audiovisual Entertainment Products*, Report by the Appellate Body, WT/DS 363/AR/R (21 December 2009). In this case, the Appellate Body found that authorization regarding public morals exclusively granted to state-owned companies discriminates against foreign-controlled operators. It fails the necessity test and is inconsistent with WTO law.

C. *The WIPO Copyright Treaty*

The TRIPS Agreement negotiations focused on "trade-related" aspects of IPRs. It was not until somewhat late in the TRIPS negotiations (which formally commenced in 1986) that it became apparent that development of the Internet and other digital media might play a significant role in international commerce. In this regard, the TRIPS Agreement was a step behind developments in the global economic arena even before the proverbial ink had dried. One step following the TRIPS Agreement would be the negotiation of new rules for the digital environment. The first set of these negotiations took place within WIPO.

1. Negotiation

In the following excerpt, Pam Samuelson describes and analyzes the final stage of negotiation of the WIPO Copyright Treaty (WCT) in 1996.

THE U.S. DIGITAL AGENDA AT WIPO
Pamela Samuelson*

I. INTRODUCTION

In December 1996, the World Intellectual Property Organization (WIPO) hosted a diplomatic conference in Geneva to consider three proposals to update world intellectual property law. The conferees considered draft treaties to revise treatment of copyright issues, legal protection for sound recordings, and legal protection for the contents of databases. Each contained provisions intended to respond to challenges that global digital networks pose for intellectual property law. . . .

The digital agenda that Clinton administration officials pursued in Geneva was almost identical to the digital agenda they had put before the U.S. Congress during roughly the same time period. Notwithstanding the fact that this digital agenda had proven so controversial in the U.S. Congress that the bills to implement it were not even reported out of committee, Clinton administration officials persisted in promoting these proposals in Geneva and pressing for an early diplomatic conference to adopt them. For a time, it appeared that administration officials might be able to get in Geneva what they could not get from the U.S. Congress, for the draft treaties published by WIPO in late August 1996 contained language that, if adopted without amendment at the diplomatic conference in December, would have substantially implemented the U.S. digital agenda, albeit with some European gloss. Had this effort succeeded in Geneva, Clinton administration officials would almost certainly have then argued to Congress that ratification of the treaties was necessary to confirm U.S. leadership in the world intellectual property community and to promote the interests of U.S. copyright industries in the world market for information products and services. . . .

III. COMPONENTS OF THE U.S. DIGITAL AGENDA AND HOW THEY FARED AT WIPO

The U.S. White Paper's digital agenda aimed to:

1. give copyright owners control over every use of copyrighted works in digital form by interpreting existing law as being violated whenever users make

* 37 VA. J. INT'L L. 369 (1997).

even temporary reproductions of works in the random access memories of their computers;

2. give copyright owners control over every transmission of works in digital form by amending the copyright statute so that digital transmissions will be regarded as distributions of copies to the public;

3. eliminate fair-use rights whenever a use might be licensed . . . ;

4. deprive the public of the "first sale" rights it has long enjoyed in the print world . . . because the White Paper treats electronic forwarding as a violation of both the reproduction and distribution rights of copyright law;

5. attach copyright management information to digital copies of a work, ensuring that publishers can track every use made of digital copies and trace where each copy resides on the network and what is being done with it at any time;

6. protect every work technologically (by encryption, for example) and make illegal any attempt to circumvent that protection; [and]

7. force online service providers to become copyright police. . . .

The only new element in the U.S. digital agenda at WIPO, as compared with the digital agenda reflected in the White Paper, was a late-added proposal by the U.S. delegation calling for a treaty to create a new form of legal protection for the contents of databases. U.S. officials submitted this in reaction to a European proposal that they apparently thought needed improvement.

. . . [W]e will see that the White Paper's high-protectionist digital agenda met with limited favor at the diplomatic conference, even though it had been substantially embodied in the draft treaties considered at that conference.

A. TEMPORARY COPIES AS REPRODUCTIONS

Echoing the White Paper's views on U.S. copyright law, a key component of the U.S. digital agenda at WIPO was the establishment of an international right in copyright owners to control temporary copies of their works in computer memory. If successful, adoption of this norm would not only lay the groundwork for giving copyright owners the right to control every access, viewing, and use of protected works in digital form; it would also help accomplish another goal set forth in the White Paper: to make intermediate institutions, such as online service providers, strictly liable for user infringements. This would, conveniently for copyright industries, have placed the bulk of the responsibility for enforcing copyright interests on these intermediate institutions.

Although representatives of the European Union (E.U.) strongly supported this aspect of the U.S. digital agenda, neither U.S. nor E.U. delegations initially submitted draft treaty language to implement this agenda item. . . .

However, Chairman Liedes decided to include a provision on temporary copying in the draft treaty he prepared for consideration at the diplomatic conference. Article 7(1) of the draft copyright treaty provided:

> The exclusive right accorded to authors of literary and artistic works in Article 9(1) of the Berne Convention of authorizing the reproduction of their works shall include direct and indirect reproduction of their works, whether permanent or temporary, in any manner or form.

Commentary on this provision explained that such a treaty provision was desirable because diverse opinions existed in the international community about whether ephemeral copies were reproductions of copyrighted works within the meaning of article 9(1) of the Berne Convention. Because "some relevant uses may, now or in the future, become totally based on a temporary reproduction," the commentary went on to say that the right to control temporary copies was of such importance that a rule on it "should be in fair and reasonable harmony all over the world."

Instead of leaving to member states the task of articulating circumstances in which temporary copies could reasonably be privileged in national laws, the draft treaty proposed a special limitation provision as article 7(2):

> Subject to the provisions of Article 9(2) of the Berne Convention, it shall be a matter for legislation in Contracting Parties to limit the right of reproduction in cases where a temporary reproduction has the sole purpose of making the work perceptible or where the reproduction is of a transient or incidental nature, provided that such reproduction takes place in the course of use of the work that is authorized by the author or permitted by law. . . .

Following the eruption of dissatisfaction with the Chairman's redraft, negotiations over the copyright treaty went into closed sessions. Chairman Liedes must have hoped these sessions would result in a consensus provision on temporary copying. However, no such consensus was achieved. On the final day of the diplomatic conference, a motion was made and carried to delete article 7 from the copyright treaty. The WIPO Copyright Treaty, as a consequence, contains no provision on temporary copying.

There are, however, some who will argue that the WIPO Copyright Treaty should be understood as regarding temporary copies as copyright-significant acts owing to a last-minute resolution that the U.S. delegation insisted be voted on in the final hour of the diplomatic conference. Like Cinderella at the fancy ball, the diplomatic conference had to end before 12:00 a.m. on December 21, 1996. Sometime after 10:30 p.m., many hours after the text of the copyright treaty had been finalized, after the unanimously acceptable agreed-upon statements of interpretation had been voted on, at a time when nearly half of the delegates had already gone home and those who remained were near exhaustion from more than twelve hours of work that day, the U.S. delegation called for a vote on a proposed three sentence statement about digital reproductions. The U.S. agreement to the deletion of article 7 from the copyright treaty, it asserted, had been contingent on the conference's acceptance of a statement on the reproduction right.

The first sentence of the U.S. proposal affirmed that article 9 of the Berne Convention and exceptions thereto applied in the digital environment. More controversial and hotly debated was a second sentence of the U.S. proposal which read: "It is understood that the storage of a protected work in digital form in an electronic medium constitutes a reproduction within the meaning of Article 9 of the Berne Convention." In an attempt to quell questions about and budding opposition to this part of the U.S. proposal, Mihaly Ficsor, a senior WIPO official, asserted that it reflected a longstanding, well-accepted principle that could not be questioned. Yet many did question it, partly because they were unsure what the term "storage" might mean. Some did so by abstaining from the vote on this statement, and others by voting against it. Still, a majority of those in attendance at that late hour did vote in favor of this second sentence. A third sentence saying that up- and downloading of works by computer was a reproduction within the meaning of the Berne Convention was, however, voted down.

Even at the time, some delegates asserted that the U.S. resolution could not be an agreed-upon statement of interpretation of the WIPO Copyright Treaty because it did not satisfy the standards for binding treaty interpretation statements set forth in the Vienna Convention on the Law of Treaties.[17] WIPO may have wrangled internally about this question for, although the Copyright Treaty went up on the WIPO website within days of the diplomatic conference's conclusion, it was almost a month before the agreed-upon statements of interpretation to the Treaty were to be found there. When finally they were, the first two sentences of the U.S.-sponsored resolution were included as an agreed-upon statement of interpretation to article 1(4) of the treaty.

Exactly what weight and scope should be given to this statement will likely be a source of contentious debate and discussion in coming years. Commissioner Lehman and others who supported article 7 will likely regard these two statements and article 9(1) of the Berne Convention as sufficient to establish that temporary copies are reproductions that copyright owners have the right to control. Others will see in the defeat of article 7 and the "up- and downloading" part of the U.S. resolution an international repudiation of the position that temporary copying is a reproduction. The most honest thing that can be said about the temporary copying of works in computer memory is that there is no international consensus on this subject. Still, it is significant that the copyright treaty signed in Geneva does not include a provision on temporary copying given how intent the U.S. and E.U. delegations had been about getting such a treaty provision.

B. DIGITAL TRANSMISSIONS . . .

Although controversies abounded at the December 1996 diplomatic conference, the proposal to treat digital transmissions as communications to the public was not among them. The U.S. delegation apparently found this approach acceptable as long as the United States could satisfy such a treaty obligation without amending U.S. law to add another exclusive rights provision. Hence, the final treaty includes as article 8 a provision that authors of literary and artistic works shall enjoy the exclusive right of authorizing any communication to the public of their works, by wire or wireless means, including the making available to the public of their works in such a way that members of the public may access these works from a place and at a time individually chosen by them. This article contains no specific reference to digital transmissions, but will nonetheless be understood as encompassing them. . . .

C. CURTAILING USER RIGHTS

Expansion of the rights of copyright owners over temporary copies and digital transmissions would not have been complete without achievement of a third component of the U.S. digital agenda at WIPO: a substantial curtailment of national authority to limit the rights accorded to copyright owners

---

17. Vienna Convention on the Law of Treaties, opened for signature May 23, 1969, U.N. Doc. A/Conf./39/27, 8 I.L.M. 679 (entered into force Jan. 27, 1980). The argument that a mere majority resolution can serve as an agreed-upon statement of interpretation relies upon the notion that the diplomatic conference's own rules may permit resolutions supported by a bare majority as being agreed-upon statements. Such a rule had been adopted at the WIPO diplomatic conference.

(for example, by providing that a particular exclusive right could only be infringed by literal copying) or to grant exceptions to those rights for certain classes of users or classes of uses (for example, enabling veteran groups to perform dramatic works without permission).

The initial aim of the U.S. delegation was not only to prevent the adoption of new limitations and exceptions to the expanded rights that the copyright treaty would recognize, but also to call into question the viability of existing limitations and exceptions, particularly as they might apply to digital works. The principal targets of this effort were the so-called "first sale" rule, under which consumers are generally free to redistribute their own copies of a protected work, and fair use and kindred privileges and doctrines, under which private or personal copying of protected works has often found shelter. . . .

Fairly soon after the diplomatic conference got down to business, considerable support emerged for conforming the text of article 12 to that of article 13 of TRIPS, as well as for an agreed-upon statement to accompany it that would preserve existing fair use-like privileges in national laws and permit evolution of new exceptions in the digital environment. . . .

Not only was there support at the diplomatic conference for recognition of national authority to grant exceptions and limitations as a means of balancing the interests of copyright owners and the public, there was also support for making the principle of balance a fundamental purpose of the treaty by adding a new clause to the treaty's preamble. The preamble to the Chairman's original draft treaty had three parts:

> Desiring to develop and maintain the protection of the rights of authors in their literary and artistic works in a manner as effective and uniform as possible,
> Recognizing the need to introduce new international rules and clarify the interpretation of certain existing rules in order to provide adequate solutions to the questions raised by new economic, social, cultural and technological developments,
> Recognizing the profound impact of the development and convergence of information and communication technologies on the creation and use of literary and artistic works[.]

To these, the final treaty added another purpose:

> Recognizing the need to maintain a balance between the rights of authors and the larger public interest, particularly education, research and access to information, as reflected in the Berne Convention[.]

This new preamble provision represents a major development in international copyright policy.[226]

If copyright policy on an international scale had seemed to be veering away from traditional purposes such as the promotion of knowledge in the public interest and toward a solely trade-oriented set of purposes, this treaty can be seen as a timely correction in the course of international copyright policy. Though the Chairman's initial draft was consistent with a trade-based approach

---

226. Another significant, although not much heralded, aspect of the WIPO Copyright Treaty is article 2, which states: "Copyright protection extends to expressions and not to ideas, procedures, methods of operation or mathematical concepts as such." Oddly enough, the idea/expression distinction as such had not been embodied in the Berne Convention or supplemental agreements to it. Agreed-upon statements of interpretation to the WIPO Copyright Treaty make it clear that article 2's proscriptions apply to computer programs and databases.

to copyright policy, the final treaty reaffirms faith in the concept of maintaining a balance between private and public interests in copyright policymaking and of recognizing that education, research, and access to information are among the important social values that a well-formed copyright law should serve.

D. REGULATING CIRCUMVENTION TECHNOLOGIES

An important part of the U.S. digital agenda at WIPO was establishment of a new international norm to regulate technologies and services likely to be used to circumvent technological protection for copyrighted works. The electronic future envisioned in the U.S. White Paper, as well as that for which many major content providers seem to be planning, contemplates broad use of technological measures, such as encryption, to protect content in digital form. As promising as such technologies are, they too pose a problem: what one technology can do, another can generally undo. Hence, the perceived need for law to regulate infringement-enabling technologies and services.

The impetus for this provision came largely from the U.S. motion picture industry, which has for many years been keen on the idea of regulating technologies that enable infringement. Although unsuccessful in previous efforts to persuade Congress to pass a broad law to allow them to sue makers of circumvention technologies, the motion picture industry saw in the Clinton administration's National Information Infrastructure (NII) intellectual property initiative a new opportunity for getting the desired legislation. As other content owners came to understand the desirability of technological solutions to the problem of protecting digital content, the motion picture industry gained new allies to support stronger regulation of circumvention technologies and services. . . .

Article 13 of Chairman Liedes' draft copyright treaty was closely modeled on the U.S. proposal: . . .

Neither the insertion of a knowledge requirement nor the Chairman's assurances regarding latitude in national implementations sufficed to overcome serious concerns about draft article 13. Many delegates to the diplomatic conference expressed deep concerns about the implications of such regulation for the public domain and for fair use. . . .

[T]here was little support for the Chairman's proposal. Some countries, such as Korea, opposed inclusion of any anti-circumvention provision in the treaty. Others, such as Singapore, proposed a "sole purpose" or "sole intended purpose" standard for regulating circumvention technologies. Some delegations wanted an explicit statement that carved out circumvention for fair use and public domain materials. The European Union emphasized the importance of a knowledge of infringement requirement in any provision regulating devices and services possessing technology-defeating purposes.

Facing the prospect of little support for the Chairman's watered-down version of the U.S. White Paper proposal, the U.S. delegation was in the uncomfortable position of trying to find a national delegation willing to introduce a compromise provision brokered by U.S. industry groups that would simply require states to have adequate and effective legal protection against circumvention technologies and services. In the end, such a delegation was found, and the final treaty embodied this provision in article 11.

This compromise was, of course, a far cry from the provision that the United States had initially promoted. Still, it was an accomplishment to get any provision on this issue in the final treaty. The inclusion of terms like "adequate" and "effective" protection in the treaty means that U.S. firms will be able to challenge national regulations that they deem deficient.

E. PROTECTING RIGHTS MANAGEMENT INFORMATION

A fifth component of the U.S. digital agenda at WIPO was acceptance of a second unprecedented norm for an international copyright treaty, namely, an agreement to protect the integrity of copyright management information (CMI) that might be attached to digital copies of protected works. In keeping with the White Paper's proposal to amend U.S. copyright law to protect CMI from depredations by would-be pirates who might strip the CMI from distributed copies of digital content, falsify, or otherwise tamper with CMI in aid of infringing activities, the U.S. delegation to WIPO recommended a virtually identical provision to the Committee of Experts for inclusion in the WIPO copyright treaty. . . .

As with the anti-circumvention provision, Chairman Liedes modeled the draft treaty provision on rights management information on the U.S. proposal, albeit with some differences in terminology and reorganization of its structure. Subsection (1) of article 14 of the draft treaty read:

> Contracting parties shall make it unlawful for any person knowingly to perform any of the following acts:
>
> (i) to remove or alter any electronic rights management information without authority;
> (ii) to distribute, import for distribution or communicate to the public, without authority, copies of works from which electronic rights management information has been removed or altered without authority.

Subsection (2) defined "rights management information" as information which identifies the work, the author of the work, the owner of any right in the work, and any numbers or codes that represent such information, when any of these items of information are attached to a copy of a work or appear in connection with the communication of a work to the public.

The commentary accompanying this subsection stated the Chairman's expectation that criminal as well as civil penalties should be available for violations of this provision. . . .

The RMI provision of the draft treaty proved to be one of the least controversial parts of the digital agenda at WIPO. But even this limited version of the U.S. proposal was further trimmed in the course of diplomatic negotiations. Concerns had arisen that the U.S. proposal would inadvertently make illegal some alterations to RMI that presented no threat to the legitimate interests of rights holders. An alteration to RMI attached to licensed copies to correct RMI after a change in copyright ownership should not be illegal, but would have been under the Chairman's original draft. To overcome this problem, the RMI provision was amended so that alterations to RMI and distributions of copies with altered RMI would only be illegal insofar as they facilitated or concealed infringing activities.

As with the anti-circumvention provision in the WIPO Copyright Treaty, the U.S. delegation did not get exactly what it had originally sought. However, it was no small achievement to get as article 12 of the final treaty a provision that will significantly protect rights management information attached to digital copies of protected works transmitted via global networks.

F. PROTECTING THE CONTENTS OF DATABASES

A late-added component of the U.S. digital agenda at WIPO was acceptance of the U.S. proposal for an international treaty to protect investments in database development by granting database makers exclusive rights to authorize or prevent extractions and uses of database contents. . . .

Widespread criticism of the Chairman's draft database treaty caused its quick removal from the conference agenda. Consideration of the draft database treaty has, however, not merely been postponed or sent back to the Committee of Experts for further refinement; it has been taken off the table. . . .

IV. REFLECTIONS ON THE OUTCOME IN GENEVA . . .

B. MEASURES OF SUCCESS FOR THE U.S. DIGITAL AGENDA AT WIPO

Whether one judges U.S. efforts to promote a digital agenda at WIPO as a success or a failure depends on what one decides to measure. By comparison with the high-protectionist agenda reflected in the White Paper and the U.S. submissions to WIPO, one would have to say that the U.S. efforts were largely unsuccessful. The conference rejected the temporary copying proposals that had initially had U.S. support. It decided to treat digital transmissions as communications to the public, rather than as distributions of copies (which may bring with it a widened possibility for some private transmissions of works). The treaty not only preserved existing user right privileges in national laws; it recognized that new exceptions might appropriately be created. The Chairman's variant on the U.S. White Paper's anti-circumvention provision garnered almost no support. Even though the treaty contains a rights management information provision, it is watered down by comparison with what the U.S. delegation had sought. Moreover, the U.S. model for a database treaty was so objectionable that it was dropped virtually without discussion from the agenda in Geneva.

Seen from another perspective, however, the U.S. digital agenda had considerable success. It is now clear that copyright law applies in the digital environment, and that storage of protected works is a reproduction that can be controlled by copyright owners. The treaty also protects copyright owners from digital transmissions insofar as they constitute communications to the public. The treaty reaffirms the three-step test that limits national authority to adopt exceptions or limitations to certain special cases that do not conflict with a normal exploitation of the work or unreasonably prejudice the legitimate interests of the author. It also requires states to have adequate protection and effective remedies against circumvention technologies and services, and to protect rights management information from alteration and removal insofar as these conceal or facilitate infringement. Finally, WIPO is to sponsor further discussions concerning a database treaty.

The copyright treaty that emerged from the diplomatic conference was a real success for the United States in part because that treaty is actually more consistent with the letter and spirit of U.S. copyright law than the digital agenda that Commissioner Lehman initially sought to promote in Geneva.

NOTES AND QUESTIONS

1. Pam Samuelson calls attention to a provision added to the WIPO Copyright Treaty preamble at the diplomatic conference that recognizes the need to maintain a balance among interests. Why might a provision in the preamble of a treaty be important? The preamble does not create specific rights or obligations. How might it be used?

2. Keep in mind Pam Samuelson's discussion of storage in temporary memory as you read the following description of the WCT from the WIPO Intellectual Property Handbook. Are the two interpretations of the result consistent?

3. Samuelson's article does not deal with the question of exhaustion of rights (other than in the context of temporary reproductions). Yet, negotiation of the WCT illustrated — as does Article 6 of the TRIPS Agreement — that governments do not agree on an approach to the exhaustion of rights in the international context. It was once again made clear in the WCT negotiations that the subject matter remains sufficiently controversial that an attempt to find common ground might have impeded the successful conclusion of the treaty. The Chairman's drafts of the Copyright Treaty and the Performances and Phonograms Treaties included alternatives that would either have precluded international exhaustion, or reserved discretion regarding the exhaustion approach to the contracting states. The Chairman's drafts did not propose an alternative mandating international exhaustion. *See* Chairman of the Committee of Experts, Basic Proposal for the Substantive Provisions of the Treaty on Certain Questions Concerning the Protection of Literary and Artistic Works to be Considered by the Diplomatic Conference, WIPO Doc. CRNR/DC/4, Aug. 30, 1996, at art. 8). Examine Article 6(2) of the WCT and Article 8(2) and 12(2) of the Performances and Phonograms Treaty. The exhaustion approach has been left again to the discretion of contracting states.

4. Telecommunications service providers played a major role in the WCT negotiations. These providers were greatly concerned over potential liability for content carried over the Internet and other digital transmission media to which they provide access. The concerns of the service providers are addressed *in extenso* in the U.S. Digital Millennium Copyright Act, see *infra*, and in the IP chapters of recent bilateral trade agreements of the United States.

2. Norms of the WCT

The following excerpt from the WIPO Intellectual Property Handbook describes the resulting WCT norms.

THE WIPO COPYRIGHT TREATY (WCT)*

INTRODUCTION . . .

5.211 After the adoption of the TRIPS Agreement under the auspices of GATT, the preparatory work of new copyright and related rights norms in

_____

* WIPO Intellectual Property Handbook (as of April 2006).

the WIPO committees was intensified to deal with problems not addressed by the TRIPS Agreement. To this end, in 1996 the WIPO Diplomatic Conference on Certain Copyright and Related Rights Questions adopted two treaties, the WIPO Copyright Treaty (WCT) and the WIPO Performances and Phonograms Treaty (WPPT). . . .

SUBSTANTIVE PROVISIONS OF THE WCT

PROVISIONS RELATING TO THE SO-CALLED "DIGITAL AGENDA"

5.217 During the preparatory work, it became clear that the most important and most urgent task was to clarify existing norms and, where necessary, create new norms to respond to the problems raised by digital technology, and particularly by the Internet. The issues addressed in this context were referred to as the "digital agenda."

5.218 The provisions of the WCT relating to the "agenda" cover the following issues — the rights applicable to the storage and transmission of works in digital systems, the limitations on and exceptions to rights in a digital environment, technological measures of protection and rights management information. As discussed below, the right of distribution may also be relevant in respect of transmissions in digital networks; its scope, however, is much broader. Also due to its relationship with the right of rental, the right of distribution is discussed, together with the former right, below.

Storage of Works in Digital Form in an Electronic Medium

5.219 In June 1982, a WIPO/Unesco Committee of Governmental Experts clarified that storage of works in an electronic medium is reproduction. The Diplomatic Conference adopted an agreed statement which reads as follows: "The reproduction right, as set out in Article 9 of the Berne Convention, and the exceptions permitted thereunder, fully apply in the digital environment, in particular to the use of works in digital form. It is understood that the storage of a protected work in digital form in an electronic medium constitutes a reproduction within the meaning of Article 9 of the Berne Convention."

5.220 It follows from this first sentence that Article 9(1) of the Convention is fully applicable. This means that the concept of reproduction under Article 9(1) of the Convention, which extends to reproduction "in any manner or form" irrespective of the duration of the reproduction, must not be restricted merely because a reproduction is in digital form through storage in an electronic memory, and just because a reproduction is of a temporary nature. It also follows from the same first sentence that Article 9(2) of the Convention is also fully applicable, which offers an appropriate basis to introduce any justified exceptions such as the above-mentioned cases of transient and incidental reproductions in national legislation, in harmony with the "three-step test" provided for in that provision of the Convention (see below, in this section, under "Limitations and Exceptions").

5.221 The second sentence of the agreed statement confirms the definition of storage of works. It is another matter that the word "storage" may still be interpreted in somewhat differing ways.

Transmission on Digital Networks

5.222 During the preparatory work, an agreement emerged that the transmission of works on the Internet and in similar networks should be the object of an exclusive right of authorization of the author or other copyright owner, with appropriate exceptions. . . .

5.225 A specific solution was therefore adopted, which provided that the act of digital transmission should be described in a neutral way, free from specific legal characterization; that such a description should not be excessively technical and, at the same time, should convey the interactive nature of digital transmissions; that, in respect of legal characterization of the exclusive right — that is, in respect of the actual choice of the right or rights to be applied — sufficient freedom should be left to national legislation; and, finally, that the gaps in the Berne Convention in the coverage of the relevant rights — the right of communication to the public and the right of distribution — should be covered. This solution was referred to as the "umbrella solution."

5.226 The WCT applies this "umbrella solution" by extending applicability of the right of communication to the public to all categories of works, and clarifies that that right also covers transmissions in interactive systems described in a manner free of legal characterization. Thus Article 8 of the Treaty reads as follows: "Without prejudice to the provisions of Articles 11(1)(ii), 11*bis*(1)(i) and (ii), 11*ter*(1)(ii), 14(1)(ii) and 14*bis*(1) of the Berne Convention, authors of literary and artistic works shall enjoy the exclusive right of authorizing any communication to the public of their works, by wire or wireless means, including the making available to the public of their works in such a way that members of the public may access these works from a place and at a time individually chosen by them." It was stated in the Diplomatic Conference that Contracting Parties are free to implement the obligation to grant an exclusive right to authorize such "making available to the public" also through the application of a right other than the right of communication to the public or through the combination of different rights. By the "other" right, first of all, the right of distribution was meant, but "other" right might also be a specific new right such as that of making available to the public as provided for in Articles 10 and 14 of the WPPT.

5.227 An agreed statement was adopted concerning this Article 8. It reads as follows: "It is understood that the mere provision of physical facilities for enabling or making a communication does not in itself amount to communication within the meaning of this Treaty or the Berne Convention. It is further understood that nothing in Article 8 precludes a Contracting Party from applying Article 11*bis*(2)." This statement is intended to clarify the issue of liability of service and access providers in digital networks like the Internet: it is evident that, if a person engages in an act not covered by a right provided in the Convention (and in corresponding national laws), such person has no direct liability for the act covered by such a right.

Limitations and Exceptions in the Digital Environment

5.228 An agreed statement was adopted in this respect, which reads as follows: "It is understood that the provisions of Article 10 [of the Treaty] permit Contracting Parties to carry forward and appropriately extend into the digital environment limitations and exceptions in their national laws which have been considered acceptable under the Berne Convention. Similarly, these provisions should be understood to permit Contracting Parties to devise new exceptions and limitations that are appropriate in the digital network environment. It is also understood that Article 10(2) [of the Treaty] neither reduces nor extends the scope of applicability of the limitations and exceptions permitted by the

Berne Convention." The provisions of Article 10 of the Treaty referred to in the agreed statement are discussed below. It is obvious that extending limitations and exceptions into the digital environment, or devising new exceptions and limitations for such environment, is subject to the three-step test included in that Article (see below, in this section, under "Limitations and Exceptions").

Technological Measures of Protection and Rights Management Information

5.229 No rights in respect of digital uses of works, particularly uses on the Internet, may be applied efficiently without the support of technological measures of protection and rights management information necessary to license and monitor uses. The application of such measures and information are left to the interested right-owners, but appropriate legal provisions are included in Articles 11 and 12 of the Treaty.

5.230 Under Article 11 of the Treaty, Contracting Parties must provide "adequate legal protection and effective legal remedies against the circumvention of effective technological measures that are used by authors in connection with the exercise of their rights under this Treaty or the Berne Convention and that restrict acts, in respect of their works, which are not authorized by the authors concerned or permitted by law."

5.231 Article 12(1) of the Treaty obliges Contracting Parties to "provide adequate and effective legal remedies against any person knowingly performing any of the following acts knowing, or with respect to civil remedies having reasonable grounds to know, that it will induce, enable, facilitate or conceal an infringement of any right covered by this Treaty or the Berne Convention, (i) to remove or alter any electronic rights management information without authority; (ii) to distribute, import for distribution, broadcast or communicate to the public, without authority, works or copies of works knowing that electronic rights management information has been removed or altered without authority." Article 12(2) defines "rights management information" as meaning "information which identifies the work, the author of the work, the owner of any right in the work, or information about the terms and conditions of use of the work, and any numbers or codes that represent such information, when any of these items of information is attached to a copy of a work or appears in connection with the communication of a work to the public."

5.232 An agreed statement was adopted by the Diplomatic Conference concerning Article 12 of the Treaty, which is in two parts. The first part reads: "It is understood that the reference to infringement of any right covered by this Treaty or the Berne Convention includes both exclusive rights and rights of remuneration." The second part reads: "It is further understood that Contracting Parties will not rely on this Article to devise or implement rights management systems that would have the effect of imposing formalities which are not permitted under the Berne Convention or this Treaty, prohibiting the free movement of goods or impeding the enjoyment of rights under this Treaty."

Other Substantive Provisions . . .

5.235 Article 3 of the Treaty, dealt with above, also prescribes the *mutatis mutandis* application of Articles 2 and 2*bis* of the Berne Convention. The scope of the subject matter covered by copyright, particularly in relation to computer programs and databases, was explored in the WCT. The Treaty shares the same concept of literary and artistic works as is found in the Berne Convention. The

Treaty also includes, however, some clarifications on the matter in common with those in the TRIPS Agreement.

5.236 First, Article 2 of the Treaty clarifies that "Copyright protection extends to expressions and not to ideas, procedures, methods of operation or mathematical concepts as such." This is virtually the same as the clarification included in Article 9.2 of the TRIPS Agreement. Nor is the principle reflected in Article 2 new in the context of the Berne Convention, since countries party to the Convention have always understood the scope of protection under the Convention in that way.

5.237 Second, Articles 4 and 5 of the Treaty contain clarifications concerning the protection of computer programs as literary works and of compilations of data (databases), which are similar to those included in Article 10 of the TRIPS Agreement. Two agreed statements specify that the scope of protection for computer programs under Article 4 of the Treaty and for compilations of data (databases) under Article 5 of the Treaty "is consistent with Article 2 of the Berne Convention and on par with the relevant provisions of the TRIPS Agreement."

Rights to Be Protected

5.238 Article 6(1) of the WCT provides an exclusive right to authorize the making available to the public of originals and copies of works through sale or other transfer of ownership, that is, an exclusive right of distribution. Under the Berne Convention, it is only in respect of cinematographic works that such a right is granted explicitly. Such a right, surviving at least until the first sale of copies, may be deduced as an indispensable corollary to the right of reproduction, and, in some legal systems, the right of distribution is in fact recognized on this basis. Article 6(1) of the WCT should be considered at least a useful clarification of the obligations under the Berne Convention (and also under the TRIPS Agreement, which includes by reference the relevant provisions of the Convention), and at the most as adding to both.

5.239 Article 6(2) of the Treaty deals with the issue of the exhaustion of the right of distribution. It does not oblige Contracting States to choose national/regional exhaustion or international exhaustion—or to regulate at all the issue of exhaustion—of the right of distribution after the first sale or other first transfer of ownership of the original or a copy of the work, with the authorization of the author.

5.240 Article 7 of the Treaty provides an exclusive right of authorizing commercial rental to the public in respect of the same categories of works—computer programs, cinematographic works and works embodied in phonograms, as determined in the national laws of Contracting Parties—as those covered by Articles 11 and 14.4 of the TRIPS Agreement, and with the same exceptions.

The exceptions are in respect of computer programs which are not themselves the essential objects of the rental, in respect of cinematographic works unless commercial rental leads to widespread copying of such works, materially impairing the exclusive right of reproduction, and in respect of a Contracting Party which, on April 15, 1994, had and still has in force a system of equitable remuneration for rental of copies of works included in phonograms, instead of an exclusive right: in the latter case the Contracting Party may maintain that system provided that commercial rental does not give rise to the material impairment of the exclusive right of authorization.

5.241 An agreed statement was adopted by the Diplomatic Conference on Articles 6 and 7 of the Treaty. It reads: "As used in these Articles, the expressions 'copies' and 'original and copies,' being subject to the right of distribution and the right of rental under the said Articles, refer exclusively to fixed copies that can be put into circulation as tangible objects."

Duration of Protection of Photographic Works

5.242 Article 9 of the WCT removes the unjustified discrimination against photographic works as to the duration of protection. It obliges Contracting Parties not to apply Article 7(4) of the Berne Convention, which, as also for works of applied art, prescribes a shorter term — 25 years — for photographic works than for the general 50-year term.

Limitations and Exceptions

5.243 Paragraph (1) of Article 10 determines the types of limitations on, or exceptions to, the rights granted under the Treaty which may be applied, while paragraph (2) of that Article provides criteria for the application of limitations of, or exceptions to, the rights under the Berne Convention.

5.244 Both paragraphs use the three-step test included in Article 9(2) of the Berne Convention to determine the limitations and exceptions allowed. That is to say, exceptions and limitations are only allowed in certain special cases:

— provided that they do not conflict with a normal exploitation of the work;
— provided that they do not unreasonably prejudice the legitimate interests of the authors.

5.245 Under Article 9(2) of the Berne Convention, this test is applicable only to the right of reproduction, while both paragraphs of Article 10 of the Treaty cover all rights provided for in the Treaty and the Berne Convention respectively. In this, the provisions of Article 10 are similar to Article 13 of the TRIPS Agreement, which applies the same test for all rights provided for in the TRIPS Agreement, either directly or through inclusion by reference to the substantive provisions of the Berne Convention.

Application in Time

5.246 Article 13 of the WCT refers simply to Article 18 of the Berne Convention to determine the works to which the Treaty applies at the moment of its entry into force for a given Contracting State, and stipulates that the provisions of that Article must also be applied to the Treaty.

Enforcement of Rights

5.247 Article 14, paragraph (1) is a *mutatis mutandis* version of Article 36(1) of the Berne Convention. It provides that "Contracting Parties undertake to adopt, in accordance with their legal systems, the measures necessary to ensure the application of this Treaty."

5.248 Paragraph (2) of Article 14 is a *mutatis mutandis* version of the first sentence of Article 41.1 of the TRIPS Agreement. It reads: "Contracting Parties shall ensure that enforcement procedures are available under their law so as to permit effective action against any act of infringement of rights covered by this Treaty, including expeditious remedies to prevent infringements and remedies which constitute a deterrent to further infringements." . . .

NOTES AND QUESTIONS

1. In the *United States — Copyright Act* decision, *supra,* the panel also addressed the issue of the role of the WCT in the interpretation of the TRIPS Agreement. The panel said:

> 6.70. In paragraph 6.66 we discussed the need to interpret the Berne Convention and the TRIPS Agreement in a way that reconciles the texts of these two treaties and avoids a conflict between them, given that they form the overall framework for multilateral copyright protection. The same principle should also apply to the relationship between the TRIPS Agreement and the WCT. The WCT is designed to be compatible with this framework, incorporating or using much of the language of the Berne Convention and the TRIPS Agreement. The WCT was unanimously concluded at a diplomatic conference organized under the auspices of WIPO in December 1996, one year after the WTO Agreement entered into force, in which 127 countries participated. Most of these countries were also participants in the TRIPS negotiations and are Members of the WTO. For these reasons, it is relevant to seek contextual guidance also in the WCT when developing interpretations that avoid conflicts within this overall framework, except where these treaties explicitly contain different obligations. The subsequent WCT was designed to be compatible with the TRIPS and the Berne Convention framework and should [be] seen as a part of the overall framework of multilateral copyright.

2. As in the TRIPS Agreement, rental rights are expressly limited to computer programs, videos, and phonograms (which include CDs). Why is the rental right limited to these three subject matters? Why is the video rental right only applicable when such rental has led to widespread copying of videos to the detriment of the author?

3. Implementation of the WCT at the National Level

In 1998, two years after conclusion of the WCT, the United States enacted the Digital Millennium Copyright Act (DMCA), which revised substantial parts of Title 17 of the U.S. Copyright Act to implement the WCT. In May 2001, the European Union adopted the European Parliament and Council Directive on the Harmonization of Certain Aspects of Copyright and Related Rights in the Information Society (the EU Information Society Directive). We discuss the features of this directive *infra* section III.A.8.

Implementation of the WCT is taking place around the globe.[11] Debate about its implementation is particularly active in the United States.

The DMCA makes certain amendments to existing copyright rules. It also adds new sections to the U.S. Copyright Act. For instance, new Section 512 creates so-called safe harbors. Online service providers are granted immunity from damage awards if they remove, upon notification by the copyright owner, allegedly infringing material (the "notice and take down" procedure).[12]

---

11. *See, e.g.,* WIPO Secretariat, Survey on Implementation Provisions of the WCT and WPPT, WIPO Doc. SCCR/9/6, April 25, 2003, http://www.wipo.int/edocs/mdocs/copyright/en/sccr_9/sccr_9_6.pdf (visited December 20, 2010).

12. *See* 17 U.S.C. §512. The procedures are detailed in subsections 512(c)(3), 512(f), and 512(g).

In addition, newly added Section 1201 of the Copyright Act makes it a copyright offense to circumvent a technological measure that effectively controls access to a copyrighted work, or to manufacture, sell, or traffic in products the only significant purpose for which is circumvention.[13] This section finds its basic premise in Article 11 of the WCT, which reads:

ARTICLE 11

OBLIGATIONS CONCERNING TECHNOLOGICAL MEASURES

Contracting Parties shall provide adequate legal protection and effective legal remedies against the circumvention of effective technological measures that are used by authors in connection with the exercise of their rights under this Treaty or the Berne Convention and that restrict acts, in respect of their works, which are not authorized by the authors concerned or permitted by law.

Article 11 of the WCT provides flexibility for implementing "adequate legal protection and effective legal remedies." Section 1201 of the U.S. Copyright Act[14] has become the subject of debate concerning the scope and limitations of the legal protection it affords.[15] Some claim the U.S. Congress went well beyond the requirements of the WCT, mainly due to the successful efforts of copyright-dependent industry interest groups seeking broad anticircumvention provisions.[16] Some legal scholars, civil liberties groups, and computer-technology interest groups have argued that DMCA's anticircumvention provisions will hinder legitimate justification for bypassing access controls, including for reverse engineering, fair use, and scientific research.

A typical technological measure is "CSS" (Content Scrambling System) copy protection encoded on DVDs. Independent programmers developed software called "DeCSS," which breaks the scrambling algorithm of the CSS system, permitting copying and access by non-authorized operating systems.

Universal Studies v. Corley, decided on November 28, 2001 by the U.S. Court of Appeals for the Second Circuit, provides background on technical issues and was the first case to address the scope and constitutionality of the DMCA's Section 1201.

UNIVERSAL CITY STUDIOS v. CORLEY
273 F.3d 429 (2d Cir. 2001)

NEWMAN, Circuit Judge.

When the Framers of the First Amendment prohibited Congress from making any law "abridging the freedom of speech," they were not thinking about computers, computer programs, or the Internet. But neither were they thinking about radio, television, or movies. Just as the inventions at the beginning and middle of the 20th century presented new First Amendment issues, so does

13. *See* 17 U.S.C. § 1201.
14. For a detailed overview of the provisions, *see* http://www.copyright.gov/title17/92chap12.html#1201 (visited December 20, 2010) and *Universal City Studios v. Corley, infra.*
15. For background, *see* Pamela Samuelson, *Intellectual Property and the Digital Economy: Why the Anti-circumvention Regulations Need to Be Revised* (1999), http://www.sims.berkeley.edu/~pam/papers/Samuelson_IP_dig_eco_htm.htm (visited December 20, 2010).
16. *Id.* at 2.

the cyber revolution at the end of that century. This appeal raises significant First Amendment issues concerning one aspect of computer technology — encryption to protect materials in digital form from unauthorized access. The appeal challenges the constitutionality of the Digital Millennium Copyright Act ("DMCA"), 17 U.S.C. § 1201 et seq. (Supp. V 1999) and the validity of an injunction entered to enforce the DMCA.

Defendant-Appellant Eric C. Corley and his company, 2600 Enterprises, Inc., (collectively "Corley," "the Defendants," or "the Appellants") appeal from the amended final judgment of the United States District Court for the Southern District of New York (Lewis A. Kaplan, District Judge), entered August 23, 2000, enjoining them from various actions concerning a decryption program known as "DeCSS." *Universal City Studios, Inc. v. Reimerdes,* 111 F. Supp. 2d 346 (S.D.N.Y. 2000) ("*Universal II*"). The injunction primarily bars the Appellants from posting DeCSS on their web site and from knowingly linking their web site to any other web site on which DeCSS is posted. *Id.* at 346-47. We affirm.

INTRODUCTION

Understanding the pending appeal and the issues it raises requires some familiarity with technical aspects of computers and computer software, especially software called "digital versatile disks" or "DVDs," which are optical media storage devices currently designed to contain movies. Those lacking such familiarity will be greatly aided by reading Judge Kaplan's extremely lucid opinion, *Universal City Studios, Inc. v. Reimerdes,* 111 F. Supp. 2d 294 (S.D.N.Y. 2000) ("*Universal I*"), beginning with his helpful section "The Vocabulary of this Case" *id.* at 305-09. . . .

In November 1999, Corley posted a copy of the decryption computer program "DeCSS" on his web site, http://www.2600.com ("2600.com"). DeCSS is designed to circumvent "CSS," the encryption technology that motion picture studios place on DVDs to prevent the unauthorized viewing and copying of motion pictures. Corley also posted on his web site links to other web sites where DeCSS could be found.

Plaintiffs-Appellees are eight motion picture studios that brought an action in the Southern District of New York seeking injunctive relief against Corley under the DMCA. Following a full non-jury trial, the District Court entered a permanent injunction barring Corley from posting DeCSS on his web site or from knowingly linking via a hyperlink to any other web site containing DeCSS. *Universal II,* 111 F. Supp. 2d at 346-47. The District Court rejected Corley's constitutional attacks on the statute and the injunction. *Universal I,* 111 F. Supp. 2d at 325-45.

Corley renews his constitutional challenges on appeal. Specifically, he argues primarily that: (1) the DMCA oversteps limits in the Copyright Clause on the duration of copyright protection; (2) the DMCA as applied to his dissemination of DeCSS violates the First Amendment because computer code is "speech" entitled to full First Amendment protection and the DMCA fails to survive the exacting scrutiny accorded statutes that regulate "speech"; and (3) the DMCA violates the First Amendment and the Copyright Clause by unduly obstructing the "fair use" of copyrighted materials. Corley also argues that the statute is susceptible to, and should therefore be given, a narrow interpretation that avoids alleged constitutional objections.

Background . . .

I. CSS

The movie studios were reluctant to release movies in digital form until they were confident they had in place adequate safeguards against piracy of their copyrighted movies. The studios took several steps to minimize the piracy threat. First, they settled on the DVD as the standard digital medium for home distribution of movies. The studios then sought an encryption scheme to protect movies on DVDs. They enlisted the help of members of the consumer electronics and computer industries, who in mid-1996 developed the Content Scramble System ("CSS"). CSS is an encryption scheme that employs an algorithm configured by a set of "keys" to encrypt a DVD's contents. The algorithm is a type of mathematical formula for transforming the contents of the movie file into gibberish; the "keys" are in actuality strings of 0's and 1's that serve as values for the mathematical formula. Decryption in the case of CSS requires a set of "player keys" contained in compliant DVD players, as well as an understanding of the CSS encryption algorithm. Without the player keys and the algorithm, a DVD player cannot access the contents of a DVD. With the player keys and the algorithm, a DVD player can display the movie on a television or a computer screen, but does not give a viewer the ability to use the copy function of the computer to copy the movie or to manipulate the digital content of the DVD. . . .

II. DeCSS

In September 1999, Jon Johansen, a Norwegian teenager, collaborating with two unidentified individuals he met on the Internet, reverse-engineered a licensed DVD player designed to operate on the Microsoft operating system, and culled from it the player keys and other information necessary to decrypt CSS. The record suggests that Johansen was trying to develop a DVD player operable on Linux, an alternative operating system that did not support any licensed DVD players at that time. In order to accomplish this task, Johansen wrote a decryption program executable on Microsoft's operating system. That program was called, appropriately enough, "DeCSS." . . .

In November 1999, Corley wrote and placed on his web site, 2600.com, an article about the DeCSS phenomenon. His web site is an auxiliary to the print magazine, 2600: The Hacker Quarterly, which Corley has been publishing since 1984. As the name suggests, the magazine is designed for "hackers," as is the web site. While the magazine and the web site cover some issues of general interest to computer users — such as threats to online privacy — the focus of the publications is on the vulnerability of computer security systems, and more specifically, how to exploit that vulnerability in order to circumvent the security systems. Representative articles explain how to steal an Internet domain name and how to break into the computer systems at Federal Express. *Universal I*, 111 F. Supp. 2d at 308-09.

Corley's article about DeCSS detailed how CSS was cracked, and described the movie industry's efforts to shut down web sites posting DeCSS. It also explained that DeCSS could be used to copy DVDs. At the end of the article, the Defendants posted copies of the object and source code of DeCSS. In Corley's words, he added the code to the story because "in a journalistic world, . . . you have to show your evidence . . . and particularly in the magazine that I work for, people want to see specifically what it is that we are referring to," including "what evidence . . . we have" that there is in fact technology that circumvents CSS. Trial Tr. at 823. Writing about DeCSS without including the DeCSS code would have been, to Corley, "analogous to printing a story about a picture and not printing the picture." *Id.* at 825. Corley also added to the article links that he explained would take the reader to other web sites where DeCSS could be found. *Id.* at 791, 826, 827, 848.

2600.com was only one of hundreds of web sites that began posting DeCSS near the end of 1999. The movie industry tried to stem the tide by sending cease-and-desist letters to many of these sites. These efforts met with only partial success; a number of sites refused to remove DeCSS. In January 2000, the studios filed this lawsuit.

III. The DMCA

The DMCA was enacted in 1998 to implement the World Intellectual Property Organization Copyright Treaty ("WIPO Treaty"), which requires contracting parties to "provide adequate legal protection and effective legal remedies against the circumvention of effective technological measures that are used by authors in connection with the exercise of their rights under this Treaty or the Berne Convention and that restrict acts, in respect of their works, which are not authorized by the authors concerned or permitted by law." WIPO Treaty, Apr. 12, 1997, art. 11, S. Treaty Doc. No. 105-17 (1997), available at 1997 WL 447232. Even before the treaty, Congress had been devoting attention to the problems faced by copyright enforcement in the digital age. Hearings on the topic have spanned several years. . . .

The Act contains three provisions targeted at the circumvention of technological protections. . . .

The DMCA contains exceptions for schools and libraries that want to use circumvention technologies to determine whether to purchase a copyrighted product, 17 U.S.C. § 1201(d); individuals using circumvention technology "for the sole purpose" of trying to achieve "interoperability" of computer programs through reverse-engineering, *id.* § 1201(f); encryption research aimed at identifying flaws in encryption technology, if the research is conducted to advance the state of knowledge in the field, *id.* § 1201(g); and several other exceptions not relevant here.

The DMCA creates civil remedies, *id.* § 1203, and criminal sanctions, *id.* § 1204. It specifically authorizes a court to "grant temporary and permanent injunctions on such terms as it deems reasonable to prevent or restrain a violation." *id.* § 1203(b)(1). . . .

Discussion . . .

III. Constitutional Challenges Based on the First Amendment

A. APPLICABLE PRINCIPLES . . .
4. The Scope of First Amendment Protection for Decryption Code

In considering the scope of First Amendment protection for a decryption program like DeCSS, we must recognize that the essential purpose of encryption code is to prevent unauthorized access. Owners of all property rights are entitled to prohibit access to their property by unauthorized persons. Homeowners can install locks on the doors of their houses. Custodians of valuables can place them in safes. Stores can attach to products security devices that will activate alarms if the products are taken away without purchase. These and similar security devices can be circumvented. Burglars can use skeleton keys to open door locks. Thieves can obtain the combinations to safes. Product security devices can be neutralized.

Our case concerns a security device, CSS computer code, that prevents access by unauthorized persons to DVD movies. . . .

DeCSS is computer code that can decrypt CSS. In its basic function, it is like a skeleton key that can open a locked door, a combination that can open a safe, or a device that can neutralize the security device attached to a store's products. DeCSS enables anyone to gain access to a DVD movie without using a DVD player.

The initial use of DeCSS to gain access to a DVD movie creates no loss to movie producers because the initial user must purchase the DVD. However, once the DVD is purchased, DeCSS enables the initial user to copy the movie in digital form and transmit it instantly in virtually limitless quantity, thereby depriving the movie producer of sales. The advent of the Internet creates the potential for instantaneous worldwide distribution of the copied material.

At first glance, one might think that Congress has as much authority to regulate the distribution of computer code to decrypt DVD movies as it has to regulate distribution of skeleton keys, combinations to safes, or devices to neutralize store product security devices. However, despite the evident legitimacy of protection against unauthorized access to DVD movies, just like any other property, regulation of decryption code like DeCSS is challenged in this case because DeCSS differs from a skeleton key in one important respect: it not only is capable of performing the function of unlocking the encrypted DVD movie, it also is a form of communication, albeit written in a language not understood by the general public. As a communication, the DeCSS code has a claim to being "speech," and as "speech," it has a claim to being protected by the First Amendment. But just as the realities of what any computer code can accomplish must inform the scope of its constitutional protection, so the capacity of a decryption program like DeCSS to accomplish unauthorized — indeed, unlawful — access to materials in which the Plaintiffs have intellectual property rights must inform and limit the scope of its First Amendment protection. *Cf. Red Lion*, 395 U.S. at 386 ("Differences in the characteristics of new media justify differences in the First Amendment standards applied to them.").

With all of the foregoing considerations in mind, we next consider the Appellants' First Amendment challenge to the DMCA as applied in the specific prohibitions that have been imposed by the District Court's injunction.

B. FIRST AMENDMENT CHALLENGE

The District Court's injunction applies the DMCA to the Defendants by imposing two types of prohibition, both grounded on the anti-trafficking provisions of the DMCA. The first prohibits posting DeCSS or any other technology for circumventing CSS on any Internet web site. *Universal II*, 111 F. Supp. 2d at 346-47, P 1 (a), (b). The second prohibits knowingly linking any Internet web site to any other web site containing DeCSS. *Id.* At 347, P 1 (c). The validity of the posting and linking prohibitions must be considered separately.

1. Posting

The initial issue is whether the posting prohibition is content-neutral, since, as we have explained, this classification determines the applicable constitutional standard. The Appellants contend that the anti-trafficking provisions of the DMCA and their application by means of the posting prohibition of the injunction are content-based. They argue that the provisions "specifically target . . . scientific expression based on the particular topic addressed by that expression—namely, techniques for circumventing CSS." . . . We disagree. The Appellants' argument fails to recognize that the target of the posting provisions of the injunction—DeCSS—has both a nonspeech and a speech component, and that the DMCA, as applied to the Appellants, and the posting prohibition of the injunction target only the nonspeech component. . . .

As a content-neutral regulation with an incidental effect on a speech component, the regulation must serve a substantial governmental interest, the interest must be unrelated to the suppression of free expression, and the incidental restriction on speech must not burden substantially more speech than is necessary to further that interest. *Turner Broadcasting*, 512 U.S. at 662. The Government's interest in preventing unauthorized access to encrypted copyrighted material is unquestionably substantial, and the regulation of DeCSS by the posting prohibition plainly serves that interest. Moreover, that interest is unrelated to the suppression of free expression. . . .

Posting DeCSS on the Appellants' web site makes it instantly available at the click of a mouse to any person in the world with access to the Internet, and such person can then instantly transmit DeCSS to anyone else with Internet access. Although the prohibition on posting prevents the Appellants from conveying to others the speech component of DeCSS, the Appellants have not suggested, much less shown, any technique for barring them from making this instantaneous worldwide distribution of a decryption code that makes a lesser restriction on the code's speech component. . . .

2. Linking

In considering linking, we need to clarify the sense in which the injunction prohibits such activity. Although the injunction defines several terms, it does not define "linking." Nevertheless, it is evident from the District Court's opinion that it is concerned with "hyperlinks," *Universal I*, 111 F. Supp. 2d at 307; *see id.* at 339. . . . With a hyperlink on a web page, the linked web site is just one click away.

In applying the DMCA to linking (via hyperlinks), Judge Kaplan recognized, as he had with DeCSS code, that a hyperlink has both a speech and a nonspeech component. It conveys information, the Internet address of the linked web page, and has the functional capacity to bring the content of the linked web page to the user's computer screen (or, as Judge Kaplan put it, to "take one almost instantaneously to the desired destination." *id.*). . . .

Applying the *O'Brien/Ward/Turner Broadcasting* requirements for content-neutral regulation, Judge Kaplan then ruled that the DMCA, as applied to the Defendants' linking, served substantial governmental interests and was unrelated to the suppression of free expression. *id.* We agree. He then carefully considered the "closer call," *id.*, as to whether a linking prohibition would satisfy the narrow tailoring requirement. In an especially carefully considered portion of his opinion, he observed that strict liability for linking to web sites containing DeCSS would risk two impairments of free expression. Web site operators would be inhibited from displaying links to various web pages for fear that a linked page might contain DeCSS, and a prohibition on linking to a web site containing DeCSS would curtail access to whatever other information was contained at the accessed site. *id.* at 340.

To avoid applying the DMCA in a manner that would "burden substantially more speech than is necessary to further the government's legitimate interests," *Turner Broadcasting,* 512 U.S. at 662 (internal quotation marks and citation omitted), Judge Kaplan adapted the standards of *New York Times Co. v. Sullivan,* 376 U.S. 254, 283, 11 L. Ed. 2d 686, 84 S. Ct. 710 (1964), to fashion a limited prohibition against linking to web sites containing DeCSS. He required clear and convincing evidence

> that those responsible for the link (a) know at the relevant time that the offending material is on the linked-to site, (b) know that it is circumvention technology that may not lawfully be offered, and (c) create or maintain the link for the purpose of disseminating that technology.

Universal I, 111 F. Supp. 2d at 341. He then found that the evidence satisfied his three-part test by his required standard of proof. *id.* . . .

Mindful of the cautious approach to First Amendment claims involving computer technology expressed in *Name.Space,* 202 F.3d at 584 n.11, we see no need on this appeal to determine whether a test as rigorous as Judge Kaplan's is required to respond to First Amendment objections to the linking provision of the injunction that he issued. It suffices to reject the Appellants' contention that an intent to cause harm is required and that linking can be enjoined only under circumstances applicable to a print medium. As they have throughout their arguments, the Appellants ignore the reality of the functional capacity of decryption computer code and hyperlinks to facilitate instantaneous unauthorized access to copyrighted materials by anyone anywhere in the world. Under the circumstances amply shown by the record, the injunction's linking prohibition validly regulates the Appellants' opportunity instantly to enable anyone anywhere to gain unauthorized access to copyrighted movies on DVDs.

At oral argument, we asked the Government whether its undoubted power to punish the distribution of obscene materials would permit an injunction prohibiting a newspaper from printing addresses of bookstore locations carrying such materials. In a properly cautious response, the Government stated that the answer would depend on the circumstances of the publication. The Appellants' supplemental papers enthusiastically embraced the arguable analogy between printing bookstore addresses and displaying on a web page links to web sites at which DeCSS may be accessed. Supplemental Brief for Appellants at 14. They confidently asserted that publication of bookstore locations carrying obscene material cannot be enjoined consistent with the First Amendment, and that a prohibition against linking to web sites containing DeCSS is similarly invalid. *id.*

Like many analogies posited to illuminate legal issues, the bookstore analogy is helpful primarily in identifying characteristics that distinguish it from the context of the pending dispute. If a bookstore proprietor is knowingly selling obscene materials, the evil of distributing such materials can be prevented by injunctive relief against the unlawful distribution (and similar distribution by others can be deterred by punishment of the distributor). And if others publish the location of the bookstore, preventive relief against a distributor can be effective before any significant distribution of the prohibited materials has occurred. The digital world, however, creates a very different problem. If obscene materials are posted on one web site and other sites post hyperlinks

to the first site, the materials are available for instantaneous worldwide distribution before any preventive measures can be effectively taken.

This reality obliges courts considering First Amendment claims in the context of the pending case to choose between two unattractive alternatives: either
tolerate some impairment of communication in order to permit Congress to
prohibit decryption that may lawfully be prevented, or tolerate some decryption in order to avoid some impairment of communication. Although the
parties dispute the extent of impairment of communication if the injunction
is upheld and the extent of decryption if it is vacated, and differ on the availability and effectiveness of techniques for minimizing both consequences, the
fundamental choice between impairing some communication and tolerating
decryption cannot be entirely avoided.

In facing this choice, we are mindful that it is not for us to resolve the issues of
public policy implicated by the choice we have identified. Those issues are for
Congress. Our task is to determine whether the legislative solution adopted by
Congress, as applied to the Appellants by the District Court's injunction, is
consistent with the limitations of the First Amendment, and we are satisfied
that it is.

IV. Constitutional Challenge Based on Claimed
Restriction of Fair Use

Asserting that fair use "is rooted in and required by both the Copyright Clause
and the First Amendment," . . . the Appellants contend that the DMCA, as
applied by the District Court, unconstitutionally "eliminates fair use" of copyrighted materials. . . . We reject this extravagant claim.

Preliminarily, we note that the Supreme Court has never held that fair use is
constitutionally required, although some isolated statements in its opinions
might arguably be enlisted for such a requirement. . . .

We need not explore the extent to which fair use might have constitutional
protection, grounded on either the First Amendment or the Copyright Clause,
because whatever validity a constitutional claim might have as to an application
of the DMCA that impairs fair use of copyrighted materials, such matters are far
beyond the scope of this lawsuit for several reasons. In the first place, the
Appellants do not claim to be making fair use of any copyrighted materials,
and nothing in the injunction prohibits them from making such fair use. They
are barred from trafficking in a decryption code that enables unauthorized
access to copyrighted materials.

Second, as the District Court properly noted, to whatever extent the anti-
trafficking provisions of the DMCA might prevent others from copying portions of DVD movies in order to make fair use of them, "the evidence as to the
impact of the anti-trafficking provisions of the DMCA on prospective fair users
is scanty and fails adequately to address the issues." *Universal I,* 111 F. Supp. 2d
at 338 n.246.

Third, the Appellants have provided no support for their premise that fair
use of DVD movies is constitutionally required to be made by copying the
original work in its original format. Their examples of the fair uses that they
believe others will be prevented from making all involve copying in a digital
format those portions of a DVD movie amenable to fair use, a copying that
would enable the fair user to manipulate the digitally copied portions. One

example is that of a school child who wishes to copy images from a DVD movie to insert into the student's documentary film. We know of no authority for the proposition that fair use, as protected by the Copyright Act, much less the Constitution, guarantees copying by the optimum method or in the identical format of the original. Although the Appellants insisted at oral argument that they should not be relegated to a "horse and buggy" technique in making fair use of DVD movies, the DMCA does not impose even an arguable limitation on the opportunity to make a variety of traditional fair uses of DVD movies, such as commenting on their content, quoting excerpts from their screenplays, and even recording portions of the video images and sounds on film or tape by pointing a camera, a camcorder, or a microphone at a monitor as it displays the DVD movie. The fact that the resulting copy will not be as perfect or as manipulable as a digital copy obtained by having direct access to the DVD movie in its digital form, provides no basis for a claim of unconstitutional limitation of fair use. A film critic making fair use of a movie by quoting selected lines of dialogue has no constitutionally valid claim that the review (in print or on television) would be technologically superior if the reviewer had not been prevented from using a movie camera in the theater, nor has an art student a valid constitutional claim to fair use of a painting by photographing it in a museum. Fair use has never been held to be a guarantee of access to copyrighted material in order to copy it by the fair user's preferred technique or in the format of the original.

CONCLUSION

We have considered all the other arguments of the Appellants and conclude that they provide no basis for disturbing the District Court's judgment. Accordingly, the judgment is affirmed.

The United Kingdom ratified the WIPO Copyright Treaty in December 2009, nine years after it was approved by the EU Council. The Treaty entered into force for the EU in 2010. The *SAS Institute v. World Programming Limited* case, argued before the UK High Court, is a recent example dealing with the interpretation of the Copyright Treaty, the TRIPS Agreement, and the EU Software Directive under UK legislation. UK law does not expressly limit the scope of copyright to the expression of ideas (not encompassing the ideas themselves). This case raised several important issues related to copyright in computer programs, including programming languages, interfaces, and program functionality. The case is important for the doctrine of consistent interpretation of domestic and international law, see *supra* Chapter 1.IV.

SAS INSTITUTE INC. v. WORLD PROGRAMMING LTD.

Before Hon. Mr. Justice Arnold
High Court of Justice Chancery Division
23 July 2010

1. The Claimant, SAS Institute Inc ("SAS Institute"), is a developer of analytical software known as SAS (referred to in these proceedings as "the

SAS System"). The SAS System is an integrated set of programs which enables users to carry out a wide range of data processing and analysis tasks, and in particular statistical analysis. The core component of the SAS System is Base SAS, which enables users to write and run application programs (also known as "scripts") to manipulate data. Such applications are written in a language known as the SAS Language. The functionality of Base SAS may be extended by the use of additional components, including three which are relevant to these proceedings called SAS/ACCESS, SAS/GRAPH and SAS/STAT (the four components being collectively referred to as "the SAS Components"). The SAS System has been developed over a period of 35 years. It is a very valuable asset, producing revenue for SAS Institute of $2.3 billion in 2009.

2. Over the years SAS Institute's customers have written, or had written on their behalf, thousands of application programs in the SAS Language. These can range from fairly short and simple programs to large and complex programs which involve many man years of effort to create. Prior to the events giving rise to this dispute, SAS Institute's customers had no alternative to continuing to license use of the necessary components in the SAS System in order to be able to run their existing SAS Language application programs, as well to create new ones. While there are many other suppliers of analytical software which compete with SAS Institute, a customer who wanted to change over to another supplier's software would be faced with re-writing its existing application programs in a different language.

3. The Defendant, World Programming Ltd ("WPL"), perceived that there would be a market demand for alternative software which would be able to execute application programs written in the SAS Language. WPL therefore created a product called World Programming System or WPS to do this. In developing WPS, WPL sought to emulate much of the functionality of the SAS Components as closely as possible in the sense that, subject to only a few minor exceptions, it tried to ensure that the same inputs would produce the same outputs. This was so as to ensure that WPL's customers' application programs executed in the same manner when run on WPS as on the SAS Components. There is no suggestion that in doing so WPL had access to the source code of the SAS Components or that WPL have copied any of the text of the source code of the SAS Components or that WPL have copied any of the structural design of the source code of the SAS Components.

4. According to two previous decisions of the courts in this country, it is not an infringement of the copyright in the source code of a computer program for a competitor of the copyright owner to study how the program functions and then to write its own program to emulate that functionality. SAS Institute challenges this view of the law. Even if it is correct, however, SAS Institute contends that WPL has both committed a series of infringements of copyright and acted in breach of contract in creating WPS and its accompanying documentation as a result of the way in which WPL has gone about those tasks.

5. SAS Institute's principal claims are as follows:

    i) A claim that WPL has copied the manuals for the SAS System published by SAS Institute ("the SAS Manuals") when creating WPS and thereby infringed the copyright in the SAS Manuals.

ii) A claim that, by copying the SAS manuals when creating WPS, WPL has indirectly copied the programs comprising the SAS Components and thereby infringed the copyright in the SAS Components.

iii) A claim that WPL has used a version of the SAS System known as the Learning Edition in contravention of the terms of its licences, and thereby both acted in breach of the relevant contracts and infringed the copyright in the Learning Edition.

iv) A claim that WPL has infringed the copyright in the SAS Manuals in creating its own documentation, namely a manual ("the WPS Manual") and some "quick reference" guides ("the WPS Guides"). . . .

THE LEGAL CONTEXT . . .

INTERNATIONAL TREATIES . . .

152. *WIPO Copyright Treaty* . . .

. . . 154. Although the WIPO Copyright Treaty was approved by the Council of the European Community on behalf of the European Community by Council Decision 2000/278/EC of 16 March 2000, the European Union and many of its Member States, including the United Kingdom, did not ratify the Treaty until 14 December 2009, although some Member States ratified it at an earlier date. The Treaty entered into force with respect to the European Union and the United Kingdom on 14 March 2010.

EUROPEAN DIRECTIVES

155. *Software Directive.* Council Directive 91/250/EEC of 14 May 1991 on the legal protection of computer programs ("the Software Directive") was recently replaced by a codified (i.e. consolidated) version, European Parliament and Council Directive 2009/24/EC of 23 April 2009 in which both the sequence of the recitals and the numbering of some of the Articles has been changed. Since the original version was in force at the time of most of the alleged infringing activity by WPL and since the case law discussed below refers to the original version, however, it is convenient to continue to refer to the original version. There is no relevant difference of substance between the two versions. . . .

161. . . . The Copyright, Designs and Patents Act 1988 was amended pursuant to section 2(2) of the 1972 Act by the Copyright (Computer Programs) Regulations 1992, SI 1992/3233, to implement the Software Directive. The 1988 Act was amended pursuant to section 2(2) of the 1972 Act by the Copyright and Related Rights Regulations 2003, SI 2003/2498, to implement the Information Society Directive. As amended by the 1992 Regulations and the 2003 Regulations, and other legislation, the 1988 Act includes the following provisions:

COPYRIGHT AND COPYRIGHT WORKS

1.(1) Copyright is a property right which subsists in accordance with this Part in the following descriptions of work —
    (a) original literary, dramatic, musical or artistic works, . . .

LITERARY, DRAMATIC AND MUSICAL WORKS

3.(1) In this Part:
"literary work" means any work, other than a dramatic or musical work, which is written, spoken or sung, and accordingly includes:
(a) a table or compilation other than a database,
(b) a computer program,
(c) preparatory design material for a computer program, and
(d) a database.

. . .

THE ACTS RESTRICTED BY COPYRIGHT IN A WORK

16.(1) The owner of the copyright in a work has, in accordance with the following provisions of this Chapter, the exclusive right to do the following acts in the United Kingdom—
(a) to copy the work (see section 17); . . .
(3) References in this Part to the doing of an act restricted by the copyright in a work are to the doing of it—
(a) in relation to the work as a whole or any substantial part of it
(b) either directly or indirectly;
and it is immaterial whether any intervening acts themselves infringe copyright.
(4) This Chapter has effect subject to—
(a) the provisions of Chapter III (acts permitted in relation to copyright works) . . .

INFRINGEMENT OF COPYRIGHT BY COPYING

17.(1) The copying of the work is an act restricted by the copyright in every description of copyright work; and references in this Part to copying and copies shall be construed as follows.
(2) Copying in relation to a literary, dramatic, musical or artistic work means reproducing the work in any material form. This includes storing the work in any medium by electronic means. . . .

CRITICISM, REVIEW AND NEWS REPORTING

30.(1) Fair dealing with a work for the purpose of criticism or review, of that or another work or of a performance of a work, does not infringe any copyright in the work provided that it is accompanied by a sufficient acknowledgement and provided that the work has been made available to the public. . . .

OBSERVING, STUDYING AND TESTING OF COMPUTER PROGRAMS

50BA.(1) It is not an infringement of copyright for a lawful user of a copy of a computer program to observe, study or test the functioning of the program in order to determine the ideas and principles which underlie any element of the program if he does so while performing any of the acts of loading, displaying, running, transmitting or storing the program which he is entitled to do.
(2) Where an act is permitted under this section, it is irrelevant whether or not there exists any term or condition in an agreement which purports to prohibit or restrict the act (such terms being, by virtue of section 296A, void).

INTERPRETATION OF DOMESTIC LEGISLATION IN THE CONTEXT OF EUROPEAN DIRECTIVES

163. It is well established that domestic legislation, and in particular legislation specifically enacted or amended to implement a European directive, must be construed so far as is possible in conformity with, and to achieve the result intended by, the directive: Case C-106/89 *Marleasing SA v La Comercial Internacional de Alimentación SA* [1990] ECR I-4135 at [8]; *Litster v Forth Dry Dock and Engineering Co Ltd* [1990] 1 AC 546, HL at 558C-H (Lord Templeman) and 576E-577D (Lord Oliver of Aylmerton); Cases C-397/01 to C-403/01 *Pfeiffer v Deutsches Rotes Kreuz, Kreisverband Waldshut eV* [2004] ECR I-8835 at [113]-[117]; and *R (IDT Card Services Ireland Ltd) v Commissioners for Her Majesty's Revenue and Customs* [2006] EWCA Civ 29, [2006] STC 1252 at [73]-[92] (Arden LJ). . . .

INTERPRETATION OF DOMESTIC LEGISLATION IN THE CONTEXT OF INTERNATIONAL TREATIES

164. The ordinary rule of statutory construction is that domestic legislation which has been enacted in order to give effect to the UK's obligations under an international convention or treaty should be construed in the same sense as the convention or treaty if the words of the statute are reasonably capable of bearing that meaning: *The Jade* [1976] 1 WLR 430 at 436 (Lord Diplock). It is generally thought that this rule imposes a weaker duty of interpretation on the courts than the *Marleasing* principle.

INTERPRETATION OF EUROPEAN DIRECTIVES

165. A European directive falls to be interpreted according to principles of interpretation of European Union legislation developed by the Court of Justice of the European Union. The basic rule of interpretation, which has been frequently reiterated by the European Court of Justice, is that stated in Case C-306/05 *Sociedad General de Autores y Editores de Españav Rafael Hoteles SA* [2006] ECR I-11519 at [34]:

> "According to settled case-law, in interpreting a provision of Community law it is necessary to consider not only its wording, but also the context in which it occurs and the objectives pursued by the rules of which it is part (see, in particular, Case C-156/98 *Germany v Commission* [2000] ECR I-6857, paragraph 50, and Case C-53/05 *Commission v Portugal* [2006] ECR I-6215, paragraph 20)."

166. As is well known, in applying this rule the ECJ routinely refers to the recitals of the measure as well as its operative provisions and frequently refers to pre-legislative materials such as the Explanatory Memoranda which accompany the Commission's legislative proposals.

167. Another rule of interpretation applied by the ECJ is that stated in *SGAE* at [35]: "Moreover, Community legislation must, so far as possible, be interpreted in a manner that is consistent with international law, in particular where its provisions are intended specifically to give effect to an international agreement concluded by the Community (see, in particular, Case C-341/95 *Bettati* [1998] ECR I-4355, paragraph 20 and the case-law cited)."

In that case the Court interpreted Article 3(1) of the Information Society Directive in accordance with Article 8 of the WIPO Copyright Treaty.

168. It follows that, in a field of intellectual property law where the European Union has legislated, national courts must interpret both European and domestic legislation as far as possible in the light of the wording and purpose of relevant international agreements to which the EU is a party, such as TRIPS and the WIPO Copyright Treaty: see Case C-53/96 *Hermès International v FHT Marketing Choice BV* [1998] ECR I-3603 at [28]; Joined Cases C-300/98 and C-392/98 *Parfums Christian Dior SA v Tuk Consultancy BV* [2000] ECR I-11307 at [47]; Case C-89/99 *Schieving-Nijstad VOF v Groeneveld* [2001] ECR I-5851 at [35]; Case C-245/02 *Anheuser-Busch Inc v Budejovicky Budvar NP* [2004] ECR I-10989 at [55]-[57]; and Case C-431/05 *Merck Genéricos — Produtos Farmacêuticos Lda v Merck & Co Inc* [2007] ECR I-7001 at [35]. . . .

DOMESTIC CASE LAW CONCERNING COPYRIGHT IN COMPUTER PROGRAMS

174. At present, the leading case on the copyright protection of computer programs in this country is the judgment of Pumfrey J in *Navitaire v easyJet* (*supra*). This was the first substantial decision on the copyright protection of computer software in this country on facts occurring after the implementation of the Software Directive.

. . .

IDEAS, PROCEDURES, METHODS OF OPERATION AND MATHEMATICAL CONCEPTS

199. Both Article 9(2) of TRIPS and Article 2 of the WIPO Copyright Treaty distinguish between "expressions," which are protected by copyright, and "ideas, procedures, methods of operation and mathematical concepts as such," which are not. Although Article 9(2) of TRIPS was referred to by Lord Hoffmann in *Designers' Guild* and by Jacob LJ in *Nova,* none of the judgments in the cases mentioned in paragraph 196 above refer to Article 2 of the WIPO Copyright Treaty. When the present case was opened, I invited the parties to consider the relevance of Article 2 of the WIPO Copyright Treaty, as well as Article 9(2) of TRIPS. By the end of the trial there was a considerable measure of common ground on these questions.

200. *Relevance of Article 9(2) of TRIPS and Article 2 of the WIPO Copyright Treaty to domestic law.* It is clear that the United Kingdom courts must interpret both the Software Directive and domestic law in conformity with both the relevant provisions of TRIPS and the relevant provisions of the WIPO Copyright Treaty. This duty arises both as a matter of EU law and as matter of domestic law. It arises as a matter of EU law as a result of the principles of interpretation laid down by the ECJ which are set out in paragraphs 167 and 168 above. In addition, it is apparent from recitals (15) and (20) and Article 1(2)(a) of the Information Society Directive that the Community legislature considered that the Software Directive was consistent with the WIPO Copyright Treaty (by contrast recital (61) of the Information Society Directive says that Directives 92/100/EEC and 93/98/EEC are being amended "in order to comply with the WIPO Performances and Phonograms Treaty"). The duty arises as a matter of domestic law under section 2(1) of the European Communities Act 1972 by virtue of the fact that, as noted in paragraph 162 above, both TRIPS and the WIPO Copyright Treaty have been designated as EU Treaties. . . .

204. *The correct approach to interpretation of Article 9(2) of TRIPS and Article 2 of the WIPO Copyright Treaty.* There is a broad consensus among scholars that both Article 9(2) of TRIPS and Article 2 of the WIPO Copyright Treaty are intended to be confirmatory of the position under Article 2 of the Berne Convention. Articles 9(2) and 10(1) of TRIPS, and Articles 2 and 4 of the WIPO Copyright Treaty, are historically linked. The inclusion of Article 10(1) in the drafts of TRIPS, requiring that computer programs be protected by copyright as literary works, led to concerns that such copyrights might be used to monopolise ideas, procedures, methods of operation or mathematical concepts. It was initially proposed that what became Article 9(2) be an exception to Article 10(1), but its application was widened to all forms of copyright protection. When the WIPO Copyright Treaty came to be drafted, it was desired to preserve the same balance between the provisions, and hence the replication of Articles 9(2) and 10(1) of TRIPS in Articles 2 and 4 of the WIPO Copyright Treaty. If Article 2 of the WIPO Copyright Treaty is compared to Article 9(2) TRIPS, it can be seen that the wording is identical, save that "shall extend to" has been replaced by "extends to." This subtle change of words is deliberate, indicating that Article 2 of the WIPO Copyright Treaty is intended to be confirmatory of an existing recognised principle, consistently with the WIPO Copyright Treaty's status as a special agreement under the Berne Convention. The linkage between Articles 2 and 4 of the WIPO Copyright Treaty, and the intention that they should re-state the effects of Articles 9(2) and 10(1) of TRIPS, is made explicit in the Agreed Statement concerning Article 4 of the WIPO Copyright Treaty. The Agreed Statement also makes it clear that Article 2 of the WIPO Copyright Treaty is intended to be consistent with Article 2 of the Berne Convention. The same point is implicit in the relationship between Article 9(1) and 9(2) in TRIPS. . . .

COPYRIGHT PROTECTION FOR PROGRAMMING LANGUAGES, INTERFACES AND FUNCTIONALITY

208. *Article 1(2) of the Software Directive.* Recital [15] of the Software Directive suggests that Article 1(2) of the Software Directive is intended to be interpreted in accordance with Article 9(2) of TRIPS and Article 2 of the WIPO Copyright Treaty, particularly now that the original version has been replaced by the codified version (in which the relevant wording is now to be found in recital (11)) which post-dates those treaties. In any event, Article 1(2) of the Software Directive must be interpreted in conformity with Article 9(2) of TRIPS and Article 2 of the WIPO Copyright Treaty for the reasons explained above. In my judgment there is no conflict between them. Although Article 1(2) of the Software Directive is differently worded, and in particular refers to "ideas and principles" rather than "ideas, procedures, methods of operation and mathematical concepts," the distinction it draws is essentially the same as that drawn by Article 9(2) of TRIPS and Article 2 of the WIPO Copyright Treaty. If and in so far as there is any difference, however, Article 9(2) of TRIPS and Article 2 of the WIPO Copyright Treaty make it clear that Article 1(2) of the Software Directive must be broadly interpreted.

209. It can be seen from the paragraphs 178-185 above that in *Navitaire* Pumfrey J interpreted Article 1(2) of the Software Directive as meaning that copyright in computer programs did not protect (i) programming languages, (ii) interfaces or (iii) the functionality of a computer program. It can be seen from paragraph 190 above that his conclusion on point (iii) was upheld by the Court of Appeal in *Nova*.

. . .

CONCLUSIONS

332. For the reasons given above, I conclude as follows:

i) Although I am not persuaded that Pumfrey J was wrong to conclude in *Navitaire* that, on the true interpretation of Article 1(2) of the Software Directive, copyright in computer programs does not protect programming languages from being copied, I agree with him that this is a question on which guidance from the ECJ is required.

ii) Although I am not persuaded that Pumfrey J was wrong to conclude in *Navitaire* that, on the true interpretation of Article 1(2) of the Software Directive, copyright in computer programs does not protect interfaces from being copied where this can be achieved without decompiling the object code, I consider this is also a question on which guidance from the ECJ is required.

iii) Although I am not persuaded that Pumfrey J was wrong to conclude in *Navitaire* that, on the true interpretation of Article 1(2) of the Software Directive, copyright in computer programs does not protect the functions of the programs from being copied, and although his decision on that point was upheld by the Court of Appeal in *Nova*, I consider that this is also a question on which guidance from the ECJ is required.

iv) On the assumption that Pumfrey J's interpretation of Article 1(2) of the Software Directive was correct, WPL has not infringed SAS Institute's copyrights in the SAS Components by producing WPS.

v) I consider that the reasoning which supports Pumfrey J's interpretation of Article 1(2) of the Software Directive also applies to Article 2(a) of the Information Society Directive, but again this is a question on which guidance from the ECJ is required.

vi) On the assumption that Article 2(a) of the Information Society Directive is to be interpreted in the same manner as Article 1(2) of the Software Directive, WPL has not infringed SAS Institute's copyright in the SAS Manuals by producing or testing WPS.

vii) WPL's use of the SAS Learning Edition falls outside the scope of the terms of the relevant licences.

viii) The interpretation of Article 5(3) of the Software Directive is another question on which guidance from the ECJ is required.

ix) On the interpretation of Article 5(3) which I favour, WPL's use of the Learning Edition is within Article 5(3), and to the extent that the licence terms prevent this they are null and void, with the result that none of WPL's acts complained of was a breach of contract or an infringement of copyright except perhaps one.

x) WPL has infringed the copyrights in the SAS Manuals by substantially reproducing them in the WPL Manual.

xi) WPL has not infringed the copyrights in the SAS Manuals by producing the WPS Guides.

NOTES AND QUESTIONS

1. In *DVD Copy Control Ass'n (DVD CCA) v. Bunner,*[17] an injunction had been issued to prevent Andrew Bunner from making available on his web page DeCSS software he had previously downloaded from the Internet. DVD CCA claimed that the publishing on or linking to web sites containing DeCSS software constituted trade secret misappropriation under California law. Bunner argued that republishing information widely available on the Internet (such as DeCSS) was protected by the First Amendment and the injunction thus violated his constitutional rights. The California Supreme Court agreed with the basic proposition that the distribution of computer code is protectable as free speech. However, in the case of publishing code protected by trade secret law, an injunction would be "content neutral" (i.e., not based on the particular content of the speech, but rather a legitimate tool to protect trade secrets), and constitutionally permissible. The California Supreme Court remanded the case to the California Court of Appeal, which found that DVD CCA failed to establish that the DeCSS code made widely available on the Internet was subject to trade secret protection (*DVD Copy Control Ass'n v. Bunner* (6th Dist. Cal. App.), 116 Cal. App. 4th 241 (2004) (*request for review by Cal. Sup. Ct. denied,* 2004 Cal. LEXIS 8697 (Cal., Sept. 15, 2004)). A portion of that decision is excerpted in the discussion of trade secrets, *infra* Chapter 5, section III.A.
2. For the purpose of interpretation of relevant provisions of the 2009 Software Directive, Justice Arnold in *SAS v. World Programming* referred a number of questions to the ECJ on August 11, 2010 for a preliminary ruling. It is possible that the ECJ will review the existing approach to the scope of "expression" and those elements of computer programs that are not subject to protection as such.

D. Neighboring Rights and the WIPO Performances and Phonograms Treaty (WPPT)

1. The Problem of Performance

Schweizerische Interpreten-Gesellschaft and Others v. X and Z, decided in 1984, illustrates why performers sought new standards of protection. This decision was rendered a decade before conclusion of the TRIPS Agreement and the WIPO Performances and Phonograms Treaty, and prior to Swiss amendments to its copyright law in 1992 (described following the decision). Though Switzerland had signed the Rome Convention in 1961, it did not ratify the Convention until September 1993.

---

17. Supreme Court of California, 2003 Cal. LEXIS 6295, 31 Cal. 4th 864, Aug. 25, 2003.

SCHWEIZERISCHE INTERPRETEN-GESELLSCHAFT
AND OTHERS v. X AND Z

Bundesgericht (Swiss Federal Court)
BGE 110 II 411, [1986] ECC 384
October 2, 1984

HEADNOTE:

Appeal from the Obergericht (Cantonal Court of Appeal), Zurich. . . .

FACTS:

A

On the evening of 2 November 1980 the Zurich Opera gave a gala performance of the opera "Tosca" by Giacomo Puccini. At that time X was still a member of the Opera chorus. That evening he sat for almost the entire performance in the second row of a so-called relatives' box, where he made sound recordings with a cassette recorder. He was seen doing this, allegedly accompanied by Mrs Z. In January 1981 he was reported by the Schweizerische Interpreten-Gesellschaft for infringement of copyrights.

In the criminal investigation, which was extended to Mrs Z, X admitted that he had made sound recordings of approximately 15 musical stage works between the middle of 1979 and December 1980 in the Zurich Opera, and had sold approximately the same number of cassettes at cost price. Mrs Z stated, as an accused, that she had advertised in the October 1980 issue of the magazine Opernwelt for people who wanted to exchange opera recordings, but only a few prospective purchasers had replied and she had sold them recordings of the opera "Tristan und Isolde" at cost price. Both accused denied that they had commercial intentions. The District Prosecutor's Office, Zurich, and, following an appeal, on 8 October 1982 the State Prosecutor of the Canton of Zurich discontinued the criminal proceedings because performances by performing artists (performers) are not protected by copyright.

Thereupon the Interpreten-Gesellschaft applied to the Single Judge of the District Court, Zurich, who on 20 October 1982 prohibited the accused, as a precautionary measure, from re-selling sound recordings of the Zurich Opera, subject to a penalty, and provisionally impounded the recordings, which had been placed in the criminal files.

B

In October 1983 the Society, together with seven musicians who had sung at the gala performance of 2 November 1980, brought an action against X and Mrs Z in the Appeal Court of the Canton of Zurich. The plaintiffs sought an injunction prohibiting the defendants from selling and exploiting commercially sound recordings originating from the Opera House, subject to a penalty; an order requiring them to disclose the volume of their sales and to surrender all receipts; and an order for the destruction of the impounded tapes and cassettes.

The defendants opposed these applications.

By judgment of 26 January 1984 the Appeal Court dismissed the action and rescinded the precautionary measures ordered by the Single Judge.

C

The plaintiffs have appealed against that judgment, maintaining their original applications. The defendants ask the Court to dismiss the appeal and to uphold the judgment appealed against.

JUDGMENT:

The plaintiffs maintain that performers also create works within the meaning of the Copyright Act and can therefore invoke the protection of the Act if their performances are to be regarded as artistic. In particular, a musical stage work is achieved only by the activity of all the performers, including the musicians of an orchestra. To refuse them protection for their performance is clearly contrary to the words and meaning of section 4(1)(2) and 4(2) of the Copyright Act, which lays down mandatory protection providing that the other requirements of copyright law are met. The Appeal Court, on the other hand, agrees with the defendants that a new work is not created by the performance of an orchestra or chorus, so that its members cannot be regarded as creators within the meaning of the Act; this applies in cases where, as here, we are not concerned with an interpretative achievement of a work, but the performance of a famous opera. . . .

However, the plaintiffs' submissions in support of their argument fail owing to the definition of a copyright-protected work. . . . A work capable of copyright protection, within the meaning of section 1(2) of the Copyright Act, presupposes an original creation, ie an achievement of creative intellectual activity with a minimum degree of its own personal character. (*See* BGE 105 II 299 and 85 II 123 para 3, with references). The plaintiffs appreciate that this also applies to the individual performance of a performer. Contrary to their objections, however, protection for a performance cannot be inferred from the wording of the Act, nor can it be acknowledged regardless of the latitude which an individual performer has within a group of musicians or singers who are attuned to each other. There can be no serious question of this at least in relation to a classical opera, as here, the performance of which is predetermined in every detail by the composer, the producer and the conductor. In such a case an exception is justified at the most in relation to the conductor and soloists, but not other participants who are members of an orchestra or choir. It is unnecessary to decide here what the position would be with regard to so-called aleatoric works by modern composers, which give the performer wide latitude, which is not the same thing, or in the case of improvisations and variations.

(b) This is also the prevailing view of legal theorists. . . . Troller (In Immaterialguterrecht 1, 3rd edition, pp 391-2) likewise now (differing from the second edition (At p 501 et seq) accepts that conductors and soloists are able to fashion musical works individually but that orchestras and choruses cannot take part in this process because they have to subordinate their view of the work to that of the conductor. He regrets that the legislature and certain theorists do not include protection for creative performers in the ambit of the Copyright Act, regardless of the power to fashion a work, and that neither the revised Berne Convention nor the Universal Copyright Convention mentions such protection, but leaves it to State Parties.

Attempts by these States to reach an objectively satisfactory solution show similar tendencies. In several European countries the rights of performing artists are protected by special legislation on the assumption that the performance does not give them a copyright in the work performed. (*See* Frank Gotzen, Das Recht des Interpreten in der Europäischen Wirtschaftsgemeinschaft, p 49 et seq). In other countries, by contrast, such protection is not given in any legislation but is left to the courts in individual cases. This applies to Switzerland, where neither the current law nor the new Copyright Bill contains, provisions for the protection of performing artists; on the contrary, according to the explanatory memorandum to the Bill, such provisions are to remain separate from copyright and incorporated in another field of law or a separate Act if necessary. (*See* BB1 [1984] III p 198 et seq).

In the present case, however, it is unnecessary to give a final answer to the question whether and, if so, to what extent qualified performers can invoke copyright protection. No doubt, there is much to be said for the proposition that conductors and soloists in particular fashion musical works individually in performance and may thereby create a work at second hand if they have enough latitude. However, this cannot be said in general of any performance of a work of classical music by elite participants, however high the qualitative level. The Court does not wish to diminish their contributions in any way, but the plaintiff members of the orchestra cannot claim copyright protection for their own contribution for this reason.

[The court subsequently rejected both the plaintiffs' allegation of unfair competition and the claim of infringement of its personality rights (*Persönlichkeitsrecht*). The court held that results of effort and labor that are not or are no longer protectable under copyright law may not be protected by means of competition law or right of personality indirectly. Exceptions to this rule should only apply if there are additional circumstances justifying the application of these provisions. Accordingly, the Federal Court dismissed the appeal and upheld the judgment of the Cantonal Appeal Court.]

NOTES AND QUESTIONS

1. Title 3 of the 1992 Federal Law on Copyright and Neighboring Rights Protection (Bundesgesetz über das Urheberrecht und verwandte Schutzrechte), adopted well after the text decision, addressed neighboring rights, and Article 33 granted performance rights to artists, including the right to authorize sound recordings (art. 33(c)). Article 34 concerned the distribution of rights among performing groups, and provided that in the case of a choral, orchestral, or theatrical performance, the rights are shared among soloists, producers, conductors, and the representative of the artists' group. It would appear that all of the aforementioned parties must consent to authorize a sound recording. May we assume that the result in the text case would be different after the changes to Swiss law brought about by the 1992 law?

2. The Rolling Stones first recorded "Satisfaction" in 1965. Since then, how many times do you think the group has performed that song live? When they performed it live during their world tour in 2006-2007, was there a creative element in the performances? Under the rules applied by the Swiss Supreme Court in the text case, would the group have been able to prevent its audiences from making sound recordings of "Satisfaction"?

2. The Rome, Geneva, and Brussels Conventions

Until the TRIPS Agreement (and subsequent WPPT), the most widely adhered-to multilateral agreement concerning rights of performers, producers, and broadcasters was the Rome Convention (1961). The following excerpt from the WIPO Intellectual Property Handbook describes the main features of the Rome Convention. This is followed by a brief description of the Geneva Convention (1971) and the Brussels Satellite Convention (1974).

SPECIAL CONVENTIONS IN THE FIELD OF RELATED RIGHTS: THE INTERNATIONAL CONVENTION FOR THE PROTECTION OF PERFORMERS, PRODUCERS OF PHONOGRAMS AND BROADCASTING ORGANIZATIONS ("THE ROME CONVENTION")*

. . . THE MINIMUM PROTECTION REQUIRED BY THE CONVENTION

5.500 The minimum protection guaranteed by the Convention to performers is provided by "the possibility of preventing certain acts" done without their consent. Instead of enumerating the minimum rights of performers, this expression was used in order to allow countries like the United Kingdom to continue to protect performers by virtue of penal statutes, determining offenses and penal sanctions under public law. It was agreed, however, that the enumerated acts which may be prevented by the performer, require his consent in advance. In fact, the possibility of preventing certain acts as defined in the Convention amounts to a distinct bundle of rights granted to performers.

5.501 The restricted acts comprise: broadcasting or communication to the public of a "live" performance; recording an unfixed performance; reproducing a fixation of the performance, provided that the original fixation was made without the consent of the performer or the reproduction is made for purposes not permitted by the Convention or the performer (Article 7).

5.502 Producers of phonograms have the right to authorize or prohibit the direct or indirect reproduction of their phonograms (Article 10). The Rome Convention does not provide for any right to authorize performances of the phonogram and does not explicitly prohibit distribution or importation of unauthorized duplicates of phonograms.

5.503 Broadcasting organizations have the right to authorize or prohibit: the simultaneous rebroadcasting of their broadcasts, the fixation of their broadcasts, the reproduction of unauthorized fixations of their broadcasts or reproduction of lawful fixations for illicit purposes and the communication to the public of their television broadcasts by means of receivers in places accessible to the public against payment. It should be noted, however, that this last-mentioned right does not extend to communication to the public of merely sound broadcasts, and that it is a matter for domestic legislation to determine the conditions under which such a right may be exercised. It should also be observed that the Rome Convention does not protect against distribution by cable of broadcasts.

PROVISIONS FOR DISCRETIONARY REGULATION OF THE EXERCISE OF RIGHTS

5.504 The Rome Convention, over and above the minimum requirements of protection, also contains provisions allowing national laws to regulate certain aspects of protection at their discretion. . . .

* WIPO Intellectual Property Handbook.

5.507 Concerning both the protection of performers and producers of phonograms, Article 12 (perhaps the most controversial part of the Convention) provides that if a phonogram published for commercial purposes is used directly for broadcasting or any communication to the public, an equitable remuneration shall be paid by the user to the performers, or to the producers of the phonogram, or to both. This Article does not grant any right to either the performers or producers of phonograms to authorize or to prohibit the secondary use of a phonogram. By guaranteeing a single remuneration for the use of the phonogram it seems to establish a sort of non-voluntary license. It does not, however, obligatorily specify the beneficiary or beneficiaries of the remuneration for the secondary use of the performance and the phonogram embodying it.

Article 12 only says that at least one of the interested parties should be paid for the use; nevertheless it provides that in the absence of agreement between these parties, domestic law may optionally lay down the conditions for the sharing of this remuneration.

5.508 The implementation of these provisions, however, can be excluded or restricted by the Contracting States at any time by an appropriate notification (Article 16(1)(a)). A State may declare that it will not apply the provisions of Article 12. A Contracting State may declare that it will not apply this article in respect of certain uses, . . .

LIMITATIONS

5.509 The Rome Convention allows for certain limitations of the rights granted and, as regards the performers, also imposes limitations on rights itself.

5.510 Any Contracting State may provide for exceptions as regards private use, use of short excerpts in connection with reporting current events, ephemeral fixation by a broadcasting organization by means of its own facilities and for its own broadcasts, and for all kinds of use solely for the purpose of teaching or scientific research (Article 15(1)). This latter possibility of introducing exceptions may be of special benefit to developing countries.

5.511 Besides the exceptions specified by the Convention, any Contracting State may also provide for the same kind of limitations with regard to the protection of performers, producers of phonograms and broadcasting organizations as it provides for in connection with copyright protection. There is, however, an important difference: compulsory licenses may be provided for only to the extent to which they are compatible with the Rome Convention (Article 15(2)).

5.512 In view of the cinematographic industry's interest in exclusively exploiting the contributions made to their productions, Article 19 of the Rome Convention provides that once a performer has consented to the incorporation of his performance in a visual or audiovisual fixation, he shall have no further rights under the Rome Convention as regards the performance concerned.

DURATION OF PROTECTION

5.513 The minimum term of protection under the Rome Convention is a period of twenty years, to be computed from the end of the year in which the fixation was made, as far as phonograms and performances incorporated therein are concerned, or the performance took place, as regards performances not incorporated in phonograms, or the broadcast took place, for broadcasts (Article 14).

RESTRICTION OF FORMALITIES

5.514 If a country requires compliance with formalities as a condition of protecting related rights in relation to phonograms, these should be considered as fulfilled if all copies in commerce of the published phonogram or their containers bear a notice consisting of the symbol P, accompanied by the year date of the first publication. If the copies of their containers do not identify the producer or his licensee, the notice shall also include the name of the owner of the rights of the producer, and if the copies or their containers do not identify the principal performers, the notice shall also include the name of the person who owns the rights of such performers (Article 11). It should be emphasized that this provision is *not* a formality requirement; it is a restriction of formalities, which may be required by some national laws. . . .

THE OTHER SPECIAL CONVENTIONS

5.524 Besides the Rome Convention of 1961, a basic legal instrument discussed in the previous section, two other international instruments have been drawn up with regard to certain related rights. These are the Convention for the Protection of Producers of Phonograms Against Unauthorized Duplication of Their Phonograms, concluded in Geneva in October 1971 and generally referred to as "the Phonograms Convention," and the Convention Relating to the Distribution of Programme-Carrying Signals Transmitted by Satellite, concluded in Brussels in May 1974 and known briefly as "the Satellites Convention." These two Conventions are also within the area of related rights, and their purpose is to protect producers of phonograms and broadcasting organizations, respectively, against certain prejudicial acts that have been widely recognized as infringements or acts of piracy.

5.525 With regard to the Rome Convention, the Phonograms Convention and the Satellites Convention may be regarded as special agreements, the conclusion of which is reserved for Contracting States insofar as the agreements grant to performers, producers of phonograms or broadcasting organizations more extensive rights than those granted by the Rome Convention, or contain other provisions not contrary to that Convention (Article 22 of the Rome Convention).

NOTES AND QUESTIONS

1. The United States did not join the Rome Convention because, *inter alia*, the United States did not recognize performers' rights, but it is a party to the Geneva Convention. The Geneva Convention provides protection to producers against unauthorized duplication of phonograms. The United States amended its copyright legislation in connection with implementation of the Uruguay Round (WTO) Agreements to recognize the rights of performers (U.S. Copyright Act, § 1101), but it has not acceded to the Rome Convention.

2. The transmission of broadcast signals by satellite has become a commonplace mode of distributing copyrighted works. The signal transmitted from a satellite to the earth creates a "footprint" or "zone of illumination" that is often larger than a single country, and it may often exceed

the geographical area for which rights to broadcast, retransmit, etc., have been secured from the copyright holder.

The Brussels Convention establishes a few basic principles regulating satellite transmissions, such as the principle obligating contracting states to take steps to prevent the misappropriation of signals within their territory. However, the rules of the Brussels Convention are limited. They do not seek to establish what country's rules should govern the interests of copyright holders. The Convention establishes obligations only with respect to satellite signals intended for retransmission to the public. It does not apply to signals that are intended for direct reception by the public. As of 2011, only 34 countries were party to the Brussels Convention.

3.   The WIPO Performances and Phonograms Treaty (WPPT)

a.   WPPT Norms

The WPPT was adopted alongside the WCT in 1996 in Geneva. Like the WCT, the WPPT was intended to make WIPO-administered rules consistent with those of the TRIPS Agreement, and to go further by addressing issues presented by digital technologies. WIPO describes the elements of the WPPT.

THE WIPO PERFORMANCES AND PHONOGRAMS TREATY (WPPT)*

INTRODUCTION

5.553 The WIPO Diplomatic Conference on Certain Copyright and Neighboring Rights Questions, held in Geneva in December 1996, adopted two treaties: the WIPO Copyright Treaty (the third section dealt with in this chapter) and the WIPO Performances and Phonograms Treaty (WPPT).

5.554 In view of the technological developments of the 1980s, as also in the field of copyright, it was recognized that guidance in the form of recommendations, guiding principles and model provisions would no longer suffice, and that binding new norms were indispensable. The WCT and the WPPT were prepared in parallel at the same Diplomatic Conference.

LEGAL NATURE OF THE WPPT AND ITS RELATIONSHIP WITH OTHER INTERNATIONAL TREATIES

5.555 The WPPT has a certain relationship with the Rome Convention which has been regulated in a way similar to the relationship between the TRIPS Agreement and the Rome Convention. . . .

---

* WIPO Intellectual Property Handbook.

SUBSTANTIVE PROVISIONS OF THE WPPT

PROVISIONS RELATING TO THE SO-CALLED "DIGITAL AGENDA"

5.559 The provisions of the WPPT relating to the "digital agenda" cover the following issues: certain definitions, rights applicable to storage and transmission of performances and phonograms in digital systems, limitations on and exceptions to rights in a digital environment, technological measures of protection and rights management information. As discussed below, the right of distribution may also be relevant in respect of transmissions in digital networks; its scope, however, is much broader. Also due to its relationship with the right of rental, the right of distribution is discussed, together with the former right, below.

Definitions

5.560 The WPPT follows the structure of the Rome Convention, in the sense that it contains, in Article 2, a series of definitions. The definitions cover more or less the same terms as those which are defined in Article 3 of the Rome Convention: "performers," "phonogram," "producer of phonograms," "publication," "broadcasting." They cover more, in the sense that the WPPT also defines "fixation" and "communication to the public," and less, in the sense that they do not define "reproduction" and "rebroadcasting."

5.561 The impact of digital technology is present in the definitions, on the basis of the recognition that phonograms do not necessarily mean the fixation of sounds of a performance or other sounds any more; now they may also include fixations of (digital) representations of sounds that have never existed, but that have been directly generated by electronic means. The reference to such possible fixations appears in the definitions of "phonogram," "fixation," "producer of phonogram," "broadcasting" and "communication to the public." It should be stressed, however, that the reference to "representations of sounds" does not expand the relevant definitions as provided under existing treaties; it only reflects the desire to offer a clarification in the face of advancing technology.

Storage of Works in Digital Form in an Electronic Medium

5.562 In June 1982, a WIPO/Unesco Committee of Governmental Experts clarified that storage of works and objects of related rights in an electronic medium is reproduction. The Diplomatic Conference adopted an agreed statement which reads: "The reproduction right, as set out in Articles 7 and 11 [of the WPPT], and the exceptions permitted thereunder through Article 16 [of the WPPT], fully apply in the digital environment, in particular to the use of performances and phonograms in digital form. It is understood that the storage of a protected performance or phonogram in digital form in an electronic medium constitutes a reproduction within the meaning of these Articles."

5.563 The first sentence states the obvious, that the provisions of the Treaty on the rights of reproduction are fully applicable in a digital environment. The concept of reproduction must not be restricted merely because a reproduction is in digital form through storage in an electronic memory, or because a reproduction is of a temporary nature. It also follows from the same first sentence that Article 16 of the Treaty is also fully applicable, offering an appropriate basis to introduce any justified exceptions, such as in respect of certain transient and incidental reproductions, in national legislation, in harmony with the "three-step test" provided for in that provision of the Treaty (see below).

5.564 The second sentence of the agreed statement simply confirms the definition of storage of works. It is another matter that the word "storage" may still be interpreted in somewhat differing ways.

Transmission in Digital Networks

5.565 The background to the provisions of the WPPT concerning transmission of works in digital networks, including the so-called "umbrella solution," can be found in the third section of this chapter.

5.566 In the WPPT, the relevant provisions regarding transmission in digital networks are Articles 10 and 14, under which performers and producers of phonograms, respectively, must enjoy "the exclusive right of authorizing the making available to the public" of their performances fixed in phonograms and of their phonograms, respectively, "by wire or wireless means, in such a way that members of the public may access them from a place and at a time individually chosen by them."

Taking into account the freedom of Contracting Parties to choose differing legal characterization of acts covered by certain rights provided for in the treaties, it is clear that, also in this case, Contracting Parties may implement the relevant provisions not only by applying such a specific right but also by applying some other rights such as the right of distribution or the right of communication to the public — providing their obligations to grant an exclusive right of authorization concerning the acts described are fully respected.

5.567 On the question of whether the mere provision of physical facilities for enabling or making a communication in itself amounts to communication within the meaning of the WCT or the Berne Convention, the agreed statement, which was adopted in relation to Article 8 of the WCT, intends to clarify the issue of the liability of service and access providers in digital networks like the Internet.

It is clear that, although this was not stated explicitly, the principle reflected in the agreed statement is also applicable, *mutatis mutandis,* to the above-mentioned provisions of Articles 10 and 14 of the WPPT concerning "making available to the public."

Limitations and Exceptions in the Digital Environment

5.568 The Diplomatic Conference affirmed that the agreed statement concerning limitations and exceptions is applicable *mutatis mutandis* also to Article 16 of the WPPT on limitations and exceptions. That provision of the WPPT is discussed below. It is obvious that any limitations and exceptions — existing or new — in the digital environment are only applicable if they are acceptable under the "three-step test" indicated in Article 16(2) of the Treaty (see below).

TECHNOLOGICAL MEASURES OF PROTECTION AND RIGHTS MANAGEMENT INFORMATION

5.569 The provisions in Articles 18 and 19 of the WPPT concerning technological measures and rights management information correspond to the similar provisions of the WCT (see the third section dealt with in this chapter).

5.570 An agreed statement was adopted by the Diplomatic Conference concerning Article 12 of the WCT, which contains provisions similar to those of Article 19 of WPPT. The first part of the agreed statement reads: "It is understood that the reference to 'infringement of any right covered by this

Treaty or the Berne Convention' includes both exclusive rights and rights of remuneration."

The second part reads: "It is further understood that Contracting Parties will not rely on this Article to devise or implement rights management systems that would have the effect of imposing formalities which are not permitted under the Berne Convention or this Treaty, prohibiting the free movement of goods or impeding the enjoyment of rights under this Treaty." The Diplomatic to Article 19 of the WPPT.

OTHER SUBSTANTIVE PROVISIONS

Criteria for Eligibility

5.571 Article 3 provides for the application of the criteria under the Rome Convention (Articles 4, 5, 17 and 18).

National Treatment

5.572 Article 4 provides for the same kind of national treatment as that prescribed by Article 3.1 of the TRIPS Agreement in respect of related rights, that is, national treatment only extends to the rights granted under the Treaty.

Coverage of the Rights of Performers

5.573 The coverage of the rights of performers is similar to that under the TRIPS Agreement; it only extends to live aural performances and performances fixed in phonograms, except for the right of broadcasting and communication to the public of live performances, which under Article 6(i) extends to all kinds of live performances, not only to aural ones (as under the second sentence of Article 14.1 of the TRIPS Agreement).

5.574 It is a question for interpretation whether the right to authorize fixation of unfixed performances under Article 6(ii) extends to all fixations or only to fixations on phonograms. The text of the provision may suggest a broader coverage; if, however, the definition of "fixation" under Article 2(c) is also taken into account, it seems that a narrower interpretation is justified. According to the said definition, "fixation" only means "the embodiment of *sounds, or the representation thereof,* from which they can be perceived, reproduced or communicated through a device" (emphasis added). Thus, Article 6(ii) seems to only extend to fixation on phonograms.

Moral Rights of Performers

5.575 Article 5(1) provides as follows: "Independently of a performer's economic rights, and even after the transfer of those rights, the performer shall, as regards his live aural performances or performances fixed in phonograms, have the right to claim to be identified as the performer of his performances, except where omission is dictated by the manner of the use of the performance, and to object to any distortion, mutilation or other modification of his performances that would be prejudicial to his reputation." This provision, in its main lines, follows Article 6*bis* of the Berne Convention (on the moral rights of authors) but it requires a somewhat lower level of protection: in respect of the right to be identified as the performer, the element of practicability is built in, and the scope of "the right to respect" is also narrower. Article 5(2) and (3), on the duration of protection of, and the means of redress for safeguarding, the rights, are *mutatis mutandis* versions of Article 6*bis*(2) and (3) of the Berne Convention.

Economic Rights of Performers

5.576 In addition to the "right of making available," discussed above under the "digital agenda," and a right of distribution, discussed below, the WPPT provides for practically the same economic rights for performers — right of broadcasting and communication to the public of unfixed performances (but in Article 6(ii) it is added: "except where the performance is already a broadcast performance"), right of reproduction and right of rental (Articles 6, 7 and 9) — as the rights granted in the TRIPS Agreement (Articles 14.1 and 14.4).

5.577 As far as the distribution right is concerned, Article 8(1) provides that performers have an exclusive right of authorizing the making available to the public of the original and copies of their performances fixed in phonograms, through sale or other transfer of ownership. Article 8(2) deals with the issue of the exhaustion of this right. It does not oblige Contracting States to choose national/regional exhaustion or international exhaustion, or to regulate at all the issue of exhaustion.

Rights of Producers of Phonograms

5.578 In addition to the right of "making available" discussed above under the "digital agenda" and a right of distribution, the WPPT provides the same rights for producers of phonograms — right of reproduction and right of rental (Articles 11 and 13) — as those granted under the TRIPS Agreement (Articles 14.2 and 14.4).

5.579 Article 12 contains, *mutatis mutandis,* the same provisions concerning a right of distribution for producers of phonograms in respect of their phonograms, as Article 8 does concerning such a right for performers in respect of their performances fixed in phonograms (see above).

Right to Remuneration for Broadcasting and Communication to the Public

5.580 Article 15 provides practically the same kind of right of remuneration to performers and producers of phonograms as Article 12 of the Rome Convention (except that, while the latter leaves it to national legislation whether this right is granted to performers, to producers or to both, the former provides that this right must be granted to both, in the form of a single equitable remuneration) and with the same extent of possible reservations as under Article 16.1(a) of the Rome Convention.

5.581 A specific feature of Article 15 appears in paragraph (4) which provides as follows: "For the purposes of this Article, phonograms made available to the public by wire or wireless means in such a way that members of the public may access them from a place and at a time individually chosen by them shall be considered as if they had been published for commercial purposes."

LIMITATIONS AND EXCEPTIONS

5.582 Under Article 16(1) of the WPPT, Contracting Parties may "provide for the same kinds of limitations or exceptions with regard to the protection of performers and producers of phonograms as they provide for, in their national legislation, in connection with the protection of copyright in literary and artistic works." This provision corresponds in substance to Article 15.2 of the Rome Convention. It is, however, an important difference that the Rome Convention, in its Article 15.1, also provides for specific limitations independent of those provided for in a given domestic law concerning copyright protection. Two of those specific limitations (use of short excerpts for reporting current events and ephemeral fixations by broadcasting organizations) are in harmony with the corresponding provisions of the Berne Convention; the third specific limitation, however, is not, since it provides for the possibility of limitations in respect of private use without any further conditions, while, in the Berne Convention, limitations for private use are also covered by the general provisions of Article 9(2) and, consequently, are subject to the "three-step test" (see under the WCT, paragraph 5.244).

5.583 If a country adheres to both the WCT and the WPPT, which is desirable, on the basis of the above-quoted Article 16(1) of the WPPT, it is obliged to apply the "three-step test" also for any limitations and exceptions to the rights provided for in the WPPT. Article 16(2) of the WPPT, however, contains a provision which prescribes this directly also (and, thus, that test is applicable irrespective of whether or not a given country also adheres to the WCT); it reads: "Contracting Parties shall confine any limitations of or exceptions to rights provided for in this Treaty to certain special cases which do not conflict with a normal exploitation of the performance or phonogram and do not unreasonably prejudice the legitimate interests of the performer or of the producer of the phonogram."

Transferability of Rights

5.584 The Treaty — similarly to the Berne Convention and the WCT — does not contain any limitation on the transferability of economic rights. The transferability of economic rights is confirmed also by the introductory phrase of Article 5(1) on moral rights of performers which reads: "Independently of a performer's economic rights and *even after the transfer of those rights. . . .*" (emphasis added).

DURATION OF PROTECTION

5.585 Under Article 17 of the WPPT, the "term of protection to be granted to performers shall last, at least, until the end of a period of 50 years computed from the end of the year in which the performance was fixed in a phonogram."

5.586 The term of protection of phonograms differs in substance from the term provided for in the TRIPS Agreement. Under Article 14.5 of the Agreement, the 50-year term is always computed from the end of the year in which the fixation was made, while under Article 17(2) of the WPPT, the term is calculated from the end of the year in which the phonogram was published, and it is only in case of absence of publication that it is calculated as under the TRIPS Agreement. Since publication normally takes place after fixation, the term under the Treaty, in general, is somewhat longer.

FORMALITIES

5.587 Under Article 20 of the WPPT, the enjoyment and exercise of rights provided for in the Treaty must not be subject to any formality. . . .

AUDIOVISUAL PERFORMANCES

5.592 The definitions of the terms "phonogram" and "fixation" in Article 2(b) and (c) of the WPPT limit the application of the Treaty to recordings of sounds. As regards audiovisual use of performances (that is use through moving images, with or without sound) the WPPT only grants protection against live broadcasting (Article 6(i)). The 1996 Diplomatic Conference which adopted the WPPT also discussed a possible extension of the scope of protection to cover such audiovisual use, but agreement was not reached at the time. . . .

NOTES AND QUESTIONS

1. The WPPT grants rights to performers and producers of phonograms that are more extensive than the rights afforded by the Rome Convention. It also addresses new technologies that enable the delivery of sound recordings over the Internet and other digital networks. The term of protection under the WPPT is 50 years as compared with the Rome term of 20 years. The 50-year term is consistent with the provisions of the TRIPS Agreement. The Rome Convention to some extent favors the interests of producers. The WPPT Treaty appears to carry forward territorial limitations with respect to the rights of performers by making their treatment subject to qualifications of the Rome Convention (*see* art. 3(2), WPPT in conjunction with art. 4, Rome). These qualifications are incorporated by reference in the TRIPS Agreement, which permits WTO Members to provide conditions and limitations on the rights of performers and producers consistent with the Rome Convention (art. 14.6, TRIPS). The rights of performers may still fall short of the rights of producers.

2. In the United States, sound recordings (e.g., phonograms) are defined by the Copyright Act as copyright subject matter.[18] Recall that in 1998, the U.S. Congress enacted the Sonny Bono Copyright Term Extension Act (CTEA), extending the term of copyright to the life of author plus 70 years (see *Eldred v. Ashcroft, supra*).[19]

3. Art. 2(b) of the WPPT defines "phonogram" as the "fixation of the sounds of a performance or of other sounds, or of a representation of sounds, other than in the form of a fixation incorporated in a cinematographic or other audiovisual work." Therefore, audiovisual use is not protected under the WPPT (with the exception of protection against live broadcasting as set forth in Article 6). As the WPPT addressed the rights of performers in respect of audiovisual performances only to a limited extent, negotiations were initiated for a treaty to protect audiovisual performances. We look at current developments on this subject *infra*.

b. *WPPT Norms and the Internet*

Business enterprises and individuals engaged in the commercial recording, distribution, and sale of copyrighted musical compositions and sound recordings were granted extensive legal protection in the WPPT. During the last several years, however, these interested groups were confronted with major challenges arising from continuously evolving technologies. New storage methods for digital data have been developed, coding audiovisual information, including movies and music, in a digital compressed format (e.g., MPEG, in

---

18. 17 U.S.C. § 102(7).
19. *See* Sonny Bono Copyright Term Extension (CTEA) Act, Pub. L. 105-298, Oct. 27, 1998, § 102.

the context of audio coding referred to as MP3).[20] The combination with broader Internet-connection bandwidth allows more efficient data exchange and storage of sound files. On the other hand, the emergence of so-called file sharing or "Peer-to-Peer" (P2P) systems provided a forum for large-scale data exchanges among Internet users.[21]

The most prominent first-generation file-sharing system was "Napster." Napster, a software application created in 1999 by a 19-year old student, facilitated the transmission of audio files between and among its users via free-download software. Napster did not store the individual user's audio files on its servers, but it stored the user's MP3 file names (i.e., personal library) and created a "collective directory" of files available for transfer during the time the user was logged onto the Napster system. The recording industry initiated legal proceedings against Napster. Eventually, the U.S. Court of Appeals for the Ninth Circuit held that Napster's service constituted both vicarious and contributory infringement of copyrighted works under the U.S. Copyright Act.[22] Yet, by the time the decision was rendered, Napster was already succeeded by myriad new P2P software. New software providers were more "copyright aware," having learned from the Napster experience. They developed more decentralized (sometimes anonymous) network systems and did not play an active role in connecting the users.

Next follows *MGM v. Grokster*, decided by the U.S. Supreme Court in 2005. The Court distinguishes Napster's and Grokster's roles in the file-sharing process. *MGM v. Grokster* does not directly apply the WPPT. There is no mention of the treaty in the opinion. Nonetheless, the decision addresses sounds that have been fixed in a digital medium for reproduction through a device, and that are accessible to individuals at a time and place of their own choosing. The Supreme Court's decision is likely to be looked at in other jurisdictions in both the copyright and neighboring rights contexts.

METRO-GOLDWYN-MAYER STUDIOS v. GROKSTER
545 U.S. 913 (2005)

Justice SOUTER delivered the opinion of the Court.

The question is under what circumstances the distributor of a product capable of both lawful and unlawful use is liable for acts of copyright infringement by third parties using the product. We hold that one who distributes a device with the object of promoting its use to infringe copyright, as shown by clear expression or other affirmative steps taken to foster infringement, is liable for the resulting acts of infringement by third parties.

I

A

Respondents, Grokster, Ltd., and StreamCast Networks, Inc., defendants in the trial court, distribute free software products that allow computer users to share electronic files through peer-to-peer networks, so called because users'

---

20. For more details, *see* http://www.chiariglione.org/mpeg/.
21. For a technical background, *see, e.g.,* http://en.wikipedia.org/wiki/Peer-to-peer.
22. *A&M Records v. Napster*, 239 F.3d 1004 (9th Cir. 2001).

computers communicate directly with each other, not through central servers. The advantage of peer-to-peer networks over information networks of other types shows up in their substantial and growing popularity. Because they need no central computer server to mediate the exchange of information or files among users, the high-bandwidth communications capacity for a server may be dispensed with, and the need for costly server storage space is eliminated. Since copies of a file (particularly a popular one) are available on many users' computers, file requests and retrievals may be faster than on other types of networks, and since file exchanges do not travel through a server, communications can take place between any computers that remain connected to the network without risk that a glitch in the server will disable the network in its entirety. Given these benefits in security, cost, and efficiency, peer-to-peer networks are employed to store and distribute electronic files by universities, government agencies, corporations, and libraries, among others.[1]

Other users of peer-to-peer networks include individual recipients of Grokster's and StreamCast's software, and although the networks that they enjoy through using the software can be used to share any type of digital file, they have prominently employed those networks in sharing copyrighted music and video files without authorization. A group of copyright holders (MGM for short, but including motion picture studios, recording companies, songwriters, and music publishers) sued Grokster and StreamCast for their users' copyright infringements, alleging that they knowingly and intentionally distributed their software to enable users to reproduce and distribute the copyrighted works in violation of the Copyright Act, 17 U.S.C. § 101 et seq. (2000 ed. and Supp. II). MGM sought damages and an injunction.

Discovery during the litigation revealed the way the software worked, the business aims of each defendant company, and the predilections of the users. . . .

Although Grokster and StreamCast do not therefore know when particular files are copied, a few searches using their software would show what is available on the networks the software reaches. . . .

But MGM's evidence gives reason to think that the vast majority of users' downloads are acts of infringement, and because well over 100 million copies of the software in question are known to have been downloaded, and billions of files are shared across the FastTrack and Gnutella networks each month, the probable scope of copyright infringement is staggering.

Grokster and StreamCast concede the infringement in most downloads, . . .

Grokster and StreamCast are not, however, merely passive recipients of information about infringing use. The record is replete with evidence that from the moment Grokster and StreamCast began to distribute their free software, each one clearly voiced the objective that recipients use it to download copyrighted works, and each took active steps to encourage infringement. . . .

In addition to this evidence of express promotion, marketing, and intent to promote further, the business models employed by Grokster and StreamCast

---

1. Peer-to-peer networks have disadvantages as well. Searches on peer-to-peer networks may not reach and uncover all available files because search requests may not be transmitted to every computer on the network. There may be redundant copies of popular files. The creator of the software has no incentive to minimize storage or bandwidth consumption, the costs of which are borne by every user of the network. Most relevant here, it is more difficult to control the content of files available for retrieval and the behavior of users.

confirm that their principal object was use of their software to download copyrighted works. . . .

Finally, there is no evidence that either company made an effort to filter copyrighted material from users' downloads or otherwise impede the sharing of copyrighted files. Although Grokster appears to have sent e-mails warning users about infringing content when it received threatening notice from the copyright holders, it never blocked anyone from continuing to use its software to share copyrighted files. . . . StreamCast not only rejected another company's offer of help to monitor infringement . . . but blocked the Internet Protocol addresses of entities it believed were trying to engage in such monitoring on its networks. . . .

B

. . . The District Court held that those who used the Grokster and Morpheus software to download copyrighted media files directly infringed MGM's copyrights, a conclusion not contested on appeal, but the court nonetheless granted summary judgment in favor of Grokster and StreamCast as to any liability arising from distribution of the then current versions of their software. Distributing that software gave rise to no liability in the court's view, because its use did not provide the distributors with actual knowledge of specific acts of infringement. . . .

The Court of Appeals affirmed. 380 F.3d 1154 (CA9 2004). In the court's analysis, a defendant was liable as a contributory infringer when it had knowledge of direct infringement and materially contributed to the infringement. But the court read *Sony Corp. of America v. Universal City Studios, Inc.,* 464 U.S. 417 . . . (1984), as holding that distribution of a commercial product capable of substantial noninfringing uses could not give rise to contributory liability for infringement unless the distributor had actual knowledge of specific instances of infringement and failed to act on that knowledge. The fact that the software was capable of substantial noninfringing uses in the Ninth Circuit's view meant that Grokster and StreamCast were not liable, because they had no such actual knowledge, owing to the decentralized architecture of their software. The court also held that Grokster and StreamCast did not materially contribute to their users' infringement because it was the users themselves who searched for, retrieved, and stored the infringing files, with no involvement by the defendants beyond providing the software in the first place.

The Ninth Circuit also considered whether Grokster and StreamCast could be liable under a theory of vicarious infringement. The court held against liability because the defendants did not monitor or control the use of the software, had no agreed-upon right or current ability to supervise its use, and had no independent duty to police infringement. We granted certiorari.

II

A

MGM and many of the amici fault the Court of Appeals's holding for upsetting a sound balance between the respective values of supporting creative pursuits through copyright protection and promoting innovation in new communication technologies by limiting the incidence of liability for copyright infringement. The more artistic protection is favored, the more technological innovation may be discouraged; the administration of copyright law is an exercise in managing the trade-off. *See Sony Corp. v. Universal City Studios, supra,* at 442, 78 L. Ed. 2d 574, 104 S. Ct. 774; *see generally* Ginsburg, Copyright and Control over New Technologies of Dissemination, 101 Colum. L. Rev. 1613 (2001); Lichtman & Landes, Indirect Liability for Copyright Infringement: An Economic Perspective, 16 Harv. J. L. & Tech. 395 (2003).

The tension between the two values is the subject of this case, with its claim that digital distribution of copyrighted material threatens copyright holders as never before, because every copy is identical to the original, copying is easy, and many people (especially the young) use file-sharing software to download copyrighted works. This very breadth of the software's use may well draw the public directly into the debate over copyright policy, . . .

The argument for imposing indirect liability in this case is, however, a powerful one, given the number of infringing downloads that occur every day using StreamCast's and Grokster's software. When a widely shared service or product is used to commit infringement, it may be impossible to enforce rights in the protected work effectively against all direct infringers, the only practical alternative being to go against the distributor of the copying device for secondary liability on a theory of contributory or vicarious infringement. *See In re Aimster Copyright Litigation,* 334 F.3d 643, 645-646 (CA7 2003).

One infringes contributorily by intentionally inducing or encouraging direct infringement, *see Gershwin Pub. Corp. v. Columbia Artists Management, Inc.,* 443 F.2d 1159, 1162 (CA2 1971), and infringes vicariously by profiting from direct infringement while declining to exercise a right to stop or limit it, *Shapiro, Bernstein & Co. v. H. L. Green Co.,* 316 F.2d 304, 307 (CA2 1963).[9] Although "the Copyright Act does not expressly render anyone liable for infringement committed by another," *Sony Corp. v. Universal City Studios,* 464 U.S., at 434, 78 L. Ed. 2d 574, 104 S. Ct. 774 these doctrines of secondary liability emerged from common law principles and are well established in the law, *id.,* at 486, 78 L. Ed. 2d 574, 104 S. Ct. 774 (Blackmun, J., dissenting). . . .

B

Despite the currency of these principles of secondary liability, this Court has dealt with secondary copyright infringement in only one recent case, and because MGM has tailored its principal claim to our opinion there, a look at our earlier holding is in order. In *Sony Corp. v. Universal City Studios, supra,* this Court addressed a claim that secondary liability for infringement can arise from the very distribution of a commercial product. There, the product, novel at the time, was what we know today as the videocassette recorder or VCR. Copyright

---

9. We stated in *Sony Corp. of America v. Universal City Studios, Inc.,* 464 U.S. 417, 78 L. Ed. 2d 574, 104 S. Ct. 774 (1984), that "'the lines between direct infringement, contributory infringement and vicarious liability are not clearly drawn'. . . . Reasoned analysis of [the *Sony* plaintiffs' contributory infringement claim] necessarily entails consideration of arguments and case law which may also be forwarded under the other labels, and indeed the parties . . . rely upon such arguments and authority in support of their respective positions on the issue of contributory infringement," *id.,* at 435, n. 17, 78 L. Ed. 2d 574, 104 S. Ct. 774 (quoting *Universal City Studios, Inc. v. Sony Corp.,* 480 F. Supp. 429, 457-458 (CD Cal. 1979)). In the present case MGM has argued a vicarious liability theory, which allows imposition of liability when the defendant profits directly from the infringement and has a right and ability to supervise the direct infringer, even if the defendant initially lacks knowledge of the infringement. *See, e.g., Shapiro, Bernstein & Co. v. H. L. Green Co.,* 316 F.2d 304, 308 (CA2 1963); *Dreamland Ball Room, Inc. v. Shapiro, Bernstein & Co.,* 36 F.2d 354, 355 (CA7 1929). Because we resolve the case based on an inducement theory, there is no need to analyze separately MGM's vicarious liability theory.

holders sued Sony as the manufacturer, claiming it was contributorily liable for infringement that occurred when VCR owners taped copyrighted programs because it supplied the means used to infringe, and it had constructive knowledge that infringement would occur. At the trial on the merits, the evidence showed that the principal use of the VCR was for "time-shifting" or taping a program for later viewing at a more convenient time, which the Court found to be a fair, not an infringing, use. . . . There was no evidence that Sony had expressed an object of bringing about taping in violation of copyright or had taken active steps to increase its profits from unlawful taping. . . . Although Sony's advertisements urged consumers to buy the VCR to " 'record favorite shows' " or " 'build a library' " of recorded programs. . . . (Blackmun, J., dissenting), neither of these uses was necessarily infringing. . . .

On those facts, with no evidence of stated or indicated intent to promote infringing uses, the only conceivable basis for imposing liability was on a theory of contributory infringement arising from its sale of VCRs to consumers with knowledge that some would use them to infringe. . . . But because the VCR was "capable of commercially significant noninfringing uses," we held the manufacturer could not be faulted solely on the basis of its distribution. . . .

This analysis reflected patent law's traditional staple article of commerce doctrine, now codified, that distribution of a component of a patented device will not violate the patent if it is suitable for use in other ways. . . .

In sum, where an article is "good for nothing else" but infringement, *Canda v. Michigan Malleable Iron Co.,* [124 F. 486 (C.A. 6 1903)], at 489, there is no legitimate public interest in its unlicensed availability, and there is no injustice in presuming or imputing an intent to infringe. . . . Conversely, the doctrine absolves the equivocal conduct of selling an item with substantial lawful as well as unlawful uses, and limits liability to instances of more acute fault than the mere understanding that some of one's products will be misused. It leaves breathing room for innovation and a vigorous commerce. . . .

The parties and many of the amici in this case think the key to resolving it is the *Sony* rule and, in particular, what it means for a product to be "capable of commercially significant noninfringing uses." *Sony Corp. v. Universal City Studios, supra,* at 442, 78 L. Ed. 2d 574, 104 S. Ct. 774. MGM advances the argument that granting summary judgment to Grokster and StreamCast as to their current activities gave too much weight to the value of innovative technology, and too little to the copyrights infringed by users of their software, given that 90% of works available on one of the networks was shown to be copyrighted. Assuming the remaining 10% to be its noninfringing use, MGM says this should not qualify as "substantial," and the Court should quantify *Sony* to the extent of holding that a product used "principally" for infringement does not qualify. . . . As mentioned before, Grokster and StreamCast reply by citing evidence that their software can be used to reproduce public domain works, and they point to copyright holders who actually encourage copying. Even if infringement is the principal practice with their software today, they argue, the noninfringing uses are significant and will grow.

We agree with MGM that the Court of Appeals misapplied *Sony,* which it read as limiting secondary liability quite beyond the circumstances to which the case applied. *Sony* barred secondary liability based on presuming or imputing intent to cause infringement solely from the design or distribution of a product capable of substantial lawful use, which the distributor knows is in fact used for infringement. The Ninth Circuit has read *Sony*'s limitation to mean that whenever a product is capable of substantial lawful use, the producer can never be held contributorily liable for third parties' infringing use of it; it read the rule as being this broad, even when an actual purpose to cause infringing use is shown by evidence independent of design and distribution of the product, unless the distributors had "specific knowledge of infringement at a time at which they contributed to the infringement, and failed to act upon that information." 380 F.3d at 1162 (internal quotation marks and alterations omitted). Because the Circuit found the StreamCast and Grokster software capable of substantial lawful use, it concluded on the basis of its reading of *Sony* that neither company could be held liable, since there was no showing that their software, being without any central server, afforded them knowledge of specific unlawful uses.

This view of *Sony*, however, was error, converting the case from one about liability resting on imputed intent to one about liability on any theory. Because *Sony* did not displace other theories of secondary liability, and because we find below that it was error to grant summary judgment to the companies on MGM's inducement claim, we do not revisit *Sony* further, as MGM requests, to add a more quantified description of the point of balance between protection and commerce when liability rests solely on distribution with knowledge that unlawful use will occur. It is enough to note that the Ninth Circuit's judgment rested on an erroneous understanding of *Sony* and to leave further consideration of the *Sony* rule for a day when that may be required.

C

Sony's rule limits imputing culpable intent as a matter of law from the characteristics or uses of a distributed product. But nothing in *Sony* requires courts to ignore evidence of intent if there is such evidence, and the case was never meant to foreclose rules of fault-based liability derived from the common law.[10] *Sony Corp. v. Universal City Studios*, 464 U.S., at 439, 78 L. Ed. 2d 574, 104 S. Ct. 774 ("If vicarious liability is to be imposed on Sony in this case, it must rest on the fact that it has sold equipment with constructive knowledge" of the potential for infringement). Thus, where evidence goes beyond a product's characteristics or the knowledge that it may be put to infringing uses, and shows statements or actions directed to promoting infringement, Sony's staple-article rule will not preclude liability.

The classic case of direct evidence of unlawful purpose occurs when one induces commission of infringement by another, or "entices or persuades another" to infringe, Black's Law Dictionary 790 (8th ed. 2004), as by advertising. . . .

The rule on inducement of infringement as developed in the early cases is no different today.[11] . . .

For the same reasons that Sony took the staple-article doctrine of patent law as a model for its copyright safe-harbor rule, the inducement rule, too, is a sensible one for copyright. We adopt it here, holding that one who distributes a device with the object of promoting its use to infringe copyright, as shown by clear expression or other affirmative steps taken to foster infringement, is liable

---

10. Nor does the Patent Act's exemption from liability for those who distribute a staple article of commerce, 35 U.S.C. § 271(c), extend to those who induce patent infringement, § 271(b).

11. Inducement has been codified in patent law. *Ibid.*

for the resulting acts of infringement by third parties. We are, of course, mindful of the need to keep from trenching on regular commerce or discouraging the development of technologies with lawful and unlawful potential. Accordingly, just as Sony did not find intentional inducement despite the knowledge of the VCR manufacturer that its device could be used to infringe, 464 U.S., at 439, n. 19, 78 L. Ed. 2d 574, 104 S. Ct. 774, mere knowledge of infringing potential or of actual infringing uses would not be enough here to subject a distributor to liability. Nor would ordinary acts incident to product distribution, such as offering customers technical support or product updates, support liability in themselves. The inducement rule, instead, premises liability on purposeful, culpable expression and conduct, and thus does nothing to compromise legitimate commerce or discourage innovation having a lawful promise.

III

A

The only apparent question about treating MGM's evidence as sufficient to withstand summary judgment under the theory of inducement goes to the need on MGM's part to adduce evidence that StreamCast and Grokster communicated an inducing message to their software users. . . .

In StreamCast's case, of course, the evidence just described was supplemented by other unequivocal indications of unlawful purpose in the internal communications and advertising designs aimed at Napster users ("When the lights went off at Napster . . . where did the users go?" . . .). . . .

Three features of th[e] evidence of intent are particularly notable. First, each company showed itself to be aiming to satisfy a known source of demand for copyright infringement, the market comprising former Napster users. StreamCast's internal documents made constant reference to Napster, it initially distributed its Morpheus software through an OpenNap program compatible with Napster, it advertised its OpenNap program to Napster users, and its Morpheus software functions as Napster did except that it could be used to distribute more kinds of files, including copyrighted movies and software programs. Grokster's name is apparently derived from Napster, it too initially offered an OpenNap program, its software's function is likewise comparable to Napster's, and it attempted to divert queries for Napster onto its own Web site. Grokster and StreamCast's efforts to supply services to former Napster users, deprived of a mechanism to copy and distribute what were overwhelmingly infringing files, indicate a principal, if not exclusive, intent on the part of each to bring about infringement.

Second, this evidence of unlawful objective is given added significance by MGM's showing that neither company attempted to develop filtering tools or other mechanisms to diminish the infringing activity using their software. While the Ninth Circuit treated the defendants' failure to develop such tools as irrelevant because they lacked an independent duty to monitor their users' activity, we think this evidence underscores Grokster's and StreamCast's intentional facilitation of their users' infringement.[12]

---

12. Of course, in the absence of other evidence of intent, a court would be unable to find contributory infringement liability merely based on a failure to take affirmative steps to prevent

Third, there is a further complement to the direct evidence of unlawful objective. It is useful to recall that StreamCast and Grokster make money by selling advertising space, by directing ads to the screens of computers employing their software. As the record shows, the more the software is used, the more ads are sent out and the greater the advertising revenue becomes. Since the extent of the software's use determines the gain to the distributors, the commercial sense of their enterprise turns on high-volume use, which the record shows is infringing.[13] This evidence alone would not justify an inference of unlawful intent, but viewed in the context of the entire record its import is clear.

The unlawful objective is unmistakable.

B

In addition to intent to bring about infringement and distribution of a device suitable for infringing use, the inducement theory of course requires evidence of actual infringement by recipients of the device, the software in this case. As the account of the facts indicates, there is evidence of infringement on a gigantic scale, and there is no serious issue of the adequacy of MGM's showing on this point in order to survive the companies' summary judgment requests. Although an exact calculation of infringing use, as a basis for a claim of damages, is subject to dispute, there is no question that the summary judgment evidence is at least adequate to entitle MGM to go forward with claims for damages and equitable relief. . . .

In sum, this case is significantly different from *Sony* and reliance on that case to rule in favor of StreamCast and Grokster was error. *Sony* dealt with a claim of liability based solely on distributing a product with alternative lawful and unlawful uses, with knowledge that some users would follow the unlawful course. The case struck a balance between the interests of protection and innovation by holding that the product's capability of substantial lawful employment should bar the imputation of fault and consequent secondary liability for the unlawful acts of others.

MGM's evidence in this case most obviously addresses a different basis of liability for distributing a product open to alternative uses. Here, evidence of the distributors' words and deeds going beyond distribution as such shows a purpose to cause and profit from third-party acts of copyright infringement. If liability for inducing infringement is ultimately found, it will not be on the basis of presuming or imputing fault, but from inferring a patently illegal objective from statements and actions showing what that objective was.

There is substantial evidence in MGM's favor on all elements of inducement, and summary judgment in favor of Grokster and StreamCast was error. On remand, reconsideration of MGM's motion for summary judgment will be in order.

---

infringement, if the device otherwise was capable of substantial noninfringing uses. Such a holding would tread too close to the *Sony* safe harbor.

13. . . . [T]he distribution of a product can itself give rise to liability where evidence shows that the distributor intended and encouraged the product to be used to infringe. In such a case, the culpable act is not merely the encouragement of infringement but also the distribution of the tool intended for infringing use.

The judgment of the Court of Appeals is vacated, and the case is remanded for further proceedings consistent with this opinion.

It is so ordered.

NOTES AND QUESTIONS

1. The successful launch of Apple's iTunes and similar pay-for-download web sites has provided some measure of relief to the recording industry and associated artists, but widespread unauthorized sharing of audio (and increasingly, video) files continues. There appears to be at least some difference in attitude among generations, with older Internet users more willing to pay for content than younger. Of course, this could simply be explained by the fact that older users are more likely to be generating income and therefore have the capacity to pay.

2. It is often pointed out that many individuals who would not contemplate "shoplifting" a CD from a brick-and-mortar store are willing to "misappropriate" copyrighted works over the Internet. What may account for these different attitudes toward misappropriation? Do individuals inherently associate "tangible" goods such as CDs with labor for which they are willing to compensate, while not associating digital bits with labor? Do people avoid shoplifting only because they fear being caught?

3. Since the earliest days of personal computing, software developers have attempted to protect against the unauthorized copying of data with technical measures. While some of these technical measures have inhibited unauthorized copying, they certainly have not controlled the problem of software "piracy," nor in the case of audio and video files do technical protection measures seem likely to keep ahead of those attempting to defeat them. Legal solutions such as recording industry litigation threats against university administrators, and searches of student dormitories (with seizure of computers) are very unpleasant and seem unlikely to generate respect for copyright protection. Historically, problems of controlling large-scale "misappropriation" of copyrighted works — such as tape recording of over-the-air music broadcasts — has been addressed by imposing a tax or royalty on the sale of the hardware that enables the copying. The tax or royalty is then distributed to copyright holders based on formulas reflecting the popularity of their works. Is this a feasible solution to problems such as peer-to-peer file sharing of audio and video files? What are the foreseeable impediments to such a system?

4. Broadcast, Cablecast, and Webcast

The WIPO Standing Committee on Copyright and Related Rights is working on a draft Treaty on the Protection of Broadcast Organizations. Information concerning the status of negotiations may be found at the WIPO web site (http://www.wipo.int). A draft as of February 2006 would extend protection to broadcasts and "cablecasts," and provide an optional Appendix for the protection of "webcasts." The term of protection would be 50 years counted from the end of the year in which the broadcast took place. The draft treaty includes protection for broadcasters with respect to retransmission, fixation, and reproduction.

E. Exhaustion and the Movement of Copyrighted Works in Trade

1. National and International Exhaustion

In Chapter 1, we introduced the subject of IPRs exhaustion and its relationship to the movement of goods in international trade. We have further examined exhaustion rules in respect of patents (Chapter 2) and trademarks (Chapter 3). It was earlier observed that countries do not necessarily follow the same rule of exhaustion with respect to all categories of intellectual property. Countries may, and do, adopt a different rule of exhaustion for copyright than they adopt with respect to patent.

Copyright affects a wide range of subject matter and its role in the international movement of goods may be broader than immediately apparent. For example, automobile producers attempt to protect the design of spare body parts with copyright, and to prevent the movement of such parts across national borders. A rule of national exhaustion of copyright may enable the producer to segregate markets. A rule of international exhaustion in copyright, on the other hand, may require the producer to make products available at roughly the same prices across world markets. Debate concerning copyright exhaustion has been quite intense in countries such as Australia and New Zealand, which have traditionally confronted higher prices based on their relative isolation from other major OECD markets.[23] Some of the best empirical studies of the impact of exhaustion rules on prices have been conducted in Australia and New Zealand.

In the United States, product labels may be protected by copyright.[24] Following the U.S. Supreme Court decision in *K mart v. Cartier, supra* Chapter 3, U.S. manufacturers increasingly turned to copyright as a means to block parallel importation of products that they (including their affiliates) had put on the market in foreign countries. This led to a division among the Courts of Appeals regarding whether the Copyright Act could be used for that purpose.

To resolve a split among the Circuits, in 1998, the Supreme Court decided *Quality King v. L'anza.* The holding of the *Quality King* decision directly applies to copyrighted subject matter produced within the United States, exported, and subsequently imported into the United States. Because of the complex construction of the U.S. Copyright Act, it cannot be assumed that the rule of exhaustion announced by the Court in *Quality King* will govern the situation in which copyrighted goods are first sold outside the United States (see discussion of *Costco v. Omega* below). Perhaps more important than the limited holding of this case is the statement of principles announced by the Court toward the end of its opinion in response to argumentation concerning the "pure" parallel imports context.

---

23. Australia and New Zealand each adopted legislation permitting parallel importation of works protected by copyright. The legislation adopted by Australia distinguishes among different types of copyrighted works. *See* Chris Creswell, *Recent Developments in Australia and New Zealand,* paper presented to ILA Trade Law Committee meeting of November 6-7, 1998, Geneva; and Abraham Van Melle, *Parallel Importing in New Zealand: Historical Origins, Recent Developments, and Future Directions,* [1999] EIPR 63. In the case of New Zealand, at least, this action led to a diplomatic protest by the U.S. government. *See* details in Frederick M. Abbott, Second Report (Final) to the Committee on International Trade Law of the International Law Association on the Subject of the Exhaustion of Intellectual Property Rights and Parallel Importation, presented in London, July 2000 at the 69th Conference of the International Law Association, rev. 1.1.

24. Recall that in *Feist v. Rural Telephone, supra,* the Supreme Court imposed a low threshold of originality.

QUALITY KING DISTRIBUTORS v. L'ANZA
RESEARCH INTERNATIONAL

523 U.S. 135 (1998)

Justice STEVENS delivered the opinion of the Court.

Section 106(3) of the Copyright Act of 1976 (Act), 17 U.S.C. § 106(3), gives the owner of a copyright the exclusive right to distribute copies of a copyrighted work. That exclusive right is expressly limited, however, by the provisions of §§ 107 through 120. Section 602(a) gives the copyright owner the right to prohibit the unauthorized importation of copies. The question presented by this case is whether the right granted by § 602(a) is also limited by §§ 107 through 120. More narrowly, the question is whether the "first sale" doctrine endorsed in § 109(a) is applicable to imported copies.

I

Respondent, L'anza Research International, Inc. (L'anza), is a California corporation engaged in the business of manufacturing and selling shampoos, conditioners, and other hair care products. L'anza has copyrighted the labels that are affixed to those products. In the United States, L'anza sells exclusively to domestic distributors who have agreed to resell within limited geographic areas and then only to authorized retailers such as barber shops, beauty salons, and professional hair care colleges. L'anza has found that the American "public is generally unwilling to pay the price charged for high quality products, such as L'anza's products, when they are sold along with the less expensive lower quality products that are generally carried by supermarkets and drug stores". . . . L'anza promotes the domestic sales of its products with extensive advertising in various trade magazines and at point of sale, and by providing special training to authorized retailers.

L'anza also sells its products in foreign markets. In those markets, however, it does not engage in comparable advertising or promotion; its prices to foreign distributors are 35% to 40% lower than the prices charged to domestic distributors. In 1992 and 1993, L'anza's distributor in the United Kingdom arranged the sale of three shipments to a distributor in Malta; each shipment contained several tons of L'anza products with copyrighted labels affixed. The record does not establish whether the initial purchaser was the distributor in the United Kingdom or the distributor in Malta, or whether title passed when the goods were delivered to the carrier or when they arrived at their destination, but it is undisputed that the goods were manufactured by L'anza and first sold by L'anza to a foreign purchaser.

It is also undisputed that the goods found their way back to the United States without the permission of L'anza and were sold in California by unauthorized retailers who had purchased them at discounted prices from Quality King Distributors, Inc. (petitioner). There is some uncertainty about the identity of the actual importer, but for the purpose of our decision we assume that petitioner bought all three shipments from the Malta distributor, imported them, and then resold them to retailers who were not in L'anza's authorized chain of distribution.

After determining the source of the unauthorized sales, L'anza brought suit against petitioner and several other defendants. The complaint alleged that the importation and subsequent distribution of those products bearing copyrighted labels violated L'anza's "exclusive rights under 17 U.S.C. §§ 106, 501 and 602 to reproduce and distribute the copyrighted material in the United States." App. 32. The District Court rejected petitioner's defense based on the "first sale" doctrine recognized by § 109 and entered summary judgment in favor of L'anza. Based largely on its conclusion that § 602 would be "meaningless" if § 109 provided a defense in a case of this kind, the Court of Appeals affirmed. 98 F.3d 1109, 1114 (CA9 1996). Because its decision created a conflict with the Third Circuit, *see Sebastian Int'l, Inc. v. Consumer Contacts (PTY) Ltd.*, 847 F.2d 1093 (1988), we granted the petition for certiorari. 520 U.S. (1997).

II

This is an unusual copyright case because L'anza does not claim that anyone has made unauthorized copies of its copyrighted labels. Instead, L'anza is primarily interested in protecting the integrity of its method of marketing the products to which the labels are affixed. Although the labels themselves have only a limited creative component, our interpretation of the relevant statutory provisions would apply equally to a case involving more familiar copyrighted materials such as sound recordings or books. Indeed, we first endorsed the first sale doctrine in a case involving a claim by a publisher that the resale of its books at discounted prices infringed its copyright on the books. *Bobbs-Merrill Co. v. Straus*, 210 U.S. 339, 52 L. Ed. 1086, 28 S. Ct. 722 (1908).[14]

In that case, the publisher, Bobbs-Merrill, had inserted a notice in its books that any retail sale at a price under $1.00 would constitute an infringement of its copyright. The defendants, who owned Macy's department store, disregarded the notice and sold the books at a lower price without Bobbs-Merrill's consent. We held that the exclusive statutory right to "vend" applied only to the first sale of the copyrighted work: . . .

. . . Under the 1976 Act, the comparable exclusive right granted in 17 U.S.C. § 106(3) is the right "to distribute copies . . . by sale or other transfer of ownership."[8] The comparable limitation on that right is provided not by judicial interpretation, but by an express statutory provision. Section 109(a) provides:

---

14. The doctrine had been consistently applied by other federal courts in earlier cases. *See Kipling v. G. P. Putnam's Sons*, 120 F. 631, 634 (CA2 1903); *Doan v. American Book Co.*, 105 F. 772, 776 (CA7 1901); *Harrison v. Maynard, Merrill & Co.*, 61 F. 689, 691 (CA2 1894); *Bobbs-Merrill Co. v. Snellenburg*, 131 F. 530, 532 (ED Pa. 1904); *Clemens v. Estes*, 22 F. 899, 900 (Mass. 1885); *Stowe v. Thomas*, 2 Wall. Jr. 547, 23 F. Cas. 201, 206-207 (ED Pa. 1853).

8. The full text of § 106 reads as follows:

"§ 106. EXCLUSIVE RIGHTS IN COPYRIGHTED WORKS
Subject to sections 107 through 120, the owner of copyright under this title has the exclusive rights to do and to authorize any of the following:
    (1) to reproduce the copyrighted work in copies or phonorecords;
    (2) to prepare derivative works based upon the copyrighted work;
    (3) to distribute copies or phonorecords of the copyrighted work to the public by sale or other transfer of ownership, or by rental, lease, or lending;
    (4) in the case of literary, musical, dramatic, and choreographic works, pantomimes, and motion pictures and other audiovisual works, to perform the copyrighted work publicly;
    (5) in the case of literary, musical, dramatic, and choreographic works, pantomimes, and pictorial, graphic, or sculptural works, including the individual images of a motion picture or other audiovisual work, to display the copyrighted work publicly; and
    (6) in the case of sound recordings, to perform the copyrighted work publicly by means of a digital audio transmission." 17 U.S.C. § 106 (1994 ed., Supp. I).

> Notwithstanding the provisions of section 106(3), the owner of a particular copy
> or phonorecord lawfully made under this title, or any person authorized by such
> owner, is entitled, without the authority of the copyright owner, to sell or
> otherwise dispose of the possession of that copy or phonorecord. . . . [9]

The *Bobbs-Merrill* opinion emphasized the critical distinction between statutory
rights and contract rights. In this case, L'anza relies on the terms of its contracts
with its domestic distributors to limit their sales to authorized retail outlets. . . .
L'anza does claim . . . that contractual provisions are inadequate to protect it
from the actions of foreign distributors who may resell L'anza's products to
American vendors unable to buy from L'anza's domestic distributors, and
that § 602(a) of the Act, properly construed, prohibits such unauthorized competition. To evaluate that submission, we must, of course, consider the text of
§ 602(a).

III

The most relevant portion of § 602(a) provides:

> Importation into the United States, without the authority of the owner of
> copyright under this title, of copies or phonorecords of a work that have
> been acquired outside the United States is an infringement of the exclusive
> right to distribute copies or phonorecords under section 106, actionable under
> section 501. . . .

It is significant that this provision does not categorically prohibit the
unauthorized importation of copyrighted materials. Instead, it provides that
such importation is an infringement of the exclusive right to distribute copies
"under section 106." Like the exclusive right to "vend" that was construed in
Bobbs-Merrill, the exclusive right to distribute is a limited right. The introductory language in § 106 expressly states that all of the exclusive rights granted by
that section — including, of course, the distribution right granted by subsection
(3) — are limited by the provisions of §§ 107 through 120. One of those limitations, as we have noted, is provided by the terms of § 109(a), which expressly
permit the owner of a lawfully made copy to sell that copy "notwithstanding the
provisions of section 106(3)."

After the first sale of a copyrighted item "lawfully made under this title," any
subsequent purchaser, whether from a domestic or from a foreign reseller, is
obviously an "owner" of that item. Read literally, § 109(a) unambiguously states
that such an owner "is entitled, without the authority of the copyright owner, to
sell" that item. Moreover, since § 602(a) merely provides that unauthorized
importation is an infringement of an exclusive right "under section 106,"
and since that limited right does not encompass resales by lawful owners, the
literal text of § 602(a) is simply inapplicable to both domestic and foreign

---

9. The comparable section in the 1909 and 1947 Acts provided that "nothing in this Act shall
be deemed to forbid, prevent, or restrict the transfer of any copy of a copyrighted work the
possession of which has been lawfully obtained." Copyright Act of 1909, ch. 320, § 41, 35 Stat.
1084; *see also* Copyright Act of 1947, ch. 391, § 27, 61 Stat. 660. It is noteworthy that § 109(a) of the
1978 Act does not apply to "any copy"; it applies only to a copy that was "lawfully made under this
title."

owners of L'anza's products who decide to import them and resell them in the United States.

Notwithstanding the clarity of the text of §§ 106(3), 109(a), and 602(a), L'anza argues that the language of the Act supports a construction of the right granted by § 602(a) as "distinct from the right under Section 106(3) standing alone," and thus not subject to § 109(a). . . . Otherwise, L'anza argues, both the § 602(a) right itself and its exceptions would be superfluous. Moreover, supported by various amici curiae, including the Solicitor General of the United States, L'anza contends that its construction is supported by important policy considerations. We consider these arguments separately.

IV

L'anza advances two primary arguments based on the text of the Act: (1) that § 602(a), and particularly its three exceptions, are superfluous if limited by the first sale doctrine; and (2) that the text of § 501 defining an "infringer" refers separately to violations of § 106, on the one hand, and to imports in violation of § 602. The short answer to both of these arguments is that neither adequately explains why the words "under section 106" appear in § 602(a). The Solicitor General makes an additional textual argument: he contends that the word "importation" in § 602(a) describes an act that is not protected by the language in § 109(a) authorizing a subsequent owner "to sell or otherwise dispose of the possession of" a copy. Each of these arguments merits separate comment.

THE COVERAGE OF § 602(A)

Prior to the enactment of § 602(a), the Act already prohibited the importation of "piratical," or unauthorized, copies. Moreover, that earlier prohibition is retained in § 602(b) of the present act.[17] L'anza therefore argues (as do the Solicitor General and other amici curiae) that § 602(a) is superfluous unless it covers non-piratical ("lawfully made") copies sold by the copyright owner, because importation nearly always implies a first sale. There are several flaws in this argument.

First, even if § 602(a) did apply only to piratical copies, it at least would provide the copyright holder with a private remedy against the importer, whereas the enforcement of § 602(b) is vested in the Customs Service. Second, because the protection afforded by § 109(a) is available only to the "owner" of a lawfully made copy (or someone authorized by the owner), the first sale doctrine would not provide a defense to a § 602(a) action against any non-owner such as a bailee, a licensee, a consignee, or one whose possession of the copy was unlawful.[19] Third,

---

17. Section 602(b) provides in relevant part: "In a case where the making of the copies or phonorecords would have constituted an infringement of copyright if this title had been applicable, their importation is prohibited. . . ." The first sale doctrine of § 109(a) does not protect owners of piratical copies, of course, because such copies were not "lawfully made."

19. In its opinion in this case, the Court of Appeals quoted a statement by a representative of the music industry expressing the need for protection against the importation of stolen motion picture prints: "We've had a similar situation with respect to motion picture prints, which are sent all over the world — legitimate prints made from the authentic negative. These prints get into illicit hands. They're stolen, and there's no contractual relationship. . . . Now those are not piratical copies." Copyright Law Revision Part 2: Discussion and Comments on Report of the Register of Copyrights on General Revision of the U.S. Copyright Law, 88th Cong., 1st Sess., 213 (H. R. Judiciary Comm. Print 1963) (statement of Mr. Sargoy), *quoted in* 98 F.3d 1109, 1116 (CA9 1996).

§ 602(a) applies to a category of copies that are neither piratical nor "lawfully made under this title." That category encompasses copies that were "lawfully made" not under the United States Copyright Act, but instead, under the law of some other country.

The category of copies produced lawfully under a foreign copyright was expressly identified in the deliberations that led to the enactment of the 1976 Act. We mention one example of such a comment in 1961 simply to demonstrate that the category is not a merely hypothetical one. In a report to Congress, the Register of Copyrights stated, in part:

> "When arrangements are made for both a U.S. edition and a foreign edition of the same work, the publishers frequently agree to divide the international markets. The foreign publisher agrees not to sell his edition in the United States, and the U.S. publisher agrees not to sell his edition in certain foreign countries. It has been suggested that the import ban on piratical copies should be extended to bar the importation of the foreign edition in contravention of such an agreement." Copyright Law Revision: Report of the Register of Copyrights on the General Revision of the U.S. Copyright Law, 87th Cong., 1st Sess., 125-126 (H. R. Judiciary Comm. Print 1961).

Even in the absence of a market allocation agreement between, for example, a publisher of the U.S. edition and a publisher of the British edition of the same work, each such publisher could make lawful copies. If the author of the work gave the exclusive U.S. distribution rights — enforceable under the Act — to the publisher of the U.S. edition and the exclusive British distribution rights to the publisher of the British edition,[20] however, presumably only those made by the publisher of the U.S. edition would be "lawfully made under this title" within the meaning of § 109(a). The first sale doctrine would not provide the publisher of the British edition who decided to sell in the American market with a defense to an action under § 602(a) (or, for that matter, to an action under § 106(3), if there was a distribution of the copies).

The argument that the statutory exceptions to § 602(a) are superfluous if the first sale doctrine is applicable rests on the assumption that the coverage of that section is co-extensive with the coverage of § 109(a). But since it is, in fact, broader because it encompasses copies that are not subject to the first sale doctrine — e.g., copies that are lawfully made under the law of another country — the exceptions do protect the traveler who may have made an isolated purchase of a copy of a work that could not be imported in bulk for purposes of resale. As we read the Act, although both the first sale doctrine embodied in § 109(a) and the exceptions in § 602(a) may be applicable in some situations, the former does not subsume the latter; those provisions retain significant independent meaning.

---

20. A participant in a 1964 panel discussion expressed concern about this particular situation. Copyright Law Revision Part 4: Further Discussion and Comments on Preliminary Draft for Revised U.S. Copyright Law, 88th Cong., 2d Sess., 119 (H. R. Judiciary Comm. Print 1964) (statement of Mrs. Pilpel) ("For example, if someone were to import a copy of the British edition of an American book and the author had transferred exclusive United States and Canadian rights to an American publisher, would that British edition be in violation so that this would constitute an infringement under this section?"); *see also id.*, at 209 (statement of Mr. Manges) (describing similar situation as "a troublesome problem that confronts U.S. book publishers frequently").

SECTION 501'S SEPARATE REFERENCES TO §§ 106 AND 602

The text of § 501 does lend support to L'anza's submission. In relevant part, it provides:

> (a) Anyone who violates any of the exclusive rights of the copyright owner as provided by sections 106 through 118 or of the author as provided in section 106A(a), or who imports copies or phonorecords into the United States in violation of section 602, is an infringer of the copyright or right of the author, as the case may be. . . .

The use of the words "or who imports," rather than words such as "including one who imports," is more consistent with an interpretation that a violation of § 602 is distinct from a violation of § 106 (and thus not subject to the first sale doctrine set out in § 109(a)) than with the view that it is a species of such a violation. Nevertheless, the force of that inference is outweighed by other provisions in the statutory text.

Most directly relevant is the fact that the text of § 602(a) itself unambiguously states that the prohibited importation is an infringement of the exclusive distribution right "under section 106, actionable under section 501." Unlike that phrase, which identifies § 602 violations as a species of § 106 violations, the text of § 106A, which is also cross-referenced in § 501, uses starkly different language. It states that the author's right protected by § 106A is "independent of the exclusive rights provided in Section 106." The contrast between the relevant language in § 602 and that in § 106A strongly implies that only the latter describes an independent right.

Of even greater importance is the fact that the § 106 rights are subject not only to the first sale defense in § 109(a), but also to all of the other provisions of "sections 107 through 120." If § 602(a) functioned independently, none of those sections would limit its coverage. For example, the "fair use" defense embodied in § 107 would be unavailable to importers if § 602(a) created a separate right not subject to the limitations on the § 106(3) distribution right. Under L'anza's interpretation of the Act, it presumably would be unlawful for a distributor to import copies of a British newspaper that contained a book review quoting excerpts from an American novel protected by a United States copyright. Given the importance of the fair use defense to publishers of scholarly works, as well as to publishers of periodicals, it is difficult to believe that Congress intended to impose an absolute ban on the importation of all such works containing any copying of material protected by a United States copyright.

In the context of this case, involving copyrighted labels, it seems unlikely that an importer could defend an infringement as a "fair use" of the label. In construing the statute, however, we must remember that its principal purpose was to promote the progress of the "useful Arts," U.S. Const., Art. I, § 8, cl. 8, by rewarding creativity, and its principal function is the protection of original works, rather than ordinary commercial products that use copyrighted material as a marketing aid. It is therefore appropriate to take into account the impact of the denial of the fair use defense for the importer of foreign publications. As applied to such publications, L'anza's construction of § 602 "would merely inhibit access to ideas without any countervailing benefit." *Sony Corp. of America v. Universal City Studios, Inc.*, 464 U.S. 417, 450-451, 78 L. Ed. 2d 574, 104 S. Ct. 774 (1984). . . .

[W]e are not persuaded by either L'anza's or the Solicitor General's textual arguments.

V

The parties and their amici have debated at length the wisdom or unwisdom of governmental restraints on what is sometimes described as either the "gray market" or the practice of "parallel importation."[28] In *K mart Corp. v. Cartier, Inc.*, 486 U.S. 281, 100 L. Ed. 2d 313, 108 S. Ct. 1811 (1988), we used those terms to refer to the importation of foreign-manufactured goods bearing a valid United States trademark without the consent of the trademark holder. *Id.*, at 285-286. We are not at all sure that those terms appropriately describe the consequences of an American manufacturer's decision to limit its promotional efforts to the domestic market and to sell its products abroad at discounted prices that are so low that its foreign distributors can compete in the domestic market.[29] But even if they do, whether or not we think it would be wise policy to provide statutory protection for such price discrimination is not a matter that is relevant to our duty to interpret the text of the Copyright Act.

Equally irrelevant is the fact that the Executive Branch of the Government has entered into at least five international trade agreements that are apparently intended to protect domestic copyright owners from the unauthorized importation of copies of their works sold in those five countries.[30] The earliest of those agreements was made in 1991; none has been ratified by the Senate. Even though they are of course consistent with the position taken by the Solicitor General in this litigation, they shed no light on the proper interpretation of a statute that was enacted in 1976.[31]

The judgment of the Court of Appeals is reversed.

It is so ordered.

Justice GINSBURG, concurring.

This case involves a "round trip" journey, travel of the copies in question from the United States to places abroad, then back again. I join the Court's opinion recognizing that we do not today resolve cases in which the allegedly infringing imports were manufactured abroad. *See* W. Patry, Copyright Law and Practice 166-170 (1997 Supp.) (commenting that provisions of Title 17 do not apply extraterritorially unless expressly so stated, hence the words "lawfully made under this title" in the "first sale" provision, 17 U.S.C. § 109(a), must mean "lawfully made in the United States"); *see generally* P. Goldstein,

---

28. Compare, for example, Gorelick & Little, The Case for Parallel Importation, 11 N.C. J. Int'l L. & Comm. Reg. 205 (1986), with Gordon, Gray Market Is Giving Hair-Product Makers Gray Hair, N.Y. Times, July 13, 1997, section 1, p. 28, col. 1.

29. Presumably L'anza, for example, could have avoided the consequences of that competition either (1) by providing advertising support abroad and charging higher prices, or (2) if it was satisfied to leave the promotion of the product in foreign markets to its foreign distributors, to sell its products abroad under a different name.

30. The Solicitor General advises us that such agreements have been made with Cambodia, Trinidad and Tobago, Jamaica, Ecuador, and Sri Lanka.

31. We also note that in 1991, when the first of the five agreements was signed, the Third Circuit had already issued its opinion in *Sebastian Int'l, Inc. v. Consumer Contacts (PTY) Ltd.*, 847 F.2d 1093 (1988), adopting a position contrary to that subsequently endorsed by the Executive Branch.

Copyright § 16.0, pp. 16:1-16:2 (2d ed. 1998) ("Copyright protection is territorial. The rights granted by the United States Copyright Act extend no farther than the nation's borders.").

NOTES AND QUESTIONS

1. In *K mart v. Cartier, supra* Chapter 3, the Supreme Court divided U.S. trademark holders into three categories (Cases 1-3, including further subdivision of Case 2). Case 1 involved foreign and domestic companies that were not economically linked. Case 2 involved commonly controlled enterprises. Case 3 involved licensees. In *Quality King*, Justice Stevens illustrates a situation that *might* allow the blocking of imports, that is, where a U.S. and British publisher are independently granted publication rights by the copyright holder. Is that closer to Case 1, 2, or 3? With what logical result?

2. In *Quality King*, a unanimous Supreme Court questions whether the policies underlying *K mart's* limited right to block parallel imports should extend to the case in which a U.S. producer is deliberately engaging in international price discrimination. Should governments encourage their producers to sell more cheaply abroad than at home? Why?

3. The Supreme Court went so far as to offer L'anza some practical business advice about protecting its U.S. marketing strategy. What is that advice, and why did the Supreme Court offer it?

4. The U.S. Justice Department argued to the Supreme Court that it should interpret the Copyright Act in a way that would not conflict with international trade agreements the United States signed with several countries. A conflicting interpretation, according to the Justice Department, would embarrass the United States in the conduct of foreign relations. A number of commentators have suggested that the Justice Department was attempting to force a change in U.S. domestic law through the "back door" of international relations. Was the executive branch attempting to bypass the Congress? How significant was it that the agreements with foreign countries had not, in the words of the Supreme Court, been "ratified by the Senate"?

5. The Supreme Court describes the statutory scheme by which the holder of a U.S. copyright may pursue a civil court action to enjoin infringing importation and/or to collect damages for infringement. In Chapter 6, we will examine another U.S. statute (Section 337 of the Tariff Act of 1930) under which the holder of a U.S. copyright may block infringing imports by petition to the U.S. International Trade Commission.

6. Subsequent to the *Quality King* case, the question whether copyrighted works first produced and sold outside the United States are subject to international exhaustion, with parallel importation into the United States permitted, was tested before the Ninth Circuit Court of Appeals in *Omega v. Costco*, 541 F.3d 982 (9th Cir. 2008). (The Ninth Circuit had rendered the decision that the Supreme Court overturned in *Quality King*.) The *Omega v. Costco* case involved luxury watches produced and first sold in Switzerland, and imported to the United States by a discount reseller. Recall that *Quality King* involved goods first produced and sold for export from the United States, and then returned. *Omega v. Costco* involved a more typical case of parallel importation.

The Ninth Circuit held that Supreme Court's holding in *Quality King* was limited to goods that had been produced in the United States (i.e., in its view, "lawfully made under this title"). The rights of a copyright holder in the United States to block importation were not exhausted by a first sale of works produced outside the United States and first sold there. The Ninth Circuit said that the Supreme Court left this question open, including by not objecting to Justice Ginsburg's concurring opinion.

The Supreme Court granted *certiorari*, was briefed by the parties and a wide range of *amicus curiae* on both sides of the issue, and heard oral argument. The U.S. government argued in favor of limiting parallel imports. In the end, however, the Supreme Court was equally divided on the outcome, with newly appointed Justice Kagan not taking part (probably because she had acted as Solicitor General for the government when its position was formulated). In *Costco v. Omega*, 562 U.S. ___ (2010), the Supreme Court issued a *per curiam* opinion that technically affirmed the decision of the Ninth Circuit because there was no majority to do otherwise. (The entire decision reads "The judgment is affirmed by an equally divided Court.") However, it is understood as a matter of U.S. federal court practice that such an equally split Supreme Court decision has no precedential value, though it leaves the Ninth Circuit Court of Appeals decision as the law for its own circuit. (*See, e.g.,* Marcia Coyle, *In* Costco, *the First 4-4 Decision of Court's Term,* NAT'L L.J., Dec. 20, 2010.) Thus, while the Ninth Circuit decision in *Omega v. Costco* is the law of the Ninth Circuit, Courts of Appeal of other circuits are left to develop their jurisprudence in a different way. As of now, the question remains to be settled either by legislation or another decision by the Supreme Court.

THE FIRST SALE DOCTRINE IN THE DIGITAL AGE
Robert H. Rotstein, Emily F. Evitt & Matthew Williams*

An English professor purchases an original edition of Rabbit Run from a quaint used bookstore. A newlywed couple holds a yard sale where the wife sells the husband's collection of "National Lampoon" and "American Pie" DVDs. A photography enthusiast purchases new editing software, loads it onto his hard drive, and lends the disc containing the software to his neighbor. An enterprising college student rips her entire CD collection onto an iPod and is inspired to start a business selling ready loaded iPods. A bookworm purchases a Kindle and dozens of e-books, decides she prefers the touch and feel of paper, and sells her Kindle — e-books and all — to a friend. On their face, these scenarios have little in common. However, each scenario raises questions concerning the applicability of copyright law's first sale doctrine and its contemporary scope.

THE FIRST SALE DOCTRINE: GENERAL BACKGROUND

Under § 106 of the U.S. Copyright Act, copyright owners have six exclusive rights: (1) reproduction; (2) preparation of derivative works; (3) distribution;

* INTELL PROP. & TECH. L.J., 22(3), 2010, at 23-28.

(4) public performance; (5) public display; and (6) digital public performance of sound recordings. The third right gives copyright owners the exclusive right to distribute copies of their works to the public, including by offering copies for sale, lease, or auction. Under the first sale doctrine, however, in most circumstances the distribution right is extinguished when a copyright owner transfers ownership of a particular legal copy of a work to another person. Specifically, § 109(a) of the Copyright Act provides:

> Notwithstanding the provisions of section 106(3), the owner of a particular copy or phonorecord lawfully made under this title, or any person authorized by such owner, is entitled, without the authority of the copyright owner, to sell or otherwise dispose of the possession of that copy or phonorecord.

The first sale doctrine provides a defense to copyright infringement. A defendant may rely on the first sale doctrine as a defense to an alleged violation of the distribution right if he overcomes the burden of proving that he lawfully owned the copy that he distributed. The first sale doctrine, however, is not universally applicable. Section 109(a) provides that the defense extends only to "the owner of a particular copy[.]" This language is clarified in § 109(d), which states, "The privileges prescribed by subsection[] (a) . . . do not, unless authorized by the copyright owner, extend to any person who has acquired possession of the copy or phonorecord from the copyright owner, by rental, lease, loan, or otherwise, without acquiring ownership of it." Under this provision, it is clear that Congress intended to allow copyright owners to enter transactions that do not involve transfers of ownership and therefore do not constitute "first sales." Moreover, Congress expressly stated in § 109(b) that there is no first sale right to rent, lease, or lend phonorecords embodying sound recordings or to rent, lease, or lend copies of a computer program for direct or indirect commercial gain. The overall first sale scheme "rest[s] on the principle that the copyright owner is entitled to realize the full value of each copy or phonorecord upon its disposition." The theory is that the price charged for the initial sale of a copyrighted book will account for the purchaser's ability to subsequently resell the book. Thus, if a book's resale value is $5, the book's initial price point can be set $5 higher, such that a book with an initial value of $7 can be sold for $12. The author captures the value of both the initial sale and the resale in the initial value, and the purchaser is then free to dispose of his or her copy as the purchaser sees fit.

. . .

THREE CONTEMPORARY FIRST SALE PARADIGMS

With the advent of modern technology, the use of many copyrighted works, such as software, has become intertwined with the reproduction of these works. This poses a challenge for the first sale doctrine, which applies to the distribution right but not to their production right. Thus, today the first sale doctrine is best understood in terms of three paradigms:

1. Traditional: cases in which transfer of possession of the physical copy of a copyrighted work does not implicate the reproduction right;

2.   Transfer of tangible/intangible property: when reproduction is necessary to attendant use of technology; and
3.   Transfer of intangible property only.

. . .

TRADITIONAL

Even today, there are still traditional applications of the first sale doctrine in which the transfer of possession of the physical copy of a copyrighted work does not implicate the reproduction right. For example, whether a hard copy book was sold or lent would not ordinarily implicate the reproduction right because one does not have to reproduce a book to use it for its primary purpose. The same is true with more advanced technology, such as a DVD. In these situations, to determine whether the first sale doctrine applies, the inquiry should generally focus on the contractual relationship between the transferor and transferee.

More recently, in *UMG Recordings, Inc. v. Augusto,* [558 F. Supp. 2d 1055 (C.D. Cal. 2008)], Judge James Otero of the Central District of California analyzed first sale in the context of an individual who repeatedly acquired and sold on eBay "promotional" copies of music CDs without authorization. Judge Otero concluded that the individual's resale of these promotional copies was protected by the first sale doctrine; the case is currently on appeal to the Ninth Circuit.

. . .

TRANSFER OF TANGIBLE/INTANGIBLE PROPERTY

The second modern first sale paradigm involves situations in which reproduction is necessary to attendant use of technology. The classic example is software, because the user not only needs the physical medium of copyrighted expression (e.g., a disc) but also must copy the intangible work of copyrighted software to another medium (e.g., a hard drive). Consequently, software transfers implicate at least two separate rights: (1) distribution, to which the first sale doctrine is relevant, and (2) reproduction, to which the first sale doctrine has no relevance. Sorting out the scope and applicability of these two rights can be difficult.

There is extensive case law from district and appellate courts across the country analyzing whether consumer transactions involving software resident on discs constitute sales or licenses for the purpose of the first sale doctrine. Two frequently cited district court cases within the Ninth Circuit, both involving Adobe software products, illustrate the issues involved.

First, in *Adobe Sys. Inc. v. One Stop Micro, Inc.,* [84 F. Supp. 2d 1086 (N.D. Cal. 2000)] a Northern District of California court concluded that the first sale doctrine did not apply. Judge Ware considered whether defendant One Stop Micro infringed Adobe's distribution rights by acquiring educational copies of Adobe software that sell at a discounted price from authorized Adobe distributors, repackaging the software to remove the "educational" labels from the products, and reselling the software. One Stop Micro argued that it was protected by the first sale doctrine because Adobe's agreements with its authorized educational distributors included words such as "purchase," "own," and "resell." Judge Ware disagreed, however, and concluded, based on "undisputed evidence submitted by Adobe regarding the intent of the parties in entering into the agreement, trade usage, the unique nature of distributing software, as well as the express restrictive language of the contract," that Adobe's end user license agreement, which was incorporated into Adobe's agreements with its distributors, clearly provided purchasers with a mere license, rather than ownership, of the software.

By contrast, in *Softman Products Co. v. Adobe Sys. Inc.,* [171 F. Supp. 2d 1075 (C.D. Cal. 2001)] a Central District of California case very similar to *One Stop Micro,* Judge Pregerson concluded that the first sale doctrine applied. Softman Products Company bought "collections" of Adobe software products that were bundled together at a discount. Softman then sold the individual products from the collections separately and made a profit. As in *One Stop,* the Adobe agreements at issue stated that Adobe was only licensing the software involved. However, Judge Pregerson concluded that these licensing agreements were mere "labels" and that "the reality of the business environment [] suggests that Adobe sells its software to distributors." He also distinguished *One Stop* as a case that was more about removing the "educational" stickers from the software than anything else. Summarizing the core issue involved, Judge Pregerson stated: "Adobe frames the issue as a dispute about the ownership of intellectual property. In fact, it is a dispute about the ownership of individual pieces of Adobe software."

TRANSFER OF INTANGIBLE PROPERTY ONLY

The third contemporary first sale scenario arises when there are multiple copyrighted works on one device, but the physical copy of each copyrighted work need not be transferred each time. This paradigm is exemplified by the Kindle and the iPod. In theory, first sale should not apply to an individual work contained on one of these devices. Some advocates, however, argue that the first sale defense applies to all copies, no matter what form. Such arguments completely ignore the fact that the reproduction right, not simply the distribution right, is implicated by the transfer of intangible property.

An interesting question is whether the sale of the Kindle itself containing lawfully downloaded material would be subject to the first sale doctrine. In this scenario, a user's right to sell a lawfully loaded Kindle might be limited because of the copyright owner's ability to limit the reproduction right. This relates to the technology used to view books on a Kindle; presumably the Kindle user makes a digital copy each time a book is loaded for reading. These digital copies, in turn, are covered by the reproduction right, which is not governed by the first sale doctrine. Courts have held that copying software from a storage medium onto hardware causes a copy to be made, and "[i]n the absence of ownership of the copyright or express permission by license, such acts constitute copyright infringement." Thus, because viewing books on a Kindle requires making a digital copy, there is no legal reason why the copyright holder cannot limit that reproduction right to the original Kindle owner and effectively bar the sale of a legally loaded Kindle.

Finally, as discussed in the context of software, ripping CDs onto an iPod and then selling the CDs and/or the iPod poses a variation of the borrow/copy problem. . . .

2.   Unique Characteristics of Audiovisual Services

The *Quality King v. L'anza* decision deals with a copyright associated with a tangible product. Yet, copyrighted works may be disseminated to the public in ways disassociated from a tangible product. We have, for example, seen the problems that arise when music files are disassociated from CDs and are shared on the Internet. *Coditel v. Cine Vog*, decided by the ECJ, is one of the earliest cases to address the difference from an exhaustion standpoint between the sale of a tangible copyrighted work and the making available to a wide public of a copyrighted work (disassociated from a tangible product). The ECJ confronts certain special characteristics of the film distribution and television broadcast industries. A film differs from a book or newspaper in that the film depends on repeated showings to generate an adequate economic return. If the initial showing of a film is treated as a "first sale" for exhaustion purposes, artists and producers of films may not recover their investments.

CODITEL v. CINE VOG FILMS

(preliminary ruling requested by the Cour d'Appel, Brussels) (Case 62/79)
European Court of Justice
[1980] ECR 881, [1981] 2 CMLR 362
18 March 1980

Panel: H. KUTSCHER, President, A. O'KEEFFE and A. TOUFFAIT, (Presidents of Chambers), J. MERTENS DE WILMARS, P. PESCATORE, Lord MACKENZIE STUART, G. BOSCO, T. KOOPMANS and O. DUE, Judges

Decision: . . .

The facts of the case bearing upon the outcome of the dispute were summarized by the Cour d'Appel as follows. By an agreement of 8 July 1969 Les Films la Boetie, acting as the owner of all the proprietary rights in the film "Le Boucher," gave Cine Vog the "exclusive right" to distribute the film in Belgium for seven years. The film was shown in cinemas in Belgium starting on 15 May 1970. However, on 5 January 1971 German television's first channel broadcast a German version of the film and this broadcast could be picked up in Belgium. Cine Vog considered that the broadcast had jeopardized the commercial future of the film in Belgium. It relied upon this ground of complaint both against Les Films la Boetie, for not having observed the exclusivity of the rights which it had transferred to it, and against the Coditel companies for having relayed the relevant broadcast over their cable diffusion networks. . . .

Believing that that submission bears upon the interpretation of the Treaty, the Cour d'Appel referred to the Court of Justice the following two questions:

1. Are the restrictions prohibited by Article 59 of the Treaty establishing the European Economic Community only those which prejudice the provision of services between nationals established in different Member States, or do they also comprise restrictions on the provision of services between nationals established in the same Member State which however concern services the substance of which originates in another Member State?

2. If the first limb of the preceding question is answered in the affirmative, is it in accordance with the provisions of the Treaty on freedom to provide services for the assignee of the performing right in a cinematographic film in one Member State to

rely upon his right in order to prevent the defendant from showing that film in that State by means of cable television where the film thus shown is picked up by the defendant in the said Member State after having been broadcast by a third party in another Member State with the consent of the original owner of the right? . . .

The second question raises the problem of whether Articles 59 and 60 of the Treaty prohibit an assignment, limited to the territory of a Member State, of the copyright in a film, in view of the fact that a series of such assignments might result in the partitioning of the Common Market as regards the undertaking of economic activity in the film industry.

A cinematographic film belongs to the category of literary and artistic works made available to the public by performances which may be infinitely repeated. In this respect the problems involved in the observance of copyright in relation to the requirements of the Treaty are not the same as those which arise in connection with literary and artistic works the placing of which at the disposal of the public is inseparable from the circulation of the material form of the works, as in the case of books or records.

In these circumstances the owner of the copyright in a film and his assigns have a legitimate interest in calculating the fees due in respect of the authorization to exhibit the film on the basis of the actual or probable number of performances and in authorizing a television broadcast of the film only after it has been exhibited in cinemas for a certain period of time. It appears from the file on the present case that the contract made between Les Films la Boetie and Cine Vog stipulated that the exclusive right which was assigned included the right to exhibit the film "Le Boucher" publicly in Belgium by way of projection in cinemas and on television but that the right to have the film diffused by Belgian television could not be exercised until 40 months after the first showing of the film in Belgium.

These facts are important in two regards. On the one hand, they highlight the fact that the right of a copyright owner and his assigns to require fees for any showing of a film is part of the essential function of copyright in this type of literary and artistic work. On the other hand, they demonstrate that the exploitation of copyright in films and the fees attaching thereto cannot be regulated without regard being had to the possibility of television broadcasts of those films. The question whether an assignment of copyright limited to the territory of a Member State is capable of constituting a restriction on freedom to provide services must be examined in this context.

Whilst Article 59 of the Treaty prohibits restrictions upon freedom to provide services, it does not thereby encompass limits upon the exercise of certain economic activities which have their origin in the application of national legislation for the protection of intellectual property, save where such application constitutes a means of arbitrary discrimination or a disguised restriction on trade between Member States. Such would be the case if that application enabled parties to an assignment of copyright to create artificial barriers to trade between Member States.

The effect of this is that, whilst copyright entails the right to demand fees for any showing or performance, the rules of the Treaty cannot in principle constitute an obstacle to the geographical limits, which the parties to a contract of assignment have agreed upon in order to protect the author and his assigns in this regard. The mere fact that those geographical limits may coincide with national frontiers does not point to a different solution in a situation where television is organized in the Member States largely on the basis of legal broadcasting monopolies, which indicates that a limitation other than the geographical field of application of an assignment is often impracticable.

The exclusive assignee of the performing right in a film for the whole of a Member State may therefore rely upon his right against cable television diffusion companies which have transmitted that film on their diffusion network having received it from a television broadcasting station established in another Member State, without thereby infringing Community law.

Consequently the answer to the second question referred to the Court by the Cour d'Appel, Brussels, should be that the provisions of the Treaty relating to the freedom to provide services do not preclude an assignee of the performing right in a cinematographic film in a Member State from relying upon his right to prohibit the exhibition of that film in that State, without his authority, by means of cable diffusion if the film so exhibited is picked up and transmitted after being broadcast in another Member State by a third party with the consent of the original owner of the right.

It is clear from the answer given to the second question that Community law, on the assumption that it applies to the activities of the cable diffusion companies which are the subject-matter of the dispute brought before the national court, has no effect upon the application by that court of the provisions of copyright legislation in a case such as this. Therefore there is no need to answer the first question. . . .

On those grounds,

THE COURT, in answer to the questions referred to it by the Cour d'Appel, Brussels, by judgment of 30 March 1979, hereby rules:

The provisions of the Treaty relating to the freedom to provide services do not preclude an assignee of the performing right in a cinematographic film in a Member State from relying upon his right to prohibit the exhibition of that film in that State, without his authority, by means of cable diffusion if the film so exhibited is picked up and transmitted after being broadcast in another Member State by a third party with the consent of the original owner of the right.

NOTES AND QUESTIONS

1. According to the CJEU, the special characteristics of the film and broadcast industries made it necessary to provide limitations on the exhaustion of copyright for these media. In what other copyright contexts do you think that limitations on the principle of exhaustion might be necessary?

2. The *Coditel* decision is addressed only to the intra-Union context. Do you think that the same policy considerations that motivated the ECJ in this decision should also apply in the international exhaustion of copyright context?

3. Issues associated with international exhaustion and intangible copyrighted works have yet to be explored in the same depth as issues of exhaustion associated with tangible products, including traditional copyrighted works such as books. The problems are similar to those associated with file-sharing networks. Copying and distribution of intangible works across national borders is conceptually similar to copying and distribution within a single country. Permission to make a single copy does not constitute permission to make an indefinite number of copies. If a single copy has

been authorized and sold, there is no special reason to confine its resale or movement within a single geographic territory, even if that movement is across a computer network. On the other hand, authorization and sale of a single copy within one country does not specially constitute authorization for indefinite replication and distribution of the work among many countries, even across a computer network. Do you see other issues associated with international exhaustion and copyrighted works disassociated from tangible products?

III.   REGIONAL COPYRIGHT SYSTEMS

A.   EU Approximation Measures

1.   Consequences of Different Rules

We have earlier examined EU approximation efforts in the fields of patent and trademark. *Warner Brothers v. Christiansen* heightened awareness that intra-EU trade distortions might arise from different member state approaches in copyright. This decision notes the emergence of a new form of right for the copyright holder — the right to control the renting out of the work — distinct from the right to sell or communicate to the public. The *Warner Brothers v. Christiansen* case helped form the background for the rental right embodied in the TRIPS Agreement.

WARNER BROTHERS INC. AND METRONOME VIDEO ApS v. ERIK VIUFF CHRISTIANSEN

Court of Justice of the European Communities
1988 ECJ CELEX LEXIS 2016
Judgment of the Court of 17 May 1988

Reference for a preliminary ruling: OEstre Landsret — Denmark
Copyright — Objection to the hiring-out of video-cassettes
Case 158/86, 686J0158

Introduction:
In Case 158/86

REFERENCE to the Court under Article 177 of the EEC Treaty by the OEstre Landsret, Copenhagen, for a preliminary ruling in the action pending before that court between

Warner Brothers Inc.,
Metronome Video ApS
and Erik Viuff Christiansen

on the interpretation of Articles 30, 36 and 222 of the EEC Treaty with regard to the action taken by an owner of exclusive rights in Denmark to restrain hiring-out in Denmark of a video-recording marketed in another Member State by the same owner of the exclusive rights or with his consent.

The Court composed of: G. Bosco, President of Chamber, for the President, O. Due and J.C. Moitinho de Almeida (Presidents of Chambers), T. Koopmans, U. Everling, K. Bahlmann, Y. Galmot, R. Joliet and F. Schockweiler, Judges,

Advocate General: G. F. Mancini . . .
Judgment by: Galmot

Judgment:

1. By order dated 11 June 1986, which was received at the Court on 1 July 1986, the OEstre Landsret referred to the Court for a preliminary ruling under Article 177 of the EEC Treaty a question on the interpretation of Articles 30 and 36 [now 34 and 36 — Eds.] of the EEC Treaty, with a view to establishing the extent to which national copyright legislation regarding the hiring-out of video-cassettes is compatible with the free movement of goods.

2. The question was raised in the context of proceedings brought by two companies, Warner Brothers Inc. (hereinafter referred to as "Warner") and Metronome Video ApS (hereinafter "Metronome"), against Mr Erik Viuff Christiansen.

3. Warner, the owner in the United Kingdom of the copyright of the film "Never Say Never Again," which it produced in that country, assigned the management of the video production rights in Denmark to Metronome.

4. The video-cassette of the film was on sale in the United Kingdom with Warner's consent. Mr Christiansen, who manages a video shop in Copenhagen, purchased a copy in London with a view to hiring it out in Denmark and imported it into that Member State for that purpose.

5. On the basis of Danish legislation, which enables the author or producer of a musical or cinematographic work to take action to restrain the hiring-out of videograms of that work until such time as he gives his consent, Warner and Metronome obtained an injunction from the Copenhagen City Court prohibiting the defendant from hiring out the video-cassette in Denmark. . . .

8. In submitting the question the national court seeks to ascertain, in essence, whether Articles 30 and 36 of the EEC Treaty preclude the application of national legislation which gives an author the right to make the hiring-out of video-cassettes conditional on his authorization, where those video-cassettes have already been put into circulation with his consent in another Member State whose legislation allows the author to control their initial sale without giving him the right to prohibit them from being hired out.

9. It should be noted that, unlike the national copyright legislation which gave rise to the judgment of 20 January 1981 in Joined Cases 55 and 57/80 *Musik Vertrieb Membran v GEMA* ((1981)) ECR 147, the legislation which gives rise to the present preliminary question does not enable the author to collect an additional fee on the actual importation of recordings of protected works which are marketed with his consent in another Member State, or to set up any further obstacle whatsoever to importation or resale. The rights and powers conferred on the author by the national legislation in question comes into operation only after importation has been carried out.

10. None the less, it must be observed that the commercial distribution of video-cassettes takes the form not only of sales but also, and increasingly, that of hiring-out to individuals who possess video-tape recorders. The right to prohibit such hiring-out in a Member State is therefore liable to influence trade in

video-cassettes in that State and hence, indirectly, to affect intra-Community trade in those products. Legislation of the kind which gave rise to the main proceedings must therefore, in the light of established case-law, be regarded as a measure having an effect equivalent to a quantitative restriction on imports, which is prohibited by Article 30 of the Treaty.

11. Consideration should therefore be given to whether such legislation may be considered justified on grounds of the protection of industrial and commercial property within the meaning of Article 36 — a term which was held by the Court, in its judgment of 6 October 1982 in Case 262/81 *Coditel v Cine-Vog* ((1982)) ECR 3381, to include literary and artistic property.

12. In that connection it should first be noted that the Danish legislation applies without distinction to video-cassettes produced in situ and video-cassettes imported from another Member State. The determining factor for the purposes of its application is the type of transaction in video-cassettes which is in question, not the origin of those video-cassettes. Such legislation does not therefore, in itself, operate any arbitrary discrimination in trade between Member States.

13. It should further be pointed out that literary and artistic works may be the subject of commercial exploitation, whether by way of public performance or of the reproduction and marketing of the recordings made of them, and this is true in particular of cinematographic works. The two essential rights of the author, namely the exclusive right of performance and the exclusive right of reproduction, are not called in question by the rules of the Treaty.

14. Lastly, consideration must be given to the emergence, demonstrated by the Commission, of a specific market for the hiring-out of such recordings, as distinct from their sale. The existence of that market was made possible by various factors such as the improvement of manufacturing methods for video-cassettes which increased their strength and life in use, the growing awareness amongst viewers that they watch only occasionally the video-cassettes which they have bought and, lastly, their relatively high purchase price. The market for the hiring-out of video-cassettes reaches a wider public than the market for their sale and, at present, offers great potential as a source of revenue for makers of films.

15. However, it is apparent that, by authorizing the collection of royalties only on sales to private individuals and to persons hiring out video-cassettes, it is impossible to guarantee to makers of films a remuneration which reflects the number of occasions on which the video-cassettes are actually hired out and which secures for them a satisfactory share of the rental market. That explains why, as the Commission points out in its observations, certain national laws have recently provided specific protection of the right to hire out video-cassettes.

16. Laws of that kind are therefore clearly justified on grounds of the protection of industrial and commercial property pursuant to Article 36 of the Treaty.

17. However, the defendant in the main proceedings, relying on the judgments of 22 January 1981 in Case 58/80 *Dansk Supermarked v Imerco* ((1981)) ECR 181 and of 20 January 1981 *Musik Vertrieb Membran v GEMA*, cited above, contends that the author is at liberty to choose the Member State in which he will market his work. The defendant in the main proceedings emphasizes that the author makes his choice according to his own interests and must, in particular, take into consideration the fact that the legislation of certain Member States, unlike that of certain others, confers on him an exclusive right

enabling him to restrain the hiring-out of the recording of the work even when that work has been offered for sale with his consent. That being so, a maker of a film who has offered the video-cassette of that film for sale in a Member State whose legislation confers on him no exclusive right of hiring it out (as in the main proceedings) must accept the consequences of his choice and the exhaustion of his right to restrain the hiring-out of that video-cassette in any other Member State.

18. That objection cannot be upheld. It follows from the foregoing considerations that, where national legislation confers on authors a specific right to hire out video-cassettes, that right would be rendered worthless if its owner were not in a position to authorize the operations for doing so. It cannot therefore be accepted that the marketing by a film-maker of a video-cassette containing one of his works, in a Member State which does not provide specific protection for the right to hire it out, should have repercussions on the right conferred on that same film-maker by the legislation of another Member State to restrain, in that State, the hiring-out of that video-cassette.

19. In those circumstances, the answer to be given to the question submitted by the national court is that Articles 30 and 36 of the Treaty do not prohibit the application of national legislation which gives an author the right to make the hiring-out of video-cassettes subject to his permission, when the video-cassettes in question have already been put into circulation with his consent in another Member State whose legislation enables the author to control the initial sale, without giving him the right to prohibit hiring-out. . . .

NOTES AND QUESTIONS

1. Christiansen points out that Warner Brothers elected to put its video cassette on the market in the United Kingdom where the law provided that a first sale exhausted the copyright holder's right to control further distribution of the cassette. Warner Brothers profited from the first sale in the United Kingdom. By enabling Warner Brothers to control the rental in Denmark, the Court is allowing Warner Brothers to obtain additional profits from the same video cassette. Has the Court persuaded you that Warner Brothers needed the additional right to control the rental of the cassette in Denmark?

2. Computer software vendors tend to characterize their transactions with consumers as "licenses." In essence, software vendors assert that their transactions with consumers are not sales, but rather rentals under restrictive conditions. As we review the EU Rental Rights Directive and Computer Software Directive, consider the potential impact of these directives on the typical vendor to end-user consumer software transaction.

2. EU Approximation in Copyright

In *Warner Brothers v. Christiansen*, the ECJ permitted differences in member state IPRs laws to act as a barrier to the free movement of goods. A primary objective of the European Union is to create a "single market" for goods and services, and it was a logical next step for EU authorities to seek removal of the barrier. The European Union has done so by adopting a series of approximation directives in copyright, including a Copyright Directive, Rental Rights Directive, Database Directive and, most recently, the Information Society Directive. With these directives, EU law has largely occupied the field in copyright law for the member states.

In this context, bear in mind the legal nature of EU directives. Unlike regulations, which are directly applicable in the national legal system and relied upon by individuals, directives "shall be binding, as to the result to be achieved, upon each Member State to which it is addressed, but shall leave to the national authorities the choice of form and methods."[25] As a general rule, directives do not automatically become part of the national legal system and are not directly applicable (self-executing).[26] Only if specific requirements are met,[27] however, might they have "direct effect," that is, giving a right to individuals to "base a claim in, and be granted relief from, the domestic courts" on the basis of the provisions of the directive.[28] If a member state does not implement (or incorrectly implements) the obligations into national law, the domestic court is still obliged to construe its law in the light of the purpose of the directive, and individuals can sue the member state for damages if the directive is not implemented on time.[29]

3. The Software Directive

As noted earlier, the German Supreme Court stimulated the approximation of computer software law in the European Union by its 1985 decision in the *Inkasso* case (*Re The Protection of Computer Programs*, (I ZR 52/83), *Bundesgerichtshof* [1986] ECC 498, 9 MAY 1985). The Court observed that there are a number of phases in the development of a computer program, and that copyright protection may be available at the various stages of development. In this Court's view, it was not necessarily — or primarily — at the level of the programming code that copyright infringement may take place. In the key passages of the decision, the Court held that copyright attaches only to program elements that reflect a substantial advance over known computer programming elements, and only if the advance embodies a skill level above that of the average programmer. "What the average composer can do, the merely workmanlike mechanical or technical combination and connection of the material, cannot be subject to any protection . . . and it presupposes a clear superiority of the compositional activity in the matter of the selection, collection, arrangement

---

25. Art. 288 Treaty on the Functioning of the European Union (ex Art. 249(3) of the Consolidated Version of the Treaty Establishing the European Community).

26. R. STREINZ, EUROPARECHT, 4th ed., Heidelberg (1999), at 135.

27. *Id.* at 142.

28. *Id.* at 141. *See also* T. Cottier/K. Nadakavukaren Schefer, *The Relationship between World Trade Organization Law, National and Regional Law*, 1 J. Int'l Econ. L. 83 (1998), at 91 for a detailed analysis of "direct effect." However, an individual can only rely on a directive's direct effect vis-à-vis the government (vertical) and not vis-à-vis other individuals (horizontal). For detailed overviews, further references and a listing of the requirements for direct effect of directives, *see* P. Craig & G. Burca (eds.), THE EVOLUTION OF EU LAW, New York (1999), at 340, and the decisions of the European Court of Justice in, *inter alia, Marshall v. Southampton and South West Hampshire Area Health Authority*, ECR (152/84), 1986, at 723 ff, and *Paola Faccini Dori v. Recreb Srl*, ECR (C-91/92), I-3325, 1994, at 3347 ff.

29. *Francovich and Bonifaci v. Italy*, ECR I-5357, 1991, at 5415 f.

and treatment of the information and instructions over the current average of achievement."

This decision was criticized by firms that invested heavily in the creation and distribution of software. The response of the European Commission was the Software Directive,[30] which rejected the approach of the German Supreme Court. In addition to eliminating any test of creativity beyond that of originality (in the sense of being the author's own creation), the Software Directive addressed the question of reverse engineering. The Software Directive gives express recognition to a right of rental that is distinct from the right of first sale.

The following excerpt from an article by Thomas Hoeren briefly summarizes some of the important provisions of the Software Directive and how the directive was implemented into national law by EU member states.

THE EUROPEAN UNION COMMISSION AND RECENT TRENDS IN EUROPEAN INFORMATION LAW

Thomas Hoeren*

. . . IV. THE IMPLEMENTATION OF THE SOFTWARE DIRECTIVE

On May 14, 1991, the European Council adopted Directive 91/250, which relates to the legal protection of computer programs (the "Software Directive"). By defining a minimum level of protection, the Software Directive was intended to harmonize Member States' legal provisions regarding the legal protection of computer programs. Before the implementation of the Software Directive, there was a disparity among Member States' laws protecting the IP rights of computer programs. In seven out of the then twelve Member States, no legislation expressly protected computer programs.

To achieve its aim of creating uniformity in copyright protection of computer programs, the Software Directive includes the following principles:

(1) computer programs are considered literary works and, as such, are provided with copyright protection (Art. 1);

(2) a protected person (or persons) is (are) specified (determination of authorship was largely left to the EU Member States) (Art. 2, 3);

(3) authorization from the copyright holder is required for restricted acts (Art. 4 and 6); and

(4) special measures of protection (e.g., remedies) against restricted acts are provided (Art. 7).

Although only three Member States — Denmark, Italy, and the U.K. — met the January 1, 1993 implementation deadline, all have now adopted the required domestic laws, regulations, and administrative provisions. The last to implement the required domestic laws was Luxembourg, on April 14, 1995. . . . [T]he Software Directive has been used as a model in a large number

---

30. Council Directive of 14 May 1991 on the legal protection of computer programs (91/250/EEC, 1991 OJ L 122, Document Date: May 14, 1991).

* 29 RUTGERS COMPUTER & TECH. L.J. 1 (2003).

of Central and Eastern European States as well as in Hong Kong, the Philippines, and Australia.

The most remarkable aspect of the Software Directive is the requisite level of originality it sets for copyright protection. The Software Directive synchronizes the level of originality necessary for a specific category of copyrightable work at the community level. Specifically, a computer program "shall be protected if it is original in the sense that it is the author's own intellectual creation." This uniform level has required twelve Member States to lower and three Member States to raise their threshold for granting protection. . . .

Article 4 of the Software Directive establishes an exclusive distribution right to a computer program, subjecting it to Community exhaustion if sold in the Community. Member States are not free to provide for [international] exhaustion with respect to computer programs since no provision in the Directive provides that a first sale outside the Community defeats the exclusive distribution right. Denmark, Finland, the Netherlands, and Portugal have not implemented this implicit restriction of parallel imports of computer programs into the Community.

Nine Member States have implemented verbatim, or in near verbatim, all the mandatory provisions concerning the exceptions to the restricted acts contained in article 5 of the Software Directive. Article 5, section 1, provides that in the absence of specific contractual provisions, the restricted acts, with the exception of distribution and rental, do not require authorization by the copyright holder when using the computer program. . . .

All Member States permit individuals to make back-up copies of computer programs for their personal use. Although private copying of computer programs was excluded from the scope of permissible exceptions by the Community legislator, some Member States have not expressly repealed their private copying exceptions. However, there is no evidence of major practical problems emanating from this omission.

The Member States have implemented article 6 of the Software Directive exception concerning the de-compilation. Only six Member States omitted article 6, which is the only exception to be omitted thus far. The possibility of de-compiling a program to make it interoperable with other programs was the subject of an intense debate, resulting in a pragmatic compromise. The compromise requires that the information for establishing interoperability be made available. To date, most licensing agreements reflect an acceptance of the Software Directive's de-compilation requirements. However, there are licence agreements from some U.S. and European sources that are inconsistent with articles 5, 6, and 9 of the Software Directive.

The duration of protection in article 8 of the Software Directive was repealed by article 11 (1) of Directive 93/98, which aimed to harmonize certain copyright protections laws ("Directive on Harmonizing Terms of Protection").[92] The standardized copyright term is now 70 years post mortem auctoris. All Member States have complied with the terms of the Directive on Harmonizing Terms of Protection.

---

92. Council Directive 93/98 of 29 October 1993 Harmonizing the Term of Protection of Copyright and Certain Related Rights, 1993 OJ L 290, Doc. Date, Oct. 29, 1993.

NOTES AND QUESTIONS

1. In light of numerous undertaken amendments, the Software Directive was replaced by a new version (Directive 2009/24/EC), incorporating the latter changes.[31]
2. Article 2(3) of the Software Directive incorporates a work made for hire doctrine, but in that regard addresses only the author's "economic rights." What rights might this leave in the hands of the author?
3. One of the key features of the Software Directive was to clarify that an off-the-shelf sale of computer software exhausts the vendor's control over resale of the product—regardless of whether the vendor attempts to characterize the sale as a "license." Under the Software Directive and Rental Rights Directive, the buyer of the program is nevertheless restricted from renting out the program. The result should be the same under Section 109 of the U.S. Copyright Act, which grants to the owner of a particular copy of a copyrighted work the right to resell or otherwise dispose of that copy without the consent of the copyright holder, provided that the owner of a copy of the computer program may not rent, lease, or lend the copy without permission of the copyright holder. Why are software developers anxious to characterize their transactions with the public as "licenses"?

4. The Rental Rights Directive

In 1992 the European Union adopted the Rental Rights Directive[32] to address the situation that gave rise to the ECJ decision in *Warner Brothers v. Christiansen*. Member states were directed to comply with the Rental Rights Directive by July 1, 1994. The directive provides at its Article 1:

> 1. In accordance with the provisions of this Chapter, Member States shall provide, subject to Article 5, a right to authorize or prohibit the rental and lending of originals and copies of copyright works, and other subject matter as set out in Article 2(1).
> 2. For the purposes of this Directive, "rental" means making available for use, for a limited period of time and for direct or indirect economic or commercial advantage.

In Article 2, the directive spells out the persons who are the beneficiaries of the rental right, including by designating the director of a film as one of its authors.

In Article 4, the directive provides that authors and performers who assign their rental right retain an "unwaivable" right to equitable remuneration for the rental.

---

31. Directive 2009/24/EC of the European Parliament and of the Council of 23 April 2009 on the legal protection of computer programs, 2009 OJ L 111, Doc. Date, May 5, 2009.
32. Council Directive 92/100/EEC of 19 November 1992 on rental right and lending right and on certain rights related to copyright in the field of intellectual property, 1992 OJ L 346, Doc. Date, Nov. 19, 1992.

5. The Satellite Broadcast Directive

The European Union has adopted "Council Directive 93/83/EEC of 27 September 1993 on the coordination of certain rules concerning copyright and rights related to copyright applicable to satellite broadcasting and cable retransmission."[33] The SBD establishes that the rights of copyright holders will be exclusively determined by the law of the EU member state from which a signal is transmitted up to a satellite (art. 1(2)(b)). The SBD provides that the author's right to authorize satellite broadcast to the public may be acquired only "by agreement" (art. 3(1)). Presumably this means that compulsory licensing of satellite transmissions is not countenanced.

6. The Copyright Directive

In 1993, the European Union adopted the Copyright Directive.[34] One of its most significant steps was to extend the general term of protection to the life of the author plus 70 years. According to the recitals of the Copyright Directive, the Berne Convention term of the author's life plus 50 years was intended to cover the average life span of an author, plus the life span of a second generation. According to the recitals, since the average life span is now longer than when the Berne norms were adopted, the copyright term should be extended. The Copyright Directive also extends the terms of protection for performers, producers, and broadcasters in line with those mandated by the TRIPS Agreement.

7. The Database Directive

In her article on the digital agenda at WIPO, Pam Samuelson referred to EU and U.S. efforts to promote an international agreement on the protection of databases. The Berne Convention included within the scope of copyrightable subject matter (art. 2(5), Berne) collections of literary and artistic works, which by reason of their selection and arrangement constitute intellectual creations. Though there was little reason to doubt that protection already existed under the Berne Convention, the TRIPS Agreement (art. 10.2) and WIPO Copyright Treaty (art. 5) went on to clarify that compilations of data in digital form that constitute intellectual creations are copyrightable subject matter. This did not put an end to the database debate.

Advances in digital technology have facilitated the extraction and reproduction of information contained in databases. Online databases may be downloaded or captured from a video screen. Database compilers contend that investment in the creation of new databases will be curtailed unless the products of this investment are granted protection. The U.S. Supreme Court in *Feist*, *supra*, illustrated the legal obstacles confronting database compilers. A party seeking to extract information from a database may have limited interest in the

---

33. 1993 OJ L 248, Doc. Date, Sept. 27, 1993.
34. Council Directive 93/98/EEC of 29 October 1993 harmonizing the term of protection of copyright and certain related rights, 1993 OJ L 290, Doc. Date, Oct. 29, 1993.

creative arrangement of that database. Rather, the information contained in the database is being sought, and reused.

The European Union sought to address the concerns of database compilers by adoption of the Database Directive.[35] The Database Directive (DBD) is comprised of two principal parts. The first part addresses, clarifies, and supplements traditional copyright protection accorded to database compilers under the general principles of the Berne Convention. The second part of the directive creates a *sui generis* form of protection for the producers of databases. This is an extensive right that attaches to a database on the basis of the level of investment by the compiler, measured by whether there has been a "substantial investment" in "qualitative" and/or "quantitative" terms in the "obtaining, verification or presentation of the contents." The holder of the *sui generis* right may prevent acts of "extraction and/or re-utilization of the whole or of a substantial part, evaluated qualitatively and/or quantitatively" (art. 7(1)). The directive contains some exceptions for fair use.

The perspective of the European Union with respect to Internet and related online services is encapsulated in a recital to the Database Directive, which provides that "every on-line service is in fact an act which will have to be subject to authorization where the copyright so provides" (para. 33, recitals, DBD).

In *British Horseracing Board v. William Hill*, which follows, the ECJ for the first time interprets the Database Directive.

BRITISH HORSERACING BOARD v. WILLIAM HILL

European Court of Justice Case C-203/02 Judgment of the Court (Grand Chamber) of 9 November 2004

THE COURT (Grand Chamber) . . . gives the following Judgment

GROUNDS

1. This reference for a preliminary ruling concerns the interpretation of Article 7 and Article 10(3) of Directive 96/9/EC of the European Parliament and of the Council of 11 March 1996 on the legal protection of databases (OJ 1996 L 77, p. 20, the directive).

2. The reference was made in the course of proceedings brought by The British Horseracing Board Ltd, the Jockey Club and Weatherbys Group Ltd (the BHB and Others) against William Hill Organization Ltd (William Hill). The litigation arose over the use by William Hill, for the purpose of organising betting on horse racing, of information taken from the BHB database.

LEGAL BACKGROUND

3. The directive, according to Article 1(1) thereof, concerns the legal protection of databases in any form. . . .

---

35. Directive 96/9/EC of the European Parliament and of the Council of the EU of March 11th, 1996 on the legal protection of databases, 1996 OJ L 077, Doc. Date, March 27, 1996.

9. The directive was implemented in United Kingdom law by the Copyright and Rights in Databases Regulations 1997 which entered into force on 1 January 1998. The terms of those regulations are identical to those of the directive.

THE MAIN PROCEEDINGS AND THE QUESTIONS REFERRED
FOR A PRELIMINARY RULING

10. The BHB and Others manage the horse racing industry in the United Kingdom and in various capacities compile and maintain the BHB database which contains a large amount of information supplied by horse owners, trainers, horse race organisers and others involved in the racing industry. The database contains information on inter alia the pedigrees of some one million horses, and prerace information on races to be held in the United Kingdom. . . .

11. Weatherbys Group Ltd, the company which compiles and maintains the BHB database, performs three principal functions, which lead up to the issue of pre-race information.

12. First, it registers information concerning owners, trainers, jockeys and horses and records the performances of those horses in each race.

13. Second, it decides on weight adding and handicapping for the horses entered for the various races.

14. Third, it compiles the lists of horses running in the races. This activity is carried out by its own call centre, manned by about 30 operators. . . .

15. The BHB database contains essential information not only for those directly involved in horse racing but also for radio and television broadcasters and for bookmakers and their clients. The cost of running the BHB database is approximately £4 million per annum. The fees charged to third parties for the use of the information in the database cover about a quarter of that amount.

16. The database is accessible on the internet site operated jointly by BHB and Weatherbys Group Ltd. Some of its contents are also published each week in the BHB's official journal. The contents of the database, or of certain parts of it, are also made available to Racing Pages Ltd, a company jointly controlled by Weatherbys Group Ltd and the Press Association, which then forwards data to its various subscribers, including some bookmakers, in the form of a "Declarations Feed," the day before a race. Satellite Information Services Limited ("SIS") is authorised by Racing Pages to transmit data to its own subscribers in the form of a "raw data feed" ("RDF"). . . .

17. William Hill, which is a subscriber to both the Declarations Feed and the RDF, is one of the leading providers of offcourse bookmaking services in the United Kingdom, to both UK and international customers. It launched an online betting service on two internet sites. Those interested can use these sites to find out what horses are running in which races at which racecourses and what odds are offered by William Hill.

18. The information displayed on William Hill's internet sites is obtained, first, from newspapers published the day before the race and, second, from the RDF supplied by SIS on the morning of the race.

19. According to the order for reference, the information displayed on William Hill's internet sites represents a very small proportion of the total amount of data on the BHB database, given that it concerns only the following matters: the names of all the horses in the race, the date, time and/or name of the race and the name of the racecourse where the race will be held. Also according to the order for reference, the horse races and the lists of runners are not arranged on William Hill's internet sites in the same way as in the BHB database.

20. In March 2000 the BHB and Others brought proceedings against William Hill in the High Court of Justice of England and Wales, Chancery Division, alleging infringement of their sui generis right. They contend, first, that each day's use by William Hill of racing data taken from the newspapers or the RDF is an extraction or re-utilisation of a substantial part of the contents of the BHB database, contrary to Article 7(1) of the directive. Secondly, they say that even if the individual extracts made by William Hill are not substantial they should be prohibited under Article 7(5) of the directive.

21. The High Court of Justice ruled in a judgment of 9 February 2001 that the action of BHB and Others was well founded. William Hill appealed to the referring court.

22. In the light of the problems of interpretation of the directive, the Court of Appeal decided to stay proceedings and refer the following questions to the Court of Justice for a preliminary ruling. . . .

83. By its 10th question, the referring court seeks to know what type of act is covered by the prohibition laid down by Article 7(5) of the directive. It also seeks to know whether acts such as those carried out by William Hill are covered by that prohibition.

84. On that point, it appears from Article 8(1) and from the 42nd recital of the preamble to the directive that, as a rule, the maker of a database cannot prevent a lawful user of that database from carrying out acts of extraction and re-utilisation of an insubstantial part of its contents. Article 7(5) of the directive, which authorises the maker of the database to prevent such acts under certain conditions, thus provides for an exception to that general rule.

85. Common Position (EC) No 20/95 adopted by the Council on 10 July 1995 (OJ 1995 C 288, p. 14) states, under point 14 of the Council's statement of reasons: to ensure that the lack of protection of the insubstantial parts does not lead to their being repeatedly and systematically extracted and/or re-utilised, paragraph 5 of this article in the common position introduces a safeguard clause.

86. It follows that the purpose of Article 7(5) of the directive is to prevent circumvention of the prohibition in Article 7(1) of the directive. Its objective is to prevent repeated and systematic extractions and/or re-utilisations of insubstantial parts of the contents of a database, the cumulative effect of which would be to seriously prejudice the investment made by the maker of the database just as the extractions and/or re-utilisations referred to in Article 7(1) of the directive would.

87. The provision therefore prohibits acts of extraction made by users of the database which, because of their repeated and systematic character, would lead to the reconstitution of the database as a whole or, at the very least, of a substantial part of it, without the authorisation of the maker of the database, whether those acts were carried out with a view to the creation of another database or in the exercise of an activity other than the creation of a database.

88. Similarly, Article 7(5) of the directive prohibits third parties from circumventing the prohibition on re-utilisation laid down by Article 7(1) of the directive by making insubstantial parts of the contents of the database available to the public in a systematic and repeated manner.

89. Under those circumstances, acts which conflict with a normal exploitation of [a] database or which unreasonably prejudice the legitimate interests of the maker of the database refer to unauthorised actions for the purpose of reconstituting, through the cumulative effect of acts of extraction, the whole or a

substantial part of the contents of a database protected by the sui generis right and/or of making available to the public, through the cumulative effect of acts of re-utilisation, the whole or a substantial part of the contents of such a database, which thus seriously prejudice the investment made by the maker of the database.

90. In the case in the main proceedings, it is clear, in the light of the information given in the order for reference, that the acts of extraction and re-utilisation carried out by William Hill concern insubstantial parts of the BHB database. . . . According to the order for reference, they are carried out on the occasion of each race held. They are thus of a repeated and systematic nature.

91. However, such acts are not intended to circumvent the prohibition laid down in Article 7(1) of the directive. There is no possibility that, through the cumulative effect of its acts, William Hill might reconstitute and make available to the public the whole or a substantial part of the contents of the BHB database and thereby seriously prejudice the investment made by BHB in the creation of that database.

92. It must be pointed out in that connection that, according to the order for reference, the materials derived from the BHB database which are published daily on William Hill's internet sites concern only the races for that day and are limited to the information mentioned in paragraph 19 of this judgment.

93. [I]t appears from the order for reference that the presence, in the database of the claimants, of the materials affected by William Hill's actions did not require investment by BHB and Others independent of the resources used for their creation.

94. It must therefore be held that the prohibition in Article 7(5) of the directive does not cover acts such as those of William Hill.

95. In the light of the foregoing, the answer to the 10th question must be that the prohibition laid down by Article 7(5) of the directive refers to unauthorised acts of extraction or re-utilisation the cumulative effect of which is to reconstitute and/or make available to the public, without the authorisation of the maker of the database, the whole or a substantial part of the contents of that database and thereby seriously prejudice the investment by the maker. . . .

OPERATIVE PART

On those grounds, the Court (Grand Chamber) rules as follows:

1. The expression "investment in . . . the obtaining . . . of the contents" of a database in Article 7(1) of Directive 96/9/EC of the European Parliament and of the Council of 11 March 1996 on the legal protection of databases must be understood to refer to the resources used to seek out existing independent materials and collect them in the database. It does not cover the resources used for the creation of materials which make up the contents of a database.

The expression "investment in . . . the . . . verification . . . of the contents" of a database in Article 7(1) of Directive 96/9 must be understood to refer to the resources used, with a view to ensuring the reliability of the information contained in that database, to monitor the accuracy of the materials collected when the database was created and during its operation. The resources used for verification during the stage of creation of materials which are subsequently collected in a database do not fall within that definition. The resources used to draw up a list of horses in a race and to carry out checks in that connection do not constitute investment in the obtaining and verification of the contents of the database in which that list appears.

2. The terms "extraction" and "re-utilisation" as defined in Article 7 of Directive 96/9 must be interpreted as referring to any unauthorised act of appropriation and distribution to the public of the whole or a part of the contents of a database. Those terms do not imply direct access to the database concerned.

The fact that the contents of a database were made accessible to the public by its maker or with his consent does not affect the right of the maker to prevent acts of extraction and/or re-utilisation of the whole or a substantial part of the contents of a database.

3. The expression "substantial part, evaluated . . . quantitatively, of the contents of [a] database" in Article 7 of Directive 96/9 refers to the volume of data extracted from the database and/or re-utilised and must be assessed in relation to the total volume of the contents of the database.

The expression "substantial part, evaluated qualitatively . . . of the contents of [a] database" refers to the scale of the investment in the obtaining, verification or presentation of the contents of the subject of the act of extraction and/or re-utilisation, regardless of whether that subject represents a quantitatively substantial part of the general contents of the protected database.

Any part which does not fulfil the definition of a substantial part, evaluated both quantitatively and qualitatively, falls within the definition of an insubstantial part of the contents of a database.

The prohibition laid down by Article 7(5) of Directive 96/9 refers to unauthorised acts of extraction or re-utilisation the cumulative effect of which is to reconstitute and/or make available to the public, without the authorisation of the maker of the database, the whole or a substantial part of the contents of that database and thereby seriously prejudice the investment by the maker.

NOTES AND QUESTIONS

1. According to the directive, permitted database uses include the extraction and reuse "for any purposes whatsoever" of "insubstantial parts" of the database (based on qualitative and/or quantitative assessment) (art. 8(1), DBD). Additional permitted uses include extraction for teaching or scientific research for noncommercial purposes (art. 9(b)). Do you think these exceptions to the rights of database producers are sufficient to protect the interests of the public, including the scientific research community?

2. One of the most controversial provisions of the Database Directive is Article 11. Under Article 11, *sui generis* database protection is afforded only to EU nationals, including companies with a commercial presence in the European Union. If a database is produced outside the European Union by a non-EU person, it will be protected within the European Union only pursuant to an agreement entered into between the European Union and the country where the database is produced. The European Union has argued that the *sui generis* right established by the directive is outside the scope of the national treatment rule of the Berne Convention (because the

sui generis database is not copyrightable subject matter, though of course many databases will be covered by both copyright and the *sui generis* right). Nevertheless, is the EU directive denying national treatment compatible with the national treatment rule of the TRIPS Agreement (art. 3.1, TRIPS)? Recall the treatment of the material reciprocity requirement in the WTO panel decision in the *EC — Geographical Indications* case, *supra*.

3. The nominal term of protection for the *sui generis* database right is 15 years. However, examine Article 10(3), which addresses ways in which this term may be extended. Does this approximate a perpetual right?

8.   The Information Society Directive

In the Information Society Directive,[36] adopted in 2001, the European Union implemented the WCT and WPPT. Except as expressly provided, the directive does not affect existing EU copyright approximation measures (art. 1). As noted in Recital 32, the directive "provides for an exhaustive enumeration of exceptions and limitations to the reproduction right and the right of communication to the public." Article 2 gives the right holder the exclusive right to "prohibit direct or indirect, temporary or permanent reproduction by any means and in any form, in whole or in part. . . ." An intra-Union exhaustion rule is incorporated (art. 4(2)). The directive addresses the protection of technological measures and rights management information (Chapter III).

9.   The Resale Rights Directive

The Resale Rights Directive,[37] adopted in 2001, requires member states to adopt legislation granting authors of original works of art a right to remuneration in the event of resale of the work (art. 1). "Original works of art" are broadly defined (art. 2). Member states may establish minimum threshold amounts below which the right will not apply (but the threshold may not be above €3,000) (art. 3). The directive sets forth the applicable royalty rates, and the total royalty due the author may not exceed €12,500 (art. 4). The right to remuneration may not be waived (art. 1), and is payable to the heirs of the author after death (art. 6). Foreign authors are entitled to benefit conditioned on reciprocity of their home country (art. 7). The resale right extends for the duration of the copyright in the work, established pursuant to the Copyright Directive (art. 8).

Recall that the Berne Convention expressly permits the droit de suite to be conditioned on reciprocity (art. 14*ter,* Berne), and this rule is incorporated by reference in the TRIPS Agreement.

---

36. European Parliament and Council Directive on the Harmonization of Certain Aspects of Copyright and Related Rights in the Information Society, Directive 2001/29/EC, O.J. 2001 No. L 167.

37. Directive on the resale right for the benefit of the author of an original work of art, Directive 2001/84/EC, O.J. 2001 No. L 272.

IV. REGIONAL AND BILATERAL TRADE AGREEMENTS

In Chapters 1 and 2, we discussed the use by the United States of bilateral and regional trade agreements to negotiate higher standards of intellectual property rights protection than are presently achievable at the WTO or WIPO. Following is an excerpt from a World Bank Trade Note that discusses this phenomenon in the context of copyright.

TIGHTENING TRIPS: THE INTELLECTUAL PROPERTY PROVISIONS OF RECENT US FREE TRADE AGREEMENTS

Carsten Fink & Patrick Reichenmiller*

COPYRIGHT PROTECTION

TRIPS requires copyright to be protected for the life of the author plus 50 years. Except for the FTAs extend this term by an additional 20 years.

Most bilateral FTAs include obligations against circumventing so-called technological protection measures—devices and software developed to prevent unauthorized copying of digital works. This issue is not covered under TRIPS. It only came to prominence with advances in information and communication technologies that greatly facilitated the copying of any literary or artistic work in digital form. The US Digital Millennium Copyright Act of 1998 strengthened standards on circumventing technologies designed to prevent unauthorized copying of digital content. These standards found their way to varying degrees into seven of the bilateral agreements. Related provisions in six of the FTAs define the liability of Internet Service Providers (ISPs) when copyright infringing content is distributed through their servers and networks. Again, these provisions are based on standards found in the US Digital Millennium Copyright Act.

In copyright infringement cases, all bilateral FTAs—except for the US-Vietnam Agreement—place the burden of proof on the defending party to show that works are in the public domain. TRIPS does not have any obligation on this question. The FTAs thus strengthen the position of copyright holders, as artistic and literary works should generally be considered as protected—unless they obviously belong to the public domain.

As in the case of pharmaceutical products, TRIPS does not mandate any rule on the permissibility of parallel imports of copyrighted works—such as books or musical CDs—that have been lawfully sold in foreign markets. Some countries, for example New Zealand, have permitted parallel importation of certain copyrighted products as a way to stimulate price competition. By contrast, the bilateral agreements with Jordan and Morocco give copyright holders the right to block parallel importation. . . .

ECONOMIC AND SOCIAL IMPLICATIONS . . .

Most countries have industries that rely on copyright protection and that may benefit from strengthened protection. And new technologies that greatly facilitate the copying of digital works pose challenges that policymakers need to

---

* World Bank, Trade Note 20, Feb. 7, 2005.

address. At the same time, copyright laws have historically sought to strike a balance between the interests of copyright producers and the interests of the general public. So-called fair use exemptions allow the copying of protected works for educational or research purposes.

There are concerns that new rules on the term of protection, technological protection measures, the liability of Internet services providers, and the burden of proof in case of copyright infringement could diminish the rights of consumers and the general public (CIPR, 2002).

Such concerns have also been voiced in the United States itself, not only by consumer rights advocates and academic institutions, but also by computer manufacturers and communications service providers that distribute copyrighted works. For example, specific amendments to the Digital Millennium Copyright Act have been proposed that would permit the circumvention of technological protection measures if such action does not result in an infringement of a copyrighted work. Ensuring fair use of copyrighted material seems particularly important for accessing educational material. The opportunities and gains from the use of digital libraries, Internet-based distance learning programs, or online databases would be limited if access to such tools is unaffordable or otherwise restricted by copyright law.

Finally, strengthening the enforcement of intellectual property rights can be a costly exercise — both in terms of budgetary outlays and the employment of skilled personnel. For developing countries that face many institutional deficiencies, a critical question is whether stronger enforcement of IPRs would draw away financial and human resources from other development priorities.

NOTES AND QUESTIONS

1. As with other areas of IPRs protection, there are reasons to question whether standards adopted by and appropriate for the United States, the European Union, and other advanced industrialized countries are equally appropriate for developing countries. The U.S. Digital Millennium Copyright Act involves complex procedural mechanisms that give a decided advantage to better-financed parties. This is a problem for individuals and small-business owners in the United States who may find it difficult to participate in litigation. When comparably complex procedural mechanisms are mandated for developing countries, the imbalance between the capacity of well-financed foreign copyright industries and local individuals and business owners is even more pronounced.

V. COPYRIGHT IN SOFTWARE AND OPEN SOURCE

A. Copyright in Software

The importance of computer software to modern economic life is self-evident. Yet, computer software entered the mainstream legal world only in the 1970s as its commercial exploitation began to be commonplace. There were many questions about computer software that lawyers confronted. It is generally quite easy to copy software. In making a program available to a purchaser, licensee, or beta-tester, how could the creator be assured that the software would not be copied, used, and/or redistributed? The commercialization of software appeared to depend upon some form of legal protection. Yet, what form?

Patents are fairly cumbersome. The application process is lengthy and technical. Both novelty and inventive step are elements that may be difficult to satisfy in the software patenting context. Moreover, commercial software is always changing. One version of a program is soon superseded by another as new features are added and bugs (or programming errors) are worked out. A single concept may be embodied in several different versions of the same program written in different programming languages. Would it be possible to draft individual patent applications in a way that would encompass the evolutionary and differentiated character of software? Would a new application need to be filed each time some substantial change to a program was made? Finally, and perhaps most important, it was unclear whether the basic algorithms underlying computer programs are patentable subject matter, because it has long been understood that mathematical formulas are not patentable as such (in that they are thought to represent laws of nature or discoveries).[38]

One potential alternative to the patent was *sui generis* protection that would take into account the unique characteristics of software. *Sui generis* protection might include several characteristics of the patent—such as a prohibition against independent creation and protection of the overall concept—while perhaps enjoying a moderate term of protection. The government of Japan advocated the development of a form of *sui generis* protection, and there was no shortage of proposals in Europe and the United States.

Ultimately, the practical needs of industry triumphed over the government policy makers. Lawyers used the tools at hand to fashion protection for their clients under the copyright laws. There were (and are) decided advantages to copyright. First, copyright laws were in place throughout most of the world, so there would be no time lost in the negotiation and implementation of new norms. Second, copyright protection is automatic. Under the Berne Convention, the absence of formalities is prescribed. (Recall that in the early 1980s the United States was not party to the Berne Convention.) Thus, assuming that software would be considered copyrightable subject matter, protection would be easy to obtain. Third, copyright law is flexible. Each addition or change to a program would automatically be the subject of protection. Fourth, copyright is of long duration, and while this long duration may not always be of practical use, it was perceived as preferable to the shorter terms generally proposed for *sui generis* protection. Finally, there was the perspective of the practicing lawyers who represented clients in the computer industry. The patent bar of each country is highly specialized, and qualification for the patent bar generally requires technical training. Many lawyers representing the computer industry

---

38. Just what is an *algorithm* has been the subject of debate. One of the authors of this book was some years ago jogging in the hills of Los Angeles with a pioneer of the personal computer industry when the author realized he needed to return to their hotel for a meeting. Not knowing how to get back to the hotel, he asked for directions from the computer scientist. "Well," queried the scientist, "Do you know what an algorithm is?" The author replied, "Perhaps, but in any event why don't you tell me?" "Allow me to explain by illustration," said the scientist. "To return to the hotel, you will always run straight, except that you will turn right at every third stoplight, and left at the only stop sign between here and the hotel. In other words," he continued, "an algorithm is a set of instructions expressed as a mathematical formula."

were not patent lawyers, and these lawyers stood to lose substantial business if representation of the software industry were channeled to the patent bar. There was an incentive for the non-patent lawyer to promote copyright protection or a form of *sui generis* protection outside the specialized patent field.

The adoption of the copyright as the accepted method for protecting computer software left myriad questions to be answered. Though some of the most basic questions have been the subject of fairly consistent legislative and judicial rule making, many questions remain unevenly answered (or not answered at all). Moreover, the computer software industry is dynamic—the "thing" that is covered by copyright protection continues to evolve. Moreover, as the "open source movement" (introduced in the next section) illustrates, shifting "business models" alter the landscape on which questions are set.

Of course, the United States over the past decade has opened the field of computer software "as such" to patent protection. Numerous difficulties have resulted.

Though almost 20 years have passed since it was decided, the *Computer Associates v. Altai* decision substantially shapes the "state of the art" in U.S. case law concerning software as copyrightable subject matter.

COMPUTER ASSOCIATES INTERNATIONAL v. ALTAI
982 F.2d 693 (2d Cir. 1992)

WALKER, Circuit Judge: . . .

Among other things, this case deals with the challenging question of whether and to what extent the "non-literal" aspects of a computer program, that is, those aspects that are not reduced to written code, are protected by copyright. While a few other courts have already grappled with this issue, this case is one of first impression in this circuit. As we shall discuss, we find the results reached by other courts to be less than satisfactory. Drawing upon long-standing doctrines of copyright law, we take an approach that we think better addresses the practical difficulties embedded in these types of cases. In so doing, we have kept in mind the necessary balance between creative incentive and industrial competition. . . .

BACKGROUND . . .

II. FACTS . . .

The subject of this litigation originates with one of CA's marketed programs entitled CA-SCHEDULER. CA-SCHEDULER is a job scheduling program designed for IBM mainframe computers. . . .

. . . ADAPTER plays an extremely important role. It is an "operating system compatibility component," which means, roughly speaking, it serves as a translator. . . .

Starting in 1982, Altai began marketing its own job scheduling program entitled ZEKE. The original version of ZEKE was designed for use in conjunction with a VSE operating system. By late 1983, in response to customer demand, Altai decided to rewrite ZEKE so that it could be run in conjunction with an MVS operating system.

At that time, James P. Williams ("Williams"), then an employee of Altai and now its President, approached Claude F. Arney, III ("Arney"), a computer programmer who worked for CA. Williams and Arney were longstanding friends, and had in fact been co-workers at CA for some time before Williams left CA to work for Altai's predecessor. Williams wanted to recruit Arney to assist Altai in designing an MVS version of ZEKE. . . .

. . . They decided to name this new component-program OSCAR. . . .

The first generation of OSCAR programs was known as OSCAR 3.4. From 1985 to August 1988, Altai used OSCAR 3.4 in its ZEKE product, as well as in programs entitled ZACK and ZEBB. In late July 1988, CA first learned that Altai may have appropriated parts of ADAPTER. After confirming its suspicions, CA secured copyrights on its 2.1 and 7.0 versions of CA-SCHEDULER. CA then brought this copyright and trade secret misappropriation action against Altai.

Apparently, it was upon receipt of the summons and complaint that Altai first learned that Arney had copied much of the OSCAR code from ADAPTER. After Arney confirmed to Williams that CA's accusations of copying were true, Williams immediately set out to survey the damage. Without ever looking at the ADAPTER code himself, Williams learned from Arney exactly which sections of code Arney had taken from ADAPTER.

Upon advice of counsel, Williams initiated OSCAR's rewrite. The project's goal was to save as much of OSCAR 3.4 as legitimately could be used, and to excise those portions which had been copied from ADAPTER. Arney was entirely excluded from the process, and his copy of the ADAPTER code was locked away. Williams put eight other programmers on the project, none of whom had been involved in any way in the development of OSCAR 3.4. Williams provided the programmers with a description of the ZEKE operating system services so that they could rewrite the appropriate code. The rewrite project took about six months to complete and was finished in mid-November 1989. The resulting program was entitled OSCAR 3.5.

From that point on, Altai shipped only OSCAR 3.5 to its new customers. Altai also shipped OSCAR 3.5 as a "free upgrade" to all customers that had previously purchased OSCAR 3.4. While Altai and Williams acted responsibly to correct Arney's literal copying of the ADAPTER program, copyright infringement had occurred. . . .

DISCUSSION . . .

I. COPYRIGHT INFRINGEMENT . . .

For the purpose of analysis, the district court assumed that Altai had access to the ADAPTER code when creating OSCAR 3.5. . . . [O]ur analysis will proceed along the same assumption.

As a general matter, and to varying degrees, copyright protection extends beyond a literary work's strictly textual form to its non-literal components. As we have said, "it is of course essential to any protection of literary property . . . that the right cannot be limited literally to the text, else a plagiarist would escape by immaterial variations." *Nichols v. Universal Pictures Co.*, 45 F.2d 119, 121 (2d Cir. 1930) (L. Hand, J.), *cert. denied*, 282 U.S. 902, 75 L. Ed. 795, 51 S. Ct. 216 (1931). Thus, where "the fundamental essence or structure of one work is duplicated in another," 3 Nimmer, § 13.03[A][1], at 13-24, courts have found copyright infringement. . . .

A. COPYRIGHT PROTECTION FOR THE NON-LITERAL ELEMENTS OF COMPUTER PROGRAMS

It is now well settled that the literal elements of computer programs, i.e., their source and object codes, are the subject of copyright protection. *See Whelan*, 797 F.2d at 1233 (source and object code). . . . Here, as noted earlier, Altai admits having copied approximately 30% of the OSCAR 3.4 program from CA's ADAPTER source code, and does not challenge the district court's related finding of infringement.

In this case, the hotly contested issues surround OSCAR 3.5. As recounted above, OSCAR 3.5 is the product of Altai's carefully orchestrated rewrite of OSCAR 3.4. After the purge, none of the ADAPTER source code remained in the 3.5 version; thus, Altai made sure that the literal elements of its revamped OSCAR program were no longer substantially similar to the literal elements of CA's ADAPTER. . . .

CA argues that, despite Altai's rewrite of the OSCAR code, the resulting program remained substantially similar to the structure of its ADAPTER program. As discussed above, a program's structure includes its nonliteral components such as general flow charts as well as the more specific organization of inter-modular relationships, parameter lists, and macros. In addition to these aspects, CA contends that OSCAR 3.5 is also substantially similar to ADAPTER with respect to the list of services that both ADAPTER and OSCAR obtain from their respective operating systems. We must decide whether and to what extent these elements of computer programs are protected by copyright law. . . .

1. Idea vs. Expression Dichotomy

It is a fundamental principle of copyright law that a copyright does not protect an idea, but only the expression of the idea. *See Baker v. Selden*, 101 U.S. 99, 25 L. Ed. 841 (1879); *Mazer v. Stein*, 347 U.S. 201, 217, 98 L. Ed. 630, 74 S. Ct. 460 (1954). This axiom of common law has been incorporated into the governing statute. Section 102(b) of the Act provides:

> In no case does copyright protection for an original work of authorship extend to any idea, procedure, process, system, method of operation, concept, principle, or discovery, regardless of the form in which it is described, explained, illustrated, or embodied in such work.

17 U.S.C. § 102(b). *See also* House Report, at 5670 ("Copyright does not preclude others from using ideas or information revealed by the author's work.").

Congress made no special exception for computer programs. To the contrary, the legislative history explicitly states that copyright protects computer programs only "to the extent that they incorporate authorship in programmer's expression of original ideas, as distinguished from the ideas themselves." *Id.* at 5667; *see also id.* at 5670 ("Section 102(b) is intended . . . to make clear that the expression adopted by the programmer is the copyrightable element in a computer program, and that the actual processes or methods embodied in the program are not within the scope of copyright law."). . . .

Drawing the line between idea and expression is a tricky business. Judge Learned Hand noted that "nobody has ever been able to fix that boundary, and nobody ever can." *Nichols*, 45 F.2d at 121. Thirty years later his convictions remained firm. "Obviously, no principle can be stated as to when an imitator has gone beyond copying the 'idea,' and has borrowed its 'expression,'" Judge Hand concluded. "Decisions must therefore inevitably be ad hoc." *Peter Pan Fabrics, Inc. v. Martin Weiner Corp.*, 274 F.2d 487, 489 (2d Cir. 1960).

The essentially utilitarian nature of a computer program further complicates the task of distilling its idea from its expression. *See SAS Inst.*, 605 F. Supp. at 829; *cf.* Englund, at 893. In order to describe both computational processes and abstract ideas, its content "combines creative and technical expression." *See Spivack,* at 755. The variations of expression found in purely creative compositions, as opposed to those contained in utilitarian works, are not directed towards practical application. For example, a narration of Humpty Dumpty's demise, which would clearly be a creative composition, does not serve the same ends as, say, a recipe for scrambled eggs—which is a more process oriented text. Thus, compared to aesthetic works, computer programs hover even more closely to the elusive boundary line described in § 102(b).

The doctrinal starting point in analyses of utilitarian works, is the seminal case of *Baker v. Selden,* 101 U.S. 99, 25 L. Ed. 841 (1879). . . .

The Supreme Court found nothing copyrightable in Selden's bookkeeping system, and rejected his infringement claim regarding the ledger sheets. The Court held that:

> The fact that the art described in the book by illustrations of lines and figures which are reproduced in practice in the application of the art, makes no difference. Those illustrations are the mere language employed by the author to convey his ideas more clearly. Had he used words of description instead of diagrams (which merely stand in the place of words), there could not be the slightest doubt that others, applying the art to practical use, might lawfully draw the lines and diagrams which were in the author's mind, and which he thus described by words in his book.
>
> The copyright of a work on mathematical science cannot give to the author an exclusive right to the methods of operation which he propounds, or to the diagrams which he employs to explain them, so as to prevent an engineer from using them whenever occasion requires.

Id. at 103.

To the extent that an accounting text and a computer program are both "a set of statements or instructions . . . to bring about a certain result," 17 U.S.C. § 101, they are roughly analogous. In the former case, the processes are ultimately conducted by human agency; in the latter, by electronic means. In either case, as already stated, the processes themselves are not protectable. But the holding in *Baker* goes farther. The Court concluded that those aspects of a work, which "must necessarily be used as incident to" the idea, system or process that the work describes, are also not copyrightable. 101 U.S. at 104. Selden's ledger sheets, therefore, enjoyed no copyright protection because they were "necessary incidents to" the system of accounting that he described. *Id.* at 103. From this reasoning, we conclude that those elements of a computer program that are necessarily incidental to its function are similarly unprotectable.

While *Baker v. Selden* provides a sound analytical foundation, it offers scant guidance on how to separate idea or process from expression, and moreover, on how to further distinguish protectable expression from that expression which "must necessarily be used as incident to" the work's underlying concept. . . .

2. *Substantial Similarity Test for Computer Program Structure*
Abstraction-Filtration-Comparison . . .

As discussed herein, we think that district courts would be well-advised to undertake a three-step procedure, based on the abstractions test utilized by the district court, in order to determine whether the non-literal elements of two or more computer programs are substantially similar. This approach breaks no new ground; rather, it draws on such familiar copyright doctrines as merger, scenes a faire, and public domain. In taking this approach, however, we are cognizant that computer technology is a dynamic field which can quickly outpace judicial decisionmaking. Thus, in cases where the technology in question does not allow for a literal application of the procedure we outline below, our opinion should not be read to foreclose the district courts of our circuit from utilizing a modified version.

In ascertaining substantial similarity under this approach, a court would first break down the allegedly infringed program into its constituent structural parts. Then, by examining each of these parts for such things as incorporated ideas, expression that is necessarily incidental to those ideas, and elements that are taken from the public domain, a court would then be able to sift out all non-protectable material. Left with a kernel, or possibly kernels, of creative expression after following this process of elimination, the court's last step would be to compare this material with the structure of an allegedly infringing program. The result of this comparison will determine whether the protectable elements of the programs at issue are substantially similar so as to warrant a finding of infringement. It will be helpful to elaborate a bit further.

Step One: Abstraction

As the district court appreciated, *see Computer Assocs.*, 775 F. Supp. at 560, the theoretic framework for analyzing substantial similarity expounded by Learned Hand in the *Nichols* case is helpful in the present context. In *Nichols,* we enunciated what has now become known as the "abstractions" test for separating idea from expression:

> Upon any work . . . a great number of patterns of increasing generality will fit equally well, as more and more of the incident is left out. The last may perhaps be no more than the most general statement of what the [work] is about, and at times might consist only of its title; but there is a point in this series of abstractions where they are no longer protected, since otherwise the [author] could prevent the use of his "ideas," to which, apart from their expression, his property is never extended.

Nichols, 45 F.2d at 121.

While the abstractions test was originally applied in relation to literary works such as novels and plays, it is adaptable to computer programs. In contrast to the *Whelan* approach, the abstractions test "implicitly recognizes that any given work may consist of a mixture of numerous ideas and expressions." 3 Nimmer § 13.03[F] at 13-62.34-63.

As applied to computer programs, the abstractions test will comprise the first step in the examination for substantial similarity. Initially, in a manner that resembles reverse engineering on a theoretical plane, a court should dissect the allegedly copied program's structure and isolate each level of abstraction contained within it. This process begins with the code and ends with an articulation of the program's ultimate function. Along the way, it is necessary essentially to retrace and map each of the designer's steps — in the opposite order in which they were taken during the program's creation. See Background: Computer Program Design, *supra*.

As an anatomical guide to this procedure, the following description is helpful:

> At the lowest level of abstraction, a computer program may be thought of in its entirety as a set of individual instructions organized into a hierarchy of modules. At a higher level of abstraction, the instructions in the lowest-level modules may be replaced conceptually by the functions of those modules. At progressively higher levels of abstraction, the functions of higher-level modules conceptually replace the implementations of those modules in terms of lower-level modules and instructions, until finally, one is left with nothing but the ultimate function of the program. . . . A program has structure at every level of abstraction at which it is viewed. At low levels of abstraction, a program's structure may be quite complex; at the highest level it is trivial. . . .

Step Two: Filtration

Once the program's abstraction levels have been discovered, the substantial similarity inquiry moves from the conceptual to the concrete. Professor Nimmer suggests, and we endorse, a "successive filtering method" for separating protectable expression from non-protectable material. *See generally* 3 Nimmer § 13.03[F]. This process entails examining the structural components at each level of abstraction to determine whether their particular inclusion at that level was "idea" or was dictated by considerations of efficiency, so as to be necessarily incidental to that idea; required by factors external to the program itself; or taken from the public domain and hence is nonprotectable expression. *See also* Kretschmer, at 844-45 [Mark T. Kretschmer, *Copyright Protection for Software Architecture: Just Say No!*, 1988 COLUM. BUS. L. REV. 823 (1988)] (arguing that program features dictated by market externalities or efficiency concerns are unprotectable). The structure of any given program may reflect some, all, or none of these considerations. Each case requires its own fact specific investigation.

Strictly speaking, this filtration serves "the purpose of defining the scope of plaintiff's copyright." *Brown Bag Software v. Symantec Corp.*, 960 F.2d 1465, 1475 (9th Cir.) (endorsing "analytic dissection" of computer programs in order to isolate protectable expression), *cert. denied*, 113 S. Ct. 198, 121 L. Ed. 2d 141 (1992). By applying well developed doctrines of copyright law, it may ultimately leave behind a "core of protectable material." 3 Nimmer § 13.03[F][5], at 13-72. Further explication of this second step may be helpful.

(a) Elements Dictated by Efficiency

The portion of *Baker v. Selden*, discussed earlier, which denies copyright protection to expression necessarily incidental to the idea being expressed, appears to be the cornerstone for what has developed into the doctrine of merger. . . .

CONTU recognized the applicability of the merger doctrine to computer programs. In its report to Congress it stated that:

> Copyrighted language may be copied without infringing when there is but a limited number of ways to express a given idea. . . . In the computer context, this means that when specific instructions, even though previously copyrighted, are the only and essential means of accomplishing a given task, their later use by another will not amount to infringement.

CONTU Report at 20. While this statement directly concerns only the application of merger to program code, that is, the textual aspect of the program, it reasonably suggests that the doctrine fits comfortably within the general context of computer programs.

Furthermore, when one considers the fact that programmers generally strive to create programs "that meet the user's needs in the most efficient manner," Menell, at 1052, [Peter S. Menell, *An Analysis of the Scope of Copyright Protection for Application Programs*, 41 STAN. L. REV. 1045 (1989)] the applicability of the merger doctrine to computer programs becomes compelling. In the context of computer program design, the concept of efficiency is akin to deriving the most concise logical proof or formulating the most succinct mathematical computation. Thus, the more efficient a set of modules are, the more closely they approximate the idea or process embodied in that particular aspect of the program's structure.

While, hypothetically, there might be a myriad of ways in which a programmer may effectuate certain functions within a program—i.e., express the idea embodied in a given subroutine—efficiency concerns may so narrow the practical range of choice as to make only one or two forms of expression workable options. *See* 3 Nimmer § 13.03[F][2], at 13-63; *see also Whelan*, 797 F.2d at 1243 n.43 ("It is true that for certain tasks there are only a very limited number of file structures available, and in such cases the structures might not be copyrightable . . ."). Of course, not all program structure is informed by efficiency concerns. *See* Menell, at 1052 (besides efficiency, simplicity related to user accommodation has become a programming priority). It follows that in order to determine whether the merger doctrine precludes copyright protection to an aspect of a program's structure that is so oriented, a court must inquire "whether the use of this particular set of modules is necessary efficiently to implement that part of the program's process" being implemented. Englund, at 902. If the answer is yes, then the expression represented by the programmer's choice of a specific module or group of modules has merged with their underlying idea and is unprotected. *Id.* at 902-03. . . .

(b) Elements Dictated by External Factors

We have stated that where "it is virtually impossible to write about a particular historical era or fictional theme without employing certain 'stock' or standard literary devices," such expression is not copyrightable. *Hoehling v. Universal City Studios, Inc.*, 618 F.2d 972, 979 (2d Cir.), *cert. denied*, 449 U.S. 841, 66 L. Ed. 2d 49, 101 S. Ct. 121 (1980). For example, the *Hoehling* case was an infringement suit stemming from several works on the Hindenberg disaster. There we concluded that similarities in representations of German beer halls, scenes depicting German greetings such as "Heil Hitler," or the singing of certain German songs would not lead to a finding of infringement because they were " 'indispensable, or at least standard, in the treatment of' " life in Nazi Germany. *Id.* (quoting *Alexander v. Haley*, 460 F. Supp. 40, 45 (S.D.N.Y. 1978)). This is known as the *scenes à faire* doctrine, and like "merger," it has its analogous application to computer programs. *Cf. Data East USA*, 862 F.2d at 208 (applying scenes a faire to a home computer video game).

Professor Nimmer points out that "in many instances it is virtually impossible to write a program to perform particular functions in a specific computing environment without employing standard techniques." 3 Nimmer § 13.03[F][3], at 13-65. This is a result of the fact that a programmer's freedom of design choice is often circumscribed by extrinsic considerations such as (1) the mechanical spe-cifications of the computer on which a particular program is intended to run; (2) compatibility requirements of other programs with which a program is designed to operate in conjunction; (3) computer manufacturers' design standards; (4) demands of the industry being serviced; and (5) widely accepted programming practices within the computer industry. *Id.* at 13-66-71.

Courts have already considered some of these factors in denying copyright protection to various elements of computer programs. . . .

Building upon this existing case law, we conclude that a court must also examine the structural content of an allegedly infringed program for elements that might have been dictated by external factors.

(c) Elements Taken from the Public Domain

Closely related to the non-protectability of *scenes à faire*, is material found in the public domain. Such material is free for the taking and cannot be appro-priated by a single author even though it is included in a copyrighted work. *See E.F. Johnson Co. v. Uniden Corp. of America*, 623 F. Supp. 1485, 1499 (D. Minn. 1985); *see also Sheldon*, 81 F.2d at 54. We see no reason to make an exception to this rule for elements of a computer program that have entered the public domain by virtue of freely accessible program exchanges and the like. *See* 3 Nimmer § 13.03[F][4]; *see also Brown Bag Software*, 960 F.2d at 1473 (affirming the district court's finding that "'plaintiffs may not claim copyright protection of an . . . expression that is, if not standard, then commonplace in the computer software industry.'"). Thus, a court must also filter out this material from the allegedly infringed program before it makes the final inquiry in its substantial similarity analysis.

Step Three: Comparison

The third and final step of the test for substantial similarity that we believe appropriate for non-literal program components entails a comparison. Once a court has sifted out all elements of the allegedly infringed program which are "ideas" or are dictated by efficiency or external factors, or taken from the public domain, there may remain a core of protectable expression. In terms of a work's copyright value, this is the golden nugget. *See Brown Bag Software*, 960 F.2d at 1475. At this point, the court's substantial similarity inquiry focuses on whether the defendant copied any aspect of this protected expression, as well as an assessment of the copied portion's relative importance with respect to the plain-tiff's overall program. . . .

3. Policy Considerations

We are satisfied that the three step approach we have just outlined not only comports with, but advances the constitutional policies underlying the Copyright Act. Since any method that tries to distinguish idea from expression ultimately impacts on the scope of copyright protection afforded to a particular type of work, "the line [it draws] must be a pragmatic one, which also keeps in consideration 'the preservation of the balance between competition and protection. . . . '" *Apple Computer* [*v. Franklin Computer Corp.*], 714 F.2d [1240] at 1253 (citation omitted). . . .

[W]e are unpersuaded that the test we approve today will lead to the dire consequences for the computer program industry that plaintiff and some amici predict. To the contrary, serious students of the industry have been highly critical of the sweeping scope of copyright protection engendered by the

Whelan rule, in that it "enables first comers to 'lock up' basic programming techniques as implemented in programs to perform particular tasks." Menell, at 1087; *see also Spivack,* at 765 (*Whelan* "results in an inhibition of creation by virtue of the copyright owner's quasi-monopoly power").

To be frank, the exact contours of copyright protection for non-literal program structure are not completely clear. We trust that as future cases are decided, those limits will become better defined. Indeed, it may well be that the Copyright Act serves as a relatively weak barrier against public access to the theoretical interstices behind a program's source and object codes. This results from the hybrid nature of a computer program, which, while it is literary expression, is also a highly functional, utilitarian component in the larger process of computing. . . .

II. TRADE SECRET PREEMPTION

[In the second part of its opinion, the Second Circuit considers the relationship between state trade secret law and federal copyright law. The court holds that state trade secret law is not preempted by federal copyright law to the extent that there is an additional substantive element to a state trade secret law cause of action. The court held: "[A] state law claim based solely upon Altai's" use, "by copying, of ADAPTER's non-literal elements could not satisfy the governing 'extra element' test, and would be preempted by section 301. However, where the use of copyrighted expression is simultaneously the violation of a duty of confidentiality established by state law, that extra element renders the state right qualitatively distinct from the federal right, thereby foreclosing preemption under section 301." Judge Altimari dissented from the court's preemption analysis.]

NOTES AND QUESTIONS

1. The second step in the court's analytical process is "filtration." The court observes that the expression in computer programs is often dictated by functional concerns — for example, the microprocessor requests that data be transmitted from the disk drive — and that there are a limited number of relatively efficient ways to frame such requests. The court does not want expression that is dictated by such functional concerns to be protected by copyright. Moreover, the court notes that some types of program instruction are commonplace — analogizing to *scenes à faire* doctrine, which precludes the copyrighting of commonplace descriptions and events (e.g., "under a clear blue sky").
2. Some courts may find it difficult to apply the tests articulated in *Computer Associates.* Is the *Computer Associates* analysis practical in the global context?
3. Recall the German Supreme Court's decision in the *Protection of Computer Programs* case, *supra* pages 482-83, that program elements dictated by functionality should be filtered out, and that originality should reflect more than the skill of the average programmer. Is that decision consistent with the decision in *Computer Associates?*

4. *Computer Associates v. Altai* is a landmark decision with respect to the question of copyright protection of computer software. It defines the "proprietary" elements of software. However, during the last decades, a new concept has emerged, altering the concept of property in the context of computer software. The "open source" movement is evolving and dynamic, creating a new software environment and innovation model.

B. Open Source and the Public Domain

Throughout this chapter the issue of public domain was mentioned several times. The importance of public domain is widely recognized—promotion of education and follow-on innovation, as well as low-cost access to information, are examples. The following excerpt from a WIPO study on the public domain explains the recent private initiatives aimed at promotion of better access to information and development of the public domain.

SCOPING STUDY ON COPYRIGHT AND RELATED RIGHTS AND THE PUBLIC DOMAIN

Prepared by Severine Dusollier
WIPO, May 7, 2010

. . .

COPYLEFT, OPEN SOURCE OR OPEN ACCESS LICENSING

1. NOTION

Unhappy with the extension of intellectual property, some creators have set up alternative regimes for exercising copyright. The first and best known is the open source software movement that was born in the 80's to counteract the proprietary exercise of copyright in software, considered by many as excessive and far-fetched and at odds with the needs of the community of software developers and users. Many licenses have been developed with common features that give some basic freedoms to the licensees, such as the right to reproduce, communicate or distribute the work to the public for free, and oblige the licensor to provide the source code of the program.

That first idea inspired and gave its name to a larger movement whose key purpose was to use the copyright to share one's works and grant large freedoms of use to the public. That movement has adopted many names. Open source is the germinal term that has embraced a myriad of licenses governing free software. It insists on the core obligation arising from such licenses—the obligation to provide the source code of the software. The movement or licenses promoting non-proprietary software are also generally dubbed as F/OSS, standing for Free/Open-Source Software (or even FLOSS, for Free, Libre, Open Source Software).

While the principles of open source have spread beyond software, these open-source initiatives have forsaken the "source" element to prefer instead "open access" or "open content." The openness of the resource, whether such openness lies in its access or use, is there emphasized. Following a body of literature applying the economic concept of the "commons" to intellectual property, many projects have also borrowed that word to signify the newly gained communality of the resources that the open access and sharing initiatives could yield. The term "commons-based initiatives" has sometimes served to designate sharing projects in copyright or patent fields.

Also taken from open-source software, the term "copyleft" gained momentum in the open-access schemes and in the literature describing them. It results from a play on words where copy *left* stands in stark contrast to copy *right*—"left" versus "right"—but also progressive versus conservative (applying to what was perceived, by the copyleft proponents, as the "right-wing" and conservative position of the proprietary copyright), "right" as legal entitlement versus "left" as relinquishment of the property. . . .

Software, works or inventions distributed to the public under an open source or copyleft licensing regime are often said to be in the public domain. This is not accurate as the decision to license the use of one's works under a copyleft license does not amount to a relinquishment of copyright, but rather as an exercise thereof, albeit different. Based on licenses granting the right to copy, distribute, communicate and sometimes modify the work to any user of the work, open access licensing can be seen as pursuing a similar objective to the public domain, i.e. promoting the free availability, use and exploitation of creative expressions.

2. PRESENTATION OF MAIN LICENSING REGIMES

(i) Open Source Software

The history of open-source software is now well known and documented. Reacting to the early development of licensing practices aimed at restricting the "rights of use" of software and of the increasing closure of the source code, Richard Stallman imagined a new model of software distribution, that would fit more closely with the habits of the programmers' community. This alternate framework was named "free software" in order to convey the freedom to access and use the software.

The history of open-source software then took different paths. Richard Stallman founded the Free Software Foundation, which has developed and continues to manage the General Public License ("GPL"), the first license embedding free software principles. The development of the operating system Linux by a student quickly gave a market pedigree to the idea of free software, demonstrating the possible commercial success of this new model. A schism occurred in 1998 when less radical programmers launched the Open Source Initiative whose objective was to develop open-source principles that could be seen not only as a confrontation to the practices of the software industry but that could be part of a business strategy. They invented the term "open source" to emphasize not the freedom to use but the necessity to make the source code of the software available. This meeting also gave birth to the Open Source Definition, which lays down the key elements and provisions that a license should include to merit the open-source label. This definition contains ten "commandments" that form a sort of label certificate. They combine the four basic freedoms that a free or open-source license should grant: (1) the freedom to run the program, for any users or purpose (e.g., for commercial purpose or not); (2) the right to obtain access to source code; (3) the freedom to redistribute copies; and (4) the freedom to improve the program and release improvements if desired.

Eventually the open source software movement gave birth to more than one hundred open-source licenses that are in use worldwide. The GPL represents the biggest share of the licenses now employed on the market. Most of them originate from a US-based legal philosophy and writing. One European license, the EUPL (European Public License) has been recently developed by the European Commission to be applied to software in a way that would be compliant with the EU regulatory framework.

(ii) Creative Commons

Lawrence Lessig, a well-known scholar in cyberspace law, has followed Richard Stallman and the overall open-source movement by imagining the transposition of the copyleft model at work in free software to other types of creation. He founded the Creative Commons ("CC") project and organization in 2001. The main objective of Creative Commons parallels that of the free software movement, i.e. to grant basic freedoms of copying and distributing a copyrighted work to users, but has devised licenses applicable to any type of literary and artistic work and not only software.

Besides developing licenses applicable outside of software, Creative Commons departs from the open-source model used in software by giving the author choices among different licenses. Each license grants diverse rights to the user. When deciding to license his/her work under Creative Commons, an author can choose whether he/she will allow the work to be modified by the user, whether he/she wants to limit uses of the work to non-commercial purposes, and whether he/she wants to oblige the user to grant the same freedom of use when the latter modifies the work and publicly communicates the derivative work. Regardless of which Creative Commons license the author chooses, a work should be attributed to its author when it is disseminated.

Creative Commons offers six different licenses for the author to choose from, divided into three basic characteristics: Commercial/Non-Commercial, Derivative Works/Non-Derivative Works, and Share Alike/Non-Share Alike. Each license grants a worldwide, royalty-free, non-exclusive, perpetual license to the user to reproduce, display, perform, communicate, and distribute copies of the work. Depending on the type of license selected, the right to create derivative works or to use the work for commercial purposes might also be granted. All rights not expressly granted by the licensor are reserved with the exception of limitations to copyright that are not prejudiced by the license. The so-called Share Alike licenses require that the further distribution of derivative works be made under the same license terms. . . .

. . . To some extent, Creative Commons can be said to provide a useful answer to the needs of some communities of creators who might consider sharing as the normal way of disseminating their creation, whether artistic, informational, scientific or functional.

Other free licenses have been developed for artistic creation such as the *Licence Art Libre*, in France in 1999, but they are less used now than Creative Commons.

(iii) Open Access to Scientific Publications

Open-access ideology has also spread to the field of scientific publications where it has been seen as a strategy for counteracting the increasing commodification of scientific publications and the reduced availability of scientific knowledge. In the realm of scientific publications, the open-access dogma has been applied by putting in place free electronic distribution of scholarly journals in almost all fields of science and by setting up central repositories of open-access journals such as the OpenDOAR (Open Directory of Open Access Repositories) that contains more than 14,000 sources of academic open access repositories or journals.

Open-access ideology in the realm of scientific publications has been aided by the fact that many research organizations, universities, libraries, research funding agencies, and publishers have signed the Berlin Declaration on Open Access to Knowledge in the Sciences and Humanities. This declaration requires authors associated with the signatories to grant to all users a free worldwide right to access their works and requires that the works be deposited in at least one online repository enabling open access, unrestricted distribution, interoperability, and long-term archiving. Publication of scientific results or articles in open access is increasingly the norm in scientific research. It does not follow any particular licensing framework for enabling open access, but rather relies on existing licensing platforms such as Creative Commons or lets the authors or the open-access repositories draft their own open-access policy.

The following excerpt by Lawrence Lessig points out that open source is not free intellectual property protection, but depends on copyright protection to remain "open."

OPEN SOURCE BASELINES: COMPARED TO WHAT?

Lawrence Lessig*

. . . [H]ere lies the puzzle: by distributing the source code with the object code, open source and free software developers give their competitors free access to any value that they might have added to the software they are distributing. A developer thus cannot capture that value for him- or herself, but rather gives at least a part of it away. How then can developers have sufficient incentive to innovate? What motivates them to develop in this way? How can developers sustain the costs of development if they must hand to their competitors all the value they have created?

My aim here is to disentangle this puzzle. Open source and free software have played an important part in the growth of the Internet. The puzzle about their existence comes from a mistaken baseline of comparison. Properly understood, these movements are completely consistent with a tradition of innovation and development outside the context of software. They may seem unique within the software industry, but they are not unique against the background of development or innovation generally. . . .

THE NATURE OF OPEN SOURCE AND FREE SOFTWARE

Open source and free software give consumers and the public something more than proprietary software does: the ability to tinker and modify. Such software

---

* GOVERNMENT POLICY TOWARD OPEN SOURCE SOFTWARE (Robert W. Hahn ed., 2003), at 50.

gives the public the benefit of the information contained within the code. Yet open source and free software don't provide these values by forfeiting public law protection. Open source and free software are not "in the public domain." Copyrights still attach to their creative content. Thus copyright law continues to control how this content can be used and distributed. Open source and free software producers use this control to impose conditions upon the use of their code. These conditions vary significantly depending upon whether the code is free or open source. But these conditions are not options. They are requirements imposed by the force of law.

Not all software-related content is protected in this way. There are important software related products that are within the public domain. The TCP/IP (Transmission Control Protocol/Internet Protocol), for example, which forms the basic protocols of the Internet, is in the public domain. Anyone is free to implement it without the permission of a copyright holder. This enabled many to build TCP/IP networks inexpensively and ensured that no one had the power to control how TCP/IP would develop.

But being in the public domain also means that TCP/IP could in principle be hijacked. A major producer of TCP/IP technology could extend the protocol in a way that benefits its own interests and weakens its competitors. It could do this because the nature of the public domain is that anyone is free to build as they wish. HTML (Hypertext Markup Language) is an example of a protocol that was in the public domain. Netscape and Microsoft each tried to extend the protocol in ways that benefited its own implementation. This competition may or may not have been beneficial to the spread of the World Wide Web. But whether or not it was, hijacking was possible because the underlying protocol was not protected.

By staying outside the public domain, open source and free software at least have the potential to protect themselves against the hijacker. Using copyright law, they have the power to require certain conditions before their code is used in ways that implicate the exclusive rights protected by copyright law. Thus, like proprietary software, open source and free software depend upon copyright; like proprietary software, open source and free software make themselves available only under certain conditions. The important difference among these three forms of software is simply the difference in conditions.

Proprietary software is made available upon the payment of a price (which sometimes is zero). In exchange for a price, the user ordinarily licenses the object code. Object code, because it is compiled into a form that is effectively opaque to humans, does not transmit the information it contains; it is simply a machine that induces another machine to function in a particular way. But attached to that machine is a license supported by copyright law. That license sets the terms according to which one may use the licensed machine. In the ordinary proprietary model, you are not permitted to sell the code you have licensed, nor are you permitted to modify and redistribute it. Proprietary code gives you the right to use the machine you've licensed, just like a rental from Hertz gives you the right to use the car you've leased.

Open source and free software impose different conditions upon users. And while the variety of open source and free software licenses is broad, we can identify essentially two sorts: copylefted software and noncopylefted software.

Copylefted software is software that is licensed under terms that require follow-on users to require others to adopt the same license terms for work derived from the copylefted code. The principle is "share and share alike." Noncopylefted open source software imposes no such condition on subsequent use. With copylefted software, the price of admission is that if you redistribute modified versions of the copylefted code, you must redistribute it under similar license terms; with noncopylefted software, no such price is demanded.

The most famous example of copylefted code is the GNU/Linux operating system. GNU/Linux is licensed under the GNU General Public License (GPL). The GPL requires that anyone who modifies and redistributes GPL-covered code do so under a GPL license. For example, if an enterprising coder modified Linux to run seamlessly Windows and Macintosh programs, he would be free to redistribute that modified GNU/Linux only if he did so under a GPL license. And since a GPL license also requires that the source code of a GPL work be made available for free, this Linux innovator would likely face competition from copycat competitors. If the coder had in fact produced an operating system that could run programs from other operating systems directly, then many would likely take it and sell it in competition with him. The GPL guarantees that "freedom."

It is for this reason that some argue that the copyleft requirement is too steep a price for developers to pay. The freedom of a single developer to build a cross-platform-compatible version of Linux, for example, might well be defeated by the copyleft condition (assuming that the costs of such a project are extremely high and that the developer would need to recover those costs from the sale of copies of the resulting operating system). But this condition is not necessarily any more expensive than the conditions imposed by proprietary code. If our Linux developer wanted to create a modified, cross-platform-compatible version of Windows, he would be no more free to redistribute the resulting Microsoft code than he would be free to distribute the modified Linux code under the GPL. If he could get the permission of Microsoft at all, no doubt he would have to pay a high price. The difference then is not that one licensing system imposes burdens while the other does not; the difference is in the nature of the burdens.

Noncopylefted open source software does not impose this condition on subsequent licensing. Not only is a user free to build upon it, but it also does not require that such building be released under similar licensing terms. . . .

No doubt, from a private perspective, the differences among these types of software are important. . . .

From the perspective of the public, however, another difference is significant. To understand this difference, however, requires a bit more explanation about the economics of software.

SOFTWARE AND PUBLIC GOODS . . .

Goods can be mixed—possessing both public and private attributes. Software is an example: it can be produced as a purely private good, but it can also be produced in a way that promotes certain public goods. These public goods might be divided between pure and "qualified" public goods. The information about how a program works—how it achieves its functionality—that is contained within its source code is a pure public good. If made available generally, then my consumption of that knowledge would leave as much for you as before. If made available generally, then it would be hard to exclude my knowledge of it to the extent that knowledge is known generally.

In contrast, the digital copy of a particular software product could be considered a qualified public good, meaning simply that it requires some resources in order to be obtained. My having a copy of your program doesn't interfere with your having a copy of your program. But it may take resources to produce that copy of your program. Likewise, an unprotected digital copy can be made available to all if it is made available to some, but it takes resources to move that content (the cost of electricity to run the network, for example). As modern digital technologies reduce these necessary resources to zero, this means in effect that software can be made available just as easily as a pure public good. . . .

Software developers, however, have tools beyond intellectual property law that they can deploy to balance the public goods nature of software. Proprietary software providers, for example, can add excludability to their software by never releasing its source code: by compiling the source code and distributing just its object code, they can make the information within the product effectively excludable. Compilation makes the source code secret, and secrecy adds to the providers' ability to recover value.

Software providers can also make software effectively rivalrous. Copy protection technologies, for example, can make particular copies of software exclusive to particular owners. Properly deployed, these technologies can make it effectively impossible for you to use my software when I am using it. This again makes it easier for the producer to recover the value of his production by eliminating another public goods aspect of the digital product.

Thus two sets of tools — one public, the other private — are available to the software provider for balancing (or defeating) the public goods character of code. These tools in turn overlap. An author doesn't have to choose between copy protection technologies and copyright or between compiled code and law — he gets both. And by combining both kinds, a producer will get more value and will, to some extent and in some contexts, increase the incentive to produce.

Yet at some point, the combination of this public and private protection may reduce, rather than increase, social welfare — at least if the protection is too strong. These protections raise the price of information above its marginal cost of production. This means less information is being distributed than is economically efficient. Economics resents a price above marginal cost. Any gap may be a necessary evil to induce production, but as with all necessary evils, it should be tolerated only so far as it is truly necessary. A gap may be justified by the need to solve the provision problem, but if the controls extend beyond the justification, they reduce social welfare. Some control is needed, but some control is far less than perfect control. And hence the problem of social policy is how best to balance a necessary evil against access to information at its marginal cost — that is, free.

These familiar ideas are presented here to remind us of a point that is too often forgotten in the debate about open source and free software: the strong bias of public policy should be to spread public goods at their marginal cost. Compromises are no doubt necessary if private actors are to contribute voluntarily to the production of public goods; but public entities, such as governments, should not indulge in these compromises unless they are necessary. Between two systems for producing a public good, one that releases the information produced by that good freely and one that does not, all things being equal, public policy should favor free access. This is not because of some egalitarian bias or because of ideals about social equality but for purely neo-classical economic reasons: free access brings the cost of information down to its marginal cost, and neoclassical economics favors price at marginal costs. If the problems of incentives have already been solved for a particular good or class of goods — no doubt a large assumption, but for some important software goods a true one — then there is no further reason to exclude access to the public goods produced. Or if the provision problem is sufficiently solved by other systems of incentive, then again there is no reason to exclude the public goods produced.

From a social perspective, this means that there is a difficult choice between these two forms of production. If social good is the sum of private and public goods, then we cannot pick between open and proprietary software in the abstract. On the one hand, open source and free software dominate proprietary software in spreading a public good. Yet on the other hand, if there is insuffi-cient incentive to produce software under the open source and free software models, then the private good from software will also be underproduced.

When society faces a difficult social choice that is usually a good reason to let both forms of production compete in the market. And thus no one sensible is calling for a requirement that all software be free or that free software be banned. Yet some do argue against open source and free software, sometimes motivated by a belief that its business model is a failure and sometimes motivated by a view that at least some forms of free software are dangerous to "software ecology."

The economics of open source and free software is just beginning to be understood. A growing body of literature increasingly demonstrates how indi-viduals could have sufficient private incentive to solve the provision problem, even though they cannot capture the full value of what they produce. . . .

CONCLUSION

There is a reason for public policy to prefer a world where software is open and free. That reason cannot trump all other considerations, and it alone does not support a general rule that would banish proprietary code. But the reason does motivate an inquiry into whether free and open source code can be adequately produced. Economists have just begun a formal inquiry into that question. That inquiry could be helped with a bit of perspective: by seeing the parallel between open source and free software production and other more familiar modes of production, we are more likely to accept the conclusion of economists that open code is often possible and often very valuable.

I have argued in favor of government neutrality regarding open and proprietary software — as long as the interests the government reckons are sufficiently broad. If they are, then the government will often arrive at the conclusion that open code is preferable to proprietary code. At the very least, such an approach would lead to the conclusion that the government should not allow software patents to tilt the competitive horizon against open code projects.

NOTES AND QUESTIONS

1. Economists have dealt extensively with the underlying question, "Why would anyone take time and effort to write software for free?" They identify several

"intrinsic" and "extrinsic" factors.[39] Motivation is extrinsic if personal needs are satisfied indirectly; for example, a certain activity is performed in order to earn money, which can then be used to address personal needs. In the case of intrinsic motivation, the activity itself satisfies personal needs (e.g., pleasure, fun, reaching self-defined goals).

Extrinsically motivated actors participate in the open source community for several reasons. For instance, they sell services using open source software (available at low cost) or sell complementary products (e.g., servers). Furthermore, publishing the source code offers the possibility that other programmers improve, maintain, and further develop the software at low cost. Finally, open software projects can be "signed" by the author, thereby "signaling" the author's abilities to potential employers.

On the other hand, participation in open source may also be motivated intrinsically. Eric S. Raymond, one of the leading figures in the open source movement, considers the joy of programming an innovative and functioning piece of code, and the respect and reputation gained from it, as a major motivation for programmers to participate in the open source movement.[40] Might it be a combination of extrinsic and intrinsic motivation that makes the open source movement a successful alternative software development model?

2.   Lessig points out that copylefted software is licensed under a General Public License (GPL). The most widely used GPL is called "GNU Public License." The GNU GPL gives the user the right to copy, re-transmit, and modify the software, and to have access to the source code. The GNU GPL must be included with each copy and alteration of the original program. Some authors refer to this effect as being "viral," since any software combined with software under GPL protection is from then on "infected" (i.e., subject to the GPL and thus open source). A number of alternative licensing systems have evolved,[41] and "open source" software licensing can be a complex endeavor.

3.   There are now many active proponents of open source. For an overview of the relationship between the public domain and copyright, see *The Public Domain: Enclosing the Commons of the Mind*, by David Boyle.[42]

39. *See, e.g.,* Lerner & Tirole, *Some Simple Economics of Open Source,* 50 J. INDUS. ECON. 197 (2002).

40. *See* Eric S. Raymond, Homesteading the Noosphere (2000), http://www.catb.org/esr/writings/cathedral-bazaar/homesteading/ (visited December 21, 2010).

41. For an illustrative overview, *see* http://www.gnu.org/philosophy/license-list.html or http://www.opensource.org/licenses/index.html (visited December 21, 2010).

42. Available at http://www.thepublicdomain.org/ (visited December 21, 2010).

CHAPTER
5

Competition Law and *Sui Generis* Systems of Intellectual Property Protection: Traditional Knowledge, Plant Variety Protection, Undisclosed Information, Industrial Designs, and Integrated Circuits

I. INTRODUCTION

The intellectual property system essentially emerged from the philosophy of protecting competitors against appropriations of costly efforts and unfair competition. Eventually, different forms of intellectual property protection discussed in previous chapters emerged. New technologies and developments have brought about new potential for unfair competition. These technologies and developments are partly addressed under existing forms of intellectual property protection, such as software under copyright or patent law, and partly addressed under laws against unfair competition; eventually, this may lead to new and specific forms of protection, often called *sui generis* forms and systems of protection. This chapter explains the foundations and the relevance of unfair competition laws and competition policy (antitrust) for the international system. It addresses emerging *sui generis* forms of protecting traditional knowledge in the context of genetic engineering, and then turns to well-established and existing forms of *sui generis* protection, in particular plant variety protection, undisclosed information, and finally, the protection of industrial designs and integrated circuits.

II. STRIKING A BALANCE — PROTECTION OF INTELLECTUAL PROPERTY AND COMPETITION LAW

Protection of intellectual property is recognized as an important precondition for competition. At the same time, it can become a barrier to trade due to the existence of exclusive rights, on which it is based. Therefore, the main challenge is to find the proper balance between the two. The following excerpts explain the existing interlinkages between these areas and their reflection in international law and domestic case law.

TEACHING INTELLECTUAL PROPERTY, UNFAIR COMPETITION AND ANTI-TRUST LAW

Thomas Cottier & Christophe Germann*

. . .

The main function of intellectual property laws is to provide incentives for innovation and creation in the form of exclusive rights that can be considered as private monopolies, either limited in time (patents, copyright, related rights etc.) or for potentially unlimited duration (indefinitely renewable trademark registrations, trade names etc.). Intellectual property works as an instrument to appropriate knowledge that is understood in a broad sense as encompassing, in particular, scientific and artistic content as well as market relevant information. The forms of protection provided by intellectual property laws range from patents for inventions over exclusive rights on industrial models, plant varieties, layout designs or integrated circuits, industrial design, to copyright and related rights. The protection of undisclosed information functions as a supplement to the patent system. Trademarks, geographical indications and, to some extent, protection of industrial designs, on the other hand, are intended to serve as identifiers and as incentives for investments in reputation (goodwill, quality). In this light, the individual user's primary interest lies in obtaining access to protected goods and services under affordable conditions, and to not be misled with respect to identifiers. The classical approach is based on a duality of paradigms where the patent paradigm typically protects functional or utilitarian achievements, whereas the copyright paradigm protects creative results that do not need to show practical applications such as artistic works. This duality has, however, been gradually eroded, for example in the area of information technology where copyright is used to protect software.

A further category of intellectual property rights to be labeled as "identifiers" protects distinctive signs such as trademarks, trade names or geographical indications. Eventually, intellectual property law traditionally also includes rules prohibiting unfair competition although these rules do not provide exclusive rights.

Unfair competition law commonly protects fair competition with a particular focus on good faith in business dealings and fair business practices. Like intellectual property rights, unfair competition law essentially aims at protecting physical and legal persons (individuals and companies) against "free riding" on investment in knowledge and the fruits of labors created by others.

Competition (anti-trust) legislation typically aims at protecting the market, and more precisely at preserving an effective competitive framework that shall promote the best quality of goods and services at the lowest cost for consumers, as well as ensure the suppliers' freedom of access to the market and the demands associated with freedom of choice. Competition rules, or anti-trust

* In Yo Takagi, Larry Allman, Mpazi A. Sinjela eds., Teaching of Intellectual Property: Principles and Methods (Cambridge University Press, 2008), at 130-66.

rules, essentially operate as legal restrictions on the freedom of contract between economic operators who are mutually placed in a competitive relationship. The law intervenes to avoid collusion and concertation which diminishes workable competition to the detriment of consumers. Also, competition law disciplines the conduct of dominant operators who otherwise need not consider other market participants. Anti-trust thus operates as a limitation on freedom of conduct to the benefit of markets and consumers.

Often, intellectual property rights are considered anathema to competition as they offer exclusive rights and thus exclude competition. However, they form as essential basis for competition. Without proper protection, investment will not be encouraged and third parties cannot be prevented from free-riding and unfairly using the fruits of investment without compensation. In operational terms, intellectual property protection and protection against unfair competition are complementary, as they essentially pursue comparable goals. Anti-trust rules, on the other hand, provide a counterbalance to the granting of exclusive rights. They assist in combating abuses of such rights detrimental to competition on markets.

. . .

In mature legal orders, the disciplines of intellectual property, competition law (anti-trust) and unfair competition rules develop in tandem and provide an appropriate balance. In many quarters of the world, such a basis does not yet exist. While international law prescribes advanced standards of intellectual property and rudimentary rules on unfair competition by means of international treaty obligations, in particular the Agreement on Trade-Related Aspects of Intellectual Property Rights (TRIPS Agreement) of the World Trade Organization (WTO), anti-trust rules have largely remained a matter of domestic law, still lacking in many countries. Vice-versa, competition law may be developed while common standards of intellectual property protection remain deficient, as has been the case in European Community law. Overall, this results in constellations of imbalance which future efforts on the national, international and regional levels need to remedy.

. . .

PROTECTION AGAINST UNFAIR COMPETITION

. . .

RELATIONSHIP TO INTELLECTUAL PROPERTY PROTECTION

Since unfair competition law and the protection of intellectual property pursue partly overlapping goals and objectives, the two areas have developed a rather complex relationship, which may vary, again, from country to country. A few general observations can be made on the basis of selected case law.

Independent Application

In many instances, unfair competition rules serve to supplement what intellectual property laws do not or cannot provide in particular circumstances. For example, according to the Swiss Federal Court, trademark legislation constitutes no special law vis-à-vis unfair competition legislation that would allow the former to prevail as *lex specialis* over the latter. This case law concludes that trademark and unfair competition laws obey different rationales. Unfair competition law aims at promoting fair and undistorted competition. As a consequence, a trademark owner may not use her exclusive rights in a way that qualifies as unfair competition. Article 3 lit. d of the Swiss Unfair Competition Act prohibits an indication or make-up and presentation of a product *(Aufmachung)* that leads to confusion in respect of older goods or services. The Court recalled that any behavior that is misleading or that otherwise infringes the principle of good faith and that influences the relationship between competitors or between supply and demand is deemed to be unfair and illicit.

Unfair competition law may substitute for protection where such protection is not available under intellectual property laws. A good example is the protection equivalent to moral rights in US law. In *Gilliam v. American Broadcasting Companies, Inc. (ABC)* ["Monty Python Case," *supra* Chapter 4], the appellants invoked the theory that the editing cuts made by the broadcaster without their consent constituted an actionable mutilation of their work. This cause of action, which seeks redress for the deformation of an artist's work, finds its roots in the continental concept of *droit moral*, or moral rights, as set forth in Article 6*bis* of the Berne Convention. US copyright law does not recognize moral rights since this law seeks to vindicate the economic, rather than the personal, rights of authors. However, the economic incentives for artistic and intellectual creation that serves as the foundation of the American Copyright Act, cannot be reconciled with the inability of artists to obtain relief for mutilation or misrepresentation of their work to the public on which the artists are financially dependent. American courts have long granted relief for misrepresentation of an artist's work by relying on theories outside the statutory law of copyright, such as contract law, or the tort of unfair competition. In the case at stake, Monty Python's members claimed that the editing done for ABC on their television programs violated the Lanham Act § 43(a), 15 U.S.C § 1125(a), the federal unfair competition act. This statute provides in particular that any person affixing, applying, annexing, or using in connection with any goods or services a false designation of origin, or any false description or representation, and causing such goods or services to enter into commerce, shall be liable to a civil action by any person who believes that he is or is likely to be damaged by the use of any such false description or representation.

Pre-Emption of Unfair Competition Rules

Protection under unfair competition law should generally not be considered as an alternative to intellectual property protection. Pursuant to the principle of pre-emption, protection under unfair competition law will be generally denied—except in certain cases of confusion—if protection under specific intellectual property rights were available, at least for a certain period of time, and expired thereafter. For example, in *Schweizerische Interpreten-Gesellschaft* [*supra* Chapter 4], the Swiss Federal Court stated that gaps in a particular law relating to intangible property rights cannot be closed by means of the general clause of the Swiss Unfair Competition Act. In principle, the results of efforts and labor which, according to the special law, are no longer protected or cannot be protected at all, may be used by anyone, even competitors. An interpretation to the contrary would amount to a monopolization of non-copyrighted content. The Court further recalled that the only exception allowed by case law related to special circumstances under which a particular conduct or measures are genuinely unfair and there-fore justify the application of the general clause of the Unfair Competition Law.

The principle of pre-emption, emanating from the principles of *lex specialis derogat legi generali,* takes its substantive legitimacy from the assumption that intellectual property law is supposed to materialize a specific balance of the various stakeholders' interests (creators, innovators, users and society) by fea-turing built-in "competitive antibodies" that promotes innovation and creation within the paradigm of monopoly-like exclusive rights. Applying unfair com-petition rules would therefore in general, undermine the balance between appropriation and public domain.

Basis for Codification of Intellectual Property

Unfair competition law often serves as a basis for intellectual property legislation. In various jurisdictions, legislators have the tendency to codify con-solidated case law on unfair competition caused by confusion and misappro-priation within their intellectual property legislation, in particular within laws on trademarks, trade names and geographical indications. In this way, intellec-tual property laws dealing with these issues are eroding the proper scope of application of unfair competition laws. This tendency is reinforced by international instruments such as the TRIPS Agreement harmonizing the approaches that deal with the prohibition of confusion and misappropriation, discussed below.

PROTECTION IN INTERNATIONAL LAW

Foundations

National legislation, divergent as it may be, has to be consistent with applic-able international instruments, such as the TRIPS Agreement and the Paris Convention. We therefore focus on common rules available in international law and thus binding on many countries being part of global law. Protection was recognized as forming part of intellectual property for more than a century. In 1900, the Brussels Diplomatic Conference for the Revision of the Paris Convention for the Protection of Industrial Property introduced Article 10*bis* that specifically addresses unfair competition. It was eventually revised in the Stockholm Act of 1967 of the Paris Convention. The provision reads as follows:

ARTICLE *10BIS*

UNFAIR COMPETITION

(1) The countries of the Union are bound to assure to nationals of such countries effective protection against unfair competition.

(2) Any act of competition contrary to honest practices in industrial or commercial matters constitutes an act of unfair competition.

(3) The following in particular shall be prohibited:

(i) all acts of such a nature as to create confusion by any means whatever with the establishment, the goods, or the industrial or commercial activities, of a competitor;

(ii) false allegations in the course of trade of such a nature as to discredit the establishment, the goods, or the industrial or commercial activities, of a competitor;

(iii) indications or allegations the use of which in the course of trade is liable to mislead the public as to the nature, the manufacturing process, the charac-teristics, the suitability for their purpose, or the quantity, of the goods.

Article 10*ter* of the Paris Convention requires providing "appropriate legal remedies" against the violation of unfair competition law as contemplated by Article 10*bis*. Pursuant to the second paragraph of this provision, member states must grant the right to be a party in judicial or administrative procedures to federations and associations representing interested industrialists, producers, or merchants who otherwise could not invoke any particular form of intellectual property protection, provided, however, that the law of the country in which protection is claimed allows such action by federations and associations of that country.

The TRIPS Agreement explicitly refers to Article 10*bis* and 10*ter* of the Paris Convention and it incorporates those provisions on the basis of its Article 2. In addition, special reference to Article 10*bis* of the Paris Convention offers the basis for particular regulation of geographical indications in Article 22, and for the protection of undisclosed information in Article 39 of the TRIPS Agreement.

With the inclusion of Article 10*bis* of the Paris Convention into the TRIPS Agreement, unfair competition law finally is made subject to effective international dispute settlement under the Dispute Settlement Understanding of the WTO. This is of particular importance as the law of unfair competition inherently builds upon case law. At this point in time Article 10*bis* of the Paris Convention has not been subject to panel or Appellate Body decisions, and little guidance exists as to how the broad principles should be interpreted on the level of international law. The field is far from settled and mature.

The provision on unfair competition in Article 10*bis* of the Paris Convention is broadly termed and refers to elusive concepts, requiring careful interpretation. The norm obliges WTO Members (and other Member States party to the Paris Convention) to provide appropriate protection in domestic jurisdictions, and to enact, if necessary, appropriate legislation. The terms primarily leave the determination of the notion of honesty in industrial and commercial matters to the national courts and administrative authorities. They are not strictly limited to producer and consumer relations. Member States of the Paris Union are free to grant protection against certain acts even if the parties involved are not competing against each other.

While leaving ample room to domestic jurisdiction, international law nevertheless provides guidance as to the scope and interpretation of these broad precepts and principles. Firstly, Members need to respect requirements emanating from other applicable regional and international treaties, in particular international instruments on human rights. Secondly, the notions of honest business practices, and the constellations addressed in the non-exhaustive list, are notions of international law. They are subject to specification in dispute settlement and fully operational in international disputes brought before the WTO. It is submitted that these specifications amount to minimal standards which Members will need to respect, irrespective of domestic definitions adopted in legislation and case law. Also, it is submitted that these minimal standards are suitable for direct effect before domestic courts and administrative authorities, where constitutional law so permits. The provision of Article 10*bis*, paragraph 1, does not imply a dualistic concept. At any rate, and once a substantial body of case law exists on the subject in WTO law, national courts should take it into account under the doctrine of consistent interpretation. Domestic terms of unfair competition should be construed in the light of minimal standards emanating from Article 10*bis* of the Paris Convention.

Protection Against Dishonest Practices, Confusion and False Allegations

Pursuant to Article 10*bis,* paragraph 2 of the Paris Convention, any act of competition contrary to honest practices in industrial or commercial matters constitutes an act of unfair competition. Unfair competition in the relationship between competitors may take various forms. Article 10*bis,* paragraph 3 of the Paris Convention mentions in particular all acts of such a nature as to create confusion by any means whatever with the establishment, the goods, or the industrial or commercial activities, of a competitor (sub-para. 1), as well as false allegations in the course of trade of such a nature as to discredit the establishment, the goods, or the industrial or commercial activities, of a competitor (sub-para. 2).

Article 10*bis,* paragraph 3 provides for a non-exhaustive list of dishonest practices that shall be prohibited including acts creating confusion by any means whatever with the establishment, the goods, or the industrial or commercial activities, of a competitor, false and discrediting or misleading indications and allegations. It aims at protecting competitors against a risk of confusion and false allegations having a discrediting effect, as well as the public against misleading information as to the nature, the manufacturing process, the characteristics, and the suitability for their purpose, or the quantity, of the goods.

Article 10*bis,* paragraph 3(1) of the Paris Convention does not make the prohibition of confusion conditional to intent or negligence in acting or omitting to act. Bad faith, however, may be taken into account in respect of the sanction for an infringement. Likelihood of confusion is sufficient. It is therefore not necessary that the confusion actually has taken place. Confusion mainly occurs in relation to indications of origin of goods and services (confusion as to affiliation or as to sponsorship and to their appearance (confusion as to product shape). Accordingly, for generic and commonplace goods and services the likelihood of confusion can normally be denied since they no longer have an original or distinctive character. Specific trademark and trade name legislation provides protection against confusion, and often makes recourse to unfair competition redundant. However, intellectual property protection may not always be appropriate and adequate, for example, in the case of protection of well-known trademarks as addressed by Article 6*bis* of the Paris Convention and Article 16 of the TRIPS Agreement. Member States may implement the prohibition to use a well-known trademark pursuant to Article 6*bis* of the Paris Convention on the national level via their unfair competition legislation, in the absence of corresponding restrictions in their trademark legislation.

Protection Against Free Riding

Undue advantage of efforts and achievement by others and recognized by consumers and other market participants may be taken by imitating products and services or their identifiers, including trade marks, trade names and other forms of commercially relevant indications. Article 10*bis* of the Paris Convention encapsulates this under the doctrine of competition contrary to honest practices in paragraph 2, while leaving it, astonishingly, without mention in the non-exclusive list of paragraph 3. Preventing and combating free riding on work and products of others is an essential and core function of unfair competition rules and of intellectual property protection alike. Whereas free riding is considered as a dishonest business practice under unfair competition law, it is deemed to hinder innovation, creativity and the supply of reliable market information under intellectual property law.

Protection against free riding amounts to one of the major functions of intellectual property and its different forms. Unfair competition rules take place where such protection is not sufficiently available or existent. They provide complementary protection. For example, a school may offer a particular curriculum or training program, composed in a particular manner. It is neither protected by trademark or copyright. Competitors nevertheless are not allowed to imitate the structure of the program without the consent of the school. As a prerequisite of the protection against free riding on a firm's identity and reputation, the indication, the good or service must have some distinctiveness. In other words, unfair competition does not protect against the imitation of mere banality. However, the degree of distinctiveness may be lower than what is required under intellectual property legislation.

The TRIPS Agreement further elaborates protection against free riding in relation to geographical indications, to undisclosed information and to test data. Today, and due to WTO law, these areas clearly pertain to the protection of intellectual property, but remain essentially informed in terms of foundations and scope to the protection of unfair competition. The respective provisions refer to Article 10*bis* of the Paris Convention.

Article 22, paragraph 2(a) of the TRIPS Agreement protects geographical indications to the extent that the designation or presentation of a product suggests that the product originates in a geographical area different from the true place of origin in a manner which misleads the public as to the geographical origin of the good. Except for wines and spirits in accordance with Articles 22 and 23 of the TRIPS Agreement, the indication of the true origin of the product protects from violating the obligation. For example, it is possible to label "Gruyere Cheese made in the US" since consumers are thus informed about the true origin of the product despite the fact that the product is based upon qualities relating to a Swiss region. Protection therefore is limited. This explains why enhanced protection applicable to wines and spirits is thought to be extended to all agricultural products in the Doha Round negotiations.

The question arises as to whether such use may otherwise constitute an act of unfair competition in accordance with paragraph 2(b) of the provision, which generally refers to Article 10*bis* of the Paris Convention. To the extent that — despite the absence of confusion as to the true origin — the product is essentially based upon free riding in terms of traditional know-how and experience and thus traditional knowledge, a case can be made under Article 10*bis* of the Paris Convention.

The same relationship is contemplated by the protection of undisclosed information (trade secrets) pursuant to Article 39 of the TRIPS Agreement. Provided that the conditions under Article 39.2 of the TRIPS Agreement regarding the secrecy and commercial value of the information are met, natural and legal persons shall have the possibility of preventing information lawfully within their control from being disclosed to, acquired by, or used by others without their consent in a manner contrary to honest commercial practices. Such practices have in common a business's attempt vis-à-vis other businesses to succeed in competition without relying on its own achievements in terms of quality and price of its products and services, but rather by taking undue advantage of the work of another (free riding) or by influencing consumer demand with false or misleading statements.

Article 39.3 of the TRIPS Agreement provides that WTO Members must protect undisclosed test or other data that took considerable effort to be generated, against unfair commercial use when they require that such data must be submitted to their agencies for the purpose of marketing approval for pharmaceutical or agricultural chemical products utilizing new chemical entities. Furthermore, WTO Members must protect such data against disclosure, except where necessary to protect the public or unless steps are taken to ensure that the data are protected against fair commercial use [further elaborated on *infra*].

Legally, the provision can be seen as an enlargement of the list of acts that are prohibited under Article 10*bis,* para. 3 of the Paris Convention. In other words, Article 39.3 of the TRIPS Agreement addresses the unfair use of undisclosed data submitted to authorities by private competitors. . . .

A recent example of linking new forms of protection to unfair competition and eventually intellectual property rights can be observed with the emerging protection of Traditional Knowledge. While currently left in the public domain, Traditional Knowledge can be freely used in the context of biotechnology as an important source of information and a basis for new products which are eligible for patent protection. . . .

Finally, a potential field of application of unfair competition rules in international law relates to the protection of Internet domain names involving more than one jurisdiction, which are dealt with by the Mediation and Arbitration Center of the WIPO. For the time being, the substantive rules only provide rules for the conflict between a domain name and a trademark, where the domain name registered by the domain name registrant is identical or confusingly similar to a trademark in which the complainant has rights (para. 4(a) UDRP). In this case, the rights of the trademark owner prevail over the interests of the domain name registrant unless the latter is in good faith. However, there is no similar dispute settlement mechanism available with respect to conflicts between domain names and trade names. These cases are essentially dealt with under the unfair competition law of national or regional jurisdictions. Corresponding judgments may be substantially more difficult and costly to enforce in foreign jurisdictions as arbitration awards under the UDRP. It would therefore be suitable to extend protection to such signs by taking recourse to Article 10*bis* of the Paris Convention, or to create appropriate additional rules under the UDRP. Again, it is a matter of refining intellectual property protection on the basis of experiences made under the case law approach of unfair competition protection.

COMPETITION (ANTI-TRUST) LAW

. . .

RELATIONSHIP TO INTELLECTUAL PROPERTY PROTECTION
Coexistence, Tensions and Balance

Intellectual property and competition law are necessary, but not sufficient, conditions of a competitive environment. Operationally, they create a dialectical tension and require mutual balancing. On the one hand, exclusive rights granted under intellectual property by definition exclude competition in a particular setting and allow excluding third parties from directly competing with the right holder. On the other hand, competition law seeks to facilitate direct competition and tends to limit the use of exclusive rights.

. . . In the United States . . . the detrimental effects of per se prohibitions were removed under the influence of the Chicago School, and eventually gave way to a case-by-case analysis, based on the rule of reason. All pertinent factors are taken into account, and licensing agreements are examined under what is called the "post-Chicago" approach. A comparable, albeit not similar, development can be observed in European Community law. As a result, competition law and intellectual property interact in a most complex manner, strongly dependent upon the case law of the courts.

Anti-Trust Guidelines and Block Exemptions for Licensing of Intellectual Property

Defining the relationship of competition law and intellectual property on a case-by-case basis responds to the needs of reality, but offers little legal security for business transactions. Authorities have, therefore, made attempts to codify pertinent principles and rules applicable to licensing of intellectual property rights. In the United States, the Justice Department and the Federal Trade Commission enacted Anti-trust Guidelines for Licensing of Intellectual Property in 1995. Building upon case law, these guidelines define allowable terms for intellectual property licensing agreements.

Similarly, the European Commission enacted Technology Transfer Block Exemptions in 1996. They were subsequently revised in 2004. These regulations define transfer agreements which are automatically exempt from the application of Article 81 of the EC Treaty where market shares do not exceed 20 per cent.

Intellectual Property Rights and the "Essential Facilities" Doctrine

Dominant positions may be based upon intellectual property rights, such as patents. Competition law breaks them by imposing compulsory licensing, i.e. the obligation to allow third parties to use such rights against compensation. Prominently, the "essential facility doctrine" serves as a legal concept, initially developed by US case law, to address such constellations. This doctrine — which is not restricted to intellectual property — may impose restrictions on companies exclusively controlling an essential facility (such as a port, a railway station, a utility, a network). In the absence of voluntarily granting reasonable access to competitors on a contractual basis, competition authorities and courts may order such access. The US Supreme Court first articulated this doctrine in *United States v. Terminal Railroad Ass'n*, 224 U.S. 383 (1912). In this case, a group of railroads controlling all railway bridges and switching yards into and out of St. Louis prevented competing railroad services from offering transportation to and through that destination. This, the court held, constituted both an illegal restraint of trade and an attempt to monopolize. Because the essential facilities doctrine represents a divergence from the general rule that even a monopolist may choose with whom to deal, courts have established widely adopted tests that parties must meet before a court will require a monopolist to grant access to an essential asset to its competitors. Specifically, to establish anti-trust liability under the essential facilities doctrine, a party must prove four factors: (1) control of the essential facility by a monopolist; (2) competitor's inability practically or reasonably to duplicate the essential facility; (3) the denial of the use of the facility to a competitor; and (4) the feasibility of providing the facility to competitors.

This test for anti-trust liability has been adopted by virtually every United States court to consider an "essential facilities" claim. Rulings of these courts also suggest that anti-trust liability under the essential facilities doctrine is particularly appropriate when denial of access is motivated by an anti-competitive animus — usually demonstrated by a change in existing business practices with the apparent intent of harming rivals.

In view of the various contexts in which the essential facilities doctrine has been applied, courts have declined to impose any artificial limit on the kinds of products, services, or other assets to which the doctrine may appropriately be applied. . . . The European Court of Justice, albeit refraining from adopting the terminology of essential facilities, adopted an essentially similar approach. It is summarized in the Advocate General's opinion of May 28, 1998 in the *Oscar Bronner* case.

In the recent *IMS* case concerning a statistical device ("brick structure") aimed at presenting sales data of pharmaceutical product and protected by copyright, the European Court of Justice recalled that, according to settled case law, refusal to grant a license, even if it is the act of an undertaking holding a dominant position, does not per se constitute an abuse of such a position. It is a legitimate exercise of intellectual property rights. However, pursuant to this case law, the exercise of an exclusive right by the owner may, in exceptional circumstances, involve abusive conduct. The Court held that such exceptional circumstances were present in a previous case dealing with intellectual property rights, namely the *Magill* case. Several television channels in a dominant position relied on the copyright conferred by national legislation on the weekly listings of their programs in order to prevent another undertaking from publishing joint information on those programs together with commentaries, on a weekly basis. In this case, the exceptional circumstances resulted from three sets of considerations. Firstly, from the fact that the refusal in question concerned a product (information on the weekly schedules of certain television channels), the supply of which was indispensable for carrying on the business in question (the publishing of a general television guide). Secondly, from the consideration that, without that information, the person wishing to produce such a guide would find it impossible to publish it and offer it for sale. Thirdly, from the fact that such refusal prevented the emergence of a new product for which there was a potential consumer demand, the fact that it was not justified by objective considerations, and was likely to exclude all competition in the secondary market. This last condition relates to the consideration that, in the balancing of the interest in protection of the intellectual property right and the economic freedom of its owner against the interest in protection of free competition, the latter can prevail only where refusal to grant a license prevents the development of the secondary market to the detriment of consumers. Therefore, the denial by an undertaking in a dominant position to allow access to a product protected by an intellectual property right, where that product is indispensable for operating on a secondary market, may be regarded as abusive only where the undertaking which requested the license does not intend to limit itself essentially to duplicating the goods or services already offered on the secondary market by the owner of the intellectual property right, but intends to produce new goods or services not offered by the owner of the right and for which there is a potential consumer demand. In the *IMS* case, the Court eventually held that the refusal to grant a license constituted an abuse of a dominant position within the meaning of Article 82 EC where the following conditions are fulfilled:

> (a) the undertaking which requested the license intends to offer, on the market at stake, new products or services not offered by the owner of the intellectual property right and for which there is a potential consumer demand;
> (b) the refusal is not justified by objective considerations;
> (c) the refusal is such as to reserve to the owner of the intellectual property right the market at stake by eliminating all competition on that market.

The Court confirmed that the application of the essential facilities doctrine to positions dominating the market based on their intellectual property rights requires the supply of a good or service that must be new. In comparison, this condition of novelty must not be fulfilled in those cases where intellectual property rights are not relevant for the essential facility. This additional requirement makes sense from the perspective of the rationale underlying the grant of intellectual property rights, i.e. the promotion of innovative and creative efforts.

THE PROTECTION AGAINST UNFAIR COMPETITION IN WTO LAW: STATUS, POTENTIAL AND PROSPECTS

Thomas Cottier & Ana Jevtic*

III. Emerging Fields of Protection Against Unfair Competition in WTO Law

Much of WTO law is dedicated to securing fair conditions of competition for foreign products, both goods and services. The basic principles of non-discrimination, most-favoured-nation (MFN) and national treatment, much as transparency, the disciplines on subsidies and on dumping, as well as the restraints imposed on trade remedies, protect legitimate expectations as to conditions of competition. The same is true for intellectual property protection. A wide variety of specialized norms assume such a function, and recourse to Article 10*bis* of the Paris Convention has been made so far. It is relevant, however, in areas still lacking specific rules or in which non-violation complaints cannot bring about relief from trade distortions induced by measures formally outside the scope of positive WTO law. . . .

THE PROTECTION OF TRADITIONAL KNOWLEDGE

Motives for providing protection to traditional knowledge (TK) are diverse and imply both legal and moral aspects. [See further information on protection of TK and relevant case law below.] TK has been widely recognized as a valuable source of information essential to the achievement of sustainable development. . . .

* Technology and Competition: Contributions in Honour of Hanns Ullrich (Josef Drexl ed., 2009), at 669-95.

The protection of traditional knowledge has been one of the major issues of intellectual property reform in the WTO. No explicit reference and recognition is given in the TRIPS Agreement, and the subject was established as a matter requiring further work and negotiations in the Doha Development Agenda of 2001. The mandate was introduced in response to the demand of countries with high biodiversity seeking to obtain a better balance of returns on bio-prospecting and recourse to modern biotechnology. It was meant to supplement mechanisms of benefit sharing under the contractual and uneven system of the Convention on Biodiversity. Negotiations so far have focused on amending patent rules relating to disclosure of sources. No agreement has so far been reached. This is even more the case for protecting TK on the basis of a *sui generis* system of intellectual property protection. Negotiations are scheduled to continue, and it is evident that all further progress on protecting innovation in genetic engineering will depend upon a solution to the problem of protecting TK.

The issue of TK is very challenging, and the establishment of a proper system of *sui generis* protection based upon traditional intellectual property rights (TIP-Rights) will take some time. . . .

Given the difficulties and complexity of the matter, recourse to Article 10*bis* of the Paris Convention currently offers the most promising avenue to address inherent problems of misappropriation and free-riding in the use of genetic materials in combination with TK. The broad concept of unfair competition, the need to assess it on a case by case basis, taking into account the context, allows experience to be gained in this field on the basis of positive law. The process may eventually support negotiations and the emergence of a *sui generis* system.

Unfair competition protection as a basis for TK protection has been particularly supported with the acknowledgement of operational legal principles by the WIPO Secretariat, whereby prohibition of unfair competition and thus protection against misappropriation is particularly emphasized. The paper contains a comprehensive list of acts of misappropriation that any applicable system of protection should be able to suppress.

Indeed, core concerns of TK protection essentially boil down to the act of misappropriation of TK and free-riding on it. Misappropriation includes any act of acquisition or appropriation of TK by unfair or illicit means. One of the most widespread examples of misappropriation of TK is related to the wrongful granting of patents covering TK. They occur in relation to either the definition of prior art which is constructed in such a way as not to recognize information available to the public through use or oral traditions outside their domestic jurisdictions; or in connection with the absence or inadequacy of the information available to patent examiners. A patent applicant may thus be conferred a monopoly right to exploit a product based on a biological resource or related TK which actually is in the public domain. It is illustrative to cite the *Enola bean* case in which the patent owner was using its exclusive right to ban the sale of imported beans with similar characteristics to the one described in the patent. Four problems may be highlighted:

a) the lack of evidence that any of the similar beans actually had the same characteristics as the actual patented *invention*, as a consequence of the broadly established claims of the patent;

b) that in the basis of the patent was a traditional way of cultivation which cannot be described as novel;

c) that no benefit sharing was organized with the original holders of this knowledge, although they themselves were no longer allowed to use it without authorization of the new patent holder in countries where the new patent holder had obtained patent protection;

d) that producers of exporting countries were prevented from trading with traditionally produced beans.

In another example, the *Hoodia case,* the patent was obtained over the plant named hoodia, which possesses ingredients with appetite-suppressing characteristics. Such plants, before a patent was claimed, were used by indigenous people, known as Khomani or San, as an appetite suppressant to help them to survive while hunting in the desert. The patent was obtained by a South African governmental institution (the South African Council for Scientific and Industrial Research—CSIR) and was meant to be developed as Africa's first best-seller drug. However, no discussion with the Khomani people, as the custodians of the knowledge, on the use of the hoodia plant had taken place prior to the patent application. It was only after being criticized by NGOs and domestic organizations that the CSIR entered into the benefit sharing agreement on the exploitation of the drug with the holders of the knowledge.

This type of situation can best be assessed under the doctrine of misappropriation under Article 10*bis* of the Paris Convention. It can be looked at on a case-by-case basis, without requiring prior registration of rights. It is available as long as the particular circumstances that trigger the protection continue to exist. It offers a basis to challenge use and effectiveness of intellectual property titles which were obtained without taking into account the legitimate interests of the stewards and custodians of TK. The remedy offered will entail a ban on commercialization of the product concerned. In doing so, it offers a strong incentive to take these interests into account prior to commercialization and to seek negotiated settlements of permission to use TK and to bring about effective benefit sharing.

The approach based upon unfair competition and misappropriation is the more important as it has been recognized and adopted in domestic law, in particular that of developed countries mainly benefiting from intellectual property protection and modern technology. Although an explicit prohibition can be found only in the Swiss law (Article 5 of the Swiss Unfair Competition Act prohibiting the unfair imitation of articles reflecting certain distinguished qualities), other jurisdictions have also broadly developed this doctrine. Importantly, Swiss law considers a pure imitation as the act of unfair competition as such. Under US law, actionable misappropriation will occur under certain conditions:

a) the claimant offers a distinctive product which has a certain value;

b) the defendant is free riding by copying the product in that he engages in direct competition;

c) which as a consequence has the impact either to the detriment of the claimant's actual or potential market or to the confusion as to the origin of the product.

Although we find here the possibility of claiming misappropriation in case of detrimental impact even on a *potential* market, or—importantly to our subject — in case of confusion as to the origin of the product; a direct competitive relationship seems nonetheless to be required.

A similar approach to that of the US has been adopted in German jurisprudence, taking into account the damage the claimant may suffer. A designation of commercial originality can be given here if the article can be attributed individuality or uniqueness. According to UK regulations, in the situation in which the infringer engages in direct competition, copying is to be considered unfair.

WTO law and dispute settlement offers the foundations to assess whether domestic regulations as applied to issues of TK comply with the standards set out in Article 10*bis* of the Paris Convention. We recall that even though the provision clearly emphasizes three examples (confusion, discrediting and misleading the public), it does not limit the protection to the listed acts of unfair behaviour. Instead, Article 10*bis* provides fertile ground for condemning *any* act of competition that is contrary to honest practices in industrial and commercial matters. Although it does not especially address acts of misappropriation, a flexible definition of unfairness in this provision allows taking misappropriation acts into account in further shaping and framing the concept of "dishonest business practice" in the context of a particular case.

Considering that the WTO Agreements are unambiguous on the issue that the international legal system prevails over national legislations, WTO Members are obliged to ensure the conformity of their laws, regulations and administrative procedures with the obligations set out in WTO Agreements. WTO Members could therefore bring a case before the Dispute Settlement Body against any Member whose unfair competition legislature is not in line with Article 10*bis*, either because the Member has not provided any protection against unfair competition at all, or if its regulations on unfair competition do not give full effect to the principle established in Article 10*bis*. When Members do maintain regulations against unfair competition, the Panel or Appellate Body will indeed have to assess whether national legislations afford comparable protection against unfair competition to that set forth in Article 10*bis* of the Paris Convention. It should be kept in mind that WTO Members do not have the obligation to provide uniform protection against unfair competition. As a consequence of a broad definition of Article 10*bis* on the basis of which many Members developed their unfair competition law, it is reasonable to expect different regulations in this area as well as different treatment of unfairness. However, irrespective of this fact, Members are compelled to have at least an equivalent level of protection securing fairness for TK holders.

NOTES AND QUESTIONS

1. Unfair competition law can be considered a common underlying policy for the different forms of IPRs. However, the relationship of the two systems is not always complementary, since they have different market outcomes as respective objectives. In the case *Frau X v. Fray Y & Z Publishing House*, discussed in Chapter 4, the Swiss Federal Court denied the subsidiary invocation of competition law after ruling out an infringement of the plaintiff's copyright for her thesis. What are different approaches to the

implementation of the two legal systems in order to create a practicable interface?

2. Following the discussion on protection of Traditional Knowledge (TK) through competition law and the possible application of Article 10*bis* of the Paris Convention, we will have a look at the possibilities for a *sui generis* system for TK in the next section. Try to identify which advantages and challenges are inherent to each of the solutions.

III. TRADITIONAL KNOWLEDGE IN THE INTERNATIONAL INTELLECTUAL PROPERTY SYSTEM

A. *Traditional Knowledge in a Modern World*

Globalization, scientific progress, and new concepts in research and development have widened the access to new fields of knowledge allotted in societies all over the world. Traditional Knowledge, gathered, developed, and passed on over generations in indigenous communities, has gradually been discovered as a vast source of know-how for public and private investment. The understanding of nature, terrain, and species behavior in certain areas has proven essential for environmental planning and engineering. Knowledge about plants and their use in farming and health is of great interest to agricultural and pharmaceutical providers.[1]

However, the trade-off between public interest in accessibility of knowledge and the protection of investment in its creation is particularly apparent in the domain of TK. The philosophical foundation of IP protection—the adequate remuneration for intellectual effort and investment—is controversial in the context of the commercial use of TK. The nature of TK, often preserved and passed on in tribal, intergenerational, and sometimes secret processes, triggers several questions: How can TK be acquired without interfering with customs and self-determination of its holders, and how can a system of fair and equitable sharing of benefits derived from that knowledge be created? How can the issue of biopiracy be addressed, and when is TK considered to be in the public domain and hence hindering patentability of inventions?

Traditional Knowledge, a good mainly available in developing countries, plays an important role in the assessment of the legitimacy of the international IP system. The interface of TK, IP, and other frameworks like the Convention on Biological Diversity (CBD) and International Convention for the Protection of New Varieties of Plants (UPOV) produced an intense debate in various fora including discussions about the integration of concepts like Prior Informed Consent (PIC), Equitable Benefit Sharing (EBS as framed by Article 8(j) CBD), and disclosure of sources into the international IP system. While some voice doubts about the need for specific legal treatment of TK,[2] others consider the creation of a *sui generis* system an adequate means for the equitable treatment of Traditional Knowledge.

---

1. *See* WIPO, Intellectual Property and Traditional Knowledge (WIPO Publication 920(E)), p. 5.
2. *See* Stephen R. Munzer & Kal Raustiala, *The Uneasy Case for Intellectual Property Rights in Traditional Knowledge*, in 27 CARDOZO ARTS & ENT. L.J. 37-97 (2009).

INTELLECTUAL PROPERTY AND TRADITIONAL KNOWLEDGE
World Intellectual Property Organization* Booklet No. 2

KEY CONCEPTS

DEFINITIONS AND USE OF TERMS

No single definition would fully do justice to the diverse forms of knowledge that are held by traditional communities; and no form of legal protection system can replace the complex social and legal systems that sustain TK within the original communities. One form of protection, but one form only, is the application of laws to prevent unauthorized or inappropriate use of TK by third parties beyond the traditional circle. This is the IP form of protection — recognition of the need to prevent third parties from misusing TK in certain ways. This has been achieved in many different ways in national laws — not necessarily by creating property rights in TK, although this approach has been taken in some cases. A common thread has been the need to refocus existing legal laws or to create new ones to clarify and strengthen the legal constraints against various forms of misuse or misappropriation of TK. . . .

WHAT KIND OF LEGAL PROTECTION FOR TK?

The protection of TK is important for communities in all countries, particularly in developing and least developed countries. First, TK plays an important role in the economic and social life of those countries. Placing value on such knowledge helps strengthen cultural identity and the enhanced use of such knowledge to achieve social and development goals, such as sustainable agriculture, affordable and appropriate public health, and conservation of biodiversity. Second, developing and least developed countries are implementing international agreements that may affect how knowledge associated with the use of genetic resources is protected and disseminated, and thus how their national interests are safeguarded. Patterns of ownership of TK, cultural, scientific and commercial interest in TK, the possibilities for beneficial partnerships in research and development, and the risk of the misuse of TK, are not neatly confined within national boundaries, so that some degree of international coordination and cooperation is essential to achieve the goals of TK protection. A comprehensive strategy for protecting TK should therefore consider the community, national, regional and international dimensions. The stronger the integration and coordination between each level, the more likely the overall effectiveness. Many communities, countries and regional organizations are working to address these levels respectively. National laws are currently the prime mechanism for achieving protection and practical benefits for TK holders. For instance, Brazil, Costa Rica, India, Peru, Panama, the Philippines, Portugal, Thailand and the United States of America have all adopted *sui generis* laws that protect at least some aspect of TK (*sui generis* measures are specialized measures aimed exclusively at addressing the characteristics of specific subject matter, such as TK). . . . Various TK holders and other stakeholders in different countries have already found existing IP rights useful and their TK protection strategies make some use of the IP system.

* WIPO Intergovernmental Committee on Intellectual Property and Genetic Resources, Traditional Knowledge and Folklore, *The Patent System and Genetic Resources*, WIPO/GRTKF/IC/9/13 (2006).

While there are diverse national and regional approaches to protection, reflecting the diversity of TK itself and its social context, some common elements arise in policy debate. For instance, it is stressed that protection should reflect the aspirations and expectations of TK holders and should promote respect for indigenous and customary practices, protocols and laws as far as possible. Several *sui generis* measures, as well as conventional IP law, have recognized elements of such customary law within a broader framework of protection. Economic aspects of development need to be addressed and the effective participation by TK holders is also important, in line with the principle of prior informed consent. TK protection should also be affordable, understandable and accessible to TK holders. The view is widely voiced that holders of TK should be entitled to fair and equitable sharing of benefits arising from the use of their knowledge. The international legal framework, within and beyond the IP system, is also an important consideration. Where TK is associated with genetic resources, the distribution of benefits should be consistent with measures established in accordance with the Convention on Biological Diversity (CBD), providing for sharing of benefits arising from the utilization of the genetic resources. Other important international instruments include the International Treaty on Plant Genetic Resources for Food and Agriculture of the Food and Agriculture Organization (FAO), the International Union for the Protection of New Varieties of Plants (UPOV), and the UN Convention to Combat Desertification (UNCCD). Other areas of international law, notably human rights and cultural policy, are also part of the context for protection of TK.

FORMS OF PROTECTION

Two key demands on the IP system in particular have arisen in policy debate: first, the call for recognition of the rights of TK holders relating to their TK, and, second, concerns about the unauthorized acquisition by third parties of IP rights over TK. Two forms of IP-related protection have therefore been developed and applied:

— positive protection: giving TK holders the right to take action or seek remedies against certain forms of misuse of TK; and
— defensive protection: safeguarding against illegitimate IP rights taken out by others over TK subject matter.

Stakeholders have stressed that these two approaches should be undertaken in a complementary way. A comprehensive approach to protection in the interests of TK holders is unlikely to rely totally on one form or the other.

B. Traditional Knowledge in the Patent System

In recent years, holders of TK have started to oppose patents containing their knowledge: The widely discussed cases of Turmeric (U.S. Patent No. 5401504) and Neem (European Patent No. 436257) involved patents that were challenged, reexamined, and annulled by the patent offices that had granted them. In both cases, evidence was put forward by the opponents that both Turmeric and Neem were used in traditional farming and agriculture for centuries, thus hindering the novelty and inventive step of the granted patents.

In the Hoodia case, the EPO came to a different conclusion in the assessment of the impact of TK on patentability.

PATENTING NEEM AND HOODIA: CONFLICTING DECISIONS ISSUED BY THE OPPOSITION BOARD OF THE EUROPEAN PATENT OFFICE

Kari Moyer-Henry, Ph.D.*

THE HOODIA PLANT

BACKGROUND

Hoodia gordonii (Hoodia) is a cactus that was used by the San People of South Africa for generations as an appetite suppressant during times of famine, low food supply, or long nomadic hunting trips. As the San remain a partially nomadic people today, Hoodia was likely used to allow them to make it on their long desert journeys with little to no supplies. South Africa's national laboratory began investigating the science behind the appetite-suppressing nature of Hoodia as part of a study of indigenous foods. In 1963, the Council for Scientific and Industrial Research (CSIR) isolated a chemical they called P57 as the active ingredient responsible for appetite suppression.

The CSIR in South Africa was established in 1945 by an act of Parliament and is the leading scientific and technology, research and development, and implementation organization in Africa. The purpose of CSIR is to engage in directed and multidisciplinary research and technological innovation, as well as industrial and scientific development to improve the quality of life of African people. But perhaps the primary goal of the organization is to improve the national competitiveness of South Africa in the global economy. Approximately 40% of the CSIR's annual income is provided by a grant from Parliament, with additional income being provided by royalties, licenses and dividends from an intellectual property portfolio and commercial companies created by the CSIR.

THE PATENT

The controversy involving Hoodia was largely twofold. The subject matter of the patent application was problematic for the EPO examiner. The Examining Division initially found that the subject matter lacked an inventive step because the traditional knowledge of the San people provided enough information to lead a person skilled in the art to use Hoodia extract as an appetite suppressant. The CSIR appealed the rejection of the patent. They argued, using prior art to demonstrate, that the traditional use of Hoodia plant parts by the San people did not disclose that "an extract from . . . Hoodia could be used [for] manufacture of a medicament" for use as an appetite suppressant.

Ultimately, the Appeal Board concluded "a skilled person, knowing that consumption of parts of a fibrous, water-storing plant of the genus Trichocaulon very efficiently 'removed the pangs of hunger,' could not obviously derive from this disclosure that an extract from the plant could be used for the manufacture of an appetite-suppressant, anti-obesity medicament." With that

* Biotechnology Law Report, February 2008, 27(1): 1-10, available at http://www.liebertonline.com/doi/abs/10.1089/blr.2008.9991.

conclusion, the subject matter included an inventive step and was therefore patentable. But this conclusion by the Board does not seem logical because even a person not skilled in the art of the invention could make the obvious connection that extracts from a plant consumed by an ancient people to stave off hunger could be used to combat obesity by piggy-backing on the appetite suppressant effects of ingesting certain plant components. Obviously, a person eating less because he/she doesn't feel hungry can lose weight. Despite this obvious lack of a true inventive step, the CSIR overcame the obstacle at the EPO, but they were not out of the woods completely.

THE REAL CONTROVERSY

The government-funded CSIR patented its discovery of P57 without communicating with the San or crediting them with the discovery of Hoodia. The CSIR then licensed use of P57 to Phytopharm, a British pharmaceutical research company. Subsequently, Phytopharm subleased the rights to P57 to Pfizer. In addition, poor public relations on the part of CSIR scientists contributed to the start of the San's opposition to the Hoodia patent. When asked how the traditional knowledge of the San aided their research of Hoodia, the scientists incorrectly stated that the San people were extinct. This errant statement, combined with the previous poor treatment of the San by CSIR, caused the South African San Council to file suit against the CSIR and its licensees.

The San first learned of the patent through a Phytopharm press release. The San felt exploited by CSIR because they had provided the national laboratory with the knowledge necessary to further their research. The San people expected the laboratory to act as advocates for them in furthering their rights and benefits in return for the information they provided to CSIR that ultimately advanced research.

THE OUTCOME

When accused of biopiracy by the San, CSIR and Phytopharm did the only thing they could do to protect their investments. The government offered a settlement to the San for use of their knowledge. Beginning in March 2003, San in four countries—South Africa, Botswana, Namibia and Angola—were guaranteed at least four payments of $30,000 during clinical testing of Hoodia. In addition, Pfizer agreed to profit sharing with the San at a rate of 6% of the royalties received on the market. Subsequently, when the Hoodia patent was granted in 2006, there was no opposition filed with the EPO. Once the Hoodia patent was granted, it provided the CSIR with protection in an array of member countries. . . . The family of patents totals 76 members derived from 58 applications to provide an expansive range of protection for the invention.

MIXED MESSAGES

CAN THE CONTRADICTORY DECISIONS BY THE EPO BE RECONCILED?

The treatment of the Hoodia patent by the EPO was in response to the mistakes made during the handling of the neem patent. The Examining Division was proceeding cautiously in its handling of another patent application based on traditional knowledge. In regard to the neem patent, some opponents accused the EPO of merely skimming over the references to traditional knowledge in the Grace application. The opponents felt a closer examination of the Indian traditional knowledge in the application would have led the Examining Division to reject the application initially for lack of inventive step, thereby avoiding the subsequent 10-year battle to invalidate the patent. Thus, the Hoodia patent was originally denied by the Examining Division "for lack of inventive step (Art. 56 EPC) in view of the traditional knowledge of the San people."

Still, there remains a simpler explanation for the outcome of these two patent applications. The response of the Indian people and the San people to the use of their respective traditional knowledge played a tremendous role in the final outcome of each controversy. The Indian government in particular attacked the neem patent with vigor. . . . It is clear that the opposition to the Grace patent was not going to stop fighting until the neem patent was defeated. In contrast, the San have largely embraced their place in the history of biotechnology, and with the signing of the licensing agreement, the San have renewed faith. The San see the commercialization of Hoodia and their part in it as a way to guarantee that the modern world recognizes the wealth to be found in the San's ancient knowledge. For a society struggling against extinction, "at least one tradition in their dying culture might be saved." . . .

The San people never filed any opposition to the granted Hoodia patent because it would only do them greater harm to do so. Under the agreement, the San people have a financial interest in the promotion of their plant and their culture. The San people are an example of how many indigenous communities could benefit from the revenue generated by profit-sharing agreements. Although it may not be the most equal division of profits for the San, the agreement still provides a significant means for them to take control over their future and plan the health and well-being of their community. Alternatively, the Indian people saw the Grace patent as another attempt to exploit their resources and steal their culture from them. Even though they were promised that the neem patent was not being sought in India, they were not willing to compromise with big industry over something they felt belonged to them entirely. Therefore, the Hoodia patent could have easily ended up revoked, just as the neem patent was, if the San people had reacted to the situation as the Indian government did.

POLICY IMPLICATIONS

The EPO's decision to reject the neem patent was a strategic one. The Opposition Board had not agreed with the opponents and their argument that the patent constituted a "de facto monopoly on a single plant variety" or that it was a violation of "public order and morality." On the other hand, they accepted the opponents' argument that patents should not be granted for common traditional knowledge, but pointed out that this argument should be used for establishing "prior art" and is not a question of morality in the sense of the European Patent Convention. This distinction was crucial for maintaining the proper role of the EPO. Rather than base their decision on standards not well defined, specifically morality, and certain to be insufficient depending on the time and societal values applied, the Board framed the decision around the long established requirement for an inventive step. In doing so, the Board set a precedent for recognizing traditional knowledge as prior art.

India has altered its policy on traditional knowledge in response to the argument that the traditional knowledge of Indian farmers does not qualify as prior art because it could not be found in printed publications prior to the filing date of the application. India has been translating ancient texts containing traditional remedies into electronic form. The sole purpose of making such records available to patent offices in English, German, French, Japanese, and Spanish is to prevent further exploitation of Indian tradition by foreign industry.

As early as 1999, Indian legislature began working to amend the Patent Act to expressly provide patent protection to indigenous peoples. Similarly, in 2000, the World Intellectual Property Organization (WIPO) General Assembly created the Intergovernmental Committee on Intellectual Property and Genetic Resources, Traditional Knowledge and Folklore (IGC) to "progress towards a shared international understanding of how best to protect TK and TCEs against misappropriation and misuse." Just last month, the member states of WIPO reaffirmed their commitment "to forging ahead with efforts to reach international consensus on the protection of traditional knowledge, genetic resources and folklore." The goal of these initiatives is to move close to stronger legal recognition of and protection for traditional knowledge in order to strengthen the rights of the member countries domestically while protecting the interest of each internationally.

The contradictory decisions by the EPO regarding the validity of the neem and Hoodia patents were based ultimately on the determination of whether the subject matter of each patent included an inventive step. However, the evidence presented by the EPO in support of their decisions does not actually fit the conclusions. Specifically, the Grace patent that was clearly based on an inventive step beyond the knowledge held by the Indian farmers was denied for lack of inventive step. The Appeals Board decided it would be easier to base their decision on the lack of inventive step rather than the more controversial, and perhaps more accurate, reason of morality that was so strongly advocated by the opponents to the patent. In regard to the Hoodia patent, the conclusion by the Appeals Board that there was an inventive step coincided with the decision by the San people to sign a licensing agreement for the use of their traditional knowledge. These seemingly unsupported decisions by the EPO result in the creation of an equally weak and unjust patent policy. The patent policy of the EPO should be fair to all applicants, not just those who can avoid opposition filings, as the CSIR and Phytopharm were able to. But until there are guidelines in place that clearly address the issue of traditional knowledge as prior art and the right of indigenous peoples to protect their traditional knowledge, the patent policy will remain unjust.

BIOTECHNOLOGY IMPLICATIONS

There needs to be a consensus about what can and cannot be patented. Currently, no such agreement exists. As a result, pharmaceutical companies feel forced to go to extraordinary lengths to gain protection for their products. Companies are filing broader patent applications in greater numbers. The EPO is suffering from a backlog of applications waiting for examination. According to Sjoerd Hoestra, director of a biotechnology department at the EPO, "[more than] 60 percent of applications are [rejected]; they are not worth [patenting because of] a lack of balance between disclosure and invention."

The need for clear regulations on biotechnology goes well beyond the EPO. An international solution is required if there is ever going to be harmony between the biotechnology industry and the patent offices. The industry will suffer and decline if there is no guarantee that the high expenditures on research costs and decades of development will be recouped. In turn, the suffering will reach the public because companies will put less capital into research and development for fear that they will never be able to recover the cost.

LEGAL PERSPECTIVES ON TRADITIONAL KNOWLEDGE: THE CASE FOR INTELLECTUAL PROPERTY PROTECTION

Thomas Cottier & Marion Panizzon*

II. A PROPOSAL FOR TRADITIONAL IP RIGHTS IN TRADITIONAL KNOWLEDGE

A. SUBJECT MATTER AND BENEFICIARIES OF THE RIGHTS

1. Subject Matter

This study suggests a . . . general term—Traditional Intellectual Property Rights ("TIP Rights")—that is left deliberately open to encompass new and changing forms of traditional knowledge. TIP rights express the concept of a *sui generis* private law entitlement vested in communities which covers data and information about plant genetic resources for food and agriculture (PGRFA) and medicinal plants. The concept encompasses methods of use and includes the seed that embodies a given community's traditional knowledge. . . .

2. Rights Holders

We believe that a TIP right should be inclusive, rather than exclusive, with respect to prospective beneficiaries of protection. It should encompass the spectrum of all relevant persons touched by such a law, ranging from individuals to communities, from associations to cooperatives. Given the strong intergenerational component of TK, it will be difficult to identify a single holder. Because TK is often held by families and even lineages, TIP rights should partake of a communitarian nature. . . .

That the TIP right as such is reserved for a collective entity hardly presents a new phenomenon in IP law. Consider, for example, that even a modern patent law deals more with teams of inventors than single persons, and "most intellectual property assets are owned by collective entities, which in many cases represent large and diffuse groups of individuals."

. . . Given that different communities [in different regions of the world] might assert parallel rights to the same traditional knowledge, cooperative efforts in assigning or transferring such knowledge to firms for industrial application would be in their mutual interests. Also beneficial might be agreements setting prices for such purposes, short of collusion running afoul of antitrust laws. In this regard, states participating in the proposed IP regime would need to adopt appropriate exceptions for collective administration of TIP rights, so as to avoid pitting different communities against one another in ways that would drive down the prices paid for their traditional knowledge. It would undermine a primary goal of establishing such rights if antitrust laws would deny traditional communities an exceptional use of monopolistic market power.

B. THE CONTENT AND SCOPE OF RIGHTS

. . . The scope of protection may range from fully developed property rights to a limited entitlement focusing on compensation without entailing powers to prevent others from using materials for commercial purposes. However, it should be clear that TIP rights only extend to commercial activities undertaken by public or private entities. The very rationale for such rights is to

* *Legal Perspective on Traditional Knowledge: The Case for Intellectual Property Protection*, 7(2) J. INT'L ECONOMIC LAW 371 (2004).

introduce a new level of economic benefits that alters the balance of power between those who possess traditional knowledge and commercial actors who seek to exploit and build upon such knowledge with a view to marketing new products.

In keeping with general principles of intellectual property law, activities partaking of private use should not be covered. Nothing therefore would bar individuals from using TK generated by others for private purposes short of engaging in commercial activities.

A difficult question arises from the need to compensate holders of rights in TK adequately when a TK component is claimed as part of a "combination patent" in jurisdictions that recognize such patents. Here the object is to prevent would-be patentees from avoiding the need to license the traditional knowledge or otherwise to compensate its holders simply because they filed for a combination patent. Similarly, policy makers must decide whether to allow potential licensees to test their products and obtain market approval prior to obtaining the consent of the right holders.

Where the TK is associated with a biological resource, as when it pertains to the effects of medicinal plants or the specific quality of a crop, the TIP right must necessarily encompass certain uses one can elicit of that plant. An open question is whether the genetic information encapsulated within the plant (or seed) should be eligible for any form of IP protection. The communities have usually neither identified the genetic sequences making up the seed nor have they matched the function of any given seed to a certain strand of the genetic code, and for contemporary international treaty law, genetic information falls under the research exemption.

. . . Logically, the poorest developing countries would prefer a strong exclusive property right in TK, unencumbered by research exceptions that required all users to be licensed. Users, especially those in developed countries, may prefer to limit the right to compensation or to adopt the compensatory liability regime (CLR) proposed by Professor Reichman.

Between an exclusive right and a clear entitlement to compensatory liability lies the possibility of adopting a misappropriation regime. Such a regime, as suggested by Professor Correa among others, seems consistent with a broader unfair competition approach, which others have proposed. The African Group within the Council for TRIPS endorsed the misappropriation approach in 2003. An approach rooted in unfair competition can benefit from Article 10bis of the Paris Convention for the Protection of Industrial Property. Just as undisclosed information has been protected on this basis by Article 39 of the TRIPS Agreement, which established a new IPR category in international law, so it can be argued that to use information and knowledge generated by others and expressed in a specific product is unfair to the extent that it serves to facilitate copies or a derived product without the consent of the creator.

All of these proposals need to be carefully evaluated in light of their potential impact on the free flow of genetic material envisaged by the FAO's International Treaty and their human rights implications.

C. THE DURATION OF RIGHTS

IPRs that stimulate innovation and creation are generally limited in time. After a period in which innovators reap their rewards, innovation enters the public domain of human knowledge and becomes freely available. With TIP rights, the process is reversed. Traditional knowledge that resides in the public domain without being privatized by law becomes, as of a particular date, subject to an intellectual property right owned by an individual or a community.

Active use of TK should constitute the required limit of protection. Rights to TK should only arise so long as the process or information exists within, and is being used by, a particular community. Once it fades into the past, it is no longer of commercial interest to the community and should no longer be granted protection.

When the use of active TK is protected, however, the period of liability for specific uses will have to be determined by law. Regardless of whether an exclusive rights regime or a compensatory liability regime is adopted, the question arises as to how long the licensee must remain liable to the licensor. The problem here is that a new product will often only be placed on the market after a number of years of research and testing, and the amount of equitable sharing of benefits cannot be properly defined during the first years of licensing.

One solution would be to differentiate the licensing fees according to a menu of options, with one charge for a period of R&D, and additional compensation to become due once the product reaches the market. Such compensation would then be limited for a certain period of time sufficient to generate adequate profit sharing. At some point, e.g. after 10 years, the duty to compensate would cease and the use of TK by that licensee would no longer trigger a duty to remunerate the right holder.

We stress that the TIP rights in traditional knowledge as such should not lapse and would again become operational if the TK were used by another economic operator or for different purposes. At this point, the process of licensing or compensatory liability would revive and additional revenues would be generated. In effect, one could envisage that TK protection could last indefinitely, so long as active use is made of the relevant information, and this solution would be consonant with the intergenerational and incremental nature of traditional knowledge.

D. THE CREATION AND REGISTRATION OF RIGHTS

1. Registration Requirements

Costly registration procedures can be avoided by linking the registration process to existing and updated inventories of knowledge. In addition to a registration requirement for TK holders, industries interested in using TK could be obliged to disclose the origin of the genetic resources in question.

This requirement, in turn, would help to foster the creation of TK inventories.

However, according to de Carvalho, a disclosure requirement seems incompatible with the TRIPS Agreement. . . .

Registration of the right itself can be either declaratory or constitutive. A declaratory registration might have the advantage that it could strengthen the claims of traditional communities against infringement prior to the vesting of a formal legal title. An examination would presuppose the creation of a core of examiners specialized in the IP rights of indigenous people.

The problem of finding the resources to apply for adequate protection and/or enforcement of a TIP right in TK is aggravated by the manner in which knowledge has often been unsystematically transmitted from one generation to another. Ideally, these rights should be registered at the international level by an international organization, in cooperation with national agencies and

NGOs. Information technology facilitates linking different sources and building a coherent system. Registered information about TK and its uses should be made publicly available, as in patent law.

An optimal solution aimed at reducing registration costs must invest a TIP right with a built in "presumption of protection" in traditional knowledge. Any user of TK would labor under a burden to disclose the origin of biological or genetic resources and to establish that he had obtained prior informed consent to their use, unless these resources were otherwise demonstrably free of claims by indigenous people or in the public domain. Such disclosure and prior informed consent requirements have not yet been included in international patent treaties. Yet, conditioning the grant of a patent on such a requirement would successfully link the objectives of the CBD access and benefit-sharing system to that of IPRs protection.

. . .

CONCLUSIONS

We contend that IP protection for traditional knowledge must be shaped by an international agreement specifically designed for this purpose. Neither the national sovereignty approach of the CBD nor the public goods approach of the FAO's International Treaty is alone sufficient effectively to empower communities whose TK has enabled them to identify, collect, develop, and conserve plant genetic resources for food and agriculture.

We, therefore, propose the creation of a traditional intellectual property right (TIP right), the scope of which will need to be more fully defined, but which at least should entail a right to compensatory liability. We support the requirements of prior informed consent and disclosure of origin as a precondition to patent applications. At the same time, we stress that existing IPRs and TIP rights are not mutually exclusive. Quite the opposite, they all need to be made part of an overall package of measures to support viable agricultural structures in developing countries. In particular, stronger protection of geographical indications of origin would further enhance the potential to develop local and international niche markets for products based on traditional knowledge.

If action is taken at the international level to implement IPRs for traditional knowledge along the lines we envision, the end results should become part of the global trading system and thus of WTO law. We maintain that it is only the WTO, which combines global trade rules with worldwide IP protection that can ensure better market access and conditions for commercially valuable assets resulting from a TK-related production process.

In an age of globalization, monetary value creates power, and trade transcends borders. Those whose traditional knowledge acquires value in identifiable plant genetic resources for food and agriculture and in the corresponding seed will not become "players" in the global market place unless these assets attract tradable IPRs. International disputes arising from the exercise of these rights should be resolved within the existing dispute settlement framework, and trade-related enforcement mechanisms should ensure that treaty rights are fully implemented. The Least Developed Countries would particularly benefit from such an arrangement, and it would thus help to rebalance the social costs of the TRIPS Agreement.

NOTES AND QUESTIONS

1. The prevention of "erroneously granted patents" is one of the measures a *sui generis* system for TK has to provide for. Other major fields of work are the disclosure of origin and source of information used in patent claims and the provision of evidence of benefit sharing and prior informed consent in patent applications. What other measures, apart from intervention in the application process of patents, would you consider suitable to enforce the rights of TK holders?
2. Patents are one form of IP that is affected by the protection of TK. Considering other fields of economic activity, for example, the tourism and souvenir industry, what other interfaces of IP and TK can you think of?

In the next section, we examine additional specific subject matter areas of intellectual property protection. For each of these areas, there is generally a combination of protective schemes available, and approaches to protection vary among countries. Nonetheless, there are multilateral rules addressing each of these subject matter areas and related forms of protection.

IV. THE INTERNATIONAL SYSTEM FOR THE PROTECTION OF PLANT VARIETIES

A. *Introduction*

Plant varieties play an enormously important role in human affairs.[2] Success or failure in producing foodstuffs is a life or death matter for large parts of the world's population. For many nations, agriculture is the dominant field of economic activity. Even in nations where agriculture is a less significant component of economic activity, there remains intense interest in maintaining farm communities and promoting food security. Disputes concerning agricultural subsidies remain at the heart of the World Trade Organization agenda. Although the protection afforded to plant varieties as a matter of intellectual property law does not receive the level of public attention accorded to pharmaceutical patents or copyrights in music, the direction of public interest should not obscure the fundamental importance of intellectual property rights in plant varieties.

Innovation in the field of agriculture has been important to human civilization since farmers first began to cultivate crops. Increasing crop yields has long been a goal of agricultural research and development (R&D). Two recent trends in agricultural R&D are rather important to understanding ongoing debates concerning the scope of plant variety protection. The first is the biotechnology revolution brought about by advances in genetic engineering. New technologies make possible comparatively rapid development of new plant varieties with yield and disease-resistance characteristics that might substantially relieve

2. *See, e.g.*, Geoff Tansey, *Trade, Intellectual Property, Food and Biodiversity[:] A Discussion Paper*, Quaker Peace and Service, London (1999).

pressures on the world food supply. Of course, concerns about the effects of genetically modified organisms (GMOs) on human health and the environment are the subject of intense public discussion, and these concerns directly and indirectly influence the IP dialogue. This is one important illustration of the general point that IP is often closely interlinked with social questions, and that IP issues must be considered in their social context.

The second recent trend is a pronounced shift in agricultural R&D from public sector institutions to the private sector. The shift toward privately funded R&D has enhanced business interest in expanding the scope of plant variety protection. Yet, farmers throughout much of the world operate with limited capital resources. For them, the introduction of better though more expensive plant varieties may be a mixed blessing. Without access to new plant varieties, the marginal farmer may be replaced by large-scale agribusiness. The social consequences could be rather dramatic.[3]

B. Plant Variety Protection as an IP Form

Plant varieties are protected by patent and by *sui generis* registration systems. In each case, there are various approaches followed by different countries. Plant varieties may be protected by more than one form of IP.

The United States today allows the protection of plant varieties by utility patent, plant patent, and *sui generis* plant variety protection. The availability of all three forms of protection for the same plant variety was recognized by the U.S. Supreme Court in *J.E.M. AG Supply v. Pioneer Hi-Bred,* decided in 2001. The decision provides a useful introduction to the different forms of protection.

J.E.M. AG SUPPLY v. PIONEER HI-BRED
534 U.S. 124 (2001)

Justice Thomas delivered the opinion of the Court.

This case presents the question whether utility patents may be issued for plants under 35 U.S.C. § 101 (1994 ed.), or whether the Plant Variety Protection Act, 84 Stat. 1542, as amended, 7 U.S.C. § 2321 et seq., and the Plant Patent Act of 1930, 35 U.S.C. §§ 161-164 (1994 ed. and Supp. V), are the exclusive means of obtaining a federal statutory right to exclude others from reproducing, selling, or using plants or plant varieties. We hold that utility patents may be issued for plants. . . .

Several years after *Chakrabarty,* the PTO Board of Patent Appeals and Interferences held that plants were within the understood meaning of "manufacture" or "composition of matter" and therefore were within the subject matter of § 101. *Ex parte Hibberd,* 227 U.S.P.Q. (BNA) 443, 444 (1985). It has been the unbroken practice of the PTO since that time to confer utility patents for plants.

---

3. The protection of plant varieties has long been controversial at the international level. A major part of agricultural research and development historically has been financed and/or undertaken by public authorities, and the results of this research have often been made freely available. There has been reluctance to apply IPRs-related limitations to the fruits of public research, and there has been some worry that private sector dominance of the agricultural research area would have adverse consequences, particularly in developing countries.

To obtain utility patent protection, a plant breeder must show that the plant he has developed is new, useful, and non-obvious. 35 U.S.C. §§ 101-103 (1994 ed. and Supp. V). In addition, the plant must meet the specifications of § 112, which require a written description of the plant and a deposit of seed that is publicly accessible. *See* 37 CFR §§ 1.801-1.809 (2001).

Petitioners do not allege that Pioneer's patents are invalid for failure to meet the requirements for a utility patent. Nor do they dispute that plants otherwise fall within the terms of § 101's broad language that includes "manufacture" or "composition of matter." Rather, petitioners argue that the PPA and the PVPA provide the exclusive means of protecting new varieties of plants, and so awarding utility patents for plants upsets the scheme contemplated by Congress. . . . We disagree. Considering the two plant specific statutes in turn, we find that neither forecloses utility patent coverage for plants.

II

A

The 1930 PPA conferred patent protection to asexually reproduced plants. Significantly, nothing within either the original 1930 text of the statute or its recodified version in 1952 indicates that the PPA's protection for asexually reproduced plants was intended to be exclusive.

Plants were first explicitly brought within the scope of patent protection in 1930 when the PPA included "plants" among the useful things subject to patents. . . .

This provision limited protection to the asexual reproduction of the plant. Asexual reproduction occurs by grafting, budding, or the like, and produces an offspring with a genetic combination identical to that of the single parent — essentially a clone.[3] The PPA also amended Revised Statutes § 4888 by adding, "No plant patent shall be declared invalid on the ground of noncompliance with this section if the description is made as complete as is reasonably possible." Id., § 2, 46 Stat. 376.

In 1952, Congress revised the patent statute and placed the plant patents into a separate chapter 15 of Title 35 entitled, "Patents for plants." 35 U.S.C. §§ 161-164.[4] This was merely a housekeeping measure that did nothing to change the substantive rights or requirements for a plant patent. A "plant patent"[5] continued to provide only the exclusive right to asexually reproduce a protected plant, § 163, and the description requirement remained relaxed, § 162.[6] Plant patents under the PPA thus have very limited coverage and less stringent requirements than § 101 utility patents.

---

3. By contrast, sexual reproduction occurs by seed and sometimes involves two different plants.

4. The PPA, as amended, provides: "Whoever invents or discovers and asexually reproduces any distinct and new variety of plant, including cultivated sports, mutants, hybrids, and newly found seedlings, other than a tuber propagated plant or a plant found in an uncultivated state, may obtain a patent therefor, subject to the conditions and requirements of this title." 35 U.S.C. § 161.

5. Patents issued under § 161 are referred to as "plant patents," which are distinguished from § 101 utility patents and § 171 design patents.

6. To obtain a plant patent under § 161 a breeder must meet all of the requirements for § 101, except for the description requirement. *See* § 162 ("No plant patent shall be declared invalid for noncompliance with section 112 [providing for written description] of this title if the description is as complete as is reasonably possible").

Importantly, chapter 15 nowhere states that plant patents are the exclusive means of granting intellectual property protection to plants. . . .

. . . [I]n 1930 Congress believed that plants were not patentable under § 101, both because they were living things and because in practice they could not meet the stringent description requirement. Yet these premises were disproved over time. As this Court held in *Chakrabarty,* "the relevant distinction" for purposes of § 101 is not "between living and inanimate things, but between products of nature, whether living or not, and human-made inventions." 447 U.S. at 313. In addition, advances in biological knowledge and breeding expertise have allowed plant breeders to satisfy § 101's demanding description requirement.

Whatever Congress may have believed about the state of patent law and the science of plant breeding in 1930, plants have always had the potential to fall within the general subject matter of § 101, which is a dynamic provision designed to encompass new and unforeseen inventions. "A rule that unanticipated inventions are without protection would conflict with the core concept of the patent law that anticipation undermines patentability." *Id.,* at 316.

Petitioners essentially ask us to deny utility patent protection for sexually reproduced plants because it was unforeseen in 1930 that such plants could receive protection under § 101. Denying patent protection under § 101 simply because such coverage was thought technologically infeasible in 1930, however, would be inconsistent with the forward-looking perspective of the utility patent statute. As we noted in *Chakrabarty,* "Congress employed broad general language in drafting § 101 precisely because [new types of] inventions are often unforeseeable." *Ibid.* . . .

B

By passing the PVPA in 1970, Congress specifically authorized limited patent-like protection for certain sexually reproduced plants. Petitioners therefore argue that this legislation evidences Congress' intent to deny broader § 101 utility patent protection for such plants. Petitioners' argument, however, is unavailing for two reasons. First, nowhere does the PVPA purport to provide the exclusive statutory means of protecting sexually reproduced plants. Second, the PVPA and § 101 can easily be reconciled. Because it is harder to qualify for a utility patent than for a Plant Variety Protection (PVP) certificate, it only makes sense that utility patents would confer a greater scope of protection.

1

The PVPA provides plant variety protection for:

> "The breeder of any sexually reproduced or tuber propagated plant variety (other than fungi or bacteria) who has so reproduced the variety. . . ." 7 U.S.C. § 2402(a).

Infringement of plant variety protection occurs, inter alia, if someone sells or markets the protected variety, sexually multiplies the variety as a step in marketing, uses the variety in producing a hybrid, or dispenses the variety without notice that the variety is protected.

Since the 1994 amendments, the PVPA also protects "any variety that is essentially derived from a protected variety," § 2541(c)(1), and "any variety whose production requires the repeated use of a protected variety," § 2541(c)(3). *See* Plant Variety Protection Act Amendments of 1994, § 9, 108

Stat. 3142. Practically, this means that hybrids created from protected plant varieties are also protected; however, it is not infringement to use a protected variety for the development of a hybrid. *See* 7 U.S.C. § 2541(a)(4).[11]

The PVPA also contains exemptions for saving seed and for research. A farmer who legally purchases and plants a protected variety can save the seed from these plants for replanting on his own farm. *See* § 2543 ("It shall not infringe any right hereunder for a person to save seed produced by the person from seed obtained, or descended from seed obtained, by authority of the owner of the variety for seeding purposes and use such saved seed in the production of a crop for use on the farm of the person . . ."); *see also Asgrow Seed Co. v. Winterboer,* 513 U.S. 179, 130 L. Ed. 2d 682, 115 S. Ct. 788 (1995). In addition, a protected variety may be used for research. *See* 7 U.S.C. § 2544 ("The use and reproduction of a protected variety for plant breeding or other bona fide research shall not constitute an infringement of the protection provided under this chapter"). The utility patent statute does not contain similar exemptions.[12]

Thus, while the PVPA creates a statutory scheme that is comprehensive with respect to its particular protections and subject matter, giving limited protection to plant varieties that are new, distinct, uniform, and stable, § 2402(a), nowhere does it restrict the scope of patentable subject matter under § 101. With nothing in the statute to bolster their view that the PVPA provides the exclusive means for protecting sexually reproducing plants, petitioners rely on the legislative history of the PVPA. They argue that this history shows the PVPA was enacted because sexually reproducing plant varieties and their seeds were not and had never been intended by Congress to be included within the classes of things patentable under Title 35.

The PVPA itself, however, contains no statement that plant variety certificates were to be the exclusive means of protecting sexually reproducing plants. The relevant statements in the legislative history reveal nothing more than the limited view of plant breeding taken by some Members of Congress who believed that patent protection was unavailable for sexually reproduced plants. This view stems from a lack of awareness concerning scientific possibilities.

Furthermore, at the time the PVPA was enacted, the PTO had already issued numerous utility patents for hybrid plant processes. Many of these patents, especially since the 1950's, included claims on the products of the patented process, i.e., the hybrid plant itself. *See* Kloppenburg 264. Such plants were protected as part of a hybrid process and not on their own. Nonetheless, these hybrids still enjoyed protection under § 101, which reaffirms that such material was within the scope of § 101.

2 . . .

To be sure, there are differences in the requirements for, and coverage of, utility patents and plant variety certificates issued pursuant to the PVPA. . . .

It is much more difficult to obtain a utility patent for a plant than to obtain a plant variety certificate because a utility patentable plant must be new, useful,

---

11. It is, however, infringement of a utility patent to use a protected plant in the development of another variety. . . .

12. The dissent argues that our "reading would destroy" the PVPA's exemptions. . . . Yet such bold predictions are belied by the facts. According to the Government, over 5,000 PVP certificates have been issued, as compared to about 1,800 utility patents for plants. Since 1985 the PTO has interpreted § 101 to include utility patents for plants and there is no evidence that the availability of such patents has rendered the PVPA and its specific exemptions obsolete.

and nonobvious, 35 U.S.C. §§ 101-103. In addition, to obtain a utility patent, a breeder must describe the plant with sufficient specificity to enable others to "make and use" the invention after the patent term expires. § 112. The disclosure required by the Patent Act is "the quid pro quo of the right to exclude." *Kewanee Oil Co. v. Bicron Corp.*, 416 U.S. 470, 484, 40 L. Ed. 2d 315, 94 S. Ct. 1879 (1974). The description requirement for plants includes a deposit of biological material, for example seeds, and mandates that such material be accessible to the public. *See* 37 CFR §§ 1.801-1.809 (2001); *see also* App. 39 (seed deposits for U.S. Patent No. 5,491,295).

By contrast, a plant variety may receive a PVP certificate without a showing of usefulness or nonobviousness. *See* 7 U.S.C. § 2402(a) (requiring that the variety be only new, distinct, uniform, and stable). Nor does the PVPA require a description and disclosure as extensive as those required under § 101. The PVPA requires a "description of the variety setting forth its distinctiveness, uniformity and stability and a description of the genealogy and breeding procedure, when known." 7 U.S.C. § 2422(2). It also requires a deposit of seed in a public depository, § 2422(4), but neither the statute nor the applicable regulation mandates that such material be accessible to the general public during the term of the PVP certificate. *See* 7 CFR § 97.6 (2001).

Because of the more stringent requirements, utility patent holders receive greater rights of exclusion than holders of a PVP certificate. Most notably, there are no exemptions for research or saving seed under a utility patent. Additionally, although Congress increased the level of protection under the PVPA in 1994, a plant variety certificate still does not grant the full range of protections afforded by a utility patent. . . .

III

We also note that the PTO has assigned utility patents for plants for at least 16 years and there has been no indication from either Congress or agencies with expertise that such coverage is inconsistent with the PVPA or the PPA. The Board of Patent Appeals and Interferences, which has specific expertise in issues of patent law, relied heavily on this Court's decision in *Chakrabarty* when it interpreted the subject matter of § 101 to include plants. *In re Hibberd,* 227 U.S.P.Q. (BNA) 443 (1985). This highly visible decision has led to the issuance of some 1,800 utility patents for plants. Moreover, the PTO, which administers § 101 as well as the PPA, recognizes and regularly issues utility patents for plants. In addition, the Department of Agriculture's Plant Variety Protection Office acknowledges the existence of utility patents for plants.

In the face of these developments, Congress has not only failed to pass legislation indicating that it disagrees with the PTO's interpretation of § 101, it has even recognized the availability of utility patents for plants. In a 1999 amendment to 35 U.S.C. § 119, which concerns the right of priority for patent rights, Congress provided: "Applications for plant breeder's rights filed in a WTO [World Trade Organization] member country . . . shall have the same effect for the purpose of the right of priority . . . as applications for patents, subject to the same conditions and requirements of this section as apply to applications for patents." 35 U.S.C. § 119(f) (1994 ed., Supp. V). Crucially, § 119(f) is part of the general provisions of Title 35, not the specific chapter of the PPA, which suggests a recognition on the part of Congress that plants are patentable under § 101.

IV

For these reasons, we hold that newly developed plant breeds fall within the terms of § 101, and that neither the PPA nor the PVPA limits the scope of § 101's coverage. As in *Chakrabarty*, we decline to narrow the reach of § 101 where Congress has given us no indication that it intends this result. 447 U.S. at 315-316. Accordingly, we affirm the judgment of the Court of Appeals.

Justice BREYER, with whom Justice STEVENS joins, dissenting.

The question before us is whether the words "manufacture" or "compositions of matter" contained in the utility patent statute, 35 U.S.C. § 101 (1994 ed.) (Utility Patent Statute), cover plants that also fall within the scope of two more specific statutes, the Plant Patent Act of 1930 (PPA), 35 U.S.C. § 161 et seq. (1994 ed. and Supp. V), and the Plant Variety Protection Act (PVPA), 7 U.S.C. § 2321 et seq. I believe that the words "manufacture" or "composition of matter" do not cover these plants. That is because Congress intended the two more specific statutes to exclude patent protection under the Utility Patent Statute for the plants to which the more specific Acts directly refer. And, as the Court implicitly recognizes, this Court neither considered, nor decided, this question in *Diamond v. Chakrabarty*, 447 U.S. 303, 65 L. Ed. 2d 144, 100 S. Ct. 2204 (1980). Consequently, I dissent. . . .

NOTES AND QUESTIONS

1. As the Supreme Court observes, a key difference between the exclusive rights accorded the utility or plant patent holder, and the holder of a plant breeder's certificate, is that the former allows the holder to prevent farmers from replanting seeds. From the standpoint of both seed vendors and farmers, there is clearly a material financial difference depending upon which form of protection is employed. Yet, patents are not a panacea for seed vendors because bringing enforcement actions against individual farmers is expensive and time-consuming, and requires monitoring of individual farmer practices. For this reason, biotechnology enterprises have sought to develop so-called terminator genes, which will physically prevent seeds generated by plants embodying the technology from reproducing. The development and employment of terminator gene technology has been highly controversial because of concerns that the genetic characteristics may inadvertently spread and result in a proliferation of non-reproducing plants.

C. Multilateral Agreements

1. The WTO TRIPS Agreement

There are 150 Members of the WTO, all of which are parties to the TRIPS Agreement. The TRIPS Agreement provisions regarding plant variety protection are therefore the most widely adopted rules in this area. Article 27.1, TRIPS Agreement, obligates Members to extend patent subject matter coverage to all fields of technology. Article 27.3 establishes certain exceptions, including the following:

> 3. Members may also exclude from patentability: . . .
>   (b) plants and animals other than micro-organisms, and essentially biological processes for the production of plants or animals other than non-biological and microbiological processes. However, Members shall provide for the protection of plant varieties either by patents or by an effective *sui generis* system or by any combination thereof. The provisions of this subparagraph shall be reviewed four years after the date of entry into force of the WTO Agreement.

Without doubt, WTO Members may exclude plant varieties from the subject matter scope of patent protection. Many Members make this exclusion. In addition, by reference to "essentially biological processes for the production of plants," Members may exclude traditional cross-breeding and related techniques from the scope of process patent protection. However, if Members do not provide patent protection for plant varieties, they must provide some form of "effective *sui generis* system," alone or in combination with patent protection. We turn to this momentarily.

Members must also provide patent protection for the production of plants through "non-biological and microbiological processes." The language of Article 27.3(b) was adapted from Article 53(b) of the European Patent Convention.[4] There has been substantial debate over the meaning of this requirement. One question is whether genes or gene sequences constitute "microbiological process[es]" that must be subject to patenting. The information contained in genetic structures does not fall within the generally accepted definition of a "micro-organism."[5] Neither genes nor the information in genes is a

---

4. Article 53(b) of the European Patent Convention, however, mandated certain exclusions from patentability, for example, plant and animal varieties, rather than merely allowing such exclusions. It provides:

ARTICLE 53
Exceptions to patentability
European patents shall not be granted in respect of:
(a) inventions the publication or exploitation of which would be contrary to "ordre public" or morality, provided that the exploitation shall not be deemed to be so contrary merely because it is prohibited by law or regulation in some or all of the Contracting States;
(b) plant or animal varieties or essentially biological processes for the production of plants or animals; this provision does not apply to microbiological processes or the products thereof.

5. The Technical Board of Appeal of the European Patent Office has defined "microorganism" as follows:

"According to the current practice of the EPO, the term "microorganism" includes not only bacteria and yeasts, but also fungi, algae, protozoa and human, animal and plant cells, i.e. all generally unicellular organisms with dimensions beneath the limits of vision which can be propagated and manipulated in a laboratory. Plasmids and viruses are also considered to fall under this definition (*cf.* Guidelines for Examination, C-IV, 3.5).

This practice is consistent with the objective teleological interpretation of Article 53(b) EPC, second half-sentence, in particular with the principle of equal treatment (*cf.* paragraph 32 *supra*), and is, therefore, fully acceptable. Furthermore, this practice takes clearly into account the developments of modern industrial microbiology (*cf.*, *for example*, A. Kocková-Kratochvilová, "Characteristics of Industrial-40-T 0356/93 1171.D . . ./ . . . Microorganisms," in "Biotechnology," 1981, Vol. 1, H.-J. Rehm and G. Reed eds., Verlag Chemie, Weinheim, Chapter 1, pages 5 to 71, in particular page 7), fulfilling thereby an objective purpose of Article 53(b) EPC, second half-sentence." (*Plant Genetic Systems/ Patentee v. Greenpeace/Opponent,* T 0356/93–3.3.4, 21 Feb. 1995).

"unicellular organism with dimensions beneath the limits of vision which can be propagated and manipulated in a laboratory." Certain WTO Members have allowed the patenting of elements of the human body isolated from it by technical means (including gene sequences). But this does not mean that such patenting is a requirement of the TRIPS Agreement. The meaning of the terminology adapted from the European Patent Convention was sufficiently ambiguous that the European Union adopted the Biotechnology Directive to address the many unanswered questions.[6] We have previously considered issues of patenting of genetic information in Chapter 2 and do not pursue that further here.

Limiting the discussion to protection of plant varieties, as such, Members may provide effective *sui generis* protection. There is no "common understanding" concerning the appropriate rules for plant variety protection. Some developed countries have argued that compliance with the latest version of the International Convention for the Protection of New Varieties of Plants (the 1991 Act, discussed *infra*) is the only acceptable effective form of *sui generis* protection. However, based on the negotiating history and terms of the TRIPS Agreement, this view is rejected by many Members, including but not limited to a number of developing countries.[7]

Article 27.3(b) of the TRIPS Agreement was adopted subject to review by the TRIPS Council beginning in 1999. That review is ongoing, and includes consideration of the disclosure of source and origin of genetic resources, as discussed in Chapters 1 and 2.

2.   The UPOV Convention

Multilateral efforts toward plant variety protection began with the 1961 Act of the International Convention for the Protection of New Varieties of Plants (UPOV).[8] This was followed by revisions, notably, a 1978 Act, and most recently, a 1991 Act of UPOV. Of 68 UPOV member countries,[9] 22 are party to the 1978 Act and 45 to the 1991 Act.[10]

---

6. See EU Biotechnology Directive:

ARTICLE 5

1. The human body, at the various stages of its formation and development, and the simple discovery of one of its elements, including the sequence or partial sequence of a gene, cannot constitute patentable inventions.

2. An element isolated from the human body or otherwise produced by means of a technical process, including the sequence or partial sequence of a gene, may constitute a patentable invention, even if the structure of that element is identical to that of a natural element.

3. The industrial application of a sequence or a partial sequence of a gene must be disclosed in the patent application.

7. For a more complete discussion, including negotiating texts, *see* UNCTAD/ICTSD Resource Book on TRIPS and Development, at 388-412.

8. Information and texts with respect to UPOV may be found at http://www.upov.int/. The UPOV web site also includes a database of national legislation with respect to plant breeder rights.

9. As of October 22, 2009.

10. The European Community is a party to the 1991 Act in addition to its individual member states.

a. 1991 Act

Under the 1991 Act, a system of plant variety protection should grant a plant "breeder's right" with respect to a "variety" that is "new," "distinct," "uniform," and "stable." These criteria differ from the criteria for the grant of a utility patent.

"Novelty" generally requires that a variety has not been sold or marketed in the country where the application is filed earlier than one year before the filing date. The variety may not have been sold or marketed in the territory of any other UPOV country earlier than four years before that same filing date (and earlier than six years for trees or vines).

"Distinctness" requires that a variety be clearly distinguishable from other commonly known varieties.

"Uniformity" that a variety must be sufficiently uniform in its relevant characteristics, subject to variation that may be expected from its propagation.

"Stability" requires that the relevant characteristics of the variety remain unchanged after repeated propagation.

"Denomination" requires that the variety be given a name that will not be misleading or confusing as to the value of the variety or the identity of the breeder.

Under the 1991 Act, the plant breeder's right extends to seven acts in respect to propagating material of a variety that requires the breeder's authorization: (1) production or reproduction (multiplication); (2) conditioning for the purpose of propagation; (3) offering for sale; (4) selling or other marketing; (5) exporting; (6) importing; and (7) stocking for any of the purposes mentioned in (1) to (6).

The breeder's right is subject to certain limited exceptions (e.g., acts done for experimental purposes). In addition, each party to the 1991 Act of UPOV *may* allow farmers certain privileges with respect to use of protected varieties for reproduction on their farm holdings. Article 15(2) ("Exceptions to the Breeder's Right") provides:

> (2) [Optional exception] Notwithstanding Article 14, each Contracting Party may, within reasonable limits and subject to the safeguarding of the legitimate interests of the breeder, restrict the breeder's right in relation to any variety in order to permit farmers to use for propagating purposes, on their own holdings, the product of the harvest which they have obtained by planting, on their own holdings, the protected variety or a variety covered by Article 14(5)(a)(i) or Article 14(5)(a)(ii).

The duration of the breeder's right must be a minimum of 20 years from the date of grant, and for trees and vines a minimum of 25 years.

The 1991 Act of UPOV provides for a one-year priority period from the date of filing the first application in a UPOV member. It also requires each country party to extend national treatment to persons of other UPOV members.

b. 1978 Act

The 1978 Act of UPOV uses a more general formula than the 1991 Act for the characteristics of plant varieties that are subject to protection. "[T]he variety must be clearly distinguishable by one or more important characteristics from any other variety whose existence is a matter of common knowledge at the time when protection is applied for. . . . The characteristics which permit a variety to be defined and distinguished must be capable of precise recognition and description." (art. 6(1)(a), UPOV 1978).

More important, the exclusive rights granted to the breeder are less extensive. The 1978 Act allows the breeder to prevent:

— the production for purposes of commercial marketing
— the offering for sale
— the marketing

of the reproductive or vegetative propagating material, as such, of the variety. (art. 5(1), UPOV 1978).

There is no prohibition against use of the reproductive material (e.g., seeds) for purposes of reproduction, planting, and harvesting of crops. Thus, parties to the 1978 Act are free to grant farmers' rights with respect to saved seed, without applying the "within reasonable limits and subject to the safeguarding of the legitimate interests of the breeder" constraint of the 1991 Act. Note that the breeders' rights under the 1978 Act are conditioned on commercial marketing or sale of seeds. Farming communities may share seed (i.e., without commercial sale). However, national law may still regulate or restrict such activity.

The breeder's right under the 1978 generally must be a minimum of 15 years from the date of the title of protection (art. 8, 1978 Act).

The reasons why some countries prefer the 1978 Act to the 1991 Act should be apparent. Countries that are net importers of plant varieties (including seed) prefer to allow their farmers wider use (e.g., replanting) of seeds that have already been purchased, and a shorter duration of protection. However, adherence to the 1978 Act is not open to new members.[11] Countries wishing to adhere to UPOV may now only opt for the 1991 Act.

D.   Regional Systems for Plant Variety Protection

1.   The EU System

The EU system for the protection of plant varieties is introduced in the following article by the President of the Community Plant Variety Office (CVPO).

**PLANT VARIETY PROTECTION
IN THE EUROPEAN COMMUNITY**

Bart Kiewiet*

1. INTRODUCTION

If breeders want to prevent the free use by others of the varieties they have developed, they can seek legal (IPR) protection for their varieties in the form of a plant variety right, also called "plant breeders' right." . . .

---

11. *See, e.g.,* UPOV Press Release No. 29, March 24, 1998, available at http://www.upov.int/en/news/pressroom/29.htm.

* World Patent Information 27 (2005) 319-27. The author is president of the Community Plant Variety Office (CPVO).

In the European Community two options for plant variety protection exist: national protection (21 national schemes with national coverage) and protection on the Community level. . . .

2. THE COMMUNITY PLANT VARIETY OFFICE

The Community Plant Variety Office, the CPVO, has been created by Council Regulation (EC) no 2100/94 of 27 July 1994 ("the Basic Regulation") "for the purpose of the implementation of" that regulation. It has its seat in Angers, France.

The core business of the CPVO encompasses:

- The formal examination of applications (article 53).
- The substantive examination of applications (article 54).
- The technical examination of candidate varieties (articles 55-58).
- The refusal of applications (article 61).
- The granting of the Community PVR (article 62).
- The approval of variety denominations (article 63).
- The declaration of nullity of Community PVRs (article 20).
- The cancellation of Community PVRs.

2.1. COMMUNITY AGENCY

The CPVO is a so-called Community agency, a body governed by European public law, distinct from the Community institutions such as Council and Commission, that has its own legal personality and, in the case of the CPVO, its own financial resources. . . .

2.4. THE BOARD OF APPEAL

Within the CPVO organization there has been established a Board of Appeal (article 45). With two exceptions, where a direct appeal to the Court of Justice of the European Communities ("the European Court") is possible, decisions of the CPVO can be challenged before its Board of Appeal. . . .

Against decisions of the Board of Appeal further appeal can be lodged to the European Court (Article 73). This task has been delegated to the Court of first instance. Until now this possibility has not been used by parties that were affected by Board decisions. . . .

3. SUBSTANTIVE MATTERS

3.1. SUBJECT MATTER

The substantive part of the Basic Regulation is based on the 1991 version of the UPOV convention.

The subject matter of a Community plant variety right, is a plant variety. In order to be eligible for protection a variety has to be distinct, uniform and stable (the DUS requirements), new and have an adequate variety denomination. . . .

3.5. RELATION TO NATIONAL SYSTEMS

As said the Community system exists in parallel with the national PVR systems of the EU Member States. All but four of these states have adopted PVR legislation. The national systems are not harmonised and based on different versions of the UPOV convention.

The Community system offers protection on a Community scale. On the basis of one application a Community plant variety right can be obtained that is valid in the territory of all the Member States of the European Community. National protection is limited of course to the territory of the state in question. It is up to the breeder seeking PVR protection in the European Community to decide what type of protection he prefers. If he sees a market for a new variety in more than two Member States the Community option is the logical choice.

As follows from article 92 of the Basic Regulation any variety which is the subject of a Community plant variety right shall not be the subject of a national plant variety right or any patent for that variety. It is nevertheless not prohibited that part of a variety, for instance a gene coding for a disease resistance, is protected by a patent whereas the variety as such is protected with a Community plant variety right.

3.6. THE SCOPE OF THE RIGHT

The scope of Community plant variety rights is to a high degree similar to that of a utility patent even though there are some differences due to the specific nature of plant variety rights. The scope of rights is mentioned in Article 13(2) of the Basic Regulation and includes the exclusive right for the holder to produce and reproduce, condition for the purpose of propagation, sell, market, import and export to the Community and stocking material (variety constituents/harvested material) of the variety. In addition to acts effected in relation to the protected variety itself, acts effected in relation to essentially derived varieties, other indistinct varieties and hybrid varieties dependent on the protected variety for their production may also constitute infringements (Article 13(2) read in conjunction with Article 13(5)).

3.7. DEROGATIONS

There are important derogations of the scope of the right laid down in Articles 14-16. Article 14 sets out the terms for the so-called agricultural exemption (farmers' privilege). This exemption gives farmers the right to use farm saved seed without the consent of the owner (right holder) of the variety in question. However, the farmer, with the exception of small farmers, must pay the holder an equitable remuneration which shall be sensibly lower than the amount charged for the licensed product (Article 14(3)). If the parties can not agree upon the level of the remuneration, such remuneration should be 50% of the amounts charged for the licensed production of propagating material (Article 5 of Council Regulation No 1768/95).

Article 15 of the Basic Regulation excludes from the exclusive rights of the PBR holder "breeding for noncommercial purposes and breeding for the purpose of discovering and developing other varieties" (the breeders exemption). Such a breeders exemption, considered as one of the important characteristics of UPOV style PVP legislation, does not exist as such in respect of patents.

3.8. COMPULSORY LICENSING

In line with the UPOV convention article 29(1) contains the provision that compulsory (exploitation) licences shall be granted only on grounds of public interest.

Recently a new paragraph has been added to this article introducing the possibility of granting a compulsory licence to the holder of a patent for a biotechnological invention incorporated in a protected variety. In order to qualify for such compulsory licence, the patent holder has to demonstrate that: (i) he/she has applied unsuccessfully to the holder of the plant variety right to obtain a contractual licence and (ii) the invention constitutes significant technical progress of considerable economic interest compared with the protected variety.

In the case a holder of a Community plant variety right has been granted — by a competent national patent authority — a compulsory licence for the non-exclusive use of a patented invention incorporated in the protected variety in question, a cross-licence shall be granted, on application, to the holder of the patent (article 29(5a)).

The competent authority for granting such compulsory licences or cross-licences is the CPVO. The new provisions laid down in article 29 as regards (cross) compulsory licences to be granted to patent holders should, as follows from article 12 of the so-called Biotech Directive find their complement in the provisions of national patent legislation in the EU member states containing provisions to grant compulsory licences in respect of patented inventions to holders of Community plant variety rights.

3.9. ENFORCEMENT

Under Community law, there is no legal system in place as regards infringement procedures for plant variety rights. The procedures in such proceedings are governed by national law. However, the Basic Regulation provides some basic conditions regarding civil claims, infringements and jurisdiction (Articles 94-107).

These rules together with the Lugano Convention ensure that there will always be a competent court to deal with infringements of Community plant variety rights (Article 101). Article 103 provides that, where jurisdiction lies with national courts, the rules of procedure of the relevant State governing the same type of action relating to corresponding national property rights shall apply.

Article 105 requires a national court or other body hearing an action relating to a community plant variety right to treat the right as valid. This provision underlines the fact that only the Office is competent with regard to the nullification or cancellation of a Community plant variety right.

Article 107 provides that Member States shall take all appropriate measures to ensure that the same provisions are made applicable to penalize infringements of Community plant rights as apply to the matter of infringements of corresponding national rights. Accordingly, even though the Basic Regulation is silent as regards the sanction of seizure and destruction of infringing material, a holder of a Community plant variety right may ask a national court for such a remedy if such remedy is provided for under national law.

The Basic Regulation states that the holder has a right to a reasonable compensation in case there is an infringement of his rights (Article 94(1)). This is the case even if the infringer was in good faith. However, if it is established that the infringement was carried out intentionally or negligently, the infringer shall be liable to compensate the holder of the CPVR for any further damage resulting from the act of infringement. In cases of slight negligence, such claims may be reduced according to the degree of such slight negligence, but not however to the extent that they are less than the advantage derived there from by the person who committed the infringement (Article 94(2)). Article 95 provides that the holder of a Community plant variety right may require reasonable compensation from any person who has, in the time between publication of the application for a Community plant variety right and grant thereof, affected an act that he would be prohibited from performing subsequent thereto. . . .

4. PROCEDURES

The procedures to be followed and the conditions required in relation to a variety submitted for Community protection can be summarized as follows.

4.1. WHERE TO APPLY?

An application for plant variety protection can be made in any of the twenty official languages of the European Community direct to the CPVO or to one of the national agencies in a Member State, which in turn will take the necessary steps to send it on to the CPVO.

4.2. WHO CAN APPLY?

Any individual or company whose domicile or headquarters is located in the European Union.

Individuals or companies from a state which is a member of the International Union for the protection of new varieties of plants (UPOV) but not a member of the European Union can also apply, provided that an agent domiciled in the Community has been nominated.

4.3. CHECKING THE APPLICATION

When an application is received, the CPVO checks to see that it is complete and eligible and that the variety is novel (see below). If no impediment is found at this stage, the CPVO arranges for a technical examination of the variety submitted.

4.4. TECHNICAL EXAMINATION

The purpose of the technical examination is to ensure that in respect of a candidate variety the criteria of distinctness, uniformity and stability, are complied with. The CPVO does not itself carry out these examinations. They are entrusted to bodies deemed competent by the CPVO Administrative Council. At present more than 20 examination offices have obtained the qualification "competent." The major ones are: the Bundessortenamt in Germany, GEVES in France, NIAB in the UK and the Raad voor het Kwekersrecht in the Netherlands. All the offices performing examinations on behalf of the CPVO render similar services in the framework of national listing and plant variety protection systems.

Examinations have to be conducted in accordance with guidelines laid down by the CPVO. Varieties submitted for protection are compared during the examination with other varieties submitted for Community protection and with appropriate varieties of common knowledge at the time of application.

4.5. GRANT OF TITLE

If the CPVO is of the opinion that the findings of the examination are sufficient to base a decision upon, it decides whether or not to grant a Community plant variety right. In the case of a successful application, the CPVO issues the title holder with a certificate attesting to the grant of protection and a copy of the decision containing an official, detailed description of the variety in question.

In the case, that the examination does not lead to clear conclusions, for instance in respect of the assessment of distinctness, an extension of the examination period, with the same sample, can be ordered. It is the responsibility of the breeder to submit sample material, that meets the relevant conditions in respect of germination, flowering, etc. Only in very exceptional cases the breeder will be offered the possibility to submit a new sample, if the first sample does not perform adequately.

Community protection may be granted as a general rule for twenty-five (25) years, or for thirty (30) years in the case of vines, potatoes and trees. These periods are maxima. For each year of protection an annual fee has to be paid. When the commercial lifetime of a variety is shorter than the maximum protection period, the breeder could decide to give up protection.

4.6. APPEALS

This subject is covered by Section 2.4 above.

4.7. STATUS INFORMATION AND PUBLICITY

Every two months the CPVO publishes an Official Gazette containing all the information appearing in its Registers, in particular applications for protection, proposals for variety denomination and grants of titles. Any other information the CPVO feels the public should be informed about may also be published in the Gazette.

Furthermore the CPVO has created a Website which contains comprehensive information about the Community system. The website contains all the information published in the Gazette. Due to legal restrictions the information published on the web has not yet an official status. Furthermore all relevant legislation, news, texts of presentations can be found on the non-confidential part of the web site.

The CPVO is in close co-operation with UPOV in the process of creating a data base for variety denominations to be fed by all the UPOV Member States. In first instance this data base will only be accessible to authorities within the European Community responsible for national PVR and listing systems. Once the data base is well established it could be made available for all the users of the Community system.

5. THE STATE OF THE SYSTEM . . .

The high number of applications for Community protection (the number of applications received by the CPVO — more than 20,000 — is higher than the sum of the national applications received by the national PVR authorities within the European Community over the same time period) shows that protection on a European scale is an attractive alternative for national protection for those varieties which have an international market. . . .

NOTES AND QUESTIONS

1. The Plant Variety Regulation assures the farmer a right to use saved seed, and except with respect to small farmers, upon payment of the reasonable royalty. Do you think this compensatory model of IP protection might have utility in other fields? Note that systems of copyright protection often make use of compensatory models.

2. The Plant Variety Regulation assures biotechnology patent holders of a license to use a protected variety, and assures the owner of a protected variety a license to use a third-party patent. What are the conditions upon which such licenses are granted? Are these conditions consistent with the provisions of Article 31 of the TRIPS Agreement—which applies only to patents? Does Article 31(l), TRIPS Agreement, apply?

V. THE INTERNATIONAL SYSTEM FOR THE PROTECTION OF TRADE SECRET AND REGULATORY DATA

A. Trade Secret as an IP Form

"Trade secret" or confidential commercial information is traditionally protected in civil and common law countries against misappropriation through dishonest practices. Prior to the TRIPS Agreement, there was no specific multilateral obligation to offer protection for trade secrets. Article 10*bis* of the Paris Convention establishes an obligation to provide protection against unfair competition, but the terms of that article leave some doubt as to whether an obligation to protect trade secrets is created.

A trade secret is generally understood as information with commercial value that has not been publicly disclosed by its holder, and that the holder has taken reasonable steps to protect. Trade secrets may include information as diverse as customer lists, manufacturing processes, and food recipes.

Trade secret and patent protection may be available for the same subject matter, and the inventor of a new product or process usually must choose the more desirable form of protection. The trade secret has two principal advantages compared with the patent. First, there is no limitation on the term of trade secret protection. Its holder is protected against misappropriation for so long as the information remains secret. The term of the patent, by way of contrast, is (generally) 20 years from the date of application. Second, the holder of a trade secret is not required to disclose that information to the public, and is, in fact, precluded from doing so in order to preserve protection. The patenting process, on the other hand, typically mandates disclosure of the invention. Perhaps the most frequently cited example of successful trade secret protection is the holding of the Coca-Cola formula for more than 100 years.

The major disadvantage of trade secret protection, as compared to patent protection, is that trade secret protection does not preclude reverse engineering and use. Anyone may attempt to replicate the information comprising the trade secret, and make use of it. The patent, by way of contrast, precludes independent creators from commercial use of an invention, and effectively precludes reverse engineering. The patent grants its holder the right to exclude others from the market, while the trade secret does not.

For many innovators, the reason for seeking patent protection (even given the limited term) is that the product can be replicated by others once it is made public. Advances in technology continue to improve the opportunities for reverse engineering even in highly technical fields. Pharmaceutical innovators traditionally have opted for patent protection because the chemical formulas for new drugs are usually subject to fairly rapid reverse engineering.

Yet, many industrial companies successfully guard production processes and methods that are critical to their competitive position with trade secret, and its importance as a tool of IP protection should not be underestimated.

KEWANEE OIL v. BICRON CORP.

416 U.S. 470 (1974)

Mr. Chief Justice BURGER delivered the opinion of the Court. . . .

Ohio has adopted the widely relied-upon definition of a trade secret found at Restatement of Torts § 757, comment b (1939). *B. F. Goodrich Co. v. Wohlgemuth*, 117 Ohio App. 493, 498, 192 N. E. 2d 99, 104 (1963); *W. R. Grace & Co. v. Hargadine*, 392 F.2d 9, 14 (CA6 1968). According to the Restatement,

> "[a] trade secret may consist of any formula, pattern, device or compilation of information which is used in one's business, and which gives him an opportunity to obtain an advantage over competitors who do not know or use it. It may be a formula for a chemical compound, a process of manufacturing, treating or preserving materials, a pattern for a machine or other device, or a list of customers."

The subject of a trade secret must be secret, and must not be of public knowledge or of a general knowledge in the trade or business. *B. F. Goodrich Co. v. Wohlgemuth, supra,* at 499, 192 N. E. 2d, at 104; *National Tube Co. v. Eastern Tube Co.,* 3 Ohio C. C. R. (n. s.) 459, 462 (1902), *aff'd,* 69 Ohio St. 560, 70 N. E. 1127 (1903). This necessary element of secrecy is not lost, however, if the holder of the trade secret reveals the trade secret to another "in confidence, and under an implied obligation not to use or disclose it." *Cincinnati Bell Foundry Co. v. Dodds,* 10 Ohio Dec. Reprint 154, 156, 19 Weekly L. Bull. 84 (Super. Ct. 1887). These others may include those of the holder's "employees to whom it is necessary to confide it, in order to apply it to the uses for which it is intended." *National Tube Co. v. Eastern Tube Co., supra,* at 462. Often the recipient of confidential knowledge of the subject of a trade secret is a licensee of its holder. *See Lear, Inc. v. Adkins,* 395 U.S. 653 (1969). The protection accorded the trade secret holder is against the disclosure or unauthorized use of the trade secret by those to whom the secret has been confided under the express or implied restriction of nondisclosure or nonuse. The law also protects the holder of a trade secret against disclosure or use when the knowledge is gained, not by the owner's volition, but by some "improper means," Restatement of Torts § 757 (a), which may include theft, wiretapping, or even aerial reconnaissance. A trade secret law, however, does not offer protection against discovery by fair and honest means, such as by independent invention, accidental disclosure, or by so-called reverse engineering, that is by starting with the known product and working backward to divine the process which aided in its development or manufacture.

Novelty, in the patent law sense, is not required for a trade secret, *W. R. Grace & Co. v. Hargadine*, 392 F.2d, at 14. "Quite clearly discovery is something less than invention." *A. O. Smith Corp. v. Petroleum Iron Works Co.*, 73 F.2d 531, 538 (CA6 1934), *modified to increase scope of injunction*, 74 F.2d 934 (1935). However, some novelty will be required if merely because that which does not possess novelty is usually known; secrecy, in the context of trade secrets, thus implies at least minimal novelty. . . .

Trade secret law and patent law have co-existed in this country for over one hundred years. Each has its particular role to play, and the operation of one does not take away from the need for the other. Trade secret law encourages the development and exploitation of those items of lesser or different invention than might be accorded protection under the patent laws, but which items still have an important part to play in the technological and scientific advancement of the Nation. Trade secret law promotes the sharing of knowledge, and the efficient operation of industry; it permits the individual inventor to reap the rewards of his labor by contracting with a company large enough to develop and exploit it. . . .

NOTES AND QUESTIONS

1. Until 1996, trade secret protection in the United States was largely a matter of state civil law. However, the Economic Espionage Act of 1996 made the theft of trade secrets a federal criminal offense, accompanied by potentially severe civil and criminal penalties (e.g., 18 U.S.C. § 1832). While the criminal offenses may be prosecuted only by federal authorities (and not by private parties in civil litigation), they nonetheless raise the stakes for those who might engage in industrial espionage. We discuss the protection of regulatory data *infra*.

2. Industrial espionage is practiced as businesses seek information about the new products, marketing campaigns, and service promotions of competitors. One of the most widely reported cases of misappropriation of trade secrets involved a senior executive of General Motors who, in accepting a senior position at Volkswagen, took with him extensive information concerning GM's arrangements with its suppliers. *See* Keith Bradsher, *Former G.M. Executive Indicted on Charges of Taking Secrets*, N.Y. Times, May 23, 2000.

3. One of the most difficult problems in trade secret law concerns the treatment of knowledge obtained by employees in the course of their employment. Even if an employee has signed a confidentiality agreement and does not intend to breach a confidence, when that employee goes to work for a rival company in the same field some "secret" information may be indirectly or directly used at the new job. Airtight protection of corporate information could not be maintained without making it difficult for employees to move between jobs. This would result in an inefficient labor market, and it would operate as a serious infringement on personal liberties. Courts have tended to address this problem by requiring the holder of trade secret information to demonstrate the misappropriation of documents or the misuse of specific product information.

4. In notes following the *Universal Studios v. Corley* excerpt, *supra* Chapter 4, section II.C.3, we referred to the decision of the California Court of Appeal in *DVD Copy Control Ass'n v. Bunner* (6th Dist. Cal. App.), 116 Cal. App. 4th 241 (2004) (*request for review by Cal. Sup. Ct. denied,* 2004 Cal. LEXIS 8697 (Cal., Sept. 15, 2004)), which held that Bunner's posting of the DeCSS program on his web site did not violate trade secret rights of the program developer. The Court of Appeal said, *inter alia:*

> DVD CCA urges us, in effect, to ignore the fact that the allegedly proprietary information may have been distributed to a worldwide audience of millions prior to Bunner's first posting. According to DVD CCA, so long as Bunner knew or should have known that the information he was republishing was obtained by improper means, he cannot rely upon the general availability of the information to the rest of the world to avoid application of the injunction to him. In support of this position, DVD CCA contends that the denial of an injunction would offend the public policies underlying trade secret law, which are to enforce a standard of commercial ethics, to encourage research and invention, and to protect the owner's moral entitlement to the fruits of his or her labors. . . . DVD CCA points out that these policies are advanced by making sure that those who misappropriate trade secrets do not avoid "judicial sanction" by making the secret widely available.
>
> The first problem with this argument is that by denying a preliminary injunction the court does not per se protect a wrongdoer from judicial sanction, which in most cases would come following trial on the merits.
>
> (8) Second, the evidence in this case is very sparse with respect to whether the offending program was actually created by improper means. Reverse engineering alone is not improper means. . . . Here the creator is believed to be a Norwegian resident who probably had to breach a Xing license in order to access the information he needed. We have only very thin circumstantial evidence of when, where, or how this actually happened or whether an enforceable contract prohibiting reverse engineering was ever formed.
>
> Finally, assuming the information was originally acquired by improper means, it does not necessarily follow that once the information became publicly available that everyone else would be liable under the trade secret laws for republishing it simply because they knew about its unethical origins. In a case that receives widespread publicity, just about anyone who becomes aware of the contested information would also know that it was allegedly created by improper means. Under DVD CCA's construction of the law, in such a case the general public could theoretically be liable for misappropriation simply by disclosing it to someone else. This is not what trade secret law is designed to do.
>
> (9) It is important to point out that we do not assume that the alleged trade secrets contained in DeCSS became part of the public domain simply by having been published on the Internet. Rather, the evidence demonstrates that in this case, the initial publication was quickly and widely republished to an eager audience so that DeCSS and the trade secrets it contained rapidly became available to anyone interested in obtaining them. Further, the record contains no evidence as to when in the course of the initial distribution of the offending program Bunner posted it. Thus, DVD CCA has not shown a likelihood that it will prevail on the merits of its claim of misappropriation against Bunner. 116 Cal. App. 4th 241, 252-53.

What implications do you see for trade secret protection from the *Bunner* decision?

B. Trade Secret and the TRIPS Agreement

The principal multilateral agreement establishing trade secret norms is the TRIPS Agreement. The TRIPS Agreement accomplishes this by specifying that Article 10*bis* of the Paris Convention applies to "undisclosed information" (art. 39.1, TRIPS Agreement), and then by defining what shall constitute protection of undisclosed information (art. 39.2, *id.*). Article 39.2 provides:

> 2. Natural and legal persons shall have the possibility of preventing information lawfully within their control from being disclosed to, acquired by, or used by others without their consent in a manner contrary to honest commercial practices [Note 10] so long as such information:
>
> (a) is secret in the sense that it is not, as a body or in the precise configuration and assembly of its components, generally known among or readily accessible to persons within the circles that normally deal with the kind of information in question;
>
> (b) has commercial value because it is secret; and
>
> (c) has been subject to reasonable steps under the circumstances, by the person lawfully in control of the information, to keep it secret.
>
> [Note 10] For the purpose of this provision, "a manner contrary to honest commercial practices" shall mean at least practices such as breach of contract, breach of confidence and inducement to breach, and includes the acquisition of undisclosed information by third parties who knew, or were grossly negligent in failing to know, that such practices were involved in the acquisition.

The terms of Article 39.2 are consistent with the traditional treatment of trade secrets in common and civil law countries. Interpretation of Article 39.2 has not been a source of controversy among WTO Members. Recall that the TRIPS Agreement provides flexibility for each Member to implement its requirements in light of their customary practices.

C. Regulatory Data Protection as an IP Form

Governments request or require the submission of data from business enterprises for a wide variety of reasons. Data may be requested (or demanded) for the purpose of:

- investigating allegations of misconduct, such as in the antitrust enforcement context
- the evaluation of merger and acquisition proposals
- in the context of monitoring economic activity
- to assess tax liability, or to assure compliance with securities regulation
- to evaluate whether products meet certain regulatory standards.

In all of these circumstances, the business enterprise may want to protect submitted data against disclosure to competitors.

It is common for national legislation to require government agencies to protect against disclosure data designated by its submitter as confidential business information, except as such disclosure is authorized by law. Disclosure may be authorized for a variety of reasons, including to protect public health or safety or to further a legitimate law enforcement objective.

Data submitted for regulatory purposes may not be "intellectual property" in the ordinary sense of that term, just as information contained in databases may not constitute intellectual property. However, that information may have commercial value because a substantial investment was required to assemble it, and because that information would have commercial value to a competitor who could use the information without repeating its assembly.

Prior to the TRIPS Agreement, there were no multilaterally agreed norms on the protection of data submitted to governments for regulatory purposes.

D.   Regulatory Data and the TRIPS Agreement

Negotiations during the GATT Uruguay Round regarding the protection of regulatory data were highly contentious, and the resulting rules of Article 39.3 have been equally contentious. The following excerpt from the UNCTAD/ICTSD Resource Book on TRIPS and Development introduces the TRIPS Agreement rules.

ARTICLE 39.3

UNCTAD/ICTSD Resource Book on TRIPS and Development*

Members, when requiring, as a condition of approving the marketing of pharmaceutical or of agricultural chemical products which utilize new chemical entities, the submission of undisclosed test or other data, the origination of which involves a considerable effort, shall protect such data against unfair commercial use. In addition, Members shall protect such data against disclosure, except where necessary to protect the public, or unless steps are taken to ensure that the data are protected against unfair commercial use.

3.3.1. Conditions for Protection of Data Submitted for Marketing Approval

A basic premise for the application of Article 39.3 is that a Member imposes an obligation to submit data as a condition to obtain the marketing approval of pharmaceutical or agrochemical products. This provision does not apply when it is not necessary to submit such data, for instance, when marketing approval is granted by the national authority relying on the existence of a prior registration elsewhere.[1034]

The subject matter of the protection under this Article is *undisclosed* information contained in written material which details the results of scientific

---

* UNCTAD/ICTSD Resource Book on TRIPS and Development (2005), available at http://www.iprsonline.org.

1034. In this case the authority does not require test data, but takes its decision on the basis of the registration granted in a foreign country.

health and safety testing of drugs and agrochemicals, in relation to human, animal and plant health, impact on the environment and efficacy of use. This information is not "invented" or "created" but developed according to standard protocols. The protected data may also include manufacturing, conservation and packaging methods and conditions, to the extent that their submission is needed to obtain marketing approval.

The data to be protected must relate to a "new chemical entity." The Agreement does not define what should be meant by "new." Members may apply a concept similar to the one applied under patent law, or consider that a chemical entity is "new" if there were no prior application for approval of the same drug. Article 39.3 does not clarify either whether newness should be absolute (universal) or relative (local).[1035]

Based on the ordinary meaning of the terms used, Article 39.3 would not apply to new uses of known products, nor to dosage forms, combinations, new forms of administration, crystalline forms, isomers, etc., of existing drugs, since there would be no novel chemical entity involved.

Article 39.3 does not define any substantive standard for granting protection (like inventive step or novelty), but simply mandates protection when obtaining the data involved "a considerable effort." The text is vague about the type of effort involved (technical, economic?) and also with respect to its magnitude. (When would it be deemed "considerable"?) The wording used here is broader than that employed in Article 70.4—where reference to "significant investment" is made. A reasonable understanding would be that the "effort" involved should not only be significant in economic terms but also from a technical and scientific point of view, including experimental activities.

3.3.2. Forms of Protection of Data Submitted for Marketing Approval

The protection to be granted under Article 39.3 is twofold: against "unfair commercial use" and against disclosure of the relevant protected information.

Considerable controversy exists about the interpretation of the extent of the obligation to protect against "unfair commercial use." According to one view, the sole or most effective method[1036] for complying with this obligation is by granting the originator of data a period of *exclusive* use thereof, as currently mandated in some developed countries. Under this interpretation, national authorities would not be permitted, during the exclusivity period, to rely on data they have received in order to assess subsequent applications for the registration of similar products.[1037]

1035. *See* T. Cook (2000). *Special Report: The protection of regulatory data in the pharmaceutical and other sectors,* Sweet & Maxwell, London, p. 6.

1036. *See, e.g.,* the Communication from the European Union and its member states on *The relationship between the provisions of the TRIPS Agreement and access to medicines,* IP/C/W/280, 12 June 2001. A similar view is expressed by R. Kampf, *Patents versus Patients?, in* Archiv des Völkerrechts, vol. 40 (2002), pp. 90-234, on p. 120, 121.

1037. The rationale behind this position is that "equity demands that protection be provided for data, which can cost the original submitter several million dollars to produce. Disclosing this data to the public or allowing its use by another applicant unfairly denies the compiler of the data the value of its efforts and grants an economic advantage to later applicants for marketing approval, enabling them to avoid the cost of developing test data for their own products. Countries that allow such unfair advantages to later applicants discourage developers of new

According to another view, Article 39.3 does not require the recognition of exclusive rights, but protection in the framework of unfair competition rules. Thus, a third party should be prevented from using the results of the test undertaken by another company as background for an independent submission for marketing approval, if the respective data had been acquired through dishonest commercial practices. However, under that provision a governmental authority would not be prevented from relying on the data presented by one company to assess submissions by other companies relating to similar products. If the regulatory body were not free, when assessing a file, to use all the knowledge available to it, including data from other files, a great deal of repetitive toxicological and clinical investigation will be required, which will be wasteful and ethically questionable. This position is also grounded on the pro-competitive effects of low entry barriers for pharmaceutical product. The early entry of generic competition is likely to increase the affordability of medicines at the lowest possible price.[1038]

On the other hand, protection is to be ensured against disclosure of the confidential data by governmental authorities, subject to the two exceptions mentioned in Article 39.3: a) when disclosure is necessary to protect the public; and b) when steps are taken to ensure that the data will not be used in a commercially unfair manner. Under these exceptions, disclosure may be permissible, for example, to allow a compulsory licensee to obtain a marketing approval, particularly when the license is aimed at remedying anti-competitive practices or at satisfying public health needs.

NOTES AND QUESTIONS

1. Rules regarding protection of data submitted for regulatory purposes may have profound effect on the functioning of the pharmaceuticals market. Innovator companies invest substantial sums in conducting clinical trials of new medicines and pursuing approval of those medicines with regulatory agencies such as the U.S. Food and Drug Administration. These innovator companies seek to protect their investment in the clinical trial process. Generic pharmaceutical producers submit applications for approval of copies of innovator medicines based on demonstrating "bioequivalence." That is, the generic producer need only demonstrate that its product is essentially the same as the innovator drug. It would be unethical to require generic producers to conduct redundant clinical trials because some of the test subjects receive placebo rather than therapy. Moreover, redundant clinical testing would be a waste of financial resources. Establishing the proper scope of protection for regulatory data in the pharmaceutical sector

---

pharmaceuticals and agricultural chemicals from seeking to introduce their state-of-the-art products in the country's market. So, not only is such protection required by the TRIPS Agreement, it is both equitable and wise from a public and health policy standpoint." *See* C. Priapantja, (2000), *Trade Secret: How does this apply to drug registration data?* Paper presented at "ASEAN Workshop on the TRIPS Agreement and its Impact on Pharmaceuticals," Department of Health and World Health Organization, May 2-4, p. 4.

1038. *See* Carlos Correa, *Protection of Data Submitted for the Registration of Pharmaceuticals: Implementing the Standards of the TRIPS Agreement*, South Centre, Geneva 2002 (available at http://www.southcentre.org/publications/protection/toc.htm).

involves striking a balance between the interests of the innovator companies in protecting investment and the interests of the general public in more rapid access to low-priced medicines. There are very large sums of money at stake in the debate over the appropriate level of protection for regulatory data in the pharmaceutical sector.

2. Similar issues arise in other regulatory sectors. For example, when the U.S. Environmental Protection Agency assesses the safety of industrial chemicals, the producer of those chemicals submits data regarding production processes. That data is of interest to competitors, but it is also of interest to nongovernmental organizations seeking to assess potential environmental impact. Should the government have a monopoly over assessment of environmental risk? How can data be made accessible to public interest groups but at the same time be protected against "unfair commercial use" by competitors?

E.   *Regional Systems for the Protection of Regulatory Data*

1.   Protection of Regulatory Data in the European Union

The *AKZO* case is the landmark decision in EU law concerning the obligation of the EC Commission to treat business secrets as confidential. In this case, the Commission asked for several sensitive documents in a competition law investigation. AKZO was obliged to produce these documents to the Commission by former Article 213 of the EC Treaty (now Article 284) as well as the corresponding provisions of Regulation No. 17 dealing with competition procedure. Later, the Commission communicated some of the documents to the intervener and only informed AKZO afterwards. In considering if this behavior of the Commission was correct, the Court of Justice of the European Union interpreted the secrecy obligation of the Commission in relation to the rights of third parties of access to the file, and it implemented a high-level duty to protect business secrets.

**AKZO CHEMIE BV AND AKZO CHEMIE UK LTD. v.
COMMISSION OF THE EUROPEAN COMMUNITIES**

Judgment of the Court (Fifth Chamber) of 24 June 1986
Case 53/85
Court of Justice of the European Communities

Prior history: application requesting the Court to declare void the decision of the Commission of the European Communities of 14 December 1984 concerning the communication to a third party of documents stated to be confidential, disposition: on those grounds, the Court (fifth chamber) hereby:

(1) Declares void the decision which the Commission notified to the applicant by letter of 18 December 1984;

(2) Dismisses the remainder of the application;

(3) Orders the Commission to pay the costs.

Introduction: In case 53/85

AKZO Chemie BV . . .

vs.

Commission of the European Communities . . .

Application requesting the Court to declare void the decision of the Commission of the European Communities of 14 December 1984 concerning the communication to a third party of documents stated to be confidential. . . .

Judgment by: JOLIET

JUDGMENT:

By an application lodged at the Court registry on 22 February 1985, AKZO Chemie BV and AKZO Chemie UK Ltd., whose registered offices are at Amersfoort (Netherlands) and Walton-on-Thames (United Kingdom) respectively, brought an action under the second paragraph of Article 173 of the EEC Treaty requesting the Court to declare void the Commission's decision of 18 December 1984 to communicate documents of a confidential nature to a third party who had submitted a complaint.

AKZO Chemie BV and AKZO Chemie UK Ltd. are part of the AKZO group which is the largest supplier in the Community of benzoyl peroxide, a chemical product which is used in the making of plastics and as a bleach for the treatment of flour. . . .

AKZO is alleged to have threatened to force ECS from the flour additives market through a policy of selective, abnormally low prices if ECS extended its activities to the market in organic peroxides for the plastics industry and to have actually carried out that threat. On 15 June 1982 ECS made a complaint to the Commission alleging an infringement of Article 86 of the EEC Treaty. As a result of that complaint, officials of the Commission carried out an investigation in December 1982 at the offices of AKZO Chemie BV and of AKZO Chemie UK Ltd. under Article 14(3) of Regulation No. 17/62. On that occasion the officials obtained various documents belonging to AKZO. . . .

On 14 December 1984 the Commission communicated to ECS certain annexes to the statement of objections and only informed AKZO that it had done so in a letter of 18 December 1984. In its letter, the Commission emphasized that it was for it to decide whether or not documents were confidential. It stated that it had followed the list drawn up by AKZO with a few exceptions in regard to which it provided a brief explanation.

By an application lodged at the Court registry on 22 February 1985, AKZO brought an action for a declaration that the Commission's decision to transmit certain confidential documents to ECS was void. In its application AKZO also sought an order from the Court requiring the Commission to demand ECS to return the documents transmitted to it.

By order of 10 July 1985, the Court granted ECS leave to intervene in the proceedings in support of the Commission's conclusions.

ADMISSIBILITY OF THE ACTION . . .

It is certainly true that the documents were transmitted with a view to facilitating the examination of the case. However, the measure adversely affecting the applicant is, as is clear from the foregoing paragraphs, the decision in which the Commission considered that the documents in question did not qualify for the confidential treatment guaranteed by Community law and could therefore be communicated. That measure is definitive in nature and is independent of any decision on the question whether Article 86 [now Article 82] of the Treaty has been infringed. The opportunity which the applicant has to bring an action against a final decision establishing that the competition rules have been infringed is not of such a nature as to provide it with an adequate degree of protection of its rights in the matter. On the one hand, it is possible that the administrative procedure will not result in a decision finding that an infringement has been committed. On the other hand, if an action is brought against that decision, it will not in any event provide the applicant with the means of preventing the irreversible consequences which would result from improper disclosure of certain of its documents.

AKZO's interest in contesting the decision in question cannot be denied on the ground that in this case the decision had already been implemented at the time when the action was brought. The annulment of such a decision is of itself capable of having legal consequences, in particular by preventing a repetition by the Commission of the practice complained of and by rendering unlawful the use by ECS of any documents improperly communicated to it.

It follows that the applicant's claim for a declaration that the contested decision is void is admissible. . . .

SUBSTANCE OF THE CASE

The applicant puts forward three submissions in support of its application. In the first place, it alleges that by communicating to ECS certain documents which were all in some way confidential, the Commission acted in breach of its obligation not to disclose information which is covered by the obligation of professional secrecy or which is subject to protection as a business secret. In the second place, by communicating to ECS certain documents which the latter could use in the legal proceedings pending in the [U]nited [K]ingdom, the Commission infringed Article 20(1) of Regulation No. 17/62 which provides that information acquired by the Commission in the exercise of its powers of investigation may be used only for the purpose for which it was obtained. Finally, the Commission has infringed Article 185 [now Article 242] of the Treaty inasmuch as, by implementing its decision before notifying it to the applicant, it deprived the latter of the possibility of applying for an order suspending the operation of that decision at the same time as it instituted proceedings for annulment.

The Commission, with whose arguments the intervener essentially agrees, considers first of all that documents constituting evidence of an infringement of Article 86 of the Treaty, such as those communicated to ECS, are not of a confidential nature. It goes on to emphasize that ECS was given access to the documents only on the express condition that it would not use them for any purpose other than the proceedings before the Commission. Finally, it denies that there was any infringement of Article 185 of the Treaty because it did not adopt any decision which could be the subject of an application for annulment.

In the first place, it must be borne in mind that Article 214 [now Article 287] of the Treaty requires the officials and other servants of the institutions of the Community not to disclose information in their possession of the kind covered by the obligation of professional secrecy. Article 20 of Regulation No. 17/62, which implements that provision in regard to the rules applicable to undertakings, contains in paragraph (2) a special provision worded as follows: "without prejudice to the provisions of Articles 19 and 21, the Commission and the competent authorities of the member states, their officials and other servants shall not disclose information acquired by them as a result of the application of this Regulation and of the kind covered by the obligation of professional secrecy."

The provisions of Articles 19 and 21, the application of which is thus reserved, deal with the Commission's obligations in regard to hearings and the publication of decisions. It follows that the obligation of professional secrecy laid down in Article 20(2) is mitigated in regard to third parties on whom Article 19(2) confers the right to be heard, that is to say in regard, in particular, to a third party who has made a complaint. The Commission may communicate to such a party certain information covered by the obligation of professional secrecy in so far as it is necessary to do so for the proper conduct of the investigation.

However, that power does not apply to all documents of the kind covered by the obligation of professional secrecy. Article 19(3) which provides for the publication of notices prior to the granting of negative clearance or exemptions, and Article 21 which provides for the publication of certain decisions, both require the Commission to have regard to the legitimate interest of undertakings in the protection of their business secrets. Business secrets are thus afforded very special protection. Although they deal with particular situations, those provisions must be regarded as the expression of a general principle which applies during the course of the administrative procedure. It follows that a third party who has submitted a complaint may not in any circumstances be given access to documents containing business secrets. Any other solution would lead to the unacceptable consequence that an undertaking might be inspired to lodge a complaint with the Commission solely in order to gain access to its competitors' business secrets.

It is undoubtedly for the Commission to assess whether or not a particular document contains business secrets. After giving an undertaking an opportunity to state its views, the Commission is required to adopt a decision in that connection which contains an adequate statement of the reasons on which it is based and which must be notified to the undertaking concerned. Having regard to the extremely serious damage which could result from improper communication of documents to a competitor, the Commission must, before implementing its decision, give the undertaking an opportunity to bring an action before the Court with a view to having the assessments made reviewed by it and to preventing disclosure of the documents in question.

In this case, the Commission gave the undertaking concerned an opportunity to make its position known and adopted a decision containing an adequate statement of the reasons on which it was based and concerning both the confidential nature of the documents at issue and the possibility of communicating them. At the same time, however, by an act which cannot be severed from that decision, the Commission decided to hand over the documents to the third party who had made the complaint even before it notified its findings to that undertaking. It thus made it impossible for the undertaking to avail itself of the means of redress provided by Article 173 [now Article 230] in conjunction with Article 185 of the Treaty with a view to preventing the implementation of a contested decision.

That being the case, the decision which the Commission notified to the applicant by letter of 18 December 1984 must be declared void without there being any need to determine whether the documents communicated to the intervener did in fact contain business secrets.

NOTES AND QUESTIONS

1. Article 287 (formerly Article 214) of the EC Treaty provides:

> The members of the institutions of the Community, the members of committees, and the officials and other servants of the Community shall be required, even after their duties have ceased, not to disclose information of the kind covered by the obligation of professional secrecy, in particular information about undertakings, their business relations or their cost components.

2. Pharmaceutical Regulatory Data in the European Union

The European Union has increasingly taken over regulation of the internal pharmaceuticals market from its member states. In 1992, the European Union adopted a regulation providing for the extension of the term of pharmaceutical patents to compensate for the period during which regulatory approval for a medicine covered by the patent was sought.[12] The patent holder is issued a "supplementary protection certificate" or "SPC," which extends the effective term of the patent. The period of supplementary protection may not be greater than five years.[13]

In 2004, in connection with the establishment of a European Medicines Agency responsible for approval of the marketing of medicines throughout the European Union,[14] the European Union adopted a common standard of data exclusivity.[15] This new system is referred to as the $8 + 2 + 1$ system. Amendments to the Community Code on Medicinal Products provide that a generic producer may seek approval of a bioequivalent product eight years following authorization of an innovator "reference" product, and in doing so may rely on the data submitted in connection with approval of the reference

---

12. Council Regulation (EEC) No 1768/92 of 18 June 1992 concerning the creation of a supplementary protection certificate for medicinal products, OJ L 182, 02/07/1992 P. 0001-0005.

13. Id., at Article 13, providing:

Duration of the certificate
   1. The certificate shall take effect at the end of the lawful term of the basic patent for a period equal to the period which elapsed between the date on which the application for a basic patent was lodged and the date of the first authorization to place the product on the market in the Community reduced by a period of five years.
   2. Notwithstanding paragraph 1, the duration of the certificate may not exceed five years from the date on which it takes effect.

14. Regulation (EC) No 726/2004 of the European Parliament and of the Council of 31 March 2004 laying down Community procedures for the authorisation and supervision of medicinal products for human and veterinary use and establishing a European Medicines Agency, OJ L 136/1, 30/4/2004.

15. Directive 2004/27/EC of the European Parliament and of the Council of 31 March 2004 amending Directive 2001/83/EC on the Community code relating to medicinal products for human use, OJ L 136/34, 30/4/2004 (Community Code Amendments).

product.[16] However, even if approval is granted earlier, the generic product may not be placed on the market until ten years following initial authorization of the "reference" product.[17] There is thus a ten-year period of marketing exclusivity in favor of the innovator product. In addition, a one-year period may be added to the ten-year marketing exclusivity period if, during the first eight years of that period, "the marketing authorization holder obtains an authorisation for one or more new therapeutic indications which, during the scientific evaluation prior to their authorisation, are held to bring a significant clinical benefit in comparison with existing therapies."[18]

All countries newly acceding to the European Union must accept the foregoing rules regarding marketing exclusivity. This has proven difficult and controversial for countries such as Hungary, which housed a successful and dynamic generic pharmaceutical sector prior to joining the European Union.

F.　Bilateral and Regional Trade Agreements and the Protection of Regulatory Data

At the urging of U.S. research-based pharmaceutical companies, the United States Trade Representative has pursued a policy of demanding extensive commitments for the protection of pharmaceutical regulatory data in bilateral and regional trade agreement negotiations. Other aspects of the FTA program are described in another excerpt from the World Bank Trade Note by Fink and Reichenmiller (see also Chapter 1, section IV.D, Chapter 4, section IV, and Chapter 6, section IV).

TIGHTENING TRIPS: THE INTELLECTUAL PROPERTY PROVISIONS OF RECENT US FREE TRADE AGREEMENTS

Carsten Fink & Patrick Reichenmiller*

. . . [O]btaining marketing approval for drugs requires the submission of test data on a drug's safety and efficacy to regulatory authorities. Such data is protected by separate legal instruments that differ from country to country. The TRIPS Agreement only requires test data to be protected against "unfair commercial use." By contrast, most of the bilateral agreements explicitly mandate test data exclusivity, as provided for under US law. Once a company has submitted original test data, no competing manufacturer is allowed to rely on these data for a period of five years to request marketing approval for its own drug. The new compilation of comparable test data by competing manufacturers may take several years and may be prohibitively expensive. Thus, test data exclusivity may pose a second obstacle for governments to effectively use compulsory licensing.

Several of the bilateral agreements go further on data exclusivity. When pharmaceutical companies seek marketing approval for previously unapproved uses of already registered drugs, regulatory authorities typically require

---

16. Art. 10(1), Community Code, as amended.
17. *Id.*
18. *Id.*
* World Bank Trade Note No. 20, Feb. 7, 2005.

the submission of "new" clinical information. The agreements with Morocco and Bahrain provide for an additional 3 year data exclusivity period triggered by such new clinical information. Drugs benefiting from this type of marketing exclusivity do not only include new patented products, but also older generic products for which the patents have expired (though generic competition for previously approved uses of such drugs would remain unaffected).

Sometimes drug regulatory authorities recognize the marketing approval decisions of foreign regulators in granting marketing approval for the same product at home. The intellectual property chapter of the US-Singapore Agreement mandates, in this case, that foreign data exclusivity also applies at home. In other words, no competing manufacturer is allowed to rely on the test data submitted to a *foreign* regulator for seeking own marketing approval at home.

The agreements with Australia, Bahrain, and the DR-CAFTA countries are still more far reaching on the cross-border application of data exclusivity. Even if regulatory authorities do not recognize foreign marketing approvals, competing manufacturers are prevented from using test data submitted to a drug regulatory agency in another territory. In other words, test data exclusivity applies automatically in all FTA jurisdictions, once a company submits test data to a drug regulator in one territory — even outside the FTA area. . . .

Are the provisions on marketing approval during the patent term, test data exclusivity, and parallel importation at odds with the Doha Declaration on TRIPS and Public Health? This Declaration — issued at the WTO Ministerial Meeting in Doha, Qatar in 2001 — recognized the gravity of the public health problems afflicting many developing countries and least developing countries. Among other things, it reaffirmed the right of WTO members to use the flexibilities of TRIPS in the area of compulsory licensing and parallel importation to ". . . *promote access to medicines for all.*" Moreover, in August 2003, WTO members created a special mechanism under the TRIPS Agreement that allows countries with insufficient manufacturing capacity to effectively use compulsory licenses by importing generic drugs (*see* Fink, 2003). Technically, the Doha Declaration and the August 2003 Decision by WTO members do not address questions of marketing approval during the patent term and test data exclusivity. However, the provisions of the FTAs in these areas can still be seen as being at odds with the spirit of these multilateral accords, to the extent that they preclude the effective use of compulsory licenses.

In side letters to the US-DR-CAFTA, US-Morocco and US-Bahrain agreements, the respective governments shared understandings that the intellectual property chapters do not affect their ability to ". . . *take necessary measures to protect public health by promoting medicines for all* [. . .]." In a recent letter to a Member of the US Congress on the US-Morocco FTA, the General Counsel of the United States Trade Representative (USTR) further clarified:

> [. . .], if circumstances ever arise in which a drug is produced under a compulsory license, and it is necessary to approve that drug to protect public health or effectively utilize the TRIPS/health solution, the data protection provision in the FTA would not stand in the way.
>
> [. . .]. As stated in the side letter, the letter constitutes a formal agreement between the Parties. It is, thus, a significant part of the interpretive context for this agreement and not merely rhetorical. According to Article 31 of the Vienna Convention on the Law of Treaties, which reflects customary rules of treaty interpretation in international law, the terms of a treaty must be interpreted "in their

context," and that "context" includes "any agreement relating to the treaty which was made between all the parties in connection with the conclusion of the treaty."

At the same time, the US Government does not view the side letters as creating any kind of exemption that would allow parties to the FTAs to ignore obligations in the agreements' intellectual property chapters. The side letters merely signal the signing governments' belief that the intellectual property rules of the FTAs will not interfere with the protection of public health.

NOTES AND QUESTIONS

1. The U.S. PhRMA campaign to promote stronger data protection and marketing exclusivity rules is not limited to developing countries. Canada and Israel were the subject of aggressive complaint from the U.S. Trade Representative for many years, and each has recently adopted an approach to protection of pharmaceutical regulatory data more consistent with U.S. preferences.

2. India is home to the developing world's most successful generic pharmaceutical sector. Having revised its patent legislation in 2005 to comply with its January 1, 2005 obligation to provide pharmaceutical product patent protection, India is under pressure from Europe and the United States to adopt a new approach to protection of regulatory data.

   In addition to seeking pharmaceutical regulatory data-based marketing exclusivity in bilateral and regional trade negotiations, the United States also bargains for such exclusivity when countries seek to join the WTO. China, for example, agreed to provide a six-year period of pharmaceutical marketing exclusivity in connection with its accession in 2001. Paragraph 284 of the Report of the Working Party on the Accession of China, WT/ACC/CHN/49, 1 Oct. 2001, provides:

   > The representative of China further confirmed that China would, in compliance with Article 39.3 of the TRIPS Agreement, provide effective protection against unfair commercial use of undisclosed test or other data submitted to authorities in China as required in support of applications for marketing approval of pharmaceutical or of agricultural chemical products which utilized new chemical entities, except where the disclosure of such data was necessary to protect the public, or where steps were taken to ensure that the data are protected against unfair commercial use. This protection would include introduction and enactment of laws and regulations to make sure that no person, other than the person who submitted such data, could, without the permission of the person who submitted the data, rely on such data in support of an application for product approval for a period of at least six years from the date on which China granted marketing approval to the person submitting the data. During this period, any second applicant for market authorization would only be granted market authorization if he submits his own data. This protection of data would be available to all pharmaceutical and agricultural products which utilize new chemical entities, irrespective of whether they were patent-protected or not. The Working Party took note of these commitments.

   The commitment in paragraph 284 of the Working Party Report should be read in conjunction with paragraph 342 of the report, and Article 1(3) of the Protocol of Accession, WT/L/432, 23 Nov. 2001, which together establish the legally binding nature of the commitment.

3. Why are pharmaceutical companies not satisfied with the protection for inventions provided by patents? What are the advantages provided by regulatory marketing exclusivity?

VI. THE INTERNATIONAL SYSTEM FOR THE PROTECTION OF INDUSTRIAL DESIGN AND INTEGRATED CIRCUIT LAYOUT DESIGN

A. Design Protection as an IP Form

The design of products, whether purely artistic or commercially useful, creates appeal for the consumer. Product design is particularly important in industries whose products are not readily differentiated on the basis of technical performance. A "designer" blouse may serve precisely the function as a plain cotton T-shirt, but consumers pay more for the designer blouse because they appreciate its aesthetic elements.

Design has an inherent relationship with function. On the one hand, design possibilities are limited by function. At a certain stage, extravagance or fantasy in design can impede function. There may be endless ways to conceive of the design of a shoe or airplane, but not all of them will result in a functional piece of footwear or a vehicle that flies. On the other hand, design can facilitate function. Certain designs of automobiles take advantage of aerodynamics and decrease air resistance to increase speed or reduce fuel consumption.

The protection of industrial designs has long been problematic. The traditional forms of IP protection — copyright, patent, and trademark — may be applicable in many cases, but their application poses problems.

Copyright protects the creative expression of artists and authors, and is not limited in respect to the media in which such expression may be embodied. Yet, copyright does not protect function or idea, and courts have faced seemingly intractable difficulties in devising methodologies for separating form from function. In addition, because designs in many fields (such as fashion) tend to be similar, it is difficult to act against "similar" works. Also, copyright does not protect against independent creation and, particularly in the international context, proving that a second-comer "copied" raises an evidentiary hurdle.

A "utility patent" may protect a functional design. However, the criteria of novelty, inventive step, and usefulness may be difficult to meet, particularly in the realm of incremental design changes. Moreover, obtaining a utility patent, particularly for a number of countries, is a costly and time-consuming enterprise. For industries where design changes are routinely introduced to stimulate consumer demand — such as textiles and automobiles — the cost and administrative obstacles to using the utility patent for protection may be insurmountable in all but rare cases.

Trademarks protect distinctive signs, and in some countries (such as the United States) trademark protection has been extended broadly to cover "trade dress," including product and packaging design. However, as with copyright, trademark (and trade dress) does not extend to function, and courts also have difficulty separating trademark-related design and function. Also, since countries follow substantially different approaches to trade dress, relying on this approach internationally presents problems.

To address the obstacles inherent in applying copyright, (utility) patent, and trademark to industrial designs, some countries have adopted approaches more uniquely suited to this subject matter. The United States has a system for the grant of "design patents" that are similar to utility patents, except that instead of demonstrating the "usefulness" of a novel design, the applicant must show that its design is "ornamental" or nonfunctional (and the term of protection is limited to 14 years). More commonly, however, countries have adopted systems of design "registration" that do not include substantive examination and that employ standards of novelty less stringent than those for patents. We will take a look at the EU registration system.

In *Best Lock v. Ilco*, the U.S. Court of Appeals for the Federal Circuit addresses the tension between form and function in relation to design patent protection. The differing views of the majority and dissent illustrate the difficulty regulators have encountered in drawing the boundaries of design protection.

BEST LOCK v. ILCO UNICAN
94 F.3d 1563 (Fed. Cir. 1996)

Lourie, Circuit Judge.

Best Lock Corporation appeals from the final decision of the United States District Court for the Southern District of Indiana in which the court held that Best Lock's U.S. Design Patent 327,636 was invalid. *Best Lock Corp. v. Ilco Unican Corp.*, 896 F. Supp. 836, 36 U.S.P.Q.2D (BNA) 1527 (S.D. Ind. 1995). Because the court did not clearly err in finding that the claimed design was functional and hence not ornamental, we affirm.

Background

This case involves a design patent for a key "blade." A typical key consists of a bow, which allows the user to turn the key in a corresponding lock, and a blade, which is the portion of the key inserted into the lock's keyway. When a key is manufactured, the key blade is "blank," i.e., the blade has not been cut or "bitted" with the combination required to operate the corresponding lock. Although a blank key blade will not operate the lock, the profile of the key blade is manufactured to fit into the corresponding lock's keyway. Subsequently, the blank key blade is cut to match the corresponding lock's combination.

In the replacement key market, a locksmith or a retail store with a key duplicating facility stocks blank key blades with various key profiles. . . . [T]he locksmith or retailer cuts the blade of the key blank with the combination required to operate the lock.

Best Lock manufactures and sells locks and keys used to maintain security at industrial, commercial, and institutional facilities. At these facilities, it is often feared that the keys used in their locks may readily be duplicated. Consequently, key and lock manufacturers, including Best Lock, have attempted to restrict unauthorized access to duplicate key blanks by obtaining utility or design patent protection on the keys. By obtaining patent protection, a company hopes to control the market for duplicate key blanks during the life of the patent.

Best Lock is the assignee of the two patents that were at issue before the district court, U.S. Patent 5,136,869 and U.S. Design Patent 327,636. The '869 patent, entitled "High Security Key and Cylinder Lock Assembly," claims an improved key blade and cylinder lock assembly that provides a wider key profile than standard keys and includes other features to deter lock picking. The '636 patent, entitled "Portion of a Key Blade Blank," claims the ornamental design for the operative portion of a key blade blank. . . . The '636 patent is the only design patent at issue on appeal. . . .

Ilco manufactures duplicate and replacement key blanks for existing locks. It sells its replacement key blanks to locksmiths and replacement key retailers. In 1993, Ilco copied the design of a Best Lock key, which had a key blade shaped like the design shown in the '636 patent. It subsequently distributed key blanks with that key blade shape at the annual convention of the Associated Locksmiths of America. In response, Best sued Ilco, alleging, *inter alia*, infringement of the '636 design patent and the '869 utility patent. Ilco counterclaimed, seeking a declaratory judgment of invalidity and noninfringement of both patents.

After a ten-day bench trial, the district court held that the '869 patent claims were invalid under 35 U.S.C. § 102 because the claims were anticipated by the prior art. *Best Lock Corp. v. Ilco Unican Corp.*, 896 F. Supp. 836, 837, 36 U.S.P.Q.2D (BNA) 1527, 1528 (S.D. Ind. 1995). Best Lock has not appealed that holding. The court also held that the '636 design patent was invalid. In particular, the court found that Best Lock's key blades were not "a matter of ornamental concern to the purchaser or the user." *Id.* at 843, 36 U.S.P.Q.2D (BNA) at 1534. The court further found that the design patent was invalid because the shape of the blank key blade was dictated by its function. *Id.* Best Lock appeals, challenging the district court's decision regarding the '636 patent.

DISCUSSION

Under 35 U.S.C. § 171, a design patent may be granted for a "new, original and ornamental design for an article of manufacture." However, if the design claimed in a design patent is dictated solely by the function of the article of manufacture, the patent is invalid because the design is not ornamental. *See Bonito Boats, Inc. v. Thunder Craft Boats, Inc.*, 489 U.S. 141, 148, 9 U.S.P.Q.2D (BNA) 1847, 1851, 103 L. Ed. 2d 118, 109 S. Ct. 971 (1989) ("To qualify for protection, a design must present an aesthetically pleasing appearance that is not dictated by function alone, and must satisfy the other criteria of patentability."); *see also In re Carletti*, 51 C.C.P.A. 1094, 328 F.2d 1020, 1022, 140 U.S.P.Q. (BNA) 653, 654 (CCPA 1964) ("It has long been settled that when a configuration is the result of functional considerations only, the resulting design is not patentable as an ornamental design for the simple reason that it is not 'ornamental'—was not created for the purpose of ornamenting."). A design is not dictated solely by its function when alternative designs for the article of manufacture are available. *See L.A. Gear, Inc. v. Thom McAn Shoe Co.,* 988 F.2d 1117, 1123, 25 U.S.P.Q.2D (BNA) 1913, 1917 (Fed. Cir.), *cert. denied,* 510 U.S. 908, 114 S. Ct. 291, 126 L. Ed. 2d 240 (1993). We review for clear error the district court's determination that the design claimed in the '636 patent is functional. *See id.* at 1124, 25 U.S.P.Q.2D (BNA) at 1917.

On appeal, Best Lock argues that the court erred in holding the '636 design patent invalid as being directed solely to a functional design. As support, it asserts that although a particular key and its corresponding lock must mate to operate the lock, an unlimited number of key blade and corresponding keyway designs are available. Choice of any particular design is arbitrary. Thus, Best Lock maintains that the key blade blank may have any number of different shapes and is therefore not dictated solely by functional concerns.

We disagree. The design shown in the claim of the '636 patent is limited to a blank key blade as shown in Figures 1-5 of the patent. Best Lock did not claim a design for the entire key.[2] See 37 C.F.R. § 1.153 (1995) (The claim of a design patent "shall be in formal terms to the ornamental design for the article . . . as shown, or as shown and described.") (emphasis added). The parties do not dispute that the key blade must be designed as shown in order to perform its intended function—to fit into its corresponding lock's keyway. An attempt to create a key blade with a different design would necessarily fail because no alternative blank key blade would fit the corresponding lock. In fact, Best Lock admitted that no other shaped key blade would fit into the corresponding keyway, and it presented no evidence to the contrary. Therefore, we find no clear error in the court's finding that the claimed key blade design was dictated solely by the key blade's function. Any aesthetic appeal of the key blade design shown in the '636 patent is the inevitable result of having a shape that is dictated solely by functional concerns.

Further, Best Lock's assertion that a variety of possible shapes of interfaces between keys and locks exists does not compel a different result. Clearly, different interfaces between key blades and corresponding lock keyways can be designed to permit the combination to function as a lock and key set. However, Best Lock's patent does not claim the combination of a lock and corresponding key. Instead, the claim in the '636 design patent is limited to a key blade, which must be designed as shown in the '636 patent in order to perform its intended function.

Moreover, the fact that Best Lock also has a design patent on the keyway that mates with the key blade shown in the '636 patent does not alter our analysis. The existence of a separate patent on the keyway is irrelevant to the construction of the '636 patent claim and to the ultimate determination that the claimed design is dictated solely by function. *See Elmer v. ICC Fabricating, Inc.,* 67 F.3d 1571, 1577, 36 U.S.P.Q.2D (BNA) 1417, 1421 (Fed. Cir. 1995) (construing design patent as limited to the article of manufacture "as shown and described"

---

2. As our predecessor court previously held, a design for an article of manufacture may be embodied in less than all of an article of manufacture . . . at *In re Zahn,* 617 F.2d 261, 267, 204 U.S.P.Q. (BNA) 988, 994 (CCPA 1980).

in the patent). The validity of a patent must be evaluated based on what it claims rather than on the totality of the claims of multiple patents.

For the foregoing reasons, the district court's finding that the claimed design is solely governed by functional concerns is not clearly erroneous. Consequently, we affirm its resulting conclusion that the '636 patent is invalid under 35 U.S.C. § 171 for failure to satisfy the statute's ornamentality requirement.

Affirmed.

NEWMAN, Circuit Judge, dissenting.

I respectfully dissent. The design of this key blade profile meets the statutory criteria of design patent subject matter. . . .

The legal principles governing design patents have their foundation in the important decision of *Gorham Co. v. White*, 81 U.S. (14 Wall.) 511, 20 L. Ed. 731 (1871), wherein the Supreme Court explained:

> The appearance may be the result of peculiarity of configuration, or of ornament alone, or of both conjointly, but, in whatever way produced, it is the new thing, or product, which the patent law regards.

81 U.S. at 525. Courts have measured the term "ornamental" by the non-functionality that distinguishes the subject of a design patent from a utility patent, while recognizing that the design of a useful article is not insulated from the utility of the article. A review of patentable designs in general illustrates the mixture of functional and non-functional features embraced in the patented design. . . .

An effective design patent law must recognize the distinction between functionality of the article and of the particular design of the article or features thereof. *See L.A. Gear, supra,* (the sneaker tongue, moustache, delta wing, and side mesh, were useful parts of the sneaker, but the overall design of these features and the shoe was not dictated by function alone). This interaction of form and function does not remove the design from the statutory scope of the design patent law, or defeat the statutory patentability of a primarily non-functional design, although it is not always easy to draw a bright line between the functionality of an article and its design, as discussed by J.H. Reichman, Design Protection and the New Technologies: The United States Experience in a Transnational Perspective, 19 Balt. L. Rev. 6 (1989), for design patents often appear on quite mundane articles of manufacture. . . .

The design of the key blade profile is primarily non-functional, as the Patent and Trademark Office recognized in granting the patent in suit. The Manual of Patent Examining Procedure defines "design" as follows for purposes of § 171:

> The design of an object consists of the visual characteristics or aspects displayed by the object. It is the appearance presented by the object which creates a visual impact upon the mind of the observer.

Since a design is manifested in appearance, the subject matter of a design patent application may relate to the configuration or shape of an object, to the surface ornamentation on an object, or both.

Design is inseparable from the object to which it is applied and cannot exist alone merely as a scheme of surface ornamentation. It must be a definite, preconceived thing, capable of reproduction and not merely the chance result of a method. MPEP § 1502 (6th ed. 1995). *See also* 1 D. Chisum, Patents § 1.04[2][a] (1996) ("[A] design rests on appearance created by the configuration of the article, surface ornamentation, or a combination of configuration and ornamentation.") (footnote omitted).

The parties to this litigation agree that there are myriad possible designs of key profiles. All keys require, of course, mating keyways. In holding that because the key must fit a keyway, the abstract design of the key profile is converted to one solely of function, the court creates an exception to design patent subject matter. An arbitrary design of a useful article is not statutorily excluded from § 171 simply because in use it interacts with an article of complementary design. Although precedent is sparse, it is contrary to this holding. In *Motorola Inc. v. Alexander Mfg. Co.*, 786 F. Supp. 808, 21 U.S.P.Q.2D (BNA) 1573 (N.D. Iowa 1991), the only United States case on this point of which we are aware, the court considered a design patent for a battery housing intended for use in a portable phone. Since the battery housing had to fit into the phone and a battery charger, the accused infringer argued that this function dictated the design. The court disagreed:

> The design of the battery housing was not dictated by the design of the battery charger because the charger did not exist when the housing was designed. The design of the phone was done concurrently with the battery housing. Therefore, the design of the battery housing cannot fairly be said to have been "dictated" by the design of the phone.

Id. at 812, 21 U.S.P.Q.2D at 1557. This reasoning is equally apt in this case. The design of the key profile was not dictated by the design of the keyway, and indeed the two share the same arbitrary design.

In sum, the fact that the key blade is the mate of a keyway does not convert the arbitrary key profile into a primarily functional design. It is not the design of the key profile that is functional, but the key itself. Thus I must, respectfully, dissent from the ruling of the panel majority that the design of the key blade profile is not patentable because the key blade requires a mating keyway.

NOTES AND QUESTIONS

1. As noted earlier, the "design patent" is one of several forms of IP used to protect designs in the United States. "Trade dress" generally refers to the distinctive appearance adopted by a business for its products or services and is a form of trademark and unfair competition protection. Trade dress may take the form of a registered trademark, but it may also be the subject of unregistered common law trademark protection. The U.S. Supreme Court has addressed the nature of trade dress protection on several occasions. *See, e.g., Traffix Devices v. Mktg. Displays*, 532 U.S. 23 (2001); *Wal-Mart Stores, Inc. v. Samara Bros.*, 529 U.S. 205 (2000); *Two Pesos v. Taco Cabana*, 505 U.S. 763 (1992). Copyright is often invoked to protect fashion and jewelry design. *See, e.g., Langman Fabrics v. Graff Californiawear*, 160 F.3d 106 (2d Cir. 1998).

2. During the Uruguay Round TRIPS Agreement negotiations, some industries actively sought improvements in design protection while other industries opposed it. The automotive industry favored lower standards for protection of designs, while the insurance industry sought to increase the required level of originality. The high-fashion design industry complained about the inefficiency of industrial design protection and called for more efficient and rapid registration systems (or improved protection through copyright). Yet, major clothing retailers were not anxious to see standards of protection raised. Why did these industries take the positions that they did?

B. The Multilateral System for Protection of Design

1. The Provisions of the TRIPs Agreement

THE AGREEMENT ON TRADE RELATED ASPECTS OF INTELLECTUAL PROPERTY RIGHTS (TRIPs)

Thomas Cottier*

INDUSTRIAL DESIGNS

NEGOTIATING HISTORY

Negotiations on industrial designs were difficult. There was controversy as to whether the standards of protection to be granted for industrial design should be based on the protection available in Europe or in the United States. The EC wanted the United States to expand coverage of its domestic design patent law. The initial U.S. proposal excluded "functional" designs from protection and was limited to designs that are "new, original, ornamental and non-obvious." One of the main practical interests at stake was trade in automobile spare parts. The automotive industry sought to obtain protection from cheaper parts produced by foreign competitors. Extension of protection was, therefore, opposed by developing countries and the car insurance industry. The interests of the textile industry, which sought enhanced protection for fashion designs, were another driving force in the negotiations and resulted in modest improvements. Overall, the minimum standard of protection that was agreed maintains a reasonable level of creativity, but allows Members to grant more extensive protection if they so wish.

THE AGREEMENT

Members are obliged by *Article 25* to provide for the protection of independently created industrial designs that are new or original. Protection can be withheld from "designs dictated essentially by technical or functional considerations." Members must ensure that the requirements for obtaining protection for textile designs do not unreasonably impair the opportunity to obtain such protection. Article 25:2 was included in recognition of the short lifecycle of such design creations due to changes in fashion and amounts to a novel instrument

* The World Trade Organization: Legal, Economic and Political Analysis, Vol. I p. 1041 (Patrick F. J. Macrory, Arthur E. Appleton, Michael G. Plummer eds., Springer 2005).

in design protection. Together with Article 62, discussed in Part III(F) below, Article 25:2 creates an obligation to, and pressures for, facilitating filing procedures in countries notoriously slow in registering designs which depend on fashion cycles. Moreover, in many countries copyright protection can also be used as a possible way for protecting designs without any registration requirements.

2. The Hague Agreement Concerning the International Registration of Industrial Designs

The Hague Agreement Concerning the International Registration of Industrial Designs provides a mechanism for registering industrial designs.[19]

The Hague Agreement is a registration mechanism and does not include substantive rules. Designs are protected only as provided for under the law of the countries where protection has been sought. Substantive examination and litigation are entirely left to the domestic entities under the national law of the parties. The system merely offers the possibility to lodge one single application for design protection for a number of countries and intergovernmental organizations. The main objective of the Hague System is to facilitate and economize the international registration of industrial designs.

There are more than 50 country parties to at least one of the three Acts of the Hague Agreement, the most recent of which (the Geneva Act) was concluded in 1999. One objective of the Geneva Act was to make the system more attractive to countries such as the United States, which do not employ design registration systems, but offer alternatives such as a design patent. The United States signed the Geneva Act, but it has not yet ratified and adhered to the Agreement. A number of EU member states are party to the Hague Agreement and in 2008, the European Union itself became party to the Geneva Act.

NOTES AND QUESTIONS

1. The following excerpt from the Federal Register sets out the U.S. position with respect to how applications under the Geneva Act of the Hague Agreement would be treated in U.S. law:

    > Given the benefits to the users of the Hague system, the United States has been actively involved in the negotiations with the goal of obtaining a suitable agreement that could engender interest and support by United States industry and designers. Although protection for industrial designs is available in the United States under various laws, including patent, trademark, copyright, and unfair competition laws, the United States has taken the position that, if adopted, implementation of the new Act of the Hague Agreement would be through United States design patent law.[20]

---

19. Information and the text of the Agreement can be found at http://www.wipo.int.

20. Patent and Trademark Office, Docket No. 990408092-0992-01, RIN 0651-ZA01, Notice of Public Hearing and Request for Comments on the Proposed New Act of the Hague Agreement Concerning the International Registration of Industrial Designs, 64 Fed. Reg. 19,135-139 (Apr. 19, 1999).

Because design patents are subject to prior examination in the United States, while many foreign design registration systems do not entail prior examination (*see, e.g.,* EU Design Regulation system, next section *infra*), U.S. participation would offer limited opportunity for registration as compared with other Geneva Act contracting states.

C.   Regional Design Protection Systems

1.   The EU Design Directive and Regulation

The European Union has adopted a directive (1998)[21] and regulation (2001)[22] on the protection of designs that effectively establish a comprehensive system for design regulation within the European Union. Similar to the situation with respect to trademarks, the European Union first adopted a directive intended to approximate the laws of the member states, but maintaining the national authority to grant design rights, and allowing some flexibility within national legal systems with respect to implementation. The subsequent regulation is directly applicable in the law of the member states and establishes a single unified design protection right throughout the European Union, embodied in a "Community Design." The unregistered Community Design (or CD) right arises when the design is first made available to the public in the European Union and has a term of three years.[23] Registered CDs have a renewal term of five years from the date of filing the application, up to a maximum of 25 years.[24] The Community Design system, like the Community Trademark System (see Chapter 3, *supra*), is administered by the Office of Harmonization in the Internal Market (OHIM), situated in Alicante, Spain.

The Design Regulation establishes "newness" and "individual character" as the criteria for design protection.[25] Registration confers significant advantages. A registered CD protects against third-party use notwithstanding independent creation.[26] An unregistered CD is only protected against "copying."[27] In addition, a registered CD enjoys a presumption of validity in an infringement action.[28] The rights of the holder are subject to limitations, such as "acts done for experimental purposes."[29] The CD right is subject to a "prior use" right in favor of a third party who can establish good-faith use or serious preparations to use within the European Union prior to the filing or priority date

---

21. Directive 98/71/EC of the European Parliament and of the Council of 13 October 1998 on the legal protection of designs, OJ L 289, 28.10.1998, p. 28, available at http://oami.europa.eu/en/design/legalaspects.htm.
22. Council Regulation (EC) No 6/2002 of 12 December 2001 on Community designs (consolidated version), available at http://oami.europa.eu/en/design/legalaspects.htm.
23. Design Regulation, art. 11(1).
24. *Id.,* art. 12.
25. *Id.,* art. 4(1).
26. *Id.,* art. 19(1).
27. *Id.,* art. 19(2).
28. *Id.,* art. 85.
29. *Id.,* art. 20(1)(b).

of the application.[30] The Design Regulation includes an express intra-Union exhaustion rule.[31]

Newness or novelty involves a modest threshold of differentiation from "identical" designs previously made available to the public (Article 5, Design Regulation). Regarding "individual character,"

> [a] design shall be considered to have individual character if the overall impression it produces on the informed user differs from the overall impression produced on such a user by any design which has been made available to the public.

(Article 6, *id.*) CDs "shall not subsist in features of appearance of a product which are solely dictated by its technical function," nor in features that are necessary to permit the product (or a connected product) to function.[32]

Applications to register CDs are submitted to the OHIM, which examines the applications for compliance with formalities. If the formal requirements are met, the design is registered and published.[33] Any natural or legal person may apply to the OHIM to invalidate the registered design.[34] An initial decision regarding invalidity is made by administrators, but may be appealed to the Board of Appeal.[35] Decisions of the Board of Appeal may be taken to the Court of Justice of the European Union.[36]

Actions for infringement of the CD are brought before national courts of the EU member states that have been designated by those states as "Community design courts," which shall include courts of both first and second instance.[37] The Community design courts also have jurisdiction over actions for declaration of noninfringement (if permitted by national law), for declarations of invalidity of unregistered CDs, and over counterclaims for invalidity regarding registered CDs.[38]

The rules established by the EU Design Regulation do not interfere with the grant by the member states of national design rights providing simultaneous protection (which remain subject to the Design Directive),[39] or with respect to unregistered designs, trademarks, patents, utility models, and unfair competition. Designs may also be protected under copyright law applicable in the member states.[40] Provision is made in the Design Regulation for treatment of parallel legal actions,[41] and for the enforcement of judgments.[42]

---

30. *Id.*, art. 22. Note that since an unregistered design is not protected against independent creation, a prior use right in favor of an independent third-party creator is not required in respect to unregistered designs.

31. *Id.*, art. 22.

32. *Id.*, art. 8.

33. *Id.*, arts 47-49. Publication is subject to deferral for up to 30 months. However, legal proceedings may only be instituted if the design had been previously communicated to the person against whom the action is brought. *Id.*, art. 50.

34. *Id.*, art. 52.

35. *Id.*, arts. 55-61.

36. *Id.*, art. 61.

37. *Id.*, art. 80.

38. *Id.*, art. 81.

39. *Id.*, art. 95.

40. *Id.*, art. 96.

41. *Id.*, art. 95.

42. *Id.*, art. 79.

OFFICE FOR HARMONIZATION IN THE INTERNAL MARKET (TRADE MARKS AND DESIGNS) DESIGNS DEPARTMENT — INVALIDITY DIVISION

**Decision of the Invalidity Division of 20/09/05
In the Proceedings for a Declaration of Invalidity
of a Registered Community Design**

File Number ICD 000000388
Community Design 000150206-0002

Applicant: LENG-D'OR, S.A. [Spain]
Holder: Crown Confectionery Co., LTD. [Republic of Korea]

The Invalidity Division,
composed of Martin SCHLÖTELBURG (rapporteur), Paul MAIER (member) and
José IZQUIERDO PERIS (member) took the following decision on 20/09/05:

1. The registered Community design No. 000150206-0002 is declared invalid.
2. The Holder shall bear the costs of the Applicant.

I. FACTS, EVIDENCE AND ARGUMENTS

(1) The Community design No. 000150206-0002 (in the following: "the CD")
has been registered in the name of the Holder with the date of filing of 20/02/04
and the date of priority of 19/01/04. In the CD, the indication of products reads
"biscuits" and the design is represented in the following views (published at
http://oami.eu.int/bulletin/rcd/2004/2004_045/000150206_0002.htm):

[Drawing 1 of several views, others omitted]
(2) On 01/07/04, the Applicant filed an application for a declaration of invalidity (in the following: "the Application") contesting the validity of the CD. . . .

(3) The Applicant, by referring to "the right recognised by article 25 point 1
section b, of the regulation in force in regard to Community Drawings and
Models," claims "lack of novelty and singularity of the challenged Community
design is lacking, prior and demanded requirements in articles 4, 5 and 6 of the
Regulations for Community Drawings and Models." He argues that the CD "does
not have any novelty and singularity necessary for its registration, given that the
distinguished features presented by same are included in the number of biscuits
and snacks located and contributed by my principal, which were made public in
this specific industrial field prior to the Community Design application."

(4) As evidence, the Applicant provided "documentation extracted from the
'Google' public database," in particular "printout extracted from the 'Google'
public database using the term referring to 'pretzels' and 'snacks' as the

parameter" and "printout extracted from the 'Google' public database using the term referring to 'pretzels'" as well as "printout of images extracted from the 'Google' public database using the term referring to 'pretzels' as the parameter." In particular, the Applicant provided a printout of an article with the title "Field Reports: New twist on environmental compliance for snack maker" published in the magazine "Food Engineering" (in the following: D1). The article bears the dating "Magazine issue date: 12/01/2002" and includes the following image (in the following: prior design):

(5) The Holder did not submit observations.

(6) For further details to the facts, evidence and arguments submitted by the Applicant and the Holder reference is made to the documents on file.

II. Grounds of the Decision

A. ADMISSIBILITY

(7) The request of the Applicant to declare the invalidity of the CD due to "lack of novelty and singularity of the challenged Community" is a statement of the grounds on which the Application is based. Therefore, the requirement of Art. 28(1)(b)(i) CDIR1 is fulfilled. Furthermore, the Application complies with Art. 28(1)(b)(v)(vi) CDIR, since the attachment contains an indication of the facts, evidence and arguments submitted in support of those grounds, in particular the "documentation extracted from the 'Google' public database" gives an indication and a reproduction of the prior design. The other requirements of Art. 28(1) CDIR are fulfilled as well. The Application is admissible. 1 Commission Regulation (EC) No 2245/2002 of 21 October 2002 implementing Council Regulation (EC) No 6/2002 on Community designs.

B. SUBSTANTIATION

B.1 Evidence

(8) D1 is a copy of an article from a magazine dated 12/01/02. Magazines are usually published and distributed. Furthermore, the Applicant submits elements that the earlier design could have been known in the normal course of business to the circles specialized in the sector concerned, operating within the Community. Therefore, D1 is considered as having been made available to the public prior to

the date of filing of the CD in accordance with Article 7(1) CDR. The Holder did not put into question any of these elements which all together constitute prima facie evidence of a disclosure of D1 according to Article 7(1) CDR.

B.2 Novelty

(9) The CD consists essentially in the shape of a pretzel. The prior design shown in D1 and the CD do not show differences except for the lines across the pretzel. Such differences are considered immaterial details. The Holder does not indicate any further differences nor has made any submission. Therefore, the Invalidity Division must conclude that both designs are identical.

C. CONCLUSION

(10) The CD lacks novelty. Therefore, it has to be declared invalid pursuant to Article 25(1)(b) CDR.

III. COSTS

(11) Pursuant to Article 70(1) CDR and Art. 79(1) CDIR, the Holder bears the costs incurred by him essential to the proceedings.

IV. RIGHT TO APPEAL

(12) An appeal shall lie from the present decision. Notice of appeal must be filed at the Office within two months after the date of notification of that decision. The notice is deemed to have been filed only when the fee for appeal has been paid. Within four months after the date of notification of the decision, a written statement setting out the grounds of appeal must be filed (Art. 57 CDR).

NOTES AND QUESTIONS

1. The text decision illustrates the effect of absence of substantive examination of CD applications by OHIM. Presumably, prior examination would have resulted in rejection of the shape of a pretzel as a biscuit for lack of novelty. At the same time, a general requirement of prior examination would result in a much more complex registration system, and would present significant problems due, *inter alia*, to the necessity of compiling a database of prior art. On the other hand, registration of a CD does not by any means guarantee the holder the right to prevent others from using the design. It does provide a presumption in litigation in favor of the holder, but that is subject to challenge by an alleged infringer. An alleged infringer may counterclaim for invalidity. There is also a prior user right. Finally, in this proceeding, the losing party (registered CD holder) bears the costs of the action. Do you think the advantages of a low-cost rapid system of registration outweigh the disadvantages of imposing on the public the burden of challenging validity in litigation? Do the holders of CDs enjoy some additional "apparent power" to threaten third parties? Is there a better alternative to this registration system?

D. Layout Designs of Integrated Circuits*

1. The Origin and Nature of the *Sui Generis* Integrated Circuit Layout Design Right

The protection of intellectual property in integrated circuit (or semiconductor device) layout design is a *sui generis* form of IPR that developed largely in the 1980s. Instead of protecting these products by means of existing forms, such as patent, copyright, or industrial designs, the view prevailed that a separate instrument should be created. The initial impetus came from the U.S. semiconductor industry, which pursued and obtained domestic legislation on the subject. Similar legislation soon followed in Japan and the European Union.[43] In 1989, the Treaty on Intellectual Property in Respect of Integrated Circuits (IC or Washington Treaty) was concluded. This treaty has never entered into force because of industry concerns over certain terms. The TRIPS Agreement, however, incorporates the substantive provisions of the IC Treaty, with amendments designed to address those concerns.

An integrated circuit (IC) or semiconductor device is produced by depositing and etching a pattern of electricity-conducting materials, for example, aluminum, and insulating material onto a semiconducting base, usually silicon. The pattern forms a series of transistors designed to perform computational functions. By designing smaller transistors and placing them closer together, engineers can produce ICs that run faster. The pattern that is deposited and etched onto a semiconducting base is embodied in a three-dimensional map, referred to as a *mask work, layout design,* or *topography,* that is used to guide the complex equipment that creates the physical end-product IC. Once such a mask work is created, it can be used by any semiconductor foundry with the requisite technical expertise to produce the subject IC. The objective of the IC producer is to assure that its competitors are not able to use a mask work it has developed to create an identical or substantially similar product.

Engineers are able to reverse engineer a mask work starting with a finished IC product. This is a complex and costly process. Nevertheless, a reverse-engineered IC may be significantly less expensive to produce than a newly developed product.

IC layout design protection is generally secured by registration of the mask work with an appropriate national or regional authority. Examination of the application by such an authority to determine whether the mask work meets the substantive requirement of originality is not a precondition of registration demanded by the terms of the IC Treaty, and a substantive examination is not ordinarily undertaken by registering authorities. However, such a substantive examination does not appear to be precluded by the terms of the IC Treaty. Whether a registered mask work or layout design meets the relevant standards for protection is generally a matter for civil litigation following registration.[44]

---

* Section D is based on FREDERICK ABBOTT, THOMAS COTTIER & FRANCIS GURRY, THE INTERNATIONAL INTELLECTUAL PROPERTY SYSTEM, (1999), and Thomas Cottier, *The Agreement on Trade Related Aspects of Intellectual Property,* in The World Trade Organization: Legal, Economic and Political Analysis, Vol. I p. 1041 (Patrick F. J. Macrory, Arthur E. Appleton, Michael G. Plummer eds., 2005).

43. For these legislative references, *see* Frederick M. Abbott, *Introductory Note to WIPO: Treaty on Intellectual Property in Respect of Integrated Circuits,* 28 International Legal Materials 1477 (1989), at note 3.

44. Note, for example, that pursuant to the U.S. Semiconductor Chip Protection Act (1984), registration with the Copyright Office establishes a presumption that a mask work is protected, thereby placing the burden of proof on a party challenging the entitlement to protection. 17 U.S.C.A. § 908(f).

2.   Integrated Circuit Protection in the TRIPS Agreement

The provisions of Articles 35 to 38 of the TRIPS Agreement implement and reinforce the Washington Treaty. They are of particular importance not only to the protection of topographies as such, but also for all products that include topographies. The provisions significantly strengthen the legal position of the right holders as they are linked with the enforcement provisions. In order to avoid distortions caused by potential abuse of border enforcement procedures, it is necessary to equally protect the interest of importers and bring about an appropriate balance of interests.

Article 35 requires Member countries to protect the layout designs of integrated circuits in accordance with the provisions of the Washington Treaty. In addition, the TRIPS Agreement clarifies several points. In Article 38, the term of protection is extended from eight to ten years from the date of filing or from the first commercial exploitation wherever it occurs. Article 36 defines the rights and their broad applicability to products containing infringing integrated circuits. The provision bans the import, sale, or distribution of unlawfully produced designs or circuits, and applies to the many products incorporating such designs or circuits. The breadth of product coverage made it imperative to limit the application to willful and negligent infringement. Article 37 excludes the *bona fide* buyer of counterfeited goods. Acts of incorporating a counterfeited layout design into an integrated circuit, or incorporating the latter into any product, are not deemed unlawful if the person performing the act did not know or had no reasonable ground to know when acquiring the product that it contained an unlawfully produced layout design. Given the number of integrated circuits contained in many products, this provision essentially limits the reach of the article to producers and traders, to the exclusion of consumers, since consumers are usually not in a position to know, and cannot be expected to know, the origin of layout designs incorporated in a product that they buy on the market.

NOTES AND QUESTIONS

1.   Integrated circuit layout design protection generally entitles the right holder to prohibit the unauthorized *reproduction* of its mask work in an IC. The use of the term "reproduction" in IC protection legislation, and in the IC Treaty, signifies that it is the copying of a protected design that is prohibited by the IC Treaty, since Article 9 of the Berne Convention uses the term "reproduction" to define the act that a copyright holder is entitled to authorize. In this regard, IC protection is more similar to copyright than patent protection. However, the term of IC layout design protection generally is ten years, which is a considerably shorter term than copyright protection, and about half that of patent protection.

CHAPTER
6

The International System for the Enforcement of Intellectual Property Rights

I. INTRODUCTION TO FORMS OF IPRs ENFORCEMENT

Judicial and administrative enforcement of intellectual property rights traditionally and exclusively pertained to the province of domestic law. States made available mechanisms of enforcement commensurate with domestic civil, administrative, and penal procedures. International constellations of rights were exclusively dealt with by domestic rules on international private law, which eventually were partly harmonized by international rules on private law. Even in European integration, enforcement of rights was not a harmonized matter. Given this tradition, perhaps the most dramatic change in focus of international IPRs rule making from the Paris and Berne Conventions of the 1880s to the TRIPS Agreement concerns the enforcement of IPRs. In fact, the shift in institutional competence from WIPO to the WTO mainly reflected the perception by industry groups in the Organisation for Economic Cooperation and Development (OECD) that the system of treaties administered by WIPO did not sufficiently compel contracting states to implement and enforce IPRs protection. The TRIPS Agreement therefore introduced minimal standards to be respected in domestic law, not limited to substantive, but also extending to and including procedural standards and obligations. Yet, despite the considerable attention paid to enforcement of IPRs in the TRIPS Agreement, and in bilateral agreements negotiated by the United States, the European Union, and other countries, the persistent lack of firm enforcement by certain countries is a priority trade and IPRs negotiation issue today. This priority manifested itself in the negotiation of a draft Anti-Counterfeiting Trade Agreement (ACTA) by a group largely comprised of developed countries that has provoked a new round of controversy regarding the role of international IPRs rules.

While governments agree to adopt and maintain standards for the protection of IPRs at international organizations in Geneva and elsewhere, enforcement ultimately takes place in national (and local) courts and administrative bodies. For many (or most) countries, enforcement of IPRs involves net royalty payments to companies based abroad (i.e., a financial outflow). In that context, whether one country can persuade another to enforce "in fact" IPRs rules depends, among other things, on their relative economic and political power. The United States, for example, may find it easier to persuade Costa Rica to enforce IPRs than to persuade China.

For the most part, enforcement of IPRs involves legal proceedings initiated by the right holder in a civil or administrative court in the country where the IPRs are held and infringement is alleged to be taking place. Depending on the circumstances, if the right holder is successful in its claim, an injunction against further acts of infringement may be obtained, a civil monetary judgment may be assessed and, in some cases, forfeiture of assets used in the infringing acts may be ordered. The execution of the judgment may require the aid of local law enforcement authorities and/or third parties, which may require further legal proceedings. If infringing goods are already in the local stream of commerce, it may be difficult to fully carry out a judgment.

Because of the difficulties inherent in pursuing remedies once infringing products have entered the local stream of commerce, IPRs holders concerned with cross-border trade have a strong preference for enforcement of "border measures." Customs authorities may be authorized or directed to prevent infringing or allegedly infringing goods from entering the stream of commerce within the national territory. In some cases, customs authorities may have standing instructions (based on IPRs "registers") to inspect and suspend (at least temporarily) the release of suspicious shipments. More generally, IPRs holders may initiate legal proceedings seeking orders directing customs authorities to prevent infringing goods from entering the country. One of the objectives of the countries negotiating the draft ACTA was to strengthen the role of customs authorities to police enforcement of IPRs at the border, including by acting on their own initiative (i.e., *ex officio*).

There is a marked trend in the enforcement of IPRs toward increased criminalization of acts of infringement. There are several reasons for this. The customary mechanism for IPRs enforcement is a civil complaint by the holder against an alleged infringer. Criminal infringement actions, on the other hand, are pursued by government authorities. This shifts the cost and responsibility for enforcement from the private sector to the public sector, saving the expense for IPRs holders. Second, the threat of incarceration and criminal fines/forfeiture is presumably a more substantial deterrent to infringement than the threat of civil fine and injunction/forfeiture. Also, and importantly, it transfers the cost and risk of enforcement to the state and public authorities, away from right holders. The increased attention to criminalization raises important public policy questions. Excerpts of the following study elaborate on these questions from the point of view of economics. They show the tensions between enhanced protection and the impact on consumer welfare, and the dilemmas society and governments face in allocating resources to IPRs enforcement.

ENFORCING INTELLECTUAL PROPERTY RIGHTS: AN ECONOMIC PERSPECTIVE
Carsten Fink*

1. Upholding the protection of intellectual property rights (IPRs) has emerged as a prominent policy issue. The year 2007 alone saw a G-8 summit

---

* Advisory Committee on Enforcement, Fifth Session, Geneva, November 2-4, 2009, WIPO/ ACE/5/6 (August 26, 2009). (Footnotes omitted.)

calling for stepped-up enforcement of IPRs, the initiation of a WTO dispute on China's IPRs enforcement regime, and the launch of inter-governmental negotiations towards an Anti-Counterfeiting Trade Agreement (ACTA). In addition, intellectual property chapters of free trade agreements (FTAs) negotiated over the past few years have introduced obligations on IPRs enforcement that go beyond multilateral standards inscribed in the WTO's Agreement on Trade Related Aspects of Intellectual Property Rights (TRIPS). Several developed countries, in turn, have called for renewed discussions on enforcement in the TRIPS Council.

2. Concerns about trademark counterfeiting, copyright piracy, and other forms of IPRs violations are not new. Already back in 1985, *Business Week* characterized counterfeiting as "*perhaps the world's fastest growing and most profitable business.*" Indeed, the desire to stem in trade in counterfeit goods was at the origin of the GATT negotiations which eventually led to the conclusion of the TRIPS Agreement. However, two developments have sharpened the policy discourse on IPRs violations in recent years.

3. First, rapid global economic integration and the fast growth of middle income countries — led by China and India — have raised the stakes for intellectual property-owning companies. They see counterfeiting and piracy as a constraint on their ability to expand sales in rapidly growing markets. More fundamentally, they also view IPRs infringements as a direct competitive threat, as firms in labor-abundant countries copy the latest technologies and undermine what is perceived to be their remaining competitive edge. In the United States, politicians have linked lax IPRs enforcement abroad to the country's persistent trade deficit, especially with China. While such a link has little economic basis — the trade balance primarily reflects the difference between domestic savings and investment — it carries political weight and is shaping US trade and foreign policy.

4. Second, counterfeiting and piracy are perceived to have reached unprecedented levels. In part, the growth of counterfeiting has been spurred by technological developments which have facilitated the copying of original products. For example, the emergence of easy-to-copy digital storage mediums has enabled the cheap reproduction of audiovisual and software products without any loss of quality. The spread of online patent databases has permitted easy access to new technologies.

5. Due to their illegal nature, there are no reliable figures on the sales of intellectual property infringing products. The OECD (2007) estimates that international trade in counterfeit and pirated goods in 2005 may have amounted to as much as 200 billion dollars, or slightly more than 2 percent of global merchandise trade. This figure understates global commerce in IPRs-infringing goods, as it excludes domestic sales and digital products distributed via the Internet. Even though there are no hard numbers on the growth of IPRs violations, anecdotal evidence suggests that their scale and scope is expanding. For example, newspaper articles and government surveys in recent years indicate that counterfeiting activity has expanded from luxury to common consumer goods, affecting products as diverse as automotive replacement parts, electrical appliances, and toys. In addition, intellectual property violations are increasingly linked to organized crime.

6. At one level, one might ask: why worry about IPRs enforcement as a matter of public policy? Governments set standards of intellectual property protection through national laws and ensuring that firms and individuals obey these laws seems only natural. To be sure, some observers have argued that the exclusive

rights granted by intellectual property laws have become overly strong (Jaffee and Lerner, 2004 and Maskus and Reichman, 2004). However, no one would seriously argue for correcting this suspected overshooting of IPRs laws by promoting illegal behavior. If laws do not serve the public interest, they ought to be changed rather than disregarded.

7. Yet there is one important reason for regarding IPRs piracy as an issue of public policy: resources needed for enforcing IPRs are invariably scarce. Counterfeiting and product piracy exist even in the richest countries which have the best staffed and best equipped law enforcement agencies. For example, the Business Software Alliance estimates that, in 2006, 45 percent of software was pirated in France, 28 percent in Germany, 25 percent in Japan, and 21 percent in the United States. Governments need to make choices about how many resources to spend on combating piracy, as opposed to enforcing other areas of law, building roads and bridges, protecting national security, and providing other public goods. Such choices are usually not stated in explicit terms, but they underlie every budgetary decision by federal and local governments. For example, greater spending on counter-terrorism in the United States after September 11, 2001 has left fewer resources for fighting crime, reportedly causing rates of crime to go up in many US cities. Deciding on appropriate spending for IPRs enforcement is especially difficult in developing countries, where many public goods are underprovided and enforcement challenges exist in many areas of law — fighting violence, guaranteeing real property rights, upholding contracts, stopping illegal logging of endangered forests, regulating traffic, and so on. This paper seeks to offer an economic perspective on policies towards IPRs enforcement. It draws on key insights from the economic literature to identify priorities for the allocation of scarce law enforcement resources. Two major themes emerge from this literature. First, different types of intellectual property infringements have different welfare effects, depending on underlying market failures and market characteristics. Past studies that have attempted to quantify the "losses" due to IPRs piracy have sometimes ignored these differences. Second, in designing an IPRs enforcement strategy, policymakers need to take into account the incentives of producers and consumers to break the law. Understanding these incentives offers important insights about the limits of government policy and the effectiveness of different types of enforcement activities.

. . .

TRADEMARK COUNTERFEITING

18. A crucial consideration for evaluating the welfare implications of trademark counterfeiting is whether consumers are misled by the falsified brand name attached to their purchases. For example, most buyers of a 10-dollar watch bearing the Rolex label know perfectly well that they acquire a fake product. Simple inspection can often reveal if a product is fake or genuine and, even if not, most consumers know that genuine Rolex watches do not sell for 10 dollars. By contrast, simple inspection may not easily reveal whether [a] pharmaceutical product is counterfeit and the purchase price alone is unlikely to offer additional information on the product's origin.

19. We will first analyze product counterfeiting assuming that buyers really do not know that they purchase a counterfeit product. We will then turn to the

case where buyers know that they are purchasing a fake. As will become clear, the welfare consequences from counterfeiting in these two cases differ markedly.

CASE 1: CONSUMERS ARE MISLED

20. If consumers cannot by themselves distinguish fakes from originals, the presence of counterfeit goods undermines the signaling function of trademarks, as described in the previous section. Consumers will invariably be worse off. Purchasers of counterfeit products will, at best, derive a value from the product which is lower than the price they paid for it and, at worst, be exposed to physical harm if counterfeit products create health or safety risks. The consumption of misbranded products may also adversely affect other individuals—for example, when the intake of drugs with no or insufficient levels of active ingredients increases the risk of disease transmission or when defect[ive] vehicle replacement parts provoke traffic accidents. In the parlance of economists, the consumption of counterfeit goods may impose "negative externalities."

21. In the long-run, if consumers know that trademarks are imperfectly enforced, markets for certain high-quality goods may not exist to begin with. Consumers would not be willing to pay the full price of a high quality original, since they fear that their purchase may be a fake. At lower prices, in turn, producers of original products would not be willing to sell. In other words, the market failure of asymmetric information strikes exactly as George Akerlof predicted more than 30 years ago.

22. The only beneficiaries of counterfeiting are the producers of counterfeits. However, the benefits accruing to those producers are bound to be lower than the losses to consumers and original producers, such that economy-wide welfare is generally lower in the presence of counterfeiting.

23. This result holds for closed economies and for the world economy at large. What if counterfeit producers are located in certain countries and export the overwhelming share of production, with domestic sales constituting a negligible share of output? For example, 90 percent of IPRs-infringing activities seized at the European border in 2006 originated in only 8 countries, with China alone accounting for 79 percent of all seizures. Even though producers in these countries invariably profit from counterfeiting activities, it is not clear how far the economies hosting such producers gain as a whole. Welfare effects will depend on patterns of comparative advantage and, in particular, how production factors in those economies would be used if counterfeiting were not feasible. Nonetheless, stronger trademark enforcement may well lead to substantial short-run employment losses in the concerned countries—an issue to which we will return below.

CASE 2: CONSUMERS ARE NOT MISLED

24. If consumers are perfectly aware that their purchases are fakes, a natural question to ask is: why do they prefer a product bearing a falsified label to a "generic" product of identical quality? The only plausible explanation is that they derive prestige or status value from the display of a particular brand name. Prestige value may be partly imaginary, for example when a consumer derives pleasure from carrying the same handbag as a Hollywood actress. More often, consumers derive status value by belonging to an exclusive club of consumers who share the same preferences and are able to afford high-end products.

Individual consumers' taste for status thus needs to be included in social welfare calculations. Such an exercise may at first seem tenuous. However, a taste for status is quite real. Why else would a consumer be ready to pay several thousand dollars for a brand-name watch, when a reliable generic timekeeper can be purchased for far less that amount? Indeed, the very presence of counterfeit status goods indicates that status matters.

25. What can we say about the welfare consequences of counterfeiting in these circumstances? To begin with, consumers who knowingly purchase fake products are likely to be better off from counterfeiting activity. They always have the option of buying either the original or a generic product of comparable quality. If they choose the fake product and are not mislead, their choice reflects a rational trade-off between price, status value, and quality.

26. For consumers of original products, a crucial question is whether and how their welfare is affected by the presence of fake goods. Suppose first that such consumers can perfectly observe whether other buyers acquire fake or original products. If so, their welfare is unaffected, as the composition of the exclusive club of original purchasers remains the same. Their welfare may even increase, as the presence of fakes may raise the status value derived from owning the "real thing."

27. However, in most cases, it is more likely that consumers of originals cannot tell whether other consumers own counterfeit or original products. For many fashion products and accessories, the difference between a fake and an original can only be ascertained by close inspection or by the fanciness of the store in which the product is bought. To the casual observer, fakes and originals are often indistinguishable. Indeed, consumers of fakes would unlikely derive much status value from counterfeit products if they could not successfully pretend that they own the genuine product.

28. Grossman and Shapiro (1988b) develop a simple model in which the prestige value a consumer derives from a given brand is negatively related to the number of consumers who own products displaying the same brand name — regardless of whether those products are fake or genuine. The presence of fake goods thus undermines the prestige of owning the genuine product, leaving buyers of those genuine products worse-off from counterfeiting. However, Grossman and Shapiro show that the economy-wide welfare consequences from stronger trademark enforcement are ambiguous: depending on demand structures, the loss suffered by consumers of counterfeits may exceed the gain to consumers of originals.

29. Trademark owners will experience an increase in profits from stronger trademark enforcement, as some consumers switch from fakes to originals. In the long term, greater profitability in the market for genuine products will induce entry of additional firms. The arrival of additional brands brings about a dual benefit to consumers of originals: each brand is purchased by fewer consumers, thus raising the prestige value associated with each brand, and greater competition between brands leads to a fall in the price of those products. Notwithstanding these additional benefits from market entry, the welfare consequences of stronger trademark enforcement remain ambiguous, as the loss to consumers of counterfeits may still outweigh any gain to consumers of originals.

30. Two additional considerations further complicate an already complex assessment of the welfare effects from counterfeiting. First, the presence of status goods may lead those consumers who cannot afford originals to be envious of those who can. Since the presence of counterfeit products may reduce this form of jealousy, there may be additional welfare losses from stronger

trademark enforcement. Second, since consumers able to afford original products are likely to have higher incomes than those unable to do so, stronger trademark enforcement may have distributional implications. A government seeking a more equal distribution of real incomes may assign a stronger weight to low income consumers in its social welfare calculations. On balance, the inclusion of distributional concerns along these lines makes it more likely that stepped-up trademark enforcement will lower economy-wide welfare — though, in the end, it remains an empirical question.

Infringements of copyright, patents, and related IPRs

31. In general, violations of copyright, patents, and related IPRs affect the policy trade-off outlined previously: they weaken incentives for investments in inventive and creative activities but benefit users of these rights by offering them access to IPRs-protected goods at competitive prices. If governments maintain socially optimal standards of protection, IPRs violations, by definition, will lead to a welfare loss. However, this is a big "if." Actual patent and copyright regimes are often the outcome of history, rules of thumb, and the influence of vested interests. Economic optimization hardly plays a role — not least because the social benefits of inventive and creative activities are unknown *ex-ante*. If the degree of protection as inscribed in laws is too strong, some levels of IPRs violations will increase welfare. If the degree of protection is too weak, any IPRs violation will invariably lower welfare.

32. An interesting question is how consumers of original products will fare upon stepped-up IPRs enforcement. Reduced competition from IPRs-infringing goods may increase the market power of the IPRs-holder, leading to higher prices for originals. However, the price effect will also depend on the price sensitivity of demand exhibited by the group of consumers that purchase originals. If their price sensitivity is lower than the average price sensitivity among all consumers in the economy, producers of originals may respond to stronger enforcement by lowering their prices. Such an outcome is consistent with consumers of originals being relatively well-off compared to consumers of illegitimate products. Indeed, original copyrighted works (e.g., audiovisual recordings) are sometimes more expensive in developing countries with higher piracy rates, as copyright holders set prices mostly reflecting demand from high-income consumers. However, possible price effects upon stronger IPRs enforcement may well be small if the distribution of income is such that only few consumers will be able to switch from IPRs-infringing to legitimate goods.

33. As in the case of trademarks, stronger enforcement of copyright, patents, and related IPRs is likely to have distributional consequences, which governments may want to take into account in their social welfare calculations. How the distribution of real incomes will be affected will, in part, depend on the average incomes of consumers of illegitimate products relative to the average incomes of workers engaged in creative and inventive activities. In a developing country context, where most intellectual property is owned by foreign residents, governments seeking to promote a more equal distribution of real incomes may attach more weight to the welfare losses suffered by low income consumers of IPRs-infringing goods relative to the strengthened incentive for investments in creative and inventive activities. Yet again, the national and global welfare effects of stronger IPRs enforcement remain ultimately an empirical question.

. . .

II.   MULTILATERAL IPRs ENFORCEMENT AGREEMENTS

A.   The TRIPS Agreement

1.   Enforcement Obligations

THE AGREEMENT ON TRADE RELATED ASPECTS OF INTELLECTUAL PROPERTY RIGHTS (TRIPs)

Thomas Cottier*

ENFORCEMENT OF INTELLECTUAL PROPERTY RIGHTS (PART III)

Effective legal protection depends both on substantive norms and the efficient and fair administration of justice. This is equally true for intellectual property rights protection. In many countries, implementation of and respect for rights fails due to lack of adequate and effective legal protection before administrative and judicial authorities. This is particularly true for intellectual property since it is a complex area of law often unfamiliar to regular courts and often alien to the legal tradition of developing countries. Efforts in the GATT prior to the Uruguay Round focused on combating counterfeiting and piracy which essentially entailed efforts to improve domestic and border enforcement. It was clear from the outset that comprehensive negotiations on trade-related aspects of intellectual property protection in the GATT, and subsequently the WTO, could not be limited to the definition of minimum substantive standards, but would need to extend to standards on judicial, administrative and even penal protection of IPRs. These efforts amounted to one of the most interesting and challenging tasks of the negotiation. None of the conventions administrated by WIPO addresses the issue of effective enforcement. A common and new ground between different legal traditions and systems had to be found. Developing countries resisted these efforts for a long time on the ground that the issue of enforcement goes far beyond aspects of international trade. Moreover, improving enforcement would not come without additional financial burdens which were not considered a priority in the process of development. Negotiations were based upon comprehensive drafts submitted by the United States, the European Communities and Switzerland. They can be characterized as a process of mutual approximation or *approchement* between common law traditions which entail party-driven instruments such as pretrial discovery, and the European-based approach leaving procedures and investigation much more in the hand of the courts. The result amounts to a first and quite substantial harmonization of civil and administrative law procedures in international law, while leaving room for alternative solutions reflecting different legal traditions. Many of the provisions are expressed in non-mandatory terms, allowing Members, but not obliging them, to authorize judicial and administrative authorities to take certain measures. These formulations demonstrate, on the one hand, the remaining divergences between judicial systems. On the other hand, they

* The World Trade Organization: Legal, Economic and Political Analysis. Vol. I p. 1041 (Patrick F. J. Macrory, Arthur E. Appleton, Michael G. Plummer eds., Springer 2005).

also prescribe and confirm that such measures as authorized, but not mandated, by the Agreement do not amount to excessive procedural requirements and, consequently, cannot give rise to violation and non-violation complaints.

As the implementation of these rules in national legislation inherently reaches beyond the realm of intellectual property protection, the provisions of Part III of the TRIPs Agreement may be described as a body of common procedural standards in international law. The norms resulting from the negotiations reflect a considerable level of detail. They are particularly apt to be referred to in the process of interpretation and application of domestic law under the doctrine of consistent interpretation. They are equally suitable for direct effect where such effect is constitutionally permitted. These points are of particular importance for the European Community. By means of the provisions on enforcement, a common regional standard in EC law was achieved for which no internal jurisdiction or competence existed in internal, domestic EC law. It is no coincidence that the provisions on enforcement resulted in a considerable expansion of the jurisdiction of the European Court of Justice in matters relating to civil procedure, and the doctrines of consistent interpretation and direct effect were first probed by the court in the field of WTO law.

While compliance with Part III only required minor, but sometimes important changes in the legislation of industrialized countries, implementing legislation was often required in developing and transitional countries, assisting the process of reinforcing the rule of law and good governance. The Agreement, however, does not oblige Members to provide additional and special resources for the protection of intellectual property rights distinct from the resources provided for the enforcement of laws in general. Article 41:5 provides a significant limitation, stating that "[n]othing in this Part creates any obligation with respect to the distribution of resources as between enforcement of intellectual property rights and the enforcement of law in general." Developing country efforts to reinforce the judicial system for the purposes of intellectual property right protection, however, have to be supported by developed country Members through technical cooperation under Article 67 of the Agreement.

GENERAL OBLIGATIONS

Article 41 of the Agreement stipulates a number of fundamental principles which apply in general and to all the subsequent, more specialized provisions of Part III. It requires Members to ensure that enforcement procedures are available under their law that permit effective action against any act of infringement of intellectual property rights covered by the TRIPs Agreement, including expeditious remedies to prevent infringements and remedies which constitute a deterrent to further infringements. The relevant test in assessing enforcement procedures is trade-related, examining whether they create barriers to legitimate trade and whether they provide safeguards against their abuse. Article 41:2 requires the procedures to be fair and equitable. Standards of fairness and equity are incorporated in the provisions throughout this Part. In addition, they need to be defined by reference to general principles of law. Procedures must not be unnecessarily complicated or costly, and must not entail unreasonable time-limits or unwarranted delays. Article 41:3 entails the fundamental principle that a decision on the merits of a case is to be reasoned, preferably in writing. Oral decisions therefore are not prohibited, and may be applied primarily in the field of rapid, provisional measures. Decisions on the merits must be based solely upon evidence in respect of which the parties were offered an opportunity to be heard.

These important provisions apply to all judicial systems alike and embody the fundamental right to be heard and the right to reasoned decision-making. They also apply, in accordance with Article 62:4, to administrative revocation and *inter-partes* procedures, such as opposition, revocation and cancellation of rights. Article 41:4 builds upon the tradition of Article X:3(b) of the GATT and prescribes the obligation to provide for appeal mechanisms. Members are required to provide for review of final administrative decisions by independent judicial authorities. As to judicial decisions in civil matters, the agreement is limited to a minimal standard. Members are free to define the jurisdictional threshold for appeal commensurate with the importance of the case (e.g., in terms of monetary thresholds). Within this range, they need to provide at least for review of legal issues on the merits. There is no obligation to provide for a second level of appeal. As to penal cases, judicial review is required for convictions, but not for acquittals.

Implementation of Part III is supported by obligations of Members to cooperate in international law enforcement in accordance with Article 69 of the Agreement. Members are obliged to establish and notify contacts point in their administrations and be ready to exchange information on infringing goods. Particular emphasis is laid on cooperation and exchange of information between customs authorities "with regard to trade in counterfeit trademark goods and pirated copyright goods."

CIVIL AND ADMINISTRATIVE PROCEDURES AND REMEDIES

The provisions of Section 2 of Part III of the TRIPs Agreement further specify the concept of fair and equitable procedural principles commensurate with well-established general rules of civil procedure. According to Article 49, they also apply to administrative procedures to the extent that "any civil remedy can be ordered as a result of administrative procedures on the merits of the case." The following requirements deserve particular emphasis:

Footnote 11 to Article 42 defines right holders entitled to civil procedures to include federations and associations having legal standing in accordance with domestic law. Parties shall be entitled to substantiate their claims. To this effect, the provision requires Members to allow representation by legal counsel. The requirement of personal appearance of right holders and defendants shall not be "overly burdensome"; an item of particular importance in transnational litigation. Defendants need to be served with sufficiently detailed and timely written notice. Subject to the constitutional law of Members, the confidential information of parties to the dispute needs to be protected, for example by making available a summary of factual evidence to the other party.

Article 43 contains important rules on evidence. Article 43:1 obliges Members to require parties to a dispute, based upon sufficiently substantiated claims, to produce evidence in administrative and judicial proceedings, subject to the protection of undisclosed information. If a party fails to produce such evidence, Article 43:2 empowers administrative and judicial authorities to make determinations based on the available evidence.

Article 44 addresses injunctions which are of particular importance in intellectual property litigation, especially in cases relating to counterfeiting or unlawful parallel trade. It requires domestic laws to grant power to local judicial authorities to prevent imminent infringements of intellectual property rights.

This provision, applicable to proceedings on the merits and to be distinguished from independent provisional measures addressed in Article 50, sets forth minimum standards for injunctions requiring a party not to commit an infringement or to cease infringement. In particular, local judicial authorities should be empowered, immediately after customs clearance of such goods, to prevent the entry into the channels of commerce of imported goods that infringe an intellectual property right and to seize the respective goods. Members are not required to extend such mechanisms to situations where the importer did not know, or did not have reasonable grounds to know that dealing in such subject matter would entail the infringement of an intellectual property right. In such cases, the right holder would need to await the judgment on the merits.

Article 45 requires that the damages awarded must constitute adequate compensation for the injury, including payment of the expenses of the right holder which, depending on the judicial system, may also (but need not) include appropriate attorney's fees. This minimum obligation is limited to willful or careless infringement. In addition, authorities may have the power to recover profits and/or the payment of pre-established damages. This possibility is available also in cases where the infringers did not knowingly, or with reasonable grounds to know, engage in infringing activity.

In addition, local authorities shall have the mandatory authority under Article 46 to seize infringing goods and to prevent the further delivery of infringing services (e.g., film screenings). Instruments ("implements") that predominantly serve to create infringing goods ("*instrumenta sceleris*"), such as production facilities and machinery, computers, etc., are also to be subject to seizure. For many countries, this amounts to an important additional obligation, reinforcing the fight against counterfeiting at its source. Judicial authorities shall have the authority to remove infringing goods and implements from the channels of commerce without compensation. Subject to the constitutional requirements of Members and the principle of proportionality, this may also involve destruction. Counterfeit goods or unlawfully imported goods in parallel trade may be used and consumed outside the channel of commerce, for example by making them available to food and support programs. Authorities are obliged to engage in a process of balancing the interests involved with a view to preventing further violations. As a result, goods may stay in the channel of commerce, even though the treaty specifies that mere removal of trademarks is generally not sufficient to comply with the TRIPs Agreement.

Article 47 provides an arguably very effective tool for detecting the sources of infringements. Provided that the measure appears to be proportionate to the infringement, the judicial authorities shall have the authority to require the infringing person to disclose (i) the identity of third persons involved in the production and distribution of the infringing goods or services, and (ii) their channels of distribution. While these obligations strongly reinforce the position of right holders, Article 48 protects defendants against abusive claims and measures. The provision is designed to deal with cases of so-called procedural harassment where measures imposing unjustified restrictions were granted. Appropriate remedies to compensate for damage must be made available. Accordingly, the judicial authorities must have authority to order the applicants to pay the defendant's expenses, which may include appropriate attorneys' fees. Members may exempt both public authorities and officials from appropriate remedial measures where unjustified actions are taken in good faith in the course of enforcing intellectual property laws.

PROVISIONAL MEASURES

Provisional measures applied for and granted beyond the ordinary civil or administrative remedies discussed above, amount to one of the most effective and important tools in enforcing intellectual property rights. Most cases against infringement or, as the case may be, unlawful importation and distribution by way of parallel trade, are settled by means of such procedures and do not reach the stage of ordinary and costly proceedings on the merits. The powers granted in Article 50 are of particular importance for trademark and copyright enforcement in the field of software protection as evidence of infringement can be easily destroyed upon notice of impending measures. A number of countries were obliged, following consultations under the DSU, to alter their legislation accordingly.

Article 50 is therefore a core provision of the TRIPs Agreement. Applying both to civil and administrative proceedings (Article 50:8), Article 50:1 obliges Members to make available prompt and effective provisional measures in order to (i) prevent an infringement from occurring, "in particular to prevent the entry into the channels of commerce in their jurisdiction or goods, including imported goods immediately after customs clearance," and (ii) "to preserve relevant evidence in regard of the alleged infringement." The Agreement sets detailed mandatory standards to this effect. In particular, according to Article 50:2 the judicial authorities shall have the authority to adopt such measures without having heard the defendant prior to taking action ("*inaudita altera parte*"). Such measures are subject to certain conditions set forth in Article 50:3 and 50:5: (i) the rights of the claimant must be reasonably established, (ii) any delay is likely to cause irreparable harm or where there is a risk of evidence being destroyed, and (iii) the goods concerned must be clearly identified and the applicant may therefore [be] required to supply additional information necessary for the identification of the goods. Upon taking measures *inaudita altera parte*, Article 50:4 requires that the defendant must be notified without delay of the measure and granted access to judicial review within a reasonable period to decide upon maintenance, revocation or modification of the measures. Article 50:6 of the Agreement requires that the provisional measures are revoked or otherwise cease to have effect upon request of the defendant, if the claimant does not initiate proceedings on the merit within a reasonable period of time. Such period is to be determined by the judicial authority ordering the provisional measure. Failing such determination, it shall not exceed 20 working days or 31 calendar days, whichever is shorter. This requirement and safeguard of linking provisional measures to proceedings on the merit amounts to a defining element of provisional measures compatible with WTO law. Article 50 gave rise to interpretation by the European Court of Justice and was applied in accordance with the doctrine of consistent interpretation with respect to both national law and the European trademark regulation. Furthermore, Article 50 is particularly suitable for direct effect when its safeguard provisions do not exist in domestic law. Under Article 50:7, courts may order the applicant to pay appropriate damages to the defendant, if the measure turns out to be unjustified.

SPECIAL REQUIREMENTS RELATED TO BORDER MEASURES

Border measures operated by customs authorities provide the second central mainstay for enforcing intellectual property rights. Counterfeit goods are best intercepted at the point of importation. Once they have reached the channels of distribution, law enforcement is more difficult and burdensome as complaints may need to be filed in different jurisdictions.

The provisions of Section 4 of Part III of the TRIPs Agreement deal[] with measures ordered by custom administrations with respect to the importation of counterfeit trademarked or pirated copyrighted goods. "Counterfeit trademark goods" (not including geographical indications) and "pirated copyright goods" (including goods protected by neighboring rights) are defined in a footnote to Article 51. There is no obligation to apply this Section to patented products, industrial designs, layout-designs, or geographical indications. However, if border measures are extended to other forms, there must be compliance with the procedures set forth in the Agreement. Furthermore, Members can also provide the same measures against infringing goods destined for export from their territories.

Article 52 requires the applicant to provide *prima facie* evidence of an impending infringement, and conditions are defined to this effect. Upon acceptance of the application, the authority informs the applicant as to the duration of the measure taken and, in accordance with Article 54, both the applicant and the importer are promptly notified of the suspension of the release of the goods at stake.

Article 53 allows authorities to require a reasonable, non-deterrent security or an equivalent assurance sufficient to protect the interests of the defendant and the authority in case wrongful actions is taken and compensation is due in accordance with Article 56. In cases other than trademark counterfeiting and copyright piracy as defined above (industrial designs, patents, layout designs and undisclosed information) the importer or consignee of such goods is entitled to their release on the posting of a sufficient security. This reflects the fact that assessing violations of IPRs in these areas is more difficult than in the field of trademarks and copyright protection.

Article 55 defines the duration of suspension of release and the relationship to proceedings on the merits. Given the powerful impact of this instrument, customs authorities are obliged to release the goods if they are not informed within ten working days that proceedings on the merits have been initiated by the applicant or that the competent judicial authority has taken provisional measures prolonging the suspension of the goods in accordance with Article 50. If proceedings on the merits have been initiated, the defendant is entitled to initiate review of the measure and to be heard. Measures may be subsequently modified, revoked or confirmed within a reasonable period of time.

Article 56 addresses the indemnification of the importer and owner of the goods for injury due to wrongful detention of goods or through detention of goods released pursuant to Article 55. The provision obligates Members to grant authorities the authority to require the applicant to pay the owner of the goods or the consignee appropriate compensation for injury caused. The Agreement does not set forth any standards and criteria to this effect and Members may base such compensation on their tort law. Also, the provision is silent on the responsibility of customs authorities. Article 53 implies that the responsibility remains exclusively with the applicant vis-à-vis the defendant. Additional remedies for *ex officio* action are required by Article 58.

Under Article 57 Members are obliged to grant the local authorities power to allow the right holder to inspect the goods in order to substantiate its claim, and the importer must also be granted the right of inspection. The Members are to authorize their authorities to inform the right holder of the names and addresses of the consignor, the importer and the consignee, and of the quantity of the goods in question if a positive determination has been made on the merits of a case.

Customs authorities are not limited to acting upon motion by the applicant. According to Article 58, Members may, but are not obligated, to empower competent authorities to order *ex officio* enforcement measures relating to the protection of intellectual property on the basis of *prima facie* evidence. Where such powers exist, a number of safeguards must be respected: (i) authorities are entitled to request additional information from the right holder at any time, (ii) the importer and right holder need to be promptly informed about the suspension of customs clearance (Article 58(b) implies that appeal procedures shaped *mutatis mutandis* in accordance with Article 55 must be available to the importer); (iii) liability of public authorities and officials for unlawful suspension must be made available and can only be excluded for acts taken or intended in good faith. The standard provides minimum protection against willful or negligent infringement.

Article 59 renders the principles and rules of Article 46 on disposal or destruction of infringing goods applicable to *ex officio* measures. Other than in exceptional circumstances, counterfeit trademark goods may not be released into a third country in an unaltered state, thus somewhat limiting the flexibility available under Article 46. Under Article 60 Members may exclude *de minimis* imports from the application of the provisions in Section 4.

CRIMINAL PROCEDURES

The TRIPs Agreement contains in Article 61 the first generation of penal provisions in the WTO system. It nevertheless leaves Members considerable flexibility in implementing the provision. Members are obligated to prosecute, at a minimum, willful trademark counterfeiting and copyright piracy (as defined in Article 51) on a commercial scale.[1] Penalties must include imprisonment and/or monetary fines. Members are obliged to set standards of punishment consistently with penalties provided for crimes of comparable gravity. In other words, they need to show consistency in their criminal policies. Penalties for other infringements, including negligent trademark or copyright violations, are permitted, but not required. Penal law must allow for the seizure, forfeiture and destruction of infringing goods and implements (defined in Article 46) in appropriate cases. The provision does allow Members to adopt extensive criminal sanctions without running the risk of facing challenges under violation or non-violation complaints, even though the threat of such sanctions may have considerable trade-restricting effects, for example in the field of internet communication.

2.   Enforcement in WTO Dispute Settlement

The TRIPS Agreement entered new international legal ground when it imposed obligations on WTO Members to adequately and effectively enforce IPRs. The difficulties inherent in establishing a breach of obligations were to some extent foreseeable. Those difficulties are on display in connection with

---

1. Even through Article 61 is framed as an alternative (by stating that criminal procedures and penalties be applied at least to trademark counterfeiting *or* copyright piracy), measures clearly need to be put in place for both trademarks *and* copyright.

U.S. efforts to require China to better implement its enforcement commitments. The first excerpt below examines some of the complications involved in pursuing an enforcement action under TRIPS Agreement rules. This is followed by an excerpt from the decision of the WTO dispute settlement panel in the *China-Enforcement* case.

CHINA IN THE WTO 2006: "LAW AND ITS LIMITATIONS" IN THE CONTEXT OF TRIPS

Frederick M. Abbott*

I. Introduction . . .

In February 2005, U.S. industry groups requested USTR to initiate a WTO dispute settlement action against China based on inadequate enforcement of intellectual property rights. USTR declined, largely on grounds that industry had not presented the kind of specific information that would be required to successfully pursue a WTO complaint. This was a significant decision reflecting a core problem the U.S. faces as it attempts to move forward at the WTO.

In April 2005, USTR announced the results of a so-called Special 301, "out of cycle review" of China's IPRs practices.[37] In addition to elevating China to "Priority Watch" country status (which is significantly less serious than designating China a priority foreign country), USTR indicated that it would invoke the provisions of Article 63 of the TRIPS Agreement which authorize a Member to formally request information from another Member regarding certain intellectual property-related matters. . . .

On October 25, 2005, in connection with a meeting of the TRIPS Council, the US Ambassador to the WTO, Peter Allgeir, transmitted a detailed request to the Chinese Ambassador to the WTO, Sun Zhenyu, regarding China's IPRs enforcement related activities. China was requested to respond on or before January 23, 2006. Japan and Switzerland made similar requests.

China's delegate questioned at the TRIPS Council meeting whether Article 63.3 of the TRIPS Agreement provides the basis for the broad request made by the United States. On December 22, 2006, the Chinese Ambassador sent a request for clarification of the legal basis of the request to the US Ambassador. As of February 2006, China had declined to formally respond to the U.S. request for information at the WTO. On February 15, 2006, USTR Robert Portman reiterated U.S. concerns with China's inadequate implementation of its IPRs-related commitments, and referred to action taken under Article 63 of the TRIPS Agreement at the WTO.

II. WTO Dispute Settlement

. . .

The TRIPS Agreement broke new ground when it established a requirement for effective enforcement of intellectual property norms. There are no

---

* In Developing Countries in the WTO: A Law and Economics Analysis (G. Bermann & P.C. Mavroidis eds., 2007).
    37. Available at http://www.ustr.gov.

comparable requirements in the WIPO Conventions. Thus, a panel and the Appellate Body would need to establish new standards under which to assess a claim for failure to permit the effective enforcement of IPRs. What quantum of enforcement failures would constitute a systemic failure? How would individual claims of judicial or administrative failure be assessed? Would a panel assess the decisions of judges in particular cases to determine whether the law was correctly applied? What would be the standard of review?

There are other trade agreements which require countries to properly apply their own law. For example, the NAFTA requires its parties to properly administer their antidumping and countervailing duty laws, and there have been a significant number of Chapter 19 panel decisions making assessments under those standards. But, the NAFTA Chapter 19 rules do not ask a systemic question. Each case is evaluated on its individual merits. The NAFTA Supplemental Agreements on Environment and Labor each require the parties to effectively enforce their respective laws in these subject matter areas, and provide mechanisms for evaluating claims of noncompliance. The mechanisms for evaluation are different than traditional state to state dispute settlement mechanisms, as in the WTO. In the environmental sector, private parties are entitled to initiate claims before the Secretariat of the NAAEC Commission for Environmental Cooperation, which may ultimately result in the preparation and publication of a factual record. There is an alternative state to state dispute settlement mechanism for allegations of failure of effective enforcement of environmental law. This mechanism has never been used and raises questions similar to that which are raised under Article 41 of the TRIPS Agreement. It is doubtful that a panel or the Appellate Body will refer to agreements outside the WTO to establish standards on effective enforcement under the TRIPS Agreement because there is no comparable context. The WTO dispute settlement system would be in uncharted jurisprudential territory.

. . .

C. REMEDIES

The Appellate Body characteristically recommends that a Member bring its measures into conformity with its WTO obligations. If it found that China was failing to implement its Article 61 obligations to provide adequate criminal sanctions against trademark counterfeiting and copyright piracy, it would presumably recommend that China remedy that failure. This could predictably lead to additional rounds of dispute settlement arbitration regarding whether China had in fact remedied the situation and, if not, what level of concessions the United States was entitled to withdraw. Such arbitrations would raise questions as difficult as those facing the panel and Appellate Body in the main dispute. How much criminal enforcement activity is required? How quickly can such a situation be remedied? Would the adequacy of the remedial measures be judged on the basis of the steps the government had taken or whether trademark counterfeiting and copyright piracy had actually been reduced? Are there reliable figures regarding the economic costs of counterfeiting and piracy?

None of this is to suggest that answers are beyond the capacity of the WTO dispute settlement system, but rather that almost any result is bound to be controversial. And this has the potential to create tensions within and for the WTO, regardless which of the main protagonists considers itself aggrieved.

NOTES AND QUESTIONS

1. The article excerpted above goes on to observe that China is likely to strengthen enforcement of IPRs as local enterprises increase their attention to innovation and branding. In other words, China will enforce IPRs when it perceives it to be in its national interest. This would be consistent with the historic pattern referred to by Keith Maskus in Chapter 1, section VIII.C. The TRIPS Agreement represents, in effect, an attempt to block this historic pattern. While the OECD countries may be successful in that effort with respect to less economically and politically powerful countries, the results are mixed with more economically and politically powerful countries like Brazil, China, and India.

2. U.S. foreign direct investors hold large stakes in China. U.S.-owned businesses produce in China for export to the United States and elsewhere. Does this restrict U.S. options for forcing China's hand with respect to IP enforcement?

3. Later in this chapter, we examine USTR's 2010 "Special 301" report with respect to China. This report sets out specific concerns with respect to IPRs practices.

As you read the following excerpt from *China — Measures Affecting the Protection and Enforcement of Intellectual Property Rights*, consider whether you accept a United States' claim that it "won" the case, recognizing that this excerpt does not address all of the issues at stake.

CHINA — MEASURES AFFECTING THE PROTECTION AND ENFORCEMENT OF INTELLECTUAL PROPERTY RIGHTS
Report of the Panel*

7.528 Part III of the TRIPS Agreement distinguishes between the treatment of wilful trademark counterfeiting and copyright piracy on a commercial scale, on the one hand, and all other infringements of intellectual property rights, on the other hand, in that only the former are subject to an obligation regarding criminal procedures and penalties. This indicates the shared view of the negotiators that the former are the most blatant and egregious acts of infringement. This view must inform the interpretation of Article 61.

7.529 The Panel recalls its findings at paragraph 7.241 above as to the circumstances of conclusion of the TRIPS Agreement with respect to enforcement procedures. Whilst some of the pre-existing international intellectual property agreements or conventions contain provisions on the characteristics of enforcement mechanisms, it is striking that none of them create any specific minimum standard for criminal enforcement procedures. Among the international intellectual property agreements with wide membership, Article 61 of the TRIPS Agreement is, in this sense, unique.

7.530 This reflects, in part, the fact that intellectual property rights are private rights, as recognized in the fourth recital of the Preamble to the TRIPS Agreement. In contrast, criminal procedures are designed to punish

* WT/DS362/R, 26 Jan. 2009.

acts that transgress societal values. This is reflected in the use of the word "penalties" in Article 61.

7.531 Bearing in mind these aspects of the context of the first sentence of Article 61, and the object and purpose of the TRIPS Agreement, the Panel now turns to the ordinary meaning of the words "on a commercial scale."

(V) "ON A COMMERCIAL SCALE"

7.532 The parties adopt different approaches to the task of interpreting the phrase "on a commercial scale." The Panel will examine each of these approaches in turn, beginning with that of the complainant.

7.533 The ordinary meaning of the word "scale" is uncontroversial. It may be defined as "relative magnitude or extent; degree, proportion. Freq. in *on a grand, lavish, small,* etc. *scale.*" The ordinary meaning of the word includes both the concept of quantity, in terms of magnitude or extent, as well as the concept of relativity. Both concepts are combined in the notions of degree and proportion. Therefore, a particular "scale" compares certain things or actions in terms of their size. Some things or actions will be of the relevant size and others will not.

7.534 The relevant size is indicated by the word "commercial." The ordinary meaning of "commercial" may be defined in various ways. The following two definitions have been raised in the course of these proceedings:

> "1. Engaged in commerce; of, pertaining to, or bearing on commerce.
> 2. (. . .)
> 3. Interested in financial return rather than artistry; likely to make a profit; regarded as a mere matter of business."

7.535 The Panel considers the first definition to be apposite. It includes the term "commerce" which may, in turn, be defined as "buying and selling; the exchange of merchandise or services, esp. on a large scale." Reading this definition into the definition of "commercial" indicates that "commercial" means, basically, engaged in buying and selling, or pertaining to, or bearing on, buying and selling. A combination of that expanded definition of "commercial" and the definition of "scale" would render a meaning in terms of a relative magnitude or extent (of those) engaged in buying and selling, or a relative magnitude or extent pertaining to, or bearing on, buying and selling. This draws a link to the commercial marketplace.

7.536 The United States also submits that the word "commercial" scale draws a link to the commercial marketplace. However, it refers to elements of the first and third meanings in definition 3., but dismisses the relevance of the second meaning, "likely to make a profit," because it is different from the other two.

7.537 . . .

7.538 Therefore, the Panel considers that the first definition set out at paragraph 7.534 above is appropriate. However, the combination of that definition of "commercial" with the definition of "scale" presents a problem in that scale is a quantitative concept whilst commercial is qualitative, in the sense that it refers to the nature of certain acts. Some acts are in fact commercial, whilst others are not. Any act of selling can be described as commercial in this primary sense, irrespective of its size or value. If "commercial" is simply read as a qualitative term, referring to all acts pertaining to, or bearing on commerce, this would read the word "scale" out of the text. Acts on a commercial scale would simply be commercial acts. The phrase "on a commercial scale" would simply mean "commercial." Such an interpretation fails to give meaning to all the terms used in the treaty and is inconsistent with the rule of effective treaty interpretation.

7.539 There are no other uses of the word "scale" in the TRIPS Agreement, besides the first and fourth sentences of Article 61. However, the wider context shows that the TRIPS Agreement frequently uses the word "commercial" with many other nouns, although nowhere else with "scale." The other uses of the word "commercial" include "commercial rental," "commercial purposes," "commercial exploitation," "commercial terms," "public non-commercial use," "first commercial exploitation," "honest commercial practices," "commercial value," "unfair commercial use," "non-commercial nature" and "legitimate commercial interests."

7.540 The provisions of the Paris Convention (1967) incorporated by Article 2.1 of the TRIPS Agreement include uses of the word "commercial" in the phrase "industrial or commercial establishment" (in the singular or plural) and in the phrases "industrial or commercial matters" and "industrial or commercial activities." . . .

7.543 . . . [T]he negotiators agreed in Article 61 to use the distinct phrase "on a commercial scale." This indicates that the word "scale" was a deliberate choice and must be given due interpretative weight. "Scale" denotes a relative size, and reflects the intention of the negotiators that the limitation on the obligation in the first sentence of the Article depended on the size of acts of counterfeiting and piracy. Therefore, whilst "commercial" is a qualitative term, it would be an error to read it solely in those terms. In context it must indicate a quantity.

7.544 A review of the uses of the word "commercial" throughout the TRIPS Agreement indicates that it links various activities, not simply selling, to the marketplace. It also shows that "commercial" activities cannot be presumed to be on a larger scale than others, such as "public non-commercial" activities, even though they would generally be larger than, say, "personal" or "domestic" use. The distinguishing characteristic of a commercial activity is that it is carried out for profit. The review of the uses of the word "commercial" also shows that, unlike all the others, Article 61 uses the word "commercial" to qualify a notion of size.

7.545 In the Panel's view, the combination of the primary definition of "commercial" and the definition of "scale" can be reconciled with the context of Article 61 if it is assessed not solely according to the nature of an activity but also in terms of relative size, as a market benchmark. As there is no other qualifier besides "commercial," that benchmark must be whatever "commercial" typically or usually connotes. In quantitative terms, the benchmark would be the magnitude or extent at which engagement in commerce, or activities pertaining to or bearing on commerce, are typically or usually carried on, in other words, the magnitude or extent of typical or usual commercial activity. Given that the phrase uses the indefinite article "a," it refers to more than one magnitude or extent of typical or usual commercial activity. The magnitude or extent will vary in the different "cases" of counterfeiting and piracy to which the obligation applies. In the Panel's view, this reflects the fact that what is typical or usual varies according to the type of commerce concerned.

7.546 Turning to the arguments of the parties and various third parties on this point, they have attempted to give due meaning to both the terms "commerce" and "scale" in different ways. Initially, the United States submitted as follows:

> "those who engage in commercial activities in order to make a 'financial return' in the marketplace . . . are, by definition, therefore operating on a commercial scale" . . .

. . .

7.559 The Panel will follow the approach explained by the Appellate Body in EC — Chicken Cuts:

> "The Appellate Body has observed that dictionaries are a 'useful starting point' for the analysis of 'ordinary meaning' of a treaty term, but they are not necessarily dispositive. The ordinary meaning of a treaty term must be ascertained according to the particular circumstances of each case. Importantly, the ordinary meaning of a treaty term must be seen in the light of the intention of the parties 'as expressed in the words used by them against the light of the surrounding circumstances.'"

7.560 The Panel recalls that the dictionary definition of "scale" (quoted at paragraph 7.533 above) includes the entry "Freq. in on a grand, lavish, small, etc. scale." These examples show that the phrase "on a . . . scale" is frequently used. Therefore, the use of the words "on a commercial scale" as a phrase appears to be relevant to their ordinary meaning.

7.561 The circumstances surrounding the inclusion of the phrase "on a commercial scale" show that the phrase has been used and, in some cases, defined in the intellectual property legislation of various countries for periods stretching back almost a century. Specifically, the patent laws of these countries refer to the working of inventions, or failure to work inventions, "on a commercial scale." The term is used in relation to the exploitation of protected subject matter, as in Article 61, but the purpose of these non-working provisions, and the considerations relevant to their operation, are distinct from those of criminal procedures and penalties as addressed in Article 61 of the TRIPS Agreement. There is insufficient indication that the meaning ascribed to the term "on a commercial scale" in such legislation was that intended by the negotiators of the TRIPS Agreement when they used the term in the first and fourth sentences of Article 61. However, this circumstance shows the phrase in use in an intellectual property context long before the negotiation of the TRIPS Agreement.

. . .

7.563 The evidence on the record includes many other uses of the words "commercial scale" and "on a commercial scale" in a variety of contexts. Accordingly, the Panel considers that the words "commercial" and "scale" provide important context for the ordinary meaning of each other when used together in the phrase "on a commercial scale" as in the first sentence of Article 61 of the TRIPS Agreement.

7.564 China submits that the phrase "on a commercial scale" refers to "a significant magnitude of infringement activity." . . .

. . .

7.570 The Panel considers that each of the uses on the record, being in the English language, reflects the understanding of the authors as to the ordinary meaning of those words and phrases in that language. That is the reason why a language allows its speakers to render themselves mutually intelligible. . . .

. . .

7.573 Simple searches of online patent databases of the Patent Cooperation Treaty, the United States Patent and Trademark Office and the European Patent Office, reveal many patent applications that use the phrase "commercial scale." China has provided abstracts of some applications that define the phrase "commercial scale" in precise, quantitative terms of volume, weight or speed. These definitions vary greatly and relate to different factors, according to the invention claimed in the application. From this evidence, China concludes that:

> "In the context of patent applications, the phrase 'commercial scale' refers to a certain level of magnitude. This magnitude is not necessarily objectively high, but it is relatively high in the context of the operation involved."

7.574 The United States finds this statement "telling" and recalls its view that:

> "[B]ased on its ordinary meaning, what qualifies as 'commercial scale' piracy or counterfeiting will vary among product and market, and therefore, what is 'commercial scale' can be determined using factors relevant to a particular situation."

7.575 The United States argues that the uses in the press releases and SEC filings must be understood in context, as in some cases:

> "[W]hether a manufacturing activity is 'commercial scale' may well mean whether the activity is undertaken on a scale, or at a level of economic efficiency, that allows that public company to make a return on investment or profit for its shareholders."

7.576 The Panel observes a certain degree of convergence between the parties' views, as compared to their initial positions, when addressing these ordinary uses of the phrase "commercial scale." The Panel considers that the contexts in which the term "on a commercial scale" or "commercial scale" is used, given their variety, indicate that each of the words "commercial" and "scale" provides important context for the interpretation of the other when used together. Their combined meaning varies greatly according to the context around them and the lack of precision in the term is apparent. However, it is clear that none of these uses refer to activities that are simply commercial. Rather, they are evidently intended to distinguish certain activities (or premises) from others that pertain to or have a bearing on commerce but which do not meet a market benchmark in terms of what is typical. The precise benchmark in each case depends on the product and the market to which the phrase relates.

7.577 The Panel recalls its view at paragraph 7.545 above and, in light of the evidence considered above, finds that a "commercial scale" is the magnitude or extent of typical or usual commercial activity. Therefore, counterfeiting or piracy "on a commercial scale" refers to counterfeiting or piracy carried on at the magnitude or extent of typical or usual commercial activity with respect to a given product in a given market. The magnitude or extent of typical or usual commercial activity with respect to a given product in a given market forms a benchmark by which to assess the obligation in the first sentence of

Article 61. It follows that what constitutes a commercial scale for counterfeiting or piracy of a particular product in a particular market will depend on the magnitude or extent that is typical or usual with respect to such a product in such a market, which may be small or large. The magnitude or extent of typical or usual commercial activity relates, in the longer term, to profitability.

7.578 The Panel observes that what is typical or usual in commerce is a flexible concept. The immediate context in the second sentence of Article 61, which is closely related to the first, refers to the similarly flexible concepts of "deterrent" and "corresponding gravity." Neither these terms nor "commercial scale" are precise but all depend on circumstances, which vary according to the differing forms of commerce and of counterfeiting and piracy to which these obligations apply.

7.579 The parties have presented certain other facts and arguments in relation to the interpretation of "a commercial scale," which the Panel will now assess.

(VI) Subsequent Practice

7.580 China refers to certain material as "subsequent practice" in the application of the TRIPS Agreement within the meaning of Article 31(3) of the Vienna Convention. The material comprises the enforcement policies of two authorities of two Members, a draft Directive of another Member and various free trade agreements entered into by the United States.

7.581 The Panel has reviewed the material and considers that it lacks the breadth to constitute a common, consistent, discernible pattern of acts or pronouncements. Further, the content of the material does not imply agreement on the interpretation of Article 61 of the TRIPS Agreement. Therefore, the Panel does not consider that it constitutes subsequent practice for the purposes of this interpretation.

(VII) Supplementary Means of Interpretation

. . .

7.589 The records of the TRIPS negotiations do not disclose any discussion of the meaning of the phrase "on a commercial scale."

. . .

(IX) Conformity of the Measures at Issue with Respect to the Level of the Thresholds

7.600 The Panel recalls its finding at paragraph 7.545 above regarding the interpretation of the phrase "wilful trademark counterfeiting or copyright piracy 'on a commercial scale,'" as used in Article 61 of the TRIPS Agreement. The Panel recalls, in particular, that this is a relative standard, which will vary when applied to different fact situations.

7.601 The Panel notes that it is the standard in the treaty obligation that varies as applied to different fact situations, and not necessarily the means by which Members choose to implement that standard. The Panel recalls that the third sentence of Article 1.1 of the TRIPS Agreement, quoted and discussed at paragraphs 7.512 and 7.513 above, provides as follows:

> "Members shall be free to determine the appropriate method of implementing the provisions of this Agreement within their own legal system and practice."

7.602 This provision confirms that the TRIPS Agreement does not mandate specific forms of legislation. The Panel may not simply assume that a Member must give its authorities wide discretion to determine what is on a commercial scale in any given case, and may not simply assume that thresholds, including numerical tests, are inconsistent with the relative benchmark in the first sentence of Article 61 of the TRIPS Agreement. As long as a Member in fact provides for criminal procedures and penalties to be applied in cases of wilful trademark counterfeiting or copyright piracy on a commercial scale, it will comply with this obligation. If it is alleged that a Member's method of implementation does not so provide in such cases, that allegation must be proven with evidence. Therefore, the Panel will assess whether the evidence shows that China fails to provide for criminal procedures and penalties to be applied in any such cases.

7.603 The Panel begins with the first limb of the claim. In the first limb of the claim, the United States challenges the levels at which certain thresholds are set. Having chosen to challenge the level of a series of numerical thresholds as compared to a relative standard, it is necessary for the United States to demonstrate that the levels are higher than that standard as applied in certain factual situations. That calls for quantitative evidence. Later, the Panel will address the second limb of the claim, in which the United States challenges the factors taken into account by the criminal thresholds. That calls for qualitative evidence.

7.604 The parties agree that the standard of "a commercial scale" will vary by product and market and that the conformity of China's criminal thresholds with that standard must be assessed by reference to China's marketplace.

7.605 The Panel recalls that a previous Panel had occasion to apply certain relative standards in the TRIPS Agreement in quantitative terms.

7.606 . . . The Panel needs to consider the specific conditions applying in China's marketplace in assessing whether the measures in question, which exclude certain acts of infringement from particular liability, conform to the relative standard in Article 61. This applies a fortiori as the relative standard is set in terms of what is "on a commercial scale," which varies not only by market but also by product within the same market.

. . .

7.609 The Panel has reviewed the measures and agrees that, on their face, they do exclude certain commercial activity from criminal procedures and penalties. For example, some of the criminal thresholds are set in terms that refer expressly to commercial activity, such as "illegal business operation volume," which is defined in terms of "manufacture, storage, transportation, or sales" of infringing products, and "illegal gains" which is defined in terms of profit. However, based solely on the measures on their face, the Panel cannot distinguish between acts that, in China's marketplace, are on a commercial scale, and those that are not.

7.610 Certain thresholds are set in monetary terms, ranging from ¥20,000 profit to ¥50,000 turnover or sales. The measures, on their face, do not indicate what these amounts represent as compared to a relevant commercial bench-mark in China. Each of these amounts represents a range of volumes of goods, which vary according to price. Another factor to take into account is the period of time over which infringements can be cumulated to satisfy these thresholds. One threshold is set not in monetary terms but rather at 500 张 (份) ("copies" for the sake of simplicity). Whilst it is reasonably clear to the Panel how many goods that comprises with respect to certain traditional media, this is not, on its face, related to any relevant market benchmark in China either.

7.611 The Panel has noted the United States' repeated assertions that certain amounts constitute counterfeiting or piracy on a commercial scale. The most recurrent example concerns 499 copyright-infringing "copies," although it is not related to the same product in all examples or, sometimes, to any product. The only facts in these examples are amounts equal to, or slightly less than, those in the measures themselves. Those amounts, in combination with the monetary thresholds and the factors used in the thresholds, demonstrate the class of acts for which China does not provide criminal procedures and penal-ties to be applied. Those numbers and factors do not, in themselves, demon-strate what constitutes a commercial scale for any product or in any market in China.

. . .

7.615 In its rebuttal of China's assertion regarding the scale of commerce in China, the United States noted that the "commercial scale" standard was a relative one. It commented on the Economic Census statistics submitted by China but at the same time dismissed their relevance as they are aggregate statistics related to undefined average economic units. It also recalled an earlier assertion that the Chinese market, including the market for many copyright and trademark-bearing goods, is fragmented and characterized by a profusion of small manufacturers, middlemen, distributors, and small outlets at the retail level.

7.616 The Panel has reviewed the evidence in support of this assertion. The evidence comprises a quote from a short article from a US newspaper, the San Francisco Chronicle, titled "30,000-Store Wholesale Mall Keeps China Com-petitive" regarding the number of stores in a particular mall in Yiwu and the physical dimensions of some stalls; a statistic quoted from an extract from a management consultant report titled "The 2005 Global Retail Development Index" that the top ten retailers in China hold less than 2 per cent of the market, and another statistic that the top 100 retailers have less than 6.4 per cent; and a quote from an article in Time magazine titled "In China, There's Priceless, and for Everything Else, There's Cash" that a shopping mall in Luohu spans six floors of small stores.

7.617 The Panel finds that, even if these sources were suitable for the purpose of demonstration of contested facts in this proceeding, the information that was provided was too little and too random to demonstrate a level that constitutes a commercial scale for any product in China.

7.618 The United States referred to Canada's third party written submission, which had provided an estimate of China's gross domestic product per capita. It did not explain specifically how this figure was comparable to China's numer-ical thresholds.

7.619 The Panel considers GDP per capita a reliable indicator of average national income but not a sufficient indicator of a commercial scale, as it is calculated with a denominator of total population. The Panel also notes that GDP is a far more aggregated figure than those in the Economic Census statistics that the United States dismissed.

7.620 China submits that the United States must provide evidence that China's laws actually function to exclude a category of infringement that meets the "commercial scale" standard. Hypothetical examples do not qualify as sufficient evidence.

7.621 In response, the United States asserts that it, and a number of third parties, have provided "numerous, concrete illustrations" of commercial-scale piracy and counterfeiting that take place underneath China's thresholds. It refers to a "Report on Copyright Complaints, Raids and Resulting Criminal Actions in China" prepared by a coalition of trade associations in 2008 (the "CCA Report").

7.622 The Panel has reviewed the CCA Report to determine whether it bears out the United States' assertion. The CCA Report was originally submitted as a case example intended to show that the criminal thresholds create a "safe harbour" (an assertion not borne out by the data) and also to show that significant quantities of retail sales of infringing product take place in China at levels below China's thresholds.

7.623 The Panel notes that the question whether retail sales of infringing product take place below the thresholds is not dispositive of the claim, as the first sentence of Article 61 does not require Members to provide for criminal procedures and penalties to be applied to all such cases.

. . .

7.627 The United States also submitted other press articles to illustrate points in its first written submission, particularly regarding the calculation of certain thresholds. China objected at the outset arguing that "[t]he Panel can afford little or no weight to such anecdotal and potentially misinformed reports." The United States was puzzled by China's concern at its recourse to newspapers or other media. It recalled its prior attempts to obtain information from China pursuant to Article 63.3 of the TRIPS Agreement. China had declined to provide information and stated instead that its competent domestic IPR authorities had also made relevant information publicly available through their official websites, newspapers, magazines and other proper channels. The United States added that the information in newspapers and magazines is "drawn from a variety of well-established and well-regarded sources."

7.628 The Panel has reviewed the press articles and notes that none of them are corroborated, nor do they refer to events or statements that would not require corroboration. Whilst the publications are reputable, most of these particular articles are brief and are quoted either for general statements or random pieces of information. Most are anecdotal in tone, some repeating casual remarks about prices of fake goods, anonymous statements or speculation. They have titles including "Fake Pens Write Their Own Ticket," "Chasing copycats in a tiger economy," "Hollywood takes on fake Chinese DVDs," "Film not out yet on DVD? You can find it in China" and "Inside China's teeming world of fake goods." Most of the press articles are printed in US or other foreign English-language media that are not claimed to be authoritative sources of information on prices and markets in China. There are four press articles from Chinese sources, one from Xinhua News Agency and three from the English-language China Daily. Two are quoted simply to demonstrate the

existence of certain goods in China; another quotes a vague statement from
unnamed "market insiders" on how illegal publishers tend to work; and the
other quotes an "insider" for the maximum and minimum prices of a range of
pirated and genuine goods. One other alleged "recent news account" is not
attributed to any source at all.

7.629 The Panel emphasizes that, in the absence of more reliable and relevant data, it has reviewed the evidence in the press articles with respect to a
central point in this claim that is highly contested. The credibility and weight of
that evidence are therefore critical to the Panel's task. For the reasons set out
above, the Panel does not ascribe any weight to the evidence in the press articles
and finds that, even if it did, the information that these press articles contain is
inadequate to demonstrate what is typical or usual in China for the purposes of
the relevant treaty obligation.

7.630 There is no indication that probative evidence on this point would be
difficult to obtain.

. . .

7.632 For the above reasons, the Panel finds that the United States has not
made a prima facie case with respect to the first limb of its claim under the first
sentence of Article 61 of the TRIPS Agreement. The Panel will now turn to the
second limb of the claim.

(X) OTHER INDICIA — PHYSICAL EVIDENCE

. . .

7.652 . . . , the Panel does not consider that the United States has made a prima
facie case with respect to other indicia of infringement, such as physical evidence
including product components, packaging and materials or implements.

(XI) OTHER INDICIA — IMPACT ON THE COMMERCIAL MARKETPLACE

7.653 With respect to the second limb of this claim, the United States also
alleges that China's thresholds are tied to finished goods and therefore ignore
other indicia of commercial scale operations, such as the impact that the piracy
or counterfeiting has on the commercial marketplace and by extension, right
holders.

. . .

7.661 For all the above reasons, the Panel does not consider that the United
States has made a prima facie case with respect to impact on the commercial
marketplace.

7.662 The Panel wishes to emphasize that its findings should not be taken to
indicate any view as to whether the obligation in the first sentence of Article 61
of the TRIPS Agreement applies to acts of counterfeiting and piracy committed
without any purpose of financial gain.

(XII) MISCELLANEOUS FACTORS

7.663 The United States asserted that the breadth of the term "on a
commercial scale" presumes that a wide range of considerations should be

probative of "commercial scale." However, it did not submit argument in support of any other considerations besides those discussed above.

. . .

7.667 Therefore, the United States did not relate these factors sufficiently to the measures at issue or to its claim to discharge its burden of proof.

7.668 The Panel recalls its findings at paragraphs 7.652, 7.661 and 7.667 above and finds that the United States has not made a prima facie case with respect to the second limb of its claim under the first sentence of Article 61 of the TRIPS Agreement.

(XIII) Conclusion with Respect to the Claim Under the First Sentence of Article 61

7.669 In light of the Panel's findings at paragraphs 7.632 and 7.668 above, the Panel concludes that the United States has not established that the criminal thresholds are inconsistent with China's obligations under the first sentence of Article 61 of the TRIPS Agreement.

. . .

6. conclusions with respect to the criminal thresholds

7.681 The Panel recalls its conclusion at paragraph 7.669 above that the United States has not established that the criminal thresholds are inconsistent with China's obligations under the first sentence of Article 61 of the TRIPS Agreement.

7.682 The Panel exercises judicial economy with respect to the claims under Article 41.1 of the TRIPS Agreement and under the second sentence of Article 61 of the TRIPS Agreement (with respect to the criminal thresholds).

. . .

8. concluding remark

. . .

8.5 In this dispute, the Panel's task was not to ascertain the existence or the level of trademark counterfeiting and copyright piracy in China in general nor to review the desirability of strict IPR enforcement. The United States challenged three specific alleged deficiencies in China's IPR legal system in relation to certain specific provisions of the TRIPS Agreement. The Panel's mandate was limited to a review of whether those alleged deficiencies, based upon an objective assessment of the facts presented by the parties, are inconsistent with those specific provisions of the TRIPS Agreement.

NOTES AND QUESTIONS

1. The United States has been pressing China for stronger enforcement of IP laws since at least the mid-1980s. Do you find it puzzling that after two decades of voicing concern, the United States could not present "better evidence" of counterfeiting on a substantial scale in China? What do you think might account for the relative paucity of evidence? Is it possible that

U.S.-based multinational companies doing business in China were not anxious to make public their specific complaints out of concern they might risk future business opportunities in China? If you find that plausible, how would you recommend pursuing stronger enforcement in China without presenting concrete evidence of TRIPS Agreement–inconsistent conduct?

3. Violation and Non-Violation Complaints

In Chapter 1, the state-to-state WTO dispute settlement mechanism was introduced. In subsequent chapters, we examined a number of WTO dispute settlement decisions involving substantive compliance, including the *Canada-Generic Pharmaceuticals, U.S.-Havana Club, U.S. — Copyright Act* and *EC — Geographic Indications* decisions (as well as a decision involving implementation of procedural obligations, *India-Mailbox,* excerpted in Chapter 1). We refer back to the introduction and the referenced cases to illustrate operation of the state-to-state WTO dispute settlement mechanism.

Each of the cases previously examined involved a claim by one WTO Member against another alleging failure to comply with an obligation expressly imposed by the WTO TRIPS Agreement. In WTO terms, these cases involved "violation" complaints. There is another type of WTO complaint that one Member may bring against another. This type does not involve failure to comply with an express obligation. Instead, one Member alleges that another deprived it of benefits it legitimately expected to receive when it entered into the agreement, even though the other Member has not failed to comply with an express obligation. This is referred to as a "non-violation nullification or impairment complaint" or, more concisely, a "non-violation complaint."

The non-violation complaint has a sensible basis in traditional trade disputes. Assume that the United States and Australia negotiate over tariff rates. The United States agrees to reduce its tariffs on imports of Australian apples in exchange for Australia's agreement to reduce its tariffs on imports of American oranges. A reciprocal bargain is struck. From the U.S. side, the benefit is that the price of U.S.-grown oranges will be lower on the Australian market (and more price-competitive with oranges grown in Australia). Following conclusion of this deal, the Australian government grants a WTO-legal domestic farm subsidy to Australian orange growers, providing them with payments for oranges they produce and sell on the Australian market. As a result of the subsidy payments, Australian growers can sell their oranges at a lower price. From the standpoint of the United States, the value of the tariff reduction previously agreed to by Australia has been "nullified or impaired." That is, the competitive gain to U.S. orange growers from the tariff reduction has been reduced or eliminated even though, technically, Australia has not violated any express WTO obligation to the United States. An action by the United States against Australia in this context would be a "non-violation" action provided for by the WTO DSU (and also by the earlier GATT dispute settlement mechanism).

Is the same type of non-violation complaint sensible in the context of TRIPS? The following paper addressed this question from the standpoint of developing countries preparing for the WTO Cancún Ministerial Conference.

NON-VIOLATION NULLIFICATION OR IMPAIRMENT CAUSES OF ACTION UNDER THE TRIPS AGREEMENT AND THE FIFTH MINISTERIAL CONFERENCE: A WARNING AND REMINDER

Frederick M. Abbott*

At the Fourth Ministerial Conference in Doha, WTO Ministers directed the TRIPS Council to continue examining the scope and modalities for bringing non-violation nullification or impairment (hereinafter "non-violation") causes of action in dispute settlement under the TRIPS Agreement. The Decision on Implementation-Related Issues and Concerns stated:

> 11. AGREEMENT ON TRADE-RELATED ASPECTS OF INTELLECTUAL PROPERTY RIGHTS (TRIPS)
>
> 11.1 The TRIPS Council is directed to continue its examination of the scope and modalities for complaints of the types provided for under subparagraphs 1(b) and 1(c) of Article XXIII of GATT 1994 and make recommendations to the Fifth Session of the Ministerial Conference. It is agreed that, in the meantime, Members will not initiate such complaints under the TRIPS Agreement.

Article 64.2, TRIPS Agreement,[1] established a five-year moratorium on the initiation of non-violation and situation[2] complaints. During that period, Members were to examine the scope and modalities for such complaints and submit recommendations to the Ministerial Conference. A decision to approve such recommendations or to extend the five-year moratorium was to be made by consensus. The question of whether failure of the TRIPS Council to submit recommendations to the Ministerial Conference acts to continue the moratorium in force is debated. Regardless of one's views on this subject, there is a *substantial risk* that should Ministers *not act* to extend the moratorium at the Fifth Ministerial Conference (or adopt rules on scope and modalities), this will enable the initiation of non-violation complaints (as a consequence of the lapse of the period stated in Article 64.2).

From the standpoint of developing countries, the possibility of non-violation causes of action being brought under the TRIPS Agreement would give rise to

---

* Quaker United Nations Office, Occasional Paper No. 11, July 2003, available at http://www.quno.org.

1. ARTICLE 64

2. Subparagraphs 1(b) and 1(c) of Article XXIII of GATT 1994 shall not apply to the settlement of disputes under this Agreement for a period of five years from the date of entry into force of the WTO Agreement.

3. During the time period referred to in paragraph 2, the Council for TRIPS shall examine the scope and modalities for complaints of the type provided for under subparagraphs 1(b) and 1(c) of Article XXIII of GATT 1994 made pursuant to this Agreement, and submit its recommendations to the Ministerial Conference for approval. Any decision of the Ministerial Conference to approve such recommendations or to extend the period in paragraph 2 shall be made only by consensus, and approved recommendations shall be effective for all Members without further formal acceptance process.

2. "Situation" complaints may be brought under GATT Article XXIII:1(c), and by cross-reference under TRIPS Agreement Article 64.1, except as limited by the moratorium. Such complaints are addressed by the DSU in a manner that makes their successful pursuit unlikely. Article 26.2, DSU, requires the consensus adoption of panel reports on "situation" grounds. Situation complaints are not considered separately in this memorandum.

serious risks. In the *India-Mailbox* decision,[3] in which the Appellate Body (AB) first interpreted the TRIPS Agreement, it stressed reliance on the express text of the agreement and discounted the significance of Member's expectations concerning its effects. Although the AB has given little indication that it would permit Members to significantly expand the agreement to encompass subject matter not expressly contemplated by the text, there remains the possibility of developing Members being forced to defend claims brought on non-violation grounds, even if for the most part such claims are ultimately rejected.

Potential Claims

Intellectual property rights (IPRs) are "negative rights" in that they entitle their holders to prevent third parties from performing acts without their consent. IPRs are not "market access" rights. However, it might be argued that granting IPRs while limiting access to the market deprives the right holder of advantages expected to be gained when the TRIPS Agreement was negotiated. Concerns over a market access theory of TRIPS in relation to the audio-visual sector motivated the European Community (EC) to support the non-violation moratorium during the Uruguay Round. The EC was concerned that the United States of America (USA) would claim that granting copyrights to authors and artists, but restricting their capacity to show films, etc., in the EC, would deprive the USA of the benefit of its TRIPS bargain.

It is not difficult to foresee Members acting on behalf of pharmaceutical patent holders claiming that price controls operate to deprive them of the benefits of patent protection. While such a claim would be unlikely to succeed in light of Article 8.1, TRIPS Agreement, and the fact that price controls were present in many countries during the TRIPS negotiations, this may not preclude a Member from threatening such action, or bringing it.

There are many forms of government regulation that could be argued to be consistent with the TRIPS Agreement, yet to nullify or impair the expectations of IPRs holders. For example, tax policies with respect to IPRs may affect the profitability of IPRs-dependent industries and nullify or impair benefits. Regulatory measures such as packaging and labelling requirements, and consumer protection rules, might be applicable to trademark holders and affect their access to the market.

Many Members maintain rules on acceptable expression, that is, they censor certain materials as against public policy. Members on behalf of copyright holders may argue that rules restricting expression are inconsistent with copyright holders' interests.

As noted above, the EC and other Members regulate access to the market for expressive works based on cultural concerns. This inhibits market access by copyright holders and might form the subject of a non-violation complaint.

Non-violation causes of action could be used to threaten developing Members' use of flexibilities inherent in the TRIPS Agreement and intellectual property law more generally. Thus, for example, Members that adopt relatively generous fair use rules in the fields of copyright or trademark might find that they are claimed against for depriving another Member of the benefit of its bargain.

---

3. *India-Patent Protection for Pharmaceutical and Agricultural Chemical Products*, AB-1997-5, WT/DS50/AB/R, 19 Dec. 1997.

Actions taken by developing Members to implement exceptions to TRIPS patent rules under Articles 30, or to grant compulsory licenses under Article 31, could be alleged to deprive patent holders of their expectations. The application of copyright rules in the area of software protection involves substantial flexibility. The use of discretion to establish permissive uses of code (for example, on hardware or software interface efficiency grounds) might be subject to challenge.

Non-violation causes of action might also be foreseen in the area of enforcement. For example, while the TRIPS Agreement requires that adequate remedial measures be provided, in most cases it leaves to Members substantial discretion to determine the level of appropriate remedies. A Member could be claimed against for nullifying or impairing benefits by imposing insufficiently stringent remedies. Although the TRIPS Agreement does not require Members to provide or enforce forms of IP protection not specified in the agreement, it might be claimed that failure to extend protection to new forms nullified or impaired the TRIPS Agreement bargain.

Non-violation causes of action might be pleaded in addition (in the alternative) to violation causes of action. It might be that in many TRIPS cases developing countries would find themselves forced to defend an additional and ambiguous claim that would raise the level of uncertainty and increase legal costs.

This is not to discount the possibility that developing Members could affirmatively use the nonviolation cause of action, for example to claim that threats or penalties imposed by certain Members concerning measures permitted under the TRIPS Agreement are nullifying or impairing the benefits of the bargain. Yet imbalance in the financial capacity of Members to pursue legal claims suggests that the balance of benefits would favour developed Members with strong IPRs holder communities.

To be clear, this brief paper is not intended to suggest that the potential claims outlined above could be successfully pursued. To the contrary, the AB would likely seek to avoid expansion of the TRIPS Agreement text through the uncertain vehicle of non-violation claims. Developing Members might nonetheless face demands and pressures to modify measures or courses of conduct under the threat of such claims.

An Issue Not to Overlook

The foregoing summary of non-violation actions that might arise suggests that the subject matter of non-violation nullification or impairment and Article 64.3, TRIPS Agreement, should not be overlooked among the myriad of issues that developing Members should address in the run-up to and at the Fifth Ministerial Conference. It is in the nature of a warning and reminder.

NOTES AND QUESTIONS

1. The moratorium on non-violation complaints under the TRIPS Agreement was continued at the Geneva Ministerial Conference in November-December 2009. The TRIPS Council recommended to the Seventh Session of the Ministerial to decide as follows:

    45. We take note of the work done by the Council for Trade-Related Aspects of Intellectual Property Rights . . . and direct it to continue its examination

of the scope and modalities for complaints of the types provided for under subparagraphs 1(b) and 1(c) of Article XXIII of GATT 1994 and make recommendations to our next Session. It is agreed that, in the meantime, Members will not initiate such complaints under the TRIPS Agreement. (WTO Ministerial Declaration, Doha Work Programme, Adopted 18 Dec. 2005, WT/MIN(05)/DEC, 22 Dec. 2005.)

The moratorium thus continues in effect until the next subsequent Ministerial Conference. The extension does not prejudge what steps are to follow.

2. The foregoing excerpt looks at non-violation complaints from the standpoint of developing countries, assuming that they are more likely to be on the "receiving end" of such complaints. Do you think the United States, the European Union, and other OECD countries may be vulnerable to such complaints? In what subject matter areas? Would it be possible to challenge, for example, price controls on pharmaceuticals by invoking non-violation in the realm of the TRIPS Agreement?

3. There is a difference in the WTO remedies available in a non-violation action as compared with a violation action. A Member against which a non-violation finding is made is not expected to modify or remove the measure against which the complaint was brought. Instead, it is expected to rebalance concessions with the complaining Member, such as by offering a compensating trade concession (art. 26, WTO DSU).

4. Non-violation complaints require that the measure at stake was not foreseeable, that is, that it was introduced only after a trade concession was made or an obligation to protect intellectual property was incurred. Practices and measures already existing at the time of negotiations do not qualify for non-violation. *See Japan — Photographic Film and Paper* (WT/DS44/R) para. 7.93 et seq.; Thomas Cottier & Matthias Oesch, International Trade Regulation: Law and Policy of the WTO, the European Union and Switzerland, London: Cameron May and Bern: Staempfli 2005, pp. 127-36. It is therefore important to distinguish the political dimension of non-violation, which explains the moratorium, from strict legal requirements, which need to be met in dispute settlement.

5. Do you think that in light of the legal requirement of non-foreseeability, the TRIPS Agreement should follow ordinary rules and the moratorium should no longer be extended?

4. Withdrawal of Concessions

Under the terms of the WTO Dispute Settlement Understanding, a Member whose measures are found to be inconsistent with the terms of the TRIPS Agreement is expected to bring those measures into conformity within a reasonable period of time.[1] If this is not done, the prevailing Member is authorized to suspend concessions "equivalent to the level of the nullification or

---

1. *See* arts. 21-22, DSU.

impairment."[2] The DSU establishes a nonbinding preference for withdrawal of concessions in the same "sector" as to which the finding of noncompliance is made. With respect to the TRIPS Agreement, "sector" is defined in terms of the categories of IP set out in Part II of the TRIPS Agreement (or Parts III or IV).[3] A finding of noncompliance in the field of patent protection preferably should lead to a withdrawal of concessions in the field of patent protection. However, the DSU also permits withdrawal of concessions more widely under the same "covered agreement" (e.g., under the TRIPS Agreement), and under other agreements (e.g., under the GATT 1994).[4]

Securing the possibility to withdraw concessions for a TRIPS violation in other areas of trade, including trade in goods and services ("cross-withdrawal" of concessions), was one reason why IP-dependent industry groups in the OECD sought to move IP subject matter protection from WIPO to the WTO. There is a practical basis for this. If a developing country tolerates the establishment of a large-scale counterfeiting industry within its borders, and the United States or the European Union seeks to penalize that country by refusing to provide patent or trademark protection to its nationals, this might result in a minor hardship. The developing country's domestic industry is not likely to be heavily IP-dependent. On the other hand, if the United States or the European Union bars importation of the main agricultural or textile products exported from that developing country, the resulting hardship might be quite serious.

The fact that WTO remedies are limited to the withdrawal of concessions establishes a significant imbalance in favor of large economy countries — both developed and developing. If the United States, the European Union, China, or Brazil suspends import concessions, this may have a material impact on any exporting country. If Nicaragua, on the other hand, suspends import concessions vis-à-vis the United States or China, the impact on the latter will be immaterial. As a practical matter, compliance with WTO obligations can be "compelled" only by the major economic powers.

CROSS-RETALIATION IN TRIPS: OPTIONS FOR DEVELOPING COUNTRIES

Frederick M. Abbott*

2. WTO JURISPRUDENCE AND EXPERIENCE IN TRIPS CROSS-RETALIATION

Cross-retaliation under the TRIPS Agreement has twice been approved by WTO dispute settlement arbitrators. Ecuador followed-up on arbitrator approval by requesting and gaining DSB authorisation for TRIPS cross-retaliation against European Communities (EC). Cross-retaliation under TRIPS has not yet been implemented by any authorised country. There has been an additional cross-retaliation request by Brazil against the United States

---

2. *Id.*, art. 22.4.
3. *Id.*, art. 22.3(f)(iii).
4. *Id.*, art. 22.3.
* *Cross-Retaliation in TRIPS: Options for Developing Countries*, ICTSD Programme on Dispute Settlement and Legal Aspects of International Trade, Issue Paper No. 8, 2009, International Centre for Trade and Sustainable Development, Geneva, Switzerland.

(US) but arbitration of that request is presently suspended by agreement of parties to the dispute.

A. EC — BANANAS III — ARTICLE 22.6 DSU ARBITRATION WITH ECUADOR

The first proceeding under the DSU in which a WTO Member requested DSB authorisation to suspend concessions under the TRIPS Agreement, which was also the first proceeding in which TRIPS suspension was requested as a matter of "cross-retaliation," involved Ecuador's claim against the EC in respect to the latter's banana trading regime. Ecuador requested authorisation pursuant to Article 22.2 of the DSU to suspend concessions or other obligations under the TRIPS Agreement, GATT and GATS, with respect to findings of inconsistencies regarding the EC's banana regime under the GATT and GATS. The EC thereupon requested arbitration pursuant to Article 22.6 of the DSU.

In the *EC — Bananas III* arbitration, Ecuador's initial request for suspension indicated the amount of its proposed suspension, and the sectors and covered agreements under which it intended to suspend concessions. Despite EC objection, the arbitrators found that this met the minimum requirements for the information needed in a request for suspension. The arbitrators indicated that Ecuador might well be required to submit additional methodological information in response to a challenge by the EC.

The arbitrators found that the EC carried the burden of proof in establishing that Ecuador was *not* justified in its request for suspension authorisation. As in other DSU proceedings, once the EC had established a *prima facie* case of inconsistency, Ecuador would be required to present evidence to rebut that *prima facie* case.

The arbitrators determined that the TRIPS Agreement does not preclude the suspension of concessions, including in light of Articles 22.3(f)(iii) and 22.3(g)(iii) that define "sector" and "covered agreement" in relation to TRIPS.

The Panel determined that although Ecuador had a certain margin of appreciation in determining whether suspension of concessions in the same sector as where the injury occurred would be practicable or effective, its discretion was limited by the requirements of Article 22.3(b)(d) with respect to the principles and procedures for making its determinations. The arbitrators are authorised to review compliance with the applicable principles and procedures. The arbitrators concluded that:

> In our view, the margin of review by the Arbitrators implies the authority to broadly judge whether the complaining party in question has considered the necessary facts objectively and whether, on the basis of these facts, it could plausibly arrive at the conclusion that it was not practicable or effective to seek suspension within the same sector under the same agreements, or only under another agreement provided that the circumstances were serious enough.

The arbitrators observed that the objective of suspending concessions is to induce the complained-against party to fulfil its obligations, and that as a practical matter this may be extremely difficult in cases where there is a great imbalance in terms of trade volume and economic power between the country seeking to suspend concessions and the complained-against country. Particularly in respect to "primary goods" and "investment goods" (referring to inputs and capital equipment), it may well be counterproductive to suspend concessions (i.e. to increase tariffs) because this will increase costs for local manufacturers. Effects on consumer goods may be less important from the standpoint of establishing the practicability or effectiveness of suspension. Because Ecuador's banana sector formed a major part of its economic activity, and because the EC's failure to implement the decision adopted by the DSB plausibly contributed to a severe disruption of Ecuador's economy, Ecuador clearly demonstrated that circumstances were "serious enough" to seek suspension of concessions under a covered agreement (i.e. under the TRIPS Agreement) other than where the violation was found.

The arbitrators said that although Article 22 of the DSU does not expressly direct the arbitrators to make suggestions regarding how to implement their decision, in light of this being the first decision to address suspension under the TRIPS Agreement and Ecuador's expressed interest in hearing the arbitrators' views, there is nothing to prevent the arbitrators from making suggestions regarding implementation of the suspension.

The arbitrators noted that Ecuador should take care that suspension of IPRs affects only nationals of Members subject to the suspension. In some circumstances it may be difficult to determine the nationality of right holders.

The arbitrators favourably noted Ecuador's stated intention to implement the suspension by a government-sanctioned licensing system for the reproduction of certain copyrighted works (i.e. phonograms), as well as geographic indications (GIs) and industrial designs, suggesting this was perhaps a better approach than "simply abolish[ing]" IP rights and placing materials in the public domain. This licensing system would permit Ecuador to monitor the level of suspended concessions and terminate the suspension when appropriate. The panel also noted that economic operators in Ecuador should be cautious about reliance on a transitory suspension regime for investments "which might not prove viable in the longer term."

The arbitrators said that authorisation of the suspension of TRIPS obligations within Ecuador does not affect IPRs in other WTO Members. In considering exports of phonograms produced under a suspension regime, the arbitrators said that Ecuador should consider footnotes 13 and 14 to Article 51 of the TRIPS Agreement. While footnote 13 provides that a Member is not under obligation to block imports of goods put on the market in another Member by or with the consent of the copyright holder, phonogram copies authorised under a suspension regime would not be put on the market with consent. Members would remain obligated to apply Article 51 border measures with respect to goods produced without consent. The panel stated:

> Distortions in third-country markets could be avoided if Ecuador would suspend the [IPRs] in question only for the purposes of supply destined for the domestic market. An authorisation of a suspension requested by Ecuador does of course not entitle other WTO Members to derogate from any of their obligations under the TRIPS Agreement. Consequently, such DSB authorisation to Ecuador cannot be construed by other WTO Members to reduce their obligations under Part III of the TRIPS Agreement in regard to imports entering their customs territories.

The arbitrators took note that implementation of the suspension of TRIPS obligations "may give rise to legal difficulties or conflicts within the domestic legal system of the Member so authorised (and perhaps even of the Member(s) affected by such suspension)." They further noted that this is a matter entirely within the prerogative of the suspending Members, and that their domestic legal situation may be influenced by the specific measures used to implement the suspension.

In the *EC—Bananas III* arbitration, the arbitrators said it is not for WTO arbitrators to pass judgment on whether Ecuador, once authorised by the DSB to suspend TRIPS commitments, might act inconsistently with obligations under relevant WIPO Conventions. This is for Ecuador and the other parties to such treaties to consider.

The arbitrators authorised Ecuador to request suspension of concessions under the TRIPS Agreement from the DSB. The DSB authorised the suspension. However, following successful negotiation of a settlement with the EC, Ecuador did not implement the suspension.

One study of the Ecuadorian experience concludes that the threat of suspension of TRIPS concessions induced the EC to reach substantially more favourable settlement terms of market access for Ecuadorian-origin bananas than would have occurred in the absence of that threat.[2] The same study suggests that the threat of suspension of TRIPS concessions may have assisted in Ecuador's renegotiation of external debt. The study's author considers that Ecuador would have had very limited negotiating power had potential retaliation been available only with respect to goods or services for reasons similar to those identified by the arbitrators in *EC—Bananas III*; namely, that asymmetry in economic and trade weight and the potentially damaging domestic consequences of raising trade barriers leaves many developing countries without a realistic prospect of inducing compliance by major developed country actors.

B. Other Multilateral Agreements on Enforcement

1. Paris and Berne Conventions

We have previously noted that the Paris and Berne Conventions each permit recourse in the event of a dispute to the International Court of Justice, and that such possibility for state-to-state enforcement of IPRs obligations has not been used. We also noted that a proposal for a WIPO dispute settlement mechanism was briefly entertained following the TRIPS negotiations, but no such WIPO mechanism was adopted.

2. Activities of the WIPO Arbitration and Mediation Center

In Chapter 3, the Uniform Domain Name Dispute Resolution Policy was addressed, including the availability of the WIPO Arbitration and Mediation Center and other dispute settlement service providers as a forum for claims regarding abusive domain name registration and use.

In addition to serving as a forum for domain name claims, the WIPO Arbitration and Mediation Center offers its services more generally in connection with mediation and arbitration of intellectual property-related disputes.[5]

---

2. McCall Smith, James. "Compliance Bargaining in the WTO: Ecuador and the Banana Dispute." In Negotiating Trade: Developing Countries in the WTO and NAFTA, ed. J. Odell, 257. Cambridge University Press, 2006.

5. Detailed information is available at http://www.wipo.int.

The WIPO Center has developed a set of Arbitration Rules (as well as Mediation Rules), and has prepared recommended clauses for insertion in contracts. The WIPO Center offers arbitration services in connection with licensing and other IP contract disputes, as well as for claims of infringement.

3. World Customs Organization

A substantial part of IP enforcement activity involves the enforcement by customs authorities of border measures. The World Customs Organization (WCO) is an intergovernmental organization based in Brussels, Belgium, which facilitates cooperation among national and regional customs authorities. The WCO has increasingly turned attention to the problem of trade in counterfeit goods. For example, in 2004, it convened a Global Congress on Combating Counterfeiting, which resulted in the adoption of the Rome Declaration.[6] That Declaration recommended increased attention by Interpol, the WCO, and WIPO to the problem of counterfeiting, including by establishing capacity-building programs for national customs authorities. It also promoted private sector cooperation with the WCO. The Cancun Declaration, adopted at the Fifth Global Congress on Combating Counterfeiting in 2009, recommended expansion of the WCO's counterfeiting and piracy database.

4. Organisation for Economic Cooperation and Development (OECD)

The OECD is also increasing its attention to the problem of counterfeiting and is preparing analytic studies. It describes its work program as follows.

OECD PROJECT ON COUNTERFEITING AND PIRACY*

OECD RESPONDS TO RISING CONCERNS ON THE IMPACT OF COUNTERFEITING AND PIRACY

Responding to concerns in governments and the business community, the OECD launched a project in 2005 to assess the magnitude and impact of counterfeiting and piracy. The objective of the project is to improve factual understanding and awareness of how large the problem is and the effects that infringements of intellectual property rights have on governments, business and consumers in member countries and non-member economies.

WHAT DOES THE PROJECT COVER?

The project covers infringements of the intellectual property rights that are described and defined in the WTO Agreement on Trade Related Aspects of Intellectual Property Rights (TRIPS).

---

6. October 21-22, 2004, available at http://www.wcoomd.org.
* http://www.oecd.org/document/50/0,3746,en_2649_34173_39542514_1_1_1_1,00.html.

In addition to assessing economic effects, the current project analyses rising concerns over the health, safety and security threats that counterfeit and pirated products pose to consumers. It also reviews trends and developments and assesses what is being done to combat the illicit practices.

How Is the Project Structured?

The project is being carried out in three separate phases.

Phase I focuses on tangible counterfeit and pirated products (*i.e.* physical products that infringe trademarks or copyrights), and to a lesser extent infringements of patents and design rights. This phase has been completed. The full report was published in June 2008. A November 2009 update on the magnitude of counterfeiting and piracy of tangible products is also available.

Phase II focused on piracy of digital content. The final report was published in July 2009.

Phase III will address infringements of other intellectual property rights.

Who Is the OECD Working With?

The project is being conducted in co-operation with international organisations that are active in the counterfeiting/piracy area, including the World Trade Organization, the World Customs Organization, the World Intellectual Property Organization, Interpol and relevant NGOs. Liaison with the business community and labour has been co-ordinated through the Business and Industry Advisory Committee to the OECD and the Trade Union Advisory Committee to the OECD.

Earlier Work

This study expands considerably on a related project on the economic impact of counterfeiting that was carried out in 1998.

NOTES AND QUESTIONS

1. As OECD governments are frustrated with their ability to negotiate stronger standards of IP protection at the WTO and WIPO, they turn their attention to alternative forums. The OECD is comprised of largely "like-minded" countries, and its agenda is often strongly supported by industry. However, as OECD governments discovered when attempting to conclude a Multilateral Agreement on Investment (MAI), failure to take into account the social consequences of a narrowly defined work program may result in considerable wasted effort. What are the potential social consequences of an aggressive anticounterfeiting program? What interests other than those of the IP-dependent industries should be taken into account?

2. Unauthorized downloading of MP3 files is considered copyright "piracy," a subcategory of counterfeiting. Should the interests of file-sharing communities be taken into account by the OECD?

3. Pharmaceutical companies typically argue that cross-border trade in medicines should be restricted because of counterfeiting concerns. Yet, the same companies have a strong economic interest in preventing cross-border trade in medicines from lower-priced markets (e.g., Canada) to higher-priced markets (e.g., the United States). How would you draw the line between legitimate public security concerns and private corporate interest?

C. Plurilateral Agreement on Enforcement

1. The Anti-Counterfeiting Trade Agreement

In 2007, Australia, Canada, the European Union, Japan, Korea, Mexico, Morocco, New Zealand, Singapore, Switzerland, and the United States began negotiations on the Anti-Counterfeiting Trade Agreement (ACTA). According to its proponents, the purpose of the draft ACTA is to "to provide a framework for countries committed to strong IPR protection to more effectively combat the challenges of IPR infringement today, particularly in the context of piracy and counterfeiting."[7] The eleventh round of the ACTA negotiations was held in Tokyo from September 23, 2010 to October 2, 2010, and culminated in the release of the latest draft text on October 6, 2010.[8] This was followed by a draft text on November 15, 2010, and a "final" text in December 3, 2010 (discussed below). The ACTA would establish an institution outside the WTO and WIPO, the existing institutions that govern the international intellectual property system, to oversee implementation of its enforcement obligations. Within the general scope of the draft ACTA are all categories of intellectual property that are the subject of Sections 1 through 7 of Part II of the TRIPS Agreement.

Although proponents of the ACTA have consistently portrayed the Agreement as concerning only enforcement mechanisms and not substantive IPRs rules, this semantic issue is certainly debatable. A wide range of public interest groups have strongly opposed the ACTA because of its likely impact on the Internet public domain. Furthermore, drafts of the ACTA raised serious concerns with respect to interference with legitimate trade in generic pharmaceuticals, extending to customs authorities rights to seize goods in transit based on IPRs (including patents) in the transit country. In mid-2010, ACTA negotiators repeatedly assured that the ACTA would not extend transit border measures to patents, and would not interfere with legitimate trade in pharmaceuticals, but the negotiating texts did not reflect such limitations. On October 2, 2010, ACTA negotiating countries announced the successful conclusion of a draft agreement, subject to resolving minor outstanding differences. This was followed by subsequent draft texts. The apparently final text of December 3, 2010 excludes patents and data protection from the scope of the chapter on border measures, thus excluding detentions of pharmaceutical products in transit based on patents and rights in data. But that appears to resolve only one of the serious issues raised by concerned stakeholders. Bear in mind that the ACTA, as of early 2011, is only a proposal for an agreement. It is not in force.

---

7. 2008 European Commission Fact Sheet.
8. USTR Oct. 2010 Fact Sheet: http://www.ustr.gov/about-us/press-office/fact-sheets/2010/acta-fact-sheet-and-guide-public-draft-text.

JOINT STATEMENT ON THE ANTI-COUNTERFEITING TRADE AGREEMENT (ACTA) FROM ALL THE NEGOTIATING PARTNERS OF THE AGREEMENT

November 15, 2010*

The participants are now publishing the finalized text of the agreement. Following legal verification of the drafting, the proposed agreement will then be ready to be submitted to the participants' respective authorities to undertake relevant domestic processes.

Participants in the negotiations include Australia, Canada, the European Union (EU) and its Member States, represented by the European Commission and the EU Presidency (Belgium), Japan, Korea, Mexico, Morocco, New Zealand, Singapore, Switzerland and the United States of America.

ACTA aims to establish a comprehensive international framework that will assist Parties to the agreement in their efforts to effectively combat the infringement of intellectual property rights, in particular the proliferation of counterfeiting and piracy, which undermines legitimate trade and the sustainable development of the world economy. It includes state-of-the-art provisions on the enforcement of intellectual property rights, including provisions on civil, criminal, border and digital environment enforcement measures, robust cooperation mechanisms among ACTA Parties to assist in their enforcement efforts, and establishment of best practices for effective IPR enforcement.

The full text of the 2010 draft of ACTA can be found at https://www.ige.ch/en/legal-info/legal-areas/counterfeiting-piracy.html (December 2010).

INTERVENTION BY THE GOVERNMENT OF INDIA IN THE WTO TRIPS COUNCIL ON THE DRAFT ACTA

October 26-27, 2010**

Members will recall that in the June TRIPS Council Meeting, the delegations of China and India had requested for an agenda item on TRIPS enforcement trends to highlight the systemic implications of the multiple TRIPS initiatives launched by a group of largely developed country members. It has been our consistent position, and we continue to hold it, that enforcement is not a permanent agenda item in TRIPS Council. However, the systemic and specific concerns compelled us to ask for an agenda item in the last TRIPS Council. The ensuing discussions demonstrated that the concerns regarding TRIPS enforcement were not only those of China and India but were echoed by a vast majority of developing countries including LDCs. In today's meeting we have requested for a discussion on "Enforcement Trends" under "Other Business" due to our continuing concerns on the issue of TRIPS. Let me elaborate on a few such systemic and specific concerns regarding the Anti Counterfeiting Trade Agreement (ACTA) in particular and TRIPS enforcement trends in general. After

---

* http://europa.eu/rapid/pressReleasesAction.do?reference=IP/10/1504&format=HTML&aged=0&language=EN&guiLanguage=en (visited December 28, 2010).
** Furnished by the Government of India.

years of negotiations in secrecy, we appreciate that negotiating text has now been released due to the unrelenting pressure of civil society, civil liberty groups and groups of parliamentarians. The ACTA text of 2nd October available in public domain has several elements which have far reaching implications for ACTA non-Members. My delegation is not sure that ACTA is TRIPS compliant but we reserve our final position till after the text is finalised.

Let me highlight some specific and systemic concerns:

1. While we are somewhat relieved that patents have been removed from the section on "border measures," we can not ignore the fact that ACTA is a plurilateral IPR enforcement agreement substantially broader than trademarks and copyrights. We are also concerned at the ambivalence of the proponents to include patents in the section on "civil enforcement" as well as in the overall scope of the agreement. This is further aggravated by the fact that "in-transit" goods is otherwise included in the overall scope of the agreement. There is no general assurance that border measures shall not apply to goods which are "in-transit," in "customs transit" and in "transhipment." Damages and injunctions also continue to be applicable to certain patent infringements as also provisions for seizures, forfeiture and destruction. Trademarks and copyrights, in any case, are covered under Border Measures. There remain provisions of the ACTA with significant implications for trade in legitimate generics, including those dealing with labelling which may affect the practice of parallel importation. Although border measures with respect to patents appear to be excluded from the scope of the agreement, including with respect to goods in transit, there remain provisions that might otherwise provide the basis for seizures of legitimate generic drug consignments. It is of interest to India that EU ACTA negotiators appear to be suggesting that non-EU countries grant rights with respect to goods in transit that its own Court of Justice has expressly denied EU customs authorities.

2. The section on "Civil Enforcements" continues to include patents. It encourages significant damages awards, e.g., damages based on "suggested retail price" of goods; valuation and lost profit presumptions in favor of right holders. This represents an inflated damages basis. The Section also extends injunctions to third-parties not directly accused as infringers and contains no time limitations for determinations or for notice to accused infringers. The United States appears to have proposed to exclude patents from this civil enforcement section, and India presumes this is because USA negotiators recognize that the provisions of that section are inconsistent with US patent law, and appear to adversely prejudge the outcome of patent reform legislation in its Congress.

3. India by no means intends to exhaust here its concerns with specific provisions of the draft ACTA. There are many areas that raise serious concern from the standpoint of developing countries in the WTO.

4. As far as systemic concerns go, first and foremost, ACTA completely bypasses the existing multilateral processes provided in particular by the WTO and WIPO. The ACTA also scales up the minimum enforcement level enshrined in TRIPS. The floor and ceiling in TRIPS conforms to a certain balance encapsulated in the Objectives and Principles of TRIPS.

The MFN provisions of TRIPS Agreement mean that any TRIPS protection secured by one trading partner via an RTA or a plurilateral agreement is *ipso facto* applicable to all other WTO Members. Therefore, ACTA will have a direct impact even on Members which are not involved in its negotiations. The trade restrictive effects of such scaling up is contrary to one of the main principles of the WTO rules based system, which is, to liberalise trade. While GATT and GATS provide for bilateral and multilateral derogations under Art XXIV and V respectively, there are no such provisions in TRIPS, which would in a sense, disallow Members to agree on higher enforcement levels since such levels will impinge on the rights and obligations on Members not party to the plurilateral negotiations.

5.   The ACTA text in Article 1.1 recognises that parties will not derogate with respect to obligations of other parties under existing agreements, including TRIPS Agreement. However, we do not see any explicit obligation regarding GATT provisions. This is a significant omission. It may be recalled that in the request for consultations on the drug seizure issue, India has raised the issue of violation of GATT Articles V and X. Our reading of TRIPS+ enforcement initiatives in general and ACTA in particular is that they can lead to serious trade distortions by creating barriers to legitimate trade in contravention of Article 41 of TRIPS. We have to bear in mind that ACTA members account for about 70% of world trade. ACTA provisions could undermine trade liberalisation when there already are several threats to the multilateral trading system in the form of trade protectionists measures in wake of the economic crisis.

6.   We call attention to the fact that ACTA negotiators have decided among themselves to overturn the decision of the WTO dispute settlement panel in the recent *China-Enforcement* case by reinterpreting the phrase "commercial scale" with respect to willful trademark counterfeiting and copyright piracy so as to refer to any activity carried out for a direct or indirect economic or commercial advantage. This is startling in light of the WTO panel's contrary decision that the term "scale" refers to a level of activity, and it highlights the risk to WTO law posed by turning enforcement matters over to small groups of plurilateral negotiators operating outside the WTO legal framework.

7.   We heard from several ACTA proponents during the last meeting that ACTA relates only to procedure while not touching on substantive IP law. It is no secret that TRIPS substantive commitments are being actively pursued through RTAs and other means. Substantive provisions like limiting grounds for CL, data exclusivity, patent linkage figure in several of US FTAs with developing countries. Therefore, ACTA is one of the prongs of efforts to make substantive and procedural changes in IP law.

8.   It also causes us concern when enforcement is seen as divorced from other obligations in the TRIPS Agreement. To recall, Article 7 and 8 bring out a balance of rights and obligations by referring to transfer of technology, socio economic development, promotion of innovation and access to knowledge. Enforcement provisions of ACTA could potentially disturb this balance. While we recognise the reference to the Doha Declaration on the TRIPS Agreement and public health in the preamble of ACTA, the provisions point to the opposite direction. In this context, let me also

share with Members the observations made by UN Special Rapporteur on right to health at an event organized by UN Human Rights Commission on 11th October. The Special Rapporteur gave concrete examples of TRIPS measures highlighting the adverse impact of such measures on access to medicines for one-third of humanity.

9.   The ACTA will substantially increase the *ex officio* activity of customs authorities in enforcing IPRs, meaning that the public will be paying more for enforcement of originator pharmaceutical industry IPRs. The draft ACTA limits the protection otherwise available to accused infringers under the TRIPS Agreement by potentially lowering knowledge thresholds, limiting due process requirements (e.g., requirements to act within particular time frames), limiting evidentiary requirements, and by not specifying the type of authority empowered to make critical decisions. This shift to summary administrative action may curtail the rights of accused infringers to defend patent infringement claims, ordinary trademark and copyright infringement claims. This represents a substantial transformation from the original concept of enforcement under the TRIPS Agreement.

10. We are also concerned at the setting up of a "plurilateral" IP enforcement body outside the purview of either WIPO or the WTO. This may undermine the role of the multilateral organizations dealing with IP.

11. ACTA also contain substantial sections on the Digital Environment. We recognise that, in a way, TRIPS Agreement belongs to the pre-digital era but we are also aware that this subject matter is being addressed in the WIPO Copyright and Performances and Phonograms Treaties. India has a direct stake in this issue due to its large and growing software and entertainment industry. In our view the best way to continue should be through existing multilateral process.

While India is committed to dealing with IPR enforcement issues in line with its TRIPS obligations, the introduction of intrusive IPRs enforcement rules in international trade does not represent a reasonable or realistic response. Agreements such as ACTA have the portents to completely upset the balance of rights and obligations of the TRIPS Agreement. They could also potentially negate decisions taken multilaterally such as the Doha Declaration on Public Health in WTO and the Development Agenda in WIPO. An enforcement response, if required, has to emerge from a multilateral and transparent process, as is available in the WTO TRIPS Council, and should fully conform to the Objectives and Principles (Art 7, 8) of TRIPS agreement and the balance of rights and obligations enshrined in the Agreement. As goods and services of developing countries are becoming competitive with those of developed country producers, TRIPS plus measures, like the ACTA, seek to introduce a new set of "non-tariff" barriers to trade that will preponderantly hinder developing country exporters. WTO cannot remain oblivious to such developments.

In conclusion, let me reiterate India's unwavering commitment to its TRIPS commitments, including, dealing with counterfeiting and piracy. But we should not miss the forest for the trees. To find an effective and enduring solution to the problem, we need to step back from a purely mercantilist approach. We also need to avoid exaggerating the issue of counterfeiting and piracy since there is lack of empirical data. Even the US Government Accountability Office (GAO) has recently raised serious questions concerning the data that has been relied on by proponents of the ACTA to support the effort. Members need to work collectively to create respect for IP and reducing the economic incentive for counterfeiting and piracy by judicious pricing of products under IPRs and working collectively towards realising the objectives of the TRIPS Agreement.

THE GLOBAL IP UPWARD RATCHET, ANTI-COUNTERFEITING AND PIRACY ENFORCEMENT EFFORTS: THE STATE OF PLAY

Susan K. Sell*

ACTA

While copyright and trademark-based industries have been concerned about enforcement for many years, the most recent push for a new approach emerged in 2004 at the first annual Global Congress on Combating Counterfeiting. The Global Business Leaders' Alliance Against Counterfeiting (GBLAAC), whose members include Coca Cola, Daimler Chrysler, Pfizer, Proctor and Gamble, American Tobacco, Phillip Morris, Swiss Watch, Nike, and Canon, sponsored the meeting in Geneva. Interpol and WIPO hosted the meeting. At the July 2005 Group of 8 (G8) meeting Japanese representatives suggested the development of a stricter enforcement regime to battle "piracy and counterfeiting." The G8 issued a post meeting statement: "Reducing IP Piracy and Counterfeiting Through More Effective Enforcement." In what would become a familiar trope, the first line claims that trade in counterfeit and pirated goods "can have links to organized crime," and threatens employment, innovation, economic growth, and public health and safety. That same year, the US Council of International Business partnered with the International Chamber of Commerce to launch the Business Coalition to Stop Counterfeiting and Piracy (BASCAP). A recently leaked discussion paper about ACTA circulated among industry insiders and government negotiators from the US, Japan, Switzerland, Canada, the European Union, Australia, Mexico, South Korea, and New Zealand included all of these negative effects and added "loss of tax revenue" to the litany.

This is no high-minded quest for the public good. As David Fewer of the Canadian Internet Policy and Public Interest Clinic and the University of Ottawa noted, "if Hollywood could order intellectual property laws for Christmas what would they look like? This is pretty close." One of the central features of ACTA's approach would be to enlist the public sector in enforcing private rights. This means that tax payers' dollars would be used to protect private profits. The opportunity costs of switching scarce resources for border enforcement of IP "crimes" is huge. There surely are more pressing problems for law enforcement in developing countries than ensuring profits for OECD-based firms. Other concerns address the lopsided nature of the ACTA approach, favoring rights holders above all else and presuming suspects to be guilty. Due process of law will be sacrificed to the interests of IP rights holders and there will be few, if any, checks on abuses of rights. It would authorize border guards and customs agents to search laptops, iPods, and cell phones for infringing content. Customs officials would have authority to take action against suspected infringers even without

* Director, Institute for Global and International Studies, Professor of Political Science and International Affairs, George Washington University, June 9, 2008. Licensed under a Creative Commons Attribution 3.0 License. [Footnotes omitted.]

complaints from rights holders; they could confiscate the laptops and iPods. Privacy issues arise over extensive data sharing and possible wire tapping that could be involved in ramped up enforcement efforts.

ACTA would require Internet Service Providers to police and control their systems for infringing content. Its one-size fits all policy exacerbates the problems that even the far more forgiving and flexible TRIPS revealed. It sharply reduces policy space for developing countries to design appropriate policies for their public policy for innovation and economic development. It also would create an additional international intellectual property governance layer atop an already remarkably complex and increasingly incoherent intellectual property regime.

NOTES AND QUESTIONS

1. The ACTA is subject to approval of ratification and acceptance in its prospective country Parties. This is almost certain to be a contentious process in the European Union and the United States. Moreover, questions arise as to how developing countries not participating in the process can be motivated to participate in this plurilateral agreement.
2. The excerpt from Susan Sells' paper highlights concerns raised by nongovernmental organizations as the ACTA text evolved. Several of the concerns she addresses were ultimately addressed in the final text, particularly with respect to obligations of Internet Service Providers, which are themselves big businesses not anxious to face significant new potential liabilities.
3. The intervention by India was based on the draft ACTA text of October 2, 2010. In a subsequent revision, application of the section on civil enforcement was made optional with respect to patents, reflecting a compromise from the U.S. proposal to exempt patents from the civil enforcement section.
4. What are the likely implications of negotiating additional obligations on enforcement in a plurilateral context, leaving important countries such as India and China outside the process? Is it feasible to implement the ACTA on the basis of critical mass of a number of industrialized countries, or does it inherently require participation of developing countries as well?

III.   REGIONAL ENFORCEMENT MECHANISMS

A.   *The EU Enforcement Regime*

As the European Union has gradually taken over from its member states responsibility for establishing substantive IPRs standards (see, e.g., Chapter 4, section III), so it has also increasingly set standards for the enforcement of IPRs.

1.   IP Border Measures Regulation

The European Union's first major effort in this area was a 1994 regulation that addressed border measures with respect to counterfeit trademarked and pirated copyrighted goods.[10] Because this measure concerned international trade, and because the European Union has exclusive competence in that area, there was a clear basis in the EC Treaty for this measure. (Recall from Chapter 1, section IV.A.1, the ECJ Advisory Opinion regarding EU membership in the WTO and the discussion of the respective competences of the European Union and its member states.)

In 2003, the original border measures regulation was replaced by a new regulation with a broader scope that extends to patents (including supplementary certificates of protection), plant variety rights, and geographical indications.[11] A right holder is entitled to file an application with the customs authorities requesting suspension of entry of infringing goods,[12] stating the period of time during which the customs authorities are expected to take action.[13] Customs authorities will suspend shipments suspected of infringing, and notify the right holder.[14] Customs authorities are also entitled to suspend shipments *ex officio* (i.e., on their own initiative) if they have reason to suspect an infringement. Generally, the right holder is expected to initiate proceedings under national law of the relevant member state seeking a determination of infringement.[15] This should occur within ten working days of notification of suspension, although the ten working day period may be extended for an additional ten working days.[16] Goods found to infringe an IPR will not be allowed to enter the European Union and may not be re-exported.[17] The member states must make provision for the destruction of infringing goods, or other removal from the stream of commerce, as appropriately determined by the national authorities.[18] The 2003 IP Border Measures regulation provided the basis for the detention of generic drugs in transit based on allegations of patent infringement discussed in Chapters 1 and 2. As of the end of 2010, the European Commission, *inter alia,* pursuant to the terms of a settlement with India arising out of WTO consultations, was preparing to submit proposed revisions to the IP Border Measures regulation to the European Parliament and Council.

2. IP Enforcement Directive

In 2004, the European Union adopted a directive on the enforcement of intellectual property rights.[19] This directive requires the member states to assure that IPRs holders have access to evidence regarding the activities of

---

10. Council Regulation (EC) No 3295/94 of 22 December 1994, laying down measures to prohibit the release for free circulation, export, re-export or entry for a suspensive procedure of counterfeit and pirated goods, 1994 OJ L 341, Dec. 22, 1994.

11. Council Regulation (EC) No 1383/2003 of 22 July 2003, concerning customs action against goods suspected of infringing certain intellectual property rights and the measures to be taken against goods found to have infringed such rights, OJ L 196/7, 2.8.2003.

12. *Id.*, art. 5. The 2003 border measures regulation allows customs authorities to suspend the release of goods suspected to infringe an intellectual property right even prior to a specific application from a right holder. *Id.*, art. 4.

13. *Id.*, arts. 5 and 8.

14. *Id.*, art. 9.

15. *Id.*, art. 13.

16. *Id.*, art. 13. This period may be extended for an additional ten working days.

17. *Id.*, art. 16.

18. *Id.*, art. 17.

19. Directive 2004/48/EC of the European Parliament and of the Council of 29 April 2004 on the enforcement of intellectual property rights, OJ L 195/16, 2.6.2004.

alleged infringers.[20] Member states must make available provisional measures, including preliminary injunctions to prevent "imminent infringement,"[21] and to make that available without the appearance of the alleged infringer, in particular when any delay would cause irreparable harm.[22] The directive specifies that member states judges must be authorized to remove from commerce and/or destroy infringing goods,[23] issue permanent injunctions,[24] and assess damages taking into account "all appropriate aspects," including lost profits.[25] The unsuccessful party shall generally bear the legal costs of the proceeding.[26] Judicial authorities may order dissemination of information concerning the decision at the expense of the infringer.[27]

The directive on enforcement is without prejudice to the criminal law applicable in the member states with respect to intellectual property rights.[28] This directive represents a significant step in consolidation in the hands of EU legislators of authority to regulate IPRs.

Along with the IP Enforcement Directive, the EU is also promoting closer cooperation between authorities for combating against counterfeiting and piracy. This was emphasized in several Resolutions, as a result of which a new platform for such collaboration was created — European Observatory on Counterfeiting and Piracy. This initiative is based on the existing Commission structures and its members represent both public and private sectors.

3. Regulation on the Recognition and Enforcement of Judgments

In 2000, the European Union adopted a regulation on jurisdiction and the recognition and enforcement of judgments in civil and commercial matters.[29] This regulation effectively supplants the Brussels Convention on Jurisdiction and the Enforcement of Judgments in Civil and Commercial Matters of 1968 (as amended) for EU member states.[30] Although this regulation is not specifically addressed to IPRs, it is important for the conduct of IP-related litigation in the European Union, including for the enforcement of judgments rendered by courts in the European Union. The regulation establishes a general rule that a person domiciled in a member state should be sued in that member state.[31] However, suits involving contracts may be brought in the place of performance, and suits in tort where the harmful event occurred.[32] Article 22 expressly addresses IPRs and establishes "exclusive" jurisdiction, regardless of domicile:

> 4. in proceedings concerned with the registration or validity of patents, trade marks, designs, or other similar rights required to be deposited or registered, the

20. *Id.*, arts. 6 and 8.
21. *Id.*, art. 9.
22. *Id.*, art. 9(4).
23. *Id.*, art. 10.
24. *Id.*, art. 11.
25. *Id.*, art. 13.
26. *Id.*, art. 14.
27. *Id.*, art. 15.
28. *Id.*, art. 2(3)(c).
29. Council Regulation (EC) No 44/2001 of 22 December 2000 on jurisdiction and the recognition and enforcement of judgments in civil and commercial matters, OJ L 12/1, 16.1.2001.
30. With the exception of Denmark, which opted out of this measure. *Id.*, art. 1(3).
31. *Id.*, art. 2.
32. *Id.*, art. 5.

courts of the Member State in which the deposit or registration has been applied for, has taken place or is under the terms of a Community instrument or an international convention deemed to have taken place.

Without prejudice to the jurisdiction of the European Patent Office under the Convention on the Grant of European Patents, signed at Munich on 5 October 1973, the courts of each Member State shall have exclusive jurisdiction, regardless of domicile, in proceedings concerned with the registration or validity of any European patent granted for that State. . . .

This provision thus reflects a territorial perspective on registration and challenges to validity, and takes into account the special character of the European Patent Convention (see Chapters 1 and 2, *supra*) further to which rights established by European patents are governed by the law of the designated member states.

The regulation provides for recognition of judgments among the member states of the European Union, "without any special procedure being required."[33] Grounds for refusal to recognize are strictly limited, and include "if such recognition is manifestly contrary to public policy in the Member State in which recognition is sought."[34] The regulation expressly precludes substantive review of a foreign member state judgment.[35] The regulation provides for enforcement by a member state of a judgment rendered in another member state when, on application of any interested party, it has been declared enforceable there.[36] The regulation includes an annex identifying the courts and competent authorities to which applications for enforcement are submitted, and provides that judgments will be declared enforceable immediately upon completion of formalities.[37] There is provision for appeal of the declaration of enforceability.[38]

The regulation's facilities for the recognition and enforcement of judgments rendered by EU member state judicial authorities are *not* made available for judgments of judicial authorities outside the European Union.[39] The absence of a recognition and enforcement mechanism for non-EU judgments is one of the drivers behind an effort to draft a new Hague Convention on jurisdiction and foreign judgments in civil and commercial law matters. That effort has not, however, yielded results. One reason for the slow progress is lack of agreement concerning the treatment of IPRs-related disputes.

4. Trade Barriers Regulation

In the next section we examine Section 301 of the U.S. Trade Act of 1974 (as amended). This controversial legislation, *inter alia*, allows interested persons to file complaints with the United States Trade Representative regarding foreign trade practices. In 1984, the European Union also adopted legislation that

33. *Id.*, art. 33(1).
34. *Id.*, art. 34(1).
35. *Id.*, art. 36.
36. *Id.*, art. 38(1).
37. *Id.*, art. 41.
38. *Id.*, arts. 43-46.
39. Except as may be provided to European Free Trade Area (EFTA) country judgments under the Lugano Convention (Lugano Convention of 1988 on jurisdiction and the enforcement of judgments in civil and commercial matters (*see* recital 5 of Regulation, *Id.*)).

permitted interested persons to seek remedial action regarding certain foreign trade practices. This legislation was superseded by legislation adopted in December 1994, which takes into account the establishment of the WTO.[40] It is commonly referred to as the "Trade Barriers Regulation" or "TBR." The TBR is less controversial than U.S. Section 301 because it is limited to actions that violate international trade rules, whereas Section 301 extends to a broad category of "unreasonable" trade practices.

Under the TBR, a person acting on behalf of an EU industry, an EU enterprise, or an EU member state,[41] may request the EU Commission to investigate an "obstacle to trade" maintained by a foreign country that causes an "adverse trade effect." An obstacle to trade may be "any trade practice adopted or maintained by a third country in respect of which international trade rules establish a right of action."[42] An "adverse trade effect" refers to a material negative impact on the economy of the European Union, a region, or a sector of economic activity.[43]

Following a threshold determination that there is sufficient evidence, the Commission will open an "examination procedure" regarding the alleged obstacle to trade, giving an affected foreign country notice and the opportunity to submit information.[44] If the Commission finds that the complaint is justified, it will initiate a procedure under the applicable legal mechanism, such as by filing a WTO dispute settlement complaint.[45]

As discussed in Chapter 1, as a general rule, WTO agreements are not directly effective in the law of the European Union or its member states. The TBR provides a mechanism to private citizens for enforcing (indirectly) WTO agreements as against foreign countries, although not against EU institutions or member states.

The TBR has been used once to address an alleged TRIPS Agreement violation.[46] It was used to initiate the WTO dispute settlement proceeding against the United States regarding the Copyright Act (see Chapter 4, section II.B.1, *supra*). The decision of the European Commission to initiate that proceeding on the basis of the TBR complaint follows.

COMMISSION DECISION OF 11 DECEMBER 1998 CONCERNING SECTION 110(5) OF THE COPYRIGHT ACT OF THE UNITED STATES OF AMERICA

(Notified Under Document Number C(1998) 4033) (98/731/EC)

THE COMMISSION OF THE EUROPEAN COMMUNITIES,
Having regard to the Treaty establishing the European Community,
Having regard to Council Regulation (EC) No 3286/94 of 22 December 1994

---

40. Council Regulation (EC) No 3286/94 of 22 December 1994 laying down Community procedures in the field of the common commercial policy in order to ensure the exercise of the Community's rights under international trade rules, in particular those established under the auspices of the World Trade Organization, OJ L 349, 31. 12. 1994.

41. *Id.*, arts. 3-4 & 6.

42. *Id.*, art. 2(1).

43. *Id.*, art. 2(4).

44. *Id.*, art 8.

45. *Id.*, arts. 12-14.

46. An important GATT dispute settlement case — the U.S. — Section 337 case (see Chapter 1, section VI.A, *supra*) — was initiated under the 1984 predecessor to the TBR.

laying down Community procedures in the field of the common commercial policy in order to ensure the exercise of the Community's right under international trade rules, in particular those established under the auspices of the World Trade Organisation,[1] as amended by Regulation (EC) No 356/95,[2] and in particular Articles 13 and 14 thereof,

After consulting the Advisory Committee,
    Whereas:

A. Procedure

(1) On 21 April 1997 the Commission received a complaint pursuant to Article 4 of Council Regulation (EC) No 3286/94 (hereafter "the Regulation"). The complaint was lodged by the Irish Music Rights Organisation (IMRO) with the unanimous support of the Groupement européen des sociétés d'auteurs et compositeurs (GESAC).

(2) The complainant alleged that Section 110(5) of the1976 Copyright Act of the United States of America is inconsistent with several provisions of the Agreement establishing the World Trade Organisation (hereafter "the WTO Agreement") and its annexes. On that basis the complainant asked the Commission to take the necessary actions to convince the United States of America to repeal this measure.

(3) The complaint contained sufficient prima facie evidence to justify the initiation of a Community examination procedure pursuant to Article 8 of the Regulation. Consequently, such procedure was initiated on 11 June 1997.[3]

(4) Following the initiation of the examination procedure the Commission conducted an in-depth legal and factual investigation into Section 110(5) of the US Copyright Act as well as into the amendments to the statute as discussed in US Congress at the time of the investigation and enacted meanwhile.

Based on the findings of this investigation the Commission reached the conclusions which are indicated below.

B. Findings Regarding the Existence of an Obstacle to Trade

(5) Although under the US Copyright Act the right holder of a musical work has the exclusive right "to perform the copyrighted work publicly," Section 110(5) of the US Copyright Act exempts certain public performances from protection. Before the recent addition of a new subparagraph widening the scope of the exemption (see further under item D) it read as follows: Notwithstanding the provisions of Section 106, the following are not infringements of copyright: (. . .) communication or transmission embodying a performance or display of a work by the public reception of the transmission on a single receiving apparatus of a kind commonly used in private homes, unless (a) a direct charge is made to see or hear the transmission or (b) the transmission thus received is further retransmitted to the public. The exemption covers the use of a radio or

---

1. OJ L 349, 31. 12. 1994, p. 71.
2. OJ L 41, 23. 2. 1995, p. 3.
3. OJ C 177, 11. 6. 1997, p. 5.

television set "of a type commonly found in private homes" in a shop, a bar, a restaurant or any other place frequented by the public. As a result of its vague and ambiguous statutory language, Section 110(5) has given rise to a very broad interpretation of what is commonly referred to as the "homestyle exemption." For example, it has been held that the exemption can also apply to companies operating large chains of stores throughout the country and using the playing of music in stores as part of their commercial policy.[4] . . .

(8) The Commission also reviewed the homestyle exemption from the point of view of "minor reservations," a category of exceptions which might be considered to apply on the exercise of the exclusive rights under the Berne Convention, but concluded that, even where "minor reservations" were applicable to the exclusive rights set out in Article 11*bis*(1)(iii) and (1)(ii), it would still remain that the homestyle exemption is clearly not a minor reservation. The exemption is widely applied on a commercial basis through the US and the economic losses incurred by Community rightholders are important, ranging between 13 to 24% of the US performing rights organisations' annual distributions to Community collecting societies representing composers and arrangers of music, lyricists and publishers.

(9) Since Article 9(1) of TRIPs imposes a mandatory obligation on WTO members to comply with Articles 1 to 21 of the Berne Convention, a WTO member is in breach of its obligations under the TRIPs Agreement where it fails to comply with the Berne Convention. Therefore, since Section 110(5) of the US Copyright Act contravenes Article 11*bis*(1), *bis*(2) and (1) of the Berne Convention, Section 110(5) of the US Copyright Act is in breach of Article 9(1) of TRIPs. Also, the Commission holds the opinion that Article 13 of TRIPs cannot be invoked by the United States to justify the homestyle exemption, as this provision limits the scope of existing exemptions under the Berne Convention to special cases which do not conflict with a normal exploitation of the work and do not unreasonably prejudice the legitimate interests of the right holder. It does not allow additional exemptions to the rights protected under the Berne Convention.

(10) Under these circumstances the Commission considers that the complainant's allegations are well-founded and that Section 110(5) of the US Copyright Act constitutes an obstacle to trade within the meaning of Article 2(1) of the Regulation, that is "a practice adopted or maintained by a third country in respect of which international trade rules establish a right of action."

(11) The Commission none the less considers that reference to the above legal bases does not rule out recourse to any other pertinent provision of the WTO Agreement and of the Agreements annexed to it, which could be of use in procedures before the WTO.

C. Findings Regarding Adverse Trade Effects

(12) Section 110(5) of the US Copyright Act curtails Community right holders in the full and normal exercise of their exclusive rights under the Berne Convention and the TRIPs Agreement. The right holders are deprived of the

---

4. *See BMI v. Edison Bros. Stores Inc.*, United States Court of Appeals for the Eighth Circuit, No 91-2115 and *BMI v. Claire's Boutiques,* United States Court of Appeals for the Seventh Circuit, No 91-1232.

possibility to license the performing right of their work (either directly or through collecting societies) and of the possibility to obtain remuneration for the communication of their works to the public. . . .

(17) Under these circumstances the Commission considers that the complainant's allegations are well-founded and that Section 110(5) of the US Copyright Act is causing adverse trade effects within the meaning of Article 2(4) of the Regulation.

D. Recent Amendments to Section 110(5) of the US Copyright Act

(18) While the Commission was investigating the homestyle exemption, US Congress was examining a bill amending Section 110(5) of the US Copyright Act in view of widening its scope.

(19) On 6 and 7 October 1998, the bill, entitled "Fairness in Music Licensing Act," was adopted by, respectively, the US House of Representatives and the US Senate. The bill consists of adding a new subparagraph B to Section 110(5) of the US Copyright Act which provides for a further exception to the rightholders' exclusive right to authorise public communication of their works, while the homestyle exemption remains unchanged under subparagraph A. The new subparagraph B now applies to a much wider range of beneficiaries, namely eating, drinking and other commercial establishments provided that they fulfil a certain number of conditions, mainly with regard to the surface of the establishment and the number of loudspeakers used. It covers the use of any type of audiovisual device, and is thus not limited to the use of a "homestyle" apparatus only.

(20) The bill was signed by the President of the United States on 27 October 1998, to enter into force 90 days after enactment. Since this means that, from a legal point of view, the bill is now part of the US legal order, although its entry into effect has been delayed for 90 days, it can already be the object of a dispute settlement procedure under WTO.

(21) From a legal point of view, the new paragraph B of Section 110(5) also deprives right holders to the protection they are entitled under Articles 11*bis*(1)(iii) and 11(1)(ii) of the Berne Convention when broadcasts of their works or cable transmissions of their works are communicated to the public. Therefore, the Commission's analysis of the 1976 version of Section 110(5) of the US Copyright Act (now under subparagraph A of the section) fully applies to the new version of the Statute, which is thus equally in breach of the Berne Convention and the TRIPs Agreement.

(22) As far as the adverse trade effects are concerned, it is clear that they will be seriously amplified by the widening of the Statute's scope in terms of beneficiaries and type of audiovisual devices used to perform music in public establishments. Whereas the Commission estimated that the 1976 homestyle exemption applied to between 20 and 35% of US business establishments categorised as small business by US Government and employing fewer than 20 persons, and to between 6 and 12% of US business of the same category employing more than 20 persons, the US collecting societies estimate that, only where eating and drinking business is concerned, the new Bill would already exempt 70% of all US bars and restaurants, as they fall below the surface thresholds under the new Section 110(5)B.

E. Community Interest

(23) Ensuring that WTO partners fully comply with their obligations is of the utmost importance for the Community which has committed itself to the same obligations. Therefore, the Community should immediately challenge Section 110(5) of the US Copyright Act.

F. Conclusions and Measures to Be Taken

(24) Meetings have been held and letters have been exchanged with the relevant US authorities to discuss this matter further and aimed at finding an amicable solution to the problems concerning the licensing of music works but the US authorities have not forwarded any proposals in view of such a solution.

(25) In these circumstances, it appears that the interests of the Community call for initiation of WTO dispute settlement proceedings, HAS DECIDED AS FOLLOWS:

Article 1

1. Section 110(5) of the Copyright Act of the United States of America appears to be inconsistent with the obligations of that country under the Marrakesh Agreement Establishing the World Trade Organisation and constitutes an "obstacle to trade" within the meaning of Article 2(1) of Regulation (EC) No. 3286/94.

2. The Community will commence action against the United States of America under the Understanding on the Rules and Procedures for the Settlement of Disputes and other relevant WTO provisions with a view to securing removal of the obstacle to trade.

Article 2

This Decision shall apply from the date of its publication in the Official Journal of the European Communities.

Done at Brussels, 11 December 1998.

For the Commission
Leon BRITTAN
Vice-President

NOTES AND QUESTIONS

1. The decision by the European Commission to initiate a proceeding at the WTO should not be confused with the WTO panel report ultimately adopted, and discussed in Chapter 4. On what aspects did the WTO panel agree with the Commission, and on what aspects did it disagree?

2. If the WTO Agreement were directly effective in the law of the European Union, private parties would be able to challenge EU trade legislation for consistency with the EU's WTO obligations. Because the WTO Agreement is not directly effective, European Union citizens have more extensive rights with respect to the trade practices of foreign states than they do with respect to the trade practices of their own government(s).

IV.   BILATERAL TRADE AGREEMENTS AND IPRs ENFORCEMENT

Throughout this book we have referred to U.S. efforts to strengthen IPRs protection through negotiation of bilateral commitments in free trade agreements. This effort extends to commitments regarding civil and criminal enforcement measures. Moreover, the WTO agreements, including the TRIPS Agreement, do not address the protection of foreign direct investment. One notable feature of the U.S. bilateral trade agreements is that IPRs are typically included within the scope of "investments" and are therefore subject to additional substantive investment rules and a supplementary dispute settlement regime. These features are briefly described by Fink and Reichenmiller below.

TIGHTENING TRIPS: THE INTELLECTUAL PROPERTY PROVISIONS OF RECENT US FREE TRADE AGREEMENTS
Carsten Fink & Patrick Reichenmiller*

. . . ENFORCEMENT OF INTELLECTUAL PROPERTY RIGHTS

The TRIPS Agreement — for the first time in an international agreement on intellectual property — introduced detailed obligations on the enforcement of IPRs. Certainly, without judicial enforcement of intellectual property laws, rules on patents, copyright and other forms of protection could be seriously undermined. However, recognizing the institutional limitations existing in many developing countries, TRIPS does not create any obligation " . . . *with respect to the distribution of resources as between enforcement of intellectual property rights and the enforcement of law in general.*"

The agreements with Vietnam, Jordan, and Australia do not explicitly allow for the same institutional flexibility. In these cases, it may therefore be difficult to defend derogations from the specific enforcement provisions of the agreements' IPRs chapters with inherent institutional constraints, such as limited budgetary or human resources. The agreements with Singapore, Chile, Morocco, DR-CAFTA, and Bahrain go further in spelling out that resource constraints cannot be invoked as an excuse for not complying with the agreements' specific enforcement obligations. Indeed, some of the specific enforcement requirements of the FTAs seem to create additional institutional obligations. For example, as in the case of TRIPS, the FTAs require customs authorities to stop trade in counterfeit and pirated goods. But TRIPS only

* World Bank Trade Note No. 20, Feb. 7, 2005.

requires these measures for imported goods, whereas most FTAs mandate border measures for imported and exported goods and, in some cases, even transiting goods.

Finally, the enforcement rules of the bilateral agreements mandate a stronger deterrent against IPRs infringement. For example, TRIPS only requires the imposition of fines adequate to compensate IPRs holders for the monetary damages they suffered. In the case of copyright piracy and trademark counterfeiting, all of the FTAs require the imposition of fines irrespective of the injury suffered by IPRs holders. TRIPS only mandates criminal procedures in cases of willful trademark counterfeiting or copyright piracy on a commercial scale. Many FTAs go beyond this broad standard and define more explicitly the scope of infringement acts subject to criminal procedures—including, for example, copyright piracy with a significant aggregate monetary value, but not necessarily for financial gain. Thus, certain forms of end-user piracy may be considered a criminal offense. . . .

INTELLECTUAL PROPERTY RIGHTS AND INVESTMENT RULES

In addition to the rules contained in the intellectual property chapters of the FTAs, IPRs are subject to separate investment disciplines. . . . [S]ix of the bilateral agreements have separate chapters on investment. The US-Bahrain and US-Jordan FTAs do not have such chapters, but the respective governments have negotiated bilateral investment treaties (BITs) with similar provisions. As no multilateral agreement on investment exists at the WTO or elsewhere, these bilateral investment rules break new ground.

A common element of the recent US FTA investment chapters and BITs is that intellectual property rights are explicitly listed in the definition of what is considered an investment. Thus, the agreements' specific investment disciplines apply, in principle, to government measures affecting the intellectual property portfolios of foreign investors. This raises, for example, the question of whether granting a compulsory license is considered an act of expropriation. Five of the FTA investment chapters explicitly remove compulsory licenses from the scope of expropriation, as long as such licenses comply with the obligations of the TRIPS Agreement and the intellectual property chapter of the respective FTA. However, the US-Vietnam FTA and the two BITs with Bahrain and Jordan do not have a comparable safeguard. Thus, as an example, if Vietnam were to issue a compulsory license in case of a national emergency, could the patent holder challenge such a decision as an act of investment expropriation?

Questions like this may be important, as these investment agreements provide for direct investor-to-state dispute settlement—going beyond the more traditional state-to-state dispute settlement procedures included in trade agreements. An exception is the investment chapter of the US-Australia FTA, which only allows for the possibility that investor-to-state dispute settlement procedures be negotiated in future. Investor-to-state dispute settlement may be more attractive to foreign investors, who can seek arbitration awards for uncompensated expropriation. By contrast, state-to-state dispute settlement can typically authorize only the imposition of punitive trade sanctions.

Notwithstanding these considerations, the reach of investment agreements into the intellectual property domain is still untested and remains in many ways legally uncertain (Correa, 2004).

NOTES AND QUESTIONS

1. The treatment of IPRs as an "investment" presupposes their characterization as a form of "property." Do IPRs have the same characteristics as real property and movable property? For example, is a trade secret a form of property? A trade secret holder may not prevent a third party from developing and using the same information. The right to exclude only arises in the event of dishonest commercial practices. How would an investment dispute arbitration panel decide on the value of an expropriated trade secret?

2. As Fink and Reichenmiller point out, provisions that exempt compulsory licensing from the rules protecting against expropriation (and requiring compensation) refer to such licensing when it complies with the TRIPS Agreement and the IPRs chapter of the relevant agreement. For example, Article 10.9 (Expropriation and Compensation) of Chapter 10 of the U.S.-Chile FTA provides:

> 5. This Article does not apply to the issuance of compulsory licenses granted in relation to intellectual property rights in accordance with the TRIPS Agreement, or to the revocation, limitation, or creation of intellectual property rights, to the extent that such revocation, limitation, or creation is consistent with Chapter Seventeen (Intellectual Property Rights).

> Does this article preclude an IPRs holder from pursuing an investment dispute settlement claim based on a compulsory license? Might not an IPRs holder argue that the license was inconsistent with the TRIPS Agreement or the bilateral IPRs chapter?

U.S.-based industry groups may be able to secure rules in bilateral trade agreements that are more favorable to them than comparable rules in domestic U.S. law. Congress routinely denies the bilateral agreements "self-executing" effect in U.S. law. Technically, changes are made to domestic law only when Congress amends it. But there is a persistent question whether the negotiation of international commitments places pressure on Congress to amend U.S. law so as to bring it in line with those commitments. In the following excerpt, some differences between remedies as provided by U.S. law and the typical bilateral trade agreement are noted.

INTELLECTUAL PROPERTY PROVISIONS OF BILATERAL AND REGIONAL TRADE AGREEMENTS IN LIGHT OF U.S. FEDERAL LAW

Frederick M. Abbott*

ENFORCEMENT . . .

2. *Damages calculation.* The provisions of the FTAs regarding calculation of damages for infringement of IPRs set forth a methodology. For example, Article 15.11 of the U.S. Morocco FTA provides:

(6)(b) in determining damages for infringement of intellectual property rights, its judicial authorities shall consider, *inter alia,* the value of the infringed-on good or

* UNCTAD-ICTSD Project on IPRs and Sustainable Development, Issue Paper No. 12, Feb. 2006.

service, measured by the suggested retail price or other legitimate measure of value submitted by the right holder.

The standard of "suggested retail price" is used in only one of the many U.S. statutes regulating intellectual property, that is, the prohibition in the Tariff Act of 1930 against the importation of goods bearing an infringing trademark.[72] U.S. courts generally have substantial discretion in determining the basis for establishing the level of damages in cases of infringement. In a trademark infringement suit, the trademark holder is ordinarily required to prove its "actual damages" which would be based on the market price of its goods. The "suggested retail price" of a good or service will be the "market price" in only a limited number of cases. The Copyright Act also uses the measure of "actual damages," providing:

> (b) Actual damages and profits. The copyright owner is entitled to recover the actual damages suffered by him or her as a result of the infringement, and any profits of the infringer that are attributable to the infringement and are not taken into account in computing the actual damages. In establishing the infringer's profits, the copyright owner is required to present proof only of the infringer's gross revenue, and the infringer is required to prove his or her deductible expenses and the elements of profit attributable to factors other than the copyrighted work.

17 USC § 504. A U.S. court might allow a trademark, copyright or patent holder to base its claim for remedies in an infringement action on the suggested retail price of its goods if there was no reasonable way to prove the actual selling price of the goods in the market. However, because the suggested retail price is a hypothetical price this would not be a first option.

The use of "suggested retail price" as the basis for calculating damages is also problematic because it suggests that the IPRs holder receives the "retail" price for its goods or services. In many cases, the IPRs holder will sell to intermediaries such as wholesalers and distributors and will receive a price substantially discounted from the suggested retail price, even assuming that the suggested retail price represents the price paid by the consuming public. The IPRs holder's "actual damages" should instead be based on the price it receives from the intermediaries.

The FTA provision does not limit courts solely to the consideration of "suggested retail price" in the calculation of damages. However, it requires the courts to take this measure into account when presented by the right holder. In doing so, it implies that using the basis of "suggested retail price" is a "safe harbor" under the FTA which can be used to avoid trade disputes.[73]

NOTES AND QUESTIONS

1. From the perspective of U.S.-IPRs-holder interest groups doing business overseas, the level of penalties for infringement can rarely be "too high." Is

---

72. 19 USCS § 1526 (f)(2)

For the first such seizure, the fine shall be not more than the value that the merchandise would have had if it were genuine, according to the manufacturer's suggested retail price, determined under regulations promulgated by the Secretary.

73. IPRs holders, similarly, are not obligated to present damage requests on the basis of "suggested retail price." They may present requests on the basis of other "legitimate measures" of value. The courts are required to consider those alternative valuations.

the same perspective reasonable within the domestic U.S. context? What are the risks associated with an enforcement system that "overpenalizes" infringement?

V. NATIONAL MECHANISMS OF INTERNATIONAL IP ENFORCEMENT

A. *United States*

1. Section 337 of the Tariff Act of 1930

The United States maintains a specific legal procedure pursuant to which holders of IPRs may obtain orders directing the Customs Service to block importation of infringing goods. This is Section 337 of the Tariff Act of 1930. Under Section 337, the holder of a U.S. IPR initiates a complaint at the International Trade Commission (ITC) in Washington, DC. The ITC is a "quasi-autonomous" agency of the federal government headed by six commissioners.[47] If threshold criteria are met, the Commission appoints an administrative law judge to make an initial determination regarding the complaint. The Section 337 procedure and available remedies are described in more detail below by the Commission.

In 1989, a GATT dispute settlement panel ruled that certain elements of Section 337, as then in force, were inconsistent with GATT national treatment rules. In effect, imported products alleged to infringe U.S. patents were treated less favorably than domestically produced products subject to patent litigation in federal court.[48] For example, a defendant in a Section 337 proceeding was not permitted to counterclaim on patent invalidity grounds, while such a counterclaim was a common defensive maneuver in federal district court patent infringement cases. Subsequent to the GATT panel decision, the United States amended Section 337 to make its procedures substantially more comparable to federal court proceedings under the Patent Act.

SECTION 337 INVESTIGATIONS AT THE U.S. INTERNATIONAL TRADE COMMISSION: ANSWERS TO FREQUENTLY ASKED QUESTIONS

U.S. International Trade Commission*

BACKGROUND ON SECTION 337

Under Section 337 of the Tariff Act of 1930 (19 U.S.C. § 1337), the Commission conducts investigations into allegations of certain unfair practices in import

---

47. Congress appoints the commissioners, with each major political party appointing three. The ITC also plays an important role in antidumping and countervailing duty cases, and in conducting studies regarding trade issues for Congress and the executive branch.

48. GATT Panel Report, United States — Section 337 of the Tariff Act of 1930, L/6439-36S/ with 345, adopted Nov. 7, 1989.

* Publication No. 3708, July 2002, U.S. International Trade Commission, Washington, D.C., available at http://hotdocs.usitc.gov/docs/pubs/trade_remedy/pub3708.pdf.

trade. Section 337 declares the infringement of certain statutory intellectual property rights and other forms of unfair competition in import trade to be unlawful practices. Most Section 337 investigations involve allegations of patent or registered trademark infringement.[1] Other forms of unfair competition, such as misappropriation of trade secrets, passing off, false advertising, and violations of the antitrust laws, may also be asserted.[2]

Section 337 investigations are initiated by the Commission following the receipt of a properly filed complaint that complies with the Commission's Rules.[3] A Commission notice announcing the institution of an investigation is published in the *Federal Register* whenever the Commission votes to institute a Section 337 investigation.

When an investigation is instituted, the Commission assigns an Administrative Law Judge to preside over the proceedings and to render an initial decision (referred to as an "Initial Determination") as to whether Section 337 has been violated. The Commission also assigns an investigative attorney from the Commission's Office of Unfair Import Investigations ("OUII"), who functions as an independent litigant representing the public interest in the investigation. The staff investigative attorney is a full party to the investigation. In the notice announcing initiation of an investigation, the Commission identifies the entities that may participate in the investigation as parties, namely, the complainant or complainants that allege a violation of Section 337, the respondent or respondents that are alleged to have violated Section 337, and the OUII staff attorney, who is formally known as the Commission Investigative Attorney.

Section 337 investigations are conducted in accordance with procedural rules that are similar in many respects to the Federal Rules of Civil Procedure. These Commission procedural rules (found in 19 C.F.R. Part 210) are typically supplemented by a set of Ground Rules issued by the presiding Administrative Law Judge. The procedural rules and Administrative Law Judge's Ground Rules provide important details regarding such matters as the taking of discovery and the handling of motions.

A formal evidentiary hearing on the merits of a Section 337 case is conducted by the presiding Administrative Law Judge in conformity with the adjudicative provisions of the Administrative Procedure Act (5 U.S.C. §§ 551 *et seq.*). Hence, parties have the right of adequate notice, cross-examination, presentation of evidence, objection, motion, argument, and other rights essential to a fair hearing.

Following a hearing on the merits of the case, the presiding Administrative Law Judge issues an Initial Determination (ID) that is certified to the Commission along with the evidentiary record. The Commission may review and adopt, modify, or reverse the Initial Determination or it may decide not to review the

---

1. Section 337 specifically declares the infringement of the following statutory rights to be unlawful import practices: a U.S. patent or a U.S. copyright registered under Title 17, a registered trademark, a mask work registered under chapter 9 of Title 17, or a boat hull design protected under chapter 13 of Title 17. 19 U.S.C. § 1337(a)(1)(B)-(E). In cases involving infringement of these intellectual property rights, there is no injury requirement.

2. In addition to unfair practices based upon infringement of certain specified statutory intellectual property rights, Section 337 also declares unlawful unfair methods of competition and unfair acts in the importation and sale of products in the United States, *the threat or effect of which* is to destroy or substantially injure a domestic industry, prevent the establishment of such an industry, or restrain or monopolize trade and commerce in the United States. Thus, in these types of investigations, threatened or actual injury must be shown.

3. Requirements for the contents of Section 337 complaints are set forth in 19 C.F.R. §§ 210.4, 210.12 and 68 Fed. Reg. 32971 (June 3, 2003).

ID. If the Commission declines to review an ID, the ID becomes the final determination of the Commission.

In the event that the Commission determines that Section 337 has been violated, the Commission may issue an exclusion order barring the products at issue from entry into the United States, as well as a cease and desist order directing the violating parties to cease certain actions. The Commission's exclusion orders are enforced by the U.S. Customs Service.

Commission orders become effective within 60 days of issuance unless disapproved by the President for policy reasons. Appeals of Commission orders entered in Section 337 investigations are heard by the U.S. Court of Appeals for the Federal Circuit.

The ordinary remedy in a Section 337 proceeding is an exclusion order barring certain products from entering the United States, and directing identified parties to cease and desist from described acts, such as repeating attempts to unlawfully import. However, one of the distinguishing characteristics of Section 337 is that it also makes available to a complaining party the possibility for obtaining a "general exclusion order." Such an order literally prevents all products described by the order from entering the United States without permission of the IPRs holder, regardless of the identity of the importer. The following proceeding involving Pfizer's Viagra illustrates this remedial option.

The first document is an initial determination and recommendation by the administrative law judge. The second is an order by the Commission.

IN THE MATTER OF CERTAIN SILDENAFIL OR ANY PHARMACEUTICALLY ACCEPTABLE SALT THEREOF, SUCH AS SILDENAFIL CITRATE, AND PRODUCTS CONTAINING SAME

United States International Trade Commission Inv. No. 337-TA-489

Order No. 19: Initial Determination Granting in Part and Denying in Part Complainant's Motion for Summary Determination Respect to Domestic Industry and Violation of Section 337 Recommended Determination on Remedy and Bonding (October 27, 2003)

On October 6, 2003, complainant Pfizer, Inc. ("Pfizer") moved (489-008) pursuant to 19 C.F.R. § 210.18 for *summary* determination on the issues of the existence of a domestic industry and violation of Section 337. On October 16, 2003, the Commission Investigative Staff ("Staff") filed a response in support of Pfizer's motion. No other responses to the motion were filed.

The instant motion is the culmination of this investigation, which began on January 29, 2003 with Pfizer's filing of a complaint with the Commission pursuant to Section 337 of the Tariff Act of 1930, as amended, 19 U.S.C. § 1337. Pfizer's complaint alleged violations of Section 337 by all named respondents in connection with the importation, sale for importation, and sale within the United States after importation of certain sildenafil or any pharmaceutically acceptable salt thereof, such as sildenafil citrate, and products containing same. On February 27, 2003, the Commission issued a Notice of Investigation that was subsequently published in the Federal Register on March 6, 2003.

The Notice of Investigation listed 15 entities as respondents. . . . Of these, eleven were found to be in default, including domestic respondent #1 Aabaaca Viagra LLC of Reno, Nevada ("Aabaaca").[1] Two more were never found to have been served with the complaint and notice of investigation, and did not otherwise participate in the investigation.[2] One more respondent was terminated from this investigation on the basis of a settlement agreement.[3] One entered into a consent order stipulation with Pfizer that remains pending.[4] Thus, none of the named respondents have contested Pfizer's allegations that they have violated and continue to violate Section 337.

Pfizer's motion seeks, in addition to a summary determination of a Section 337 violation and the existence of a domestic industry, the entry of a general exclusion order against all infringing imports of accused sildenafil products. . . . Pfizer also seeks the entry of a cease and desist order against Respondent Aabaaca, the only domestic defaulting respondent in this case. . . .

The Legal Framework of Pfizer's Motion

The standards for granting a motion for summary determination under 19 C.F.R. § 210.18(a) are well-recognized and need no repetition here. . . . It is only useful to note for the purposes of the instant motion that the Commission's Rules require an appropriate, properly supported, unopposed motion for summary determination to be granted. . . .

The Elements of a Section 337 Investigation Are Satisfied by Pfizer's Motion

Turning, then, to the matter at hand, Pfizer has amply established by "substantial, reliable, and probative evidence" that a violation has occurred and continues to occur, and that the *Spray Pumps* conditions [Certain Airless Paint Spray Pumps and Components Thereof, Inv. No. 337-TA-90, USITC Pub. No. 1199, Commission Opinion, 216 U.S.P.Q. 465 (U.S.I.T.C., November 1981)] for issuing a general exclusion order are present in this case.

Infringement of the '534 Patent

Concerning violation of Section 337, Pfizer's motion establishes, and the Staff concurs, that there is a violation by reason of the Respondents' importation into the United States, sale for importation in the United States, or sale within the

1. The 11 defaulting respondents are as follows: Planet Pharmacy; LTMC, Ltd.; Aleppo Pharmaceutical Industries; #1 Aabaaca Viagra LLC; Zhejiang Medicines & Health Products Import & Export Co., Ltd.; Tianjin Shuaike Chemical Co., Ltd.; Sino Health Care Company of Sichuan; China Jiangsu International; Yiho Export & Import Co., Ltd.; and EBC Corporation.

2. The two respondents that were never found to have been formally served were Investment and Future Development Corp. SA, of Nicaragua; and Jiangxi Jilin Chemical Corp. Ltd., of China. . . .

3. The terminated respondent is Ezee Soulnature Healthcare Pvt. Ltd., of India ("Ezee"). . . .

4. The respondent that executed the pending consent order stipulation with Pfizer is Biovea. . . .

United States after importation, of certain sildenafil and pharmaceutically acceptable sales thereof, including sildenafil citrate, and products containing the same, that infringe one or more of claims 1-5 of Pfizer's U.S. Patent No. 5,250,534 (the "'534 patent"). . . . Pfizer's complaint includes a declaration of Rubie Ann Mages, Pfizer's Manager of Corporate Security, which details the instances of importation and sale of Respondents' accused products and identifies the chemical analysis of each product that was performed by Dr. John W. Thomas, Pfizer's Senior Research Scientist. The complaint also includes a declaration from Dr. Thomas demonstrating that the products imported into the United States by the Respondents contain sildenafil citrate and therefore infringe the '534 patent. Dr. Thomas" declaration includes detailed chemical analysis reports prepared by Pfizer that show the presence of sildenafil citrate in each defaulting respondent's product. Chemical analyses also demonstrate the presence of sildenafil citrate in the products of settling respondents Biovea and Ezee. Additionally, the Thomas declaration includes a claim chart demonstrating that the sildenafil citrate present in respondents' products is covered by claims 1-5 of the '534 patent.

DOMESTIC INDUSTRY

Pfizer's motion, with Staff concurrence, also demonstrates that a domestic industry exists that practices the '534 patent in accordance with Section 337(a)(2) and (3). . . . Under Section 337(a)(3), a domestic industry exists: (1) if the domestic articles are "protected by the patent . . . concerned," i.e., practice one or more of the claims of the patent; and (2) if there exist in the United States with respect to those articles one or more of the following:

1. Significant investment in plant and equipment;
2. Significant employment of labor or capital; or
3. Substantial investment in the exploitation of the patent, including engineering, research and development, or licensing.

See 19 U.S.C. § 1337(a)(3). Pfizer's motion satisfies both the first, so-called "technical prong" and the second, so-called "economic prong" of the domestic industry requirements.

Regarding the technical prong, the declaration of Dr. Thomas shows that each of claims 1-5 of the '534 patent embraces sildenafil, and pharmaceutically acceptable salts thereof, including sildenafil citrate. Sildenafil is the active ingredient in Viagra, Pfizer's domestic drug for the treatment of erectile dysfunction. Viagra contains sildenafil in the form of its citrate salt. . . . The Staff concurs with Pfizer's assertions. . . . With regard to the economic prong, Pfizer has submitted with its motion the declarations of Jose Torres and Sheldon Epstein, two Pfizer employees, stating that Viagra is manufactured at two Pfizer facilities in the United States. . . . One facility is located in Barceloneta, Puerto Rico, and the other in Brooklyn, New York. In both plants, according to the declarations, bulk sildenafil citrate manufactured in Ireland is blended with various excipients to produce Viagra blend, which is then processed into Viagra tablets. The Staff concurs with these assertions as well. . . . Further in connection with the economic prong, the Torres and Epstein declarations state that Pfizer's total investment in plant and equipment used for the production of

Viagra in the United States is approximately $5.756 million. . . . In addition, Pfizer employs approximately 2500 employees in the United States who are involved at least part-time in manufacturing and packaging activities relating to Viagra. Pfizer's annual labor costs relating to Viagra are approximately $11.066 million. The Staff also concurs with these statements.

In connection with Pfizer's research and development activities connected with exploitation of the '534 patent, Pfizer asserts in its motion, but does not support by any declaration or other evidence, that it has conducted extensive pre-market clinical testing of Viagra in the United States in order to ensure the safety and efficacy of Viagra, as well as to satisfy U.S. regulatory requirements. In 1995 and 1996, Pfizer asserts, it conducted eight major clinical trials of Viagra on human males in the United States, evaluating hundreds of subjects at numerous testing centers. Pfizer further states that since the approval of Viagra by the FDA in 1998, it has conducted, and continues to conduct, numerous additional clinical trials of Viagra throughout the United States. These tests, according to Pfizer, cost it several hundreds of millions of dollars.[15] . . .

VALIDITY OF THE '534 PATENT

As for the validity of the '534 patent, its validity is presumed by law and has not been challenged in this proceeding by the Staff or by any Respondent. . . .

IMPORTATION OF ACCUSED PRODUCTS

Concerning importation of the accused products, the Mages declaration attached to the complaint demonstrates that each of the defaulting Respondents has imported accused sildenafil products into the United States. . . . The Staff concurs with these findings. . . .

CONCLUSION ON VIOLATION OF SECTION 337

In accordance with the foregoing reasons, Pfizer has demonstrated by "substantial, reliable, and probative evidence," with the concurrence of the Staff, that there is a violation of Section 337 by reason of the defaulting Respondents' importation into the United States, sale for importation, and sale within the United States after importation, of certain sildenafil or pharmaceutically acceptable salts thereof, such as sildenafil citrate, and products containing the same, that infringe claims 1-5 of the '534 patent.

RECOMMENDED DETERMINATION ON REMEDY AND BONDING

Finally, following the issuance of an initial determination on violation of Section 337, the administrative law judge must also issue a recommended

---

15. Although the Staff does not endorse Pfizer's research and development allegations solely because they have not been accompanied by a declaration under oath, it does not question their truthfulness.

termination concerning the appropriate remedy in the event that the Commission finds a violation of Section 337 and the amount of the bond to be posted by the respondents during the 60-day period of Presidential review of the Commission's action under Section 337(j). 19 C.F.R. § 210.42(a)(l)(ii).

PROPRIETY OF A GENERAL EXCLUSION ORDER

In the case of a finding of violation of Section 337 by defaulting respondents under Section 337(g)(2), a general exclusion order may issue if the requirements of Section 337(d)(2) are met. 19 U.S.C. § 1337(g)(2)(C). As mentioned earlier, these are the *Spray Pumps* factors, under which a general exclusion order is warranted if: "(A) a general exclusion from entry of articles is necessary to prevent circumvention of an exclusion order limited to products of named persons; or (B) there is a pattern of violation of this section and it is difficult to identify the source of infringing products." 19 U.S.C. § 1337(d)(2).

Under *Spray Pumps,* a two-pronged test must be satisfied for issuance of a general exclusion order. There must be (1) "a widespread pattern of unauthorized use of [the] patented invention"; and (2) "certain business conditions from which one might reasonably infer that foreign manufacturers other than respondents to the investigation may attempt to enter the U.S. market with infringing articles." The following factors are considered relevant to demonstrating a widespread pattern of unauthorized use:

1.   Commission determination of unauthorized importation into the United States of infringing articles by numerous foreign manufacturers; and
2.   other evidence which demonstrates a history of unauthorized foreign use of the patented invention.

The Commission has also identified a number of factors relevant to showing "certain business conditions," including:

1.   an established market for the patented product in the U.S. market and conditions of the world market; and
2.   the availability of marketing and distribution networks in the United States for potential foreign manufacturers.

Both Pfizer and the Staff agree that there is a "widespread pattern of unauthorized use" in that numerous entities in India and China manufacture sildenafil citrate, and possibly Thailand as well. . . . They also agree that infringing sildenafil citrate is widely available on the Internet and through unsolicited bulk e-mail (also known colloquially as "spam"). Pfizer further asserts that "Customs and FDA have been overwhelmed by 'massive quantities' of pharmaceutical shipments that the [Customs Service Miami International Mail Branch] receives routinely from South and Central America, Canada, Europe, the Bahamas, and Mexico and many foreign prescription drugs have improperly entered the U.S. as a result." . . . As an example for this case, Pfizer cites a letter from a member of Congress to the Commissioner of the U.S. Food and Drug Administration stating that on May 6, 2003, the Miami Customs facility improperly released 1,233 packages labeled as "Sildenafil" or "generic Viagra" to consignees in the United States. *Id.,* citing Motion Exhibit 5 (Letter from W.J. "Billy" Tauzin, et al. to The

Honorable Mark B. McClellan, M.D., Ph.D. (June 5, 2003)).[19] [William Tauzin subsequently became President of PhRMA—Eds.]

Concerning the presence of "business conditions" influencing such unfair imports, Pfizer and the Staff agree that Viagra is a popular drug, sales of which were in excess of $1.5 billion in 2001. . . . Infringers offer their versions of Viagra over the Internet at significantly lower prices than Pfizer, often without requiring a prescription. *See id.* It is not difficult for foreign entities to gain access to the U.S. market, Pfizer notes, citing numerous foreign manufacturers of infringing sildenafil citrate products and ready access to the market through Internet sales.

Concerning the possibility of circumvention, Pfizer and the Staff note the difficulty of identifying and shutting down individual suppliers. . . . Both note that infringers operating through Internet web sites typically offer very limited contact information, making it difficult to take effective action against individual suppliers.

Based on these considerations, it is readily apparent that the *Spray Pumps* factors have been satisfied by Pfizer in this case and that a general exclusion order is, therefore, warranted. . . .

RESPONDENTS' BOND

In accordance with Section 337(j), the accused products are entitled to entry under bond during the 60-day period of Presidential review. 19 U.S.C. § 1337(j). To the extent possible, the bond should be an amount that would be sufficient to protect the complainant from any injury. 19 C.F.R. § 210.50(a)(3).

Although the Commission frequently sets the bond on the basis of a difference in sales prices between the patented domestic product and the infringing product, . . . there is only limited evidence here of prices charged by the defaulting Respondents because they did not participate in the investigation. As Pfizer and the Staff both point out, the evidence that does exist is based on Pfizer's investigation and demonstrates a wide range of prices charged by the Respondents, generally well below the retail price charged for Pfizer's Viagra product. . . .

Where it has been difficult or impossible to calculate a bond based upon price differentials, and particularly where the respondents fail to provide discovery, the Commission has set the bond at 100 percent of the entered value of the infringing imported product. . . . Pfizer and Staff concur, and the undersigned recommends as appropriate, that the bond in this instance should be set at 100 percent of the entered value of Respondents' accused products during the Presidential review period.

Accordingly, Motion No. 489-008 is granted in part and denied in part to the extent set forth herein.

Pursuant to 19 C.F.R. § 210.38(d), the Administrative Law Judge hereby CERTIFIES to the Commission the record in this investigation.

---

19. The difficulties faced by Customs in stemming the tide of unauthorized drug imports raises a question of whether Customs is any more equipped to enforce a general exclusion order of this kind than it is to enforce FDA notices of detention for drugs that violate the Food, Drug and Cosmetic Act. Such "public interest" issues, however, cannot be addressed in this Initial Determination.

Pursuant to 19 C.F.R. § 210.42(h), this Initial Determination shall become the determination of the Commission unless a party files a petition for review pursuant to 19 C.F.R. § 210.43(a) or the Commission, pursuant to 19 C.F.R § 210.44, orders on its own motion a review of the Initial Determination or certain issues therein.

So Ordered.

Charles E. Bullock
Administrative Law Judge

IN THE MATTER OF CERTAIN SILDENAFIL OR ANY PHARMACEUTICALLY ACCEPTABLE SALT THEREOF, SUCH AS SILDENAFIL CITRATE, AND PRODUCTS CONTAINING SAME

United States International Trade Commission Inv. No. 337-TA-489
General Exclusion Order

The Commission has determined that there is a violation of section 337 of the Tariff Act of 1930 (19 U.S.C. § 1337) in the unlawful importation and sale of certain sildenafil, or any pharmaceutically acceptable salt thereof, such as sildenafil citrate, and products containing same that infringe one or more of claims 1-5 of U.S. Patent No. 5,250,534 ("the '534 patent").

Having reviewed the record in this investigation, including the recommended determination of the presiding administrative law judge and the written submissions of the parties, the Commission has made its determination on the issues of remedy, the public interest, and bonding. The Commission has determined that the appropriate form of relief is a general exclusion order issued under section 337(d)(2) prohibiting the unlicensed importation of sildenafil, or any pharmaceutically acceptable salt thereof, such a sildenafil citrate, and products containing same covered by one or more of claims 1-5 of the '534 patent.

The Commission has also determined that the public interest factors enumerated in 19 U.S.C. § 1337(d) do not preclude issuance of the general exclusion order, and that the bond during the Presidential review period shall be in the amount of 100 percent of the entered value of the products subject to this order.

Accordingly, the Commission hereby ORDERS THAT:

1. Sildenafil, or any pharmaceutically acceptable salt thereof, such as sildenafil citrate, and products containing same covered by one or more of claims 1-5 of U.S. Patent No. 5,250,534 are excluded from entry for consumption into the United States, entry for consumption from a foreign trade zone, or withdrawal from warehouse for consumption, for the remaining term of the patent, except under license of the patent owner or as provided by law.

2. Sildenafil, or any pharmaceutically acceptable salt thereof, such as sildenafil citrate, and products containing same that are excluded by paragraph 1 of this Order are entitled to entry for consumption into the United States, entry for consumption from a foreign trade zone, or withdrawal from warehouse for consumption, under bond in the amount of 100 percent of entered value pursuant to subsection (j) of section 337 of the Tariff Act

of 1930, as amended, 19 U.S.C. § 1337(j), from the day after this Order is received by the President until such time as the President notifies the Commission that he approves or disapproves this action but, in any event, not later than sixty (60) days after the date of receipt of this action.

3. In accordance with 19 U.S.C. § 1337(l), the provisions of this Order shall not apply to products otherwise covered by this Order that are imported by and for the use of the United States, or imported for, and to be used for, the United States with the authorization or consent of the Government.

4. The Commission may modify this Order in accordance with the procedures described in section 210.76 of the Commission's Rules of Practice and Procedure, 19 C.F.R. § 210.76.

5. The Secretary shall serve copies of this Order upon each party of record in this investigation and upon the Department of Health and Human Services, the Department of Justice, the Federal Trade Commission, and the Bureau of Customs and Border Protection.

6. Notice of this Order shall be published in the *Federal Register*.

By Order of the Commission.

NOTES AND QUESTIONS

1. The issuance of the general exclusion order does not prevent a third party from challenging the validity of Pfizer's patent in a reexamination proceeding before the USPTO or in an ordinary federal court patent invalidity proceeding. If the patent were found to be invalid, the ITC could be petitioned to remove the general exclusion order.

2. Because it has obtained a general exclusion order, Pfizer does not need to bring individual claims for patent infringement — seeking injunction (and damages) against third parties attempting to import Viagra into the United States. Based on the general exclusion order, the Customs Service will routinely block imports by any third party. Note, however, that Section 337 does not include a means for securing monetary damages such as are available in a patent infringement proceeding (although the ITC may assess civil fines in the event an order is violated). We saw earlier (in *Jazz Photo v. Fuji Film, supra* Chapter 2, section II.A.4.b) a patent holder bring a suit for infringement and damages following a successful Section 337 action. Based on *Jazz Photo,* it would appear that a Section 337 determination does not preclude a further Patent Act cause of action on the same subject matter.

3. The ITC's general exclusion order does not apply to the federal government. This is consistent with 28 U.S.C. § 1498, which generally exempts the federal government from patent infringement injunctions, permitting only claims for compensation before the Court of Claims.

2. Other Statutory Authority Regarding Importation

In Chapter 3, we examined *K mart v. Cartier* and *Lever Brothers v. United States,* each of which involved actions to block imports into the United States of products bearing trademarks alleged to infringe the rights of U.S. trademark holders. The *K mart* case was initiated under Section 526 of the Tariff Act of 1930 (19 U.S.C. § 1526), while the *Lever Brothers* case was initiated under Section 42 of the Lanham Act (15 U.S.C. § 1124). In Chapter 4, we examined *Quality King v. L'Anza* and *Omega S.A. v. Costco Wholesale Corporation,* both of which involved an attempt to block import into the United States of goods embodying copyrighted material. The *Quality King* and *Omega S.A.* cases were initiated pursuant to Section 602 of the Copyright Act. We refer to these cases for explanation of the statutory authority — in addition to Section 337 — pursuant to which private litigants in the United States may seek to block importation of goods infringing U.S. copyright and trademark (as well as seek damages for unlawful importation).

These same statutes provide the basis for recording U.S. registered trademarks and copyrights, as well as unregistered trade names, with the U.S. Customs Service (part of the Department of Homeland Security), and for detention by U.S. Customs authorities of goods infringing them. The relevant rules of the Customs Service are codified at 19 C.F.R. Part 133. Upon detention of goods, the importer is notified and may provide evidence of authorization to import, pursuant to which evidence the goods will be released. If the importer does not, within 30 days of notice, obtain release of the goods, the Customs Service commences proceedings for forfeiture. The Customs Service has the authority to levy fines in respect of counterfeit trademark imports, and may refer trademark counterfeiting and copyright piracy cases to the Department of Justice for criminal prosecution.

The Customs Service compiles data with respect to seizures of IPRs-infringing goods, broken down by commodity type and country of origin, and makes that data available online.[49] In fiscal year 2009, it reported approximately $260.7 million in IPRs-related seizures. China was by far the largest source of seized goods.

3.   Section 301 and Special 301

U.S. trade legislation provides a mechanism — Section 301 of the Trade Act of 1974 (as amended) — under which interested persons may initiate administrative proceedings at the Office of the United States Trade Representative (USTR) that may lead to a finding that a foreign country is engaging in unlawful or unreasonable trade practices.[50] Such administrative proceedings may also be self-initiated by USTR. Depending upon the nature of the finding, USTR may be obligated to negotiate a satisfactory resolution with the foreign country and, if unsuccessful, initiate a dispute settlement action at the WTO or under another applicable trade agreement. If the complained-against country is found to have violated an agreement and fails to remedy the problem, USTR is obligated to impose trade sanctions (unless USTR determines that this would be against the national interest).

Section 301 actions are not limited to situations in which a foreign country is engaging in acts that violate a trade agreement. Such actions also extend to "unreasonable" foreign trade practices that, even if not illegal, are "otherwise

---

49. http://www.cbp.gov/linkhandler/cgov/trade/priority_trade/ipr/pubs/seizure/fy09_stats.ctt/fy09_stats.pdf.
50. 19 U.S.C. §§ 2411 et seq.

unfair and inequitable."[51] Unreasonable practices are expressly defined to include acts or practices that deny fair and equitable "provision of adequate and effective protection of intellectual property rights notwithstanding the fact that the foreign country may be in compliance with the specific obligations of the Agreement on Trade-Related Aspects of Intellectual Property Rights."[52] While a determination that a foreign trade practice is unlawful mandates (subject to exceptions) that USTR take action to remedy the situation, a determination that a practice is unreasonable leaves USTR with discretion regarding whether and what action to take.

From the standpoint of foreign countries that are members of the WTO, it is a matter of concern that U.S. legislation expressly contemplates remedial action notwithstanding the lack of TRIPS Agreement violation. However, the United States might argue that some intellectual property issues fall outside the scope of the TRIPS Agreement, and that any remedial action it proposes will not necessarily contravene its WTO obligations.

Section 301, like the EU Trade Barriers Regulation (which post-dates it), provides a means for private enterprises and individuals to pursue redress of WTO-inconsistent measures (and measures inconsistent with other foreign trade agreements). Because the U.S. Congress commonly denies self-executing effect to trade agreements, private parties in the United States may not sue the U.S. government directly on the basis of rights that might be established by those agreements.

In 1988, Congress evidenced heightened attention to IPRs-related trade practices when it adopted, as part of the Omnibus Trade and Competitiveness Act, provisions referred to as "Special 301." Special 301, among other things, requires USTR to prepare an annual report regarding foreign IP-related practices and, as appropriate, identify the most serious violators of U.S. interests as "priority" countries. Priority countries are subject to an accelerated Section 301 process. While not provided for in Special 301 legislation, USTR from the outset of its implementation chose to establish a "priority watch list" and "watch list" to identify countries of particular concern. Placement on a "watch list" does not trigger the same statutory obligations for USTR as does a country's designation as "priority" country. Following is part of USTR's 2010 Special 301 Report, which includes a brief description of USTR's Special 301 mandate, and its 2010 discussion and identification of China and Russia as priority watch list countries.

OFFICE OF UNITED STATES TRADE REPRESENTATIVE 2010 SPECIAL 301 REPORT*

BACKGROUND ON SPECIAL 301

Pursuant to Section 182 of the Trade Act of 1974, as amended by the Omnibus Trade and Competitiveness Act of 1988 and the Uruguay Round Agreements Act (enacted in 1994) ("Special 301"), under Special 301 provisions, USTR must identify those countries that deny adequate and effective protection for IPR or deny fair and equitable market access for persons that rely on intellectual

---

51. 19 U.S.C. § 2411(b) & (d).
52. 19 U.S.C. § 2411(d)(3)(B)(i)(II).
* Available at http://www.ustr.gov.

property protection. Countries that have the most onerous or egregious acts, policies, or practices and whose acts, policies, or practices have the greatest adverse impact (actual or potential) on the relevant U.S. products must be designated as "Priority Foreign Countries."

Priority Foreign Countries are potentially subject to an investigation under the Section 301 provisions of the Trade Act of 1974. USTR may not designate a country as a Priority Foreign Country if it is entering into good faith negotiations or making significant progress in bilateral or multilateral negotiations to provide adequate and effective protection of IPR.

USTR must decide whether to identify countries within 30 days after issuance of the annual National Trade Estimate Report. In addition, USTR may identify a trading partner as a Priority Foreign Country or remove such identification whenever warranted.

USTR has created a "Priority Watch List" and "Watch List" under Special 301 provisions. Placement of a trading partner on the Priority Watch List or Watch List indicates that particular problems exist in that country with respect to IPR protection, enforcement, or market access for persons relying on intellectual property. Countries placed on the Priority Watch List are the focus of increased bilateral attention concerning the problem areas.

Additionally, under Section 306, USTR monitors a country's compliance with bilateral intellectual property agreements that are the basis for resolving an investigation under Section 301. USTR may apply sanctions if a country fails to satisfactorily implement an agreement.

The interagency Trade Policy Staff Committee, in advising USTR on the implementation of Special 301, obtains information from and holds consultations with the private sector, U.S. embassies, the United States' trading partners, the U.S. Congress, and the National Trade Estimates report, among other sources.

PRIORITY WATCH LIST

CHINA

China will remain on the Priority Watch List in 2010 and will remain subject to Section 306 monitoring. China's enforcement of IPR and implementation of its TRIPS Agreement obligations remain top priorities for the United States. The United States is heartened by many positive steps the Chinese government took in 2009 with respect to these issues, including the largest software piracy prosecution in Chinese history, and an increase in the numbers of civil IP cases in the courts. The U.S. Government welcomes the continued and constructive discussions of these matters in the Joint Commission on Commerce and Trade (JCCT) and the JCCT Intellectual Property Rights Working Group. However, the overall level of IPR theft in China remains unacceptable.

The United States is also deeply troubled by the development of policies that may unfairly disadvantage U.S. rights holders by promoting "indigenous innovation" including through, among other things, preferential government procurement and other measures that could severely restrict market access for foreign technology and products.

China's IPR enforcement regime remains largely ineffective and non-deterrent. Widespread IPR infringement continues to affect products, brands and technologies from a wide range of industries, including movies, music, publishing, entertainment software, apparel, athletic footwear, textile fabrics and floor coverings, consumer goods, chemicals, electrical equipment, and information technology, among many others. The share of IPR-infringing product seizures at the U.S. border that were of Chinese origin was 79 percent in 2009, a small decrease from 81 percent in 2008.

The U.S. copyright industries report severe losses due to piracy in China. Trade in pirated optical discs continues to thrive, supplied by both licensed and unlicensed factories as well as by smugglers. These pirated optical discs are exported to markets across the region, impacting legitimate sales outside of China as well. Small retail shops continue to be the major commercial outlets for pirated movies and music. The theft of software, books and journals also remain key concerns. Business software theft by enterprises is particularly troubling as it not only results in lost revenues to software companies but also lowers the business costs of offending enterprises, and may give these firms an unfair advantage against their law-abiding competitors.

Strong action to curb trademark counterfeiting and copyright piracy on the Internet is critical to the future of IPR enforcement in China. China should significantly increase criminal prosecutions and other enforcement actions against Internet-based piracy and counterfeiting operations through a sustained national effort backed by appropriate resources. A recent internet enforcement campaign in which 558 cases were investigated and 375 websites were shut down demonstrates that when the Chinese government chooses to utilize its enforcement resources and personnel to deal with an IPR problem, it can produce results. The United States notes that at times particular enforcement actions are directed not only at copyright or trademark infringement, but also include infringement activities that may be considered more serious under the Chinese legal system. There is a concern that such actions lead to the public perception that the enforcement authorities are not focused on enforcing intellectual property specifically. This perception can be reinforced when effective enforcement measures are not taken against well-known infringers. The United States urges the Chinese government to demonstrate consistent resolve when fighting piracy and counterfeiting on the Internet by taking firm action against such infringers, so that they will adjust their business models to respect intellectual property laws, and thereby send a strong signal throughout the country.

Additionally, in October 2009, in response to allegations that some state-run libraries were providing unauthorized electronic copies of scientific and medical journal articles to for-profit entities, the NCAC, the Ministry of Education, the Ministry of Culture, and the National Anti-Pornography Office issued the *Notice on Strengthening Library Protection of Copyright*, which directs libraries to strictly adhere to the disciplines of the *Copyright Law*. This was a welcome step, and the United States will monitor implementation of this directive in 2010. In particular, the United States will look to the Chinese authorities to implement this directive through unannounced audits and inspections. Emphasis should be placed on preventing the unauthorized commercial sale of journals, either directly to consumers or through online intermediaries. Counterfeiting remains pervasive in many retail and wholesale markets. This problem continues in spite of significant attention and resources from brand owners, administrative supervision, civil lawsuits, agreements with landlords, and attention from China's central government and from foreign governments. There have been some improvements, including judicial enforcement related to infringing activities in retail markets in Beijing and Shanghai. Other welcome steps include judicial authorities sentencing wholesalers to prison terms, and holding retail market landlords liable for failing to take appropriate measures to prevent infringement. Unfortunately, outside Beijing and Shanghai, there have been limited efforts to hold landlords liable for infringement that occurs on their premises. Even in Beijing and Shanghai, the relatively minor penalties levied by courts, and examples of landlords and infringers ignoring applicable court rulings, indicate that additional measures, including criminal sanctions, will be necessary to bring this problem under control.

There are a number of other obstacles to effective enforcement. These include high value and volume thresholds that must be met in order to initiate criminal prosecution of IPR infringement. U.S. trademark and copyright industries report that administrative fines are too low, and imposed too infrequently, to provide deterrence. Consequently, infringers view administrative seizures and fines merely as a cost of doing business. Civil damages for infringement are likewise inadequate.

Exacerbating its enforcement difficulties, China maintains market access barriers, such as import restrictions and restrictions on wholesale and retail distribution, which can discourage and delay the introduction into China's market of a number of legitimate foreign products that rely on IPR. The United States challenged certain restrictions in connection with a WTO dispute filed in April 2007. (See Section I above for further information.)

China's market access barriers create additional incentives to infringe products such as movies, video games, and books, and lead consumers to the black market, thereby compounding the severe problems already faced by China's enforcement authorities. An example of such a barrier is a Ministry of Culture circular regarding digital music [that] was issued in September 2009. That circular bars providers of imported—but not domestic—digital music from distributing their content online unless they obtain content approval, and meet unrealistic obligations, such as a entering into mandatory exclusive licensing arrangement with a wholly Chinese-owned entity. The United States is also very concerned about a troubling trend whereby China adopts policies that unfairly advantage domestic or "indigenous" innovation over foreign innovation and technologies. In November 2009, Chinese government agencies issued the Circular on *Launching the 2009 National Indigenous Innovation Product Accreditation Work*, requiring companies to file applications by December 2009 for their products to be considered for accreditation as "indigenous innovation products." This Circular, and revisions to it issued in April 2010, provides for subsequent catalogs to be issued that provide preferential treatment in government procurement to any products that are granted this accreditation. Provinces and municipal governments have also reportedly issued their own "indigenous innovation" catalogs related to government procurement. The Circular, and the April 2010 revisions, contain provisions that allow Chinese authorities to require that R&D on products receiving accreditation be conducted, at least partially, in China. The United States has raised concerns regarding this and other problematic criteria with Chinese authorities.

Draft *Regulations for the Administration of the Formulation and Revision of Patent-Involving National Standards,* released for public comment in November 2009 by the Standardization Administration of China (SAC), raise concerns regarding their expansive scope, the feasibility of certain patent disclosure requirements, and the possible use of compulsory licensing for essential patents included in national standards. If adopted in their current form, these provisions may have the unintended effect of undermining the incentives for innovation and, by discouraging foreign rights holders from participating in the development of standards in China, depriving the standard setting process of potentially superior technology.

With respect to patents, on October 1, 2009, the *Third Amendment to China's Patent Law,* passed in December 2008, went into effect. While many provisions of the Patent Law were clarified and improved, rights holders have raised a number of concerns about the new law and implementing regulations, including the effect of disclosure of origin requirements on patent validity, inventor remuneration, and the scope of and procedures related to compulsory licensing, among other matters. The United States will closely follow the implementation of these measures in 2010.

The United States encourages China to provide an effective system to expeditiously address patent issues in connection with applications to market pharmaceutical products. Additionally, the United States continues to have concerns about the extent to which China provides effective protection against unfair commercial use, as well as unauthorized disclosure, of undisclosed test or other data generated to obtain marketing approval for pharmaceutical products.

The United States believes that continued bilateral dialogue and cooperation can lead to further progress in these and other areas. The United States will continue to work with China on IPR enforcement and protection strategies, innovation policies, and the range of other important IPR-related matters in our bilateral economic relationship, including through the Joint Commission on Commerce and Trade (JCCT) and other fora.

Provincial and Local Issues

Progress, or lack thereof, in protecting and enforcing IPR in China can vary greatly by region. For example, industry stakeholders continue to identify Shanghai municipality as a bright spot in China's IPR landscape. Stakeholders hope that additional improvements may result from Shanghai's hosting of the 2010 World Expo. Neighboring Zhejiang province has also shown progress. Zhejiang courts have set an example of transparency by publishing IPR decisions on the Internet. In 2009, Zhejiang undertook more trademark infringement investigations than any other Chinese province, thereby highlighting both the increasing responsiveness of officials to industry requests for enforcement, and the scale of the problem in the province.

Jiangsu province, with its focus on promoting high technology, has demonstrated its recognition of the importance of IPR protection, including through a Suzhou court's criminal sentences in a high-profile software piracy case. However, right holders continue to express frustration at the level and scale of counterfeit manufacturing in Guangzhou province, one of China's largest manufacturing hubs. Enforcement is undermined by inconsistencies with respect to matters such as the valuation methodologies for calculating damages, fines, and penalties. Moreover, fines and penalties are not deterrent and the numbers of criminal IPR cases that are initiated is too low to bring about measurable improvements in the region.

Generally, IPR enforcement at the local level is hampered by poor coordination among Chinese government ministries and agencies, local protectionism and corruption, high thresholds for initiating investigations and prosecuting criminal cases, lack of training, and inadequate and non-transparent processes.

As in the past, the United States will continue to review the policies and enforcement situation in China at the sub-national levels of government.

Russia will remain on the Priority Watch List in 2010. While Russia has made some progress over the past several years in improving IPR protection and enforcement, concerns remain, particularly with respect to Russia's continued failure to implement fully its commitments in the November 2006 Bilateral Agreement on Protection and Enforcement of Intellectual Property Rights ("IPR Bilateral Agreement").

In the IPR Bilateral Agreement, Russia committed to fight optical disc and Internet piracy, enact legislation to protect against unfair commercial use of undisclosed test or other data generated to obtain marketing approval for pharmaceutical products, deter piracy and counterfeiting through enhanced criminal penalties, strengthen border enforcement, and conform its laws to international IPR norms. Russia's continued delays in fully implementing this Agreement are particularly troubling, since, with respect to several of the obligations, the IPR Bilateral Agreement established an agreed-upon deadline of June 1, 2007. While the amendments to the Civil Code and Customs Code have been introduced into the Duma they have not yet become law. Amendments to the Law on Medicines were enacted in 2010; they did not implement the provisions of the IPR Bilateral Agreement on protection of pharmaceutical test data.

The United States urges Russia to strengthen its enforcement efforts against piracy and counterfeiting, which remain major concerns. . . .

NOTES AND QUESTIONS

1. U.S. bilateral trade pressure applied under Section 301 and Special 301 has been the source of political tension with foreign governments and nongovernmental organizations for many years, and the subject of numerous academic papers. The most thoughtful defense of Section 301 and U.S. action pursuant to it was written by Professor Bob Hudec during the GATT 1947 era: Robert E. Hudec, *Thinking About the New Section 301: Beyond Good and Evil*, in AGGRESSIVE UNILATERALISM: AMERICA'S 301 TRADE POLICY AND THE WORLD TRADING SYSTEM 113-22 (J. Bhagwati & H. Patrick eds., 1990). In his paper, Hudec argued that the GATT legal system included some significant gaps that governments were unwilling to address. Under certain circumstances, the United States was justified to engage in "disobedience" under the prevailing rules in order to force the system to change. Hudec posited five substantive guidelines for the use of extralegal GATT measures.

    "1. The objective of the disobedient act must be to secure recognition of the legal change that is consistent with the general objectives of the Agreement. . . .
    2. Disobedience undertaken in support of a claim must be preceded by a good-faith effort to achieve the desired legal change by negotiation. This is a minimum condition of necessity.
    3. Disobedience must be accompanied by an offer to continue negotiating in good faith, with a pledge to terminate the disobedient action upon satisfactory completion of such negotiations. . . .
    4. The extent of the disobedience must be limited to that which is necessary to achieve the negotiated legal reform of the kind needed to solve the problem. . . .

5. Finally, governments acting out of a concern to improve GATT law must necessarily respect that law as fully as possible, even when disobeying it. Accordingly, they must except the power of the legal process to judge their disobedient behavior, and must accept the consequences imposed by law. . . ." (*Id.*, Hudec, at 137-38).

Hudec's defense of Section 301 was written before transformation of the GATT into the more comprehensive WTO legal system. Do you think Hudec's theory of justified disobedience retains its validity?

2.   U.S. Special 301 reports are prepared almost wholly on the basis of data supplied by U.S. industry groups. USTR's Special 301 negotiating agenda is essentially established through consultation with those groups. Of course, U.S. industry has a major stake in foreign IPRs policy. What other U.S. interest groups have a stake in that policy?

4.   Civil Litigation

The most commonly used mechanism for enforcement of IPRs — following consultation and negotiation — is civil litigation. The holder of the IPR files a complaint with judicial or administrative authorities seeking, typically, an injunction to prevent an alleged infringer from continuing its activities. In addition, the IPRs holder usually seeks monetary damages and, as appropriate, forfeiture or destruction of infringing goods and the equipment used to make them. Up until now, almost all civil litigation to enforce IPRs has involved conduct within the territory of the country where the IPRs holder's rights are granted. This is because IPRs are granted with respect to specific national or regional territories and, generally speaking, do not establish rights in foreign territories.[53] Judgments may be enforced abroad on the basis of rules of international private law and the recognition of foreign rulings. Basically, the principle of territoriality applies. However, we examined in Chapter 1 the *NTP v. Research in Motion* case, where the U.S. Court of Appeals for the Federal Circuit imposed liability for infringement of a U.S. software patent on the basis of processing activities taking place in Canada. This type of decision may be opening the door to further civil litigation based on activities taking place outside the country where the IPR is granted. *NTP v. Research in Motion* is not the only case in which liability for infringement of an IPR has been based on activities taking place outside the United States. The following decision by the U.S. Court of Appeals for the Eleventh Circuit, *Babbit Electronics v. Dynascan*, bases liability for U.S. trademark infringement on consumer confusion and injury in various Latin American markets. There are physical jurisdictional links with the United States, including the transit of infringing goods through a U.S. "free trade zone" (where goods transit the United States without passing through customs and entering the stream of commerce), as well as the presence of the parties to the dispute.[54]

The *Babbit Electronics v. Dynascan* decision is included here not only to illustrate the potential extraterritorial reach of U.S. trademark law, but also to show

---

53. There are exceptions, for example, in the case of well-known trademarks.
54. Babbit is a Florida corporation. Dynascan is a Delaware corporation.

that the penalties for trademark infringement may be rather severe. It is a lesson in strong enforcement of IP law.

BABBIT ELECTRONICS v. DYNASCAN
38 F.3d 1161 (11th Cir. 1994)

PER CURIAM . . .

II. CONCLUSIONS OF LAW . . .

B. DYNASCAN'S COUNTERCLAIM . . .

2. Trademark Infringement

Dynascan's trademark infringement claim, pursuant to 15 U.S.C. § 1114(1)(a),[3] rests on the notion that a particular use of a registered trademark is likely to cause confusion. In this case, the registration of the trademarks is not an issue, because Dynascan presented certificates of registration for each of the "Cobra" trademarks owned by Dynascan. The Court must therefore determine whether Babbit's use of the Cobra trademark is likely to cause confusion in the minds of potential buyers as to the source, affiliation or sponsorship of the products. *Interstate Battery System v. Wright*, 811 F. Supp. 237, 241 (N.D. Tex. 1993).

In determining whether there is a likelihood of confusion, the Court may consider a variety of factors, including similarity of design, similarity of the products, identity of retail outlets and purchasers, similarity of advertising media, the defendant's intent and actual confusion. *Jaguar Cars Ltd. v. Skandrani*, 771 F. Supp. 1178, 1183 (S.D. Fla. 1991). Application of these elements to the facts of this case compels the conclusion that Babbit's sale of Cobra cordless telephones is likely to confuse the public into believing that Babbit's products are associated with Dynascan or that Dynascan sponsored, licensed or consented to the manufacture and sale of Babbit's products. The marks used by Babbit are identical to the Cobra trademarks owned by Dynascan, and the Model SA-660s telephones sold by Babbit containing a Cobra label are nearly identical to Dynascan's Model SA-620s cordless telephones.

In addition, although there is no evidence of actual confusion,[4] this Court has found that Babbit intentionally infringed upon Dynascan's trademark rights and intentionally breached the Agreement. . . .

---

3. Section 1114 provides, in pertinent part:

> (1) Any person who shall, without the consent of the registrant—
> · (a) use in commerce any reproduction, counterfeit, copy or colorable imitation of a registered mark in connection with the sale, offering for sale, distribution, or advertising of any goods or services on or in connection with which such use is likely to cause confusion, or to cause mistake, or to deceive; or
> (b) reproduce, counterfeit, copy or colorably imitate a registered mark and apply such reproduction, counterfeit, copy or colorable imitation to labels, signs, prints, packages, wrappers, receptacles or advertisements intended to be used in commerce upon or in connection with the sale, offering for sale, distribution, or advertising of goods or services on or in connection with which such use is likely to cause confusion, or to cause mistake, or to deceive, shall be liable in a civil action by the registrant.

4. "Evidence of confusion is not a prerequisite to a finding of likely confusion." *Jaguar Cars Ltd.*, 771 F. Supp. 1178, 1184, citing *E. Remy Martin & Co. v. Shaw-Ross Internat'l Imports, Inc.*, 756 F.2d 1525, 1529 (11th Cir. 1985).

In fact, a likelihood of confusion can be found as a matter of law if the defendant intended to derive benefit from the plaintiff's trademark. . . . Babbit intended to improve sales of MCE telephones by relabeling them with Cobra labels because Babbit was having difficulty selling MCE telephones. Based on the foregoing discussion, the Court concludes that there has been trademark infringement as determined by the likelihood of confusion analysis.

. . . Direct competition between the parties is not a prerequisite to relief under the Lanham Act. In fact, the Court would not expect to find substantial evidence demonstrating that Dynascan was in competition with Babbit in South America because Babbit was already selling Cobra telephones in that geographic territory with Dynascan's permission. Regardless of Dynascan's activities at the time of the infringement, its name continued to be a marketable commodity and it has the right to use it on other goods or to grant such a license to other companies. *Bowmar Instrument Co. v. Continental Microsystems, Inc.*, 497 F. Supp. 947, 208 U.S.P.Q. 496, 503 (S.D.N.Y. 1980).

As a corollary to this argument, Babbit contends that United States copyright laws and the Lanham Act do not apply to Babbit's sales of cordless telephones because the sales occurred outside of the United States. This argument is not compelling because this Court has already found that Lanham Act jurisdiction exists because Babbit imported cordless telephones into the United States to a free trade zone before shipping the products to South America. Babbit presses this argument, however, by presenting the Court with *Zenger-Miller, Inc. v. Training Team, GmbH*, 757 F. Supp. 1062 (N.D. Cal. 1991).

In *Zenger-Miller*, the court concluded that there was no subject matter jurisdiction over Lanham Act claims where all of the defendant's sales occurred in Germany. A close examination of the underlying rationale of *Zenger-Miller*, however, clearly supports this Court's conclusion that the Lanham Act can apply where sales occur outside of the United States. Specifically, the *Zenger-Miller* court found that the defendant was a foreign corporation and all negotiations leading to the contract in that case occurred abroad. In the instant case, Babbit is an American corporation, and the negotiations leading to the Agreement occurred primarily in the United States. In addition, the defendant in *Zenger-Miller* did not allege that any infringing activity took place in the United States. Babbit, however, imported labels and telephones into a free trade zone in the United States, and Babbit orchestrated sales from a Florida office.

In *Reebok Internat'l v. American Sales Corp.*, 11 U.S.P.Q.2D (BNA) 1229 [1989 WL 418625] (E.D. Wash. 1989), the court upheld the invocation of Lanham Act jurisdiction where the defendant, a California corporation, imported counterfeit shoes from Taiwan to a free trade zone in Los Angeles and then exported the goods to Belgium. The court noted that "the Lanham Act imposes upon this court the duty to protect the entire gamut of purchasers, including non-English speaking purchasers, in various countries throughout the world to which the defendants intend to export their products." *Id.* at 1231. Consequently, this Court concludes that it has jurisdiction to address the trademark infringement counterclaim, even though Babbit's sales of cordless telephones occurred outside of the United States. *See also Ocean Garden, Inc. v. Marktrade Co., Inc.*, 953 F.2d 500, 505 (9th Cir. 1991) (Court held that "entry of infringing goods into a foreign trade zone is a sufficient act in commerce to trigger subject matter jurisdiction in federal courts under the Lanham Act.").

Babbit also argues that Dynascan has engaged in "naked licensing" and thereby forfeits all rights to the Cobra mark in the geographic and product markets where use of the mark has not been adequately protected. In this instance, there is substantial evidence that a number of counterfeiters were active in South America during the mid-1980s. "The existence of third party infringers, however, does not constitute an abandonment of a mark where the trademark owner does not consent to the use of the mark by these others but rather, vigorously pursues these third party infringers." *Visa International v. Bankcard Holders of America*, 211 U.S.P.Q. 28, 41 [1981 WL 40539] (N.D. [Cal.] 1981). In addition, the party seeking to prove abandonment must prove intent to abandon on the part of the trademark owner. *Id.* Although Dynascan did not act with particular vigor against third party infringers in South America, failure to institute legal action against an infringer is insufficient to establish abandonment of a trademark. *Playboy Enterprises v. P.K. Sorren Export Co.*, 546 F. Supp. 987, 996 (S.D. Fla. 1982). Babbit has utterly failed to prove that Dynascan intentionally abandoned its Cobra mark or ceased use of the Cobra trademark.

Finally, Babbit argues that there is no violation of the Lanham Act because the articles that are alleged to be counterfeits are actually genuine goods, produced in the same factory as the approved Cobra telephones. It is true that the unauthorized sale of a genuine trademarked product does not in itself constitute trademark infringement, but Babbit fails to appreciate that identical goods sold in an unauthorized manner are not necessarily genuine for purposes of the Lanham Act. *Hunting World, Inc. v. Reboans, Inc.*, 1992 U.S. Dist. LEXIS 21477, 24 U.S.P.Q.2D (BNA) 1844, 1849 [1992 WL 361741] (N.D. [Cal.] 1992), citing, *H.L. Hayden Co. v. Siemens Medical Systems, Inc.*, 879 F.2d 1005, 1023 (2nd Cir. 1989). . . . Although there is no evidence suggesting that the Model SA-660s cordless telephones are inferior to authorized Cobra products, inferiority is not a prerequisite to a finding of a Lanham Act violation. *Tanning Research Lab. v. Worldwide Import and Export*, 803 F. Supp. 606, 609 (E.D.N.Y. 1992). "Congress hardly intended to step through the looking glass into a world in which valid trademark owners were only protected from inartful counterfeiters." *Id.*

3. Counterfeiting

In order for Dynascan to prevail on its counterfeiting claim, it must demonstrate that Babbit infringed a registered trademark in violation of 15 U.S.C. § 1114(1)(a), and it must prove that Babbit "intentionally used a mark, knowing such mark is a counterfeit mark." 15 U.S.C. § 1117(b).[5] The Court has determined that Babbit infringed registered marks in violation of 15 U.S.C. § 1114(1)(a). The Court has also found that Babbit intentionally used the

---

5. Section 1117 provides, in pertinent part:

(b) Treble damages for use of counterfeit mark
In assessing damages under subsection (a) of this section, the court shall, unless the court finds extenuating circumstances, enter judgment for three times such profits or damages, whichever is greater, together with a reasonable attorney's fee, in the case of any violation of section 1114(1)(a) of this title or section 380 of Title 36 that consists of intentionally using a mark or designation, knowing such mark or designation is a counterfeit mark (as defined in section 1116(d) of this title), in connection with the sale, offering for sale, or distribution of goods or services.

marks in question. "The analysis therefore focuses on whether [Babbit] used the marks knowing that they were counterfeit."[6]

In the Agreement, Babbit and Dynascan agreed that Babbit could use the Cobra trademark in connection with the distribution and sale of certain models of cordless telephones in South America, as long as Babbit ordered the products through Dynascan. . . . [I]t is clear that Babbit used Dynascan's trademarks knowing that they were counterfeit. Babbit is therefore liable for trademark counterfeiting.

4. Unfair Competition, False Designation & Dilution

Dynascan also presents an allegation of false designation of origin under Section 43(a) of the Lanham Act, 15 U.S.C. § 1125(a), state law causes of action for dilution, pursuant to Fla. Stat. § 495.151, and unfair and deceptive trade practices, pursuant to Fla. Stat. § 501.204(1), and a common law cause of action for unfair competition. The same set of facts enabling Dynascan to prevail under Section 1114(a)(1) will result in recovery pursuant to Section 1125. *Marathon Mfg. Co. v. Enerlite Products Corp.*, 767 F.2d 214, 217 (5th Cir. 1985). This is because Section 1125(a) is broader than Section 1114 in that it covers false advertising or description whether or not it involves trademark infringement. . . . This Court's analysis is therefore equally conclusive of these issues.

Finally, Dynascan is entitled to relief under the state cause of action for dilution. *See Jaguar Cars Ltd. v. Skandrani*, 771 F. Supp. 1178, 1185 (S.D. Fla. 1991). Section 495.151 provides that any person using a mark is entitled to an injunction enjoining:

> Subsequent use by another of the same or similar mark if it appears to the court that there exists a likelihood of injury to business reputation or of dilution of the distinctive quality of the mark, notwithstanding the absence of competition between the parties or of confusion as to the source of goods or services.

Fla. Stat. § 495.151. There is a strong likelihood of dilution in the present case because purchasers may associate Babbit's telephones with Dynascan telephones.[7]

C. DAMAGES AND INJUNCTIVE RELIEF

Dynascan argues that it is entitled to a plethora of damages pursuant to the Lanham Act, including a permanent injunction, treble damages, attorney's fees and costs, and prejudgment interest.[8] The Lanham Act provides for recovery by

---

6. A "counterfeit" mark means "a spurious mark which is identical with, or substantially indistinguishable from, a registered mark." 15 U.S.C. § 1127.

7. . . . . The Court also notes that Dynascan has presented no case law, nor can the Court find any case law, suggesting that the Tariff Act of 1930, 19 U.S.C § 1526, applies to a standard trademark infringement case. Although the plain language of the Tariff Act suggests that a party may not import trademarked merchandise into the United States without the consent of the trademark owner, this Court concludes that "there is no evidence that Congress intended such a sweeping scope to § 1526(a)." *See Vivitar Corp. v. United States,* 595 [593] F. Supp. 420, 435 (Ct. Int'l Trade 1984) (Court held that "construing § 1526 to apply when a foreign source of imports is related to, or the agent of, the American trademark owner could lead to results that Congress could not reasonably have intended when it enacted the section.").

8. Babbit's sales of Model SA-660s cordless telephones bearing a Cobra trademark have infringed Dynascan's trademark registrations in violation of the Lanham Act, 15 U.S.C. § 1114(1) and 15 U.S.C. § 1125(a). Consequently, Dynascan is entitled to an injunction enjoining Babbit and its corporated affiliates and subsidiaries, officers, agents, servants, employees, attorneys and those in active concert and participation with them from the unauthorized use or employment in connection with buying, advertising, promoting, displaying, offering for sale or

a successful plaintiff of: "(1) defendants profits; (2) any damages sustained by the plaintiff; and (3) the costs of this action." 15 U.S.C. § 1117. This recovery is cumulative, that is, the Court may award Dynascan both its damages and Babbit's profits. *Playboy Enterprises*, 546 F. Supp. at 997. There are, however, different standards for the awarding of each measure of damages.

1. Babbit's Profits

Where the defendant's infringement is deliberate and willful, as in this case, an accounting for profits is proper under a theory of unjust enrichment. *Maltina Corp. v. Cawy Bottling Co. Inc.*, 613 F.2d 582, 585 (5th Cir. 1980). This accounting serves to deter future infringement, and is thus appropriate even where the plaintiff is not in direct competition with the defendant. *Id.* In this instance, Babbit has demonstrated and the Court has found that Babbit's profits averaged 25% on all sales of Cobra products. Babbit's sales of infringing products to South America amounted to a total sum of $561,868.30. Babbit's profits on these sales, calculated consistent with Babbit's 25% profit margin, totaled $140,467.08.

2. Dynascan's Damages

In order to recover damages (apart from Babbit's profits), Dynascan must demonstrate that it suffered actual damages. *Id.* at 587. "The mark owners royalties are normally used as the measure of damages, but the plaintiff must prove both lost sales and that the loss was caused by defendants' actions." *Playboy Enterprises*, 546 F. Supp. at 998. Dynascan has not demonstrated that it would have made any of the sales that Babbit has made, but the Court concludes that it has demonstrated that Babbit would have purchased authentic Cobra telephones had they not acquired the counterfeit telephones. The Court draws this conclusion because Babbit was unable to sell its MCE labelled telephones, and the sales of Cobra telephones were still highly profitable, as demonstrated by the sale of the counterfeit telephones. Thus, Dynascan is entitled to an award of damages for Babbit's failure to pay the required five percent royalty on cordless telephone sales of $561,868.30. Consequently, Dynascan is entitled to damages totalling $28,093.42.[9]

3. Trebling of Damages

The Court may, in its discretion, reduce or enhance the resulting award up to three times the amount of profits or damages, whichever is greater, as justice shall require. 15 U.S.C. § 1117(a). Such an award is discretionary, but it may not be punitive, and must be based on a showing of actual harm. *Donsco, Inc. v. Casper Corp.*, 587 F.2d 602 (3rd Cir. 1978). If the infringement is intentional, however, and the use of a counterfeit trademark has been proven, then § 1117(b) governs, and the Court is required to treble damages and award attorney's fees unless the Court finds extenuating circumstances. *Chanel, Inc.*, 931 F.2d at 1476. *See also Louis Vuitton S.A. v. Lee*, 875 F.2d 584, 588 (7th Cir. 1989).

---

distributing of goods or merchandise containing or having attached or having in association therewith Dynascan's Cobra trademarks and trade name or colorable imitations thereof and specifically including cordless telephones manufactured by Hyundai or any related companies. 15 U.S.C. § 1116(a). *See Jaguar Cars, Ltd.*, 771 F. Supp. at 1185.

9. Dynascan is also entitled to damages in the form of lost royalties pursuant to Babbit's breach of contract.

Dynascan has demonstrated and this Court has found that Babbit intentionally infringed the Cobra trademark and used a counterfeit Cobra trademark. Consequently, the Court finds that a trebling of damages is required. Pursuant to this conclusion, Dynascan is entitled to a trebling of Lanham Act damages from Babbit for lost profits in the amount of $421,401.24.

4. Costs

Dynascan is entitled to recover its costs. 15 U.S.C. § 1117; Fed. R. Civ. P. 54(d). Dynascan is directed to submit a bill of costs to the Court within fifteen (15) calendar days of the date of this Order.

5. Attorney's Fees

In an exceptional case, the Court may award attorney's fees. 15 U.S.C. § 1117. This is an exceptional case because Babbit intentionally arranged to obtain counterfeit goods from Hyundai, intentionally avoided contractual obligations, and intentionally passed off such goods as Cobra products. Consequently, attorney's fees are awarded to Dynascan.[10] Dynascan is directed to submit a detailed affidavit describing the work done, the time involved, and the amount claimed for each such item of work within fifteen (15) calendar days of the date of this Order.

6. Prejudgment Interest

The Court may, in its discretion, award prejudgment interest on the total amount of the damages award. 15 U.S.C. § 1117. For the reasons stated above, Dynascan is awarded prejudgment interest, beginning with the date that Dynascan filed its counterclaims, filed May 24, 1991, to the conclusion of the trial of this matter, November 13, 1992.

7. Personal Guarantee of Damages Award

Dynascan has requested that all relief awarded in this case be applied jointly and severally to Defendants Babbit, Robert Steinmetz and Sol Steinmetz. Robert Steinmetz is President of Babbit and Sol Steinmetz is Chairman of Babbit. Both officers testified that they were personally involved in the unauthorized purchase and sale of Cobra products, even after receiving notification from Dynascan that the sale of any Model SA-660s cordless telephones was a violation of the Agreement and trademark statutes. . . . Robert Steinmetz and Sol Steinmetz are jointly and personally liable for their participation in Babbit's counterfeiting activities.

III. Conclusion

For the preceding reasons, it is hereby

ORDERED AND ADJUDGED that judgment shall be entered in favor of Defendant Dynascan and against Plaintiff Babbit as to Babbit's Complaint,

---

10. The Court notes that Dynascan is also entitled to attorney's fees pursuant to the Agreement. Specifically, Babbit's breach of the Agreement entitles Dynascan to attorney's fees pursuant to the personal guarantees executed by Robert and Sol Steinmetz in connection with the Agreement.

and in favor of Counter-plaintiff Dynascan and against Counter-defendant Babbit as to Dynascan's Counterclaim, by separate order, pursuant to Fed.R. Civ. P. 58.

NOTES AND QUESTIONS

1. What if the cordless telephones at issue in *Babbit* had been shipped directly from the manufacturer/supplier in South Korea to Latin America and the "counterfeit" labels had been placed on the goods in Latin America? Could trademark infringement subject matter jurisdiction be predicated on the facts that the distribution and trademark licensing agreement was negotiated in the United States, that the domicile of the contracting parties is in the United States and that sales were "orchestrated" from Florida? While this might involve sufficient contact with the forum state to establish jurisdiction over a breach of contract claim, should infringement of a U.S. registered trademark be predicated on so little contact with the forum? Can this decision be reconciled with the strong presumption against extraterritorial effect of U.S. law confirmed by the U.S. Supreme Court in *Microsoft v. AT&T*, excerpted in Chapter 1.VI.D.1?.

2. Note that the officers of Babbit are held personally liable for the damages in this case, despite the fact that they were acting on behalf of a corporation. The imposition of personal liability should act as an extraordinary deterrent to potential trademark infringers. Yet, do you think the court would have imposed personal liability on the officers of a major multinational corporation who directed their employees to breach a distribution contract and continue using a trademark without the permission of the trademark holder? Should it matter that Babbit is a closely held corporation?

5. Criminal Enforcement

Some of the most serious issues confronting the international intellectual property system are raised by the increased focus on criminal prosecution for infringement. There are legitimate law enforcement objectives in seeking to prevent trademark counterfeiting and copyright piracy from being used as mechanisms for financing broader criminal enterprises such as trafficking in narcotics and funding terrorist activities. Yet, there are serious risks involved in shifting responsibility for enforcing intellectual property laws to criminal enforcement authorities. First, the threat of criminal penalties may have a deterrent or "chilling" effect on the willingness of researchers to pursue innovation and on freedom of expression. Second, industry groups seeking to solidify their control over IPRs tend to view "balancing mechanisms" with suspicion, and seek to limit those mechanisms, including through the imposition of criminal liability. The U.S. Department of Justice Task Force on Intellectual Property, for example, has recommended that U.S. free trade agreements "restrict[] the ability of FTA partners to order compulsory licensing of patents."[55] This recommendation implies that compulsory licensing constitutes

---

55. U.S. Department of Justice, *Progress Report of the Department of Justice's Task Force on Intellectual Property*, June 2006, at 35.

a form of theft or criminal activity, which is contrary to the letter and spirit of the Paris Convention, the TRIPS Agreement, and the WTO Doha Declaration on the TRIPS Agreement and Public Health. One of the more difficult policy problems confronting intellectual property lawyers and the international intellectual property system is achieving a socially appropriate balance between affording access to knowledge, on one hand, and providing fair compensation to innovators, on the other. The introduction of severe criminal penalties for IP violations may make achieving this balance more difficult.

The United States is moving increasingly in the direction of adopting criminal penalties for infringement of IPRs, and it is strongly encouraging other countries to follow its lead. The following is a list of the penalties established under U.S. law with respect to "IP" crimes and that may be sought by the U.S. Department of Justice in criminal enforcement proceedings.

FEDERAL CRIMINAL LAWS
PROTECTING INTELLECTUAL PROPERTY*

COPYRIGHT

17 U.S.C. § 506(a)(1)(A) [(formerly § 506(a)(1))] & 18 U.S.C. § 2319(b) *Copyright Infringement for Profit (Felony)*

Statutory maximum penalty of 5 years in prison and a $250,000 fine or twice the gain/loss for an individual first-time offender (10 years for second offense); $500,000 fine or twice the gain/loss for a corporate offender. Civil and criminal forfeiture available.

17 U.S.C. § 506(a)(1)(B) [(formerly § 506(a)(2))] & 18 U.S.C. § 2319(c) *Large-Scale Copyright Infringement Without Profit Motive (Felony)*

Statutory maximum penalty of 3 years in prison and $250,000 fine or twice the gain/loss for an individual first-time offender (6 years for second offense); $500,000 fine or twice gain/loss for corporate offender. Civil and criminal forfeiture available.

17 U.S.C. § 506(a)(1)(C) & 18 U.S.C. § 2319(d) *Distribution of Pre-Release Copyrighted Works or Material over Publicly-Accessible Computer Network*

If infringement is effected for commercial purpose: Statutory maximum penalty of 5 years in prison and a $250,000 fine or twice the gross gain/loss for an individual first-time offender (10 years for second offense); $500,000 fine or twice the gain/loss for a corporate offender. Civil and criminal forfeiture available.

If infringement is not effected for commercial purpose: Statutory maximum penalty of 3 years in prison and $250,000 fine or twice the gain/loss for an individual first-time offender (6 years for second offense); $500,000 fine or twice the gain/loss for a corporate offender. Civil and criminal forfeiture available.

---

* U.S. Department of Justice, *Progress Report of the Department of Justice's Task Force on Intellectual Property,* June 2006, at 11-12.

17 U.S.C. § 1204 *Technology to Circumvent Anti-Piracy Protections Digital Millennium Copyright Act ("DMCA")*

Statutory maximum penalty of 5 years in prison and a $500,000 fine or twice the gain/loss for an individual and corporate first-time offender. Statutory maximum penalty of 10 years in prison for a second offense and a $1 million fine or twice the gain/loss. No forfeiture available.

18 U.S.C. § 2318 *Counterfeit/Illicit Labels and Counterfeit Documentation and Packaging for Copyrighted Works*

Statutory maximum penalty of 5 years in prison and a $250,000 fine or twice the gross gain/loss for an individual; $500,000 fine or twice the gain/loss for a corporate offender. Criminal and civil forfeiture available.

18 U.S.C. § 2319A *Bootleg Recordings of Live Musical Performances*

Statutory maximum penalty of 5 years in prison and a $250,000 fine or twice the gain/loss for an individual first-time offender (10 years for second offense); $500,000 or twice the gain/loss for a corporate offender. Civil and criminal forfeiture available.

18 U.S.C. § 2319B *Camcording*

Statutory maximum penalty of 3 years in prison and $250,000 fine or twice the gain/loss for an individual first-time offender (6 years for second offense); $500,000 fine or twice the gain/loss for a corporate offender. Criminal forfeiture available.

TRADEMARKS, SERVICE MARKS, AND CERTIFICATION MARKS

Counterfeit Trademarks, Service Marks, and Certification Marks

Statutory maximum penalty of 10 years in prison and a $2 million fine or twice the gain/loss for an individual first-time offender; $5 million fine or twice the gain/loss for corporate offender. For second-time offenders statutory maximum penalty of 20 years in prison and a $5 million fine or twice the gain/loss for an individual; $15 million fine or twice the gain/loss for corporate offender. Civil and criminal forfeiture available.

TRADE SECRETS

Economic Espionage to Benefit a Foreign Government

Statutory maximum of 15 years in prison and a $500,000 fine or twice the gain/loss for an individual offender, $10 million fine or twice the gain/loss for a corporate offender. Criminal forfeiture is available.

Commercial Theft of Trade Secrets

Statutory maximum penalty of 10 years in prison and a $250,000 fine or twice the gain/loss for an individual first-time offender (10 years for second offense); $5 million fine or twice the gain/loss for a corporate offender. Criminal forfeiture available.

NOTES AND QUESTIONS

1. Note that there are no U.S. statutes that impose criminal liability for patent infringement. Recall that a substantial proportion of patents subject to challenge are found to be invalid. Recall also that major U.S. corporations frequently are involved in patent disputes. Might these factors explain why criminalization of patent infringement has not yet taken place? But see the following note regarding an EU proposal for criminalization of patent infringement. If such legislation is adopted in the European Union, will the United States again be facing a "protection gap"? Will IP-dependent industry groups urge Congress to criminalize patent infringement lest research and development teams move to Europe to take advantage of criminal prosecution of infringers?

2. The European Commission in July 2005 presented a proposal that would include criminalization of patent infringement. *See* Proposal for a European Parliament and Council Directive on criminal measures aimed at ensuring the enforcement of intellectual property rights and Proposal for a Council Framework Decision to strengthen the criminal law framework to combat intellectual property offences (SEC(2005)848) (presented by the Commission), Brussels, 12.7.2005, COM(2005)276 final, 2005/0127(COD), 2005/0128(CNS).

In order to appreciate the trend toward stronger enforcement of IPRs, including through criminalization, it may be instructive to examine the recommendations of the US Intellectual Property Enforcement Coordinator (the so-called IP Czar[ina] appointed pursuant to the Prioritizing Resources and Organization for Intellectual Property Act (PRO-IP Act) of October 2008 (Pub. L. No. 110-403).

2010 JOINT STRATEGIC PLAN ON INTELLECTUAL PROPERTY ENFORCEMENT[6]

U.S. INTELLECTUAL PROPERTY ENFORCEMENT COORDINATOR

ENFORCING OUR RIGHTS INTERNATIONALLY

[A]ddressing infringement in other countries is a critical component of protecting and enforcing our rights. To that end, the U.S. Government will work

---

6. Federal agencies, including the U.S. Departments of Agriculture (USDA), Commerce (DOC), Health and Human Services (HHS), Homeland Security (DHS), Justice (DOJ), and State (DOS), the Office of the U.S. Trade Representative (USTR) and the U.S. Copyright Office participated in the development of the Joint Strategic Plan.

collectively to strengthen enforcement of intellectual property rights internationally.

Combat Foreign-Based and Foreign-Controlled Websites That Infringe American Intellectual Property Rights

The use of foreign-based and foreign-controlled websites and web services to infringe American intellectual property rights is a growing problem that undermines our national security, particularly our national economic security. Despite the scope and increasing prevalence of such sites, enforcement is complicated because of the limits of the U.S. Government's jurisdiction and resources in foreign countries. To help better address these enforcement issues, Federal agencies, in coordination with the IPEC, will expeditiously assess current efforts to combat such sites and will develop a coordinated and comprehensive plan to address them that includes: (1) U.S. law enforcement agencies vigorously enforcing intellectual property laws; (2) U.S. diplomatic and economic agencies working with foreign governments and international organizations; and (3) the U.S. Government working with the private sector.

Enhance Foreign Law Enforcement Cooperation

International law enforcement cooperation is a critical part of combating the global nature of piracy and counterfeiting. Federal law enforcement agencies will encourage cooperation with their foreign counterparts to: (1) enhance efforts to pursue domestic investigations of foreign intellectual property infringers; (2) encourage foreign law enforcement to pursue those targets themselves; and (3) increase the number of criminal enforcement actions against intellectual property infringers in foreign countries in general. Federal law enforcement agencies will also use, as appropriate, formal cooperative agreements or arrangements with foreign governments as a tool to strengthen cross-border intellectual property enforcement efforts.

Promote Enforcement of U.S. Intellectual Property Rights Through Trade Policy Tools

The U.S. Government has traditionally sought to use the tools of trade policy to seek strong intellectual property enforcement. Examples include bilateral trade dialogues and problem-solving, communicating U.S. concerns clearly through reports such as the Special 301 Report, committing our trading partners to protect American intellectual property through trade agreements such as the Anti-Counterfeiting Trade Agreement (ACTA) and the Trans-Pacific Partnership (TPP), and, when necessary, asserting our rights through the World Trade Organization (WTO) dispute settlement process. USTR, in coordination with the IPEC and relevant Federal agencies, will continue the practice of using these tools to seek robust intellectual property enforcement, including protection of patents, copyrights, trade secrets and trademarks including geographical indications, as well as strong civil, criminal and border measures. Furthermore, USTR will be vigilant in enforcing U.S. trade rights under its trade agreements. These efforts will be conducted in a manner consistent with the balance found in U.S. law and the legal traditions of U.S. trading partners.

Special 301 "Action Plans"

USTR conducts annual reviews of intellectual property protection and market access practices in foreign countries. Through an extensive Special

301 interagency process, USTR publishes a report annually, designating countries of concern on different watch lists, referred to as "priority watch list" (PWL), "watch list" and "priority foreign country." Countries placed on the PWL are the focus of increased bilateral attention concerning the problem areas. The 2010 Special 301 report countries on the PWL included Algeria, Argentina, Canada, Chile, China, India, Indonesia, Pakistan, Russia, Thailand and Venezuela.

USTR also develops action plans and similar documents to establish benchmarks, such as legislative, policy or regulatory action, and as a tool to encourage improvements by countries in order to be removed from the Special 301 list. In order to work with foreign governments to improve their practices related to intellectual property and market access, USTR, in coordination with the IPEC, will initiate an interagency process to increase the effectiveness of, and strengthen implementation of, Special 301 action plans. The action plans, or other appropriate measures, will focus on selected trading partners for which targeted efforts could produce desired results.

Strengthen Intellectual Property Enforcement Through International Organizations

Numerous international organizations have an interest in and focus on intellectual property rights. The IPEC will work with relevant Federal agencies and the IPR Center to raise awareness of intellectual property enforcement and to increase international collaborative efforts through international organizations, such as the World Intellectual Property Organization (WIPO), the WTO, the World Customs Organization (WCO), the World Health Organization (WHO), the Group of Twenty Finance Ministers and Central Bank Governors (G-20), the International Criminal Police Organization (INTERPOL), the Asia-Pacific Economic Cooperation (APEC) Forum, and the Organization for Economic Co-operation and Development (OECD). By working with such organizations, the U.S. Government can strengthen international intellectual property enforcement efforts and increase cross-border diplomatic and law enforcement cooperation. In particular, the U.S. Government will explore opportunities for joint training, sharing of best practices and lessons learned and coordinated law enforcement action.

NOTES AND QUESTIONS

1. In an increasingly competitive and "flat" economic world, is the United States obliged to differentiate among the IP interests of countries at different stages of economic development? Do the recommendations set out above reflect such differentiation?

TABLE OF CASES

Italics indicate principal cases.

INDEX